The Longman Anthology of British Literature

VOLUME 1C

THE RESTORATION AND THE EIGHTEENTH CENTURY

David Damrosch
HARVARD UNIVERSITY

Kevin J. H. Dettmar
POMONA COLLEGE

Christopher Baswell
BARNARD COLLEGE AND COLUMBIA UNIVERSITY

Clare Carroll
QUEENS COLLEGE, CITY UNIVERSITY OF NEW YORK

Andrew Hadfield
UNIVERSITY OF SUSSEX

Heather Henderson

Peter J. Manning
STATE UNIVERSITY OF NEW YORK, STONY BROOK

Anne Howland Schotter
WAGNER COLLEGE

William Chapman Sharpe
BARNARD COLLEGE

Stuart Sherman
FORDHAM UNIVERSITY

Susan J. Wolfson
PRINCETON UNIVERSITY

The Longman Anthology of British Literature
Fourth Edition

David Damrosch and Kevin J. H. Dettmar

General Editors

VOLUME 1C

THE RESTORATION AND THE EIGHTEENTH CENTURY
Stuart Sherman

Longman

New York   San Francisco   Boston
London   Toronto   Sydney   Tokyo   Singapore   Madrid
Mexico City   Munich   Paris   Cape Town   Hong Kong   Montreal

Editor-in-Chief: *Joseph Terry*
Associate Development Editor: *Erin Reilly*
Executive Marketing Manager: *Joyce Nilsen*
Senior Supplements Editor: *Donna Campion*
Production Manager: *Ellen MacElree*
Project Coordination, Text Design, and Page Makeup: GGS Higher Education Resources, a
    Division of PreMedia Global, Inc.
Cover Design Manager: *Nancy Danahy*
On the Cover: *Joshua Reynolds*, Mrs. Abington as "Miss Prue." *1771. Yale Center for British Art,
    Paul Mellon Collection.*
Photo Researcher: *Julie Tesser*
Senior Manufacturing Buyer: *Dennis J. Para*
Printer and Binder: *Quebecor-World/Taunton*
Cover Printer: *Lehigh-Phoenix Color/Hagerstown*

For permission to use copyrighted material, grateful acknowledgment is made to the copyright
holders on page 2839, which is hereby made part of this copyright page.

Library of Congress Cataloging-in-Publication Data
The Longman anthology of British literature / David Damrosch and Kevin J.H. Dettmar,
general editors.—4th ed.
    p. cm.
  Includes bibliographical references and index.
  ISBN–13: 978–0–205–65524–3 (v. 1 : alk. paper)
  ISBN–10: 0–205–65524–6 (v. 1 : alk. paper)
  ISBN–13: 978–0–205–65519–9 (v. 2 : alk. paper)
  ISBN–10: 0–205–65519–X (v. 2 : alk. paper) 1. English literature. 2. Great Britain—Literary
collections. I. Damrosch, David. II. Dettmar, Kevin J. H., 1958–
  PR1109.L69 2010
  820.8—dc22
                                                                          2009020241

Single Volume Edition, Volume 1: ISBN-13: 978-0-205-65524-3; ISBN-10: 0-205-65524-6

Volume 1A, *The Middle Ages*: ISBN-13: 978-0-205-65530-4; ISBN-10: 0-205-65530-0
    A la Carte Edition: ISBN-13: 978-0-13-450877-1; ISBN-10: 0-13-450877-7

Volume 1B, *The Early Modern Period*: ISBN-13: 978-0-205-65532-8; ISBN-10: 0-205-65532-7
    A la Carte Edition: ISBN-13: 978-0-13-450876-4; ISBN-10: 0-13-450876-9

Volume 1C, *The Restoration and the 18th Century*: ISBN-13: 978-0-205-65527-4;
ISBN-10: 0-205-65527-0
    A la Carte Edition: ISBN-13: 978-0-13-450873-3; ISBN-10: 0-13-450873-4

CONTENTS

⟺ PERSPECTIVES ⟸
Mind and God   2613

ADDITIONAL RESOURCES

Cultural Editions

Longman Cultural Editions present major texts along with a generous selection of contextual material that reveal the conversations and controversies of its historical moment. Taken together, our new edition and the Longman Cultural Editions offer an unparalleled set of materials for the enjoyment and study of British literary culture from its earliest beginnings to the present. One Longman Cultural Edition is available at no additional cost when packaged with the anthology. Contact your local Pearson Publisher's Representative for packaging details. Some titles of interest for Volume One include the following works:

Beowulf, Anonymous. Translated by Alan Sullivan and Timothy Murphy & ed. Anderson
ISBN-10: 0-321-10720-9 | ISBN-13: 978-0-321-10720-6

Julius Caesar. Shakespeare. ed. Arnold.
ISBN-10: 0-321-20943-5 | ISBN-13: 978-0-321-20943-6

Henry IV, Parts One and Two. Shakespeare. ed. Levao
ISBN-10: 0-321-18274-X | ISBN-13: 978-0-321-18274-6

The Merchant of Venice, Shakespeare. ed. Danson
ISBN-10: 0-321-16419-9 | ISBN-13: 978-0-321-16419-3

Antony and Cleopatra, Shakespeare, ed. Quint
ISBN-10: 0-321-19874-3 | ISBN-13: 978-0-321-19874-7

Hamlet, Shakespeare. ed. Jordan
ISBN-10: 0-321-31729-7 | ISBN-13: 978-0-321-31729-2

King Lear, Shakespeare. ed. McEachern
ISBN-10: 0-321-10722-5 | ISBN-13: 978-0-321-10722-0

Othello and *The Tragedy of Mariam*, Shakespeare and Cary. ed. Carroll and Damrosch
ISBN-10: 0-321-09699-1 | ISBN-13: 978-0-321-09699-9

The History of the Adventures of Joseph Andrews, Fielding. ed. Potkay
ISBN-10: 0-321-20937-0 | ISBN-13: 978-0-321-20937-5

The Castle of Otranto and *The Man of Feeling*, Walpole and MacKenzie. ed. Mandell
ISBN-10: 0-321-39892-0 | ISBN-13: 978-0-321-39892-5

For a complete listing of Longman Cultural Edition titles, please visit www.pearsonhighered.com/literature.

WEB SITE FOR *THE LONGMAN ANTHOLOGY OF BRITISH LITERATURE*

www.myliteraturekit.com

The fourth edition makes connections beyond its covers as well as within them. The Web site we have developed for the course provides a wealth of resources:

Student Resources

- **Discussion Questions for Major Selections and Perspectives Sections.** Designed to prepare students for the kind of deeper-level analysis expected in class discussions, these compelling prompts are available for each period introduction and for major selections and Perspectives groupings.

- **Self-Grading Multiple Choice Practice Questions.** Available for each period introduction and for all major authors and Perspectives groupings, these objective practice quizzes are designed to help students review their basic understanding of the reading.

- **An Interactive Timeline.** Our interactive timeline helps students visualize the key literary, political, and cultural events of an era. Each event is accompanied by a detailed explanation, usually including references to relevant texts that can be found in the anthology, links to helpful sites, and colorful pictures and illustrations.

- **Links to Valuable British Literature Resources.** Our Online Research Guide provides a wealth of annotated links to excellent Web resources on major authors, texts, and related historical and cultural movements and events.

- **An Archive of Additional Texts.** Our new online archive contains a wealth of selections that could not fit within the bounds of the print anthology. A listing of many of these works can be found in context in our table of contents.

- **Additional Reference Materials.** The Web site also features an extensive glossary of literary and cultural terms, useful summaries of British political and religious organizations, and of money, weights, and measures. For further reading, we provide carefully selected, up-to-date bibliographies for each period and author.

Instructor's Section

- **An Online Instructor's Manual (0-205-67976-5).** The online version of our print manual uses a hyperlink format to allow instructors to jump directly to the author or selection they want to access.

- **PowerPoint Presentations.** A visually rich presentation is available for each period.

- **Sample Syllabi.** Our collection of syllabi include samples of a wide variety of approaches to both the survey-level and period-specific courses.

PREFACE

Literature has a double life. Born in one time and place and read in another, literary works are at once products of their age and independent creations, able to live on long after their original world has disappeared. The goal *The Longman Anthology of British Literature* is to present a wealth of poetry, prose, and drama from the full sweep of the literary history of Great Britain and its empire, and to do so in ways that will bring out both the works' original cultural contexts and their lasting aesthetic power. These aspects are in fact closely related: form and content, verbal music and social meanings, go hand in hand. This double life makes literature, as Aristotle said, "the most philosophical" of all the arts, intimately connected to ideas and to realities that the writer transforms into moving patterns of words. The challenge is to show these works in the contexts in which, and for which, they were written, while at the same time not trapping them within those contexts. The warm response this anthology has received from the hundreds of teachers who have adopted it in its first three editions reflects the growing consensus that we are not forced to choose between the literature's aesthetic and cultural dimensions. Our users' responses have now guided us in seeing how we can improve our anthology further, so as to be most pleasurable and stimulating to students, most useful to teachers, and most responsive to ongoing developments in literary studies. This preface can serve as a road map to this book's goals and structure.

NEW TO THIS EDITION

- **Period at a Glance features.** These informative illustrated features open each volume, providing thumbnail sketches of daily life during each period.

- **Enhanced Web site.** A new fourth edition site includes an archive of valuable texts from previous editions, detailed bibliographies, an interactive timeline, discussion questions, and Web resources for major selections and authors.

- **New major, classic texts.** In response to instructors' requests, major additions of important works frequently taught in the British Literature course have been added, including the following selections:

  - A selection from the Irish epic *The Táin Bó Cuailnge*
  - William Baldwin's *Beware the Cat* (sometimes called the first English novel)
  - Edmund Spenser's *The Faerie Queene*, Book 6 and *the Cantos of Mutabilitie*
  - William Shakespeare's *Othello* and *King Lear*

- **New selections across the anthology.** We have continued to refine our contents, adding new selections to established units across the anthology, including authors such as John Skelton, Fynes Moryson, Edmund Spenser, and John Donne.

- **Penguin Classics editions of *Beowulf* translated by Michael Alexander and *Sir Gawain and the Green Knight* translated by Brian Stone.** The *Longman Anthology of British Literature* now includes authoritative Penguin Classic translations, trusted throughout the world as editions of classics texts that are both riveting and scholarly.

- **New Perspectives groupings of works in cultural context.** "Perspectives" groupings new to this edition include *The English Sonnet and Sonnet Sequences in the Sixteenth Century*, *Early Modern Books*, and *England, Britain, and the World*.

- **New Response pairings.** A selection from Sir Francis Bacon's *New Atlantis* is paired with Sir Thomas More's *Utopia*.

LITERATURE IN ITS TIME—AND IN OURS

When we engage with a rich literary history that extends back over a thousand years, we often encounter writers who assume their readers know all sorts of things that are little known today: historical facts, social issues, literary and cultural references. Beyond specific information, these works will have come out of a very different literary culture than our own. Even the contemporary British Isles present a cultural situation—or a mix of cultures—very different from what North American readers encounter at home, and these differences only increase as we go farther back in time. A major emphasis of this anthology is to bring the works' original cultural moment to life: not because the works simply or naively reflect that moment of origin, but because they do refract it in fascinating ways. British literature is both a major heritage for modern North America and, in many ways, a very distinct culture; reading British literature will regularly give an experience both of connection and of difference. Great writers create imaginative worlds that have their own compelling internal logic, and a prime purpose of this anthology is to help readers to understand the formal means—whether of genre, rhetoric, or style—with which these writers have created works of haunting beauty. At the same time, as Virginia Woolf says in *A Room of One's Own*, the gossamer threads of the artist's web are joined to reality "with bands of steel."

   The Longman Anthology pursues a range of strategies to bring out both the beauty of these webs of words and their points of contact with reality and to bring related authors and works together in several ways:

☞ PERSPECTIVES: **Broad groupings that illuminate underlying issues in a variety of the major works of a period.**

☞ AND ITS TIME: **A focused cluster that illuminates a specific cultural moment or a debate to which an author is responding.**

☞ RESPONSES: **One or more texts in which later authors in the tradition respond creatively to the challenging texts of their forebears.**

These groupings provide a range of means of access to the literary culture of each period. The Perspectives sections do much more than record what major writers thought about an issue: they give a variety of views in a range of voices, to illustrate the wider culture within which the literature was being written. Theological reflections by the pioneering scientist Isaac Newton; these and many other vivid readings featured in Volume One give rhetorical as well as social contexts for the poems, plays, and stories around them. Perspectives sections typically relate to several major authors of the period, as with a section on the sixteenth-century sonnet that brings the poetry of Edmund Spenser and Sir Philip Sidney into conversation with less widely read figures like Sir Thomas Wyatt and Henry Howard, Earl of Surrey. Most of the writers included in Perspectives sections are important figures of the period who might be neglected if they were listed on their own with just a few pages each; grouping them together has proved to be useful pedagogically as well as intellectually. Perspectives sections may also include work by a major author whose primary listing appears elsewhere in the period; thus, a Perspective section on the Civil War features a selection from Milton's *Eikonoklastes*, and a section on British perceptions of other lands includes a selection from Spenser's *View of the State of Ireland*, so as to give a rounded presentation of the issue in ways that can inform the reading of those authors in their individual sections.

When we present a major work "And Its Time," we give a cluster of related materials to suggest the context within which the work was written. Thus Sir Philip Sidney's great *Apology for Poetry* is accompanied by readings showing the controversy that was raging at the time concerning the nature and value of poetry. Some of the writers in these groupings and in our Perspectives sections have not traditionally been seen as literary figures, but all have produced lively and intriguing works, from medieval clerics writing about saints and sea monsters, to a polemical seventeenth-century tract giving *The Arraignment of Lewd, Idle, Froward, and Unconstant Women*, to economic writings by William Petty—of the type parodied by Swift in his "Modest Proposal."

We also include "Responses" to significant texts in the British literary tradition, demonstrating the sometimes far-reaching influence these works have had over the decades and centuries, and sometimes across oceans and continents. *Beowulf* and John Gardner's *Grendel* are separated by the Atlantic ocean, perhaps eleven hundred or twelve hundred years—and, most notably, by their attitude toward the poem's monster. The *Morte Darthur* is reinterpreted comically by the 1970s British comedy troupe Monty Python's Flying Circus.

WHAT IS BRITISH LITERATURE?

Stepping back from the structure of the book, let us define our basic terms: What is "British" literature? What is literature itself? And just what should an anthology of this material look like at the present time? The term "British" can mean many things, some of them contradictory, some of them even offensive to people on whom the name has been imposed. If the term "British" has no ultimate essence, it does have a history. The first British were Celtic people who inhabited the British Isles and the northern coast of France (still called Brittany) before various Germanic tribes of Angles and Saxons moved onto the islands in the fifth and sixth centuries. Gradually the Angles and Saxons amalgamated into the Anglo-Saxon culture that became dominant in the southern and eastern regions of Britain and then spread outward; the old British people were pushed west, toward what became known as Cornwall,

Wales, and Ireland, which remained independent kingdoms for centuries, as did Celtic Scotland to the north. By an ironic twist of linguistic fate, the Anglo-Saxons began to appropriate the term "British" from the Britons they had displaced, and they took as a national hero the early, semimythic Welsh King Arthur. By the seventeenth century, English monarchs had extended their sway over Wales, Ireland, and Scotland, and they began to refer to their holdings as "Great Britain." Today, Great Britain includes England, Wales, Scotland, and Northern Ireland, but does not include the Republic of Ireland, which has been independent since 1922.

This anthology uses "British" in a broad sense, as a geographical term encompassing the whole of the British Isles. For all its fraught history, it seems a more satisfactory term than to speak simply of "English" literature, for two reasons. First, most speakers of English live in countries that are not the focus of this anthology (for instance, the United States and Canada); second, while the English language and its literature have long been dominant in the British Isles, other cultures in the region have always used other languages and have produced great literature in these languages. Important works by Irish, Welsh, and Scots writers appear regularly in the body of this anthology, some of them written directly in their languages and presented here in translation, and others written in an English inflected by the rhythms, habits of thought, and modes of expression characteristic of these other languages and the people who use them.

We use the term "literature" in a similarly capacious sense, to refer to a range of artistically shaped works written in a charged language, appealing to the imagination at least as much as to discursive reasoning. It is only relatively recently that creative writers have been able to make a living composing poems, plays, and novels, and only in the past hundred years or so has creating "belles lettres" or high literary art been thought of as a sharply separate sphere of activity from other sorts of writing that the same authors would regularly produce. Sometimes, early modern poets wrote sonnets to reflect and honor loves won and lost; at other times, they wrote sonnets to realize courtly ambition and material gain; and always, they wrote their sonnets with an eye to posterity, and with the goal of a poetic form of immortality ("Not marble, nor the gilded monuments / Of princes, shall outlive this pow'rful rhyme"—Shakespeare, *Sonnet 55*).

VARIETIES OF LITERARY EXPERIENCE

Above all, we have strived to give as full a presentation as possible to the varieties of great literature produced from the eighth to the eighteenth centuries in the British Isles, by women as well as by men, in outlying regions as well as in the metropolitan center of London, and in prose, drama, and verse alike. For these earlier periods, we include More's entire *Utopia*, Baldwin's *Beware the Cat*, and Milton's *Paradise Lost*, and we give major space to narrative poetry by Chaucer and Spenser, and to Swift's *Gulliver's Travels*, among others. Drama appears throughout the anthology, from the medieval *Second Play of the Shepherds* and *Mankind* to a range of early modern and restoration plays: Marlowe's *The Tragical History of Dr. Faustus*, Shakespeare's *Twelfth Night, Othello*, and *King Lear*, Jonson's *The Alchemist*, William Wyncherly's *The Country Wife*, and John Gay's *The Beggar's Opera*. Finally, lyric poetry appears in profusion throughout the anthology, from early lyrics by anonymous Middle English poets and the trenchantly witty Dafydd ap Gwilym to the great flowering of lyric poetry in the early modern period in the writings of Shakespeare, Sidney, and Spenser—to name just the "S's"—to the formal perfection and august rhetoric of Restoration and eighteenth-century poets like Swift, Dryden, Pope, and Johnson. Prose fiction always struggles for space in a literary anthology, but we close this volume with a selection from some of the most vital novelistic writing of the eighteenth century. We hope that this anthology will show that the great works of earlier centuries can speak to us compellingly today, their value only increased by the resistance they offer to our views of ourselves and our world. To read and reread the full sweep of this literature is to be struck anew by the degree to which the most radically new works are rooted in centuries of prior innovation.

ILLUSTRATING VISUAL CULTURE

Another important context for literary production has been a different kind of culture: the visual. This edition includes a suite of color plates in each volume, along with hundreds of black-and-white illustrations throughout the anthology, chosen to show artistic and cultural images that figured importantly for literary creation. Sometimes, a poem refers to a specific painting, or more generally emulates qualities of a school of visual art. At other times, more popular materials like frontispieces may illuminate scenes in early modern writing. In some cases, visual and literary creation have merged, as in William Hogarth's series *A Rake's Progress*, included in Volume One. Thumbnail portraits of many major authors mark the beginning of author introductions.

AIDS TO UNDERSTANDING

We have attempted to contextualize our selections in suggestive rather than exhaustive ways, trying to enhance rather than overwhelm the experience of reading the texts themselves. Thus, when difficult or archaic words need defining in poems, we use glosses in the margins, so as to disrupt the reader's eye as little as possible; footnotes are intended to be concise and informative, rather than massive or interpretive. Important literary and social terms are defined when they are used. For convenience of reference, new Period at a Glance features appear at the beginning of each period, providing a thumbnail sketch of daily life during the period. With these informative, illustrated features readers can begin to connect with the world that the anthology is illuminating. Sums of money, for instance, can be understood better when one knows what a loaf of bread cost at the time; the symbolic values attached to various articles of clothing are sometimes difficult for today's readers to decipher, without some information about contemporary apparel and its class associations. And the gradual shift of the Empire's population from rural regions to urban centers is graphically presented in charts for each period.

LOOKING—AND LISTENING—FURTHER

Beyond the boundaries of the anthology itself, we have expanded our Web site, available to all readers at www.myliteraturekit.com; this site gives a wealth of information, annotated links to related sites, and an archive of texts for further reading. For reference, there is also an extensive glossary of literary and cultural terms available there, together with useful summaries of British political and religious organization, and of money, weights, and measures. For further reading, carefully selected, up-to-date bibliographies for each period and for each author can be found in on the

Web site. A guide to our media resources can be found at the end of the table of contents.

For instructors, we have revised and expanded our popular companion volume, *Teaching British Literature*, written directly by the anthology editors, 600 pages in length, available free to everyone who adopts the anthology.

David Damrosch & Kevin J. H. Dettmar

ACKNOWLEDGMENTS

In planning and preparing the fourth edition of our anthology, the editors have been fortunate to have the support, advice, and assistance of many committed and gifted people. Our editor, Joe Terry, has been unwavering in his enthusiasm for the book and his commitment to it; he and his associates Roth Wilkofsky, Mary Ellen Curley, and Joyce Nilsen have supported us in every possible way throughout the process, ably assisted by Katy Needle, Rosie Ellis, and Annie England. Our developmental editor Erin Reilly guided us and our manuscript from start to finish with unfailing acuity and seemingly unwavering patience. Our copyeditor Stephanie Magean seamlessly integrated the work of a dozen editors. Erin Reilly, Elizabeth Bravo and Stefanie Liebman have devoted enormous energy and creativity to revising our Web site. Karyn Morrison cleared our many permissions, and Julie Tesser tracked down and cleared our many new illustrations. Finally, Nancy Wolitzer and Ellen MacElree oversaw the production with sunny good humor and kept the book successfully on track on a very challenging schedule, working closely with Doug Bell at GGS Higher Education Resources.

Our plans for the new edition have been shaped by comments and suggestions from many faculty who have used the book over the years. We are specifically grateful for the thoughtful advice of our reviewers for this edition, Jesse T. Airaudi (Baylor University), Thomas Crofts (East Tennessee State University), Lois Feuer (California State University, Dominguez Hills), Daniel P. Galvin (Clemson University), S. E. Gontarski (Florida State University), Stephen Harris (University of Massachusetts), Roxanne Kent-Drury (Northern Kentucky University), Carol A. Lowe (McLennan Community College), Darin A Merrill (Brigham Young University—Idaho), David G. Miller (Mississippi College), Crystal L. Mueller (University of Wisconsin Oshkosh), and Gary Schneider (University of Texas—Pan American).

We remain grateful as well for the guidance of the many reviewers who advised us on the creation of the first three editions, the base on which this new edition has been built. In addition to the people named above, we would like to thank Lucien Agosta (California State University, Sacramento), Anne W. Astell (Purdue University), Derek Attridge (Rutgers University), Linda Austin (Oklahoma State University), Arthur D. Barnes (Louisiana State University), Robert Barrett (University of Pennsylvania), Candice Barrington (Central Connecticut State University), Joseph Bartolomeo (University of Massachusetts, Amherst), Mary Been (Clovis Community College), Stephen Behrendt (University of Nebraska), Todd Bender (University of Wisconsin, Madison), Bruce Boehrer (Florida State University), Bruce Brandt (South Dakota State University), Joel J. Brattin (Worcester Polytechnic Institute), James Campbell (University of Central Florida), J. Douglas Canfield (University of Arizona), Paul A. Cantor (University of Virginia), George Allan Cate (University of Maryland, College Park), Philip Collington (Niagra University), Linda McFerrin

Cook (McLellan Community College), Eugene R. Cunnar (New Mexico State University), Earl Dachslager (University of Houston), Elizabeth Davis (University of California, Davis), Andrew Elfenbein (University of Minnesota), Hilary Englert (New Jersey City University), Margaret Ferguson (University of California, Davis), Sandra K. Fisher (State University of New York, Albany), Sandra C. Fowler (The University of Alabama), Allen J. Frantzen (Loyola University, Chicago), Kevin Gardner (Baylor University), Kate Gartner Frost (University of Texas), Leon Gottfried (Purdue University), Leslie Graff (University at Buffalo), Mark L. Greenberg (Drexel University), Peter Greenfield (University of Puget Sound), Natalie Grinnell (Wofford College), James Hala (Drew University), Wayne Hall (University of Cincinnati), Donna Hamilton (University of Maryland), Wendell Harris (Pennsylvania State University), Richard H. Haswell (Washington State University), Susan Sage Heinzelman (University of Texas, Austin), Standish Henning (University of Wisconsin, Madison), Noah Heringman (University of Missouri—Columbia), Jack W. Herring (Baylor University), Carrie Hintz (Queens College), Romana Huk (University of Notre Dame), Maurice Hunt (Baylor University), Mary Anne Hutchison (Utica College), Patricia Clare Ingham (Indiana University), Kim Jacobs (University of Cincinnati Clermont College), Carol Jamison (Armstrong Atlantic State University), Eric Johnson (Dakota State College), Mary Susan Johnston (Minnesota State University), Eileen A. Joy (Southern Illinois University—Edwardsville), Colleen Juarretche (University of California, Los Angeles), George Justice (University of Missouri), Roxanne Kent-Drury (Northern Kentucky University), R. B. Kershner (University of Florida), Lisa Klein (Ohio State University), Adam Komisaruk (West Virginia University), Rita S. Kranidis (Radford University), Leslie M. LaChance (University of Tennessee at Martin), John Laflin (Dakota State University), Lisa Lampert (University of California, San Diego), Dallas Liddle (Augsburg College), Paulino Lim (California State University, Long Beach), Elizabeth B. Loizeaux (University of Maryland), Ed Malone (Missouri Western State College), John J. Manning (University of Connecticut), William W. Matter (Richland College), Evan Matthews (Navarro College), Michael Mays (University of Southern Mississippi), Lawrence McCauley (College of New Jersey), Michael B. McDonald (Iowa State University), James J. McKeown Jr. (McLennan Community College), Kathryn McKinley (Florida International University), Peter E. Medine (University of Arizona), Barry Milligan (Wright State University), Celia Millward (Boston University), Charlotte Morse (Virginia Commonwealth University), Mary Morse (Rider University), Thomas C. Moser, Jr. (University of Maryland), James Najarian (Boston College), Deborah Craig Wester (Worcester State College), Jude V. Nixon (Baylor University), Richard Nordquist (Armstrong Atlantic State University), Daniel Novak (Tulane University), John Ottenhoff (Alma College), Violet O'Valle (Tarrant County Junior College, Texas), Joyce Cornette Palmer (Texas Women's University), Leslie Palmer (University of North Texas), Richard Pearce (Wheaton College), Rebecca Phillips (West Virginia University), Renée Pigeon (California State University, San Bernardino), Tadeusz Pioro (Southern Methodist University), Deborah Preston (Dekalb College), William Rankin (Abilene Christian University), Sherry Rankin (Abilene Christian University), Luke Reinsma (Seattle Pacific University), Elizabeth Robertson (University of Colorado), Deborah Rogers (University of Maine), David Rollison (College of Marin), Brian Rosenberg (Allegheny College), Charles Ross (Purdue University), Kathryn Rummel (California Polytechnic), Harry Rusche (Emory University), Laura E. Rutland (Berry College), Kenneth D. Shields

(Southern Methodist University), R. G. Siemens (Malaspina University-College), Clare A. Simmons (Ohio State University), Sally Slocum (University of Akron), Phillip Snyder (Brigham Young University), Isabel Bonnyman Stanley (East Tennessee University), Brad Sullivan (Florida Gulf Coast University), Margaret Sullivan (University of California, Los Angeles), Herbert Sussmann (Northeastern University), Mary L. Tanter (Tarleton State University), Ronald R. Thomas (Trinity College), Theresa Tinkle (University of Michigan), William A. Ulmer (University of Alabama), Jennifer A. Wagner (University of Memphis), Anne D. Wallace (University of Southern Mississippi), Brett Wallen (Cleveland Community College), Jackie Walsh (McNeese State University, Louisiana), Daniel Watkins (Duquesne University), John Watkins (University of Minnesota), Martin Wechselblatt (University of Cincinnati), Arthur Weitzman (Northeastern University), Bonnie Wheeler (Southern Methodist University), Jan Widmayer (Boise State University), Dennis L. Williams (Central Texas College), William A. Wilson (San Jose State University), Paula Woods (Baylor University), and Julia Wright (University of Waterloo).

Other colleagues brought our developing book into the classroom, teaching from portions of the work-in-progress. Our thanks go to Lisa Abney (Northwestern State University), Charles Lynn Batten (University of California, Los Angeles), Brenda Riffe Brown (College of the Mainland, Texas), John Brugaletta (California State University, Fullerton), Dan Butcher (Southeastern Louisiana University), Lynn Byrd (Southern University at New Orleans), David Cowles (Brigham Young University), Sheila Drain (John Carroll University), Lawrence Frank (University of Oklahoma), Leigh Garrison (Virginia Polytechnic Institute), David Griffin (New York University), Rita Harkness (Virginia Commonwealth University), Linda Kissler (Westmoreland County Community College, Pennsylvania), Brenda Lewis (Motlow State Community College, Tennessee), Paul Lizotte (River College), Wayne Luckman (Green River Community College, Washington), Arnold Markely (Pennsylvania State University, Delaware County), James McKusick (University of Maryland, Baltimore), Eva McManus (Ohio Northern University), Manuel Moyrao (Old Dominion University), Kate Palguta (Shawnee State University, Ohio), Paul Puccio (University of Central Florida), Sarah Polito (Cape Cod Community College), Meredith Poole (Virginia Western Community College), Tracy Seeley (University of San Francisco), Clare Simmons (Ohio State University), and Paul Yoder (University of Arkansas, Little Rock).

As if all this help weren't enough, the editors also drew directly on friends and colleagues in many ways, for advice, for information, sometimes for outright contributions to headnotes and footnotes, even (in a pinch) for aid in proofreading. In particular, we wish to thank David Ackiss, Marshall Brown, James Cain, Cathy Corder, Jeffrey Cox, Michael Coyle, Pat Denison, Tom Farrell, Andrew Fleck, Jane Freilich, Laurie Glover, Lisa Gordis, Joy Hayton, Ryan Hibbet, V. Lauryl Hicks, Nelson Hilton, Jean Howard, David Kastan, Stanislas Kemper, Andrew Krull, Ron Levao, Carol Levin, David Lipscomb, Denise MacNeil, Jackie Maslowski, Richard Matlak, Anne Mellor, James McKusick, Melanie Micir, Michael North, David Paroissien, Stephen M. Parrish, Peter Platt, Cary Plotkin, Desma Polydorou, Gina Renee, Alan Richardson, Esther Schor, Catherine Siemann, Glenn Simshaw, David Tresilian, Shasta Turner, Nicholas Watson, Michael Winckleman, Gillen Wood, and Sarah Zimmerman for all their guidance and assistance.

The pages on the Restoration and the eighteenth century are the work of many collaborators, diligent and generous. Michael F. Suarez, S. J. (Campion Hall,

Oxford) edited the Swift and Pope sections; Mary Bly (Fordham University) edited Sheridan's *School for Scandal*; Michael Caldwell (University of Chicago) edited the portions of "Reading Papers" on *The Craftsman* and the South Sea Bubble. Steven N. Zwicker (Washington University) co-wrote the period introduction, and the headnotes for the Dryden section. Bruce Redford (Boston University) crafted the footnotes for Dryden, Gay, Johnson, and Boswell. Susan Brown, Janice Cable, Christine Coch, Marnie Cox, Tara Czechowski, Susan Greenfield, Mary Nassef, Paige Reynolds, and Andrew Tumminia helped with texts, footnotes, and other matters throughout; William Pritchard gathered texts, wrote notes, and prepared the bibliography. To all, abiding thanks.

It has been a pleasure to work with all of these colleagues in the ongoing collaborative process that has produced this book and brought it to this new stage of its life and use. This book exists for its readers, whose reactions and suggestions we warmly welcome, as these will in turn reshape this book for later users in the years to come.

David Damrosch
HARVARD UNIVERSITY

Kevin J. H. Dettmar
POMONA COLLEGE

Christopher Baswell
BARNARD COLLEGE AND COLUMBIA UNIVERSITY

Clare Carroll
QUEENS COLLEGE, CITY UNIVERSITY OF NEW YORK

Andrew Hadfield
UNIVERSITY OF SUSSEX

Heather Henderson

Peter J. Manning
STATE UNIVERSITY OF NEW YORK, STONY BROOK

Anne Howland Schotter
WAGNER COLLEGE

William Chapman Sharpe
BARNARD COLLEGE

Stuart Sherman
FORDHAM UNIVERSITY

Susan J. Wolfson
PRINCETON UNIVERSITY

ABOUT THE EDITORS

David Damrosch is Professor Comparative Literature at Harvard University. He is past President of the American Comparative Literature Association, and has written widely on world literature from antiquity to the present. His books include *What is World Literature?* (2003), *The Buried Book: The Loss and Rediscovery of the Great Epic of Gilgamesh* (2007), and *How to Read World Literature* (2009). He is the founding general editor of the six-volume *The Longman Anthology of World Literature, 2/e* (2009) and the editor of *Teaching World Literature* (2009).

Kevin J. H. Dettmar is W.M. Keck Professor and Chair of the Department of English at Pomona College, and Past President of the Modernist Studies Association. He is the author of *The Illicit Joyce of Postmodernism and Is Rock Dead?*, and the editor of *Rereading the New: A Backward Glance at Modernism; Marketing Modernisms: Self-Promotion, Canonization, and Rereading; Reading Rock & Roll: Authenticity, Appropriation, Aesthetics*; the Barnes & Noble Classics edition of James Joyce's *A Portrait of the Artist as a Young Man and Dubliners*; and *The Blackwell Companion to Modernist Literature and Culture*, of *The Cambridge Companion to Bob Dylan*.

❧

Christopher Baswell is A.W. Olin Chair of English at Barnard College, and Professor of English and Comparative Literature at Columbia University. His interests include classical literature and culture, medieval literature and culture, and contemporary poetry. He is author of *Virgil in Medieval England: Figuring the "Aeneid" from the Twelfth Century to Chaucer*, which won the 1998 Beatrice White Prize of the English Association. He has held fellowships from the NEH, the National Humanities Center, and the Institute for Advanced Study, Princeton.

Clare Carroll is Director of Renaissance Studies at The Graduate Center, City University of New York and Professor of Comparative Literature at Queens College, CUNY. Her research is in Renaissance Studies, with particular interests in early modern colonialism, epic poetry, historiography, and translation. She is the author of *The Orlando Furioso: A Stoic Comedy*, and editor of Richard Beacon's humanist dialogue on the colonization of Ireland, *Solon His Follie*. Her most recent book is *Circe's Cup: Cultural Transformations in Early Modern Ireland*. She has received Fulbright Fellowships for her research and the Queens College President's Award for Excellence in Teaching.

Andrew Hadfield is Professor of English at The University of Sussex. He is the author of a number of books, including *Shakespeare and Republicanism* (2005), which was awarded the 2006 Sixteenth-Century Society Conference Roland H. Bainton Prize for Literature; *Literature, Travel and Colonialism in the English Renaissance, 1540–1625* (1998); and Spenser's *Irish Experience: Wild Fruyt and Salvage Soyl* (1997). He has also edited a number of texts, most recently, with Matthew Dimmock, *Religions of the Book: Co-existence and Conflict, 1400–1660* (2008), and with Raymond Gillespie, *The Oxford History of the Irish Book, Vol. III: The Irish Book in English, 1550–1800* (2006). He is a regular reviewer for the TLS.

Heather Henderson is a freelance writer and former Associate Professor of English Literature at Mount Holyoke College. A specialist in Victorian literature, she is the recipient of a fellowship from the National Endowment for the Humanities. She is the author of *The Victorian Self: Autobiography and Biblical Narrative*. Her current interests include homeschooling, travel literature, and autobiography.

Peter J. Manning is Professor at Stony Brook University. He is the author of *Byron and His Fictions* and *Reading Romantics*, and of numerous essays on the British Romantic poets and prose writers. With Susan J. Wolfson, he has co-edited *Selected Poems of Byron*, and *Selected Poems of Beddoes, Hood, and Praed*. He has received fellowships from the National Endowment for the Humanities and the John Simon Guggenheim Memorial Foundation, and the Distinguished Scholar Award of the Keats-Shelley Association.

Anne Schotter is Professor of English at Wagner College. She is the co-editor of *Ineffability: Naming the Unnamable from Dante to Beckett* and author of articles on Middle English poetry, Dante, and medieval Latin poetry. Her current interests include the medieval reception of classical literature, particularly the work of Ovid. She has held fellowships from the Woodrow Wilson and Andrew W. Mellon foundations.

William Sharpe is Professor of English Literature at Barnard College. A specialist in Victorian poetry and the literature of the city, he is the author of *Unreal Cities: Urban Figuration in Wordsworth, Baudelaire, Whitman, Eliot, and Williams*. He is also co-editor of *The Passing of Arthur* and *Visions of the Modern City*. He is the recipient of Guggenheim, National Endowment of the Humanities, Fulbright, and Mellon fellowships, and recently published *New York Nocturne: The City After Dark in Literature, Painting, and Photography*.

Stuart Sherman is Associate Professor of English at Fordham University. He received the Gottschalk Prize from the American Society for Eighteenth-Century Studies for his book *Telling Time: Clocks, Diaries, and English Diurnal Form, 1660–1775*, and is currently at work on a study called "News and Plays: Evanescences of Page and Stage, 1620–1779." He has received the Quantrell Award for Undergraduate Teaching, as well as fellowships from the American Council of Learned Societies and the Chicago Humanities Institute.

Susan J. Wolfson teaches at Princeton University and is general editor of Longman Cultural Editions. She has also produced editions of Felicia Hemans, Lord Byron, Thomas L. Beddoes, William M. Praed, and Thomas Hood. She is the editor of the innovative Longman Cultural Editions of John Keats, and of Mary Shelley's *Franken-stein*, and coeditor (with Barry V. Qualls) of *Three Tales of Doubles*, and (with Claudia Johnson) of Jane Austen's *Pride and Prejudice*. She is author of *The Questioning Presence* (1986), *Formal Charges: The Shaping of Poetry in British Romanticism* (1997), and *Border-lines: The Shiftings of Gender* (2007).

The Longman Anthology of British Literature

VOLUME 1C

THE RESTORATION AND THE EIGHTEENTH CENTURY

Thomas Bowles, *The Bubblers' Medley, or a Sketch of the Times*, 1720.

The Restoration and the Eighteenth Century

Population[1]

National Populations (in millions)[2]

	England and Wales	Scotland	Ireland
1661	5.5	—	2.2
1701	5.6	1.0	1.8–2.0
1751	6.5	1.3	3.2
1791	8.3	1.4	4.8

Urban Populations[3]

	London	Manchester	Edinburgh
1650	400,000	4,500	35,000
1700	75,000	8,000	40,000
1750	675,000	18,000	57,000
1801	959,000	89,0000	83,000

Life Expectancy

Life expectancy at birth is about 36 years. In London expectancy is shorter (perhaps 25 years); more than half of the children born in London die by the age of 10; London burials consistently outnumber London christenings.

Daily Life

Currency[4]

4 farthings	1d. (1 penny)	One penny (a 240th of a pound) in 1750 would be worth 85 U.S. cents today.
12d.	1s. (1 shilling)	One shilling (a 20th of a pound) would be worth $10.20 today.
5s.	1 crown	One crown (a 4th of a pound) would be worth $51 today.
20s.	1£ (1 pound)	One pound in 1750 would be worth $204 today.
21s.	1 guinea	One guinea in 1750 would be worth $214.20 today.

Social Structure and Income in England and Wales in 1696[5]

	Number of Persons	Annual Income per Family
Lords Temporal (secular peers)	6,400	£12,800
Gentlemen Freeholders (i.e., property owners): the "better sort"	96,000 / 280,000	£1280 / £184
Shopkeepers and tradesmen	180,000	£145
Farmers	750,000	£144
Artisans	240,000	£140
Laborers and servants	1,275,000	£115
Cottagers and paupers	1,300,000	£16
Vagrants	30,000	£12

1. Any population figures before 1801, when the first official census was taken, are only speculations, grounded in very fragmentary data.
2. The population of today's United Kingdom is 60,493,912 (July 2008 est.).
3. The population of today's London is over 7.6 million (October 2008 est.).
4. Historical equivalences for the purchasing power of a given sum are very approximate. Different types of calculations provide quite different results. A calculation based on wages, for instance, yields a different figure from a calculation based on the prices of basic consumer goods; and those consumer goods thought essential to daily life change drastically over time. These conversions, then, are meant only to be suggestive.
5. The chart represents selected groups from the much more comprehensive table, A Scheme of the Income and Expense of the Several Families of England, produced by the statistician Gregory King (1648–1712).

Cost of Goods[6]

1d. A bun at the Chelsea Bun House, London 1711; enough gin to get drunk on
4d. One pound of butcher's meat in London
1s. 6d. Price of a chicken in London, 1755
2s. 3d. Price of a chicken in London, 1785
2d. Cost per night of a bed in a gin-shop, 1751
£3 House rent for an Oxfordshire rural laborer, last quarter of the century
£22 Annual rent on James Boswell's modest but comfortable London lodgings
£20–60 Approximate annual rent of "handsome large houses" in Stratford in the early 1720s
3d. Duty per gallon on gin sales, midcentury
18s. 2d. Tax on a shopkeeper with seven windows and an annual rent of £6 in 1797
£1 Duty per gallon on gin sales between 1736 and 1743
£1 5s. Average Englishman's tax bill c.1776
£12 14s. Tax on a shopkeeper with 23 windows, an annual rent of £50, a dog, and a servant, in 1797

Cost of Bread (in pence, per four-pound loaf)

1660 – 1664	5.8
1700 – 1704	4.8
1750 – 1754	5.1
1800 – 1804	11.7

Food and Drink

For the London poor, the cheapest foods are bread (often heavily adulterated), bacon, occasional beef and thin beef soup, tripe, and fish sold at discount price because past its first freshness; narrow apartments offer no opportunities for cooking, but the ovens of local bakeshops are sometimes made available on Sundays for the heating of a meal.

For the middling ranks and wealthy, dinners are served between three and five o'clock, and they are elaborate: two large courses, each composed of multiple items (as many as 25 per course). First course: peas, broccoli, salad, calf's head . . . ; second course: pheasant, hare, pig snipe . . . ; and dessert: apple pie, spun sugar, ices, syllabub (sherry with sugar, cream, and nutmeg).

Estimates of Per Capita Consumption of Beer and Spirits in London (pints per annum)

	1700	1750
Strong beer	512	417
Small beer	307	207
Spirits	4	22

Cocoa, coffee, sugar, and tobacco, all cultivated by slave labor on colonial plantations, are relatively inexpensive and widely consumed; tea, initially more expensive, becomes a ritual component of middle-class life beginning in the 1750s.

During the early 1700s, the craze for gin, pervasively and cheaply sold in impoverished neighborhoods, grows to be regarded as a dangerous blight on city life. "That poison," wrote the London magistrate and novelist Henry Fielding, "is the principal sustenance (if so it may be called) of more than 100,000 people in this metropolis."

Apparel

Men of the middle and higher ranks would don the following, in sequence: drawers (underpants) tied at the waist and knee; a linen shirt with jabots (frills) down the front; breeches that descend to the knee, and stockings either rolled over or tucked under the breeches' bottom edge; a waistcoat of silk or satin; a close-fitting coat with large buttons of the same material; a third "greatcoat" for outerwear; shoes or boots with large buckles; a wig and (outdoors) a hat in one of many widely varied styles.

Women of the middle and higher ranks would don the following, in sequence: a knee-length chemise (shirt) that functioned as undergarment; "stays"—a bodice, stiffened with whalebone but covered in costly and elegant materials and often left visible in the completed outfit; a petticoat, often elaborately decorated with flounces, embroidery, and even jewelry; an overskirt left open at the front to display the elegancies of the petticoat; shoes of silk or satin; and for outdoor wear, a cloak, or a tippet (a small fur cape) and muff. Wigs are worn less often by women than by men; hairstyles vary in intricacy, but by the 1760s they have achieved both height and elaboration to a notorious degree, and display a variety of cumbersome ornamentations: model ships, flower baskets, mini-gardens, and platters of fresh produce. Headwear ranges widely: elegant caps, large soft hats, luxuriantly lined hoods.

The clothing of the poor entails fewer items (often cast-off or second-hand), and only one of each, kept until worn out: for women, stays, a skirt, a wool-and-flax petticoat, a woolen gown, and a white, close-fitting cap; for men, a linen shirt, breeches, stockings, strong shoes, hat, and foul-weather overcoat.

---

6. Adapted from Kristen Olsen, *Daily Life in Eighteenth-Century England*. Westport, CT.: Greenwood Press, 1999.

RULERS

MONARCHS	PARTIES AND PREEMINENT MINISTERS
THE STUARTS	Tories: originally, during the Exclusion Crisis (1678–1682), they supported the hereditary succession, by which the Catholic James, Duke of York, succeeded (1685) his older brother Charles II. After James's abdication (1688), many Tories became Jacobites, supporting the hereditary claims of James and his descendants—an allegiance that excluded them from office throughout the first three decades (1714–1742) of Hanoverian rule.
Charles II, King of England, Scotland, and Ireland (1660–1685)	
James II, King of England, Scotland, and Ireland (1685–1688)	
William III, King of England, Scotland, and Ireland (1689–1702); and Mary II, Queen of England, Scotland, and Ireland (1689–1694)	Whigs: originally, during the Exclusion Crisis, they argued against James's succession and for parliamentary rather than monarchical prerogative; the "Glorious Revolution" of 1688, which supplanted James with the Protestant William of Orange, constituted their first triumph; the establishment of the Hanoverian line in 1714 enabled them to monopolize power over the ensuing decades.
Anne, Queen of Great Britain and Ireland (1702–1714)	
THE HANOVERIANS	
George I, King of Great Britain and Ireland (1714–1727)	
George II, King of Great Britain and Ireland (1727–1760)	Robert Walpole (1721–1742) Whig
George III, King of the United Kingdom of Great Britain and Ireland (1760–1820)	William Pitt the Elder (1766–1768) Whig
	William Pitt the Younger (1804–1806) Tory

Queen Anne

Robert Walpole

TIMELINE

1660 Charles II restored as king; the Act of Indemnity and Oblivion extends a general pardon to nearly all participants in the Civil War and the Interregnum administrations.

1664–1667 The Second Anglo-Dutch War, fought over trade routes and rights, ends with Dutch ships entering the Thames and destroying much of the English fleet.

1660 Pepys begins his diary (page 2010).

1660 The Royal Society is founded (page 2039).

1665–1666 Bubonic Plague breaks out in London one last time, killing approximately 57,000 (some 14% of the city's population).

1666 The Great Fire of London destroys 13,200 houses, 87 churches, and most municipal and guild buildings in the city, but leaves western London (site of the royal palace, government buildings, and fashionable town life) intact.

1668 Aphra Behn's *Oroonoko* (page 2137)

1673 The First Test Act excludes nonmembers of the Church of England (i.e., Catholics and Dissenters) from holding public office.

1675 William Wycherley's *The Country Wife* (page 2215)

1679 The Popish Plot, an adroitly fabricated conspiracy theory, propagates the conviction that Jesuits are planning, by means of assassination and invasion, to establish Catholic rule in England.

1679–1681 In the Exclusion Crisis, a large parliamentary faction attempts (unsuccessfully) to bar the king's Catholic brother from succession.

1681 John Dryden's *Absalom and Achitophel* (page 2077)

1685 Charles II dies; accession of James II.

1687 Sir Isaac Newton publishes *Principia Mathematica*, the founding text of modern physics.

1688–1689 The "Glorious Revolution": William of Orange conducts a virtually bloodless invasion-by-invitation; James II's escape to France enables Parliament to construe his throne as "vacant" and to ratify the accession of William and his wife Mary (James's daughter) as William III and Mary II.

1689 The Toleration Act permits dissenters (but not Catholics or Unitarians) to worship in authorized meeting houses.

1690 John Locke's *Essay Concerning Human Understanding* (page 2618)

1694 Founding of the Bank of England. Mary II dies.

1700 Mary Astell's *Reflections on Marriage* (page 2284)

1701–1713 The War of the Spanish Succession is fought by the British, Dutch, and Germans against the French and Spanish in hopes of preventing an expansion of French hegemony.

1701 The Act of Settlement bypasses 50 Catholic claimants to the English throne, and grants the succession to Sophia, Electress of Hanover (first cousin to Charles II) and her heirs; James II dies in exile.

1702 William III dies; accession of Queen Anne (Mary II's younger sister)

1707 The Act of Union unites the kingdoms of England and Scotland under the name of Great Britain.

1708 Sir Christopher Wren designs St. Paul's Cathedral, and about 50 new churches, to replace the 86 destroyed by the Great Fire.

1711 Alexander Pope's *An Essay on Criticism* (page 2441)

1713 The Treaty of Utrecht concludes the War of the Spanish Succession, and grants Britain the *asiento*—the exclusive right to supply slaves to the Spanish empire.

1714 Queen Anne dies; accession of George I, Elector of Hanover.

1715 The Jacobite rebellion in support of James II's son ("The Old Pretender") fails.

1717 Lady Mary Wortley Montagu's *Turkish Embassy Letters* (page 2544)

1719 Daniel Defoe's *Robinson Crusoe* (page 2793)

1720 Stock in the South Sea Company rises sharply, then plummets; the bursting of the "Bubble" plunges many into ruin.

1721 Robert Walpole, credited with engineering a post-Bubble recovery and appointed First Lord of the Treasury and Chancellor of the Exchequer, creates the Whig administrative "machine" that will enable him to monopolize power for the next two decades.

1726 Jonathan Swift's *Gulliver's Travels* (page 2371)

1727 George I dies; accession of George II.

1728 John Gay's *Beggar's Opera*, a pioneering piece of musical theater that unexpectedly becomes one of the most successful and enduring entertainments of the century (page 2557)

1735 William Hogarth's *Rake's Progress* (page 2605)

1739–1748 The War of the Austrian Succession is fought on fronts in Europe, America, and India.

1742 Walpole resigns.

1745 The "Forty-Five," a sustained Jacobite uprising led by the "Young Pretender" Charles Edward Stuart (James II's grandson), ends in defeat at the Battle of Culloden.

1750s Strawberry Hill, designed by Horace Walpole and friends, helps spark the Gothic revival.

1755 Samuel Johnson's *Dictionary of the English Language* (page 2704)

1756–1763 The Seven Years' War entailing for the British considerable conquest in Europe, Canada, and India

1757 Robert Clive, a leading force of the East India Company, defeats the army of the Bengali leader Siraj ud-Daula at the Battle of Plassey, consolidating the Empire's hold on India.

1760 George II dies; accession of George III.

1772 The practice of slavery is declared illegal within Britain, but continues legally within the British Empire until the Slave Trade Act of 1807.

1776 The American War of Independence begins.

1778 The Roman Catholic Relief Act permits Catholic worship.

1780 Lord George Gordon, petitioning for the repeal of the Catholic Relief Act, triggers the most violent riots in British history.

1781 The American War of Independence ends.

1787–1795 The impeachment and trial of Warren Hastings, governor-general of Bengal, focuses attention on questions of ethics, exploitation, and empire in British India.

1789 The French Revolution begins.

The Restoration and the Eighteenth Century

On 25 May 1660, Charles II set foot on the shore of Dover and brought his eleven-year exile to an end. The arrival was recorded by the great diarist Samuel Pepys, and his words preserve for us a form of the event:

> I went, and Mr. Mansell, and one of the King's footmen, with a dog that the King loved (which beshat the boat, which made us laugh, and methink that a king and all that belong to him are but just as others are), in a boat by ourselves, and so got on shore when the King did, who was received . . . with all imaginable love and respect at his entrance upon the land of Dover. Infinite the crowd of people and the horsemen, citizens, and noblemen of all sorts. The Mayor of the town came and gave him his white staff, the badge of his place, which the King did give him again. The Mayor also presented him from the town a very rich Bible, which he took and said it was the thing that he loved above all things in the world. . . . The shouting and joy expressed by all is past imagination.

Pepys captures and creates a brilliant mix of materials and experiences: his words compound jubilation and skepticism, images of authority and obeisance, tropes of spirituality and irony, and they remind us of the elements and passions by which all mortals live. Every gesture and exchange in this scene forecast the world to come, but what most signals the future is the paradox of remembering and forgetting that the diarist performs even as he records this scene. And all who witnessed the King's descent at Dover committed similar acts of memory and oblivion. Many of those (Pepys included) who were drunk with pleasure at the return of Charles Stuart had endorsed the destruction of his father eleven years before. The entire Restoration and the events that would follow over the ensuing years would prove a complex unfolding of memory and forgetfulness.

The jubilant crowds at Dover thought to make flux stop here: forever to banish the turbulence of civil war and political innovation, to restore all the old familiar forms, utterly to erase what had come between the death of the father and the restoration of the son. Charles II would soon institute an Act of Oblivion to those ends, forgiving proponents of rebellion by officially forgetting their misdeeds. But civil war and revolution would not be erased, nor could monarchy, the Anglican Church, aristocratic privilege, political patronage, and the old social hierarchies be revived as though nothing had intervened. Much of the old was brought back with the return of the Stuart monarchy, but the consequence of layering the present over a willfully suppressed past was an instability of feelings and forms that ensured the ever-changing triumph of different memories and different oblivions during the ensuing decades. No one celebrating the return of ancient ways in 1660 could have foreseen the ruptures and innovations that lay ahead in the next half of the century, when crises of conspiracy and the birth of party politics would produce further shifts in monarchy through a sequence of

No one celebrating the return of ancient ways in 1660 could have foreseen the ruptures and innovations that lay ahead in the next half of the century . . .

three ruling houses from three different countries. But even in 1660 the innocent acclaim on the shores of Dover was accompanied by hidden guilts and ironies, by vindictive desires, even for some by millenarian hopes. And while such stresses and tensions were unacknowledged in May 1660, they soon enough surfaced, and they unsettled not only the pleasures of this king's rule but the politics of an entire age.

MONARCHS, MINISTERS, EMPIRE

The coronation of Charles II in May 1661 marked the beginning of both the first and the eleventh year of his rule. The King's laws were named as if he had taken possession of the crown at the moment of his father's execution in 1649. And fictions, legal and not so legal, were to prove a hallmark of Stuart rule. The King openly proclaimed his love of parliaments, his devotion to the immemorial constitution of balance and moderation, his Protestant fervor, and his pious hopes for a national church. Yet he often postponed his parliaments; he claimed a tender conscience for Protestant dissenters, but he maneuvered for the toleration of Roman Catholics; he conducted an aggressive, nationalist program against European powers, but he signed a secret and deeply compromising treaty with Louis XIV; he took communion in the Anglican Church, but on his deathbed he sealed his own conversion to Catholicism; he was tenderly affectionate to his barren queen, yet he publicly flaunted his whoring tastes; he repeatedly exiled his unpopular brother James, Duke of York, while promoting and indulging his own bastard sons, yet he staunchly resisted any effort to displace his brother from the line of succession. The dominance of masquerade surely derived from Charles's temper, but fiction and falsehood were also the structural principles and aesthetic features of an entire world.

> *. . . fictions, legal and not so legal, were to prove a hallmark of Stuart rule.*

In December 1678, a series of events started to unfold that proved the very emblem of the masking, the fears, and the psychology of Charles II's rule. It began with legal depositions: one Titus Oates, a baker's son and self-anointed savior of a Protestant people, claimed to have knowledge of a secret plot to kill the King, crown his Catholic brother, and begin the wholesale conversion of English souls—and, just as frightening, English properties—to Rome. Oates offered to a public hungry for scandal and change a Popish plot and a familiar mix of images and idioms: priests and idols, the Roman Antichrist, conspiracy, murder, and mayhem. His depositions and fabrications played brilliantly on memories of the past and on fears of a future under a Catholic king. Nor did it help that the Duke of York's private secretary, Edward Coleman, was caught with treasonous correspondence in his chamber. The plot seemed compounded of sufficient truths to challenge the stability of the Crown. From the midst of the plot, and under the hand of the Earl of Shaftesbury, a political party emerged that took advantage of Popish facts and fears by proposing the Bill of Exclusion in Parliament, which would have barred the Duke of York and any future Catholic monarchs from the English throne. In the event, the bill failed, Charles died of natural causes, and the Duke succeeded his brother in February 1685.

During James's brief reign, no plots, conspiracies, or political parties proved so costly to his rule as did the new king himself. He succeeded his brother in a mood of surprising public affirmation. At his accession, James returned the embrace of

Anglican England by promising to honor the national church and that most beloved of Protestant properties, a tender conscience. There would be no forcing of religious uniformity in this reign. But soon enough James began to move against Anglican interests: he staffed his army with Catholic officers, he imposed Catholic officials on Oxford University, and he insisted that his Declarations of Toleration be read aloud from the pulpits of Anglican churches. Such a program challenged interest, property, and propriety, and it spelled the quick demise of Catholic rule.

As Duke of York, James had been famed for martial valor. But now, when confronted in November 1688 by the army of his Dutch son-in-law, William of Orange, he fled under cover of night to France. What had in part provoked James's flight were memories of the past—of civil war and of the execution of his father, Charles I. What had provoked the invasion by William of Orange was not merely the specter of Louis XIV hovering behind James's rule or the open presence of Jesuits at James's court. It was the birth of James Francis Edward Stuart, son of James II and Mary of Modena. Protestants would suffer not only the inconvenience of one Catholic monarch but the possibility of an endless Catholic succession. The prospect was too much to bear. Secret negotiations were begun between powerful English artistocrats—Whigs and Tories alike—and William, the governor (stadholder) of Holland, resulting in what many called the Glorious Revolution. But the deceits and pretenses—the gaps and silences—of this palace coup did not strike all contemporaries as glorious. The stadholder who chased a Catholic king from England was not only an invading hero (though some did call him William the Conqueror), he

> . . . the deceits and pretenses—the gaps and silences—of this palace coup did not strike all contemporaries as glorious.

was also the son-in-law of James II. Those who clung to the binding ties of loyalty and gratitude accused William and Mary of deep impiety, indeed, of parricide.

But the astonishing invitation to William of Orange produced no bloodshed. What it did produce was a Protestant monarchy under the rule of King William III and Queen Mary. Members of Parliament, meeting to invent the laws that would sanctify this revolutionary change, decided that it would be best to say they had discovered the throne of England mysteriously vacant and that this William was no conqueror but a rightful claimant on a vacant throne. Of course, not everyone was pleased by such a revolution—sacred oaths had been broken, binding ties were cast aside, vows were juggled as mere words. Those who would not accept a convenient revolution were called Jacobites, that is, supporters of King James (*Jacobus* in Latin); they remained a force that would trouble British political life by threatening a Stuart restoration in the fervent but failed Jacobite rebellions of 1715 and 1745.

Most of William's subjects, though, were content with the evasions of this Glorious Revolution. Many were not content, though, with the program of European war in which the English were now plunged by their new king, intent on thwarting the ambitions of Louis XIV, his lifelong nemesis. The ruinous expense of war demanded taxes and fiscal innovation; it produced a stream of grumbling satire, complaint against Dutch favorites, and more than one conspiracy and attempted assassination. No such disaffection or turbulence disturbed the reign (1702–1714) of William's successor, Queen Anne. Her years were the twilight of Stuart monarchy, a time of political nostalgia and commercial confidence whose mood the young

Alexander Pope captured in the lines of *Windsor-Forest* (1713), where softened memories and strategic elisions of the years of Stuart rule are mingled with images of triumph—of imperial expansion and a swelling commerce of domestic and foreign trade.

But luxury was not England's only import. At the death of Queen Anne, an entire court and new ruling house were shipped to England from the German state of Hanover. George I was the grandson of James I; beyond lineage, George's communion in a Protestant church was the virtue that most recommended his succession. He spoke no English, knew nothing of his new subjects, and could not be bothered to learn. Nor was he much implicated in the management of a state whose rule would successively become less the prerogative of kings than the business of ministers and the function of parties, interest, and corruption. This displacement of monarch by minister was cemented during the period caustically nicknamed "Robin's Reign": two decades (1721–1742), transversing the reigns of George I and George II, when politics were dominated by Robert Walpole, who bought loyalties, managed kings, and ran the state with such ruthless efficiency as to earn him the new label "prime minister" (the phrase was meant as an insult, aimed at the perceived excess of his power in a government where ministers were only supposed to advise their colleagues and their king). The South Sea Bubble, a state-endorsed investment scheme that ruined many, was the making of Robert Walpole. As the only cabinet minister untainted by the scandal (he had initially argued against the scheme, then lost money in it), he was put in charge of the subsequent governmental housecleaning. Once empowered, he cheerfully shed his scruples, devising a political machine fueled by patronage that made his cronies rich, his opposition apoplectic. By the firmness of his rule and the prudence of his policies, Walpole consolidated a long period of Whig supremacy that supplanted the party contest of the preceding decades, when Whigs and Tories had seesawed more swiftly in and out of power.

> *. . . politics were dominated by Robert Walpole, who bought loyalties, managed kings, and ran the state with such ruthless efficiency as to earn him the new label "prime minister" . . .*

The parties had begun to crystallize during the Exclusion crisis of the early 1680s, when Whigs fought to bar the king's Catholic brother from the throne and Tories upheld the established continuity of the Stuart line. Like "prime minister," the two party names began as insult, "Tory" denoting an Irish-Catholic bandit, "Whigs" identifying a group of Scottish rebels during the civil wars. Late in the eighteenth century, Samuel Johnson summed up their polarities: "The prejudice of the Tory is for establishment; the prejudice of the Whig is for innovation." "Establishment" meant preserving monarchic prerogatives, upholding the Anglican church, lamenting the advent of the Hanoverians, and—for some Tories, not all—actively yearning for the restoration of the Stuart line and abetting the attempts to achieve this in the Jacobite rebellions of 1715 and 1745. Whig "innovation" entailed enthusiastic support for both the Glorious Revolution and the House of Hanover, for policies of religious tolerance, and for all measures that advanced the interests of the newly prosperous and powerful merchant class. In the late seventeenth century, party politics had begun for the first time to supplant long-running religious conflicts as the main articulation of interest and power. For all its noise and rage, the new structure produced a paradoxical calm, not by the suppression of difference but by its recognition. The division into parties amounted to a sanctioned fragmentation of the whole. Even during the reign of Anne, when party conflict was at its most feverish, what the machinery of party seemed to ensure was the containment of partisan interest within the dynamic, even organic, coherence of the state.

During Walpole's "reign," portions of the two parties coalesced in an uneasy alliance. The arrogance, obstinacy, and efficacy of Walpole's methods galvanized an opposition consisting of both Tories and alienated Whigs; their endeavors acquired luster from the contributions of a remarkable array of writers (the Tories Jonathan Swift, Alexander Pope, John Gay, and Henry Fielding, and the Whig James Thomson) who opposed the prime minister on grounds of personality, principle, and of course self-interest. Walpole, recognizing that the best writers worked for the opposition, strove to suppress them by all the strategies of censorship he could devise. But by his greatness as a character and his force as an opponent, Walpole loomed for a long while as both literature's nemesis and its muse.

In fact, Walpole enforced the policies endorsed by only a fraction of his party—those moderate Whigs deeply interested in cultivating the country's wealth by commerce, deeply resistant to waging war. "My *politics*," he once wrote emphatically, "*are to keep free from all engagements, as long as we possibly can*"; by "engagements," he meant military commitments abroad. By the late 1730s, he discovered that he could keep free from them no longer. Britons feared that powers on the Continent—Spain, Austria, and above all France—were encroaching on their rights, and the popular clamor to wage European war prevailed. "When trade is at stake," the oppositionist William Pitt warned the British, "it is your last retrenchment; you must defend it or perish." Under the pressure of such sentiments Walpole eventually resigned, having led the state through two decades of comparative peace, growing national prosperity, and a new stability in government, but leaving behind him an army and a

> . . . with trade at stake and the navy rebuilt, Britain embarked on a series of wars that ran almost unbroken for the rest of the century.

navy debilitated by disuse. Nonetheless, with trade at stake and the navy rebuilt, Britain embarked on a series of wars that ran almost unbroken for the rest of the century. Pitt presided brilliantly over many of them, wars waged directly or indirectly against France for trading privileges and territories abroad. By 1763, Britain had secured possession of Bengal in India, many islands and coastal territories in the Caribbean, and virtually all of North America (including Canada) east of the Mississippi, as well as half of all the international trade transpiring on the planet. So great was the impetus toward empire that even Britain's humiliating defeat in the American War of Independence (1775–1783) could not really halt the momentum; territories in India were still expanding, and settlement of Australia lay in the offing.

By now, the throne was occupied by the first Hanoverian monarch born in Britain—George III. His long reign (1760–1820) teemed with troubles: the popular scorn for his chosen ministers, the loss of the American war, the aftershocks of the French Revolution, the defiance of his heirs, the torments of his own slow-encroaching madness. But almost from beginning to end he ruled over the richest nation and the widest empire in the world. In 1740, a new song could be heard with a catchy refrain: "Rule, Britannia, rule the waves / Britons never will be slaves." The words were the work of the Scots-born poet James Thomson, now a proud adherent of "Britannia" by virtue of the Act of Union (1707), which had fused Scotland with England and Wales into a new nation, newly named: Great Britain. Over the ensuing years the song took hold partly because of the seductively prophetic ways in which it forecast Britain's greatness and partly because of the proud but peculiar resonances of the refrain's last line. There, Thomson contrasts British liberties with the slave-like constraints supposedly suffered by subjects of absolute monarchy elsewhere. Less directly, "slaves" also points to those peoples upon whose subjugation British privilege and British prosperity were increasingly to depend. Throughout the century, Britons profited spectacularly from the capture, transport, sale, and labor of African slaves in current and former colonies; "no nation," William Pitt the Younger proclaimed in 1792, had "plunged so deeply into this guilt as Great Britain."

There were also whole populations whose condition often evoked the analogy of slavery in the minds of the few who paid reformist attention to their plight: the oppressed indigenous peoples of the colonies, and women and the poor at home. Conversation about such issues became louder and more purposeful near the end of the eighteenth century, as particular champions began to turn social questions into moral causes: John Wilkes on the widening of liberties and voting rights; Mary Wollstonecraft on the rights of women; William Blake (and later, William Cobbett) on the economic inequities of the whole social structure. The problems themselves did not even begin to find redress until the following century, but the emergence of such advocacies, quickened by the audacities of the French Revolution, marked a turning point toward the Romanticism that seized poetic and political imaginations in the 1790s. For most Britons of the eighteenth century, however, the new prosperity produced no special promptings of conscience. As their Restoration forebears had actively encouraged oblivion in an effort to anesthetize themselves to their past, men and women now sustained a moral and social oblivion that eased their use of others and their pleasure in new wealth. Out of such adroitly managed oscillations, Britons fabricated a new sense of themselves as a nation and an empire.

. . . particular champions began to turn social questions into moral causes . . .

This new construct was in large measure the work of a prominent breed of economic architects: the capital-wielding middle classes. For centuries, wealth had derived primarily from land: tenant farmers performed the labor; the landed gentry collected the often enormous profits. The new wealth was amassed, even created, by people situated between these two extremes, constituting what was often referred to as "the middling rank," "the middling station," or "the middling orders." What set the middling orders apart was the comparatively new way in which they made their money: not by landed inheritance, not by tenancy or wage work, but by the adroit deployment of money itself. Having acquired a sum by inheritance, wage, or loan, they used it as capital, investing it, along with their own efforts, in potentially lucrative enterprises: in shops, in factories, and in the enormous new financial structures (banks, stocks) that underwrote the nation's economic expansiveness. They hired helpers, reinvested profits, and when their schemes succeeded, they made their money grow. With wealth, of course, grew clout. The interests of the "City"—that is, of the eastern half of London where bustling merchants made their deals—increasingly shaped the affairs of state, the appetites for empire. Empire also shaped the progress of the arts.

Members of the middle class became the chief consumers and energetic producers of the period's most conspicuous new forms of literature: newspapers and novels. But nowhere were the new powers of the burgeoning bourgeoisie more striking than in the theater, that cultural site they often visited and ultimately revised.

MONEY, MANNERS, AND THEATRICS

No event more exactly and more economically signals the return of an aristocratic court to the center of English culture than the reopening of the London theaters in 1660. The intimacy, indeed the complicity, of court with theater throughout the early modern period was such that when in the 1640s Parliament took aim at monarchy, aristocracy, and privilege, it not only struck off the heads of the Earl of Strafford and Archbishop Laud, it also banished play acting and shut tight the doors of the London stage. But Puritans could not banish the theater from the English imagination, and no sooner were the playhouses closed than publishers issued new editions of old plays and the theater made a secret return in domestic spaces and before private audiences. Print and memory would be the preservative of an entire culture. In 1660, monarchy and theater were restored in tandem. But this artistic restoration, like the political one that made it possible, irresistibly mingled the old with the new. Pepys captured all the excitement and splendor of this restoration; as usual he proves adroit at reckoning innovation:

> [T]he stage is now . . . a thousand times better and more glorious than heretofore. Now, wax-candles, and many of them; then, not above three pounds of tallow. Now, all things civil, no rudeness anywhere; then, as in a bear garden. Then, two or three fiddlers; now, nine or ten of the best. Then, nothing but rushes upon the ground and everything mean; and now all otherwise. Then the Queen seldom and the King never would come; now not the King only for state but all civil people do think they may come as well as any.

One reason that "all civil people" thought so was a matter of simple geography. Whereas the theaters of Shakespeare's day had been located in seedy districts on the outskirts of the city, this new and sumptuous theatrical world was ensconced in new neighborhoods strategically located for maximum social confluence, on the border between Westminster—home of the court—and the City of London, dwelling place of a "mighty band of citizens and prentices" whose sudden convergence with royalty seemed a dramatic innovation. They had all gathered to witness the most astonishing new spectacle of all: women on stage in a public theater.

Before the Restoration, aristocratic women had tantalized the court in private and privileged masquing; now the pleasures of display and consumption were democratized in several ways. For women, theatricality was no longer a pastime reserved for the very few but a plausible—though precarious—profession. For audiences at the new theaters, actresses represented the possibility of erotic spectacle for the price of a ticket—a chance to gaze on women who everyone knew were managing the pleasures, and often the policies, of kings and courtiers. Inevitably new strategies of theatricality suffused this audience, where women might model seductive conduct on the teasing combinations of concealment and display enacted before them. Pepys eavesdropped on the libertine Sir Charles Sedley in urgent banter with two women: "And one of the women would and did sit with her mask on, all the play. He would fain know who she was, but she would not tell; yet did give him many pleasant hints of her knowledge of him, by

The traffic between revelation and concealment defined this theater.

that means setting his brains at work to find out who she was, and did give him leave to use all means but pulling off her mask." Display and disguise not only animated the stage, they quickened social exchange in the intimate spaces of stalls and boxes. The traffic between revelation and concealment defined this theater. It drove the plots of plays and galvanized audiences, modeling and scripting their fashions, their language, their lives.

In such a world the theater provided a national mask, a fantasy of empire and heroism, and yet at the same time sustained a critique of masquerade, a brutal exposure of deceptions rampant in the culture. On the one hand, the heroic drama displayed, indeed reveled in, outsized acts of conquest in exotic lands, valor, and virtue: on stage, princes slaughtered infidels by the thousands; virgins sustained honor through impossible ordeals of abduction and assault. Yet in 1667, at the same moment such dramas were thriving in the king's and the duke's playhouses, the royal fleet was being burned and sunk by a Dutch navy that breached all defenses, invading the very precincts and privacy of London's docks and shipyards. And while the fleet burned, the king busied himself with other depredations, sustaining a series of intrigues, some with the very actresses who wore such incomparable honor and virtue on the stage. (The mix of myth and mischief was popular in pictures too—for example, in the portrait of Barbara Villiers, Countess of Castlemaine, perhaps the most notorious of all the king's mistresses, gotten up in the guise of Minerva, Roman goddess of wisdom; see Color Plate 20.) The heroic drama celebrated military conquest and colonial glory, and displayed them at a moment in national history that produced nothing so much as shame and humiliation: defeat at the hands of Dutch ships and Dutch commerce.

At the same time, but in a far different dramatic mode, the stage sustained a brilliant critique of a whole culture of incongruity, masquerade, and self-delusion. Restoration comedy took as its subject appetite and opportunism, social hypocrisy and sexual power play. The London audience watched scenes of seduction and connivance set in the very vicinities they had traversed to reach the playhouse: St. James's Park, Covent Garden. Such aristocratic libertines as Sir Charles Sedley and Lord Rochester, intent on their own intrigues, might admire themselves in a theatrical mirror, where the rake-hero conducted endless parry-and-thrust with his equals, brutalized his inferiors, and laid hands and claim on any moveable object of desire: fruits and foodstuffs, silks and sonnets, housemaids and women of high estate. But the rakes in the playhouse might see themselves mocked as well. The best comic writers—Wycherley, Etherege, Behn, Congreve—showed the libertines equaled and often bested in cunning by the women they pursued, baffled where they would be most powerful, enslaved where they would be most free. In brilliant volleys of dialogue, these lovers mixed passion and poison in

. . . Restoration comedy, in an astounding fugue of excesses and depravities, laid bare the turbulence and toxins of this culture.

volatile measures, chasing one another through a maze of plots, counterplots, and subplots so convoluted as to suggest a world of calculation run mad. Over the thirty years of its triumphs, Restoration comedy, in an astounding fugue of excesses and depravities, laid bare the turbulence and toxins of this culture.

That the heroic drama, with all its exaggerations and flatteries, found a market is hardly surprising; what is more puzzling is the commercial triumph of Restoration comedy, a theatrical mode that entertained by punishing and humiliating its audience—though it is hardly surprising that this theater should itself have fallen victim in the 1690s to prudery and what would come to be called "taste." In the wake of the Protestant revolution of 1688, which typed Stuart rule as the very emblem of self-indulgence, agents of moral improvement and social propriety made their assault on Restoration comedy the stalking horse for a broad program of Christian reform. Restoration comedy, which had erupted as a repudiation of Puritan prohibitions, now seemed to prompt a new wave of moral rectitude.

Under such pressures, the playhouse redirected its mirror away from the aristocracy toward the upper strata of the "middling sort": London merchants, colonial profiteers. During the Restoration, the newly prosperous mercantile classes who converged with courtiers at the theater had watched themselves either derided or ignored on stage, their social pretensions and ineptitudes put down in the comedies, their commercial concerns absent from the heroic drama. In the early eighteenth century, they saw themselves glorified instead, in "domestic tragedy," which displayed the tribulations of commercial households, and in sentimental comedy, which sought by a mix of tears and modest laughter to inculcate family values and to portray the merchant class as the nation's moral core. Richard Steele's *The Conscious Lovers* (1722) sounded the fanfare for a newly theatric social self-conception. "We merchants," a businessman informs an aristocrat, "are a species of gentry that have grown into the world this last century, and are as honorable and almost as useful as you landed folk, that have always thought yourself so much above us."

Nor was the stage the only venue to promulgate this new cultural self-awareness. By its very title *The Spectator* (1711–1713), one of the most widely read periodicals of the century, assured its largely middle-class audience that they moved under the constant, thoughtful scrutiny of a virtual playgoer, the paper's fictive author, "Mr. Spectator," who made all London a kind of theater, in which he (and his eagerly imitative readers) might perpetually enjoy the privileges of making observations and forming judgments. The very energies that had been drained away from the stage now found a new home in the theatricalized world of commerce, fashion, manners, taste.

The cast members in this new theater were numerous, varied, and eager for direction, mostly because, as a "new species of gentry," they aspired to roles for which they had formerly been deemed unfit. Terms like "esquire" and "gentleman" had operated in previous centuries as proof of literal "entitlement." They were secured by registration with the College of Heralds, and they calibrated not merely monetary wealth but lineage, landholdings, education, and social standing. In the eighteenth century, men and women with sufficient money and nerve assumed these titles for themselves, confident enough that they might learn to play the part. "In our days," noted a 1730 dictionary, "all are accounted gentlemen that have money." But since the "money" was now so variously attainable—by shopkeeping, by manufacture, by international trade—the "middle station" was itself subdivided into many strata, and since the very point of capital was accumulation and improvement, ascent by emulation became a master plot in the new social theater. "Everyone," observed one commentator, "is flying from his inferiors in pursuit of his superiors, who fly from him with equal alacrity."

Wigs, fans, scarves, silks, petticoats, and jewels; china, silver, family portraits—these were the costumes, these the props of the new commercial theater . . .

Amid the flux, fashion and commodity—what one wore, what one owned—mattered enormously. Wigs, fans, scarves, silks, petticoats, and jewels; china, silver, family portraits—these were the costumes, these the props of the new commercial theater, by which members of the middle orders pleased themselves and imitated the gentry. The commercial classes who had begun by catering to the aristocracy gradually became, in their waxing prosperity, their own best customers, selling garb and goods to one another. Shrewd marketers saw that novelty itself possessed an intrinsic and urgent appeal for people constantly in social flight, tirelessly engaged in remaking themselves. Advertising came into its own, filling the pages and underwriting the costs of the daily, weekly, and monthly periodicals. The listing of consumables became a prevalent mode of print, in everything from auction catalogues (the still-dominant houses of Christie's and Sotheby's got their start near the middle of the century) to poems and novels, where long lists of products and possessions became a means of recording the culture's appetites, and at times of satirizing them. In the hands of Swift and Pope, the catalogue itself became a form of art. The taste in literary miscellany reflected a more general taste for omnivorous consumption: variety indexed abundance and proved power. Tea from China, coffee from the Caribbean, tobacco from Virginia—all were relatively new, comparatively inexpensive, and enormously popular. In daily rituals of drink and smoke, the middling orders imbibed and inhaled a pleasing sense of their global reach, their comfortable centrality on a planet newly commercialized.

Commodities formed part of a larger discourse, involving speech and gesture as well as prop and costume. A cluster of precepts, gathered under the umbrella-term

A cluster of precepts, gathered under the umbrella-term "politeness," supplied the stage directions, even at times the script, for the new social theater . . .

"politeness," supplied the stage directions, even at times the script, for the new social theater in which everyone was actor and everyone was audience. Eager to shine in their recently acquired roles, the merchant classes pursued the polish implicit in the word "polite." They hired "dancing masters" to teach them graceful motions and proper manners, "bear leaders" (tutors) to guide their sons on the Grand Tour of France and Italy in the footsteps of the nobility, elocution coaches to help them purge inappropriate accents, teachers of painting and music to supply their daughters with marriageable competence. For the newly prosperous, politeness was the epitome of distinction: it went beyond gesture and accomplishment to suggest a state of mind, a refinement of perception, a mix of knowledge, responsiveness, and judgment often summarized as "taste." "The man of polite imagination," said the *Spectator*, "is let into a great many pleasures that the vulgar are not capable of receiving." Eager to gain access, middle-class readers avidly sought instruction.

Politeness (which Samuel Johnson once defined as "fictitious benevolence") required considerable self-control; the passions (rage, greed, lust) were to be contained and channeled into the appearance of abundant and abiding goodwill. The middle classes embraced such constraints partly to allay widespread suspicion of their

Color Plate 20 Theatricality Disseminated. Sir Peter Lely, *Barbara Villiers, Countess of Castlemaine*, c. 1665. Charles II's favorite painter portrays Charles II's favorite mistress, in costume as Minerva, Roman goddess of wisdom, against a stormy background. Castlemaine's countenance was reproduced in less costly ways as well, in engravings from Lely's portraits that made the visage of the King's mistress possessible by ordinary mortals. The diarist Samuel Pepys records a visit to Lely's sumptuous studio, where he "saw the so-much-by-me-desired picture of my Lady Castlemaine, which is a most blessed picture and that I must have a copy of." (*The Royal Collection* © 2005, Her Majesty Queen Elizabeth II.)

Color Plate 21 Theatricality Domesticated. Johann Zoffany, *Queen Charlotte with Her Two Eldest Sons*, 1764. A century after Lely painted the king's mistress in the garb of the goddess of wisdom (Color Plate 20), such mythological trappings are reduced to dress-up for George III's two young sons at play. Amid sumptuous furnishings, Zoffany's conversation piece emphasizes not the grandeur of the royal family but its intimacy and affection; a new era of majesty as "good example" has commenced. (*The Royal Collection* © 2005, Her Majesty Queen Elizabeth II.)

Color Plate 22 Restoration Theatricality Transposed and Transformed. Joshua Reynolds, *Mrs. Abington as "Miss Prue,"* 1771. The comic actress Frances Abington (1737–1815) here traverses time and rank, reincarnating Miss Prue, an "awkward country girl" in William Congreve's late-17th-century comedy *Love for Love* (1695), in garb that epitomizes late-18th-century high fashion. Abington later scored her greatest triumph in a similar role, modeled on Restoration antecedents and crafted especially for her: Lady Teazle, the country wife ardent for London life in Richard Brinsley Sheridan's *School for Scandal. (The Royal Collection © 2005, Her Majesty Queen Elizabeth II.)*

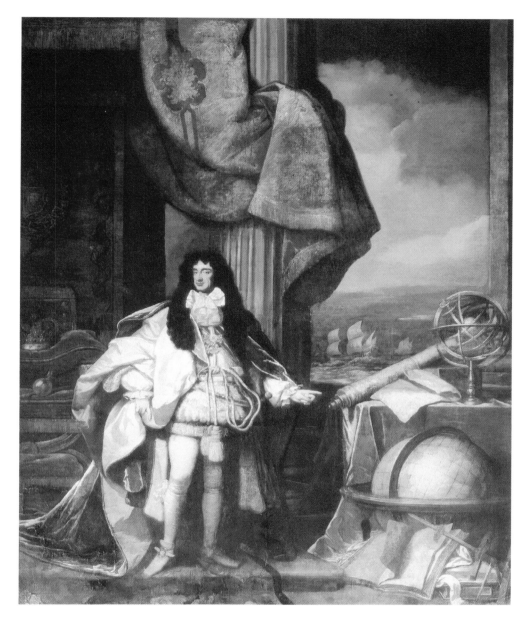

Color Plate 23   Science Enthroned.   Marcellus Laroon, *Charles II as President of the Royal Society*, 1684. In this portrait of the King painted a year before his death, the traditional trappings of royalty—crown, throne, and orb—literally take a back seat (in the background at left) to the advancements of the new science. Charles gestures toward the instruments of seeing, modeling, mapping, and calibrating that the Royal Society he sponsored had done much to devise and develop. By their placement, the painter suggests that these tools make possible the naval commerce and conquest depicted in the distance—as though the telescope were the world's new scepter, and the globe the monarch's proper sphere. *(Picture Desk, Inc./Kobal Collection.)*

Color Plate 24 Science Popularized. Joseph Wright, *A Philosopher Giving That Lecture on the Orrery, in Which a Lamp Is Put in Place of the Sun,* 1766. The experimental philosophy and new science pioneered during the 17th century provided both pleasure and instruction in the 18th, as teachers and textbooks strove to distill and redistribute recondite discoveries as common knowledge. The orrery, a working model of the solar system, figured prominently in this new educational endeavor; it could supply, wrote Richard Steele, "the pleasures of science to any one." The spheres within the circle, coordinated by clockwork, enacted the orbits of the planets and their moons. The sun's stand-in was often a brass ball, but more rarely (as here) a lit oil lamp at the center of the machine. In Wright's painting, the flame sheds light on the lecturer and his listeners, each of them different, all of them enthralled. *(Derby Museums and Art Gallery.)*

Color Plate 25   Science Interrogated.   Joseph Wright, *An Experiment on a Bird in the Air Pump*, 1768. The experiment's purpose is to demonstrate the effects of a vacuum on a breathing creature; its outcome, unless the experimenter restores air to the glass chamber, will be the death of the bird. Such experiments, though widely performed, were deemed by one lecturer "too shocking to every spectator who has the least degree of humanity." This time, Wright depicts a mixture of reactions. The lecturer, gesturing like a conjurer, stares out at the viewer as though in a kind of trance, oblivious both to the bird and to his audience, whose faces and forms variously evince absorption, meditation, distraction, and distress. (*Copyright © National Gallery, London/Art Resource, New York.*)

Color Plate 26 Theatricality Encompasses All. William Hogarth, *The Beggar's Opera*, Act 3, Scene 11, 1792. Audience and actors encounter each other on stage. Hogarth here replicates icons of art history much as *The Beggar's Opera*, a theatrical sensation of 1728, echoed popular ballads. Macheath, the criminal-hero of the play, is shown poised in the center between Lucy (left) and Polly (right)—a grouping that evokes the hero Hercules at his mythic moment of choosing between Virtue and Vice. Meanwhile, Polly and her father, Mr. Peachum (in black at right), strike poses bizarrely reminiscent of Christ and Mary Magdalen. Another kind of pairing is in play too. Lavinia Fenton, the actress playing Polly, gestures not so much toward her stage father as to the audience member standing starstruck just beyond him: the Duke of Bolton, so taken with her in the role that he became her lover and eventually her husband. In this, the fifth version he painted of the same scene, Hogarth has expanded the scope of the stage set so that the prison walls appear to enclose the spectators too within the *Opera*'s bright, bleak world, where everything and everyone have become commodities—objects of desire and items of exchange engulfed in intricate, energetic, precarious transactions. *(The Bridgeman Art Library International.)*

Color Plate 27   Satire Suspended.   William Hogarth, *Hogarth's Servants*, mid-1750s. In this late painting, Hogarth's lifelong brilliancies of satire cede place to an approach both documentary and tender, as he traces, with painstaking attention and evident affection, the faces of six people deeply familiar to him. *(Copyright © Tate Gallery, London/Art Resource, New York.)*

Color Plate 28 Doubled Vision.   Thomas Gainsborough, *Cottage Door with Children Playing*, c. 1788. As the critic John Barrell has pointed out, Gainsborough's painting mingles two different perceptions of the rural poor. The gracious women and boisterous children basking in the day's last light conjure up the sort of sentimental idealization of pastoral joys that also found expression in such poems as Oliver Goldsmith's *The Deserted Village*. George Crabbe's contrapuntal insistence on the misery of the laborer's lot in such works as *The Village* and *The Parish Register* is figured here in the form of the returning husband at bottom left, bent with his burden of firewood and nearly buried by the shadows. *(Cincinnati Art Museum, Given in honor of Mr. and Mrs. Charles F. Williams by their children. Accession #: 1948.173.)*

commercial aggressions, their social ambitions. Their preoccupation with politeness has helped to foster a recurrent misimpression of the period: that, setting aside the occasional rake or wench, it was all manners and morals, dignity and decorum, fuss and formality, reason and enlightenment. Not so. Even among the merchant classes, politeness afforded only provisional concealment for roiling energies; amid the impoverished and the gentry, it held less purchase still. In no succeeding epoch until our own was language so openly and energetically obscene, drunkenness so rampant, sexual conduct so various and unapologetic. Even among the "officially" polite, the very failure of containment could produce a special thrill. In one of the century's most often-used phrases, a speaker announces that "I cannot forbear"—that is, cannot restrain myself—from saying or doing what the verb itself suggests were better left unsaid or undone. The formula declares helpless and pleasurable surrender to an unmastered impulse, and the condition was apparently endemic. James Boswell records the memorable self-summary of an elderly lawyer: "I have tried . . . in my time to be a philosopher, but—I don't know how—cheerfulness was always breaking in." Such "breakings-in" (and breakings-out) of feeling were common, even cherished. The scholar Donald Greene has argued well that the eighteenth century was less an "age of reason" (as has often been said) than an age of exuberance. Certainly much of what the middle classes read and wrote is a literature of outburst: of hilarity, of lament, of rage, of exaltation. The copious diaries that the century brought forth deal in all such exclamations; they are the prose of people who have chosen to write rather than repress the thoughts and actions that strict politeness might proscribe. Even the *Spectator*, that manual of polished taste, presents itself as the daily outpouring of a writer who, after maintaining an eccentric lifelong silence, has found that he can no longer keep his "discoveries"—moral, social, experiential—to himself.

Such self-publicizing was more complex for women than for men. When women represented their own lives—in manuscript (letters, journals) and increasingly in print—they sometimes chafed at the paradoxical mix of tantalizing possibilities and painful limitations that their privilege produced. Post-Restoration prosperity and politeness supplied women with many new venues for self-display and sociability, in playhouses and pleasure gardens, ballrooms, spas, and shops. Society exalted and paraded women as superior consumers: wearing the furs, fragrances, and fabrics of distant climes, they furnished evidence of empire, proud proof of their fathers' and husbands' economic attainments. They consumed print, too; near the start of the eighteenth century, male editors invented the women's periodical and found the new genre immensely profitable. Increasingly, women not only purchased print but produced it, deploying their words and wit as a kind of cultural capital, which when properly expended might reap both cash and fame. During the eighteenth century, for the first time, books by women—of poems, of precepts, and above all of fiction-became not exotic but comparatively commonplace.

Still, books by women remained controversial, as did all manifestations of female autonomy and innovation. The very excitement aroused by women's new conspicuousness in the culture provoked counter-efforts at containment. Preachers and moralists argued endlessly that female virtue resided in domesticity. Marriage itself offered an

Post-Restoration prosperity and politeness supplied women with many new venues for self-display and sociability . . .

age-old instrument of social control, newly retooled to meet the needs of ambitious merchants, for whom daughters were the very currency of social mobility. If parents could arrange the right marriage, the whole family's status promptly rose. The dowry that the bride brought with her was an investment in future possibilities: in the rank and connections that the union secured, in the inheritance that would descend to its heirs, in the annual income ("jointure") that the wife herself would receive following the death of the husband. Financially, a widow (or for that matter, a well-born woman who never married) was often far more independent than a wife, whose wedding led to a kind of sanctioned erasure. She possessed little or no control over marital property (including the wealth she had brought to the union); "in marriage," wrote the codifier of English law William Blackstone, "husband and wife are one person, and that person is the husband." The sums that the husband undertook to hand over to his wife were dubbed "pin money" (a suggestive trivialization): funds for managing the household, that sphere wherein, as the moral literature insisted, a woman might best deploy her innate talents and find her sanctioned satisfactions. These consisted first and foremost in producing children and in shaping their manners and morals. In a time of improvisatory birth control, precarious obstetrics, and high infant mortality, the bearing of children was a relentless, dangerous, and emotionally exhausting process. The upbringing of children provided more pleasure and possessed a new cachet: the conduct literature endorsed busy, attentive child-rearing as the highest calling possible for women whose prosperity freed them from the need to work for wages. (Guidebooks for parents and pleasure books for children both had their origins in the eighteenth century.) Apart from the duties of motherhood and household management—the supervision of servants, meals, shopping, and social occasions—the woman of means was encouraged to pursue those pleasures for which her often deliberately constricted education had prepared her: music, embroidery, letter writing, and talk at the tea table—the domestic counterpart of the clubs and coffeehouses, where women were not permitted to appear.

In the late seventeenth century, the possibilities for women had seemed at moments more various and more audacious. In the plays of Aphra Behn, female characters pursued their pleasures with an almost piratical energy and ingenuity; in *A Serious Proposal to the Ladies* (1694), the feminist Mary Astell imagined academies where women could withdraw to pursue the pleasures of learning and escape the drudgeries of marriage. In the eighteenth century, though, despite women's increasing authorial presence, these early audacities tended to go underground. Protests by women against their secondary status are most overt in manuscript—in the acerbic poems and letters that Mary Wortley Montagu circulated among her friends, in the journal entries wherein the brewer's wife Hester Thrale vented her frustrations. In print, women's desire for autonomy became a tension in the text, rather than its explicit point or outcome. Novelists explored women's psyches with subtlety; their plots, however, nearly always culminated in marriage, and more rarely in catastrophe, as though those were the only alternatives. Even the Bluestocking Circle, an eminent late-century group of intellectual women, preached tenets of essential sexual difference and subordination; they argued (for example) in favor of improving girls' educations, but as a way of preparing them for better and happier

> *In print, women's desire for autonomy became a tension in the text, rather than its explicit point or outcome.*

work within the home rather than for adventures abroad. During the eighteenth century, the middle classes did much to spell out the gendered divison of labor—father as the family's champion in the marketplace, mother as cheerfully efficient angel in the house—that remained a cultural commonplace, among families who could afford it, for the next two hundred years.

Among the poor, such divisions were not tenable; most manual labor paid so little that everyone in the family had to work if all were to survive. Wives not only managed their frugal households, they also worked for wages, in fields, in shops, or in cottage manufacture of fabrics, gloves, basketry. Children often began wage work at age four or five, treading laundry, scaring crows, sweeping chimneys; boys began the more promising role of apprenticeships around the age of ten. For many of the poor, domestic service offered employment comparatively secure and endlessly demanding. Darker prospects included prostitution and crime: shoplifting was punishable by death. In the case of the helplessly indigent, local government was responsible for providing relief, but the Poor Law provided large loop-holes by which the parish could drive out any unwanted supplicant—an unwed mother, for example—who could not meet the intricate and restrictive criteria for legal residence. The poor had no vote, no voice in government; as the century progressed, their predicament attracted increasing attention and advocacy. Philanthropists instituted charity schools designed, in the words of their proponent Hannah More, "to train up the lower classes in habits of industry and piety." Two convictions informed even the most ambitious philanthropy: that poverty was part of a divine plan and that it was the fault of the indolent poor themselves; they thus found themselves caught between the rock of providence and the hard place of reproach. Yet charity schools did increase literacy, and with it perhaps the sense of possibilities. Other late-century developments, too, were mixed. Improvements in sanitation, medicine, and hygiene contributed to a surge in population, which in turn produced among the rural poor a labor surplus: too many people, too little work. At the same time, wealthy landholders increased the practice of "enclosure," acquiring and sequestering acreage formerly used by the poor for common pasturage and family farming. As a result, many rural families left the land on which they had worked for centuries and traveled to alien terrain: the textile mills that capitalists had newly built and the industrial cities developing rapidly around them.

As the poor became poorer, the very rich—landowning lords and gentry—became very much richer, both by the means they now shared with the middle class (capital investment in banks and stocks) and through their own long-held resources. Land increased in value, partly because there were now so many merchant families passionately eager to buy into the landscape and the life of their aristocratic betters, among whom the spectacle of emulation provoked amusement and revulsion. The landed gentry preserved their distance by many means: social practices (they often flaunted their adulteries, for example, as contrast to middle-class proprieties), artistic allegiance (with the advent of the bourgeois drama, aristocratic audiences defected from the theater to the opera house, where elaborate productions and myth-based plots sustained the aristocratic values of the heroic drama), and the sheer ostentation of their leisure and magnitude of their consumption. But the pivotal difference remained political: by the

As the poor became poorer, the very rich—landowning lords and gentry—became very much richer . . .

award of offices, by the control of elections, landowners maintained their stranglehold on local and national power, despite all the waxing wealth of trade.

At the same time, their very absorption in pleasure and power demanded a continual traffic with their inferiors. Merchants and shopkeepers catered to them; professionals managed their transactions; household servants contrived their comforts; aspiring artists sought to cultivate their taste and profit by their patronage. Transactions among the aristocracy and the middle classes took other forms as well. A lord low on money often found it lucrative to marry the daughter of a thriving merchant. And middle-class modes of life could exert a subtler magnetism, too—particularly for George III, who prized mercantile decorum over aristocratic swagger. In the portrait of his queen and her two eldest sons in Color Plate 21, the artist Johann Zoffany (himself an expensive German import) celebrates not their royal state but their domestic felicity: the heroic trappings (helmet, spear, turban) so conspicuous in Lely's portrait of the scandalous Lady Castlemaine (see Color Plate 20) are here reduced to the props of child's play in the domestic theater of family relations.

King George had commissioned Johann Zoffany in pursuit of precisely this effect. By his eager emulation of the middling orders, George III broke with monarchic traditions, but he inaugurated a new one that would be sustained and expanded in various ways by Queen Victoria in the nineteenth century and her successors in the twentieth. During George's reign, too, the middle classes began to pursue more practical convergence with the aristocracy: a wider distribution of voting rights, a firmer political power base. For the first time, the phrase "middle classes" itself came into use, as a way of registering this cohort's recognition of its own coherence and interests, its unique, often combative relations with the classes above and below; the plural ("classes") registered the abiding diversity—of income, of lifestyle—within the cohesion. In the years since the Restoration, the middle classes had moved themselves energetically in the theater of social and economic relations from a place in the audience toward center stage, exerting enormous power over the working lives of the poor, posing challenges to the elite. Increasingly, their money, manners, appetites, and tastes came to be perceived as the essence of national life, as the part that might stand for the whole. "Trade," Henry Fielding remarked in 1751, "has indeed given a new face to the nation."

It gave the nation new momentum, too, literal as well as figurative. The engineering marvels of the eighteenth century—the harnessing of steam power, the innovations in factory design, the acceleration of production—were instruments of capital. So were improvements in the rate of transport. Over the course of the century, the government collaborated with private investors to construct a proliferating network of smooth turnpikes and inland waterways: canal boats delivered coal and other cargo with new celerity; stagecoaches sped between cities on precise schedules with crowded timetables. Timekeeping itself became a source of national wealth and pride. During the 1660s, British clockmakers established themselves as the best in Europe. A century later, the clockmaker John Harrison invented the "marine chronometer," a large watch so sturdy and so precise that it could keep time to the minute throughout a voyage around the world, amid all

The engineering marvels of the eighteenth century—the harnessing of steam power, the innovations in factory design, the acceleration of production—were instruments of capital.

vicissitudes of wind and weather. Harrison's invention made it possible to calculate a ship's longitude accurately, thus solving a problem that had bedeviled navigation for centuries (and sometimes sunk whole fleets). The innovation further paved the way for trade and empire-building, and did much to establish Greenwich, a town just east of London, as the reference point for world timekeeping. Trade was giving a new face—a new distribution of power and priority—not only to the nation but also to the globe, placing Britain (so Britons liked to think) at its center.

FAITH AND KNOWLEDGE, THOUGHT AND FEELING

Clockwork functioned another way too: as a new, theologically unsettling metaphor for the relations between God and his creation. In his *Principia Mathematica* (1687), Isaac Newton set forth the mathematical principles—the laws of motion, the workings of gravity—by which, it turned out, the universe could be seen to operate more consistently and efficiently than even the finest clockwork. What need had this flawless mechanism for any further adjustments by its divine clockmaker? Some of Newton's admirers—though never the pious scientist himself—found in his discoveries the cue for a nearly omnivorous skepticism. The boldest deists and "freethinkers" dismissed Christianity as irrational fiction, to be supplanted by the stripped-down doctrine of "natural religion." In the intricate design of nature they found the proof of a creator whose existence and infinite wisdom, they argued, are all we know on earth and all we need to know. The fashion for such thought—at least in its purest form—proved fleeting. To most minds, the "argument from design" simply furnished further proof of God's benevolence. Amid such comfortable conviction, the blasphemies of a virtuoso skeptic like David Hume appeared an aberration, even an entertainment, rather than a trend. "There is a great cry about infidelity," Samuel Johnson remarked in 1775, "but there are, in reality, very few infidels." From deep belief and ingrained habit, Christianity retained its hold over the entire culture; though a few pietists voiced alarm, science tended to enhance faith, not destroy it.

Still, the relation of religion to public life had changed. In the mid-seventeenth century, politics was inevitably suffused with spirituality. Charles I had gone to the scaffold as an Anglican martyr; he had ruled according to the dictum "No bishop, no king." For many English men and women, the war of Parliament against the king was a holy war: Puritans had typed Charles I as that "man of blood"; Cromwell's army had gone to battle singing David's psalms. By the eighteenth century, ardors had cooled: no one went to war for creed alone. But that is not to say that these were lives bereft of the spiritual; deep religious feeling remained, even as violence of expression abated. The Restoration had reinstated Anglicanism as the national faith; its adherents were admitted to the full privileges of education and office. Over the ensuing century, the Church of England pursued a strategic but controversial mix of old exclusions and new accommodations. For dissenters (offspring of the Puritans), new laws proffered certain permissions (to teach, to congregate for public worship) in exchange for certain oaths. Catholics, by contrast, were kept beyond the pale; they received no such concessions until late in the eighteenth century, when even a limited act provoked angry Protestant riots. Early in the century, the Anglican

> By the eighteenth century, ardors had cooled: no one went to war for creed alone.

faithful were divided between the "high flyers," who perennially claimed that the church was in danger of dilution, and the Latitudinarians, who argued that all kinds of dissent might finally be accommodated within the structure of the church. Latitudinarians prevailed, but as the Church of England broadened, it began to lose the force of its exclusiveness; attendance at services shrank markedly as the century advanced, but alternative forms of communal worship flourished. In the eighteenth century, evangelical religions came to occupy the crucial space of fervent spirituality that the church of Donne and Herbert had once claimed as its own. By midcentury, in the new movement called Methodism, John Wesley expressed a vehement response against the skeptical rationalism of the freethinkers and the monied complacency of the established church. Wesley preached the truth of scriptural revelation. He urged his followers to purge their sins methodically—by a constant self-monitoring, partly modeled on earlier Puritan practices—and enthusiastically, by attending revival meetings, hearing electrifying sermons. Wesley delivered some 40,000 sermons over the course of a phenomenally energetic life, and his no less relentless brother Charles composed some 6,000 hymns to quicken evangelical spirits. Methodism found its most ardent following among the poor, who discovered in the doctrine a sympathy for their condition and a recognition of their worth, epitomized in one of Charles Wesley's verses: "Our Savior by the rich unknown / Is worshipped by the poor alone." Their worship was loud and fervent; intensity of feeling attested authenticity of faith.

The middle class and gentry located their own fervor in the more polished idioms of sentiment and sensibility. The terms named a code of conduct and of feeling current in the mid-eighteenth century, when men and women increasingly came to pride themselves on an emotional responsiveness highly cultivated and conspicuously displayed: tears of pity at the spectacle of suffering, admiration for the achievements of art or the magnificence of nature. For many in the middle class, the cult of sentiment held out the appealing prospect of a democratization of manners; the elaborate protocols of the aristocracy might remain elusive, but pure *feeling* was surely more accessible, to anyone with the leisure and the training. For many women, the cult afforded the added attraction of honoring that very susceptibility to feeling and that renunciation of reason that had long and pejoratively been gendered female. The sufferings of the poor, of children, of animals, became a testing ground for empathy; majestic mountains became favorite proving grounds for heightened response.

The fashion for benevolence helped focus attention on the plight of the poor and the oppressed . . .

The fashion for benevolence helped focus attention on the plight of the poor and the oppressed, prompting new charities and social movements. For many of the conventionally religious, sentimentality became an adjunct article of faith. They found their scriptures in treatises that posited proper feeling as a chief measure of human worth—Adam Smith's *Theory of Moral Sentiments* (1759); in sentimental dramas that modeled the cultivation (and the performance) of elaborate emotion; in novels that paid minute attention to the protagonist's every emotional nuance—Samuel Richardson's *Pamela* (1740–1741) and *Clarissa* (1747–1749), Laurence Sterne's *Life and Opinions of Tristram Shandy* (1759–1767) and *A Sentimental Journey* (1768), Henry Mackenzie's *The Man of Feeling* (1771); in travel books that transported readers geographically and emotionally by charged descriptions of mighty vistas. For both deists and pietists earlier in the century, nature had testified the existence of a God; for connoisseurs of the sublime near century's end, nature itself was beginning to serve as surrogate for the divine.

In the articulation of eighteenth-century faith and science, thought and feeling, the most conspicuous and continuous voice was that of the first person. The "I" was omnipresent, observing world and self alike: in the experiment-reports of the scientists and the thought-experiments of the philosophers; in the Methodists' self-monitoring, the sentimentalist's self-approbation, the sublimity-seekers' recorded raptures; in the copious autobiographical writings—diaries, letters, memoirs—of characters in novels and people in the real world. Always and everywhere, it seems, someone was setting down the nuances of his or her experience. The self-reckoning promulgated in the past by dissenters was now a broad cultural preoccupation. Its dominion may help to explain why the literature of this era famed for the dominance and delight of its conversation returns us, again and again, to a sense of fundamental solitude.

WRITERS, READERS, CONVERSATIONS

The century and a half from the English Civil Wars to the brink of the French Revolution brought startling change to the structures of politics, social relations, scientific knowledge, and the economy, and no change was more intimate to all these revolutions than the transformations in the relations between writers and readers. From our present perspective, perhaps no scene seems more familiar, even eternal, than that of reader with book in hand. We imagine Virgil's readers and Dante's, Austen's and Wilde's, Pound's and Pynchon's similarly situated, alone with a book, communing silently with an oracular author. But these configurations have changed radically from age to age—sometimes driven by shifts in technology, at other times by social changes. In the eighteenth century, the sea change in relations between writers and readers derived from new social transactions and a new marketplace of letters. And this change did much to shape the modern reckoning of the mix of the solitary and the social, the commercial and the therapeutic within the act of reading. In its refiguring of the social contract between writers and readers, the eighteenth century was nearly as eruptive as our own time with its marketplace of e-mail and Internet, where everyone can potentially operate as both consumer and purveyor—and no one knows for sure the shape of literary things to come.

In 1661, the Earl of Argyle wrote to his son with advice on books, their acquisition, and their proper use:

> Think no cost too much in purchasing rare books; next to that of acquiring good friends I look upon this purchase; but buy them not to lay by or to grace your library, with the name of such a manuscript, or by such a singular piece, but read, revolve him, and lay him up in your memory where he will be far the better ornament. Read seriously whatever is before you, and reduce and digest it to practice and observation, otherwise it will be Sisyphus's labor to be always revolving sheets and books at every new occurence which will require the oracle of your reading. Trust not to your memory, but put all remarkable, notable things you shall meet with in your books *sub salva custodia* [under the sound care] of pen and ink, but so alter the property by your own scholia and annotations on it, that your memory may speedily recur to the place it was committed to.

The earl's account displays all the elements of the traditional reading program of Renaissance humanism: book or manuscript as surrogate friend, as "ornament" of the gentleman's mind and library, as "oracle" of enduring truths, as "property" to be possessed, marked, transcribed, and committed to memory. In the decades that followed, all these constructions remained in play, yet every one of the earl's crucial terms broadened in application to include print genres and transactions that Argyle would not have imagined: the periodical review, the monthly miscellany; epistolary fiction; the three-volume novel; as well as the coffeehouses and penny lending libraries that broadly circulated these new forms of print. With these new genres and modes of distribution, the text's status as friend, ornament, oracle, and property changed markedly.

Nothing had demonstrated (some even thought created) the material force and oracular authority of print so much as the English Civil Wars. Sermons and prophecies bearing the names of "oracles" and "revelations" forecast the demise of the Beast, the triumph of Parliament, indeed the imminence of the thousand-year rule of Christ on earth. Nor had the restoration of the Stuart monarchy wholly denatured print as prophecy—royalists and radicals continued to publish apocalyptic claims. And yet, over the ensuing decades the repeated threat of contest and rebellion began to exhaust both the authority of print as prophecy and the appetite of readers for a textual diet of frenzy and apocalypse—not that party warfare in print forms declined, but rather that partisanship yoked political contest to forms of confrontation that cooled apocalyptic tempers and supplanted military combat with paper controversy. The uneven course of government censorship, the issuing and lapsing of the licensing laws that governed press freedom, meant that paper wars with their full armory of ephemera—pamphlets, broadsides, pasquinades—raged at moments of crisis and parliamentary inattention when printers might cash in on the market for opposition and confrontation.

> Satire, that most venerable mode of attack and advocacy, flourished in England as it had in Augustan Rome.

But not all the action of print contest was situated in the gutter of journalism. Satire, that most venerable mode of attack and advocacy, flourished in England as it had in Augustan Rome. Horace and Juvenal were indeed the models for Dryden, Pope, and Swift, who not only translated the forms of Roman satire into native idioms but were themselves possessed by all the Roman delight in outrage and invective, in civic engagement and political contest. But the genius of satire is never solely political. Satirists always score their most important points by wit, by cool savagery, by the thrust and parry of language, by the most brilliant and damaging metaphors and rhymes. Their peers, their rivals, even their enemies ruefully conceded that Dryden, Pope, and Swift had brought the verse couplet and the prose sentence to an unprecedented suppleness and precision. Satire in the years of civil war and Stuart agitations had begun in politics; pamphlet wars, swelled by periodicals, continued to rage through the Georgian age. But the classic verse satire had moved to a more exalted ground where the aesthetic often overwhelmed the political, and satire itself became an object of admiration, even of theorizing, and of the most vivid and polite conversation.

"Conversation" had once meant the entire conduct of life itself; now, "conversation" had narrowed to signify social exchange; yet social exchange in its turn had expanded to govern the conduct of life itself. Many of the most striking literary developments in the period—its poetic modes and tastes, the popularity and prominence of letter and journal writing, the advent of the newspaper and the novel—can perhaps best be understood as new ways devised by writers for performing conversation on the page—conversation with readers, with other writers, and within the texts themselves. The cultural critic Mikhail Bakhtin has pinpointed as one key feature of the novel its "heteroglossia": its capacity to speak, almost concurrently, many different languages, in the various voices and viewpoints of its characters and narrators; the range of its concerns (across social ranks and geographical spaces); even the variabilities of its style (each with its own cultural connotations) from page to page, paragraph to paragraph. But in this respect as in so many, the novel, usually reckoned the greatest literary invention of the period, is the product of a time when virtually all modes of writing were involved with diversity and dialogue.

One of the most popular ways of buying and reading poetry, for example, was in the form of "miscellanies"—anthologies of work by many hands ancient and modern in many modes, brought together in intriguing juxtapositions. Such juxtapositions could also take place within a single poem. For poets, a crucial procedure was the "imitation"—a poem in English that closely echoes the tone, structure, and sequence of a classical model while applying the predecessor's form and thought to contemporary topics. Where the Roman poet Juvenal, for example, begins his tenth Satire by declaring that wise men are hard to find even if you search every country from Spain to India (roughly the extent of the known Roman world), Samuel Johnson begins his imitation of Juvenal's poem (*The Vanity of Human Wishes*) this way:

> Let Observation, with extensive view,
> Survey mankind, from China to Peru . . .

The known world, Johnson tacitly reminds his knowing reader, is much larger than it was when Juvenal wrote (and hence the rarity of discerning mortals will be all the more striking). The opening couplet prepares us for the poem's close, where it will turn out that moral possibilities are larger too: there, Johnson will supplant Juvenal's characteristically Roman resignation to "Fortune" with an expressly Christian reliance on the cardinal virtues (faith, hope, charity) as a means of protection from the delusions of desire. The writer of a poetic imitation always conducts at least a double dialogue: between poet and predecessor, and between the present writer and the ideal reader who knows enough of the "original" to savor the poetic exchange, the cultural cross-talk, in all its echoes, divergences, and diversions.

Johnson here practices a more general kind of imitation as well, by casting his poem in heroic couplets: iambic pentameter lines paired in a sequence of successive rhymes. The rhymed pairs are often "closed," so that the moment of the rhyme coincides with and clinches the completion of a sentence and a thought. The verse form was called "heroic" because of its frequent use in the heroic drama and other high-aspiring poetry of the Restoration; the rhymed, closed pentameter was also thought to imitate, as closely as English allowed, the grandeur and the sonority of the lines in which ancient poets composed their epics. Throughout the century following the Restoration, the heroic couplet prevailed as the most commonly used poetic structure, adaptable to all genres and occasions, deployed by every sort of poet from hacks to John Dryden and Alexander Pope, the supreme masters of the mode. It was in this form that Dryden translated Virgil's *Aeneid* (1697) and Pope translated Homer's *Iliad* (1715–1720) and *Odyssey* (1725–1726),

. . . the mesh of mighty ancient models with trivial modern subjects produced a new mode of satire . . .

it was in this form that they wrote original poems of high seriousness and savage satire, and it was in this form that they aspired (like many of their contemporaries) to write new epics of their own. Neither ever did; both complained intermittently that they lived in an unheroic age. But the mesh of mighty ancient models with trivial modern subjects produced a new mode of satire, the mock-heroic, and disclosed astonishing suppleness in the heroic couplet itself.

In the hands of Dryden, Pope, and many others, the mock mode—high style, low subject matter—performed brilliant accommodations and solved large problems. It allowed poets to turn what they perceived as the crassness of modern culture to satiric advantage. If the triviality of modern life prevented them from recapturing epic grandeur whole, they could at least strive to match the epic's inclusiveness, its capacity to encompass all the things and actions of the world: the accessories of a young woman's dressing table (Pope's *Rape of the Lock*), the clutter in a gutter after rain (Swift's *Description of a City Shower*), the glut of print itself and the folly of those who produce so much bad writing (Pope's *Dunciad*). After Pope's death, though, this vein of mockery seemed exhausted. The heroic couplet persisted in poetry to the end of the century, but other verse forms became prominent too, partly in the service of an even wider inclusiveness, of paying new kinds of attention to modes of life and literature that lay outside the heroic and the mock: the predicament of the poor, the pleasures of domesticity, the discoveries of science, the tones and textures of medieval English balladry, the modalities of melancholy, the improvisatory motions of human thought and feeling. Blank verse—iambic pentameter without rhyme—offered one manifestation of the impulse to open-endedness. James Thomson's *The Seasons* (1730) and William Cowper's *The Task* (1785), huge works in blank verse, are epic in their own kind: they mingle genres and move from topic to topic with the improvisatory energy of a barely stoppable train of thought. They perform the world's miscellany, the mind's conversation with itself and others, in a new poetic language—one that Wordsworth had absorbed by century's end, when he cast his *Prelude* in a capacious blank verse and praised in the preface to *Lyrical Ballads* that kind of poetry which deploys "the real language" of "a man speaking to men."

In the new prose forms of the eighteenth century—both nonfiction and fiction— the dominion of miscellany, the centrality of conversation, is if anything more palpable than in poetry. The first daily newspaper and the first magazines both appeared early in the century, providing a regularly recurrent compendium of disparate items intended to appeal to a variety of tastes and interests. These periodicals formed part of a larger and highly visible print mix: coffeehouses attracted a burgeoning clientele of urbanites by laying out copies of the current gazettes, mercuries, newsletters, playbooks, and satiric verses. Customers took pleasure in the literary montage, the ever-shifting anthology on the tabletops (of which the pictorial medley on page 1980 conveys a vivid visual idea). Coffeehouse customers

Coffeehouse customers gathered to consume new drink and new print in a commerce of pleasure, intellect, and gossip.

gathered to consume new drink and new print in a commerce of pleasure, intellect, and gossip. Some read silently, others aloud to listeners who eagerly seized on texts and topics. Habits of social reading that would have been familiar to Chaucer and his audience (even to Virgil performing his epic at the court of Augustus Caesar) contributed to sociable debate on the persons and personalities of public life, foreign potentates, military campaigns, theatrical rivalries, monsters, and prodigies. In the eighteenth century, the papers and the consequent conversations broadened to encompass questions of personal conduct, relations between the sexes, manner and fashion. Writers of papers still claimed oracular authority: "Isaac Bickerstaff" of the *Tatler* dubbed himself the Censor of Great Britain, Mr. Spectator claimed to watch everyone who read his paper, and the *Athenian Gazette* dispensed advice as though with the authority of a supremely learned society. But writers made such claims at least partly with tongue in cheek; they knew that their oracular "truths" would trickle down into the commerce of conversation.

The press not only stimulated but also simulated conversation. Newspapers had always depended on "correspondents"—not (as now) professional reporters, but local letter writers who sent in the news of their parish and county in exchange for free copies of the paper. To read a newspaper was to read in part the work of fellow readers. Other periodicals—the scientific monthly as well as the journal of advice and the review of arts—adopted the practice of printing letters as a reliable source of copy and as an act and model of sociability. Printed correspondence ran longer, more ambitiously, and more lucratively. For the first time, the collected letters of the eminent became an attractive commercial genre (Pope was a pioneer), and travel books in the form of copious letters home sold by the thousands.

The printed letter would prove crucial too to the development of the newest form of all, the novel. Aphra Behn had pioneered epistolary fiction in the Restoration, and Samuel Richardson recast the mode on an epic scale in *Pamela* and *Clarissa,* among the most important and talked-about fictions of the eighteenth century. In discussing the fate of his characters, Richardson's readers joined a conversation already in progress; Richardson's characters, in their lively exchange of letters, performed and modeled what their creator called "the converse of the pen."

Yet letters were only one among the many kinds of conversation that novelists contrived to carry on. "The rise of the novel"—the emergence over the course of the eighteenth century of so curious, capacious, and durable a genre—has long excited interest and controversy among scholars, who explain the phenomenon in various ways: by the emergence of a large middle-class readership with the money to obtain, the leisure to read, and the eagerness to absorb long narratives that mirrored their circumstances, their aspirations, and their appetites; by a tension between the aristocratic virtues central to older forms of fiction and the constructs of human merit prized by a proud commercial culture; by the passion for journalistic and experiential fact (in newspapers, criminal autobiographies, scientific experiments, etc.), shading over imperceptibly into new practices of fiction.

All of these explanations are true, and each is revelatory when applied to particular clusters of novels. Still, definition and explanation remain elusive, as they clearly were for the genre's early readers and practitioners. The very word "novel"—identifying the genre by no other marks than newness itself—performs a kind of surrender in the face of a form whose central claim to novelty was its

> Mimicry, motion, and metamorphosis are the genre's stock in trade.

barely definable breadth. Mimicry, motion, and metamorphosis are the genre's stock in trade. Novels absorbed all the modes of literature around them: letters, diaries, memoirs, news items, government documents, drawings, verses, even sheet music all crop up within the pages of the early novels, one representational mode supplanting another with often striking speed. Novelists moved with equal alacrity through space: through England (Henry Fielding's *Tom Jones*), Britain more broadly (Tobias Smollett's *Humphry Clinker*), Europe (Smollett's *Roderick Random*), the entire globe as it is ordinarily mapped (Behn's *Oroonoko*, Defoe's *Robinson Crusoe*) or as it could be extraordinarily imagined (Swift's *Gulliver's Travels*). Traversing geographies, the genre crossed cultures too, mostly by means of mimicry, and parroted a range of accents, for purposes either of mockery—the malapropisms of a semiliterate housemaid, the fulminations of a Scots soldier, the outrage of an Irish cuckold— or of pathos: the lamentations of the African slave Oroonoko, the delirium of the violated Clarissa. Many novels, too, made a point of spanning the social spectrum, often compassing destitution and prosperity, labor and luxury within the career of a single ambitious character. Social mobility was perhaps the one plot element that novel readers savored most.

But the novel's supplest means of self-conveyance, its subtlest modes of conversation, were grounded in its attention to the workings of the mind. In his *Essay Concerning Human Understanding* (1690), the philosopher John Locke had explained the mind as a capacious, absorptive instrument engaged in constant motion, linking mixed memories, impressions, and ideas in a ceaseless chain of "associations." In the eighteenth century, novelists took Locke's cue: their works both mimicked the mind's capacity, heterogeneity, and associativeness, and explored them too, tracking over many pages the subtlest modulations in the characters' thoughts and feelings. Richardson famously boasted that his epistolary mode, featuring "familiar letters written as it were to the moment" by characters in their times of crisis, enabled him to track the course of their "hopes and fears" with unprecedented precision—and he trusted that the value of such a process would surely excuse the "bulk" of the huge novels themselves. In the nine volumes of Laurence Sterne's *Life and Opinions of Tristram Shandy*, the title narrator is so committed to following his digressive trains of thought wherever they may lead that the pronouncement of his opinions leaves him preposterously little time to narrate his life. Moving widely over space, freely through society, minutely through time, and deeply into mind, the novelists devised new strategies for achieving that epic inclusiveness that writers sought, in various ways, throughout the century.

The new tactics of miscellany, the new conversations conducted by means of pen and printing press, poetry and prose, refigured the practices of reading that the Earl of Argyle had wished to transmit to his son. In the aristocratic world of Renaissance letters, the book as friend had intimated a sphere of male pedagogy and sociability. The grammar school classroom, the college lecture hall, the estate library, the world of the tutor and his high-born protégé, all these figured reading principally as the privilege and the pleasure of a limited few, mostly males in positions of some leisure, comfort, and power. The links between reading and power were sustained through patterns of production and consumption in which authors received benefits from aristocratic patrons, and manuscripts passed from hand to hand. Donne refused to imagine his verse circulating in any other fashion. After the Restoration, Dryden, Behn, and Pope all pursued the compensations of print, but they nonetheless remained eager to participate in patronage and coterie circulation. Even when printed, their satires purveyed the pleasurable sense of shared knowledge that had constituted the *frisson* of coterie reading. Printers and poets understood that concealing a public name behind initials and dashes provided safety from censors and litigants, at the same time garnering a market share among readers who pleased themselves by decoding "dangerous matter."

By the middle of the eighteenth century, the patronage model of literary production and the coterie mode of distribution had been complicated (some thought ruined) by the commerce of print, for print had become the principal mode of literary distribution. Samuel Johnson, a bookseller's son, thought of literature as print and rarely circulated a manuscript as a gesture of literary sociability. ("None but a blockhead," he famously intoned, "ever wrote except for money.") As a consequence of the dominance of print and its broad distribution, the audiences for texts proliferated into new mixtures. Readers from many strata could afford a penny paper; apprentices and merchants' daughters might read the same novel. Assumptions of commonality that had underwritten the intimate sociability of Renaissance reading had been exploded by civil conflict in the mid-seventeenth century, by the profusion of print and the proliferation of genres that drove and were driven by the appetite of contest and conversation. During the eighteenth century, the print marketplace generated audiences on a scale vaster than ever before, circulating widely across the boundaries of class and gender. Print may have canceled some of the intimacies of the coterie, but it generated new convergences, even new consciousness—a public sphere in which aesthetics, politics, conduct, and taste were all objects of perpetual, often pleasurable debate. To an unprecedented extent, print furnished its readers with the substance for sustained conversation and continual contact.

It also kept them apart. Nothing was more evident to eighteenth-century men and women than the burgeoning of their domestic economy, the vastness of their colonial empire, and the growth in wealth and population which both entailed. The proliferation of consumables was evident in the village market, the Royal Exchange, and the bookstalls of country towns and capitol. The sheer bulk and variety of these consumables were strikingly evident in the length and scope of that capacious new genre, the novel. But even in the midst of abundance and sociability, eighteenth-century consumers were instructed in their paradoxical solitude. Defoe inscribes the condition of the novel as isolation—Robinson Crusoe, a man alone on an island, opines that human life "is, or ought to be, one universal act of solitude." And in novel after novel the very transactions of commerce produce isolation, as ambition and acquisition drive each character into the solitary, often melancholy corner of his or her own self-interest. The novel itself as a reading experience produced comparable sensations. Readers might now empathize with an entire world of fictional characters, but in order to savor such imaginative pleasures, they spent long hours in the privacy of their own quarters, in silent acts of reading.

A sense of solitude underwrote all this century's celebrated gregariousness. This held true even for sociable transactions that might take place between a

A sense of solitude underwrote all this century's celebrated gregariousness.

reader and a text. In the Renaissance, it had long been a practice to annotate texts with comments echoing and endorsing the author's oracular wisdom. Under the pressure of civil war, the dialogue between author and reader often became more heated as the manuscript marginalia expressed anger and outrage at the partisan zeal of the printed text. But one form of textual reverence persisted. Throughout the seventeenth century readers took pleasure in writing marginalia that epitomized the text, making its wisdom portable. They filled blank books with pithy sentences, "commonplaces" drawn from their favorite works and organized in ways that would allow them to recirculate these sayings in their own writing and conversation.

By the eighteenth century, print had managed to appropriate all these modes of study and sociability. Through print, the manuscript collation of wit and wisdom turned into popular commodities—the printed commonplace book, the miscellany, the anthology. Even annotation itself migrated from manuscript markings into print, as Swift and Pope (among others) found ways of exploding scholarly pretension and of rendering the breath of gossip and scandal in the elaborate apparatus of the printed page. By century's end, all of manuscript's august authority and its most cherished genres—letters and memoirs—had been commandeered by print. In the mid-1730s, Pope alarmed and outraged his contemporaries by publishing his letters as if they deserved to partake of eternity with Cicero's. By the early nineteenth century, even that most secretive mode of self-communion, the private journal, had made its way into the marketplace. In 1825, Pepys's *Diary* appeared in two large printed folios, laying bare the elaborate machinery of public life, the secrets and scandals of the Restoration court, and the diarist's own experiences, transgressions, and sequestered musings, which he had written in shorthand code and shown to no one. The communal and commodified medium of print had found yet another way to market signal acts of solitude.

CODA

Mrs. Abington as "Miss Prue" (1771), by the pre-eminent portraitist Sir Joshua Reynolds (see Color Plate 22), shows a solitary figure engaged in intricate conversation with the viewer. Some of the intricacy inheres in the life history of the sitter, whose career many of the painting's first viewers would have known well. The daughter of a cobbler, Frances Abington had worked in childhood as a flower seller and in her teens as an actress, quickly establishing herself as "by far the most eminent performer in comedy of her day" (these words, and others to follow, are the testimony of contemporaries); she would eventually score one of her greatest hits in the role of that latter-day country wife Lady Teazle, in Richard Brinsley Sheridan's *The school for Scandal* (1777). When an unknown, Abington had married her music teacher; as fame increased, she carried on several well-publicized affairs with members of parliament and the aristocracy. By her sexual frankness, she scandalized—and of course fascinated—the multitudes. By her grace and taste, she became "a favorite of the public" and "the high priestess of fashion"; her costumes on stage instantly set new trends among her audience. Reynolds, who greatly

Joshua Reynolds, *Mrs. Abington as "Miss Prue,"* 1771. Restoration theatricality transposed and transformed.

admired her, here captures the complexity of her character and reputation. Her dress is supremely stylish, her pose deliberately provocative. For a woman to lean casually over the back of a chair this way violated all propriety; in earlier portraits, only men had struck such a pose. The thumb at her lips suggests vulgarity verging on the lascivious. The portrait's title purports to explain such seeming aberrations: the actress here appears in her celebrated role as Miss Prue, the "silly, awkward country girl" in William Congreve's Restoration comedy *Love for Love* (1695), who comes to London with the intention, frankly lustful and loudly declared, of getting herself a husband. In Reynolds's painting, of course, Mrs. Abington plays a role more layered: a hybrid of Miss Prue, of the matchlessly fashionable figure into which the actress had transformed herself, and of the whole range of experiences, the prodigious lifelong motion from poverty to polish, which formed part of her self-creation and her fame. Impersonating Miss Prue some seventy-five years after the comedy's first production, Mrs. Abington here infuses Restoration wantonness with Georgian elegance, transgression with high taste, theatricality with self-assertive authenticity. Like the century she inhabits, she is miscellany incarnate.

Stuart Sherman
and Steven N. Zwicker

 For additional resources on the Restoration and the eighteenth century, including a timeline of the period, go to *The Longman Anthology of British Literature* Web site at www.myliteraturekit.com.

Samuel Pepys
1633–1703

John Hayls, *Samuel Pepys*, 1666.

Twice in his life, Samuel Pepys embarked on long projects that allowed him to fuse the methods of the bureaucrat with an inventiveness that amounted to genius. The longer project, which occupied him from his mid-twenties through his mid-fifties, was a fundamental restructuring of the Royal Navy. The shorter project began just a few months earlier. Starting on 1 January 1660, and continuing for the next nine years, Pepys devised the diary form as we know it today: a detailed, private, day-by-day account of daily doings.

Halfway through the diary, Pepys delights to describe himself as "a very rising man," and he wrote the diary in part to track his ascent. The rise began slowly. Born in London to a tailor and a butcher's sister, Pepys studied at Puritan schools; he then attended Magdalene College, Cambridge, as a scholarship student. His B.A. left him well educated but short on cash. A year later he married the fifteen-year-old Elizabeth St. Michel, a French Protestant whose poverty surpassed his own. By his mid-twenties (when the diary commences), neither his accomplishments nor his prospects were particularly striking: he was working as factotum for two powerful men, one of them his high-born cousin Edward Mountagu, First Earl of Sandwich, an important naval officer once devoted to Cromwell but recently turned Royalist.

The diary begins at a calendrical turning point (the first day of a new week, a new year, and a new decade) and on a kind of double bet: that the coming time would bring changes worth writing up, both in the life of the diarist and in the history of the state. The two surmises quickly proved true. As a schoolboy taught by Puritans, Pepys had attended and applauded the execution of Charles I, but the Restoration of Charles II was the making of him, and he recalibrated his loyalties readily enough. His cousin secured for him the Clerkship of the Acts in the Navy Office, a secretarial post that Pepys transformed into something more. By mastering the numberless details of shipbuilding and supplying—from the quality of timber to the composition of tar and hemp—he contrived to control costs and produce results to an extent unmatched by any predecessor.

He managed all these matters so carefully that he soon became the ruler of the Royal Navy, in effect if not in name. When the Test Act of 1673 forced Charles's Catholic brother James to resign as Lord High Admiral, Pepys took his place (in the newly created post of Admiralty Secretary) and ran the operation. He immediately launched a systematic reform of the institution, which he had come to see as dangerously slipshod. By devising (in the words of one biographer) "a rule for all things, great or small" and by enforcing the new disciplines through a method of tireless surveillance and correspondence with ports extending from the Thames to Tangier, Pepys made the navy immeasurably more efficient than ever before. His efforts were interrupted by the political tribulations of his patron James: Pepys spent two brief terms in prison on trumped-up charges of Catholic sympathies, and in 1688 the Glorious Revolution drove him from office into a prosperous retirement. At the height of his power, though, as his biographer Richard Ollard observes, Pepys was the "master builder" of the permanent, professional navy that made possible the expansion of trade and the conquest of colonies over the ensuing century. Energetic in his king's service and in his own (the taking of bribes was one of the perquisites of office that Pepys mastered most adroitly), the tailor's son functioned formidably as an early architect of empire.

Pepys's schooling and profession had immersed him in the two practices most central to earlier English diaries, Puritanism and financial bookkeeping. But where account books and religious diaries emphasize certain kinds of moment—exchanges of money and goods, instances of moral redemption and relapse—Pepys tries for something more comprehensive. He implicitly commits himself to tracking the whole day's experience: the motions of the body as it makes its way through the city in boats, in coaches, and on foot, and the motions of the mind as it shuttles between business and pleasure. He sustained his narrative over a virtually unbroken series of daily entries before stopping out of fear that his work on the diary had helped to damage his eyesight to the brink of blindness. "None of Pepys's contemporaries," writes his editor Robert Latham, "attempted a diary in the all-inclusive Pepysian sense and on the Pepysian scale." To the efficiency of the bookkeeper and the discipline of the Puritan, Pepys added the ardor of the virtuoso, eager (as he observes at one point) "to see any strange thing" and capable of finding wonder in ordinary things: music, plays, books, food, clothes, conversation. The phrase "with great pleasure" recurs in the diary as a kind of leitmotiv, and superlatives play leapfrog through the pages: many, many experiences qualify in turn as the "best" thing that the diarist ever ate, read, thought, saw, heard. To achieve the diary's seeming immediacy, Pepys put his entries through as many as five stages of revision, sometimes days or even months after the events recorded. Even at the final stage, in the bound, elegantly formatted volumes of the diary manuscript, he often crammed new detail or comment into margins and between the lines. Comparable pressures operated in connection with the diary's complex privacy. Pepys took pains to secure secrecy for his text. He hid it from view in drawers or in cabinets. He wrote most of it in a secretarial shorthand, and where he most wanted secrecy, as in the accounts of his many flirtations and infidelities, he obscured things further by an improvised language made up of Spanish, French, Latin, and other tongues. (Elizabeth Pepys figures throughout the diary as a kind of muse and countermuse, the narrative's most recurrent and obsessive subject, and the person most urgently to be prevented from reading it.) At the same time, the manuscript makes notable gestures toward self-display. Pepys frequently shifts to a readily readable longhand, especially for names, places, titles of books, plays, and persons; at times even his secret sexual language opens out into longhand.

This ambivalent secrecy persisted past the diarist's death. Pepys bequeathed the manuscript to Magdalene College without calling any special attention to it. It was included among his many collections: of naval books and papers, of broadsheet ballads, and of instruction manuals on shorthand methods—including the one Pepys used to write the diary. The manuscript kept its secrets long. In the early nineteenth century, the diary was discovered and painstakingly decoded (by a transcriber who, missing the connection between the manuscript and the shorthand manuals on adjacent shelves, treated the text as a million-word cryptogram); it was finally published, in a severely shortened and expurgated version, in 1825. Readers and reviewers soon called for more, recognizing that Pepys possessed (in the words of one reviewer) "the most indiscriminating, insatiable, and miscellaneous curiosity, that ever . . . supplied the pen, of a daily chronicler." Expanded (but still bowdlerized) editions appeared throughout the century, and only in the 1970s did the semisecret manuscript make its way wholly into print.

from **The Diary**
[First Entries][1]
$16\dfrac{59}{60}$

Blessed be God, at the end of the last year I was in very good health, without any sense of my old pain[2] but upon taking of cold.

---

1. England still adhered to the Old Style calendar, in which the new year officially began on March 25, Pepys wrote this "prolude" in early January 1659 according to the English reckoning, but 1660 (New Style) in the rest of Europe.

2. Pepys had suffered from stones in the bladder from babyhood until 1658, when he under went a risky but successful operation.

I lived in Axe Yard,[3] having my wife and servant Jane, and no more in family than us three.

My wife, after the absence of her terms[4] for seven weeks, gave me hopes of her being with child, but on the last day of the year she hath them again. The condition of the state was thus. *Viz.* the Rump, after being disturbed by my Lord Lambert, was lately returned to sit again.[5] The officers of the army all forced to yield. Lawson lies still in the river and Monck is with his army in Scotland.[6] Only my Lord Lambert is not yet come in to the Parliament; nor is it expected that he will, without being forced to it.

The new Common Council of the City doth speak very high; and hath sent to Monck their sword-bearer, to acquaint him with their desires for a free and full Parliament, which is at present the desires and the hopes and expectation of all—22 of the old secluded members having been at the House door the last week to demand entrance; but it was denied them, and it is believed that they nor the people will not be satisfied till the House be filled.[7]

My own private condition very handsome; and esteemed rich, but indeed very poor, besides my goods of my house and my office, which at present is somewhat uncertain. Mr Downing master of my office.[8]

1 January 1659/60. Lord's Day. This morning (we lying lately in the garret) I rose, put on my suit with great skirts,[9] having not lately worn any other clothes but them.

Went to Mr. Gunning's church at Exeter House, where he made a very good sermon upon these words: that in the fullness of time God sent his Son, made of a woman, etc., showing that by "made under the law" is meant his circumcision, which is solemnized this day.[1]

Dined at home in the garret, where my wife dressed the remains of a turkey, and in the doing of it she burned her hand.

I stayed at home all the afternoon, looking over my accounts.

Then went with my wife to my father's; and in going, observed the great posts which the City hath set up[2] at the Conduit in Fleet Street.

Supped at my father's, where in came Mrs. Theophila Turner and Madam Morris[3] and supped with us. After that, my wife and I went home with them, and so to our own home.

3. In Westminster.

4. Menstrual periods.

5. John Lambert, a skilled general under Oliver Cromwell, now opposed the convening of the Rump Parliament, which had governed England since the fall of Cromwell's son Richard in 1659.

6. At this point, the political intentions and allegiance of General George Monck were the object of much speculation; he led his army back from Scotland into England on January 1 and became one of the principal engineers of the Restoration. Vice-Admiral John Lawson supported the rump.

7. A Parliament that would include the "old secluded members"—the representatives expelled in 1648—was

understood to be a first step toward restoration of the monarchy.

8. Pepys was at this point a clerk in the office of the Exchequer.

9. I.e., with a long coat.

1. Peter Gunning had held illegal Anglican services during the Commonwealth. His sermon text is Galatians 4.4; "But, when the fullness of the time was come, God sent forth his Son, made of a woman, made under the law."

2. As defesive barriers during its opposition to the Rump Parliament.

3. A relative and a friend, respectively, "Mistress" ("Mrs.") was applied to unmarried as well as to married women; Theophila was eight years old.

[THE CORONATION OF CHARLES II][4]

[23 April 1661] I lay with Mr. Shiply,[5] and about 4 in the morning I rose.

Coronation Day.

And got to the Abbey,[6] where I followed Sir J. Denham the surveyor with some company that he was leading in. And with much ado, by the favor of Mr. Cooper his man, did get up into a great scaffold across the north end of the Abbey—where with a great deal of patience I sat from past 4 till 11 before the King came in. And a pleasure it was to see the Abbey raised in the middle, all covered with red and a throne (that is a chair) and footstool on the top of it. And all the officers of all kinds, so much as the very fiddlers, in red vests.

At last comes in the Dean and prebends of Westminster with the Bishops (many of them in cloth-of-gold copes); and after them the nobility all in their Parliament robes, which was a most magnificent sight. Then the Duke[7] and the King with a scepter (carried by my Lord of Sandwich) and sword and mond before him, and the crown too.

The King in his robes, bare-headed, which was very fine. And after all had placed themselves, there was a sermon and the service. And then in the choir at the high altar he passed all the ceremonies of the coronation—which, to my very great grief, I and most in the Abbey could not see. The crown being put upon his head, a great shout begun. And he came forth to the throne and there passed more ceremonies: as, taking the oath and having things read to him by the Bishop, and his lords (who put on their caps as soon as the King put on his crown) and bishops came and kneeled before him.

And three times the King-at-Arms went to the three open places on the scaffold and proclaimed that if any one could show any reason why Charles Stuart should not be King of England, that now he should come and speak.

And a general pardon also was read by the Lord Chancellor;[8] and medals flung up and down by my Lord Cornwallis—of silver; but I could not come by any.

But so great a noise, that I could make but little of the music; and indeed, it was lost to everybody. But I had so great a list[9] to piss, that I went out a little while before the King had done all his ceremonies and went round the Abbey to Westminster Hall, all the way within rails, and 10,000 people, with the ground covered with blue cloth—and scaffolds all the way. Into the hall I got—where it was very fine with hangings and scaffolds, one upon another, full of brave[1] ladies. And my wife in one little one on the right hand.

Here I stayed walking up and down; and at last, upon one of the side-stalls, I stood and saw the King come in with all the persons (but the soldiers) that were yesterday in the cavalcade;[2] and a most pleasant sight it was to see them in their several robes. And the King came in with his crown on and his scepter in his hand—under a canopy borne up by six silver staves, carried by Barons of the Cinqueports—and little bells at every end.

And after a long time he got up to the farther end, and all set themselves down at their several tables—and that was also a rare sight. And the King's first course

4. Charles II had returned to England in May 1660; he scheduled his coronartion for St. George's Day, honoring England's patron saint.
5. Edward Shipley was steward to Pepys's cousin Edward Mountagu.
6. Westminster Abbey, site of English coronations.
7. Charles's brother James, Duke of York, later James II.

8. Charles II's Act of Oblivion forgave the crimes of all those on the parliamentary side, with the principal exception of those who had participated in the trial, sentencing, and execution of his father.
9. Desire.
1. Splendid.
2. The previous day's procession.

carried up by the Knights of the Bath. And many fine ceremonies there was of the heralds leading up people before him and bowing; and my Lord of Albemarle's[3] going to the kitchen and eat[4] a bit of the first dish that was to go to the King's table.

But above all was these three Lords, Northumberland and Suffolk and the Duke of Ormond, coming before the courses on horseback and staying so all dinner-time; and at last, to bring up Dymock the King's champion, all in armor on horseback, with his spear and target carried before him. And a herald proclaim that if any dare deny Charles Stuart to be lawful King of England, here was a champion that would fight with him; and with those words the champion flings down his gauntlet; and all this he doth three times in his going up toward the King's table. At last, when he is come, the King drinks to him and then sends him the cup, which is of gold; and he drinks it off and then rides back again with the cup in his hand.

I went from table to table to see the bishops and all others at their dinner, and was infinite pleased with it. And at the lords' table I met with Will Howe and he spoke to my Lord for me and he did give him four rabbits and a pullet; and so I got it, and Mr. Creed and I got Mr. Mitchell to give us some bread and so we at a stall eat it, as everybody else did what they could get.[5]

I took a great deal of pleasure to go up and down and look upon the ladies—and to hear the music of all sorts; but above all, the 24 violins.

About 6 at night they had dined; and I went up to my wife and there met with a pretty lady (Mrs. Franklin, a doctor's wife, a friend of Mr. Bowyer's) and kissed them both—and by and by took them down to Mr. Bowyer's. And strange it is, to think that these two days have held up fair till now that all is done and the King gone out of the Hall; and then it fell a-raining and thundering and lightening as I have not seen it do some years—which people did take great notice of God's blessing of the work of these two days—which is a foolery, to take too much notice of such things.

I observed little disorder in all this; but only the King's footmen had got hold of the canopy and would keep it from the Barons of the Cinqueports; which they endeavored to force from them again but could not do it till my Lord Duke of Albemarle caused it to be put into Sir R. Pye's hand till tomorrow to be decided.

At Mr. Bowyer's, a great deal of company; some I knew, others I did not. Here we stayed upon the leads[6] and below till it was late, expecting to see the fireworks; but they were not performed tonight. Only, the City had a light like a glory round about it, with bonfires.

At last I went to King Street; and there sent Crockford to my father's and my house to tell them I could not come home tonight, because of the dirt and a coach could not be had.

And so after drinking a pot of ale alone at Mrs. Harper's, I returned to Mr. Bowyer's; and after a little stay more, I took my wife and Mrs. Franklin (who I proferred the civility of lying with my wife at Mrs. Hunt's tonight) to Axe Yard. In which, at the further end, there was three great bonfires and a great many great gallants, men and women; and they laid hold of us and would have us drink the King's health upon our knee, kneeling upon a fagot; which we all did, they drinking to us one after another—which we thought a strange frolic. But these gallants continued thus a great while, and I wondered to see how the ladies did tipple.

3. In 1660 Charles II had made George Monck Duke of Albemarle as a reward for his role in the Restoration.
4. Ate (pronounced "ett"), to test for poison.
5. Will Howe and John Creed served as clerks to Sandwich, whom the diarist invariably refers to as "my Lord." Miles Mitchell was a local bookseller.
6. Rooftop.

At last I sent my wife and her bedfellow to bed, and Mr. Hunt and I went in with Mr. Thornbury (who did give the company all their wines, he being yeoman of the wine-cellar to the King) to his house; and there, with his wife and two of his sisters and some gallant sparks that were there, we drank the King's health and nothing else, till one of the gentlemen fell down stark drunk and there lay spewing. And I went to my Lord's pretty well. But no sooner a-bed with Mr. Shiply but my head begun to turn and I to vomit, and if ever I was foxed[7] it was now—which I cannot say yet, because I fell asleep and sleep till morning—only, when I waked I found myself wet with my spewing. Thus did the day end, with joy everywhere; and blessed be God, I have not heard of any mischance to anybody through it all, but only to Sergeant Glynne, whose horse fell upon him yesterday and is like to kill him; which people do please themselves with, to see how just God is to punish that rogue at such a time as this—he being now one of the King's sergeants and rode in the cavalcade with Maynard, to whom people wished the same fortune.[8]

There was also this night, in King Street, a woman had her eye put out by a boy's flinging of a firebrand into the coach.

Now after all this, I can say that besides the pleasure of the sight of these glorious things, I may now shut my eyes against any other objects, or for the future trouble myself to see things of state and show, as being sure never to see the like again in this world.

[24 April 1661] Waked in the morning with my head in a sad taking through the last night's drink, which I am very sorry for. So rise and went out with Mr. Creed to drink our morning draught, which he did give me in chocolate to settle my stomach. And after that to my wife, who lay with Mrs. Franklin at the next door to Mrs. Hunt's.

And they were ready, and so I took them up in a coach and carried the lady to Paul's[9] and there set her down; and so my wife and I home—and I to the office.

That being done, my wife and I went to dinner to Sir W. Batten;[1] and all our talk about the happy conclusion of these last solemnities.

After dinner home and advised with my wife about ordering things in my house; and then she went away to my father's to lie, and I stayed with my workmen, who do please me very well with their work.

At night set myself to write down these three days' diary; and while I am about it, I hear the noise of the chambers and other things of the fireworks, which are now playing upon the Thames before the King. And I wish myself with them, being sorry not to see them.

So to bed.

[THE PLAGUE YEAR]

[7 June 1665] This morning my wife and mother rose about 2 a-clock, and with Mercer, Mary, the boy, and W. Hewer,[2] as they had designed, took boat and down to refresh themselves on the water to Gravesend. I lay till 7 a-clock; then up, and to the office upon Sir G. Carteret's accounts again—where very busy.[3] Thence abroad and to the Change, no news of certainty being yet come from the fleet.[4] Thence to the

---

7. Drunk.
8. Sir John Glynne and Sir John Maynard were lawyers who had served under Cromwell.
9. St. Paul's Cathedral.
1. Surveyor of the Navy.
2. Mary Mercer was Elizabeth Pepys's paid companion; Will Hewer was Pepys's office clerk and lifelong friend;

Mary and "the boy" are household servants.
3. George Carteret was Navy Treasurer.
4. The Royal Exchange was the City's central location for luxury shopping, business dealings, and news gathering. Pepys wanted news of the ongoing Second Dutch War; his patron Sandwich was in command of the fleet.

Dolphin Tavern, where Sir J. Mennes, Lord Brouncker, Sir Thomas Harvey and myself dined upon Sir G. Carteret's charge—and very merry we were, Sir Thomas Harvey being a very droll.[5] Thence to the office; and meeting Creed, away with him to my Lord Treasurer's, there thinking to have met the goldsmiths, or at Whitehall; but did not, and so appointed another time for my lord to speak to them to advance us some money. Thence, it being the hottest day that ever I felt in my life, and it is confessed so by all other people the hottest they ever knew in England in the beginning of June—we to the New Exchange and there drunk whey; with much entreaty, getting it for our money, and would not be entreated to let us have one glass more. So took water, and to Foxhall[6] to the Spring Garden and there walked an hour or two with great pleasure, saving our minds ill at ease concerning the fleet and my Lord Sandwich, that we have no news of them, and ill reports run up and down of his being killed, but without ground. Here stayed, pleasantly walking and spending but 6d, till 9 at night; and then by water to Whitehall, and there I stopped to hear news of the fleet, but none come, which is strange; and so by water home—where, weary with walking and with the mighty heat of the weather, and for my wife's not coming home—I staying walking in the garden till 12 at night, when it begun to lighten exceedingly through the greatness of the heat. Then, despairing of her coming home, I to bed.

This day, much against my will, I did in Drury Lane see two or three houses marked with a red cross upon the doors, and "Lord have mercy upon us" writ there[7]—which was a sad sight to me, being the first of that kind that to my remembrance I ever saw. It put me into an ill conception of myself and my smell, so that I was forced to buy some roll-tobacco to smell to and chaw—which took away the apprehension.[8]

[30 July 1665] Lord's Day. Up, and in my nightgown, cap, and neck-cloth, undressed all day long; lost not a minute, but in my chamber setting my Tangier accounts to rights, which I did by night, to my very heart's content; not only that it is done, but I find everything right and even beyond what, after so long neglecting them, I did hope for. The Lord of Heaven be praised for it.

Will was with me today and is very well again. It was a sad noise to hear our bell to toll and ring so often today, either for deaths or burials; I think five or six times.

At night, weary with the day's work but full of joy at my having done it—I to bed, being to rise betimes tomorrow to go to the wedding at Dagnams.

So to bed—fearing I have got some cold sitting in my loose garment all this day.

[31 July 1665[9]] Up, and very betimes, by 6 a-clock, at Deptford; and there find Sir G. Carteret and my lady ready to go—I being in my new colored-silk suit and coat, trimmed with gold buttons and gold broad lace round my hands, very rich and fine. By water to the ferry, where, when we came, no coach there—and tide of ebb so far spent as the horse-boat could not get off on the other side the river to bring away the coach. So we were fain to stay there in the unlucky Isle of Dogs—in a chill place, the morning cool and wind fresh, above two if not three hours, to our great discontent. Yet being upon a pleasant errand, and seeing that could not be helped, we did bear it

---

5. All these men were colleagues on the Navy Board. *Droll*: jester.
6. Vauxhall, a cluster of riverside gardens, immensely popular for its avenues, covered walks, and wine stalls.
7. The red cross marked houses infected by plague.

8. Tobacco was thought to prevent infection.
9. The wedding day of Lady Jemimah Mountagu, Sandwich's eldest daughter, and Philip Carteret, eldest son of Pepys's colleague Sir George. Pepys had helped to arrange the match.

very patiently; and it was worth my observing, I thought as ever anything, to see how upon these two scores, Sir G. Carteret, the most passionate man in the world and that was in greatest haste to be gone, did bear with it, and very pleasant all the while, at least not troubled much so as to fret and storm at it.

Anon the coach comes—in the meantime there coming a citizen thither with his horse to go over, that told us he did come from Islington this morning, and that Proctor the vintner of the Mitre in Wood Street, and his son, is dead this morning there—of the plague. He having laid out abundance of money there—and was the greatest vintner for some time in London for great entertainments.

We, fearing the canonical hour would be past before we got thither,[1] did with a great deal of unwillingness send away the license and wedding ring. So that when we came, though we drove hard with six horses, yet we found them gone from home; and going toward the church, met them coming from church—which troubled us. But however, that trouble was soon over—hearing it was well done—they being both in their old clothes. My Lord Crew giving her—there being three coach-fulls of them. The young lady mighty sad, which troubled me; but yet I think it was only her gravity, in a little greater degree than usual. All saluted her,[2] but I did not till my Lady Sandwich did ask me whether I had not saluted her or no. So to dinner, and very merry we were; but yet in such a sober way as never almost any wedding was in so great families—but it was much better. After dinner, company divided, some to cards—others to talk. My Lady Sandwich and I up to settle accounts and pay her some money—and mighty kind she is to me, and would fain have had me gone down for company with her to Hinchingbrooke—but for my life I cannot.

At night to supper, and so to talk and, which methought was the most extraordinary thing, all of us to prayers as usual, and the young bride and bridegroom too. And so after prayers, soberly to bed; only, I got into the bridegroom's chamber while he undressed himself, and there was very merry—till he was called to the bride's chamber and into bed they went. I kissed the bride in bed, and so the curtains drawn with the greatest gravity that could be, and so good-night.

But the modesty and gravity of this business was so decent, that it was to me, indeed, ten times more delightful than if it had been twenty times more merry and jovial.

Whereas I feared I must have sat up all night, we did here all get good beds—and I lay in the same I did before, with Mr. Brisband, who is a good scholar and sober man; and we lay in bed, getting him to give me an account of Rome, which is the most delightful talk a man can have of any traveler. And so to sleep—my eyes much troubled already with the change of my drink.

Thus I ended this month with the greatest joy that ever I did any in my life, because I have spent the greatest part of it with abundance of joy and honor, and pleasant journeys and brave entertainments, and without cost of money. And at last live to see that business ended[3] with great content on all sides.

This evening with Mr. Brisband speaking of enchantments and spells, I telling him some of my charms,[4] he told me this of his own knowledge at Bourdeaux in France. The words these—

---

1. Church law stipulated that weddings could be performed only during certain hours of the day.
2. Greeted her with a kiss.
3. The marriage concluded.

4. At the end of the previous year, Pepys had written into his diary a set of incantations ("charms") for healing cuts, burns, etc.

Voicy un corps mort
Royde comme un baston
Froid comme marbre
Leger comme un esprit,
Levons te au nom de Jesus Christ.[5]

He saw four little girls, very young ones, all kneeling, each of them upon one knee; and one begin the first line, whispering in the ear of the next, and the second to the third, and the third to the fourth, and she to the first. Then the first begun the second line, and so round quite through. And putting each one finger only to a boy that lay flat upon his back on the ground, as if he was dead. At the end of the words they did with their four fingers raise this boy as high as they could reach. And he being there and wondering at it (as also being afeared to see it—for they would have had him to have bore a part in saying the words in the room of one of the little girls, that was so young that they could hardly make her learn to repeat the words), did, for fear there might be some sleight used in it by the boy, or that the boy might be light, called the cook of the house, a very lusty fellow, as Sir G. Carteret's cook, who is very big, and they did raise him just in the same manner.

This is one of the strangest things I ever heard, but he tells it me of his own knowledge and I do heartily believe it to be true. I inquired of him whether they were Protestant or Catholic girls, and he told me they were Protestant—which made it the more strange to me.

Thus we end this month, as I said, after the greatest glut of content that ever I had; only, under some difficulty because of the plague, which grows mightily upon us, the last week being about 1,700 or 1,800 [dead] of the plague.

My Lord Sandwich, at sea with a fleet of about 100 sail to the Norward, expect De Ruyter or the Dutch East-India fleet.

My Lord Hinchingbrooke[6] coming over from France, and will meet his sister at Scott's Hall.

Myself having obliged both these families in this business very much, as both my lady and Sir G. Carteret and his lady do confess exceedingly; and the latter two also now call me cousin, which I am glad of.

So God preserve us all friends long, and continue health among us.

[15 August 1665] Up by 4 a-clock and walked to Greenwich, where called at Captain Cocke's[7] and to his chamber, he being in bed—where something put my last night's dream into my head, which I think is the best that ever was dreamed—which was, that I had my Lady Castlemaine[8] in my arms and was admitted to use all the dalliance I desired with her, and then dreamed that this could not be awake but that it was only a dream. But that since it was a dream and that I took so much real pleasure in it, what a happy thing it would be, if when we are in our graves (as Shakespeare resembles it),[9] we could dream, and dream but such dreams as this—that then we should not need to be so fearful of death as we are this plague-time. * * *

5. Here is a dead body / Stiff as a rod / Cold as marble / Light as a spirit, / We raise thee in the name of Jesus Christ.
6. Sandwich's son.
7. George Cocke, supplier to the navy and Pepys's colleague on the board.
8. Barbara Palmer, Countess of Castlemaine, was a celebrated beauty and at this point the foremost among the King's mistresses. See Color Plate 20.
9. Shakespeare compares ("resembles") death to sleep in Hamlet's famous soliloquy, though Hamlet fears what he might dream when dead: "To die, to sleep; / To sleep, perchance to dream. Ay, there's the rub, / For in that sleep of death what dreams may come, / When we have shuffled off this mortal coil, / Must give us pause." (*Hamlet* 3.1.65–69).

It was dark before I could get home; and so land at church-yard-stairs, where to my great trouble I met a dead corpse, of the plague, in the narrow ally, just bringing down[1] a little pair of stairs—but I thank God I was not much disturbed at it. However, I shall beware of being late abroad again.

[10 September 1665] *Lord's day*. Walked home, being forced thereto by one of my watermen falling sick yesterday; and it was God's great mercy I did not go by water with them yesterday, for he fell sick on Saturday night and it is to be feared of the plague. So I sent him away to London with his fellow.

But another boat came to me this morning, whom I sent to Blackwell for Mr. Andrews; I walked to Woolwich,[2] and there find Mr. Hill, and he and I all the morning at music and a song he hath set, of three parts; methinks very good. Anon comes Mr. Andrews, though it be a very ill day. And so after dinner we to music and sang till about 4 or 5 a-clock, it blowing very hard, and now and then raining—and, wind and tide being against us, Andrews and I took leave and walked to Greenwich—my wife before I came out telling me the ill news that she hears, that her father is very ill; and then I told her I feared of the plague, for that the house is shut up.[3] And so, she much troubled, she did desire me to send them something, and I said I would, and will do so.

But before I came out, there happened news to come to me by an express from Mr. Coventry, telling me the most happy news of my Lord Sandwich's meeting with part of the Dutch; his taking two of their East India ships and six or seven others, and very good prize—and that he is in search of the rest of the fleet, which he hopes to find upon the Well Bank—with the loss only of the *Hector*, poor Captain Cuttle. This news doth so overjoy me, that I know not what to say enough to express it; but the better to do it, I did walk to Greenwich;[4] and there sending away Mr. Andrews, I to Captain Cocke's, where I find my Lord Brouncker and his mistress and Sir J. Mennes—where we supped (there was also Sir W. Doyly and Mr. Evelyn);[5] but the receipt of this news did put us all into such an ecstasy of joy, that it inspired into Sir J. Mennes and Mr. Evelyn such a spirit of mirth, that in all my life I never met with so merry a two hours as our company this night was. Among other humors, Mr. Evelyn's repeating of some verses made up of nothing but the various acceptations of May and Can, and doing it so aptly, upon occasion of something of that nature, and so fast, did make us all die almost with laughing, and did so stop the mouth of Sir J. Mennes in the middle of all his mirth (and in a thing agreeing with his own manner of genius) that I never saw any man so outdone in all my life; and Sir J. Mennes's mirth too, to see himself outdone, was the crown of all our mirth.

In this humor we sat till about 10 at night; and so my Lord and his mistress home, and we to bed—it being one of the times of my life wherein I was the fullest of true sense of joy.

[14 September 1665] Up, and walked to Greenwich and there fitted myself in several businesses to go to London, where I have not been now a pretty while. But before I

---

1. Being carried down.
5. A navy yard on the Thames, east of London, where Pepys, his wife, and their servants had taken lodgings in an effort to avoid the plague.
3. Quarantined.
4. A town on the Thames, east of London, where the Navy

Office had temporarily relocated during plague time.
5. John Evelyn (1620–1706), author, virtuoso, and fellow diarist. During the Second Dutch War, both Evelyn and William Doyly served the Navy as Commissioners for the Sick and Wounded.

went from the office, news is brought by word of mouth that letters are now just now brought from the Fleet of our taking a great many more of the Dutch fleet—in which I did never more plainly see my command of my temper, in my not admitting myself to receive any kind of joy from it till I had heard the certainty of it. And therefore went by water directly to the Duke of Albemarle, where I find a letter of the 12th from Solebay, from my Lord Sandwich, of the fleet's meeting with about 18 more of the Dutch fleet and his taking of most of them; and the messenger says they had taken three after the letter was wrote and sealed; which being 21, and the 14 took the other day, is 45 sail—some of which are good, and others rich ships—which is so great a cause of joy in us all, that my Lord and every body is highly joyed thereat. And having taken a copy of my Lord's letter, I away back again to the Bear at the bridge-foot, being full of wind and out of order, and there called for a biscuit and a piece of cheese and gill of sack[6]—being forced to walk over the bridge toward the Change, and the plague being all thereabouts. Here my news was highly welcome, and I did wonder to see the Change so full, I believe 200 people; but not a man or merchant of any fashion, but plain men all. And Lord, to see how I did endeavor all I could to talk with as few as I could, there being now no observation of shutting up of houses infected, that to be sure we do converse and meet with people that have the plague upon them. I to Sir Robert Viners, where my main business was about settling the business of Debusty's 5000*l* tallies—which I did for the present to enable me to have some money. And so home, buying some things for my wife in the way. So home and put up several things to carry to Woolwich—and upon serious thoughts, I am advised by W. Griffin to let my money and plate[7] rest there, as being as safe as any place, nobody imagining that people would leave money in their houses now, when all their families are gone. So for the present, that being my opinion, I did leave them there still. But Lord, to see the trouble that it puts a man to to keep safe what with pain a man hath been getting together; and there is good reason for it. Down to the office, and there wrote letters to and again about this good news of our victory, and so by water home late—

Where when I came home, I spent some thoughts upon the occurrences of this day, giving matter for as much content on one hand and melancholy on another as any day in all my life—for the first, the finding of my money and plate and all safe at London and speeding in my business of money this day—the hearing of this good news, to such excess after so great a despair of my Lord's doing anything this year— adding to that, the decrease of 500 and more, which is the first decrease we have yet had in the sickness since it begun—and great hopes that the next week it will be greater. Then on the other side—my finding that though the Bill[8] in general is abated, yet the City within the walls[9] is increased and likely to continue so and is close to our house there—my meeting dead corpses of the plague, carried to be buried close to me at noonday through the City in Fanchurch Street—to see a person sick of the sores carried close by me by Grace Church in a hackney-coach—my finding the Angel Tavern at the lower end of Tower Hill shut up; and more than that, the ale- house at the Tower stairs; and more than that, that the person was then dying of the plague when I was last there, a little while ago at night, to write a short letter there,

---

6. Quarter pint of white wine.
7. Silver.
8. The Bill of Mortality, a weekly, parish-by-parish

account of the deaths in London.
9. London had spread beyond its original walls, but the area within those walls was still known as "the City."

and I overheard the mistress of the house sadly saying to her husband somebody was very ill, but did not think it was of the plague—to hear that poor Payne my waterman hath buried a child and is dying himself—to hear that a laborer I sent but the other day to Dagnams to know how they did there is dead of the plague; and that one of my own watermen, that carried me daily, fell sick as soon as he had landed me on Friday morning last, when I had been all night upon the water (and I believed he did get his infection that day at Brainford) is now dead of the plague—to hear that Captain Lambert and Cuttle are killed in the taking these ships and that Mr. Sidney Mountagu is sick of a desperate fever at my Lady Carteret's at Scott's Hall—to hear that Mr. Lewes hath another daughter sick—and lastly, that both my servants, W. Hewer and Tom Edwards, have lost their fathers, both in St. Sepulcher's parish, of the plague this week—doth put me into great apprehensions of melancholy, and with good reason. But I put off the thoughts of sadness as much as I can; and the rather to keep my wife in good heart, and family also. After supper (having eat nothing all this day) upon a fine tench[1] of Mr. Sheldon's taking, we to bed.

[THE FIRE OF LONDON]

[2 September 1666] Lord's Day. Some of our maids sitting up late last night to get things ready against our feast today, Jane called us up, about 3 in the morning, to tell us of a great fire they saw in the City. So I rose, and slipped on my nightgown and went to her window, and thought it to be on the back side of Mark Lane at the furthest; but being unused to such fires as followed, I thought it far enough off, and so went to bed again and to sleep. About 7 rose again to dress myself, and there looked out at the window and saw the fire not so much as it was, and further off. So to my closet[2] to set things to rights after yesterday's cleaning. By and by Jane comes and tells me that she hears that above 300 houses have been burned down tonight by the fire we saw, and that it was now burning down all Fish Street by London Bridge. So I made myself ready presently, and walked to the Tower and there got up upon one of the high places, Sir J. Robinson's little son going up with me; and there I did see the houses at that end of the bridge all on fire, and an infinite great fire on this and the other side the end of the bridge—which, among other people, did trouble me for poor little Mitchell and our Sarah on the bridge.[3] So down, with my heart full of trouble, to the Lieutenant of the Tower, who tells me that it begun this morning in the King's baker's house in Pudding Lane, and that it hath burned down St. Magnus's Church and most part of Fish Street already. So I down to the water-side and there got a boat and through bridge,[4] and there saw a lamentable fire. Poor Mitchell's house, as far as the Old Swan, already burned that way and the fire running further, that in a very little time it got as far as the Steelyard while I was there. Everybody endeavoring to remove their goods, and flinging into the river or bringing them into lighters[5] that lay off. Poor people staying in their houses as long as till the very fire touched them, and then running into boats or clambering from one pair of stair by the water-side to another. And among other things, the poor pigeons I perceive were loath to leave their houses, but hovered about the windows and balconies till they were some of them burned, their wings, and fell down.

1. A kind of fish.
2. Private room, study.
3. London Bridge was lined with shops and houses, including the liquor shop of Pepys's friend Michael

Mitchell and the residence of his former servant Sarah.
4. Under the bridge.
5. Barges.

Having stayed, and in an hour's time seen the fire rage every way, and nobody to my sight endeavoring to quench it, but to remove their goods and leave all to the fire; and having seen it get as far as the Steelyard, and the wind mighty high and driving it into the City, and everything, after so long a drought, proving combustible, even the very stones of churches, and among other things, the poor steeple by which pretty Mrs. Horsley lives, and whereof my old school-fellow Elborough is parson, taken fire in the very top and there burned till it fall down—I to Whitehall with a gentleman with me who desired to go off from the Tower to see the fire in my boat—to Whitehall, and there up to the King's closet in the chapel, where people came about me and I did give them an account dismayed them all; and word was carried in to the King, so I was called for and did tell the King and Duke of York what I saw, and that unless his Majesty did command houses to be pulled down, nothing could stop the fire. They seemed much troubled, and the King commanded me to go to my Lord Mayor from him and command him to spare no houses but to pull down before the fire every way. The Duke of York bid me tell him that if he would have any more soldiers, he shall; and so did my Lord Arlington afterward, as a great secret. Here meeting with Captain Cocke, I in his coach, which he lent me, and Creed with me, to Paul's; and there walked along Watling Street as well as I could, every creature coming away loaden with goods to save—and here and there sick people carried away in beds. Extraordinary good goods carried in carts and on backs. At last met my Lord Mayor in Canning Street, like a man spent, with a hankercher about his neck. To the King's message, he cried like a fainting woman, "Lord, what can I do? I am spent! People will not obey me. I have been pulling down houses. But the fire overtakes us faster than we can do it." That he needed no more soldiers; and that for himself, he must go and refresh himself, having been up all night. So he left me, and I him, and walked home—seeing people all almost distracted and no manner of means used to quench the fire. The houses too, so very thick thereabouts, and full of matter for burning, as pitch and tar, in Thames Street—and warehouses of oil and wines and brandy and other things. Here I saw Mr. Isaac Houblon, that handsome man—prettily dressed and dirty at his door at Dowgate, receiving some of his brothers' things whose houses were on fire; and as he says, have been removed twice already, and he doubts (as it soon proved) that they must be in a little time removed from his house also—which was a sad consideration. And to see the churches all filling with goods, by people who themselves should have been quietly there at this time.

By this time it was about 12 a-clock, and so home and there find my guests, which was Mr. Wood and his wife, Barbary Shelden, and also Mr. Moone—she mighty fine, and her husband, for aught I see, a likely man. But Mr. Moone's design and mine, which was to look over my closet and please him with the sight thereof, which he hath long desired, was wholly disappointed, for we were in great trouble and disturbance at this fire, not knowing what to think of it. However, we had an extraordinary good dinner, and as merry as at this time we could be.

While at dinner, Mrs. Batelier came to inquire after Mr. Woolfe and Stanes (who it seems are related to them), whose houses in Fish Street are all burned, and they in a sad condition. She would not stay in the fright.

As soon as dined, I and Moone away and walked through the City, the streets full of nothing but people and horses and carts loaden with goods, ready to run over one another, and removing goods from one burned house to another—they now removing out of Canning Street (which received goods in the morning) into Lombard Street and further; and among others, I now saw my little goldsmith Stokes receiving some friend's goods, whose house itself was burned the day after. We parted at Paul's, he home and I to Paul's Wharf, where I had appointed a boat to attend me; and took in Mr. Carkesse and his brother, whom I met in the street, and carried them below and above bridge, to and again, to see the fire, which was now got further, both below and above, and no likelihood of stopping it. Met with the King and Duke of York in their barge, and with them to Queenhithe and there called Sir Richard Browne to them. Their order was only to pull down houses apace, and so below bridge at the water-side; but little was or could be done, the fire coming upon them so fast. Good hopes there was of stopping it at the Three Cranes above, and at Buttolph's Wharf below bridge, if care be used; but the wind carries it into the City, so as we know not by the water-side what it doth there. River full of lighters and boats taking in goods, and good goods swimming in the water; and only, I observed that hardly one lighter or boat in three that had the goods of a house in, but there was a pair of virginals[6] in it. Having seen as much as I could now, I away to Whitehall by appointment, and there walked to St. James's Park, and there met my wife and Creed and Wood and his wife and walked to my boat, and there upon the water again, and to the fire up and down, it still increasing and the wind great. So near the fire as we could for smoke; and all over the Thames, with one's face in the wind you were almost burned with a shower of firedrops—this is very true—so as houses were burned by these drops and flakes of fire, three or four, nay five or six houses, one from another. When we could endure no more upon the water, we to a little alehouse on the Bankside over against the Three Cranes, and there stayed till it was dark almost and saw the fire grow; and as it grow darker, appeared more and more, and in corners and upon steeples and be-tween churches and houses, as far as we could see up the hill of the City, in a most horrid malicious bloody flame, not like the fine flame of an ordinary fire. Barbary and her husband away before us. We stayed till, it being darkish, we saw the fire as only one entire arch of fire from this to the other side the bridge, and in a bow up the hill, for an arch of above a mile long. It made me weep to see it. The churches, houses, and all on fire and flaming at once, and a horrid noise the flames made, and the cracking of houses at their ruin. So home with a sad heart, and there find everybody discoursing and lamenting the fire; and poor Tom Hayter[7] came with some few of his goods saved out of his house, which is burned upon Fish Street Hill. I invited him to lie at my house, and did receive his goods: but was deceived in his lying there, the noise coming every moment of the growth of the fire, so as we were forced to begin to pack up our own goods and prepare for their removal. And did by moonshine (it being brave,[8] dry, and moonshine and warm weather) carry much of my goods into the garden, and Mr. Hayter and I did remove my money and iron-chests into my cellar—as thinking that the safest place. And got my bags of gold into my office ready to carry away, and my chief papers of accounts also there, and my tallies into a box by themselves. So great was our fear, as Sir W. Batten had carts come out of the country to fetch away his goods this night. We did put Mr. Hayter, poor man, to bed a little; but he got but very little rest, so much noise being in my house, taking down of goods.

[3 September 1666] About 4 a-clock in the morning, my Lady Batten sent me a cart to carry away all my money and plate and best things to Sir W. Rider's at Bethnell

---

6. A small harpsichord.
7. One of Pepys's clerks in the Navy Office.

8. Pleasant.

Green; which I did, riding myself in my nightgown in the cart; and Lord, to see how the streets and the highways are crowded with people, running and riding and getting of carts at any rate to fetch away things. I find Sir W. Rider tired with being called up[9] all night and receiving things from several friends. His house full of goods—and much of Sir W. Batten and Sir W. Penn's.[1] I am eased at my heart to have my treasure so well secured. Then home with much ado to find a way. Nor any sleep all this night to me nor my poor wife. But then, and all this day, she and I and all my people laboring to get away the rest of our things, and did get Mr. Tooker to get me a lighter to take them in, and we did carry them (myself some) over Tower Hill, which was by this time full of people's goods, bringing their goods thither. And down to the lighter, which lay at the next quay above the Tower Dock. And here was my neighbor's wife, Mrs. Buckworth, with her pretty child and some few of her things, which I did willingly give way to be saved with mine. But there was no passing with anything through the postern,[2] the crowd was so great.

The Duke of York came this day by the office and spoke to us, and did ride with his guard up and down the City to keep all quiet (he being now general, and having the care of all).

This day, Mercer being not at home, but against her mistress's order gone to her mother's, and my wife going thither to speak with W. Hewer, met her there and was angry; and her mother saying that she was not a prentice girl, to ask leave every time she goes abroad, my wife with good reason was angry, and when she came home, bid her be gone again. And so she went away, which troubled me; but yet less than it would, because of the condition we are in fear of coming into in a little time, of being less able to keep one in her quality. At night, lay down a little upon a quilt of W. Hewer in the office (all my own things being packed up or gone); and after me, my poor wife did the like—we having fed upon the remains of yesterday's dinner, having no fire nor dishes, nor any opportunity of dressing anything.

[4 September 1666] Up by break of day to get away the remainder of my things, which I did by a lighter at the Iron Gate; and my hands so few, that it was the afternoon before we could get them all away.

Sir W. Penn and I to Tower Street, and there met the fire burning three or four doors beyond Mr. Howell's; whose goods, poor man (his trays and dishes, shovels, etc., were flung all along Tower Street in the kennels, and people working therewith from one end to the other), the fire coming on in that narrow street, on both sides, with infinite fury. Sir W. Batten, not knowing how to remove his wine, did dig a pit in the garden and laid it in there; and I took the opportunity of laying all the papers of my office that I could not otherwise dispose of. And in the evening Sir W. Penn and I did dig another and put our wine in it, and I my parmesan cheese as well as my wine and some other things.

The Duke of York was at the office this day at Sir W. Penn's, but I happened not to be within. This afternoon, sitting melancholy with Sir W. Penn in our garden and thinking of the certain burning of this office without extraordinary means, I did propose for the sending up of all our workmen from Woolwich and Deptford yards (none whereof yet appeared), and to write to Sir W. Coventry to have the Duke of York's

---

9. Called on, woken.
1. William Penn, Pepys's colleague on the Navy Board

(and father of the founder of Pennsylvania).
2. Back or side gate.

permission to pull down houses rather then lose this office, which would much hinder the King's business. So Sir W. Penn he went down this night, in order to the sending them up tomorrow morning; and I wrote to Sir W. Coventry about the business, but received no answer.

This night Mrs. Turner (who, poor woman, was removing her goods all this day—good goods, into the garden, and knew not how to dispose of them)—and her husband supped with my wife and I at night in the office, upon a shoulder of mutton from the cook's, without any napkin or anything, in a sad manner but were merry. Only, now and then walking into the garden and saw how horridly the sky looks, all on a fire in the night, was enough to put us out of our wits; and indeed it was extremely dreadful—for it looks just as if it was at us, and the whole heaven on fire. I after supper walked in the dark down to Tower Street, and there saw it all on fire at the Trinity House on that side and the Dolphin Tavern on this side, which was very near us—and the fire with extraordinary vehemence. Now begins the practice of blowing up of houses in Tower Street, those next the Tower, which at first did frighten people more than anything; but it stopped the fire where it was done—it bringing down the houses to the ground in the same places they stood, and then it was easy to quench what little fire was in it, though it kindled nothing almost. W. Hewer this day went to see how his mother did, and comes late home, but telling us how he hath been forced to remove her to Islington, her house in Pye Corner being burned. So that it is got so far that way and all the Old Bailey, and was running down to Fleet Street. And Paul's is burned, and all Cheapside. I wrote to my father this night; but the post-house being burned, the letter could not go.

❧ PEPYS'S DIARY AND ITS TIME ❧
John Evelyn: from *Kalendarium*[1]

[2 September 1666] This fatal night about ten, began that deplorable fire, near Fish Street in London. 2: I had public prayers at home: after dinner the fire continuing, with my wife and son took coach and went to the Bankside in Southwark,[2] where we beheld that dismal spectacle, the whole City in dreadful flames near the water-side, and had now consumed all the houses from the bridge all Thames Street and upwards towards Cheapside, down to the Three Cranes, and so returned exceedingly astonished, what would become of the rest. 3: The fire having continued all this night (if I may call that night, which was as light as day for 10 miles round about after a dreadful manner) when conspiring with a fierce eastern wind, in a very dry season, I went on foot to the same place, when I saw the whole south part of the City burning from Cheapside to the Thames, and all along Cornhill (for it likewise kindled back against the wind, as well as forward) Tower Street, Fenchurch Street, Gracious Street and so along to Baynard Castle, and was now taking hold of St. Paul's Church, to which the

---

1. John Evelyn (1620–1706), versatile author (on air pollution, architecture, gardening, forestry, and other subjects), wrote up his life on a plan very different from that of his friend Pepys. Evelyn's vantage on the Fire of London (as on much else) contrasts with Pepys's. A landowning gentleman, Evelyn dwelt at a remove from the City on a country estate across the river. A devout Anglican,

he saw the catastrophe as an apocalypse steeped in biblical precedent and prophecy. For another account of the fire, see the selection from the *London Gazette* in Perspectives: Reading Papers, page 2310.
2. The southern bank of the Thames, across the river from the fire.

scaffolds contributed exceedingly. The conflagration was so universal, and the people so astonished, that from the beginning (I know not by what desponding or fate), they hardly stirred to quench it, so as there was nothing heard or seen but crying out and lamentation, and running about like distracted creatures, without at all attempting to save even their goods; such a strange consternation there was upon them, so as it burned both in breadth and length, the churches, public halls, Exchange, hospitals, monuments, and ornaments, leaping after a prodigious manner from house to house and street to street, at great distance one from the other, for the heat (with a long set of fair and warm weather) had even ignited the air, and prepared the materials to conceive the fire, which devoured after an incredible manner, houses, furniture, and everything. Here we saw the Thames covered with goods floating, all the barges and boats laden with what some had time and courage to save, as on the other, the carts etc. carrying out to the fields, which for many miles were strewed with moveables of all sorts, and tents erecting to shelter both people and what goods they could get away: O the miserable and calamitous spectacle, such as haply the whole world had not seen the like since the foundation of it, nor to be outdone, till the universal conflagration of it. All the sky were of a fiery aspect, like the top of a burning oven, and the light seen above 40 miles round about for many nights. God grant mine eyes may never behold the like, who now saw above ten thousand houses all in one flame, the noise and crackling and thunder of the impetuous flames, the shrieking of women and children, the hurry of people, the fall of towers, houses and churches was like an hideous storm, and the air all about so hot and inflamed that at the last one was not able to approach it, so as they were forced to stand still, and let the flames consume on which they did for near two whole miles in length and one in breadth. The clouds also of smoke were dismal, and reached upon computation near 50 miles in length. Thus I left it this afternoon burning, a resemblance of Sodom, or the last day.[3] It called to mind that of 4 Heb: *non enim hic habemus stabilem Civitatem:*[4] the ruins resembling the picture of *Troy: London* was,[5] but is no more. Thus I returned.

[4 September 1666] The burning still rages; I went now on horseback, and it was now gotten as far as the Inner Temple; all Fleet Street, Old Bailey, Ludgate Hill, Warwick Lane, Newgate, Paul's Chain, Watling Street now flaming and most of it reduced to ashes, the stones of Paul's flew like granados,[6] the lead melting down the streets in a stream, and the very pavements of them glowing with fiery redness, so as nor horse nor man was able to tread on them, and the demolitions had stopped all the passages, so as no help could be applied; the eastern wind still more impetuously driving the flames forwards. Nothing but the almighty power of God was able to stop them, for vain was the help of man. On the fourth it crossed towards Whitehall, but O the confusion was then at that court. It pleased his Majesty to command me among the rest to look after the quenching of Fetter Lane end, to preserve (if possible) that part of Holborn, whilst the rest of the gentlemen took their several posts, some at one part, some at another, for now they began to bestir themselves, and not till now, who till

---

3. In Genesis, the Lord destroys the sinful city of Sodom by raining "fire and brimstone . . . out of heaven" (19.24). "The last day" is the Day of Judgment, when the city of Babylon (emblem of the corrupt world) "shall be utterly burned with fire" (Revelation 18.8).
4. For here we have no lasting city (Hebrews 13.14; the sentence continues: "but we seek one to come").
5. Echoing the account of the fall of Troy in the *Aeneid* (2.325): on the night the Greeks burn the city, a Trojan priest declares *fuit Ilium* ("Troy was").
6. Grenades.

now had stood as men interdict, with their hands a cross,[7] and began to consider that nothing was like to put a stop, but the blowing up of so many houses, as might make a wider gap, than any had yet been made by the ordinary method of pulling them down with engines.[8] This some stout seamen proposed early enough to have saved the whole City; but some tenacious and avaricious men, aldermen etc., would not permit, because their houses must have been of the first. It was therefore now commanded to be practiced, and my concern being particularly for the Hospital of St. Bartholomew's near Smithfield, where I had many wounded and sick men, made me the more diligent to promote it;[9] nor was my care for the Savoy less. So as it pleased Almighty God by abating of the wind, and the industry of people, now when all was lost, infusing a new spirit into them (and such as had if exerted in time undoubtedly preserved the whole) that the fury of it began sensibly to abate, about noon, so as it came no farther than the Temple westward, nor than the entrance of Smithfield north; but continued all this day and night so impetuous toward Cripplegate, and the Tower, as made us even all despair. It also brake out again in the Temple: but the courage of the multitude persisting, and innumerable houses blown up with gunpowder, such gaps and desolations were soon made, as also by the former three days' consumption, as the back fire did not so vehemently urge upon the rest, as formerly. There was yet no standing near the burning and glowing ruins near a furlong's space. The coal and wood wharves and magazines of oil, rosin, chandler, etc.[1] did infinite mischief; so as the invective I but a little before dedicated to his Majesty and published, giving warning what might probably be the issue of suffering those shops to be in the City, was looked on as prophetic.[2] But there I left this smoking and sultry heap, which mounted up in dismal clouds night and day, the poor inhabitants dispersed all about St. George's, Moorfields, as far as Highgate, and several miles in circle, some under tents, others under miserable huts and hovels, without a rag, or any necessary utensils, bed or board, who from delicateness, riches and easy accommodations in stately and well-furnished houses, were now reduced to extremest misery and poverty. In this calamitous condition I returned with a sad heart to my house, blessing and adoring the distinguishing mercy of God, to me and mine, who in the midst of all this ruin, was like Lot, in my little Zoar, safe and sound.[3]

END OF PEPYS'S DIARY AND ITS TIME

※

[THE ROYAL SOCIETY][4]

[14 November 1666] Up, and by water to Whitehall; and thence to Westminister, where I bought several things—as, a hone—ribband—gloves—books. And then took coach and to Knepp's[5] lodging, whom I find not ready to go home with me, so I away to do a little business; among others, to call upon Mr. Osborne for my Tangier warrant for the last quarter, and so to the New Exchange for some things for my wife, and

---

7. Immobilized, with their arms crossed (a conventional posture of passivity).
8. Machines.
9. Evelyn served on the Navy Board as a commissioner, charged with the care of sick and wounded seamen.
1. Different sorts of fuel, stored and sold in shops along the Thames.
2. In 1661 Evelyn had warned of these dangers in a pamphlet entitled *Fumifugium: or the Inconvenciency of the Air*

and Smoke of London Dissipated. Together with Some Remedies Humbly Proposed by J. E., Esq; to His Sacred Majesty, and to the Parliament Now Assembled.
3. Lot, a prosperous inhabitant of Sodom, is warned by angels of the city's impending destruction. He escapes to Zoar, a small city nearby (Genesis 19.20–22).
4. This next selection from Pepys was written two months after the fire, when life had begun to return to normal.
5. Elizabeth Knepp, actress, singer, and friend of Pepys.

then to Knepp again and there stayed, reading of Waller's[6] verses while she finished her dressing—her husband being by, I had no other pastime. Her lodging very mean, and the condition she lives in; yet makes a show without doors, God bless us. I carried him along with us into the City, and set him down in Bishopsgate Street and then home with her. She tells me how Smith of the Duke's house hath killed a man upon a quarrel in play—which makes everybody sorry, he being a good actor, and they say a good man, however this happens. The ladies of the court do much bemoan him, she says. Here she and we alone at dinner, to some good victuals that we could not put off,[7] that was intended for the great dinner of my Lord Hinchingbrooke, if he had come. After dinner, I to teach her my new recitative of *It is decreed*[8]—of which she learnt a good part; and I do well like it, and believe shall be well pleased when she hath it all, and that it will be found an agreeable thing. Then carried her home, and my wife and I intended to have seen my Lady Jemima at Whitehall; but the Exchange street was so full of coaches, everybody as they say going thither to make themselves fine against tomorrow night,[9] that after half an hour's stay we could not do any; but only, my wife to see her brother, and I to go speak one word with Sir G. Carteret about office business. And talk of the general complexion of matters; which he looks upon, as I do, with horror, and gives us all for an undone people—that there is no such thing as a peace in hand, nor a possibility of any without our begging it, they[1] being as high, or higher, in their terms than ever. And tells me that just now my Lord Hollis had been with him, and wept to think in what a condition we are fallen. He showed me my Lord Sandwich's letter to him, complaining of the lack of money; which Sir G. Carteret is at a loss how in the world to get the King to supply him[2] with—and wishes him for that reason here, for that he fears he will be brought to disgrace there, for want of supplies. He says the House is yet in a bad humor; and desiring to know whence it is that the King stirs not, he says he minds it not, nor will be brought to it—and that his servants of the House do, instead of making the Parliament better, rather play the rogue one with another, and will put all in fire.[3] So that upon the whole, we are in a wretched condition, and I went from him in full apprehensions of it. So took up my wife, her brother being yet very bad, and doubtful whether he will recover or no; and so to St. Ellen's and there sent my wife home, and myself to the Pope's Head, where all the Houblons were, and Dr. Croone;[4] and by and by to an exceeding pretty supper—excellent discourse of all sorts; and indeed, are a set of the finest gentlemen that ever I met withal in my life. Here Dr. Croone told me that at the meeting[5] at Gresham College tonight (which it seems they now have every Wednesday again) there was a pretty experiment, of the blood of one dog let out (till he died) into the body of another on one side, while all his own run out on the other side. The first died upon the place, and the other very well, and likely to do well. This did give occasion to many pretty wishes, as of the blood of a Quaker to be let into an archbishop, and such like. But, as Dr. Croone says, may if it takes be of

---

6. Sir Edmund Waller (1606–1687), widely read poet and pioneer of the heroic couplet; he wrote much love poetry in praise of "Sacharissa," a woman he wooed without success.
7. Delay (because the food would spoil).
8. Pepys enjoyed composing music (here setting words from Ben Jonson's play *Catiline*).
9. When a court ball was to be held for the queen's birthday.
1. The Dutch.

2. Sandwich, now ambassador to Spain.
3. Into ruin.
4. The Houblons were a merchant family—a father and five sons—whom Pepys and others admired for their affection and generosity. Dr. William Croone, a specialist in anatomy, was an original Fellow and First Secretary of the Royal Society for the Improving of Natural Knowledge.
5. Of the Royal Society.

mighty use to man's health, for the amending of bad blood by borrowing from a better body.

After supper James Houblon and another brother took me aside, and to talk of some businesses of their own, where I am to serve them, and will. And then to talk of public matters; and I do find that they, and all merchants else, do give over trade and the nation for lost—nothing being done with care or foresight—no convoys[6] granted, nor anything done to satisfaction. But do think that the Dutch and French will master us the next year, do what we can; and so do I, unless God Almighty makes the King to mind his business; which might yet save all.

Here we sat talking till past one in the morning, and then home—where my people sat up for me, my wife and all; and so to bed.

[30 May 1667] Up, and to the office, where all the morning. At noon dined at home; being, without any words, friends with my wife, though last night I was very angry, and do think I did give her as much cause to be angry with me. After dinner I walked to Arundel House, the way very dusty (the day of meeting of the Society being changed from Wednesday to Thursday; which I knew not before because the Wednesday is a Council day and several of the Council are of the Society, and would come but for their attending the King at Council); where I find much company, indeed very much company, in expectation of the Duchess of Newcastle,[7] who had desired to be invited to the Society, and was, after much debate pro and con, it seems many being against it, and we do believe the town will be full of ballets[8] of it. Anon comes the Duchess, with her women attending her; among others, that Ferrabosco[9] of whom so much talk is, that her lady would bid her show her face and kill the gallants. She is indeed black[1] and hath good black little eyes, but otherwise but a very ordinary woman I do think; but they say sings well. The Duchess hath been a good comely woman; but her dress so antic and her deportment so unordinary, that I do not like her at all, nor did I hear her say anything that was worth hearing, but that she was full of admiration, all admiration.[2] Several fine experiments were shown her of colors, lodestones, microscope, and of liquors: among others, of one that did while she was there turn a piece of roasted mutton into pure blood—which was very rare. Here was Mr. Moore of Cambridge, whom I had not seen before, and I was glad to see him—as also a very pretty black boy that run up and down the room, somebody's child in Arundel House. After they had shown her many experiments, and she cried still she was "full of admiration," she departed, being led out and in by several lords that were there; among others, Lord George Berkeley and the Earl of Carlisle and a very pretty young man, the Duke of Somerset.

She gone, I by coach home and there busy at my letters till night; and then with my wife in the evening, singing with her in the garden with great pleasure. And so home to supper and to bed.

[21 November 1667] Up, and to the office, where all the morning; and at noon home, where my wife not very well, but is to go to Mr. Mill's child's christening, where she is godmother, Sir. J. Mennes and Sir R. Brookes her companions. I left

---

6. Protective escort for merchant ships.
7. Margaret Cavendish, Duchess of Newcastle, had published poems, plays, and treatises on natural philosophy highly critical of the Society's methods (see pages 2068–70.)

8. Ballads (Evelyn wrote one on Cavendish's visit).
9. An Italian family of this name was eminent in England for its musical talents.
1. I.e., of dark complexion and hair.
2. Wonder, amazement.

her after dinner (my clerks dining with me) to go with Sir J. Mennes, and I to the office, where did much business till after candlelight; and then, my eyes beginning to fail me, I out and took coach and to Arundel House, where the meeting of Gresham College was broke up; but there meeting Creed, I with him to the tavern in St. Clement's churchyard, where was Dean Wilkins, Dr. Whistler[3] * * * and others. * * * Among the rest, they discourse of a man that is a little frantic (that hath been a kind of minister, Dr. Wilkins saying that he hath read for him in his church) that is a poor and debauched man, that the college have hired for 20s[4] to have some of the blood of a sheep let into his body; and it is to be done on Saturday next. They purpose to let in about twelve ounces, which they compute is what will be let in in a minute's time by a watch. They differ in the opinion they have of the effects of it; some think that it may have a good effect upon him as a frantic man, by cooling his blood; others, that it will not have any effect at all. But the man is a very healthy man, and by this means will be able to give an account what alteration, if any, he doth find in himself, and so may be useful. On this occasion Dr. Whistler told a pretty story related by Muffett, a good author, of Dr. Caius that built Key's College: that being very old and lived only at that time upon woman's milk, while he fed upon the milk of an angry fretful woman, was so himself; and then being advised to take of a good-natured patient woman, he did become so, beyond the common temper of his age. Thus much nutriment, they observed, might do. Their discourse was very fine; and if I should be put out of my office,[5] I do take great content in the liberty I shall be at of frequenting these gentlemen's companies. Broke up thence and home, and there to my wife in her chamber, who is not well (of those[6]); and there she tells me great stories of the gossiping women of the parish, what this and what that woman was; and among the rest, how Mrs. Hollworthy is the veriest confident bragging gossip of them all, which I should not have believed—but that Sir R. Brookes, her partner,[7] was mighty civil to her and taken with her and what not. My eyes being bad, I spent the evening with her in her chamber, talking and inventing a cipher to put on a piece of plate[8] which I must give, better than ordinary, to the parson's child; and so to bed, and through my wife's illness had a bad nght of it, and she a worse, poor wretch.

[30 November 1667] Then to Cary House, a house now of entertainment, * * * next my Lord Ashly's; and there, where I have heretofore heard Common Prayer in the time of Dr. Mossum,[9] we after two hours' stay, sitting at the table with our napkins open, had our dinners brought; but badly done. But here was good company, I choosing to sit next Dr. Wilkins, Sir George Ent, and others whom I value. And there talked of several things; among others, Dr. Wilkins, talking of the universal speech, of which he hath a book coming out,[1] did first inform me how man was certainly

3. The mathematician John Wilkins was one of the founders of the Royal Society; the physician Daniel Whistler was a Fellow.

4. Twenty shillings.

5. Pepys's position was in jeopardy because of a parliamentary investigation into Navy Office mismanagement during the Second Dutch War.

6. Her menstrual period.

7. As godfather at the christening.

8. I.e., a coded message to be engraved on a silver dish (so that the gift includes a kind of game).

9. Robert Mossum had conducted illegal Anglican services (using the forbidden Book of Common Prayer) during the Interregnum.

1. In his Essay toward a Real Character, and a Philosophical Language (1668), Wilkins argued for (and attempted) the creation of a newly precise and logical language based not on an arbitrary alphabet but on written symbols representing ideas and things.

made for society, he being of all creatures the least armed for defense; and of all creatures in the world, the young ones are not able to do anything to help themselves, nor can find the dug without being put to it, but would die if the mother did not help it. And he says were it not for speech, man would be a very mean creature. Much of this good discourse we had. But here above all, I was pleased to see the person who had his blood taken out. He speaks well, and did this day give the Society a relation thereof in Latin, saying that he finds himself much better since, and as a new man. But he is cracked a little in his head, though he speaks very reasonably and very well. He had but 20s for his suffering it, and is to have the same again tried upon him—the first sound man that ever had it tried on him in England, and but one that we hear of in France, which was a porter hired by the virtuosi.

[THEATER AND MUSIC]

[5 October 1667] Up, and to the office and there all the morning, none but my Lord Anglesey and myself. But much surprised with the news of the death of Sir W. Batten, who died this morning, having been but two days sick. Sir W. Penn and I did dispatch a letter this morning to Sir W. Coventry[2] to recommend Colonel Middleton, who we think a most honest and understanding man, and fit for that place. Sir G. Carteret did also come this morning, and walked with me in the garden and concluded not to concern or have any advice made to Sir W. Coventry in behalf of my Lord Sandwich's business; so I do rest satisfied, though I do think they are all mad,[3] that they will judge Sir W. Coventry an enemy, when he is indeed no such man to anybody, but is severe and just, as he ought to be, where he sees things ill done. At noon home, and by coach to Temple Bar to a India shop[4] and there bought a gown and sash, which cost me 26s. And so she and Willett[5] away to the Change, and I to my Lord Crew and there met my Lord Hinchingbrooke and Lady Jemima, and there dined with them and my Lord—where pretty merry. And after dinner, my Lord Crew and Hinchingbrooke and myself went aside to discourse about my Lord Sandwich's business, which is in a very ill state for want of money; and so parted, and I to my tailor's and there took up my wife and Willet, who stayed there for me, and to the Duke of York's playhouse;[6] but the House so full, it being a new play *The Coffee-House*, that we could not get in, and so to the King's House; and there going in, met with Knepp and she took us up into the tiring-rooms and to the women's shift,[7] where Nell[8] was dressing herself and was all unready; and is very pretty, prettier than I thought; and so walked all up and down the house above, and then below into the scene-room, and there sat down and she gave us fruit; and here I read the Qu's[9] to Knepp while she answered me, through all her part of *Flora's Figarys*, which was acted today. But Lord, to see how they were both painted would make a man mad—and did make me loathe them—and what base company of men comes among them, and how lewdly they talk—and how poor the men are in clothes, and yet what a show they make on the stage by candlelight, is very

2. A commissioner on the Navy Board.
3. "They" are the Parliament investigators looking into the Board's (and Sandwich's) conduct during the Second Dutch War.
4. Dealing in goods imported from India.
5. Deborah Willett, recently hired as Elizabeth Pepys's companion.

6. There were only two licensed theater companies in Restoration London, one officially sponsored by the duke, the other by the king.
7. Attiring rooms; women's dressing room.
8. Nell Gwyn, a popular comic actress; she would later become the king's mistress.
9. Cues.

observable. But to see how Nell cursed for having so few people in the pit was pretty, the other house carrying away all the people at the new play, and is said nowadays to have generally most company, as being better players. By and by into the pit and there saw the play; which is pretty good, but my belly was full of what I had seen in the house; and so after the play done, away home and there to the writing my letters; and so home to supper and to bed.

[27 February 1668] All the morning at the office, and at noon home to dinner; and thence with my wife and Deb[1] to the King's House to see *Virgin Martyr*,[2] the first time it hath been acted a great while, and it is mighty pleasant; not that the play is worth much, but it is finely acted by Becke Marshall; but that which did please me beyond anything in the whole world was the wind-music when the angel comes down, which is so sweet that it ravished me; and indeed, in a word, did wrap up my soul so that it made me really sick, just as I have formerly been when in love with my wife; that neither then, nor all the evening going home and at home, I was able to think of anything, but remained all night transported, so as I could not believe that ever any music hath that real command over the soul of a man as this did upon me; and makes me resolve to practice wind-music and to make my wife do the like.

[20 January 1669], Up, and my wife and I and W. Hewer to White-hall, where she set us down. * * * Thence to my wife at Unthankes and with her and W. Hewer to Hercules-Pillars, calling to do two or three things by the way, and there dined; and thence to the Duke of York's House[3] and saw *Twelfth Night*, as it is now revived, but I think one of the weakest plays that ever I saw on the stage.[4] [This afternoon, before the play, I called with my wife at Dancre's[5] the great lanskip-painter, by Mr. Povy's advice, and have bespoke him to come to take measure of my dining-room panels; and there I met with the pretty daughter of the Coate-seller's that lived in Cheapside, and now in Covent-garden, who hath her picture drawn here, but very poorly; but she is a pretty woman, and now I perceive married, a very pretty black[6] woman.][7] So the play done, we home, my wife letting fall some words of her observing my eyes too mightily employed in the playhouse; meaning, upon women, which did vex me; but however, when we came home we were good friends; and so to read and to supper, and so to bed.

[Elizabeth Pepys and Deborah Willett]

[25 October 1668] *Lord's Day*. Up, and discoursing with my wife about our house and many new things we are doing of; and so to church I, and there find Jack Fen come, and his wife, a pretty black woman; I never saw her before, nor took notice of her now. So home and to dinner; and after dinner, all the afternoon got my wife and boy to read to me. And at night W. Batelier comes and sups with us; and after supper, to have my head combed by Deb, which occasioned the greatest sorrow to me that ever I knew in this world; for my wife, coming up suddenly, did find me embracing the girl con my

---

1. Deborah Willett.
2. A tragedy by Thomas Dekker and Philip Massinger, first performed c. 1620.
3. I.e., playhouse.
4. Pepys had already seen the play twice, and set down similar opinions both times: "the play [was] a burthen to me, and I took no pleasure at all in it" (11 September 1661); "saw *Twelfth Night* acted well, though it be but a

silly play and not relating at all to the name or day"—i.e., to the Twelfth Night festivities celebrated on this date (6 January 1663).
5. Hendrick Danckerts, Dutch-born painter of portraits and landscapes.
6. Dark-haired.
7. Pepys squeezed these bracketed sentences into the margin of the entry's pages as an afterthought.

hand sub su coats; and indeed, I was with my main in her cunny.[8] I was at a wonderful loss upon it, and the girl also; and I endeavored to put it off, but my wife was struck mute and grew angry, and as her voice came to her, grew quite out of order; and I do say little, but to bed; and my wife said little also, but could not sleep all night; but about 2 in the morning waked me and cried, and fell to tell me as a great secret that she was a Roman Catholic and had received the Holy Sacrament; which troubled me but I took no notice of it, but she went on from one thing to another, till at last it appeared plainly her trouble was at what she saw; but yet I did not know how much she saw and therefore said nothing to her. But after her much crying and reproaching me with inconstancy and preferring a sorry girl before her, I did give her no provocations but did promise all fair usage to her, and love, and foreswore any hurt that I did with her—till at last she seemed to be at ease again; and so toward morning, a little sleep; [26][9] and so I, with some little repose and rest, rose, and up and by water to Whitehall, but with my mind mightily troubled for the poor girl, whom I fear I have undone by this, my wife telling me that she would turn her out of door. However, I was obliged to attend the Duke of York, thinking to have had a meeting of Tangier today, but had not; but he did take me and Mr. Wren into his closet, and there did press me to prepare what I had to say upon the answers of my fellow-officers to his great letter; which I promised to do against his coming to town again the next week; and so to other discourse, finding plainly that he is in trouble and apprehensions of the reformers, and would be found to do what he can towards reforming himself.[1] And so thence to my Lord Sandwich; where after long stay, he being in talk with others privately, I to him; and there he taking physic and keeping his chamber, I had an hour's talk with him about the ill posture of things at this time, while the King gives countenance to Sir Charles Sedley and Lord Buckhurst,[2] telling him their late story of running up and down the streets a little while since all night, and their being beaten and clapped up all night by the constable, who is since chid and imprisoned for his pains.

He tells me that he thinks his matters do stand well with the King—and hopes to have dispatch to his mind; but I doubt it, and do see that he doth fear it too. He told me my Lady Carteret's trouble about my writing of that letter[3] of the Duke of York's lately to the office; which I did not own, but declared to be of no injury to G. Carteret, and that I would write a letter to him to satisfy him therein. But this I am in pain how to do without doing myself wrong, and the end I had, of preparing a justification to myself hereafter, when the faults of the Navy come to be found out. However, I will do it in the best manner I can.

Thence by coach home and to dinner, finding my wife mightily discontented and the girl sad, and no words from my wife to her. So after dinner, they out with me about two or three things; and so home again, I all the evening busy and my wife full of trouble in her looks; and anon to bed—where about midnight, she wakes me and there falls foul on me again, affirming that she saw me hug and kiss the girl; the latter I denied, and truly; the other I confessed and no more. And upon her pressing me,

---

8. I.e., with his hand under her petticoats and his hand in her vagina. Here as often, Pepys reports his illicit sexual activities in a "secret" language compounded of Latin, French, Spanish, and English.

9. Pepys wedges the new date into the margin, beside the run-on narrative.

1. The duke was Lord High Admiral of the navy; on his behalf Pepys had composed a letter to the Navy Board proposing reforms in response to parliamentary investigations of the disastrous Second Dutch War.

2. Notorious libertines (Buckhurst was Nell Gwyn's current lover).

3. The "great letter" on naval reform.

did offer to give her under my hand that I would never see Mrs. Pearse[4] more, nor Knepp, but did promise her particular demonstrations of my true love to her, owning some indiscretion in what I did, but that there was no harm in it. She at last on these promises was quiet, and very kind we were, and so to sleep; [27] and in the morning up, but with my mind troubled for the poor girl, with whom I could not get opportunity to speak; but to the office, my mind mighty full of sorrow for her, where all the morning, and to dinner with my people and to the office all the afternoon; and so at night home and there busy to get some things ready against tomorrow's meeting of Tangier; and that being done and my clerks gone, my wife did toward bedtime begin to be in a mighty rage from some new matter that she had got in her head, and did most part of the night in bed rant at me in most high terms, of threats of publishing my shame; and when I offered to rise, would have rose too, and caused a candle to be lit, to burn by her all night in the chimney while she ranted; while I, that knew myself to have given some grounds for it, did make it my business to appease her all I could possibly, and by good words and fair promises did make her very quiet; and so rested all night and rose with perfect good peace, being heartily afflicted for this folly of mine that did occasion it; but was forced to be silent about the girl, which I have no mind to part with, but much less that the poor girl should be undone by my folly. [28] So up, with mighty kindness from my wife and a thorough peace; and being up, did by a note advise the girl what I had done and owned, which note I was in pain for till she told me that she had burned it. This evening, Mr. Spong came and sat late with me, and first told me of the instrument called parrallogram, which I must have one of, showing me his practice thereon by a map of England.[5]

So by coach with Mr. Gibson[6] to Chancery Lane, and there made oath before a master of chancery to my Tangier account of fees; and so to Whitehall, where by and by a committee met; my Lord Sandwich there, but his report was not received, it being late; but only a little business done, about the supplying the place with victuals; but I did get, to my great content, my account allowed of fees, with great applause by my Lord Ashley and Sir W. Penn. Thence home, calling at one or two places, and there about our workmen, who are at work upon my wife's closet and other parts of my house, that we are all in dirt. So after dinner, with Mr. Gibson all the afternoon in my closet; and at night to supper and to bed, my wife and I at good peace, but yet with some little grudgings of trouble in her, and more in me, about the poor girl.

[14 November 1668] Up, and had a mighty mind to have seen or given a note to Deb or to have given her a little money; to which purpose I wrapped up 40s in a paper, thinking to give her; but my wife rose presently, and would not let me be out of her sight; and went down before me into the kitchen, and came up and told me that she was in the kitchen, and therefore would have me go round the other way; which she repeating, and I vexed at it, answered her a little angrily; upon which she instantly flew out into a rage, calling me dog and rogue, and that I had a rotten heart; all which, knowing that I deserved it, I bore with; and word being brought presently up that she was gone away by coach with her things, my wife was friends; and so all quiet, and I to the office with my heart sad, and find that I cannot forget the girl, and vexed I know not where to look for her—and more troubled to see how my wife is by this means likely for ever to have her hand over me, that I shall for ever be a slave to her;

4. Elizabeth Pearse, wife of a naval surgeon.
5. The parallelogram was a device for making copies of
diagrams and maps on the same or on a different scale.
6. A favorite assistant of Pepys's.

that is to say, only in matters of pleasure, but in other things she will make her business, I know, to please me and to keep me right to her—which I will labor to be indeed, for she deserves it of me, though it will be I fear a little time before I shall be able to wear Deb out of my mind. At the office all the morning, and merry at noon at dinner; and after dinner to the office, where all the afternoon and doing much business late; my mind being free of all troubles, I thank God, but only for my thoughts of this girl, which hang after her. And so at night home to supper, and there did sleep with great content with my wife. I must here remember that I have lain with my moher[7] as a husband more times since this falling-out than in I believe twelve months before—and with more pleasure to her than I think in all the time of our marriage before.

[20 November 1668] This morning up, with mighty kind words between my poor wife and I; and so to Whitehall by water, W. Hewer with me, who is to go with me everywhere until my wife be in condition to go out along with me herself; for she doth plainly declare that she dares not trust me out alone, and therefore made it a piece of our league that I should alway take somebody with me, or her herself; which I am mighty willing to, being, by the grace of God resolved never to do her wrong more.[8]

We landed at the Temple, and there I did bid him call at my cousin Roger Pepys's lodgings, and I stayed in the street for him; and so took water again at the Strand stairs and so to Whitehall, in my way I telling him plainly and truly my resolutions, if I can get over this evil, never to give new occasion for it. He is, I think, so honest and true a servant to us both, and one that loves us, that I was not much troubled at his being privy to all this, but rejoiced in my heart that I had him to assist in the making us friends; which he did do truly and heartily, and with good success—for I did get him to go to Deb to tell her that I had told my wife all of my being with her the other night, that so, if my wife should send, she might not make the business worse by denying it. While I was at Whitehall with the Duke of York doing our ordinary business with him, here being also the first time the new treasurers, W. Hewer did go to her and come back again; and so I took him into St. James's Park, and there he did tell me he had been with her and found what I said about my manner of being with her true, and had given her advice as I desired. I did there enter into more talk about my wife and myself, and he did give me great assurance of several particular cases to which my wife had from time to time made him privy of her loyalty and truth to me after many and great temptations, and I believe them truly. I did also discourse the unfitness of my leaving of my employment now in many respects, to go into the country as my wife desires—but that I would labor to fit myself for it; which he thoroughly understands, and doth agree with me in it; and so, hoping to get over this trouble, we about our business to Westminster Hall to meet Roger Pepys; which I did, and did there discourse of the business of lending him 500l to answer some occasions of his, which I believe to be safe enough; and so took leave of him and away by coach home, calling on my coach-maker by the way, where I like my little coach mightily. But when I came home, hoping for a further degree of peace and quiet, I find my wife upon her bed in a horrible rage afresh, calling me all the bitter names; and rising, did

7. Spanish *mujer*: wife. For the first time, Pepys applies his secret language to Elizabeth.
8. Two nights earlier, Pepys had traced Deborah Willett to her new lodgings, and caressed her in his coach. The next day, Elizabeth told him that she knew about the assignation, and he signed a pledge "never to see or speak with Deb while I live."

fall to revile me in the bitterest manner in the world, and could not refrain to strike me and pull my hair; which I resolved to bear with, and had good reason to bear it. So I by silence and weeping did prevail with her a little to be quiet, and she would not eat her dinner without me; but yet by and by into a raging fit she fell again worse than before, that she would slit the girl's nose; and at last W. Hewer came in and came up, who did allay her fury, I flinging myself in a sad desperate condition upon the bed in the blue room, and there lay while they spoke together; and at last it came to this, that if I would call Deb "whore" under my hand,[9] and write to her that I hated her and would never see her more, she would believe me and trust in me— which I did agree to; only, as to the name of "whore" I would have excused, and therefore wrote to her sparing that word; which my wife thereupon tore it, and would not be satisfied till, W. Hewer winking upon me, I did write so, with the name of a whore, as that I did fear she might too probably have been prevailed upon to have been[1] a whore by her carriage to me, and therefore, as such, I did resolve never to see her more. This pleased my wife, and she gives it W. Hewer to carry to her, with a sharp message from her. So from that minute my wife begun to be kind to me, and we to kiss and be friends, and so continued all the evening and fell to talk of other matters with great comfort, and after supper to bed.

This evening comes Mr. Billup to me to read over Mr. Wren's alterations of my draft of a letter for the Duke of York to sign, to the board; which I like mighty well, they being not considerable, only in mollifying some hard terms which I had thought fit to put in. From this to other discourse; I do find that the Duke of York and his servant Mr. Wren do look upon this service of mine as a very seasonable service to the Duke of York, as that which he will have to show to his enemies in his own justification of his care of the King's business. And I am sure I am heartily glad of it—both for the King's sake and the Duke of York's, and my own also—for if I continue, my work, by this means, will be the less, and my share in the blame[2] also.

He being gone, I to my wife again and so spent the evening with very great joy, and the night also, with good sleep and rest, my wife only troubled in her rest, but less than usual—for which the God of Heaven be praised. I did this night promise to my wife never to go to bed without calling upon God upon my knees by prayer; and I begun this night, and hope I shall never forget to do the like all my life—for I do find that it is much the best for my soul and body to live pleasing to God and my poor wife—and will ease me of much care, as well as much expense.

[31 May 1669] Up very betimes, and so continued all the morning, with W. Hewer, upon examining and stating my accounts, in order to the fitting myself to go abroad beyond sea,[3] which the ill condition of my eyes, and my neglect for a year or two, hath kept me behindhand in, and so as to render it very difficult now, and troublesome to my mind to do it; but I this day made a satisfactory entrance therein.[4] Dined at home, and in the afternoon by water to Whitehall, calling by the way at Mitchell's,[5] where I have not been many a day till just the other day; and now I met her mother there and knew her husband to be out of town. And here yo did besar

---

9. In writing.
1. Become.
2. For Navy Board misconduct.
3. Pepys and his wife planned a tour of Holland, Flanders, and France. Near journey's end, Elizabeth Pepys caught a fever; she died in London on 10 November 1669.

4. Pepys suffered from a painful combination of farsightedness and astigmatism which doctors did not know how to diagnose or to treat; he feared (mistakenly) that he was going blind.
5. Michael Mitchell sold liquor in a shop on London Bridge; his wife Betty is the "her" of the ensuing clauses.

ella, but have not opportunity para hazer mas[6] with her as I would have offered if yo had had it. And thence had another meeting with the Duke of York at Whitehall with the Duke of York on yesterday's work, and made a good advance; and so being called by my wife, we to the park, Mary Batelier, a Dutch gentleman, a friend of hers, being with us. Thence to the World's End, a drinking-house by the park, and there merry; and so home late.

And thus ends all that I doubt I shall ever be able to do with my own eyes in the keeping of my journal, I being not able to do it any longer, having done now so long as to undo my eyes almost every time that I take a pen in my hand; and therefore, whatever comes of it, I must forbear; and therefore resolve from this time forward to have it kept by my people in longhand, and must therefore be contented to set down no more than is fit for them and all the world to know; or if there be anything (which cannot be much, now my amours to Deb are past, and my eyes hindering me in almost all other pleasures), I must endeavor to keep a margin in my book open, to add here and there a note in shorthand with my own hand.[7] And so I betake myself to that course which is almost as much as to see myself go into my grave—for which, and all the discomforts that will accompany my being blind, the good God prepare me.

May. 31. 1669.   S.P.

⎯⎯⎯⎯⎯⎯

RESPONSE

Robert Louis Stevenson (1850–1894): from Samuel Pepys[1]

Pepys was a young man for his age, came slowly to himself in the world, sowed his wild oats late, took late to industry, and preserved till nearly forty the headlong gusto of a boy. So, to come rightly at the spirit in which the Diary was written, we must recall a class of sentiments which with most of us are over and done before the age of twelve. In our tender years we still preserve a freshness of surprise at our prolonged existence; events make an impression out of all proportion to their consequence; we are unspeakably touched by our own past adventures, and look forward to our future personality with sentimental interest. It was something of this, I think, that clung to Pepys. Although not sentimental in the abstract, he was sweetly sentimental about himself. His own past clung about his heart, an evergreen. He was the slave of an association. He could not pass by Islington, where his father used to carry him to cakes and ale, but he must light at the "King's Head" and eat and drink "for rememberance

---

6. I did kiss her but had no chance to do more.
7. Pepys never produced the continuation of his journal that he envisions here.
1. Pepys's diary, written in the seventeenth century, made its way into print only in the nineteenth. Readers were at once fascinated by his distance from them in time and by what they regarded as his proximity to them in temperament; they resurrected him, as readers always will, partly in their own image. When a new, unprecedentedly full but still partly expurgated edition of the diary appeared in 1881, it was greeted with mixed emotion (praise for the fullness, exasperation at the expurgation) by a prolific literary journalist who would achieve

his own global fame just a few years later: Robert Louis Stevenson. After a single paragraph, Stevenson's review of the edition gives way to a long, perceptive essay on the diarist, in whom he finds forecast many of the energies and endeavors that had preoccupied his own century: the self-absorbed self-revelations of the Romantics; a countervailing devotion to proto-Victorian "respectability"; and a recurrent, almost sensual devotion to the memories and pleasures of childhood that would soon mark much of Stevenson's own most enduring work: Treasure Island, Kidnapped, and A Child's Garden of Verses (1885). The essay first appeared in Cornhill Magazine 44 (July 1881).

of the old house sake." He counted it good fortune to lie at night at Epsom to renew his old walks, "where Mrs. Hely and I did use to walk and talk, with whom I had the first sentiments of love and pleasure in a woman's company, discourse and taking her by the hand, she being a pretty woman." He goes about weighing up the *Assurance*, which lay near Woolwich under water, and cries in a parenthesis, "Poor ship, that I have been twice merry in, in Captain Holland's time"; and after revisiting the *Naseby*, now changed into the *Charles*, he confesses "it was a great pleasure to myself to see the ship that I began my good fortune in." The stone that he was cut for[2] he preserved in a case; and to the Turners he kept alive such gratitude for their assistance that for years, and after he had begun to mount himself into higher zones, he continued to have that family to dinner on the anniversary of the operation. Not Hazlitt[3] nor Rousseau[4] had a more romantic passion for their past, although at times they might express it more romantically; and if Pepys shared with them this childish fondness, did not Rousseau, who left behind him the *Confessions*, or Hazlitt, who wrote the *Liber Amoris*, and loaded his essays with loving personal detail, share with Pepys in his unwearied egotism? For the two things go hand in hand; or, to be more exact, it is the first that makes the second either possible or pleasing.

But, to be quite in sympathy with Pepys, we must return once more to the experience of children. I can remember to have written, in the flyleaf of more than one book, the date and the place where I was then—if, for instance, I was ill in bed or sitting in a certain garden; these were jottings for my future self; if I should chance on such a note in after years, I thought it would cause me a particular thrill to recognize myself across the intervening distance. Indeed, I might come upon them now, and not be moved one tittle—which shows that I have comparatively failed in life, and grown older than Samuel Pepys. For in the Diary we can find more than one such note of perfect childish egotism; as when he explains that his candle is going out, "which makes me write thus slobberingly"; or as in this incredible particularity, "To my study, where I only wrote thus much of this day's passages to this,[5] and so out again"; or lastly, as here, with more of circumstance: "I staid up till the bellman came by with his bell under my window, *as I was writing of this very line,* and cried, 'Past one of the clock, and a cold, frosty, windy morning.'" Such passages are not to be misunderstood. The appeal to Samuel Pepys years hence is unmistakable. He desires that dear, though unknown, gentleman keenly to realize his predecessor; to remember why a passage was uncleanly written; to recall (let us fancy, with a sigh) the tones of the bellman, the chill of the early, windy morning, and the very line his own romantic self was scribing at the moment. The man, you will perceive, was making reminiscences—a sort of pleasure by ricochet, which comforts many in distress, and turns some others into sentimental libertines: and the whole book, if you will but look at it in that way, is seen to be a work of art to[6] Pepys's own address.

Here, then, we have the key to that remarkable attitude preserved by him throughout his Diary, to that unflinching—I had almost said, that unintelligent—sincerity which makes it a miracle among human books. * * *

1881

⌒⌒

2. See Pepys's first diary entry, p. 2011.
3. William Hazlitt (1778–1830), journalist, essayist, critic, and author of *Liber Amoris* (1823), an autobiographical account of his feverish, futile love affair with his landlady's daughter.

4. Jean-Jacques Rousseau (1712–1788), political philosopher, novelist, and author of the matchlessly unabashed and copious autobiography *Confessions* (1781).
5. I.e., to this point in the entry.
6. I.e., posted to.

══╬ PERSPECTIVES ╬══

The Royal Society and the New Science

In the late 1600s, the antiquarian John Aubrey looked back to the middle of his century as a turning point in intellectual history: "Till about the year 1649, when experimental philosophy was first cultivated by a club at Oxford, 'twas held a strange presumption for a man to attempt an innovation in learnings; and not to be good manners, to be more knowing than his neighbors and forefathers." The "club" consisted of a group of inquirers for whom the university at Oxford offered a place of retreat in time of civil war. As Aubrey implies, their "innovation" consisted in a kind of bad manners. They refused to take the word of their intellectual "forefathers" (notably Aristotle) for how the natural world worked, and instead pursued knowledge of it through direct experiment, preferring new data to old theory, the testimony of the senses over the constructs of the intellect; the works of Francis Bacon, who had articulated such a method a half-century earlier, served for these investigators as something akin to scripture. The members continued to meet during the Interregnum. In 1662, Charles II granted the group (which had relocated to London) a charter, a seal, and with his patronage, a new prominence. The informal club had become the "Royal Society for the Improving of Natural Knowledge."

That "Improving" was to take place on many fronts. The Society's charter stipulated that its experiments should be aimed at "promoting the knowledge of natural things and useful arts": science and technology. In its first decades, its members made enormous advances in both realms, producing (among innumerable innovations) new explanations of heat, cold, and light; an air pump capable of creating a vacuum; a newly efficient pocket watch; and a newly coherent and durable account of the universe. A Fellow of the Society might work simultaneously at many endeavors that have since become specialties, investigating biology, physics, and astronomy, inventing scientific instruments and domestic appliances, advancing inquiries into theology, astrology, even demonology.

The group liked to portray itself as inclusive demographically too. Its Fellows represented many religious views, political persuasions, and social strata, from dukes to merchants to "mechanicks." Still, the early records evince an initial emphasis on high rank: aristocrats, courtiers, politicians, and "gentlemen" made up more than half the original membership (women were excluded altogether). Many of these men were mere names on the rolls, enlisted to bolster the respectability of the new enterprise; others were occasional spectators, intermittently attending the meetings to observe (amused, amazed, often baffled) the experiments performed there. But the Society also fostered a new category of inquirer: the "Christian virtuoso," a man of birth, means, merit, brains, and leisure, whose dissociation from any one profession was taken to guarantee the objectivity of his investigations, and whose rank and goodness underwrote the integrity of his findings. The Honorable Robert Boyle, who coined the phrase, was also its epitome. Well-born, devout, and dazzlingly gifted at science, he was the Society's prime mover and first star. But the type also found a less rarified, more popular incarnation in a new kind of amateur: the prosperous person who read, contemplated, talked the new philosophy, and kept a "cabinet of curiosities"—a closet or small room in which were arranged, and proudly displayed, antiquarian objects, scientific specimens, anything whose strangeness might arouse interest. The Society was amassing comparable collections on a much larger scale; the history of museums begins within the cabinets of the virtuosi.

The Society's emphasis on gentlemanly virtuosity was partly a form of self-defense against attacks from many quarters, where the "experimental philosophy" was regarded as ludicrous or dangerous or both. The influential wits of the day scoffed at the earnestness of the investigators and the seeming preposterousness of their findings (even Charles II laughed out loud when he learned that the members were busy weighing air); some clergymen and politicians saw in the new enterprise a threat to religion and to social hierarchy, a challenge against past, present, and divine authority, mounted by persons so presumptuous as to suppose that the truths of the world could be determined by human investigation rather than by Christian revelation.

The Society answered (again in the language of its charter) that it was intent upon serving "the glory of God and the good of mankind." The "good of mankind" was to be enhanced by technological improvements, which would make work more productive, life easier, and commerce more abundant, in contrast to the dark old days when (as Aubrey reminisces) "even to attempt an improvement in husbandry [agriculture], though it succeeded with profit, was looked upon with an ill eye." The "glory of God" would be served by a new form of attention to the world God made. A long tradition ascribed to the Deity two sacred texts: the Book of Scripture, and the Book of Nature. The faithful had long pondered the first; the Society now undertook to read the second anew and aright. "Each page in the great volume of nature," observed Boyle, "is full of real hieroglyphs, where (by an inverted way of expression) things stand for words"—objects and actions incarnate truths. To disclose the divine intricacy in the Book of Nature (so the Society's advocates argued) could only enlarge wonder and increase worship.

The new reading of that old text reshaped other texts as well. In the 1660s and after, manuscripts, periodicals, and printed books all explored new forms, as writers attempted to render in language what Michel Foucault has called "the prose of the world," to grapple with new relations between words and things, and to make the written or the printed page (like the closet and the cabinet) a copious repository of newfound curiosities.

✦ ≔✦⚊ ✦

Thomas Sprat
1635–1713

Given the date of its first appearance, the *History of the Royal Society* seems puzzlingly titled. The Oxford-educated clergyman Thomas Sprat wrote much of it in 1663, just a year after the Society received its charter, and published it (after delays caused by fire, plague, and other distractions) in 1667. Both title and timing reflect the pressures that produced the book in the first place. As he acknowledges at the outset, Sprat has produced not so much a "plain history" of the Society as an "apology," in the Greek-based sense of the word current in the seventeenth century: an energetic defense of the new institution's policies and methods.

From its inception, the Society's directors felt the need for such a defense, and they brought Sprat in specifically to provide it, appointing him a Founding Fellow and anxiously inquiring after his progress on the book. They had chosen him not for his knowledge of science (negligible) but for his status as a divine and for his skill as a rhetorician. In response to its detractors, Sprat insists that the Society will enhance piety (by detailing the wonders of Creation); will uphold hierarchy (as evidenced by the predominance of gentlemen and aristocrats among the Fellowship); and will cultivate community (in order to appease fears that the Fellows will revive "disputation" when the new Restoration needs it least, Sprat downplays the importance of argument in the new science and stresses instead the accumulation of raw data). Above all, Sprat focuses on the Society's capacity to improve ordinary life by producing "new inventions and shorter ways of labor" that will make possible an easier and more prosperous existence for the English, whose national "Genius" is uniquely suited to such advances.

As Michael Hunter notes, Sprat's "generalized attempt to appeal to everybody and antagonize nobody" fell short. It appealed mainly to adherents, and provided critics with a new target for their attacks. In the selection printed here, Sprat navigates a particularly delicate portion of his argument. He sets forth the Fellows' attempts to simplify the prose style in which they wrote up their inquiries and discoveries. The degree to which the Society actually sought and managed to implement a new "mathematical plainness" has long remained a matter of dispute. In contemporary writing, clarity and "ornament" were often seen as mutually supportive; even when Sprat is arguing for a "naked" prose, he intermittently resorts to the very "amplifications, digressions, and swellings of style" that he is ruling out. As its sponsors intended, Sprat's *History* applies a polished rhetoric to a pointed claim: that the Royal Society was creating a "common-stock" of knowledge on which all might draw, and from which all might profit.

from The History of the Royal Society of London, for the Improving of Natural Knowledge

Thus they have directed, judged, conjectured upon, and improved experiments. But lastly, in these and all other businesses that have come under their care, there is one thing more about which the Society has been most solicitous, and that is the manner of their discourse, which unless they have been watchful to keep in due temper, the whole spirit and vigor of their design had been soon eaten out by the luxury and redundance of speech. The ill effects of this superfluity of talking have already overwhelmed most other arts and professions, insomuch that when I consider the means of happy living and the causes of their corruption, I can hardly forbear recanting what I said before, and concluding that eloquence ought to be banished out of all civil societies as a thing fatal to peace and good manners. To this opinion I should wholly incline, if I did not find that it is a weapon which may be as easily procured by bad men as good, and that, if these should only cast it away and those retain it, the naked innocence of virtue would be upon all occasions exposed to the armed malice of the wicked. This is the chief reason that should now keep up the ornaments of speaking in any request, since they are so much degenerated from their original usefulness. They were at first, no doubt, an admirable instrument in the hands of wise men, when they were only employed to describe goodness, honesty, obedience, in larger, fairer, and more moving images; to represent truth, clothed with bodies; and to bring knowledge back again to our very senses, from whence it was at first derived to our understandings. But now they are generally changed to worse uses. They make the fancy disgust[1] the best things, if they come sound and unadorned. They are in open defiance against reason, professing not to hold much correspondence with that, but with its slaves, the passions. They give the mind a motion too changeable and bewitching to consist with right practice. Who can behold, without indignation, how many mists and uncertainties these specious tropes and figures[2] have brought on our knowledge? How many rewards, which are due to more profitable and difficult arts, have been still snatched away by the easy vanity of fine speaking? For now I am warmed with this just anger, I cannot withhold myself from betraying the shallowness of all these seeming mysteries upon which we writers and speakers look so big. And, in few words, I dare say that of all the studies of men, nothing may be sooner obtained than this vicious abundance of phrase, this trick of metaphors, this volubility of tongue, which makes so great a noise in the world. But I spend words in vain; for the evil is now so inveterate that it is hard to know whom to blame or where to begin to reform. We all value one another so much upon this beautiful deceit and labor so long after it in the years of our education that we cannot but ever after think kinder of it than it deserves. And indeed, in most other

---

1. They make the imagination reject.   2. Figures of speech.

parts of learning, I look on it to be a thing almost utterly desperate in its cure. And I think it may be placed amongst those general mischiefs such as the dissension of Christian princes,[3] the want[4] of practice in religion and the like, which have been so long spoken against, that men are become insensible about them, every one shifting off the fault from himself to others, and so they are only made bare commonplaces of complaint. It will suffice my present purpose to point out what has been done by the Royal Society towards the correcting of its[5] excesses in natural philosophy, to which it is, of all others, a most professed enemy.

They have therefore been most rigorous in putting in execution the only remedy that can be found for this extravagance. And that has been a constant resolution to reject all the amplifications, digressions, and swellings of style; to return back to the primitive purity and shortness, when men delivered so many *things*, almost in an equal number of *words*. They have exacted from all their members a close, naked, natural way of speaking; positive expressions; clear senses; a native easiness; bringing all things as near the mathematical plainness as they can and preferring the language of artisans, countrymen, and merchants before that of wits or scholars.[6]

And here there is one thing not to be passed by, which will render this established custom of the Society well nigh everlasting; and that is, the general constitution of the minds of the English. I have already often insisted on some of the prerogatives of England, whereby it may justly lay claim to be the head of a philosophical league, above all other countries in Europe. I have urged its situation,[7] its present genius, and the disposition of its merchants, and many more such arguments to encourage us still remain to be used. But of all others, this, which I am now alleging, is of the most weighty and important consideration. If there can be a true character given of the universal temper of any nation under heaven, then certainly this must be ascribed to our countrymen: that they have commonly an unaffected sincerity; that they love to deliver their minds with a sound simplicity; that they have the middle qualities between the reserved, subtle southern and the rough, unhewn northern people; that they are not extremely prone to speak; that they are more concerned what others will think of the strength, than of the fineness of what they say; and that an universal modesty possesses them. These qualities are so conspicuous and proper to our soil that we often hear them objected to us by some of our neighbor satirists in more disgraceful expressions. For they are wont to revile the English with a want of familiarity; with a melancholy dumpishness,[8] with slowness, silence, and with the unrefined sullenness of their behavior. But these are only the reproaches of partiality or ignorance. For they ought rather to be commended for an honorable integrity; for a neglect of circumstances and flourishes; for regarding things of greater moment,[9] more than less; for a scorn to deceive as well as to be deceived, which are all the best endowments that can enter into a philosophical mind. So that even the position of our climate, the air, the influence of the heaven, the composition of the English blood, as well as the embraces of the ocean, seem to join with the labors of the Royal Society to render our country a land of experimental

3. Disputes between Christian monarchs.
4. Lack.
5. I.e., eloquence's.
6. For a parody of this position, see Swift's depiction of the Academy in *Gulliver's Travels*, Part 3. ch.5.
7. I.e., its location. Sprat has earlier emphasized that

England's status as an island, and as "mistress of the Ocean," gives it a privileged position from which to supervise international scientific experiments and correspondence.
8. Tendency to depression.
9. Importance.

knowledge. And it is a good sign that nature will reveal more of its secrets to the English than to others because it has already furnished them with a genius so well proportioned for the receiving and retaining its mysteries.

And now to come to a close of the second part of the narration. The Society has reduced its principal observations into one common-stock[1] and laid them up in public registers to be nakedly transmitted to the next generation of men, and so from them to their successors. And as their purpose was to heap up a mixed mass of experiments, without digesting them into any perfect model, so to this end, they confined themselves to no order of subjects; and whatever they have recorded, they have done it, not as complete schemes of opinions, but as bare, unfinished histories.

Philosophical Transactions

Philosophical Transactions first appeared in 1665 and continues to the present day; it is the longest running periodical in English and the oldest scientific journal in the world. It was created by Henry Oldenburg (1618–1677), a German-born diplomat who came to England in 1653 as an emissary to Oliver Cromwell and found himself powerfully drawn to the ideas and the company of the practitioners of the new science at Oxford. His gift for copious, accurate reporting on scientific matters prompted the Royal Society to enlist him as Fellow and Secretary, charged with attending the meetings, keeping the minutes, and managing the new institution's huge correspondence with scientific inquirers in England and abroad. Oldenburg produced the monthly *Transactions* as a private venture, but he drew its material from the documents in which his Society work immersed him, particularly from the correspondence that provided so plentiful an account (in the words of the journal's subtitle) "of the present undertakings, studies, and labors of the ingenious in many considerable parts of the world." The *Transactions'* content ranged wide conceptually as well as geographically, readily shifting from systematic searches for natural laws, to reports on technological innovations, to eager surmises about random oddities: monstrous births, human and otherwise, were a recurrent favorite. The new journal combined in text the attractions of the scientific treatise and the cabinet of curiosities; the insatiable curiosity of the journal's most assiduous contributor, Oldenburg's patron Robert Boyle, helped to ensure this variety and texture.

More than any other instrument, the *Transactions* established the Royal Society as central to the new philosophy and fostered the conviction that the advancement of learning was a communal pursuit of truth to which (as Francis Bacon had predicted) everyone from a mariner to a virtuoso could contribute indispensable information. The *Transactions* influenced nonscientific journalism as well: with its topical headlines, variegated matter, and detailed tables of contents, it resembled no periodical of its time, but many that came after.

from **Philosophical Transactions**
[THE INTRODUCTION][1]

Whereas there is nothing more necessary for promoting the improvement of philosophical matters than the communicating, to such as apply their studies and

---

1. Property and resource for the use of all.   Vol 1., No.1, 6 March 1665.
1. This and the following two selections appeared in

endeavors that way, such things as are discovered or put in practice by others, it is therefore thought fit to employ the press as the most proper way to gratify those whose engagement in such studies and delight in the advancement of learning and profitable discoveries doth entitle them to the knowledge of what this kingdom or other parts of the world do from time to time afford, as well of the progress of the studies, labors, and attempts of the curious and learned in things of this kind, as of their complete discoveries and performances. To the end that, such productions being clearly and truly communicated, desires after solid and useful knowledge may be further entertained, ingenious endeavors and undertakings cherished, and those addicted to and conversant in such matters may be invited and encouraged to search, try, and find out new things, impart their knowledge to one another, and contribute what they can to the grand design of improving natural knowledge and perfecting all philosophical arts and sciences. All for the glory of God, the honor and advantage of these kingdoms, and the universal good of mankind.

* * *

An Account of a Very Odd Monstrous Calf

By the same noble person[2] was lately communicated to the Royal Society an account of a very odd, monstrous birth produced at Limmington in Hampshire, where a butcher, having caused a cow (which calved her first calf the year before) to be covered that she might the sooner be fatted, killed her when fat, and opening the womb, which he found heavy to admiration, saw in it a calf, which had begun to have hair, whose hinderlegs had no joints and whose tongue was, Cerebus-like,[3] triple—to each side of his mouth one, and one in the midst. Between the forelegs and the hinderlegs was a great stone, on which the calf rid.[4] The *sternum*, or that part of the breast where the ribs lie, was also perfect stone. And the stone on which it rid weighed twenty pounds and a half. The outside of the stone was of greenish color, but some small parts being broken off, it appeared a perfect free-stone. The stone, according to the letter of Mr. David Thomas, who sent this account to Mr. Boyle, is with Dr. Haughten of Salisbury, to whom he also refers for further information.

* * *

An observation imparted to the noble Mr. Boyle by Mr. David Thomas touching some particulars further considerable in the monster mentioned in the first papers of these Philosophical Transactions.[5]

Upon the strictest inquiry, I find by one that saw the monstrous calf and stone, within four hours after it was cut out of the cow's belly, that the breast of the calf was not stony (as I wrote) but that the skin of the breast and between the legs and of the neck (which parts lay on the smaller end of the stone) was very much thicker than on any other part, and that the feet of the calf were so parted as to be like the claws of a dog. The stone I have since seen. It is bigger at one end than the other, of no plain *superficies*,[6] but full of little cavities. The stone, when broken, is full of

---

2. Robert Boyle.
3. Resembling the mythical three-headed dog that guarded the entrance to Hades, the underworld of the dead.

4. Rode (i.e., straddled).
5. A "follow-up" from Vol. 1, No. 2.
6. Smooth surface.

small pebble stones of an oval figure. Its color is gray—like free-stone, but intermixed with veins of yellow and black. A part of it I have begged of Dr. Haughten for you, which I have sent to Oxford, whither a more exact account will be conveyed by the same person.

* * *

A letter of the honorable Robert Boyle of Sept. 13, 1673, to the publisher concerning Amber Greece and its being a vegetable production[7]

Sir,

Some occasions calling me this afternoon up to London, I was met there with a very intelligent gentleman, who was ready to go out of it. But before he did so, he willingly spared me some time to discourse with him about some of the affairs of our East Indian Company,[8] of which he was very lately Deputy Governor, and, his year being expired, is still one of the chief of the Court of Committees, which a foreigner would call Directors that manage all the affairs of that considerable society. And among other things, talking with him about some contents of a journal lately taken in a Dutch East Indian prize,[9] I learned from him that he, who understands that language very well, is now perusing that manuscript; and among many things recorded there that concern the economical and political affairs of the said Dutch company, he met with one physical observation which he thought so rare that, remembering the curiosity I had expressed for such things, he put it into English and transcribed it for me; and immediately drawing it out of his pocket, he presented me the short paper, whereof I now show you the copy. Upon perusal of which, you will very easily believe, that not only his civility obliged me, but the information it brought me surprised me too. For the several trials and observations of my own about amber greece have long kept me from acquiescing either in the vulgar opinions[1] or those of some learned men concerning it. Yet I confess, my experiments did much less discover what it is than this paper has done, in case we may safely and entirely give credit to its information, and that it reach to all kinds of amber greece. And probably you will be invited to look on this account, though not as complete, yet as very sincere, and on that score credible if you consider that this was not written by a philosopher to broach[2] a paradox or serve a hypothesis, but by a merchant or factor[3] for his superiors to give them an account of a matter of fact. And that this passage is extant in an authentic journal, wherein the affairs of the company were by public order from time to time registered at their chief colony Batavia.[4] And it appears by the paper itself that the relation was not looked upon as a doubtful thing, but as a thing from which a practical way may be deduced to make this discovery easily lucriferous[5] to the Dutch Company. And I could heartily wish that in those countries that are addicted to long navigations, more notice than is usual were taken and given of the natural rarities

7. Ambergris (Latin, "gray amber") is a gray waxy substance formed in the intestines of sperm whales; it was valued as a component in perfumes and medicines. Because ambergris, once emitted by the whale, often floats along the sea coast, traders and scientists were uncertain about its orgins. (Boyle's letter appeared in Vol. 8 No. 97).
8. A company chartered by Elizabeth 1 in 1600 to develop trade with India and the Far East.
9. I.e., the ship's log of a Dutch trading vessel recently captured by the English.
1. Received ideas of ordinary people.
2. Penetrate, untangle.
3. Company agent. Boyle reaffirms the Royal Society's interest in raw data over cooked theory, in the testimony of experienced "mechanics" over that of abstract "philosophers."
4. A seaport on the island of Java.
5. Profitable.

that occur to merchants and seamen. On which occasion I remember when I had in compliance with my curiosity put myself into our East Indian Company and had by their civility to me been chosen of their Committee as long as my health allowed me to continue so, I had the opportunity in some register books of merchants English and Dutch to observe some things which would easily justify this wish of mine, if my haste and their interest would permit me to acquaint others with them. But to return to our account of amber greece I think you will easily believe that if I had received it not by a paper but immediately from the writer,[6] I should by proposing diverse questions, have been enabled to give you a much more satisfactory account than this short one contains. But the obliging person that gave it me, being just going out of town, I could not civilly stay him to receive my queries about it, which though (God permitting) I may propose ere long, if I can light on him again, yet I fear he has given me in these few lines all that he found about this matter. However, this relation, as short as it is, being about the nature of a drug so precious and so little known will not, I hope, be unwelcome to the curious. To whom none is so like to convey it so soon and so well as Mr. O,[7] whose forwardness to oblige others by his various communications challenges returns of the like nature from others and particularly from his affectionate humble servant.

Follows the extract itself out of a Dutch journal belonging to the Dutch East Indian Company:

> Amber greece is not the scum or excrement of the whale, etc., but issues out of the root of a tree, which tree how far soever it stands on the land, always shoots forth its roots towards the sea, seeking the warmth of it, thereby to deliver the fattest gum that comes out of it, which tree otherwise by its copious fatness might be burnt and destroyed. Wherever that fat gum is shot into the sea, it is so tough that it is not easily broken from the root, unless its own weight and the working of the warm sea doth it,[8] and so it floats on the sea.
>
> There was found by a soldier 7/8 of a pound and by the chief two pieces weighing five pounds. If you plant the trees where the stream sets to the shore, then the stream will cast it up to great advantage. March 1, 1672, in Batavia.

Robert Hooke
1635–1703

In a long life, Robert Hooke got little sleep. From the age of twenty-eight until his death, he lived in rooms at Gresham College, the Royal Society headquarters, in order to make himself maximally available to meet the ceaseless demands of his many concurrent employments, as the Society's first Curator of Experiments, as the College's lecturer in geometry, as surveyor and rebuilder of London after the Great Fire, and as restless, relentless inventor and improver of scientific instruments. Hooke's friend John Aubrey described him as "the greatest mechanick this day in the world"; the jostle between the high superlative and the equivocal noun captures Hooke's uncertain status in the Society to which he devoted his prodigiously productive working life. The mechanical arts were in many ways the lifeblood of the Society's enterprise,

---

6. I.e., in conversation.   8. I.e., breaks it off.
7. Henry Oldenburg, editor of the *Transactions*.

but "mechanicks" were not gentry. In an institution founded and headed by aristocrats and gentlemen, this gifted son of a provincial clergyman was often treated (in Stephen Shapin's words) "as a tradesman, as a servant." Hooke's contract as Curator required that he prepare and perform "three or four substantial experiments" at each of the Society's weekly meetings, as well as any other experiments the Fellows might (in the recurrent wording of the meeting minutes) "order" or "direct" him to undertake. The empirical life of the Society during its first four decades would have been unimaginable without Hooke, but the Fellows registered his indispensability by irritation at the outside interests through which he pursued autonomy and income. "I could wish," wrote Sir Robert Moray, "he had finished the task laid upon him rather than to learn a dozen trades." Hooke's variegated pursuits, though, produced dozens of inventions and discoveries: newly efficient lenses, lamps, telescopes, watches; new theories of optics, chemistry, and gravity that in some cases anticipated Issac Newton's. Constitutionally irascible, Hooke spent much energy asserting, angrily but often accurately, the priority and/or superiority of his many innovations.

Hooke produced *Micrographia* at the Society's behest. The book doubled as a work of science and a piece of institutional propaganda, designed to promote the Society's methods. It fulfilled both purposes. In Hooke's sixty word-and-picture "Observations" of magnified objects, readers could see for the first time how far the useful artifice of the microscope had extended the "knowledge of natural things" into realms unreachable by the eye and mind alone. At the same time, the book touched a cultural pulse point. At its Greek root, Hooke's title suggests "the writing down of small things," and this is what many of his fellow Fellows— Pepys, Oldenburg, Evelyn, Aubrey—were in their different ways newly up to. (Pepys thought *Micrographia* "the most ingenious book that I ever read in my life.") Small things, it had been discovered, could produce large amazements when written up.

from Micrographia
Or Some Physiological Description of Minute Bodies Made by Magnifying Glasses with Observations and Inquiries thereupon
To the King

Sir,

I do here most humbly lay this small present at your Majesty's royal feet. And though it comes accompanied with two disadvantages, the meanness of the author and of the subject; yet in both I am encouraged by the greatness of your mercy and your knowledge. By the one I am taught, that you can forgive the most presumptuous offenders. And by the other, that you will not esteem the least work of nature or art unworthy of your observation. Amidst the many felicities that have accompanied your Majesty's happy restoration and government, it is none of the least considerable that philosophy and experimental learning have prospered under your royal patronage.[1] And as the calm prosperity of your reign has given us the leisure to follow these studies of quiet and retirement, so it is just that the fruits of them should, by way of acknowledgment, be returned to your Majesty. There are, Sir, several other of your subjects, of your Royal Society, now busy about nobler matters: the improvement of manufactures and agriculture, the increase of commerce, the advantage of navigation—in all which they are assisted by your Majesty's encouragement and example. Amidst all those greater designs, I here presume to bring in that which is

---

1. Charles II had granted the Society a royal charter in 1662.

more proportional to the smallness of my abilities and to offer some of the least of all visible things to that mighty king that has established an empire over the best of all invisible things of this world, the minds of men. Your Majesty's most humble and most obedient subject and servant,

Robert Hooke

TO THE ROYAL SOCIETY

After my address to our great founder and patron, I could not but think myself obliged, in consideration of those many engagements you have laid upon me, to offer these my poor labors to this most illustrious assembly. You have been pleased formerly to accept of these rude drafts.[2] I have since added to them some descriptions and some conjectures of my own. And therefore, together with your acceptance, I must also beg your pardon. The rules you have prescribed yourselves in your philosophical progress do seem the best that have ever yet been practiced. And particularly that of avoiding dogmatizing and the espousal of any hypothesis not sufficiently grounded and confirmed by experiments. This way seems the most excellent and may preserve both philosophy and natural history from its former corruptions. In saying which, I may seem to condemn my own course in this treatise, in which there may perhaps be some expressions, which may seem more positive than your prescriptions will permit. And though I desire to have them understood only as conjectures and queries (which your method does not altogether disallow) yet if even in those I have exceeded, 'tis fit that I should declare that it was not done by your directions. For it is most unreasonable that you should undergo the imputation of the faults of my conjectures, seeing you can receive so small advantage of reputation by the slight observations of Your most humble and most faithful servant,

Robert Hooke

from *The Preface*

[A]ll the uncertainty and mistakes of human actions proceed either from the narrowness and wandering of our senses, from the slipperiness or delusion of our memory, from the confinement or rashness of our understanding, so that 'tis no wonder that our power over natural causes and effects is so slowly improved, seeing we are not only to contend with the obscurity and difficulty of the things whereon we work and think, but even the forces of our own minds conspire to betray us.

These being the dangers in the process of human reason, the remedies of them all can only proceed from the real, the mechanical, the experimental philosophy, which has this advantage over the philosophy of discourse and disputation, that whereas that chiefly aims at the subtlety of its deductions and conclusions, without much regard to the first groundwork, which ought to be well laid on the sense and memory, so this intends the right ordering of them all and the making them serviceable to each other.

The first thing to be undertaken in this weighty work is a watchfulness over the failings and an enlargement of the dominion of the senses.

To which end it is requisite, first, that there should be a scrupulous choice and a strict examination of the reality, constancy, and certainty of the particulars that we

---

2. Hooke had originally drawn many of the book's illustrations for use in the public presentation of experiments, which, as the Society's Curator of Experiments, he was obliged to perform regularly.

admit.[3] This is the first rise[4] whereon truth is to begin, and here the most severe and most impartial diligence must be employed. The storing up of all, without any regard to evidence or use, will only tend to darkness and confusion. We must not therefore esteem the riches of our philosophical treasure by the number only, but chiefly by the weight. The most vulgar instances[5] are not to be neglected, but above all, the most instructive are to be entertained.[6] The footsteps of Nature are to be traced, not only in her ordinary course, but when she seems to be put to her shifts,[7] to make many doublings and turnings, and to use some kind of art in endeavoring to avoid our discovery.

The next care to be taken, in respect of the senses, is a supplying of their infirmities with instruments, and as it were, the adding of artificial organs to the natural; this in one of them has been of late years accomplished with prodigious benefit to all sorts of useful knowledge by the invention of optical glasses. By the means of telescopes, there is nothing so far distant but may be represented to our view; and by the help of microscopes, there is nothing so small as to escape our inquiry; hence there is a new visible world discovered to the understanding. By this means the heavens are opened, and a vast number of new stars and new motions and new productions appear in them to which all the ancient astronomers were utterly strangers. By this the earth itself, which lies so near us under our feet, shows quite a new thing to us; and in every little particle of its matter, we now behold almost as great a variety of creatures as we were able before to reckon up in the whole universe itself. * * *

I here present to the world my imperfect endeavors, which though they shall prove no other way considerable, yet I hope they may be in some measure useful to the main design of a reformation in philosophy, if it be only by showing that there is not so much required towards it any strength of imagination or exactness of method or depth of contemplation (though the addition of these, where they can be had, must needs produce a much more perfect composure) as[8] a sincere hand and a faithful eye to examine and to record the things themselves as they appear.

And I beg my reader to let me take the boldness to assure him that in this present condition of knowledge, a man so qualified as I have endeavored to be, only with resolution and integrity and plain intentions of employing his senses aright, may venture to compare the reality and the usefulness of his services towards the true philosophy with those of other men that are of much stronger and more acute speculations that shall not make uses of the same method by the senses. * * *

from Observation 1. Of the Point of a Sharp Small Needle

As in geometry, the most natural way of beginning is from a mathematical point, so is the same method in observations and natural history the most genuine, simple, and instructive. We must first endeavor to make letters, and draw single strokes true, before we venture to write whole sentences, or to draw large pictures. And in physical inquiries, we must endeavor to follow Nature in the more plain and easy ways she treads in the most simple and uncompounded bodies, to trace her steps, and be acquainted with her manner of walking there, before we venture ourselves into the multitude of meanders she has in bodies of a more complicated nature; lest, being

3. I.e., as experimental data.
4. Elevation (with "truth" imagined as a progressive ascent).
5. Familiar particulars.

6. Considered.
7. Up to her tricks.
8. But only.

Robert Hooke, *Schema ii: Needle Point and Period,* from *Micrographia,* 1665.

unable to distinguish and judge of our way, we quickly lose both Nature our guide, and ourselves too, and are left to wander in the labyrinth of groundless opinions; wanting both judgment, that light, and experience, that clue, which should direct our proceedings.

We will begin these our inquiries therefore with the observations of bodies of the most simple nature first, and so gradually proceed to those of a more compounded one. In prosecution of which method, we shall begin with a physical point; of which kind the point of a needle is commonly reckoned for one, and is indeed, for the most part, made so sharp, that the naked eye cannot distinguish any parts of it. It very easily pierces and makes its way through all kinds of bodies softer than itself. But if viewed with a very good microscope, we may find that the top of a needle (though as to the sense very sharp) appears a broad, blunt, and very irregular end; not resembling a cone, as is imagined, but only a piece of a tapering body, with a great part of the top removed, or deficient. The points of pins are yet more blunt, and the points of the most curious mathematical instruments so very seldom arrive at so great a sharpness. How much therefore can be built upon demonstrations made only by the productions of the ruler and compasses, he will be better able to consider that shall but view those points and lines with a microscope.

* * *

The image we have here exhibited in the first figure, was the top of a small and very sharp needle, whose point *aa* nevertheless appeared through the microscope above a quarter of an inch broad, not round nor flat, but irregular and uneven; so that it seemed to have been big enough to have afforded a hundred armed mites room enough to be ranged by each other without endangering the breaking one another's necks, by being thrust off on either side. The surface of which, though appearing to the naked eye very smooth, could not nevertheless hide a multitude of holes and scratches and ruggednesses from being discovered by the microscope to invest it, several of which inequalities (as A, B, C, seemed holes made by some small specks of rust; and D some adventitious[9] body, that stuck very close to it) were casual.[1] All the rest that roughen the surface, were only so many marks of the rudeness and bungling of art.[2] So unaccurate is it, in all its productions, even in those which seem most neat, that if examined with an organ more acute than that by which they were made, the more we see of their shape, the less appearance will there be of their beauty; whereas in the works in nature, the deepest discoveries show us the greatest excellencies. An evident argument, that He that was the author of all these things, was no other than omnipotent; being able to include as great a variety of parts and contrivances in the yet smallest discernible point, as in those vaster bodies (which comparatively are called also points) such as the earth, sun, or planets. Nor need it seem strange that the earth itself may be by an analogy called a physical point: for as its body, though now so near us as to fill our eyes and fancies with a sense of the vastness of it, may by a little distance, and some convenient diminishing glasses, be made vanish into a scarce visible speck, or point (as I have often tried on the moon, and—when not too bright—on the sun itself), so, could a mechanical contrivance successfully answer our theory, we might see the least spot as big as the earth itself; and discover, as Descartes also conjectures,[3] as great a variety of bodies in the moon, or planets, as in the earth.

But leaving these discoveries to future industries, we shall proceed to add one observation more of a point commonly so called, that is, the mark of a full stop, or period. And for this purpose I observed many both printed ones and written; and among multitudes I found few of them more round or regular than this which I have delineated in the * * * second scheme, but very many abundantly more disfigured; and for the most part if they seemed equally round to the eye, I found those points that had been made by a copper plate, and roll-press, to be as misshapen as those which had been made with types, the most curious and smoothly engraven strokes and points looking but as so many furrows and holes, and their printed impressions but like smutty daubings on a mat or uneven floor with a blunt extinguished brand[4] or stick's end. And as for points made with a pen they were much more rugged and deformed. Nay, having viewed certain pieces of exceeding curious writing of the kind (one of which in the breadth of a two-pence comprised the Lord's Prayer, the Apostles' Creed, the Ten Commandments, and about half a dozen verses besides of the Bible[5]), whose lines were so small and near together, that I was unable to number them with my naked eye, a very ordinary microscope, I had then about me, enabled me to see that what the writer of it had asserted was true, but withal discovered of what pitiful bungling scribbles and scrawls it was composed, Arabian and China characters being almost as well shaped; yet thus much I must say for the man, that it was for the most part legible enough, though in some places there wanted a good fantasy well prepossessed[6] to help one through. If this manner of

9. Chance-encountered.
1. Accidental.
2. Artifice; human (as opposed to natural) creation.
3. René Descartes (1596–1650); French mathematician and philosopher.

4. Torch.
5. In the mid-17th century, this minuscule writing was practiced as a craft; specimens (often of the scriptural texts Hooke lists here) were prized by collectors.
6. Imagination kindly disposed.

small writing were made easy and practicable (and I think I know such a one,[7] but have never yet made trial of it, whereby one might be enabled to write a great deal with much ease, and accurately enough in a very little room) it might be of very good use to convey secret intelligence without any danger of discovery or mistrusting. But to come again to the point. The irregularies of it are caused by three or four coadjutors,[8] one of which is the uneven surface of the paper, which at best appears no smoother than a very coarse piece of shagged cloth; next the irregularity of the type of engraving; and a third is the rough daubing of the printing ink that lies upon the instrument that makes the impression; to all which, add the variation made by the different lights and shadows, and you may have sufficient reason to guess that a point may appear much more ugly than this, which I have here presented, which though it appeared through the microscope gray, like a great splatch of London dirt, about three inches over; yet to the naked eye it was black, and no bigger than that in the midst of the Circle A. And could I have found room in this plate to have inserted an O you should have seen that the letters were not more distinct than the points of distinction, nor a drawn circle more exactly so, than we have now shown a point to be a point.

from *Observation 53. Of a Flea*

The strength and beauty of this small creature, had it no other relation at all to man, would deserve a description.

For its strength, the microscope is able to make no greater discoveries of it than the naked eye, but only the curious contrivance of its legs and joints, for the exerting that strength, is very plainly manifested, such as no other creature I have yet observed has anything like it; for the joints of it are so adapted, that he can, as 'twere, fold them short one within another, and suddenly stretch, or spring them out to their whole length, that is, of the forelegs. The part A * * * lies within B, and B within C, parallel to, or side by side each other; but the parts of the two next lie quite contrary, that is, D without E, and E without F, but parallel also; but the parts of the hinder legs G, H, and I, bend one within another, like the parts of a double jointed ruler, or like the foot, leg, and thigh of a man; these six legs he clitches[9] up altogether, and when he leaps, springs them all out, and thereby exerts his whole strength at once.

But, as for the beauty of it, the microscope manifests it to be all over adorned with a curiously polished suit of sable armor, neatly jointed, and beset with multitudes of sharp pins, shaped almost like porcupine's quills, or bright conical steel bodkins[1]; the head is either side beautified with a quick and round black eye K, behind each of which also appears a small cavity, L, in which he seems to move to and fro a certain thin film beset with many small transparent hairs, which probably may be his ears. In the forepart of his head, between the two forelegs, he has two small long jointed feelers, or rather smellers, M M, which have four joints, and are hairy, like those of several other creatures. Between these, it has a small proboscis, or probe, N N O, that seems to consist of a tube N N, and a tongue or sucker O, which I have perceived him to flip in and out. Besides these, it has also two chaps or biters P P, which are somewhat like those of an ant, but

---

7. I.e., an instrument.
8. Factors.
9. Clutches.

1. "A instrument with a small blade and sharp point used to bore holes" (Johnson's *Dictionary*).

Robert Hooke, *Schema xxxiv: A Flea*, from *Micrographia*, 1665.

I could not perceive them toothed; and were opened and shut just after the same manner. With these instruments does this little busy creature bite and pierce the skin, and suck out the blood of an animal, leaving the skin inflamed with a small round red spot. These parts are very difficult to be discovered, because for the most part, they lie covered between the forelegs. There are many other particulars, which, being more obvious, and affording no great matter of information, I shall pass by, and refer the reader to the figure.

1663–1665   1665

John Aubrey
1626–1697

One of the original Fellows of the Royal Society, John Aubrey possessed in abundance two of its defining characteristics: an omnivorous curiosity and a reluctance to impose arbitrary order on collections of raw data. Prosperous by birth, sickly throughout his life, and prevented by the Civil Wars from completing the Oxford education he craved, Aubrey devoted himself to the study of natural history, folklore, and archaeology. His discovery of the prehistoric stone circle at Avebury remains one of the most important finds in Britain, but he is now best known as an innovator in biography. In the 1670s he agreed to help his friend Anthony à Wood with research for a "history of all the writers and bishops" educated at Oxford since

1500. He began compiling a cluster of manuscripts he called "Minutes of Lives": notes on eminent men and women of the century, dealing in data gathered from documents, conversation, and correspondence with the subjects and their survivors, and from Aubrey's own prodigious (if at times unreliable) memory.

The life stories thus produced display an obsessive particularity, an abiding preference for the telling detail over the big picture (which in the conventional biographies of Aubrey's time took the form of hagiography: pious summations of pious lives). Aubrey's *Lives*, notes his editor Oliver Lawson Dick, "were the first biographies that did not point a moral."

Throughout his "Minutes," Aubrey performs a kind of textual archaeology. He dwells on the physical objects, natural and manufactured, which marked the early seventeenth-century world inhabited by most of his subjects, and by his younger self. The Civil Wars, destroying buildings, communities, and bodies, had rendered that world as remote in some respects as the ancient tribes elusively commemorated at Avebury. Aubrey writes the *Lives* out of a passion for recovery and an awareness of the precariousness of his whole enterprise. "'Tis pity," he observed to Wood, "that such minutes had not been taken 100 years since or more: for want whereof many worthy men's names and notions are swallowed up in oblivion." This urgency infuses the *Lives'* odd form. Aubrey cares more to get the facts down than to set them in order: he repeatedly describes himself as writing his notes "tumultuarily," that is, "as they occurred to my thoughts or as occasionally I had information" or (more succinctly) as if "tumbled out of a sack." Such an unmethodical method sorted well with the Royal Society's program as Sprat had elaborated it: "to heap up a mixed mass of experiments, without digesting them into any perfect model"; to record findings not "as complete schemes of opinions, but as bare unfinished histories."

Aubrey's notes have outlasted their original purpose as preparatory adjuncts to Wood's more "finished" history. Rediscovered and published over the course of the nineteenth century, they have exerted considerable influence over the twentieth, primarily through their talky, energetic language and their unabashed attention to bodily functions and ignoble motives as defining elements in the course of a human life. Lytton Strachey and James Joyce both display distinctly Aubreyan characteristics, as do more recent practitioners of the tell-all biography and the contemporary novel. In the "bare unfinished histories" of Aubrey's "Minutes," the techniques and protocols of the new science begin to infuse the craft of biography.

from **Brief Lives**
[FRANCIS BACON][1]

* * * He came often to Sir John Danvers[2] at Chelsea. Sir John told me that when his lordship had wrote the *History of Henry 7*, he sent the manuscript copy to him to desire his opinion of it before 'twas printed. Qd.[3] Sir John, "Your lordship knows that I am no scholar." "'Tis no matter," said my lord, "I know what a scholar can say; I would know what *you* can say." Sir John read it, and gave his opinion what he misliked which Tacitus[4] did not omit (which I am sorry I have forgot) which my lord acknowledged to be true, and mended it: "Why," said he, "a scholar would never have told me this."

---

1. Statesman, scholar, philosopher, and writer (1561–1626); in his *Advancement of Learning* (1605) and *Novum Organum* (1620) he articulated the experimental methods that would later be championed by the Royal Society.
2. Danvers was a relative of Aubrey's and "a great acquaintance and favorite" of Bacon's.
3. *Quod*: said (Latin).
4. Publius Tacitus (c. 56–c.117 C.E.), Roman historian; the sense here seems to be that Bacon has left out some element in history that Tacitus would have included.

Mr. Thomas Hobbes (Malmesburiensis[5]) was beloved by his lordship, who was wont to have him walk with him in his delicate groves where he did meditate: and when a notion darted into his mind, Mr. Hobbes was presently to write it down, and his lordship was wont to say that he did it better than anyone else about him; for that many times, when he read their[6] notes he scarce understood what they writ, because they understood it not clearly themselves.

In short, all that were *great* and *good* loved and honored him. * * *

His lordship would many times have music in the next room where he meditated.

The aviary at York House[7] was built by his lordship; it did cost £300.

At every meal, according to the season of the year, he had his table strewn with sweet herbs and flowers, which he said did refresh his spirits and memory.

When his lordship was at his country house at Gorhambery,[8] St. Albans seemed as if the Court were there, so nobly did he live. His servants had liveries with his crest (a boar . . .[9]); his watermen[1] were more employed by gentlemen than any other, even the King's.

King James sent a buck to him, and he gave the keeper fifty pounds.

He was wont to say to his servant Hunt (who was a notable thrifty man, and loved this world, and the only servant he had that he could never get to become bound for[2] him), "The world was made for man, Hunt; and not man for the world." Hunt left an estate of £1000 per annum in Somerset.

None of his servants durst appear before him without Spanish leather boots:[3] for he would smell the neat's leather which offended him. * * *

He was a παιδεροτής.[4] His Ganimeds[5] and favorites took bribes; but his lordship always gave judgment *secundum aequum et bonum.*[6] His decrees in Chancery[7] stand firm, i.e., there are fewer of his decrees reversed than any other Chancellor.

His dowager[8] married her gentleman-usher,[9] Sir (Thomas, I think) Underhill, whom she made deaf and blind with too much of Venus.[1] She was living since the beheading of the late King.—Quaere[2] where and when she died.

He had a delicate, lively hazel eye; Dr. Harvey told me it was like the eye of a viper. I have now forgot what Mr. Bushnell said, whether his lordship enjoyed his Muse[3] best at night, or in the morning.

Apothegmata[4]

His lordship being in York House garden looking on fishers as they were throwing their net, asked them what they would take for their draught;[5] they answered *so*

---

5. Of Malmeshury (Hobbes's birthplace). Hobbes was a close friend of Aubrey's, and his is the longest and the fullest of the *Brief Lives.*

6. Anyone else's.

7. In London; Bacons's birthplace and residence.

8. Gornhambry, Bacon's estate on the river Ver, near the city of St. Albans.

9. Aubrey inserts this ellipsis, presumably for filling in later.

1. Ferrymen, busy bringing guests to and from the house.

2. I.e., legaly committed to serve.

3. Cordovan leather from Spain was more highly processed than ordinary English "neat's (cattle) leather."

4. Greek: pederast, a homosexual lover of boys.

5. Beloved boys (so called after the Trojan youth Ganymede, Zeus's cupbearer).

6. "Fairly and well." Bacon had served as attorney-general and Lord Chancellor until he was impeached for taking bribes.

7. The law court presided over by the Lord Chancellor.

8. Widow.

9. A gentleman acting as attendant to a person of superior rank.

1. Sex.

2. "Find out" (Aubrey's most frequent instruction to himself in his notes).

3. I.e., wrote and thought.

4. Witty sayings.

5. Catch.

much: his lordship would offer them no more but *so much*. They drew up their net, and in it were only 2 or 3 little fishes: his lordship then told them it had been better for them to have taken his offer. They replied, they hoped to have had a better draught. "But," said his lordship, "hope is a good breakfast, but an ill supper." * * *

The Bishop of London did cut down a noble cloud of trees at Fulham. The Lord Chancellor told him that he was *a good expounder of dark places.*[6]

Upon his being in disfavor his servants suddenly went away; he compared them to the flying of the vermin when the house was falling.

One told his lordship it was now time to look about him. He replied, "I do not look *about* me, I look *above* me." * * *

His lordship would often drink a good draught of strong beer (March beer) to-bedwards, to lay his working fancy[7] asleep: which otherwise would keep him from sleeping great part of the night. * * *

Mr. Hobbes told me that the cause of his lordship's death was trying an experiment: viz., as he was taking the air in a coach with Dr. Witherborne (a Scotchman, physician to the king) towards Highgate, snow lay on the ground, and it came into my lord's thought, why flesh might not be preserved in snow, as in salt. They were resolved they would try the experiment presently. They alighted out of the coach, and went into a poor woman's house at the bottom of Highgate Hill, and bought a hen, and made the woman exenterate[8] it, and then stuffed the body with snow, and my lord did help to do it himself. The snow so chilled him, that he immediately fell so extremely ill, that he could not return to his lodgings (I suppose then at Gray's Inn), but went to the Earl of Arundel's house at Highgate, where they put him into a good bed warmed with a pan, but it was a damp bed that had not been lain in in about a year before, which gave him such a cold that in 2 or 3 days, as I remember he told me, he died of suffocation.

[William Harvey][9]

He was always very contemplative, and the first that I hear of that was curious in anatomy in England. He had made dissections of frogs, toads, and a number of other animals, and had curious observations on them, which papers, together with his goods, in his lodgings at Whitehall, were plundered at the beginning of the Rebellion, he being for the King, and with him at Oxon;[1] but he often said, that of all the losses he sustained, no grief was so crucifying to him as the loss of these papers, which for love or money he could never retrieve or obtain. When Charles I by reason of the tumults left London, he attended him, and was at the fight of Edgehill with him; and during the fight, the Prince and Duke of York were committed to his care. He told me that he withdrew with them under a hedge, and took out of his pocket a book and read; but he had not read very long before a bullet of a great gun grazed on the ground near him, which made him remove his station. He told me that Sir Adrian Scrope was dangerously wounded there, and left for dead amongst the dead men, stripped; which happened to be the saving of his life. It was cold,

---

6. Bacon puns on the Bishop's duty to shed light on obscure passages in scripture.
7. Busy mind.
8. Clean it; remove its innards.

9. Physician and anatomist (1578–1657); he discovered the circulation of the blood, and set forth his findings in *De Motu Cordis* ("on the heart's motion"), 1628.
1. Oxford, to which Charles I removed himself and his Court in 1643.

clear weather, and a frost that night; which staunched his bleeding, and about midnight, or some hours after his hurt, he awaked, and was fain to draw a dead body upon him for warmth-sake * * *

He did delight to be in the dark, and told me he could then best contemplate. He had a house heretofore at Combe, in Surrey, a good air and prospect, where he had caves made in the earth, in which in summer time he delighted to meditate.— He was pretty well versed in the mathematics, and had made himself master of Mr. Oughtred's *Clavis Math.*[2] in his old age; and I have seen him perusing it, and working problems, not long before he died, and that book was always in his meditating apartment. * * *

At Oxford, he grew acquainted with Dr. Charles Scarborough,[3] then a young physician (since by King Charles II knighted), in whose conversation he much delighted; and whereas before he marched up and down with the army, he took him to him and made him lie in his chamber, and said to him, "Prithee leave off thy gunning, and stay here; I will bring thee into practice."[4]

I remember he kept a pretty young wench to wait on him, which I guess he made use of for warmth-sake as King David did,[5] and took care of her in his will, as also of his man servant. * * *

He was, as all the rest of the brothers, very choleric;[6] and in his young days wore a dagger (as the fashion then was, nay I remember my old schoolmaster, old Mr. Latimer, at 70, wore a dudgeon, with a knife, and bodkin, as also my old grandfather Lyte, and alderman Whitson of Bristowe, which I suppose was the common fashion in their young days), but this Dr. would be too apt to draw out his dagger upon every slight occasion.

He was not tall; but of the lowest stature, round faced, olivaster[7] complexion; little eye, round, very black, full of spirit; his hair was black as a raven, but quite white 20 years before he died. * * *

He was much and often troubled with the gout,[8] and his way of cure was thus: he would then sit with his legs bare, if it were frost, on the leads[9] of Cockaine house, put them into a pail of water, till he was almost dead with cold, and betake himself to the stove, and so 'twas gone.

He was hot-headed, and his thoughts working would many times keep him from sleeping; he told me that then his way was to rise out of his bed and walk about his chamber in his shirt till he was pretty cool, i.e., till he began to have a horror,[1] and then return to bed, and sleep very comfortably.

I remember he was wont to drink coffee; which he and his brother Eliab did, before coffeehouses were in fashion in London.[2] * * *

It is now fit, and but just, that I should endeavor to undeceive the world in a scandal that I find strongly runs of him, which I have met amongst some learned young men: viz. that he made himself away[3] to put himself out of his pain, by opium; not but that, had he labored under great pains, he had been ready enough to have done it; I do not deny that it was not according to his principles upon certain

2. William Oughtred (1575–1660), mathematician; his *Clavis Mathematicae* ("the key of mathematics") was a widely used textbook on algebra and arithmetic (it introduced the symbol "3" for multiplication).
3. Charles Scarburgh (1616–1694) assisted Harvey with his work on the generation of animals.
4. I.e., medical practice.
5. In his old age David was warmed in bed at night by a young woman (1 Kings 1.1–4).

6. Prone to anger.
7. Olive-colored.
8. Inflammation of the joints in the hands and feet.
9. Rooftop (lined with lead).
1. Shiver.
2. The drink was rare in England before midcentury, hugely popular thereafter; London's first coffeehouse opened in 1652.
3. Killed himself.

occasions to . . . .[4] But the manner of his dying was really, and *bona fide*, thus, viz.: The morning of his death about 10 a clock, he went to speak, and found he had the dead palsy[5] in his tongue; then he saw what was to become of him, he knew there was then no hopes of his recovery, so presently sends for his young nephews to come up to him, to whom he gives one his watch ('twas a minute watch with which he made his experiments);[6] to another, another remembrance, etc.; made sign to . . .[7] Sambroke, his apothecary (in Blackfriars), to let him blood in[8] the tongue, which did little or no good; and so he ended his days. His practice was not very great towards his later end; he declined it, unless to a special friend—e.g. my Lady Howland, who had a cancer in her breast, which he did cut off and seared, but at last she died of it.

* * *

I was at his funeral, and helped to carry him into the vault.

1680s   1813

≈→   END OF PERSPECTIVES: THE ROYAL SOCIETY AND THE NEW SCIENCE   ←≈

━━◆━━

Margaret Cavendish, Duchess of Newcastle
1623–1674

The youngest child in a wealthy family whose social arrogance and Royalist sympathies brought it near ruin during the Civil Wars, Margaret Lucas combined a near immobilizing shyness with a passion for fame. She spent the years of war and Interregnum on the continent, first as maid of honor to Charles's exiled queen, then as wife to the Royalist general William Cavendish, Marquis of Newcastle; he was made Duke by Charles II after the couple returned to England at the Restoration. Neglected by the Court, they lived far from London on their northern estates, where they cultivated their passions: his, riding and fencing; hers, reading and writing. Words poured from her pen into a variety of genres: verse (*Poems and Fancies*, 1653), fiction (*Nature's Pictures*, 1656), plays (*Love's Adventure*, *The Matrimonial Trouble*, *The Female Academy*, and some fifteen others: all printed, none performed); essays (*The World's Olio*, 1655); scientific speculations (*Philosophical and Physical Opinions*, 1663; *Observations upon Experimental Philosophy*, 1665); biography (of her husband); and autobiography (*A True Relation*, 1656; *Sociable Letters*, 1664). Cavendish and her husband published much of her work (and some of his) in sumptuous editions at their own expense.

It was rare for a woman to write and publish, rarer still for an aristocrat to write so revealingly and emphatically about her own fears, desires, opinions, and aspirations. The combination of her gender, rank, and work brought the Duchess an equivocal celebrity, a mix of amazement and derision which her occasional trips to London did much to animate. After one such visit, Mary Evelyn (wife of the diarist John) tried to capture Cavendish's impact in a letter to a friend: "I was surprised to find so much extravagancy and vanity in any person not confined within four walls" (of a madhouse). Her clothing, Evelyn reported, was "fantastical"; her behavior outstripped "the imagination of poets, or the descriptions of a romance heroine's

---

4. Aubrey leaves the blank, perhaps intending a phrase like "commit suicide."
5. Paralysis caused by stroke.
6. At this time, most clocks and watches told only the

hour, not the minutes.
7. Aubrey's blank.
8. Draw blood from.

greatness; her gracious bows, seasonable nods, courteous stretching out of hands, twinkling of her eyes, and various gestures of approbation, show what may be expected from her discourse, which is as airy, empty, whimsical, and rambling as her books, aiming at science, difficulties, high notions . . ." Evelyn voices a satiric hostility shared by many London onlookers, but she also pinpoints some of Cavendish's range and intensity: her idiosyncratic engagement with the new science of her day, and her variable, highly conscious self-presentation.

At letter's end, Evelyn despairs of description. The Duchess "is not of mortal race, and therefore cannot be defined." Cavendish, though, knew herself mortal. She repeatedly made clear that the threat of oblivion impelled her pen, and she worked constantly and inventively to define herself, sometimes in familiar genres, sometimes in modes of her own making—most notably that mix of fantasy, science fiction, argument, and autobiography she called *The Blazing World* (1665). The Duchess's extraordinary energies and kaleidoscopic output have transmuted seventeenth-century ridicule into late twentieth-century fascination with a woman's voice in relentless pursuit of (a favorite Cavendish term) "singularity."

from POEMS AND FANCIES[1]

The Poetress's Hasty Resolution

Reading my verses, I liked them so well,
Self-love did make my judgment to rebel;
And thinking them so good, thought more to make,
Considering not how others would them take.
5   I writ so fast, thought, lived I many a year,
A pyramid of fame thereon to rear.[2]
Reason, observing which way I was bent,
Did stay my hand, and asked me what I meant.
"Will you," said he, "thus waste your time in vain,
10   On that which in the world small praise shall gain?
For shame leave off, and do the printer spare:
He'll lose by your ill poetry, I fear.
Besides, the world already hath great store
Of useless books, wherefore do write no more,
15   But pity take, do the world a good turn,
And all you write cast in the fire and burn."
Angry I was, and Reason struck away,
When I did hear what he to me did say.
Then all in haste I to the press it sent,
20   Fearing persuasion might my book prevent.
But now 'tis done, repent with grief do I,
Hang down my head with shame, blush, sigh, and cry.
Take pity, and my drooping spirits raise,
Wipe off my tears with handkerchiefs of praise.

---

1. This was Cavendish's first publication; the first three pieces presented here functioned as a verse preface to the collection. The texts are taken from the second edition (1664), "much altered and corrected."

2. I.e., I thought that if I were to live a long time I would be able to create a poetic monument to myself.

The Poetress's Petition

Like to a fever's pulse my heart doth beat,
For fear my book some great repulse should meet.
If it be naught, let it in silence lie;
Disturb it not; let it in quiet die;
5   Let not the bells of your dispraise ring loud,
But wrap it up in silence as a shroud;
Cause black oblivion on its hearse to lie,
Instead of tapers, let dark night stand by;
Instead of flowers, on its grave to strew,
10   Before its hearse, sleepy, dull poppy throw;
Instead of scutcheons,[3] let my tears be hung,
Which grief and sorrow from my eyes out wrung.
Let those that bear its corpse no jesters be,
But sober, sad, and grave mortality.
15   No satyr° poets by its grave appear,   satirical
No altars raised, to write inscriptions there.
Let dust of all forgetfulness be cast
Upon its corpse, there let it lie and waste.
Nor let it rise again, unless some know,
20   At Judgments some good merits it can show;
Then shall it live in Heavens of high praise,
And for its glory, garlands have of bays.[4]

An Apology for Writing So Much upon This Book

Condemn me not, I make so much ado
About this book; it is my child, you know;
Just like a bird, when her young are in nest,
Goes in, and out, and hops, and takes no rest;
5   But when their young are fledged,[5] their heads out peep,
Lord! what a chirping does the old one keep.
So I, for fear my strengthless child should fall
Against a door, or stool, aloud I call,
Bid have a care of such a dangerous place.
10   Thus write I much, to hinder all disgrace.

The Hunting of the Hare

Betwixt two ridges of plowed land sat Wat,[6]
Whose body, pressed to the earth, lay close and squat;
His nose upon his two forefeet did lie,
With his gray eyes he glared obliquely;
5   His head he always set against the wind,
His tail when turned, his hair blew up behind,
And made him to get cold; but he being wise,

---

3. Escutcheons: funeral ornaments, shield-shaped, exhibiting the deceased's coat of arms.
4. Wreaths of laurel leaves, awarded for military victory

or literary excellence.
5. Feathered; ready to fly.
6. Conventional nickname for a hare.

Doth keep his coat still down, so warm he lies.
Thus rests he all the day, til th' sun doth set,
10 Then up he riseth his relief to get,
And walks about, until the sun doth rise,
Then coming back in's° former posture lies.   *in his*
At last poor Wat was found, as he there lay,
By huntsmen, which came with their dogs that way,
15 Whom seeing, he got up, and fast did run,
Hoping some ways the cruel dogs to shun;
But they by nature had so quick a scent,
That by their nose they traced what way he went,
And with their deep wide mouths set forth a cry,
20 Which answered was by echo in the sky;
Then Wat was struck with terror and with fear,
Seeing each shadow thought the dogs were there,
And running out some distance from their cry,
To hide himself, his thoughts he did employ;
25 Under a clod of earth in sand pit wide
Poor Wat sat close, hoping himself to hide,
There long he had not been, but straight in's ears
The winding° horns and crying dogs he hears;   *blowing*
Then starting up with fear, he leaped, and such
30 Swift speed he made, the ground he scarce did touch;
Into a great thick wood straight ways he got,
And underneath a broken bough he sat,
Where every leaf that with the wind did shake
Brought him such terror, that his heart did ache;
35 That place he left, to champaign° plains he went,   *open*
Winding about, for to deceive their scent,
And while they snuffling were to find his track,
Poor Wat being weary, his swift pace did slack;
On his two hinder legs for ease he sat;
40 His forefeet rubbed his face from dust and sweat;
Licking his feet, he wiped his ears so clean
That none could tell that Wat had hunted been;
But casting round about his fair gray eyes,
The hounds in full career he near him 'spies;
45 To Wat it was so terrible a sight,
Fear gave him wings and made his body light;
Though he was tired before by running long,
Yet now his breath he never felt more strong—
Like those that dying are, think health returns,
50 When 'tis but a faint blast which life out-burns;
For spirits seek to guard the heart about,
Striving with death, but death doth quench them out.
The hounds so fast came on, and with such cry,
That he no hopes had left, nor help could 'spy;
55 With that the winds did pity poor Wat's case,
And with their breath the scent blew from that place;

Then every nose was busily employed,
And every nostril was set open wide,
And every head did seek a several way,
60   To find the grass or track where the scent lay;
For witty industry° is never slack,   *cunning diligence*
'Tis like to witchcraft, and brings lost things back;
But though the wind had tied the scent up close,
A busy dog thrust in his snuffling nose
65   And drew it out, with that did foremost run,
Then horns blew loud, the rest to follow on;
The great slow hounds their throats did set a base,
The fleet, swift hounds, as tenors next in place,
The little beagles did a treble sing,
70   And through the air their voices round did ring,
Which made such consort as they ran along,
That, had they spoken words, 't had been a song;
The horns kept time, the men did shout for joy,
And seemed most valiant, poor Wat to destroy;
75   Spurring their horses to a full career,
Swum rivers deep, leaped ditches without fear,
Endangered life and limbs, so fast they'd ride,
Only to see how patiently Wat died;
At last the dogs so near his heels did get,
80   That their sharp teeth they in his breech did set;
Then tumbling down he fell, with weeping eyes
Gave up his ghost; and thus poor Wat he dies.
Men whooping loud, such acclamations made,
As if the Devil they imprisoned had,
85   When they but did a shiftless creature kill;
To hunt, there needs no valiant soldier's skill;
But men do think that exercise and toil,
To keep their health, is best, which makes most spoil,
Thinking that food and nourishment so good,
90   Which doth proceed from others' flesh and blood.
When they do lions, wolves, bears, tigers see
Kill silly sheep, they say, they cruel be,
But for themselves all creatures think too few,
For luxury, wish God would make more new;
95   As if God did make creatures for man's meat,
And gave them life and sense for man to eat,
Or else for sport or recreation's sake
For to destroy those lives that God did make,
Making their stomachs graves, which full they fill
100   With murdered bodies, which in sport they kill;
Yet man doth think himself so gentle and mild,
When of all creatures he's most cruel, wild,
Nay, so proud, that he only⁷ thinks to live,

7. Alone, with no other creature.

That God a God-like nature him did give,
105   And that all creatures for his sake alone
Were made, for him to tyrannize upon.

1653, 1664

from A True Relation of My Birth, Breeding, and Life[1]

My father was a gentleman,[2] which title is grounded and given by merit, not by princes; and 'tis the act of time, not favor. And though my father was not a peer of the realm, yet there were few peers who had much greater estates, or lived more noble therewith. * * *

As for my breeding, it was according to my birth and the nature of my sex, for my birth was not lost in my breeding; for as my sisters was or had been bred, so was I in plenty, or rather with superfluity. Likewise we were bred virtuously, modestly, civilly, honorably, and on honest principles. As for plenty, we had not only for necessity, conveniency, and decency, but for delight and pleasure to a superfluity. 'Tis true, we did not riot, but we lived orderly; for riot, even in kings' courts and princes' palaces, brings ruin without content or pleasure, when order in less fortune shall live more plentifully and deliciously than princes that lives in a hurly-burly, as I may term it, in which they are seldom well served, for disorder obstructs. Besides, it doth disgust life,[3] distract the appetites, and yield no true relish to the senses; for pleasure, delight, peace, and felicity live in method and temperance.

As for our garments, my mother[4] did not only delight to see us neat and cleanly, fine and gay, but rich and costly, maintaining us to the height of her estate, but not beyond it. For we were so far from being in debt, before the wars,[5] as we were rather beforehand with the world, buying all with ready money, not on the score.[6] For although after my father's death the estate was divided between my mother and her sons, paying such a sum of money for portions to her daughters either at the day of their marriage or when they should come to age, yet by reason she and her children agreed with a mutual consent, all their affairs were managed so well as she lived not in a much lower condition than when my father lived. 'Tis true my mother might have increased her daughters' portions by a thrifty sparing, yet she chose to bestow it on our breeding, honest pleasures, and harmless delights, out of an opinion that if she bred us with needy necessity it might chance to create in us sharking[7] qualities, mean[8] thoughts, and base actions, which she knew my father as well as herself did abhor. Likewise we were bred tenderly, for my mother naturally did strive to please and delight her children, not to cross or torment them, terrifying them with threats or lashing them with slavish whips. But instead of threats, reason was used to persuade us, and instead of lashes, the deformities of vices was discovered, and the

1. Cavendish published her autobiography as the closing piece in a collection of her fiction called *Nature's Pictures* (1656), which she wrote while living in exile at Antwerp during the years of Cromwell's commonwealth. This work (like many of her others) was privately printed, at the author's expense, in a lavish folio, whose title page suggests the autobiography's particular place in the scheme: "In this volume there are several feigned stories . . . comical, tragical, and tragicomical, poetical, romantical, philosophical, and historical. . . . And a true story at the latter end, wherein there is no feignings." In a later edition (1671), published after she and her husband had returned to England, Cavendish omitted the autobiography.
2. Thomas Lucas (c. 1573–1625), whose forebears had risen to the gentry in the 16th century. He died when Margaret was two years old.
3. I.e., makes life unpleasant.
4. Elizabeth Lucas, née Leighton (?–1647).
5. The English Civil Wars, begun in 1642.
6. On credit.
7. Greedy.
8. Ignoble.

graces and virtues were presented unto us. Also we were bred with respectful attendance, every one being severally waited upon. And all her servants in general used
the same respect to her children (even those that were very young) as they did to
herself, for she suffered not her servants either to be rude before us or to domineer
over us, which all vulgar servants are apt and ofttimes have leave to do. Likewise she
never suffered the vulgar servingmen to be in the nursery amongst the nursemaids,
lest their rude lovemaking[9] might do unseemly actions, or speak unhandsome words
in the presence of her children, knowing that youth is apt to take infection by ill examples, having not the reason of distinguishing good from bad. Neither were we suffered to have any familiarity with the vulgar servants, or conversation; yet caused us
to demean ourselves[1] with an humble civility towards them, as they with a dutiful respect to us. Not because they were servants were we so reserved, for many noble persons are forced to serve through necessity, but by reason the vulgar sort of servants
are as ill bred as meanly born, giving children ill examples, and worse counsel. * * *

But some time after this war began, I knew not how they[2] lived. For though
most of them were in Oxford, where the King was, yet after the Queen went from
Oxford, and so out of England, I was parted from them.[3] For when the Queen was in
Oxford, I had a great desire to be one of her Maids of Honor, hearing the Queen had
not the same number she was used to have. Whereupon I wooed and won my
mother to let me go, for my mother being fond of all her children was desirous to
please them, which made her consent to my request. But my brothers and sisters
seemed not very well pleased, by reason I had never been from home, nor seldom
out of their sight; for though they knew I would not behave myself to their or my
own dishonor, yet they thought I might to my disadvantage, being inexperienced in
the world. Which indeed I did, for I was so bashful when I was out of my mother's,
brothers', and sisters' sight, whose presence used to give me confidence, thinking I
could not do amiss while any one of them were by, for I knew they would gently reform me if I did. Besides, I was ambitious they should approve of my actions and behavior, that when I was gone from them I was like one that had no foundation to
stand, or guide to direct me, which made me afraid lest I should wander with ignorance out of the ways of honor so that I knew not how to behave myself. Besides, I
had heard the world was apt to lay aspersions even on the innocent, for which
I dared neither look up with my eyes, nor speak, nor be any way sociable, insomuch
as I was thought a natural fool.[4] Indeed I had not much wit, yet I was not an idiot;
my wit was according to my years. And though I might have learned more wit, and
advanced my understanding by living in a court, yet being dull, fearful, and bashful,
I neither heeded what was said or practiced, but just what belonged to my loyal duty
and my own honest reputation. And indeed I was so afraid to dishonor my friends
and family by my indiscreet actions that I rather chose to be accounted a fool than
to be thought rude or wanton. In truth my bashfulness and fears made me repent my
going from home to see the world abroad, and much I did desire to return to my
mother again, or to my sister Pye,[5] with whom I often lived when she was in
London, and loved with a supernatural affection. But my mother advised me there
to stay, although I put her to more charges than if she had kept me at home, and the

9. Flirtation.
1. To behave.
2. Her mother and siblings.
3. In 1643, Charles I had moved his family, court, and
military base to Oxford as the Civil Wars rendered Lon-

don unsafe. In 1644 his queen, Henrietta Maria, escaped
to her native Paris in hopes of raising money and support
for the Royalist cause.
4. I.e., born mentally defective.
5. Catherine, wife of Edmond Pye.

more, by reason she and my brothers were sequestered from their estates and plundered of all their goods.[6] Yet she maintained me so, that I was in a condition rather to lend than to borrow, which courtiers usually are not, being always necessitated by reason of great expenses courts put them to. But my mother said it would be a disgrace for me to return out of the court so soon after I was placed.

So I continued almost two years, until such time as I was married from thence. For my Lord the Marquis of Newcastle[7] did approve of those bashful fears which many condemned, and would choose such a wife as he might bring to his own humors,[8] and not such an one as was wedded to self-conceit, or one that had been tempered to the humors of another, for which he wooed me for his wife. And though I did dread marriage, and shunned men's companies as much as I could, yet I could not nor had not the power to refuse him, by reason my affections were fixed on him, and he was the only person I ever was in love with. Neither was I ashamed to own it, but gloried therein, for it was not amorous love. I never was infected therewith—it is a disease, or a passion, or both, I know by relation, not by experience. Neither could title, wealth, power, or person entice me to love. But my love was honest and honorable, being placed upon merit; which affection joyed at the fame of his worth, pleased with delight in his wit, proud of the respects he used to me, and triumphing in the affections he professed for me; which affections he hath confirmed to me by a deed[9] of time, sealed by constancy, and assigned by an unalterable decree of his promise, which makes me happy in despite of Fortune's frowns. For though misfortunes may and do oft dissolve base, wild, loose, and ungrounded affections, yet she hath no power of those that are united either by merit, justice, gratitude, duty, fidelity, or the like. And though my Lord hath lost his estate, and banished out of his country for his loyalty to his King and country, yet neither despised poverty nor pinching necessity could make him break the bonds of friendship, or weaken his loyal duty to his King or country.

But not only the family I am linked to is ruined, but the family from which I sprung, by these unhappy wars—which ruin my mother lived to see, and then died, having lived a widow many years, for she never forgot my father so as to marry again. Indeed he remained so lively in her memory, and her grief was so lasting, as she never mentioned his name, though she spoke often of him, but love and grief caused tears to flow, and tender sighs to rise, mourning in sad complaints. She made her house her cloister, enclosing herself as it were therein, for she seldom went abroad, unless to church, but these unhappy wars forced her out by reason she and her children were loyal to the King, for which they plundered her and my brothers of all their goods, plate, jewels, money, corn, cattle, and the like, cut down their woods, pulled down their houses, and sequestered them from their lands and livings. But in such misfortunes my mother was of an heroic spirit, in suffering patiently where there is no remedy, or to be industrious where she thought she could help. She was of a grave behavior, and had such a majestic grandeur, as it were continually hung about her, that it would strike a kind of an awe to the beholders, and command respect from the rudest. I mean the rudest of civilized people; I mean not such

6. The Lucas family took the king's side in the Civil Wars; its property was raided during anti-Royalist riots in 1642.
7. William Cavendish (1593–1676), a general in the king's army. In 1644, after suffering defeat in a pivotal battle, he departed for the Continent. He married Margaret (his second wife) at Paris in 1645.
8. Inclinations, ways of thinking.
9. A legal document (here used metaphorically).

barbarous people as plundered her and used her cruelly, for they would have pulled God out of Heaven, had they had power, as they did royalty out of his throne. Also her beauty was beyond the ruin of time, for she had a well-favored loveliness in her face, a pleasing sweetness in her countenance, and a well-tempered complexion, as neither too red nor too pale, even to her dying hour, although in years. And by her dying, one might think death was enamored with her, for he embraced her in a sleep, and so gently, as if he were afraid to hurt her. Also she was an affectionate mother, breeding her children with a most industrious care and tender love. * * * Likewise my mother was a good mistress to her servants, taking care of her servants in their sickness, not sparing any cost she was able to bestow for their recovery. Neither did she exact more from them in their health than what they with ease or rather like pastime could do. She would freely pardon a fault, and forget an injury. Yet sometimes she would be angry, but never with her children; the sight of them would pacify her. Neither would she be angry with others but when she had cause, as with negligent or knavish servants that would lavishly or unnecessarily waste, or subtly and thievishly steal. And though she would often complain that her family was too great for her weak management, and often pressed my brother to take it upon him, yet I observe she took a pleasure and some little pride in the governing thereof. * * *

But howsoever our fortunes are, we are both content, spending our time harm-lessly, for my Lord pleaseth himself with the management of some few horses, and exercises himself with the use of the sword. Which two arts he hath brought by his studious thoughts to an absolute perfection. And though he hath taken as much pains in those arts, both by study and practice, as chemists[1] for the philosopher's stone, yet he hath this advantage of them, that he hath found the right and the truth thereof and therein, which chemists never found in their art and I believe never will. Also he recreates himself with his pen, writing what his wit dictates to him. But I pass my time rather with scribbling than writing, with words than wit. Not that I speak much, because I am addicted to contemplation, unless I am with my Lord; yet then I rather attentively listen to what he says, than impertinently speak. Yet when I am writing any sad feigned stories or serious humors or melan-choly passions, I am forced many times to express them with the tongue before I can write them with the pen, by reason those thoughts that are sad, serious, and melan-choly are apt to contract and to draw too much back, which oppression doth as it were overpower or smother the conception in the brain. But when some of those thoughts are sent out in words, they give the rest more liberty to place themselves in a more methodical order, marching more regularly with my pen on the ground of white paper. But my letters seem rather as a ragged rout, than a well-armed body, for the brain being quicker in creating than the hand in writing, or the memory in re-taining, many fancies are lost by reason they ofttimes outrun the pen. Where I, to keep speed in the race, write so fast as I stay not so long as to write my letters plain, insomuch as some have taken my handwriting for some strange character.[2] And being accustomed so to do, I cannot now write very plain. When I strive to write my best, indeed my ordinary handwriting is so bad as few can read it so as to write it fair for the press. But however that[3] little wit I have, it delights me to scribble it out and

1. Alchemists, who devoted themselves to the search for the "philosopher's stone"—the substance that would turn base metals into gold.

2. Code, cryptography.
3. Whatever.

disperse it about. For I being addicted from my childhood to contemplation rather than conversation, to solitariness rather than society, to melancholy rather than mirth, to write with the pen than to work with a needle, passing my time with harmless fancies, their company being pleasing, their conversation innocent, in which I take such pleasure as I neglect my health. For it is as great a grief to leave their society, as a joy to be in their company. My only trouble is lest my brain should grow barren, or that the root of my fancies should become insipid, withering into a dull stupidity, for want of maturing subjects to write on. * * *

But since I have writ in general thus far of my life, I think it fit I should speak something of my humor, particular practice, and disposition. As for my humor, I was from my childhood given to contemplation, being more taken or delighted with thoughts than in conversation with a society. * * * Also I did dislike any should follow my fashions, for I always took delight in a singularity, even in accoutrements of habits. But whatsoever I was addicted to, either in fashions of clothes, contemplation of thoughts, actions of life, they were lawful, honest, honorable, and modest, of which I can avouch to the world with a great confidence, because it is a pure truth. * * * Likewise I am neither spiteful, envious, nor malicious. I repine not at[4] the gifts that Nature or Fortune bestows upon others, yet I am a great emulator. For though I wish none worse than they are, nor fear any should be better than they are, yet it is lawful for me to wish myself the best, and to do my honest endeavor thereunto. For I think it no crime to wish myself the exactest[5] of Nature's works, my thread of life the longest, my chain of destiny the strongest, my mind the peaceablest, my life the pleasantest, my death the easiest, and the greatest saint in Heaven. * * * As I am not covetous, so I am not prodigal.[6] But of the two I am inclining to be prodigal, yet I cannot say to a vain prodigality, because I imagine it is to a profitable end; for perceiving the world is given or apt to honor the outside more than the inside, worshipping show more than substance; and I am so vain, if it be a vanity, as to endeavor to be worshipped rather than not to be regarded. Yet I shall never be so prodigal as to impoverish my friends,[7] or go beyond the limits or facility of our estate. And though I desire to appear at the best advantage whilst I live in the view of the public world, yet I could most willingly exclude myself, so as never to see the face of any creature but my Lord as long as I live, enclosed myself like an anchorite,[8] wearing a frieze gown[9] tied with a cord about my waist. But I hope my readers will not think me vain for writing my life, since there have been many that have done the like, as Caesar, Ovid,[1] and many more, both men and women, and I know no reason I may not do it as well as they. But I verily believe some censuring readers will scornfully say, "Why hath this lady writ her own life, since none cares to know whose daughter she was or whose wife she is, or how she was bred, or what fortunes she had, or how she lived, or what humor or disposition she was of?" I answer that it is true, that 'tis to no purpose, to the readers, but it is to the authoress, because I write it for my own sake, not theirs. Neither did I intend this piece for to delight, but to divulge, not to please the fancy, but to tell the truth, lest after-ages should mistake, in not knowing I was daughter to one Master Lucas of St. Johns near Colchester in Essex, second wife to

---

4. Do not fret about.
5. Most perfected.
6. Spendthrift, lavish.
7. Family members.
8. Religious recluse.

9. Coarse woolen robe.
1. Julius Caesar (c. 100–44 B.C.E.), Roman general and statesman, wrote memoirs of his military campaigns; the Roman poet Ovid (43 B.C.E.–17 C.E.) wrote many autobiographical poems.

the Lord Marquis of Newcastle; for my Lord having had two wives, I might easily have been mistaken, especially if I should die, and my Lord marry again.

1656

from Observations upon Experimental Philosophy. To which is added, The Description of a New Blazing World[1]
Of Micrography, and of Magnifying and Multiplying Glasses[2]

Although I am not able to give a solid judgment of the art of micrography and the several dioptrical[3] instruments belonging thereto, by reason I have neither studied nor practiced that art, yet of this I am confident: that this same art, with all its instruments, is not able to discover the interior natural motions of any part or creature of nature. Nay, the question is whether it can represent yet the exterior shapes and motions so exactly as naturally they are, for art[4] doth more easily alter than inform. As, for example, art makes cylinders, concave and convex glasses, and the like, which represent the figure of an object in no part exactly and truly, but very deformed and misshaped. Also a glass that is flawed, cracked, or broke, or cut into the figure of lozenges, triangles, squares, or the like, will present numerous pictures of one object. Besides, there are so many alterations made by several lights, their shadows, refractions, reflections, as also several lines, points, mediums, interposing and intermixing parts, forms, and positions, as the truth of an object will hardly be known.[5] For the perception of sight, and so of the rest of the senses, goes no further than the exterior parts of the object presented, and though the perception may be true when the object is truly presented, yet when the presentation is false, the information must be false also. And it is to be observed that art for the most part makes hermaphroditical,[6] that is, mixed figures, as partly artificial and partly natural. For art may make some metal as pewter, which is between tin and lead, as also brass, and numerous other things of mixed natures; in the like manner may artificial glasses present objects partly natural and partly artificial. Nay, put the case they can present the natural figure of an object; yet that natural figure may be presented in as monstrous a shape as it may appear misshapen rather than natural. For example, a louse by the help of a magnifying glass appears like a lobster,[7] where the microscope enlarging and magnifying each part of it makes them bigger and rounder than naturally they are. The truth is, the more the figure by art is magnified, the more it appears misshapen from the natural, inasmuch as each joint will appear as a diseased, swelled and tumid body, ready and ripe for incision. But mistake me not; I do not say that no glass presents the true picture of an object, but only that magnifying, multiplying, and the like optic glasses may and do oftentimes present falsely the picture of an

---

1. The *Observations* is a critique of science, the *Blazing World* a work of fantasy; Cavendish published them together in a single volume as complementary texts. The "experimental philosophy" was that method and outlook pursued and exalted by the Royal Society; the group itself makes a sustained parodic appearance in the *Blazing World*. The Society held that copious experiment was the necessary basis for reliable study of the natural world. Cavendish challenges any such investigation grounded in human perceptions and the machines (microscopes, telescopes) contrived to enhance them; in the excerpt here she specifically takes on the work of Robert Hooke (see page 2046), whose *Micrographia* (1665) may well have prompted her to write the *Observations*, which includes the first selection given here.

2. Lenses.

3. Vision-enhancing (by means of refraction).

4. Artifice, like that of the lens-makers.

5. Early microscopes in England used simple lenses that blurred the image.

6. Composed of two opposite qualities.

7. As in Hooke's *Micrographia* illustration.

exterior object. I say the picture because it is not the real body of the object which the glass presents, but the glass only figures or patterns out the picture presented in and by the glass, and there may easily mistakes be committed in taking copies from copies. Nay, artists[8] do confess themselves that flies and the like will appear of several figures or shapes, according to the several reflections, refractions, mediums, and positions of several lights. Which if so, how can they tell or judge which is the truest light, position, or medium, that doth present the object naturally as it is? And if not, then an edge may very well seem flat, and a point of a needle a globe;[9] but if the edge of a knife, or point of a needle were naturally and really so as the microscope presents them, they would never be so useful as they are, for a flat or broad plain-edged knife would not cut, nor a blunt globe pierce so suddenly another body. Neither would or could they pierce without tearing and rending, if their bodies were so uneven. And if the picture of a young beautiful lady should be drawn according to the representation of the microscope, or according to the various refraction and reflection of light through such like glasses, it would be so far from being like her, as it would not be like a human face, but rather a monster than a picture of nature.

Wherefore those that invented microscopes and suchlike dioptrical glasses at first did, in my opinion, the world more injury than benefit. For this art has intoxicated so many men's brains, and wholly employed their thoughts and bodily actions about phenomena, or the exterior figures of objects, as[1] all better arts and studies are laid aside. Nay, those that are not as earnest and active in such employments as they, are by many of them accounted unprofitable subjects to the commonwealth of learning. But though there be numerous books written of the wonders of these glasses, yet I cannot perceive any such; at best, they are but superficial wonders, as I may call them.

But could experimental philosophers find out more beneficial arts than our forefathers have done, either for the better increase of vegetables and brute animals to nourish our bodies, or better and commodious contrivances in the art of architecture to build us houses, or for the advancing of trade and traffic to provide necessaries for us to live, or for the decrease of nice[2] distinctions and sophistical[3] disputes in churches, schools, and courts of judicature, to make men live in unity, peace, and neighborly friendship, it would not only be worth their labor, but of as much praise as could be given to them. But as boys that play with watery bubbles, or sling dust into each other's eyes, or make a hobbyhorse of snow, are worthy of reproof rather than praise, for wasting their time with useless sports, so those that addict themselves to unprofitable arts spend more time than they reap benefit thereby. Nay, could they benefit men either in husbandry, architecture, or the like necessary and profitable employments, yet before the vulgar sort[4] would learn to understand them, the world would want bread to eat, and houses to dwell in, as also clothes to keep them from the inconveniences of the inconstant weather. But truly, although spinsters[5] were most experienced in this art, yet they will never be able to spin silk, thread, or wool, etc., from loose atoms; neither will weavers weave a web of light from the sun's rays, nor an architect build a house of the bubbles of water and air,

8. Technicians.
9. Cavendish evidently refers to Hooke's micrographic depiction of a needle's point, a printed period (her "globe"), and (in the original illustration) a razor's edge; see page 2050.
1. That.

2. Minute, subtle, trivial.
3. Complicatedly and falsely argued.
4. Common people.
5. People who spin yarn or thread (possibly, here, with the additional sense of "unmarried woman").

unless they be poetical spinsters, weavers, and architects. And if a painter should draw a louse as big as a crab, and of that shape as the microscope presents, can anybody imagine that a beggar would believe it to be true?[6] But if he did, what advantage would it be to the beggar? For it doth neither instruct him how to avoid breeding them, or how to catch them, or to hinder them from biting. Again, if a painter should paint birds according to those colors the microscope presents, what advantage would it be for fowlers to take them? Truly, no fowler will be able to distinguish several birds through a microscope, neither by their shapes nor colors; they will be better discerned by those that eat their flesh than by micrographers that look upon their colors and exterior figures through a magnifying glass.

In short, magnifying glasses are like a high heel to a short leg, which if it be made too high, it is apt to make the wearer fall, and at the best can do no more than represent exterior figures in a bigger, and so in a more deformed shape and posture than naturally they are. But as for the interior form and motions of a creature, as I said before, they can no more represent them, than telescopes can the interior essence and nature of the sun, and what matter it consists of. For if one that never had seen milk before should look upon it through a microscope, he would never be able to discover the interior parts of milk by that instrument, were it the best that is in the world—neither the whey, nor the butter, nor the curds. Wherefore the best optic[7] is a perfect natural eye, and a regular sensitive perception, and the best judge is reason, and the best study is rational contemplation joined with the observations of regular sense, but not deluding arts. For art is not only gross[8] in comparison to nature, but for the most part deformed and defective, and at best produces mixed or hermaphroditical figures—that is, a third figure between nature and art. Which proves that natural reason is above artificial sense, as I may call it. Wherefore those arts are the best and surest informers that alter nature least, and they the greatest deluders that alter nature most—I mean, the particular nature of each particular creature. (For art is so far from altering infinite Nature that it is no more in comparison to it than a little fly to an elephant;[9] no, not so much, for there is no comparison between finite and infinite.) But wise Nature taking delight in variety, her parts, which are her creatures, must of necessity do so too.

from The Description of a New Blazing World
from To the Reader

If you wonder that I join a work of fancy[1] to my serious philosophical contemplations, think not that it is out of a disparagement to philosophy, or out of an opinion as if this noble study were but a fiction of the mind * * * The end of reason is truth, the end of fancy is fiction. But mistake me not when I distinguish fancy from reason; I mean not as if fancy were not made by the rational parts of matter, but by "reason" I understand a rational search and inquiry into the causes of natural effects, and by "fancy" a voluntary creation or production of the mind, both being effects, or rather actions, of the rational part of matter, of which, as that[2] is a more profitable and useful study than this,

---

6. Beggars were assumed to be most familiar (because most often afflicted) with lice.
7. Lens.
8. Rough, approximate.

9. Cavendish probably refers to Hooke's illustration of a flea (see page 2053).
1. Imagination.
2. Philosophy.

so it is also more laborious and difficult, and requires sometimes the help of fancy to recreate the mind and withdraw it from its more serious contemplations.

And this is the reason, why I added this piece of fancy to my philosophical observations, and joined them as two worlds at the ends of their poles; both for my own sake, to divert my studious thoughts, which I employed in the contemplation thereof, and to delight the reader with variety, which is always pleasing. But lest my fancy should stray too much, I chose such a fiction as would be agreeable to the subject treated of in the former parts; it is a description of a new world, not such as Lucian's, or the Frenchman's world in the moon;[3] but a world of my own creating, which I call the Blazing World: the first part whereof is romancical, the second philosophical, and the third is merely fancy, or (as I may call it) fantastical, which if it add any satisfaction to you, I shall account myself a happy creatoress.[4] If not, I must be content to live a melancholy life in my own world; I cannot call it a poor world, if poverty be only want of gold, silver, and jewels; for there is more gold in it than all the chemists ever did, and (as I verily believe) will ever be able to make.[5] As for the rocks of diamonds, I wish with all my soul they might be shared amongst my noble female friends, and upon that condition, I would willingly quit my part;[6] and of the gold I should only desire so much as might suffice to repair my noble Lord and husband's losses:[7] for I am not covetous, but as ambitious as ever any of my sex was, is, or can be; which makes, that though I cannot be Henry the Fifth, or Charles the Second,[8] yet I endeavor to be Margaret the First; and although I have neither power, time, nor occasion to conquer the world as Alexander and Caesar did; yet rather than not to be mistress of one, since Fortune and the Fates would give me none, I have made a world of my own: for which nobody, I hope, will blame me, since it is in everyone's power to do the like.

[CREATING WORLDS]

At last, when the Duchess[9] saw that no patterns would do her any good in the framing of her world, she resolved to make a world of her own invention, * * * which world after it was made, appeared so curious and full of variety, so well ordered and wisely governed, that it cannot possibly be expressed by words, nor the delight and pleasure which the Duchess took in making this world of her own.

In the meantime the Empress was also making and dissolving several worlds in her own mind, and was so puzzled, that she could not settle in any of them; wherefore she sent for the Duchess, who being ready to wait on the Empress, carried her

3. The *True History*, by the Greek satirist Lucian (2nd century C.E.), initiated a long literary tradition of imaginary voyages, to which the French writer Savinien Cyrano de Bergerac's account of a trip to the moon (*Histoire comique contenant les états et empires de la lune* [1657]) was a recent, celebrated contribution.
4. In the first part of *The Blazing World*, a "virtuous lady" survives her abduction at sea and is transported into a "Blazing World" that touches Earth at the North Pole; quickly wooed and wedded by the Emperor of this utopia, she becomes its Empress. In the second, "philosophical," section, she hears the testimony of various scholars, scientists, theologians, and philosophers; in the third, "fantastical," section, the Empress summons the soul of Margaret Cavendish to travel from England to the Blazing World, in order to serve as her companion and

secretary. The excerpts that follow are from the third part of the narrative.
5. Alchemists sought to turn base metals into gold.
6. Give up my share.
7. During the civil wars, William Cavendish had lost much wealth and property, of which he had recovered only part since the Restoration.
8. Henry V of England (1387–1422) was celebrated for his conquest of France; Charles II for his restoration of the monarchy after the Interregnum.
9. Cavendish herself, whose soul has been transported to the Blazing World at the Empress's request. At this point in the story she and the Empress have been experimenting with creating worlds in accordance with the theories established by various experts, ancient and modern (Pythagoras, Plato, Aristotle, Descartes, Hobbes).

beloved world along with her, and invited the Empress's soul to observe the frame, order, and government of it. Her Majesty was so ravished with the perception of it, that her soul desired to live in the Duchess's world; but the Duchess advised her to make such another world in her own mind; for, said she, your Majesty's mind is full of rational corporeal motions, and the rational motions of my mind shall assist you by the help of sensitive expressions, with the best instructions they are able to give you.

The Empress being thus persuaded by the Duchess to make an imaginary world of her own, followed her advice; and after she had quite finished it, and framed all kinds of creatures proper and useful for it, strengthened it with good laws, and beautified it with arts and sciences; having nothing else to do, unless she did dissolve her imaginary world, or made some alterations in the Blazing World she lived in, which yet she could hardly do, by reason it was so well ordered that it could not be mended.[1]

[EMPRESS, DUCHESS, DUKE]

At last, they entered into the Duke's house,[2] an habitation not so magnificent, as useful; and when the Empress saw it, "Has the Duke," said she, "no other house but this?" "Yes," answered the Duchess, "some five miles from this place, he has a very fine castle, called Bolsover."[3] "That place then," said the Empress, "I desire to see." "Alas!" replied the Duchess, "it is but a naked house, and unclothed of all furniture." "However," said the Empress, "I may see the manner of its structure and building." "That you may," replied the Duchess. And as they were thus discoursing, the Duke came out of the house into the court, to see his horses of manage;[4] whom when the Duchess's soul perceived, she was so overjoyed, that her aerial vehicle[5] became so splendorous, as if it had been enlightened by the sun; by which we may perceive, that the passions of souls or spirits can alter their bodily vehicles. Then these two ladies' spirits went close to him, but he could not perceive them; and after the Empress had observed the art of manage, she was much pleased with it, and commended it as a noble pastime, and an exercise fit and proper for noble and heroic persons; but when the Duke was gone into the house again, those two souls followed him; where the Empress observing, that he went to the exercise of the sword, and was such an excellent and unparalleled master thereof, she was as much pleased with that exercise, as she was with the former. But the Duchess's soul being troubled, that her dear lord and husband used such a violent exercise before meat, for fear of overheating himself, without any consideration of the Empress's soul, left her aerial vehicle, and entered into her lord. The Empress's soul perceiving this, did the like: and then the Duke had three souls in one body; and had there been but some such souls more, the Duke would have been like the Grand Signior in his seraglio,[6] only it would have been a Platonic seraglio.[7] But the Duke's soul being wise, honest, witty, complaisant, and noble, afforded such delight and pleasure to the Empress's soul by

---

1. Instead, the Empress resolves "to see the world the Duchess came from," and so "those two female souls" travel together "as lightly as two thoughts," into England.
2. Welbeck Abbey, north-country birthplace and family seat of Cavendish's husband the Duke of Newcastle.
3. The Duke's favorite residence.
4. Well-disciplined in the actions and paces of *ménage*, or systematic horse training. The Duke, an expert equestrian, had published two books on the subject; when Charles II was a boy, Newcastle had taught him how to ride.
5. Form made out of air.
6. Harem.
7. One where the pleasures of the flesh would be repudiated in favor of the contemplation of pure, disembodied Ideas.

her conversation, that these two souls became enamored of each other; which the Duchess's soul perceiving, grew jealous at first, but then considering that no adultery could be committed amongst Platonic lovers, and that Platonism was divine, as being derived from divine Plato, cast forth of her mind that idea of jealousy. Then the conversation of these three souls was so pleasant, that it cannot be expressed; for the Duke's soul entertained the Empress's soul with scenes, songs, music, witty discourses, pleasant recreations, and all kinds of harmless sports; so that the time passed away faster than they expected. At last, a spirit came and told the Empress, that although neither the Emperor, nor any of his subjects knew that her soul was absent; yet the Empress's soul was so sad and melancholy, for want of his own beloved soul, that all the imperial court took notice of it. Wherefore he advised the Empress's soul to return into the Blazing World, into her own body she left there; which both the Duke's and Duchess's soul was very sorry for, and wished, that if it had been possible, the Empress's soul might have stayed a longer time with them; but seeing it could not be otherwise, they pacified themselves. * * *

Epilogue
TO THE READER

By this poetical description, you may perceive, that my ambition is not only to be Empress, but Authoress of a whole world; and that the worlds I have made, both the Blazing and the other Philosophical World, mentioned in the first part of this description, are framed and composed of the most pure, that is, the rational parts of matter, which are the parts of my mind; which creation was more easily and suddenly effected than the conquests of the two famous monarchs of the world, Alexander and Caesar. Neither have I made such disturbances, and caused so many dissolutions of particulars,[8] otherwise named deaths, as they did; for I have destroyed but some few men in a little boat,[9] which died through the extremity of cold, and that by the hand of Justice, which was necessitated to punish their crime of stealing away a young and beauteous lady. And in the formation of those worlds, I take more delight and glory, than ever Alexander or Caesar did in conquering this terrestrial world; and though I have made my Blazing World a peaceable world, allowing it but one religion, one language, and one government; yet could I make another world, as full of factions, divisions, and wars, as this is of peace and tranquility; and the rational figures of my mind might express as much courage to fight, as Hector and Achilles had; and be as wise as Nestor, as eloquent as Ulysses, and as beautiful as Helen.[1] But I esteeming peace before war, wit before policy, honesty before beauty; instead of the figures of Alexander, Caesar, Hector, Achilles, Nestor, Ulysses, Helen, etc. chose rather the figure of honest Margaret Newcastle, which now I would not change for all this terrestrial world; and if any should like the world I have made, and be willing to be my subjects, they may imagine themselves such, and they are such, I mean, in their minds, fancies, or imaginations; but if they cannot endure to be subjects, they may create worlds of their own, and govern themselves as they please: but yet let them have a care, not to prove unjust usurpers, and to rob me of mine; for concerning the Philosophical World, I am Empress of it myself; and as for the Blazing World, it having an Empress already, who rules it with great wisdom

8. Individuals.
9. The sailor-abductors of the "virtuous lady," who die during the boat's passage through the North Pole to the

Blazing World.
1. Characters in the *Iliad*, Homer's epic poem about the Trojan War.

and conduct, which Empress is my dear Platonic friend; I shall never prove so unjust, treacherous, and unworthy to her, as to disturb her government, much less to depose her from her imperial throne, for the sake of any other; but rather choose to create another world for another friend.

1666

John Dryden
1631–1700

Godfrey Kneller, *John Dryden*, 1693.

In his last years, John Dryden often felt the need to defend his morals, his religion, his politics, even his writing. For nearly a quarter of a century, he had held high literary office and mingled with the great; he had curried royal favor and aristocratic patronage, bolstering officialdom, aiming to injure the Crown's enemies and to caress its friends. He wrote about politics and religion, about trade and empire; he wrote for the theater and for public occasions; he composed songs, fables, odes, and panegyrics, brilliant satire and savage polemic; he translated from many languages and formulated an idiomatic, familiar, and fluent prose style. Dryden virtually invented the idea of a commercial literary career; and through all the turns of a difficult public life, he fashioned from his own unlikely personality—from his privacy, self-doubts, and hesitations—a public figure of literary distinction. But he attained this celebrity at the cost of gossip and scandal, and in the last decade of his life (after the Glorious Revolution and his deposition from the Poet Laureateship) he faced suspicion and scorn.

The poet's beginnings give no hint of literary greatness or the likelihood of fame. He was born in 1631 in a country town and to comfortable circumstance; he was educated at Westminster School and graduated from Trinity College, Cambridge. He held minor public office in the 1650s but had written almost nothing before he was twenty-seven. Dryden then began his long career as public poet. He mourned the Lord Protector in 1659 (*Heroic Stanzas*) and then, in what looks like a convenient turn of allegiance, he celebrated the return of monarchy in 1660, writing poems to Charles II, to the Lord Chancellor, and to the Duchess of York; he praised the Royal Society (*To Doctor Charleton*) and defended the Royal Navy and its aristocratic high command (*Annus Mirabilis*, 1667).

The first years seem a series of calculated moves; and the combination of talent, application, and opportunity was crowned when Dryden was named Poet Laureate in 1667. But in addition to fashioning a career in the 1660s, Dryden also forged a new drama—an epic theater whose themes and language echoed the idioms of heroic verse—and a body of literary criticism that itself would have made his lasting reputation. Indeed, the great text of the first decade was the *Essay of Dramatic Poesy* (1668), Dryden's formulation of a pointedly English poetics and theater. Along with Sir Philip Sidney's *Apology for Poetry*, and Samuel Johnson's *Lives of the Poets*, Dryden's *Essay* is central to the long-standing canon of English literary criticism. Some of Dryden's early plays have been forgotten, but he worked steadily at a craft that would enable him to turn Milton's *Paradise Lost* into theater (*The State of Innocence*, 1677), create a superb adaptation of Shakespeare's *Antony and Cleopatra* in *All for Love* (1678), the finest of Restoration tragedies in *Don Sebastian* (1690), and the texts of one of England's first operas, *King Arthur* (1691), and last masques, *The Pilgrim* (1700).

By the late 1670s Dryden was famed as publicist for the Crown, and his theatrical work had come to dominate the stage; but he had hardly begun the career as satirist by which he is now best known. Its opening move was *Mac Flecknoe* (1676), and in the next few years Dryden fashioned masterpieces of literary mockery and political invective, poems that virtually created literary genres and dominated satire for decades to come. *Mac Flecknoe* allowed Dryden to ridicule and crush his rivals, all the while conjuring the suave tones and elegant manners of literary supremacy. In the abuse of rivals, only Pope surpasses Dryden as a master of scorn. But *Mac Flecknoe* was only the first act in a theater of invective. In the fall of 1681 Dryden wrote *Absalom and Achitophel,* a biblical allegory occasioned by the crisis of succession. The king had failed to beget a legitimate heir, and the king's Catholic brother waited ominously in the wings. It was Dryden's job to defend the Crown, to extenuate royal indulgence, and, especially, to defuse anxieties. With *Absalom and Achitophel,* Dryden wove together the Bible and contemporary politics with such deftness that mere diversionary tactics were spun into an incomparable allegory of envy, ambition, and misdeed. The satire was read, marked, circulated, and treasured as a masterpiece and a menace.

The masterpiece secured Dryden's fame; the menace exacted a cost. The poet had attacked powerful men: aristocrats, politicans, and their partisan hacks who intrigued against the Crown. They failed in the early 1680s to foment rebellion, but by 1688 they were able to effect a revolution that deposed Catholic monarchy and the Poet Laureate himself. Dryden was reputed a brilliant and damaging advocate of Stuart rule; he had collaborated with court publicity and polemic; he had even converted to Roman Catholicism after James ascended the throne. Indeed, Dryden wrote his longest and most elaborate original poem—*The Hind and the Panther* (1687)—in defense of that king's rule and religion, and of his own conversion to Roman Catholicism. Once James II had been chased into exile, the poet felt he had nowhere to turn. In 1688 Dryden was fifty-seven, an old man by contemporary standards. He was forced from office, his pension was canceled, and he was driven back to the venues of commercial writing: the theater, translation, publication by subscription, even editing and anthologizing. He often expressed a keen sense of loss and abandonment in the 1690s, yet the decade would prove to be a remarkable phase of his career. Between his loss of the laureateship in 1689 and his death in 1700, Dryden wrote a series of superb translations that included selections from the satires of Juvenal and Persius, Ovid's *Metamorphoses* and *Amores*, Boccaccio's and Chaucer's tales. In these same years he wrote odes and epitaphs, and collaborated with his publisher Jacob Tonson in the new fashion for literary anthologies. Most remarkably, he produced *The Works of Virgil,* which set the standard for the translation of Latin poetry. He had come to his project late, and more than once he wrote of his inadequacy for this daunting task: "What Virgil wrote in the vigor of his age, in plenty and at ease, I have undertaken to translate in my declining years, struggling with wants, oppressed with sickness, curbed in my genius, liable to be misconstrued in all I write; and my judges . . . already prejudiced against me, by the lying character which has been given them of my morals." But Dryden's *Virgil* was a resounding, rehabilitating commercial and artistic success.

Nor were the twelve thousand lines of translated Virgil the close of this career. What followed was *Fables Ancient and Modern,* an anthology of original verse and new translations that included Ovid, Boccaccio, and Chaucer as well as a trial for what Dryden hoped would be his English Homer. He saw commercial opportunity in this new collection; but he must also have understood it as a crowning achievement in this life of theatricality and ventriloquism. He had begun by seeking a voice in the idioms and gestures of other poets; he now belonged wholly to himself as he casually turned their verse into his own. It is something of a paradox that a life of literary self-assertion, of aggressive, even calculating, careerism, should have closed with Dryden rummaging among other poets' verse, pausing over favorite lines, translating Ovid's Latin and Boccaccio's Italian into what was unmistakably his own voice. And the paradox of self-assertion ending in translation helps us to identify what is so particularly and so brilliantly Dryden's art. In the early modern world, writing meant belonging to others—to the authority of antiquity, to the opinions and fickle pleasure of patrons, to favor, to obligation, to taste, even to the emerging appetites of a reading public. Many of Dryden's contemporaries—Donne, Milton, Rochester—appeal to us by their seeming defiance of such self-denying ordinances. We read Dryden today not just for the skill with which he picked his way through political dangers or negotiated social minefields, not even for the savage cartooning of enemies or baroque praise of friends, but for the achievement of belonging to others as he became more exactly and more generously himself.

 For additional resources on Dryden, including the ode "To the Pious Memory of the Accomplished Young Lady Mrs. Anne Killigrew," go to *The Longman Anthology of British Literature* Web site at www.myliteraturekit.com.

ABSALOM AND ACHITOPHEL   Dryden wrote *Absalom and Achitophel* as a piece of propaganda; he was, after all, Poet Laureate. He may even have written it at the personal request of Charles II, and he surely intended to please the king, to entertain his friends, to embarrass their enemies. He performed these offices amidst tangled circumstances and under extraordinary partisan and civic pressures.

Charles had sired many children by many mistresses, but no heir by his wife. These habits and accidents of royal procreation had created a succession crisis: in the absence of a legitimate heir, the crown would pass to Charles's brother James, an openly professed Roman Catholic. This prospect excited every fear of absolute rule—of Popery, slavery, subjugation to France and to Rome. The crisis, in turn, helped crystallize an opposition of Protestants, rebels, republicans, and opportunists who mustered support for an audacious proposal: exclude the duke from succession and appoint as substitute the dim but charming, Protestant but (alas) bastard offspring of the king, James, Duke of Monmouth.

To bolster its program, the opposition made ingenious use of a conspiracy theory, widely entertained though largely false. In 1678 the mysterious murder of an eminent judge, a cloud of perjured witnesses, and a blizzard of broadsides, rumors, and innuendos persuaded many that the Queen, the Duke of York, and a band of Jesuits had conspired in a "Popish Plot" to kill the king and inaugurate Catholic rule. At the height of the mania, thirty-five Catholics were executed for their supposed complicity in this "plot." After the bloodletting, and in the face of much evidence to suggest that the plot itself was fiction, the rage subsided. The Whig opposition, now emerging from thuggery and faction into England's first organized political party, tested its powers by parliamentary maneuver. In 1680 its leader, the Earl of Shaftesbury, tried twice to pass a bill excluding Charles's brother James from the succession. In 1681 Shaftesbury publicly urged Charles to legitimate Monmouth. The king had had enough: he dismissed Parliament in March, and on 2 July had Shaftesbury imprisoned on charges of high treason. Four months later, a packed jury produced the verdict *ignoramus* ("we don't know").

Dryden's poem, appearing the week before the trial, told these busy stories in terms both daring and familiar. He cast the crisis as biblical drama: Charles became King David, Monmouth was David's wayward son Absalom, Shaftesbury the wily counselor Achitophel. Of course, factions of all sorts had long deployed parallels between England and Israel for instruction, for prophecy and exhortation, for mockery and even scandal. But no one had set all the possibilities of irony and celebration simultaneously in motion. Against the king's enemies Dryden turned their own rhetoric of scriptural sanctimony; in support of the king's friends he wrote hymns of praise; but on behalf of that complex client the king himself, Dryden discovered a way of portraying monarchy in a spirit at once appreciative, ironic, and delicately abrasive. In the poem's mischievous opening lines we hear these possibilities fully orchestrated. Charles's sexual energies, mapped as Davidic fecundity, are simultaneously grand and titillating, munificent and comic. Such mixtures of tone suffuse all the actions and arguments of Dryden's poem—its images of authority, its satiric portraits, its theories of governance, its monologues and declamations—all its traffic with the dangerous world of politics, plots, and promiscuity.

Absalom and Achitophel: A Poem.

—Si propiùes stes
Te capiet magis—[1]

TO THE READER

'Tis not my intention to make an apology for my poem: some will think it needs no excuse, and others will receive none. The design, I am sure, is honest, but he who draws his pen for one party must expect to make enemies of the other. For wit and fool are consequents of Whig and Tory, and every man is a knave or an ass to the contrary side. There's a treasury of merits in the fanatic church, as well as in the Papist, and a pennyworth to be had of saintship, honesty, and poetry, for the lewd, the factious, and the blockheads.[2] But the longest chapter in Deuteronomy has not curses enough for an anti-Bromingham.[3] My comfort is, their manifest prejudice to my cause will render their judgment of less authority against me. Yet if a poem have a genius, it will force its own reception in the world. For there's a sweetness in good verse, which tickles even while it hurts, and no man can be heartily angry with him who pleases him against his will. The commendation of adversaries is the greatest triumph of a writer, because it never comes unless extorted. But I can be satisfied on more easy terms: if I happen to please the more moderate sort, I shall be sure of an honest party and, in all probability, of the best judges, for the least concerned are commonly the least corrupt. And, I confess, I have laid in for those, by rebating[4] the satire (where justice would allow it) from carrying too sharp an edge. They who can criticize so weakly as to imagine I have done my worst may be convinced, at their own cost, that I can write severely with more ease than I can gently. I have but laughed at some men's follies, when I could have declaimed against their vices; and other men's virtues I have commended as freely as I have taxed[5] their crimes. And now, if you are a malicious reader, I expect you should return upon me that I affect to be thought more impartial than I am. But if men are not to be judged by their professions,[6] God forgive you commonwealthsmen[7] for professing so plausibly for the government. You cannot be so unconscionable as to charge me for not subscribing of my name, for that would reflect too grossly upon your own party, who never dare, though they have the advantage of a jury to secure them.[8] If you like not my poem, the fault may, possibly, be in my writing (though 'tis hard for an author to judge

1. "If you stand closer, it will capture you more readily" (Horace, *Ars Poetica* 361–62); Horace is here developing his argument that a poem works like a picture (*ut pictura poesis*).
2. Roman Catholic doctrine posited the existence in heaven of a fund of surplus "merits," accumulated through the goodness of Christ and the saints, on which ordinary mortals might draw for absolution. Dryden suggests that the dissenting Protestant sects ("the fanatic church"), like the Catholic ("Papist") church, confer forgiveness (even "saintship") too freely, and too cheaply.
3. Tory (Royalist). Deuteronomy 28 includes a long list of curses against those who "shall not enter into the congregation of the Lord" because they have disobeyed his law.
4. Abating, softening.
5. Denounced.
6. What they say (profess).
7. Here and throughout the poem, Dryden conflates the supporters of Monmouth with the supporters of Cromwell, as enemies of the monarchy.
8. Dryden published his politically volatile poem anonymously. He accuses Whig writers of similar caution, and hence of greater cowardice, because the London juries that adjudicated cases of seditious libel were handpicked by Whig sheriffs for their bias in the party's favor.

against himself); but, more probably, 'tis in your morals, which cannot bear the truth of it. The violent on both sides will condemn the character of Absalom as either too favorably or too hardly drawn. But they are not the violent whom I desire to please. The fault, on the right hand, is to extenuate, palliate, and indulge; and, to confess freely, I have endeavored to commit it. Besides the respect which I owe his birth, I have a greater for his heroic virtues; and David himself could not be more tender of the young man's life than I would be of his reputation. But since the most excellent natures are always the most easy,[9] and, as being such, are the soonest perverted by ill counsels, especially when baited with fame and glory, 'tis no more a wonder that he withstood not the temptations of Achitophel than it was for Adam not to have resisted the two devils, the serpent and the woman. The conclusion of the story I purposely forbore to prosecute, because I could not obtain from myself to show Absalom unfortunate.[1] The frame of it was cut out but for a picture to the waist; and if the draught be so far true, 'tis as much as I designed.

Were I the inventor, who am only the historian, I should certainly conclude the piece with the reconcilement of Absalom to David. And who knows but this may come to pass? Things were not brought to an extremity where I left the story. There seems yet to be room left for a composure;[2] hereafter, there may only be for pity. I have not so much as an uncharitable wish against Achitophel, but am content to be accused of a good-natured error and to hope with Origen[3] that the Devil himself may, at last, be saved. For which reason, in this poem he is neither brought to set his house in order nor to dispose of his person afterwards as he in wisdom shall think fit.[4] God is infinitely merciful, and his vicegerent[5] is only not so because he is not infinite.

The true end of satire is the amendment of vices by correction. And he who writes honestly is no more an enemy to the offender than the physician to the patient, when he prescribes harsh remedies to an inveterate disease; for those are only in order to prevent the surgeon's work of an *ense rescindendum*,[6] which I wish not to my very enemies. To conclude all, if the body politic have any analogy to the natural, in my weak judgment, an Act of Oblivion were as necessary in a hot, distempered state as an opiate would be in a raging fever.

Absalom and Achitophel: A Poem

    In pious times, ere priestcraft did begin,
    Before polygamy was made a sin;[7]
    When man on many multiplied his kind,
    Ere one to one was cursedly confined;
5   When Nature prompted, and no law denied
    Promiscuous use of concubine and bride;
    Then Israel's monarch, after Heaven's own heart,
    His vigorous warmth did variously impart
    To wives and slaves; and, wide as his command,

---

9. Easily persuaded.

1. I.e., Dryden decided to leave off the end of the biblical story (in which Absalom is killed), because he could not bring himself to show Absalom's misfortune.

2. Reconciliation.

3. An early Christian theologian.

4. Dryden insinuatingly echoes the biblical account of Achitophel's disappointment and suicide (2 Samuel 23).

5. The king.

6. "Something to be cut out" in order to prevent infection of the whole organism. Dryden next suggests that an "Act of Oblivion" forgiving the rebels, like the one Charles II enacted at his Restoration, might constitute a gentler remedy.

7. "Priestcraft" is "religious fraud" (Johnson's *Dictionary*); Dryden mimics the anti-Catholicism of the Whigs, while insinuating that monogamy is an unnatural restriction imposed by power-hungry priests.

10	Scattered his Maker's image through the land.
	Michal,[8] of royal blood, the crown did wear,
	A soil ungrateful to the tiller's care:
	Not so the rest, for several mothers bore
	To godlike David several sons before.
15	But since like slaves his bed they did ascend,
	No true succession could their seed attend.[9]
	Of all this numerous progeny was none
	So beautiful, so brave as Absolon:
	Whether, inspired by some diviner lust,
20	His father got° him with a greater gust,° *begot / pleasure*
	Or that his conscious destiny made way
	By manly beauty to imperial sway.
	Early in foreign fields he won renown,
	With kings and states allied to Israel's crown:
25	In peace the thoughts of war he could remove,
	And seemed as he were only born for love.
	Whate'er he did was done with so much ease,
	In him alone 'twas natural to please.
	His motions all accompanied with grace;
30	And paradise was opened in his face.
	With secret joy indulgent David viewed
	His youthful image in his son renewed:
	To all his wishes nothing he denied,
	And made the charming Annabel[1] his bride.
35	What faults he had (for who from faults is free?)
	His father could not, or he would not see.
	Some warm excesses, which the law forbore,
	Were construed youth that purged by boiling o'er:
	And Amnon's murder,[2] by a specious name,
40	Was called a just revenge for injured fame.
	Thus praised and loved the noble youth remained,
	While David, undisturbed, in Sion[3] reigned.
	But life can never be sincerely blest:
	Heaven punishes the bad, and proves° the best. *tests*
45	The Jews,[4] a headstrong, moody, murmuring race,
	As ever tried th' extent and stretch of grace;
	God's pampered people whom, debauched with ease,
	No king could govern, nor no God could please
	(Gods they had tried of every shape and size
50	That god-smiths could produce, or priests devise);
	These Adam-wits, too fortunately free,
	Began to dream they wanted° liberty; *lacked, desired*
	And when no rule, no precedent was found

8. Daughter of David's predecessor King Saul; here she represents Charles's childless wife, Catherine of Braganza.
9. Their offspring could not succeed to the throne because of their illegitimacy.
1. Anne, Countess of Buccleuch.

2. In 2 Samuel 8, Amnon rapes Absalom's half sister, and Absalom orders his murder; the correspondence with events in Monmouth's life is uncertain.
3. Jerusalem (hence, London).
4. The English.

Of men by laws less circumscribed and bound,

55 They led their wild desires to woods and caves,
And thought that all but savages were slaves.
They who when Saul was dead, without a blow,
Made foolish Ishbosheth⁵ the crown forgo;
Who banished David did from Hebron bring,⁶

60 And with a general shout proclaimed him King:
Those very Jews, who, at their very best,
Their humor more than loyalty expressed,
Now wondered why so long they had obeyed
An idol monarch which their hands had made;

65 Thought they might ruin him they could create,
Or melt him to that golden calf, a state.
But these were random bolts; no formed design,
Nor interest made the factious crowd to join:
The sober part of Israel, free from stain,

70 Well knew the value of a peaceful reign:
And, looking backward with a wise afright,
Saw seams of wounds, dishonest to the sight;
In contemplation of whose ugly scars
They cursed the memory of Civil Wars.

75 The moderate sort of men, thus qualified,
Inclined the balance to the better side:
And David's mildness managed it so well,
The bad found no occasion to rebel.
But when to sin our biased nature leans,

80 The careful Devil is still° at hand with means;   *always*
And providently pimps for ill desires:
The Good Old Cause⁷ revived, a Plot requires.
Plots, true or false, are necessary things,
To raise up commonwealths and ruin kings.

85   Th' inhabitants of old Jerusalem
Were Jebusites:⁸ the town so called from them;
And theirs the native right—
But when the chosen people grew more strong,
The rightful cause at length became the wrong:

90 And every loss the men of Jebus bore,
They still were thought God's enemies the more.
Thus, worn and weakened, well or ill content,
Submit they must to David's government:
Impoverished, and deprived of all command,

95 Their taxes doubled as they lost their land,
And, what was harder yet to flesh and blood,
Their gods disgraced, and burnt like common wood.⁹

5. Ishbosheth briefly succeeded his father Saul; correspondingly, Richard Cromwell was Protector for a few months after the death of his father, Oliver.
6. David ruled in Hebron seven years before becoming king of Israel. Charles had been crowned in Scotland in 1651.

7. Popular name for the Cromwellian opposition to the monarchy.
8. Jebusites inhabited Jerusalem before the Israelites; here, they represent the Catholics.
9. Dryden alludes to a variety of anti-Catholic penal laws.

This set the heathen priesthood in a flame;
For priests of all religions are the same:
100   Of whatsoe'er descent their godhead be,
Stock, stone, or other homely pedigree,
In his defense his servants are as bold
As if he had been born of beaten gold.
The Jewish rabbins,[1] though their enemies,
105   In this conclude them honest men and wise:
For 'twas their duty, all the learned think,
T' espouse his cause by whom they eat and drink.
From hence began that Plot,[2] the nation's curse,
Bad in itself, but represented worse:
110   Raised in extremes, and in extremes decried;
With oaths affirmed, with dying vows denied:
Not weighed or winnowed by the multitude,
But swallowed in the mass, unchewed and crude.
Some truth there was, but dashed and brewed with lies,
115   To please the fools, and puzzle all the wise.
Succeeding times did equal folly call
Believing nothing, or believing all.
Th' Egyptian rites the Jebusites embraced,
Where gods were recommended by their taste.[3]
120   Such savory deities must needs be good,
As served at once for worship and for food.
By force they could not introduce these gods,
For ten to one[4] in former days was odds.
So fraud was used (the sacrificer's trade):
125   Fools are more hard to conquer than persuade.
Their busy teachers mingled with the Jews,
And raked, for converts, even the court and stews:°   *brothels*
Which Hebrew priests the more unkindly took,
Because the fleece[5] accompanies the flock.
130   Some thought they God's anointed[6] meant to slay
By guns, invented since full many a day:[7]
Our author swears it not; but who can know
How far the Devil and Jebusites may go?
This Plot, which failed for want of common sense,
135   Had yet a deep and dangerous consequence:
For, as when raging fevers boil the blood,
The standing lake soon floats into a flood,
And every hostile humor,[8] which before
Slept quiet in its channels, bubbles o'er;
140   So several factions from this first ferment
Work up to foam, and threat the government.

---

1. Anglican clergy.
2. The Popish Plot.
3. Here, and in the lines following, Dryden mocks the Catholic belief in transubstantiation.
4. Protestants to Catholics.

5. Tithe, paid by the "flock" (the parishioners).
6. The king.
7. Long since; Dryden playfully acknowledges this anachronism.
8. Bodily fluid, thought to determine temperament.

Some by their friends, more by themselves thought wise,
Opposed the power to which they could not rise.
Some had in courts been great, and thrown from thence,
145   Like fiends were hardened in impenitence.
Some, by their monarch's fatal mercy, grown,
From pardoned rebels, kinsmen to the throne,
Were raised in power and public office high:
Strong bands, if bands ungrateful men could tie.
150   Of these the false Achitophel⁹ was first:
A name to all succeeding ages cursed:
For close° designs and crooked counsels fit;   secret
Sagacious, bold, and turbulent of wit:
Restless, unfixed in principles and place;
155   In power unpleased, impatient of disgrace:
A fiery soul, which working out its way,
Fretted the pygmy body to decay:
And o'er-informed the tenement of clay.¹
A daring pilot in extremity;
160   Pleased with the danger, when the waves went high
He sought the storms; but for a calm unfit,
Would steer too nigh the sands, to boast his wit.
Great wits are sure to madness near allied;
And thin partitions do their bounds divide:
165   Else why should he, with wealth and honor blessed,
Refuse his age² the needful hours of rest?
Punish a body which he could not please;
Bankrupt of life, yet prodigal of ease?
And all to leave what with his toil he won,
170   To that unfeathered, two-legged thing, a son:
Got while his soul did huddled notions try;
And born a shapeless lump, like anarchy.
In friendship false, implacable in hate:
Resolved to ruin or to rule the state.
175   To compass this the triple bond³ he broke,
The pillars of the public safety shook,
And fitted Israel for a foreign yoke.
Then, seized with fear, yet still affecting° fame,   desiring
Usurped a patriot's all-atoning name.⁴
180   So easy still it proves in factious times,
With public zeal to cancel private crimes:
How safe is treason, and how sacred ill,
Where none can sin against the people's will:
Where crowds can wink,⁵ and no offense be known,

9. David's counselor, who encourages Absalom to rebel against his father; here representing Anthony Ashley Cooper, first Earl of Shaftesbury, counselor to both Cromwell and Charles II.
1. The body; Dryden contrasts Shaftesbury's large ambition with his small and sickly body.
2. Shaftesbury was 60 in 1681.
3. England's 1668 alliance with Sweden and Holland (against France).
4. Name that excuses anything.
5. Turn a blind eye.

185 Since in another's guilt they find their own.
Yet fame deserved no enemy can grudge;
The statesman we abhor, but praise the judge.
In Israel's courts ne'er sat an Abbethdin[6]
With more discerning eyes, or hands more clean:
190 Unbribed, unsought, the wretched to redress,
Swift of dispatch, and easy of access.
Oh, had he been content to serve the crown,
With virtues only proper to the gown;
Or had the rankness of the soil been freed
195 From cockle,° that oppressed the noble seed: weeds
David for him his tuneful harp had strung,
And heaven had wanted one immortal song.[7]
But wild ambition loves to slide, not stand,
And fortune's ice prefers to virtue's land:
200 Achitophel, grown weary to possess°   of possessing
A lawful fame and lazy happiness,
Disdained the golden fruit to gather free,
And lent the crowd his arm to shake the tree.
Now, manifest° of crimes contrived long since,   clearly guilty
205 He stood at bold defiance with his prince:
Held up the buckler° of the people's cause   shield
Against the crown; and skulked behind the laws.
The wished occasion of the Plot he takes,
Some circumstances finds, but more he makes;
210 By buzzing emissaries fills the ears
Of list'ning crowds with jealousies and fears
Of arbitrary counsels brought to light,
And proves the King himself a Jebusite:
Weak arguments! which yet he knew full well
215 Were strong with people easy to rebel.
For, governed by the moon, the giddy Jews
Tread the same track when she the prime renews;[8]
And once in twenty years, their scribes record,
By natural instinct they change their lord.
220 Achitophel still wants a chief, and none
Was found so fit as warlike Absolon:
Not that he wished his greatness to create
(For politicians neither love nor hate),
But for he knew his title not allowed,
225 Would keep him still depending on the crowd,
That kingly power, thus ebbing out, might be
Drawn to the dregs of a democracy.[9]
Him he attempts with studied arts to please,

6. Chief justice of the Jewish supreme court.
7. David would have composed one psalm fewer because he would be employed in writing praise of Achitophel.
8. A lunar cycle lasts about 20 years; Dryden alludes to the constitutional crises of 1640, 1660, and 1680.
9. Like "commonwealth" and "state," a pejorative term used to suggest a government of mob rule.

And sheds his venom in such words as these.
230   "Auspicious Prince! at whose nativity
    Some royal planet ruled the southern sky;
    Thy longing country's darling and desire;
    Their cloudy pillar, and their guardian fire:
    Their second Moses, whose extended wand
235   Divides the seas and shows the promised land:[1]
    Whose dawning day, in every distant age,
    Has exercised the sacred prophet's rage:
    The people's prayer, the glad diviners' theme,
    The young men's vision, and the old men's dream!
240   Thee, savior, thee, the nation's vows confess,
    And, never satisfied with seeing, bless:
    Swift, unbespoken pomps° thy steps proclaim,   unsought honors
    And stammering babes are taught to lisp thy name.
    How long wilt thou the general joy detain,
245   Starve and defraud the people of thy reign?
    Content ingloriously to pass thy days
    Like one of virtue's fools that feeds on praise;
    Till thy fresh glories, which now shine so bright,
    Grow stale and tarnish with our daily sight.
250   Believe me, royal youth, thy fruit must be
    Or° gathered ripe, or rot upon the tree.   either
    Heav'n has to all allotted, soon or late,
    Some lucky revolution of their fate:
    Whose motions, if we watch and guide with skill
255   (For human good depends on human will),
    Our Fortune rolls as from a smooth descent,
    And from the first impression takes the bent:
    But, if unseized, she glides away like wind,
    And leaves repenting folly far behind.[2]
260   Now, now she meets you with a glorious prize,
    And spreads her locks before her as she flies.
    Had thus old David, from whose loins you spring,
    Not dared, when Fortune called him, to be King,
    At Gath[3] an exile he might still remain,
265   And heaven's anointing oil had been in vain.
    Let his successful youth your hopes engage,
    But shun the example of declining age:
    Behold him setting in his western skies,
    The shadows length'ning as the vapors rise.
270   He is not now as when on Jordan's sand
    The joyful people thronged to see him land,
    Cov'ring the beach, and black'ning all the strand:[4]
    But, like the Prince of Angels[5] from his height,

---

1. On the way to Canaan, God's "promised land," Moses
led the Israelites across the Red Sea and through the
desert; they followed a pillar of cloud by day and a pillar
of fire by night.
2. Fortune, represented as a woman with streaming hair,
needs to be grasped at the first opportunity.

3. Brussels, where Charles spent the last phase of his exile.
4. Dryden refers to Charles's triumphant landing at
Dover in May of 1660.
5. Lucifer (light-bearer) rebelled against God and was
cast out from heaven.

Comes tumbling downward with diminished light;
275 Betrayed by one poor plot to public scorn
(Our only blessing since his curst return),
Those heaps of people which one sheaf did bind,
Blown off and scattered by a puff of wind.
What strength can he to your designs oppose,
280 Naked of friends, and round beset with foes?
If Pharaoh's doubtful succor he should use,[6]
A foreign aid would more incense the Jews:
Proud Egypt would dissembled friendship bring,
Foment the war, but not support the King:
285 Nor would the royal party e'er unite
With Pharaoh's arms t' assist the Jebusite;
Or if they should, their interest soon would break,
And with such odious aid make David weak.
All sorts of men by my successful arts,
290 Abhorring kings, estrange their altered hearts
From David's rule; and 'tis the general cry,
'Religion, Commonwealth, and Liberty.'[7]
If you, as champion of the public good,
Add to their arms a chief of royal blood,
295 What may not Israel hope, and what applause
Might such a general gain by such a cause?
Not barren praise alone, that gaudy flower,
Fair only to the sight, but solid power:
And nobler is a limited command,
300 Giv'n by the love of all your native land,
Than a successive° title, long and dark,   *inherited*
Drawn from the moldy rolls of Noah's ark."
    What cannot praise effect in mighty minds,
When flattery soothes, and when ambition blinds!
305 Desire of power, on earth a vicious weed,
Yet, sprung from high, is of celestial seed:
In God 'tis glory, and when men aspire,
'Tis but a spark too much of heavenly fire.
Th' ambitious youth, too covetous of fame,
310 Too full of angel's metal[8] in his frame,
Unwarily was led from virtue's ways,
Made drunk with honor, and debauched with praise.
Half loath, and half consenting to the ill
(For royal blood within him struggled still),
315 He thus replied: "And what pretense have I
To take up arms for public liberty?
My father governs with unquestioned right;

6. I.e., if Charles should turn for assistance to Louis XIV, Catholic king of France.
7. A slogan of the Good Old Cause.

8. Dryden puns on "angel" (a coin as well as a supernatural being) and on "metal" / "mettle" ("spriteliness, courage"—Johnson's *Dictionary*).

The faith's defender, and mankind's delight:
Good, gracious, just, observant of the laws;
320   And heav'n by wonders has espoused his cause.
Whom has he wronged in all his peaceful reign?
Who sues for justice to his throne in vain?
What millions has he pardoned[9] of his foes,
Whom just revenge did to his wrath expose!
325   Mild, easy, humble, studious of our good,
Inclined to mercy, and averse from blood.
If mildness ill with stubborn Israel suit,
His crime is God's beloved attribute.
What could he gain, his people to betray,
330   Or change his right for arbitrary sway?
Let haughty Pharaoh curse, with such a reign,
His fruitful Nile, and yoke a servile train.
If David's rule Jerusalem displease,
The dog star[1] heats their brains to this disease.
335   Why then should I, encouraging the bad,
Turn rebel and run popularly mad?
Were he a tyrant who, by lawless might,
Oppressed the Jews and raised the Jebusite,
Well might I mourn; but nature's holy bands
340   Would curb my spirits and restrain my hands:
The people might assert their liberty,
But what was right in them were crime in me.
His favor leaves me nothing to require,
Prevents my wishes, and outruns desire.
345   What more can I expect while David lives?
All but his kingly diadem he gives;
And that—" But there he paused; then sighing said,
"Is justly destined for a worthier head.
For when my father from his toils shall rest,
350   And late augment the number of the blest,
His lawful issue shall the throne ascend,
Or the collateral line[2] where that shall end.
His brother, though oppressed with vulgar spite,[3]
Yet dauntless and secure of native right,
355   Of every royal virtue stands possessed;
Still dear to all the bravest and the best.
His courage foes, his friends his truth proclaim;
His loyalty the King, the world his fame.
His mercy ev'n th' offending crowd will find,
360   For sure he comes of a forgiving kind.°   *family*
Why should I then repine at Heaven's decree,
Which gives me no pretense to royalty?
Yet O that Fate, propitiously inclined,

9. By the Act of Oblivion of 1660.
1. Sirius, which presides over the madness-inducing "dog
days" of summer.

2. That which passed through Charles's brother, James.
3. The hostility of the common people.

Had raised my birth, or had debased my mind;
365   To my large soul not all her treasure lent,
And then betrayed it to a mean descent.
I find, I find my mounting spirits bold,
And David's part disdains my mother's mold.
Why am I scanted by a niggard[4] birth?
370   My soul disclaims the kindred of her earth:
And, made for empire, whispers me within,
'Desire of greatness is a godlike sin.' "
     Him staggering so when Hell's dire agent found,[5]
While fainting Virtue scarce maintained her ground,
375   He pours fresh forces in, and thus replies:
     "Th' eternal God, supremely good and wise,
Imparts not these prodigious gifts in vain;
What wonders are reserved to bless your reign?
Against your will, your arguments have shown
380   Such virtue's only given to guide a throne.
Not that your father's mildness I condemn;
But manly force becomes the diadem.
'Tis true, he grants the people all they crave,
And more perhaps than subjects ought to have:
385   For lavish grants suppose° a monarch tame,   *suggest*
And more his goodness than his wit proclaim.
But when should people strive their bonds to break,
If not when kings are negligent or weak?
Let him give on till he can give no more,
390   The thrifty Sanhedrin[6] shall keep him poor:
And every shekel° which he can receive,   *coin*
Shall cost a limb of his prerogative.[7]
To ply him with new plots shall be my care,
Or plunge him deep in some expensive war;
395   Which when his treasure can no more supply,
He must with the remains of kingship buy.
His faithful friends our jealousies and fears
Call Jebusites, and Pharaoh's pensioners:
Whom, when our fury from his aid has torn,
400   He shall be naked left to public scorn.
The next successor,[8] whom I fear and hate,
My arts have made obnoxious to the state;
Turned all his virtues to his overthrow,
And gained our elders[9] to pronounce a foe.
405   His right, for sums of necessary gold,
Shall first be pawned, and afterwards be sold:
Till time shall ever-wanting David draw,

---

4. Stingy; i.e., Monmouth's illegitimacy prevents him from acquiring all he desires.
5. The Miltonic inversion of syntax helps to link Achitophel's speech to the temptation of Eve by Satan in Book 9 of *Paradise Lost.*
6. The Jewish council; here the English Parliament.
7. Royal privileges (which Parliament sought to limit).
8. James, Duke of York.
9. Shaftesbury's supporters, who included members of both the gentry and the aristocracy.

To pass your doubtful title into law:
If not, the people have a right supreme
410   To make their kings, for kings are made for them.
All empire is no more than power in trust,
Which, when resumed, can be no longer just.
Succession, for the general good designed,
In its own wrong a nation cannot bind:
415   If altering that the people can relieve,
Better one suffer than a nation grieve.
The Jews well know their power: ere Saul they chose,
God was their King, and God they durst depose.[1]
Urge now your piety, your filial name,
420   A father's right, and fear of future fame;
The public good, that universal call
To which even Heav'n submitted, answers all.
Nor let his love enchant your generous mind;
'Tis Nature's trick to propagate her kind.
425   Our fond begetters, who would never die,
Love but themselves in their posterity.
Or let his kindness by th' effects be tried,
Or let him lay his vain pretense aside.
God said he loved your father; could he bring
430   A better proof than to anoint him King?
It surely showed he loved the shepherd well,
Who gave so fair a flock as Israel.
Would David have you thought his darling son?
What means he then to alienate° the crown?   *give away*
435   The name of godly he may blush to bear:
'Tis after God's own heart to cheat his heir.
He to his brother gives supreme command;
To you a legacy of barren land,[2]
Perhaps th' old harp on which he thrums his lays,[3]
440   Or some dull Hebrew ballad in your praise.
Then the next heir, a prince severe and wise,
Already looks on you with jealous eyes;
Sees through the thin disguises of your arts,
And marks your progress in the people's hearts.
445   Though now his mighty soul its grief contains,
He meditates revenge who least complains;
And like a lion, slumbering in the way,
Or sleep dissembling, while he waits his prey,
His fearless foes within his distance draws,
450   Constrains his roaring, and contracts his paws;
Till at the last, his time for fury found,
He shoots with sudden vengeance from the ground:
The prostrate vulgar passes o'er and spares,

1. The prophet Samuel warned the Israelites that in choosing a king they would displace their true king, God (1 Samuel 8).

2. In 1678 Charles had promoted James and in the following year banished Monmouth.
3. David was said to have composed the Psalms.

But with a lordly rage his hunters tears.
455 Your case no tame expedients will afford;
Resolve on death, or conquest by the sword,
Which for no less a stake than life you draw;
And self-defense is nature's eldest law.
Leave the warm people no considering time,
460 For then rebellion may be thought a crime.
Prevail° yourself of what occasion gives,   *avail*
But try your title while your father lives:
And that your arms may have a fair pretense,
Proclaim you take them in the King's defense,
465 Whose sacred life each minute would expose
To plots from seeming friends and secret foes.
And who can sound the depth of David's soul?
Perhaps his fear his kindness may control.
He fears his brother, though he loves his son,
470 For plighted vows too late to be undone.
If so, by force he wishes to be gained,
Like women's lechery, to seem constrained:
Doubt not, but when he most affects the frown,
Commit a pleasing rape upon the crown.
475 Secure his person to secure your cause;
They who possess the prince, possess the laws."
    He said, and this advice above the rest,
With Absalom's mild nature suited best;
Unblamed of° life (ambition set aside),   *blameless in*
480 Not stained with cruelty, nor puffed with pride;
How happy had he been, if destiny
Had higher placed his birth, or not so high!
His kingly virtues might have claimed a throne,
And blessed all other countries but his own:
485 But charming greatness, since so few refuse,
'Tis juster to lament him than accuse.
Strong were his hopes a rival to remove,
With blandishments to gain the public love;
To head the faction while their zeal was hot,
490 And popularly prosecute the Plot.
To farther this, Achitophel unites
The malcontents of all the Israelites;
Whose differing parties he could wisely join,
For several ends, to serve the same design:
495 The best, and of the princes some were such,
Who thought the power of monarchy too much:
Mistaken men, and patriots in their hearts;
Not wicked, but seduced by impious arts.
By these the springs of property were bent,
500 And wound so high they cracked the government.
The next for interest sought t' embroil the state,
To sell their duty at a dearer rate;

And make their Jewish markets of the throne,
Pretending public good, to serve their own.
505   Others thought kings an useless heavy load,
Who cost too much, and did too little good.
These were for laying honest David by,
On principles of pure good husbandry.°   *economy*
With them joined all th' haranguers of the throng,
510   That thought to get preferment by the tongue.
Who follow next a double danger bring,
Not only hating David, but the King;
The Solymaean rout,[4] well versed of old
In godly faction, and in treason bold;
515   Cowering and quaking at a conqueror's sword,
But lofty° to a lawful prince restored;   *arrogant*
Saw with disdain an ethnic[5] plot begun,
And scorned by Jebusites to be outdone.
Hot Levites[6] headed these; who, pulled before
520   From th' ark, which in the judges' days they bore,[7]
Resumed their cant, and with a zealous cry
Pursued their old beloved theocracy:[8]
Where Sanhedrin and priest enslaved the nation,
And justified their spoils by inspiration;[9]
525   For who so fit for reign as Aaron's race,[1]
If once dominion they could found in grace?
These led the pack; though not of surest scent,
Yet deepest-mouthed against the government.
A numerous host of dreaming saints succeed;
530   Of the true old enthusiastic[2] breed:
'Gainst form and order they their power employ,
Nothing to build and all things to destroy.
But far more numerous was the herd of such
Who think too little, and who talk too much.
535   These out of mere instinct, they knew not why,
Adored their fathers' God and property:
And, by the same blind benefit of fate,
The Devil and the Jebusite did hate:
Born to be saved, even in their own despite,°   *despite themselves*
540   Because they could not help believing right.
Such were the tools, but a whole Hydra[3] more
Remains, of sprouting heads too long to score.
Some of their chiefs were princes of the land:

---

4. Solymas was another name for Jerusalem, hence, "the London mob."
5. Here, Catholic.
6. Dissenting clergymen.
7. The 1662 Act of Uniformity deprived Presbyterian clergy of their livings which they had acquired during the commonwealth (the judges' days, when they bore the ark).
8. I.e., sought to restore the commonwealth.

9. Members of dissenting sects sometimes claimed to be inspired directly by God.
1. Priests (who, in Jewish law, had to be descendants of Moses's brother Aaron).
2. A pejorative term, applied to those who claimed special inspiration.
3. Many-headed monster, who would sprout new heads every time one was cut off.

In the first rank of these did Zimri[4] stand:
545   A man so various, that he seemed to be
Not one, but all mankind's epitome.
Stiff in opinions, always in the wrong;
Was everything by starts, and nothing long:
But, in the course of one revolving moon,
550   Was chemist, fiddler, statesman, and buffoon:
Then all for women, painting, rhyming, drinking;
Besides ten thousand freaks° that died in thinking.   *whims*
Blest madman, who could every hour employ,
With something new to wish, or to enjoy!
555   Railing° and praising were his usual themes;   *criticizing*
And both (to show his judgment) in extremes:
So over-violent, or over-civil,
That every man, with him, was god or devil.
In squand'ring wealth was his peculiar art:
560   Nothing went unrewarded but desert.°   *true worth*
Beggared by fools, whom still he found° too late: *found out*
He had his jest, and they had his estate.
He laughed himself from court, then sought relief
By forming parties, but could ne'er be chief:
565   For, spite of him, the weight of business fell
On Absalom and wise Achitophel:
Thus, wicked but in will, of means bereft,
He left not faction, but of that was left.
    Titles and names 'twere tedious to rehearse
570   Of lords below the dignity of verse.
Wits, warriors, commonwealthsmen, were the best:
Kind husbands and mere nobles all the rest.
And therefore, in the name of dullness, be
The well-hung Balaam[5] and cold Caleb free.
575   And canting Nadab[6] let oblivion damn,
Who made new porridge for the paschal lamb.[7]
Let friendship's holy band some names assure:
Some their own worth, and some let scorn secure.
Nor shall the rascal rabble here have place,
580   Whom kings no titles gave, and God no grace:
Not bull-faced Jonas,[8] who could statutes draw

4. An Old Testament conspirator and regicide (1 Kings 16.9–20); here, George Villiers, Second Duke of Buckingham, a prominent Whig. He had satirized the playwright Dryden in *The Rehearsal* (1671).
5. Balaam was a prophet who first resisted and then accepted God's will (Numbers 22–24); here, he probably represents Theophilus Hastings, Earl of Huntingdon, who initially supported Shaftesbury but was subsequently forgiven by Charles. *Well-hung:* Eloquent, or sexually impressive ("Lord Huntingdon," wrote one of the poem's early readers in a marginal inscription, "is said to have a swinging p——"). Caleb (a spy in Numbers 13) has been identified as either Lord Grey, whose wife was reputedly Monmouth's mistress, or Arthur Capel, an efficient administrator and ally of Shaftesbury.
6. The priest Nadab tries to institute improper rites of worship, and is slain by God (Leviticus 10); probably William, Lord Howard of Escrick, a dissenting preacher.
7. Howard was said to have celebrated communion (the commemoration of Christ's sacrifice as "paschal lamb") not with bread and wine but with ale and roasted apples—a concoction known as "lamb's wool." Dissenters such as Howard referred disparagingly to the Anglican Book of Common Prayer as "porridge."
8. Sir William Jones, attorney general and fierce prosecutor of alleged Popish plotters.

To mean rebellion, and make treason law.
But he, though bad, is followed by a worse,
The wretch who heaven's anointed dared to curse:
585   Shimei,[9] whose youth did early promise bring
Of zeal to God, and hatred to his King;
Did wisely from expensive sins refrain,
And never broke the Sabbath, but for gain:
Nor ever was he known an oath to vent,
590   Or curse, unless against the government.
Thus heaping wealth by the most ready way
Among the Jews, which was to cheat and pray;
The city, to reward his pious hate
Against his master, chose him magistrate:
595   His hand a vare° of justice did uphold;   staff
His neck was loaded with a chain of gold.
During his office, treason was no crime;
The sons of Belial[1] had a glorious time:
For Shimei, though not prodigal of pelf,[2]
600   Yet loved his wicked neighbor as himself: ⎫
When two or three were gathered to declaim[3] ⎬
Against the monarch of Jerusalem,   ⎭
Shimei was always in the midst of them:
And, if they cursed the King when he was by,
605   Would rather curse than break good company.
If any durst his factious friends accuse,
He packed a jury of dissenting Jews,
Whose fellow-feeling in the godly cause
Would free the suff'ring saint from human laws.
610   For laws are only made to punish those
Who serve the King, and to protect his foes.
If any leisure time he had from power
(Because 'tis sin to misemploy an hour),
His business was, by writing, to persuade
615   That kings were useless, and a clog to trade:
And that his noble style he might refine,
No Rechabite[4] more shunned the fumes of wine.
Chaste were his cellars, and his shrieval board[5]
The grossness of a city feast abhorred:
620   His cooks, with long disuse, their trade forgot;
Cool was his kitchen, though his brains were hot.
Such frugal virtue malice may accuse,
But sure 'twas necessary to the Jews:
For towns once burnt[6] such magistrates require

9. Shimei cursed David as he fled Absalom's rebellion. Here, he is Slingsby Bethel, one of London's sheriffs.
1. Rebellious, debauched men.
2. Free with money.
3. The description of Shimei echoes two of Christ's pronouncements: "Thou shalt love thy neighbor as thyself"

(Matthew 22.39); "When two or three are gathered together in my name, there am I in the midst of them" (Matthew 18.20).
4. Rechabites drank no wine.
5. Sheriff's hospitality.
6. A reference to the Fire of London (1666).

625 As dare not tempt God's providence by fire.
     With spiritual food he fed his servants well,
     But free from flesh that made the Jews rebel:
     And Moses's laws he held in more account,
     For forty days of fasting in the mount.[7]
630 To speak the rest, who better are forgot,
     Would tire a well-breathed witness of the Plot:
     Yet, Corah,[8] thou shalt from oblivion pass;
     Erect thyself, thou monumental brass,°   *shamelessness*
     High as the serpent of thy metal made,[9]
635 While nations stand secure beneath thy shade.
     What though his birth were base, yet comets rise
     From earthy vapors ere they shine in skies.
     Prodigious actions may as well be done
     By weaver's issue,[1] as by prince's son.
640 This arch-attestor for the public good
     By that one deed ennobles all his blood.
     Who ever asked the witnesses' high race,
     Whose oath with martyrdom did Stephen[2] grace?
     Ours was a Levite, and as times went then,
645 His tribe were God Almighty's gentlemen.
     Sunk were his eyes, his voice was harsh and loud,
     Sure signs he neither choleric° was, nor proud: *hot-tempered*
     His long chin proved his wit; his saintlike grace
     A church vermilion, and a Moses's face;[3]
650 His memory, miraculously great,
     Could plots, exceeding man's belief, repeat;
     Which therefore cannot be accounted lies,
     For human wit could never such devise.
     Some future truths are mingled in his book;
655 But where the witness failed, the prophet spoke:
     Some things like visionary flights appear;
     The spirit caught him up, the Lord knows where,
     And gave him his rabbinical degree
     Unknown to foreign university.[4]
660 His judgment yet his memory did excel;
     Which pieced his wondrous evidence so well,
     And suited to the temper of the times,
     Then groaning under Jebusitic crimes.
     Let Israel's foes suspect his heav'nly call,
665 And rashly judge his writ apocryphal;[5]

---

7. Shimei attempts to justify his frugality by citing the precedent of Moses, who fasted on Mount Sinai before receiving the Ten Commandments.
8. A rebellious Levite; here, Titus Oates, the ambitious informer who did more than anyone to arouse suspicions of a "Popish Plot."
9. Moses set up a brass serpent that saved the Jews from dying of snakebite (Numbers 21).

1. Oates's father was a weaver.
2. The first Christian martyr, sworn against and stoned by false witness (Acts 6–7).
3. After Moses received the tables of the law on Mount Sinai, his face shone with divine illumination; Oates's face, by contrast, is flushed with debauchery.
4. Oates pretended to hold a doctorate of divinity from the University of Salamanca.
5. Not part of the canon of biblical texts.

Our laws for such affronts have forfeits made:
He takes his life, who takes away his trade.
Were I myself in witness Corah's place,
The wretch who did me such a dire disgrace
670   Should whet my memory, though once forgot,
To make him an appendix of my plot.
His zeal to heav'n made him his prince despise,
And load his person with indignities:
But zeal peculiar privilege affords,
675   Indulging latitude to deeds and words;
And Corah might for Agag's murder[6] call,
In terms as coarse as Samuel used to Saul.
What others in his evidence did join
(The best that could be had for love or coin)
680   In Corah's own predicament will fall:
For *witness* is a common name to all.
　　Surrounded thus with friends of every sort,
Deluded Absalom forsakes the court:
Impatient of high hopes, urged with renown,
685   And fired with near possession of a crown:
Th' admiring crowd are dazzled with surprise,
And on his goodly person feed their eyes:
His joy concealed, he sets himself to show,
On each side bowing popularly low:
690   His looks, his gestures, and his words he frames,
And with familiar ease repeats their names.
Thus, formed by nature, furnished out with arts,
He glides unfelt into their secret hearts:
Then with a kind compassionating look,
695   And sighs bespeaking pity ere he spoke,
Few words he said, but easy those and fit:
More slow than Hybla° drops, and far more sweet.　　　　　　　　*honey*
　　"I mourn, my countrymen, your lost estate,
Though far unable to prevent your fate:
700   Behold a banished man, for your dear cause
Exposed a prey to arbitrary laws!
Yet O! that I alone could be undone,
Cut off from empire, and no more a son!
Now all your liberties a spoil are made,
705   Egypt and Tyrus° intercept your trade,　　　　　　　　　　*France and Holland*
And Jebusites your sacred rites invade. ⎦
My father, whom with reverence yet I name,
Charmed into ease, is careless of his fame:
And bribed with petty sums of foreign gold,
710   Is grown in Bathsheba's[7] embraces old:
Exalts his enemies, his friends destroys,

6. Oates denounced Lord Stafford, who was then executed, as Samuel denounced Agag, who was murdered by
Saul (1 Samuel 15).

7. Louise de Kéroualle, Duchess of Portsmouth, Charles's
French, Catholic mistress.

And all his pow'r against himself employs.
He gives, and let him give, my right away:
But why should he his own, and yours betray?
715 He only, he can make the nation bleed,
And he alone from my revenge is freed.
Take then my tears" (with that he wiped his eyes)
"'Tis all the aid my present power supplies:
No court informer can these arms accuse,
720 These arms may sons against their fathers use,
And 'tis my wish, the next successor's reign
May make no other Israelite complain."
        Youth, beauty, graceful action seldom fail:
But common interest always will prevail:
725 And pity never ceases to be shown
To him, who makes the people's wrongs his own.
The crowd (that still believe their kings oppress)
With lifted hands their young Messiah bless:
Who now begins his progress to ordain,[8]
730 With chariots, horsemen, and a numerous train:
From east to west his glories he displays:
And, like the sun, the promised land surveys.
Fame runs before him, as the morning star,
And shouts of joy salute him from afar:
735 Each house receives him as a guardian god,
And consecrates the place of his abode:
But hospitable treats did most commend
Wise Issachar,[9] his wealthy western friend.
This moving court, that caught the people's eyes,
740 And seemed but pomp, did other ends disguise:
Achitophel had formed it, with intent
To sound the depths, and fathom, where it went,
The people's hearts; distinguish friends from foes,
And try their strength before they came to blows:
745 Yet all was colored with a smooth pretense
Of specious love, and duty to their prince.
Religion, and redress of grievances,
Two names that always cheat and always please,
Are often urged, and good King David's life
750 Endangered by a brother and a wife.[1]
Thus, in a pageant show, a plot is made,
And peace itself is war in masquerade.
O foolish Israel! never warned by ill,
Still the same bait, and circumvented still!
755 Did ever men forsake their present ease,
In midst of health imagine a disease;
Take pains contingent mischiefs to foresee,

---

8. Monmouth traveled through the west of England in 1680, rallying popular support.
9. Thomas Thynne, a wealthy Whig.

1. Both James and Catherine were Catholic and were thought by some to be implicated in Popish plotting.

Make heirs for monarchs, and for God decree?
What shall we think! can people give away,
760   Both for themselves and sons, their native sway?
Then they are left defenseless to the sword
Of each unbounded, arbitrary lord:
And laws are vain, by which we right enjoy,
If kings unquestioned can those laws destroy.
765   Yet, if the crowd be judge of fit and just,
And kings are only officers in trust,
Then this resuming cov'nant was declared
When kings were made, or is forever barred:
If those who gave the scepter could not tie
770   By their own deed their own posterity,
How then could Adam bind his future race?
How could his forfeit on mankind take place?
Or how could heavenly justice damn us all,
Who ne'er consented to our father's fall?
775   Then kings are slaves to those whom they command,
And tenants to their people's pleasure stand.
Add, that the pow'r for property[2] allowed
Is mischievously seated in the crowd:
For who can be secure of private right,
780   If sovereign sway may be dissolved by might?
Nor is the people's judgment always true:
The most may err as grossly as the few,
And faultless kings run down by common cry
For vice, oppression, and for tyranny.
785   What standard is there in a fickle rout,
Which, flowing to the mark,° runs faster out?   *high-water mark*
Nor only crowds, but Sanhedrins may be
Infected with this public lunacy,
And share the madness of rebellious times,
790   To murder monarchs for imagined crimes.
If they may give and take whene'er they please,
Not kings alone (the Godhead's images),
But government itself at length must fall
To nature's state, where all have right to all.
795   Yet, grant our lords the people kings can make,
What prudent men a settled throne would shake?
For whatsoe'er their sufferings were before,
That change they covet makes them suffer more.
All other errors but disturb a state,
800   But innovation is the blow of fate.
If ancient fabrics nod, and threat to fall,
To patch the flaws, and buttress up the wall,
Thus far 'tis duty; but here fix the mark:
For all beyond it is to touch our ark.[3]

2. Political influence derived from ownership of land.   3. To touch the ark was to commit sacrilege.

805   To change foundations, cast the frame anew,
    Is work for rebels who base ends pursue,
    At once divine and human laws control,
    And mend the parts by ruin of the whole.
    The tampering world is subject to this curse,
810   To physic their disease into a worse.
       Now what relief can righteous David bring?
    How fatal 'tis to be too good a king!
    Friends he has few, so high the madness grows;
    Who dare be such, must be the people's foes:
815   Yet some there were, ev'n in the worst of days;
    Some let me name, and naming is to praise.
       In this short file Barzillai[4] first appears;
    Barzillai crowned with honor and with years:
    Long since, the rising rebels he withstood
820   In regions waste, beyond the Jordan's flood:[5]
    Unfortunately brave to buoy the state,
    But sinking underneath his master's fate:
    In exile with his godlike prince he mourned;
    For him he suffered, and with him returned.
825   The court he practiced, not the courtier's art:
    Large was his wealth, but larger was his heart:
    Which well the noblest objects knew to choose,
    The fighting warrior, and recording Muse.[6]
    His bed could once a fruitful issue boast:
830   Now more than half a father's name is lost:
    His eldest hope,[7] with every grace adorned,
    By me (so Heaven will have it) always mourned,
    And always honored, snatched in manhood's prime
    By unequal Fates, and Providence's crime:
835   Yet not before the goal of honor won,
    All parts fulfilled of subject and of son;
    Swift was the race, but short the time to run.
    Oh narrow circle, but of pow'r divine,
    Scanted in space, but perfect in thy line!
840   By sea, by land, thy matchless worth was known;
    Arms thy delight, and war was all thy own:
    Thy force, infused, the fainting Tyrians[8] propped:
    And haughty Pharaoh found his fortune stopped.
    O ancient honor, O unconquered hand,
845   Whom foes unpunished never could withstand!
    But Israel was unworthy of thy name;
    Short is the date of all immoderate fame.
    It looks as Heaven our ruin had designed,
    And durst not trust thy fortune and thy mind.

---

4. James Butler, Duke of Ormonde, loyal to Charles I and II.
5. I.e., in Ireland.
6. I.e., he gave money to support the Stuart cause and was also a patron to authors.
7. Ormonde's eldest son, who died in 1680.
8. The Dutch, whom Ormonde's son had aided against the French.

850 Now, free from earth, thy disencumbered soul
Mounts up, and leaves behind the clouds and starry pole:
From thence thy kindred legions mayst thou bring,
To aid the guardian angel of thy King.
Here stop, my Muse, here cease thy painful flight;
855 No pinions° can pursue immortal height: *wings*
Tell good Barzillai thou canst sing no more,
And tell thy soul she should have fled before;
Or fled she with his life, and left this verse
To hang on her departed patron's hearse?
860 Now take thy steepy flight from heaven, and see
If thou canst find on earth another *he;*
Another *he* would be too hard to find,
See then whom thou canst see not far behind:
Zadock[9] the priest, whom, shunning power and place,
865 His lowly mind advanced to David's grace:
With him the Sagan[1] of Jerusalem,
Of hospitable soul and noble stem;
Him of the western dome,[2] whose weighty sense
Flows in fit words and heavenly eloquence.
870 The prophets' sons[3] by such example led,
To learning and to loyalty were bred:
For colleges on bounteous kings depend,
And never rebel was to arts a friend.
To these succeed the pillars of the laws,
875 Who best could plead and best can judge a cause.
Next them a train of loyal peers ascend:
Sharp-judging Adriel,[4] the Muses' friend,
Himself a Muse—in Sanhedrin's debate
True to his prince, but not a slave of state:
880 Whom David's love with honors did adorn,
That from his disobedient son were torn.[5]
Jotham[6] of piercing wit and pregnant thought,
Indued° by nature, and by learning taught   *endowed*
To move assemblies, who but only tried
885 The worse awhile, then chose the better side;
Nor chose alone, but turned the balance too;
So much the weight of one brave man can do.
Hushai,[7] the friend of David in distress,
In public storms of manly steadfastness;
890 By foreign treaties he informed his youth,

9. William Sancroft, Archbishop of Canterbury.
1. Henry Compton, Bishop of London.
2. John Dolben, Dean of Westminster ("the western dome").
3. Students of the Westminster School.
4. John Sheffield, Earl of Mulgrave, poet and a patron of Dryden.
5. In 1679 Mulgrave received two offices that had previously belonged to Monmouth.
6. George Savile, Marquis of Halifax, formerly a critic but now a supporter of Charles's policies, was instrumental in defeating the exclusion bill.
7. Laurence Hyde, Earl of Rochester, negotiated several European treaties and became the first Lord of the Treasury.

And joined experience to his native truth.
His frugal care supplied the wanting throne,
Frugal for that, but bounteous of his own:
'Tis easy conduct when exchequers[8] flow,
895 But hard the task to manage well the low:
For sovereign power is too depressed or high,
When kings are forced to sell, or crowds to buy.
Indulge one labor more, my weary Muse,
For Amiel,[9] who can Amiel's praise refuse?
900 Of ancient race by birth, but nobler yet
In his own worth, and without title great:
The Sanhedrin long time as chief he ruled,
Their reason guided and their passion cooled;
So dexterous was he in the crown's defense,
905 So formed to speak a loyal nation's sense,
That, as their band was Israel's tribes in small,
So fit was he to represent them all.
Now rasher charioteers the seat ascend,
Whose loose careers his steady skill commend:
910 They like th' unequal ruler of the day,[1]
Misguide the seasons and mistake the way;
While he, withdrawn, at their mad labor smiles,
And safe enjoys the sabbath of his toils.
      These were the chief, a small but faithful band ⎤
915 Of worthies, in the breach who dared to stand, ⎬
And tempt th' united fury of the land.   ⎦
With grief they viewed such powerful engines bent,
To batter down the lawful government:
A numerous faction with pretended frights,
920 In Sanhedrins to plume° the regal rights: *pluck away*
The true successor from the court removed:[2]
The Plot by hireling witnesses improved.
These ills they saw, and as their duty bound,
They showed the King the danger of the wound:
925 That no concessions from the throne would please,
But lenitives fomented[3] the disease:
That Absalom, ambitious of the crown,
Was made the lure to draw the people down:
That false Achitophel's pernicious hate
930 Had turned the Plot to ruin Church and State:
The council violent, the rabble worse:
That Shimei taught Jerusalem to curse.

---

8. Treasurers/treasuries.
9. Edward Seymour, Speaker of the Commons (1673–1678) and Treasurer of the Navy (1673–1681); opponent of exclusion.
1. Phaëthon, who drove (with disastrous results) the chariot of the sun that belonged to his father, Apollo.

2. In 1679, at the height of the furor over the Popish Plot, Charles II had ordered his brother to withdraw to the Continent, where James remained for six months.
3. I.e., soothing measures/medicines only encouraged the disease.

With all these loads of injuries oppressed,
And long revolving, in his careful breast,
935 Th' event of things, at last, his patience tired,
Thus from his royal throne by Heav'n inspired,
The godlike David spoke: with awful fear
His train their Maker in their master hear.
"Thus long have I, by native mercy swayed,
940 My wrongs dissembled, my revenge delayed:
So willing to forgive th' offending age,
So much the father did the king assuage.
But now so far my clemency they slight,
Th' offenders question my forgiving right.
945 That one was made for many, they contend:
But 'tis to rule, for that's a monarch's end.
They call my tenderness of blood my fear:
Though manly tempers can the longest bear.
Yet, since they will divert my native course,
950 'Tis time to show I am not good by force.
Those heaped affronts that haughty subjects bring,
Are burdens for a camel, not a king:
Kings are the public pillars of the state,
Born to sustain and prop the nation's weight:
955 If my young Samson[4] will pretend a call
To shake the column, let him share the fall:
But O that yet he would repent and live!
How easy 'tis for parents to forgive!
With how few tears a pardon might be won
960 From Nature, pleading for a darling son!
Poor pitied youth, by my paternal care
Raised up to all the height his frame could bear:
Had God ordained his fate for empire born,
He would have given his soul another turn:
965 Gulled with a patriot's name, whose modern sense
Is one that would by law supplant his prince:
The people's brave,° the politicians' tool;   *bully*
Never was patriot yet, but was a fool.
Whence comes it that religion and the laws
970 Should more be Absalom's than David's cause?
His old instructor,[5] ere he lost his place,
Was never thought indued with so much grace.
Good heavens, how faction can a patriot paint!
My rebel ever proves my people's saint:
975 Would they impose an heir upon the throne?
Let Sanhedrins be taught to give their own.
A king's at least a part of government,

4. Monmouth, who threatens, Samson-like, to bring   5. Achitophel/Shaftesbury.
down the nation.

And mine as requisite as their consent:
Without my leave a future king to choose,
980 Infers a right the present to depose:
True, they petition me t' approve their choice,
But Esau's hands suit ill with Jacob's voice.[6]
My pious subjects for my safety pray,
Which to secure they take my power away.
985 From plots and treasons Heaven preserve my years,
But save me most from my petitioners.
Unsatiate as the barren womb or grave;
God cannot grant so much as they can crave.
What then is left but with a jealous eye
990 To guard the small remains of royalty?
The law shall still direct my peaceful sway,
And the same law teach rebels to obey:
Votes shall no more established pow'r control,
Such votes as make a part exceed the whole:
995 No groundless clamors shall my friends remove,
Nor crowds have power to punish ere they prove:
For gods, and godlike kings, their care express,
Still to defend their servants in distress.
O that my power to saving were confined: ⎤
1000 Why am I forced, like Heaven, against my mind, ⎬
To make examples of another kind? ⎦
Must I at length the sword of justice draw?
O cursed effects of necessary law!
How ill my fear they by my mercy scan;[7]
1005 Beware the fury of a patient man.
Law they require, let law then show her face;
They could not be content to look on Grace,
Her hinder parts, but with a daring eye
To tempt the terror of her front, and die.
1010 By their own arts, 'tis righteously decreed,
Those dire artificers of death shall bleed.
Against themselves their witnesses will swear,
Till viper-like their mother Plot they tear:
And suck for nutriment that bloody gore
1015 Which was their principle of life before.
Their Belial with their Belzebub[8] will fight;
Thus on my foes, my foes shall do me right:
Nor doubt th' event: for factious crowds engage,
In their first onset, all their brutal rage;
1020 Then let 'em take an unresisted course,

6. In Genesis 27, Esau is a hunter and a "hairy man"; his younger brother Jacob steals his birthright by impersonating him before their blind father Isaac, covering his own smooth hands with rough goatskin. David/Charles here accuses his opposition of Esau-like violence and Jacob-like deception.
7. How wrong ("ill") they are to see ("scan") fear in my mercy.
8. Both devils.

Retire and traverse, and delude their force:
But when they stand all breathless, urge the fight,
And rise upon 'em with redoubled might:
For lawful pow'r is still superior found,
1025   When long driven back, at length it stands the ground."
    He said. Th' Almighty, nodding, gave consent;
And peals of thunder shook the firmament.
Henceforth a series of new time began,
The mighty years in long procession ran:
1030   Once more the godlike David was restored,
And willing nations knew their lawful lord.

1681   1681

⚙ For a companion text, *His Majesty's Declaration to All His Loving Subjects*, go to *The Longman Anthology of British Literature* Web site at www.myliteraturekit.com.

MAC FLECKNOE   In *Mac Flecknoe*, Dryden put on display a literary culture dangerously debased. The poem's title ("Son of Flecknoe") announces a royal succession in the kingdom of bad writing. A literary "father," the priest and minor poet Richard Flecknoe (c. 1605–c. 1677), anoints as his true heir Thomas Shadwell (1640–1692), a playwright whom Dryden loathed as a tiresome controversialist and an ardent (worse, successful) rival for public favor and aristocratic patronage. Dryden wages his attack in an idiom at once elevated and scandalous, in language whose allegiance alternates (even within a single line) between epic poetry and the privy. Like much libelous and bawdy verse, Dryden's demolitionary masterpiece circulated in manuscript for several years; it was eventually printed in a pirated edition (1682) by a publisher seeking to capitalize on the recent success of *Absalom and Achitophel*. Like that poem, *Mac Flecknoe* plays upon the question of monarchic succession, but stages it in such a way as to implicate bad politics in bad taste. Dryden maps a City of London where foul writing chokes the streets, and dim-witted citizens get—and applaud—the poet-monarchs they deserve.

Mac Flecknoe

All human things are subject to decay,
And, when Fate summons, monarchs must obey.
This Flecknoe found, who, like Augustus, young
Was called to empire,[1] and had governed long:
5   In prose and verse was owned, without dispute,
Through all the realms of Nonsense, absolute.
This aged prince, now flourishing in peace,
And blest with issue of a large increase,
Worn out with business, did at length debate
10   To settle the succession of the state:
And, pondering which of all his sons was fit
To reign, and wage immortal war with wit,
Cried, "'Tis resolved; for Nature pleads that he
Should only rule, who most resembles me:
15   Sh——alone my perfect image bears,
Mature in dullness from his tender years.

1. Augustus became the first Roman emperor at the age of 32.

Sh——alone, of all my sons, is he
Who stands confirmed in full stupidity.
The rest to some faint meaning make pretense,
20   But Sh——never deviates into sense.
Some beams of wit on other souls may fall,
Strike through and make a lucid interval,
But Sh——'s genuine night admits no ray,
His rising fogs prevail upon the day.
25   Besides, his goodly fabric° fills the eye,   *large body*
And seems designed for thoughtless majesty:
Thoughtless as monarch oaks that shade the plain,
And, spread in solemn state, supinely reign.
Heywood and Shirley were but types of thee,[2]
30   Thou last great prophet of tautology:
Even I, a dunce of more renown than they,
Was sent before but to prepare thy way;
And coarsely clad in Norwich drugget[3] came
To teach the nations in thy greater name.[4]
35   My warbling lute, the lute I whilom° strung   *once*
When to King John of Portugal I sung,[5]
Was but the prelude to that glorious day
When thou on silver Thames didst cut thy way,
With well-timed oars before the royal barge,
40   Swelled with the pride of thy celestial charge;
And big with hymn, commander of an host,
The like was ne'er in Epsom blankets tossed.[6]
Methinks I see the new Arion[7] sail,
The lute still trembling underneath thy nail.
45   At thy well-sharpened thumb from shore to shore
The treble squeaks for fear, the basses roar:
Echoes from Pissing Alley[8] 'Sh——' call,
And 'Sh——' they resound from A——Hall.[9]
About thy boat the little fishes throng,
50   As at the morning toast° that floats along.   *sewage*
Sometimes as prince of thy harmonious band
Thou wield'st thy papers in thy threshing hand.
St. André's feet[1] ne'er kept more equal time,
Not ev'n the feet of thy own *Psyche's* rhyme,
55   Though they in number as in sense excel;
So just, so like tautology they fell,

2. Thomas Heywood and James Shirley, popular and prolific playwrights from the first half of the 17th century.
As "types," they foreshadow or prepare for Shadwell, just
as Old Testament figures such as Moses or Isaac were interpreted in Christian theology as forerunners of Jesus.
3. Woolen cloth; Shadwell came from Norwich.
4. Here, Flecknoe is John the Baptist ("coarsely clad" in
camel's hair) to Shadwell's Jesus.
5. Flecknoe claimed that, during his travels in Europe, he
had been summoned to perform before the king of Portugal.
6. A glance at two of Shadwell's plays: *Epsom Wells* and

The Virtuoso, in which Sir Samuel Hearty is tossed in a
blanket; tossing in blankets was also a means of inducing
childbirth.
7. Greek musician-poet rescued from drowning by music-
loving dolphins.
8. West of Temple Bar, it led from the Strand down to
the Thames.
9. Unidentified.
1. St. André, a French dancer who choreographed the
opera *Psyche* (1675), for which Shadwell wrote the li-
bretto.

That, pale with envy, Singleton foreswore
The lute and sword which he in triumph bore,
And vowed he ne'er would act Villerius[2] more."
60 Here stopped the good old sire, and wept for joy
In silent raptures of the hopeful boy.
All arguments, but most his plays, persuade,
That for anointed dullness he was made.
    Close to the walls which fair Augusta bind[3]
65 (The fair Augusta much to fears inclined[4]),
An ancient fabric,[5] raised t' inform the sight,
There stood of yore, and Barbican it hight:[6]
A watchtower once, but now, so Fate ordains,
Of all the pile an empty name remains.
70 From its old ruins brothel-houses rise,
Scenes of lewd loves and of polluted joys;
Where their vast courts the mother-strumpets keep
And, undisturbed by watch,° in silence sleep.[7]   *police*
Near these a nursery[8] erects its head,
75 Where queens[9] are formed and future heroes bred;
Where unfledged actors learn to laugh and cry,
Where infant punks° their tender voices try,   *prostitutes*
And little Maximins[1] the gods defy.
Great Fletcher never treads in buskins here,
80 Nor greater Jonson dares in socks appear.[2]
But gentle Simkin[3] just reception finds
Amid this monument of vanished minds:
Pure clinches° the suburbian Muse[4] affords,   *puns*
And Panton[5] waging harmless war with words.
85 Here Flecknoe, as a place to fame well known,
Ambitiously designed his Sh———'s throne.
For ancient Dekker[6] prophesied long since,
That in this pile should reign a mighty prince,
Born for a scourge of wit, and flail of sense:
90 To whom true dullness should some *Psyches* owe,
But Worlds of *Misers* from his pen should flow;

---

2. John Singleton, one of the king's musicians; Villerius, a character in William Davenant's opera, *The Siege of Rhodes*.
3. The old wall of the City of London (Augusta).
4. Fears aroused by the Popish Plot.
5. Structure.
6. Was named; the Barbican, a medieval gatehouse, gave its name to a disreputable district of gaming and prostitution; adjoining it was Grub Street, the center of hack journalism.
7. Parodying Abraham Cowley, *Davideis* (1656), "Where their vast court the mother-waters keep, / And undisturbed by moons in silence sleep."
8. A training theater for the two main playhouses.
9. Dryden puns on queen (stage-monarch)/quean (prosti-

tute). During the Restoration, actresses were often thought to moonlight as sexual companions.
1. Maximin is the fulminating protagonist of Dryden's *Tyrannic Love*.
2. John Fletcher and Ben Jonson, major playwrights of the previous generations. The buskin is the symbol of tragedy (Fletcher's forte) and the sock of comedy (Jonson's). Shadwell promoted himself as Jonson's successor in the tradition of "humors" comedy.
3. A clownish character in a series of popular farces.
4. I.e., the muse presiding over the disreputable area outside the City walls.
5. Another farce character.
6. Thomas Dekker (1570?–1632), prolific dramatist whose plays focused on London life.

Humorists and *Hypocrites*[7] it should produce,
Whole Raymond families, and tribes of Bruce.
   Now Empress Fame had published the renown
95   Of Sh————'s coronation through the town.
Roused by report of Fame, the nations meet,
From near Bunhill, and distant Watling Street.[8]
No Persian carpets spread th' imperial way,
But scattered limbs of mangled poets lay:
100   From dusty shops neglected authors come,
Martyrs of pies, and relics of the bum.[9]
Much Heywood, Shirley, Ogilby[1] there lay,
But loads of Sh————almost choked the way.
Bilked stationers for yeomen stood prepared,
105   And H————[2] was captain of the guard.
The hoary prince in majesty appeared,
High on a throne of his own labors reared.
At his right hand our young Ascanius[3] sate,
Rome's other hope, and pillar of the state.
110   His brows thick fogs, instead of glories, grace,
And lambent° dullness played around his face.   *glowing*
As Hannibal did to the altars come,
Sworn by his sire a mortal foe to Rome,[4]
So Sh————swore, nor should his vow be vain,
115   That he till death true dullness would maintain;
And in his father's right, and realm's defense,
Ne'er to have peace with wit, nor truce with sense.
The king himself the sacred unction[5] made,
As king by office, and as priest by trade:
120   In his sinister° hand, instead of ball,   *left*
He placed a mighty mug of potent ale;
Love's Kingdom[6] to his right he did convey,
At once his scepter and his rule of sway,[7]
Whose righteous lore the prince had practiced young,
125   And from whose loins[8] recorded Psyche sprung.
His temples last with poppies[9] were o'erspread,
That nodding seemed to consecrate his head:
Just at that point of time, if Fame not lie,

7. Shadwell was the author of *The Miser* (1672), *The Humorists* (1671), and *The Hypocrite* (1669). Raymond and Bruce appear in *The Humorists* and *The Virtuoso*, respectively.
8. Fame draws her crowd both from cemeteries (like Bunhill Fields) and from mercantile districts (like Watling Street); thus, these devotees of Shadwell include both the dead and the living.
9. Unsold books might be recycled as pie wrappers or as toilet paper; the bones of martyrs were often venerated as relics.
1. John Ogilby, printer, cartographer, and translator (like Dryden) of Virgil.
2. Henry Herringman, a prominent bookseller-publisher;

he had published both Shadwell and Dryden.
3. The son of Aeneas, marked for greatness by a heaven-sent flame about his head.
4. According to Livy, Hannibal's father made the young boy swear himself Rome's enemy.
5. The oil with which the king was anointed during the coronation ceremony.
6. A play by Flecknoe.
7. Dryden parodies the rituals and props of the coronation ceremony.
8. Pronounced "lines" (a fact that permits Dryden a significant pun).
9. Symbolizing sleep.

On his left hand twelve reverend owls[1] did fly.
130   So Romulus,[2] 'tis sung, by Tiber's brook,
Presage of sway from twice six vultures took.
Th' admiring throng loud acclamations make,
And omens of his future empire take.
The sire then shook the honors[3] of his head,
135   And from his brows damps of oblivion shed ⎫
Full on the filial dullness: long he stood,   ⎪
Repelling from his breast the raging God;   ⎬
At length burst out in this prophetic mood: ⎭
    "Heavens bless my son, from Ireland let him reign
140   To far Barbados on the western main;[4]
Of his dominion may no end be known,
And greater than his father's be his throne.
Beyond *Love's Kingdom* let him stretch his pen!"
He paused, and all the people cried, "Amen."
145   "Then thus," continued he, "my son, advance
Still in new impudence, new ignorance.
Success let others teach, learn thou from me
Pangs without birth, and fruitless industry.
Let *Virtuosos* in five years be writ,
150   Yet not one thought accuse thy toil of wit.
Let gentle George[5] in triumph tread the stage,
Make Dorimant betray, and Loveit rage;
Let Cully, Cockwood, Fopling charm the pit,
And in their folly show the writer's wit.
155   Yet still thy fools shall stand in thy defense,
And justify° their author's want of sense.   prove
Let 'em be all by thy own model made
Of dullness, and desire no foreign aid:
That they to future ages may be known,
160   Not copies drawn, but issue[6] of thy own.
Nay let thy men of wit too be the same,
All full of thee, and differing but in name;
But let no alien S–dl–y[7] interpose
To lard with wit thy hungry *Epsom* prose.
165   And when false flowers of rhetoric thou would'st cull,
Trust nature, do not labor to be dull;
But write thy best, and top; and in each line,
Sir Formal's[8] oratory will be thine.
Sir Formal, though unsought, attends thy quill,
170   And does thy northern dedications[9] fill.

---

1. Symbols of ignorance and darkness (because nocturnal).
2. Cofounder of Rome (through which the Tiber runs).
3. Ornaments, and by extension, hair—a Virgilian expression.
4. His kingdom will be the Atlantic Ocean.
5. Sir George Etherege, comic playwright; characters from his plays follow.
6. A pun: both progeny and printing.

7. Sir Charles Sedley, courtier, poet, and intimate of Dryden's circle; he wrote a prologue for *Epsom Wells*.
8. Sir Formal Trifle, a character in Shadwell's *The Virtuoso*, described by Shadwell as "the Orator, a florid coxcomb."
9. Both Flecknoe and Shadwell dedicated several of their works to the Duke and Duchess of Newcastle (a town in the north of England).

Nor let false friends seduce thy mind to fame,
By arrogating Jonson's hostile name.
Let father Flecknoe fire thy mind with praise,
And uncle Ogilby thy envy raise.
175   Thou art my blood, where Jonson has no part;
What share have we in nature or in art?
Where did his wit on learning fix a brand,
And rail at arts he did not understand?
Where made he love in Prince Nicander's[1] vein,
180   Or swept the dust in Psyche's humble strain?
Where sold he bargains,[2] 'whip-stitch, kiss my arse,'
Promised a play and dwindled to a farce?
When did his Muse from Fletcher scenes purloin,
As thou whole Eth'rege dost transfuse to thine?
185   But so transfused as oil on waters flow,
His always floats above, thine sinks below.
This is thy province, this thy wondrous way,
New humors to invent for each new play:[3]
This is that boasted bias of thy mind,
190   By which one way, to dullness, 'tis inclined;
Which makes thy writings lean on one side still,
And in all changes that way bends thy will.
Nor let thy mountain belly make pretense
Of likeness; thine's a tympany[4] of sense.
195   A tun of man in thy large bulk is writ,
But sure thou'rt but a kilderkin[5] of wit.
Like mine thy gentle numbers feebly creep;
Thy tragic Muse gives smiles, thy comic sleep.
With whate'er gall thou sett'st thyself to write,
200   Thy inoffensive satires never bite.
In thy felonious heart, though venom lies,
It does but touch thy Irish[6] pen, and dies.
Thy genius calls thee not to purchase fame
In keen iambics,[7] but mild anagram:
205   Leave writing plays, and choose for thy command
Some peaceful province in acrostic land.
There thou may'st wings display and altars[8] raise,
And torture one poor word ten thousand ways.
Or if thou would'st thy diff'rent talents suit,

---

1. A character in *Psyche*.
2. "To sell bargains" is to respond to an innocent question with a coarse phrase, as in this line. Dryden sharpens the insult by quoting the slangy nonsense phrase "whip-stitch" from Shadwell's own play, *The Virtuoso*.
3. I.e., by these contemptible means, you purport to outdo Ben Jonson.
4. A swelling of the abdomen, caused by air or gas.
5. A tun was a large cask of wine; a kilderkin a quarter of a tun.

6. Neither Flecknoe nor Shadwell was actually Irish; Ireland was regarded in England as an abode of savages.
7. Sharp satire (written in iambic meter by classical satirists).
8. Dryden here mocks the practice of writing emblematic verse, poems in the shape of their subjects (e.g., George Herbert's *Easter Wings* and *The Altar*). He lumps this practice together with other forms of empty ingenuity.

210   Set thy own songs, and sing them to thy lute."
       He said, but his last words were scarcely heard, ⎤
       For Bruce and Longvil had a trap prepared,[9] ⎬
       And down they sent the yet declaiming bard.   ⎦
       Sinking he left his drugget robe behind,
215   Borne upward by a subterranean wind.
       The mantle fell to the young prophet's part,[1]
       With double portion of his father's art.

c. 1676   1682

To the Memory of Mr. Oldham[1]

       Farewell, too little and too lately known,
       Whom I began to think and call my own;
       For sure our souls were near allied; and thine
       Cast in the same poetic mold with mine.[2]
5   One common note on either lyre did strike,
       And knaves and fools[3] we both abhorred alike:
       To the same goal did both our studies drive,
       The last set out the soonest did arrive.
       Thus Nisus[4] fell upon the slippery place,
10   While his young friend performed and won the race.
       O early ripe! to thy abundant store
       What could advancing age have added more?
       It might (what Nature never gives the young)
       Have taught the numbers[5] of thy native tongue.
15   But satire needs not those, and wit will shine
       Through the harsh cadence of a rugged line:
       A noble error, and but seldom made,
       When poets are by too much force betrayed.
       Thy generous fruits, though gathered ere their prime, ⎤
20   Still showed a quickness;[6] and maturing time   ⎬
       But mellows what we write to the dull sweets of rhyme. ⎦
       Once more, hail and farewell;[7] farewell thou young,
       But ah too short, Marcellus of our tongue;
       Thy brows with ivy, and with laurels bound;
25   But fate and gloomy night encompass thee around.[8]

                                                              1684

---

9. In Shadwell's The Virtuoso, Bruce and Longvil open a trap door beneath the long-winded Sir Formal Trifle.

1. A burlesque of 2 Kings 2.8–14, in which the prophet Elijah is borne up to heaven, while his mantle falls to his successor, Elisha.

1. John Oldham (1653–1683) achieved fame at age 28 with his Satires upon the Jesuits (1681). Three years later, an aging Dryden mourned him in a tribute that prefaced the Remains of Mr. John Oldham in Verse and Prose. Within his poem's brief compass, Dryden echoes many poets—Virgil, Catullus, Milton, and Oldham himself— and invokes several modes: satire, celebration, elegy.

2. An echo of Oldham's poem David's Lamentation: "Oh, dearer than my soul! if I can call it mine, / For sure we had the same, 'twas very thine."

3. Satire's traditional targets.

4. In Book 5 of Virgil's Aeneid, Nisus slips near the finish line during a footrace, falling in a manner that permits "his young friend" Euryalus to win.

5. Metrical patterns and harmonies.

6. Liveliness; also, sharpness of taste.

7. Dryden echoes a phrase in Catullus's elegy for his brother: "Ave atque vale" (101.10).

8. In Book 6 of Virgil's Aeneid, the hero visits the underworld, where his dead father shows him a vision of Rome's future. This vision concludes with a sight of Augustus Caesar's adopted son and heir Marcellus, who after a glorious military career died at the age of 20. The last line of Dryden's elegy reworks Virgil's conclusion:"But hov'ring mists around his brows are spread, / And night, with sable shades, involves his head" (Aeneid 6.866; Dryden's translation).

Alexander's Feast

or, The Power of Music
An Ode in Honor of St. Cecilia's Day[1]

1

'Twas at the royal feast, for Persia won
      By Philip's warlike son:[2]
    Aloft in awful state
    The godlike hero sate
5   On his imperial throne:
His valiant peers were placed around;
Their brows with roses and with myrtles bound
    (So should desert in arms be crowned).
The lovely Thais[3] by his side
10 Sat like a blooming Eastern bride
In flow'r of youth and beauty's pride.
      Happy, happy, happy pair!
      None but the brave
      None but the brave
15   None but the brave deserves the fair.

       CHORUS

Happy, happy, happy pair!
None but the brave
None but the brave
None but the brave deserves the fair.

2

20 Timotheus,[4] placed on high
    Amid the tuneful choir,
    With flying fingers touched the lyre:
The trembling notes ascend the sky,
        And heav'nly joys inspire.
25 The song began from Jove,
Who left his blissful seats above
(Such is the power of mighty love).
A dragon's fiery form belied[5] the god:
Sublime on radiant spires° he rode,   *coils*
30   When he to fair Olympia pressed:
    And while he sought her snowy breast:
Then, round her slender waist he curled,

---

1. The early martyr Cecilia is the patron saint of music and musicians. Her feast day (22 November) was annually celebrated in London by a concert featuring a new piece with words by an eminent poet and music by a distinguished composer. The musical society in charge of the occasion commissioned two odes from Dryden, ten years apart: *A Song for St. Cecilia's Day* (1687) and *Alexander's Feast*. Dryden undertook the commission with some reluctance, but after the piece's successful premiere, he noted with pleasure that *Alexander's Feast* "is esteemed the best of all my poetry, by all the town. I thought so myself when I writ it, but being old, I mistrusted my own judgment."

2. Alexander the Great, son of Philip of Macedon; Dryden depicts the feast that Alexander held after defeating the Persians and their emperor Darius in 331 B.C.E.
3. Alexander's Greek concubine.
4. Celebrated poet and musician.
5. Timotheus tells the alternative story of Alexander's parentage, that he was begotten by Jove—disguised ("belied") as a serpent—upon Philip's wife Olympias.

And stamped an image of himself, a sov'reign of the world.
The listening crowd admire the lofty sound:
35   "A present deity," they shout around:
"A present deity," the vaulted roofs rebound.
     With ravished ears
     The monarch hears,
     Assumes the god,[6]
40   Affects to nod,
And seems to shake the spheres.

       CHORUS

*   With ravished ears*
*   The monarch hears,*
*   Assumes the god,*
45 *   Affects to nod,*
And seems to shake the spheres.

       3

The praise of Bacchus then the sweet musician sung,
  Of Bacchus ever fair and ever young:
     The jolly god in triumph comes;
50   Sound the trumpets; beat the drums:
     Flushed with a purple grace
     He shows his honest face,
Now give the hautboys° breath; he comes, he comes.   *oboes*
     Bacchus, ever fair and young,
55   Drinking joys did first ordain:
Bacchus' blessings are a treasure;
Drinking is the soldier's pleasure;
     Rich the treasure,
     Sweet the pleasure;
60   Sweet is pleasure after pain.

       CHORUS

Bacchus' blessings are a treasure;
Drinking is the soldier's pleasure;
*   Rich the treasure,*
*   Sweet the pleasure;*
65 *   Sweet is pleasure after pain.*

       4

Soothed with the sound, the king grew vain;
  Fought all his battles o'er again;
And thrice he routed all his foes, and thrice he slew the slain.
     The master saw the madness rise,
70   His glowing cheeks, his ardent eyes;
     And, while he heav'n and earth defied,
     Changed his hand, and checked his pride.[7]

---

6. Behaves like Jove, whose nod is said by Virgil to cause earthquakes.

7. Timotheus ("the master") changes the music in order to restrain Alexander's swelling pride.

He chose a mournful Muse
Soft pity to infuse:
75   He sung Darius great and good,
By too severe a fate
Fallen, fallen, fallen, fallen,
Fallen from his high estate
And welt'ring in his blood:
80 Deserted at his utmost need,
By those his former bounty fed:
On the bare earth exposed he lies,
With not a friend to close his eyes.

With downcast looks the joyless victor sat,
85   Revolving° in his altered soul   *pondering*
The various turns of chance below;
And, now and then, a sigh he stole,
And tears began to flow.

CHORUS

Revolving in his altered soul
90   *The various turns of chance below;*
And, now and then, a sigh he stole;
And tears began to flow.

5

The mighty master smiled to see
That love was in the next degree:
95 'Twas but a kindred sound to move;[8]
For pity melts the mind to love.
Softly sweet, in Lydian measures,[9]
Soon he soothed his soul to pleasures.
"War," he sung, "is toil and trouble,
100 Honor but an empty bubble.
Never ending, still° beginning,   *always*
Fighting still, and still destroying,
If the world be worth thy winning,
Think, O think, it worth enjoying.
105 Lovely Thais sits beside thee,
Take the good the gods provide thee."

The many[1] rend the skies with loud applause;
So love was crowned, but music won the cause.
The prince, unable to conceal his pain,
110 Gazed on the fair
Who caused his care,
And sighed and looked, sighed and looked,

---

8. All it took to "move" Alexander to the "next degree" of feeling was to shift ("move") musical registers.

9. In ancient Greek music, the mode associated with pathos.
1. The retinue or company.

Sighed and looked, and sighed again:
At length, with love and wine at once oppressed,
115   The vanquished victor sunk upon her breast.

CHORUS

The prince, unable to conceal his pain,
Gazed on the fair
Who caused his care,
And sighed and looked, sighed and looked,
120   *Sighed and looked, and sighed again:*
At length, with love and wine at once oppressed,
The vanquished victor sunk upon her breast.

6

Now strike the golden lyre again:
A louder yet, and yet a louder strain.
125   Break his bands of sleep asunder,
And rouse him, like a rattling peal of thunder.
                    Hark, hark, the horrid sound
                    Has raised up his head,
                    As awaked from the dead,
130   And, amazed, he stares around.
"Revenge, revenge," Timotheus cries,
                "See the Furies[2] arise!
See the snakes that they rear,
How they hiss in their hair,
135   And the sparkles that flash from their eyes!
                Behold a ghastly band,
                Each a torch in his hand!
Those are Grecian ghosts, that in battle were slain,
                                And unburied remain
140   Inglorious on the plain.
                Give the vengeance due
                To the valiant crew.
Behold how they toss their torches on high,
                How they point to the Persian abodes,
145   And glitt'ring temples of their hostile gods!"
The princes applaud, with a furious joy;
And the king seized a flambeau,[3] with zeal to destroy;
                Thais led the way,
                To light him to his prey,
150   And, like another Helen, fired another Troy.[4]

CHORUS

And the king seized a flambeau, with zeal to destroy;
Thais led the way,

---

2. Spirits of punishment.
3. Torch.

4. Stolen away to Troy by Paris, Helen was blamed for
setting in motion the chain of events that led to the
burning of the city by the Greeks.

To light him to his prey,
And, like another Helen, fired another Troy.

7

155　　　　　Thus, long ago,
　　　Ere heaving bellows learned to blow,
　　　　While organs yet were mute,
　　Timotheus, to his breathing flute,
　　　　　And sounding lyre,
160　Could swell the soul to rage, or kindle soft desire.
　　　At last divine Cecilia came,
　　　Inventress of the vocal frame;[5]
　The sweet enthusiast,[6] from her sacred store,
　　　Enlarged the former narrow bounds,
165　　　And added length to solemn sounds,
With nature's mother wit, and arts unknown before.
　　　Let old Timotheus yield the prize,
　　　　Or both divide the crown;
　　　He raised a mortal to the skies;
170　　　She drew an angel down.[7]

GRAND CHORUS

At last divine Cecilia came,
Inventress of the vocal frame;
The sweet enthusiast, from her sacred store,
　　Enlarged the former narrow bounds,
175　　*And added length to solemn sounds,*
With nature's mother wit, and arts unknown before.
　Let old Timotheus yield the prize,
　　　Or both divide the crown;
　He raised a mortal to the skies;
　　She drew an angel down.

1697　　　　　　　　　　　　　　　　　　　　　1697

from Fables Ancient and Modern[1]
from Preface

'Tis with a poet as with a man who designs to build, and is very exact, as he supposes, in casting up the cost beforehand. But generally speaking, he is mistaken in his account, and reckons short of the expense he first intended. He alters his mind

5. Cecilia was believed to have invented the organ.
6. One possessed by spirits or by a god.
7. Dryden alludes to his earlier ode to music, *A Song for St. Cecilia's Day* (1687): as Cecilia plays the organ, "An angel heard and straight appear'd, / Mistaking earth for heaven."
1. Following the triumph of his *Virgil* (1697), Dryden turned again to translation. He had frequently collaborated with others in the assembly of anthologies; now he undertook to make one of his own, containing poets both "Ancient"—Ovid and Homer—and "Modern"—Boccaccio, Chaucer, and Dryden himself. In the *Fables*, Dryden's

pleasure and assurance in his own technical mastery are everywhere on display: in the expansiveness of his translations; in the bravado with which he plunders his own works as a treasury of echo and allusion; in the arrangement of his materials, so that fable talks to fable in an almost calculated sequence; and in his preface, where he lays out the history of his book's development with a conspicuous delight in the improvisatory logic of his creative process, and then proudly argues for the greatness of Chaucer, whose career and craft he celebrates in such a way as to suggest parallels with his own.

as the work proceeds, and will have this or that convenience more, of which he had not thought when he began. So has it happened to me; I have built a house where I intended but a lodge, yet with better success than a certain nobleman,[2] who beginning with a dog kennel, never lived to finish the palace he had contrived.

From translating the first of Homer's *Iliads* (which I intended as an essay to[3] the whole work) I proceeded to the translation of the twelfth book of Ovid's *Metamorphoses*,[4] because it contains, among other things, the causes, the beginning, and ending, of the Trojan War. Here I ought in reason to have stopped; but the speeches of Ajax and Ulysses lying next in my way, I could not balk 'em. When I had compassed them, I was so taken with the former part of the fifteenth book[5] (which is the masterpiece of the whole *Metamorphoses*) that I enjoined myself the pleasing task of rendering it into English. And now I found, by the number of my verses, that they began to swell into a little volume; which gave me an occasion of looking backward on some beauties of my author, in his former books: there occurred to me the hunting of the boar, Cinyras and Myrrha, the good-natured story of Baucis and Philemon, with the rest, which I hope I have translated closely enough, and given them the same turn of verse, which they had in the original; and this, I may say without vanity, is not the talent of every poet. He who has arrived the nearest to it, is the ingenious and learned Sandys,[6] the best versifier of the former age, if I may properly call it by that name, which was the former part of this concluding century. For Spenser and Fairfax[7] both flourished in the reign of Queen Elizabeth: great masters in our language, and who saw much farther into the beauties of our numbers than those who immediately followed them. Milton was the poetical son of Spenser, and Mr. Waller[8] of Fairfax; for we have our lineal descents and clans, as well as other families. Spenser more than once insinuates that the soul of Chaucer was transfused into his body, and that he was begotten by him two hundred years after his decease. Milton has acknowledged to me that Spenser was his original, and many besides myself have heard our famous Waller own that he derived the harmony of his numbers from the *Godfrey of Bulloign*, which was turned into English by Mr. Fairfax.

But to return: having done with Ovid for this time, it came into my mind that our old English poet Chaucer in many things resembled him, and that with no disadvantage on the side of the modern author, as I shall endeavor to prove when I compare them. And as I am and always have been studious to promote the honor of my native country, so I soon resolved to put their merits to the trial, by turning some of the *Canterbury Tales* into our language, as it is now refined, for by this means, both the poets being set in the same light, and dressed in the same English habit, story to be compared with story, a certain judgment may be made betwixt them by the reader, without obtruding my opinion on him: or if I seem partial to my countryman, and predecessor in the laurel, the friends of antiquity are not few. And besides many of the learned, Ovid has almost all the beaux,[9] and the whole fair sex,

---

2. Probably the Duke of Buckingham (whom Dryden had ridiculed as Zimri in *Absalom and Achitophel* line 544), and Buckingham's house at Cliveden.
3. First attempt at, and "taste of" (Johnson's *Dictionary*).
4. Ovid (43 B.C.E.–17 C.E.), Roman poet who spent the last decade of his life in exile. His *Metamorphoses* is a collection of ancient legends; in many, the characters undergo bodily transformations, from one form of life into another.
5. In which Ovid puts into verse the philosophy of the Greek mystic Pythagoras, who propounded a doctrine of reincarnation, arguing that "all things are but altered, nothing dies."
6. George Sandys (1578–1644), poet and translator, whose *Ovid's Metamorphosis Englished* was issued in 1626 and often republished.
7. Edward Fairfax (c. 1580–1635), poet and translator.
8. Edmund Waller (1606–1687), poet, early practitioner of the heroic couplet; Dryden praised him as "the father" of English versification.
9. Fashionable gentlemen.

his declared patrons. Perhaps I have assumed somewhat more to myself than they allow me, because I have adventured to sum up the evidence. But the readers are the jury; and their privilege remains entire to decide according to the merits of the cause or, if they please, to bring it to another hearing before some other court. In the meantime, to follow the thread of my discourse (as thoughts, according to Mr. Hobbes,[1] have always some connection) so from Chaucer I was led to think on Boccace,[2] who was not only his contemporary, but also pursued the same studies; wrote novels in prose, and many works in verse; particularly is said to have invented the octave rhyme, or stanza of eight lines, which ever since has been maintained by the practice of all Italian writers who are, or at least assume the title of, heroic poets. He and Chaucer, among other things, had this in common, that they refined their mother tongues; but with this difference, that Dante had begun to file their language,[3] at least in verse, before the time of Boccace, who likewise received no little help from his master Petrarch.[4] But the reformation of their prose was wholly owing to Boccace himself, who is yet the standard of purity in the Italian tongue, though many of his phrases are become obsolete, as in process of time it must needs happen. Chaucer (as you have formerly been told by our learned Mr. Rymer) first adorned and amplified our barren tongue from the Provençal, which was then the most polished of all the modern languages.[5] But this subject has been copiously treated by that great critic, who deserves no little commendation from us his countrymen. For these reasons of time, and resemblance of genius, in Chaucer and Boccace, I resolved to join them in my present work, to which I have added some original papers of my own, which whether they are equal or inferior to my other poems, an author is the most improper judge; and therefore I leave them wholly to the mercy of the reader. I will hope the best, that they will not be condemned; but if they should, I have the excuse of an old gentleman, who mounting on horseback before some ladies, when I was present, got up somewhat heavily, but desired of the fair spectators that they would count fourscore and eight before they judged him. By the mercy of God, I am already come within twenty years of his number, a cripple in my limbs, but what decays are in my mind, the reader must determine. I think myself as vigorous as ever in the faculties of my soul, excepting only my memory, which is not impaired to any great degree; and if I lose not more of it, I have no great reason to complain. What judgment I had increases rather than diminishes; and thoughts, such as they are, come crowding in so fast upon me that my only difficulty is to choose or to reject; to run them into verse, or to give them the other harmony of prose. I have so long studied and practiced both that they are grown into a habit, and become familiar to me. In short, though I may lawfully plead some part of the old gentleman's excuse, yet I will reserve it till I think I have greater need, and ask no grains of allowance for the faults of this my present work but those which are given of course to human frailty. I will not trouble my reader with the shortness of time in which I writ it, or the several intervals of sickness. They who think too well of their own performances are apt to boast in their prefaces how little time their

1. In his *Leviathan* (1651), Thomas Hobbes includes a chapter on "The Consequence or Train of Imaginations" (1.3).
2. Giovanni Boccaccio (1313–1375), Italian writer, authored *The Decameron* (a collection of 100 tales) and was one of Chaucer's chief influences.
3. Dante Alighieri (1265–1321), author of *The Divine Comedy*, was the first great vernacular poet in Italy; *to file*: to smooth (into graceful verse).

4. Italian poet (1304–1374), whose cycle of love sonnets exerted enormous influence over English writers.
5. In his *Short View of Tragedy* (1693), Thomas Rymer writes that Chaucer seized "all Provençal [Old French], French, or Latin that came in his way, gives them a new garb . . . and mingles them amongst our English."

works have cost them, and what other business of more importance interfered. But the reader will be as apt to ask the question, why they allowed not a longer time to make their works more perfect? and why they had so despicable an opinion of their judges, as to thrust their indigested stuff upon them, as if they deserved no better?

With this account of my present undertaking, I conclude the first part of this discourse. In the second part, as at a second sitting, though I alter not the draught, I must touch the same features over again, and change the dead-colorings[6] of the whole.

* * *

It remains that I say somewhat of Chaucer in particular.

In the first place, as he is the father of English poetry, so I hold him in the same degree of veneration as the Grecians held Homer, or the Romans Virgil. He is a perpetual fountain of good sense; learned in all sciences; and therefore speaks properly on all subjects. As he knew what to say, so he knows also when to leave off, a continence which is practiced by few writers, and scarcely by any of the Ancients, excepting Virgil and Horace. One of our late great poets[7] is sunk in his reputation, because he could never forgive any conceit which came in his way, but swept like a dragnet, great and small. There was plenty enough, but the dishes were ill sorted; whole pyramids of sweet-meats for boys and women, but little of solid meat for men. All this proceeded not from any want of knowledge, but of judgment; neither did he want that in discerning the beauties and faults of other poets, but only indulged himself in the luxury of writing; and perhaps knew it was a fault, but hoped the reader would not find it. For this reason, though he must always be thought a great poet, he is no longer esteemed a good writer; and for ten impressions,[8] which his works have had in so many successive years, yet at present a hundred books are scarcely purchased once a twelvemonth. For, as my last Lord Rochester said, though somewhat profanely, "Not being of God, he could not stand."

Chaucer followed Nature everywhere, but was never so bold to go beyond her. And there is a great difference of being *poeta* and *nimis poeta*,[9] if we may believe Catullus, as much as betwixt a modest behavior and affectation. The verse of Chaucer, I confess, is not harmonious to us; but 'tis like the eloquence of one whom Tacitus commends: it was *auribus istius temporis accommodata*.[1] They who lived with him, and some time after him, thought it musical, and it continues so even in our judgment, if compared with the numbers of Lydgate and Gower, his contemporaries. There is the rude sweetness of a Scotch tune in it, which is natural and pleasing, though not perfect. 'Tis true, I cannot go so far as he who published the last edition of him,[2] for he would make us believe the fault is in our ears, and that there were really ten syllables in a verse where we find but nine. But this opinion is not worth confuting; 'tis so gross and obvious an error that common sense (which is a rule in everything but matters of faith and revelation) must convince the reader that equality of numbers, in every verse which we call heroic,[3] was either not known or not always practiced in Chaucer's age. It were an easy matter to produce some thousands of his verses which are lame for want of half a foot, and sometimes a whole one, and

---

6. The prepatory layer of paint applied to a canvas.
7. Abraham Cowley (1618–1667), whom Dryden admired and imitated.
8. Printings.
9. "A poet" and "too much a poet"; the Latin poet Martial, and not his predecessor Catullus, made this observation.

1. "Suited to the ears of those times": Cornelius Tacitus, Roman historian.
2. Thomas Speght, who argued (correctly) that Chaucer's versification was skillful and smooth but misrepresented by transcribers and misunderstood by readers.
3. I.e., consistent iambic pentameter.

which no pronunciation can make otherwise. We can only say that he lived in the infancy of our poetry, and that nothing is brought to perfection at the first. We must be children before we grow men. There was an Ennius, and in process of time a Lucilius and a Lucretius, before Virgil and Horace; even after Chaucer there was a Spenser, a Harrington, a Fairfax, before Waller and Denham were in being.[4] And our numbers were in their nonage[5] till these last appeared. I need say little of his parentage, life, and fortunes. They are to be found at large in all the editions of his works. He was employed abroad, and favored by Edward the Third, Richard the Second, and Henry the Fourth, and was poet, as I suppose, to all three of them. In Richard's time, I doubt, he was a little dipped in the rebellion of the Commons, and being brother-in-law to John of Gaunt, it was no wonder if he followed the fortunes of that family, and was well with Henry the Fourth when he had deposed his predecessor.[6] Neither is it to be admired[7] that Henry, who was a wise as well as a valiant prince, who claimed by succession, and was sensible that his title was not sound, but was rightfully in Mortimer, who had married the heir of York—it was not to be admired, I say, if that great politician should be pleased to have the greatest wit of those times in his interests, and to be the trumpet of his praises. Augustus had given him the example, by the advice of Maecenas,[8] who recommended Virgil and Horace to him; whose praises helped to make him popular while he was alive, and after his death have made him precious to posterity. As for the religion of our poet, he seems to have some little bias toward the opinions of Wyclif,[9] after John of Gaunt his patron; somewhat of which appears in the *Tale of Piers Plowman*.[1] Yet I cannot blame him for inveighing so sharply against the vices of the clergy in his age. Their pride, their ambition, their pomp, their avarice, their worldly interest deserved the lashes which he gave them, both in that, and in most of his *Canterbury Tales*. Neither has his contemporary Boccace spared them. Yet both those poets lived in much esteem, with good and holy men in orders, for the scandal which is given by particular priests reflects not on the sacred function. Chaucer's Monk, his Canon, and his Friar took not[2] from the character of his Good Parson. A satirical poet is the check of the laymen on bad priests. We are only to take care that we involve not the innocent with the guilty in the same condemnation. The good cannot be too much honored, nor the bad too coarsely used, for the corruption of the best becomes the worst. When a clergyman is whipped, his gown is first taken off, by which the dignity of his order is secured. If he be wrongfully accused, he has his action of slander, and 'tis at the poet's peril if he transgress the law. But they will tell us that all kind of satire, though never so well deserved by particular priests, yet brings the whole order into contempt. Is then the peerage of England any thing dishonored, when a peer suffers for his treason? If he be libeled, or any way defamed, he has his *scandalum magnatum* [legal recourse] to punish the offender. They who use this kind of argument seem to be conscious to themselves of somewhat which has deserved the poet's lash, and are less concerned for their public capacity than for their private. At least, there is pride at the bottom of their reasoning. If the faults of men in orders are only to be judged among themselves, they are all in some sort parties. For, since they say the honor of

4. Dryden traces a "descent and lineage" of influence first in Latin and then in English poetry.
5. Early youth.
6. Henry Bolingbroke (son to John of Gaunt) deposed his cousin Richard II in 1399; Chaucer survived political upheaval and received patronage from both kings.
7. Wondered at.

8. Roman patron of the poets Virgil, Horace, and Propertius.
9. John Wyclif (c. 1330–1384), theologian and religious reformer.
1. This tale had been mistakenly attributed to Chaucer; there is no evidence that he was a follower of Wyclif.
2. I.e., did not detract.

their order is concerned in every member of it, how can we be sure that they will be impartial judges? How far I may be allowed to speak my opinion in this case I know not, but I am sure a dispute of this nature caused mischief in abundance betwixt a King of England and an Archbishop of Canterbury; one standing up for the laws of his land, and the other for the honor (as he called it) of God's Church; which ended in the murder of the prelate, and in the whipping of his Majesty from post to pillar for his penance.[3] The learned and ingenious Dr. Drake[4] has saved me the labor of inquiring into the esteem and reverence which the priests have had of old; and I would rather extend than diminish any part of it. Yet I must needs say that when a priest provokes me without any occasion given him, I have no reason, unless it be the charity of a Christian, to forgive him. *Prior laesit*[5] is justification sufficient in the civil law. If I answer him in his own language, self-defense, I am sure, must be allowed me, and if I carry it farther, even to a sharp recrimination, somewhat may be indulged to human frailty. Yet my resentment has not wrought so far, but that I have followed Chaucer in his character of a holy man, and have enlarged on that subject with some pleasure, reserving to myself the right, if I shall think fit hereafter, to describe another sort of priests, such as are more easily to be found than the Good Parson; such as have given the last blow to Christianity in this age, by a practice so contrary to their doctrine. But this will keep cold till another time.

In the meanwhile, I take up Chaucer where I left him. He must have been a man of a most wonderful comprehensive nature, because, as it has been truly observed of him, he has taken into the compass of his *Canterbury Tales* the various manners and humors (as we now call them) of the whole English nation in his age. Not a single character has escaped him. All his pilgrims are severally distinguished from each other; and not only in their inclinations, but in their very physiognomies and persons. Baptista Porta[6] could not have described their natures better than by the marks which the poet gives them. The matter and manner of their tales, and of their telling, are so suited to their different educations, humors, and callings, that each of them would be improper in any other mouth. Even the grave and serious characters are distinguished by their several sorts of gravity: their discourses are such as belong to their age, their calling, and their breeding; such as are becoming of them, and of them only. Some of his persons are vicious, and some virtuous; some are unlearned, or (as Chaucer calls them) *lewd*, and some are learned. Even the ribaldry of the low characters is different: the Reeve, the Miller, and the Cook, are several men, and distinguished from each other, as much as the mincing Lady Prioress and the broad-speaking gap-toothed Wife of Bath. But enough of this: there is such a variety of game springing up before me that I am distracted in my choice, and know not which to follow. 'Tis sufficient to say according to the proverb, that here is God's plenty. We have our forefathers and great grand-dames all before us, as they were in Chaucer's days; their general characters are still remaining in mankind, and even in England, though they are called by other names than those of monks, and friars, and canons, and lady abbesses, and nuns. For mankind is ever the same, and nothing lost out of nature, though everything is altered. May I have leave to do myself the justice (since my enemies will do me none, and are

---

3. Thomas à Becket, Archbishop of Canterbury, was murdered in 1170 on the orders of his king, Henry II, after a long dispute over the powers and rights of the church. (The pilgrims in *The Canterbury Tales* are traveling to Becket's shrine.)
4. James Drake (1667–1707), physician, dramatist, and

ally of Dryden in literary controversies.
5. He injured first (i.e., "he started it").
6. Giambattista della Porta (c. 1538–1615), a physician whose book *De humana physiognomia* catalogued the effects of the emotional life on the look of the face.

so far from granting me to be a good poet that they will not allow me so much as to be a Christian, or a moral man) may I have leave, I say, to inform my reader, that I have confined my choice to such tales of Chaucer as savor nothing of immodesty.[7] If I had desired more to please than to instruct, the Reeve, the Miller, the Shipman, the Merchant, the Summoner, and above all, the Wife of Bath, in the Prologue to her Tale, would have procured me as many friends and readers as there are beaux and ladies of pleasure in the town. But I will no more offend against good manners. I am sensible as I ought to be of the scandal I have given by my loose writings;[8] and make what reparation I am able, by this public acknowledgment. If anything of this nature, or of profaneness, be crept into these poems, I am so far from defending it, that I disown it. *Totum hoc indictum volo.*[9] Chaucer makes another manner of apology for his broad speaking, and Boccace makes the like; but I will follow neither of them. Our countryman, in the end of his characters, before the *Canterbury Tales*, thus excuses the ribaldry, which is very gross, in many of his novels.

> But first, I pray you, of your courtesy,
> That ye ne arrete it nought my villany,
> Though that I plainly speak in this mattere
> To tellen you her words, and eke her chere:
> 5 Ne though I speak her words properly,
> For this ye knowen as well as I,
> Who shall tellen a tale after a man
> He mote rehearse as nye as ever he can:
> Everich word of it been in his charge,
> 10 *All speke he never so rudely, ne large.*
> Or else he mote tellen his tale untrue,
> Or feine things, or find words new:
> He may not spare, altho he were his brother,
> He mote as well say o word as another.
> 15 Christ spake himself full broad in holy writ,
> And well I wote no villany is it.
> Eke Plato saith, who so can him rede,
> The words mote been cousin to the dede.[1]

Yet if a man should have inquired of Boccace or of Chaucer, what need they had of introducing such characters, where obscene words were proper in their mouths, but very undecent to be heard, I know not what answer they could have made. For that reason, such tales shall be left untold by me. You have here a specimen of Chaucer's language, which is so obsolete that his sense is scarce to be understood; and you have likewise more than one example of his unequal numbers, which were mentioned before. Yet many of his verses consist of ten syllables, and the words not much behind our present English, as for example, these two lines, in the description of the carpenter's young wife:

> Wincing she was, as is a jolly colt,
> Long as a mast, and upright as a bolt.[2]

7. The *Fables* includes Dryden's translations of *The Knight's Tale*, *The Nun's Priest's Tale* (*The Cock and the Fox*), *The Wife of Bath's Tale*, and the portrait of the Parson from the *General Prologue* (*The Character of a Good Parson; Imitated from Chaucer and Inlarg'd*).

8. Throughout his career, Dryden had found it necessary to defend his plays against charges of immorality.
9. I wish all this unsaid.
1. *The General Prologue*, lines 727–744.
2. *The Miller's Tale*, lines 155–156.

I have almost done with Chaucer, when I have answered some objections relating to my present work. I find some people are offended that I have turned these tales into modern English, because they think them unworthy of my pains, and look on Chaucer as a dry, old-fashioned wit, not worth receiving. I have often heard the late Earl of Leicester[3] say that Mr. Cowley himself was of that opinion, who having read him over at my Lord's request, declared he had no taste of him. I dare not advance my opinion against the judgment of so great an author. But I think it fair, however, to leave the decision to the public. Mr. Cowley was too modest to set up for a dictator, and being shocked perhaps with his old style, never examined into the depth of his good sense. Chaucer, I confess, is a rough diamond, and must first be polished ere he shines. I deny not likewise, that living in our early days of poetry, he writes not always of a piece; but sometimes mingles trivial things with those of greater moment. Sometimes also, though not often, he runs riot, like Ovid, and knows not when he has said enough. But there are more great wits, beside Chaucer, whose fault is their excess of conceits, and those ill sorted. An author is not to write all he can, but only all he ought. Having observed this redundancy in Chaucer (as it is an easy matter for a man of ordinary parts to find a fault in one of greater) I have not tied myself to a literal translation, but have often omitted what I judged unnecessary, or not of dignity enough to appear in the company of better thoughts. I have presumed farther in some places, and added somewhat of my own where I thought my author was deficient, and had not given his thoughts their true luster, for want of words in the beginning of our language. And to this I was the more emboldened, because (if I may be permitted to say it of myself) I found I had a soul congenial to his, and that I had been conversant in the same studies. Another poet, in another age, may take the same liberty with my writings, if at least they live long enough to deserve correction. It was also necessary sometimes to restore the sense of Chaucer, which was lost or mangled in the errors of the press. Let this example suffice at present; in the story of Palamon and Arcite,[4] where the Temple of Diana is described, you find these verses in all the editions of our author:

> There saw I Danè turned unto a tree,
> I mean not the goddess Diane,
> But Venus daughter, which that hight Danè.

Which after a little consideration I knew was to be reformed into this sense, that Daphne the daughter of Peneus was turned into a tree. I durst not make thus bold with Ovid, lest some future Milbourne[5] should arise, and say I varied from my author because I understood him not.

But there are other judges who think I ought not to have translated Chaucer into English, out of a quite contrary notion. They suppose there is a certain veneration due to his old language, and that it is little less than profanation and sacrilege to alter it. They are farther of opinion that somewhat of his good sense will suffer in this transfusion, and much of the beauty of his thoughts will infallibly be lost, which appear with more grace in their old habit. Of this opinion was that excellent person whom I mentioned, the late Earl of Leicester, who valued Chaucer as much as

3. Philip Sidney (1619–1698), patron of Dryden, to whom the poet had dedicated his tragedy *Don Sebastian* (1690).

4. *The Knight's Tale*.
5. Luke Milbourne (1649–1720), a clergyman and translator who had attacked Dryden's *Virgil*.

Mr. Cowley despised him. My Lord dissuaded me from this attempt (for I was thinking of it some years before his death) and his authority prevailed so far with me as to defer my undertaking while he lived, in deference to him. Yet my reason was not convinced with what he urged against it. If the first end of a writer be to be understood, then as his language grows obsolete, his thoughts must grow obscure: *multa renascentur quae nunc cecidere; cadentque quae nunc sunt in honore vocabula, si volet usus, quem penes arbitrium est & jus & norma loquendi.*[6] When an ancient word for its sound and significancy deserves to be revived, I have that reasonable veneration for antiquity to restore it. All beyond this is superstition. Words are not like landmarks, so sacred as never to be removed. Customs are changed, and even statutes are silently repealed when the reason ceases for which they were enacted. As for the other part of the argument, that his thoughts will lose of their original beauty by the innovation of words: in the first place, not only their beauty, but their being is lost, where they are no longer understood, which is the present case. I grant that something must be lost in all transfusion, that is, in all translations; but the sense will remain, which would otherwise be lost, or at least be maimed, when it is scarce intelligible, and that but to a few. How few are there who can read Chaucer so as to understand him perfectly? And if imperfectly, then with less profit, and no pleasure. 'Tis not for the use of some old Saxon friends[7] that I have taken these pains with him. Let them neglect my version, because they have no need of it. I made it for their sakes who understand sense and poetry as well as they, when that poetry and sense is put into words which they understand. I will go farther, and dare to add, that what beauties I lose in some places, I give to others which had them not originally. But in this I may be partial to myself; let the reader judge, and I submit to his decision. Yet I think I have just occasion to complain of them who, because they understand Chaucer, would deprive the greater part of their countrymen of the same advantage, and hoard him up, as misers do their grandam gold,[8] only to look on it themselves, and hinder others from making use of it. In sum, I seriously protest that no man ever had, or can have, a greater veneration for Chaucer than myself. I have translated some part of his works, only that I might perpetuate his memory, or at least refresh it, amongst my countrymen. If I have altered him anywhere for the better, I must at the same time acknowledge that I could have done nothing without him. *Facile est inventis addere*[9] is no great commendation, and I am not so vain to think I have deserved a greater. I will conclude what I have to say of him singly, with this one remark: a lady of my acquaintance, who keeps a kind of correspondence with some authors of the fair sex in France, has been informed by them, that Mademoiselle de Scudery,[1] who is as old as Sibyl,[2] and inspired like her by the same god of poetry, is at this time translating Chaucer into modern French. From which I gather, that he has been formerly translated into the old Provençal (for how she should come to understand old English, I know not). But the matter of fact being true, it makes me think that there is something in it like fatality; that after certain periods of time, the fame and memory of great wits should be renewed, as Chaucer is both in France and England.

---

6. Many terms that have fallen out of use shall be born again, and those shall fall which that are now in use, if usage so will it, in whose hands lies the judgment, the right, and the rule of speech (Horace, *Ars Poetica* 70–72).
7. Friends who were scholars of Anglo-Saxon literature.
8. Long-stored-up wealth.

9. It is easy to add to what has already been discovered.
1. Madeleine de Scudéry (1607–1701), author of chivalric romances.
2. The Sybil of Cumae was a prophetess who served Apollo, god of poetry; he granted her wish to live a thousand years.

If this be wholly chance, 'tis extraordinary; and I dare not call it more, for fear of being taxed with superstition. * * *

The Secular Masque[1]
[*Enter Janus.*[2]]

JANUS: Chronos,[3] Chronos, mend thy pace,
        A hundred times the rolling sun.
        Around the radiant belt[4] has run
        In his revolving race.
5   Behold, behold, the goal in sight,
        Spread thy fans,[5] and wing thy flight.
          [*Enter Chronos, with a scythe in his hand, and a great globe on his back, which he sets down at his entrance.*]
CHRONOS: Weary, weary of my weight,
        Let me, let me drop my freight,
          And leave the world behind.
10   I could not bear
           Another year
        The load of humankind.
          [*Enter Momus*[6] *laughing.*]
MOMUS: Ha! ha! ha! ha! ha! ha! well hast thou done,
        To lay down thy pack,
15   And lighten thy back,
        The world was a fool, e'er since it begun,
        And since neither Janus, nor Chronos, nor I,
         Can hinder the crimes,
         Or mend the bad times,
20   'Tis better to laugh than to cry.
          [*Chorus of all three.*]
        'Tis better to laugh than to cry.
JANUS: Since Momus comes to laugh below,
        Old Time, begin the show,
        That he may see, in every scene,
25   What changes in this age have been.
CHRONOS: Then, goddess of the silver bow, begin.
        [*Horns, or hunting music, within. Enter Diana.*[7]]

---

1. "Within this month," Dryden wrote a friend in April 1700, "there will be played for my profit, an old play . . . called *The Pilgrim*, . . . to which I have added a new masque." Dryden called this new portion *The Secular Masque*, because it marked the turn of the century (Latin *saeculum*: age, period, century). Through its nostalgic form, he looked back to the start of the 17th century, and to the courts of Elizabeth, James, and Charles I, where just such masques, dominated by pagan gods mirroring and musing on present events, exerted a hypnotic appeal. In the *Masque*'s short span, Dryden sought both to compass the century—its pursuits and pleasures, its wars and loves—and to dispatch it, in a tone compounded of affection and scorn. The *Masque* proved valedictory in one

other way as well. On 1 May, a few days after the piece's first performance, Dryden died.
2. The Roman god of openings (gates, doors) and beginnings, possessing two faces pointed in opposite directions (past, future). January is named for him.
3. Time, traditionally depicted as described in the ensuing stage direction.
4. The zodiac.
5. Wings.
6. Greek god (the name means "blame") of ridicule, mockery, satire.
7. Roman goddess of chastity and of hunting, here reminiscent of Elizabeth I, the Virgin Queen, and of James I, enthusiastic hunter.

DIANA: With horns and with hounds, I waken the day,
              And hie to the woodland walks away;
              I tuck up my robe, and am buskined soon,
30   And tie to my forehead a waxing moon,
              I course the fleet stag, unkennel the fox,
              And chase the wild goats o'er summits of rocks,
              With shouting and hooting we pierce through the sky,
              And Echo turns hunter, and doubles the cry.
                       [*Chorus of all.*]
35   With shouting and hooting we pierce through the sky,
              And Echo turns hunter, and doubles the cry.
JANUS: Then our age was in its prime:
CHRONOS: Free from rage,
DIANA: And free from crime.
MOMUS: A very merry, dancing, drinking,
40   Laughing, quaffing, and unthinking time.
                    [*Chorus of all.*]
              Then our age was in its prime,
              Free from rage, and free from crime;
              A very merry, dancing, drinking,
              Laughing, quaffing, and unthinking time.
             [*Dance of Diana's attendants. Enter Mars.*[8]]
MARS: Inspire the vocal brass,[9] inspire;
              The world is past its infant age:
                Arms and honor,
                Arms and honor,
              Set the martial mind on fire,
50   And kindle manly rage.
              Mars has looked the sky[1] to red;
              And peace, the lazy good, is fled.
              Plenty, peace, and pleasure fly;
                The sprightly green,
55   In woodland walks, no more is seen;
              The sprightly green has drunk the Tyrian dye.[2]
                   [*Chorus of all.*]
              Plenty, peace, etc.
MARS: Sound the trumpet, beat the drum;
              Through all the world around,
60   Sound a reveille, sound, sound,
              The warrior god is come.
                    [*Chorus of all.*]
                Sound the trumpet, etc.
MOMUS: Thy sword within the scabbard keep,

8. Roman god of war, here incarnating the midcentury
civil wars.
9. Sound the speaking trumpet, the call to arms.
1. I.e., has by his stare changed the color of the sky.

2. An ancient purple hue: the color of the soldiers' garments (here displacing the green of the hunters') and of
the blood they shed.

And let mankind agree;
65   Better the world were fast asleep,
            Than kept awake by thee.
        The fools are only thinner,
            With all our cost and care;
        But neither side a winner,
70   For things are as they were.
                        [*Chorus of all.*]
                    The fools are only, etc.
                        [*Enter Venus*[3]]
VENUS: Calms appear, when storms are past;
        Love will have his hour at last:
        Nature is my kindly care;
75   Mars destroys, and I repair;
        Take me, take me, while you may,
        Venus comes not every day.
                        [*Chorus of all.*]
                    Take her, take her, etc.
CHRONOS: The world was then so light,
80   I scarcely felt the weight;
        Joy ruled the day, and love the night.
        But since the queen of pleasure left the ground,
            I faint, I lag,
            And feebly drag
85   The ponderous orb around.
MOMUS: All, all of a piece throughout;
        Thy chase had a beast in view;
                    [*Pointing to Diana.*]
        Thy wars brought nothing about;
                        [*To Mars.*]
        Thy lovers were all untrue.
                        [*To Venus.*]
JANUS: 'Tis well an old age is out,
CHRONOS: And time to begin a new.
                    [*Chorus of all.*]
        All, all of a piece throughout;
        Thy chase had a beast in view;
        Thy wars brought nothing about;
95   Thy lovers were all untrue.
        'Tis well an old age is out,
        And time to begin a new.
        [*Dance of huntsmen, nymphs, warriors and lovers.*]

                                            1700

---

3. Roman goddess of love, here presiding over the amorous court of Charles II.

Aphra Behn
1640?–1689

Robert White, after John Riley, line engraving of *Aphra Behn (née Johnson)*, 1716.

Aphra Behn's career was unprecedented, her output prodigious, her fame extensive, and her voice distinctive. Her origins, though, remain elusive. We know nothing certain about her birth, family, education, or marriage. She may have been born at the start or at the end of the 1640s, to parents of low or "gentle" station, named Johnson, Amies, or Cooper. Her Catholicism and her firm command of French suggest the possibility of a prosperous upbringing in a convent at home or abroad; the running argument against marriage for money that she sustains through much of her work suggests that her own marriage, to the otherwise unidentifiable "Mr. Behn," may have been obligatory and unhappy. In any case it was brief—and just possibly fictitious, since a widow could pursue a profession more freely than a spinster.

Behn's first appearances in the historical record suggest a propensity for self-invention. In 1663–1664, during a short stay with her family in the South American sugar colony of Surinam, a government agent there reported that she was conducting a flirtation with William Scott, an antimonarchist on the run from the Restoration. The agent referred to Scott as "Celadon" and Aphra as "Astraea," names the lovers may well have chosen for themselves from a popular French romance; Behn kept hers, as a *nom de plume*, for the whole of her writing life. Within two years, her loyalties had shifted and her self-invention had grown more intricate. In 1666 Behn herself became the king's spy, sent from London to Antwerp to persuade her old flame Scott to turn informer against his fellow Republicans and to apprise King Charles of rebellious plots. She did useful but costly work, garnering good information that her handlers ignored and spending much money that they were slow to reimburse. Returning to England later that year, and threatened with imprisonment for debt, she wrote her supervisor, "I have cried myself dead and could find in my heart to break through all and get to the King and never rise till he were pleased to pay this, but I am sick and weak and unfit for it or a prison . . . Sir, if I have not the money tonight you must send me something to keep [sustain] me in prison, for I will not starve." The king paid up, and Behn forestalled any further threat of starvation by writing plays for money—the first woman in England to earn a living by her pen. She had been "forced to write for bread," she later declared, and she was "not ashamed to own it."

Throughout her career Behn transmuted such "shamelessness" into a positive point of pride and a source of literary substance. Many of her plays, poems, and fictions focus on the difficulty with which intelligent, enterprising women pursue their desires against the current of social convention. In the prologues, prefaces, postscripts, and letters by which she provided a running commentary on her work, Behn sometimes aligned herself with the large fraternity of male authors who "like good tradesmen" sell whatever is "in fashion," but she often stood apart to muse acerbically on her unique position as a *female* purveyor of literary product. Once, surveying the panoply of contemporary male playwrights, she declared that "except for our most unimitable Laureate [Dryden], I dare say I know of none that write at such a formidable rate, but that a woman may well hope to reach their greatest heights." "Formidable rate" suggests both speed and skill; Behn made good on both boasts, producing twenty plays in twenty years, along with much poetry (including fervent pro-Stuart propaganda), copious translations, one of the earliest epistolary novels in English, and a cluster of innovative shorter fiction. In her range and her dexterity, she approached the stature of the "unimitable Laureate" himself, who knew her and praised her repeatedly. With her greatest successes—the comedy *The Rover* (1677), the novella *Oroonoko* (1688)—she secured both an audience and a reputation that continued without pause well into the following century.

Other pieces worked less well. Changes in literary fashion often obliged Behn to try new modes; she switched to fiction, for example, in the 1680s, when plays became less lucrative. Out of her vicissitudes—professional and personal, amorous, financial, literary—she fashioned a formidable celebrity, becoming the object of endless speculation in talk and in ink. "I value fame," she once wrote, and she cultivated it by what seemed an unprecedented frankness. ("All women together," wrote Virginia Woolf, "ought to let flowers fall upon the grave of Aphra Behn . . . for it was she who earned them the right to speak their minds.") In an age of libertines, when men like Rochester paraded their varied couplings in verse couplets, Behn undertook to proclaim and to analyze women's sexual desire, as manifested in her characters and in herself. Her disclosures, though, were intricately orchestrated. Living and writing at the center of a glamorous literary circle, Behn may have fostered, as the critic Janet Todd suggests, the "fantasy of a golden age of sexual and social openness," but she performed it for her readers rather than falling for it herself. Throughout her work Behn adroitly conceals the "self" that she purports to show and sell. She sometimes likens herself to those other female denizens of the theater, the mask-wearing prostitutes who roamed the audience in search of customers. The critic Catherine Gallagher has argued that Behn's literary persona—defiant, vulnerable, hypnotic—functions like the prostitute's vizard, promising the woman's "availability" as commodity while at the same time implying "the impenetrability of the controlling mind" behind the mask.

In Gallagher's reckoning, as in Woolf's, Behn's total career is more important than any particular work it produced. This is fitting tribute to a writer who, in an era of spectacular self-performers (Charles II, Dryden, Rochester), brought off, by virtue of her gender and her art, one of the most intricate performances of all. That performance now looks set for a long second run. After a hiatus in the nineteenth century, when both the writer and the work were dismissed as indecent, Behn's fame has undergone extraordinary revival. She dominates cultural-studies discourse as both a topic and a set of texts. The texts in particular are worth attending to: many are as astonishing as the career that engendered them.

 For additional resources on Behn, go to *The Longman Anthology of British Literature* Web site at www.myliteraturekit.com.

The Disappointment[1]

One day the amorous Lysander,
By an impatient passion swayed,
Surprised fair Cloris, that loved maid,
Who could defend herself no longer.
5   All things did with his love conspire;
The gilded planet of the day,
In his gay chariot drawn by fire,
Was now descending to the sea,
And left no light to guide the world,
10   But what from Cloris' brighter eyes was hurled.

1. Behn based this poem partly on a French source, *Sur une impuissamce* (1661), itself dervied in part from Ovid's poem on impotence in *Amores*, which also provided the model for Rochester's *Imperfect Enjoyment* (see page 2205). Behn's poem and Rochester's first appeared in the same volume, *Poems on Several Occasions* (1680); she later included hers, with alterations, in her own collection, *Poems on Several Occasions* (1684).

In a lone thicket made for love,
Silent as yielding maid's consent,
She with a charming languishment
Permits his force, yet gently strove;
15   Her hands his bosom softly meet,
But not to put him back designed,
Rather to draw 'em² on inclined;
Whilst he lay trembling at her feet,
Resistance 'tis in vain to show;
20   She wants° the power to say, "Ah! What d'ye do?"   *lacks*

Her bright eyes sweet, and yet severe,
Where love and shame confusedly strive,
Fresh vigor to Lysander give;
And breathing faintly in his ear,
25   She cried, "Cease, cease your vain desire,
Or I'll call out—what would you do?
My dearer honor even to you
I cannot, must not give—retire,
Or take this life, whose chiefest part
30   I gave you with the conquest of my heart."

But he as much unused to fear,
As he was capable of love,
The blessed minutes to improve,
Kisses her mouth, her neck, her hair;
35   Each touch her new desire alarms,
His burning trembling hand he pressed
Upon her swelling snowy breast,
While she lay panting in his arms.
All her unguarded beauties lie
40   The spoils and trophies of the enemy.

And now without respect or fear,
He seeks the object of his vows,
(His love no modesty allows)
By swift degrees advancing—where
45   His daring hand that altar seized,
Where gods of love do sacrifice:
That awful° throne, that paradise   *awe-inspiring*
Where rage is calmed, and anger pleased;
That fountain where delight still flows,
50   And gives the universal world repose.

Her balmy lips encountering his,
Their bodies, as their souls, are joined;
Where both in transports unconfined
Extend themselves upon the moss.
55   Cloris half dead and breathless lay;

2. Behn's earlier version reads "him."

Her soft eyes cast a humid light,
Such as divides the day and night;
Or falling stars, whose fires decay:
And now no signs of life she shows,
60   But what in short-breathed sighs returns and goes.

He saw how at her length she lay;
He saw her rising bosom bare;
Her loose thin robes, through which appear
A shape designed for love and play;
65   Abandoned by her pride and shame,
She does her softest joys dispense,
Offering her virgin innocence
A victim to love's sacred flame;
While the o'er-ravished shepherd lies
70   Unable to perform the sacrifice.

Ready to taste a thousand joys,
The too transported hapless swain[3]
Found the vast pleasure turned to pain;
Pleasure which too much love destroys.
75   The willing garments by he laid,
And Heaven all opened to his view,
Mad to possess, himself he threw
On the defenseless lovely maid.
But oh what envying god conspires
80   To snatch his power, yet leave him the desire!

Nature's support[4] (without whose aid
She can no human being give)
Itself now wants the art to live.
Faintness its slackened nerves invade.
85   In vain the enraged youth essayed
To call its fleeting vigor back,
No motion 'twill from motion take.
Excess of love his love betrayed.
In vain he toils, in vain commands;
90   The insensible[5] fell weeping in his hand.

In this so amorous cruel strife,
Where love and fate were too severe,
The poor Lysander in despair
Renounced his reason with his life.
95   Now all the brisk and active fire
That should the nobler part inflame,
Served to increase his rage and shame,
And left no spark for new desire.
Not all her naked charms could move

---

3. In English pastoral poetry, this is the conventional term for the shepherd/lover.

4. I.e., the erect penis.

5. The unfeeling object.

100   Or calm that rage that had debauched° his love.   *corrupted*

       Cloris returning from the trance
       Which love and soft desire had bred,
       Her timorous hand she gently laid
       (Or° guided by design or chance)   *either*
105   Upon that fabulous Priapus,[6]
       That potent god, as poets feign;
       But never did young shepherdess,
       Gathering of fern upon the plain,
       More nimbly draw her fingers back,
110   Finding beneath the verdant leaves a snake,

       Than Cloris her fair hand withdrew,
       Finding that god of her desires
       Disarmed of all his awful fires,
       And cold as flowers bathed in the morning dew.
115   Who can the nymph's confusion guess?
       The blood forsook the hinder place,
       And strewed with blushes all her face,
       Which both disdain and shame expressed.
       And from Lysander's arms she fled,
120   Leaving him fainting on the gloomy bed.

       Like lightning through the grove she hies,
       Or Daphne from the Delphic god,[7]
       No print upon the grassy road
       She leaves, to instruct pursuing eyes.
125   The wind that wantoned in her hair,
       And with her ruffled garments played,
       Discovered in the flying maid
       All that the gods e'er made, if fair.
       So Venus, when her love was slain,
130   With fear and haste flew o'er the fatal plain.[8]

       The nymph's resentments none but I
       Can well imagine or condole.
       But none can guess Lysander's soul,
       But those who swayed his destiny.
135   His silent griefs swell up to storms,
       And not one god his fury spares;
       He cursed his birth, his fate, his stars;
       But more the shepherdess's charms,
       Whose soft bewitching influence
140   Had damned him to the hell of impotence.

       1680

---

6. Greek god of male fertility, often depicted as possessing a permanent erection.

7. Apollo, who pursued the nymph Daphne until she was turned into a laurel tree in order to escape his advances.

8. When her beloved Adonis was wounded by a boar, the goddess of love rushed to help him, but in vain.

To Lysander,[1] on Some Verses He Writ, and Asking More for His Heart than 'Twas Worth

Take back that heart you with such caution give,
    Take the fond[2] valued trifle back;
I hate love-merchants that a trade would drive;
    And meanly cunning bargains make.

5   I care not how the busy market goes,
    And scorn to chaffer° for a price: *bargain*
Love does one staple° rate on all impose,   *fixed*
    Nor leaves it to the trader's choice.

A heart requires a heart unfeigned and true,
10   Though subtly you advance the price,
And ask a rate that simple love ne'er knew:
    And the free trade monopolize.

An humble slave the buyer must become,
    She must not bate[3] a look or glance,
15   You will have all, or you'll have none;
    See how love's market° you enhance.°   *price / increase*

Is't not enough, I gave you heart for heart,
    But I must add my lips and eyes?
I must no friendly smile or kiss impart;
20   But you must dun[4] me with advice?

And every hour still more unjust you grow.
    Those freedoms you my life deny,
You to Adraste[5] are obliged to show,
    And give her all my rifled° joy.   *stolen*

25   Without control she gazes on that face,
    And all the happy envied night,
In the pleased circle of your fond embrace:
    She takes away the lover's right.

From me she ravishes those silent hours,
30   That are by sacred love my due;
Whilst I in vain accuse the angry powers,
    That make me hopeless love pursue.

Adraste's ears with that dear voice are blest,
    That charms my soul at every sound,
35   And with those love-enchanting touches pressed:
    Which I ne'er felt without a wound.

1. "Lysander," the addressee of several of Behn's poems (and, in name at least, the male lover in *The Disappointment*), has not been identified; the poem suggests that he was a married man.
2. The word meant both "foolish" and "affectionate."
3. Withhold (by way of reducing love's "price").
4. Badger, demand payment from.
5. Apparently his wife.

She has thee all: whilst I with silent grief,
    The fragments of thy softness feel,
Yet dare not blame the happy licensed[6] thief:
40   That does my dear-bought pleasures steal.

Whilst like a glimmering taper still I burn,
    And waste myself in my own flame,
Adraste takes the welcome rich return:
    And leaves me all the hopeless pain.

45   Be just, my lovely swain, and do not take
    Freedoms you'll not to me allow;
Or give Amynta[7] so much freedom back:
    That she may rove as well as you.

Let us then love upon the honest square,[8]
50   Since interest neither have designed.[9]
For the sly gamester,[1] who ne'er plays me fair,
    Must trick for trick expect to find.

1684

To Lysander at the Music-Meeting

It was too much, ye gods, to see and hear,
Receiving wounds both from the eye and ear.
One charm might have secured a victory;
Both, raised the pleasure even to ecstasy.
5 So ravished lovers in each other's arms,
Faint with excess of joy, excess of charms.
Had I but gazed and fed my greedy eyes,
Perhaps you'd pleased no farther than surprise.
That heav'nly form might admiration move,
10 But, not without the music, charmed° with love: *have charmed*
At least so quick the conquest had not been;
You stormed without, and harmony within.
Nor could I listen to the sound alone,
But I alas must look—and was undone:
15 I saw the softness that composed your face,
While your attention heightened every grace:
Your mouth all full of sweetness and content,
And your fine killing eyes of languishment:
Your bosom now and then a sigh would move,
20 (For music has the same effects with love).
Your body easy and all tempting lay,
Inspiring wishes which the eyes betray,

---

6. Permitted (by the marriage license).
7. I.e., the poem's speaker.
8. I.e., by rules that apply to both sides equally.

9. Neither of us has intended to make a profit (on our investment in each other).
1. Trickster or gambler.

In all that have the fate to glance that way.
A careless and a lovely negligence,
25   Did a new charm to every limb dispense.
So look young angels, listening to the sound,
When the tuned spheres glad[1] all the heav'ns around:
So raptured lie amidst the wondering crowd,
So charmingly extended on a cloud.
30   When from so many ways love's arrows storm,
Who can the heedless heart defend from harm?
Beauty and music must the soul disarm;
Since harmony, like fire to wax, does fit
The softened heart impressions to admit:
35   As the brisk sounds of war the courage move,
Music prepares and warms the soul to love.
But when the kindling sparks such fuel meet,
No wonder if the flame inspired be great.

1684

A Letter to Mr. Creech at Oxford[1]
Written in the Last Great Frost[2]

Daphnis, because I am your debtor,   ⎫
(And other causes which are better)   ⎬
I send you here by debt of letter.   ⎭
You should have had a scrap of nonsense,
5   You may remember left at Tonson's.[3]
(Though by the way that's scurvy rhyme Sir,
But yet 'twill serve to tag° a line Sir.)   *round off*
A *billet-doux°* I had designed then,   *sweet note*
But you may think I was in wine then;
10   Because it being cold, you know
We warmed it with a glass—or so.
I grant you that shy° wine's the devil,   *cheap*
To make one's memory uncivil;
But, when, 'twixt every sparkling cup,
15   I so much brisker wit took up;
Wit, able to inspire a thinking;
And make one solemn even in drinking;
Wit that would charm and stock a poet,
Even instruct ———[4] who has no wit;

1. Gladden. In the Ptolematic view of the universe that Behn invokes here, the heavens were composed of concentice crystalline spheres, whose motion produced a sublime music. Angels could hear it, humans could not.
1. Thomas Creech (1659–1700), classicist and translator. Behn had praised his work in a previous poem, in which (as here) she addresses him by the pastoral name "Daphnis." Here she produces a less solemn piece, explaining why a love letter from her has failed to reach him, and conveying (in the postscript) a compliment from an unnamed will-wisher.
2. The winter of 1683–1684 was so severe that the surface of the river Thames froze solid.
3. The eminent bookseller Jacob Tonson (1656–1737) had published several of Behn's plays and her *Poems on Several Occasions* (1684). The route through London that Behn traces in this poem would have taken her past Tonson's shop.
4. An in-joke, probabaly referring or some mutually despised Whig poet.

20 Wit that was hearty, true, and loyal,
    Of wit, like Bays'[5] Sir, that's my trial;
    I say 'twas most impossible,
    That after that one should be dull.
    Therefore because you may not blame me,
25 Take the whole truth as —— shall sa'me.[6]
        From Whitehall[7] Sir, as I was coming,
    His sacred Majesty from dunning—
    Who oft in debt is, truth to tell,
    For Tory farce, or doggerel—[8]
30 When every street as dangerous was,
    As ever the Alpian hills° to pass,   *the Alps*
    When melted snow and ice confound one,
    Whether to break one's neck or drown one,
    And *billet-doux* in pocket lay,
35 To drop as° coach should jolt that way,   *whenever*
    Near to that place of fame called Temple,[9] ⎤
    (Which I shall note by sad example)   ⎬
    Where college dunce is cured of simple,[1] ⎦
    Against that sign of whore called scarlet,[2]
40 My coachman fairly laid pilgarlic.[3]
        Though scribbling fist was out of joint,
    And every limb made great complaint;
    Yet missing the dear assignation,[4]
    Gave me most cause of tribulation.
45 To honest H—le[5] I should have shown ye,
    A wit that would be proud t'have known ye;
    A wit uncommon, a facetious,
    A great admirer of Lucretius.[6]
    But transitory hopes do vary,
50 And high designments oft miscarry.
    Ambition never climbed so lofty,
    But may descend too fair and softly.
    But would you'd seen how sneakingly
    I looked with this catastrophe.
55 So saucy Whig, when plot broke out,

5. John Dryden, Poet Laureate (so nicknamed because in ancient Rome the laureate wore a wreath of bay leaves); Behn here implies that Dryden sets the standard ("trial") for true wit.
6. As Christ shall save me.
7. The royal palace in London; Behn has apparently been trying to collect payment from the king for a poem she wrote in his support.
8. I.e., Charles II frequently owes money to the partisan poets who write for him.
9. A cluster of buildings on Fleet Street containing residences, offices, and lecture halls for lawyers and students.
1. Simplicity, foolishness.
2. The Pope's Head tavern, so nicknamed because

anti-Catholic literature identified the Roman church with the "whore . . . in scarlet" of Revelation 17.
3. The word originally denoted baldness (with "a head like peeled garlic"), but had become slang for any unfortunate person.
4. I.e., with Creech.
5. John Hoyle, a rakish lawyer with whom Aphra Behn had carried on a much-talked-about amorous relationship and to whom she had addressed many poems.
6. Roman author of *De rerum natura* (*On the Nature of Things*), which Creech had translated (1683). Lucretius's insistence on worldly pleasure had established him as the patron philosopher of Restoration libertines.

Dejected hung his sniveling snout;[7]
So Oxford member looked, when Rowley
Kicked out the rebel crew so foully;[8]
So Perkin, once that god of Wapping,
60   Whom slippery turn of state took napping,
From hopes of James the Second fell
Into the native scoundrel.[9]
So lover looked of joy defeated,
When too much fire his vigor cheated.[1]
65   Even so looked I, when bliss-depriving
Was caused by over-hasty driving.
Who saw me could not choose but think,
I looked like brawn in sousing drink,[2]
Or Lazarello[3] who was showed
70   For a strange fish, to the gaping crowd.
    Thus you by fate (to me, sinister)
At shop of book my *billet* missed Sir.
And home I went as discontent, ⎤
As a new routed° Parliament, ⎬   *dismissed*
75   Not seeing Daphnis ere he went. ⎦
And sure his grief beyond expressing,
Of joy proposed to want the blessing.[4]
Therefore to pardon pray incline,
Since disappointment all was mine.
80   Of Hell we have no other notion,
Than all the joys of Heaven's privation;
So Sir with recommendations fervent,
I rest your very humble servant.

Postscript

On Twelfth Night Sir, by that good token,
85   When lamentable cake was broken,[5]
You had a friend, a man of wit,
A man whom I shall ne'er forget,
For every word he did impart,

---

7. Behn imagines a partisan disappointed by the exposure (and hence the failure) of the Rye House plot, an alleged Whig scheme to assassinate the king and his brother in 1683.

8. In March 1681, Charles II (often dubbed "Rowley" in casual talk and satiric ballads) dismissed the Parliament at Oxford to frustrate the ambitions of the Whig faction.

9. "Perkin" is Charles II's illegitimate son James, Duke of Monmouth, who (like the medieval pretender Perkin Warbeck) claimed that he was the legitimate heir to the crown; his cause was at one point popular in the rough neighborhood of Wapping. Had he made good on his claim, he (rather than his like-named uncle the Duke of York) would have become James II. Disappointed of that prospect, Behn suggests, he has now "fallen back" into what he truly is: a born rascal.

1. I.e., because of premature ejaculation.

2. Like pickled pig's flesh, bruised and discolored.

3. Hero of Juan de Luna's picaresque narrative *Lazarillo de Tormes*, who is rescued in fishermen's nets after a shipwreck and displayed as a sea monster.

4. Certainly he, having missed out on a promised pleasure, suffers inexpressible grief.

5. On the Twelfth Night of Christmas (6 January, "lamentable," perhaps, because it marked the holiday's conclusion), the traditional festivities included the cutting of a cake in which a pea and bean had been concealed. The recipients of the "prize" pieces presided over the celebration as king and queen (cf. the poem's final line, where Behn and Creech are linked in praise).

'Twas worth the keeping in a heart.
90   True Tory all! and when he spoke,
A god of wit, though man in look.
"To this your friend Daphnis, address
The humblest of my services.
Tell him how much—yet do not, too.
95   My vast esteem no words can show.
Tell him—that he is worthy—you."

1685

To the Fair Clarinda, Who Made Love to Me, Imagined More than Woman

Fair lovely maid, or if that title be
Too weak, too feminine for nobler thee,
Permit a name that more approaches truth,
And let me call thee, lovely charming youth.
5   This last will justify my soft complaint,
While that may serve to lessen my constraint;
And without blushes I the youth pursue,
When so much beauteous woman is in view.
Against thy charms we struggle but in vain,
10   With thy deluding form thou giv'st us pain,
While the bright nymph betrays us to the swain.[1]
In pity to our sex sure thou wert sent,
That we might love, and yet be innocent:
For sure no crime with thee we can commit;
15   Or if we should—thy form excuses it.
For who that gathers fairest flowers believes
A snake lies hid beneath the fragrant leaves.
    Thou beauteous wonder of a different kind,
Soft Cloris with the dear Alexis[2] joined;
20   Whene'er the manly part of thee would plead
Thou tempts us with the image of the maid,
While we the noblest passions do extend
The love to Hermes, Aphrodite the friend.[3]

1688

OROONOKO   "I am very ill and have been dying this twelve month," Behn wrote an acquaintance late in 1687; she suffered from degenerative arthritis and had some eighteen months' dying still to do. Now, near the end of her writing career, she set down a narrative of events that had predated its beginnings, a story that she claimed to recall from the months she spent in 1663–1664 as a young woman in Surinam, an English colony on the northeastern coast of South America. A friend records that during the intervening decades Behn had often told the

---

1. The conventional pastoral term for a male lover or a country lad.
2. "Cloris" is female, "Alexis" male.

3. Named after the offspring of these two gods, a hermaphrodite combines the characteristics of both sexes.

story of an African prince enslaved on the plantation where she dwelt; prompted by his love for a slave from his own country, he mounted a rebellion against his English masters. In *Oroonoko*, Behn displayed Surinam as a world where the appetites of trade and empire had brought several cultures—indigenous "Indians," colonizing Europeans, abducted Africans—into violent and precarious fusion.

Writing the narrative, Behn undertook volatile fusions of her own. On the title page, the single name "Oroonoko" sits above two subtitles in which both hero and text are implicitly split in two. The hero is both "royal" and a "slave"; the text's "true history" is so suffused with fictional conventions that for a long while historians suspected that Behn had never been to Surinam and had made the whole thing up (the truth of many of the story's details has been neither established nor refuted). Oroonoko and his beloved Imoinda play out the love-and-loss plot of a heroic romance—a genre favored by Restoration aristocracy—within the far more realistic context of a world driven by bourgeois imperatives and political aspirations. Behn's boldest fusion involves not only cultures, identities, and modes but also times. Oroonoko, "the chief actor in this history," comes to embody the history of Stuart sovereignty, playing the roles of all three kings to whom Behn had devoted her own obsessive loyalties: Charles I, whose 1649 execution haunts the narrative, particularly in its last few pages; Charles II, whose 1660 Restoration Behn pointedly invokes at the celebratory moment of the African prince's arrival at Surinam; and James II, the beleaguered Catholic king whose three-year reign was hurtling toward its close at the very moment of *Oroonoko*'s publication, and whose predicament as the embattled champion of an oppressed minority finds many echoes in the royal slave's rebellion and his fate.

Mapping all these convergences—of culture with culture, of monarch with slave, of man with woman—Behn places herself as narrator problematically near their center. The story is driven by her empathy for the slave couple, for whom she acts as mentor, friend, and advocate. Yet her empathy is complicated, perhaps even compromised. She shows less pity for less "royal" slaves, she acknowledges the possibility of her own complicity (however inadvertent) in her hero's pain, and she is oddly absent at the height of his suffering. She also participates in the profitable systems that enmesh him. Even before she tells his story, she presents herself as a kind of trader, who has brought back from Surinam butterflies for the Royal Society and exotic feathers for the dress of the "Indian Queen" in the popular heroic tragedy of that name. As the scholar Laura Brown points out, Behn's "treatment of slavery . . . is neither coherent nor fully critical." The narrative is by turns empathetic with the oppressed and complicit with the powerful; the crossing vectors of Behn's allegiance produce no conclusive sum.

In *Oroonoko*, cultural compounds prove unstable. Again and again in the story, human bodies are torn apart, and these sunderings foretell other dissolutions. Behn repeatedly reminds her readers that shortly after the events she narrates, the entire colony at Surinam disappeared: the English traded it away to the Dutch (they got New York in return). As colonist she laments this loss; as Tory, she anticipates another: the loss of James II in the parliamentary overthrow that would soon supplant the English Catholic with the Dutch Protestant William of Orange. Stuart rule, which had "ended" once with regicide, would end again (like the world of her youth in Surinam) with revolution.

Behn died shortly after publishing her narrative; she was buried in Westminster Abbey, where William would be crowned just five days later. In *Oroonoko*, amid all its intricacies, she had mingled energies of reminiscence with intimations of ruin, to produce one of the earliest and most abiding interrogations of the colonial commerce in human beings. Hugh Thomas, historian of the slave trade and of abolition, reads Behn as a pivotal figure between the two. She was "more influential than popes and missionaries," he writes, in preparing "people for a change on humanitarian grounds"—a change of thought and feeling that would beget, well over a century later, a change of law and practice.

Oroonoko
Or
The Royal Slave A True History

I do not pretend, in giving you the history of this royal slave, to entertain my reader with the adventures of a feigned hero, whose life and fortunes Fancy may manage at the poet's pleasure; nor in relating the truth, design to adorn it with any accidents, but such as arrived in earnest to him. And it shall come simply into the world, recommended by its own proper merits, and natural intrigues; there being enough of reality to support it, and to render it diverting, without the addition of invention.

I was myself an eyewitness to a great part of what you will find here set down; and what I could not be witness of, I received from the mouth of the chief actor in this history, the hero himself, who gave us the whole transactions of his youth; and though I shall omit, for brevity's sake, a thousand little accidents of his life, which, however pleasant to us, where history was scarce, and adventures very rare, yet might prove tedious and heavy to my reader, in a world where he finds diversions for every minute, new and strange. But we who were perfectly charmed with the character of this great man were curious to gather every circumstance of his life.

The scene of the last part of his adventures lies in a colony in America called Surinam, in the West Indies.

But before I give you the story of this gallant slave, 'tis fit I tell you the manner of bringing them to these new colonies; for those they make use of there, are not natives of the place; for those we live with in perfect amity, without daring to command them; but on the contrary, caress them with all the brotherly and friendly affection in the world, trading with them for their fish, venison, buffaloes, skins, and little rarities; as marmosets, a sort of monkey as big as a rat or weasel, but of a marvelous and delicate shape, and has face and hands like an human creature; and cousheries,[1] a little beast in the form and fashion of a lion, as big as a kitten; but so exactly made in all parts like that noble beast, that it is it in miniature. Then for little parakeets, great parrots, macaws, and a thousand other birds and beasts of wonderful and surprising forms, shapes, and colors. For skins of prodigious snakes, of which there are some threescore yards in length; as is the skin of one that may be seen at His Majesty's Antiquaries,[2] where are also some rare flies,[3] of amazing forms and colors, presented to them by myself, some as big as my fist, some less; and all of various excellencies, such as art cannot imitate. Then we trade for feathers, which they order into all shapes, make themselves little short habits of them, and glorious wreaths for their heads, necks, arms, and legs, whose tinctures are inconceivable. I had a set of these presented to me, and I gave them to the King's Theater, and it was the dress of the *Indian Queen*,[4] infinitely admired by persons of quality, and were inimitable. Besides these, a thousand little knacks and rarities in nature, and some of art; as their baskets, weapons, aprons, etc. We dealt with them with beads of all colors, knives, axes, pins, and needles, which they used only as tools to drill holes with in their ears, noses, and lips, where they hang a great many little things; as long beads, bits of tin, brass, or silver, beat thin, and any shining trinket. The beads they weave into aprons about a quarter of an ell[5] long, and of the same breadth, working

---

1. Other writers mention this animal, but its identity remains uncertain.
2. Probably the "Repository" (museum) of the Royal Society.
3. Butterflies.
4. A heroic drama (1664) by Robert Howard and John Dryden, celebrated for its sumptuous costumes and design.
5. Forty-five inches.

them very prettily in flowers of several colors of beads; which apron they wear just before them, as Adam and Eve did the fig leaves; the men wearing a long strip of linen, which they deal with us for. They thread these beads also on long cotton threads, and make girdles to tie their aprons to, which come twenty times or more about the waist and then cross, like a shoulder-belt, both ways, and round their necks, arms, and legs. This adornment, with their long black hair, and the face painted in little specks or flowers here and there, makes them a wonderful figure to behold. Some of the beauties which indeed are finely shaped, as almost all are, and who have pretty features, are very charming and novel; for they have all that is called beauty except the color, which is a reddish yellow; or after a new oiling, which they often use to themselves, they are of the color of a new brick, but smooth, soft, and sleek. They are extreme modest and bashful, very shy, and nice[6] of being touched. And though they are all thus naked, if one lives forever among them, there is not to be seen an indecent action or glance; and being continually used to see one another so unadorned, so like our first parents before the Fall, it seems as if they had no wishes; there being nothing to heighten curiosity, but all you can see, you see at once, and every moment see; and where there is no novelty, there can be no curiosity. Not but I have seen a handsome young Indian, dying for love of a very beautiful young Indian maid; but all his courtship was, to fold his arms, pursue her with his eyes, and sighs were all his language; while she, as if no such lover were present, or rather, as if she desired none such, carefully guarded her eyes from beholding him; and never approached him, but she looked down with all the blushing modesty I have seen in the most severe and cautious of our world. And these people represented to me an absolute idea of the first state of innocence, before man knew how to sin; and 'tis most evident and plain, that simple Nature is the most harmless, inoffensive, and virtuous mistress. 'Tis she alone, if she were permitted, that better instructs the world than all the inventions of man; religion would here but destroy that tranquility they possess by ignorance, and laws would but teach them to know offense, of which now they have no notion. They once made mourning and fasting for the death of the English governor, who had given his hand to come on such a day to them, and neither came, nor sent; believing, when once a man's word was past, nothing but death could or should prevent his keeping it. And when they saw he was not dead, they asked him, what name they had for a man who promised a thing he did not do? The governor told them, such a man was a liar, which was a word of infamy to a gentleman. Then one of them replied, "Governor, you are a liar, and guilty of that infamy." They have a native justice which knows no fraud, and they understand no vice, or cunning, but when they are taught by the white men. They have plurality of wives which, when they grow old, they serve those that succeed them, who are young; but with a servitude easy and respected; and unless they take slaves in war, they have no other attendants.

Those on that continent where I was had no king; but the oldest war captain was obeyed with great resignation.

A war captain is a man who has led them on to battle with conduct[7] and success, of whom I shall have occasion to speak more hereafter, and of some other of their customs and manners, as they fall in my way.

With these people, as I said, we live in perfect tranquility and good understanding, as it behooves us to do; they knowing all the places where to seek the best food

6. Shy.   7. Skillful management.

of the country, and the means of getting it; and for very small and invaluable trifles, supply us with what 'tis impossible for us to get; for they do not only in the wood, and over the savannahs, in hunting, supply the parts of hounds, by swiftly scouring through those almost impassable places, and by the mere activity of their feet, run down the nimblest deer, and other eatable beasts; but in the water, one would think they were gods of the rivers, or fellow citizens of the deep, so rare an art they have in swimming, diving, and almost living in water, by which they command the less swift inhabitants of the floods. And then for shooting, what they cannot take, or reach with their hands, they do with arrows, and have so admirable an aim, that they will split almost a hair; and at any distance that an arrow can reach, they will shoot down oranges and other fruit, and only touch the stalk with the darts' points, that they may not hurt the fruit. So that they being, on all occasions, very useful to us, we find it absolutely necessary to caress them as friends, and not to treat them as slaves; nor dare we do other, their numbers so far surpassing ours in that continent.

Those then whom we make use of to work in our plantations of sugar are Negroes, black slaves altogether, which are transported thither in this manner.

Those who want slaves make a bargain with a master, or captain of a ship, and contract to pay him so much apiece, a matter of twenty pound a head for as many as he agrees for, and to pay for them when they shall be delivered on such a plantation. So that when there arrives a ship laden with slaves, they who have so contracted go aboard, and receive their number by lot; and perhaps in one lot that may be for ten, there may happen to be three or four men; the rest, women and children; or be there more or less of either sex, you are obliged to be contented with your lot.

Coramantien,[8] a country of blacks so called, was one of those places in which they found the most advantageous trading for these slaves, and thither most of our great traders in that merchandise trafficked; for that nation is very warlike and brave, and having a continual campaign, being always in hostility with one neighboring prince or other, they had the fortune to take a great many captives; for all they took in battle were sold as slaves, at least, those common men who could not ransom themselves. Of these slaves so taken, the general only has all the profit; and of these generals, our captains and masters of ships buy all their freights.

The King of Coramantien was himself a man of a hundred and odd years old, and had no son, though he had many beautiful black wives; for most certainly, there are beauties that can charm of that color. In his younger years he had had many gallant men to his sons, thirteen of which died in battle, conquering when they fell; and he had only left him for his successor one grandchild, son to one of these dead victors; who, as soon as he could bear a bow in his hand, and a quiver at his back, was sent into the field, to be trained up by one of the oldest generals to war; where, from his natural inclination to arms, and the occasions given him, with the good conduct of the old general, he became, at the age of seventeen, one of the most expert captains, and bravest soldiers, that ever saw the field of Mars; so that he was adored as the wonder of all that world, and the darling of the soldiers. Besides, he was adorned with a native beauty so transcending all those of his gloomy race, that he struck an awe and reverence, even in those that knew not his quality; as he did in me, who beheld him with surprise and wonder, when afterwards he arrived in our world.

---

8. Koromantyn, a fort and trading post on the western coast of Africa (in modern Ghana).

He had scarce arrived at his seventeenth year when, fighting by his side, the general was killed with an arrow in his eye, which the Prince Oroonoko (for so was this gallant Moor[9] called) very narrowly avoided; nor had he, if the general, who saw the arrow shot, and perceiving it aimed at the Prince, had not bowed his head between, on purpose to receive it in his own body rather than it should touch that of the Prince, and so saved him.

'Twas then, afflicted as Oroonoko was, that he was proclaimed general in the old man's place; and then it was, at the finishing of that war, which had continued for two years, that the Prince came to court, where he had hardly been a month together, from the time of his fifth year to that of seventeen; and 'twas amazing to imagine where it was he learned so much humanity or, to give his accomplishments a juster name, where 'twas he got that real greatness of soul, those refined notions of true honor, that absolute generosity, and that softness that was capable of the highest passions of love and gallantry, whose objects were almost continually fighting men, or those mangled or dead; who heard no sounds but those of war and groans. Some part of it we may attribute to the care of a Frenchman of wit and learning, who finding it turn to very good account to be a sort of royal tutor to this young black, and perceiving him very ready, apt, and quick of apprehension, took a great pleasure to teach him morals, language, and science, and was for it extremely beloved and valued by him. Another reason was, he loved, when he came from war, to see all the English gentlemen that traded thither, and did not only learn their language but that of the Spaniards also, with whom he traded afterwards for slaves.

I have often seen and conversed with this great man, and been a witness to many of his mighty actions, and do assure my reader, the most illustrious courts could not have produced a braver man, both for greatness of courage and mind, a judgment more solid, a wit more quick, and a conversation more sweet and diverting. He knew almost as much as if he had read much: he had heard of, and admired the Romans; he had heard of the late Civil Wars in England, and the deplorable death of our great monarch,[1] and would discourse of it with all the sense, and abhorrence of the injustice imaginable. He had an extreme good and graceful mien, and all the civility of a well-bred great man. He had nothing of barbarity in his nature, but in all points addressed himself as if his education had been in some European court.

This great and just character of Oroonoko gave me an extreme curiosity to see him, especially when I knew he spoke French and English, and that I could talk with him. But though I had heard so much of him, I was as greatly surprised when I saw him as if I had heard nothing of him, so beyond all report I found him. He came into the room, and addressed himself to me, and some other women, with the best grace in the world. He was pretty tall, but of a shape the most exact that can be fancied; the most famous statuary[2] could not form the figure of a man more admirably turned from head to foot. His face was not of that brown, rusty black which most of that nation are, but a perfect ebony, or polished jet. His eyes were the most awful that could be seen, and very piercing, the white of them being like snow, as were his teeth. His nose was rising and Roman, instead of African and flat; his mouth, the finest shaped that could be seen, far from those great turned lips which are so natural to the rest of

9. The word originally meant "Moroccan," but was often used more generally for any person of African descent. Oroonoko's name may echo the river Orinoco in Venezuela, or the African god Oro.

1. Charles I, whose beheading in 1649 by sentence of the House of Commons marked the culmination of the wars between Royalists and Parliament.
2. Sculptor.

the Negroes. The whole proportion and air of his face was so noble and exactly formed that, bating[3] his color, there could be nothing in nature more beautiful, agreeable, and handsome. There was no one grace wanting that bears the standard of true beauty. His hair came down to his shoulders by the aids of art, which was, by pulling it out with a quill and keeping it combed, of which he took particular care. Nor did the perfections of his mind come short of those of his person, for his discourse was admirable upon almost any subject; and whoever had heard him speak, would have been convinced of their errors, that all fine wit is confined to the white men, especially to those of Christendom; and would have confessed that Oroonoko was as capable even of reigning well, and of governing as wisely, had as great a soul, as politic maxims,[4] and was as sensible of power as any prince civilized in the most refined schools of humanity and learning, or the most illustrious courts.

This Prince, such as I have described him, whose soul and body were so admirably adorned, was (while yet he was in the court of his grandfather) as I said, as capable of love as 'twas possible for a brave and gallant man to be; and in saying that, I have named the highest degree of love; for sure, great souls are most capable of that passion.

I have already said the old general was killed by the shot of an arrow, by the side of this Prince, in battle; and that Oroonoko was made general. This old dead hero had one only daughter left of his race; a beauty that, to describe her truly, one need say only, she was female to the noble male; the beautiful black Venus to our young Mars; as charming in her person as he, and of delicate virtues. I have seen an hundred white men sighing after her, and making a thousand vows at her feet, all vain and unsuccessful; and she was, indeed, too great for any but a prince of her own nation to adore.

Oroonoko coming from the wars (which were now ended) after he had made his court to his grandfather, he thought in honor he ought to make a visit to Imoinda, the daughter of his foster-father, the dead general; and to make some excuses to her, because his preservation was the occasion of her father's death; and to present her with those slaves that had been taken in this last battle, as the trophies of her father's victories. When he came, attended by all the young soldiers of any merit, he was infinitely surprised at the beauty of this fair Queen of Night, whose face and person was so exceeding all he had ever beheld; that lovely modesty with which she received him, that softness in her look and sighs, upon the melancholy occasion of this honor that was done by so great a man as Oroonoko, and a prince of whom she had heard such admirable things; the awfulness[5] wherewith she received him, and the sweetness of her words and behavior while he stayed, gained a perfect conquest over his fierce heart, and made him feel the victor could be subdued. So that having made his first compliments, and presented her a hundred and fifty slaves in fetters, he told her with his eyes that he was not insensible of her charms; while Imoinda, who wished for nothing more than so glorious a conquest, was pleased to believe she understood that silent language of new-born love; and from that moment, put on all her additions to beauty.

The Prince returned to court with quite another humor[6] than before; and though he did not speak much of the fair Imoinda, he had the pleasure to hear all his followers speak of nothing but the charms of that maid; insomuch that, even in

3. Excepting.
4. Shrewd principles or sayings.

5. Respect.
6. Frame of mind.

the presence of the old king, they were extolling her, and heightening, if possible, the beauties they had found in her; so that nothing else was talked of, no other sound was heard in every corner where there were whisperers, but "Imoinda! Imoinda!"

'Twill be imagined Oroonoko stayed not long before he made his second visit; nor, considering his quality, not much longer before he told her he adored her. I have often heard him say that he admired by what strange inspiration he came to talk things so soft and so passionate, who never knew love, nor was used to the conversation of women; but (to use his own words) he said, most happily, some new, and till then unknown power instructed his heart and tongue in the language of love, and at the same time, in favor of him, inspired Imoinda with a sense of his passion. She was touched with what he said, and returned it all in such answers as went to his very heart, with a pleasure unknown before. Nor did he use those obligations ill that love had done him; but turned all his happy moments to the best advantage; and as he knew no vice, his flame aimed at nothing but honor, if such a distinction may be made in love; and especially in that country, where men take to themselves as many as they can maintain, and where the only crime and sin with woman is to turn her off, to abandon her to want, shame, and misery. Such ill morals are only practiced in Christian countries, where they prefer the bare name of religion; and, without virtue or morality, think that's sufficient. But Oroonoko was none of those professors; but as he had right notions of honor, so he made her such propositions as were not only and barely such; but, contrary to the custom of his country, he made her vows she should be the only woman he would possess while he lived; that no age or wrinkles should incline him to change, for her soul would be always fine, and always young; and he should have an eternal idea in his mind of the charms she now bore, and should look into his heart for that idea, when he could find it no longer in her face.

After a thousand assurances of his lasting flame, and her eternal empire over him, she condescended to receive him for her husband; or rather, received him, as the greatest honor the gods could do her.

There is a certain ceremony in these cases to be observed, which I forgot to ask him how performed; but 'twas concluded on both sides that, in obedience to him, the grandfather was to be first made acquainted with the design; for they pay a most absolute resignation to the monarch, especially when he is a parent also.

On the other side, the old king, who had many wives, and many concubines, wanted not court flatterers to insinuate in his heart a thousand tender thoughts for this young beauty; and who represented her to his fancy as the most charming he had ever possessed in all the long race of his numerous years. At this character his old heart, like an extinguished brand, most apt to take fire, felt new sparks of love and began to kindle; and now grown to his second childhood, longed with impatience to behold this gay thing, with whom, alas, he could but innocently play. But how he should be confirmed she was this wonder, before he used his power to call her to court (where maidens never came, unless for the King's private use) he was next to consider; and while he was so doing, he had intelligence brought him, that Imoinda was most certainly mistress to the Prince Oroonoko. This gave him some chagrin; however, it gave him also an opportunity, one day, when the Prince was a-hunting, to wait on a man of quality, as his slave and attendant, who should go and make a present to Imoinda, as from the Prince; he should then, unknown, see this fair maid, and have an opportunity to hear what message she would return the

Prince for his present; and from thence gather the state of her heart, and degree of her inclination. This was put in execution, and the old monarch saw, and burned; he found her all he had heard, and would not delay his happiness, but found he should have some obstacle to overcome her heart; for she expressed her sense of the present the Prince had sent her, in terms so sweet, so soft and pretty, with an air of love and joy that could not be dissembled, insomuch that 'twas past doubt whether she loved Oroonoko entirely. This gave the old king some affliction, but he salved it with this, that the obedience the people pay their king was not at all inferior to what they paid their gods, and what love would not oblige Imoinda to do, duty would compel her to.

He was therefore no sooner got to his apartment, but he sent the royal veil to Imoinda, that is, the ceremony of invitation; he sends the lady, he has a mind to honor with his bed, a veil, with which she is covered and secured for the King's use; and 'tis death to disobey; besides, held a most impious disobedience.

'Tis not to be imagined the surprise and grief that seized this lovely maid at this news and sight. However, as delays in these cases are dangerous, and pleading worse than treason, trembling and almost fainting, she was obliged to suffer herself to be covered and led away.

They brought her thus to court; and the King, who had caused a very rich bath to be prepared, was led into it, where he sat under a canopy in state, to receive this longed for virgin; whom he having commanded should be brought to him, they (after disrobing her) led her to the bath and, making fast the doors, left her to descend. The King, without more courtship, bade her throw off her mantle and come to his arms. But Imoinda, all in tears, threw herself on the marble on the brink of the bath, and besought him to hear her. She told him, as she was a maid, how proud of the divine glory she should have been of having it in her power to oblige her king; but as by the laws he could not, and from his royal goodness would not take from any man his wedded wife, so she believed she should be the occasion of making him commit a great sin, if she did not reveal her state and condition, and tell him she was another's, and could not be so happy to be his.

The King, enraged at this delay, hastily demanded the name of the bold man that had married a woman of her degree without his consent. Imoinda, seeing his eyes fierce and his hands tremble, whether with age or anger I know not, but she fancied the last, almost repented she had said so much, for now she feared the storm would fall on the Prince; she therefore said a thousand things to appease the raging of his flame, and to prepare him to hear who it was with calmness; but before she spoke, he imagined who she meant, but would not seem to do so, but commanded her to lay aside her mantle and suffer herself to receive his caresses; or by his gods, he swore, that happy man whom she was going to name should die, though it were even Oroonoko himself. "Therefore," said he, "deny this marriage, and swear thyself a maid." "That," replied Imoinda, "by all our powers I do, for I am not yet known to my husband." "'Tis enough," said the King, "'tis enough to satisfy both my conscience and my heart." And rising from his seat, he went and led her into the bath, it being in vain for her to resist.

In this time the Prince, who was returned from hunting, went to visit his Imoinda, but found her gone; and not only so, but heard she had received the royal veil. This raised him to a storm, and in his madness they had much ado to save him from laying violent hands on himself. Force first prevailed, and then reason. They urged all to him that might oppose his rage; but nothing weighed so greatly with him as the King's old age, incapable of injuring him with Imoinda. He would give way to that hope, because it pleased him most, and flattered best his heart. Yet this served not altogether to make him cease his different passions, which sometimes raged within him, and sometimes softened into showers. 'Twas not enough to appease him, to tell him his grandfather was old, and could not that way injure him, while he retained that awful[7] duty which the young men are used there to pay to their grave relations. He could not be convinced he had no cause to sigh and mourn for the loss of a mistress he could not with all his strength and courage retrieve. And he would often cry, "O my friends! Were she in walled cities, or confined from me in fortifications of the greatest strength; did enchantments or monsters detain her from me, I would venture through any hazard to free her. But here, in the arms of a feeble old man, my youth, my violent love, my trade in arms, and all my vast desire of glory avail me nothing. Imoinda is as irrecoverably lost to me as if she were snatched by the cold arms of death. Oh! she is never to be retrieved. If I would wait tedious years, till fate should bow the old King to his grave, even that would not leave me Imoinda free; but still that custom that makes it so vile a crime for a son to marry his father's wives or mistress would hinder my happiness; unless I would either ignobly set an ill precedent to my successors, or abandon my country and fly with her to some unknown world, who never heard our story."

But it was objected to him that his case was not the same; for Imoinda being his lawful wife, by solemn contract, 'twas he was the injured man, and might, if he so pleased, take Imoinda back, the breach of the law being on his grandfather's side; and that if he could circumvent him, and redeem her from the otan, which is the palace of the King's women, a sort of seraglio, it was both just and lawful for him so to do.

This reasoning had some force upon him, and he should have been entirely comforted, but for the thought that she was possessed by his grandfather. However, he loved so well that he was resolved to believe what most favored his hope, and to endeavor to learn from Imoinda's own mouth what only she could satisfy him in: whether she was robbed of that blessing, which was only due to his faith and love. But as it was very hard to get a sight of the women, for no men ever entered into the otan but when the King went to entertain himself with some one of his wives or mistresses, and 'twas death at any other time for any other to go in, so he knew not how to contrive to get a sight of her.

While Oroonoko felt all the agonies of love, and suffered under a torment the most painful in the world, the old king was not exempted from his share of affliction. He was troubled for having been forced by an irresistible passion to rob his son of a treasure he knew could not but be extremely dear to him, since she was the most beautiful that ever had been seen; and had besides all the sweetness and innocence of youth and modesty, with a charm of wit surpassing all. He found that however she was forced to expose her lovely person to his withered arms, she could only sigh and weep there, and think of Oroonoko; and oftentimes could not forbear speaking of him, though her life were, by custom, forfeited by owning her passion. But she spoke not of a lover only, but of a prince dear to him to whom she spoke; and of the praises of a man, who, till now, filled the old man's soul with joy at every recital of his bravery, or even his name. And 'twas this dotage on our young hero that gave Imoinda a thousand privileges to speak of him without offending, and this

---

7. Reverential.

condescension in the old king that made her take the satisfaction of speaking of him so very often.

Besides, he many times inquired how the Prince bore himself; and those of whom he asked, being entirely slaves to the merits and virtues of the Prince, still answered what they thought conduced best to his service; which was, to make the old king fancy that the Prince had no more interest in Imoinda, and had resigned her willingly to the pleasure of the king; that he diverted himself with his mathematicians, his fortifications, his officers, and his hunting.

This pleased the old lover, who failed not to report these things again to Imoinda, that she might, by the example of her young lover, withdraw her heart and rest better contented in his arms. But however she was forced to receive this unwelcome news, in all appearance, with unconcern and content, her heart was bursting within, and she was only happy when she could get alone, to vent her griefs and moans with sighs and tears.

What reports of the Prince's conduct were made to the King, he thought good to justify as far as possibly he could by his actions; and when he appeared in the presence of the King, he showed a face not at all betraying his heart; so that in a little time the old man, being entirely convinced that he was no longer a lover of Imoinda, he carried him with him, in his train to the otan, often to banquet with his mistress. But as soon as he entered one day into the apartment of Imoinda with the King, at the first glance from her eyes, notwithstanding all his determined resolution, he was ready to sink in the place where he stood; and had certainly done so, but for the support of Aboan, a young man who was next to him; which, with his change of countenance, had betrayed him, had the King chanced to look that way. And I have observed, 'tis a very great error in those who laugh when one says a Negro can change color; for I have seen them as frequently blush, and look pale, and that as visibly as ever I saw in the most beautiful white. And 'tis certain that both these changes were evident, this day, in both these lovers. And Imoinda, who saw with some joy the change in the Prince's face, and found it in her own, strove to divert the King from beholding either, by a forced caress, with which she met him, which was a new wound in the heart of the poor dying Prince. But as soon as the King was busied in looking on some fine thing of Imoinda's making, she had time to tell the Prince with her angry but love-darting eyes, that she resented his coldness, and bemoaned her own miserable captivity. Nor were his eyes silent, but answered hers again, as much as eyes could do, instructed by the most tender and most passionate heart that ever loved. And they spoke so well, and so effectually, as Imoinda no longer doubted but she was the only delight, and the darling of that soul she found pleading in them its right of love, which none was more willing to resign than she. And 'twas this powerful language alone that in an instant conveyed all the thoughts of their souls to each other, that they both found there wanted but opportunity to make them both entirely happy. But when he saw another door opened by Onahal, a former old wife of the King's who now had charge of Imoinda, and saw the prospect of a bed of state made ready with sweets and flowers for the dalliance of the King, who immediately led the trembling victim from his sight into that prepared repose, what rage, what wild frenzies seized his heart! Which forcing to keep within bounds, and to suffer without noise, it became the more insupportable and rent his soul with ten thousand pains. He was forced to retire to vent his groans, where he fell down on a carpet, and lay struggling a long time, and only breathing now and then, "O Imoinda!" When Onahal had finished her necessary affair within, shutting the door, she came forth to wait till the King called; and hearing some one sighing in the other room, she passed on, and found the Prince in that deplorable condition which she thought needed her aid. She gave him cordials but all in vain, till finding the nature of his disease by his sighs, and naming Imoinda, she told him he had not so much cause as he imagined to afflict himself; for if he knew the King so well as she did, he would not lose a moment in jealousy, and that she was confident that Imoinda bore, at this minute, part in his affliction. Aboan was of the same opinion; and both together persuaded him to reassume his courage; and all sitting down on the carpet, the Prince said so many obliging things to Onahal, that he half persuaded her to be of his party. And she promised him she would thus far comply with his just desires, that she would let Imoinda know how faithful he was, what he suffered, and what he said.

This discourse lasted till the King called, which gave Oroonoko a certain satisfaction; and with the hope Onahal had made him conceive, he assumed a look as gay as 'twas possible a man in his circumstances could do; and presently after, he was called in with the rest who waited without. The King commanded music to be brought, and several of his young wives and mistresses came all together by his command, to dance before him, where Imoinda performed her part with an air and grace so passing all the rest as her beauty was above them, and received the present ordained as a prize. The Prince was every moment more charmed with the new beauties and graces he beheld in this fair one; and while he gazed and she danced, Onahal was retired to a window with Aboan.

This Onahal, as I said, was one of the past mistresses of the old king; and 'twas these (now past their beauty) that were made guardians, or governants, to the new and the young ones; and whose business it was, to teach them all those wanton arts of love with which they prevailed and charmed heretofore in their turn; and who now treated the triumphing happy ones with all the severity, as to liberty and freedom, that was possible, in revenge of those honors they rob them of; envying them those satisfactions, those gallantries and presents, that were once made to themselves, while youth and beauty lasted, and which they now saw pass regardless by, and paid only to the bloomings. And certainly, nothing is more afflicting to a decayed beauty than to behold in itself declining charms that were once adored, and to find those caresses paid to new beauties to which once she laid a claim; to hear them whisper as she passes by, "That once was a delicate woman." These abandoned ladies therefore endeavor to revenge all the despites and decays of time on these flourishing happy ones. And 'twas this severity that gave Oroonoko a thousand fears he should never prevail with Onahal to see Imoinda. But, as I said, she was now retired to a window with Aboan.

This young man was not only one of the best quality, but a man extremely well made and beautiful; and coming often to attend the King to the otan, he had subdued the heart of the antiquated Onahal, which had not forgot how pleasant it was to be in love. And though she had some decays in her face, she had none in her sense and wit; she was there agreeable still, even to Aboan's youth, so that he took pleasure in entertaining her with discourses of love. He knew also, that to make his court to these she-favorites was the way to be great; these being the persons that do all affairs and business at court. He had also observed that she had given him glances more tender and inviting than she had done to others of his quality. And now, when he saw that her favor could so absolutely oblige the Prince, he failed not to sigh in her ear, and to look with eyes all soft upon her, and give her hope that she had made some impressions on his heart. He found her pleased at this, and making a thousand advances to him; but the ceremony ending, and the King departing, broke up the company for that day, and his conversation.

Aboan failed not that night to tell the Prince of his success, and how advantageous the service of Onahal might be to his amour with Imoinda. The Prince was overjoyed with this good news, and besought him, if it were possible, to caress her, so as to engage her entirely; which he could not fail to do, if he complied with her desires. "For then," said the Prince, "her life lying at your mercy, she must grant you the request you make in my behalf." Aboan understood him, and assured him he would make love so effectually, that he would defy the most expert mistress of the art to find out whether he dissembled it or had it really. And 'twas with impatience they waited the next opportunity of going to the otan.

The wars came on, the time of taking the field approached, and 'twas impossible for the Prince to delay his going at the head of his army to encounter the enemy; so that every day seemed a tedious year, till he saw his Imoinda, for he believed he could not live if he were forced away without being so happy. 'Twas with impatience therefore that he expected the next visit the King would make; and, according to his wish, it was not long.

The parley of the eyes of these two lovers had not passed so secretly, but an old jealous lover could spy it; or rather, he wanted not flatterers who told him they observed it. So that the Prince was hastened to the camp, and this was the last visit he found he should make to the otan; he therefore urged Aboan to make the best of this last effort, and to explain himself so to Onahal, that she, deferring her enjoyment of her young lover no longer, might make way for the Prince to speak to Imoinda.

The whole affair being agreed on between the Prince and Aboan, they attended the King, as the custom was, to the otan; where, while the whole company was taken up in beholding the dancing and antic[8] postures the women royal made to divert the King, Onahal singled out Aboan, whom she found most pliable to her wish. When she had him where she believed she could not be heard, she sighed to him, and softly cried, "Ah, Aboan! When will you be sensible of my passion? I confess it with my mouth, because I would not give my eyes the lie; and you have but too much already perceived they have confessed my flame. Nor would I have you believe that because I am the abandoned mistress of a king I esteem myself altogether divested of charms. No, Aboan; I have still a rest of beauty enough engaging, and have learned to please too well, not to be desirable. I can have lovers still, but will have none but Aboan." "Madam," replied the half-feigning youth, "you have already, by my eyes, found you can still conquer; and I believe 'tis in pity of me, you condescend to this kind confession. But, Madam, words are used to be so small a part of our country courtship, that 'tis rare one can get so happy an opportunity as to tell one's heart; and those few minutes we have are forced to be snatched for more certain proofs of love than speaking and sighing; and such I languish for."

He spoke this with such a tone that she hoped it true, and could not forbear believing it; and being wholly transported with joy, for having subdued the finest of all the King's subjects to her desires, she took from her ears two large pearls and commanded him to wear them in his. He would have refused them, crying, "Madam, these are not the proofs of your love that I expect; 'tis opportunity, 'tis a lone hour

8. Fantastic or grotesque.

only, that can make me happy." But forcing the pearls into his hand, she whispered softly to him, "Oh! Do not fear a woman's invention when love sets her a-thinking." And pressing his hand she cried, "This night you shall be happy. Come to the gate of the orange groves, behind the otan, and I will be ready, about midnight, to receive you." 'Twas thus agreed, and she left him, that no notice might be taken of their speaking together.

The ladies were still dancing, and the King, laid on a carpet, with a great deal of pleasure was beholding them, especially Imoinda, who that day appeared more lovely than ever, being enlivened with the good tidings Onahal had brought her of the constant passion the Prince had for her. The Prince was laid on another carpet at the other end of the room, with his eyes fixed on the object of his soul; and as she turned or moved so did they; and she alone gave his eyes and soul their motions. Nor did Imoinda employ her eyes to any other use than in beholding with infinite pleasure the joy she produced in those of the Prince. But while she was more regarding him than the steps she took, she chanced to fall, and so near him as that leaping with extreme force from the carpet, he caught her in his arms as she fell; and 'twas visible to the whole presence, the joy wherewith he received her. He clasped her close to his bosom, and quite forgot that reverence that was due to the mistress of a king, and that punishment that is the reward of a boldness of this nature; and had not the presence of mind of Imoinda (fonder of his safety than her own) befriended him in making her spring from his arms and fall into her dance again, he had at that instant met his death; for the old king, jealous to the last degree, rose up in rage, broke all the diversion, and led Imoinda to her apartment, and sent out word to the Prince to go immediately to the camp; and that if he were found another night in court, he should suffer the death ordained for disobedient offenders.

You may imagine how welcome this news was to Oroonoko, whose unseasonable transport and caress of Imoinda was blamed by all men that loved him; and now he perceived his fault, yet cried that for such another moment, he would be content to die.

All the otan was in disorder about this accident; and Onahal was particularly concerned, because on the Prince's stay depended her happiness, for she could no longer expect that of Aboan. So that e'er they departed, they contrived it so that the Prince and he should come both that night to the grove of the otan, which was all of oranges and citrons, and that there they should wait her orders.

They parted thus, with grief enough, till night, leaving the King in possession of the lovely maid. But nothing could appease the jealousy of the old lover. He would not be imposed on, but would have it that Imoinda made a false step on purpose to fall into Oroonoko's bosom, and that all things looked like a design on both sides, and 'twas in vain she protested her innocence. He was old and obstinate, and left her more than half assured that his fear was true.

The King going to his apartment, sent to know where the Prince was, and if he intended to obey his command. The messenger returned and told him he found the Prince pensive, and altogether unpreparing for the campaign; that he lay negligently on the ground, and answered very little. This confirmed the jealousy of the King, and he commanded that they should very narrowly and privately watch his motions; and that he should not stir from his apartment, but one spy or other should be employed to watch him. So that the hour approaching, wherein he was to go to the citron grove, and taking only Aboan along with him, he leaves his apartment, and was watched to the very gate of the otan, where he was seen to enter, and where they left him, to carry back the tidings to the King.

Oroonoko and Aboan were no sooner entered but Onahal led the Prince to the apartment of Imoinda, who, not knowing anything of her happiness, was laid in bed. But Onahal only left him in her chamber to make the best of his opportunity, and took her dear Aboan to her own, where he showed the height of complaisance[9] for his prince, when, to give him an opportunity, he suffered himself to be caressed in bed by Onahal.

The Prince softly wakened Imoinda, who was not a little surprised with joy to find him there, and yet she trembled with a thousand fears. I believe he omitted saying nothing to this young maid that might persuade her to suffer him to seize his own and take the rights of love; and I believe she was not long resisting those arms where she so longed to be; and having opportunity, night and silence, youth, love and desire, he soon prevailed, and ravished in a moment what his old grandfather had been endeavoring for so many months.

'Tis not to be imagined the satisfaction of these two young lovers; nor the vows she made him, that she remained a spotless maid till that night; and that what she did with his grandfather had robbed him of no part of her virgin honor, the gods in mercy and justice having reserved that for her plighted lord, to whom of right it belonged. And 'tis impossible to express the transports he suffered while he listened to a discourse so charming from her loved lips, and clasped that body in his arms for whom he had so long languished; and nothing now afflicted him but his sudden departure from her; for he told her the necessity and his commands; but should depart satisfied in this, that since the old king had hitherto not been able to deprive him of those enjoyments which only belonged to him, he believed for the future he would be less able to injure him. So that abating the scandal of the veil, which was no otherwise so than that she was wife to another, he believed her safe even in the arms of the King, and innocent; yet would he have ventured at the conquest of the world, and have given it all, to have had her avoided that honor of receiving the royal veil. 'Twas thus, between a thousand caresses, that both bemoaned the hard fate of youth and beauty, so liable to that cruel promotion; 'twas a glory that could well have been spared here, though desired and aimed at by all the young females of that kingdom.

But while they were thus fondly employed, forgetting how time ran on and that the dawn must conduct him far away from his only happiness, they heard a great noise in the otan, and unusual voices of men; at which the Prince, starting from the arms of the frighted Imoinda, ran to a little battle-ax he used to wear by his side; and having not so much leisure as to put on his habit, he opposed himself against some who were already opening the door; which they did with so much violence that Oroonoko was not able to defend it, but was forced to cry out with a commanding voice, "Whoever ye are that have the boldness to attempt to approach this apartment thus rudely, know that I, the Prince Oroonoko, will revenge it with the certain death of him that first enters. Therefore stand back, and know this place is sacred to love and me this night; tomorrow 'tis the King's."

This he spoke with a voice so resolved and assured that they soon retired from the door, but cried, "'Tis by the King's command we are come; and being satisfied by thy voice, O Prince, as much as if we had entered, we can report to the King the truth of all his fears, and leave thee to provide for thy own safety, as thou art advised by thy friends."

---

9. Desire to please.

At these words they departed, and left the Prince to take a short and sad leave of his Imoinda; who trusting in the strength of her charms, believed she should appease the fury of a jealous king by saying she was surprised, and that it was by force of arms he got into her apartment. All her concern now was for his life, and therefore she hastened him to the camp, and with much ado prevailed on him to go. Nor was it she alone that prevailed; Aboan and Onahal both pleaded, and both assured him of a lie that should be well enough contrived to secure Imoinda. So that at last, with a heart sad as death, dying eyes, and sighing soul, Oroonoko departed, and took his way to the camp.

It was not long after the King in person came to the otan, where beholding Imoinda with rage in his eyes, he upbraided her wickedness and perfidy, and threatening her royal lover, she fell on her face at his feet, bedewing the floor with her tears and imploring his pardon for a fault which she had not with her will committed, as Onahal, who was also prostrate with her, could testify that, unknown to her, he had broke into her apartment, and ravished her. She spoke this much against her conscience; but to save her own life, 'twas absolutely necessary she should feign this falsity. She knew it could not injure the Prince, he being fled to an army that would stand by him against any injuries that should assault him. However, this last thought of Imoinda's being ravished changed the measures of his revenge, and whereas before he designed to be himself her executioner, he now resolved she should not die. But as it is the greatest crime in nature amongst them to touch a woman after having been possessed by a son, a father, or a brother, so now he looked on Imoinda as a polluted thing, wholly unfit for his embrace; nor would he resign her to his grandson, because she had received the royal veil. He therefore removes her from the otan, with Onahal, whom he put into safe hands, with order they should be both sold off as slaves to another country, either Christian or heathen; 'twas no matter where.

This cruel sentence, worse than death, they implored might be reversed; but their prayers were vain, and it was put in execution accordingly, and that with so much secrecy that none, either without or within the otan, knew anything of their absence or their destiny.

The old king, nevertheless, executed this with a great deal of reluctance; but he believed he had made a very great conquest over himself when he had once resolved, and had performed what he resolved. He believed now that his love had been unjust, and that he could not expect the gods, or Captain of the Clouds (as they call the unknown power) should suffer a better consequence from so ill a cause. He now begins to hold Oroonoko excused and to say he had reason for what he did; and now everybody could assure the King, how passionately Imoinda was beloved by the Prince; even those confessed it now who said the contrary before his flame was abated. So that the King being old and not able to defend himself in war, and having no sons of all his race remaining alive but only this to maintain him on the throne; and looking on this as a man disobliged, first by the rape of his mistress, or rather, wife, and now by depriving him wholly of her, he feared, might make him desperate, and do some cruel thing, either to himself, or his old grandfather the offender; he began to repent him extremely of the contempt he had, in his rage, put on Imoinda. Besides, he considered he ought in honor to have killed her for this offense, if it had been one. He ought to have had so much value and consideration for a maid of her quality, as to have nobly put her to death, and not to have sold her like a common slave, the greatest revenge, and the most disgraceful of any, and to which they a thousand times prefer death, and implore it as Imoinda did, but could not obtain that honor. Seeing therefore it was certain that Oroonoko would highly resent this affront, he thought good to make some excuse for his rashness to him, and to that end he sent a messenger to the camp with orders to treat with him about the matter, to gain his pardon, and to endeavor to mitigate his grief; but that by no means he should tell him she was sold, but secretly put to death; for he knew he should never obtain his pardon for the other.

When the messenger came, he found the Prince upon the point of engaging with the enemy, but as soon as he heard of the arrival of the messenger he commanded him to his tent, where he embraced him and received him with joy; which was soon abated, by the downcast looks of the messenger, who was instantly demanded the cause by Oroonoko, who, impatient of delay, asked a thousand questions in a breath, and all concerning Imoinda. But there needed little return, for he could almost answer himself of all he demanded from his sighs and eyes. At last, the messenger casting himself at the Prince's feet and kissing them with all the submission of a man that had something to implore which he dreaded to utter, he besought him to hear with calmness what he had to deliver to him, and to call up all his noble and heroic courage to encounter with his words, and defend himself against the ungrateful things he must relate. Oroonoko replied, with a deep sigh and a languishing voice, "I am armed against their worst efforts—for I know they will tell me, Imoinda is no more—and after that, you may spare the rest." Then, commanding him to rise, he laid himself on a carpet under a rich pavilion, and remained a good while silent, and was hardly heard to sigh. When he was come a little to himself, the messenger asked him leave to deliver that part of his embassy which the Prince had not yet divined, and the Prince cried, "I permit thee." Then he told him the affliction the old king was in for the rashness he had committed in his cruelty to Imoinda, and how he deigned to ask pardon for his offense, and to implore the Prince would not suffer that loss to touch his heart too sensibly which now all the gods could not restore him, but might recompense him in glory which he begged he would pursue; and that death, that common revenger of all injuries, would soon even the account between him and a feeble old man.

Oroonoko bade him return his duty to his lord and master, and to assure him there was no account of revenge to be adjusted between them; if there were, 'twas he was the aggressor, and that death would be just, and, maugre[1] his age, would see him righted; and he was contented to leave his share of glory to youths more fortunate, and worthy of that favor from the gods. That henceforth he would never lift a weapon, or draw a bow, but abandon the small remains of his life to sighs and tears, and the continual thoughts of what his lord and grandfather had thought good to send out of the world, with all that youth, that innocence, and beauty.

After having spoken this, whatever his greatest officers and men of the best rank could do, they could not raise him from the carpet, or persuade him to action and resolutions of life, but commanding all to retire, he shut himself into his pavilion all that day, while the enemy was ready to engage; and wondering at the delay, the whole body of the chief of the army then addressed themselves to him, and to whom they had much ado to get admittance. They fell on their faces at the foot of his carpet, where they lay, and besought him with earnest prayers and tears to lead them forth to battle, and not let the enemy take advantages of them; and implored him to have regard to his glory, and to the world that depended on his courage and

---

1. In spite of; i.e., despite Oroonoko's youth, death will avenge the king by taking Oroonoko first.

conduct. But he made no other reply to all their supplications but this, that he had now no more business for glory; and for the world, it was a trifle not worth his care. "Go," continued he, sighing, "and divide it amongst you; and reap with joy what you so vainly prize, and leave me to my more welcome destiny."

They then demanded what they should do, and whom he would constitute in his room, that the confusion of ambitious youth and power might not ruin their order, and make them a prey to the enemy. He replied, he would not give himself the trouble; but wished them to choose the bravest man amongst them, let his quality or birth be what it would. "For, O my friends!" said he, "it is not titles make men brave, or good; or birth that bestows courage and generosity, or makes the owner happy. Believe this, when you behold Oroonoko, the most wretched, and abandoned by fortune of all the creation of the gods." So turning himself about, he would make no more reply to all they could urge or implore.

The army beholding their officers return unsuccessful, with sad faces and ominous looks that presaged no good luck, suffered a thousand fears to take possession of their hearts, and the enemy to come even upon them, before they would provide for their safety by any defense; and though they were assured by some, who had a mind to animate them, that they should be immediately headed by the Prince, and that in the meantime Aboan had orders to command as general, yet they were so dismayed for want of that great example of bravery that they could make but a very feeble resistance, and at last downright fled before the enemy, who pursued them to the very tents, killing them. Nor could all Aboan's courage, which that day gained him immortal glory, shame them into a manly defense of themselves. The guards that were left behind about the Prince's tent, seeing the soldiers flee before the enemy and scatter themselves all over the plain in great disorder, made such outcries as roused the Prince from his amorous slumber, in which he had remained buried for two days without permitting any sustenance to approach him. But in spite of all his resolutions, he had not the constancy of grief to that degree as to make him insensible of the danger of his army; and in that instant he leapt from his couch and cried, "Come, if we must die, let us meet death the noblest way; and 'twill be more like Oroonoko to encounter him at an army's head, opposing the torrent of a conquering foe, than lazily, on a couch, to wait his lingering pleasure, and die every moment by a thousand wrecking thoughts; or be tamely taken by an enemy and led a whining, love-sick slave, to adorn the triumphs of Jamoan, that young victor, who already is entered beyond the limits I had prescribed him."

While he was speaking, he suffered his people to dress him for the field; and sallying out of his pavilion, with more life and vigor in his countenance than ever he showed, he appeared like some divine power descended to save his country from destruction; and his people had purposely put him on all things that might make him shine with most splendor, to strike a reverend awe into the beholders. He flew into the thickest of those that were pursuing his men, and being animated with despair, he fought as if he came on purpose to die, and did such things as will not be believed that human strength could perform, and such as soon inspired all the rest with new courage and new order. And now it was that they began to fight indeed, and so, as if they would not be outdone even by their adored hero, who turning the tide of the victory, changing absolutely the fate of the day, gained an entire conquest; and Oroonoko having the good fortune to single out Jamoan, he took him prisoner with his own hand, having wounded him almost to death.

This Jamoan afterwards became very dear to him, being a man very gallant and of excellent graces and fine parts, so that he never put him amongst the rank of captives, as they used to do, without distinction, for the common sale or market, but kept him in his own court, where he retained nothing of the prisoner but the name, and returned no more into his own country, so great an affection he took for Oroonoko; and by a thousand tales and adventures of love and gallantry, flattered his disease of melancholy and languishment, which I have often heard him say had certainly killed him, but for the conversation of this prince and Aboan, [and] the French governor he had from his childhood, of whom I have spoken before, and who was a man of admirable wit, great ingenuity and learning, all which he had infused into his young pupil. This Frenchman was banished out of his own country for some heretical notions he held; and though he was a man of very little religion, he had admirable morals, and a brave soul.

After the total defeat of Jamoan's army, which all fled, or were left dead upon the place, they spent some time in the camp, Oroonoko choosing rather to remain a while there in his tents, than enter into a palace, or live in a court where he had so lately suffered so great a loss. The officers therefore, who saw and knew his cause of discontent, invented all sorts of diversions and sports to entertain their prince: so that what with those amusements abroad and others at home, that is, within their tents, with the persuasions, arguments, and care of his friends and servants that he more peculiarly prized, he wore off in time a great part of that chagrin and torture of despair which the first effects of Imoinda's death had given him; insomuch as having received a thousand kind embassies from the King, and invitations to return to court, he obeyed, though with no little reluctance; and when he did so, there was a visible change in him, and for a long time he was much more melancholy than before. But time lessens all extremes, and reduces them to mediums and unconcern; but no motives or beauties, though all endeavored it, could engage him in any sort of amour, though he had all the invitations to it, both from his own youth and others' ambitions and designs.

Oroonoko was no sooner returned from this last conquest, and received at court with all the joy and magnificence that could be expressed to a young victor, who was not only returned triumphant but beloved like a deity, when there arrived in the port an English ship.

This person had often before been in these countries, and was very well known to Oroonoko, with whom he had trafficked for slaves, and had used to do the same with his predecessors.

This commander was a man of a finer sort of address and conversation, better bred and more engaging than most of that sort of men are; so that he seemed rather never to have been bred out of a court than almost all his life at sea. This captain therefore was always better received at court than most of the traders to those countries were; and especially by Oroonoko, who was more civilized, according to the European mode, than any other had been, and took more delight in the white nations, and, above all, men of parts and wit. To this captain he sold abundance of his slaves, and for the favor and esteem he had for him made him many presents, and obliged him to stay at court as long as possibly he could. Which the captain seemed to take as a very great honor done him, entertaining the Prince every day with globes and maps, and mathematical discourses and instruments; eating, drinking, hunting, and living with him with so much familiarity that it was not to be doubted but he had gained very greatly upon the heart of this gallant young man. And the captain, in return of all these mighty favors, besought the Prince to honor his vessel with his presence, some day or other, to dinner, before he should set sail; which he condescended to accept, and appointed his day. The captain, on his part, failed not to have all things in a readiness, in the most magnificent order he could possibly. And the day being come, the captain, in his boat richly adorned with carpets and velvet cushions, rowed to the shore to receive the Prince; with another longboat, where was placed all his music and trumpets, with which Oroonoko was extremely delighted, who met him on the shore, attended by his French governor, Jamoan, Aboan, and about an hundred of the noblest of the youths of the court. And after they had first carried the Prince on board, the boats fetched the rest off; where they found a very splendid treat, with all sorts of fine wines, and were as well entertained as 'twas possible in such a place to be.

The Prince having drunk hard of punch, and several sorts of wine, as did all the rest (for great care was taken they should want nothing of that part of the entertainment) was very merry, and in great admiration of the ship, for he had never been in one before; so that he was curious of beholding every place where he decently might descend. The rest, no less curious, who were not quite overcome with drinking, rambled at their pleasure fore and aft, as their fancies guided them: so that the captain, who had well laid his design before, gave the word and seized on all his guests; they clapping great irons suddenly on the Prince when he was leaped down in the hold to view that part of the vessel, and locking him fast down, secured him. The same treachery was used to all the rest; and all in one instant, in several places of the ship, were lashed fast in irons and betrayed to slavery. That great design over, they set all hands to work to hoist sail; and with as treacherous and fair a wind they made from the shore with this innocent and glorious prize, who thought of nothing less than such an entertainment.

Some have commended this act, as brave in the captain; but I will spare my sense of it, and leave it to my reader to judge as he pleases.

It may be easily guessed in what manner the Prince resented this indignity, who may be best resembled to a lion taken in a toil; so he raged, so he struggled for liberty, but all in vain; and they had so wisely managed his fetters that he could not use a hand in his defense, to quit himself of a life that would by no means endure slavery; nor could he move from the place where he was tied to any solid part of the ship against which he might have beat his head, and have finished his disgrace that way; so that being deprived of all other means, he resolved to perish for want of food. And pleased at last with that thought, and toiled and tired by rage and indignation, he laid himself down, and sullenly resolved upon dying, and refused all things that were brought him.

This did not a little vex the captain, and the more so because he found almost all of them of the same humor; so that the loss of so many brave slaves, so tall and goodly to behold, would have been very considerable. He therefore ordered one to go from him (for he would not be seen himself) to Oroonoko, and to assure him he was afflicted for having rashly done so inhospitable a deed, and which could not be now remedied, since they were far from shore; but since he resented it in so high a nature, he assured him he would revoke his resolution, and set both him and his friends ashore on the next land they should touch at; and of this the messenger gave him his oath, provided he would resolve to live. And Oroonoko, whose honor was such as he never had violated a word in his life himself, much less a solemn asseveration, believed in an instant what this man said, but replied he expected for a confirmation of this to have his shameful fetters dismissed. This demand was carried to the captain, who returned him answer that the offense had been so great which he had put upon the Prince, that he durst not trust him with liberty while he remained in the ship, for fear lest by a valor natural to him, and a revenge that would animate that valor, he might commit some outrage fatal to himself and the King his master, to whom his vessel did belong. To this Oroonoko replied, he would engage his honor to behave himself in all friendly order and manner, and obey the command of the captain, as he was lord of the King's vessel, and general of those men under his command.

This was delivered to the still doubting captain, who could not resolve to trust a heathen he said, upon his parole,[2] a man that had no sense or notion of the God that he worshipped. Oroonoko then replied he was very sorry to hear that the captain pretended to the knowledge and worship of any gods who had taught him no better principles, than not to credit as he would be credited; but they told him the difference of their faith occasioned that distrust: for the captain had protested to him upon the word of a Christian, and sworn in the name of a great God, which if he should violate, he would expect eternal torment in the world to come. "Is that all the obligation he has to be just to his oath?" replied Oroonoko. "Let him know I swear by my honor, which to violate, would not only render me contemptible and despised by all brave and honest men, and so give myself perpetual pain, but it would be eternally offending and diseasing all mankind, harming, betraying, circumventing, and outraging all men; but punishments hereafter are suffered by oneself; and the world takes no cognizances whether this god have revenged them, or not, 'tis done so secretly, and deferred so long; while the man of no honor suffers every moment the scorn and contempt of the honester world, and dies every day ignominiously in his fame, which is more valuable than life. I speak not this to move belief, but to show you how you mistake, when you imagine that he who will violate his honor will keep his word with his gods." So turning from him with a disdainful smile, he refused to answer him when he urged him to know what answer he should carry back to his captain; so that he departed without saying any more.

The captain pondering and consulting what to do, it was concluded that nothing but Oroonoko's liberty would encourage any of the rest to eat, except the Frenchman, whom the captain could not pretend to keep prisoner, but only told him he was secured because he might act something in favor of the Prince, but that he should be freed as soon as they came to land. So that they concluded it wholly necessary to free the Prince from his irons that he might show himself to the rest, that they might have an eye upon him, and that they could not fear a single man.

This being resolved, to make the obligation the greater, the captain himself went to Oroonoko; where, after many compliments, and assurances of what he had already promised, he receiving from the Prince his parole, and his hand, for his good behavior, dismissed his irons, and brought him to his own cabin; where, after having treated and reposed him a while, for he had neither eaten nor slept in four days before, he besought him to visit those obstinate people in chains, who refused all manner of sustenance; and entreated him to oblige them to eat, and assure them of their liberty the first opportunity.

2. Word of honor.

Oroonoko, who was too generous not to give credit to his words, showed himself to his people, who were transported with excess of joy at the sight of their darling prince, falling at his feet, and kissing and embracing them, believing, as some divine oracle, all he assured them. But he besought them to bear their chains with that bravery that became those whom he had seen act so nobly in arms; and that they could not give him greater proofs of their love and friendship, since 'twas all the security the captain (his friend) could have against the revenge, he said, they might possibly justly take, for the injuries sustained by him. And they all, with one accord, assured him they could not suffer enough when it was for his repose and safety.

After this they no longer refused to eat, but took what was brought them and were pleased with their captivity, since by it they hoped to redeem the Prince, who, all the rest of the voyage, was treated with all the respect due to his birth, though nothing could divert his melancholy; and he would often sigh for Imoinda, and think this a punishment due to his misfortune, in having left that noble maid behind him that fatal night in the otan, when he fled to the camp.

Possessed with a thousand thoughts of past joys with this fair young person, and a thousand griefs for her eternal loss, he endured a tedious voyage, and at last arrived at the mouth of the river of Surinam, a colony belonging to the King of England, and where they were to deliver some part of their slaves. There the merchants and gentlemen of the country going on board to demand those lots of slaves they had already agreed on, and amongst those the overseers of those plantations where I then chanced to be, the captain, who had given the word, ordered his men to bring up those noble slaves in fetters, whom I have spoken of; and having put them, some in one, and some in other lots, with women and children (which they call pickaninnies), they sold them off as slaves to several merchants and gentlemen; not putting any two in one lot, because they would separate them far from each other; not daring to trust them together, lest rage and courage should put them upon contriving some great action, to the ruin of the colony.

Oroonoko was first seized on and sold to our overseer, who had the first lot, with seventeen more of all sorts and sizes, but not one of quality with him. When he saw this, he found what they meant; for, as I said, he understood English pretty well; and being wholly unarmed and defenseless, so as it was in vain to make any resistance, he only beheld the captain with a look all fierce and disdainful; upbraiding him with eyes that forced blushes on his guilty cheeks, he only cried in passing over the side of the ship, "Farewell, Sir! 'Tis worth my suffering to gain so true a knowledge both of you and of your gods by whom you swear." And desiring those that held him to forbear their pains, and telling them he would make no resistance, he cried, "Come, my fellow slaves, let us descend, and see if we can meet with more honor and honesty in the next world we shall touch upon." So he nimbly leapt into the boat, and showing no more concern, suffered himself to be rowed up the river with his seventeen companions.

The gentleman that bought him was a young Cornish gentleman, whose name was Trefry, a man of great wit and fine learning, and was carried into those parts by the Lord——, Governor, to manage all his affairs.[3] He reflecting on the last words of

---

3. John Treffry (?–1674) supervised the plantation at Parham for Francis, Lord Willoughby (1613?–1686), a nobleman long involved with colonization, who received from Charles II both the governorship and a grant of land in Surinam; his appointment of Behn's father to the post of lieutenant-governor appears to account for her sojourn in the colony (though her father died en route).

Oroonoko to the captain, and beholding the richness of his vest,[4] no sooner came into the boat, but he fixed his eyes on him; and finding something so extraordinary in his face, his shape and mien, a greatness of look, and haughtiness in his air, and finding he spoke English, had a great mind to be inquiring into his quality and fortune; which, though Oroonoko endeavored to hide by only confessing he was above the rank of common slaves, Trefry soon found he was yet something greater than he confessed; and from that moment began to conceive so vast an esteem for him, that he ever after loved him as his dearest brother, and showed him all the civilities due to so great a man.

Trefry was a very good mathematician and a linguist, could speak French and Spanish, and in the three days they remained in the boat (for so long were they going from the ship to the plantation) he entertained Oroonoko so agreeably with his art and discourse, that he was no less pleased with Trefry, than he was with the Prince; and he thought himself, at least, fortunate in this, that since he was a slave, as long as he would suffer himself to remain so, he had a man of so excellent wit and parts for a master. So that before they had finished their voyage up the river, he made no scruple of declaring to Trefry all his fortunes and most part of what I have here related, and put himself wholly into the hands of his new friend, whom he found resenting all the injuries were done him, and was charmed with all the greatnesses of his actions, which were recited with that modesty and delicate sense, as wholly vanquished him, and subdued him to his interest. And he promised him on his word and honor, he would find the means to reconduct him to his own country again; assuring him, he had a perfect abhorrence of so dishonorable an action; and that he would sooner have died, than have been the author of such a perfidy. He found the Prince was very much concerned to know what became of his friends, and how they took their slavery; and Trefry promised to take care about the inquiring after their condition, and that he should have an account of them.

Though, as Oroonoko afterwards said, he had little reason to credit the words of a backeararary,[5] yet he knew not why, but he saw a kind of sincerity and awful truth in the face of Trefry; he saw an honesty in his eyes, and he found him wise and witty enough to understand honor; for it was one of his maxims, "A man of wit could not be a knave or villain."

In their passage up the river they put in at several houses for refreshment, and ever when they landed numbers of people would flock to behold this man; not but their eyes were daily entertained with the sight of slaves, but the fame of Oroonoko was gone before him, and all people were in admiration of his beauty. Besides, he had a rich habit on, in which he was taken, so different from the rest, and which the captain could not strip him of because he was forced to surprise his person in the minute he sold him. When he found his habit made him liable, as he thought, to be gazed at the more, he begged Trefry to give him something more befitting a slave; which he did, and took off his robes. Nevertheless, he shone through all and his osenbrigs (a sort of brown holland suit he had on)[6] could not conceal the graces of his looks and mien; and he had no less admirers than when he had his dazzling habit on. The royal youth appeared in spite of the slave, and people could not help treating him after a different manner without designing it; as soon as they approached him they venerated and esteemed him; his eyes insensibly commanded respect, and his

4. Robe.
5. An African-derived term for "white master."

6. Osnaburg and holland were thick cotton or linen fabrics.

behavior insinuated it into every soul. So that there was nothing talked of but this young and gallant slave, even by those who yet knew not that he was a prince.

I ought to tell you, that the Christians never buy any slaves but they give them some name of their own, their native ones being likely very barbarous, and hard to pronounce; so that Mr. Trefry gave Oroonoko that of Caesar, which name will live in that country as long as that (scarce more) glorious one of the great Roman, for 'tis most evident, he wanted no part of the personal courage of that Caesar, and acted things as memorable, had they been done in some part of the world replenished with people and historians that might have given him his due. But his misfortune was to fall in an obscure world, that afforded only a female pen to celebrate his fame, though I doubt not but it had lived from others' endeavors, if the Dutch, who immediately after his time took that country,[7] had not killed, banished, and dispersed all those that were capable of giving the world this great man's life, much better than I have done. And Mr. Trefry, who designed it, died before he began it, and bemoaned himself for not having undertook it in time.

For the future therefore, I must call Oroonoko Caesar, since by that name only he was known in our western world, and by that name he was received on shore at Parham House, where he was destined a slave. But if the King himself (God bless him) had come ashore, there could not have been greater expectations by all the whole plantation, and those neighboring ones, than was on ours at that time; and he was received more like a governor than a slave. Notwithstanding, as the custom was, they assigned him his portion of land, his house, and his business, up in the plantation. But as it was more for form than any design to put him to his task, he endured no more of the slave but the name, and remained some days in the house, receiving all visits that were made him, without stirring towards that part of the plantation where the Negroes were.

At last, he would needs go view his land, his house, and the business assigned him. But he no sooner came to the houses of the slaves, which are like a little town by itself, the Negroes all having left work, but they all came forth to behold him, and found he was that prince who had, at several times, sold most of them to these parts; and, from a veneration they pay to great men, especially if they know them, and from the surprise and awe they had at the sight of him, they all cast themselves at his feet, crying out, in their language, "Live, O King! Long live, O King!" And kissing his feet, paid him even divine homage.

Several English gentlemen were with him; and what Mr. Trefry had told them was here confirmed, of which he himself before had no other witness than Caesar himself. But he was infinitely glad to find his grandeur confirmed by the adoration of all the slaves.

Caesar, troubled with their over-joy, and over-ceremony, besought them to rise, and to receive him as their fellow slave, assuring them, he was no better. At which they set up with one accord a most terrible and hideous mourning and condoling, which he and the English had much ado to appease. But at last they prevailed with them, and they prepared all their barbarous music, and everyone killed and dressed something of his own stock (for every family has their land apart, on which, at their leisure times, they breed all eatable things) and clubbing it together, made a most magnificent supper, inviting their grandee captain, their

---

7. In 1667 Surinam twice changed hands. The Dutch briefly captured the colony and the English won it back, but immediately ceded it to the Dutch (in exchange for New York) at the Treaty of Breda.

prince, to honor it with his presence, which he did, and several English with him, where they all waited on him, some playing, others dancing before him all the time, according to the manners of their several nations, and with unwearied industry endeavoring to please and delight him.

While they sat at meat Mr. Trefry told Caesar that most of these young slaves were undone in love, with a fine she-slave, whom they had had about six months on their land. The Prince, who never heard the name of love without a sigh, nor any mention of it without the curiosity of examining further into that tale which of all discourses was most agreeable to him, asked, how they came to be so unhappy, as to be all undone for one fair slave? Trefry, who was naturally amorous, and loved to talk of love as well as anybody, proceeded to tell him, they had the most charming black that ever was beheld on their plantation, about fifteen or sixteen years old, as he guessed; that, for his part, he had done nothing but sigh for her ever since she came; and that all the white beauties he had seen never charmed him so absolutely as this fine creature had done; and that no man of any nation ever beheld her, that did not fall in love with her; and that she had all the slaves perpetually at her feet; and the whole country resounded with the fame of Clemene, "for so," said he, "we have christened her. But she denies us all with such a noble disdain, that 'tis a miracle to see that she, who can give such eternal desires, should herself be all ice, and all unconcern. She is adorned with the most graceful modesty that ever beautified youth; the softest sigher—that, if she were capable of love, one would swear she languished for some absent happy man; and so retired, as if she feared a rape even from the God of Day,[8] or that the breezes would steal kisses from her delicate mouth. Her task of work some sighing lover every day makes it his petition to perform for her, which she accepts blushing, and with reluctance, for fear he will ask her a look for a recompense, which he dares not presume to hope, so great an awe she strikes into the hearts of her admirers." "I do not wonder," replied the Prince, "that Clemene should refuse slaves, being as you say so beautiful, but wonder how she escapes those who can entertain her as you can do. Or why, being your slave, you do not oblige her to yield." "I confess," said Trefry, "when I have, against her will, entertained her with love so long as to be transported with my passion even above decency, I have been ready to make use of those advantages of strength and force nature has given me. But oh! she disarms me, with that modesty and weeping so tender and so moving, that I retire, and thank my stars she overcame me." The company laughed at his civility to a slave, and Caesar only applauded the nobleness of his passion and nature, since that slave might be noble, or, what was better, have true notions of honor and virtue in her. Thus passed they this night, after having received from the slaves all imaginable respect and obedience.

The next day Trefry asked Caesar to walk, when the heat was allayed, and designedly carried him by the cottage of the fair slave, and told him, she whom he spoke of last night lived there retired. "But, " says he, "I would not wish you to approach, for I am sure you will be in love as soon as you behold her." Caesar assured him he was proof against all the charms of that sex, and that if he imagined his heart could be so perfidious to love again after Imoinda, he believed he should tear it from his bosom. They had no sooner spoke, but a little shock dog,[9] that Clemene had presented her, which she took great delight in, ran out, and she, not knowing anybody was there, ran to get it in again, and bolted out on those who were just speaking of

8. The sun.   9. A thick-haired dog.

her. When seeing them she would have run in again, but Trefry caught her by the hand and cried, "Clemene, however you fly a lover, you ought to pay some respect to this stranger" (pointing to Caesar). But she, as if she had resolved never to raise her eyes to the face of a man again, bent them the more to the earth when he spoke, and gave the Prince the leisure to look the more at her. There needed no long gazing or consideration to examine who this fair creature was. He soon saw Imoinda all over her; in a minute he saw her face, her shape, her air, her modesty, and all that called forth his soul with joy at his eyes, and left his body destitute of almost life. It stood without motion, and, for a minute, knew not that it had a being. And I believe he had never come to himself, so oppressed he was with overjoy, if he had not met with this allay,[1] that he perceived Imoinda fall dead in the hands of Trefry. This awakened him, and he ran to her aid, and caught her in his arms, where, by degrees, she came to herself; and 'tis needless to tell with what transports, what ecstasies of joy, they both a while beheld each other, without speaking, then snatched each other to their arms, then gaze again, as if they still doubted whether they possessed the blessing they grasped. But when they recovered their speech, 'tis not to be imagined what tender things they expressed to each other, wondering what strange fate had brought them again together. They soon informed each other of their fortunes, and equally bewailed their fate; but at the same time, they mutually protested that even fetters and slavery were soft and easy, and would be supported with joy and pleasure, while they could be so happy to possess each other, and to be able to make good their vows. Caesar swore he disdained the empire of the world while he could behold his Imoinda, and she despised grandeur and pomp, those vanities of her sex, when she could gaze on Oroonoko. He adored the very cottage where she resided, and said, that little inch of the world would give him more happiness than all the universe could do, and she vowed, it was a palace, while adorned with the presence of Oroonoko.

Trefry was infinitely pleased with this novel,[2] and found this Clemene was the fair mistress of whom Caesar had before spoke; and was not a little satisfied, that Heaven was so kind to the Prince as to sweeten his misfortunes by so lucky an accident, and leaving the lovers to themselves, was impatient to come down to Parham House (which was on the same plantation) to give me an account of what had happened. I was as impatient to make these lovers a visit, having already made a friendship with Caesar, and from his own mouth learned what I have related, which was confirmed by his Frenchman, who was set on shore to seek his fortunes, and of whom they could not make a slave because a Christian, and he came daily to Parham Hill to see and pay his respects to his pupil prince. So that concerning and interesting myself in all that related to Caesar, whom I had assured of liberty as soon as the governor arrived, I hasted presently to the place where the lovers were, and was infinitely glad to find this beautiful young slave (who had already gained all our esteems, for her modesty and her extraordinary prettiness) to be the same I had heard Caesar speak so much of. One may imagine then, we paid her a treble respect; and though from her being carved in fine flowers and birds all over her body, we took her to be of quality before, yet, when we knew Clemene was Imoinda, we could not enough admire her.

I had forgot to tell you, that those who are nobly born of that country are so delicately cut and raced[3] all over the fore part of the trunk of their bodies, that it

1. Reduction; release.   3. Carved.
2. New development.

looks as if it were japanned;[4] the works being raised like high point[5] round the edges of the flowers. Some are only carved with a little flower or bird at the sides of the temples, as was Caesar; and those who are so carved over the body resemble our ancient Picts,[6] that are figured in the chronicles, but these carvings are more delicate.

From that happy day Caesar took Clemene for his wife, to the general joy of all people, and there was as much magnificence as the country would afford at the celebration of this wedding. And in a very short time after she conceived with child; which made Caesar even adore her, knowing he was the last of his great race. This new accident made him more impatient of liberty, and he was every day treating with Trefry for his and Clemene's liberty; and offered either gold, or a vast quantity of slaves, which should be paid before they let him go, provided he could have any security that he should go when his ransom was paid. They fed him from day to day with promises, and delayed him, till the Lord Governor should come, so that he began to suspect them of falsehood, and that they would delay him till the time of his wife's delivery, and make a slave of that too, for all the breed is theirs to whom the parents belong. This thought made him very uneasy, and his sullenness gave them some jealousies[7] of him, so that I was obliged, by some persons who feared a mutiny (which is very fatal sometimes in those colonies that abound so with slaves that they exceed the whites in vast numbers), to discourse with Caesar, and to give him all the satisfaction I possibly could. They knew he and Clemene were scarce an hour in a day from my lodgings, that they ate with me, and that I obliged them in all things I was capable of: I entertained him with the lives of the Romans, and great men, which charmed him to my company, and her, with teaching her all the pretty works that I was mistress of, and telling her stories of nuns, and endeavoring to bring her to the knowledge of the true God. But of all discourses Caesar liked that the worst, and would never be reconciled to our notions of the Trinity, of which he ever made a jest; it was a riddle, he said, would turn his brain to conceive, and one could not make him understand what faith was. However, these conversations failed not altogether so well to divert him, that he liked the company of us women much above the men, for he could not drink, and he is but an ill companion in that country that cannot. So that obliging him to love us very well, we had all the liberty of speech with him, especially myself, whom he called his Great Mistress; and indeed my word would go a great way with him. For these reasons, I had opportunity to take notice to him, that he was not well pleased of late, as he used to be, was more retired and thoughtful, and told him, I took it ill he should suspect we would break our words with him, and not permit both him and Clemene to return to his own kingdom, which was not so long away, but when he was once on his voyage he would quickly arrive there. He made me some answers that showed a doubt in him, which made me ask him, what advantage it would be to doubt? It would but give us a fear of him, and possibly compel us to treat him so as I should be very loath to behold: that is, it might occasion his confinement. Perhaps this was not so luckily spoke of me, for I perceived he resented that word, which I strove to soften again in vain. However, he assured me, that whatsoever resolutions he should take, he would act nothing upon the white people. And as for myself, and those upon that plantation where he was, he would sooner forfeit his eternal liberty, and life itself, than lift his

---

4. Varnished with a glossy black lacquer.
5. Intricate lace.
6. Ancient inhabitants of northern Britain, possibly so

named by the Romans because of the "pictures" (tattoos and other ornaments) they bore on their skin.
7. Suspicions.

hand against his greatest enemy on that place. He besought me to suffer no fears upon his account, for he could do nothing that honor should not dictate, but he accused himself for having suffered slavery so long; yet he charged that weakness on love alone, who was capable of making him neglect even glory itself, and for which now he reproaches himself every moment of the day. Much more to this effect he spoke, with an air impatient enough to make me know he would not be long in bondage, and though he suffered only the name of a slave, and had nothing of the toil and labor of one, yet that was sufficient to render him uneasy, and he had been too long idle, who used to be always in action, and in arms. He had a spirit all rough and fierce, and that could not be tamed to lazy rest, and though all endeavors were used to exercise himself in such actions and sports as this world afforded, as running, wrestling, pitching the bar,[8] hunting and fishing, chasing and killing tigers of a monstrous size, which this continent affords in abundance; and wonderful snakes, such as Alexander[9] is reported to have encountered at the river of Amazons, and which Caesar took great delight to overcome; yet these were not actions great enough for his large soul, which was still panting after more renowned action.

Before I parted that day with him, I got, with much ado, a promise from him to rest yet a little longer with patience, and wait the coming of the Lord Governor, who was every day expected on our shore. He assured me he would, and this promise he desired me to know was given perfectly in complaisance to me, in whom he had an entire confidence.

After this, I neither thought it convenient to trust him much out of our view, nor did the country who feared him; but with one accord it was advised to treat him fairly, and oblige him to remain within such a compass, and that he should be permitted as seldom as could be to go up to the plantations of the Negroes; or if he did, to be accompanied by some that should be rather in appearance attendants than spies. This care was for some time taken, and Caesar looked upon it as a mark of extraordinary respect, and was glad his discontent had obliged them to be more observant to him. He received new assurance from the overseer, which was confirmed to him by the opinion of all the gentlemen of the country, who made their court to him. During this time that we had his company more frequently than hitherto we had had, it may not be unpleasant to relate to you the diversions we entertained him with, or rather he us.

My stay was to be short in that country, because my father died at sea, and never arrived to possess the honor was designed him (which was lieutenant-general of six and thirty islands, besides the continent[1] of Surinam), nor the advantages he hoped to reap by them, so that though we were obliged to continue on our voyage, we did not intend to stay upon the place. Though, in a word, I must say thus much of it, that certainly had his late Majesty,[2] of sacred memory, but seen and known what a vast and charming world he had been master of in that continent, he would never have parted so easily with it to the Dutch. 'Tis a continent whose vast extent was never yet known, and may contain more noble earth than all the universe besides; for they say it reaches from east to west, one way as far as China, and another to Peru. It affords all things both for beauty and use; 'tis there eternal spring, always the very months of April, May, and June. The shades are perpetual, the trees, bearing at once all degrees

8. Hurling a heavy rod for purposes of exercise or sport.
9. Legends surrounding Alexander the Great included his encounter with the mythical woman warriors called Amazons, and with the formidable snakes inhabiting their territories.
1. Mainland.
2. Charles II.

of leaves and fruit from blooming buds to ripe autumn, groves of oranges, lemons, citrons, figs, nutmegs, and noble aromatics, continually bearing their fragrancies. The trees appearing all like nosegays adorned with flowers of different kind; some are all white, some purple, some scarlet, some blue, some yellow; bearing, at the same time, ripe fruit and blooming young, or producing every day new. The very wood of all these trees have an intrinsic value above common timber, for they are, when cut, of different colors, glorious to behold, and bear a price considerable, to inlay withal. Besides this, they yield rich balm and gums, so that we make our candles of such an aromatic substance as does not only give a sufficient light but, as they burn, they cast their perfumes all about. Cedar is the common firing, and all the houses are built with it. The very meat we eat, when set on the table, if it be native, I mean of the country, perfumes the whole room, especially a little beast called an armadillo, a thing which I can liken to nothing so well as a rhinoceros. 'Tis all in white armor so jointed that it moves as well in it as if it had nothing on. This beast is about the bigness of a pig of six weeks old. But it were endless to give an account of all the diverse wonderful and strange things that country affords, and which we took a very great delight to go in search of, though those adventures are oftentimes fatal and at least dangerous. But while we had Caesar in our company on these designs we feared no harm, nor suffered any.

As soon as I came into the country, the best house in it was presented me, called St. John's Hill. It stood on a vast rock of white marble, at the foot of which the river ran a vast depth down, and not to be descended on that side. The little waves still dashing and washing the foot of this rock made the softest murmurs and purlings in the world, and the opposite bank was adorned with such vast quantities of different flowers eternally blowing,[3] and every day and hour new, fenced behind them with lofty trees of a thousand rare forms and colors, that the prospect was the most ravishing that sands can create. On the edge of this white rock, toward the river, was a walk or grove of orange and lemon trees, about half the length of the Mall[4] here, whose flowery and fruity branches meet at the top, and hindered the sun, whose rays are very fierce there, from entering a beam into the grove, and the cool air that came from the river made it not only fit to entertain people in at all the hottest hours of the day, but refreshed the sweet blossoms, and made it always sweet and charming, and sure the whole globe of the world cannot show so delightful a place as this grove was. Not all the gardens of boasted Italy can produce a shade to out-vie this, which Nature had joined with Art to render so exceeding fine. And 'tis a marvel to see how such vast trees, as big as English oaks, could take footing on so solid a rock, and in so little earth, as covered that rock, but all things by nature there are rare, delightful, and wonderful. But to our sports.

Sometimes we would go surprising,[5] and in search of young tigers in their dens, watching when the old ones went forth to forage for prey, and oftentimes we have been in great danger, and have fled apace for our lives, when surprised by the dams. But once, above all other times, we went on this design, and Caesar was with us, who had no sooner stolen a young tiger from her nest, but going off, we encountered the dam, bearing a buttock of a cow, which he[6] had torn off with his mighty paw, and going with it towards his den. We had only four women, Caesar, and an English

---

3. Blossoming.
4. A walk extending alongside London's St. James's Park.
5. I.e., surprise-attacking.
6. The "dam" is the cub's mother, but Behn has surprisingly

shifted the gender of the pronoun from "she" to "he"; she will do so again in reference to another tiger in the next paragraph.

gentleman, brother to Harry Martin, the great Oliverian.[7] We found there was no escaping this enraged and ravenous beast. However, we women fled as fast as we could from it, but our heels had not saved our lives if Caesar had not laid down his cub, when he found the tiger quit her prey to make the more speed towards him, and taking Mr. Martin's sword desired him to stand aside, or follow the ladies. He obeyed him, and Caesar met this monstrous beast of might, size, and vast limbs, who came with open jaws upon him, and fixing his awful stern eyes full upon those of the beast, and putting himself into a very steady and good aiming posture of defense, ran his sword quite through his breast down to his very heart, home to the hilt of the sword. The dying beast stretched forth her paw, and going to grasp his thigh, surprised with death in that very moment, did him no other harm than fixing her long nails in his flesh very deep, feebly wounded him, but could not grasp the flesh to tear off any. When he had done this, he hollowed to us to return, which, after some assurance of his victory, we did, and found him lugging out the sword from the bosom of the tiger, who was laid in her blood on the ground. He took up the cub, and with an unconcern, that had nothing of the joy or gladness of a victory, he came and laid the whelp at my feet. We all extremely wondered at his daring, and at the bigness of the beast, which was about the height of an heifer, but of mighty, great, and strong limbs.

Another time, being in the woods, he killed a tiger, which had long infested that part, and borne away abundance of sheep and oxen and other things, that were for the support of those to whom they belonged. Abundance of people assailed this beast, some affirming they had shot her with several bullets quite through the body, at several times, and some swearing they shot her through the very heart, and they believed she was a devil rather than a mortal thing. Caesar had often said he had a mind to encounter this monster, and spoke with several gentlemen who had attempted her, one crying, I shot her with so many poisoned arrows, another with his gun in this part of her, and another in that. So that he remarking all these places where she was shot, fancied still he should overcome her, by giving her another sort of a wound than any had yet done, and one day said (at the table), "What trophies and garlands, ladies, will you make me, if I bring you home the heart of this ravenous beast that eats up all your lambs and pigs?" We all promised he should be rewarded at all our hands. So taking a bow, which he chose out of a great many, he went up in the wood, with two gentlemen, where he imagined this devourer to be. They had not passed very far in it, but they heard her voice, growling and grumbling, as if she were pleased with something she was doing. When they came in view, they found her muzzling in the belly of a new ravished sheep which she had torn open, and seeing herself approached, she took fast hold of her prey with her forepaws, and set a very fierce raging look on Caesar, without offering to approach him, for fear, at the same time, of losing what she had in possession. So that Caesar remained a good while, only taking aim, and getting an opportunity to shoot her where he designed. 'Twas some time before he could accomplish it, and to wound her and not kill her would but have enraged her more, and endangered him. He had a quiver of arrows at his side, so that if one failed he could be supplied. At last, retiring a little, he gave her opportunity to eat, for he found she was ravenous, and fell to as soon as she saw him retire, being more eager of her prey than of doing new mischiefs. When he going softly to one side of her, and hiding his person behind certain herbage that grew high and thick, he took so good aim that, as he intended, he shot her just into the eye, and the arrow was sent with so

---

7. Supporter of Oliver Cromwell.

good a will, and so sure a hand, that it stuck in her brain, and made her caper and become mad for a moment or two, but being seconded by another arrow, he fell dead upon the prey. Caesar cut him open with a knife, to see where those wounds were that had been reported to him, and why he did not die of them. But I shall now relate a thing that possibly will find no credit among men, because 'tis a notion commonly received with us that nothing can receive a wound in the heart and live; but when the heart of this courageous animal was taken out, there were seven bullets of lead in it, and the wounds seamed up with great scars, and she lived with the bullets a great while, for it was long since they were shot. This heart the conqueror brought up to us, and 'twas a very great curiosity, which all the country came to see; and which gave Caesar occasion of many fine discourses, of accidents in war and strange escapes.

At other times he would go a-fishing, and discoursing on that diversion, he found we had in that country a very strange fish, called a numb eel[8] (an eel of which I have eaten), that while it is alive, it has a quality so cold that those who are angling, though with a line of never so great a length, with a rod at the end of it, it shall, in the same minute the bait is touched by this eel, seize him or her that holds the rod with be-numbedness, that shall deprive them of sense for a while. And some have fallen into the water, and others dropped as dead on the banks of the rivers where they stood, as soon as this fish touches the bait. Caesar used to laugh at this, and believed it impossible a man could lose his force at the touch of a fish; and could not understand that philosophy, that a cold quality should be of that nature. However, he had a great curiosity to try whether it would have the same effect on him it had on others, and often tried, but in vain. At last, the sought-for fish came to the bait as he stood angling on the bank; and instead of throwing away the rod, or giving it a sudden twitch out of the water, whereby he might have caught both the eel and have dismissed the rod before it could have too much power over him for experiment sake, he grasped it but the harder, and fainting fell into the river. And being still possessed of the rod, the tide carried him senseless as he was a great way, till an Indian boat took him up, and perceived, when they touched him, a numbness seize them, and by that knew the rod was in his hand, which with a paddle (that is, a short oar) they struck away, and snatched it into the boat, eel and all. If Caesar were almost dead with the effect of this fish, he was more so with that of the water, where he had remained the space of going a league, and they found they had much ado to bring him back to life. But at last they did, and brought him home, where he was in a few hours well recovered and refreshed, and not a little ashamed to find he should be overcome by an eel, and that all the people who heard his defiance would laugh at him. But we cheered him up and he, being convinced, we had the eel at supper, which was a quarter of an ell about, and most delicate meat, and was of the more value, since it cost so dear as almost the life of so gallant a man.

About this time we were in many mortal fears about some disputes the English had with the Indians, so that we could scarce trust ourselves, without great numbers, to go to any Indian towns or place where they abode, for fear they should fall upon us, as they did immediately after my coming away, and that it was in the possession of the Dutch, who used them not so civilly as the English, so that they cut in pieces all they could take, getting into houses, and hanging up the mother, and all her children about her, and cut a footman I left behind me all in joints, and nailed him to trees.

This feud began while I was there, so that I lost half the satisfaction I proposed, in not seeing and visiting the Indian towns. But one day, bemoaning of our misfortunes

8. An electric eel.

upon this account, Caesar told us we need not fear, for if we had a mind to go he would undertake to be our guard. Some would, but most would not venture. About eighteen of us resolved, and took barge, and after eight days arrived near an Indian town. But approaching it, the hearts of some of our company failed, and they would not venture on shore, so we polled who would, and who would not. For my part, I said, if Caesar would, I would go. He resolved, so did my brother and my woman, a maid of good courage. Now none of us speaking the language of the people, and imagining we should have a half diversion in gazing only and not knowing what they said, we took a fisherman that lived at the mouth of the river, who had been a long inhabitant there, and obliged him to go with us. But because he was known to the Indians, as trading among them, and being, by long living there, become a perfect Indian in color, we, who resolved to surprise them, by making them see something they never had seen (that is, white people) resolved only myself, my brother, and woman should go. So Caesar, the fisherman, and the rest, hiding behind some thick reeds and flowers, that grew on the banks, let us pass on towards the town, which was on the bank of the river all along. A little distant from the houses, or huts, we saw some dancing, others busied in fetching and carrying of water from the river. They had no sooner spied us but they set up a loud cry, that frighted us at first. We thought it had been for those that should kill us, but it seems it was of wonder and amazement. They were all naked, and we were dressed, so as is most commode for the hot countries, very glittering and rich, so that we appeared extremely fine. My own hair was cut short, and I had a taffeta cap, with black feathers, on my head. My brother was in a stuff[9] suit, with silver loops and buttons, and abundance of green ribbon. This was all infinitely surprising to them, and because we saw them stand still, till we approached them, we took heart and advanced, came up to them, and offered them our hands, which they took, and looked on us round about, calling still for more company; who came swarming out, all wondering, and crying out *tepeeme*, taking their hair up in their hands, and spreading it wide to those they called out to, as if they would say (as indeed it signified) "numberless wonders," or not to be recounted, no more than to number the hair of their heads. By degrees they grew more bold, and from gazing upon us round, they touched us, laying their hands upon all the features of our faces, feeling our breasts and arms, taking up one petticoat, then wondering to see another, admiring our shoes and stockings, but more our garters, which we gave them, and they tied about their legs, being laced with silver lace at the ends, for they much esteem any shining things. In fine, we suffered them to survey us as they pleased, and we thought they would never have done admiring us. When Caesar and the rest saw we were received with such wonder, they came up to us, and finding the Indian trader whom they knew (for 'tis by these fishermen, called Indian traders, we hold a commerce with them; for they love not to go far from home, and we never go to them), when they saw him therefore they set up a new joy, and cried, in their language, "Oh! here's our *tiguamy*, and we shall now know whether those things can speak." So advancing to him, some of them gave him their hands, and cried, "*Amora tiguamy*," which is as much as, "How do you," or "Welcome friend," and all, with one din, began to gabble to him, and asked, If we had sense, and wit? If we could talk of affairs of life, and war, as they could do? If we could hunt, swim, and do a thousand things they use? He answered them, we could. Then they invited us into their houses, and dressed venison and buffalo for us; and, going out, gathered a leaf of a tree, called a sarumbo leaf, of six yards long, and spread it on the ground for a

---

9. Woolen.

tablecloth, and cutting another in pieces instead of plates, setting us on little bow Indian stools, which they cut out of one entire piece of wood, and paint in a sort of japan work. They serve everyone their mess on these pieces of leaves, and it was very good, but too high seasoned with pepper. When we had eaten, my brother and I took out our flutes and played to them, which gave them new wonder, and I soon perceived, by an admiration that is natural to these people, and by the extreme ignorance and simplicity of them, it were not difficult to establish any unknown or extravagant religion among them, and to impose any notions or fictions upon them. For seeing a kinsman of mine set some paper afire with a burning-glass, a trick they had never before seen, they were like to have adored him for a god, and begged he would give them the characters or figures of his name, that they might oppose it against winds and storms, which he did, and they held it up in those seasons, and fancied it had a charm to conquer them, and kept it like a holy relic. They are very superstitious, and called him the great *peeie*, that is, prophet. They showed us their Indian *peeie*, a youth of about sixteen years old, as handsome as Nature could make a man. They consecrate a beautiful youth from his infancy, and all arts are used to complete him in the finest manner, both in beauty and shape. He is bred to all the little arts and cunning they are capable of, to all the legerdemain tricks and sleight of hand whereby he imposes upon the rabble, and is both a doctor in physic and divinity. And by these tricks makes the sick believe he sometimes eases their pains, by drawing from the afflicted part little serpents, or odd flies, or worms, or any strange thing; and though they have besides undoubted good remedies for almost all their diseases, they cure the patient more by fancy than by medicines, and make themselves feared, loved, and reverenced. This young *peeie* had a very young wife, who seeing my brother kiss her, came running and kissed me; after this, they kissed one another, and made it a very great jest, it being so novel, and new admiration and laughing went round the multitude, that they never will forget that ceremony, never before used or known. Caesar had a mind to see and talk with their war captains, and we were conducted to one of their houses, where we beheld several of the great captains, who had been at council. But so frightful a vision it was to see them no fancy can create; no such dreams can represent so dreadful a spectacle. For my part I took them for hobgoblins, or fiends, rather than men. But however their shapes appeared, their souls were very humane and noble, but some wanted their noses, some their lips, some both noses and lips, some their ears, and others cut through each cheek, with long slashes, through which their teeth appeared; they had several other formidable wounds and scars, or rather dismemberings. They had *comitias*, or little aprons before them, and girdles of cotton, with their knives naked, stuck in it, a bow at their backs, and a quiver of arrows on their thighs, and most had feathers on their heads of diverse colors. They cried "*Amora tiguamy*" to us at our entrance, and were pleased we said as much to them. They feted us, and gave us drink of the best sort, and wondered, as much as the others had done before, to see us. Caesar was marveling as much at their faces, wondering how they should all be so wounded in war; he was impatient to know how they all came by those frightful marks of rage or malice, rather than wounds got in noble battle. They told us, by our interpreter, that when any war was waging, two men chosen out by some old captain, whose fighting was past, and who could only teach the theory of war, these two men were to stand in competition for the generalship, or Great War Captain, and being brought before the old judges, now past labor, they are asked, what they dare do to show they are worthy to lead an army? When he who is first asked, making no reply, cuts off his nose, and throws it contemptibly[1] on the ground, and the other does something to himself that he thinks surpasses him, and perhaps deprives himself of lips and an eye. So they slash on till one gives out, and many have died in this debate. And 'tis by a passive valor they show and prove their activity, a sort of courage too brutal to be applauded by our black hero; nevertheless he expressed his esteem of them.

In this voyage Caesar begot so good an understanding between the Indians and the English, that there were no more fears or heartburnings during our stay, but we had a perfect, open, and free trade with them. Many things remarkable, and worthy reciting, we met with in this short voyage, because Caesar made it his business to search out and provide for our entertainment, especially to please his dearly adored Imoinda, who was a sharer in all our adventures; we being resolved to make her chains as easy as we could, and to compliment the Prince in that manner that most obliged him.

As we were coming up again, we met with some Indians of strange aspects, that is, of a larger size, and other sort of features, than those of our country. Our Indian slaves, that rowed us, asked them some questions, but they could not understand us, but showed us a long cotton string with several knots on it, and told us, they had been coming from the mountains so many moons as there were knots. They were habited in skins of a strange beast, and brought along with them bags of gold dust, which, as well as they could give us to understand, came streaming in little small channels down the high mountains, when the rains fell, and offered to be the convoy to anybody, or persons, that would go to the mountains. We carried these men up to Parham, where they were kept till the Lord Governor came. And because all the country was mad to be going on this golden adventure, the governor, by his letters, commanded (for they sent some of the gold to him) that a guard should be set at the mouth of the river of Amazons (a river so called, almost as broad as the river of Thames), and prohibited all people from going up that river, it conducting to those mountains of gold. But we going off for England before the project was further prosecuted, and the Governor being drowned in a hurricane, either the design died, or the Dutch have the advantage of it. And 'tis to be bemoaned what His Majesty lost by losing that part of America.

Though this digression is a little from my story, however since it contains some proofs of the curiosity and daring of this great man, I was content to omit nothing of his character.

It was thus, for some time we diverted him. But now Imoinda began to show she was with child, and did nothing but sigh and weep for the captivity of her lord, herself, and the infant yet unborn, and believed, if it were so hard to gain the liberty of two, 'twould be more difficult to get that for three. Her griefs were so many darts in the great heart of Caesar, and taking his opportunity one Sunday, when all the whites were overtaken in drink, as there were abundance of several trades, and slaves for four years,[2] that inhabited among the Negro houses, and Sunday was their day of debauch (otherwise they were a sort of spies upon Caesar), he went pretending out of goodness to them, to feast amongst them, and sent all his music, and ordered a great treat for the whole gang, about three hundred Negroes. And about a hundred and fifty were able to bear arms, such as they had, which were sufficient to do execution with spirits accordingly. For the English had none but rusty swords, that no strength could draw from a scabbard, except the people of particular quality, who took care to oil them and keep them in good order. The guns also, unless here and there one, or those newly carried from England, would do no good or harm, for 'tis the nature of that

---

1. Contemptuously.

2. I.e., whites who, as punishment for crime or debt, had been forced into service for fixed periods of time.

country to rust and eat up iron, or any metals but gold and silver. And they are very inexpert at the bow, which the Negroes and Indians are perfect masters of.

Caesar, having singled out these men from the women and children, made a harangue to them of the miseries and ignominies of slavery; counting up all their toils and sufferings, under such loads, burdens, and drudgeries as were fitter for beasts than men, senseless brutes than human souls. He told them it was not for days, months, or years, but for eternity; there was no end to be of their misfortunes. They suffered not like men who might find a glory and fortitude in oppression, but like dogs that loved the whip and bell,[3] and fawned the more they were beaten. That they had lost the divine quality of men, and were become insensible asses, fit only to bear. Nay worse, an ass, or dog, or horse, having done his duty, could lie down in retreat, and rise to work again, and while he did his duty endured no stripes; but men, villainous, senseless men such as they, toiled on all the tedious week till black Friday, and then, whether they worked or not, whether they were faulty or meriting, they promiscuously, the innocent with the guilty, suffered the infamous whip, the sordid stripes, from their fellow slaves till their blood trickled from all parts of their body, blood whose every drop ought to be revenged with a life of some of those tyrants that impose it. "And why," said he, "my dear friends and fellow sufferers, should we be slaves to an unknown people? Have they vanquished us nobly in fight? Have they won us in honorable battle? And are we, by the chance of war, become their slaves? This would not anger a noble heart, this would not animate a soldier's soul. No, but we are bought and sold like apes, or monkeys, to be the sport of women, fools, and cowards, and the support of rogues, runagades, that have abandoned their own countries, for raping, murders, thefts, and villainies. Do you not hear every day how they upbraid each other with infamy of life below the wildest savages, and shall we render obedience to such a degenerate race, who have no one human virtue left to distinguish them from the vilest creatures? Will you, I say, suffer the lash from such hands?" They all replied, with one accord, "No, no, no; Caesar has spoke like a great captain, like a great king."

After this he would have proceeded, but was interrupted by a tall Negro of some more quality than the rest. His name was Tuscan, who bowing at the feet of Caesar, cried, "My lord, we have listened with joy and attention to what you have said, and, were we only men, would follow so great a leader through the world. But oh! consider, we are husbands and parents too, and have things more dear to us than life: our wives and children unfit for travel, in these impassable woods, mountains, and bogs. We have not only difficult lands to overcome, but rivers to wade, and monsters to encounter, ravenous beasts of prey—" To this, Caesar replied, that honor was the first principle in nature that was to be obeyed; but as no man would pretend to that, without all the acts of virtue, compassion, charity, love, justice, and reason, he found it not inconsistent with that, to take an equal care of their wives and children, as they would of themselves, and that he did not design, when he led them to freedom and glorious liberty, that they should leave that better part of themselves to perish by the hand of the tyrant's whip. But if there were a woman among them so degenerate from love and virtue to choose slavery before the pursuit of her husband, and with the hazard of her life to share with him in his fortunes, that such an one ought to be abandoned, and left as a prey to the common enemy.

To which they all agreed—and bowed. After this, he spoke of the impassable woods and rivers, and convinced them, the more danger, the more glory. He told

3. Because rigorous training has taught them to cherish their punishment.

them that he had heard of one Hannibal, a great captain, had cut his way through mountains of solid rocks,[4] and should a few shrubs oppose them, which they could fire before them? No, 'twas a trifling excuse to men resolved to die, or overcome. As for bogs, they are with a little labor filled and hardened, and the rivers could be no obstacle, since they swam by nature, at least by custom, from their first hour of their birth. That when the children were weary they must carry them by turns, and the woods and their own industry would afford them food. To this they all assented with joy.

Tuscan then demanded, what he would do? He said, they would travel towards the sea; plant a new colony, and defend it by their valor; and when they could find a ship, either driven by stress of weather, or guided by Providence that way, they would seize it, and make it a prize, till it had transported them to their own countries. At least, they should be made free in his kingdom, and be esteemed as his fellow sufferers, and men that had the courage and the bravery to attempt, at least, for liberty. And if they died in the attempt it would be more brave than to live in perpetual slavery.

They bowed and kissed his feet at this resolution, and with one accord vowed to follow him to death. And that night was appointed to begin their march; they made it known to their wives, and directed them to tie their hamaca[5] about their shoulder, and under their arm like a scarf; and to lead their children that could go, and carry those that could not. The wives, who pay an entire obedience to their husbands, obeyed, and stayed for them where they were appointed. The men stayed but to furnish themselves with what defensive arms they could get, and all met at the rendezvous, where Caesar made a new encouraging speech to them, and led them out.

But, as they could not march far that night, on Monday early, when the overseers went to call them all together to go to work, they were extremely surprised to find not one upon the place, but all fled with what baggage they had. You may imagine this news was not only suddenly spread all over the plantation, but soon reached the neighboring ones, and we had by noon about six hundred men, they call the militia of the county, that came to assist us in the pursuit of the fugitives. But never did one see so comical an army march forth to war. The men of any fashion would not concern themselves, though it were almost the common cause, for such revoltings are very ill examples, and have very fatal consequences oftentimes in many colonies. But they had a respect for Caesar, and all hands were against the Parhamites, as they called those of Parham Plantation, because they did not, in the first place, love the Lord Governor, and secondly, they would have it that Caesar was ill used, and baffled with.[6] And 'tis not impossible but some of the best in the country was of his counsel in this flight, and depriving us of all the slaves, so that they of the better sort would not meddle in the matter. The deputy governor,[7] of whom I have had no great occasion to speak, and who was the most fawning fair-tongued fellow in the world, and one that pretended the most friendship to Caesar, was now the only violent man against him, and though he had nothing, and so need fear nothing, yet talked and looked bigger than any man. He was a fellow whose character is not fit to be mentioned with the worst of the slaves. This fellow would lead his army forth to meet Caesar, or rather to pursue him. Most of their arms were

---

4. The Carthaginian general (247–182 B.C.E.) had accomplished this while crossing the Alps to invade Rome.
5. Hammock.

6. Cheated.
7. William Byam, who during a decade as administrator in Surinam had acquired a reputation for arrogance and severity.

of those sort of cruel whips they call cat-with-nine-tails; some had rusty useless guns for show; others old basket-hilts, whose blades had never seen the light in this age, and others had long staffs, and clubs. Mr. Trefry went along rather to be a mediator than a conqueror in such a battle, for he foresaw and knew, if by fighting they put the Negroes into despair, they were a sort of sullen fellows that would drown or kill themselves before they would yield, and he advised that fair means was best. But Byam was one that abounded in his own wit, and would take his own measures.

It was not hard to find these fugitives, for as they fled they were forced to fire and cut the woods before them, so that night or day they pursued them by the light they made, and by the path they had cleared. But as soon as Caesar found he was pursued, he put himself in a posture of defense, placing all the women and children in the rear, and himself, with Tuscan by his side, or next to him, all promising to die or conquer. Encouraged thus, they never stood to parley, but fell on pell-mell upon the English, and killed some, and wounded a good many, they having recourse to their whips, as the best of their weapons. And as they observed no order, they perplexed the enemy so sorely, with lashing them in the eyes. And the women and children, seeing their husbands so treated, being of fearful cowardly dispositions, and hearing the English cry out, "Yield and live, yield and be pardoned," they all ran in amongst their husbands and fathers, and hung about them, crying out, "Yield, yield, and leave Caesar to their revenge," that by degrees the slaves abandoned Caesar, and left him only Tuscan and his heroic Imoinda, who, grown big as she was, did nevertheless press near her lord, having a bow, and a quiver full of poisoned arrows, which she managed with such dexterity that she wounded several, and shot the governor into the shoulder, of which wound he had like to have died but that an Indian woman, his mistress, sucked the wound, and cleansed it from the venom. But however, he stirred not from the place till he had parleyed with Caesar, who he found was resolved to die fighting, and would not be taken; no more would Tuscan, or Imoinda. But he, more thirsting after revenge of another sort, than that of depriving him of life, now made use of all his art of talking and dissembling, and besought Caesar to yield himself upon terms which he himself should propose, and should be sacredly assented to and kept by him. He told him, it was not that he any longer feared him, or could believe the force of two men, and a young heroine, could overcome all them, with all the slaves now on their side also, but it was the vast esteem he had for his person, the desire he had to serve so gallant a man, and to hinder himself from the reproach hereafter of having been the occasion of the death of a prince, whose valor and magnanimity deserved the empire of the world. He protested to him, he looked upon this action as gallant and brave, however tending to the prejudice of his lord and master, who would by it have lost so considerable a number of slaves, that this flight of his should be looked on as a heat of youth, and rashness of a too forward courage, and an unconsidered impatience of liberty, and no more; and that he labored in vain to accomplish that which they would effectually perform, as soon as any ship arrived that would touch on his coast. "So that if you will be pleased," continued he, "to surrender yourself, all imaginable respect shall be paid you; and yourself, your wife, and child, if it be here born, shall depart free out of our land." But Caesar would hear of no composition, though Byam urged, if he pursued and went on in his design, he would inevitably perish, either by great snakes, wild beasts, or hunger, and he ought to have regard to his wife, whose condition required ease, and not the fatigues of tedious travel, where she could not be secured from being devoured. But Caesar told him, there was no faith in the white men, or the gods they adored, who instructed them in principles so false that honest men could not live amongst them; though no people professed so much, none performed so little; that he knew what he had to do, when he dealt with men of honor, but with them a man ought to be eternally on his guard, and never to eat and drink with Christians without his weapon of defense in his hand, and, for his own security, never to credit one word they spoke. As for the rashness and inconsiderateness of his action he would confess the governor is in the right, and that he was ashamed of what he had done, in endeavoring to make those free, who were by nature slaves, poor wretched rogues, fit to be used as Christians' tools; dogs, treacherous and cowardly, fit for such masters, and they wanted only but to be whipped into the knowledge of the Christian gods to be the vilest of all creeping things, to learn to worship such deities as had not power to make them just, brave, or honest. In fine, after a thousand things of this nature, not fit here to be recited, he told Byam, he had rather die than live upon the same earth with such dogs. But Trefry and Byam pleaded and protested together so much, that Trefry believing the governor to mean what he said, and speaking very cordially himself, generously put himself into Caesar's hands, and took him aside, and persuaded him, even with tears, to live, by surrendering himself, and to name his conditions. Caesar was overcome by his wit and reasons, and in consideration of Imoinda, and demanding what he desired, and that it should be ratified by their hands in writing, because he had perceived that was the common way of contract between man and man amongst the whites. All this was performed, and Tuscan's pardon was put in, and they surrender to the governor, who walked peaceably down into the plantation with them, after giving order to bury their dead. Caesar was very much toiled with the bustle of the day, for he had fought like a Fury, and what mischief was done he and Tuscan performed alone, and gave their enemies a fatal proof that they durst do anything, and feared no mortal force.

But they were no sooner arrived at the place where all the slaves receive their punishments of whipping, but they laid hands on Caesar and Tuscan, faint with heat and toil; and surprising them, bound them to two several stakes, and whipped them in a most deplorable and inhumane manner, rending the very flesh from their bones; especially Caesar, who was not perceived to make any moan, or to alter his face, only to roll his eyes on the faithless governor, and those he believed guilty, with fierceness and indignation. And, to complete his rage, he saw every one of those slaves, who, but a few days before, adored him as something more than mortal, now had a whip to give him some lashes, while he strove not to break his fetters, though if he had, it were impossible. But he pronounced a woe and revenge from his eyes, that darted fire, that 'twas at once both awful and terrible to behold.

When they thought they were sufficiently revenged on him, they untied him, almost fainting with loss of blood from a thousand wounds all over his body, from which they had rent his clothes, and led him bleeding and naked as he was, and loaded him all over with irons, and then rubbed his wounds, to complete their cruelty, with Indian pepper, which had like to have made him raving mad, and in this condition made him so fast to the ground that he could not stir, if his pains and wounds would have given him leave. They spared Imoinda, and did not let her see this barbarity committed towards her lord, but carried her down to Parham, and shut her up, which was not in kindness to her, but for fear she should die with the sight, or miscarry, and then they should lose a young slave, and perhaps the mother.

You must know, that when the news was brought on Monday morning, that Caesar had betaken himself to the woods, and carried with him all the Negroes, we were possessed with extreme fear, which no persuasions could dissipate, that he would secure himself till night, and then, that he would come down and cut all our throats. This apprehension made all the females of us fly down the river, to be secured, and while we were away, they acted this cruelty. For I suppose I had authority and interest enough there, had I suspected any such thing, to have prevented it, but we had not gone many leagues, but the news overtook us that Caesar was taken, and whipped like a common slave. We met on the river with Colonel Martin, a man of great gallantry, wit, and goodness, and, whom I have celebrated in a character of my new comedy,[8] by his own name, in memory of so brave a man. He was wise and eloquent, and, from the fineness of his parts, bore a great sway over the hearts of all the colony. He was a friend to Caesar, and resented this false dealing with him very much. We carried him back to Parham, thinking to have made an accommodation; when we came, the first news we heard was that the governor was dead of a wound Imoinda had given him, but it was not so well. But it seems he would have the pleasure of beholding the revenge he took on Caesar, and before the cruel ceremony was finished, he dropped down, and then they perceived the wound he had on his shoulder was by a venomed arrow, which, as I said, his Indian mistress healed, by sucking the wound.

We were no sooner arrived, but we went up to the plantation to see Caesar, whom we found in a very miserable and inexpressible condition, and I have a thousand times admired how he lived, in so much tormenting pain. We said all things to him that trouble, pity, and good nature could suggest, protesting our innocence of the fact, and our abhorrence of such cruelties; making a thousand professions of services to him, and begging as many pardons for the offenders, till we said so much, that he believed we had no hand in his ill treatment, but told us, he could never pardon Byam. As for Trefry, he confessed he saw his grief and sorrow for his suffering, which he could not hinder, but was like to have been beaten down by the very slaves, for speaking in his defense. But for Byam, who was their leader, their head—and should, by his justice, and honor, have been an example to them—for him, he wished to live, to take a dire revenge of him, and said, "It had been well for him if he had sacrificed me, instead of giving me the contemptible whip." He refused to talk much, but begging us to give him our hands, he took them, and protested never to lift up his, to do us any harm. He had a great respect for Colonel Martin, and always took his counsel, like that of a parent, and assured him, he would obey him in anything but his revenge on Byam. "Therefore," said he, "for his own safety, let him speedily dispatch me, for if I could dispatch myself, I would not, till that justice were done to my injured person, and the contempt of a soldier. No, I would not kill myself, even after a whipping, but will be content to live with that infamy, and be pointed at by every grinning slave, till I have completed my revenge; and then you shall see that Oroonoko scorns to live with the indignity that was put on Caesar." All we could do could get no more words from him, and we took care to have him put immediately into a healing bath, to rid him of his pepper, and ordered a chirurgeon[9] to anoint him with healing balm, which he suffered, and in some time he began to be able to walk and eat. We failed not to visit him every day, and, to that end, had him brought to an apartment at Parham.

The governor was no sooner recovered, and had heard of the menaces of Caesar, but he called his council, who (not to disgrace them, or burlesque the government

---

8. *The Younger Brother: or the Amorous Jilt*, produced posthumously in 1696.   9. Surgeon.

there) consisted of such notorious villains as Newgate[1] never transported, and possibly originally were such, who understood neither the laws of God or man, and had no sort of principles to make them worthy the name of men, but at the very council table would contradict and fight with one another, and swear so bloodily that 'twas terrible to hear and see them. (Some of them were afterwards hanged, when the Dutch took possession of the place; others sent off in chains.) But calling these special rulers of the nation together, and requiring their counsel in this weighty affair, they all concluded that (damn them) it might be their own cases, and that Caesar ought to be made an example to all the Negroes, to fright them from daring to threaten their betters, their lords and masters, and, at this rate, no man was safe from his own slaves, and concluded, *nemine contradicente*,[2] that Caesar should be hanged.

Trefry then thought it time to use his authority, and told Byam his command did not extend to his lord's plantation, and that Parham was as much exempt from the law as Whitehall; and that they ought no more to touch the servants of the Lord—(who there represented the King's person) than they could those about the King himself; and that Parham was a sanctuary, and though his lord were absent in person, his power was still in being there, which he had entrusted with him, as far as the dominions of his particular plantations reached, and all that belonged to it; the rest of the country, as Byam was lieutenant to his lord, he might exercise his tyranny upon. Trefry had others as powerful, or more, that interested themselves in Caesar's life, and absolutely said he should be defended. So turning the governor, and his wise council, out of doors (for they sat at Parham House) we set a guard upon our landing place, and would admit none but those we called friends to us and Caesar.

The governor having remained wounded at Parham till his recovery was completed, Caesar did not know but he was still there, and indeed, for the most part, his time was spent there, for he was one that loved to live at other people's expense, and if he were a day absent, he was ten present there, and used to play, and walk, and hunt, and fish, with Caesar. So that Caesar did not at all doubt, if he once recovered strength, but he should find an opportunity of being revenged on him. Though, after such a revenge, he could not hope to live, for if he escaped the fury of the English mobile,[3] who perhaps would have been glad of the occasion to have killed him, he was resolved not to survive his whipping, yet he had, some tender hours, a repenting softness, which he called his fits of coward, wherein he struggled with love for the victory of his heart, which took part with his charming Imoinda there; but, for the most part, his time was passed in melancholy thought, and black designs. He considered, if he should do this deed, and die either in the attempt, or after it, he left his lovely Imoinda a prey, or at best a slave, to the enraged multitude; his great heart could not endure that thought. "Perhaps," said he, "she may be first ravished by every brute, exposed first to their nasty lusts, and then a shameful death." No, he could not live a moment under that apprehension, too insupportable to be borne. These were his thoughts, and his silent arguments with his heart, as he told us afterwards, so that now resolving not only to kill Byam, but all those he thought had enraged him, pleasing his great heart with the fancied slaughter he should make over the whole face of the plantation, he first resolved on a deed that (however horrid it at first appeared to us all), when we had heard his reasons, we thought it brave and just. Being able to walk and, as he believed, fit for the execution of his great design, he begged Trefry to trust him

1. London prison from which convicts were sent to work in the colonies.

2. No one disagreeing.

3. Mob.

into the air, believing a walk would do him good, which was granted him, and taking Imoinda with him, as he used to do in his more happy and calmer days, he led her up into a wood where, after (with a thousand sighs, and long gazing silently on her face, while tears gushed, in spite of him, from his eyes), he told her his design first of killing her, and then his enemies, and next himself, and the impossibility of escaping, and therefore he told her the necessity of dying. He found the heroic wife faster pleading for death than he was to propose it, when she found his fixed resolution, and on her knees besought him not to leave her a prey to his enemies. He (grieved to death) yet pleased at her noble resolution, took her up, and embracing her with all the passion and languishment of a dying lover, drew his knife to kill this treasure of his soul, this pleasure of his eyes. While tears trickled down his cheeks, hers were smiling with joy she should die by so noble a hand, and be sent in her own country (for that's their notion of the next world) by him she so tenderly loved, and so truly adored in this, for wives have a respect for their husbands equal to what any other people pay a deity, and when a man finds any occasion to quit his wife, if he love her, she dies by his hand; if not, he sells her, or suffers some other to kill her. It being thus, you may believe the deed was soon resolved on, and 'tis not to be doubted, but the parting, the eternal leave-taking of two such lovers, so greatly born, so sensible,[4] so beautiful, so young, and so fond, must be very moving, as the relation of it was to me afterwards.

All that love could say in such cases being ended, and all the intermitting irresolutions being adjusted, the lovely, young, and adored victim lays herself down before the sacrificer, while he, with a hand resolved, and a heart breaking within, gave the fatal stroke, first cutting her throat, and then severing her yet smiling face from that delicate body, pregnant as it was with fruits of tenderest love. As soon as he had done, he laid the body decently on leaves and flowers, of which he made a bed, and concealed it under the same coverlid of nature, only her face he left yet bare to look on. But when he found she was dead, and past all retrieve, never more to bless him with her eyes and soft language, his grief swelled up to rage; he tore, he raved, he roared, like some monster of the wood, calling on the loved name of Imoinda. A thousand times he turned the fatal knife that did the deed toward his own heart, with a resolution to go immediately after her, but dire revenge, which now was a thousand times more fierce in his soul than before, prevents him, and he would cry out, "No, since I have sacrificed Imoinda to my revenge, shall I lose that glory which I have purchased so dear, as at the price of the fairest, dearest, softest creature that ever Nature made? No, no!" Then, at her name, grief would get the ascendant of rage, and he would lie down by her side, and water her face with showers of tears, which never were wont to fall from those eyes. And however bent he was on his intended slaughter, he had not power to stir from the sight of this dear object, now more beloved and more adored than ever.

He remained in this deploring condition for two days, and never rose from the ground where he had made his sad sacrifice. At last, rousing from her side, and accusing himself with living too long now Imoinda was dead, and that the deaths of those barbarous enemies were deferred too long, he resolved now to finish the great work; but offering to rise, he found his strength so decayed, that he reeled to and fro, like boughs assailed by contrary winds, so that he was forced to lie down again, and try to summon all his courage to his aid. He found his brains turn round, and his eyes were dizzy, and objects appeared not the same to him as they were wont to do; his breath was short, and all his limbs surprised with a faintness he had never felt

4. Sensitive.

before. He had not eaten in two days, which was one occasion of this feebleness, but excess of grief was the greatest; yet still he hoped he should recover vigor to act his design, and lay expecting it yet six days longer, still mourning over the dead idol of his heart, and striving every day to rise, but could not.

In all this time you may believe we were in no little affliction for Caesar and his wife. Some were of opinion he was escaped never to return; others thought some accident had happened to him. But however, we failed not to send out a hundred people several ways to search for him. A party of about forty went that way he took, among whom was Tuscan, who was perfectly reconciled to Byam. They had not gone very far into the wood, but they smelt an unusual smell, as of a dead body, for stinks must be very noisome that can be distinguished among such a quantity of natural sweets, as every inch of that land produces. So that they concluded they should find him dead, or somebody that was so. They passed on towards it, as loathsome as it was, and made such a rustling among the leaves that lie thick on the ground, by continual falling, that Caesar heard he was approached, and though he had, during the space of these eight days, endeavored to rise, but found he wanted strength, yet looking up, and seeing his pursuers, he rose, and reeled to a neighboring tree, against which he fixed his back. And being within a dozen yards of those that advanced and saw him, he called out to them, and bid them approach no nearer, if they would be safe; so that they stood still, and hardly believing their eyes, that would persuade them that it was Caesar that spoke to them, so much was he altered, they asked him what he had done with his wife, for they smelt a stink that almost struck them dead. He, pointing to the dead body, sighing, cried, "Behold her there." They put off the flowers that covered her with their sticks, and found she was killed, and cried out, "Oh monster! that hast murdered thy wife." Then asking him, why he did so cruel a deed, he replied, he had no leisure to answer impertinent questions. "You may go back," continued he, "and tell the faithless governor he may thank Fortune that I am breathing my last, and that my arm is too feeble to obey my heart in what it had designed him." But his tongue faltering, and trembling, he could scarce end what he was saying. The English taking advantage by his weakness, cried, "Let us take him alive by all means." He heard them; and, as if he had revived from a fainting, or a dream, he cried out, "No, gentlemen, you are deceived, you will find no more Caesars to be whipped, no more find a faith in me. Feeble as you think me, I have strength yet left to secure me from a second indignity." They swore all anew, and he only shook his head, and beheld them with scorn. Then they cried out, "Who will venture on this single man? Will nobody?" They stood all silent while Caesar replied, "Fatal will be the attempt to the first adventurer, let him assure himself," and, at that word, held up his knife in a menacing posture. "Look ye, ye faithless crew," said he, "'tis not life I seek, nor am I afraid of dying," and, at that word, cut a piece of flesh from his own throat, and threw it at them, "yet still I would live if I could, till I had perfected my revenge. But oh! it cannot be. I feel life gliding from my eyes and heart, and, if I make not haste, I shall yet fall a victim to the shameful whip." At that, he ripped up his own belly, and took his bowels and pulled them out, with what strength he could, while some, on their knees imploring, besought him to hold his hand. But when they saw him tottering, they cried out, "Will none venture on him?" A bold English cried, "Yes, if he were the Devil" (taking courage when he saw him almost dead) and swearing a horrid oath for his farewell to the world he rushed on. Caesar with his armed hand met him so fairly, as stuck him to the heart, and he fell dead at his feet. Tuscan seeing that, cried out, "I love thee, oh Caesar, and therefore will not let thee die, if possible." And, running to him, took him in his arms, but at the same time, warding a blow that Caesar made at his bosom, he received it quite through his arm, and Caesar having not the strength to pluck the knife forth, though he attempted it, Tuscan neither pulled it out himself, nor suffered it to be pulled out, but came down with it sticking in his arm, and the reason he gave for it was because the air should not get into the wound. They put their hands across, and carried Caesar between six of them, fainted as he was, and they thought dead, or just dying, and they brought him to Parham, and laid him on a couch, and had the chirurgeon immediately to him, who dressed his wounds, and sewed up his belly, and used means to bring him to life, which they effected. We ran all to see him; and, if before we thought him so beautiful a sight, he was now so altered that his face was like a death's head blacked over, nothing but teeth and eye-holes. For some days we suffered nobody to speak to him, but caused cordials to be poured down his throat, which sustained his life, and in six or seven days he recovered his senses. For you must know, that wounds are almost to a miracle cured in the Indies, unless wounds in the legs, which rarely ever cure.

When he was well enough to speak, we talked to him, and asked him some questions about his wife, and the reasons why he killed her. And he then told us what I have related of that resolution, and of his parting, and he besought us we would let him die, and was extremely afflicted to think it was possible he might live. He assured us, if we did not dispatch him, he would prove very fatal to a great many. We said all we could to make him live, and gave him new assurances, but he begged we would not think so poorly of him, or of his love to Imoinda, to imagine we could flatter him to life again; but the chirurgeon assured him he could not live, and therefore he need not fear. We were all (but Caesar) afflicted at this news; and the sight was gashly.[5] His discourse was sad; and the earthly smell about him so strong, that I was persuaded to leave the place for some time (being myself but sickly, and very apt to fall into fits of dangerous illness upon any extraordinary melancholy). The servants, and Trefry, and the chirurgeons, promised all to take what possible care they could of the life of Caesar, and I, taking boat, went with other company to Colonel Martin's, about three days' journey down the river; but I was no sooner gone, but the governor taking Trefry about some pretended earnest business a day's journey up the river, having communicated his design to one Banister, a wild Irishman, and one of the council, a fellow of absolute barbarity, and fit to execute any villainy, but was rich, he came up to Parham, and forcibly took Caesar, and had him carried to the same post where he was whipped, and causing him to be tied to it, and a great fire made before him, he told him he should die like a dog, as he was. Caesar replied, this was the first piece of bravery that ever Banister did, and he never spoke sense till he pronounced that word, and, if he would keep it, he would declare, in the other world, that he was the only man, of all the whites, that ever he heard speak truth. And turning to the men that bound him, he said, "My friends, am I to die, or to be whipped?" And they cried, "Whipped! no; you shall not escape so well." And then he replied, smiling, "A blessing on thee," and assured them, they need not tie him, for he would stand fixed, like a rock, and endure death so as should encourage them to die. "But if you whip me," said he, "be sure you tie me fast."

He had learned to take tobacco, and when he was assured he should die, he desired they would give him a pipe in his mouth, ready lighted, which they did, and the executioner came, and first cut off his members,[6] and threw them into the fire.

5. Ghastly.   6. Genitals.

After that, with an ill-favored knife, they cut his ears and his nose, and burned them; he still smoked on, as if nothing had touched him. Then they hacked off one of his arms, and still he bore up, and held his pipe. But at the cutting off the other arm, his head sunk, and his pipe dropped, and he gave up the ghost, without a groan, or a reproach. My mother and sister were by him all the while, but not suffered to save him, so rude and wild were the rabble, and so inhuman were the justices, who stood by to see the execution, who after paid dearly enough for their insolence. They cut Caesar in quarters, and sent them to several of the chief plantations. One quarter was sent to Colonel Martin, who refused it, and swore he had rather see the quarters of Banister and the governor himself than those of Caesar on his planta-tions, and that he could govern his Negroes without terrifying and grieving them with frightful spectacles of a mangled king.

Thus died this great man, worthy of a better fate, and a more sublime wit than mine to write his praise. Yet, I hope, the reputation of my pen is considerable enough to make his glorious name to survive to all ages, with that of the brave, the beautiful, and the constant Imoinda.

1688

◦⬥◦

RESPONSE
Thomas Southerne: from *Oroonoko: A Tragedy*[1]
[DEBATING REBELLION][2]

OROONOKO: What would you do?
ABOAN: Cut our oppressors' throats.
OROONOKO: And you would have me join in your design
          Of murder?
ABOAN: It deserves a better name.
          But be it what it will, 'tis justified
5   By self-defense, and natural liberty.
OROONOKO: I'll hear no more on't.
ABOAN: I am sorry for't.

---

1. After Behn's death, *Oroonoko* did more than any of her other works to sustain her fame, partly in print and partly in the theater. In 1696, the Irish-born, intermittently successful playwright Thomas Southerne (1660–1746) found cause to praise Behn's story but to puzzle over her choice of genre. "She had great command of the stage," he remarked in the dedication to the play he based on her book, "and I have often wondered that she would bury her favorite hero in a *novel*, when she might have revived him in the *scene*."

In *Oroonoko: A Tragedy*, Southerne undertook just such a revival, relocating Oroonoko from the printed page to the playhouse. The playwright added an erotic subplot about a pair of English sisters who have traveled to Surinam to seek rich husbands. More strikingly, he changed the race of the play's heroine. Imoinda is here not African but European, the daughter of a white "stranger in my father's court" who died protecting Oroonoko in battle. The play shifts timings, too: this Imoinda marries Oroonoko and becomes pregnant by him in Africa, shortly before the two are separately sold

into slavery. Their mixed-race marriage becomes one of several motifs by which Southerne echoes yet another 17th-century source: Shakespeare's *Othello*.

Audience response confirmed Southerne's faith in the theatrical power of Behn's protagonists. His play, re-staged and re-adapted many times, became a touchstone text for the antislavery movement that grew in England and America over the next century and a half. Only with the appearance of *Uncle Tom's Cabin* in the 1850s did the advocates of abolition find a more contemporary narra-tive to take *Oroonoko's* place. Southerne's tragedy abet-ted the alchemy by which Behn's intricately fictionalized "true history" survived its initial moment, and helped shape history thereafter.

2. From Act 3, Scene 2. Oroonoko and Imoinda, freshly reunited, hear Aboan make his case for insurrection. Southerne retains Behn's complex view of slavery: Oroonoko briefly defends the slaveholders as "innocent"; Aboan's arguments, in their tone and phrasing, some-times echo those of *Othello's* arch-villain Iago.

OROONOKO: Nor shall you think of it.

ABOAN: Not think of it!

OROONOKO: No, I command you not.

ABOAN: Remember, Sir,
    You are a slave yourself, and to command
10 Is now another's right. Not think of it!
    Since the first moment they put on my chains,
    I've thought of nothing but the weight of 'em,
    And how to throw 'em off. Can yours sit easy?

OROONOKO: I have a sense of my condition,
15 As painful, and as quick, as yours can be.
    I feel for my Imoinda and myself;
    Imoinda much the tenderest part of me.
    But though I languish for my liberty,
    I would not buy it at the Christian price
20 Of black ingratitude. They shannot say
    That we deserved our fortune by our crimes.
    Murder the innocent!

ABOAN: The innocent!

OROONOKO: These men are so, whom you would rise against.
    If we are slaves, they did not make us slaves,
25 But bought us in an honest way of trade:
    As we have done before 'em, bought and sold
    Many a wretch, and never thought it wrong.[3]
    They paid our price for us, and we are now
    Their property, a part of their estate,
30 To manage as they please. Mistake me not,
    I do not tamely say, that we should bear
    All they could lay upon us. But we find
    The load so light, so little to be felt
    (Considering they have us in their power,
35 And may inflict what grievances they please)
    We ought not to complain.

ABOAN: My Royal Lord!
    You do not know the heavy grievances,
    The toil, the labors, weary drudgeries,
    Which they impose; burdens more fit for beasts,
40 For senseless beasts to bear, than thinking men.
    Then if you saw the bloody cruelties
    They execute on every slight offense—
    Nay sometimes in their proud, insulting sport—
    How worse than dogs they lash their fellow-creatures:
45 Your heart would bleed for 'em. O could you know
    How many wretches lift their hands and eyes
    To you, for their relief.

OROONOKO: I pity 'em.
    And wish I could with honesty do more.

---

3. "We" here are Africans, who (as Behn's story also emphasizes) sold slaves to each other, and to Europeans.

ABOAN: You must do more, and may, with honesty.
50   O Royal Sir, remember who you are,
        A prince, born for the good of other men,
        Whose god-like office is to draw the sword
        Against oppression, and set free mankind;
        And this, I'm sure, you think oppression now.
55   What though you have not felt these miseries,
        Never believe you are obliged to them.
        They have their selfish reasons, maybe, now,
        For using of you well. But there will come
        A time, when you must have your share of 'em.
OROONOKO: You see how little cause I have to think so:
        Favored in my own person, in my friends;
        Indulged in all that can concern my care,
        In my Imoinda's soft society. [*Embracing her*]
ABOAN: And therefore would you lie contented down,
65   In the forgetfulness, and arms of love,
        To get young princes for 'em?
OROONOKO: Say'st thou! ha!
ABOAN: Princes, the heirs of empire, and the last
        Of your illustrious lineage, to be born
        To pamper up their pride, and be their slaves?
OROONOKO: Imoinda! Save me, save me from that thought.
IMOINDA: There is no safety from it. I have long
        Suffered with a mother's laboring pains,
        And can no longer. Kill me, kill me now,
        While I am blessed, and happy in your love,
75   Rather than let me live to see you hate me
        As you must hate me: me, the only cause,
        The fountain of these flowing miseries.
        Dry up this spring of life, this poisonous spring,
        That swells so fast, to overwhelm us all.
OROONOKO: Shall the dear babe, the eldest of my hopes,
        Whom I begot a prince, be born a slave?
        The treasure of this temple was designed
        T' enrich a kingdom's fortune; shall it here
        Be seized upon by vile unhallowed hands,
85   To be employed in uses most profane?
ABOAN: Nay, grant this man, you think so much your friend,
        Be honest, and intends all that he says.[4]
        He is but one, and in a government
        Where, he confesses, you have enemies
90   That watch your looks. What looks can you put on
        To please these men, who are before resolved
        To read 'em their own way? alas! my Lord!
        If they incline to think you dangerous,

---

4. Aboan refers to Blanford, the play's counterpart to Behn's character Trefry: a young Englishman who has professed friendship for Oroonoko and promised that the governor, due soon in Surinam, will grant his freedom.

They have their knavish arts to make you so.
95   And then who knows how far their cruelty
May carry their revenge?
IMOINDA: To everything
That does belong to you, your friends, and me;
I shall be torn from you, forced away,
Helpless and miserable. Shall I live
100   To see that day again?[5]
OROONOKO: That day shall never come.
ABOAN: I know you are persuaded to believe
The governor's arrival will prevent
These mischiefs, and bestow your liberty.
But who is sure of that? I rather fear
105   More mischiefs from his coming. He is young,
Luxurious, passionate, and amorous.
Such a complexion, and made bold by power
To countenance all he is prone to do,
Will know no bounds, no law against his lusts.
110   If, in a fit of his intemperance,
With a strong hand he should resolve to seize
And force my royal mistress from your arms,
How can you help yourself?
OROONOKO: Ha! thou hast roused
The lion in his den; he stalks abroad,
115   And the wide forest trembles at his roar.
I feel the danger now: my spirits start
At the alarm and from all quarters come
To man my heart, the citadel of love.
Is there a power on earth to force you from me?
120   And shall I not resist it? Not strike first
To keep, to save you—to prevent that curse?
This is your cause, and shall it not prevail?
O! your were born all ways to conquer me.
[*to* ABOAN] Now I am fashioned to thy purpose. Speak:
125   What combination, what conspiracy,
Would'st thou engage me in? I'll undertake
All thou would'st have me now for liberty,
For the great cause of love and liberty.
ABOAN: Now, my great master, you appear yourself.
130   And since we have you joined in our design,
It cannot fail us. I have mustered up
The choicest slaves, men who are sensible
Of their condition, and seem most resolved.
They have their several parties.
OROONOKO: Summon 'em,

---

5. The lovers have been sundered once before, by the African king (in Southerne's play he is Oroonoko's father rather than grandfather) who wanted Imoinda for himself.

135   Assemble 'em. I will come forth and show
            Myself amongst 'em. If they are resolved,
            I'll lead their foremost resolutions.
ABOAN: I have provided those will follow you.
OROONOKO: With this reserve in our proceeding still:
140   The means that lead us to our liberty
            Must not be bloody.
ABOAN: You command in all.
            We shall expect you, Sir.
OROONOKO: You shannot long.
            [*Exeunt* OROONOKO *and* IMOINDA *at one door,* ABOAN *at another.*]

["THUS 'TIS FINISHED"][6]

OROONOKO: I see 'em coming.
            They shannot overtake us. This last kiss.
145   And now farewell.
IMOINDA: Farewell, farewell forever.
OROONOKO: I'll turn my face away, and do it so.
            Now, are you ready?
IMOINDA: Now. But do not grudge me
            The pleasure in my death of a last look.
            Pray look upon me—now I'm satisfied.
OROONOKO: So fate must be by this—
            [*Going to stab her, he stops short; she lays her hands on his, in order to give the blow.*]
IMOINDA: Nay then I must assist you.
            And since it is the common cause of both,
            'Tis just that both should be employed in it,
            Thus, thus 'tis finished, and I bless my fate, [*Stabs herself.*]
155   That where I lived, I die, in these loved arms. [*Dies.*]
OROONOKO: She's gone. And now all's at an end with me.
            [*Throws himself by her.*]
            But let me pay the tribute of my grief,
            A few sad tears to thy loved memory,
            And then I follow—
            [*Weeps over her. A noise again.*]
                                But I stay too long.
160   The noise comes nearer. Hold, before I go,
            There's something would be done. It shall be so.
            And then, Imoinda, I'll come all to thee. [*Rises.*]
            [BLANFORD, *and his party, enter before the* GOVERNOR *and his party, swords drawn on both sides.*][7]
GOVERNOR: You strive in vain to save him. He shall die.
BLANFORD: Not while we can defend him with our lives.
GOVERNOR: Where is he?
OROONOKO: Here's the wretch whom you would have.

---

6. From Act 5, Scene 5. In Southerne's play as in Behn's story the rebellion fails. Anticipating capture, Oroonoko and Imoinda opt instead for death.

7. Blanford, having tried earlier to mediate between the governor and the rebel slaves, has witnessed the colonist's cruelty and now seeks to rescue Oroonoko.

> Put up your swords, and let not civil broils
> Engage you in the cursed cause of one
> Who cannot live, and now entreats to die.
> This object will convince you.
> [*They gather about the body.*]

BLANFORD: 'Tis his wife!
170   Alas! there was no other remedy.

GOVERNOR: Who did the bloody deed?

OROONOKO: The deed was mine:
> Bloody I know it is, and I expect
> Your laws should tell me so. Thus self-condemned
> I do resign myself into your hands,
175   The hands of justice—but I hold the sword
> For you—and for myself.

[*Stabs the* GOVERNOR, *and himself, then throws himself by* IMOINDA's *body.*]

STANMORE: He has killed the governor, and stabbed himself.

OROONOKO: 'Tis as it should be now. I have sent his ghost
> To be a witness of that happiness
180   In the next world, which he has denied us here. [*Dies.*]

BLANFORD: I hope there is a place of happiness
> In the next world for such exalted virtue.
> Pagan, or unbeliever, yet he lived
> To all he knew. And if he went astray,
185   There's mercy still above to set him right.
> But Christians, guided by the heavenly ray,
> Have no excuse if we mistake our way.
> [*Exeunt omnes.*]

FINIS.

1695   1696

⇒⇥ PERSPECTIVES ⇥⇐
Coterie Writing

To Lysander, To the Fair Clarinda, A Letter to Mr. Creech: Some of Behn's poetry, like much other verse in the seventeenth and eighteenth centuries, proffered its readers the voyeuristic sense that they were being let in on the poet's correspondence. Sometimes this was so. In literary families and in friendships, verse often served as a medium of communication. A poem might make its way first from the writer to a designated recipient, then to a larger circle of acquaintances, and finally (with or without the author's consent) to the printing press. The practice of circulating manuscripts has come to be called "coterie writing," and its antecedents were ancient. Theocritus, the Greek poet credited with inventing pastoral verse, cast many of his poems as expressions of love and friendship (sung rather than written) among shepherds and nymphs living in a Golden Age. The Greek names of these ardent Arcadians—all those swooning "Lysanders" and "Clarindas"—came down to the English poets through the *Eclogues* of Virgil, Theocritus's immeasurably influential Roman imitator. Another Roman, Horace, had pioneered the durable paradigm of the verse epistle, a wittily self-conscious poetic performance addressed to a real-life, explicitly identified contemporary. In the seventeenth century, the resurgence of coterie writing began with the work of Katherine Philips, who celebrated her friendships with women in poems published to great acclaim shortly after her early death. (Behn admired Philips enormously, but reworked the tradition by addressing many of her poems to men—lovers and literary colleagues—in a boldly specific, often sexual language that contrasted sharply with Philips's celebrated chastity.) Both men and women produced poems of friendship in great numbers, but for women writers the practice appears to have held a particular attraction. In addressing other women, they could enact a solidarity, cultivate a self-discovery, define and develop a resistance otherwise muted in a male-dominated world; they often depict themselves as building from female friendship what the critic Janet Todd calls "the last buttress against the irrationality always implied in the female condition." The equivocal "privacy" of the coterie poem made it a particularly supple medium, capable of combining fact and fiction, disguise and revelation, intimacy and declamation. The three practitioners sampled here worked many variations in this pliable, powerful mode of writing.

⊷ ⊷ ⊷

Mary, Lady Chudleigh

Born Mary Lee, and wed at age 17 into a family as aristocratic as her own, Lady Chudleigh (1656–1710) lived and wrote in the west coast county of Devon. After years of dispatching manuscript verses among a widening circle of writing friends (including the laureate John Dryden and the pioneering feminist Mary Astell), Chudleigh made her first foray into print with *The Ladies Defense* (1701), a satiric retort to a parson who had exhorted all women (in her mocking paraphrase) to "give up their reason, and their wills resign" to the dictates of their husbands. In her *Defense*, and in the two collections of shorter poems that followed (1703, 1710), Chudleigh sought to expand her coterie into a larger collective readership consisting of "all ingenious ladies": women willing, in defiance of male presumption and social convention, "to read and think, and think and read again," and thereby to "make it our whole business to be wise."

To the Ladies

Wife and servant are the same,
But only differ in the name:

For when that fatal knot is tied,
Which nothing, nothing can divide:
5   When she the word *obey* has said,
And man by law supreme has made,
Then all that's kind is laid aside,
And nothing left but state° and pride: dignity
Fierce as an Eastern Prince he grows,
10   And all his innate rigor shows:
Then but to look, to laugh, or speak,
Will the nuptial contract break.
Like mutes she signs alone must make,
And never any freedom take:
15   But still be governed by a nod,
And fear her husband as her God:
Him still must serve, him still obey,
And nothing act, and nothing say,
But what her haughty lord thinks fit,
20   Who with the power, has all the wit.°   intelligence
Then shun, oh! shun that wretched state,
And all the fawning flatterers hate:
Value your selves, and men despise,
You must be proud, if you'll be wise.

                                                              1703

To Almystrea[1]

1

Permit Marissa[2] in an artless lay
To speak her wonder, and her thanks repay:
Her creeping Muse can ne'er like yours ascend;
She has not strength for such a towering flight.
5   Your wit, her humble fancy does transcend;
She can but gaze at your exalted height:
Yet she believed it better to expose
     Her failures, than ungrateful prove;
          And rather chose
10   To show a want of sense, than want of love:
But taught by you, she may at length improve,
And imitate those virtues she admires.
Your bright example leaves a tract divine,
She sees a beamy brightness in each line,
15   And with ambitious warmth aspires,
Attracted by the glory of your name,
To follow you in all the lofty roads of fame.

---

1. The name is an anagram for Mary Astell, feminist au-   2. Chudleigh's pen name.
thor of *Some Reflections upon Marriage* (see page 2284).

2

Merit like yours can no resistance find,
But like a deluge overwhelms the mind;
20 Gives full possession of each part,
Subdues the soul, and captivates the heart.
Let those whom wealth, or interest[3] unite,
  Whom avarice, or kindred sway,[4]
  Who in the dregs of life delight,
25 And every dictate of their sense° obey,   *appetites*
Learn here to love at a sublimer rate,
To wish for nothing but exchange of thoughts,
  For intellectual joys,
  And pleasures more refined
30 Than earth can give, or fancy can create.
Let our vain sex be fond of glittering toys,
Of pompous titles, and affected noise,
Let envious men by barb'rous custom led
  Descant° on faults,   *expound*
35 And in detraction° find   *criticisms*
Delights unknown to a brave generous mind,
While we resolve a nobler path to tread,
  And from tyrannic custom free,
View the dark mansions of the mighty dead,
40 And all their close recesses see;
  Then from those awful shades retire,
   And take a tour above,
  And there, the shining scenes admire,
  The opera of eternal love;
45 View the machines,[5] on the bright actors gaze,
Then in a holy transport, blest amaze,
To the great Author our devotion raise,
And let our wonder terminate in praise.

1703

Anne Finch, Countess of Winchilsea

In the early 1680s, while serving as Maid of Honor to Mary of Modena (wife of the future James II), Anne Kingsmill (1661–1720) met and married Colonel Heneage Finch, and savored the splendors of the Stuart court. When that world vanished in the Revolution of 1688, she and her husband withdrew to his country estate, where she suffered recurrent depression, cultivated friendships, wrote poetry, and saw her work published in several miscellanies. In 1713, despite her wariness of the censures heaped on women writers, she published anonymously a collection of her own, *Miscellany Poems on Several Occasions*. (The *Introduction*, in

---

3. Self-interest, desire for power and material prosperity.
4. I.e., who are motivated by greed or desire for family status.

5. The stage mechanisms used to move scenery and produce striking effects (including the appearances of gods and angels).

which she most memorably confronts the censurers, remained like much of her verse unpublished until the twentieth century.) The book brought her some fame in her own time and much more a century later, when William Wordsworth proclaimed his admiration for her work. Her poetry moves adroitly among polarities: city and country, satire and affection, solitude and friendship.

The Introduction

Did I my lines intend for public view,
How many censures would their faults pursue!
Some would, because such words they do affect,
Cry they're insipid, empty, uncorrect.
5   And many have attained, dull and untaught,
The name of wit, only by finding fault.
True judges might condemn their want of wit,
And all might say they're by a woman writ.
Alas! A woman that attempts the pen,
10   Such an intruder on the rights of men,
Such a presumptuous creature is esteemed,
The fault can by no virtue be redeemed.
They tell us we mistake our sex and way;
Good breeding, fashion, dancing, dressing, play
15   Are the accomplishments we should desire;
To write, or read, or think, or to inquire
Would cloud our beauty, and exhaust our time,
And interrupt the conquests of our prime;
Whilst the dull manage of a servile house
20   Is held by some our utmost art, and use.
    Sure 'twas not ever thus, nor are we told
Fables,° of women that excelled of old;   *false stories*
To whom, by the diffusive° hand of heaven   *scattering*
Some share of wit and poetry was given.
25   On that glad day, on which the Ark returned,[1]
The holy pledge for which the land had mourned,
The joyful tribes attend it on the way,
The Levites do the sacred charge convey,
Whilst various instruments before it play;
30   Here, holy virgins in the concert join,
The louder notes to soften, and refine,
And with alternate verse,[2] complete the hymn divine.
Lo! The young poet,[3] after God's own heart,
By Him inspired, and taught the Muse's art,
35   Returned from conquest, a bright chorus meets,
That sing his slain ten thousand in the streets.

---

1. The Ark of the Covenant was a chest containing the stone tablets of the Ten Commandments. Recovered by King David, it was carried into Jerusalem by members of the Levite tribe (1 Chronicles 15).
2. Responsive singing: the male and the female choruses sing by turns, answering line with line.
3. David, who in his youth was skilled both as a fighter, conquering the Philistines, and as a harper, credited with composing the Psalms.

In such loud numbers° they his acts declare,   *verses*
Proclaim the wonders of his early war,
That Saul upon the vast applause does frown,
40 And feels its mighty thunder shake the crown.[4]
What can the threatened judgment now prolong?[5]
Half of the kingdom is already gone:
The fairest half, whose influence guides the rest,
Have David's empire o'er their hearts confessed.
45   A woman[6] here leads fainting Israel on,
She fights, she wins, she triumphs with a song,
Devout, majestic, for the subject fit,
And far above her arms, exalts her wit,
Then to the peaceful, shady palm withdraws,
50 And rules the rescued nation with her laws.
How are we fal'n, fal'n by mistaken rules?
And education's, more than nature's fools,
Debarred from all improvements of the mind,
And to be dull, expected and designed;°   *intended*
55 And if someone would soar above the rest,
With warmer fancy[7] and ambition pressed,
So strong the opposing faction still appears,
The hopes to thrive can ne'er outweigh the fears.
Be cautioned then my Muse, and still retired;
60 Nor be despised, aiming to be admired;
Conscious of wants, still with contracted wing,
To some few friends and to thy sorrows sing;
For groves of laurel[8] thou wert never meant;
Be dark enough thy shades, and be thou there content.

1903

Friendship Between Ephelia and Ardelia[1]

Eph.   What friendship is, Ardelia, show.
Ard.   'Tis to love, as I love you.
Eph.   This account, so short (though kind)
        Suits not my inquiring mind.
5   Therefore farther now repeat:
        What is friendship when complete?
Ard.   'Tis to share all joy and grief;
        'Tis to lend all due relief
        From the tongue, the heart, the hand;
10   'Tis to mortgage house and land;
        For a friend be sold a slave;

---

4. Saul, first king of Israel, had made David his general but tried to kill him after hearing the women of Israel singing, "Saul has slain his thousands, and David his ten thousands" (1 Samuel 18.7).
5. Postpone; the prophet Samuel had foretold an untimely end to Saul's reign.

6. Deborah, judge and prophet who led the Israelites to victory over the Canaanites (Judges 4–5).
7. Livelier imagination.
8. Tree whose leaves were used to crown celebrated poets.
1. "Ardelia" is Finch's pastoral pen name.

'Tis to die upon a grave,
If a friend therein do lie.
Eph.   This indeed, though carried high,
15   This, though more than e'er was done
          Underneath the rolling sun,
          This has all been said before.
          Can Ardelia say no more?
Ard.   Words indeed no more can show:
20   But 'tis to love, as I love you.

1713

A Nocturnal Reverie

In such a night,[1] when every louder wind
Is to its distant cavern safe confined;
And only gentle Zephyr° fans his wings,   *the west wind*
And lonely Philomel,° still waking, sings;   *the nightingale*
5 Or from some tree, famed for the owl's delight,
She, hollowing clear, directs the wanderer right:
In such a night, when passing clouds give place,
Or thinly veil the heavens' mysterious face;
When in some river, overhung with green,
10 The waving moon and trembling leaves are seen;
When freshened grass now bears itself upright,
And makes cool banks to pleasing rest invite,
Whence springs the woodbind, and the bramble-rose,
And where the sleepy cowslip sheltered grows;
15 Whilst now a paler hue the foxglove takes,
Yet checkers still with red the dusky brakes:°   *thickets*
When scattered glow-worms, but in twilight fine,
Show trivial beauties, watch their hour to shine;
Whilst Salisbury[2] stands the test of every light,
20 In perfect charms, and perfect virtue bright;
When odors, which declined repelling day,
Through temperate air uninterrupted stray;
When darkened groves their softest shadows wear,
And falling waters we distinctly hear;
25 When through the gloom more venerable shows
Some ancient fabric,° awful in repose,   *building*
While sunburnt hills their swarthy looks conceal,
And swelling haycocks thicken up the vale;
When the loosed horse now, as his pasture leads,

1. Finch takes her opening words from the evocation of night in Shakespeare's *Merchant of Venice* (5.1.1–21), where the lovers Lorenzo and Jessica speak the phrase repeatedly to each other, as they retell old tales of nocturnal passion and betrayal. This time, though, Finch reverses the sociable impulses implicit in the poems above and below. What Shakespeare casts as conversation, she transmutes into soliloquy.
2. Anne Tufton, Countess of Salisbury, daughter of one of Finch's close friends.

30 Comes slowly grazing through th' adjoining meads,
    Whose stealing pace, and lengthened shade we fear,
    Till torn up forage in his teeth we hear;
    When nibbling sheep at large pursue their food,
    And unmolested kine rechew the cud;
35 When curlews cry beneath the village-walls,
    And to her straggling brood the partridge calls;
    Their short-lived jubilee the creatures keep,
    Which but endures, whilst tyrant-man does sleep;
    When a sedate content the spirit feels,
40 And no fierce light disturbs, whilst it reveals;
    But silent musings urge the mind to seek
    Something, too high for syllables to speak;
    Till the free soul to a compos'dness charmed,
    Finding the elements of rage disarmed,
45 O'er all below a solemn quiet grown,
    Joys in th' inferior° world, and thinks it like her own: *lower*
    In such a night let me abroad remain,
    Till morning breaks, and all's confused again;
    Our cares, our toils, our clamors are renewed,
50 Or pleasures, seldom reached, again pursued.

                                                                    1713

A Ballad to Mrs. Catherine Fleming in London from Malshanger Farm in Hampshire

    From me, who whilom° sung the town,   *formerly*
        This second ballad comes;
    To let you know we are got down
        From hurry, smoke, and drums:
5   And every visitor that rolls
    In restless coach from Mall to Paul's,[1]
        With a fa-la-la-la-la-la.

    And now were I to paint the seat[2]
        (As well-bred poets use°)   *do*
10 I should embellish our retreat,
        By favor of the Muse:
    Though to no villa we pretend,
    But a plain farm at the best end,
        With a fa-la etc.

15 Where innocence and quiet reigns,
        And no distrust is known;
    His nightly safety none maintains,
        By ways they do in town,
    Who rising loosen bolt and bar;

1. From Pall Mall, a fashionable promenade in London,   2. The "country seat": the farm.
to St. Paul's Cathedral.

20   We draw the latch and out we are,
            With a fa-la etc.

        For jarring sounds in London streets,
            Which still are passing by;
        Where "Cowcumbers"³ with "Sand ho" meets,
25   And for loud mastery vie:
        The driver whistling to his team
        Here wakes us from some rural dream,
            With a fa-la etc.

        From rising hills through distant views,
30   We see the sun decline;
        Whilst everywhere the eye pursues
            The grazing flocks and kine:
        Which home at night the farmer brings,
        And not the post's but sheep's bell rings,
35   With a fa-la etc.

        We silver trouts and crayfish eat,
            Just taken from the stream;
        And never think our meal complete,
            Without fresh curds and cream:
40   And as we pass by the barn floor,
        We choose our supper from the door,
            With a fa-la etc.

        Beneath our feet the partridge springs,
            As to the woods we go;
45   Where birds scarce stretch their painted wings,
            So little fear they show:
        But when our outspread hoops° they spy,   hoop skirts
        They look when we like them should fly,
            With a fa-la etc.

50   Through verdant circles as we stray,
            To which no end we know;
        As we o'erhanging boughs survey,
            And tufted grass below:
        Delight into the fancy falls,
55   And happy days and verse recalls,
            With a fa-la etc.

        Oh! Why did I these shades forsake,
            And shelter of the grove;
        The flowering shrub, the rustling brake,°   thicket
60   The solitude I love:
        Where emperors have fixed their lot,
        And greatly chose to be forgot,
            With a fa-la etc.

3. Cucumbers; these are the cries of street peddlers.

    Then how can I from hence depart,
65   Unless my pleasing friend
    Should now her sweet harmonious art
       Unto these shades extend:
    And, like old Orpheus' powerful song,[4]
    Draw me and all my woods along,
70   With a fa-la etc.

    So charmed like Birnam's they would rise,
       And march in goodly row,[5]
    But since it might the town surprise
       To see me travel so,
75   I must from soothing joys like these,
    Too soon return in open chaise°   *carriage*
       With a fa-la etc.

    Meanwhile accept what I have writ,
       To show this rural scene;
80   Nor look for sharp satiric wit
       From off the balmy plain:
    The country breeds no thorny bays,
       But mirth and love and honest praise,
       With a fa-la etc.

c. 1719   1929

Mary Leapor

The daughter of a gardener, Mary Leapor (1722–1746) worked as a kitchen maid, read voraciously, wrote plentifully, and sustained the tradition of the social poem (complete with pastoral pseudonyms) into a new era and a new register. Her manuscripts, circulating among neighbors, brought her the attention, friendship, and support of Bridget Freemantle, who undertook to arrange their publication. Leapor died of measles at age 24 before she could see her work in print. *Her Poems upon Several Occasions* appeared in 1748; its success prompted an additional volume three years later. Though the books were marketed as (in the words of one contemporary) the work of "a most extraordinary, uncultivated genius," the poems themselves prove otherwise. They display influences absorbed from Greek and Roman classics, Restoration drama, and Augustan literature—particularly Swift and Pope. Leapor transports these elements across boundary lines of class and gender to produce a new, arresting voice speaking from an old position: that of the woman who must labor in order to live.

The Headache. To Aurelia

    Aurelia, when your zeal makes known
    Each woman's failing but your own,
    How charming Silvia's teeth decay,
    And Celia's hair is turning grey;

---

4. The mythological poet's music charmed trees and stones into motion.
5. In Shakespeare's *Macbeth*, the forest of Birnam "comes" to Dunsinane (fulfilling the witches' prophecy) when soldiers carry boughs as camouflage.

5 Yet Celia gay has sparkling eyes,
 But (to your comfort) is not wise:
 Methinks you take a world of pains
 To tell us Celia has no brains.

  Now you wise folk, who make such a pother°   *fuss*
10 About the wit of one another,
 With pleasure would your brains resign,
 Did all your noddles° ache like mine.   *heads*

  Not cuckolds half my anguish know,
 When budding horns[1] begin to grow;
15 Nor battered skull of wrestling Dick,
 Who late was drubbed at singlestick;[2]
 Nor wretches that in fevers fry,
 Not Sappho[3] when her cap's awry,
 E'er felt such torturing pangs as I;
20 Not forehead of Sir Jeffrey Strife,
 When smiling Cynthio kissed his wife.

  Not lovesick Marcia's languid eyes,
 Who for her simpering Corin dies,
 So sleepy look or dimly shine,
25 As these dejected eyes of mine:
 Not Claudia's brow such wrinkles made
 At sight of Cynthia's new brocade.

  Just so, Aurelia, you complain
 Of vapors, rheums, and gouty pain;
30 Yet I am patient, so should you,
 For cramps and headaches are our due:
 We suffer justly for our crimes,
 For scandal you, and I for rhymes;
 Yet we (as hardened wretches do)
35 Still the enchanting vice pursue;
 Our reformation ne'er begin
 But fondly hug the darling sin.

  Yet there's a mighty difference too
 Between the fate of me and you;
40 Though you with tottering age shall bow,
 And wrinkles scar your lovely brow,
 Your busy tongue may still proclaim
 The faults of every sinful dame:
 You still may prattle nor give o'er,
45 When wretched I must sin no more.
 The sprightly Nine° must leave me then,   *Muses*
 This trembling hand resign its pen:
 No matron ever sweetly sung,

---

1. Folklore held that the husband of an unfaithful wife would sprout horns from his forehead.
2. Beaten in a fencing match using short, heavy sticks.

3. Apparently a mutual friend; the ensuing names, too, refer to either real or imaginary people, otherwise unidentified.

Apollo° only courts the young.   *god of poetry*
50   Then who would not (Aurelia, pray)
Enjoy his favors while they may?
Nor cramps nor headaches shall prevail:
I'll still write on, and you shall rail.

1748

Mira To Octavia

Fair one, to you this monitor[1] I send;
Octavia, pardon your officious friend.
You think your conduct merits only praise,
But outlawed poets censure whom they please.
Thus we begin: your servant[2] has been told
That you (despising settlements and gold)
Determine Florio witty, young and gay,
To have and hold for ever and for ay;[3]
And view that person as your mortal foe
Who dares object against your charming beau.
But now, to furnish meter for my song,
Let us suppose Octavia may be wrong:
'Tis true, you're lovely; yet the learn'd aver
That even beauties like the rest may err.
    I know, to shun, you hold it as a rule,
The arrant coxcomb and the stupid fool.
No such is Florio, he has wit—'tis true:
Enough, Octavia, to impose on you.
Yet such a wit you'll by experience find
Worse than a fool that's complaisant and kind.
It only serves to gild his vices o'er,
And teach his malice how to wound the more.
    I need not tell you, most ingenious fair,
That hungry mortals are not fed with air,
But solid food: And this voracious clay
Asks drink and victuals more than once a day:
Now, could your Florio by his wit inspire
The chilly hearth to blaze with lasting fire;
Or, when his children round the table throng,
By an allusion or a sprightly song,
Adorn the board, i'th'twinkling of an eye,
With a hot pasty or a warden pie,[4]
There might be reason on Octavia's side,
And not a sage could blame the prudent bride.
    Yet (or some authors often deal in lies)
Lovers may live on nuts and blackberries;
For roving knights, bewildered in their way,

1. Advice; warning.
2. I.e., "your humble servant": Leapor herself.
3. Always.
4. Pasty: a meat pie. Warden: a kind of pear.

Who in black forests half a season stray,
Unless they find provision on the trees,
Must sup on grass and breakfast on the breeze.[5]
But as you've long been used to nicer fare,
Your constitution would but hardly bear
Such food as this. And therefore I advise
That you'd consider (for you're mighty wise)
If sober Dusterandus would not make
A better husband than your darling rake.
Grave Dusterandus: He whose steadfast mind
Is yet untainted, though not much refined;
Whose soul ne'er roves beyond his native fields,
Nor asks for joys but what his pasture yields;
On life's dull cares with patience can attend,
A gentle master and a constant friend;
Who in soft quiet spends the guiltless days,
His servants' blessing and his neighbors' praise.
Say, would you, in his happy mansion, reign,
Toast of the village and the rural plain?
With honest friends your cheerful days beguile,
While peace and plenty on your table smile?
Or cold and hungry writhe your tired jaws,
And dine with Florio upon hips and haws?[6]
In troth I think there's little room for pause.
    In spite of all romantic poets sing,
This gold, my dearest, is an useful thing.
Not that I'd have you hoard the precious store—
For not a wretch is like the miser poor.
Enjoy your fortune with a cheerful mind,
And let the blessing spread amongst the kind.
But if there's none but Florio that will do,
Write ballads both, and you may thrive. Adieu.

1748

An Epistle to Artemisia.[1] On Fame

Say, Artemisia, do the slaves of fame
Deserve our pity, or provoke our blame?
Whose airy hopes, like some new-kindled fire,
A moment blaze, and then in smoke expire;
5   Or like a babe i'th'midst of plenty cry,
And leave their supper for a painted fly[2]

---

5. Leapor parodies the ordeals of deprivation often suffered by heroes of romance.
6. Wild berries.
1. "Artemisia" is the name of an ancient ruler celebrated as a patron of literature; Leapor applies it to her friend and patron, Bridget Freemantle. The poem's topics (the hopes entailed in writing, the pains of being read—and visited) and its tone (affectionate to its addressee, exasperated with everyone else) show affinities with Pope's *Epistle to Dr. Arbuthnot* (see pages 2509–21).
2. I.e., a colorful (and distracting) bug.

Bold Maro[3] paints her of gigantic size,
And makes her forehead prop the lofty skies;
With eyes and ears he hung the lady round,
10   And her shrill clarion shook the heavens around.
Then worthy names the trembling notes prolong,
And actions blazing in immortal song;
But, weary now, and grown an ancient maid,
Her strength exhausted, and her lungs decayed,
15   Her unspread wings resign their plumy pride,
And her hoarse trumpet dangles by her side.
A handmaid leads the purblind dame along,
Black Slander called, with never-ceasing tongue;
And when this servant whispers in her ears,
20   She to her mouth the heavy trumpet rears.
The rattling concave[4] sends a horrid cry,
And smoking scandals hiss along the sky;
Yet round her still the supple vot'ries[5] crowd,
And pay devotion to a painted cloud.
25   The fond Ixions[6] spread their longing arms,
And grasp a vapor for a Juno's charms.
     The hero brave, that never knew to shun
The pointed canon, or the bursting gun,
Of bruises vain, and prodigal of scars,
30   Returns from pillage, and successful wars.
But if the sullen rout[7] refuse to pay
The vulgar triumphs of a noisy day,[8]
To his sad bosom pale despondence creeps,
And the stern soldier like an infant weeps.
35   Caballing skeptics shake the frighted gown,[9]
And poets tremble at an idiot's frown.
The scorn of fools can pierce a noble heart,
And wound an author in the tend'rest part.
     Rich Merrio thought, like eastern kings, to raise
40   By lofty columns everlasting praise.
His broad foundations half the field surround,
And piles of timber load the sinking ground.
This Heav'n beheld, and smiled at seeing Man,
Whose joy is vapor, and whole life a span,[1]
45   Who Death's black warrant every moment fears,
Still building castles for a thousand years.

---

3. The Roman epic poet Virgil, who in Book 4 of his *Aeneid* portrays Fama (Rumor) as an immense goddess, who wears a garment studded with functioning eyes and ears.
4. The trumpet's horn.
5. Votaries: those who worship and desire fame.
6. In Greek mythology, a king named Ixion hopes to seduce Zeus's wife Hera (the "Juno" of the next line). Zeus tricks him by sculpting a cloud-likeness of the goddess, which Ixion deludedly embraces.

7. Crowd.
8. The celebration, called a "triumph," traditionally held in honor of military victory.
9. The gown was an emblem of both church and university; here it stands for the clergyman or scholar alarmed by those who mock his argument. A "cabal" is any powerful and secret conspiracy.
1. A small distance: the space, with the hand outstretched. "from the end of the thumb to the end of the little finger" (Johnson's *Dictionary*).

On this grand wretch was passed an early doom;
And Merrio, summoned to the silent gloom,
Feels, ere his eyes behold the glowing spires,
50   The stroke of fate, and with a sigh expires.
    All reas'ning creatures, though by different ways,
Would prove their titles to a share of praise.
Cornelia's praise consists in plaiting well;[2]
Pastora's fingers at a Knot excel;
55   Her gaudy ribbons gay Sabina furls;
But looks with Envy on Aurelia's curls.
    Unhappy Delia thought a shining gown
Would gain respect, and win the gazing town.
But Envy rose, to clip her rising wings,
60   And, grinning ghastly (as the poet sings),
In Claudia's shape dissolved the lady's pride,[3]
And slily whispered, "Delia's gown is dyed."
    Even Mira's self, presuming on the bays,[4]
Appears among the candidates for praise:
65   Has watched applause, as from the lips it fell;
With what success? Why, that the Muse shall tell.
May Artemisia not refuse to hear!
For praise could ne'er offend her gentle ear.
I count the patrons of my early song,
70   And pay the tributes to their shares belong.[5]
What sorrows too oppressed the Muse's wing,
Till your good nature gave her strength to sing!
    Once Delpho read—sage Delpho,[6] learn'd and wise,
O'er the scrawled paper cast his judging eyes,
75   Whose lifted brows confessed a critic's pride,
While his broad thumb moved nimbly down the side.
His form was like some oracle profound:
The listening audience formed a circle round:
But Mira, fixing her presuming eyes
80   On the stern image, thus impatient cries:
Sir, will they prosper? Speak your judgment, pray.
Replies the statue, "Why, perhaps they may."
For further answers we in vain implore:
The charm was over, and it spoke no more.
85   Cressida comes,[7] the next unbidden guest.
Small was her top-knot,[8] and her judgment less.
A decent virgin, blest with idle time,

---

2. I.e., in skillfully braiding hair.
3. I.e., Envy incarnates itself in Claudia, who whispers the couplet's punchline.
4. I.e., Leapor herself (the name is a near-anagram of "Mary," and may echo the Latin *mirari*: to wonder at), here aspiring to the crown of bay leaves traditionally bestowed on poets laureate.
5. Here Leapor lays out her plan for the rest of the poem: to recount the reactions of the early readers to whom she

showed her work.
6. A critic, whom Leapor renames for the ancient oracle of Delphi, which delivered hard truths in obscure language.
7. Another reader, here named for the fickle Trojan heroine of Chaucer's poem and Shakespeare's play.
8. "A knot [of hair] worn by women on the top of their head" (Johnson's *Dictionary*).

Now jingles bobbins,[9] and now ponders rhyme:
Not ponders—reads—not reads—but looks 'em o'er
90   To little purpose, like a thousand more.
     "Your servant, Molly."[1]
                          "I am yours the same."
"I pay this visit, Molly, to your fame:
'Twas that that brought me here—or let me die."[2]
"My fame's obliged—and truly, so am I."
95   "Then fetch me something, for I must not stay
Above four hours."
                  "But you'll drink some tea?"[3]
We sip, and read; we laugh, and chat between.
"The air is pleasant, and the fields are green.
Well, Molly, sure, there never was thy fellow.[4]
100   But don't my ruffles look exceeding yellow?
My apron's dirty—Mira, well, I vow,
This thought of yours was very pretty now.
I've read the like, though I forget the place.
But, Mrs. Mira, how d'ye like my lace?"
105   Afflicted Mira, with a languid eye,
Now views the clock, and now the western sky.
"The sun grows lower. Will you please to walk?"
"No, read some more."
               "But I had rather talk."
"Perhaps you're tired."
                "Truly, that may be."
110   "Or think me weak."
             "Why, Cressy, thoughts are free."[5]
At last we part, with congees[6] at the door.
"I'd thank you, Mira, but my thanks are poor.
I wish, alas! But wishes are in vain.
I like your garden; and I'll come again.
115   Dear, how I wish—I do, or let me die!—
That we lived near."
           Thinks Mira, "So don't I."
  This nymph, perhaps, as some had done before,
Found the cold welcome, and returned no more.
    Then Vido[7] next to Mira's cot appears,
120   And with soft praise salutes her list'ning ears;
Whose maxim was, with truth not to offend,
And, right or wrong, his business to commend.
"Look here," cries Mira, "pray peruse this song.
Even I, its parent, see there's something wrong."

---

9. "A small pin of wood, with a notch, to wind the thread about when women weave lace" (Johnson's *Dictionary*).
1. Cressida greets Leapor ("Molly" was a nickname for Mary) with a traditional formula of politeness: [I am] your servant.
2. I.e., "I swear."
3. Pronounced *tay*.

4. I.e., "no one equals you" (Cressida offhandedly praises her poetry).
5. Proverbial: I may think what I please.
6. Formal farewells.
7. A friend whom Leapor depicts in other poems ("Celadon to Mira" and "The Disappointment") as a shameless flatterer, skilled in the "well-bred lie."

125　　"But you mistake: 'Tis excellent indeed."
　　　　"Then I'll correct it."
　　　　　　　　　　　　　　"No, there is no need."
　　　　"Pray, Vido, look on these: methinks they smell
　　　　Too much of Grub Street;[8] that myself can tell."
　　　　"Not so indeed; they're easy and polite."
130　　"And can you bear 'em?"
　　　　　　　　　　　　　　"I could read till night."
　　　　But Mira, though too partial to the bays
　　　　And, like her brethren, not averse to praise,
　　　　Had learned this lesson: praise, if planted wrong,
　　　　Is more destructive than a spiteful tongue.
135　　　　Comes Codrus next, with talents to offend;
　　　　A simple tutor, and a saucy friend,
　　　　Who poured thick sonnets like a troubled spring,
　　　　And such as Butler's wide-mouthed mortals sing:[9]
　　　　In shocking rhymes a nymph's perfections tells,
140　　Like the harsh ting-tong of some village bells.
　　　　Then a rude quarrel sings through either ear,
　　　　And Mira's levee[1] once again is clear.
　　　　　　Now the dull Muses took their usual rest.
　　　　The babes[2] slept soundly in their tiny chest.
145　　Not so their parent: Fortune still[3] would send
　　　　Some proud director,[4] or ill-meaning friend.
　　　　At least we thought their sour meanings ill,
　　　　Whose lectures strove to cross a stubborn will.
　　　　　　Parthenia cries, "Why, Mira, you are dull,
150　　And ever musing till you crack your skull.
　　　　Still poking o'er your what-d'ye-call—your Muse.
　　　　But prithee, Mira, when dost clean thy shoes?"
　　　　　　Then comes Sophronia, like a barb'rous Turk:
　　　　"You thoughtless baggage, when d'ye mind your work?
155　　Still o'er a table leans your bending neck.
　　　　Your head will grow prepost'rous, like a peck.[5]
　　　　Go, ply your needle. You might earn your bread;
　　　　Or who must feed you when your father's dead?"
　　　　She sobbing answers, "Sure, I need not come
160　　To you for lectures; I have store at home.
　　　　What can I do?"
　　　　　　　　　　　　"Not scribble."
　　　　　　　　　　　　　　　　　　"But I will."
　　　　"Then get thee packing—and be awkward still."
　　　　　　Thus wrapped in sorrow wretched Mira lay,

---

8. The proverbial London habitat of hack writers.
9. Leapor echoes the mocking description, by Samuel Butler (1612–1680) in his satiric poem *Hudibras* (1663–1678), of a vacuous-minded astrologer's assistant named Whachum, whose "sonnets charmed th' attentive crowd / By wide-mouthed mortal trolled aloud" (2.3.383–4).

1. "Royal reception"; here self-mockingly invoked to describe the gathering of Leapor's friends, who now disperse in order to avoid hearing Codrus's ponderous poems.
2. "Her poems" [editor's note, 1751].
3. Always; repeatedly.
4. Pedantic instructor.
5. A two-gallon container.

Till Artemisia swept the gloom away.
165 The laughing Muse, by her example led,
Shakes her glad wings, and quits the drowsy bed.
   Yet some impertinence pursues me still;
And so I fear it ever must, and will.
So soft Pappilia[6] o'er the table bends
170 With her small circle of insipid friends,
Who wink, and stretch, and rub their drowsy eyes,
While o'er their heads imperial Dullness flies.[7]
"What can we do? We cannot stir for show'rs;[8]
Or what invent, to kill the irksome hours?
175 Why, run to Leapor's, fetch that idle play[9]
'Twill serve to laugh at all the livelong day."
   Preferment great! To beat one's weary brains,
To find diversion only when it rains!
   Methinks I feel this coward bosom glow[1]
180 Say, Artemisia, shall I speak, or no?
The Muse shall give herself no fancy airs,
But only bid 'em[2] softly, read their prayers.

1751

Advice to Sophronia

   When youth and charms have ta'en their wanton flight,
And transient beauty bids the fair good-night;
When once her sparkling eyes shall dimly roll,
Then let the matron dress her lofty soul;
5 Quit affectation, partner of her youth,
For goodness, prudence, purity, and truth.
These virtues will her lasting peace prepare,
And give a sanction to her silver hair.
These precepts let the fond Sophronia prove,
10 Nor vainly dress her blinking eyes with love.
Can roses flourish on a leafless thorn,
Or dewy woodbines grace a wintry morn?
The weeping Cupids languish in your eye;
On your brown cheek the sickly beauties die.
15 Time's rugged hand has stroked your visage o'er;
The gay vermilion stains your lip no more.
None can with justice now your shape admire;
The drooping lilies on your breast expire.
Then, dear Sophronia, leave thy foolish whims:
20 Discard your lover with your favorite sins.
Consult your glass; then prune your wanton mind,

---

6. *Papilio* (Latin): butterfly. Pope gives the same name to a whim-driven woman in "Epistle 2: To a Lady" (ll. 37–40; see page 2522).
7. Torpor, stupidity; here personified as the apocalyptic goddess of Pope's *Dunciad* (see pages 2531–43).

8. I.e., the rain prevents their going out.
9. Leapor wrote plays as well as poems.
1. I.e., kindle with sudden courage.
2. I.e., the "small circle of insipid friends" (line 170) who seek to divert themselves with Leapor's play.

Nor furnish laughter for succeeding time.
'Tis not your own; 'tis gold's all-conquering charms
Invite Myrtillo to your shrivelled arms:
25   And shall Sophronia, whose once-lovely eyes
Beheld those triumphs which her heart despised,
Who looked on merit with a haughty frown,
At five-and-fifty take a beardless clown?
Ye pitying Fates, this withered damsel save,
30   And bear her safely to her virgin grave.

                                              1751

The Epistle of Deborah Dough

Dearly beloved Cousin, these
Are sent to thank you for your cheese;
The price of oats is greatly fell:
I hope your children all are well
5   (Likewise the calf you take delight in),
As I am at this present writing.
But I've no news to send you now;
Only I've lost my brindled° cow,   *spotted*
And that has greatly sunk my dairy.
10   But I forgot our neighbor Mary;
Our neighbor Mary—who, they say,
Sits scribble-scribble all the day,
And making—what—I can't remember;
But sure 'tis something like December;
15   A frosty morning—let me see—
O! Now I have it to a T:
She throws away her precious time
In scrawling nothing else but rhyme;[1]
Of which, they say, she's mighty proud,
20   And lifts her nose above the crowd;
Though my young daughter Cicely
Is taller by a foot than she,
And better learned (as people say);
Can knit a stocking in a day;
25   Can make a pudding, plump and rare;
And boil her bacon to an hair;
Will coddle° apples nice and green,   *cook*
And fry her pancakes—like a queen.

     But there's a man, that keeps a dairy,
30   Will clip the wings of neighbor Mary:
Things wonderful they talk of him,
But I've a notion 'tis a whim.
Howe'er, 'tis certain he can make

---

1. A pun on "rime" (frost), which is why her work is "like December."

Your rhymes as thick as plums in cake;
35   Nay more, they say that from the pot
He'll take his porridge, scalding hot,
And drink 'em down;—and yet they tell ye
Those porridge shall not burn his belly;
A cheesecake o'er his head he'll throw,
40   And when 'tis on the stones below,
It shan't be found so much as quaking,
Provided 'tis of his wife's making.
From this some people would infer
That this good man's a conjuror:
45   But I believe it is a lie;
I never thought him so, not I,
Though Win'fred Hobble who, you know,
Is plagued with corns on every toe,
Sticks on his verse with fastening spittle,
50   And says it helps her feet a little.
Old Frances too his paper tears,
And tucks it close behind his ears;
And (as she told me t'other day)
It charmed her toothache quite away.

55   Now as thou'rt better learned than me,
Dear Cos', I leave it all to thee
To judge about this puzzling man,
And ponder wisely—for you can.

Now Cousin, I must let you know
60   That, while my name is Deborah Dough,
I shall be always glad to see ye,
And what I have, I'll freely gi' ye.

'Tis one o'clock, as I'm a sinner;
The boys are all come home to dinner,
65   And I must bid you now farewell.
I pray remember me to Nell;
And for your friend I'd have you know
Your loving Cousin,
                    DEBORAH DOUGH

1751

꜡ END OF PERSPECTIVES: COTERIE WRITING ꜡

꜡꜡꜡

John Wilmot, Earl of Rochester
1647–1680

In one of his many notorious escapades, John Wilmot, Earl of Rochester, drunkenly smashed to
pieces one of the king's costliest timekeepers. He always lived at odds with ordinary time, mostly
ahead of it: he became Earl at age ten, when his father died; received his M.A. from Oxford at

fourteen; conducted a Grand Tour of Europe during the next three years; tried to abduct his future wife Elizabeth Malet (a much-sought woman of wealth, wit, and beauty) when he was eighteen, and was briefly imprisoned for the attempt; married her at twenty; and died, after long libertinage and precipitate piety, at thirty-three. Rochester's wit and beauty, the stupendous energies of his mind (erudite, inventive), of his language (adroit, obscene), of his body (alcoholic, bisexual), and of his convictions (hedonistic, atheistic) made him the fascination of the Restoration court, whose proclivities for theatrics, for combat, and for amorous entanglement he pushed to matchless extremes. Theatrics: Rochester wrote plays of his own and produced plays by others; he tutored the stage novice Elizabeth Barry, soon to become the greatest actress of the age (they carried on a volatile affair, and had a daughter); at times he could don a disguise himself and play a role so successfully (in order to go underground, to escape punishment, to bring off a seduction) that close friends could not recognize him. Combat: Rochester distinguished himself for courage by plunging into the thick of the fighting during several sea battles; he once disgraced himself for cowardice in running away during a nocturnal street brawl, "frighted" (he later wrote) "at my own mischiefs" and leaving one of his own defenders dead. In the lesser combats of the court, those endless verbal cutting contests of improvised insult and impromptu verse, Rochester was virtually unbeatable (though the king, when cut, could cut back: the earl's status shifted often and quickly between favorite and outcast). Amorous entanglement: Rochester's letters to his wife bespeak a marriage of extraordinary tenderness; his poems boast a career of fornication scarcely credible in its range and ferocity. In 1680, ill and exhausted, Rochester left London for his ancestral country estate where, frighted by his own mischiefs on a grander scale, he pursued a highly publicized course of penitence under the tutelage of the clergyman Gilbert Burnet, who later published a detailed account of their conversations. The authenticity of this deathbed conversion was questioned then, and has been questioned since, but its results were real enough: Rochester asked his mother to burn his papers, and she did. Fewer than a hundred poems survive. Rochester had never troubled to publish any of them himself; a pirated collection appeared a few months after his death. Yet these pieces, and the conflicting accounts of the life that produced them, have been enough to make him last. Soon after his death, the poet Aphra Behn claimed in verse to have received a visit from his "lovely phantom." "The great, the god-like Rochester" comes before her in order both to praise and to correct her poetry. Since then he has haunted many—pietists, poets, and others—as object of veneration, or reproach, or both together: as admonitory example, verbal virtuoso, extraordinary mortal.

Against Constancy

Tell me no more of constancy,
   The frivolous pretense
Of cold age, narrow jealousy,
   Disease, and want of sense.

5   Let duller fools, on whom kind chance
   Some easy heart has thrown,
Despairing higher to advance,
   Be kind to one alone.

Old men and weak, whose idle flame
10   Their own defects discovers,
Since changing can but spread their shame,
   Ought to be constant lovers.

But we, whose hearts do justly swell
   With no vainglorious pride,

15 Who know how we in love excel,
    Long to be often tried.

Then bring my bath, and strew my bed,
    As each kind night returns;
I'll change a mistress till I'm dead—
20   And fate change me to worms.

1676

The Disabled Debauchee

As some brave admiral, in former war
    Deprived of force, but pressed with courage still,
Two rival fleets appearing from afar,
    Crawls to the top of an adjacent hill;

5 From whence, with thoughts full of concern, he views
    The wise and daring conduct of the fight,
Whilst each bold action to his mind renews
    His present glory and his past delight;

From his fierce eyes flashes of fire he throws,
10   As from black clouds when lightning breaks away;
Transported, thinks himself amidst the foes,
    And absent, yet enjoys the bloody day;

So, when my days of impotence approach,
    And I'm by pox and wine's unlucky chance
15 Forced from the pleasing billows of debauch
    On the dull shore of lazy temperance,

My pains at least some respite shall afford
    While I behold the battles you maintain
When fleets of glasses sail about the board,[1]
20   From whose broadsides volleys of wit shall rain.

Nor let the sight of honorable scars,
    Which my too forward valor did procure,
Frighten new-listed soldiers from the wars:
    Past joys have more than paid what I endure.

25 Should any youth (worth being drunk) prove nice,
    And from his fair inviter meanly shrink,
'Twill please the ghost of my departed Vice[2]
    If, at my counsel, he repent and drink.

Or should some cold-complexioned sot forbid,
30   With his dull morals, our bold night-alarms,
I'll fire his blood by telling what I did
    When I was strong and able to bear arms.

1. I.e., wine glasses passed around the table.
2. A character bearing this name had been a staple figure in medieval morality plays, as the comic, scoffing incarnation of depravity.

I'll tell of whores attacked, their lords at home;
   Bawds' quarters beaten up, and fortress won;
35   Windows demolished, watches overcome;
   And handsome ills by my contrivance done.

Nor shall our love-fits, Chloris,[3] be forgot,
   When each the well-looked linkboy[4] strove t' enjoy,
And the best kiss was the deciding lot
40   Whether the boy fucked you, or I the boy.

With tales like these I will such thoughts inspire
   As to important mischief shall incline:
I'll make him long some ancient church to fire,
   And fear no lewdness he's called to by wine.

45   Thus, statesmanlike, I'll saucily impose,
   And safe from action, valiantly advise;
Sheltered in impotence, urge you to blows,
   And being good for nothing else, be wise.

1675?   1680

Song

Love a woman? You're an ass!
   'Tis a most insipid passion
To choose out for your happiness
   The silliest part of God's creation.

5   Let the porter and the groom,
   Things designed for dirty slaves,
Drudge in fair Aurelia's womb
   To get supplies for age and graves.

Farewell, woman! I intend
10   Henceforth every night to sit
With my lewd, well-natured friend,
   Drinking to engender wit.

Then give me health, wealth, mirth, and wine,
   And, if busy love entrenches,
15   There's a sweet, soft page of mine
   Does the trick worth forty wenches.

                                        1680

The Imperfect Enjoyment

Naked she lay, clasped in my longing arms,
I filled with love, and she all over charms;
Both equally inspired with eager fire,
Melting through kindness, flaming in desire.

---

3. A woman's name, common in pastoral verse (and in Rochester's).
4. A boy employed to accompany walkers on the city streets at night, lighting their way by means of a torch ("link").

5   With arms, legs, lips close clinging to embrace,
     She clips me to her breast, and sucks me to her face.
     Her nimble tongue, Love's lesser lightning, played
     Within my mouth, and to my thoughts conveyed
     Swift orders that I should prepare to throw
10   The all-dissolving thunderbolt below.
     My fluttering soul, sprung with the pointed kiss,
     Hangs hovering o'er her balmy brinks of bliss.
     But whilst her busy hand would guide that part
     Which should convey my soul up to her heart,
15   In liquid raptures I dissolve all o'er,
     Melt into sperm, and spend at every pore.
     A touch from any part of her had done 't:
     Her hand, her foot, her very look's a cunt.
       Smiling, she chides in a kind murmuring noise,
20   And from her body wipes the clammy joys,
     When, with a thousand kisses wandering o'er
     My panting bosom, "Is there then no more?"
     She cries. "All this to love and rapture's due;
     Must we not pay a debt to pleasure too?"
25   But I, the most forlorn, lost man alive,
     To show my wished obedience vainly strive:
     I sigh, alas! and kiss, but cannot swive.°   *screw*
     Eager desires confound my first intent,
     Succeeding shame does more success prevent,
30   And rage at last confirms me impotent.
     Ev'n her fair hand, which might bid heat return
     To frozen age, and make cold hermits burn,
     Applied to my dead cinder, warms no more
     Than fire to ashes could past flames restore.
35   Trembling, confused, despairing, limber, dry,
     A wishing, weak, unmoving lump I lie.
     This dart of love, whose piercing point, oft tried,
     With virgin blood ten thousand maids have dyed,
     Which nature still directed with such art
40   That it through every cunt reached every heart—
     Stiffly resolved, 'twould carelessly invade
     Woman or man, nor ought° its fury stayed:°   *anything / stopped*
     Where'er it pierced, a cunt it found or made—
     Now languid lies in this unhappy hour,
45   Shrunk up and sapless like a withered flower.
       Thou treacherous, base deserter of my flame,
     False to my passion, fatal to my fame,
     Through what mistaken magic dost thou prove
     So true to lewdness, so untrue to love?
50   What oyster-cinder-beggar-common whore
     Didst thou e'er fail in all thy life before?
     When vice, disease, and scandal lead the way,
     With what officious haste doest thou obey!

	Like a rude, roaring hector° in the streets	*bully*
55	Who scuffles, cuffs, and justles all he meets,	
	But if his king or country claim his aid,	
	The rakehell villain shrinks and hides his head;	
	Ev'n so thy brutal valor is displayed,	
	Breaks every stew,° does each small whore invade,	*brothel*
60	But when great Love the onset does command,	
	Base recreant to thy prince, thou dar'st not stand.	
	Worst part of me, and henceforth hated most,	
	Through all the town a common fucking post,	
	On whom each whore relieves her tingling cunt	
65	As hogs on gates do rub themselves and grunt,	
	Mayst thou to ravenous chancres° be a prey,	*syphilis sores*
	Or in consuming weepings waste away;	
	May strangury and stone¹ thy days attend;	
	May'st thou never piss, who didst refuse to spend	
70	When all my joys did on false thee depend.	
	And may ten thousand abler pricks agree	
	To do the wronged Corinna right for thee.	

1680

Upon Nothing

Nothing! thou elder brother even to Shade:
Thou hadst a being ere the world was made,
And well fixed, art alone of ending not afraid.

Ere Time and Place were, Time and Place were not,
5 When primitive Nothing Something straight begot;
Then all proceeded from the great united What.

Something, the general attribute of all,
Severed from thee, its sole original,
Into thy boundless self must undistinguished fall;

10 Yet Something did thy mighty power command,
And from thy fruitful Emptiness's hand
Snatched men, beasts, birds, fire, water, air, and land.

Matter, the wicked'st offspring of thy race,
By Form assisted, flew from thy embrace,
15 And rebel Light obscured thy reverend dusky face.

With Form and Matter, Time and Place did join;
Body, thy foe, with these did leagues combine
To spoil thy peaceful realm, and ruin all thy line;

But turncoat Time assists the foe in vain,
20 And bribed by thee, destroys their short-lived reign,
And to thy hungry womb drives back thy slaves again.

---

1. Painful diseases of the bladder and urinary tract that block the flow of urine.

Though mysteries are barred from laic° eyes,   *uninitiated*
And the divine alone with warrant pries
Into thy bosom, where the truth in private lies,

25   Yet this of thee the wise may truly say:
Thou from the virtuous nothing dost delay,
And to be part of thee the wicked wisely pray.

Great Negative, how vainly would the wise
Inquire, define, distinguish, teach, devise,
30   Didst thou not stand to point their blind philosophies!

Is or Is Not, the two great ends of Fate,
And True or False, the subject of debate,
That perfect or destroy the vast designs of state—

When they have racked the politician's breast,
35   Within thy bosom most securely rest,
And when reduced to thee, are least unsafe and best.

But Nothing, why does Something still permit
That sacred monarchs should in council sit
With persons highly thought at best for nothing fit,

40   While weighty Something modestly abstains
From princes' coffers, and from statesmen's brains,
And Nothing there like stately Nothing reigns?

Nothing! who dwellst with fools in grave disguise,
For whom they reverend shapes and forms devise,
45   Lawn[1] sleeves and furs and gowns, when they like thee look wise:

French truth, Dutch prowess, British policy,
Hibernian learning, Scotch civility,
Spaniards' dispatch, Danes' wit are mainly seen in thee;

The great man's gratitude to his best friend,
50   Kings' promises, whores' vows—towards thee they bend,
Flow swiftly into thee, and in thee ever end.

1678   1679

A Satyr[1] Against Reason and Mankind

Were I (who to my cost already am
One of those strange, prodigious creatures, man)
A spirit free to choose, for my own share,
What case of flesh and blood I pleased to wear,
5   I'd be a dog, a monkey, or a bear,
Or anything but that vain animal
Who is so proud of being rational.
The senses are too gross, and he'll contrive

---

1. Linen; worn (like the furs and gowns) as a mark of rank
by eminent professionals: lawyers, scholars, statesmen, etc.

1. Possibly a pun, identifying both the genre (satire) and
the speaker (a satyr: half-man, half-animal).

A sixth, to contradict the other five,
10   And before certain instinct, will prefer
Reason, which fifty times for one does err;
Reason, an *ignis fatuus*[2] in the mind,
Which, leaving light of nature, sense, behind,
Pathless and dangerous wandering ways it takes
15   Through error's fenny bogs and thorny brakes;
Whilst the misguided follower climbs with pain
Mountains of whimseys, heaped in his own brain;
Stumbling from thought to thought, falls headlong down
Into doubt's boundless sea, where, like to drown,
20   Books bear him up awhile, and make him try
To swim with bladders of philosophy;
In hopes still to o'ertake th' escaping light,
The vapor dances in his dazzling sight
Till, spent, it leaves him to eternal night.
25   Then old age and experience, hand in hand,
Lead him to death, and make him understand,
After a search so painful and so long,
That all his life he has been in the wrong.
Huddled in dirt the reasoning engine lies,
30   Who was so proud, so witty, and so wise.
    Pride drew him in, as cheats their bubbles° catch,   *victims*
And made him venture to be made a wretch.
His wisdom did his happiness destroy,
Aiming to know that world he should enjoy.
35   And wit was his vain, frivolous pretense
Of pleasing others at his own expense,
For wits are treated just like common whores:
First they're enjoyed, and then kicked out of doors.
The pleasure past, a threatening doubt remains
40   That frights th' enjoyer with succeeding pains.
Women and men of wit are dangerous tools,
And ever fatal to admiring fools:
Pleasure allures, and when the fops escape,
'Tis not that they're belov'd, but fortunate,
45   And therefore what they fear at heart, they hate.
    But now, methinks, some formal band and beard[3]
Takes me to task. Come on, sir; I'm prepared.
    "Then, by your favor, anything that's writ
Against this gibing, jingling knack called wit
50   Likes° me abundantly; but you take care   *pleases*
Upon this point, not to be too severe.
Perhaps my muse were fitter for this part,

---

2. Literally "foolish fire": a marshland phosphorescence that, appearing now here and now there, was thought to be created by sprites to mislead night travelers.
3. I.e., clergyman, wearing these marks of office. In 1675 one clergyman in particular, the king's chaplain Edward Stillingfleet, had denounced in a sermon an earlier version of Rochester's *Satyr,* prompting the poet to alter and add some portions of the dialogue that follows.

For I profess I can be very smart
On wit, which I abhor with all my heart.
55   I long to lash it in some sharp essay,
But your grand indiscretion bids me stay
And turns my tide of ink another way.
      "What rage ferments in your degenerate mind
To make you rail at reason and mankind?
60   Blest, glorious man! to whom alone kind heaven
An everlasting soul has freely given,
Whom his great Maker took such care to make
That from himself he did the image take
And this fair frame in shining reason dressed
65   To dignify his nature above beast;
Reason, by whose aspiring influence
We take a flight beyond material sense,
Dive into mysteries, then soaring pierce
The flaming limits of the universe,
70   Search heaven and hell, find out what's acted there,
And give the world true grounds of hope and fear."
      Hold, mighty man, I cry, all this we know
From the pathetic pen of Ingelo,
From Patrick's *Pilgrim*, Stillingfleet's replies,[4]
75   And 'tis this very reason I despise:
This supernatural gift, that makes a mite
Think he's the image of the infinite,
Comparing his short life, void of all rest,
To the eternal and the ever blest;
80   This busy, puzzling stirrer-up of doubt
That frames deep mysteries, then finds 'em out,
Filling with frantic crowds of thinking fools
Those reverend bedlams,° colleges and schools;   *madhouses*
Borne on whose wings, each heavy sot can pierce
85   The limits of the boundless universe;
So charming ointments make an old witch fly
And bear a crippled carcass through the sky.
'Tis this exalted power, whose business lies
In nonsense and impossibilities,
90   This made a whimsical philosopher
Before the spacious world, his tub prefer,[5]
And we have modern cloistered coxcombs who
Retire to think, 'cause they have nought to do.
      But thoughts are given for action's government;
95   Where action ceases, thought's impertinent.
Our sphere of action is life's happiness,

---

4. Rochester names three pious inspirational writers: Nathaniel Ingelo (?1621–1683); Simon Patrick, whose *Parable of the Pilgrim* appeared in 1664; and Stillingfleet, Rochester's clerical critic.

5. Diogenes (c. 400–325 B.C.E.), Greek philosopher who supposedly lived in an earthenware tub, as an emblem of his scorn for the shallowness of more opulent modes of life.

And he who thinks beyond, thinks like an ass.
Thus, whilst against false reasoning I inveigh,
I own[6] right reason, which I would obey:
100 That reason which distinguishes by sense
And gives us rules of good and ill from thence,
That bounds desires with a reforming will
To keep 'em more in vigor, not to kill.
Your reason hinders, mine helps to enjoy,
105 Renewing appetites yours would destroy.
My reason is my friend, yours is a cheat;
Hunger calls out, my reason bids me eat;
Perversely, yours your appetite does mock:
This asks for food, that answers, "What's o'clock?"
110 This plain distinction, sir, your doubt secures:
'Tis not true reason I despise, but yours.
　　Thus I think reason righted, but for man,
I'll ne'er recant; defend him if you can.
For all his pride and his philosophy,
115 'Tis evident beasts are, in their degree,
As wise at least, and better far than he.
Those creatures are the wisest who attain,
By surest means, the ends at which they aim.
If therefore Jowler[7] finds and kills his hares
120 Better than Meres[8] supplies committee chairs,
Though one's a statesman, th' other but a hound,
Jowler, in justice, would be wiser found.
　　You see how far man's wisdom here extends;
Look next if human nature makes amends:
125 Whose principles most generous are, and just,
And to whose morals you would sooner trust.
Be judge yourself, I'll bring it to the test:
Which is the basest creature, man or beast?
Birds feed on birds, beasts on each other prey,
130 But savage man alone does man betray.
Pressed by necessity, they kill for food;
Man undoes man to do himself no good.
With teeth and claws by nature armed, they hunt
Nature's allowance, to supply their want.
135 But man, with smiles, embraces, friendship, praise,
Inhumanly his fellow's life betrays;
With voluntary pains works his distress,
Not through necessity, but wantonness.
　　For hunger or for love they fight and tear,
140 Whilst wretched man is still in arms for fear.
For fear he arms, and is of arms afraid,

---

6. Acknowledge. "Right reason" refers to natural instinct or common sense, as opposed to the more elaborate modes of thought Rochester is attacking.
7. A dog's name, emphasizing the animal's appetites.

8. Sir Thomas Meres (1634–1715), politician noted for his energy, efficacy, and self-serving flexibility in questions of party allegiance.

By fear to fear successively betrayed;
Base fear, the source whence his best passions came:
His boasted honor, and his dear-bought fame;
145   That lust of power, to which he's such a slave,
And for the which alone he dares be brave;
To which his various projects are designed;
Which makes him generous, affable, and kind;
For which he takes such pains to be thought wise,
150   And screws his actions in a forced disguise,
Leading a tedious life in misery
Under laborious, mean hypocrisy.
Look to the bottom of his vast design,
Wherein man's wisdom, power, and glory join:
155   The good he acts, the ill he does endure,
'Tis all from fear, to make himself secure.
Merely for safety, after fame we thirst,
For all men would be cowards if they durst.
        And honesty's against all common sense:
160   Men must be knaves, 'tis in their own defense.
Mankind's dishonest; if you think it fair
Amongst known cheats to play upon the square,
You'll be undone.
Nor can weak truth your reputation save:
165   The knaves will all agree to call you knave.
Wronged shall he live, insulted o'er, oppressed,
Who dares be less a villain than the rest.
        Thus, sir, you see what human nature craves:
Most men are cowards, all men should be knaves.
170   The difference lies, as far as I can see,
Not in the thing itself, but the degree,
And all the subject matter of debate
Is only: Who's a knave of the first rate?
        All this with indignation have I hurled
175   At the pretending part of the proud world,
Who, swollen with selfish vanity, devise
False freedoms, holy cheats, and formal lies
Over their fellow slaves to tyrannize.
But if in court so just a man there be
180   (In court a just man, yet unknown to me)
Who does his needful flattery direct,
Not to oppress and ruin, but protect
(Since flattery, which way soever laid,
Is still a tax on that unhappy trade);
185   If so upright a statesman you can find,
Whose passions bend to his unbiased mind,
Who does his arts and policies apply
To raise his country, not his family,
Nor, whilst his pride owned avarice withstands,
190   Receives close bribes through friends' corrupted hands—

Is there a churchman who on God relies;
Whose life, his faith and doctrine justifies?
Not one blown up with vain prelatic pride,
Who, for reproof of sins, does man deride;
195   Whose envious heart makes preaching a pretense,
With his obstreperous, saucy eloquence,
To chide at kings, and rail at men of sense;
None of that sensual tribe whose talents lie
In avarice, pride, sloth, and gluttony;
200   Who hunt good livings, but abhor good lives;
Whose lust exalted to that height arrives
They act adultery with their own wives,
And ere a score of years completed be,
Can from the lofty pulpit proudly see
205   Half a large parish their own progeny;
Nor doting bishop who would be adored
For domineering at the council board,
A greater fop in business at fourscore,
Fonder of serious toys, affected more,
210   Than the gay, glittering fool at twenty proves
With all his noise, his tawdry clothes, and loves;
    But a meek, humble man of honest sense,
Who, preaching peace, does practice continence;
Whose pious life's a proof he does believe
215   Mysterious truths, which no man can conceive.
If upon earth there dwell such God-like men,
I'll here recant my paradox to them,
Adore those shrines of virtue, homage pay,
And, with the rabble world, their laws obey.
220   If such there be, yet grant me this at least:
Man differs more from man, than man from beast.

1674–1676   1679

——— ❄❖❄ ———

William Wycherley
1641–1715

The plot of *The Country Wife* turns on a trick. The rakish Harry Horner devises a tactic calcu-lated to secure both a cover-story and a kinky enhancement for his future seductions of other men's wives. He starts a rumor going round to the effect that he has become a eunuch; hus-bands will henceforth not suspect him, and wives, he trusts, will be intrigued. Early in the play, it becomes clear that Horner has tested his new disguise by making a visit to the theater. "Come," one of his friends remarks, "your appearance at the play yesterday has, I hope, hard-ened you for the future" as to the social consequences of his sexless new reputation. "Did I not bear it bravely?" asks Horner, pleased. "With a most theatrical impudence," answers his friend.

    In London playhouses of the 1660s and the 1670s, theatrical impudence was in high sup-ply. People came to watch not only the performers, but also each other. Pepys records a telling anecdote (so telling that it is cited also, more compactly, within a fuller discussion of

Restoration theater in the introduction to this section, page 1991). Attending a play one evening, he found himself distracted throughout the performance by the libertine Sir Charles Sedley, seated nearby in conversation with two women.

> And one of the ladies would and did sit with her mask on, all the play and, being exceedingly witty as ever I heard woman, did talk most pleasantly with him; but was, I believe, a virtuous woman and of quality. He would fain know who she was, but she would not tell; yet did give him many pleasant hints of her knowledge of him, by that means setting his brains at work to find out who she was, and did give him leave to use all means to find out who she was but pulling off her mask. He was mighty witty and she also, making sport of him very inoffensively, that a more pleasant rencontre I never heard. By that means lost the pleasure of the play wholly...

But that loss hardly seems to matter, in comparison with the pleasure of the playlet Pepys has witnessed within the audience. Masks of the kind this woman wears were a widespread item of Restoration fashion. Characters in the *Country Wife* mention them obsessively, in part because they were worn both by "virtuous" women and by prostitutes, with the tantalizing effect of rendering those two human categories not quite distinguishable from one another. In Pepys's anecdote, man and woman engage in a contest for power grounded in wit, concealment, and artifice; the new plays on stage during the Restoration teemed with just such sexually charged encounters and combats. For purposes of theatrical impudence and strategic experiment, Horner could not have picked for himself a better venue.

Neither could William Wycherley. He wrote four comedies while in his early thirties. The last two—*The Country Wife* (1675) and *The Plain Dealer* (1676)—brought him to the early high point of a career that sloped rather steeply on either side. Before these successes he had been a law-student, soldier, courtier, traveler in France, and convert to Catholicism. In their wake he was widely celebrated as the deftest wielder alive of those gifts that Dryden enumerated in a single memorable line: "The satire, wit, and strength of manly Wycherley." "Manly" was the name of the forthright protagonist in *The Plain Dealer*; the adjective alternated with "brawny" as the most popular epithets for this vigorous and accomplished playwright in his prime. But by the time Dryden wrote the line, in 1694, it applied more readily to the work than to the man. Before Wycherley turned forty, a serious illness had left his memory permanently damaged and an imprudent marriage with a widowed countess had cost him much in money, serenity, and the patronage of Charles II and his court. He spent years mired in debt, received temporary relief in the form of a pension from that temporary king James II, and found more reliable respite in the estate he inherited from his father in 1697. In old age he published a failed book of ungainly poems, held literary court at Will's Coffee House (where Dryden had previously presided), and basked in the attention of the young, ambitious Alexander Pope. Eleven days before his death he married a second time. His estate passed to his young widow and hence to his cousin, her secret lover; they had spent his last days scheming to secure it.

In the *Country Wife*, alliances prove comparably shifty. The wits (Horner and his friends), though ostensibly relentless in their pursuit of women, nonetheless seem often more interested in their transactions with each other. They array themselves against the "cits"—the prudent, prosperous businessmen of London—and chase after their desirable, precariously domesticated spouses and sisters. Horner the London rake works his charms on Margery the country wife, who proves cheerfully, even ingeniously susceptible. A group of erotically agitated women—headed by the aptly named Lady Fidget—collude with Horner in his deceit, disappear behind closed doors to savor his emphatically non-eunuchoid sexuality while pretending to sample his china, and finally team up, as a suddenly "virtuous gang," to reproach him for his perfidies. Throughout the play, Wycherley works a running comparison between sex and gambling (and, in the famous china scene, a second parallel between sex and shopping). Most of the amorous gamesters play their hands with witty fervor, but the playwright deliberately leaves unclear what exactly is at stake. Deep feelings, real risks, sturdy allegiances seem hard to come by. Most bets are placed instead on power, on cunning, on conquest, perhaps on momentary pleasure; in the end it can be hard to tell who's won, who's lost, and why. *Comedy* takes its name from *komos*, the dance of communal harmony with which so many such plays close. *The Country Wife*, by contrast, ends with a "dance of cuckolds": music for a world where fidelities are faint, and even betrayals, transpiring for muddled motives behind closed doors, are not fully comprehensible.

The Country Wife
PROLOGUE, SPOKEN BY MR. HART[1]

Poets, like cudgeled bullies, never do
At first or second blow submit to you;
But will provoke you still, and ne'er have done,
Till you are weary first with laying on.
5 The late so baffled scribbler[2] of this day,
Though he stands trembling, bids me boldly say,
What we before most plays are used to do,
For poets out of fear first draw on you;
In a fierce prologue the still pit defy
10 And ere you speak, like Castril,[3] give the lie.
But though our Bayes's battles[4] oft I've fought,
And with bruised knuckles their dear conquests bought;
Nay, never yet feared odds upon the stage,
In prologue dare not hector with the age,
15 But would take quarter from your saving hands,
Though Bayes within[5] all yielding countermands,
Says you confederate wits[6] no quarter give,
Therefore his play shan't ask your leave to live.
Well, let the vain rash fop, by huffing[7] so,
20 Think to obtain the better terms of you;
But we the actors humbly will submit,
Now, and at any time, to a full pit;
Nay, often we anticipate your rage,
And murder poets for you on our stage.
25 We set no guards upon our tiring-room,[8]
But when with flying colors there you come,
We patiently, you see, give up to you
Our poets, virgins, nay, our matrons too.

---

1. Charles Hart, who starred as Horner in the first production, was famous both as actor and as lover. As actor, he achieved some of his greatest successes playing the preternaturally virile and virtuous protagonists in Dryden's heroic tragedies. As lover, he had been linked with eminent beauties, including Nell Gwyn and Lady Castlemaine (for Pepys's comments on both, see pages 2018 and 2031).
2. Refers to the cold reception of *The Gentleman Dancing Master*, which Wycherley himself recognized as a trivial work.
3. An angry character in Ben Jonson's *The Alchemist* (1610), who impulsively challenges ("gives the lie" to) others.
4. The battles that Hart had "fought" onstage in his roles as soldier-hero in Dryden's tragedies, and also the struggles of writers in general (and Wycherley in particular) to secure approval of their work. Bayes was the central character in the Duke of Buckingham's comedy *The Rehearsal* (1671): a foolish, preening playwright, he incarnated in every particular a merciless, hilarious parody of Dryden. His name soon became a mocking designation for any ambitious poet.
5. I.e., Wycherley, backstage.
6. Critics conjoined to condemn the play.
7. Blustering.
8. Dressing-room.

The Persons

MR. HORNER
MR. HARCOURT
MR. DORILANT
MR. PINCHWIFE
MR. SPARKISH
SIR JASPAR FIDGET
MRS. MARGERY PINCHWIFE
MRS. ALITHEA
MY LADY FIDGET

MRS. DAINTY FIDGET
MRS. SQUEAMISH
OLD LADY SQUEAMISH
WAITERS, SERVANTS, AND ATTENDANTS
A BOY
A QUACK
LUCY, ALITHEA'S MAID
[CLASP]
[A PARSON]

The Scene: London

ACT 1

Scene 1

[Enter Horner, and Quack following him at a distance.]

HORNER *[aside]*: A quack is as fit for a pimp as a midwife for a bawd;[1] they are still[2] but in their way both helpers of nature.—Well, my dear doctor, hast thou done what I desired?

QUACK: I have undone you forever with the women, and reported you throughout the whole town as bad as an eunuch, with as much trouble as if I had made you one in earnest.

HORNER: But have you told all the midwives you know, the orange-wenches[3] at the playhouses, the city husbands,[4] and old fumbling keepers[5] of this end of the town? For they'll be the readiest to report it.

QUACK: I have told all the chambermaids, waiting-women, tire-women[6] and old women of my acquaintance; nay, and whispered it as a secret to 'em, and to the whisperers of Whitehall;[7] so that you need not doubt, 'twill spread, and you will be as odious to the handsome young women as—

HORNER: As the smallpox. Well—

QUACK: And to the married women of this end of the town as—

HORNER: As the great ones;[8] nay, as their own husbands.

QUACK: And to the city dames as aniseed Robin[9] of filthy and contemptible memory; and they will frighten their children with your name, especially their females.

HORNER: And cry, "Horner's coming to carry you away." I am only afraid 'twill not be believed. You told 'em 'twas by an English–French disaster and an English–French chirurgeon,[1] who has given me at once, not only a cure, but an antidote[2] for the future against that damned malady, and that worse distemper, love, and all other women's evils.

---

1. Brothel-keeper.
2. Always.
3. Orange-sellers.
4. Respectable men of business who (according to stereotype) would loathe the likes of Horner.
5. Men who keep mistresses.
6. Ladies' maids, also dressmakers.
7. The royal residence, a center for news and gossip.
8. Syphilis.

9. A famous hermaphrodite; hence (from the vantage of respectable "city dames") a repellent monster.
1. In muddled phrasing, Horner appears to blame both English and French personnel (women, doctors) for both his supposed illness (syphilis, often called "the French pox") and its drastic cure. The muddle may be intentional; Horner is, after all, making up the whole story.
2. I.e., his purported impotence.

QUACK: Your late journey into France has made it the more credible and your being here a fortnight before you appeared in public looks as if you apprehended the shame, which I wonder you do not. Well, I have been hired by young gallants to belie 'em t' other way, but you are the first would be thought a man unfit for women.

HORNER: Dear Mr. Doctor, let vain rogues be contented only to be thought abler men than they are, generally 'tis all the pleasure they have; but mine lies another way.

QUACK: You take, methinks, a very preposterous way to it and as ridiculous as if we operators in physic should put forth bills to disparage our medicaments, with hopes to gain customers.

HORNER: Doctor, there are quacks in love as well as physic, who get but the fewer and worse patients for their boasting; a good name is seldom got by giving it one-self, and women no more than honor are compassed[3] by bragging. Come, come, doctor, the wisest lawyer never discovers[4] the merits of his cause till the trial; the wealthiest man conceals his riches, and the cunning gamester his play. Shy husbands and keepers, like old rooks,[5] are not to be cheated but by a new unpracticed trick; false friendship will pass now no more than false dice upon 'em; no, not in the city. [Enter Boy.]

BOY: There are two ladies and a gentleman coming up.

[Exit.]

HORNER: A pox! Some unbelieving sisters of my former acquaintance, who, I am afraid, expect their sense should be satisfied of the falsity of the report. No—this formal[6] fool and women!

[Enter Sir Jaspar Fidget, Lady Fidget, and Mrs. Dainty Fidget.]

QUACK: His wife and sister.

SIR JASPAR: My coach breaking just now before your door, sir, I look upon as an occasional[7] reprimand to me, sir, for not kissing your hands, sir, since your coming out of France, sir; and so my disaster, sir, has been my good fortune, sir; and this is my wife, and sister, sir.

HORNER: What then, sir?

SIR JASPAR: My lady, and sister, sir.—Wife, this is Master Horner.

LADY FIDGET: Master Horner, husband!

SIR JASPAR: My lady, my Lady Fidget, sir.

HORNER: So, sir.

SIR JASPAR: Won't you be acquainted with her, sir? [Aside.] So the report is true, I find, by his coldness or aversion to the sex; but I'll play the wag with him.—Pray salute my wife, my lady, sir.

HORNER: I will kiss no man's wife, sir, for him, sir; I have taken my eternal leave, sir, of the sex already, sir.

SIR JASPAR [aside]: Hah, hah, hah! I'll plague him yet.—Not know my wife, sir?

HORNER: I do know your wife, sir; she's a woman, sir, and consequently a monster, sir, a greater monster than a husband, sir.

SIR JASPAR: A husband! How, sir?

HORNER [makes horns[8]]: So, sir; but I make no more cuckolds, sir.

3. Won.
4. Reveals.
5. Cheats, swindlers.

6. Unduly ceremonious, stiff.
7. Opportune.
8. With forefingers on the forehead, the cuckold sign.

SIR JASPAR: Hah, hah, hah! Mercury, Mercury![9]

LADY FIDGET: Pray, Sir Jaspar, let us be gone from this rude fellow.

DAINTY: Who, by his breeding, would think he had ever been in France?

LADY FIDGET: Foh, he's but too much a French fellow,[1] such as hate women of quality and virtue for their love to their husbands, Sir Jaspar; a woman is hated by 'em as much for loving her husband as for loving their money. But pray, let's be gone.

HORNER: You do well, madam, for I have nothing that you came for; I have brought over not so much as a bawdy picture, new postures,[2] nor the second part of the *École des Filles*,[3] nor—

QUACK [*apart to Horner*]: Hold, for shame, sir! What d'ye mean? You'll ruin yourself forever with the sex—

SIR JASPAR: Hah, hah, hah, he hates women perfectly, I find.

DAINTY: What a pity 'tis he should.

LADY FIDGET: Ay, he's a base, rude fellow for't; but affectation makes not a woman more odious to them than virtue.

HORNER: Because your virtue is your greatest affectation madam.

LADY FIDGET: How, you saucy fellow! Would you wrong my honor?

HORNER: If I could.

LADY FIDGET: How d'ye mean, sir?

SIR JASPAR: Hah, hah, hah! No, he can't wrong your ladyship's honor, upon my honor; he, poor man—hark you in your ear—a mere eunuch.

LADY FIDGET: O filthy French beast, foh, foh! Why do we stay? Let's be gone; I can't endure the sight of him.

SIR JASPAR: Stay but till the chairs[4] come; they'll be here presently.

LADY FIDGET: No, no.

SIR JASPAR: Nor can I stay longer. 'Tis—let me see, a quarter and a half quarter of a minute past eleven; the Council[5] will be sat, I must away. Business must be preferred always before love and ceremony with the wise, Mr. Horner.

HORNER: And the impotent, Sir Jaspar.

SIR JASPAR: Ay, ay, the impotent, Master Horner, hah, ha, ha!

LADY FIDGET: What, leave us with a filthy man alone in his lodgings?

SIR JASPAR: He's an innocent man now, you know. Pray stay, I'll hasten the chairs to you.—Mr. Horner, your servant; I should be glad to see you at my house. Pray come and dine with me, and play at cards with my wife after dinner; you are fit for women at that game yet, hah, ha! [*Aside.*] 'Tis as much a husband's prudence to provide innocent diversion for a wife as to hinder her unlawful pleasures, and he had better employ her than let her employ herself.—Farewell. [*Exit Sir Jaspar.*]

HORNER: Your servant, Sir Jaspar.

LADY FIDGET: I will not stay with him, foh!

HORNER: Nay, madam, I beseech you stay, if it be but to see I can be as civil to ladies yet as they would desire.

LADY FIDGET: No, no, foh, you cannot be civil to ladies.

9. Both the messenger-god, whose winged hat Horner's "horns" may call to mind, and the chemical often used in treating syphilis.
1. Fop.
2. Pornographic engravings.
3. A pornographic dialogue between a virgin and an experienced woman (1655); Pepys called it "the most bawdy, lewd book that I ever saw."
4. Sedan chairs, in which two bearers carried a single passenger.
5. Privy Council.

DAINTY: You as civil as ladies would desire?

LADY FIDGET: No, no, no, foh, foh, foh!

[*Exeunt Lady Fidget and Dainty.*]

QUACK: Now, I think, I, or you yourself rather, have done your business[6] with the women.

HORNER: Thou art an ass. Don't you see already, upon the report and my carriage,[7] this grave man of business leaves his wife in my lodgings, invites me to his house and wife, who before would not be acquainted with me out of jealousy?

QUACK: Nay, by this means you may be the more acquainted with the husbands, but the less with the wives.

HORNER: Let me alone; if I can but abuse the husbands, I'll soon disabuse the wives. Stay—I'll reckon you up the advantages I am like to have by my stratagem: first, I shall be rid of all my old acquaintances, the most insatiable sorts of duns,[8] that invade our lodgings in a morning. And next to the pleasure of making a new mistress is that of being rid of an old one; and of all old debts, love, when it comes to be so, is paid the most unwillingly.

QUACK: Well, you may be so rid of your old acquaintances; but how will you get any new ones?

HORNER: Doctor, thou wilt never make a good chemist, thou art so incredulous and impatient. Ask but all the young fellows of the town if they do not lose more time, like huntsmen, in starting the game than in running it down; one knows not where to find 'em, who will or will not. Women of quality are so civil, you can hardly distinguish love from good breeding and a man is often mistaken; but now I can be sure, she that shows an aversion to me loves the sport, as those women that are gone, whom I warrant to be right.[9] And then the next thing is, your women of honor, as you call 'em, are only chary[1] of their reputations, not their persons, and 'tis scandal they would avoid, not men. Now may I have, by the reputation of an eunuch, the privileges of one and be seen in a lady's chamber in a morning as early as her husband, kiss virgins before their parents or lovers and may be, in short, the *passe partout*[2] of the town. Now, doctor.

QUACK: Nay, now you shall be the doctor; and your process is so new that we do not know but it may succeed.

HORNER: Not so new neither; *probatum est*,[3] doctor.

QUACK: Well, I wish you luck and many patients whilst I go to mine. [*Exit Quack.*] [*Enter Harcourt and Dorilant to Horner.*]

HARCOURT: Come, your appearance at the play yesterday has, I hope, hardened you for the future against the women's contempt and the men's raillery and now you'll abroad as you were wont.

HORNER: Did I not bear it bravely?

DORILANT: With a most theatrical impudence; nay, more than the orange-wenches show there or a drunken vizard-mask[4] or a great-bellied actress; nay, or the most impudent of creatures, an ill poet; or what is yet more impudent, a second-hand critic.

6. Spoiled your reputation.

7. Conduct.

8. Persistent creditors.

9. Ripe for play, promiscuous.

1. Careful, wary.

2. One who may go anywhere.

3. "It has been proved or tested," a phrase used in prescriptions.

4. A prostitute; many of them wore masks, as emblems of their trade.

HORNER: But what say the ladies? Have they no pity?

HARCOURT: What ladies? The vizard-masks, you know, never pity a man when all's gone, though in their service.

DORILANT: And for the women in the boxes, you'd never pity them when 'twas in your power.

HARCOURT: They say, 'tis pity, but all that deal with common women should be served so.

DORILANT: Nay, I dare swear, they won't admit you to play at cards with them, go to plays with 'em, or do the little duties which other shadows of men are wont to do for 'em.

HORNER: Who do you call shadows of men?

DORILANT: Half-men.

HORNER: What, boys?

DORILANT: Ay, your old boys, old *beaux garçons*,[5] who, like superannuated[6] stallions, are suffered to run, feed and whinny with the mares as long as they live, though they can do nothing else.

HORNER: Well, a pox on love and wenching! Women serve but to keep a man from better company; though I can't enjoy them, I shall you the more. Good fellowship and friendship are lasting, rational and manly pleasures.

HARCOURT: For all that, give me some of those pleasures you call effeminate too; they help to relish one another.

HORNER: They disturb one another.

HARCOURT: No, mistresses are like books. If you pore upon them too much, they doze[7] you and make you unfit for company; but if used discreetly, you are the fitter for conversation by 'em.

DORILANT: A mistress should be like a little country retreat near the town, not to dwell in constantly, but only for a night and away, to taste the town the better when a man returns.

HORNER: I tell you, 'tis as hard to be a good fellow, a good friend and a lover of women, as 'tis to be a good fellow, a good friend and a lover of money. You cannot follow both, then choose your side. Wine gives you liberty, love takes it away.

DORILANT: Gad, he's in the right on't.

HORNER: Wine gives you joy; love, grief and tortures, besides the chirurgeon's. Wine makes us witty; love, only sots. Wine makes us sleep; love breaks it.

DORILANT: By the world, he has reason,[8] Harcourt.

HORNER: Wine makes—

DORILANT: Ay, wine makes us—makes us princes; love makes us beggars, poor rogues, egad—and wine—

HORNER: So, there's one converted.—No, no, love and wine, oil and vinegar.

HARCOURT: I grant it; love will still be uppermost.

HORNER: Come, for my part I will have only those glorious, manly pleasures of being very drunk and very slovenly. [*Enter Boy.*]

BOY: Mr. Sparkish is below, sir. [*Exit.*]

HARCOURT: What, my dear friend! A rogue that is fond of me only, I think, for abusing him.

DORILANT: No, he can no more think the men laugh at him than that women jilt[9] him, his opinion of himself is so good.

---

5. Old gallants.
6. Old and infirm.
7. Stupefy.

8. Speaks truth (French *il a raison:* "he is right").
9. Reject.

HORNER: Well, there's another pleasure by drinking I thought not of: I shall lose his acquaintance, because he cannot drink; and you know 'tis a very hard thing to be rid of him, for he's one of those nauseous offerers at wit, who, like the worst fiddlers, run themselves into all companies.

HARCOURT: One that, by being in the company of men of sense, would pass for one.

HORNER: And may so to the short-sighted world, as a false jewel amongst true ones is not discerned at a distance. His company is as troublesome to us as a cuckold's when you have a mind to his wife's.

HARCOURT: No, the rogue will not let us enjoy one another, but ravishes our conversation, though he signifies no more to't than Sir Martin Mar-all's[1] gaping and awkward thrumming upon the lute does to his man's voice and music.

DORILANT: And to pass for a wit in town shows himself a fool every night to us that are guilty of the plot.

HORNER: Such wits as he are, to a company of reasonable men, like rooks[2] to the gamesters, who only fill a room[3] at the table, but are so far from contributing to the play that they only serve to spoil the fancy of those that do.

DORILANT: Nay, they are used like rooks too, snubbed, checked and abused; yet the rogues will hang on.

HORNER: A pox on 'em, and all that force nature and would be still what she forbids 'em! Affectation is her greatest monster.

HARCOURT: Most men are the contraries to that they would seem. Your bully, you see, is a coward with a long sword; the little, humbly fawning physician, with his ebony cane, is he that destroys men.

DORILANT: The usurer, a poor rogue possessed of moldy bonds and mortgages, and we they call spendthrifts are only wealthy, who lay out his money upon daily new purchases of pleasure.

HORNER: Ay, your arrantest cheat is your trustee or executor; your jealous man, the greatest cuckold; your churchman, the greatest atheist; and your noisy, pert rogue of a wit, the greatest fop, dullest ass and worst company, as you shall see: for here he comes.

[Enter Sparkish to them.]

SPARKISH: How is't, sparks,[4] how is't? Well, faith, Harry, I must rally[5] thee a little, ha, ha, ha, upon the report in town of thee, ha, ha, ha, I can't hold i'faith; shall I speak?

HORNER: Yes, but you'll be so bitter then.

SPARKISH: Honest Dick and Frank here shall answer for me, I will not be extreme bitter, by the universe.

HARCOURT: We will be bound in ten thousand pound bond, he shall not be bitter at all.

DORILANT: Nor sharp, nor sweet.

HORNER: What, not downright insipid?

SPARKISH: Nay then, since you are so brisk and provoke me, take what follows. You must know, I was discoursing and rallying with some ladies yesterday, and they happened to talk of the fine new signs[6] in town.

---

1. Foolish title character of Dryden's comedy (1667) who lip-synchs and fake-strums a serenade to his mistress while his "man" (servant), hidden, actually performs the song. When his servant finishes playing, Sir Martin fails to quit miming. Harcourt regards Sparkish as such another empty fraud.

2. Here, simpletons, fools.
3. Space.
4. Fashionable young men; the term is usually derogatory, but Sparkish speaks it in fellowship.
5. Mock, tease.
6. Indicating the business of a shop.

HORNER: Very fine ladies, I believe.

SPARKISH: Said I, "I know where the best new sign is." "Where?" says one of the ladies. "In Covent Garden,"[7] I replied. Said another, "In what street?" "In Russell Street," answered I. "Lord," says another, "I'm sure there was ne'er a fine new sign there yesterday." "Yes, but there was," said I again, "and it came out of France and has been there a fortnight."

DORILANT: A pox, I can hear no more, prithee.

HORNER: No, hear him out; let him tune his crowd[8] a while.

HARCOURT: The worst music, the greatest preparation.

SPARKISH: Nay, faith, I'll make you laugh. "It cannot be," says a third lady. "Yes, yes," quoth I again. Says a fourth lady—

HORNER: Look to't, we'll have no more ladies.

SPARKISH: No—then mark, mark, now. Said I to the fourth, "Did you never see Mr. Horner? He lodges in Russell Street, and he's a sign of a man, you know, since he came out of France." Heh, hah, he!

HORNER: But the devil take me, if thine be the sign of a jest.

SPARKISH: With that they all fell a-laughing, till they bepissed themselves. What, but it does not move you, methinks? Well, I see one had as good go to law without a witness as break a jest without a laugher on one's side. Come, come, sparks, but where do we dine? I have left at Whitehall an earl to dine with you.

DORILANT: Why, I thought thou hadst loved a man with a title better than a suit with a French trimming to't.

HARCOURT: Go, to him again.

SPARKISH: No, sir, a wit to me is the greatest title in the world.

HORNER: But go dine with your earl, sir; he may be exceptious.[9] We are your friends and will not take it ill to be left, I do assure you.

HARCOURT: Nay, faith, he shall go to him.

SPARKISH: Nay, pray, gentlemen.

DORILANT: We'll thrust you out, if you wo'not. What, disappoint anybody for us?

SPARKISH: Nay, dear gentlemen, hear me.

HORNER: No, no, sir, by no means; pray go, sir.

SPARKISH: Why, dear rogues—

DORILANT: No, no.

[They all thrust him out of the room.]

ALL: Ha, ha, ha!

[Sparkish returns.]

SPARKISH: But, sparks, pray hear me. What, d'ye think I'll eat then with gay, shallow fops and silent coxcombs? I think wit as necessary at dinner as a glass of good wine, and that's the reason I never have any stomach when I eat alone.—Come, but where do we dine?

HORNER: Even where you will.

SPARKISH: At Chateline's?[1]

DORILANT: Yes, if you will.

SPARKISH: Or at the Cock?[2]

---

7. The most fashionable area of London, teeming with theaters, taverns, and shops.
8. Fiddle.
9. Peevish.

1. A famous French ordinary, or restaurant, in Covent Garden.
2. Probably the Cock Tavern in Bow Street, where Wycherley himself spent time.

DORILANT: Yes, if you please.

SPARKISH: Or at the Dog and Partridge?[3]

HORNER: Ay, if you have a mind to't, for we shall dine at neither.

SPARKISH: Pshaw, with your fooling we shall lose the new play; and I would no more miss seeing a new play the first day than I would miss setting in the wits' row. Therefore I'll go fetch my mistress and away.

[*Exit Sparkish. Manent*[4] *Horner, Harcourt, Dorilant. Enter to them Mr. Pinchwife.*]

HORNER: Who have we here? Pinchwife?

PINCHWIFE: Gentlemen, your humble servant.

HORNER: Well, Jack, by the long absence from the town, the grumness of thy countenance and the slovenliness of thy habit, I should give thee joy, should I not, of marriage?

PINCHWIFE [*aside*]: Death! Does he know I'm married too? I thought to have concealed it from him at least.—My long stay in the country will excuse my dress and I have a suit of law, that brings me up to town, that puts me out of humor, besides, I must give Sparkish tomorrow five thousand pound[5] to lie with my sister.

HORNER: Nay, you country gentlemen, rather than not purchase, will buy anything; and he is a cracked title,[6] if we may quibble. Well, but am I to give thee joy? I heard thou wert married.

PINCHWIFE: What then?

HORNER: Why, the next thing that is to be heard is thou'rt a cuckold.

PINCHWIFE [*aside*]: Insupportable name!

HORNER: But I did not expect marriage from such a whoremaster[7] as you, one that knew the town so much and women so well.

PINCHWIFE: Why, I have married no London wife.

HORNER: Pshaw, that's all one; that grave circumspection in marrying a country wife is like refusing a deceitful, pampered Smithfield jade[8] to go and be cheated by a friend in the country.

PINCHWIFE [*aside*]: A pox on him and his simile.—At least we are a little surer of the breed there, know what her keeping has been, whether foiled[9] or unsound.

HORNER: Come, come, I have known a clap[1] gotten in Wales; and there are cozens,[2] justices, clerks and chaplains in the country, I won't say coachmen. But she's handsome and young?

PINCHWIFE [*aside*]: I'll answer as I should do.—No, no, she has no beauty but her youth; no attraction but her modesty; wholesome, homely and house-wifely; that's all.

DORILANT: He talks as like a grazier[3] as he looks.

PINCHWIFE: She's too awkward, ill-favored and silly to bring to town.

HARCOURT: Then methinks you should bring her, to be taught breeding.

PINCHWIFE: To be taught! No, sir! I thank you. Good wives and private soldiers should be ignorant. [*Aside.*] I'll keep her from your instructions, I warrant you.

HARCOURT [*aside*]: The rogue is as jealous as if his wife were not ignorant.

---

3. A tavern in Fleet Street; the least fashionable of the places Sparkish suggests.
4. Remain.
5. As a dowry.
6. I.e., Sparkish owns shoddy property, has a weak claim to it, and is himself a bad bargain.
7. A man who consorts with whores and is given to lechery.
8. Broken-down horse bought at Smithfield Market, where the sellers were often swindlers; here a metaphor for disreputable women purchased at far too high a price.
9. With reference to a horse, injured; to a woman, deflowered.
1. Gonorrhea.
2. Cheaters.
3. One who feeds cattle for market.

HORNER: Why, if she be ill-favoured, there will be less danger here for you than by leaving her in the country; we have such variety of dainties that we are seldom hungry.

DORILANT: But they have always coarse, constant, swingeing stomachs[4] in the country.

HARCOURT: Foul feeders indeed.

DORILANT: And your hospitality is great there.

HARCOURT: Open house, every man's welcome.

PINCHWIFE: So, so, gentlemen.

HORNER: But, prithee, why wouldst thou marry her? If she be ugly, ill-bred and silly, she must be rich then.

PINCHWIFE: As rich as if she brought me twenty thousand pound out of this town, for she'll be as sure not to spend her moderate portion as a London baggage would be to spend hers, let it be what it would; so 'tis all one. Then, because she's ugly, she's the likelier to be my own; and being ill-bred, she'll have conversation; and since silly and innocent, will not know the difference betwixt a man of one-and-twenty and one of forty.

HORNER: None—to my knowledge; but if she be silly, she'll expect as much from a man of forty-nine as from him of one-and-twenty. But methinks wit is more necessary than beauty, and I think no young woman ugly that has it, and no handsome woman agreeable without it.

PINCHWIFE: 'Tis my maxim, he's a fool that marries, but he's a greater that does not marry a fool. What is wit in a wife good for, but to make a man a cuckold?

HORNER: Yes, to keep it from his knowledge.

PINCHWIFE: A fool cannot contrive to make her husband a cuckold.

HORNER: No, but she'll club[5] with a man that can; and what is worse, if she cannot make her husband a cuckold, she'll make him jealous and pass for one, and then 'tis all one.

PINCHWIFE: Well, well, I'll take care for one, my wife shall make me no cuckold, though she had your help, Mr. Horner; I understand the town, sir.

DORILANT [aside]: His help!

HARCOURT [aside]: He's come newly to town, it seems, and has not heard how things are with him.

HORNER: But tell me, has marriage cured thee of whoring, which it seldom does?

HARCOURT: 'Tis more than age can do.

HORNER: No, the word is, I'll marry and live honest; but a marriage vow is like a penitent gamester's oath and entering into bonds and penalties to stint himself to such a particular small sum at play for the future, which makes him but the more eager and, not being able to hold out, loses his money again and his forfeit to boot.

DORILANT: Ay, ay, a gamester will be a gamester whilst his money lasts, and a whoremaster whilst his vigor.

HARCOURT: Nay, I have known 'em, when they are broke and can lose no more, keep a-fumbling with the box[6] in their hands to fool with only and hinder other gamesters.

---

4. Immense appetites.
5. Associate.

6. For throwing dice in gaming; also slang for vagina. Parallels between gambling and sex recur throughout the play.

DORILANT: That had wherewithal to make lusty stakes.

PINCHWIFE: Well, gentlemen, you may laugh at me, but you shall never lie with my wife; I know the town.

HORNER: But prithee, was not the way you were in better? Is not keeping better than marriage?

PINCHWIFE: A pox on't! The jades would jilt me; I could never keep a whore to myself.

HORNER: So, then you only married to keep a whore to yourself. Well, but let me tell you, women, as you say, are like soldiers, made constant and loyal by good pay rather than by oaths and covenants. Therefore I'd advise my friends to keep rather than marry, since too, I find, by your example, it does not serve one's turn, for I saw you yesterday in the eighteen-penny place[7] with a pretty country wench.

PINCHWIFE [*aside*]: How the devil! Did he see my wife then? I sat there that she might not be seen. But she shall never go to a play again.

HORNER: What, dost thou blush at nine-and-forty, for having been seen with a wench?

DORILANT: No, faith, I warrant 'twas his wife, which he seated there out of sight, for he's a cunning rogue and understands the town.

HARCOURT: He blushes. Then 'twas his wife, for men are now more ashamed to be seen with them in public than with a wench.

PINCHWIFE [*aside*]: Hell and damnation! I'm undone, since Horner has seen her and they know 'twas she.

HORNER: But prithee, was it thy wife? She was exceedingly pretty; I was in love with her at that distance.

PINCHWIFE: You are like never to be nearer to her. Your servant, gentlemen. [*Offers to go.*]

HORNER: Nay, prithee stay.

PINCHWIFE: I cannot, I will not.

HORNER: Come, you shall dine with us.

PINCHWIFE: I have dined already.

HORNER: Come, I know thou hast not. I'll treat thee, dear rogue; thou shalt spend none of thy Hampshire[8] money today.

PINCHWIFE [*aside*]: Treat me! So, he uses me already like his cuckold.

HORNER: Nay, you shall not go.

PINCHWIFE: I must, I have business at home. [*Exit Pinchwife.*]

HARCOURT: To beat his wife; he's as jealous of her as a Cheapside[9] husband of a Covent Garden wife.

HORNER: Why, 'tis as hard to find an old whoremaster without jealousy and the gout, as a young one without fear or the pox.

As gout in age from pox in youth proceeds,
So wenching past, then jealousy succeeds,
The worst disease that love and wenching breeds.

[*Exeunt.*]

---

7. The middle gallery of the playhouse occupied by (among others) clerks, merchants, and prostitutes.
8. The rural county in south-central England where Pinchwife now lives.
9. City-merchant (Cheapside was a center of finance).

ACT 2

Scene 1

[*Mrs. Margery Pinchwife and Alithea. Mr. Pinchwife peeping behind at the door.*]

MRS. PINCHWIFE: Pray, sister, where are the best fields and woods to walk in, in London?

ALITHEA: A pretty question! Why, sister, Mulberry Garden and St. James's Park[1] and, for close walks, the New Exchange.[2]

MRS. PINCHWIFE: Pray, sister, tell me why my husband looks so grum[3] here in town and keeps me up so close and will not let me go a-walking, nor let me wear my best gown yesterday.

ALITHEA: Oh, he's jealous, sister.

MRS. PINCHWIFE: Jealous? What's that?

ALITHEA: He's afraid you should love another man.

MRS. PINCHWIFE: How should he be afraid of my loving another man, when he will not let me see any but himself?

ALITHEA: Did he not carry you yesterday to a play?

MRS. PINCHWIFE: Ay, but we sat amongst ugly people; he would not let me come near the gentry, who sat under us, so that I could not see 'em. He told me none but naughty women sat there, whom they toused and moused.[4] But I would have ventured for all that.

ALITHEA: But how did you like the play?

MRS. PINCHWIFE: Indeed, I was a-weary of the play, but I liked hugeously the actors; they are the goodliest, properest men, sister!

ALITHEA: O, but you must not like the actors, sister.

MRS. PINCHWIFE: Ay, how should I help it, sister? Pray, sister, when my husband comes in, will you ask leave for me to go a-walking?

ALITHEA [*aside*]: A-walking, hah, ha! Lord, a country gentlewoman's leisure is the drudgery of a foot-post;[5] and she requires as much airing as her husband's horses.

[*Enter Mr. Pinchwife to them.*]

But here comes your husband; I'll ask, though I'm sure he'll not grant it.

MRS. PINCHWIFE: He says he won't let me go abroad for fear of catching the pox.

ALITHEA: Fie! The smallpox you should say.

MRS. PINCHWIFE: O my dear, dear bud, welcome home! Why dost thou look so fropish? Who has nangered[6] thee?

PINCHWIFE: You're a fool.

[*Mrs. Pinchwife goes aside and cries.*]

ALITHEA: Faith, so she is, for crying for no fault, poor tender creature!

PINCHWIFE: What, you would have her as impudent as yourself, as arrant a jill-flirt, a gadder, a magpie[7] and, to say all, a mere notorious town-woman?

ALITHEA: Brother, you are my only censurer; and the honor of your family shall sooner suffer in your wife there than in me, though I take the innocent liberty of the town.

---

1. Popular places for gathering, strolling and savoring sights, talk, and entertainment.
2. This elegant arcade, with its covered ("close") walkways, served as *the* center for fashionable London shopping. The second scene in Act 3 takes place there.

3. Gloomy, surly.
4. Pulled about good-naturedly, but roughly.
5. A walking message-carrier.
6. Baby-talk: *fropish*, irritable; *nangered*, angered.
7. A wanton girl, a rover, a chatterer.

PINCHWIFE: Hark you, mistress, do not talk so before my wife. The innocent liberty of the town!

ALITHEA: Why, pray, who boasts of any intrigue with me? What lampoon[8] has made my name notorious? What ill women frequent my lodgings? I keep no company with any women of scandalous reputations.

PINCHWIFE: No, you keep the men of scandalous reputations company.

ALITHEA: Where? Would you not have me civil? Answer 'em in a box at the plays? In the drawing room at Whitehall? In St. James's Park? Mulberry Gardens? Or—

PINCHWIFE: Hold, hold! Do not teach my wife where the men are to be found! I believe she's the worse for your town documents[9] already. I bid you keep her in ignorance, as I do.

MRS. PINCHWIFE: Indeed, be not angry with her, bud; she will tell me nothing of the town, though I ask her a thousand times a day.

PINCHWIFE: Then you are very inquisitive to know, I find!

MRS. PINCHWIFE: Not I, indeed, dear; I hate London. Our place-house[1] in the country is worth a thousand of 't; would I were there again!

PINCHWIFE: So you shall, I warrant. But were you not talking of plays and players when I came in? [To Alithea.] You are her encourager in such discourses.

MRS. PINCHWIFE: No, indeed, dear; she chid me just now for liking the playermen.

PINCHWIFE [aside]: Nay, if she be so innocent as to own to me her liking them, there is no hurt in't.—Come, my poor rogue, but thou lik'st none better than me?

MRS. PINCHWIFE: Yes, indeed, but I do; the playermen are finer folks.

PINCHWIFE: But you love none better than me?

MRS. PINCHWIFE: You are mine own dear bud, and I know you; I hate a stranger.

PINCHWIFE: Ay, my dear, you must love me only and not be like the naughty town-women, who only hate their husbands and love every man else, love plays, visits, fine coaches, fine clothes, fiddles, balls, treats, and so lead a wicked town-life.

MRS. PINCHWIFE: Nay, if to enjoy all these things be a town-life, London is not so bad a place, dear.

PINCHWIFE: How! If you love me, you must hate London.

ALITHEA [aside]: The fool has forbid me discovering to her the pleasures of the town and he is now setting her agog upon them himself.

MRS. PINCHWIFE: But, husband, do the town-women love the playermen too?

PINCHWIFE: Yes, I warrant you.

MRS. PINCHWIFE: Ay, I warrant you.

PINCHWIFE: Why, you do not, I hope?

MRS. PINCHWIFE: No, no, bud; but why have we no playermen in the country?

PINCHWIFE: Ha—Mrs. Minx, ask me no more to go to a play.

MRS. PINCHWIFE: Nay, why, love? I did not care for going; but when you forbid me, you make me, as 'twere, desire it.

ALITHEA [aside]: So 'twill be in other things, I warrant.

MRS. PINCHWIFE: Pray let me go to a play, dear.

PINCHWIFE: Hold your peace, I wo'not.

MRS. PINCHWIFE: Why, love?

PINCHWIFE: Why, I'll tell you.

8. Scurrilous satire.   1. Grand home.
9. Teachings about fashionable life.

ALITHEA [aside]: Nay, if he tell her, she'll give him more cause to forbid her that place.

MRS. PINCHWIFE: Pray, why, dear?

PINCHWIFE: First, you like the actors and the gallants may like you.

MRS. PINCHWIFE: What, a homely country girl? No, bud, nobody will like me.

PINCHWIFE: I tell you, yes, they may.

MRS. PINCHWIFE: No, no, you jest—I won't believe you, I will go.

PINCHWIFE: I tell you then that one of the lewdest fellows in town, who saw you there, told me he was in love with you.

MRS. PINCHWIFE: Indeed! Who, who, pray, who was't?

PINCHWIFE [aside]: I've gone too far and slipped before I was aware. How overjoyed she is!

MRS. PINCHWIFE: Was it any Hampshire gallant, any of our neighbors? I promise you, I am beholding to him.

PINCHWIFE: I promise you, you lie, for he would but ruin you, as he has done hundreds. He has no other love for women but that; such as he look upon women, like basilisks,[2] but to destroy 'em.

MRS. PINCHWIFE: Ay, but if he loves me, why should he ruin me? Answer me to that. Methinks he should not; I would do him no harm.

ALITHEA: Hah, ha, ha!

PINCHWIFE: 'Tis very well; but I'll keep him from doing you any harm, or me either.
    [Enter Sparkish and Harcourt.]
    But here comes company; get you in, get you in.

MRS. PINCHWIFE: But pray, husband, is he a pretty gentleman that loves me?

PINCHWIFE: In, baggage, in. [Thrusts her in, shuts the door.] What, all the lewd libertines of the town brought to my lodging by this easy coxcomb! 'Sdeath, I'll not suffer it.

SPARKISH: Here, Harcourt, do you approve my choice? [To Alithea.] Dear little rogue, I told you I'd bring you acquainted with all my friends, the wits, and—
    [Harcourt salutes her.]

PINCHWIFE [aside]: Ay, they shall know her, as well as you yourself will, I warrant you.

SPARKISH: This is one of those, my pretty rogue, that are to dance at your wedding tomorrow; and him you must bid welcome ever to what you and I have.

PINCHWIFE [aside]: Monstrous!

SPARKISH: Harcourt, how dost thou like her, faith?—Nay, dear, do not look down; I should hate to have a wife of mine out of countenance at anything.

PINCHWIFE [aside]: Wonderful!

SPARKISH: Tell me, I say, Harcourt, how dost thou like her? Thou hast stared upon her enough to resolve me.

HARCOURT: So infinitely well that I could wish I had a mistress too, that might differ from her in nothing but her love and engagement to you.

ALITHEA: Sir, Master Sparkish has often told me that his acquaintance were all wits and railleurs[3] and now I find it.

SPARKISH: No, by the universe, madam, he does not rally now; you may believe him. I do assure you, he is the honestest, worthiest, true-hearted gentleman—a man of such perfect honor, he would say nothing to a lady he does not mean.

2. Mythical reptiles whose gaze dealt death.   3. Mockers, banterers.

PINCHWIFE [*aside*]: Praising another man to his mistress!

HARCOURT: Sir, you are so beyond expectation obliging that—

SPARKISH: Nay, egad, I am sure you do admire her extremely; I see't in your eyes.—He does admire you, madam.—By the world, don't you?

HARCOURT: Yes, above the world, or the most glorious part of it, her whole sex; and till now I never thought I should have envied you, or any man about to marry, but you have the best excuse for marriage I ever knew.

ALITHEA: Nay, now, sir, I'm satisfied you are of the society of the wits and railleurs, since you cannot spare your friend, even when he is but too civil to you; but the surest sign is since you are an enemy to marriage, for that, I hear, you hate as much as business or bad wine.

HARCOURT: Truly, madam, I never was an enemy to marriage till now, because marriage was never an enemy to me before.

ALITHEA: But why, sir, is marriage an enemy to you now? Because it robs you of your friend here? For you look upon a friend married as one gone into a monastery, that is dead to the world.

HARCOURT: 'Tis indeed because you marry him; I see, madam, you can guess my meaning. I do confess heartily and openly, I wish it were in my power to break the match; by heavens I would.

SPARKISH: Poor Frank!

ALITHEA: Would you be so unkind to me?

HARCOURT: No, no, 'tis not because I would be unkind to you.

SPARKISH: Poor Frank! No, gad, 'tis only his kindness to me.

PINCHWIFE [*aside*]: Great kindness to you indeed! Insensible fop, let a man make love to his wife to his face!

SPARKISH: Come, dear Frank, for all my wife there that shall be, thou shalt enjoy me sometimes, dear rogue. By my honor, we men of wit condole for our deceased brother in marriage as much as for one dead in earnest. I think that was prettily said of me, ha, Harcourt? But come, Frank, be not melancholy for me.

HARCOURT: No, I assure you I am not melancholy for you.

SPARKISH: Prithee, Frank, dost think my wife that shall be there a fine person?

HARCOURT: I could gaze upon her till I became as blind as you are.

SPARKISH: How, as I am? How?

HARCOURT: Because you are a lover and true lovers are blind, stock blind.[4]

SPARKISH: True, true; but by the world, she has wit too, as well as beauty. Go, go with her into a corner and try if she has wit; talk to her anything; she's bashful before me.

HARCOURT: Indeed, if a woman wants[5] wit in a corner, she has it nowhere.

ALITHEA [*aside to Sparkish*]: Sir, you dispose of me a little before your time—

SPARKISH: Nay, nay, madam, let me have an earnest[6] of your obedience, or—go, go, madam—

[*Harcourt courts Alithea aside.*]

PINCHWIFE: How, sir! If you are not concerned for the honor of a wife, I am for that of a sister; he shall not debauch her. Be a pander[7] to your own wife, bring men to her, let 'em make love before your face, thrust 'em into a corner together, then leave 'em in private! Is this your town wit and conduct?

---

4. As blind as any lifeless object.
5. Lacks.

6. Foretaste, pledge.
7. Pimp, procurer.

SPARKISH: Hah, ha, ha, a silly wise rogue would make one laugh more than a stark fool, hah, ha! I shall burst. Nay, you shall not disturb 'em; I'll vex thee, by the world. [*Struggles with Pinchwife to keep him from Harcourt and Alithea.*]

ALITHEA: The writings are drawn, sir, settlements made; 'tis too late, sir, and past all revocation.

HARCOURT: Then so is my death.

ALITHEA: I would not be unjust to him.

HARCOURT: Then why to me so?

ALITHEA: I have no obligation to you.

HARCOURT: My love.

ALITHEA: I had his before.

HARCOURT: You never had it; he wants, you see, jealousy, the only infallible sign of it.

ALITHEA: Love proceeds from esteem; he cannot distrust my virtue. Besides, he loves me, or he would not marry me.

HARCOURT: Marrying you is no more sign of his love than bribing your woman, that he may marry you, is a sign of his generosity. Marriage is rather a sign of interest than love, and he that marries a fortune covets a mistress, not loves her. But if you take marriage for a sign of love, take it from me immediately.

ALITHEA: No, now you have put a scruple in my head; but, in short, sir, to end our dispute, I must marry him; my reputation would suffer in the world else.

HARCOURT: No, if you do marry him, with your pardon, madam, your reputation suffers in the world and you would be thought in necessity for a cloak.[8]

ALITHEA: Nay, now you are rude, sir.—Mr. Sparkish, pray come hither, your friend here is very troublesome, and very loving.

HARCOURT [*aside to Alithea*]: Hold, hold!—

PINCHWIFE: D'ye hear that?

SPARKISH: Why, d'ye think I'll seem to be jealous, like a country bumpkin?

PINCHWIFE: No, rather be a cuckold, like a credulous cit.[9]

HARCOURT: Madam, you would not have been so little generous as to have told him.

ALITHEA: Yes, since you could be so little generous as to wrong him.

HARCOURT: Wrong him! No man can do't, he's beneath an injury; a bubble,[1] a coward, a senseless idiot, a wretch so contemptible to all the world but you that—

ALITHEA: Hold, do not rail at him, for since he is like to be my husband, I am resolved to like him. Nay, I think I am obliged to tell him you are not his friend.— Master Sparkish, Master Sparkish.

SPARKISH: What, what?—Now, dear rogue, has not she wit?

HARCOURT [*speaks surlily*]: Not so much as I thought and hoped she had.

ALITHEA: Mr. Sparkish, do you bring people to rail at you?

HARCOURT: Madam—

SPARKISH: How! No, but if he does rail at me, 'tis but in jest, I warrant; what we wits do for one another and never take any notice of it.

ALITHEA: He spoke so scurrilously of you, I had no patience to hear him; besides, he has been making love to me.

---

8. I.e., to hide your secrets: perhaps pregnancy or love affairs.
9. "A pert low townsman, a pragmatical trader" (Johnson's

Dictionary); contemptuous abbreviation of "citizen."
1. Dupe.

HARCOURT [*aside*]: True, damned, telltale woman!

SPARKISH: Pshaw, to show his parts[2]—we wits rail and make love often but to show our parts; as we have no affections, so we have no malice. We—

ALITHEA: He said you were a wretch, below an injury.

SPARKISH: Pshaw!

HARCOURT [*aside*]: Damned, senseless, impudent, virtuous jade! Well, since she won't let me have her, she'll do as good, she'll make me hate her.

ALITHEA: A common bubble.

SPARKISH: Pshaw!

ALITHEA: A coward.

SPARKISH: Pshaw, pshaw!

ALITHEA: A senseless, driveling idiot.

SPARKISH: How! Did he disparage my parts? Nay, then my honor's concerned; I can't put up that, sir, by the world. Brother, help me to kill him. [*Aside.*] I may draw now, since we have the odds of him. 'This a good occasion, too, before my mistress—[*Offers to draw.*]

ALITHEA: Hold, hold!

SPARKISH: What, what?

ALITHEA [*aside*]: I must not let 'em kill the gentleman neither, for his kindness to me; I am so far from hating him that I wish my gallant had his person and understanding.—Nay, if my honor—

SPARKISH: I'll be thy death.

ALITHEA: Hold, hold! Indeed, to tell the truth, the gentleman said after all that what he spoke was but out of friendship to you.

SPARKISH: How! say I am—I am a fool, that is, no wit, out of friendship to me?

ALITHEA: Yes, to try whether I was concerned enough for you and made love to me only to be satisfied of my virtue, for your sake.

HARCOURT [*aside*]: Kind, however—

SPARKISH: Nay, if it were so, my dear rogue, I ask thee pardon; but why would not you tell me so, faith?

HARCOURT: Because I did not think on't, faith.

SPARKISH: Come, Horner does not come, Harcourt, let's be gone to the new play.—Come, madam.

ALITHEA: I will not go if you intend to leave me alone in the box and run into the pit, as you use to do.

SPARKISH: Pshaw! I'll leave Harcourt with you in the box to entertain you, and that's as good; if I sat in the box, I should be thought no judge but of trimmings.[3]—Come away, Harcourt, lead her down.

[*Exeunt Sparkish, Harcourt and Alithea.*]

PINCHWIFE: Well, go thy ways, for the flower of the true town fops, such as spend their estates before they come to 'em and are cuckolds before they're married. But let me go look to my own freehold.—How!—

[*Enter Lady Fidget, Mrs. Dainty Fidget and Mrs. Squeamish.*]

LADY FIDGET: Your servant, sir; where is your lady? We are come to wait upon her to the new play.

PINCHWIFE: New play!

---

2. Abilities, talents.

3. Clothes, fashions. The "wits," who came to criticize the play, customarily occupied not the boxes but the "pit."

LADY FIDGET: And my husband will wait upon you presently.

PINCHWIFE [*aside*]: Damn your civility.—Madam, by no means; I will not see Sir Jaspar here till I have waited upon him at home; nor shall my wife see you till she has waited upon your ladyship at your lodgings.

LADY FIDGET: Now we are here, sir—

PINCHWIFE: No, madam.

DAINTY: Pray, let us see her.

SQUEAMISH: We will not stir till we see her.

PINCHWIFE [*aside*]: A pox on you all! [*Goes to the door, and returns.*]—She has locked the door and is gone abroad.

LADY FIDGET: No, you have locked the door and she's within.

DAINTY: They told us below she was here.

PINCHWIFE [*aside*]: Will nothing do?—Well, it must out then. To tell you the truth, ladies, which I was afraid to let you know before, lest it might endanger your lives, my wife has just now the smallpox come out upon her. Do not be frightened but pray, be gone, ladies; you shall not stay here in danger of your lives. Pray get you gone, ladies.

LADY FIDGET: No, no, we have all had 'em.

SQUEAMISH: Alack, alack.

DAINTY: Come, come, we must see how it goes with her; I understand the disease.

LADY FIDGET: Come.

PINCHWIFE [*aside*]: Well, there is no being too hard for[4] women at their own weapon, lying; therefore I'll quit the field. [*Exit Pinchwife.*]

SQUEAMISH: Here's an example of jealousy.

LADY FIDGET: Indeed, as the world goes, I wonder there are no more jealous, since wives are so neglected.

DAINTY: Pshaw, as the world goes, to what end should they be jealous?

LADY FIDGET: Foh, 'tis a nasty world.

SQUEAMISH: That men of parts, great acquaintance and quality should take up with and spend themselves and fortunes in keeping little playhouse creatures, foh!

LADY FIDGET: Nay, that women of understanding, great acquaintance and good quality should fall a-keeping too of little creatures, foh!

SQUEAMISH: Why, 'tis the men of quality's fault; they never visit women of honor and reputation, as they used to do and have not so much as common civility for ladies of our rank, but use us with the same indifferency and ill-breeding as if we were all married to 'em.

LADY FIDGET: She says true; 'tis an arrant shame women of quality should be so slighted. Methinks birth, birth should go for something. I have known men admired, courted, and followed for their titles only.

SQUEAMISH: Ay, one would think men of honor should not love, no more than marry, out of their own rank.

DAINTY: Fie, fie upon 'em! They are come to think crossbreeding for themselves best, as well as for their dogs and horses.

LADY FIDGET: They are dogs and horses for't.

SQUEAMISH: One would think, if not for love, for vanity a little.

DAINTY: Nay, they do satisfy their vanity upon us sometimes and are kind to us in their report, tell all the world they lie with us.

---

4. Too clever for.

LADY FIDGET: Damned rascals! That we should be only wronged by 'em! To report a man has had a person, when he has not had a person, is the greatest wrong in the whole world that can be done to a person.

SQUEAMISH: Well, 'tis an arrant shame noble persons should be so wronged and neglected.

LADY FIDGET: But still 'tis an arranter shame for a noble person to neglect her own honor and defame her own noble person with little inconsiderable fellows, foh!

DAINTY: I suppose the crime against our honor is the same with a man of quality as with another.

LADY FIDGET: How! No, sure, the man of quality is likest one's husband and therefore the fault should be the less.

DAINTY: But then the pleasure should be the less.

LADY FIDGET: Fie, fie, fie, for shame, sister! Whither shall we ramble? Be continent[5] in your discourse, or I shall hate you.

DAINTY: Besides, an intrigue is so much the more notorious for the man's quality.

SQUEAMISH: 'Tis true, nobody takes notice of a private man and therefore with him 'tis more secret, and the crime's the less when 'tis not known.

LADY FIDGET: You say true; i'faith, I think you are in the right on't. 'Tis not an injury to a husband till it be an injury to our honors; so that a woman of honor loses no honor with a private person; and to say truth—

DAINTY [apart to Squeamish]: So, the little fellow is grown a private person—with her—

LADY FIDGET: But still my dear, dear honor.
[Enter Sir Jaspar, Horner, Dorilant.]

SIR JASPAR: Ay, my dear, dear of honor, thou hast still so much honor in thy mouth—

HORNER [aside]: That she has none elsewhere.

LADY FIDGET: Oh, what d'ye mean to bring in these upon us?

DAINTY: Foh, these are as bad as wits.

SQUEAMISH: Foh!

LADY FIDGET: Let us leave the room.

SIR JASPAR: Stay, stay; faith, to tell you the naked truth—

LADY FIDGET: Fie, Sir Jaspar, do not use that word "naked."

SIR JASPAR: Well, well, in short, I have business at Whitehall and cannot go to the play with you, therefore would have you go—

LADY FIDGET: With those two to a play?

SIR JASPAR: No, not with t'other but with Mr. Horner; there can be no more scandal to go with him than with Mr. Tattle or Master Limberham.[6]

LADY FIDGET: With that nasty fellow! No—no!

SIR JASPAR: Nay, prithee, dear, hear me.
[Whispers to Lady Fidget.]

HORNER: Ladies—
[Horner, Dorilant drawing near Squeamish and Dainty.]

DAINTY: Stand off.

SQUEAMISH: Do not approach us.

DAINTY: You herd with the wits, you are obscenity all over.

5. Restrained.   6. I.e., Horner and Dorilant.

SQUEAMISH: And I would as soon look upon a picture of Adam and Eve, without fig leaves, as any of you, if I could help it; therefore keep off and do not make us sick.

DORILANT: What a devil are these?

HORNER: Why, these are pretenders to honor, as critics to wit, only by censuring others; and as every raw, peevish, out-of-humored, affected, dull, tea-drinking, arithmetical[7] fop sets up for a wit by railing at men of sense, so these for honor by railing at the Court and ladies of as great honor as quality.

SIR JASPAR: Come, Mr. Horner, I must desire you to go with these ladies to the play, sir.

HORNER: I, sir!

SIR JASPAR: Ay, ay, come, sir.

HORNER: I must beg your pardon, sir, and theirs; I will not be seen in women's company in public again for the world.

SIR JASPAR: Ha, ha, strange aversion!

SQUEAMISH: No, he's for women's company in private.

SIR JASPAR: He—poor man—he! Hah, ha, ha!

DAINTY: 'Tis a greater shame amongst lewd fellows to be seen in virtuous women's company than for the women to be seen with them.

HORNER: Indeed, madam, the time was I only hated virtuous women, but now I hate the other too; I beg your pardon, ladies.

LADY FIDGET: You are very obliging, sir, because we would not be troubled with you.

SIR JASPAR: In sober sadness, he shall go.

DORILANT: Nay, if he wo'not, I am ready to wait upon the ladies; and I think I am the fitter man.

SIR JASPAR: You, sir, no, I thank you for that—Master Horner is a privileged man amongst the virtuous ladies; 'twill be a great while before you are so; heh, he, he! He's my wife's gallant, heh, he, he! No, pray withdraw, sir, for as I take it, the virtuous ladies have no business with you.

DORILANT: And I am sure he can have none with them. 'Tis strange a man can't come amongst virtuous women now but upon the same terms as men are admitted into the Great Turk's seraglio;[8] but heavens keep me from being an ombre[9] player with 'em! But where is Pinchwife?

[*Exit Dorilant.*]

SIR JASPAR: Come, come, man; what, avoid the sweet society of womankind? that sweet, soft, gentle, tame, noble creature, woman, made for man's companion—

HORNER: So is that soft, gentle, tame and more noble creature a spaniel, and has all their tricks: can fawn, lie down, suffer beating and fawn the more; barks at your friends when they come to see you; makes your bed hard; gives you fleas, and the mange sometimes. And all the difference is, the spaniel's the more faithful animal and fawns but upon one master.

SIR JASPAR: Heh, he, he!

SQUEAMISH: Oh, the rude beast!

DAINTY: Insolent brute!

LADY FIDGET: Brute! Stinking, mortified, rotten French wether,[1] to dare—

SIR JASPAR: Hold, an't please your ladyship.—For shame, Master Horner, your mother was a woman. [*Aside.*] Now shall I never reconcile 'em. [*Aside to Lady*

---

7. Precise, fussy.
8. The Sultan's harem.

9. Three-person card game (with a pun on *hombre*: man).
1. Castrated ram.

Fidget.] Hark you, madam, take my advice in your anger. You know you often want one to make up your drolling[2] pack of ombre players; and you may cheat him easily, for he's an ill gamester and consequently loves play. Besides, you know, you have but two old civil gentlemen, with stinking breaths too, to wait upon you abroad; take in the third into your service. The other are but crazy; and a lady should have a supernumerary gentleman-usher,[3] as a supernumerary coach-horse, lest sometimes you should be forced to stay at home.

LADY FIDGET: But are you sure he loves play and has money?

SIR JASPAR: He loves play as much as you and has money as much as I.

LADY FIDGET: Then I am contented to make him pay for his scurrility; money makes up in a measure all other wants in men. [*Aside.*] Those whom we cannot make hold for gallants, we make fine.[4]

SIR JASPAR [*aside*]: So, so; now to mollify, to wheedle him.—Master Horner, will you never keep civil company? Methinks 'tis time now, since you are only fit for them. Come, come, man, you must e'en fall to visiting our wives, eating at our tables, drinking tea with our virtuous relations after dinner, dealing cards to 'em, reading plays and gazettes[5] to 'em, picking fleas out of their shocks[6] for 'em, collecting receipts,[7] new songs, women, pages and footmen for 'em.

HORNER: I hope they'll afford me better employment, sir.

SIR JASPAR: Heh, he, he! 'Tis fit you know your work before you come into your place; and since you are unprovided of a lady to flatter and a good house to eat at, pray frequent mine and call my wife mistress and she shall call you gallant, according to the custom.

HORNER: Who, I?

SIR JASPAR: Faith, thou shalt for my sake; come, for my sake only.

HORNER: For your sake—

SIR JASPAR [*to Lady Fidget*]: Come, come, here's a gamester for you; let him be a little familiar sometimes. Nay, what if a little rude? Gamesters may be rude with ladies, you know.

LADY FIDGET: Yes, losing gamesters have a privilege with women.

HORNER: I always thought the contrary, that the winning gamester had most privilege with women, for when you have lost your money to a man, you'll lose anything you have, all you have, they say, and he may use you as he pleases.

SIR JASPAR: Heh, he, he! Well, win or lose, you shall have your liberty with her.

LADY FIDGET: As he behaves himself; and for your sake I'll give him admittance and freedom.

HORNER: All sorts of freedom, madam?

SIR JASPAR: Ay, ay, ay, all sorts of freedom thou canst take, and so go to her, begin thy new employment; wheedle[8] her, jest with her and be better acquainted one with another.

HORNER [*aside*]: I think I know her already, therefore may venture with her, my secret for hers.

[*Horner and Lady Fidget whisper.*]

SIR JASPAR: Sister, cuz, I have provided an innocent playfellow for you there.

DAINTY: Who, he!

2. Jesting, silly.
3. Extra attendant, servant.
4. Compensate, especially by way of money.
5. Newspapers.

6. Poodles.
7. Recipes.
8. Entice.

SQUEAMISH: There's a playfellow indeed!

SIR JASPAR: Yes, sure; what, he is good enough to play at cards, blindman's buff,[9] or the fool with sometimes.

SQUEAMISH: Foh, we'll have no such playfellows.

DAINTY: No, sir, you shan't choose playfellows for us, we thank you.

SIR JASPAR: Nay, pray hear me. [*Whispering to them.*]

LADY FIDGET [*aside to Horner*]: But, poor gentleman, could you be so generous, so truly a man of honor, as for the sakes of us women of honor, to cause yourself to be reported no man? No man! And to suffer yourself the greatest shame that could fall upon a man, that none might fall upon us women by your conversation? But indeed, sir, as perfectly, perfectly the same man as before your going into France, sir? As perfectly, perfectly, sir?

HORNER: As perfectly, perfectly, madam. Nay, I scorn you should take my word; I desire to be tried only, madam.

LADY FIDGET: Well, that's spoken again like a man of honor; all men of honor desire to come to the test. But, indeed, generally you men report such things of yourselves, one does not know how or whom to believe and it is come to that pass we dare not take your words, no more than your tailors,[1] without some staid servant of yours be bound with you. But I have so strong a faith in your honor, dear, dear, noble sir, that I'd forfeit mine for yours at any time, dear sir.

HORNER: No, madam, you should not need to forfeit it for me; I have given you security already to save you harmless, my late reputation being so well known in the world, madam.

LADY FIDGET: But if upon any future falling out or upon a suspicion of my taking the trust out of your hands to employ some other, you yourself should betray your trust, dear sir? I mean, if you'll give me leave to speak obscenely, you might tell, dear sir.

HORNER: If I did, nobody would believe me; the reputation of impotency is as hardly recovered again in the world as that of cowardice, dear madam.

LADY FIDGET: Nay then, as one may say, you may do your worst, dear, dear sir.

SIR JASPAR: Come, is your ladyship reconciled to him yet? Have you agreed on matters? For I must be gone to Whitehall.

LADY FIDGET: Why, indeed, Sir Jaspar, Master Horner is a thousand, thousand times a better man than I thought him. Cousin Squeamish, Sister Dainty, I can name him now; truly, not long ago, you know, I thought his very name obscenity and I would as soon have lain with him as have named him.

SIR JASPAR: Very likely, poor madam.

DAINTY: I believe it.

SQUEAMISH: No doubt on't.

SIR JASPAR: Well, well—that your ladyship is as virtuous as any she, I know, and him all the town knows—heh, he, he! Therefore, now you like him, get you gone to your business together; go, go to your business, I say, pleasure, whilst I go to my pleasure, business.

LADY FIDGET: Come then, dear gallant.

HORNER: Come away, my dearest mistress.

SIR JASPAR: So, so. Why, 'tis as I'd have it.   [*Exit Sir Jaspar.*]

---

9. Game in which a blindfolded player is pushed about as he guesses other players' identities.

1. Tailors often went unpaid by their customers, and so had reason to mistrust them.

HORNER: And as I'd have it.
LADY FIDGET: Who for his business from his wife will run,
Takes the best care to have her business done.   [*Exeunt omnes.*]

ACT 3

Scene 1

[*Alithea and Mrs. Pinchwife.*]
ALITHEA: Sister, what ails you? You are grown melancholy.
MRS. PINCHWIFE: Would it not make anyone melancholy to see you go every day fluttering about abroad, whilst I must stay at home like a poor, lonely, sullen bird in a cage?
ALITHEA: Ay, sister, but you came young and just from the nest to your cage, so that I thought you liked it and could be as cheerful in't as others that took their flight themselves early and are hopping abroad in the open air.
MRS. PINCHWIFE: Nay, I confess I was quiet enough till my husband told me what pure[1] lives the London ladies live abroad, with their dancing, meetings and junketings,[2] and dressed every day in their best gowns, and, I warrant you, play at ninepins[3] every day of the week, so they do.
[*Enter Mr. Pinchwife.*]
PINCHWIFE: Come, what's here to do? You are putting the town pleasures in her head and setting her a-longing.
ALITHEA: Yes, after ninepins; you suffer none to give her those longings, you mean, but yourself.
PINCHWIFE: I tell her of the vanities of the town like a confessor.
ALITHEA: A confessor! Just such a confessor as he that, by forbidding a silly ostler to grease the horse's teeth,[4] taught him to do't.
PINCHWIFE: Come, Mistress Flippant, good precepts are lost when bad examples are still before us; the liberty you take abroad makes her hanker after it, and out of humor at home, poor wretch! She desired not to come to London; I would bring her.
ALITHEA: Very well.
PINCHWIFE: She has been this week in town and never desired, till this afternoon, to go abroad.
ALITHEA: Was she not at a play yesterday?
PINCHWIFE: Yes, but she ne'er asked me; I was myself the cause of her going.
ALITHEA: Then, if she ask you again, you are the cause of her asking, and not my example.
PINCHWIFE: Well, tomorrow night I shall be rid of you and the next day, before 'tis light, she and I'll be rid of the town, and my dreadful apprehensions. [*To Mrs. Pinchwife.*] Come, be not melancholy, for thou shalt go into the country after tomorrow, dearest.
ALITHEA: Great comfort!
MRS. PINCHWIFE: Pish, what d'ye tell me of the country for?

---

1. Splendid.
2. Merrymakings.
3. A game like bowling, more common in the country than in London high society.

4. The groomsmen ("ostlers") at inns reputedly played this lucrative trick: they would grease the horse's teeth to discourage its eating, but charge the owner nonetheless for the uneaten feed.

PINCHWIFE: How's this! What, pish at the country!

MRS. PINCHWIFE: Let me alone, I am not well.

PINCHWIFE: Oh, if that be all—what ails my dearest?

MRS. PINCHWIFE: Truly I don't know; but I have not been well since you told me there was a gallant at the play in love with me.

PINCHWIFE: Ha—

ALITHEA: That's by my example too!

PINCHWIFE: Nay, if you are not well, but are so concerned because a lewd fellow chanced to lie and say he liked you, you'll make me sick too.

MRS. PINCHWIFE: Of what sickness?

PINCHWIFE: O, of that which is worse than the plague, jealousy.

MRS. PINCHWIFE: Pish, you jeer! I'm sure there's no such disease in our receipt-book[5] at home.

PINCHWIFE: No, thou never met'st with it, poor innocent. [*Aside.*] Well, if thou cuckold me, 'twill be my own fault—for cuckolds and bastards are generally makers of their own fortune.

MRS. PINCHWIFE: Well, but pray, bud, let's to go a play tonight.

PINCHWIFE: 'Tis just done, she comes from it. But why are you so eager to see a play?

MRS. PINCHWIFE: Faith, dear, not that I care one pin for their talk there; but I like to look upon the playermen and would see, if I could, the gallant you say loves me; that's all, dear bud.

PINCHWIFE: Is that all, dear bud?

ALITHEA: This proceeds from my example.

MRS. PINCHWIFE: But if the play be done, let's go abroad, however, dear bud.

PINCHWIFE: Come, have a little patience and thou shalt go into the country on Friday.

MRS. PINCHWIFE: Therefore I would see first some sights, to tell my neighbors of. Nay, I will go abroad, that's once.[6]

ALITHEA: I'm the cause of this desire too.

PINCHWIFE: But now I think on't, who was the cause of Horner's coming to my lodging today? That was you.

ALITHEA: No, you, because you would not let him see your handsome wife out of your lodging.

MRS. PINCHWIFE: Why, O Lord! Did the gentleman come hither to see me indeed?

PINCHWIFE: No, no.—You are not cause of that damned question too, Mistress Alithea? [*Aside.*] Well, she's in the right of it. He is in love with my wife—and comes after her—'tis so—but I'll nip his love in the bud, lest he should follow us into the country and break his chariot-wheel near our house on purpose for an excuse to come to't. But I think I know the town.

MRS. PINCHWIFE: Come, pray, bud, let's go abroad before 'tis late, for I will go, that's flat and plain.

PINCHWIFE [*aside*]: So! the obstinacy already of a town-wife, and I must, whilst she's here, humor her like one.—Sister, how shall we do, that she may not be seen or known?

ALITHEA: Let her put on her mask.

---

5. Book of medical recipes.   6. I.e., That's that.

PINCHWIFE: Pshaw, a mask makes people but the more inquisitive and is as ridiculous a disguise as a stage-beard; her shape, stature, habit will be known and if we should meet with Horner, he would be sure to take acquaintance with us, must wish her joy, kiss her, talk to her, leer upon her, and the devil and all. No, I'll not use her to a mask, 'tis dangerous, for masks have made more cuckolds than the best faces that ever were known.

ALITHEA: How will you do then?

MRS. PINCHWIFE: Nay, shall we go? The Exchange will be shut, and I have a mind to see that.

PINCHWIFE: So—I have it—I'll dress her up in the suit we are to carry down to her brother, little Sir James; nay, I understand the town tricks. Come, let's go dress her. A mask! No—a woman masked, like a covered dish, gives a man curiosity and appetite, when, it may be, uncovered, 'twould turn his stomach; no, no.

ALITHEA: Indeed your comparison is something a greasy[7] one. But I had a gentle gallant used to say, "A beauty masked, like the sun in eclipse, gathers together more gazers than if it shined out."

[*Exeunt.*]

Scene 2

[*The scene changes to the New Exchange. Enter Horner, Harcourt, Dorilant.*]

DORILANT: Engaged to women, and not sup with us?

HORNER: Ay, a pox on 'em all!

HARCOURT: You were much a more reasonable man in the morning and had as noble resolutions against 'em as a widower of a week's liberty.

DORILANT: Did I ever think to see you keep company with women in vain?

HORNER: In vain! No—'tis, since I can't love 'em, to be revenged on 'em.

HARCOURT: Now your sting is gone, you looked in the box amongst all those women, like a drone in the hive, all upon you, shoved and ill-used by 'em all, and thrust from one side to t'other.

DORILANT: Yet he must be buzzing amongst 'em still, like other old beetle-headed,[8] liquorish[9] drones. Avoid 'em, and hate 'em as they hate you.

HORNER: Because I do hate 'em, and would hate 'em yet more, I'll frequent 'em; you may see by marriage, nothing makes a man hate a woman more than her constant conversation. In short, I converse with 'em, as you do with rich fools, to laugh at 'em and use 'em ill.

DORILANT: But I would no more sup with women, unless I could lie with 'em, than sup with a rich coxcomb, unless I could cheat him.

HORNER: Yes, I have known thee sup with a fool for his drinking; if he could set out your hand[1] that way only, you were satisfied, and if he were a wine-swallowing mouth 'twas enough.

HARCOURT: Yes, a man drinks often with a fool, as he tosses with a marker,[2] only to keep his hand in ure.[3] But do the ladies drink?

HORNER: Yes, sir, and I shall have the pleasure at least of laying 'em flat with a bottle, and bring as much scandal that way upon 'em as formerly t'other.

HARCOURT: Perhaps you may prove as weak a brother amongst 'em that way as t'other.

7. Filthy or obscene.
8. Stupid.
9. Lecherous.

1. Provide you with food and drink.
2. Plays dice with a score-keeper.
3. In practice.

DORILANT: Foh, drinking with women is as unnatural as scolding with 'em; but 'tis a pleasure of decayed fornicators, and the basest way of quenching love.

HARCOURT: Nay, 'tis drowning love instead of quenching it. But leave us for civil women too!

DORILANT: Ay, when he can't be the better for 'em. We hardly pardon a man that leaves his friend for a wench, and that's a pretty lawful call.

HORNER: Faith, I would not leave you for 'em, if they would not drink.

DORILANT: Who would disappoint his company at Lewis's[4] for a gossiping?

HARCOURT: Foh, wine and women, good apart, together as nauseous as sack and sugar.[5] But hark you, sir, before you go, a little of your advice; an old maimed general, when unfit for action, is fittest for counsel. I have other designs upon women than eating and drinking with them. I am in love with Sparkish's mistress, whom he is to marry tomorrow. Now how shall I get her?
  [*Enter Sparkish, looking about.*]

HORNER: Why, here comes one will help you to her.

HARCOURT: He! He, I tell you, is my rival, and will hinder my love.

HORNER: No, a foolish rival and a jealous husband assist their rival's designs, for they are sure to make their women hate them, which is the first step to their love for another man.

HARCOURT: But I cannot come near his mistress but in his company.

HORNER: Still the better for you, for fools are most easily cheated when they themselves are accessories; and he is to be bubbled[6] of his mistress, as of his money, the common mistress, by keeping him company.

SPARKISH: Who is that, that is to be bubbled? Faith, let me snack,[7] I han't met with a bubble since Christmas. Gad, I think bubbles are like their brother woodcocks,[8] go out with the cold weather.

HARCOURT [*apart to Horner*]: A pox! He did not hear all, I hope.

SPARKISH: Come, you bubbling rogues you, where do we sup?—Oh, Harcourt, my mistress tells me you have been making fierce love to her all the play long, hah, ha! But I—

HARCOURT: I make love to her?

SPARKISH: Nay, I forgive thee, for I think I know thee, and I know her, but I am sure I know myself.

HARCOURT: Did she tell you so? I see all women are like these of the Exchange, who, to enhance the price of their commodities, report to their fond customers offers which were never made 'em.

HORNER: Ay, women are as apt to tell before the intrigue as men after it, and so show themselves the vainer sex. But hast thou a mistress, Sparkish? 'Tis as hard for me to believe it as that thou ever hadst a bubble, as you bragged just now.

SPARKISH: Oh, your servant, sir; are you at your raillery, sir? But we were some of us beforehand with you today at the play. The wits were something bold with you, sir; did you not hear us laugh?

HORNER: Yes, but I thought you had gone to plays to laugh at the poet's wit, not at your own.

SPARKISH: Your servant, sir; no, I thank you. Gad, I go to a play as to a country treat;[9] I carry my own wine to one and my own wit to t'other, or else I'm sure I

4. A London restaurant.
5. Sack, white wine from Spain or the Canary Islands, was often drunk with sugar.
6. Cheated, fooled.

7. Have a share.
8. Migratory birds; also fools.
9. Reception.

should not be merry at either. And the reason why we are so often louder than the players is because we think we speak more wit and so become the poet's rivals in his audience. For to tell you the truth, we hate the silly rogues, nay, so much that we find fault even with their bawdy upon the stage, whilst we talk nothing else in the pit as loud.

HORNER: But why shouldst thou hate the silly poets? Thou hast too much wit to be one, and they, like whores, are only hated by each other—and thou dost scorn writing, I'm sure.

SPARKISH: Yes, I'd have you to know I scorn writing; but women, women, that make men do all foolish things, make 'em write songs too. Everybody does it. 'Tis even as common with lovers as playing with fans; and you can no more help rhyming to your Phyllis[1] than drinking to your Phyllis.

HARCOURT: Nay, poetry in love is no more to be avoided than jealousy.

DORILANT: But the poets damned your songs, did they?

SPARKISH: Damn the poets! They turned 'em into burlesque, as they call it. That burlesque[2] is a hocus-pocus trick they have got, which, by virtue of *hictius doctius*,[3] *topsy-turvy*, they make a wise and witty man in the world a fool upon the stage, you know not how; and 'tis therefore I hate 'em too, for I know not but it may be my own case, for they'll put a man into a play for looking asquint.[4] Their predecessors were contented to make serving-men only their stage-fools, but these rogues must have gentlemen, with a pox to 'em, nay, knights; and, indeed, you shall hardly see a fool upon the stage but he's a knight and, to tell you the truth, they have kept me these six years from being a knight in earnest, for fear of being knighted in a play, and dubbed a fool.

DORILANT: Blame 'em not; they must follow their copy,[5] the age.

HARCOURT: But why shouldst thou be afraid of being in a play, who expose yourself every day in the play-houses, and as public places?

HORNER: 'Tis but being on the stage, instead of standing on a bench in the pit.

DORILANT: Don't you give money to painters to draw you like? And are you afraid of your pictures at length in a playhouse, where all your mistresses may see you?

SPARKISH: A pox! Painters don't draw the smallpox or pimples in one's face. Come, damn all your silly authors whatever, all books and booksellers, by the world, and all readers, courteous or uncourteous.

HARCOURT: But who comes here, Sparkish?

[*Enter Mr. Pinchwife and his wife in man's clothes, Alithea, Lucy her maid.*]

SPARKISH: Oh, hide me! There's my mistress too. [*Sparkish hides himself behind Harcourt.*]

HARCOURT: She sees you.

SPARKISH: But I will not see her. 'Tis time to go to Whitehall and I must not fail the drawing room.

HARCOURT: Pray, first carry me, and reconcile me to her.

SPARKISH: Another time; faith, the King will have supped.

HARCOURT: Not with the worse stomach for thy absence; thou art one of those fools that think their attendance at the King's meals as necessary as his physicians', when you are more troublesome to him than his doctors, or his dogs.

---

1. I.e., "sweetheart"; beloved women were often so named in pastoral poetry.
2. I.e., they wrote parodies of Sparkish's songs.
3. Like hocus-pocus.

4. I.e., they'll make him a comic character in a play, mocking even the tiniest fault.
5. The original from which a copy is made.

SPARKISH: Pshaw, I know my interest, sir. Prithee hide me.

HORNER: Your servant, Pinchwife.—What, he knows us not!

PINCHWIFE [to his wife aside]: Come along.

MRS. PINCHWIFE: Pray, have you any ballads? Give me sixpenny worth.

CLASP: We have no ballads.

MRS. PINCHWIFE: Then give me *Covent Garden Drollery*,[6] and a play or two— Oh, here's *Tarugo's Wiles*, and *The Slighted Maiden*;[7] I'll have them.

PINCHWIFE [apart to her]: No, plays are not for your reading. Come along; will you discover yourself?

HORNER: Who is that pretty youth with him, Sparkish?

SPARKISH: I believe his wife's brother, because he's something like her, but I never saw her but once.

HORNER: Extremely handsome; I have seen a face like it too. Let us follow 'em.

[Exeunt Pinchwife, Mrs. Pinchwife, Alithea, Lucy; Horner, Dorilant following them.]

HARCOURT: Come, Sparkish, your mistress saw you and will be angry you go not to her. Besides, I would fain be reconciled to her, which none but you can do, dear friend.

SPARKISH: Well, that's a better reason, dear friend, I would not go near her now, for hers or my own sake, but I can deny you nothing, for though I have known thee a great while, never go,[8] if I do not love thee as well as a new acquaintance.

HARCOURT: I am obliged to you indeed, dear friend. I would be well with her, only to be well with thee still, for these ties to wives usually dissolve all ties to friends. I would be contented she should enjoy you a-nights, but I would have you to myself a-days, as I have had, dear friend.

SPARKISH: And thou shalt enjoy me a-days, dear, dear friend, never stir, and I'll be divorced from her sooner than from thee. Come along.

HARCOURT [aside]: So, we are hard put to't when we make our rival our procurer; but neither she nor her brother would let me come near her now. When all's done, a rival is the best cloak to steal to a mistress under, without suspicion, and when we have once got to her as we desire, we throw him off like other cloaks.

[Exit Sparkish, and Harcourt following him. Re-enter Mr. Pinchwife, Mrs. Pinchwife in man's clothes.]

PINCHWIFE [to Alithea (off-stage)]: Sister, if you will not go, we must leave you. [Aside.] The fool her gallant and she will muster up all the young saunterers of this place, and they will leave their dear seamstresses to follow us. What a swarm of cuckolds and cuckold-makers are here!—Come, let's be gone, Mistress Margery.

MRS. PINCHWIFE: Don't you believe that; I ha'n't half my bellyful of sights yet.

PINCHWIFE: Then walk this way.

MRS. PINCHWIFE: Lord, what a power of brave signs are here! Stay—the Bull's-Head, the Ram's-Head and the Stag's-Head, dear—

PINCHWIFE: Nay, if every husband's proper sign[9] here were visible, they would be all alike.

MRS. PINCHWIFE: What d'ye mean by that, bud?

PINCHWIFE: 'Tis no matter—no matter, bud.

6. A collection of songs, prologues, epilogues, and poetry by various authors, including Wycherley, believed to have been edited by Aphra Behn (1672).
7. Two theatrical "oldies," no longer current: a comedy by Thomas St. Serfe (1668) and a tragicomedy by Robert Stapleton (1663).
8. Worry not.
9. I.e., a cuckold's horns.

MRS. PINCHWIFE: Pray tell me; nay, I will know.

PINCHWIFE: They would be all bulls', stags', and rams' heads.

[*Exeunt Mr. Pinchwife, Mrs. Pinchwife. Re-enter Sparkish, Harcourt, Alithea, Lucy, at t'other door.*]

SPARKISH: Come, dear madam, for my sake you shall be reconciled to him.

ALITHEA: For your sake I hate him.

HARCOURT: That's something too cruel, madam, to hate me for his sake.

SPARKISH: Ay indeed, madam, too, too cruel to me, to hate my friend for my sake.

ALITHEA: I hate him because he is your enemy; and you ought to hate him too, for making love to me, if you love me.

SPARKISH: That's a good one! I hate a man for loving you! If he did love you, 'tis but what he can't help and 'tis your fault, not his, if he admires you. I hate a man for being of my opinion! I'll ne'er do't by the world.

ALITHEA: Is it for your honor or mine, to suffer a man to make love to me, who am to marry you tomorrow?

SPARKISH: Is it for your honor or mine, to have me jealous? That he makes love to you is a sign you are handsome and that I am not jealous is a sign you are virtuous. That, I think, is for your honor.

ALITHEA: But 'tis your honor too I am concerned for.

HARCOURT: But why, dearest madam, will you be more concerned for his honor than he is himself? Let his honor alone, for my sake and his. He, he has no honor—

SPARKISH: How's that?

HARCOURT: But what my dear friend can guard himself.

SPARKISH: O ho—that's right again.

HARCOURT: Your care of his honor argues his neglect of it, which is no honor to my dear friend here; therefore once more, let his honor go which way it will, dear madam.

SPARKISH: Ay, ay, were it for my honor to marry a woman whose virtue I suspected and could not trust her in a friend's hands?

ALITHEA: Are you not afraid to lose me?

HARCOURT: He afraid to lose you, madam! No, no—you may see how the most estimable and most glorious creature in the world is valued by him. Will you not see it?

SPARKISH: Right, honest Frank, I have that noble value for her that I cannot be jealous of her.

ALITHEA: You mistake him, he means you care not for me, nor who has me.

SPARKISH: Lord, madam, I see you are jealous.[1] Will you wrest a poor man's meaning from his words?

ALITHEA: You astonish me, sir, with your want of jealousy.

SPARKISH: And you make me giddy, madam, with your jealousy and fears and virtue and honor. Gad, I see virtue makes a woman as troublesome as a little reading or learning.

ALITHEA: Monstrous!

LUCY [*behind*]: Well, to see what easy husbands these women of quality can meet with; a poor chambermaid can never have such lady-like luck. Besides, he's

1. Here, vehement, fearful.

thrown away upon her; she'll make no use of her fortune, her blessing. None to[2] a gentleman for a pure cuckold, for it requires good breeding to be a cuckold.

ALITHEA: I tell you then plainly, he pursues me to marry me.

SPARKISH: Pshaw!

HARCOURT: Come, madam, you see you strive in vain to make him jealous of me; my dear friend is the kindest creature in the world to me.

SPARKISH: Poor fellow.

HARCOURT: But his kindness only is not enough for me, without your favor; your good opinion, dear madam, 'tis that must perfect my happiness. Good gentleman, he believes all I say—would you would do so. Jealous of me! I would not wrong him nor you for the world.

SPARKISH: Look you there; hear him, hear him, and do not walk away so.
    [Alithea walks carelessly to and fro.]

HARCOURT: I love you, madam, so—

SPARKISH: How's that! Nay—now you begin to go too far indeed.

HARCOURT: So much, I confess, I say I love you, that I would not have you miserable and cast yourself away upon so unworthy and inconsiderable a thing as what you see here. [Clapping his hand on his breast, points at Sparkish.]

SPARKISH: No, faith, I believe thou wouldst not; now his meaning is plain. But I knew before thou wouldst not wrong me nor her.

HARCOURT: No, no, heavens forbid the glory of her sex should fall so low as into the embraces of such a contemptible wretch, the last of mankind—my dear friend here—I injure him! [Embracing Sparkish.]

ALITHEA: Very well.

SPARKISH: No, no, dear friend, I knew it.—Madam, you see he will rather wrong himself than me, in giving himself such names.

ALITHEA: Do not you understand him yet?

SPARKISH: Yes, how modestly he speaks of himself, poor fellow.

ALITHEA: Methinks he speaks impudently of yourself, since—before yourself too; insomuch that I can no longer suffer his scurrilous abusiveness to you, no more than his love to me. [Offers to go.]

SPARKISH: Nay, nay, madam, pray stay—his love to you! Lord, madam, he has not spoke yet plain enough?

ALITHEA: Yes, indeed, I should think so.

SPARKISH: Well then, by the world, a man can't speak civilly to a woman now but presently she says he makes love to her. Nay, madam, you shall stay, with your pardon, since you have not yet understood him, till he has made an éclaircissement[3] of his love to you, that is, what kind of love it is. [To Harcourt.] Answer to thy catechism. Friend, do you love my mistress here?

HARCOURT: Yes, I wish she would not doubt it.

SPARKISH: But how do you love her?

HARCOURT: With all my soul.

ALITHEA: I thank him; methinks he speaks plain enough now.

SPARKISH [to Alithea]: You are out still.—But with what kind of love, Harcourt?

HARCOURT: With the best and truest love in the world.

SPARKISH: Look you there then, that is with no matrimonial love, I'm sure.

ALITHEA: How's that? Do you say matrimonial love is not best?

2. There's no one like.   3. Explanation.

SPARKISH: Gad, I went too far ere I was aware. But speak for thyself, Harcourt; you said you would not wrong me nor her.

HARCOURT: No, no, madam, e'en take him for heaven's sake—

SPARKISH: Look you there, madam.

HARCOURT: Who should in all justice be yours, he that loves you most. [*Claps his hand on his breast.*]

ALITHEA: Look you there, Mr. Sparkish, who's that?

SPARKISH: Who should it be?—Go on, Harcourt.

HARCOURT: Who loves you more than women titles or fortune fools. [*Points at Sparkish.*]

SPARKISH: Look you there, he means me still, for he points at me.

ALITHEA: Ridiculous!

HARCOURT: Who can only match your faith and constancy in love.

SPARKISH: Ay.

HARCOURT: Who knows, if it be possible, how to value so much beauty and virtue.

SPARKISH: Ay.

HARCOURT: Whose love can no more be equaled in the world than that heavenly form of yours.

SPARKISH: No.

HARCOURT: Who could no more suffer a rival than your absence, and yet could no more suspect your virtue than his own constancy in his love to you.

SPARKISH: No.

HARCOURT: Who, in fine,[4] loves you better than his eyes that first made him love you.

SPARKISH: Ay—nay, madam, faith, you shan't go till—

ALITHEA: Have a care, lest you make me stay too long—

SPARKISH: But till he has saluted you, that I may be assured you are friends, after his honest advice and declaration. Come, pray, madam, be friends with him.

[*Enter Mr. Pinchwife, Mrs. Pinchwife*]

ALITHEA: You must pardon me, sir, that I am not yet so obedient to you.

PINCHWIFE: What, invite your wife to kiss men? Monstrous! Are you not ashamed? I will never forgive you.

SPARKISH: Are you not ashamed that I should have more confidence in the chastity of your family than you have? You must not teach me. I am a man of honor, sir, though I am frank[5] and free; I am frank, sir—

PINCHWIFE: Very frank, sir, to share your wife with your friends.

SPARKISH: He is an humble, menial[6] friend, such as reconciles the differences of the marriage bed. You know man and wife do not always agree; I design him for that use, therefore would have him well with my wife.

PINCHWIFE: A menial friend!—you will get a great many menial friends by showing your wife as you do.

SPARKISH: What then? It may be I have a pleasure in't, as I have to show fine clothes at a playhouse the first day and count money before poor rogues.

PINCHWIFE: He that shows his wife or money will be in danger of having them borrowed sometimes.

4. In short.
5. Unreserved, open.

6. Household.

SPARKISH: I love to be envied and would not marry a wife that I alone could love; loving alone is as dull as eating alone. Is it not a frank age? And I am a frank person. And to tell you the truth, it may be I love to have rivals in a wife; they make her seem to a man still but as a kept mistress. And so good night, for I must to Whitehall.—Madam, I hope you are now reconciled to my friend and so I wish you a good night, madam, and sleep if you can, for tomorrow you know I must visit you early with a canonical gentleman. Good night, dear Harcourt. [*Exit Sparkish.*]

HARCOURT: Madam, I hope you will not refuse my visit tomorrow, if it should be earlier, with a canonical gentleman, than Mr. Sparkish's.

PINCHWIFE [*coming between Alithea and Harcourt*]: This gentlewoman is yet under my care; therefore you must yet forbear your freedom with her, sir.

HARCOURT: Must, sir!

PINCHWIFE: Yes, sir, she is my sister.

HARCOURT: 'Tis well she is, sir—for I must be her servant, sir.—Madam—

PINCHWIFE: Come away, sister; we had been gone, if it had not been for you, and so avoided these lewd rake-hells,[7] who seem to haunt us.
[*Enter Horner, Dorilant to them.*]

HORNER: How now, Pinchwife?

PINCHWIFE: Your servant.

HORNER: What, I see a little time in the country makes a man turn wild and unsociable and only fit to converse with his horses, dogs and his herds.

PINCHWIFE: I have business, sir, and must mind it; your business is pleasure, therefore you and I must go different ways.

HORNER: Well, you may go on, but this pretty young gentleman—[*Takes hold of Mrs. Pinchwife.*]

HARCOURT: The lady—

DORILANT: And the maid—

HORNER: Shall stay with us, for I suppose their business is the same with ours, pleasure.

PINCHWIFE [*aside*]: 'Sdeath, he know her, she carries it so sillily! Yet if he does not, I should be more silly to discover it first.

ALITHEA: Pray, let us go, sir.

PINCHWIFE: Come, come—

HORNER [*to Mrs. Pinchwife*]: Had you not rather stay with us?—Prithee, Pinchwife, who is this pretty young gentleman?

PINCHWIFE: One to whom I'm a guardian. [*Aside.*] I wish I could keep her out of your hands.

HORNER: Who is he? I never saw anything so pretty in all my life.

PINCHWIFE: Pshaw, do not look upon him so much. He's a poor bashful youth, you'll put him out of countenance.—Come away, brother. [*Offers to take her away.*]

HORNER: Oh, your brother!

PINCHWIFE: Yes, my wife's brother.—Come, come, she'll stay supper for us.

HORNER: I thought so, for he is very like her I saw you at the play with, whom I told you I was in love with.

MRS. PINCHWIFE [*aside*]: O jeminy! Is this he that was in love with me? I am glad on't, I vow, for he's a curious fine gentleman, and I love him already too. [*To Mr. Pinchwife.*] Is this he, bud?

7. Scoudrels.

PINCHWIFE [*to his wife.*]: Come away, come away.

HORNER: Why, what haste are you in? Why won't you let me talk with him?

PINCHWIFE: Because you'll debauch him; he's yet young and innocent and I would not have him debauched for anything in the world. [*Aside.*] How she gazes on him! The devil!

HORNER: Harcourt, Dorilant, look you here; this is the likeness of that dowdy[8] he told us of, his wife. Did you ever see a lovelier creature? The rogue has reason to be jealous of his wife since she is like him, for she would make all that see her in love with her.

HARCOURT: And as I remember now, she is as like him here as can be.

DORILANT: She is indeed very pretty, if she be like him.

HORNER: Very pretty? A very pretty commendation! She is a glorious creature, beautiful beyond all things I ever beheld.

PINCHWIFE: So, so.

HARCOURT: More beautiful than a poet's first mistress of imagination.

HORNER: Or another man's last mistress of flesh and blood.

MRS. PINCHWIFE: Nay, now you jeer, sir; pray don't jeer me.

PINCHWIFE: Come, come. [*Aside.*] By heavens, she'll discover herself!

HORNER: I speak of your sister, sir.

PINCHWIFE: Ay, but saying she was handsome, if like him, made him blush. [*Aside.*] I am upon a rack!

HORNER: Methinks he is so handsome he should not be a man.

PINCHWIFE [*aside*]: Oh, there 'tis out! He has discovered her! I am not able to suffer any longer. [*To his wife.*] Come, come away, I say.

HORNER: Nay, by your leave, sir, he shall not go yet.—[*To them.*] Harcourt, Dorilant, let us torment this jealous rogue a little.

HARCOURT:⎱
DORILANT:⎰ How?

HORNER: I'll show you.

PINCHWIFE: Come, pray, let him go, I cannot stay fooling any longer. I tell you his sister stays supper for us.

HORNER: Does she? Come then, we'll all go sup with her and thee.

PINCHWIFE: No, now I think on't, having stayed so long for us, I warrant she's gone to bed. [*Aside.*] I wish she and I were well out of their hands.—Come, I must rise early tomorrow, come.

HORNER: Well, then, if she be gone to bed, I wish her and you a good night. But pray, young gentleman, present my humble service to her.

MRS. PINCHWIFE: Thank you heartily, sir.

PINCHWIFE [*aside*]: 'Sdeath! she will discover herself yet in spite of me.—He is something more civil to you, for your kindness to his sister, than I am, it seems.

HORNER: Tell her, dear sweet little gentleman, for all your brother there, that you have revived the love I had for her at first sight in the playhouse.

MRS. PINCHWIFE: But did you love her indeed, and indeed?

PINCHWIFE [*aside*]: So, so.—Away, I say.

HORNER: Nay, stay. Yes, indeed, and indeed, pray do you tell her so, and give her this kiss from me. [*Kisses her.*]

---

8. Shabby, dull woman.

PINCHWIFE [*aside*]: O heavens! What do I suffer! Now 'tis too plain he knows her, and yet—

HORNER: And this, and this—[*Kisses her again.*]

MRS. PINCHWIFE: What do you kiss me for? I am no woman.

PINCHWIFE [*aside*]: So—there, 'tis out.—Come, I cannot, nor will stay any longer.

HORNER: Nay, they shall send your lady a kiss too. Here, Harcourt, Dorilant, will you not? [*They kiss her.*]

PINCHWIFE [*aside*]: How! Do I suffer this? Was I not accusing another just now for this rascally patience, in permitting his wife to be kissed before his face? Ten thousand ulcers gnaw away their lips!—Come, come.

HORNER: Good night, dear little gentleman. Madam, good night. Farewell, Pinchwife. [*Apart to Harcourt and Dorilant.*] Did not I tell you I would raise his jealous gall? [*Exeunt Horner, Harcourt, and Dorilant.*]

PINCHWIFE: So, they are gone at last; stay, let me see first if the coach be at this door.   [*Exit.*]

   [*Horner, Harcourt, Dorilant return.*]

HORNER: What, not gone yet? Will you be sure to do as I desired you, sweet sir?

MRS. PINCHWIFE: Sweet sir, but what will you give me then?

HORNER: Anything. Come away into the next walk.

                              [*Exit Horner, haling away Mrs. Pinchwife.*]

ALITHEA: Hold, hold! What d'ye do?

LUCY: Stay, stay, hold—

HARCOURT: Hold, madam, hold! Let him present[9] him, he'll come presently. Nay, I will never let you go till you answer my question.

LUCY: For God's sake, sir, I must follow 'em.

DORILANT: No, I have something to present you with too; you shan't follow them.

   [*Alithea, Lucy struggling with Harcourt and Dorilant. Pinchwife returns.*]

PINCHWIFE: Where?—how?—what's become of?—gone!—whither?

LUCY: He's only gone with the gentleman, who will give him something, an't please your worship.

PINCHWIFE: Something—give him something, with a pox!—where are they?

ALITHEA: In the next walk only, brother.

PINCHWIFE: Only, only! Where, where?

   [*Exit Pinchwife and returns presently, then goes out again.*]

HARCOURT: What's the matter with him? Why so much concerned? But dearest madam—

ALITHEA: Pray let me go, sir; I have said and suffered enough already.

HARCOURT: Then you will not look upon nor pity my sufferings?

ALITHEA: To look upon 'em, when I cannot help 'em, were cruelty, not pity; therefore I will never see you more.

HARCOURT: Let me then, madam, have my privilege of a banished lover, complaining or railing, and giving you but a farewell reason why, if you cannot condescend to marry me, you should not take that wretch, my rival.

ALITHEA: He only, not you, since my honor is engaged so far to him, can give me a reason why I should not marry him; but if he be true and what I think him to me, I must be so to him. Your servant, sir.

----

9. Offer a gift to.

HARCOURT: Have women only constancy when 'tis a vice and, like fortune, only true to fools?

DORILANT [to Lucy, who struggles to get from him]: Thou shalt not stir, thou robust creature; you see I can deal with you, therefore you should stay the rather, and be kind.

[Enter Pinchwife.]

PINCHWIFE: Gone, gone, not to be found! Quite gone! Ten thousand plagues go with 'em! Which way went they?

ALITHEA: But into t'other walk, brother.

LUCY: Their business will be done presently sure, an't please your worship; it can't be long in doing, I'm sure on't.

ALITHEA: Are they not there?

PINCHWIFE: No; you know where they are, you infamous wretch, eternal shame of your family, which you do not dishonor enough yourself, you think, but you must help her to do it too, thou legion of bawds!

ALITHEA: Good brother—

PINCHWIFE: Damned, damned sister!

ALITHEA: Look you here, she's coming.

[Enter Mrs. Pinchwife in man's clothes, running, with her hat under her arm, full of oranges and dried fruit; Horner following.]

MRS. PINCHWIFE: O dear bud, look you here what I have got, see!

PINCHWIFE [aside, rubbing his forehead]: And what I have got here too, which you can't see.

MRS. PINCHWIFE: The fine gentleman has given me better things yet.

PINCHWIFE: Has he so? [Aside.] Out of breath and colored! I must hold yet.

HORNER: I have only given your little brother an orange, sir.

PINCHWIFE [to Horner]: Thank you, sir. [Aside.] You have only squeezed my orange, I suppose, and given it me again; yet I must have a city patience. [To his wife.] Come, come away.

MRS. PINCHWIFE: Stay, till I have put up my fine things, bud.

[Enter Sir Jaspar Fidget.]

SIR JASPAR: O Master Horner, come, come, the ladies stay for you; your mistress, my wife, wonders you make not more haste to her.

HORNER: I have stayed this half hour for you here and 'tis your fault I am not now with your wife.

SIR JASPAR: But pray, don't let her know so much; the truth on't is, I was advancing a certain project to his Majesty about—I'll tell you.

HORNER: No, let's go and hear it at your house.—Good night, sweet little gentleman. One kiss more, you'll remember me now, I hope. [Kisses her.]

DORILANT: What, Sir Jaspar, will you separate friends? He promised to sup with us; and if you take him to your house, you'll be in danger of our company too.

SIR JASPAR: Alas, gentlemen, my house is not fit for you; there are none but civil women there, which are not fit for your turn. He, you know, can bear with the society of civil women now, ha, ha, ha! Besides, he's one of my family—he's— heh, heh, heh!

DORILANT: What is he?

SIR JASPAR: Faith, my eunuch, since you'll have it, heh, he, he!

[Exeunt Sir Jaspar Fidget and Horner.]

DORILANT: I rather wish thou wert his, or my cuckold. Harcourt, what a good cuckold is lost there for want of a man to make him one! Thee and I cannot have Horner's privilege, who can make use of it.

HARCOURT: Ay, to poor Horner 'tis like coming to an estate at threescore, when a man can't be the better for't.

PINCHWIFE: Come.

MRS. PINCHWIFE: Presently, bud.

DORILANT: Come, let us go too. [*To Alithea.*] Madam, your servant. [*To Lucy.*] Good night, strapper.[1]

HARCOURT: Madam, though you will not let me have a good day or night, I wish you one; but dare not name the other half of my wish.

ALITHEA: Good night, sir, forever.

MRS. PINCHWIFE: I don't know where to put this here, dear bud; you shall eat it; nay, you shall have part of the fine gentleman's good things, or treat as you call it, when we come home.

PINCHWIFE: Indeed, I deserve it, since I furnished the best part of it. [*Strikes away the orange.*]

> The gallant treats, presents, and gives the ball
> But 'tis the absent cuckold pays for all.

[*Exeunt.*]

ACT 4

Scene 1

[*In Pinchwife's house in the morning. Lucy, Alithea dressed in new clothes.*]

LUCY: Well—madam, now have I dressed you and set you out with so many ornaments and spent upon you ounces of essence and pulvilio,[1] and all this for no other purpose but as people adorn and perfume a corpse for a stinking secondhand grave[2]—such or as bad I think as Master Sparkish's bed.

ALITHEA: Hold your peace.

LUCY: Nay, madam, I will ask you the reason why you would banish poor Master Harcourt forever from your sight. How could you be so hardhearted?

ALITHEA: 'Twas because I was not hardhearted.

LUCY: No, no, 'twas stark love and kindness, I warrant.

ALITHEA: It was so; I would see him no more because I love him.

LUCY: Hey-day, a very pretty reason!

ALITHEA: You do not understand me.

LUCY: I wish you may yourself.

ALITHEA: I was engaged to marry, you see, another man, whom my justice will not suffer me to deceive or injure.

LUCY: Can there be a greater cheat or wrong done to a man than to give him your person without your heart? I should make a conscience of[3] it.

ALITHEA: I'll retrieve it for him after I am married a while.

LUCY: The woman that marries to love better will be as much mistaken as the wencher that marries to live better. No, madam, marrying to increase love is like gaming to become rich; alas, you only lose what little stock you had before.

---

1. Robust woman.
1. Perfume and tragrant powder.

2. I.e., a grave newly opened for a second burial.
3. Have scruples about.

ALITHEA: I find by your rhetoric you have been bribed to betray me.

LUCY: Only by his merit, that has bribed your heart, you see, against your word and rigid honor. But what a devil is this honor! 'Tis sure a disease in the head, like the megrim, or falling sickness,[4] that always hurries people away to do themselves mischief. Men lose their lives by it; women what's dearer to 'em, their love, the life of life.

ALITHEA: Come, pray talk you no more of honor, nor Master Harcourt. I wish the other would come to secure my fidelity to him and his right in me.

LUCY: You will marry him then?

ALITHEA: Certainly. I have given him already my word and will my hand too, to make it good when he comes.

LUCY: Well, I wish I may never stick pin more if he be not an arrant natural to[5] t'other fine gentleman.

ALITHEA: I own he wants the wit of Harcourt, which I will dispense withal for another want he has, which is want of jealousy, which men of wit seldom want.

LUCY: Lord, madam, what should you do with a fool to your husband? You intend to be honest, don't you? Then that husbandly virtue, credulity, is thrown away upon you.

ALITHEA: He only that could suspect my virtue should have cause to do it; 'tis Sparkish's confidence in my truth that obliges me to be so faithful to him.

LUCY: You are not sure his opinion may last.

ALITHEA: I am satisfied 'tis impossible for him to be jealous after the proofs I have had of him. Jealousy in a husband—Heaven defend me from it! It begets a thousand plagues to a poor woman, the loss of her honor, her quiet and her—

LUCY: And her pleasure.

ALITHEA: What d'ye mean, impertinent?

LUCY: Liberty is a great pleasure, madam.

ALITHEA: I say, loss of her honor, her quiet, nay, her life sometimes, and what's as bad almost, the loss of this town; that is, she is sent into the country, which is the last ill usage of a husband to a wife, I think.

LUCY [aside]: Oh, does the wind lie there?—Then, of necessity, madam, you think a man must carry his wife into the country, if he be wise. The country is as terrible, I find, to our young English ladies as a monastery to those abroad, and, on my virginity, I think they would rather marry a London jailer than a high sheriff of a county, since neither can stir from his employment. Formerly women of wit married fools for a great estate, a fine seat, or the like, but now 'tis for a pretty seat only in Lincoln's Inn Fields, St James's Fields, or the Pall Mall.[6]

[Enter to them Sparkish and Harcourt dressed like a parson.]

SPARKISH: Madam, your humble servant, a happy day to you, and to us all.

HARCOURT: Amen.

ALITHEA: Who have we here?

SPARKISH: My chaplain, faith. O madam, poor Harcourt remembers his humble service to you and, in obedience to your last commands, refrains coming into your sight.

---

4. Migraine headache, or epilepsy.
5. An utter fool in comparison to.
6. Fashionable residential areas of London, distinguished by their famous inhabitants and expensive shops, as well as their grand houses.

ALITHEA: Is not that he?

SPARKISH: No, fie, no; but to show that he ne'er intended to hinder our match, has sent his brother here to join our hands. When I get me a wife, I must get her a chaplain, according to the custom; this is his brother, and my chaplain.

ALITHEA: His brother?

LUCY [aside]: And your chaplain, to preach in your pulpit then.

ALITHEA: His brother!

SPARKISH: Nay, I knew you would not believe it.—I told you, sir, she would take you for your brother Frank.

ALITHEA: Believe it!

LUCY [aside]: His brother! hah, ha, he! He has a trick left still, it seems.

SPARKISH: Come, my dearest, pray let us go to church before the canonical hour[7] is past.

ALITHEA: For shame, you are abused still.

SPARKISH: By the world, 'tis strange now you are so incredulous.

ALITHEA: 'Tis strange you are so credulous.

SPARKISH: Dearest of my life, hear me. I tell you this is Ned Harcourt of Cambridge; by the world, you see he has a sneaking college look. 'Tis true he's something like his brother Frank and they differ from each other no more than in their age, for they were twins.

LUCY: Hah, ha, he!

ALITHEA: Your servant, sir; I cannot be so deceived, though you are. But come, let's hear; how do you know what you affirm so confidently?

SPARKISH: Why, I'll tell you all. Frank Harcourt coming to me this morning, to wish me joy and present his service to you, I asked him if he could help me to a parson, whereupon he told me he had a brother in town who was in orders and he went straight away and sent him you see there to me.

ALITHEA: Yes, Frank goes and puts on a black coat, then tells you he is Ned; that's all you have for't.

SPARKISH: Pshaw, pshaw, I tell you by the same token, the midwife put her garter about Frank's neck to know 'em asunder, they were so like.

ALITHEA: Frank tells you this too.

SPARKISH: Ay, and Ned there too; nay, they are both in a story.

ALITHEA: So, so; very foolish!

SPARKISH: Lord, if you won't believe one, you had best try him by your chambermaid there, for chambermaids must needs know chaplains from other men, they are so used to 'em.

LUCY: Let's see; nay, I'll be sworn he has the canonical smirk and the filthy, clammy palm of a chaplain.

ALITHEA: Well, most reverend doctor, pray let us make an end of this fooling.

HARCOURT: With all my soul, divine, heavenly creature, when you please.

ALITHEA: He speaks like a chaplain indeed.

SPARKISH: Why, was there not "soul," "divine," "heavenly," in what he said?

---

7. Church law permitted the marriage ceremony only in the morning; it could be performed at any time between 8 A.M. and noon.

ALITHEA: Once more, most impertinent black coat, cease your persecution and let us have a conclusion of this ridiculous love.

HARCOURT [aside]: I had forgot. I must suit my style to my coat, or I wear it in vain.

ALITHEA: I have no more patience left; let us make once an end of this troublesome love, I say.

HARCOURT: So be it, seraphic lady, when your honor shall think it meet and convenient so to do.

SPARKISH: Gad, I'm sure none but a chaplain could speak so, I think.

ALITHEA: Let me tell you, sir, this dull trick will not serve your turn; though you delay our marriage, you shall not hinder it.

HARCOURT: Far be it from me, munificent patroness, to delay your marriage. I desire nothing more than to marry you presently, which I might do, if you yourself would, for my noble, good-natured and thrice generous patron here would not hinder it.

SPARKISH: No, poor man, not I, faith.

HARCOURT: And now, madam, let me tell you plainly, nobody else shall marry you; by heavens, I'll die first, for I'm sure I should die[8] after it.

LUCY [aside]: How his love has made him forget his function, as I have seen it in real parsons!

ALITHEA: That was spoken like a chaplain too! Now you understand him, I hope.

SPARKISH: Poor man, he takes it heinously to be refused. I can't blame him; 'tis putting an indignity upon him not to be suffered. But you'll pardon me, madam, it shan't be, he shall marry us. Come away, pray, madam.

LUCY [aside]: Hah, ha, he! More ado! 'Tis late.

ALITHEA: Invincible stupidity! I tell you he would marry me as your rival, not as your chaplain.

SPARKISH [pulling her away]: Come, come, madam.

LUCY: Ay, pray, madam, do not refuse this reverend divine the honor and satisfaction of marrying you, for I dare say he has set his heart upon't, good doctor.

ALITHEA: What can you hope or design by this?

HARCOURT [aside]: I could answer her, a reprieve for a day only often revokes a hasty doom; at worst, if she will not take mercy on me and let me marry her, I have at least the lover's second pleasure, hindering my rival's enjoyment, though but for a time.

SPARKISH: Come, madam, 'tis e'en twelve o'clock, and my mother charged me never to be married out of the canonical hours. Come, come. Lord, here's such a deal of modesty, I warrant, the first day.

LUCY: Yes, an't please your worship, married women show all their modesty the first day, because married men show all their love the first day.

[Exeunt Sparkish, Alithea, Harcourt, and Lucy.]

---

8. Harcourt plays on literal death and sexual "death": orgasm.

Scene 2

[The scene changes to a bedchamber, where appear Pinchwife, Mrs. Pinchwife.]

PINCHWIFE: Come, tell me, I say.

MRS. PINCHWIFE: Lord, ha'n't I told it an hundred times over?

PINCHWIFE *[aside]*: I would try if, in the repetition of the ungrateful[9] tale, I could find her altering it in the least circumstance, for if her story be false, she is so too.—Come, how was't, baggage?

MRS. PINCHWIFE: Lord, what pleasure you take to hear it, sure!

PINCHWIFE: No, you take more in telling it, I find; but speak, how was't?

MRS. PINCHWIFE: He carried me up into the house next to the Exchange.

PINCHWIFE: So, and you two were only in the room.

MRS. PINCHWIFE: Yes, for he sent away a youth that was there, for some dried fruit and China oranges.[1]

PINCHWIFE: Did he so? Damn him for it—and for—

MRS. PINCHWIFE: But presently came up the gentle-woman of the house.

PINCHWIFE: O, 'twas well she did; but what did he do whilst the fruit came?

MRS. PINCHWIFE: He kissed me an hundred times and told me he fancied he kissed my fine sister, meaning me, you know, whom he said he loved with all his soul and bid me be sure to tell her so and to desire her to be at her window by eleven of the clock this morning and he would walk under it at that time.

PINCHWIFE *[aside]*: And he was as good as his word, very punctual—a pox reward him for't.

MRS. PINCHWIFE: Well, and he said if you were not within, he would come up to her, meaning me, you know, bud, still.

PINCHWIFE *[aside]*: So—he knew her certainly; but for this confession, I am obliged to her simplicity.—But what, you stood very still when he kissed you?

MRS. PINCHWIFE: Yes, I warrant you; would you have had me discovered myself?

PINCHWIFE: But you told me he did some beastliness to you, as you called it; what was't?

MRS. PINCHWIFE: Why, he put—

PINCHWIFE: What?

MRS. PINCHWIFE: Why, he put the tip of his tongue between my lips and so mousled[2] me—and I said, I'd bite it.

PINCHWIFE: An eternal canker seize it, for[3] a dog!

MRS. PINCHWIFE: Nay, you need not be so angry with him neither, for to say truth, he has the sweetest breath I ever knew.

PINCHWIFE: The devil!—you were satisfied with it then, and would do it again.

MRS. PINCHWIFE: Not unless he should force me.

PINCHWIFE: Force you, changeling![4] I tell you no woman can be forced.

MRS. PINCHWIFE: Yes, but she may, sure, by such a one as he, for he's a proper, goodly strong man; 'tis hard, let me tell you, to resist him.

PINCHWIFE: So, 'tis plain she loves him, yet she has not love enough to make her conceal it from me; but the sight of him will increase her aversion for me and love for him and that love instruct her how to deceive me and satisfy him, all idiot as

9. Unpleasant.
1. Sweet oranges, regarded in the seventeenth century as an exotic delicacy.
2. A variation on "muzzled": kissed deeply.
3. I.e., for acting like.
4. Fool.

she is. Love! 'Twas he gave women first their craft, their art of deluding; out of nature's hands they came plain, open, silly and fit for slaves, as she and Heaven intended 'em; but damned love—well—I must strangle that little monster[5] whilst I
can deal with him.—Go fetch pen, ink and paper out of the next room.

MRS. PINCHWIFE: Yes, bud.   [*Exit Mrs. Pinchwife.*]

PINCHWIFE [*aside*]: Why should women have more invention in love than
men? It can only be because they have more desires, more soliciting passions,
more lust, and more of the devil. [*Mrs. Pinchwife returns.*] Come, minx, sit down
and write.

MRS. PINCHWIFE: Ay, dear bud, but I can't do't very well.

PINCHWIFE: I wish you could not at all.

MRS. PINCHWIFE: But what should I write for?

PINCHWIFE: I'll have you write a letter to your lover.

MRS. PINCHWIFE: O Lord, to the fine gentleman a letter!

PINCHWIFE: Yes, to the fine gentleman.

MRS. PINCHWIFE: Lord, you do but jeer; sure, you jest.

PINCHWIFE: I am not so merry. Come, write as I bid you.

MRS. PINCHWIFE: What, do you think I am a fool?

PINCHWIFE [*aside*]: She's afraid I would not dictate any love to him, therefore
she's unwilling.—But you had best begin.

MRS. PINCHWIFE: Indeed, and indeed, but I won't, so I won't.

PINCHWIFE: Why?

MRS. PINCHWIFE: Because he's in town; you may send for him if you will.

PINCHWIFE: Very well, you would have him brought to you; is it come to this? I
say, take the pen and write, or you'll provoke me.

MRS. PINCHWIFE: Lord, what d'ye make a fool of me for? Don't I know that letters are never writ but from the country to London and from London into the
country? Now he's in town and I am in town too; therefore I can't write to him,
you know.

PINCHWIFE [*aside*]: So, I am glad it is no worse; she is innocent enough yet.—
Yes, you may, when your husband bids you, write letters to people that are in
town.

MRS. PINCHWIFE: O, may I so? Then I'm satisfied.

PINCHWIFE: Come, begin.—[*Dictates.*] "Sir"—

MRS. PINCHWIFE: Shan't I say, "Dear Sir"? You know one says always something
more than bare "Sir."

PINCHWIFE: Write as I bid you, or I will write "whore" with this penknife in your
face.

MRS. PINCHWIFE: Nay, good bud—[*She writes.*] "Sir"—

PINCHWIFE: "Though I suffered last night your nauseous, loathed kisses and embraces"—Write.

MRS. PINCHWIFE: Nay, why should I say so? You know I told you he had a sweet
breath.

PINCHWIFE: Write.

MRS. PINCHWIFE: Let me but put out "loathed."

PINCHWIFE: Write, I say.

5. Cupid.

MRS. PINCHWIFE: Well then. [*Writes.*]

PINCHWIFE: Let's see, what have you writ? [*Takes the paper and reads.*] "Though I suffered last night your kisses and embraces"—Thou impudent creature, where is "nauseous" and "loathed"?

MRS. PINCHWIFE: I can't abide to write such filthy words.

PINCHWIFE: Once more write as I'd have you, and question it not, or I will spoil thy writing with this. [*Holds up the penknife.*] I will stab out those eyes that cause my mischief.

MRS. PINCHWIFE: O Lord, I will!

PINCHWIFE: So—so—let's see now! [*Reads.*] "Though I suffered last night your nauseous, loathed kisses and embraces"—go on—"yet I would not have you presume that you shall ever repeat them"—So—[*She writes.*]

MRS. PINCHWIFE: I have writ it.

PINCHWIFE: On then.—"I then concealed myself from your knowledge to avoid your insolencies"—[*She writes.*]

MRS. PINCHWIFE: So—

PINCHWIFE: "The same reason, now I am out of your hands"—[*She writes.*]

MRS. PINCHWIFE: So—

PINCHWIFE: "Makes me own to you my unfortunate, though innocent, frolic, of being in man's clothes"—[*She writes.*]

MRS. PINCHWIFE: So—

PINCHWIFE: "That you may for evermore cease to pursue her, who hates and detests you"—[*She writes on.*]

MRS. PINCHWIFE: So—h—[*Sighs.*]

PINCHWIFE: What, do you sigh?—"detests you—as much as she loves her husband and her honour."

MRS. PINCHWIFE: I vow, husband, he'll ne'er believe I should write such a letter.

PINCHWIFE: What, he'd expect a kinder from you? Come, now your name only.

MRS. PINCHWIFE: What, shan't I say, "Your most faithful, humble servant till death"?

PINCHWIFE: No, tormenting fiend! [*Aside.*] Her style, I find, would be very soft.—Come, wrap it up now, whilst I go fetch wax and a candle, and write on the backside, "For Mr. Horner."   [*Exit Pinchwife.*]

MRS. PINCHWIFE: "For Mr. Horner."—So, I am glad he has told me his name. Dear Mr. Horner! But why should I send thee such a letter that will vex thee and make thee angry with me?—Well, I will not send it—Ay, but then my husband will kill me—for I see plainly he won't let me love Mr. Horner—but what care I for my husband?—I won't, so I won't send poor Mr. Horner such a letter—But then my husband—But oh—What if I writ at bottom, my husband made me write it?—Ay, but then my husband would see't—Can one have no shift?[6] Ah, a London woman would have had a hundred presently. Stay—what if I should write a letter, and wrap it up like this, and write upon't too? Ay, but then my husband would see't—I don't know what to do—But yet y'vads[7] I'll try, so I will—for I will not send this letter to poor Mr. Horner, come what will on't.

[*She writes, and repeats what she hath writ.*]

---

6. Expedient; trick.   7. In faith.

"Dear, sweet Mr. Horner"—so—"my husband would have me send you a base, rude, unmannerly letter—but I won't"—so—"and would have me forbid you loving me—but I won't"—so—"and would have me say to you, I hate you, poor Mr. Horner—but I won't tell a lie for him"—there—"for I'm sure if you and I were in the country at cards together"—so—"I could not help treading on your toe under the table"—so—"or rubbing knees with you and staring in your face till you saw me"—very well—"and then looking down and blushing for an hour together"—so—"but I must make haste before my husband comes; and now he has taught me to write letters, you shall have longer ones from me, who am, Dear, dear, poor, dear Mr. Horner, Your most humble friend, and servant to command till death, Margery Pinchwife." Stay, I must give him a hint at bottom—so—now wrap it up just like t'other—so—now write, "For Mr. Horner"—But, oh now, what shall I do with it? For here comes my husband. [Enter Pinchwife.]

PINCHWIFE [aside]: I have been detained by a sparkish coxcomb, who pretended a visit to me; but I fear 'twas to my wife.—What, have you done?

MRS. PINCHWIFE: Ay, ay, bud, just now.

PINCHWIFE: Let's see't. What d'ye tremble for? What, you would not have it go?

MRS. PINCHWIFE: Here. [Aside.] No, I must not give him that; so I had been served if I had given him this.

PINCHWIFE [He opens, and reads the first letter]: Come, where's the wax and seal?

MRS. PINCHWIFE [aside]: Lord, what shall I do now? Nay, then, I have it.— Pray let me see't. Lord, you think me so arrant a fool I cannot seal a letter. I will do't, so I will. [Snatches the letter from him, changes it for the other, seals it and delivers it to him.]

PINCHWIFE: Nay, I believe you will learn that, and other things too, which I would not have you.

MRS. PINCHWIFE: So, han't I done it curiously?[8] [Aside.] I think I have; there's my letter going to Mr. Horner, since he'll needs have me send letters to folks.

PINCHWIFE: 'Tis very well; but I warrant you would not have it go now?

MRS. PINCHWIFE: Yes, indeed, but I would, bud, now.

PINCHWIFE: Well, you are a good girl then. Come, let me lock you up in your chamber, till I come back, and be sure you come not within three strides of the window when I am gone, for I have a spy in the street.

[Exit Mrs. Pinchwife. Pinchwife locks the door.]

At least, 'tis fit she think so. If we do not cheat women, they'll cheat us, and fraud may be justly used with secret enemies, of which a wife is the most dangerous, and he that has a handsome one to keep, and a frontier town, must provide against treachery rather than open force. Now I have secured all within, I'll deal with the foe without with false intelligence. [Holds up the letter. Exit Pinchwife.]

Scene 3

[The scene changes to Horner's lodging. Quack and Horner.]

QUACK: Well, sir, how fadges[9] the new design? Have you not the luck of all your brother projectors,[1] to deceive only yourself at last?

8. Adroitly; cleverly.   1. Designers, schemers.
9. Progresses.

HORNER: No, good domine[2] doctor, I deceive you, it seems, and others too, for the grave matrons and old, rigid husbands think me as unfit for love as they are but their wives, sisters and daughters know some of 'em better things already.

QUACK: Already!

HORNER: Already, I say. Last night I was drunk with half a dozen of your civil persons, as you call 'em, and people of honor, and so was made free of their society and dressing-rooms forever hereafter, and am already come to the privileges of sleeping upon their pallets,[3] warming smocks,[4] tying shoes and garters, and the like, doctor, already, already, doctor.

QUACK: You have made use of your time, sir.

HORNER: I tell thee, I am now no more interruption to 'em when they sing or talk bawdy than a little squab[5] French page who speaks no English.

QUACK: But do civil persons and women of honor drink and sing bawdy songs?

HORNER: O, amongst friends, amongst friends. For your bigots in honor are just like those in religion; they fear the eye of the world more than the eye of Heaven and think there is no virtue but railing at vice and no sin but giving scandal. They rail at a poor, little, kept player and keep themselves some young, modest pulpit comedian[6] to be privy to their sins in their closets, not to tell 'em of them in their chapels.

QUACK: Nay, the truth on't is, priests among the women now have quite got the better of us lay confessors, physicians.

HORNER: And they are rather their patients, but— [Enter Lady Fidget, looking about her.]

Now we talk of women of honor, here comes one. Step behind the screen there and but observe if I have not particular privileges with the women of reputation already, doctor, already.

[Quack steps behind screen.]

LADY FIDGET: Well, Horner, am not I a woman of honor? You see I'm as good as my word.

HORNER: And you shall see, madam, I'll not be behindhand with you in honor and I'll be as good as my word too, if you please but to withdraw into the next room.

LADY FIDGET: But first, my dear sir, you must promise to have a care of my dear honor.

HORNER: If you talk a word more of your honor, you'll make me incapable to wrong it. To talk of honor in the mysteries of love is like talking of heaven or the deity in an operation of witchcraft, just when you are employing the devil; it makes the charm impotent.

LADY FIDGET: Nay, fie, let us not be smooty.[7] But you talk of mysteries and bewitching to me; I don't understand you.

HORNER: I tell you, madam, the word "money" in a mistress's mouth, at such a nick of time, is not a more disheartening sound to a younger brother[8] than that of "honor" to an eager lover like myself.

LADY FIDGET: But you can't blame a lady of my reputation to be chary.

HORNER: Chary! I have been chary of it already, by the report I have caused of myself.

LADY FIDGET: Ay, but if you should ever let other women know that dear secret, it would come out. Nay, you must have a great care of your conduct, for my acquaintance are so censorious (oh, 'tis a wicked, censorious world, Mr. Horner!), I say, are so censorious and detracting that perhaps they'll talk, to the prejudice of my honor, though you should not let them know the dear secret.

HORNER: Nay, madam, rather than they shall prejudice your honor, I'll prejudice theirs, and, to serve you, I'll lie with 'em all, make the secret their own, and then they'll keep it. I am a Machiavel in love, madam.

LADY FIDGET: Oh, no, sir, not that way.

HORNER: Nay, the devil take me if censorious women are to be silenced any other way.

LADY FIDGET: A secret is better kept, I hope, by a single person than a multitude; therefore pray do not trust anybody else with it, dear, dear Mr. Horner. [Embracing him.]
    [Enter Sir Jaspar Fidget.]

SIR JASPAR: How now!

LADY FIDGET [aside]: Oh, my husband—prevented—and what's almost as bad, found with my arms about another man—that will appear too much—what shall I say?—Sir Jaspar, come hither, I am trying if Mr. Horner were ticklish, and he's as ticklish as can be; I love to torment the confounded toad. Let you and I tickle him.

SIR JASPAR: No, your ladyship will tickle him better without me, I suppose. But is this your buying china? I thought you had been at the china house.[9]

HORNER [aside]: China house! That's my cue, I must take it.—A pox, can't you keep your impertinent wives at home? Some men are troubled with the husbands, but I with the wives. But I'd have you to know, since I cannot be your journeyman[1] by night, I will not be your drudge by day, to squire your wife about and be your man of straw, or scarecrow, only to pies and jays,[2] that would be nibbling at your forbidden fruit; I shall be shortly the hackney gentleman-usher[3] of the town.

SIR JASPAR [aside]: Heh, heh, he! Poor fellow, he's in the right on't, faith; to squire women about for other folks is as ungrateful an employment as to tell[4] money for other folks.—Heh, he, he! Ben't angry, Horner—

LADY FIDGET: No, 'tis I have more reason to be angry, who am left by you to go abroad indecently alone; or, what is more indecent, to pin myself upon such ill-bred people of your acquaintance as this is.

SIR JASPAR: Nay, prithee, what has he done?

LADY FIDGET: Nay, he has done nothing.

SIR JASPAR: But what d'ye take ill, if he has done nothing?

LADY FIDGET: Hah, hah, hah! Faith, I can't but laugh, however; why d'ye think the unmannerly toad would not come down to me to the coach? I was fain to come up to fetch him, or go without him, which I was resolved not to do, for he knows china very well and has himself very good, but will not let me see it lest I should beg some. But I will find it out and have what I came for yet.

9. China shop, sometimes used by lovers as a secret meeting place.
1. One who works for another.
2. Crafty fellows and fools.
3. Hired escort.
4. Count.

[*Exit Lady Fidget and locks the door, followed by Horner to the door.*]

HORNER [*apart to Lady Fidget*]: Lock the door, madam.—So, she has got into my chamber, and locked me out. Oh, the impertinency of womankind! Well, Sir Jaspar, plain-dealing is a jewel; if ever you suffer your wife to trouble me again here, she shall carry you home a pair of horns, by my Lord Mayor she shall; though I cannot furnish you myself, you are sure, yet I'll find a way.

SIR JASPAR [*aside*]: Hah, ha, he! At my first coming in and finding her arms about him, tickling him it seems, I was half jealous, but now I see my folly.— Heh, he, he! Poor Horner.

HORNER: Nay, though you laugh now, 'twill be my turn ere long. Oh, women, more impertinent, more cunning and more mischievous than their monkeys,[5] and to me almost as ugly! Now is she throwing my things about and rifling all I have, but I'll get into her the back way and so rifle her for it.

SIR JASPAR: Hah, ha, ha, poor angry Horner.

HORNER: Stay here a little; I'll ferret her out to you presently, I warrant.

[*Exit Horner at t'other door.*]

SIR JASPAR: Wife! My Lady Fidget! Wife! He is coming into you the back way.

[*Sir Jaspar calls through the door to his wife; she answers from within.*]

LADY FIDGET: Let him come, and welcome, which way he will.

SIR JASPAR: He'll catch you and use you roughly and be too strong for you.

LADY FIDGET: Don't you trouble yourself; let him if he can.

QUACK [*behind*]: This indeed I could not have believed from him, nor any but my own eyes.

[*Enter Mrs. Squeamish.*]

SQUEAMISH: Where's this woman-hater, this toad, this ugly, greasy, dirty sloven?

SIR JASPAR [*aside*]: So, the women all will have him ugly; methinks he is a comely person, but his wants make his form contemptible to 'em and 'tis e'en as my wife said yesterday, talking of him, that a proper handsome eunuch was as ridiculous a thing as a gigantic coward.

SQUEAMISH: Sir Jaspar, your servant. Where is the odious beast?

SIR JASPAR: He's within in his chamber, with my wife; she's playing the wag with him.

SQUEAMISH: Is she so? And he's a clownish beast, he'll give her no quarter;[6] he'll play the wag with her again, let me tell you. Come, let's go help her.—What, the door's locked?

SIR JASPAR: Ay, my wife locked it.

SQUEAMISH: Did she so? Let us break it open then.

SIR JASPAR: No, no, he'll do her no hurt.

SQUEAMISH: No. [*Aside.*] But is there no other way to get in to 'em? Whither goes this? I will disturb 'em. [*Exit Squeamish at another door.*]

OLD LADY SQUEAMISH: Where is this harlotry, this impudent baggage, this rambling tomrig?[7] O Sir Jaspar, I'm glad to see you here. Did you not see my vild[8] grandchild come in hither just now?

SIR JASPAR: Yes.

---

5. Which ladies sometimes kept as pets.
6. No mercy.

7. Strumpet.
8. Vile.

OLD LADY SQUEAMISH: Ay, but where is she then? Where is she? Lord, Sir Jaspar, I have e'en rattled myself to pieces in pursuit of her. But can you tell what she makes here? They say below, no woman lodges here.

SIR JASPAR: No.

OLD LADY SQUEAMISH: No! What does she here then? Say, if it be not a woman's lodging, what makes she here? But are you sure no woman lodges here?

SIR JASPAR: No, nor no man neither; this is Mr. Horner's lodging.

OLD LADY SQUEAMISH: Is it so, are you sure?

SIR JASPAR: Yes, yes.

OLD LADY SQUEAMISH: So then there's no hurt in't, I hope. But where is he?

SIR JASPAR: He's in the next room with my wife.

OLD LADY SQUEAMISH: Nay, if you trust him with your wife, I may with my Biddy.[9] They say he's a merry harmless man now, e'en as harmless a man as ever came out of Italy with a good voice,[1] and as pretty harmless company for a lady as a snake without his teeth.

SIR JASPAR: Ay, ay, poor man.

[Enter Mrs. Squeamish.]

SQUEAMISH: I can't find 'em.—Oh, are you here, Grandmother? I followed, you must know, my Lady Fidget hither; 'tis the prettiest lodging and I have been staring on the prettiest pictures.

[Enter Lady Fidget with a piece of china in her hand, and Horner following.]

LADY FIDGET: And I have been toiling and moiling[2] for the prettiest piece of china, my dear.

HORNER: Nay, she has been too hard for me, do what I could.

SQUEAMISH: O Lord, I'll have some china too. Good Mr. Horner, don't think to give other people china and me none; come in with me too.

HORNER: Upon my honor, I have none left now.

SQUEAMISH: Nay, nay, I have known you deny your china before now, but you shan't put me off so. Come—

HORNER: This lady had the last there.

LADY FIDGET: Yes, indeed, madam, to my certain knowledge he has no more left.

SQUEAMISH: O, but it may be he may have some you could not find.

LADY FIDGET: What, d'ye think if he had had any left, I would not have had it too? For we women of quality never think we have china enough.

HORNER: Do not take it ill. I cannot make china for you all, but I will have a roll-wagon[3] for you too, another time.

SQUEAMISH: Thank you, dear toad.

LADY FIDGET [to Horner aside]: What do you mean by that promise?

HORNER [apart to Lady Fidget]: Alas, she has an innocent, literal understanding.

OLD LADY SQUEAMISH: Poor Mr. Horner, he has enough to do to please you all, I see.

HORNER: Ay, madam, you see how they use me.

OLD LADY SQUEAMISH: Poor gentleman, I pity you.

---

9. Abbreviation of Bridget; also, a general term for a young woman.
1. I.e., as a castrato, a male singer castrated in boyhood so as to preserve his soprano voice.

2. Working hard.
3. A cylindrical vase; here (of course) with phallic connotations.

HORNER: I thank you, madam. I could never find pity but from such reverend ladies as you are; the young ones will never spare a man.

SQUEAMISH: Come, come, beast, and go dine with us, for we shall want a man at ombre after dinner.

HORNER: That's all their use of me, madam, you see.

SQUEAMISH: Come, sloven, I'll lead you, to be sure of you: [*Pulls him by the cravat.*]

OLD LADY SQUEAMISH: Alas, poor man, how she tugs him! Kiss, kiss her; that's the way to make such nice[4] women quiet.

HORNER: No, madam, that remedy is worse than the torment; they know I dare suffer anything rather than do it.

OLD LADY SQUEAMISH: Prithee, kiss her and I'll give you her picture in little,[5] that you admired so last night; prithee do.

HORNER: Well, nothing but that could bribe me; I love a woman only in effigy and good painting, as much as I hate them. I'll do't, for I could adore the devil well painted. [*Kisses Mrs. Squeamish.*]

SQUEAMISH: Foh, you filthy toad! Nay, now I've done jesting.

OLD LADY SQUEAMISH: Ha, ha, ha, I told you so.

SQUEAMISH: Foh, a kiss of his—

SIR JASPAR: Has no more hurt in't than one of my spaniel's.

SQUEAMISH: Nor no more good neither.

QUACK [*behind*]: I will now believe anything he tells me.
    [*Enter Mr. Pinchwife.*]

LADY FIDGET: O Lord, here's a man! Sir Jaspar, my mask, my mask! I would not be seen here for the world.

SIR JASPAR: What, not when I am with you?

LADY FIDGET: No, no, my honor—let's be gone.

SQUEAMISH: Oh, Grandmother, let us be gone; make haste, make haste, I know not how he may censure us.

LADY FIDGET: Be found in the lodging of anything like a man! Away!
        [*Exeunt Sir Jaspar, Lady Fidget, Old Lady Squeamish, Mrs. Squeamish.*]

QUACK [*behind*]: What's here? Another cuckold? He looks like one, and none else sure have any business with him.

HORNER: Well, what brings my dear friend hither?

PINCHWIFE: Your impertinency.

HORNER: My impertinency!—Why, you gentlemen that have got handsome wives think you have a privilege of saying anything to your friends and are as brutish as if you were our creditors.

PINCHWIFE: No, sir, I'll ne'er trust you any way.

HORNER: But why not, dear Jack? Why diffide[6] in me thou knowest so well?

PINCHWIFE: Because I do know you so well.

HORNER: Han't I been always thy friend, honest Jack, always ready to serve thee, in love or battle, before thou wert married, and am so still?

PINCHWIFE: I believe so; you would be my second now indeed.

HORNER: Well then, dear Jack, why so unkind, so grum, so strange to me? Come, prithee kiss me, dear rogue. Gad, I was always, I say, and am still as much thy servant as—

4. Fastidious; also, in an older sense, wanton.   6. Distrust.
5. Miniature.

PINCHWIFE: As I am yours, sir. What, you would send a kiss to my wife, is that it?

HORNER: So, there 'tis—a man can't show his friendship to a married man but presently he talks of his wife to you. Prithee, let thy wife alone and let thee and I be all one, as we were wont. What, thou art as shy of my kindness as a Lombard Street[7] alderman of a courtier's civility at Locket's.[8]

PINCHWIFE: But you are overkind to me, as kind as if I were your cuckold already; yet I must confess you ought to be kind and civil to me, since I am so kind, so civil to you, as to bring you this. Look you there, sir. [*Delivers him a letter.*]

HORNER: What is't?

PINCHWIFE: Only a love-letter, sir.

HORNER: From whom?—how! this is from your wife—hum—and hum—[*Reads.*]

PINCHWIFE: Even from my wife, sir. Am I not wondrous kind and civil to you now too? [*Aside.*] But you'll not think her so.

HORNER [*aside*]:   Ha, is this a trick of his or hers?

PINCHWIFE: The gentleman's surprised, I find. What, you expected a kinder letter?

HORNER: No, faith, not I, how could I?

PINCHWIFE: Yes, yes, I'm sure you did; a man so well made as you are must needs be disappointed if the women declare not their passion at first sight or opportunity.

HORNER [*aside*]:   But what should this mean? Stay, the postscript. [*Reads aside.*] "Be sure you love me, whatsoever my husband says to the contrary, and let him not see this, lest he should come home and pinch me, or kill my squirrel.[9]" [*Aside.*] It seems he knows not what the letter contains.

PINCHWIFE: Come, ne'er wonder at it so much.

HORNER: Faith, I can't help it.

PINCHWIFE: Now, I think, I have deserved your infinite friendship and kindness and have showed myself sufficiently an obliging kind friend and husband; am I not so, to bring a letter from my wife to her gallant?

HORNER: Ay, the devil take me, art thou the most obliging, kind friend and husband in the world, ha, ha!

PINCHWIFE: Well, you may be merry, sir; but in short I must tell you, sir, my honor will suffer no jesting.

HORNER: What dost thou mean?

PINCHWIFE: Does the letter want a comment? Then know, sir, though I have been so civil a husband as to bring you a letter from my wife, to let you kiss and court her to my face, I will not be a cuckold, sir, I will not.

HORNER: Thou art mad with jealousy. I never saw thy wife in my life but at the play yesterday, and I know not if it were she or no. I court her, kiss her!

PINCHWIFE: I will not be a cuckold, I say; there will be danger in making me a cuckold.

HORNER: Why, wert thou not well cured of thy last clap?

PINCHWIFE: I wear a sword.

HORNER: It should be taken from thee lest thou shouldst do thyself a mischief with it; thou art mad, man.

---

7. Banking center of London.
8. In Charing Cross, a celebrated restaurant and popular

post-theater meeting place.
9. A fashionable pet.

PINCHWIFE: As mad as I am, and as merry as you are, I must have more reason from you ere we part. I say again, though you kissed and courted last night my wife in man's clothes, as she confesses in her letter—

HORNER [*aside*]:   Ha!

PINCHWIFE: Both she and I say, you must not design it again, for you have mistaken your woman, as you have done your man.

HORNER [*aside*]:   Oh—I understand something now.—Was that thy wife? Why wouldst thou not tell me 'twas she? Faith, my freedom with her was your fault, not mine.

PINCHWIFE [*aside*]:   Faith, so 'twas.

HORNER: Fie, I'd never do't to a woman before her husband's face, sure.

PINCHWIFE: But I had rather you should do't to my wife before my face than behind my back, and that you shall never do.

HORNER: No—you will hinder me.

PINCHWIFE: If I would not hinder you, you see by her letter, she would.

HORNER: Well, I must e'en acquiesce then and be contented with what she writes.

PINCHWIFE: I'll assure you 'twas voluntarily writ; I had no hand in't, you may believe me.

HORNER: I do believe thee, faith.

PINCHWIFE: And believe her too, for she's an innocent creature, has no dissembling in her; and so fare you well, sir.

HORNER: Pray, however, present my humble service to her and tell her I will obey her letter to a tittle and fulfill her desires, be what they will, or with what difficulty soever I do't, and you shall be no more jealous of me, I warrant her and you.

PINCHWIFE: Well, then, fare you well, and play with any man's honor but mine, kiss any man's wife but mine, and welcome. [*Exit Mr. Pinchwife.*]

HORNER: Ha, ha, ha, doctor.

QUACK: It seems he has not heard the report of you, or does not believe it.

HORNER: Ha, ha! Now, doctor, what think you?

QUACK: Pray let's see the letter—hum— [*Reads the letter.*] "for—dear—love you—"

HORNER: I wonder how she could contrive it! What say'st thou to't? 'Tis an original.

QUACK: So are your cuckolds, too, originals, for they are like no other common cuckolds, and I will henceforth believe it not impossible for you to cuckold the Grand Signior[1] amidst his guards of eunuchs, that I say.

HORNER: And I say for the letter, 'tis the first love-letter that ever was without flames, darts, fates, destinies, lying and dissembling in't.

[*Enter Sparkish, pulling in Mr. Pinchwife.*]

SPARKISH: Come back, you are a pretty brother-in-law, neither go to church, nor to dinner with your sister bride!

PINCHWIFE: My sister denies her marriage and you see is gone away from you dissatisfied.

---

1. Sultan of Turkey, whose eunuchs guarded his harem.

SPARKISH: Pshaw, upon a foolish scruple, that our parson was not in lawful or-ders and did not say all the Common Prayer; but 'tis her modesty only, I believe. But let women be never so modest the first day, they'll be sure to come to them-selves by night, and I shall have enough of her then. In the meantime, Harry Horner, you must dine with me; I keep my wedding at my aunt's in the Piazza.²

HORNER: Thy wedding! What stale maid has lived to despair of a husband, or what young one of a gallant?

SPARKISH: Oh, your servant, sir—this gentleman's sister then—no stale maid.

HORNER: I'm sorry for't.

PINCHWIFE [aside]:   How comes he so concerned for her?

SPARKISH: You sorry for't? Why, do you know any ill by her?

HORNER: No, I know none but by thee; 'tis for her sake, not yours, and another man's sake that might have hoped, I thought.

SPARKISH: Another man, another man! What is his name?

HORNER: Nay, since 'tis past he shall be nameless. [Aside.] Poor Harcourt, I am sorry thou hast missed her.

PINCHWIFE [aside]:   He seems to be much troubled at the match.

SPARKISH: Prithee tell me—nay, you shan't go, brother.

PINCHWIFE: I must of necessity, but I'll come to you to dinner.   [Exit Pinchwife.]

SPARKISH: But, Harry, what, have I a rival in my wife already? But with all my heart, for he may be of use to me hereafter, for though my hunger is now my sauce and I can fall on heartily without, but the time will come when a rival will be as good sauce for a married man to a wife as an orange to veal.

HORNER: O thou damned rogue! Thou hast set my teeth on edge with thy orange.

SPARKISH: Then let's to dinner—there I was with³ you again. Come.

HORNER: But who dines with thee?

SPARKISH: My friends and relations, my brother Pinchwife, you see, of your acquaintance.

HORNER: And his wife?

SPARKISH: No, gad, he'll ne'er let her come amongst us good fellows. Your stingy country coxcomb keeps his wife from friends, as he does his little firkin⁴ of ale for his own drinking, and a gentleman can't get a smack⁵ on't; but his servants, when his back is turned, broach⁶ it at their pleasures and dust it away,⁷ ha, ha, ha! Gad, I am witty, I think, considering I was married today, by the world. But come—

HORNER: No, I will not dine with you, unless you can fetch her too.

SPARKISH: Pshaw, what pleasure canst thou have with women now, Harry?

HORNER: My eyes are not gone; I love a good prospect yet and will not dine with you unless she does too. Go fetch her, therefore, but do not tell her husband 'tis for my sake.

SPARKISH: Well, I'll try what I can do. In the mean-time come away to my aunt's lodging; 'tis in the way to Pinchwife's.

HORNER: The poor woman has called for aid and stretched forth her hand, doc-tor; I cannot but help her over the pale⁸ out of the briars.

[Exeunt Sparkish, Horner, Quack.]

2. An elegant arcade near Covent Garden; Act 5, Scene 3 is set there.
3. Caught.
4. Small cask.
5. Taste.
6. Tap.
7. Finish it off.
8. Fence; here, figuratively, the constraints of marital fidelity.

Scene 4

[The scene changes to Pinchwife's house. Mrs. Pinchwife alone, leaning on her elbow. A table, pen, ink and paper.]

MRS. PINCHWIFE: Well, 'tis e'en so, I have got the London disease they call love; I am sick of my husband and for my gallant. I have heard this distemper[9] called a fever, but methinks 'tis liker an ague, for when I think of my husband, I tremble and am in a cold sweat and have inclinations to vomit but when I think of my gallant, dear Mr. Horner, my hot fit comes and I am all in a fever, indeed, and as in other fevers my own chamber is tedious to me and I would fain be removed to his and then methinks I should be well. Ah, poor Mr. Horner! Well, I cannot, will not stay here; therefore I'd make an end of my letter to him, which shall be a finer letter than my last, because I have studied it like anything. O, sick, sick!

[Takes the pen and writes.]

[Enter Mr. Pinchwife, who, seeing her writing, steals softly behind her and, looking over her shoulder, snatches the paper from her.]

PINCHWIFE: What, writing more letters?

MRS. PINCHWIFE: O Lord, bud, why d'ye fright me so?

[She offers to run out; he stops her and reads.]

PINCHWIFE: How's this! Nay, you shall not stir, madam. "Dear, dear, dear Mr. Horner"—very well—I have taught you to write letters to good purpose—but let's see't. "First, I am to beg your pardon for my boldness in writing to you, which I'd have you to know I would not have done had not you said first you loved me so extremely, which if you do, you will never suffer me to lie in the arms of another man, whom I loathe, nauseate and detest."—Now you can write these filthy words. But what follows?—"Therefore I hope you will speedily find some way to free me from this unfortunate match, which was never, I assure you, of my choice, but I'm afraid 'tis already too far gone. However, if you love me, as I do you, you will try what you can do, but you must help me away before tomorrow, or else, alas, I shall be forever out of your reach, for I can defer no longer our—our" *[The letter concludes.]*—What is to follow "our"?—Speak, what? Our journey into the country, I suppose—Oh, woman, damned woman and love, damned love, their old tempter! For this is one of his miracles; in a moment he can make all those blind that could see and those see that were blind, those dumb that could speak and those prattle who were dumb before; nay, what is more than all, make these dough-baked,[1] senseless, indocile animals, women, too hard for us, their politic[2] lords and rulers, in a moment. But make an end of your letter and then I'll make an end of you thus, and all my plagues together.

[Draws his sword.]

MRS. PINCHWIFE: O Lord, O Lord, you are such a passionate man, bud!

[Enter Sparkish.]

SPARKISH: How now, what's here to do?

PINCHWIFE: This fool here now!

SPARKISH: What, drawn upon your wife? You should never do that but at night in the dark, when you can't hurt her. This is my sister-in-law, is it not?

[Pulls aside her handkerchief.]

---

9. Disease.
1. Half-baked, feeble-minded.

2. Sagacious, judicious.

Ay, faith, e'en our country Margery; one may know her. Come, she and you must go
   dine with me; dinner's ready, come. But where's my wife? Is she not come home
   yet? Where is she?
PINCHWIFE: Making you a cuckold; 'tis that they all do, as soon as they can.
SPARKISH: What, the wedding day? No, a wife that designs to make a cully[3] of
   her husband will be sure to let him win the first stake of love, by the world. But
   come, they stay dinner for us. Come, I'll lead down our Margery.
PINCHWIFE: No—sir, go, we'll follow you.
SPARKISH: I will not wag[4] without you.
PINCHWIFE [aside]:   This coxcomb is a sensible[5] torment to me amidst the great-
   est in the world.
SPARKISH: Come, come, Madam Margery.
PINCHWIFE: No, I'll lead her my way. What, would you treat your friends with
   mine, for want of your own wife? [Leads her to t'other door and locks her in and
   returns. Aside.] I am contented my rage should take breath.
SPARKISH [aside]:   I told Horner this.
PINCHWIFE: Come now.
SPARKISH: Lord, how shy[6] you are of your wife! But let me tell you, brother, we
   men of wit have amongst us a saying that cuckolding, like the smallpox, comes
   with a fear, and you may keep your wife as much as you will out of danger of infection but if her constitution incline her to't, she'll have it sooner or later, by
   the world, say they.
PINCHWIFE [aside]:   What a thing is a cuckold, that every fool can make him
   ridiculous!—Well, sir—but let me advise you, now you are come to be concerned,
   because you suspect the danger, not to neglect the means to prevent it, especially
   when the greatest share of the malady will light upon your own head, for—

   Hows'e'er the kind wife's belly comes to swell,
   The husband breeds for her[7] and first is ill.

                                          [Exeunt Pinchwife and Sparkish.]

ACT 5

Scene 1

   [Mr. Pinchwife's house. Enter Mr. Pinchwife and Mrs. Pinchwife. A table and
   candle.]
PINCHWIFE: Come, take the pen and make an end of the letter, just as you in-
   tended; if you are false in a tittle, I shall soon perceive it and punish you with this
   as you deserve. [Lays his hand on his sword.] Write what was to follow—let's see—
   "You must make haste and help me away before tomorrow, or else I shall be for-
   ever out of your reach, for I can defer no longer our—" What follows "our"?
MRS. PINCHWIFE: Must all out then, bud?
   [Mrs. Pinchwife takes the pen and writes.] Look you there then.
PINCHWIFE: Let's see—"For I can defer no longer our—wedding—Your slighted
   Alithea."—What's the meaning of this? My sister's name to't. Speak, unriddle!

3. Dupe, gull.
4. Stir.
5. Keenly felt.
6. Distrustful.
7. Grows cuckhold's horns in consequence of her behavior.

MRS. PINCHWIFE: Yes, indeed, bud.

PINCHWIFE: But why her name to't? Speak—speak, I say!

MRS. PINCHWIFE: Ay, but you'll tell her then again; if you would not tell her again—

PINCHWIFE: I will not—I am stunned, my head turns round. Speak.

MRS. PINCHWIFE: Won't you tell her, indeed, and indeed?

PINCHWIFE: No, speak, I say.

MRS. PINCHWIFE: She'll be angry with me, but I had rather she should be angry with me than you, bud; and to tell you the truth, 'twas she made me write the letter and taught me what I should write.

PINCHWIFE [aside]: Ha! I thought the style was somewhat better than her own.—But how could she come to you to teach you, since I had locked you up alone?

MRS. PINCHWIFE: O, through the keyhole, bud.

PINCHWIFE: But why should she make you write a letter for her to him, since she can write herself?

MRS. PINCHWIFE: Why, she said because—for I was unwilling to do it.

PINCHWIFE: Because what—because?

MRS. PINCHWIFE: Because, lest Mr. Horner should be cruel and refuse her or vain afterwards and show the letter, she might disown it, the hand not being hers.

PINCHWIFE [aside]: How's this? Ha!—then I think I shall come to myself again. This changeling could not invent this lie; but if she could, why should she? She might think I should soon discover it—stay—now I think on't too, Horner said he was sorry she had married Sparkish, and her disowning her marriage to me makes me think she has evaded it for Horner's sake. Yet why should she take this course? But men in love are fools; women may well be so.—But hark you, madam, your sister went out in the morning and I have not seen her within since.

MRS. PINCHWIFE: Alackaday, she has been crying all day above, it seems, in a corner.

PINCHWIFE: Where is she? Let me speak with her.

MRS. PINCHWIFE [aside]: O Lord, then he'll discover all!—Pray hold, bud. What, d'ye mean to discover me? She'll know I have told you then. Pray, bud, let me talk with her first.

PINCHWIFE: I must speak with her, to know whether Horner ever made her any promise and whether she be married to Sparkish or no.

MRS. PINCHWIFE: Pray, dear bud, don't, till I have spoken with her and told her that I have told you all, for she'll kill me else.

PINCHWIFE: Go then, and bid her come out to me.

MRS. PINCHWIFE: Yes, yes, bud.

PINCHWIFE: Let me see—

MRS. PINCHWIFE [aside]: I'll go, but she is not within to come to him. I have just got time to know of Lucy her maid, who first set me on work, what lie I shall tell next, for I am e'en at my wit's end. [Exit Mrs. Pinchwife.]

PINCHWIFE: Well, I resolve it; Horner shall have her. I'd rather give him my sister than lend him my wife and such an alliance will prevent his pretensions to my wife, sure. I'll make him of kin to her and then he won't care for her.
    [Mrs. Pinchwife returns.]

MRS. PINCHWIFE: O Lord, bud, I told you what anger you would make me with my sister.

PINCHWIFE: Won't she come hither?

MRS. PINCHWIFE: No, no, alackaday, she's ashamed to look you in the face, and she says, if you go in to her, she'll run away downstairs and shamefully go herself to Mr. Horner, who has promised her marriage, she says, and she will have no other, so she won't—

PINCHWIFE: Did he so—promise her marriage—then she shall have no other. Go tell her so, and if she will come and discourse with me a little concerning the means, I will about it immediately. Go.   [Exit Mrs. Pinchwife.]

His estate is equal to Sparkish's, and his extraction as much better than his as his parts are; but my chief reason is, I'd rather be of kin to him by the name of brother-in-law than that of cuckold.

  [Enter Mrs. Pinchwife.]

Well, what says she now?

MRS. PINCHWIFE: Why, she says she would only have you lead her to Horner's lodging—with whom she first will discourse the matter before she talk with you, which yet she cannot do, for alack, poor creature, she says she can't so much as look you in the face, therefore she'll come to you in a mask, and you must excuse her if she make you no answer to any question of yours, till you have brought her to Mr. Horner, and if you will not chide her, nor question her, she'll come out to you immediately.

PINCHWIFE: Let her come. I will not speak a word to her, nor require a word from her.

MRS. PINCHWIFE: Oh, I forgot; besides, she says, she cannot look you in the face though through a mask, therefore would desire you to put out the candle.

PINCHWIFE: I agree to all; let her make haste—there, 'tis out. [Puts out the candle.]
                                                                        [Exit Mrs. Pinchwife.]

My case is something better. I'd rather fight with Horner for not lying with my sister than for lying with my wife, and of the two I had rather find my sister too forward than my wife; I expected no other from her free education, as she calls it, and her passion for the town. Well—wife and sister are names which make us expect love and duty, pleasure and comfort, but we find 'em plagues and torments, and are equally, though differently, troublesome to their keeper, for we have as much ado to get people to lie with our sisters as to keep 'em frm lying with our wives.

  [Enter Mrs. Pinchwife masked and in hoods and scarves, and a nightgown[1] and petticoat of Alithea's, in the dark.]

What, are you come, sister? Let us go then—but first let me lock up my wife.— Mrs. Margery, where are you?

MRS. PINCHWIFE: Here, bud.

PINCHWIFE: Come hither, that I may lock you up; get you in. [Locks the door.] Come, sister, where are you now?

  [Mrs. Pinchwife gives him her hand but, when he lets her go, she steals softly on t'other side of him, and is led away by him for his sister Alithea.]

Scene 2

[The scene changes to Horner's lodging. Quack, Horner.]

QUACK: What, all alone? Not so much as one of your cuckolds here, nor one of their wives! They use to take their turns with you, as if they were to watch you.

1. A loose gown, usually (but not exclusively) worn at night.

HORNER: Yes, it often happens that a cuckold is but his wife's spy and is more upon family duty when he is with her gallant abroad, hindering his pleasure, than when he is at home with her, playing the gallant. But the hardest duty a married woman imposes upon a lover is keeping her husband company always.

QUACK: And his fondness wearies you almost as soon as hers.

HORNER: A pox, keeping a cuckold company, after you have had his wife, is as tiresome as the company of a country squire to a witty fellow of the town, when he has got all his money.

QUACK: And as at first a man makes a friend of the husband to get the wife, so at last you are fain to fall out with the wife to be rid of the husband.

HORNER: Ay, most cuckold-makers are true courtiers; when once a poor man has cracked[2] his credit for 'em, they can't abide to come near him.

QUACK: But at first, to draw him in, are so sweet, so kind, so dear, just as you are to Pinchwife. But what becomes of that intrigue with his wife?

HORNER: A pox, he's as surly as an alderman that has been bit[3] and, since he's so coy, his wife's kindness is in vain, for she's a silly innocent.

QUACK: Did she not send you a letter by him?

HORNER: Yes, but that's a riddle I have not yet solved. Allow the poor creature to be willing, she is silly too, and he keeps her up so close—

QUACK: Yes, so close that he makes her but the more willing and adds but revenge to her love, which two, when met, seldom fail of satisfying each other one way or other.

HORNER: What, here's the man we are talking of, I think.

    [Enter Mr. Pinchwife, leading in his wife masked, muffled, and in her sister's gown.]
    Pshaw!

QUACK: Bringing his wife to you is the next thing to bringing a love-letter from her.

HORNER: What means this?

PINCHWIFE: The last time, you know, sir, I brought you a love-letter; now, you see, a mistress. I think you'll say I am a civil man to you.

HORNER: Ay, the devil take me, will I say thou art the civilest man I ever met with, and I have known some! I fancy I understand thee now better than I did the letter. But hark thee, in thy ear—

PINCHWIFE: What?

HORNER: Nothing but the usual question, man: is she sound,[4] on thy word?

PINCHWIFE: What, you take her for a wench and me for a pimp?

HORNER: Pshaw, wench and pimp, paw[5] words. I know thou art an honest fellow and hast a great acquaintance among the ladies and perhaps hast made love for me rather than let me make love to thy wife—

PINCHWIFE: Come, sir, in short, I am for no fooling.

HORNER: Nor I neither; therefore, prithee, let's see her face presently. Make her show, man. Art thou sure I don't know her?

PINCHWIFE: I am sure you do know her.

HORNER: A pox, why dost thou bring her to me then?

PINCHWIFE: Because she's a relation of mine.

---

2. Ruined.
3. A city official who's been tricked.

4. Free from venereal disease.
5. Naughty.

HORNER: Is she, faith, man? Then thou art still more civil and obliging, dear rogue.

PINCHWIFE: Who desired me to bring her to you.

HORNER: Then she is obliging, dear rogue.

PINCHWIFE: You'll make her welcome for my sake, I hope.

HORNER: I hope she is handsome enough to make herself welcome. Prithee, let her unmask.

PINCHWIFE: Do you speak to her; she would never be ruled by me.

HORNER: Madam—

[*Mrs. Pinchwife whispers to Horner.*]

She says she must speak with me in private. Withdraw, prithee.

PINCHWIFE [*aside*]: She's unwilling, it seems, I should know all her undecent conduct in this business.—Well then, I'll leave you together and hope when I am gone you'll agree; if not, you and I shan't agree, sir.

HORNER [*aside*]: What means the fool?—If she and I agree, 'tis no matter what you and I do.

[*Whispers to Mrs. Pinchwife, who makes signs with her hand for him (Pinchwife) to be gone.*]

PINCHWIFE: In the meantime, I'll fetch a parson and find out Sparkish and disabuse him. You would have me fetch a parson, would you not? Well then—now I think I am rid of her, and shall have no more trouble with her. Our sisters and daughters, like usurers' money, are safest when put out; but our wives, like their writings,[6] never safe but in our closets under lock and key.   [*Exit Mr. Pinchwife.*]

[*Enter Boy.*]

BOY: Sir Jaspar Fidget, sir, is coming up.   [*Exit.*]

HORNER: Here's the trouble of a cuckold, now, we are talking of. A pox on him! Has he not enough to do to hinder his wife's sport but he must other women's too?—Step in here, madam.   [*Exit Mrs. Pinchwife.*]

[*Enter Sir Jaspar.*]

SIR JASPAR: My best and dearest friend.

HORNER [*aside to Quack*]: The old style, doctor.—Well, be short, for I am busy. What would your impertinent wife have now?

SIR JASPAR: Well guessed, i'faith, for I do come from her.

HORNER: To invite me to supper. Tell her I can't come; go.

SIR JASPAR: Nay, now you are out, faith, for my lady and the whole knot of the virtuous gang, as they call themselves, are resolved upon a frolic of coming to you tonight in a masquerade and are all dressed already.

HORNER: I shan't be at home.

SIR JASPAR [*aside*]: Lord, how churlish he is to women!—Nay, prithee don't disappoint 'em; they'll think 'tis my fault. Prithee don't. I'll send in the banquet and the fiddles. But make no noise on't, for the poor virtuous rogues would not have it known for the world that they go a-masquerading, and they would come to no man's ball but yours.

HORNER: Well, well—get you gone and tell 'em, if they come, 'twill be at the peril of their honor and yours.

6. Legal and financial documents.

SIR JASPAR: Heh, he, he!—we'll trust you for that; farewell. [*Exit Sir Jaspar.*]

HORNER: Doctor, anon you too shall be my guest, But now I'm going to a private feast.

[*Exeunt.*]

Scene 3

[*The scene changes to the Piazza of Covent Garden. Sparkish, Pinchwife.*]

SPARKISH [*with the letter in his hand*]: But who would have thought a woman could have been false to me? By the world, I could not have thought it.

PINCHWIFE: You were for giving and taking liberty; she has taken it only, sir, now you find in that letter. You are a frank person and so is she you see there.

SPARKISH: Nay, if this be her hand—for I never saw it.

PINCHWIFE: 'Tis no matter whether that be her hand or no; I am sure this hand, at her desire, led her to Mr. Horner, with whom I left her just now, to go fetch a parson to 'em, at their desire too, to deprive you of her forever, for it seems yours was but a mock marriage.

SPARKISH: Indeed, she would needs have it that 'twas Harcourt himself in a parson's habit that married us, but I'm sure he told me 'twas his brother Ned.

PINCHWIFE: Oh, there 'tis out, and you were deceived, not she, for you are such a frank person—but I must be gone. You'll find her at Mr. Horner's; go and believe your eyes. [*Exit Mr. Pinchwife.*]

SPARKISH: Nay, I'll to her and call her as many crocodiles, sirens, harpies and other heathenish names as a poet would do a mistress who had refused to hear his suit, nay more, his verses on her.—But stay, is not that she following a torch at t'other end of the Piazza? And from Horner's certainly—'tis so.

[*Enter Alithea, following a torch,*[7] *and Lucy behind.*]

You are well met, madam, though you don't think so. What, you have made a short visit to Mr. Horner, but I suppose you'll return to him presently; by that time the parson can be with him.

ALITHEA: Mr. Horner, and the parson, sir!

SPARKISH: Come, madam, no more dissembling, no more jilting, for I am no more a frank person.

ALITHEA: How's this?

LUCY [*aside*]: So, 'twill work, I see.

SPARKISH: Could you find out no easy country fool to abuse? None but me, a gentleman of wit and pleasure about the town? But it was your pride to be too hard for a man of parts, unworthy false woman, false as a friend that lends a man money to lose, false as dice who undo those that trust all they have to 'em.

LUCY [*aside*]: He has been a great bubble by his similes, as they say.

ALITHEA: You have been too merry, sir, at your wedding dinner, sure.

SPARKISH: What, d'ye mock me too?

ALITHEA: Or you have been deluded.

SPARKISH: By you.

ALITHEA: Let me understand you.

SPARKISH: Have you the confidence—I should call it something else, since you know your guilt—to stand my just reproaches? You did not write an impudent

7. A boy carrying a torch.

letter to Mr. Horner, who I find now has clubbed with you in deluding me with his aversion for women, that I might not, forsooth, suspect him for my rival.

LUCY [*aside*]: D'ye think the gentleman can be jealous now, madam?

ALITHEA: I write a letter to Mr. Horner!

SPARKISH: Nay, madam, do not deny it; your brother showed it me just now and told me likewise he left you at Horner's lodging to fetch a parson to marry you to him, and I wish you joy, madam, joy, joy, and to him too, much joy, and to myself more joy for not marrying you.

ALITHEA [*aside*]: So, I find my brother would break off the match, and I can consent to't, since I see this gentleman can be made jealous.—O Lucy, by his rude usage and jealousy, he makes me almost afraid I am married to him. Art thou sure 'twas Harcourt himself and no parson that married us?

SPARKISH: No, madam, I thank you. I suppose that was a contrivance too of Mr. Horner's and yours, to make Harcourt play the parson; but I would as little as you have him one now, no, not for the world, for shall I tell you another truth? I never had any passion for you till now, for now I hate you. 'Tis true I might have married your portion, as other men of parts of the town do sometimes, and so your servant, and to show my unconcernedness, I'll come to your wedding and resign you with as much joy as I would a stale wench to a new cully, nay, with as much joy as I would after the first night, if I had been married to you. There's for you, and so your servant, servant.   [*Exit Sparkish.*]

ALITHEA: How was I deceived in a man!

LUCY: You'll believe, then, a fool may be made jealous now? For that easiness in him that suffers him to be led by a wife will likewise permit him to be persuaded against her by others.

ALITHEA: But marry Mr. Horner! My brother does not intend it, sure; if I thought he did, I would take thy advice and Mr. Harcourt for my husband. And now I wish that if there be any over-wise woman of the town who, like me, would marry a fool for fortune, liberty or title; first, that her husband may love play and be a cully to all the town but her and suffer none but fortune to be mistress of his purse; then, if for liberty, that he may send her into the country under the conduct of some housewifely mother-in-law, and, if for title, may the world give 'em none but that of cuckold.

LUCY: And for her greater curse, madam, may he not deserve it.

ALITHEA: Away, impertinent!—Is not this my old Lady Lanterlu's?[8]

LUCY: Yes, madam. [*Aside.*] And here I hope we shall find Mr. Harcourt.

[*Exeunt Alithea, Lucy.*]

Scene 4

[*The scene changes again to Horner's lodging. Horner, Lady Fidget, Mrs. Dainty Fidget, Mrs. Squeamish. A table, banquet, and bottles.*]

HORNER [*aside*]: A pox! They are come too soon—before I have sent back my new—mistress. All I have now to do is to lock her in, that they may not see her.

---

8. The lady is comically named after a popular card game, "loo" for short.

LADY FIDGET: That we may be sure of our welcome, we have brought our entertainment with us and are resolved to treat thee, dear toad.

DAINTY: And that we may be merry to purpose, have left Sir Jaspar and my old Lady Squeamish quarrelling at home at backgammon.

SQUEAMISH: Therefore let us make use of our time, lest they should chance to interrupt us.

LADY FIDGET: Let us sit then.

HORNER: First, that you may be private, let me lock this door and that, and I'll wait upon you presently.

LADY FIDGET: No, sir, shut 'em only and your lips forever, for we must trust you as much as our women.

HORNER: You know all vanity's killed in me; I have no occasion for talking.

LADY FIDGET: Now, ladies, supposing we had drank each of us our two bottles, let us speak the truth of our hearts.

DAINTY: . } Agreed.
SQUEAMISH: }

LADY FIDGET: By this brimmer,⁹ for truth is nowhere else to be found. [*Aside to Horner.*] Not in thy heart, false man!

HORNER [*aside to Lady Fidget*]: You have found me a true man, I'm sure.

LADY FIDGET [*aside to Horner*]: Not every way.—But let us sit and be merry. [*Lady Fidget sings.*]

1

> Why should our damned tyrants oblige us to live
> On the pittance of pleasure which they only give?
> We must not rejoice
> With wine and with noise.
> In vain we must wake in a dull bed alone,
> Whilst to our warm rival, the bottle, they're gone.
> They lay aside charms
> And take up these arms.¹

2

> 'Tis wine only gives 'em their courage and wit;
> Because we live sober, to men we submit.
> If for beauties you'd pass,
> Take a lick of the glass;
> 'Twill mend your complexions and, when they are gone,
> The best red we have is the red of the grape.
> Then, sisters, lay't on,
> And damn a good shape.

DAINTY: Dear brimmer! Well, in token of our openness and plain-dealing, let us throw our masks over our heads.

HORNER: So, 'twill come to the glasses anon.

---

9. Brimming cup.   1. I.e., the glasses.

SQUEAMISH: Lovely brimmer! Let me enjoy him first.

LADY FIDGET: No, I never part with a gallant till I've tried him. Dear brimmer, that mak'st our husbands shortsighted.

DAINTY: And our bashful gallants bold.

SQUEAMISH: And for want of a gallant, the butler lovely in our eyes.—Drink, eunuch.

LADY FIDGET: Drink, thou representative of a husband. Damn a husband!

DAINTY: And, as it were a husband, an old keeper.

SQUEAMISH: And an old grandmother.

HORNER: And an English bawd and a French chirurgeon.[2]

LADY FIDGET: Ay, we have all reason to curse 'em.

HORNER: For my sake, ladies?

LADY FIDGET: No, for our own, for the first spoils all young gallants' industry.

DAINTY: And the other's art makes 'em bold only with common women.

SQUEAMISH: And rather run the hazard of the vile distemper amongst them than of a denial amongst us.

DAINTY: The filthy toads choose mistresses now as they do stuffs,[3] for having been fancied and worn by others.[4]

SQUEAMISH: For being common and cheap.

LADY FIDGET: Whilst women of quality, like the richest stuffs, lie untumbled and unasked for.

HORNER: Ay, neat and cheap and new often they think best.

DAINTY: No, sir, the beasts will be known by a mistress longer than by a suit.

SQUEAMISH: And 'tis not for cheapness neither.

LADY FIDGET: No, for the vain fops will take up druggets[5] and embroider 'em. But I wonder at the depraved appetites of witty men; they use to be out of the common road and hate imitation. Pray tell me, beast, when you were a man, why you rather chose to club with a multitude in a common house[6] for an entertainment than to be the only guest at a good table!

HORNER: Why, faith, ceremony and expectation are unsufferable to those that are sharp bent;[7] people always eat with the best stomach at an ordinary, where every man is snatching for the best bit.

LADY FIDGET: Though he get a cut over the fingers.—But I have heard people eat most heartily of another man's meat, that is, what they do not pay for.

HORNER: When they are sure of their welcome and freedom, for ceremony in love and eating is as ridiculous as in fighting; falling on briskly is all should be done in those occasions.

LADY FIDGET: Well, then, let me tell you, sir, there is nowhere more freedom than in our houses and we take freedom from a young person as a sign of good breeding, and a person may be as free as he pleases with us, as frolic, as gamesome, as wild as he will.

HORNER: Han't I heard you all declaim against wild men?

---

2. The supposed causes of Horner's fictitious plight (see Act 1, Scene 1, page 2216).
3. Garments.
4. Second-hand trade was commonplace in Restoration England.
5. Cheap woolen fabric.
6. A restaurant or brothel.
7. Hungry.

LADY FIDGET: Yes, but for all that, we think wildness in a man as desirable a quality as in a duck or rabbit; a tame man, foh!

HORNER: I know not, but your reputations frightened me, as much as your faces invited me.

LADY FIDGET: Our reputation! Lord, why should you not think that we women make use of our reputation, as you men of yours, only to deceive the world with less suspicion? Our virtue is like the statesman's religion, the Quaker's word, the gamester's oath and the great man's honor—but to cheat those that trust us.

SQUEAMISH: And that demureness, coyness and modesty that you see in our faces in the boxes at plays is as much a sign of a kind woman as a vizard-mask in the pit.

DAINTY: For, I assure you, women are least masked when they have the velvet vizard on.

LADY FIDGET: You would have found us modest women in our denials only.

SQUEAMISH: Our bashfulness is only the reflection of the men's.

DAINTY: We blush when they are shamefaced.

HORNER: I beg your pardon, ladies; I was deceived in you devilishly. But why that mighty pretense to honor?

LADY FIDGET: We have told you. But sometimes 'twas for the same reason you men pretend business often, to avoid ill company, to enjoy the better and more privately those you love.

HORNER: But why would you ne'er give a friend a wink then?

LADY FIDGET: Faith, your reputation frightened us as much as ours did you, you were so notoriously lewd.

HORNER: And you so seemingly honest.

LADY FIDGET: Was that all that deterred you?

HORNER: And so expensive—you allow freedom, you say—

LADY FIDGET: Ay, ay.

HORNER: That I was afraid of losing my little money, as well as my little time, both which my other pleasures required.

LADY FIDGET: Money, foh! You talk like a little fellow now; do such as we expect money?

HORNER: I beg your pardon, madam; I must confess, I have heard that great ladies, like great merchants, set but the higher prizes[8] upon what they have, because they are not in necessity of taking the first offer.

DAINTY: Such as we make sale of our hearts?

SQUEAMISH: We bribed for our love? Foh!

HORNER: With your pardon, ladies, I know, like great men in offices, you seem to exact flattery and attendance only from your followers; but you have receivers[9] about you and such fees to pay, a man is afraid to pass your grants.[1] Besides, we must let you win at cards, or we lose your hearts, and if you make an assignation, 'tis at a goldsmith's, jeweller's or china house, where, for your honor you deposit to him, he must pawn his to the punctual cit, and so paying for what you take up, pays for what he takes up.[2]

---

8. Prices.
9. Collectors.
1. Accept your favors (because in the end they are so expensive).

2. I.e., you arrange to meet your lover at an expensive shop, where he in effect pays for your favors by purchasing for you the shopkeeper's ("punctual cit's") costly merchandise.

DAINTY: Would you not have us assured of our gallant's love?

SQUEAMISH: For love is better known by liberality than by jealousy.

LADY FIDGET: For one may be dissembled, the other not. [*Aside*.] But my jealousy can be no longer dissembled, and they are telling ripe.[3]—Come, here's to our gallants in waiting, whom we must name, and I'll begin. This is my false rogue. [*Claps him on the back.*]

SQUEAMISH: How!

HORNER: So all will out now.

SQUEAMISH [*aside to Horner*]: Did you not tell me, 'twas for my sake only you reported yourself no man?

DAINTY [*aside to Horner*]: Oh, wretch! Did you not swear to me, 'twas for my love and honor you passed for that thing you do?

HORNER: So, so.

LADY FIDGET: Come, speak, ladies; this is my false villain.

SQUEAMISH: And mine too.

DAINTY: And mine.

HORNER: Well then, you are all three my false rogues too, and there's an end on't.

LADY FIDGET: Well then, there's no remedy; sister sharers, let us not fall out, but have a care of our honor. Though we get no presents, no jewels of him, we are savers of our honor, the jewel of most value and use, which shines yet to the world unsuspected, though it be counterfeit.

HORNER: Nay, and is e'en as good as if it were true, provided the world think so, for honor, like beauty now, only depends on the opinion of others.

LADY FIDGET: Well, Harry Common, I hope you can be true to three. Swear— but 'tis to no purpose to require your oath, for you are as often forsworn as you swear to new women.

HORNER: Come, faith, madam, let us e'en pardon one another, for all the difference I find betwixt we men and you women, we forswear ourselves at the beginning of an amour, you as long as it lasts.

[*Enter Sir Jaspar Fidget and Old Lady Squeamish.*]

SIR JASPAR: Oh, my Lady Fidget, was this your cunning, to come to Mr. Horner without me? But you have been nowhere else, I hope.

LADY FIDGET: No, Sir Jaspar.

OLD LADY SQUEAMISH: And you came straight hither, Biddy?

SQUEAMISH: Yes, indeed, Lady Grandmother.

SIR JASPAR: 'Tis well, 'tis well; I knew when once they were thoroughly acquainted with poor Horner, they'd ne'er be from him. You may let her masquerade it with my wife and Horner and I warrant her reputation safe.

[*Enter Boy.*]

BOY: Oh, sir, here's the gentleman come whom you bid me not suffer to come up without giving you notice, with a lady too, and other gentlemen—

HORNER: Do you all go in there, whilst I send 'em away, and, boy, do you desire 'em to stay below till I come, which shall be immediately.

[*Exeunt Sir Jaspar, Old Lady Squeamish, Lady Fidget, Mrs. Dainty, Squeamish.*]

BOY: Yes, sir.   [*Exit.*]

[*Exit Horner at t'other door and returns with Mrs. Pinchwife.*]

3. Ripe for the telling.

HORNER: You would not take my advice to be gone home before your husband came back; he'll now discover all. Yet pray, my dearest, be persuaded to go home and leave the rest to my management. I'll let you down the back way.

MRS. PINCHWIFE: I don't know the way home, so I don't.

HORNER: My man shall wait upon you.

MRS. PINCHWIFE: No, don't you believe that I'll go at all. What, are you weary of me already?

HORNER: No, my life, 'tis that I may love you long, 'tis to secure my love, and your reputation with your husband; he'll never receive you again else.

MRS. PINCHWIFE: What care I? D'ye think to frighten me with that? I don't intend to go to him again; you shall be my husband now.

HORNER: I cannot be your husband, dearest, since you are married to him.

MRS. PINCHWIFE: Oh, would you make me believe that? Don't I see every day, at London here, women leave their first husbands and go and live with other men as their wives? Pish, pshaw, you'd make me angry, but that I love you so mainly.[4]

HORNER: So, they are coming up—in again, in, I hear 'em.

[Exit Mrs. Pinchwife.]

Well, a silly mistress is like a weak place, soon got, soon lost, a man has scarce time for plunder; she betrays her husband first to her gallant and then her gallant to her husband.

[Enter Pinchwife, Alithea, Harcourt, Sparkish, Lucy and a Parson.]

PINCHWIFE: Come, madam, 'tis not the sudden change of your dress, the confidence of your asseverations and your false witness there, shall persuade me I did not bring you hither just now; here's my witness, who cannot deny it, since you must be confronted.—Mr. Horner, did not I bring this lady to you just now?

HORNER [aside]: Now must I wrong one woman for another's sake, but that's no new thing with me, for in these cases I am still on the criminal's side, against the innocent.

ALITHEA: Pray, speak, sir.

HORNER [aside]: It must be so—I must be impudent and try my luck; impudence uses to be too hard for truth.

PINCHWIFE: What, you are studying an evasion or excuse for her. Speak, sir.

HORNER: No, faith, I am something backward only to speak in women's affairs or disputes.

PINCHWIFE: She bids you speak.

ALITHEA: Ay, pray, sir, do; pray satisfy him.

HORNER: Then truly, you did bring that lady to me just now.

PINCHWIFE: O ho!

ALITHEA: How, sir!

HARCOURT: How, Horner!

ALITHEA: What mean you, sir? I always took you for a man of honor.

HORNER [aside]: Ay, so much a man of honor that I must save my mistress, I thank you, come what will on't.

SPARKISH: So, if I had had her, she'd have made me believe the moon had been made of a Christmas pie.

4. Mightily.

LUCY [aside]: Now could I speak, if I durst, and solve the riddle, who am the author of it.

ALITHEA: O unfortunate woman! A combination against my honor, which most concerns me now, because you share in my disgrace, sir, and it is your censure, which I must now suffer, that troubles me, not theirs.

HARCOURT: Madam, then have no trouble, you shall now see 'tis possible for me to love too, without being jealous; I will not only believe your innocence myself, but make all the world believe it. [Apart to Horner.] Horner, I must now be concerned for this lady's honor.

HORNER: And I must be concerned for a lady's honor too.

HARCOURT: This lady has her honor and I will protect it.

HORNER: My lady has not her honor but has given it me to keep and I will preserve it.

HARCOURT: I understand you not.

HORNER: I would not have you.

MRS. PINCHWIFE [peeping in behind]: What's the matter with 'em all?

PINCHWIFE: Come, come, Mr. Horner, no more disputing. Here's the parson; I brought him not in vain.

HARCOURT: No, sir, I'll employ him, if this lady please.

PINCHWIFE: How! What d'ye mean?

SPARKISH: Ay, what does he mean?

HORNER: Why, I have resigned your sister to him; he has my consent.

PINCHWIFE: But he has not mine, sir; a woman's injured honor, no more than a man's, can be repaired or satisfied by any but him that first wronged it; and you shall marry her presently, or—[Lays his hand on his sword.]
[Enter to them Mrs. Pinchwife.]

MRS. PINCHWIFE [aside]: O Lord, they'll kill poor Mr. Horner! Besides, he shan't marry her whilst I stand by and look on; I'll not lose my second husband so.

PINCHWIFE: What do I see?

ALITHEA: My sister in my clothes!

SPARKISH: Ha!

MRS. PINCHWIFE [to Mr. Pinchwife]: Nay, pray now don't quarrel about finding work for the parson; he shall marry me to Mr. Horner, for now, I believe, you have enough of me.

HORNER: Damned, damned, loving changeling!

MRS. PINCHWIFE: Pray, sister, pardon me for telling so many lies of you.

HARCOURT: I suppose the riddle is plain now.

LUCY: No, that must be my work. Good sir, hear me.
[Kneels to Mr. Pinchwife, who stands doggedly, with his hat over his eyes.]

PINCHWIFE: I will never hear woman again, but make 'em all silent, thus—
[Offers to draw upon his wife.]

HORNER: No, that must not be.

PINCHWIFE: You then shall go first; 'tis all one to me [Offers to draw on Horner; stopped by Harcourt.]

HARCOURT: Hold!
[Enter Sir Jaspar Fidget, Lady Fidget, Old Lady Squeamish, Mrs. Dainty Fidget, Mrs. Squeamish.]

SIR JASPAR: What's the matter, what's the matter, pray, what's the matter, sir? I beseech you communicate, sir.

PINCHWIFE: Why, my wife has communicated[5], sir, as your wife may have done too, sir, if she knows him, sir.

SIR JASPAR: Pshaw, with him? Ha, ha, he!

PINCHWIFE: D'ye mock me, sir? A cuckold is a kind of a wild beast; have a care, sir.

SIR JASPAR: No, sure, you mock me, sir—he cuckold you! It can't be, ha, ha, he! Why, I tell you, sir—[Offers to whisper.]

PINCHWIFE: I tell you again, he has whored my wife, and yours too, if he knows her, and all the women he comes near; 'tis not his dissembling, his hypocrisy can wheedle me.

SIR JASPAR: How! does he dissemble? Is he a hypocrite? Nay, then—how—wife—sister, is he an hypocrite?

OLD LADY SQUEAMISH: An hypocrite, a dissembler! Speak, young harlotry, speak, how?

SIR JASPAR: Nay, then—O, my head too!—O thou libidinous lady!

OLD LADY SQUEAMISH: O thou harloting harlotry! Hast thou done't then?

SIR JASPAR: Speak, good Horner, art thou a dissembler, a rogue? Hast thou—

HORNER: Soh—

LUCY [apart to Horner]: I'll fetch you off, and her too, if she will but hold her tongue.

HORNER [apart to Lucy]: Canst thou? I'll give thee—

LUCY [to Mr. Pinchwife]: Pray have but patience to hear me, sir, who am the unfortunate cause of all this confusion. Your wife is innocent, I only culpable, for I put her upon telling you all these lies concerning my mistress, in order to the breaking off the match between Mr. Sparkish and her, to make way for Mr. Harcourt.

SPARKISH: Did you so, eternal rotten tooth? Then, it seems, my mistress was not false to me, I was only deceived by you.—Brother that should have been, now man of conduct, who is a frank person now? To bring your wife to her lover—ha!

LUCY: I assure you, sir, she came not to Mr. Horner out of love, for she loves him no more—

MRS. PINCHWIFE: Hold, I told lies for you, but you shall tell none for me, for I do love Mr. Horner with all my soul, and nobody shall say me nay. Pray, don't you go to make poor Mr. Horner believe to the contrary; 'tis spitefully done of you, I'm sure.

HORNER [aside to Mrs. Pinchwife]: Peace, dear idiot.

MRS. PINCHWIFE: Nay, I will not peace.

PINCHWIFE: Not till I make you.

[Enter Dorilant, Quack.]

DORILANT: Horner, your servant; I am the doctor's guest, he must excuse our intrusion.

QUACK: But what's the matter, gentlemen? For heaven's sake, what's the matter?

HORNER: Oh, 'tis well you are come. 'Tis a censorious world we live in; you may have brought me a reprieve, or else I had died for a crime I never committed, and

5. Fornicated.

these innocent ladies had suffered with me. Therefore pray satisfy these worthy, honorable, jealous gentlemen—that—[*Whispers.*]

QUACK: O, I understand you; is that all?
     [*Whispers to Sir Jaspar.*]
Sir Jaspar, by heavens and upon the word of a physician, sir—

SIR JASPAR: Nay, I do believe you truly.—Pardon me, my virtuous lady and dear of honor.

OLD LADY SQUEAMISH: What, then all's right again?

SIR JASPAR: Ay, ay, and now let us satisfy him too.
     [*They whisper with Mr. Pinchwife.*]

PINCHWIFE: An eunuch! Pray, no fooling with me.

QUACK: I'll bring half the chirurgeons in town to swear it.

PINCHWIFE: They!—they'll swear a man that bled to death through his wounds died of an apoplexy.[6]

QUACK: Pray hear me, sir—why, all the town has heard the report of him.

PINCHWIFE: But does all the town believe it?

QUACK: Pray inquire a little, and first of all these.

PINCHWIFE: I'm sure when I left the town he was the lewdest fellow in't.

QUACK: I tell you, sir, he has been in France since; pray, ask but these ladies and gentlemen, your friend Mr. Dorilant.—Gentlemen and ladies, han't you all heard the late sad report of poor Mr. Horner?

ALL THE LADIES: Ay, ay, ay.

DORILANT: Why, thou jealous fool, dost thou doubt it? He's an arrant French capon.[7]

MRS. PINCHWIFE: 'Tis false, sir, you shall not disparage poor Mr. Horner, for to my certain knowledge—

LUCY: Oh, hold!

SQUEAMISH [*aside to Lucy*]: Stop her mouth!

LADY FIDGET [*to Pinchwife*]: Upon my honor, sir, 'tis as true—

DAINTY: D'ye think we would have been seen in his company?

SQUEAMISH: Trust our unspotted reputations with him!

LADY FIDGET [*aside to Horner*]: This you get, and we too, by trusting your secret to a fool.

HORNER: Peace, madam. [*Aside to Quack.*] Well, doctor, is not this a good design, that carries a man on unsuspected and brings him off safe?

PINCHWIFE [*aside*]: Well, if this were true, but my wife—[*Dorilant whispers with Mrs. Pinchwife.*]

ALITHEA: Come, brother, your wife is yet innocent, you see; but have a care of too strong an imagination, lest like an overconcerned, timorous gamester, by fancying an unlucky cast, it should come. Women and fortune are truest still to those that trust 'em.

LUCY: And any wild thing grows but the more fierce and hungry for being kept up and more dangerous to the keeper.

ALITHEA: There's doctrine for all husbands, Mr. Harcourt.

6. A convenient fiction since dueling was now illegal   7. Eunuch.
(1679).

HARCOURT: I edify, madam, so much that I am impatient till I am one.

DORILANT: And I edify so much by example I will never be one.

SPARKISH: And because I will not disparage my parts I'll ne'er be one.

HORNER: And I, alas, can't be one.

PINCHWIFE: But I must be one—against my will, to a country wife, with a country murrain[8] to me.

MRS. PINCHWIFE [aside]: And I must be a country wife still too, I find, for I can't, like a city one, be rid of my musty husband and do what I list.

HORNER: Now, sir, I must pronounce your wife innocent, though I blush whilst I do it, and I am the only man by her now exposed to shame, which I will straight drown in wine, as you shall your suspicion, and the ladies' troubles we'll divert with a ballet.—Doctor, where are your maskers?

LUCY: Indeed, she's innocent, sir, I am her witness; and her end of coming out was but to see her sister's wedding and what she has said to your face of her love to Mr. Horner was but the usual innocent revenge on a husband's jealousy—was it not, madam? Speak.

MRS. PINCHWIFE [aside to Lucy and Horner]: Since you'll have me tell more lies—Yes, indeed, bud.

PINCHWIFE: For my own sake fain I would all believe; Cuckolds, like lovers, should themselves deceive. But—[Sighs.]

> His honor is least safe, too late I find,
> Who trusts it with a foolish wife or friend.

[A Dance of Cuckolds.[9]]

HORNER: Vain fops but court and dress and keep a puther,[1]
            To pass for women's men with one another,
5   But he who aims by women to be priz'd,
            First by the men, you see, must be despis'd.

EPILOGUE, SPOKEN BY MRS. KNEPP[2]

Now, you the vigorous,[3] who daily here
O'er vizard-mask in public domineer,
And what you'd do to her if in place where,
Nay, have the confidence to cry, "Come out,"
5   Yet when she says "Lead on," you are not stout,
But to your well-dressed brother straight turn round
And cry, "Pox on her, Ned, she can't be sound,"
Then slink away, a fresh one to engage,
With so much seeming heat and loving rage,
10 You'd frighten listening actress on the stage,
Till she at last has seen you huffing come
And talk of keeping in the tiring-room,
Yet cannot be provok'd to lead her home.

---

8. Pestilence.
9. This dance was performed to the then-familiar tune called "Cuckolds All [in] a Row."
1. Make a fuss.
2. Elizabeth Knepp, actress and singer, created the role of

Lady Fidget. Pepys held her in high regard; see page 2031.
3. The epilogue derisively addresses two categories of males who, unlike Horner, pretend to sexual potency: the young (lines 1–13) and the old (14–17).

	Next, you Falstaffs[4] of fifty, who beset
15	Your buckram[5] maidenheads, which your friends get,
	And while to them you of achievements boast,
	They share the booty and laugh at your cost.
	In fine, you essenced boys, both old and young,
	Who would be thought so eager, brisk and strong,
20	Yet do the ladies, not their husbands, wrong,
	Whose purses for your manhood make excuse,
	And keep your Flanders mares[6] for show, not use:
	Encouraged by our woman's man today,
	A Horner's part may vainly think to play
25	And may intrigues so bashfully disown
	That they may doubted be by few or none,[7]
	May kiss the cards at picquet, ombre, loo,[8]
	And so be thought to kiss the lady too;
	But, gallants, have a care, faith, what you do.
30	The world, which to no man his due will give,
	You by experience know you can deceive
	And men may still believe you vigorous,
	But then we women—there's no cozening[9] us.

1675   1675

---

‡‡‡‡‡‡‡

Mary Astell
1666–1731

The pioneering feminist Mary Astell was born in Newcastle to a merchant who dealt in coal, and she was tutored early by an uncle who immersed himself in literature and philosophy. From him she absorbed a lifelong affinity for the ideas of the Cambridge Platonists, who held that reason was the sole route to truth and to the proper love of God; out of this conviction she developed her defiant argument that, despite centuries of cultural practice to the contrary, women's powers of reason were as worth cultivating as men's. At age twenty Astell moved to London, where eight years later she published the book that made her fame. In *A Serious Proposal to the Ladies* (1694), Astell argued for the founding of an all-female academy, where unmarried women might develop their reason, deepen their knowledge, and nurture their faith free from the distractions imposed by social conventions. Astell's idea for such a school exerted a lasting influence: Daniel Defoe enthusiastically revived it in his *Essay upon Projects* (1697), Samuel Johnson wove it into his philosophical tale *Rasselas* (1759), and Sarah Scott made it the premise of her feminist novel *Millenium Hall* (1762). More important, perhaps, was the *Proposal*'s immediate effect on contemporary

---

4. I.e., you who resemble the immense, aged, comic liar Shakespeare created in *Henry IV*.
5. A stiff fabric. Falstaff at one point pretends to have killed some "rogues in buckram suits" during a robbery (*1 Henry IV* 2.4). In truth he killed no one, and his younger accomplices made off with the loot.
6. Costly coach horses; here a metaphor for kept mistresses

or prostitutes.
7. I.e., Horner's example may encourage "you" fakers to reverse tactics, and to seek a rake's reputation by feigning "bashfulness."
8. Card games; kissing the cards was a way of flirting with fellow-players.
9. Fooling.

women writers and thinkers (Ladies Mary Chudleigh and Mary Wortley Montagu among them), who found in it a template and an endorsement for their own most cherished pursuits and for their sense of possibilities.

Dwelling abstemiously in the Thames-side town of Chelsea, Astell began to enjoy the consequences of celebrity. She received tributes and visits from admiring readers, and she assembled a circle of women like herself—well-educated, pious, unmarried—whose friendships she deeply valued and with whose help she later founded a charity school for girls. Still, the *Proposal* itself was never implemented in her time, in part because the imagined academy for women sounded too much like a Catholic convent to find ready acceptance in Protestant England, and in part because the argument's point—that women could find intellectual, moral, and spiritual self-sufficiency outside marriage—was so unsettling as to rouse energetic opposition.

Astell pushed the argument further in *Some Reflections upon Marriage* (1700), a hundred-page tract written, she reported, in the white heat of an angry and inspired afternoon. Starting from a conservative premise—that as the monarch rightfully possesses absolute authority over the state, so does the husband over his wife—Astell develops a breathtakingly skeptical line of inquiry: why, then, would a woman wish to enter into so self-immolating a contract as marriage in the first place? The question ultimately brings her back to the theme of the *Serious Proposal*: the importance for women of a good education, one that will enable them to see their choices clearly, to make those choices discerningly, and to lead, whether married or not, a Christian life grounded in the cultivation of their own intellect and faith (though Astell strongly implies that within marriage female virtue will produce a grim martyrdom; outside marriage, a richer fulfillment). In limning the alternatives, Astell deploys the directness, the sarcasm, and the urgency that made her famous in her own day and again in ours. She was, as her biographer Ruth Perry notes, "probably the first person to consider the rights and duties of women as a political question"; the prose in which she couched the question gave it an often hypnotic pugnacity.

from Some Reflections upon Marriage

But how can a man respect his wife when he has a contemptible opinion of her and her sex? When from his own elevation he looks down on them as void of understanding, and full of ignorance and passion, so that folly and a woman are equivalent terms with him? Can he think there is any gratitude due to her whose utmost services he exacts as strict duty? Because she was made to be a slave to his will, and has no higher end than to serve and obey him? Perhaps we arrogate too much to ourselves when we say this material world was made for our sakes; that its glorious maker has given us the use of it is certain, but when we suppose that over which we have dominion to be made purely for our sakes, we draw a false conclusion, as he who should say the people were made for the prince who is set over them, would be thought to be out of his senses as well as his politics. Yet even allowing that He who made everything in number, weight and measure, who never acts but for some great and glorious end, an end agreeable to His majesty, allowing that He created such a number of rational spirits merely to serve their fellow creatures, yet how are these lords and masters helped by the contempt they show of their poor humble vassals? Is it not rather an hindrance to that service they expect, as being undeniable and constant proof how unworthy they are to receive it?

None of God's creatures absolutely considered are in their own nature contemptible; the meanest fly, the poorest insect has its use and virtue. Contempt is scarce a human passion; one may venture to say it was not in innocent man, for till sin came into the world, there was nothing in it to be condemned. But pride, which makes everything serve its purposes, wrested this passion from its only use, so that instead of being an antidote against sin, it is become a grand promoter of it, nothing making us more worthy of that contempt we show, than when (poor, weak, dependent creatures as we are!) we look down with scorn and disdain on others.

There is not a surer sign of a noble mind, a mind very far advanced towards perfection, than the being able to bear contempt and an unjust treatment from one's superiors evenly and patiently. For inward worth and real excellency are the true ground of superiority, and one person is not in reality better than another, but as he is more wise and good. But this world being a place of trial and governed by general laws, just retributions being reserved for hereafter, respect and obedience many times become due for order's sake to those who don't otherwise deserve them. Now though humility keeps us from over-valuing ourselves or viewing our merit through a false and magnifying medium, yet it does not put out our eyes; it does not, it ought not to deprive us of that pleasing sentiment which attends our acting as we ought to act, which is as it were a foretaste of heaven, our present reward for doing what is just and fit. And when a superior does a mean and unjust thing, as all contempt of one's neighbor is, and yet this does not provoke his inferiors to refuse that observance which their stations in the world require, they cannot but have an inward sense of their own real superiority, the other having no pretense to it, at the same time that they pay him an outward respect and deference, which is such a flagrant testimony of the sincerest love of order as proves their souls to be of the highest and noblest rank.

A man therefore for his own sake, and to give evidence that he has a right to those prerogatives he assumes, should treat women with a little more humanity and regard than is usually paid them. Your whiffling wits may scoff at them, and what then? It matters not, for they rally[1] everything though ever so sacred, and rail at the women commonly in very good company. Religion, its priests, and these its most constant and regular professors, are the usual subjects of their manly, mannerly, and surprising jests. Surprising indeed! not for the newness of the thought, the brightness of the fancy, or nobleness of expression, but for the good assurance with which such threadbare jests are again and again repeated. But that your grave dons, your learned men, and which is more your men of sense as they would be thought, should stoop so low as to make invectives against the women, forget themselves so much as to jest with their slaves, who have neither liberty nor ingenuity to make reprisals! that they should waste their time and debase their good sense which fits them for the most weighty affairs, such as are suitable to their profound wisdoms and exalted understandings! to render those poor wretches more ridiculous and odious who are already in their opinion sufficiently contemptible, and find no better exercise of their wit and satire than such as are not worth their pains, though it were possible to reform them—this, this indeed may justly be wondered at!

I know not whether or no women are allowed to have souls. If they have, perhaps it is not prudent to provoke them too much, lest silly as they are, they at last recriminate, and then what polite and well-bred gentleman, though himself is concerned, can forbear taking that lawful pleasure which all who understand raillery must taste, when they find his jests who insolently began to peck at his neighbor, returned with interest upon his own head? And indeed men are too humane, too wise

1. Mock.

to venture at it did they not hope for this effect, and expect the pleasure of finding their wit turn to such account; for if it be lawful to reveal a secret, this is without doubt the whole design of those fine discourses which have been made against the women from our great forefathers to this present time. Generous man has too much bravery, he is too just and too good to assault a defenseless enemy, and if he did inveigh against the women it was only to do them service. For since neither his care of their education, his hearty endeavors to improve their minds, his wholesome precepts, nor great example could do them good, as his last and kindest essay he resolved to try what contempt would do, and chose rather to expose himself by a seeming want of justice, equity, ingenuity, and good nature, than suffer women to remain such vain and insignificant creatures as they have hitherto been reckoned. And truly women are some degrees beneath what I have thus far thought them, if they do not make the best use of his kindness, improve themselves, and like Christians return it.

Let us see then what is their part, what must they do to make the matrimonial yoke tolerable to themselves as well as pleasing to their lords and masters? That the world is an empty and deceitful thing, that those enjoyments which appear so desirable at a distance, which raised our hopes and expectations to such a mighty pitch, which we so passionately coveted and so eagerly pursued, vanish at our first approach, leaving nothing behind them but the folly of delusion, and the pain of disappointed hopes, is a common outcry; and yet as common as it is, though we complain of being deceived this instant, we do not fail of contributing to the cheat the very next. Though in reality it is not the world that abuses us, 'tis we abuse ourselves, it is not the emptiness of that, but our own false judgments, our unreasonable desires and expectations that torment us; for he who exerts his whole strength to lift a straw, ought not to complain of the burden but of his own disproportionate endeavor which gives him the pain he feels. The world affords us all that pleasure a sound judgment can expect from it, and answers all those ends and purposes for which it was designed. Let us expect no more than is reasonable, and then we shall not fail of our expectations.

It is even so in the case before us: a woman who has been taught to think marriage her only preferment, the sum-total of her endeavors, the completion of all her hopes, that which must settle and make her happy in this world, and very few, in their youth especially, carry a thought steadily to a greater distance; she who has seen a lover dying at her feet, and can't therefore imagine that he who professes to receive all his happiness from her can have any other design or desire than to please her; whose eyes have been dazzled with all the glitter and pomp of a wedding, and who hears of nothing but joy and congratulation; who is transported with the pleasure of being out of pupillage, and mistress not only of herself but of a family too; she who is either so simple or so vain as to take her lover at his word either as to the praises he gave her, or the promises he made for himself. In sum, she whose expectation has been raised by courtship, by all the fine things that her lover, her governess, and domestic flatterers say, will find a terrible disappointment when the hurry is over, and when she comes calmly to consider her condition, and views it no more under a false appearance, but as it truly is.

I doubt in such a view it will not appear over-desirable if she regards only the present state of things. Hereafter may make amends for what she must be prepared to suffer here; then will be her reward, this is her time of trial, the season of exercising and improving her virtues. A woman that is not mistress of her passions, that cannot patiently submit even when reason suffers with her, who does not practice passive obedience[2] to the utmost, will never be acceptable to such an absolute sovereign as a husband. Wisdom ought to govern without contradiction, but strength however will be obeyed. There are but few of those wise persons who can be content to be made yet wiser by contradiction; the most will have their will, and it is right because it is theirs. Such is the vanity of human nature that nothing pleases like an entire subjection; what imperfections won't a man overlook where this is not wanting! Though we live like brutes, we would have incense offered us that is only due to heaven itself, would have an absolute and blind obedience paid us by all over whom we pretend authority. We were not made to idolize one another, yet the whole strain of courtship is little less than rank idolatry. But does a man intend to give and not receive his share in this religious worship? No such matter; pride and vanity and self-love have their designs, and if the lover is so condescending as to set a pattern in the time of his addresses, he is so just as to expect his wife should strictly copy after it all the rest of her life.

But how can a woman scruple entire subjection, how can she forbear to admire the worth and excellency of the superior sex, if she at all considers it? Have not all the great actions that have been performed in the world been done by them? Have not they founded empires and overturned them? Do not they make laws and continually repeal them and amend them? Their vast minds lay kingdoms waste; no bounds or measures can be prescribed to their desires. War and peace depend on them, they form cabals[3] and have the wisdom and courage to get over all these rubs[4] which may lie in the way of their desired grandeur. What is it they cannot do? They make worlds and ruin them, form systems of universal nature and dispute eternally about them, their pen gives worth to the most trifling controversy, nor can a fray be inconsiderable if they have drawn their swords in't. All that the wise man pronounces is an oracle, and every word the witty speaks a jest. It is a woman's happiness to hear, admire, and praise them, especially if a little ill-nature keeps them at anytime from bestowing due applause on each other. And if she aspires no further she is thought to be in her proper sphere of action; she is as wise and as good as can be expected from her.

She then who marries ought to lay it down for an indisputable maxim, that her husband must govern absolutely and entirely, and that she has nothing else to do but to please and obey. She must not attempt to divide his authority, or so much as dispute it (to struggle with her yoke will only make it gall the more) but must believe him wise and good and in all respects the best, at least he must be so to her. She who can't do this is no way fit to be a wife; she may set up for that peculiar coronet the ancient fathers talked of, but is not qualified to receive that great reward,[5] which attends the eminent exercise of humility and self-denial, patience and resignation—the duties that a wife is called to.

---

2. The term denoted the Tory policy of obeying Whig monarchs and of refraining from rebellion despite their "usurpation" of the Stuart throne, on the principle that rebellion itself would run contrary to divine and human law.

3. Small, secretive groups formed to wield power.
4. Obstacles.
5. Salvation. The "peculiar coronet" is that of martyrdom, often imaged as a crown in the writings of early Christian theologians.

But some refractory woman perhaps will say how can this be? Is it possible for her to believe him wise and good who by a thousand demonstrations convinces her and all the world of the contrary? Did the bare name of husband confer sense on a man, and the mere being in authority infallibly qualify him for government, much might be done. But since a wise man and a husband are not terms convertible, and how loath soever one is to own it, matter of fact won't allow us to deny that the head many times stands in need of the inferior's brains to manage it, she must beg leave to be excused from such high thoughts of her sovereign, and if she submits to his power, it is not so much reason as necessity that compels her.

Now of how little force soever this objection may be in other respects, methinks it is strong enough to prove the necessity of a good education, and that men never mistake their true interest more than when they endeavor to keep women in ignorance. Could they indeed deprive them of their natural good sense at the same time they deny them the due improvement of it, they might compass their end; otherwise natural sense unassisted may run into a false track, and serve only to punish him justly, who would not allow it to be useful to himself or others. If man's authority be justly established, the more sense a woman has the more reason she will find to submit to it; if according to the tradition of our fathers (who having had *possession* of the pen, thought they had also the best *right* to it), women's understanding is but small, and men's partiality adds no weight to the observation, ought not the more care to be taken to improve them? How it agrees with the justice of men we inquire not, but certainly Heaven is abundantly more equitable than to enjoin women the hardest task and give them the least strength to perform it. And if men, learned, wise, and discreet as they are, who have as is said all the advantages of nature, and without controversy have or may have all the assistance of art, are so far from acquitting themselves as they ought, from living according to that reason and excellent understanding they so much boast of, can it be expected that a woman who is reckoned silly enough in herself, at least comparatively, and whom men take care to make yet more so, can it be expected that she should constantly perform so difficult a duty as entire subjection, to which corrupt nature is so averse?

If the great and wise Cato,[6] a *man*, a man of no ordinary firmness and strength of mind, a man who was esteemed as an oracle, and by the philosophers and great men of his nation equaled even to the gods themselves; if he with all his stoical principles was not able to bear the sight of a triumphant conqueror (who perhaps would have insulted and perhaps would not), but out of a cowardly fear of an insult, ran to death to secure him from it; can it be thought that an ignorant weak woman should have patience to bear a continual outrage and insolence all the days of her life? Unless you will suppose her a very ass, but then remember what the Italians say, to quote them once more, since being very husbands they may be presumed to have some authority in this case: *L'asino pur pigro, stimulato tira quelche calcio*; an ass though slow if provoked will kick.

We never see or perhaps make sport with the ill effects of a bad education, till it come to touch us home in the ill conduct of a sister, a daughter, or wife. Then the women must be blamed, their folly is exclaimed against, when all this while it was the wise man's fault who did not set a better guard on those who according to him

---

6. Cato of Utica (95–46 B.C.E.), Stoic Roman senator and commander, whose devotion to the ideal of a Republic prompted him to commit suicide rather than accede to the growing power of Julius Caesar; his death was traditionally represented as heroic.

stand in so much need of one. A young gentleman, as a celebrated author tells us, ought above all things to be acquainted with the state of the world, the ways and humors, the follies, the cheats, the faults of the age he is fallen into; he should by degrees be informed of the vice of fashion, and warned of the application and design of those who will make it their business to corrupt him, should be told the arts they use and the trains they lay, be prepared to be shocked by some and caressed by others; warned who are like to oppose, who to mislead; who to undermine and who to serve him. He should be instructed how to know and distinguish them, where he should let them see, and when dissemble the knowledge of them and their aims and workings. Our author is much in the right, and not to disparage any other accomplishments which are useful in their kind, this will turn to more account than any language or philosophy, art or science, or any other piece of good-breeding and fine education that can be taught him, which are no otherwise excellent than as they contribute to this, as this does above all things to the making him a wise, virtuous, and useful man.

And it is not less necessary that a young lady should receive the like instructions; whether or no her temptations be fewer, her reputation and honor however are to be more nicely preserved; they may be ruined by a little ignorance or indiscretion, and then though she has kept her innocence, and so is secured as to the next world, yet she is in a great measure lost to this. A woman cannot be too watchful, too apprehensive of her danger, nor keep at too great a distance from it, since man, whose wisdom and ingenuity is so much superior to hers, condescends for his interest sometimes, and sometimes by way of diversion, to lay snares for her. For though men are virtuous, philosophers and politicians in comparison of the ignorant and illiterate women, yet they don't all pretend to be saints, and 'tis no great matter to them if women, who were born to be their slaves, be now and then ruined for their entertainment.

But according to the rate that young women are educated; according to the way their time is spent; they are destined to folly and impertinence, to say no worse, and which is yet more inhuman, they are blamed for that ill conduct they are not suffered to avoid, and reproached for those faults they are in a manner forced into; so that if heaven has bestowed any sense on them, no other use is made of it than to leave them without excuse. So much and no more of the world is shown them, as serves to weaken and corrupt their minds, to give them wrong notions, and busy them in mean pursuits; to disturb, not to regulate their passions, to make them timorous and dependent, and in a word, fit for nothing else but to act a farce for the diversion of their governors.

Even men themselves improve no otherwise than according to the aim they take, and the end they propose; and he whose designs are but little and mean, will be the same himself. Though ambition, as 'tis usually understood, is a foolish, not to say a base and pitiful vice, yet the aspirings of the soul after true glory are so much its nature, that it seems to have forgot itself and to degenerate, if it can forbear; and perhaps the great secret of education lies in affecting the soul with a lively sense of what is truly its perfection, and exciting the most ardent desires after it.

But, alas! what poor woman is ever taught that she should have a higher design than to get her a husband? Heaven will fall in of course; and if she make but an obedient and dutiful wife, she cannot miss of it. A husband indeed is thought by both sexes so very valuable, that scarce a man who can keep himself clean and make a bow, but thinks he is good enough to pretend to any woman, no matter for the difference of birth or fortune, a *husband* is such a wonder-working name as to make an equality, or something more, whenever it is pronounced. * * *

To wind up this matter, if a woman were duly principled and taught to know the world, especially the true sentiments that men have of her, and the traps they lay for her under so many gilded compliments, and such a seemingly great respect, that disgrace would be prevented which is brought upon too many families, women would marry more discreetly, and demean[7] themselves better in a married state than some people say they do. The foundation indeed ought to be laid deep and strong: she should be made a good Christian, and understand why she is so, and then she will be everything else that is good. Men need keep no spies on a woman's conduct, need have no fear of her virtue, or so much as of her prudence and caution, were but a due sense of true honor and virtue awakened in her, were her reason excited and prepared to consider the sophistry of those temptations which would persuade her from her duty, and were she put in a way to know that it is both her wisdom and interest to observe it. She would then duly examine and weigh all the circumstances, the good and evil of a married state, and not be surprised with unforeseen inconveniences, and either never consent to be a wife, or make a good one when she does. This would show her what human nature *is*, as well as what it *ought* to be, and teach her not only what she may justly expect, but what she must be content with; would enable her to cure some faults, and patiently to suffer what she cannot cure.

Indeed nothing can assure obedience, and render it what it ought to be, but the confidence of duty, the paying it for God's sake. Superiors don't rightly understand their own interest when they attempt to put out their subjects' eyes to keep them obedient. A blind obedience is what a rational creature should never pay, nor would such an one receive it did he rightly understand its nature. For human actions are no otherwise valuable than as they are conformable to reason, but blind obedience is an obeying *without reason*, for ought we know, *against it*. God himself does not require our obedience at this rate; He lays before us the goodness and reasonableness of His laws, and were there anything in them whose equity we could not readily comprehend, yet we have this clear and sufficient reason on which to found our obedience, that nothing but what's just and fit can be enjoined by a just, a wise, and gracious God. But this is a reason will never hold in respect of men's commands unless they can prove themselves infallible, and consequently impeccable too.

It is therefore very much a man's interest that women should be good Christians, in this as in every other instance; he who does his duty finds his own account[8] in it. Duty and true interest are one and the same thing, and he who thinks otherwise is to be pitied for being so much in the wrong; but what can be more the duty of the head, than to instruct and improve those who are under government? She will freely leave him the quiet dominion of this world whose thoughts and expectations are placed on the next. A prospect of heaven, and that only, will cure that ambition which all generous minds are filled with, not by taking it away but by placing it on a right object. She will discern a time when her sex shall be no bar to the best employments, the highest honor; a time when that distinction, now so much used to her prejudice, shall be no more, but provided she is not wanting to herself, her soul shall shine as bright as the greatest hero's. This is a true, and indeed the only consolation, this makes her a sufficient compensation for all the neglect

7. Behave (though the meaning "to lower herself" was also current).   8. I.e., is amply compensated.

and contempt the ill-grounded customs of the world throw on her, for all the injuries brutal power may do her, and is a sufficient cordial to support her spirits, be her lot in this world what it may.

But some sage persons may perhaps object that were women allowed to improve themselves, and not amongst other discouragements driven back by those wise jests and scoffs that are put upon a woman of sense or learning, a philosophical lady as she is called by way of ridicule, they would be too wise and too good for the men. I grant it, for vicious and foolish men. Nor is it to be wondered that he is afraid he should not be able to govern them were their understandings improved, who is resolved not to take too much pains with his own. But these 'tis to be hoped are no very considerable number, the foolish at least; and therefore this is so far from being an argument against their improvement, that it is a strong one for it, if we do but suppose the men to be as capable of improvement as the women, but much more if according to tradition we believe they have greater capacities. This, if anything, would stir them up to be what they ought, not permit them to waste their time and abuse their faculties in the service of their irregular appetites and unreasonable desires, and to let poor contemptible women who have been their slaves excel them in all that is truly excellent. This would make them blush at employing an immoral mind no better than in making provision for the flesh to fulfill the lusts thereof, since women by a wiser conduct have brought themselves to such a reach of thought, to such exactness of judgment, such clearness and strength of reasoning, such purity and elevation of mind, such command of their passions, such regularity of will and affection, and in a word to such a pitch of perfection as the human soul is capable of attaining even in this life by the grace of God, such true wisdom, such real greatness, as though it does not qualify them to make a noise in this world, to found or overturn empires, yet it qualifies them for what is infinitely better, a kingdom that cannot be moved, an incorruptible crown of glory.

Besides, it were ridiculous to suppose that a woman, were she ever so much improved, could come near the topping genius of men, and therefore why should they envy or discourage her? Strength of mind goes along with strength of body, and 'tis only for some odd accidents which philosophers have not yet thought worthwhile to inquire into, that the sturdiest porter is not the wisest man. As therefore the men have the power in their hands, so there's no dispute of their having the brains to manage it. There is no such thing as good judgment and sense upon earth, if it is not to be found among them. Do not they generally speaking do all the great actions and considerable business of this world, and leave that of the next to the women? Their subtlety in forming cabals and laying deep designs, their courage and conduct in breaking through all ties sacred and civil to effect them, not only advances them to the post of honor and keeps them securely in it for twenty or thirty years, but gets them a name, and conveys it down to posterity for some hundreds, and who would look any further? Justice and injustice are administered by their hands; courts and schools are filled with these sages; 'tis men who dispute for truth as well as men who argue against it; histories are writ by them, they recount each others' great exploits, and have always done so. All famous arts have their original from men, even from the invention of guns to the mystery of good eating. And to show that nothing is beneath their care, any more than above their reach, they have brought *gaming*[9] to an

9. Gambling.

art and science, and a more profitable and honorable one too, than any of those that used to be called *liberal*. Indeed what is it they can't perform, when they attempt it? This strength of their brains shall be every whit as conspicuous at their cups as in a Senate house, and when they please they can make it pass for as sure a mark of wisdom to drink deep as to reason profoundly; a greater proof of courage and consequently of understanding to dare the vengeance of heaven itself than to stand the raillery of some of the worst of their fellow creatures!

Again, it may be said, if a wife's case be as it is here represented, it is not good for a woman to marry, and so there's an end of human race. But this is no fair consequence, for all that can justly be inferred from hence is that a woman has no mighty obligations to the man who makes love to her, she has no reason to be fond of being a wife, or to reckon it a piece of preferment when she is taken to be a man's upper-servant; it is no advantage to her in this world, if rightly managed it may prove one as to the next. For she who marries purely to do good, to educate souls for heaven, who can be so truly mortified as to lay aside her own will and desires, to pay such an entire submission for life, to one whom she cannot be sure will always deserve it, does certainly perform a more heroic action than all the famous masculine heroes can boast of; she suffers a continual martyrdom to bring glory to God and benefit to mankind, which consideration indeed may carry her though all difficulties, I know not what else can, and engage her to love him who proves perhaps so much more worse than a brute, as to make this condition yet more grievous than it needed to be. She has need of a strong reason, of a truly Christian and well-tempered spirit, of all the assistance the best education can give her, and ought to have some good assistance of her own firmness and virtue, who ventures on such a trial; and for this reason 'tis less to be wondered at that women marry off in haste, for perhaps if they took time to consider and reflect upon it, they seldom would.

To conclude, perhaps I've said more than most men will thank me for; I cannot help it, for how much soever I may be their friend and humble servant, I am more a friend to truth. Truth is strong, and some time or other will prevail; nor is it for their honor, and therefore one would think not for their interest, to be partial to themselves and unjust to others. They may fancy I have made some discoveries which like *arcana imperii*[1] ought to be kept secret, but in good earnest I do them more honor than to suppose their lawful prerogatives need any mean arts to support them. If they have usurped, I love justice too much to wish success and continuance to usurpations, which though submitted to out of prudence and for quietness' sake, yet leave everybody free to regain their lawful right whenever they have power and opportunity. I don't say that tyranny *ought*, but we find in *fact*, that it provokes the oppressed to throw off even a lawful yoke that fits too heavy. And if he who is freely elected, after all his fair promises and the fine hopes he raised, proves a tyrant, the consideration that he was one's own choice will not render more submissive and patient, but I fear more refractory. For though it is very unreasonable, yet we see 'tis the course of the world not only to return injury for injury, but crime for crime; both parties indeed are guilty, but the aggressors have a double guilt; they have not only their own, but their neighbor's ruin to answer for.

As to the female reader, I hope she will allow I've endeavored to do her justice, nor betrayed her cause as her advocates usually do, under pretense of defending it: a practice too mean for any to be guilty of who have the least sense of honor, and who

---

1. The secrets of power.

do any more than merely pretend to it. I think I have held the balance even, and not being conscious of partiality I ask no pardon for it. To plead for the oppressed and to defend the weak seemed to me a generous undertaking; for though it may be secure, 'tis not always honorable to run over to the strongest party. And if she infers from what has been said that marriage is a very happy state for men, if they think fit to make it so; that they govern the world, they have prescription on their side, women are too weak to dispute it with them, therefore they, as all other governors, are most, if not only, accountable for what's amiss. For whether other governments in their original were or were not conferred according to the merit of the person, yet certainly in this case Heaven would not have allotted the man to govern, but because he was best qualified for it. So far I agree with him. But if she goes on to infer, that therefore he has not these qualifications, where is his right? If he misemploys, does he not abuse it? And if he abuses, according to modern deduction, he forfeits it; I must leave her there. A peaceable woman indeed will not carry it so far, she will neither question her husband's right nor his fitness to govern, but how? Not as an absolute lord and master, with an arbitrary and tyrannical sway, but as reason governs and conducts a man, by proposing what is just and fit. And the man who acts according to that wisdom he assumes, who would have that superiority he pretends to acknowledged just, will receive no injury by anything that has been offered here. A woman will value him the more who is so wise and good, when she discerns how much he excels the rest of his noble sex; the less he requires, the more will he merit that esteem and deference, which those who are so forward to exact seem conscious they don't deserve. So then the man's prerogative is not at all infringed, whilst the woman's privileges are secured; and if any woman think herself injured, she has a remedy in reserve which few men will envy or endeavor to rob her of, the exercise and improvement of her virtue here, and the reward of it hereafter.
1700   1700

━━ ⬥ ━━

Daniel Defoe
1660–1731

At the age of fifty-two, Daniel Defoe summed up his life in a couplet:

> No man has tasted differing fortunes more,
> And thirteen times I have been rich or poor.

Vicissitude marked his career until the very end, and money, though a constant preoccupation, was not the only medium of change. Deeply engaged in politics, and phenomenally skilled at promoting causes with his pen, Defoe switched allegiances several times among the most conspicuous factions of his day. What's more, since he was prized by each side in turn for his efficiency as a secret agent, his political work often required him to present himself—in person and in print—as someone or something he was not, to incur hostilities from the very factions he was secretly working to support. His accomplishments, late in life, as a pioneer of English fiction partly originate in the fictions he manipulated as a consummate political journalist and spy obliged to "taste" in imagination and performance the "differing fortunes" of the person he pretended, for one purpose or another, to be. Out of all these oscillations—financial, political, imaginative—came one of the most prolific and inventive careers in British literature.

Defoe was born in the City of London in the year of the Restoration to a family whose fortunes were on the rise. His father James Foe manufactured and sold candles, and over the ensuing decades attained positions of increasing eminence in his trade (Defoe himself later added the French prefix to his family surname). Under the influence of their pastor, the Foes left the Church of England to become Dissenters, at a time when to do so was to incur certain exclusion—from attending universities, from holding public office—and possible persecution (violence, imprisonment). At around the age of ten, shortly after his mother's early death, Defoe began a decade in the schools of the Dissenters. The curriculum, underplaying the Greek and Latin of conventional Anglican education, focused instead on new science and philosophy, on clear argument and public speaking, as well as on two forms of thought and composition that cultivated the student's ability to imagine "differing fortunes": prose imper-sonation, where the student was asked to "play" a given figure (for example, a secretary of state) in a particular situation, and to write a letter or give a speech suitable to the occasion; and casuistry, a kind of moral and theological game of "What if?": if I were to find myself in such and such a predicament, such a dilemma, what should I do? The question recurs, explic-itly and implicitly, throughout Defoe's prose.

As Defoe entered his twenties, the question became personally pressing. Many of his classmates were preparing for the ministry; he opted instead to enter his father's world of trade, though with a taste for range and risk that his prudent forebear had never displayed. Defoe dealt at one time or another in men's clothing, tobacco, wine; opened and operated a brick and tile factory, and invested capital so audaciously and ill-advisedly that in 1692 he was forced to declare bankruptcy, having incurred the enormous debt of £17,000. "The God that gave me brains will give me bread," Defoe remarked at one point, with characteristic confidence in both the deity and himself. From his late thirties onward, he used those brains to earn bread, for himself and his large family, by writing. He worked with astonishing speed and efficiency, producing by his life's end more than 500 separate works, as well as several pe-riodical series that he wrote (at the rate of two or three essays a week) over the course of many years. Nonetheless, he never quite escaped the financial distresses that had first pushed him into print.

His pen's other impetus was politics. As a Whig and a Dissenter eager to end the reign of the Catholic James II, Defoe had fought as soldier in the abortive Monmouth Rebellion of 1685, and in 1688 celebrated the advent of the Glorious Revolution and William III. He served his new king as secret agent and as author, publishing the phenomenally popular poem *The True-Born Englishman* (1701), whose title sarcastically identifies those "natives" hostile to William on the grounds of his foreign birth (the poem argues, among other things, that their own lineage is far more complex and corrupt than they admit). Defoe's powers as a political advocate were now near full stride, and his knack for irony soon brought him trouble. In his parodic pamphlet *The Shortest Way with Dissenters,* published anonymously in 1702 at the height of Tory hopes for a new assault on Nonconformists, Defoe impersonates a rabid Tory eager to mete out extravagant punishments on the Nonconformists (to whom Defoe himself had felt a lifelong loyalty and tenderness). Neither faction appreciated the joke. After four months in hiding, Defoe was arrested, convicted of libel, and sentenced to prison and to three separate sessions in the pillory, where the crowds (to his surprise) celebrated him as a hero, pelting him with fresh flowers rather than rotten vegetables. The episode initiated a sea change in his affiliations. Disillusioned with Whigs and Dissenters, Defoe secretly aligned himself with the ambitious Tory politician Robert Harley, who in an inspired move had arranged to pay some of Defoe's fines and debts after his release from jail. Commissioned by Harley to create and manage a kind of personal secret service, Defoe traveled extensively, often under assumed names, advocating Tory causes (most notably the Union with Scotland) and reporting on the opposition; he also wrote the widely read *Review* (1704–1713), a thrice-weekly periodical essay intricately calculated to further Harley's interests. After the fall of the

Tories, the intricacy deepened. Under threat of punishment by the new Whig government, Defoe agreed to work as double agent for *them*, by moving among Tory journalists and contributing to Tory papers, but in such ways as to undermine the Tory cause. For the seasoned ironist and impersonator this was irony enough: having worked brilliantly for years to devise Tory propaganda, he was now at pains to dilute it.

At the age of fifty-nine, Defoe hit upon a new way to make impersonation pay. His book *The Strange, Surprising Adventures of Robinson Crusoe* (1719) was the first in a series of long fictions that present themselves as historical fact, as the written reminiscences of people who had actually lived the extraordinary experiences they relate, in books that often bear their fictive names as titles: *Captain Singleton* (1720); *Moll Flanders* (1722); *Colonel Jack* (1722); *Roxana* (1724). In creating these memoirists, Defoe drew on his decades as a journalist. He saturated his stories with particulars (clothing, furniture, tools); his memoirists write a prose that often reads like talk—digressive, fervent, improvisatory. By such strategies he made his tales persuasive. As a genre, the novel has no one inventor, because it absorbs so much (and so variously) from other kinds of texts: newspapers, essays, diaries, financial accounts, religious devotions, conduct manuals. Defoe, though, was perhaps the most astute early orchestrator of such absorptions. Having written in most of his culture's modes, he melded them into a form of fiction that still seems (in keeping with the genre's name) new.

Vicissitude persisted. Having written his last long fiction (*Roxana*) in 1724, Defoe turned his hand to another project. In his *Tour through the Whole Island of Great Britain* (three volumes, 1724–1726), and in other late works, he celebrated British trade as a source of present prosperity and a seedbed of future empire. He died while hiding out from his creditors in the neighborhood of his birth, once again on the run from debt and cut off from his contentious family. The ending feels emblematic. In many ways the most communicative of writers, Defoe often used his powers to study solitude. "Between me and thee there is a great gulf fixed," remarks Robinson Crusoe on his island, quoting scripture: "thee" is the whole world, from which he finds himself definitively sundered. But the phrase might be invoked by almost any speaker in Defoe—characters talking to characters, ghosts to the living, narrators to readers—as they survey the landscape of their own isolation, even in crowded cities. Defoe devoted his writing life to mapping these "great gulfs," to chronicling the energies—political, social, and commercial—by which the mortals of his time and place tried to bridge them, and to seeking out the work of God and Providence in all these prolific, troubled transactions.

 For additional resources on Defoe, go to *The Longman Anthology of British Literature* Web site at www.myliteraturekit.com.

A TRUE RELATION   *A True Relation* was long thought to be Defoe's earliest foray into fiction; it was then discovered to have a firm basis in fact. The original pamphlet was published anonymously; Defoe was not identified as author until 1790. For most of the nineteenth century it was assumed that he had made up the entire story, possibly as publicity for Charles Drelincourt's *Defense against the Fears of Death*, the book that Mrs. Veal repeatedly recommends to her friend Mrs. Bargrave. Shortly after the *Apparition's* first appearance as a pamphlet, in fact, Defoe's text and Drelincourt's were combined into a single, popular volume which went through many printings. In 1895 the Defoe scholar George Aitken published the first independent evidence for the authenticity of the story, if not of the ghost: a Latin memorandum from 1714 recording an interview with the actual Mrs. Bargrave, who adhered (and added) to her narrative nearly a decade after it took place. Other contemporary accounts of her and her story have since been discovered. Defoe, then, was practicing not fiction but journalism, sifting, selecting, and arranging testimony then in circulation, presenting it in the voice of Mrs. Bargrave's "intimate friend," the "very intelligent" Justice of the Peace who professes himself very "affected" by his interview with her (his own status, as historical person or fabricated narrator, has never been established). Mingling "matter of fact" (a recurrent phrase) with matters of mystery, Defoe here manages (as Leslie Stephen once remarked) to embody "in a few lines all the essential particularities of his art."

A True Relation of the Apparition of One Mrs. Veal the Next Day after Her Death to One Mrs. Bargrave at Canterbury the 8th of September, 1705

The Preface

This relation is matter of fact, and attended with such circumstances as may induce any reasonable man to believe it. It was sent by a gentleman, a Justice of Peace at Maidstone in Kent and a very intelligent person, to his friend in London, as it is here worded. Which discourse is attested by a very sober and understanding gentlewoman, a kinswoman of the said gentleman's, who lives in Canterbury within a few doors of the house in which the within named Mrs. Bargrave lives; who believes his kinswoman to be of so discerning a spirit, as not to be put upon by any fallacy. And who positively assured him that the whole matter, as it is here related and laid down, is what is really true, and what she herself had in the same words (as near as may be) from Mrs. Bargrave's own mouth, who she knows had no reason to invent and publish such a story, nor any design to forge and tell a lie, being a woman of much honesty and virtue, and her whole life a course as it were of piety. The use which we ought to make of it is to consider that there is a life to come after this, and a just God who will retribute to everyone according to the deeds done in the body; and therefore, to reflect upon our past course of life we have led in the world, that our time is short and uncertain, and that if we would escape the punishment of the ungodly and receive the reward of the righteous, which is the laying hold of eternal life, we ought for the time to come to turn to God by a speedy repentance, ceasing to do evil and learning to do well: to seek after God early, if happily he may be found of us, and lead such lives for the future as may be well pleasing in his sight.

A Relation of the Apparition of Mrs. Veal

This thing is so rare in all its circumstances, and on so good authority, that my reading and conversation has not given me anything like it; it is fit to gratify the most ingenious and serious inquirer. Mrs. Bargrave is the person to whom Mrs. Veal appeared after her death. She is my intimate friend, and I can avouch for her reputation for these last fifteen or sixteen years on my own knowledge; and I can confirm the good character she had from her youth, to the time of my acquaintance. Though since this relation she is calumniated by some people that are friends to the brother of Mrs. Veal who appeared, who think the relation of this appearance to be a reflection,[1] and endeavor what they can to blast Mrs. Bargrave's reputation and to laugh the story out of countenance. But the circumstances

---

1. I.e., injurious to the family's reputation.

thereof, and the cheerful disposition of Mrs. Bargrave, notwithstanding the un-heard of ill usage of a very wicked husband, there is not the least sign of dejection in her face; nor did I ever hear her let fall a desponding or murmuring expression; nay, not when actually under her husband's barbarity, which I have been witness to, and several other persons of undoubted reputation.[2]

Now you must know that Mrs. Veal was a maiden gentlewoman[3] of about thirty years of age, and for some years last past had been troubled with fits, which were per-ceived coming on her by her leaving off from her discourse very abruptly to some impertinence.[4] She was maintained by an only brother, and kept his house in Dover. She was a very pious woman, and her brother a very sober man to all appearance. But now he does all he can to null or quash the story. Mrs. Veal was intimately ac-quainted with Mrs. Bargrave from her childhood. Mrs. Veal's circumstances were then mean; her father did not take care of his children as he ought, so that they were exposed to hardships. And Mrs. Bargrave in those days had as unkind a father, though she wanted for neither food nor clothing, while Mrs. Veal wanted for both. So that it was in the power of Mrs. Bargrave to be very much her friend in several instances, which mightily endeared Mrs. Veal; insomuch that she would often say, "Mrs. Bargrave, you are not only the best, but the only friend I have in the world, and no circumstances of life shall ever dissolve my friendpship." They would often condole each other's adverse fortunes, and read together *Drelincourt upon Death*[5] and other good books. And so like two Christian friends they comforted each other under their sorrow.

Sometime after, Mr. Veal's friends got him a place in the custom house at Dover, which occasioned Mrs. Veal by little and little to fall off from her intimacy with Mrs. Bargrave, though there was never any such thing as a quarrel; but an in-difference came on by degrees, till at last Mrs. Bargrave had not seen her in two years and a half; though above a twelve month of the time Mrs. Bargrave had been absent from Dover, and this last half year has been in Canterbury about two months of the time, dwelling in a house of her own.

In this house, on the eighth of September last, viz. 1705, she was sitting alone in the forenoon, thinking over her unfortunate life and arguing herself into a due resignation to Providence, though her condition seemed hard. And said she, "I have been provided for hitherto, and doubt not but I shall be still, and am well satisfied that my afflictions shall end when it is most fit for me." And then took up her sewing work, which she had no sooner done but she hears a knocking at the door. She went to see who it was there, and this proved to be Mrs. Veal, her old friend, who was in a riding habit. At that moment of time, the clock struck twelve at noon.

"Madam," says Mrs. Bargrave, "I am surprised to see you, you have been so long a stranger," but told her she was glad to see her and offered to salute[6] her, which Mrs. Veal complied with till their lips almost touched, and then Mrs. Veal drew her hand cross her own eyes and said, "I am not very well," and so waived it. She told Mrs. Bargrave she was going a journey, and had a great mind to see her first. "But," says Mrs. Bargrave, "how came you to take a journey alone? I am amazed at it, because I know you have so fond a brother." "O!" says Mrs. Veal, "I

---

2. The sentence is grammatically incomplete (Defoe sup-plies no verb for the initial subject "the circumstances").
3. "Mrs." (pronounced "Mistress") designated any adult woman, married or unmarried.
4. Irrelevance; digression.

5. I.e., *The Christian's Defense against the Fears of Death*, by Charles Drelincourt, a French Protestant pastor and prolific devotional writer who published the book in 1651; the first English translation appeared in 1675.
6. Kiss.

gave my brother the slip and came away, because I had so great a mind to see you before I took my journey." So Mrs. Bargrave went in with her, into another room within the first, and Mrs. Veal sat herself down in an elbow-chair, in which Mrs. Bargrave was sitting when she heard Mrs. Veal knock. Then says Mrs. Veal, "My dear friend, I am come to renew our old friendship again, and to beg your pardon for my breach of it, and if you can forgive me you are one of the best of women." "O!" says Mrs. Bargrave, "don't mention such a thing. I have not had an uneasy thought about it; I can easily forgive it." "What did you think of me?" says Mrs. Veal. Says Mrs. Bargrave, "I thought you were like the rest of the world, and that prosperity had made you forget yourself and me." Then Mrs. Veal reminded Mrs. Bargrave of the many friendly offices she did her in former days, and much of the conversation they had with each other in the time of their adversity: what books they read, and what comfort in particular they received from *Drelincourt's Book of Death*, which was the best, she said, on that subject ever wrote. She also mentioned Dr. Sherlock,[7] and two Dutch books which were translated, wrote upon death, and several others. But Drelincourt, she said, had the clearest notions of death and of the future state of any who have handled that subject. Then she asked Mrs. Bargrave whether she had Drelincourt. She said, "Yes." Says Mrs. Veal, "Fetch it," and so Mrs. Bargrave goes upstairs and brings it down. Says Mrs. Veal, "Dear Mrs. Bargrave, if the eyes of our faith were as open as the eyes of our body, we should see numbers of angels about us for our guard. The notions we have of Heaven now are nothing like what it is, as Drelincourt says. Therefore be comforted under your afflictions, and believe that the Almighty has a particular regard to you, and that your afflictions are marks of God's favor. And when they have done the business they were sent for, they shall be removed from you. And believe me, my dear friend, believe what I say to you, one minute of future happiness will infinitely reward you for all your sufferings. For I can never believe" (and claps her hand upon her knee, with a great deal of earnestness, which indeed ran through all her discourse) "that ever God will suffer you to spend all your days in this afflicted state. But be assured that your afflictions shall leave you, or you them, in a short time." She spake in that pathetical and heavenly manner, that Mrs. Bargrave wept several times, she was so deeply affected with it. Then Mrs. Veal mentioned Dr. Horneck's *Ascetic*,[8] at the end of which he gives an account of the lives of the primitive Christians. Their pattern she recommended to our imitation, and said their conversation was not like this of our age. "For now" (says she) "there is nothing but frothy vain discourse, which is far different from theirs. Theirs was to edification, and to build one another up in the faith. So that they were not as we are, nor are we as they are. But," said she, "we might do as they did. There was a hearty friendship among them, but where is it now to be found?" Says Mrs. Bargrave, "'Tis hard indeed to find a true friend in these days." Says Mrs. Veal, "Mr. Norris[9] has a fine copy of verses called *Friendship in Perfection*, which I wonderfully admire. Have you seen the book?" says Mrs. Veal. "No," says Mrs. Bargrave, "but I have the verses of my own writing out." "Have you?" says Mrs. Veal, "then fetch them." Which she did from above stairs, and offered them to Mrs. Veal to read,

---

7. William Sherlock, Protestant divine and author of the widely read *Practical Discourse upon Death* (1689).

8. Anthony Horneck, clergyman and author of *The Happy Ascetic* (1681).
9. John Norris, a clergyman, philosopher, and poet.

who refused, and waived the thing, saying holding down her head would make it ache, and then desired Mrs. Bargrave to read them to her, which she did. As they were admiring friendship, Mrs. Veal said, "Dear Mrs. Bargrave, I shall love you forever. In the verses, there is twice used the word Elysium. Ah!" says Mrs. Veal, "these poets have such names for heaven." She would often draw her hand cross her own eyes, and say, "Mrs. Bargrave, don't you think I am mightily impaired by my fits?" "No," says Mrs. Bargrave, "I think you look as well as ever I knew you."

After all this discourse, which the apparition put in words much finer than Mrs. Bargrave said she could pretend to, and was much more than she can remember (for it cannot be thought that an hour and three quarters' conversation could all be retained, though the main of it she thinks she does), she said to Mrs. Bargrave she would have her write a letter to her brother, and tell him she would have him give rings to such and such, and that there was a purse of gold in her cabinet, and that she would have two broad pieces given to her cousin Watson. Talking at this rate, Mrs. Bargrave thought that a fit was coming upon her,[1] and so placed herself in a chair just before her knees, to keep her from falling to the ground if her fits should occasion it; for the elbow chair she thought would keep her from falling on either side. And to divert Mrs. Veal, as she thought, she took hold of her gown sleeve several times, and commended it. Mrs. Veal told her it was a scoured[2] silk, and newly made up. But for all this Mrs. Veal persisted in her request, and told Mrs. Bargrave she must not deny her. And she would have her tell her brother all their conversation, when she had an opportunity. "Dear Mrs. Veal," says Mrs. Bargrave, "this seems so impertinent that I cannot tell how to comply with it; and what a mortifying story will our conversation be to a young gentleman?" "Well," says Mrs. Veal, "I must not be denied." "Why," says Mrs. Bargrave, "'tis much better methinks to do it yourself." "No," says Mrs. Veal, "though it seems impertinent to you now, you will see more reason for it hereafter." Mrs. Bargrave then, to satisfy her importunity, was going to fetch a pen and ink; but Mrs. Veal said, "Let it alone now, and do it when I am gone; but you must be sure to do it." Which was one of the last things she enjoined her at parting; and so she promised her.

Then Mrs. Veal asked for Mrs. Bargrave's daughter. She said she was not at home. "But if you have a mind to see her," says Mrs. Bargrave, "I'll send for her." "Do," says Mrs. Veal. On which she left her, and went to a neighbor's to send for her. And by the time Mrs. Bargrave was returning, Mrs. Veal was got without the door in the street, in the face of the beast-market on a Saturday (which is market day), and stood ready to part as soon as Mrs. Bargrave came to her. She asked her why she was in such haste. She said she must be going, though perhaps she might not go her journey till Monday. And told Mrs. Bargrave she hoped she should see her again at her cousin Watson's before she went whither she was a-going. Then she said she would take her leave of her, and walked from Mrs. Bargrave in her view till a turning interrupted the sight of her, which was three quarters after one in the afternoon.

Mrs. Veal died the 7th of September at 12 o'clock at noon, of her fits, and had not above four hours' senses before her death, in which time she received the

---

1. I.e., Mrs. Veal.   2. Polished; cleaned with detergent.

sacrament. The next day after Mrs. Veal's appearing being Sunday, Mrs. Bargrave was mightily indisposed with a cold and a sore throat, that she could not go out that day. But on Monday morning she sends a person to Captain Watson's to know if Mrs. Veal were there. They wondered at Mrs. Bargrave's inquiry, and sent her word that she was not there, nor was she expected. At this answer Mrs. Bargrave told the maid she had certainly mistook the name, or made some blunder. And though she was ill, she put on her hood and went herself to Captain Watson's, though she knew none of the family, to see if Mrs. Veal was there or not. They said they wondered at her asking, for that she had not been in town; they were sure, if she had, she would have been there. Says Mrs. Bargrave, "I am sure she was with me on Saturday almost two hours." They said it was impossible, for they must have seen her if she had. In comes Captain Watson, while they were in dispute, and said that Mrs. Veal was certainly dead, and her escutcheons were making.[3] This strangely surprised Mrs. Bargrave, who went to the person immediately who had the care of them, and found it true. Then she related the whole story to Captain Watson's family, and what gown she had on, and how striped. And that Mrs. Veal told her it was scoured. Then Mrs. Watson cried out, "You have seen her indeed, for none knew but Mrs. Veal and myself that the gown was scoured." And Mrs. Watson owned that she described the gown exactly; "for," said she, "I helped her to make it up." This, Mrs. Watson blazed all about the town, and avouched the demonstration of the truth of Mrs. Bargrave's seeing Mrs. Veal's apparition. And Captain Watson carried two gentlemen immediately to Mrs. Bargrave's house, to hear the relation from her own mouth. And then it spread so fast that gentlemen and persons of quality, the judicious and skeptical part of the world, flocked in upon her, which at last became such a task that she was forced to go out of the way. For they were, in general, extremely satisfied of the truth of the thing, and plainly saw that Mrs. Bargrave was no hypochondriac, for she always appears with such a cheerful air and pleasing mien that she has gained the favor and esteem of all the gentry. And it's thought a great favor if they can but get the relation from her own mouth. I should have told you before that Mrs. Veal told Mrs. Bargrave that her sister and brother-in-law were just come down from London to see her. Says Mrs. Bargrave, "How came you to order matters so strangely?" "It could not be helped," said Mrs. Veal. And her sister and brother did come to see her, and entered the town of Dover just as Mrs. Veal was expiring. Mrs. Bargrave asked her whether she would drink some tea. Says Mrs. Veal, "I do not care if I do. But I'll warrant this mad fellow" (meaning Mrs. Bargrave's husband) "has broke all your trinkets." "But," says Mrs. Bargrave, "I'll get something to drink in for all that." But Mrs. Veal waived it, and said, "It is no matter, let it alone," and so it passed.

All the time I sat with Mrs. Bargrave, which was some hours, she recollected fresh sayings of Mrs. Veal. And one material thing more she told Mrs. Bargrave, that old Mr. Breton allowed Mrs. Veal ten pounds a year, which was a secret, and unknown to Mrs. Bargrave till Mrs. Veal told it her. Mrs. Bargrave never varies in her story, which puzzles those who doubt of the truth, or are unwilling to believe it. A servant in a neighbor's yard adjoining to Mrs. Bargrave's house heard her talking to somebody an hour of the time Mrs. Veal was with her. Mrs. Bargrave went out to her next neighbors the very moment she parted with Mrs. Veal, and told her what

---

3. Funeral ornaments were being prepared.

ravishing conversation she had with an old friend, and told the whole of it. *Drelincourt's Book of Death* is, since this happened, bought up strangely. And it is to be observed that notwithstanding all this trouble and fatigue Mrs. Bargrave has undergone upon this account, she never took the value of a farthing, nor suffered her daughter to take anything of anybody, and therefore can have no interest in telling the story.

But Mr. Veal does what he can to stifle the matter, and said he would see Mrs. Bargrave. But yet it is certain matter fact that he has been at Captain Watson's since the death of his sister, and yet never went near Mrs. Bargrave. And some of his friends report her to be a great liar, and that she knew of Mr. Breton's ten pounds a year. But the person who pretends to say so has the reputation of a notorious liar among persons which I know to be of undoubted repute. Now Mr. Veal is more a gentleman than to say she lies, but says a bad husband has crazed her. But she needs only to present herself, and it will effectually confute that pretense. Mr. Veal says he asked his sister on her deathbed whether she had a mind to dispose of anything, and she said, "No." Now, what the things which Mrs. Veal's apparition would have disposed of were so trifling, and nothing of justice aimed at in their disposal, that the design of it appears to me to be only in order to make Mrs. Bargrave, so to demonstrate the truth of her appearance as to satisfy the world of the reality thereof, as to what she had seen and heard, and to secure her reputation among the reasonable and understanding part of mankind. And then again, Mr. Veal owns that there was a purse of gold; but it was not found in her cabinet, but in a comb box. This looks improbable, for that Mrs. Watson owned that Mrs. Veal was so very careful of the key of her cabinet that she would trust nobody with it. And if so, no doubt she would not trust her gold out of it. And Mrs. Veal's often drawing her hand over her eyes, and asking Mrs. Bargrave whether her fits had not impaired her, looks to me as if she did it on purpose to remind Mrs. Bargrave of her fits, to prepare her not to think it strange that she should put her upon writing to her brother to dispose of rings and gold, which looked so much like a dying person's bequest. And it took accordingly with Mrs. Bargrave, as the effect of her fits coming upon her, and was one of the many instances of her wonderful love to her, and care of her, that she should not be affrighted. Which indeed appears in her whole management; particularly in her coming to her in the daytime, waiving the salutation, and when she was alone; and then the manner of her parting, to prevent a second attempt to salute her.

Now, why Mr. Veal should think this relation a reflection (as 'tis plain he does by his endeavoring to stifle it), I can't imagine, because the generality believe her to be a good spirit, her discourse was so heavenly. Her two great errands were to comfort Mrs. Bargrave in her affliction and to ask her forgiveness for her breach of friendship, and with a pious discourse to encourage her. So that after all, to suppose that Mrs. Bargrave could hatch such an invention as this from Friday noon till Saturday noon (supposing that she knew of Mrs. Veal's death the very first moment) without jumbling circumstances, and without any interest too—she must be more witty, fortunate, and wicked too than any indifferent person, I dare say, will allow. I asked Mrs. Bargrave several times if she was sure she felt the gown. She answered modestly, "If my senses be to be relied on, I am sure of it." I asked her if she heard a sound when she clapped her hand upon her knee. She said she did not remember she did. And she said, "She appeared to be as much a substance as I did, who talked with her. And I may," said she, "be as soon persuaded that your apparition is talking to me now, as that I did not really see her. For I was under no manner of fear; I received her as a friend, and parted with her as such. I would not," says she, "give one farthing to make anyone believe it. I have no interest in it; nothing but trouble is entailed upon me for a long time for aught that I know. And had it not come to light by accident, it would never have been made public." But now, she says, she will make her own private use of it, and keep herself out of the way as much as she can. And so she has done since. She says she had a gentleman who came thirty miles to her to hear the relation, and that she had told it to a room full of people at a time. Several particular gentlemen have had the story from Mrs. Bargrave's own mouth.

This thing has very much affected me, and I am as well satisfied as I am of the best grounded matter of fact. And why should we dispute matter of fact, because we cannot solve things of which we can have no certain or demonstrative notions, seems strange to me. Mrs. Bargrave's authority and sincerity alone would have been undoubted in any other case.

1706   1706

from A Journal of the Plague Year
Being Observations or Memorials of the Most Remarkable Occurrences, as Well Public as Private, Which Happened in London during the Last Great Visitation in 1665[1]

[AT THE BURIAL PIT]

I went all the first part of the time freely about the streets, though not so freely as to run myself into apparent danger, except when they dug the great pit in the church-yard of our parish of Aldgate; a terrible pit it was, and I could not resist my curiosity to go and see it. As near as I may judge, it was about 40 foot in length, and about 15 or 16 foot broad; and at the time I first looked at it, about nine foot deep; but it was said they dug it near 20 foot deep afterwards, in one part of it, till they could go no deeper for the water: for they had, it seems, dug several large pits before this, for though the plague was long a-coming to our parish, yet when it did come, there was no parish in or about London where it raged with such violence as in the two parishes of Aldgate and Whitechapel.

I say they had dug several pits in another ground, when the distemper began to spread in our parish, and especially when the dead carts began to go about, which was not in our parish till the beginning of August. Into these pits they had put perhaps 50 or 60 bodies each; then they made larger holes, wherein they buried all that the cart brought in a week, which by the middle to the end of August, came to from 200 to 400 a week; and they could not well dig them larger, because of the order of the magistrates, confining them to leave no bodies within six foot of the surface; and the water coming on, at about 17 or 18 foot, they could not well, I say, put more in

---

1. In the early 1720s, London found itself once again threatened with the prospect of bubonic plague. Defoe responded with two long pieces of prose: a manual of preventive measures called *Due Preparations for the Plague* (1720), and a histor-ical fiction thoroughly researched and deeply grounded in historical facts. The text's purported narrator—already dead by the time his book is published—presents himself as recasting in retrospect the journal entries he wrote during that terrible year, in the hope that they may benefit future generations. Designated only by his initials, "H. F.," he is probably modeled in part on the author's uncle Henry Foe, who like "H. F." was a London saddler who lived in the parish of Aldgate.

one pit; but now at the beginning of September, the plague raging in a dreadful manner, and the number of burials in our parish increasing to more than was ever buried in any parish about London of no larger extent, they ordered this dreadful gulf to be dug; for such it was, rather than a pit.

They had supposed this pit would have supplied them for a month or more, when they dug it, and some blamed the church wardens for suffering such a frightful thing, telling them they were making preparations to bury the whole parish, and the like; but time made it appear, the church wardens knew the condition of the parish better than they did; for the pit being finished the 4th of September, I think, they began to bury in it the 6th, and by the 20th, which was just two weeks, they had thrown into it 1,114 bodies, when they were obliged to fill it up, the bodies being then come to lie within six foot of the surface: I doubt not but there may be some ancient persons alive in the parish, who can justify the fact of this, and are able to show even in what part of the churchyard the pit lay, better than I can; the mark of it also was many years to be seen in the churchyard on the surface lying in length, parallel with the passage which goes by the west wall of the churchyard, out of Houndsditch, and turns east again into Whitechapel, coming out near the Three Nuns Inn.

It was about the 10th of September, that my curiosity led, or rather drove me to go and see this pit again, when there had been near 400 people buried in it; and I was not content to see it in the daytime, as I had done before; for then there would have been nothing to have been seen but the loose earth; for all the bodies that were thrown in were immediately covered with earth, by those they called the buriers, which at other times were called bearers;[2] but I resolved to go in the night and see some of them thrown in.

There was a strict order to prevent people coming to those pits, and that was only to prevent infection: but after some time, that order was more necessary, for people that were infected, and near their end, and delirious also, would run to those pits wrapped in blankets or rugs and throw themselves in and, as they said, bury themselves: I cannot say that the officers suffered any willingly to lie there; but I have heard that in a great pit in Finsbury, in the parish of Cripplegate, it lying open then to the fields (for it was not then walled about) came and threw themselves in, and expired there, before they threw any earth upon them; and that when they came to bury others, and found them there, they were quite dead, though not cold.

This may serve a little to describe the dreadful condition of that day, though it is impossible to say anything that is able to give a true idea of it to those who did not see it, other than this; that it was indeed very, very, very dreadful, and such as no tongue can express.

I got admittance into the churchyard by being acquainted with the sexton[3] who attended, who though he did not refuse me at all, yet earnestly persuaded me not to go; telling me very seriously, for he was a good religious and sensible man, that it was indeed their business and duty to venture, and to run all hazards; and that in it they might hope to be preserved; but that I had no apparent call to it, but my own curios-

2. H. F. combines two categories: the buriers put the dead bodies into the pits, arranging them in order to conserve space, and covering them with lime in order to quicken decomposition. The bearers, by contrast, handled bodies living and dead: during the day they delivered the infected to the plague-hospitals; by night they collected corpses for the pits.
3. Caretaker of the church and graveyard.

ity, which, he said, he believed I would not pretend was sufficient to justify my running that hazard. I told him I had been pressed in my mind to go, and that perhaps it might be an instructing sight that might not be without its uses. "Nay," says the good man, "if you will venture upon that score, '*Name of God go in*; for depend upon it, 'twill be a sermon to you, it may be, the best that ever you heard in your life. 'Tis a speaking sight," says he, "and has a voice with it, and a loud one, to call us all to repentance." And with that he opened the door and said, "Go, if you will."

His discourse had shocked my resolution a little, and I stood wavering for a good while; but just at that interval I saw two links[4] come over from the end of the Minories,[5] and heard the bellman,[6] and then appeared a dead cart, as they called it, coming over the streets so I could no longer resist my desire of seeing it, and went in: there was nobody, as I could perceive at first, in the churchyard or going into it, but the buriers and the fellow that drove the cart, or rather led the horse and cart; but when they came up to the pit, they saw a man go to and again, muffled up in a brown cloak and making motions with his hands, under his cloak, as if he

4. I.e., boys carrying torches ("links"), who for a fee led people through the streets at night.
5. A street.

6. In ordinary times, the bellman announced the time and weather as he made his way through the streets at night; in plague time, he rang his bell to alert people that the cart burying the dead was approaching.

John Dunstall, *Scenes from the Plague in London*, 1665. The sequence tracks the course of corpses, from death within the city to burial in the plague-pits outside the city's walls.

was in a great agony; and the buriers immediately gathered about him, supposing he was one of those poor delirious or desperate creatures that used to pretend,[7] as I have said, to bury themselves. He said nothing as he walked about, but two or three times groaned very deeply, and loud, and sighed as he would break his heart.

When the buriers came up to him they soon found he was neither a person infected and desperate, as I have observed above, or a person distempered in mind, but one oppressed with a dreadful weight of grief indeed, having his wife and several of his children, all in the cart that was just come in with him, and he followed in an agony and excess of sorrow. He mourned heartily, as it was easy to see, but with a kind of masculine grief that could not give itself vent by tears, and calmly desiring the buriers to let him alone, said he would only see the bodies thrown in, and go away, so they left importuning him; but no sooner was the cart turned round, and the bodies shot into the pit promiscuously, which was a surprise to him, for he at least expected they would have been decently laid in, though indeed he was afterwards convinced that was impractible; I say, no sooner did he see the sight, but he cried out aloud unable to contain himself; I could not hear what he said, but he went backward two or three steps, and fell down in a swoon: the buriers ran to him and took him up, and in a little while he came to himself, and they led him away to the Pye Tavern over-against the end of Houndsditch, where, it seems, the man was known, and where they took care of

7. Attempt.

him. He looked into the pit again, as he went away, but the buriers had covered the bodies so immediately with throwing in earth that, though there was light enough, for there were lanterns and candles in them placed all night round the sides of the pit, upon the heaps of earth, seven or eight, or perhaps more, yet nothing could seen.

This was a mournful scene indeed, and affected me almost as much as the rest; but the other was awful, and full of terror. The cart had in it sixteen or seventeen bodies; some were wrapped up in linen sheets, some in rugs, some little other than naked, or so loose that what covering they had fell from them in the shooting out of the cart, and they fell quite naked among the rest; but the matter was not much to them, or the indecency much to anyone else, seeing they were all dead, and were to be huddled together into the common grave of mankind, as we may call it, for here was no difference made, but poor and rich went together; there was no other way of burials, neither was it possible there should, for coffins were not to be had for the prodigious numbers that fell in such a calamity as this.

[Encounter with a Waterman]

Much about the same time I walked out into the fields towards Bow; for I had a great mind to see how things were managed in the river, and among the ships; and as I had some concern in shipping, I had a notion that it had been one of the best ways of securing oneself from the infection to have retired into a ship, and musing how to satisfy my curiosity in that point, I turned away over the fields, from Bow to Bromley, and down to Blackwall, to the Stairs, which are there for landing or taking water.[8]

Here I saw a poor man walking on the bank, or seawall, as they call it, by himself. I walked a while also about, seeing the houses all shut up;[9] at last I fell into some talk, at a distance, with this poor man; first I asked him, how people did thereabouts? "Alas, Sir!" says he, "almost all desolate; all dead or sick: here are very few families in this part, or in that village," pointing at Poplar, "where half of them are not dead already, and the rest sick." Then he pointed to one house. "There they are all dead," said he, "and the house stands open; nobody dares go into it. A poor thief," says he, "ventured in to steal something, but he paid dear for his theft; for he was carried to the churchyard too last night." Then he pointed to several other houses. "There," says he, "they are all dead; the man and his wife, and five children. There," says he, "they are shut up; you see a watchman at the door," and so of other houses. "Why," says I, "What do you here all alone?" "Why," says he, "I am a poor desolate man; it has pleased God I am not yet visited,[1] though my family is, and one of my children dead." "How do you mean then," said I, "that you are not visited?" "Why," says he, "that's my house," pointing to a very little low boarded house, "and there my poor wife and two children live," said he, "if they may be said to live; for my wife and one of the children are visited, but I do not come at them." And with

---

8. H.F.'s walk takes him to the bank of the river Thames.
9. By London ordinances, all houses in which an inhabitant had become infected were "shut up," with the surviving

residents confined inside.
1. Infected.

that word I saw the tears run very plentifully down his face; and so they did down mine too, I assure you.

But said I, "Why do you not come at them? How can you abandon your own flesh, and blood?" "Oh, Sir!" says he, "the Lord forbid; I do not abandon them; I work for them as much as I am able, and blessed be the Lord, I keep them from want," and with that I observed, he lifted up his eyes to Heaven, with a countenance that presently told me, I had happened on a man that was no hypocrite, but a serious, religious good man, and his ejaculation was an expression of thankfulness, that in such a condition as he was in, he should be able to say his family did not want. "Well," says I, "honest man, that is a great mercy as things go now with the poor: but how do you live then, and how are you kept from the dreadful calamity that is now upon us all?" "Why Sir," says he, "I am a waterman,[2] and there's my boat," says he, "and the boat serves me for a house; I work in it in the day, and I sleep in it in the night; and what I get, I lay down upon that stone," says he, showing me a broad stone on the other side of the street, a good way from his house, "and then," says he, "I halloo, and call to them till I make them hear; and they come and fetch it."

"Well friend," says I, "but how can you get any money as a waterman? Does anybody go by water these times?" "Yes Sir," says he, "in the way I am employed there does. Do you see there," says he, "five ships lie at anchor," pointing down the river, a good way below the town, "and do you see," says he, "eight or ten ships lie at the chain, there, and at anchor yonder," pointing above the town. "All those ships have families on board, of their merchants and owners, and such like, who have locked themselves up, and live on board, close shut in, for fear of the infection; and I tend on them to fetch things for them, carry letters, and do what is absolutely necessary, that they may not be obliged to come on shore; and every night I fasten my boat on board one of the ship's boats, and there I sleep by myself, and blessed be God, I am preserved hitherto."

"Well," said I, "friend, but will they let you come on board, after you have been on shore here, when this is such a terrible place, and so infected as it is?"

"Why, as to that," said he, "I very seldom go up the ship side, but deliver what I bring to their boat, or lie by the side, and they hoist it on board; if I did, I think they are in no danger from me, for I never go into any house on shore, or touch anybody, no, not of my own family; but I fetch provisions for them."

"Nay," says I, "but that may be worse, for you must have those provisions of somebody or other; and since all this part of the town is so infected, it is dangerous so much as to speak with anybody; for this village," said I, "is as it were, the beginning of London, though it be at some distance from it."

"That is true," added he, "but you do not understand me right, I do not buy provisions for them here; I row up to Greenwich and buy fresh meat there, and sometimes I row down the river to Woolwich and buy there; then I go to single farm houses on the Kentish side, where I am known, and buy fowls and eggs and butter, and bring to the ships, as they direct me, sometimes one, sometimes the other; I seldom come on shore here; and I came now only to call to my wife, and

2. Ferryman.

hear how my little family do, and give them a little money, which I received last night."

"Poor man!" said I, "and how much hast thou gotten for them?"

"I have gotten four shillings," said he, "which is a great sum, as things go now with poor men; but they have given me a bag of bread too, and a salt fish and some flesh; so all helps out."

"Well," said I, "and have you given it them yet?"

"No," said he, "but I have called, and my wife has answered, that she cannot come out yet, but in half an hour she hopes to come, and I am waiting for her: poor woman!" says he, "she is brought sadly down; she has a swelling, and it is broke, and I hope she will recover;[3] but I fear the child will die; but *it is the Lord!*"—Here he stopped, and wept very much.

"Well, honest friend," said I, "thou hast a sure comforter, if thou hast brought thyself to be resigned to the will of God; He is dealing with us all in judgment."

"Oh, Sir," says he, "it is infinite mercy, if any of us are spared; and who am I to repine!"

"Sayest thou so," said I, "and how much less is my faith than thine?" And here my heart smote me, suggesting how much better this poor man's foundation was, on which he stayed in the danger, than mine; that he had nowhere to fly; that he had a family to bind him to attendance, which I had not; and mine was mere presumption, his a true dependence, and a courage resting on God: and yet, that he used all possible caution for his safety.

I turned a little way from the man, while these thoughts engaged me, for indeed, I could no more refrain from tears than he.

At length, after some farther talk, the poor woman opened the door, and called, "Robert, Robert." He answered and bid her stay a few moments, and he would come; so he ran down the common stairs to his boat, and fetched up a sack in which was the provisions he had brought from the ships; and when he returned, he hallooed again; then he went to the great stone which he showed me, and emptied the sack, and laid all out, everything by themselves, and then retired; and his wife came with a little boy to fetch them away; and he called, and said, such a captain had sent such a thing, and such a captain such a thing, and at the end adds, "God has sent it all, give thanks to Him." When the poor woman had taken up all, she was so weak, she could not carry it at once in, *though the weight was not much neither*; so she left the biscuit which was in a little bag and left a little boy to watch it till she came again.

"Well, but," says I to him, "did you leave her the four shillings too, which you said was your week's pay?"

"YES, YES," says he, "you shall hear her own it." So he calls again, "Rachel, Rachel,"[4] which it seems was her name, "did you take up the money?" "YES," said she. "How much was it?" said he. "Four shillings and a groat," said she. "Well, well," says he, "the Lord keep you all"; and so he turned to go away.

As I could not refrain contributing tears to this man's story, so neither could I refrain my charity for his assistance; so I called him. "Hark thee friend," said I, "come hither; for I believe thou art in health, that I may venture thee." So I pulled

---

3. The plague afflicted its victims with painful swellings ("buboes"); if the swelling broke open, it was thought to presage recovery.

4. The name evokes Jeremiah 31.15: "Rachel weeping for her children refused to be comforted."

out my hand, which was in my pocket before. "Here," says I, "go and call thy Rachel once more, and give her a little more comfort from me. God will never forsake a family that trust in him as thou dost." So I gave him four other shillings, and bade him go lay them on the stone and call his wife.

I have not words to express the poor man's thankfulness, neither could he express it himself, but by tears running down his face; he called his wife, and told her God had moved the heart of a stranger, upon hearing their condition, to give them all that money; and a great deal more such as that he said to her. The woman too made signs of the like thankfulness, as well to Heaven, as to me, and joyfully picked it up; and I parted with no money all that year that I thought better bestowed.

1722

PERSPECTIVES
Reading Papers

Shakespeare never read a newspaper. In the early seventeenth century, the news was purveyed irregularly and improvisatorily. A breaking story or a sensational event might prompt a spate of ballads, broadsides, and bulletins, which would then abate until the next big thing hove into view. The news periodical, nascent on the Continent during Shakespeare's lifetime, arrived in England in 1620 in the form of English-language news sheets dispatched from Amsterdam. London publishers quickly took up the enterprise, to their considerable profit. Shakespeare's caustic contemporary Ben Jonson lived to witness their innovation; he promptly forecast an imminent glut of cheap and worthless information—fearing, with reason, that the new medium would supplant the theater as the public's favored oracle.

Even Jonson, though, could not have foreseen the quantities of print that would pour from presses decades later during the Civil Wars, when the instability of authority allowed innumerable newsbooks to appear, supporting every party in the conflict. During the Interregnum and Restoration, government tried through strict licensing laws to limit the flow and narrow the range of newsprint, but whenever those laws lapsed, innovations abounded: the first daily reports on proceedings in the House of Commons (1680), the first English newspaper outside London (1701), the first daily newspaper (1702), the first weekly journals (1713), melding the news with a miscellany of other departments. At the centennial of Shakespeare's death, London was producing some sixteen newspapers; a century later Britain possessed more than 350, in addition to legions of other periodicals purveying opinion and advice. The newspaper, the periodical essay, and the magazine had become confirmed habits in the lives of almost everyone who could read, and even of many who could not, since the papers were often read aloud, their contents discussed and debated, in public gathering places and household circles.

The periodical was a creature of the seventeenth century and a staple of the eighteenth. It punctuated the calendar with a new print pulse, and imparted to its readership a new sense of moving together in synchrony, in a rhythm that paradoxically combined the solitary and the social, the private and the public. The "mass ceremony" of reading the newspaper is generally performed (as the historian Benedict Anderson has observed) in "privacy, in the lair of the skull. Yet each communicant is well aware that the ceremony he performs is being replicated simultaneously by thousands (or millions) of others, of whose existence he is confident, yet of whose identity he has not the slightest notion." The periodical press, then, gave its readers a new way of seeing the world, and of seeing themselves in the world, as private beings and public entities; it prompted them (in Anderson's phrase) to imagine themselves as a community.

Monarchs and politicians tried hard to control the press, to dictate its views and to contain its criticisms, but in Britain the phenomenon proved too large for such arrant limitation. The news sheets and the essays helped create a new arena of political thought and action, separate from the older power centers of Court and Parliament, a public sphere of newly engaged readers who increasingly valued and deployed their own capacity to form collective opinions, and who increasingly expected their opinions to affect events. The freedom and copiousness of the press became a national boast, and abetted Britons in a conviction they were already cultivating: that they were participants in an ongoing narrative of commerce and taste, politeness, politics, and empire, protagonists in a story with numberless installments and no foreseeable end, unfolding at the center of the world.

Each newspaper in this section is introduced at its first appearance.

 For additional selections from seventeenth-and eighteenth-century newspapers and periodicals, go to *The Longman Anthology of British Literature* Web site at www.myliteraturekit.com.

⦁—⦁ ⌦◆⌫ ⦁—⦁

News and Comment

If the seventeenth century gave birth to the seething enterprise of print journalism, it also ushered in still-lingering distinctions and confusions as to what newspapers ought to be, and do. Most papers proudly declared their objectivity, yet at the same time they plainly manifested their partisan sympathies in their reportage and their prose. The division between news and opinion was rarely sharp, but in the early 1700s, opinion found fuller expression in periodicals like Defoe's *Review*, which more or less took for granted that readers had gathered their news elsewhere, and offered instead a running commentary on events.

MERCURIUS PUBLICUS (1660–1663) During the Civil Wars, journalism gave voice to different factions; afterwards, it became the instrument of consolidated power. During the Interregnum, Cromwell controlled the news through his chief journalist Marchamont Nedham; strict licensing laws ensured that Nedham's *Public Intelligencer* (published every Monday) and *Mercurius Politicus* (every Thursday) were virtually the sole print sources for fresh information. (Mercury, the speedy messenger-god, remained throughout the century the favorite titular deity of the English press; more than a hundred periodicals bore his name). In 1660 the chief architects of the Restoration dismissed Nedham and supplanted him with their own advocate, Henry Muddiman (1629–1692). Taking over Nedham's newsbooks (now pointedly renamed the *Kingdom's Intelligencer* and *Mercurius Publicus*), Muddiman denounced the old regime and heralded the new with the zeal that would maintain him for nearly three decades, despite stiff competition from rival newsmen, as a favored journalist with the House of Stuart, right up to its fall from power in the 1688 Revolution.

from Mercurius Publicus
24–31 January 1661
[ANNIVERSARY OF THE REGICIDE]

London

This day January 30 (we need say no more but name the day of the month) was doubly observed, not only by a solemn fast, sermons, and prayers at every parish church, for the precious blood of our late pious sovereign King Charles the First, of ever glorious memory; but also by public dragging of those odious carcasses of Oliver Cromwell, Henry Ireton, and John Bradshaw to Tyburn.[1] On Monday night Cromwell and Ireton in two several carts were drawn to Holborn from Westminster, after they were digged up on Saturday last, and the next morning Bradshaw; today they were drawn upon sledges to Tyburn, all the way (as before from Westminster) the outcry of the people went along with them. When these their carcasses were at Tyburn, they were pulled out of their coffins and hanged at the several angles of the triple tree,[2] where they hung till the sun was set; after which they were taken down,

---

1. Ireton (1611–1651) and Bradshaw (1602–1659) had played key roles in the trial, condemnation, and execution of Charles I. Tyburn had been for nearly three centuries the site for the public execution of common criminals (Charles had been dispatched on the grounds of the royal palace at Whitehall).
2. Tyburn's notorious "triangular gallows," whose three long horizontal beams could support as many as 21 hangings at a time.

their heads cut off, and their loathsome trunks thrown into a deep hole under the gallows. And now we cannot forget how at Cambridge when Cromwell first set up for a rebel, he rode under the gallows where, his horse just curvetting,[3] threw his cursed Highness out of the saddle just under the gallows (as if he had been turned off[4] the ladder), the spectators then observing the place, and rather presaging the present work of this day, than the monstrous villainies of this day twelve years.[5] But he is now again thrown under the gallows (never more to be digged up) and there we leave him.

LONDON GAZETTE (1665–PRESENT) New media are often modeled on old. In its first decades, English print journalism took the shape of a newsbook (actually a pamphlet) because that was a format with which printers and consumers had been long familiar. The *London Gazette* was something visibly different: the first news*paper*, a single sheet printed in double columns. Containment was the paper's whole point, not only in format but in content. Published twice weekly, "by authority" (as it proclaimed on its masthead), it remained for thirteen years the only printed news source the English were legally permitted to read, and it presented only that news which its government masters deemed fit for wide publication: full accounts of Continental politics, carefully trimmed treatments of domestic doings, all couched in a dry prose that deliberately eschewed the popular (and sometimes rabble-rousing) effects of the paper's midcentury forebears. The *Gazette* broke briefly from its self-constraints in the number for 10 September 1666, when the Great Fire of London had forced the printer to set up his press in the open air, and the correspondents reported very local events with considerable accuracy and unaccustomed fervor.

from The London Gazette
10 September 1666
[THE FIRE OF LONDON[1]]

Whitehall, September 8

The ordinary course of this paper having been interrupted by a sad and lamentable accident of fire lately happened in the City of London, it hath been thought fit for satisfying the minds of so many of His Majesty's good subjects, who must needs be concerned for the issue of so great an accident, to give this short, but true account of it.

On the second instant[2] at one of the clock in the morning there happened to break out a sad and deplorable fire, in Pudding Lane near New Fish Street, which falling out at that hour of the night, and in a quarter of the town so close-built with wooden pitched[3] houses, spread itself so far before day, and with such distraction to the inhabitants and neighbors, that care was not taken for the timely preventing the further diffusion of it by pulling down houses, as ought to have been; so that this lamentable fire in a short time became too big to be mastered by any engines or working near it. It fell out most unhappily too, that a violent easterly wind fomented it, and kept it burning all that day, and the night following spreading itself up to Gracechurch Street, and downwards from Cannon Street to the waterside as far as the Three Cranes in the Vintry.

---

3. Leaping, frisking.
4. Dropped from.
5. Ago. I.e., they foresaw that he would eventually be hung, but not that he would accomplish the regicide of 30 January 1649.

1. Compare the accounts of Pepys (page 2021) and Evelyn (page 2025).
2. On 2 September.
3. Covered with pitch (distilled tar) in order to keep out water.

The people in all parts about it distracted by the vastness of it, and their particular care to carry away their goods, many attempts were made to prevent the spreading of it, by pulling down houses, and making great intervals, but all in vain, the fire seizing upon the timber and rubbish, and so continuing itself, even through those spaces, and raging in a bright flame all Monday and Tuesday, notwithstanding His Majesty's own, and his Royal Highness's[4] indefatigable and personal pains to apply all possible remedies to prevent it, calling upon and helping the people with their Guards;[5] and a great number of nobility and gentry unweariedly assisting therein, for which they were requited with a thousand blessings from the poor distressed people. * * *

And we cannot but observe, to the confutation of all His Majesty's enemies, who endeavor to persuade the world abroad of great parties and disaffection at home against His Majesty's government, that a greater instance of the affections of this City could never be given than hath been now given in this sad and deplorable accident, when if at any time disorder might have been expected from the losses, distraction, and almost desperation of some persons in their private fortunes, thousands of people not having had habitations to cover them. And yet in all this time it hath been so far from any appearance of designs or attempts against His Majesty's government, that His Majesty and his royal brother, out of their care to stop and prevent the fire, frequently exposing their persons with very small attendance in all parts of the town, sometimes even to be intermixed with those who labored in the business, yet nevertheless there hath not been observed so much as a murmuring word to fall from any, but on the contrary, even those persons whose losses rendered their conditions most desperate, and to be fit objects of other prayers, beholding those frequent instances of His Majesty's care of this people, forgot their own misery, and filled the streets with their prayers for His Majesty, whose trouble they seemed to compassionate before their own.

THE DAILY COURANT (1702–1735) The *Daily Courant's* title announced its innovation. Its editor-publisher, Samuel Buckley (d. 1741), was the first in England to put out a paper every day (except for Sunday, which had no paper of its own until the 1770s); before now, papers had appeared thrice weekly at most. In his opening number, Buckley made clear both his dependence on "foreign prints" (newspapers from the Continent) and his distrust of them; his faith in his readers' capacity to winnow bias and interpret information; and his perhaps defensive condescension to his journalistic rivals as he embarked on the audacious enterprise of a daily paper.

from **The Daily Courant No. 1**
Wednesday, 11 March 1702

[EDITORIAL POLICY]

It will be found from the foreign prints, which from time to time, as occasion offers, will be mentioned in this paper, that the author has taken care to be duly furnished with all that comes from abroad in any language. And for an assurance that he will not, under pretense of having private intelligence, impose any additions of feigned circumstances to an action, but give his extracts fairly and impartially, at the beginning

---

4. The King's brother James, Duke of York.

5. The royal brothers deployed their soldiers to aid the fire's victims.

of each article he will quote the foreign paper from whence 'tis taken, that the public, seeing from what country a piece of news comes with the allowance of that government, may be better able to judge of the credibility and fairness of the relation. Nor will he take upon him to give any comments or conjectures of his own, but will relate only matter of fact, supposing other people to have sense enough to make reflections for themselves.

The *Courant* (as the title shows) will be published daily, being designed to give all the material[1] news as soon as every post arrives; and is confined to half the compass,[2] to save the public at least half the impertinences[3] of ordinary newspapers.

A REVIEW OF THE STATE OF THE BRITISH NATION (1704–1713) Of the periodical commentators on the news, none was more formidable than Daniel Defoe, who single-handedly wrote his *Review* twice and sometimes thrice a week for nine years. The paper changed its name, its format, and its ostensible focus several times during its long run, but its general purposes remained the same throughout. Defoe wrote to celebrate trade, and to propose strategies for its improvement; to teach a rigorous piety and morality to a readership he saw as lax; and to advance by adroit advocacy the favorite programs of the paper's secret sponsor, Secretary of State Robert Harley (1661–1724). One of these was the Treaty of Union, whereby Scotland would merge under a single government with England and Wales to form the new national entity of Great Britain. Advocates of the measure construed it as a fair exchange, providing expanded trade for Scotland, enhanced security for England. In support of the cause, Defoe not only wrote copiously (pamphlets and essays as well as *Reviews*), he also persuaded Harley to send him to Scotland (where the prospect of Union was far from popular) to serve as chief strategist and propagandist. There, he argued energetically and successfully for passage of the treaty, while keeping his affiliation with Harley a close secret. When the Treaty of Union was ratified, the *Review* indulged in a moment of exultation, in the characteristic voice its creator had devised during his sustained periodic enterprise: that of a writer enmeshed in actual and volatile circumstance, deeply engaged with the politics, conduct, and commerce of the real world, sometimes embattled, often exasperated, occasionally exhausted, but ultimately indefatigable.

For more about Defoe, see his principal listing on page 2293.

Daniel Defoe: *from* A Review of the State of the British Nation, Vol. 4, No. 21
Saturday, 29 March 1707

[THE NEW UNION]

I have a long time dwelt on the subject of a Union; I have happily seen it transacted in the kingdom of Scotland; I have seen it carried on there through innumerable oppositions, both public and private, peaceable and unpeaceable; I have seen it perfected there, and ratified, sent up to England, debated, opposed, and at last passed in both houses, and having obtained the royal assent, I have the pleasure, just while I am writing these lines, to hear the guns proclaiming the happy conjunction from Edinburgh Castle. And though it brings an unsatisfying childish custom in play, and exposes me to a vain and truly ridiculous saying in England,

---

1. Relevant.
2. Space. Most newspapers printed on both sides of the sheet. At first, Buckley printed on only one side, unsure

that his sources would supply him with enough matter to fill two sides daily (they soon did).
3. Irrelevancies; filler.

"as the fool thinks, etc.," yet 'tis impossible to put the lively sound of the cannon just now firing into any other note to my ear than the articulate expression of Union, Union. Strange power of imagination, strange incoherence of circumstances that fills the mind so with the thing that it makes even the thunder of warlike engines cry peace; and what is made to divide and destroy, speaks out the language of this glorious conjunction!

I have hardly room to introduce the various contemplations of the consequences of this mighty transaction; 'tis a sea of universal improvement, every day it discovers new mines of treasure, and when I launch out in the bark of my own imagination, I every minute discover new success, new advantages, and the approaching happiness of both kingdoms. Nor am I an idle spectator here; I have told Scotland of improvements in trade, wealth, and shipping that shall accrue to them on the happy conclusion of this affair, and I am pleased double with this, that I am like to be one of the first men that shall give them the pleasure of the experiment. I have told them of the improvement of their coal trade, and 'tis their own fault if they do not particularly engage 20 or 25 sail of ships immediately from England on that work. I have told them of the improvement of their salt, and I am now contracting for English merchants for Scots salt to the value of about ten thousand pounds per annum. I have told them of linen manufactures, and I have now above 100 poor families at work, by my procuring and direction, for the making such sorts of linen, and in such manner as never was made here before, and as no person in the trade will believe could be made here, till they see it.

This has been my employment in Scotland, and this my endeavor to do that nation service, and convince them by the practice that what I have said of the Union has more weight in it than some have endeavored to persuade them. Those that have charged me with missions and commissions from neither they nor I know who, shall blush at their rashness, and be ashamed for reflecting on a man come hither on purpose to do them good.[1] Have I had a hand in the Union, have I been maltreated by the tongues of the violent, threatened to be murdered, and insulted, because I have pleaded for it and pressed you to it—gentlemen, in Scotland, I refer you to Her Majesty's speech; there's my claim, and you do me too much honor to entitle me to a share in what Her Majesty says shall be their due that have done so. Hearken to the words of your sovereign: "I make no doubt but it will be remembered and spoke of hereafter to the honor of those that have been instrumental to bring it to such an happy conclusion." (Queen's Speech to the Parliament, 6 March 1707.)

Pray, gentlemen, have a care how you charge me with having any hand in bringing forward this matter *to such an happy conclusion*, lest you build that monument upon me which Her Majesty has foretold, and honor the man you would debase. I plead no merit, I do not raise the value of what I have done; and I know some that are gone to London to solicit the reward of what they have had no hand in—I might have said, are gone to claim the merit of what I have been the single author of—but as this has been the constant way of the world with me, so I have no repinings on that account. Nor am I pleading any other merit than that I may have it wrote on my grave that I did my duty in promoting the Union, and consequently the happiness of these nations. * * *

---

1. In both England and Scotland, Defoe had been accused (with reason) of conducting a kind of espionage on behalf of Harley and the Union.

Periodical Personae

In print journalism it was primarily the news that sold the paper; in the periodical essay it was the voice: the idiosyncratic mix of assertion and deference, comedy and charisma, with which author addressed audience. Political writers had long known the advantages of using a mask or *persona*—a pen name, a fictitious character—as a means of both concealing their identity and expanding the appeal of their controversial arguments. In the early 1700s, the inventors of the periodical essay extended the tactic of the fictitious self into new territory. While collaborating on *The Tatler* and *The Spectator*, Richard Steele and Joseph Addison devised strategies for making the unreal author a real arbitrator in the culture, a teacher of taste and conduct, manners and morality, someone whom readers found it pleasurable to learn from, to identify with, even to "believe in," despite (and because of) his comically exaggerated quirks, his patent nonexistence. Working behind their carefully crafted masks, Addison and Steele sold so many papers and impressed so many readers that their mark became indelible. For the rest of the century, the periodical essayist's first task was to devise a persona unusual enough to define the paper, and engaging enough to sustain it.

THE TATLER (1709–1711) At age thirty-five, after a checkered career as soldier, poet, playwright, popular moralist, and Whig propagandist, Captain Richard Steele (1672–1729) was appointed editor of the *London Gazette*, the government's long-running newspaper. Evidently even this task did not sufficiently absorb his energies. Two years later, while still supervising the *Gazette*, he launched *The Tatler*, a periodical of his own that outstripped all its predecessors in commercial success and enduring appeal. It appeared three times a week, ran for two years and 271 numbers, spawned many imitators, and continued to sell (in a four-volume collected edition) for the rest of the century. The *Tatler's* appeal derived in large measure from its putative author, Isaac Bickerstaff, Esquire, whose name Steele had borrowed from one of Swift's satires, but whose character he elaborated into that of a genial, perceptive, and comically self-congratulatory old man. The paper's commodious structure mirrored the gregariousness of its "author." Bickerstaff datelined his dispatches from the coffeehouses around London where papers were distributed, read, and discussed; he included letters (fictitious and authentic) from readers all over the country. The *Tatler's* audience thus found itself absorbed into the paper several ways: they were its constant topic, they sometimes supplied its text, they constituted both its origin and its end point, and they gave it their unprecedented devotion. Steele soon made further discoveries of form under the influence of his school friend Joseph Addison (1672–1719), whom he had brought in (so one contemporary put it) as his "great and constant assistant." Addison and Steele found that Bickerstaff's private musings, dispatched "From my Own Apartment," were the most pleasing items of all, and so they often devoted whole papers to reprinting what their character was pleased to call his "lucubrations" (meditations by candlelight, late at night). John Gay summed up the strategy's success. Coffeehouse owners, Gay reported, "began to be sensible that the Esquire's lucubrations alone had brought them more customers than all their other newspapers put together." Bickerstaff's other "departments" diminished or disappeared, and "the Esquire's lucubrations," now running the full length of the paper, created the format and the fashion for the periodical essay, a unified piece on a single topic as opposed to the fragmentary "miscellany" from which Steele had started. By the time he stopped *The Tatler* (probably because of political pressures following the Whigs' fall from power), he and Addison had devised means and achieved ends with which they would experiment anew in the *Spectator*: ways of creating community shot through with solitude, of mixing sociability and meditation, morality and mirth.

Richard Steele: *from* Tatler No. 1
Tuesday, 12 April 1709

[INTRODUCING MR. BICKERSTAFF]

Quicquid agunt homines nostri farrago libelli.[1]

Though the other papers which are published for the use of the good people of England have certainly very wholesome effects, and are laudable in their particular kinds, they do not seem to come up to the main design of such narrations, which, I humbly presume, should be principally intended for the use of politic persons, who are so public-spirited as to neglect their own affairs to look into transactions of state. Now these gentlemen, for the most part, being persons of strong zeal and weak intellects,[2] it is both a charitable and necessary work to offer something whereby such worthy and well-affected members of the commonwealth may be instructed, after their reading, *what to think:* which shall be the end and purpose of this my paper, wherein I shall from time to time report and consider all matters of what kind soever that shall occur to me, and publish such my advices and reflections every Tuesday, Thursday, and Saturday in the week, for the convenience of the post.[3] I resolve also to have something which may be of entertainment to the fair sex, in honor of whom I have invented the title of this paper. I therefore earnestly desire all persons, without distinction, to take it in for the present *gratis,*[4] and hereafter at the price of one penny, forbidding all hawkers to take more for it at their peril. And I desire all persons to consider, that I am at a very great charge for proper materials for this work, as well as that before I resolved upon it, I had settled a correspondence in all parts of the known and knowing world. And forasmuch as this globe is not trodden upon by mere drudges of business only, but that men of spirit and genius are justly to be esteemed as considerable agents in it, we shall not upon a dearth of news present you with musty foreign edicts, or dull proclamations, but shall divide our relations of the passages which occur in action or discourse throughout this town, as well as elsewhere, under such dates of places as may prepare you for the matter you are to expect, in the following manner.

All accounts of gallantry,[5] pleasure, and entertainment shall be under the article of White's Chocolate House; poetry, under that of Will's Coffeehouse; learning, under the title of Grecian; foreign and domestic news you will have from St. James's Coffeehouse; and what else I have to offer on any other subject, shall be dated from my own apartment.[6]

I once more desire my reader to consider, that as I cannot keep an ingenious man to go daily to Will's, under two-pence each day merely for his charges; to White's, under sixpence; nor to the Grecian, without allowing him some Plain Spanish,[7] to be as able as others at the learned table; and that a good observer

---

1. "Whatever people do [will furnish] the variety of our little book" (Juvenal, *Satires* 1.85–86); or (in the freer and more apt 18th-century translation by Thomas Percy) "Whate'er men do, or say, or think, or dream, / Our motley paper seizes for its theme."

2. Bickerstaff mocks that category of men known as the "coffeehouse politicians," who spent long hours together discussing news. For a more sustained satire of them, see *Tatler* No. 155 (pages 2324–25).

3. These were the days on which the postal system carried mail from London to the provinces.

4. Steele distributed his first four numbers free, as a way of attracting readers.

5. Flirtation and self-display.

6. Steele exploits associations between topic and venue long familiar to his readers. Each of the coffeehouses he names catered to a clientele "specializing" in the pursuits he names. A journalist himself, Steele parodies the newspaper format that headed each item by the name of its (usually foreign) city of origin.

7. A kind of snuff, used as a stimulant to induce sneezing.

cannot speak with even Kidney[8] at St. James's without clean linen. I say, these considerations will, I hope, make all persons willing to comply with my humble request (when my *gratis* stock is exhausted) of a penny apiece; especially since they are sure of some proper amusement, and that it is impossible for me to want means to entertain 'em, having, besides the force of my own parts, the power of divination, and that I can, by casting a figure, tell you all that will happen before it comes to pass.[9]

But this last faculty I shall use very sparingly, and speak but of few things 'till they are passed, for fear of divulging matters which may offend our superiors.[1] * * *

From my own apartment

I am sorry I am obliged to trouble the public with so much discourse, upon a matter which I at the very first mentioned as a trifle, *viz.* the death of Mr. Partridge, under whose name there is an almanac come out for the year 1709.[2] In one page of which, it is asserted by the said John Partridge, that he is still living, and not only so, but that he was also living some time before, and even at the instant when I writ of his death. I have in another place, and in a paper by itself, sufficiently convinced this man that he is dead, and if he has any shame, I don't doubt but that by this time he owns it to all his acquaintance: for though the legs and arms, and whole body, of that man may still appear and perform their animal functions; yet since, as I have elsewhere observed, his art is gone, the man is gone. I am, as I said, concerned that this little matter should make so much noise; but since I am engaged, I take myself obliged in honor to go on in my lucubrations, and by the help of these arts of which I am master, as well as my skill in astrological speculations, I shall, as I see occasion, proceed to confute other dead men, who pretend to be in being, that they are actually deceased. I therefore give all men fair warning to mend their manners, for I shall from time to time print bills of mortality; and I beg the pardon of all such who shall be named therein, if they who are good for nothing shall find themselves in the number of the deceased.

THE SPECTATOR (1711–1713) In the weeks of the *Spectator*'s first appearance, readers marveled at both its contents and its pace. "We had at first . . . no manner of notion," the wit John Gay reported from London, "how a diurnal paper could be continued in the spirit and style of our present *Spectators*; but to our no small surprise we find them still rising upon us, and can only wonder from whence so prodigious a run of wit and learning can proceed." It proceeded (as Gay guessed) from the minds and pens of the same two writers who had shut down the *Tatler* just a few months before. For their second periodical collaboration, Addison and Steele considerably upped the ante. Not only did they undertake to publish a new number every day (something no essayist had hitherto attempted), they also devised a new persona, intricately linked with their triumphant earlier creation Isaac Bickerstaff. Where the *Tatler* had begun in gregariousness and modulated towards solitude (at "my own apartment"), the new paper started from an even farther remove, in the eccentric silence of Mr. Spectator, who declares at the outset that he has not spoken "three sentences together" since birth. Mr. Spectator carries

---

8. A waiter.
9. To "cast a figure" is to work out a horoscope, an ability that the *Tatler*'s first readers would readily associate with the character "Isaac Bickerstaff." Jonathan Swift had originally created the character (in a series of pamphlets in 1708) as a way of satirizing the fashion for astrological almanacs, which purported to foretell the important events of the coming year. In Swift's first pamphlet, the fictitious astrologer Isaac Bickerstaff forecast the imminent

death of the real (and very successful) astrologer John Partridge; in the second pamphlet, Bickerstaff declared blithely that his prophecy had come to pass. Partridge's subsequent, frantic protestations added relish to the joke.
1. Bickerstaff proceeds to supply first dispatches from White's, Will's, and St. James's coffeehouses.
2. In the 1709 issue of his annual almanac *Merlinus Liberatus*, Partridge had insisted that he was "still alive."

his "own apartment"—his state of psychological apartness—with him, not at his residence but in his head; "the working of my own mind," he announces early on, "is the chief entertainment of my life."

In his focused interiority, Mr. Spectator played out the principles of psychology that John Locke had propounded, but his extreme self-possession turned out to possess enormous rhetorical impact and commercial cachet as well. More than any other periodical persona, Mr. Spectator managed to embody and to allegorize the operations of the paper he inhabited. Like the paper he was everywhere, at once silent and articulate, fictitious in substance but impressive in effect, observant and absorbent of the culture, able to move into his readers' minds by the mysterious osmosis of reading itself, and to remain there, a disembodied monitor with a rapidly growing portfolio of daily essays. An anonymous pamphleteer reproached Mr. Spectator for the presumptuous "tyranny" of his surveillance, but the paper's tactics of reform remained in power for most of the century. It was read (and imitated) on the Continent, in the American colonies, and in remoter outposts like Sumatra, from whence a British trader wrote home to his daughter in London, admonishing her "to study the *Spectators*, especially those which relate to religion and domestic life. Next to the Bible you cannot read any writings so much to your purpose for the improvement of your mind and the conduct of your actions." The *Spectator*, Gay noted soon after the paper's debut, "is in everyone's hands, and a constant topic for our morning conversation at tea tables and coffeehouses." More than sixty years later, the Scots rhetorician Hugh Blair could only echo and elaborate on Gay's phrasing, in accordance with the paper's now long-established place in the British canon: "The *Spectator* . . . is a book which is in the hands of everyone, and which cannot be praised too highly. The good sense, and good writing, the useful morality, and the admirable vein of humor which abound in it, render it one of those standard books which have done the greatest honor to the English nation."

Joseph Addison: *from* Spectator No. 1
Thursday, 1 March 1711

[INTRODUCING MR. SPECTATOR]

Non fumum ex fulgore, sed ex fumo dare lucem
Cogitat, ut speciosa debinc miracula promat.[1]

I have observed, that a reader seldom peruses a book with pleasure 'till he knows whether the writer of it be a black or a fair man,[2] of a mild or choleric disposition, married or a bachelor, with other particulars of the like nature, that conduce very much to the right understanding of an author. To gratify this curiosity, which is so natural to a reader, I design this paper, and my next, as prefatory discourses to my following writings, and shall give some account in them of the several persons that are engaged in this work. As the chief trouble of compiling, digesting, and correcting will fall to my share, I must do myself the justice to open the work with my own history.

I was born to a small hereditary estate, which, according to the tradition of the village where it lies, was bounded by the same hedges and ditches in William

1. "He intends to produce not smoke from fire, but light from smoke, so that he may then put forth striking and amazing things" (Horace, *Ars Poetica* 143–44).
2. Of dark or light complexion.

the Conqueror's time[3] that it is at present, and has been delivered down from father to son whole and entire, without the loss or acquisition of a single field or meadow, during the space of six hundred years. There runs a story in the family, that when my mother was gone with child of me about three months, she dreamt that she was brought to bed of[4] a judge. Whether this might proceed from a lawsuit which was then depending in the family, or my father's being a justice of the peace, I cannot determine; for I am not so vain as to think it presaged any dignity that I should arrive at in my future life, though that was the interpretation which the neighborhood put upon it. The gravity of my behavior at my very first appearance in the world, and all the time that I sucked, seemed to favor my mother's dream: for, as she has often told me, I threw away my rattle before I was two months old, and would not make use of my coral[5] 'till they had taken away the bells from it.

As for the rest of my infancy, there being nothing in it remarkable, I shall pass it over in silence. I find that, during my nonage,[6] I had the reputation of a very sullen youth, but was always a favorite of my schoolmaster, who used to say, *that my parts were solid and would wear well.* I had not been long at the university before I distinguished myself by a most profound silence: for during the space of eight years, excepting in the public exercises of the college, I scarce uttered the quantity of an hundred words; and indeed do not remember that I ever spoke three sentences together in my whole life. Whilst I was in this learned body I applied myself with so much diligence to my studies that there are very few celebrated books, either in the learned or the modern tongues, which I am not acquainted with.

Upon the death of my father I was resolved to travel into foreign countries, and therefore left the university, with the character[7] of an odd unaccountable fellow that had a great deal of learning, if I would but show it. An insatiable thirst after knowledge carried me into all the countries of Europe, in which there was anything new or strange to be seen; nay, to such a degree was my curiosity raised, that having read the controversies of some great men concerning the antiquities of Egypt, I made a voyage to Grand Cairo, on purpose to take the measure of a pyramid; and as soon as I had set myself right in that particular, returned to my native country with great satisfaction.

I have passed my latter years in this city, where I am frequently seen in most public places, though there are not above half a dozen of my select friends that know me; of whom my next paper shall give a more particular account. There is no place of general resort, wherein I do not often make my appearance.[8] Sometimes I am seen thrusting my head into a round of politicians at Will's, and listening with great attention to the narratives that are made in those little circular audiences. Sometimes I smoke a pipe at Child's; and whilst I seem attentive to nothing but the *Post-Man,*[9] overhear the conversation of every table in the room. I appear on Sunday nights at St. James's Coffeehouse, and sometimes join the little committee of politics in the

---

3. The late 11th century, when William ruled as king of England.
4. Had given birth to. The silence of judges was proverbial.
5. Another sound maker for infants.
6. Childhood.
7. Reputation.

8. With a conspicuous openness to all parties and pursuits, Mr. Spectator distributes his visitations among some of London's favorite meeting places, including ones popular with Whigs (St. James's), Tories (the Cocoa Tree), authors (Child's), lawyers (the Grecian), and the news-obsessives he calls "politicians" (Will's).
9. A thrice-weekly newspaper, favored by Whigs.

inner-room, as one who comes there to hear and improve. My face is likewise very well known at the Grecian, the Cocoa Tree, and in the theaters both of Drury Lane, and the Haymarket. I have been taken for a merchant upon the Exchange[1] for above these ten years, and sometimes pass for a Jew in the assembly of stock-jobbers at Jonathan's.[2] In short, wherever I see a cluster of people I always mix with them, though I never open my lips but in my own club.

Thus I live in the world, rather as a spectator of mankind than as one of the species; by which means I have made myself a speculative statesman, soldier, merchant, and artisan, without ever meddling with any practical part in life. I am very well versed in the theory of an husband or a father, and can discern the errors in the economy, business, and diversion of others, better than those who are engaged in them; as standers-by discover blots,[3] which are apt to escape those who are in the game. I never espoused any party with violence, and am resolved to observe an exact neutrality between the Whigs and Tories,[4] unless I shall be forced to declare myself by the hostilities of either side. In short, I have acted in all the parts of my life as a looker-on, which is the character I intend to preserve in this paper.

I have given the reader just so much of my history and character as to let him see I am not altogether unqualified for the business I have undertaken. As for other particulars in my life and adventures, I shall insert them in following papers as I shall see occasion. In the mean time, when I consider how much I have seen, read, and heard, I begin to blame my own taciturnity; and since I have neither time nor inclination to communicate the fullness of my heart in speech, I am resolved to do it in writing; and to print my self out, if possible, before I die. I have been often told by my friends that it is pity so many useful discoveries which I have made should be in the possession of a silent man. For this reason therefore, I shall publish a sheet-full of thoughts every morning, for the benefit of my contemporaries; and if I can any way contribute to the diversion or improvement of the country in which I live, I shall leave it, when I am summoned out of it, with the secret satisfaction of thinking that I have not lived in vain. * * *

THE FEMALE SPECTATOR (APRIL 1744–MAY 1746)

The Female Spectator was the first periodical written by a woman for women. Its author, Eliza Haywood (c. 1693–1756), had been an actress, a playwright, and the writer of some sixty romances, novels, and other narratives, many of them scandalous and some of them wildly successful. In the mid-1740s, after a long eclipse prompted in part by Alexander Pope's derision of her in the *Dunciad*, Haywood emerged in a new guise: no longer a purveyor of exotic thrills, she set up instead as a teacher of morality. *The Female Spectator* differed from its namesake in calendar (monthly rather than daily) and format: a pamphlet and not a sheet, each number presented an essay focused on a single topic with several illustrative fictional stories interspersed. The biggest difference, though, was in the new paper's point of view. Mr. Spectator had observed, described, and instructed "the fair sex" from without, as supremely self-confident male mentor. Haywood

---

1. The Royal Exchange was a large building containing many shops and serving as a meeting place for merchants. (For Addison's paean to the place, see *Spectator* No. 69, page 2330).
2. Jonathan's coffeehouse, near the Royal Exchange, was a principal meeting place of merchants and stockbrokers ("stock-jobbers").

3. In backgammon, a blot is a piece whose position puts it at risk of being taken.
4. Addison and Steele maintained "neutrality" more strictly in the *Spectator* than they had in the *Tatler*, which had incurred much controversy by its Whig partisanship.

offered instead a running report from the interior of women's lives. Her vantage point proved popular. *The Female Spectator* continued to sell, in a four-volume collected edition, for more than two decades after its periodical run had ceased.

from **The Female Spectator Vol. 1, No. 1**

[THE AUTHOR'S INTENT]

It is very much by the choice we make of subjects for our entertainment that the refined taste distinguishes itself from the vulgar and more gross. Reading is universally allowed to be one of the most improving as well as agreeable amusements; but then to render it so, one should, among the number of books which are perpetually issuing from the press, endeavor to single out such as promise to be most conducive to those ends. In order to be as little deceived as possible, I, for my own part, love to get as well acquainted as I can with an author, before I run the risk of losing my time in perusing his work; and as I doubt not but most people are of this way of thinking, I shall, in imitation of my learned brother of ever precious memory,[1] give some account of what I am, and those concerned with me in this undertaking; and likewise of the chief intent of the lucubrations[2] hereafter communicated, that the reader, on casting his eye over the four or five first pages, may judge how far the book may or may not be qualified to entertain him, and either accept or throw it aside as he thinks proper. And here I promise that in the pictures I shall give of myself and associates, I will draw no flattering lines, assume no perfection that we are not in reality possessed of, nor attempt to shadow over any defect with an artificial gloss.

As a proof of my sincerity, I shall in the first place assure him that for my own part I never was a beauty, and am now very far from being young (a confession he will find few of my sex ready to make). I shall also acknowledge that I have run through as many scenes of vanity and folly as the greatest coquette of them all. Dress, equipage,[3] and flattery were the idols of my heart. I should have thought that day lost which did not present me with some new opportunity of showing myself. My life, for some years, was a continued round of what I then called pleasure, and my whole time engrossed by a hurry of promiscuous diversions. But whatever inconveniences such a manner of conduct has brought upon myself, I have this consolation, to think that the public may reap some benefit from it. The company I kept was not, indeed, always so well chosen as it ought to have been, for the sake of my own interest or reputation; but then it was general, and by consequence furnished me not only with the knowledge of many occurrences, which otherwise I had been ignorant of, but also enabled me, when the too great vivacity of my nature became tempered with reflection, to see into the secret springs which gave rise to the actions I had either heard or been witness of—to judge of the various passions of the human mind, and distinguish those imperceptible degrees by which they become masters of the heart, and attain the dominion over reason. A thousand odd adventures, which at the time they happened made slight impression on me, and seemed to dwell no longer on my mind than the wonder they occasioned, now rise fresh to my remembrance,

---

1. Addison and Steele's Mr. Spectator.
2. Writings by candlelight; Haywood pointedly picks up

Isaac Bickerstaff's catchword for his essays in the *Tatler*.
3. Fancy carriages, servants, and furniture.

with this advantage, that the mystery I then, for want of attention, imagined they contained, is entirely vanished, and I find it easy to account for the cause by the consequence.

With this experience, added to a genius[4] tolerably extensive, and an education more liberal than is ordinarily allowed to persons of my sex, I flattered myself that it might be in my power to be in some measure both useful and entertaining to the public; and this thought was so soothing to those remains of vanity not yet wholly extinguished in me, that I resolved to pursue it, and immediately began to consider by what method I should be most likely to succeed. To confine myself to any one subject, I knew could please but one kind of taste, and my ambition was to be as universally read as possible. From my observations of human nature, I found that curiosity had more or less a share in every breast; and my business, therefore, was to hit this reigning humor in such a manner as that the gratification it should receive from being made acquainted with other people's affairs should at the same time teach every one to regulate their own.

Having agreed within myself on this important point, I commenced author, by setting down many things which, being pleasing to myself, I imagined would be so to others; but on examining them the next day, I found an infinite deficiency both in matter and style, and that there was an absolute necessity for me to call in to my assistance such of my acquaintance as were qualified for that purpose. The first that occurred to me, I shall distinguish by the name of Mira, a lady descended from a family to which wit seems hereditary, married to a gentleman every way worthy of so excellent a wife, and with whom she lives in so perfect a harmony, that having nothing to ruffle the composure of her soul, or disturb those sparkling ideas she received from nature and education, left me no room to doubt if what she favored me with would be acceptable to the public. The next is a widow of quality, who not having buried her vivacity in the tomb of her lord, continues to make one in all the modish diversions of the times, so far, I mean, as she finds them consistent with innocence and honor; and as she is far from having the least austerity in her behavior, nor is rigid to the failings she is wholly free from herself, those of her acquaintance who had been less circumspect scruple not to make her the confidante of secrets they conceal from all the world beside. The third is the daughter of a wealthy merchant, charming as an angel, but endued with so many accomplishments that to those who know her truly, her beauty is the least distinguished part of her. This fine young creature I shall call Euphrosyne, since she has all the cheerfulness and sweetness ascribed to that goddess.[5]

These three approved my design, assured me of all the help they could afford, and soon gave a proof of it in bringing their several essays; but as the reader, provided the entertainment be agreeable, will not be interested from which quarter it comes, whatever productions I shall be favored with from these ladies, or any others I may hereafter correspond with, will be exhibited under the general title of *The Female Spectator,* and how many contributors soever there may happen to be to the work, they are to be considered only as several members of one body, of which I am the mouth. * * *

4. Talent, ability.
5. Euphrosyne is one of the three Graces, sister goddesses in Greek mythology who possess (and bestow) the gift of beauty.

Richard Steele: *from* Tatler No. 18
21 May 1709

[The News Writers in Danger[1]]

St. James's Coffeehouse, May 20.

* * * It being therefore visible, that our society[2] will be greater sufferers by the peace than the soldiery itself; insomuch, that the *Daily Courant* is in danger of being broken, my friend Dyer of being reformed,[3] and the very best of the whole band of being reduced to half-pay; might I presume to offer anything in the behalf of my distressed brethren, I would humbly move, that an appendix of proper apartments furnished with pen, ink, and paper, and other necessaries of life should be added to the Hospital of Chelsea,[4] for the relief of such decayed news writers as have served their country in the wars; and that for their exercise, they should compile the annals of their brother-veterans, who have been engaged in the same service, and are still obliged to do duty after the same manner.

I cannot be thought to speak this out of an eye to any private interest; for, as my chief scenes of action are coffeehouses, playhouses, and my own apartment, I am in no need of camps, fortifications, and fields of battle, to support me; I don't call out for heroes and generals to my assistance. Though the officers are broken, and the armies disbanded, I shall still be safe as long as there are men or women, or politicians, or lovers, or poets, or nymphs, or swains, or cits,[5] or courtiers, in being.

Joseph Addison: *from* Tatler No. 155
Thursday, 6 April 1710

[The Political Upholsterer]

—*Aliena negotia curat*
Excussus propriis.[1]

From My Own Apartment, April 5

There lived some years since within my neighborhood a very grave person, an upholsterer, who seemed a man of more than ordinary application to business. He was a very early riser, and was often abroad two or three hours before any of his neighbors. He had a particular carefulness in the knitting of his brows, and a kind of impatience in all his motions, that plainly discovered he was always intent on matters of importance. Upon my enquiry into his life and conversation, I found him to be the greatest newsmonger in our quarter;[2] that he rose before day to read the *Post-Man*;[3] and that

---

1. Papers often defined themselves by contrasting their methods and achievements with those of their rivals. For the essayists, the newspapers afforded the readiest foil. Steele was a seasoned journalist, but he and Addison devised many ways of mocking the vacuity of the newsmongers, and of flattering those readers who preferred essays to mere journalism. In this early *Tatler*, Bickerstaff announces that England will soon be victorious in its foreign wars, observes that "the approach of peace strikes a panic through our armies," who will have nowhere left to fight, and worries that peace will prove even more costly to the journalists, who will have nothing left to write about.
2. I.e., the "brotherhood" of news writers.

3. John Dyer's fervently Tory newsletter often denounced the Whigs for (among other things) mismanaging the wars abroad.
4. Where disabled soldiers were given care and lodging.
5. City dwellers, tradespeople.
1. "He minds others' concerns, since he has lost his own" (Horace, *Satires* 2.3.19–20).
2. "Monger" not because he sells news but because he tells it, to anyone who will listen; Addison's news-addicted upholsterer became one of the *Tatler*'s most popular comic creations, reappearing in several later numbers.
3. The leading Whig newspaper (1695–1730).

he would take two or three turns to the other end of the town before his neighbors were up, to see if there were any Dutch mails[4] come in. He had a wife and several children; but was much more inquisitive to know what passed in Poland than in his own family, and was in greater pain and anxiety of mind for King Augustus's[5] welfare than that of his nearest relations. He looked extremely thin in a dearth of news, and never enjoyed himself in a westerly wind.[6] This indefatigable kind of life was the ruin of his shop; for about the time that his favorite prince left the crown of Poland, he broke and disappeared.

This man and his affairs had been long out of my mind, till about three days ago, as I was walking in St. James's Park, I heard somebody at a distance hemming after me: and who should it be but my old neighbor the upholsterer? I saw he was reduced to extreme poverty, by certain shabby superfluities in his dress: for notwithstanding that it was a very sultry day for the time of the year, he wore a loose great coat and a muff, with a long campaign-wig out of curl;[7] to which he had added the ornament of a pair of black garters buckled under the knee. Upon his coming up to me, I was going to inquire into his present circumstances; but was prevented by his asking me, with a whisper, whether the last letters brought any accounts that one might rely upon from Bender?[8] I told him, none that I heard of; and asked him, whether he had yet married his eldest daughter? He told me, No. But pray, says he, tell me sincerely, what are your thoughts of the King of Sweden? For though his wife and children were starving, I found his chief concern at present was for this great monarch. I told him, that I looked upon him as one of the first heroes of the age. But pray, says he, do you think there is anything in the story of his wound? And finding me surprised at the question, Nay, says he, I only propose it to you. I answered, that I thought there was no reason to doubt of it. But why in the heel, says he, more than in any other part of the body? Because, says I, the bullet chanced to light there. * * *

We were now got to the upper end of the Mall,[9] where were three or four very odd fellows sitting together upon the bench. These I found were all of them politicians, who used to sun themselves in that place every day about dinner time.[1]* * *

I at length took my leave of the company, and was going away; but had not been gone thirty yards before the upholsterer hemmed again after me. Upon his advancing towards me, with a whisper, I expected to hear some secret piece of news, which he had not thought fit to communicate to the bench; but instead of that, he desired me in my ear to lend him half a crown. In compassion to so needy a statesman, and to dissipate the confusion I found he was in, I told him, if he pleased, I would give him five shillings, to receive five pounds of him when the Great Turk was driven out of Constantinople; which he very readily accepted, but not before he had laid down to me the impossibility of such an event, as the affairs of Europe now stand.

This paper I design for the particular benefit of those worthy citizens who live more in a coffeehouse than in their shops, and whose thoughts are so taken up with the affairs of the Allies, that they forget their customers.

4. Mailboats from the Netherlands, bringing fresh news.
5. Frederick Augustus I of Poland, whose loss and recovery of power had filled the papers for several years.
6. Which prevented the arrival of the "Dutch mails."
7. A "campaign wig" was used when traveling and was remarkable for its decorative curls (here flattened and disordered).
8. A town in modern Bessarabia, where Charles XII of Sweden (1682–1718) had sought refuge after a long string of military victories and a final catastrophic defeat (see Samuel Johnson, The Vanity of Human Wishes, lines 191–222, page 2682).
9. The public walk in St. James's Park, near the royal residence.
1. Bickerstaff proceeds to eavesdrop, astonished, on the conversation of these news-obsessives.

Joseph Addison: *from* Spectator No. 10
Monday, 12 March 1711

[THE SPECTATOR AND ITS READERS[1]]

Non aliter quam qui adverso vix flumine lembum
Remigiis subigit: si brachia forte remisit,
Atque illum in praeceps prono rapit alveus amni.[2]

It is with much satisfaction that I hear this great city inquiring day by day after these my papers, and receiving my morning lectures with a becoming seriousness and attention. My publisher tells me, that there are already three thousand of them distributed every day: so that if I allow twenty readers to every paper, which I look upon as a modest computation, I may reckon about three-score thousand disciples in London and Westminster, who I hope will take care to distinguish themselves from the thoughtless herd of their ignorant and inattentive brethren. Since I have raised to myself so great an audience, I shall spare no pains to make their instruction agreeable, and their diversion useful. For which reasons I shall endeavor to enliven morality with wit, and to temper wit with morality, that my readers may, if possible, both ways find their account in the speculation of the day. And to the end that their virtue and discretion may not be short transient intermitting starts of thought, I have resolved to refresh their memories from day to day, till I have recovered them out of that desperate state of vice and folly into which the age is fallen. The mind that lies fallow but a single day sprouts up in follies that are only to be killed by a constant and assiduous culture. It was said of Socrates, that he brought philosophy down from heaven, to inhabit among men;[3] and I shall be ambitious to have it said of me, that I have brought philosophy out of closets and libraries, schools and colleges, to dwell in clubs and assemblies, at tea tables, and in coffeehouses.

I would therefore in a very particular manner recommend these my speculations to all well-regulated families, that set apart an hour in every morning for tea and bread and butter; and would earnestly advise them for their good to order this paper to be punctually served up, and to be looked upon as a part of the tea equipage.

Sir Francis Bacon observes that a well-written book, compared with its rivals and antagonists, is like Moses's serpent, that immediately swallowed up and devoured those of the Egyptians.[4] I shall not be so vain as to think that where the *Spectator* appears, the other public prints will vanish; but shall leave it to my readers' consideration whether, is it not much better to be let into the knowledge of oneself, than to hear what passes in Muscovy[5] or Poland; and to amuse ourselves with such writings as tend to the wearing out of ignorance, passion, and prejudice, than such as naturally conduce to inflame hatreds and make enmities irreconcilable?

---

1. The *Spectator* bore a close resemblance to the *Daily Courant*: both papers were a single sheet produced by the same printer (Samuel Buckley) for the same price (a penny), and both appeared every day except Sunday. In this number, Addison elaborates on the ways in which his new essay—less than two weeks old and already very successful—is not a newspaper.
2. "As if one, whose oars can scarce force his skiff against the stream, should by chance slacken his arms, and lo!

headlong down the current the channel sweeps it away" (Virgil, *Georgics* 1.201–3).
3. Addison paraphrases a remark by the Roman orator Cicero (*Tusculan Disputations* 5.4.10).
4. Bacon makes this point in his *Advancement of Learning* (2.14), alluding to Exodus 7.10–12.
5. A territory in west-central Russia (Moscow was its capital).

In the next place, I would recommend this paper to the daily perusal of those gentlemen whom I cannot but consider as my good brothers and allies, I mean the fraternity of spectators who live in the world without having anything to do in it; and either by the affluence of their fortunes, or laziness of their dispositions, have no other business with the rest of mankind but to look upon them. Under this class of men are comprehended all contemplative tradesmen, titular physicians, Fellows of the Royal Society,[6] Templers[7] that are not given to be contentious, and statesmen that are out of business. In short, everyone that considers the world as a theater, and desires to form a right judgment of those who are the actors on it.

There is another set of men that I must likewise lay a claim to, whom I have lately called the Blanks of society, as being altogether unfurnished with ideas, till the business and conversation of the day has supplied them. I have often considered these poor souls with an eye of great commiseration, when I have heard them asking the first man they have met with, whether there was any news stirring? and by that means gathering together materials for thinking. These needy persons do not know what to talk of, till about twelve a clock in the morning; for by that time they are pretty good judges of the weather, know which way the wind sits, and whether the Dutch mail[8] be come in. As they lie at the mercy of the first man they meet, and are grave or impertinent all the day long, according to the notions which they have imbibed in the morning, I would earnestly entreat them not to stir out of their chambers till they have read this paper, and do promise them that I will daily instill into them such sound and wholesome sentiments as shall have a good effect on their conversation for the ensuing twelve hours.

But there are none to whom this paper will be more useful than to the female world. I have often thought there has not been sufficient pains taken in finding out proper employments and diversions for the fair ones. Their amusements seem contrived for them rather as they are women, than as they are reasonable creatures; and are more adapted to the sex, than to the species. The toilet[9] is their great scene of business, and the right adjusting of their hair the principal employment of their lives. The sorting of a suit of ribbons is reckoned a very good morning's work; and if they make an excursion to a mercer's[1] or a toy shop,[2] so great a fatigue makes them unfit for anything else all the day after. Their more serious occupations are sewing and embroidery, and their greatest drudgery the preparation of jellies and sweetmeats. This, I say, is the state of ordinary women; though I know there are multitudes of those of a more elevated life and conversation, that move in an exalted sphere of knowledge and virtue, that join all the beauties of the mind to the ornaments of dress, and inspire a kind of awe and respect, as well as love, into their male beholders. I hope to increase the number of these by publishing this daily paper, which I shall always endeavor to make an innocent if not an improving entertainment, and by that means at least divert the minds of my female readers from greater trifles. At the same time, as I would fain give some finishing touches to those which are already the most beautiful pieces in human nature, I shall endeavor to point out all those imperfections that are the

6. The London group chartered in the 1660s for the advancement of scientific inquiry.
7. Lawyers.
8. The boat bearing letters and newspapers from Holland.

9. Dressing tables.
1. Fabric sellers.
2. Where they might buy ornamental accessories—fans, silks, ribbons, laces—as well as playthings.

blemishes, as well as those virtues which are the embellishments, of the sex. In the meanwhile I hope these my gentle readers, who have so much time on their hands, will not grudge throwing away a quarter of an hour in a day on this paper, since they may do it without any hindrance to business.

I know several of my friends and well-wishers are in great pain for me, lest I should not be able to keep up the spirit of a paper which I oblige myself to furnish every day: but to make them easy in this particular, I will promise them faithfully to give it over as soon as I grow dull. This I know will be matter of great raillery to the small wits; who will frequently put me in mind of my promise, desire me to keep my word, assure me that it is high time to give over, with many other little pleasantries of the like nature, which men of a little smart genius cannot forbear throwing out against their best friends, when they have such a handle given them of being witty. But let them remember, that I do hereby enter my caveat against this piece of raillery.

⊷⊷ ⊠⧫⊠ ⊶⊶

Getting, Spending, Speculating

The periodical essay was one commodity among many, in an economy whose energies were evident almost everywhere: in shops stocked with new (often exotic) goods; at outposts in remote countries where trade was gradually being transmuted into empire; at London banks, where the apparatus of transaction (loans, bills, draughts) was rapidly being refined; in nearby coffeehouses, where the agents and accumulators of wealth paused during busy days to absorb substances imported from abroad (coffee, tobacco, chocolate) as well as that home-crafted item of consumption, the periodical essay itself. The essayists often construed their audience as though it consisted *primarily* of merchants, shopkeepers, and customers—of people profoundly concerned with the course of commerce, whatever their gender or occupation. Defoe, Addison, and Steele all wrote to celebrate trade (its new profusions and possibilities), but also to regularize it, to render it respectable, to reconcile it with notions of human excellence originating in an earlier culture centered on aristocracy. The *Review*, the *Tatler*, and the *Spectator* all undertook (as the historian J. G. A. Pocock has elegantly argued) to redefine the idea of "virtue," to shift its focus of application from the classically defined obligations of the hereditary landowner to the prudent calculation of the urban merchant, alert to realities and probabilities in an economy awash with speculation and controlled by credit, where "what one owned was promises": promises by entrepreneurs in search of capital; by stock-jobbers selling hopes of future prosperity; by the government whose operations depended on intricately structured loans from its own citizens. One central concern of the periodicals was how to commute promise into actual prosperity, rather than mere air.

In the selections in this section, Addison rejoices in the commercial and cultural confluence at the Royal Exchange (London's shopping center). In a more sentimental vein, Steele tracks the consequences of foreign trade in the lives and feelings of two lovers. Defoe, by contrast, is harder-headed, more closely analytic. Unlike the authors of the *Spectator*, he had spent years in business, making and losing fortunes. Surveying the shops of London, Defoe declares (as in virtually every *Review*) his passion for trade, but he asks what prospects the *present* patterns of consumption actually hold forth.

Where the *Review, Tatler,* and *Spectator* defined themselves *against* their print contemporaries, other periodicals took a different tack. With so much information, instruction, and entertainment flowing from so many sources, a desire developed for a digest that might organize it all. No one catered more adroitly to this new market than did Edward Cave, founder and editor of *Gentleman's Magazine,* a monthly pamphlet whose title coined a pivotal new term for print. "Magazine" meant a military storehouse of provisions and artillery; the *Gentleman's Magazine* promised an intellectual storehouse similarly well stocked. Cave promised "more in quantity, and greater variety, than any book of the kind and price." He delivered on the promise by publishing extracts and abstracts from many periodicals, but he soon cultivated a stable of his own writers (including the young Samuel Johnson) who furnished his readers with an ever-widening range of fresh materials: biographies, poetry, parliamentary debates. The *Magazine's* logo presents it as a compendium of other papers, but Cave had in fact produced a true original, "one of the most successful and lucrative pamphlets" (wrote Johnson, whose observation still holds true) "which literary history has upon record." The title page depicts the 200-year-old gatehouse where the *Gentleman's Magazine* was composed, printed, and sold (the building's fortress-like appearance may entail a visual pun, conjuring up the military meaning of "magazine"). The building is flanked by the names of papers that the *Magazine* has incorporated, one way or another, into its own pages (London papers on the left, provincial and foreign ones on the right). The fictitious name "Sylvanus Urban" conjures up both countryside (*sylvanus,* "wooded") and city; as the bottom lines make clear, Cave aimed his appeal at audiences in both domains.

Joseph Addison: Spectator No. 69
Saturday, 19 May 1711

[ROYAL EXCHANGE[1]]

Hic segetes, illic veniunt felicius uvae:
Arborei foetus alibi, atque injussa virescunt
Gramina. Nonne vides, croceos ut Tmolus odores,
India mittit ebur, molles sua thura Sabaei?
At Chalybes nudi ferrum, virosaque Pontus
Castorea, Eliadum palmas Epirus equarum?
Continuo has leges aeternaque foedera certis
Imposuit Natura locis . . .[2]

There is no place in the town which I so much love to frequent as the Royal Exchange. It gives me a secret satisfaction, and in some measure gratifies my vanity, as I am an Englishman, to see so rich an assembly of countrymen and foreigners consulting together upon the private business of mankind, and making this metropolis a kind of emporium for the whole earth. I must confess I look upon high-change[3] to be a great council, in which all considerable nations have their representatives. Factors[4] in the trading world are what ambassadors are in the politic world; they negotiate affairs, conclude treaties, and maintain a good correspondence between those wealthy societies of men that are divided from one another by seas and oceans, or live on the different extremities of a continent. I have often been pleased to hear disputes adjusted between an inhabitant of Japan and an alderman of London, or to see a subject of the Great Mogul[5] entering into a league with one of the Czar of Muscovy.[6] I am infinitely delighted in mixing with these several ministers of commerce, as they are distinguished by their different walks and different languages. Sometimes I am jostled among a body of Armenians: sometimes I am lost in a crowd of Jews, and sometimes make one in a group of Dutchmen. I am a Dane, Swede, or Frenchman at different times, or rather fancy myself like the old philosopher,[7] who upon being asked what countryman he was, replied that he was a citizen of the world.

Though I very frequently visit this busy multitude of people, I am known to nobody there but my friend, Sir Andrew,[8] who often smiles upon me as he sees me bustling in the crowd, but at the same time connives at my presence without taking any

---

1. The Exchange, a quadrangle of arcades and shops surrounding a huge courtyard, had functioned as a crucial site of London commerce since its creation in 1570. Destroyed in the Great Fire, it was rebuilt from a new design in 1669. The illustration on page 2331 depicts both the original building by Thomas Gresham (upper right corner) and the later structure with its more intricate, Baroque ornamentation. Statues of English kings occupy the second-floor arches. At the center of the courtyard, the statue of Charles II in the garb of a Roman emperor enacts that favored comparison (echoed by Addison in his essay's epigraph from Virgil) between contemporary Britain and the ancient Roman Empire.

2. "Corn grows more plentifully here, grapes there. In other places grow trees laden with fruit, and grasses unbidden. Do you not see how Tmolus sends us its saffron perfumes; India her ivory; the soft Sabaens their frankincense; but the naked Chalybes send us iron, the Pontus

pungent beaver-oil, and Epirus prize-winning Olympic horses? These perpetual laws and eternal covenants Nature has imposed on certain places" (Virgil, *Georgics* 1.54–61).

3. In addition to housing shops, the Exchange was a central meeting place for international merchants, who frequently closed deals in the courtyard. "High change" was that period when trading was at its peak.

4. Commercial agents.

5. The Indian emperor.

6. A territory in west-central Russia (Moscow was its capital).

7. Diogenes the Cynic, credited for developing the concept of "cosmopolitanism" (citizenship in the universe), in which all beings are parts of a single whole.

8. Sir Andrew Freeport, a member of Mr. Spectator's club: Whig merchant and ardent advocate (as his name implies) of free trade.

Sutton Nicholls, *The Royal Exchange*, 1712

further notice of me. There is indeed a merchant of Egypt, who just knows me by sight, having formerly remitted me some money to Grand Cairo;[9] but as I am not versed in the modern Coptic, our conferences go no further than a bow and a grimace.[1]

This grand scene of business gives me an infinite variety of solid and substantial entertainments. As I am a great lover of mankind, my heart naturally overflows with pleasure at the sight of a prosperous and happy multitude, insomuch that at many public solemnities I cannot forbear expressing my joy with tears that have stolen down my cheeks. For this reason I am wonderfully delighted to see such a body of men thriving in their own private fortunes, and at the same time promoting the public stock; or in other words, raising estates for their own families, by bringing into their country whatever is wanting, and carrying out of it whatever is superfluous.

Nature seems to have taken a particular care to disseminate her blessings among the different regions of the world, with an eye to this mutual intercourse and traffic among mankind, that the natives of the several parts of the globe might have a kind of dependence upon one another, and be united together by their common interest. Almost every degree produces something peculiar to it. The food often grows in one country, and the sauce in another. The fruits of Portugal are corrected by the

9. Where Mr. Spectator spent some time as a young man (see *Spectator* No. 1, page 2319).

1. The word denoted an expression of politeness.

products of Barbados; the infusion of a China plant sweetened with the pith of an Indian cane; the Philippic islands give a flavor to our European bowls. The single dress of a woman of quality is often the product of an hundred climates. The muff and the fan come together from the different ends of the Earth. The scarf is sent from the torrid zone, and the tippet from beneath the pole. The brocade petticoat rises out of the mines of Peru, and the diamond necklace out of the bowels of Indostan.

If we consider our own country in its natural prospect, without any of the benefits and advantages of commerce, what a barren uncomfortable spot of earth falls to our share! Natural historians tell us that no fruit grows originally among us, besides hips and haws, acorns and pig-nuts, with other delicacies of the like nature; that our climate of itself, and without the assistances of art, can make no further advances towards a plum than to a sloe,[2] and carries an apple to no greater a perfection than a crab;[3] that our melons, our peaches, our figs, our apricots, and cherries, are strangers among us, imported in different ages, and naturalized in our English gardens; and that they would all degenerate and fall away into the trash of our own country, if they were wholly neglected by the planter, and left to the mercy of our sun and soil. Nor has traffic more enriched our vegetable world, than it has improved the whole face of nature among us. Our ships are laden with the harvest of every climate; our tables are stored with spices, and oils, and wines; our rooms are filled with pyramids of China, and adorned with the workmanship of Japan; our morning's draught[4] comes to us from the remotest corners of the earth; we repair our bodies by the drugs of America, and repose ourselves under Indian canopies. My friend Sir Andrew calls the vineyards of France our gardens; the Spice Islands[5] our hotbeds; the Persians our silk weavers, and the Chinese our potters. Nature indeed furnishes us with the bare necessaries of life, but traffic gives us a great variety of what is useful, and at the same time supplies us with everything that is convenient and ornamental. Nor is it the least part of this our happiness, that whilst we enjoy the remotest products of the north and south, we are free from those extremities of weather which give them birth; that our eyes are refreshed with the green fields of Britain, at the same time that our palates are feasted with fruits that rise between the tropics.

For these reasons there are not more useful members in a commonwealth than merchants. They knit mankind together in a mutual intercourse of good offices, distribute the gifts of nature, find work for the poor, add wealth to the rich, and magnificence to the great. Our English merchant converts the tin of his own country into gold, and exchanges his wool for rubies. The Mahometans are clothed in our British manufacture, and the inhabitants of the frozen zone warmed with the fleeces of our sheep.

When I have been upon the 'Change, I have often fancied one of our old kings[6] standing in person, where he is represented in effigy, and looking down upon the wealthy concourse of people with which that place is every day filled. In this case, how would he be surprised to hear all the languages of Europe spoken in this little spot of his former dominions, and to see so many private men, who in his time would have been the vassals of some powerful baron, negotiating like princes for greater sums of money than were formerly to be met with in the Royal Treasury! Trade, without enlarging the British territories, has given us a kind of additional empire: it has multiplied the number of the rich, made our landed estates infinitely more

---

2. The berry of the blackthorn.
3. Crabapple.
4. Drink.

5. A cluster of islands in modern Indonesia.
6. As depicted in the statues on the second story (see illustration on page 2331).

valuable than they were formerly, and added to them an accession of other estates as valuable as the lands themselves.

Richard Steele: Spectator No. 11
Tuesday, 13 March 1711

[INKLE AND YARICO[1]]

Dat veniam corvis, vexat censura columbas.[2]

Arietta is visited by all persons of both sexes who have any pretense to wit and gallantry. She is in that time of life which is neither affected with the follies of youth or infirmities of age; and her conversation is so mixed with gaiety and prudence that she is agreeable both to the young and the old. Her behavior is very frank, without being in the least blameable; and as she is out of the tract of any amorous or ambitious pursuits of her own, her visitants entertain her with accounts of themselves very freely, whether they concern their passions or their interests. I made her a visit this afternoon, having been formerly introduced to the honor of her acquaintance by my friend Will. Honeycomb,[3] who has prevailed upon her to admit me sometimes into her assembly, as a civil, inoffensive man. I found her accompanied with one person only, a commonplace talker who, upon my entrance, rose, and after a very slight civility sat down again; then turning to Arietta, pursued his discourse, which I found was upon the old topic of constancy in love. He went on with great facility in repeating what he talks every day of his life; and with the ornaments of insignificant laughs and gestures, enforced his arguments by quotations out of plays and songs, which allude to the perjuries of the fair, and the general levity[4] of women. Methought he strove to shine more than ordinarily in his talkative way, that he might insult my silence, and distinguish himself before a woman of Arietta's taste and understanding. She had often an inclination to interrupt him, but could find no opportunity, 'till the larum[5] ceased of itself; which it did not 'till he had repeated and murdered the celebrated story of the Ephesian matron.[6]

Arietta seemed to regard this piece of raillery as an outrage done to her sex, as indeed I have always observed that women, whether out of a nicer[7] regard to their honor, or what other reason I cannot tell, are more sensibly touched with those general aspersions which are cast upon their sex, than men are by what is said of theirs.

When she had a little recovered herself from the serious anger she was in, she replied in the following manner.

"Sir, when I consider, how perfectly new all you have said on this subject is, and that the story you have given us is not quite two thousand years old, I cannot but think it a piece of presumption to dispute with you: but your quotations put me in mind of the fable of the lion and the man.[8] The man, walking with that noble

---

1. Steele here elaborates on a 60-year-old traveler's tale, in such a way as to combine two of the *Spectator*'s central concerns: the transactions of love and power between men and women, and the impact of commerce on human conduct.
2. "Their verdict goes easy on the raven, but is severe on the dove" (Juvenal, *Satires* 2.63). The speaker, a woman, is complaining of how leniently men assess themselves, and how harshly they criticize women.
3. An aged member of Mr. Spectator's club, proud of his long-ago days as a Restoration rake, and still deeply interested in matters of the heart.

4. Lightness, fickleness.
5. The long-ringing alarm bell (of his talk).
6. The Roman story (told in Petronius's *Satyricon*, pt. 2) of a widow who, while mourning at the tomb of her newly deceased husband, succumbs to the attractions of a soldier standing nearby, and makes love with him on her husband's tomb.
7. More precise.
8. In Aesop's *Fables* (No. 219).

animal, showed him, in the ostentation of human superiority, a sign of a man killing a lion. Upon which the lion said very justly, 'We lions are none of us painters, else we could show a hundred men killed by lions, for one lion killed by a man.' You men are writers, and can represent us women as unbecoming as you please in your works, while we are unable to return the injury. You have twice or thrice observed in your discourse that hypocrisy is the very foundation of our education; and that an ability to dissemble our affections is a professed part of our breeding. These, and such other reflections, are sprinkled up and down the writings of all ages, by authors who leave behind them memorials of their resentment against the scorn of particular women, in invectives against the whole sex. Such a writer, I doubt not, was the celebrated Petronius, who invented the pleasant aggravations of the frailty of the Ephesian lady; but when we consider this question between the sexes, which has been either a point of dispute or raillery ever since there were men and women, let us take facts from plain people, and from such as have not either ambition or capacity to embellish their narrations with any beauties of imagination. I was the other day amusing myself with Ligon's *Account of Barbados*; and, in answer to your well-wrought tale, I will give you (as it dwells upon my memory) out of that honest traveler, in his fifty-fifth page, the History of Inkle and Yarico.[9]

"Mr. Thomas Inkle[1] of London, aged 20 years, embarked in the Downs[2] on the good ship called the Achilles, bound for the West Indies, on the 16th of June 1647, in order to improve his fortune by trade and merchandise. Our adventurer was the third son of an eminent citizen, who had taken particular care to instill into his mind an early love of gain, by making him a perfect master of numbers, and consequently giving him a quick view of loss and advantage, and preventing the natural impulses of his passions, by prepossession towards his interests. With a mind thus turned, young Inkle had a person every way agreeable, a ruddy vigor in his counteance, strength in his limbs, with ringlets of fair hair loosely flowing on his shoulders. It happened, in the course of the voyage, that the Achilles, in some distress, put into a creek on the main of America, in search of provisions. The youth, who is the hero of my story, among others, went ashore on this occasion. From their first landing they were observed by a party of Indians, who hid themselves in the woods for that purpose. The English unadvisedly marched a great distance from the shore into the country, and were intercepted by the natives, who slew the greatest number of them. Our adventurer escaped among others, by flying into a forest. Upon his coming into a remote and pathless part of the wood, he threw himself, tired and breathless, on a little hillock, when an Indian maid rushed from a thicket behind him. After the first surprise, they appeared mutually agreeable to each other. If the European was highly charmed with the limbs, features, and wild graces of the naked American, the American was no less taken with the dress, complexion, and shape of an European, covered from head to foot. The Indian grew immediately enamored of him, and consequently solicitous for his preservation. She therefore conveyed him to a cave, where she gave him a delicious repast of fruits, and led him to a stream to slake his thirst. In the midst of these good offices, she would sometimes play with his hair, and delight in the opposition of its color to that of her fingers; then open his bosom, then laugh at him for covering it. She was, it

---

9. Richard Ligon's *True and Exact History of the Island of Barbados* (1657) includes a paragraph on a slave named Yarico and her misadventures in love, which Steele elaborates into the tale that follows.

1. Steele invents the name for this character; it means (perhaps prophetically) "linen tape," a common commodity.
2. A harbor on the southeastern coast of England.

seems, a person of distinction, for she every day came to him in a different dress, of the most beautiful shells, bugles, and bredes.[3] She likewise brought him a great many spoils, which her other lovers had presented to her; so that his cave was richly adorned with all the spotted skins of beasts, and most parti-colored feathers of fowls, which that world afforded. To make his confinement more tolerable, she would carry him in the dusk of the evening, or by the favor of moonlight, to unfrequented groves and solitudes, and show him where to lie down in safety, and sleep amidst the falls of waters, and melody of nightingales. Her part was to watch and hold him in her arms, for fear of her countrymen, and wake him on occasions to consult his safety. In this manner did the lovers pass away their time, till they had learned a language of their own, in which the voyager communicated to his mistress, how happy he should be to have her in his country, where she should be clothed in such silks as his waistcoat was made of, and be carried in houses drawn by horses, without being exposed to wind or weather. All this he promised her the enjoyment of, without such fears and alarms as they were there tormented with. In this tender correspondence these lovers lived for several months, when Yarico, instructed by her lover, discovered a vessel on the coast, to which she made signals, and in the night, with the utmost joy and satisfaction accompanied him to a ship's crew of his countrymen, bound for Barbados. When a vessel from the main arrives in that island, it seems the planters come down to the shore, where there is an immediate market of the Indians and other slaves, as with us of horses and oxen.

"To be short, Mr. Thomas Inkle, now coming into English territories, began seriously to reflect upon his loss of time, and to weigh with himself how many days' interest of his money he had lost during his stay with Yarico. This thought made the young man very pensive, and careful what account he should be able to give his friends of his voyage. Upon which considerations, the prudent and frugal young man sold Yarico to a Barbadian merchant; notwithstanding that the poor girl, to incline him to commiserate her condition, told him that she was with child by him; but he only made use of that information, to rise in his demands upon the purchaser."

I was so touched with this story, (which I think should be always a counterpart to the Ephesian matron) that I left the room with tears in my eyes; which a woman of Arietta's good sense did, I am sure, take for greater applause, than any compliments I could make her.

Daniel Defoe: *from* A Review of the State of the British Nation, Vol. 1, No. 43
Thursday, 8 January 1713

[WEAK FOUNDATIONS]

The subject of trade which I am now entered upon has this one excellency in it, for the benefit of the author, that really it can never be exhausted. * * * I remember some time ago I gave you a hint about the mighty alteration in the face of trade in this city; I cannot but touch it again on this occasion, because it relates to what I am upon. Let any man who remembers the glorious state of our trade about thirty or forty years past view but the streets of this opulent city and even the Exchange of London—nay, even our courts of law. It must of necessity put him in mind of Ezra 3.12,

---

3. Tube-shaped glass beads and braiding.

where the ancient men who had seen the old temple wept when they saw the weak foundations of the new.

However, to go on as I began and examine our new increase of commerce which we so must boast of: let me note a little to you with what mighty advantages the chasms, gaps, and breaches of our trade are filled up of late, and let us see it, I say, in the streets. Here, in the room of a trifling banker, or goldsmith, we are supplied with a most eminent brandy shop (Cheapside). There in the room of ditto you have a flaming shop[1] for white tea pots and luted earthen mugs (Cornhill), the most excellent offspring of that most valuable manufacture of earthenware. It is impossible that coffee, tea, and chocolate can be so advanced in their consumption without an eminent increase of those trades that attend them; whence we see the most noble shops in the city taken up with the valuable utensils of the tea table. The china warehouses are little marts within themselves (and by the way, are newly become markets of clandestine trade, of which I shall say more very quickly), and the eminent corner houses in the chief streets of London are chosen out by the town tinkers to furnish us with tea kettles and chocolate pots—vide Catherine Street and Bedford Buildings. Two thousand pound is reckoned a small stock in copper pots and lacquered kettles, and the very fitting up one of these brazen people's shops with fine sashes,[2] etc., to set forth his ware, costs above 500£ sterling, which is more by half than the best draper or mercer's shop in London requires.

This certainly shows the increase of our trade. Brass locks for our chambers and parlors, brass knockers for our doors, and the like add to the luster of those shops, of which hereafter. And the same sash works, only finer and larger, are now used to range[3] your brass and copper, that the goldsmiths had always to set out their less valuable silver and gold plate. From hence, be pleased to look upon the druggists of the town who are the merchants of these things. Bucklers-Bury and Little Lombard Street were the places which a few years ago held the whole number, a very few excepted, of that difficult nice employment, whose number is now spread over the whole town and with the most capital stocks, whose whole employ is the furnishing us by wholesale and retail with these most valuable of all drugs, coffee, tea, and chocolate—the general furniture of a druggist's shop being now three bales of coffee, twelve boxes of chocolate, six large canisters of tea, and an hundred and fifty empty gilded boxes. In like manner the rest of the town—how gloriously it is supplied! How do pastry cooks and periwig makers, brandy shops and toy shops, succeed linen drapers, mercers, upholsterers, and the like. A hundred pounds to rent for a house to sell jellies and apple pies; two hundred pounds to fit up a brandy shop, and afterwards not a hundred pound stock to put into it. These I can show many instances of.

Look, gentlemen, upon the particular parts of your town, formerly eminent for the best of tradesmen! View the famous churchyard of St. Paul's where so many aldermen and lord mayors have been raised by the trade of broadcloth and mere woolen manufactures,[4] and on whose trades so many families of poor always depended, that Sir William Turner used to say his shop alone employed 50,000 poor people! What succeeds him? A most noble, and to be sure, a much more valuable vintner's warehouse, *Anglice*,[5] a tavern, more vulgarly a bawdyhouse. And the next draper's shop, a coffee house; what takes up the whole row there? and supplies the place of eighteen or nineteen topping drapers? Who can but observe it! Cane chair

---

1. A shop with a kiln for making earthenware.
2. Windows made up of two sliding frames (common now, new and fancy at this time).
3. Display.

4. The trade in textiles had provided the foundation for many family fortunes and (hence) political careers.
5. In English.

makers, gilders of leather, looking-glass shops, and peddlers or toy shops—manifold improvements of trade! and an eminent instance of the growth of our manufactures!

* * *

Advertisements from the *Spectator* [1]

At the Lace Chamber on Ludgate Hill, kept by Mary Parsons, is a great quantity of Flanders lace, lately come over, to be sold off at great pennyworths[2] by wholesale or retail. She bought them there herself. [No. 200; Friday, 19 October 1711]

This day is published *The Court and City Vagaries,* being some late (and real) intrigues of several gentlemen and ladies. Written by one of the fair sex, price 6d. Sold by J. Baker in Paternoster Row. [No. 255; Saturday, 22 December 1711]

The famous Italian water, for dying red and gray hairs of the head and eyebrows into a lasting brown or black; at 1, 2, or 4s. the bottle, with printed directions for the use of it. To be had at Mrs. Hannam's toyshop, at the sign of the Three Angels near the Half-Moon Tavern in Cheapside. [Vol. 8, No. 634; Friday, 17 December 1714]

The ladies that called at Mr. Charles Lillie's at the corner of Beauford Buildings,[3] in a hackney coach on Wednesday night, the 6th of this instant, about 10 o'clock, are desired to let him know where to direct to them, he being now able to give a particular account of what they enquired after. [No. 305; Tuesday, 19 February 1712]

For a collection of periodical pieces on gender, manners, and marriage, go to *The Longman Anthology of British Literature* Web site at www.myliteraturekit.com.

⊱ END OF PERSPECTIVES: READING PAPERS ⊰

Jonathan Swift
1667–1745

Charles Jervas, *Jonathan Swift.*

Arguably the greatest prose satirist in the history of English literature, Jonathan Swift was born in Dublin, the only son of English parents, seven months after his father died. In his infancy he was kidnapped by his nurse and did not see his mother for three years. With the future dramatist William Congreve he attended the Kilkenny School (Ireland's best), and in 1682 he began six years of study at Trinity College, Dublin. He received his BA degree in 1686. From 1689, Swift served as secretary to Sir William Temple (1628–1699), a retired diplomat whose father had befriended Swift's family. Swift worked at Temple's estate at Moor Park in Surrey for most of the next ten years. It was at Moor Park that Swift first experienced the vertigo, nausea, and hearing impairment of Ménière's syndrome, a disturbance of the inner ear that would plague him for the rest of his life and sometimes wrongly led

---

1. Periodicals did not merely comment on commerce, they participated in it, earning much of their revenue from the advertisements that they printed at the conclusion of their main editorial matter.
2. At a terrific bargain.

3. Charles Lillie, a close associate of Addison's and Steele's, owned a perfume shop in the Strand. He had been one of the publishers and distributors of the *Tatler,* and sold the *Spectator* at his shop, where he also accepted advertisements for inclusion in the paper.

him (and others) to question his mental stability. While working for Temple, Swift also wrote his first poems, undistinguished compositions that do not presage the literary acclaim that was to come.

Not content with his station in life, Swift took an M.A. degree from Oxford University in 1692; three years later, he was ordained a priest in the (Anglican) Church of Ireland and appointed to the undesirable prebendary of Kilroot, where he found the local Presbyterians unsympathetic and the salary meager. Added to professional discontent was personal disappointment: Swift was rejected in his marriage proposal to Jane "Varina" Waring, the daughter of an Anglican clergyman. Swift returned to Moor Park in 1696, and, after Temple died in 1699, held a series of ecclesiastical posts in Ireland, none of which fulfilled his ambition for an important position in England. In 1702 he was made Doctor of Divinity by his alma mater, Trinity College, Dublin.

While at Moor Park, Swift began to tutor an eight-year-old girl, Esther "Stella" Johnson, daughter of Sir William's late steward. Though she was nearly fourteen years Swift's junior, "Stella" would in time become his beloved companion and his most trusted friend. When she was eighteen, Swift described her as "one of the most beautiful, graceful, and agreeable young women in London." In 1701, at Swift's request, Stella and Sir William's spinster cousin, Rebecca Dingley, moved to Dublin, where they remained for the rest of their lives. Swift and Stella met regularly, but never alone. Although there has been much debate about the nature of their relationship, it is clear that Swift and Stella loved, trusted, and valued each other, whether or not they were ever secretly married (the evidence suggests they were not). Swift's *Journal to Stella* (composed 1710 to 1713) and the series of poems he composed for her birthdays reveal a playful intimacy and affection not seen in his more public writings.

Moor Park not only led him to Stella but was also the cradle of Swift's first major literary work: *A Tale of a Tub* (composed 1697 to 1698, published 1704), a brilliant satire on "corruptions in religion and learning," published with *The Battle of the Books*, Swift's mock-epic salvo in the debate between the Ancients and the Moderns. Like most of his subsequent works, *A Tale of a Tub* did not appear under Swift's name, though its ironic treatment of the church subsequently damaged his prospects for ecclesiastical preferment when his authorship became widely known.

In the first decade of the new century Swift placed his hopes for preferment with the Whigs, then in power, and became associated with the Whig writers Joseph Addison and Richard Steele, founder of the *Tatler*, a London periodical in which two of Swift's important early poems, *A Description of the Morning* (1709) and *A Description of a City Shower* (1710), first appeared. Swift's career as a political polemicist began when he rose to the defense of three Whig lords facing impeachment with his allegorical *Discourse of the Contests and Dissentions between the Nobles and Commons in Athens and Rome* (1701). His *Bickerstaff Papers* (1708–1709), witty parodies of the cobbler-turned-astrologer John Partridge, occasioned much laughter regardless of party allegiances. More important, Swift began to write a series of pamphlets on church affairs, including his ironical *Argument against Abolishing Christianity* (1708) and *A Letter . . . Concerning the Sacramental Test* (1709), which damaged his relationship with the Whigs.

While in London as an emissary for the Irish clergy in 1708, Swift met Esther "Vanessa" Vanhomrigh (pronounced "Vanummry") and, as with "Stella," acted as her mentor. Although his feelings for this attractive young woman (twenty-one years younger than he) clearly became more than paternal, Swift was eventually put off by her declaration of "inexpressible passion" and wrote *Cadenus and Vanessa* (composed 1713, published 1726) to cool the relationship.

Vehemently disagreeing with the Whig policies supporting the Dissenters (Protestants who were not members of the established church) because he feared they would weaken the Anglican church, Swift shifted his allegiance to the Tories in 1710 and soon became their principal spokesman and propagandist, taking charge of their weekly periodical the *Examiner* (1710–1711) and producing a series of highly effective political pamphlets, such as *The Conduct of the Allies* (1712), which called for an end to the War of Spanish Succession (1701–1713). Swift's years in London from 1710 to 1714, when he was an important lobbyist for the Church of Ireland and an influential agent of the Tory government, were the most exciting of his life.

In 1713 Swift was installed as Dean of Saint Patrick's Cathedral, Dublin—a prestigious appointment, but far short of the English bishopric he felt he deserved. Returning quickly to London, Swift became a vital presence in the Scriblerus Club—with Alexander Pope, John Arbuthnot, John Gay, Thomas Parnell, and Robert Harley, Earl of Oxford—which met in 1714. The influence of this group, with its love of parody, literary hoaxes, and the ridicule of false learning, is evident in *Gulliver's Travels*. Upon the death of Queen Anne in 1714 and the resultant fall of the Tory Ministry, Swift's hopes for further advancement were dashed, and he took up permanent residence in Ireland, where he conscientiously carried out his duties as Dean.

When Swift successfully defended Irish interests by writing *The Drapier's Letters* (1724–1725)—attacking a government plan to impose a new coin, "Wood's halfpence," that would devalue Ireland's currency and seriously damage the economy—he became a national hero. Thereafter, the people lit bonfires on his birthday and hailed him as a champion of Irish liberty, though he never ceased to regard Ireland as the land of his exile. From Dublin, he corresponded with Pope, Gay, Arbuthnot, and Henry St. John, Lord Bolingbroke; he enjoyed a long visit with his friends in England in 1726. While there, he encouraged Gay's *The Beggar's Opera* and Pope's *The Dunciad,* and arranged for the publication of his own masterpiece, *Gulliver's Travels* (1726).

When the death of George I the following year briefly created hopes of unseating "Prime Minister" Robert Walpole, Swift paid his final visit to England, where he assisted Pope in editing their joint *Miscellanies* in three volumes (1727, 1728, 1732). The years that followed in Dublin saw the production of many of Swift's finest poems, including *The Lady's Dressing Room* (1732), *A Beautiful Young Nymph Going to Bed* (1734), and *Verses on the Death of Dr. Swift* (composed 1731–1732, published 1739), his most celebrated poem. Swift continued to champion the cause of Irish political and economic freedom; with his like-minded friend Thomas Sheridan, he conducted a weekly periodical, the *Intelligencer* (1728). In 1729, he published his most famous essay, *A Modest Proposal*. Some years later, he supervised the publication of the first four volumes of his *Works* (1735) by the Dublin publisher George Faulkener.

When Swift reached his early seventies, his infirmities made him incapable of carrying out his clerical duties at Saint Patrick's; at seventy-five, he was found "of unsound mind and memory," and guardians were appointed to manage his affairs. In addition to ongoing debilities from Ménière's syndrome, he suffered from arteriosclerosis, aphasia, memory loss, and other diseases of old age; he was not insane, however, as many of his contemporaries believed. A devoted clergyman, Swift practiced the Christian charity he preached, giving more than half of his income to the needy; the founding of Ireland's first mental hospital through a generous provision in his will was the most famous of Swift's many benefactions.

Voltaire hailed Swift as the "English Rabelais," while Henry Fielding lauded him as the "English Lucian." Although the more delicate sensibilities of the nineteenth century eschewed his writings for their coarseness and truculence, twentieth-century readers have prized Swift's work for its intelligence, wit, and inventiveness. A committed champion of social justice and an untiring enemy of pride, Swift was a brilliant satirist in part because he was a thoroughgoing humanist.

 For additional resources on Swift, go to *The Longman Anthology of British Literature* Web site at www.myliteraturekit.com.

A DESCRIPTION OF THE MORNING   Introducing this poem in the ninth number of his new periodical, the *Tatler* (for 30 April 1709), Richard Steele wrote that Swift, "has . . . run into a way [of writing] perfectly new, and described things exactly as they happen." *A Description of the Morning* is an early and important example of the "town eclogue," or urban pastoral, a poetic style further popularized by John Gay's *Trivia, or The Art of Walking the Streets of London* (1716). Traditionally, the eclogue—Virgil's bucolic poems are the most famous example—has no appreciable action or characterization, but depends on the thorough and evocative depiction of a pastoral scene. Swift's *Morning* imitates the conventions of pastoral description, not to portray the idealized natural harmony of Arcadia but rather to present the reality of social disorder masquerading under the appearance of order as day breaks over London. Remarkably, Alexander Pope's *Pastorals*, his first published poems, went on sale in the same week that Swift's pioneering mock-pastoral appeared, though the two future friends would not meet for several years.

A Description of the Morning

Now hardly° here and there a hackney coach[1]   *harshly*
Appearing, showed the ruddy morn's approach.
Now Betty[2] from her master's bed has flown,
And softly stole to discompose her own.
5   The slipshod 'prentice from his master's door
Had pared° the dirt, and sprinkled round the floor.[3]   *reduced*
Now Moll had whirled her mop with dexterous airs,
Prepared to scrub the entry and the stairs.
The youth with broomy stumps began to trace
10   The kennel edge, where wheels had worn the place.[4]
The smallcoal man was heard with cadence deep;[5]
Till drowned in shriller notes of chimney sweep.
Duns° at his Lordship's gate began to meet;   *creditors*
And brickdust[6] Moll had screamed through half a street.
15   The turnkey now his flock returning sees,
Duly let out a-nights to steal for fees.[7]
The watchful bailiffs take their silent stands;
And schoolboys lag with satchels in their hands.[8]

1709   1709

A DESCRIPTION OF A CITY SHOWER   "They say 'tis the best thing I ever writ, and I think so too," boasted Swift of his *Description of a City Shower* in 1710. It was first published in the *Tatler*, No. 238, on 17 October 1710, soon after its composition. Swift's closely observed rendering of London street life playfully mocks the English imitators of Virgil, especially John Dryden and his celebrated translation, *The Works of Virgil* (1697). We see, for example, Swift's

---

1. A hired coach, drawn by two horses and seating six people; here, equated with the chariot of Phoebus Apollo, Greek god of the sun.
2. Like "Moll" (line 7), a typical maidservant's name.
3. Fresh sawdust was used to absorb mud.
4. Scavenging in the gutters (kennels) "to find old nails" [Swift's note] was common.
5. Small pieces of coal or charcoal used to light fires; like many other products and services, they were sold by street vendors who advertised, or "cried," their wares by

calling or singing as they walked the streets. The smallcoal man has a deep voice; sweeps were always small boys.
6. An abrasive, used for cleaning or for sharpening knives.
7. As prisoners had to pay the jailer for food and for other comforts, the jailer has let them out overnight to steal.
8. Cf. the second "age of man" in Shakespeare's *As You Like It*: "Then the whining schoolboy, with his satchel / And shining morning face, creeping like snail / Unwillingly to school" (2.7.145–47).

mock-heroic effects based on Virgil's *Aeneid* (29–19 B.C.E.), most notably in comparing the timorous "beau" trapped in his sedan chair to the fierce Greek warriors hiding inside the Trojan Horse, and in calling to mind the storm that led to Queen Dido's seduction and eventual ruin (Dryden's translation 4.231–238). More important, just as Swift invoked the mock-pastoral in *A Description of the Morning*, so too does he create a mock-georgic mode in his *City Shower*. The division of the poem into portents, preliminaries, and deluge closely parallels the tempest scene in Virgil's *Georgics* (36–29 B.C.E.; bk. 1, 431–458, 483–538 in Dryden), so that Swift uses structural and verbal elements from a classical poem extolling the virtues of agriculture and rural life to depict the teeming diversity of the contemporary urban scene.

A Description of a City Shower

Careful observers may foretell the hour
(By sure prognostics) when to dread a shower.
While rain depends,° the pensive cat gives o'er   *is impending*
Her frolics, and pursues her tail no more.
5   Returning home at night you find the sink[1]
Strike your offended sense with double stink.
If you be wise, then go not far to dine,
You spend in coach-hire more than save in wine.
A coming shower your shooting corns[2] presage,
10 Old aches[3] throb, your hollow tooth will rage:
Sauntering in coffee-house is Dulman seen;
He damns the climate, and complains of spleen.[4]

Meanwhile the South,° rising with dabbled° wings,   *south wind / muddy*
A sable cloud athwart the welkin° flings;   *sky*
15 That swilled more liquor than it could contain,
And like a drunkard gives it up again.
Brisk Susan whips her linen from the rope,[5]
While the first drizzling shower is borne aslope:°   *at a slant*
Such is that sprinkling which some careless quean°   *hussy*
20 Flirts° on you from her mop, but not so clean: *flicks*
You fly, invoke the gods; then turning, stop
To rail; she singing, still whirls on her mop.
Nor yet the dust had shunned th' unequal strife,
But aided by the wind, fought still for life;
25 And wafted with its foe by violent gust,
'Twas doubtful which was rain, and which was dust.[6]
Ah! Where must needy poet seek for aid,
When dust and rain at once his coat invade?
Sole coat, where dust cemented by the rain
30 Erects the nap, and leaves a cloudy stain.

1. Sewer. The poem is built upon Swift's experiences in London: on 8 November 1710, Swift wrote to his beloved Stella (Esther Johnson) that "I will give ten shillings a week for my lodging; for I am almost stunk out of this with the sink, and it helps me to verses in my Shower." The parsimonious Swift normally spent around half this amount for lodgings.
2. The shooting pain in your corns.

3. Pronounced "aitches."
4. Dulman (a descriptive name) complains of melancholy or depression, then attributed to the spleen.
5. The typically named maid brings in her washing from the line.
6. Swift here parallels a line from Samuel Garth's popular satirical poem, *The Dispensary* (1699): "'Tis doubtful which is sea, and which is sky" (5.176).

Now in contiguous drops the flood comes down,
Threatening with deluge this devoted° town.   *doomed*
To shops in crowds the daggled° females fly,   *muddied*
Pretend to cheapen° goods, but nothing buy.   *bargain for*
35 The Templer spruce,[7] while every spout's abroach,[8]
Stays till 'tis fair, yet seems to call a coach.
The tucked-up seamstress walks with hasty strides,
While streams run down her oiled umbrella's sides.
Here various kinds by various fortunes led,
40 Commence acquaintance underneath a shed.°   *shelter*
Triumphant Tories, and desponding Whigs,[9]
Forget their feuds, and join to save their wigs.
Boxed° in a chair[1] the beau impatient sits,   *confined*
While spouts run clattering o'er the roof by fits;
45 And ever and anon with frightful din
The leather sounds; he trembles from within.
So when Troy chairmen bore the wooden steed,
Pregnant with Greeks, impatient to be freed;
(Those bully Greeks, who, as the moderns do,
50 Instead of paying chairmen, run them through[2])
Laocoon struck the outside with his spear,
And each imprisoned hero quaked for fear.[3]

Now from all parts the swelling kennels[4] flow,
And bear their trophies with them as they go:
55 Filths of all hues and odors, seem to tell
What streets they sailed from, by the sight and smell.
They, as each torrent drives with rapid force
From Smithfield, or St. Pulchre's shape their course;[5]
And in huge confluent join at Snow Hill ridge,
60 Fall from the conduit prone to Holborn Bridge.[6]
Sweepings from butchers' stalls, dung, guts, and blood, ⎤
Drowned puppies, stinking sprats,° all drenched in mud, ⎬ *small fish*
Dead cats and turnip tops come tumbling down the flood.[7]⎦

1710   1710

STELLA'S BIRTHDAY Between 1719 and 1727 Swift wrote seven birthday poems to "Stella," his dear Esther Johnson. The two reprinted here are his first and last. Swift's earliest use of the name "Stella" in verse was in the first of this series of celebratory verses, which

7. Well-dressed lawyer.
8. Drainpipe pouring water.
9. 1710, the year this poem was written, was the first year of the Tory ministry under Queen Anne.
1. A sedan chair, carried by two men; this one has a leather roof.
2. With their swords.
3. When the Trojans carried the Greek's wooden horse into Troy, thinking that the opposing army had given up their siege, the priest Laocoon was suspicious, and struck the horse. See *Aeneid* 2.50–53.
4. Gutters, which were also open sewers.
5. Respectively, the cattle market and the parish west of the Newgate prison.

6. Snow Hill ridge extended down to Holborn Bridge, which spanned Fleet ditch, used as an open sewer; from 1343, local butchers had been given permission to dump entrails in the Fleet.
7. These last three lines were intended against the licentious manner of modern poets, in making three rhymes together, which they call *Triplets*; and the last of the three was two, or sometimes more syllables longer, called an *Alexandrian*. These *Triplets* and *Alexandrians* were brought in by Dryden, and other poets in the reign of Charles II. They were the mere effect of haste, idleness, and want of money, and have been wholly avoided by the best poets since these verses were written [Swift's note].

play on the obligation of the Poet Laureate to write an official "birthday ode" for the monarch every year. Placing himself in the role of her laureate, Swift may have chosen the name "Stella" to highlight the difference between his own uncontrived expressions of affection and those of the courtly Sir Philip Sidney in *Astrophil and Stella* (1591). Like Shakespeare's Sonnet 130 ("My mistress' eyes are nothing like the sun"), Swift's first poem on Stella's birthday violates the traditions of the conventional love lyric by calling attention to his beloved's considerable weight and age, only to suggest that his admiration of her lies in her deeper virtues. In his last birthday poem, Swift attempts to escape from the prospect of Stella's impending death, first by humor and then by the power of reason; when these fail, he tenderly acknowledges how much she means to him. Swift was to sail for England less than a month after he gave those verses to her—both knew that they might never see each other again. Though more formal than the *Journal to Stella*, Swift's birthday verses were written primarily for Stella's enjoyment and for the entertainment of their small circle of intimate friends. Despite the private nature of these poems, Swift nevertheless authorized their publication in the third and last volume of the Pope-Swift *Miscellanies*, which appeared in March 1728.

Stella's Birthday, 1719
WRITTEN IN THE YEAR 1718/9[1]

Stella this day is thirty-four,[2]
(We shan't dispute a year or more):
However, Stella, be not troubled,
Although thy size and years are doubled,
5   Since first I saw thee at sixteen,[3]
The brightest virgin on the green.[4]
So little is thy form° declined;   *figure*
Made up° so largely in thy mind.   *compensated*

   Oh, would it please the gods to *split*
10   Thy beauty, size, and years, and wit,
No age could furnish out a pair
Of nymphs so graceful, wise, and fair:
With half the luster of your eyes,
With half your wit, your years, and size:
15   And then before it grew too late,
How should I beg of gentle fate,
(That either nymph might have her swain),
To split my worship too in twain.

1719   1728

---

1. Until the calendar was reformed in 1751, the new year legally began on the Feast of the Annunciation (sometimes called "Lady Day") on March 25th, though January 1st was also commonly recognized as the start of the new year. Therefore, to avoid confusion, it was a widely accepted practice to write dates between January 1 and March 24 according to both methods of reckoning: 1718/19. Since Swift's poem was composed in February or March, we would say it was written in 1719.

2. Stella (Esther Johnson) actually celebrated her thirty-eighth birthday on 13 March 1719.
3. Swift first met Stella when she was eight years old; he may have "seen" her only when she grew from child to woman.
4. The village green, or common land, here implies a pastoral simplicity that suggests the natural innocence of their relationship.

Stella's Birthday, 1727

This day, whate'er the fates decree,
Shall still be kept with joy by me:
This day then, let us not be told,
That you are sick, and I grown old,
5   Nor think on our approaching ills,
And talk of spectacles and pills.
Tomorrow will be time enough
To hear such mortifying stuff.[1]
Yet, since from reason may be brought
10   A better and more pleasing thought,
Which can in spite of all decays,
Support a few remaining days:
From not the gravest of divines,°   clergymen
Accept for once some serious lines.

15   Although we now can form no more
Long schemes of life, as heretofore;
Yet you, while time is running fast,
Can look with joy on what is past.

Were future happiness and pain[2]
20   A mere contrivance of the brain,
As atheists argue, to entice
And fit their proselytes° for vice   converts
(The only comfort they propose,
To have companions in their woes);
25   Grant this the case, yet sure 'tis hard,
That virtue, styled its own reward,
And by all sages understood
To be the chief of human good,
Should acting, die, nor leave behind
30   Some lasting pleasure in the mind;
Which by remembrance will assuage
Grief, sickness, poverty, and age;
And strongly shoot a radiant dart
To shine through life's declining part.

35   Say, Stella, feel you no content,
Reflecting on a life well spent?
Your skillful hand employed to save
Despairing wretches from the grave;[3]
And then supporting with your store,
40   Those whom you dragged from death before
(So Providence on mortals waits,
Preserving what it first creates);
Your generous boldness to defend

---

1. Both humbling and leading to death. Stella died less than a year later.
2. I.e., heaven and hell.

3. Swift often praised Stella's charity, not only for nursing him in his bouts of illness, but also for attending to the poor in her neighborhood.

An innocent and absent friend;
45 That courage which can make you just,
To merit humbled in the dust;
The detestation you express
For vice in all its glittering dress;
That patience under torturing pain,
50 Where stubborn Stoics would complain.

Shall these like empty shadows pass,
Or forms reflected from a glass?
Or mere chimeras° in the mind,   *imaginary creatures or notions*
That fly and leave no marks behind?
55 Does not the body thrive and grow
By food of twenty years ago?
And had it not been still supplied,
It must a thousand times have died.
Then, who with reason can maintain
60 That no effects of food remain?
And is not virtue in mankind
The nutriment that feeds the mind?
Upheld by each good action past,
And still continued by the last:
65 Then who with reason can pretend,
That all effects of virtue end?

Believe me, Stella, when you show
That true contempt for things below,
Nor prize your life for other ends
70 Than merely to oblige your friends;
Your former actions claim their part,
And join to fortify your heart.
For Virtue in her daily race,
Like Janus⁴ bears a double face;
75 Looks back with joy where she has gone,
And therefore goes with courage on.
She at your sickly couch will wait,
And guide you to a better state.

O then, whatever Heaven intends,
80 Take pity on your pitying friends;
Nor let your ills affect your mind,
To fancy they can be unkind.
Me, surely me, you ought to spare,
Who gladly would your sufferings share;
85 Or give my scrap of life to you,
And think it far beneath your due;
You, to whose care so oft I owe
That I'm alive to tell you so.

1727   1728

4. The god of doorways and of the rising and setting sun, whose two-faced head looks forward and backward, and after whom the month of January is named.

THE LADY'S DRESSING ROOM   The first of Swift's so-called scatological poems, which have attracted much critical attention and amateur psychoanalysis, these verses enjoyed considerable popularity in Swift's lifetime, though some contemporaries condemned them as "deficient in point of delicacy, even to the highest degree." One of Swift's friends recorded in her memoirs that *The Lady's Dressing Room* made her mother "instantly" lose her lunch. Sir Walter Scott found in this poem (and other pieces by Swift) "the marks of an incipient disorder of the mind, which induced the author to dwell on degrading and disgusting subjects." If Pope's *The Rape of the Lock* describes Belinda at the "altar" of her dressing table undergoing "the sacred rites of pride" as she and her maid apply all manner of cosmetics to make her a beautiful "goddess" and arm her for the battle of the sexes, then *The Lady's Dressing Room* reveals the coarse realities of Celia's embodiment—a humorous and disturbing corrective to the pretense and false appearances on which her glorification depends. Although Swift assails the social and literary conventions that celebrate women for their superficial qualities, there is also a misogynistic quality to the poem, which may be attributable to his anger and disappointment over his beloved Stella's death in January 1728. Nevertheless, Strephon is ridiculed for being so naively idealistic about his lover and so easily deceived by appearances; once his secret investigations free him from his illusions, Strephon's permanent revulsion and rejection of all women show his inability to follow a middle course by appreciating women in their complex reality.

The Lady's Dressing Room

Five hours (and who can do it less in?)
By haughty Celia spent in dressing;
The goddess from her chamber issues,
Arrayed in lace, brocade, and tissues:
5   Strephon,[1] who found the room was void,
And Betty[2] otherwise employed,
Stole in, and took a strict survey,
Of all the litter as it lay:
Whereof, to make the matter clear,
10   An *inventory* follows here.

And first, a dirty smock appeared,
Beneath the arm-pits well besmeared;
Strephon, the rogue, displayed it wide,
And turned it round on every side.
15   In such a case few words are best,
And Strephon bids us guess the rest;
But swears how damnably the men lie,
In calling Celia sweet and cleanly.

Now listen while he next produces
20   The various combs for various uses,
Filled up with dirt so closely fixed,
No brush could force a way betwixt;
A paste of composition rare,
Sweat, dandruff, powder, lead,[3] and hair,

1. Strephon and Celia are names usually associated with pastoral poetry, and are therefore used mockingly here.

2. A typical maidservant's name.
3. White lead face paint, used to whiten the skin.

A forehead cloth with oil upon't
To smooth the wrinkles on her front;
Here alum flour[4] to stop the steams,
Exhaled from sour, unsavory streams;
There night-gloves made of Tripsy's[5] hide,
Bequeathed by Tripsy when she died;
With puppy water,[6] beauty's help,
Distilled from Tripsy's darling whelp.
Here gallipots° and vials placed,   *ointment jars*
Some filled with washes, some with paste;
Some with pomatum,° paints, and slops,   *hair ointment*
And ointments good for scabby chops.°   *lips or cheeks*
Hard° by a filthy basin stands,   *close*
Fouled with the scouring of her hands;
The basin takes whatever comes,
The scrapings of her teeth and gums,
A nasty compound of all hues,
For here she spits, and here she spews.

    But oh! it turned poor Strephon's bowels,
When he beheld and smelt the towels;
Begummed, bemattered, and beslimed;
With dirt, and sweat, and ear-wax grimed.
No object Strephon's eye escapes,
Here, petticoats in frowzy° heaps;   *unkempt*
Nor be the handkerchiefs forgot,
All varnished o'er with snuff[7] and snot.
The stockings why should I expose,
Stained with the moisture of her toes;
Or greasy coifs and pinners° reeking,   *night caps*
Which Celia slept at least a week in?
A pair of tweezers next he found
To pluck her brows in arches round,
Or hairs that sink the forehead low,
Or on her chin like bristles grow.

    The virtues we must not let pass
Of Celia's magnifying glass;
When frighted Strephon cast his eye on't,
It showed the visage of a giant:[8]
A glass that can to sight disclose
The smallest worm in Celia's nose,

25
30
35
40
45
50
55
60

4. Powdered alum used like modern antiperspirant.
5. Celia's lapdog; no fashionable lady was without such a pet.
6. A recipe for this cosmetic, made from the innards of a pig or a fat puppy, was given in the "Fop's Dictionary" in *Mundus Muliebris* [Womanly Make-up]: *Or, the Ladies' Dressing Room Unlocked* (1690), which Swift also used for other terms.

7. Powdered tobacco, sniffed by fashionable men and women alike.
8. Cf. *Gulliver's Travels*, Part 2, "A Voyage to Brobdingnag," ch. 1: "This made me reflect upon the fair skins of our *English* ladies, who appear so beautiful to us, only because they are of our own size, and their defects not to be seen but through magnifying glass, where we find by experiment that the smoothest and whitest skins look rough and coarse, and ill colored."

65   And faithfully direct her nail
        To squeeze it out from head to tail;
        For catch it nicely by the head,
        It must come out alive or dead.

        Why, Strephon, will you tell the rest?
70   And must you needs describe the chest?
        That careless wench! no creature warn her
        To move it out from yonder corner,
        But leave it standing full in sight,
        For you to exercise your spite!
75   In vain the workman showed his wit
        With rings and hinges counterfeit
        To make it seem in this disguise
        A cabinet to vulgar eyes;
        Which Strephon ventured to look in,
80   Resolved to go through *thick and thin;*
        He lifts the lid: there need no more,
        He smelt it all the time before.

        As, from within Pandora's box,
        When Epimethus oped the locks,
85   A sudden universal crew
        Of human evils upward flew;[9]
        He still was comforted to find
        That hope at last remained behind.

        So, Strephon, lifting up the lid
90   To view what in the chest was hid,
        The vapors flew from out the vent,
        But Strephon cautious never meant
        The bottom of the pan to grope,
        And foul his hands in search of hope.

95   O! ne'er may such a vile machine°   construction
        Be once in Celia's chamber seen!
        O! may she better learn to keep
        "Those secrets of the hoary deep."[1]

        As mutton cutlets, prime of meat,
100   Which though with art you salt and beat
        As laws of cookery require,
        And roast them at the clearest fire;
        If from adown the hopeful chops
        The fat upon a cinder drops,
105   To stinking smoke it turns the flame

9. In Greek mythology, Epimethus, acting against advice, opened the box Jove had given his wife Pandora, and all the evils and vices of the world flew out, leaving only hope in the box.
1. Quoting Milton's *Paradise Lost* 2.891, in which Sin is unleashing the chaotic forces of her infernal realm.

Poisoning the flesh from whence it came;
And up exhales a greasy stench
For which you curse the careless wench:
So things which must not be expressed,
110   When *plumped*° into the reeking chest,   *dropped*
Send up an excremental smell
To taint the parts from which they fell:
The petticoats and gown perfume,
And waft a stink round every room.

115   Thus finishing his grand survey,
The swain disgusted slunk away,
Repeating in his amorous fits,
"Oh! Celia, Celia, Celia shits!"

         But Vengeance, goddess never sleeping,
120   Soon punished Strephon for his peeping.
His foul imagination links
Each dame he sees with all her stinks:
And if unsavory odors fly,
Conceives a lady standing by:
125   All women his description fits,
And both ideas jump° like wits   *join together*
By vicious fancy coupled fast,
And still appearing in contrast.

         I pity wretched Strephon, blind
130   To all the charms of womankind;
Should I the queen of love refuse,
Because she rose from stinking ooze?²
To him that looks behind the scene,
Statira's but some pocky quean.³

135   When Celia in her glory shows,
If Strephon would but stop his nose,
Who now so impiously blasphemes
Her ointments, daubs, and paints and creams;
Her washes, slops, and every clout,⁴
140   With which she makes so foul a rout;⁵
He soon would learn to think like me,
And bless his ravished eyes to see
Such order from confusion sprung,
Such gaudy *tulips* raised from *dung*.

c. 1730   1732

---

2. Venus, Roman goddess of sexual love and physical
beauty, rose from the sea.
3. One of the heroines of Nathaniel Lee's highly popular
tragedy *The Rival Queens* (1677); Swift's common slat-
tern (quean) has had either smallpox or venereal disease.

4. Washes were either treated water used for the complexion or stale urine used as a detergent; clouts were
rags.
5. Both of her skin and, presumably, of the men.

⟨✿⟩

RESPONSE
Lady Mary Wortley Montagu: The Reasons that Induced Dr. S. to write a Poem called The Lady's Dressing Room[1]

The Doctor in a clean starched band,
His golden snuff box in his hand,
With care his diamond ring displays
And artful shows its various rays,
5　While grave he stalks down —— street
His dearest Betty —— to meet.[2]
　　Long had he waited for this hour,
Nor gained admittance to the bower,
Had joked and punned, and swore and writ,
10　Tried all his gallantry and wit,[3]
Had told her oft what part he bore
In Oxford's schemes in days of yore,[4]
But bawdy,° politics, nor satire　　　　　　　　　　　*obscenity*
Could move this dull hard hearted creature.
15　Jenny her maid could taste° a rhyme　　　　　　　　*enjoy*
And, grieved to see him lose his time,
Had kindly whispered in his ear,
"For twice two pound you enter here;
My lady vows without that sum
20　It is in vain you write or come."
　　The destined offering now he brought,
And in a paradise of thought,
With a low bow approached the dame,
Who smiling heard him preach his flame.
25　His gold she takes (such proofs as these
Convince most unbelieving shes)
And in her trunk rose up to lock it
(Too wise to trust it in her pocket)
And then, returned with blushing grace,
30　Expects the doctor's warm embrace.
　　But now this is the proper place
Where morals stare me in the face,
And for the sake of fine expression
I'm forced to make a small digression.
35　Alas for wretched humankind,
With learning mad, with wisdom blind!

1. Lady Mary Wortley Montagu, energetic traveler and versatile writer, found in Swift an object of recurrent scorn. *Gulliver's Travels* (and particularly its fourth book) she dismissed as filth, perpetrated upon a "mad" and inexplicably admiring readership. When "The Lady's Dressing Room" appeared, Montagu crafted her own verse retort. Here, with formidable mimicry, she echoes Swift's method (the catalogue of disconcerting physical particulars), his meter, his phrasings, and his thoughts in such a way that they recoil upon their maker. What Swift depicts as disillusion (Strephon's), Montagu re-reckons as self-delusion (Swift's). The trauma that he derives from Celia's fabrications, she ascribes instead to the Dean's own fears and failures. (For more on Montagu, see page 2543.)

2. In Swift's poem, Betty is the maid's name, Celia the mistress's.

3. Montagu echoes Swift's poem *Cadenus and Vanessa*, where the clumsy lover "Had sighed and languished, / vowed and writ, / For pastime, or to show his wit" (542–43).

4. Swift had collaborated closely in the political schemes of Robert Harley, first Earl of Oxford (1661–1724).

The ox thinks he's for saddle fit
(As long ago friend Horace writ[5])
And men their talents still mistaking,[6]
40   The stutterer fancies his is speaking.
With admiration oft we see
Hard features heightened by toupée,
The beau affects° the politician,   *pretends to be*
Wit is the citizen's ambition,
45   Poor Pope philosophy displays on
With so much rhyme and little reason,
And though he argues ne'er so long
That all is right, his head is wrong.[7]
        None strive to know their proper merit
50   But strain for wisdom, beauty, spirit,
And lose the praise that is their due
While they've th' impossible in view.
So have I seen the injudicious heir
To add one window the whole house impair.
55   Instinct the hound does better teach,
Who never undertook to preach;
The frighted hare from dogs does run
But not attempts to bear a gun.
Here many noble thoughts occur
60   But I prolixity abhor,
And will pursue th' instructive tale
To show the wise in some things fail.
        The reverend lover with surprise ⎫
Peeps in her bubbies, and her eyes,   ⎬
65   And kisses both, and tries—and tries. ⎭
The evening in this hellish play,
Beside his guineas thrown away,
Provoked the priest to that degree
He swore, "The fault is not in me.
70   Your damned close stool° so near my nose,   *chamber pot*
Your dirty smock, and stinking toes
Would make a Hercules as tame
As any beau that you can name."[8]
        The nymph grown furious roared, "By God
75   The blame lies all in sixty odd,"[9]
And scornful pointing to the door
Cried, "Fumbler, see my face no more."
"With all my heart I'll go away,
But nothing done, I'll nothing pay.
80   Give back the money." "How," cried she,

---

5. "The ox desires the saddle" (Horace, *Epistles* 1.14.43).
6. In this line, Montague echoes an idea, and a way of wording it, that Swift used often in his work.
7. Montagu ridicules Pope's conclusion to Epistle 1 of *An Essay on Man*: "Whatever IS, is RIGHT" (see page 2509). Over the previous few years, her long, ardent friendship with Pope had dissolved in rancor.

8. In these four lines, Montagu compacts some scattered particulars and the sustained conclusion of Swift's poem: ll. 11–14, 51–52, 69 ff.
9. I.e., Swift's impotence derives not from her odors but from his age (65 at the time the poem was written).

"Would you palm such a cheat on me!
For poor four pound to roar and bellow—
Why sure you want some new Prunella?"[1]
"I'll be revenged, you saucy quean"°   *whore*
85   (Replies the disappointed Dean)
"I'll so describe your dressing room
The very Irish shall not come."
She answered short, "I'm glad you'll write.
You'll furnish paper when I shite."[2]

VERSES ON THE DEATH OF DR. SWIFT   "I have been several months writing near five hundred lines on a pleasant subject," wrote Swift to his friend John Gay in December 1731, "only to tell what my friends and enemies will say on me after I am dead." Swift completed what was to become his most celebrated poem by adding explanatory notes in the early months of 1732. It seems that Swift intended the *Verses* to be published after his death but showed the poem in manuscript to various friends. When the reputation of his *Verses* spread, Swift used the opportunity to publish a different autobiographical poem, *The Life and Genuine Character of Dr. Swift* (1733), which would satisfy public demand and make the eventual appearance of the *Verses* all the more surprising. Six years later, believing they were doing their friend a service, Alexander Pope and William King (1685–1763) published a version of the poem in which they edited out some of Swift's most self-aggrandizing and controversial lines. Swift was "much dissatisfied" with this London edition and responded by supervising the speedy publication of an unexpurgated text of the work in Dublin, though even he had the prudence to leave blank spaces for some of the names in his poem. Among the most controversial elements in the *Verses* were its direct attack on Prime Minister Robert Walpole and his government; the unflattering depiction of the court and singling out of Lady Suffolk and Queen Caroline for ridicule; and Swift's praise of Bolingbroke and Pulteney, leading opposition politicians. Swift's jaunty tetrameter carries an admixture of self-fashioning for posterity and moral instruction, a spirited apologia for his life and writings, and an idealized account of the principles by which he strove to live. *Verses on the Death of Dr. Swift* reveals its subject as a champion of liberty and embattled self-promoter, a humanistic preacher and an unsparing satirist.

Verses on the Death of Dr. Swift, D.S.P.D.[1]
Occasioned by Reading a Maxim in Rochefoucauld

*Dans l'adversité de nos meilleurs amis nous trouvons quelque
chose, qui ne nous deplaist pas.*[2]

"In the adversity of our best friends, we find something that
doth not displease us."

As Rochefoucauld his maxims drew
From Nature, I believe 'em true:
They argue° no corrupted mind   *suggest*
In him; the fault is in mankind.

---

1. "Prunella" is both a fabric used in clergy vestments (Swift was a clergyman), and the name of the promiscuous, low-born heroine in Richard Estcourt's comic interlude, *Prunella* (1708).
2. Compare line 118 of Swift's poem.

1. Dean of St. Patrick's, Dublin.
2. François, duc de La Rochefoucauld, *Réflexions ou Sentences et Maximes Morales* ("Reflections or Moral Aphorisms and Maxims," 1665).

5   This maxim more than all the rest
           Is thought too base for human breast;
           "In all distresses of our friends
           We first consult our private ends,
           While Nature kindly bent to ease us,
10   Points out some circumstance to please us."

           If this perhaps your patience move°   *strains*
           Let reason and experience prove.

           We all behold with envious eyes,
           Our equal raised above our size;
15   Who would not at a crowded show,
           Stand high himself, keep others low?
           I love my friend as well as you,
           But would not have him stop my view;
           Then let me have the higher post;
20   I ask but for an inch at most.

           If in a battle you should find,
           One, whom you love of all mankind,
           Had some heroic action done,
           A champion killed, or trophy won;
25   Rather than thus be overtopped,
           Would you not wish his laurels[3] cropped?

           Dear honest Ned is in the gout,[4]
           Lies racked with pain, and you without:[5]
           How patiently you hear him groan!
30   How glad the case is not your own!

           What poet would not grieve to see,
           His brethren write as well as he?
           But rather than they should excel,
           He'd wish his rivals all in Hell.

35   Her end when emulation misses,
           She turns to envy, stings, and hisses:
           The strongest friendship yields to pride,
           Unless the odds be on our side.

           Vain humankind! Fantastic race!
40   Thy various follies, who can trace?
           Self-love, ambition, envy, pride,
           Their empire in our hearts divide:
           Give others riches, power, and station,
           'Tis all on me a usurpation.
45   I have no title to aspire;

3. In ancient times, laurel wreaths were given to poets, athletes, and war heroes to signify their preeminence.
4. A disease characterized by an inflammation of small joints, especially in the feet and hands.
5. Outside his room.

Yet, when you sink, I seem the higher.
In Pope,[6] I cannot read a line,
But with a sigh, I wish it mine:
When he can in one couplet fix
50   More sense than I can do in six:
It gives me such a jealous fit,
I cry, "Pox take him, and his wit."

Why must I be outdone by Gay,[7]
In my own humorous, biting way?

55   Arbuthnot[8] is no more my friend,
Who dares to irony pretend;
Which I was born to introduce,
Refined it first, and showed its use.

St. John, as well as Pulteney[9] knows,
60   That I had some repute for prose;
And till they drove me out of date,
Could maul a minister of state:
If they have mortified my pride,
And made me throw my pen aside;
65   If with such talents Heaven hath blest 'em,
Have I not reason to detest 'em?

To all my foes, dear fortune, send
Thy gifts, but never to my friend:
I tamely can endure the first,
70   But, this with envy makes me burst.

Thus much may serve by way of proem,°   preface
Proceed we therefore to our poem.

The time is not remote, when I
Must by the course of nature die:
75   When I foresee my special friends,
Will try to find their private ends:
Though it is hardly understood,[1]
Which way my death can do them good;
Yet, thus methinks, I hear 'em speak;
80   "See, how the Dean begins to break:°   weaken
Poor gentleman, he droops apace,°   quickly
You plainly find it in his face:
That old vertigo in his head
Will never leave him, till he's dead:

---

6. Alexander Pope, poet, satirist, and friend of Swift.
7. John Gay, poet and playwright, author of *The Beggar's Opera* (1728), friend of Swift, Pope, and Arbuthnot.
8. John Arbuthnot (1667–1735), physician to Queen Anne and member of Scriblerus Club along with Swift, Pope, and Gay; he was the principal author of *Memoirs of . . . Martinus Scriblerus* (1741).

9. Henry St. John Bolingbroke (1678–1751) and William Pulteney; both politicians—one a Tory, the other a Whig—were united in their opposition to Robert Walpole. See Swift's notes to lines 194 and 196.
1. Hard to understand.

85 Besides, his memory decays,
    He recollects not what he says;
    He cannot call his friends to mind;
    Forgets the place where last he dined:
    Plies you with stories o'er and o'er,
90 He told them fifty times before.
    How does he fancy we can sit
    To hear his out-of-fashioned wit?
    But he takes up with younger folks,
    Who for his wine will bear his jokes:
95 Faith,° he must make his stories shorter,   *in truth*
    Or change his comrades once a quarter:
    In half the time, he talks them round;[2]
    There must another set be found.

        "For poetry, he's past his prime,
100 He takes an hour to find a rhyme:
    His fire° is out, his wit decayed,   *creative fire*
    His fancy sunk, his muse a jade.[3]
    I'd have him throw away his pen;
    But there's no talking to some men."

105   And then their tenderness appears,
    By adding largely to my years:
    "He's older than he would be reckoned,
    And well remembers Charles the Second."[4]

        "He hardly° drinks a pint of wine;   *barely*
110 And that, I doubt,° is no good sign.   *suspect*
    His stomach° too begins to fail: *appetite*
    Last year we thought him strong and hale;
    But now, he's quite another thing;
    I wish he may hold out till spring."

115   Then hug themselves, and reason thus:
    "It is not yet so bad with us."

        In such a case they talk in tropes,°   *figuratively*
    And by their fears express their hopes:
    Some great misfortune to portend,°   *predict*
120 No enemy can match a friend;
    With all the kindness they profess,
    The merit of a lucky guess
    (When daily "Howd'y's"[5] come of course,°   *routinely*
    And servants answer: "Worse and worse")
125 Would please 'em better than to tell
    That, God be praised, the Dean is well.

---

2. Runs through his stock of stories and has to begin again.
3. The poet's muse—his inspiration (always female)—is here a worn-out horse or a disreputable or shrewish woman.
4. King Charles II died in 1685, when Swift was 18.
5. How does [is] he?

Then he who prophesied the best,
Approves° his foresight to the rest: *confirms*
"You know, I always feared the worst,
130   And often told you so at first":
He'd rather choose that I should die
Than his prediction prove a lie.
No one foretells I shall recover;
But, all agree to give me over.°   *give up hope*

135   Yet should some neighbor feel a pain
Just in the parts where I complain;
How many a message would he send?
What hearty prayers that I should mend?
Inquire what regimen[6] I kept;
140   What gave me ease, and how I slept?
And more lament, when I was dead,
Than all the snivellers round my bed.

My good companions, never fear,
For though you may mistake a year;
145   Though your prognostics run too fast,
They must be verified at last.

"Behold the fatal day arrive!
How is the Dean? He's just alive.
Now the departing prayer is read:
150   He hardly breathes. The Dean is dead.
Before the passing bell[7] begun,
The news through half the town has run.
O, may we all for death prepare!
What has he left? And who's his heir?
155   I know no more than what the news is,
'Tis all bequeathed to public uses.[8]
To public use! A perfect whim!
What had the public done for him?
Mere envy, avarice, and pride!
160   He gave it all.—But first he died.
And had the Dean, in all the nation,
No worthy friend, no poor relation?
So ready to do strangers good,
Forgetting his own flesh and blood?"

165   Now Grub Street wits[9] are all employed;
With elegies, the town is cloyed:

6. Prescribed pattern of living, exercising, and eating.
7. Death bell, rung to obtain prayers for the passing soul.
8. In fact, when Swift died he left a number of small personal bequests in addition to his large gifts to public

charities.
9. Hack writers, paid to produce (often libelous) materials for London journals.

Some paragraph in every paper,
To curse the Dean, or bless the Drapier.[1]

The doctors tender of their fame,
170 Wisely on me lay all the blame:
"We must confess his case was nice,°   *difficult*
But he would never take advice;
Had he been ruled, for aught appears,
He might have lived these twenty years:
175 For when we opened him we found
That all his vital parts were sound."

From Dublin soon to London spread,[2]
'Tis told at court, the Dean is dead.

Kind Lady Suffolk[3] in the spleen,[4]
180 Runs laughing up to tell the Queen.
The Queen, so gracious, mild, and good,
Cries, "Is he gone? 'Tis time he should.
He's dead you say, why let him rot;
I'm glad the medals were forgot.[5]
185 I promised them, I own;° but when?   *admit*
I only was a princess then;
But now as consort of the King,
You know 'tis quite a different thing."

Now, Chartres[6] at Sir Robert's levee,[7]
190 Tells, with a sneer, the tidings heavy:
"Why, is he dead without his shoes?"[8]
(Cries Bob)[9] "I'm sorry for the news;
Oh, were the wretch but living still,

1. The Author imagines, that the Scribblers of the prevailing Party, which he always opposed, will libel him after his Death; but that others will remember him with gratitude, who consider the service he had done to Ireland, under the name of M. B. Drapier [Swift's note, referring to *The Drapier's Letters* (1724–1725), a series of essays he wrote to defend Ireland from the British government's plan to impose a new coin, "Wood's halfpence," that would have devastated Ireland's economy].
2. The Dean supposeth himself to die in Ireland [Swift's note]; he did.
3. Mrs. Howard, afterwards Countess of Suffolk, then of the Bedchamber to the Queen, professed much friendship for the Dean. The Queen, then Princess, sent a dozen times to the Dean (then in London) with her command to attend her; which at last he did, by advice of all his friends. She often sent for him afterwards, and always treated her with a present worth ten pounds, which she promised before he should return to Ireland, but on his taking leave, the medals were not ready" [Swift's note].
4. The 18th-century equivalent of "depression."
5. The medals were to be sent to the Dean in four months, but she forgot them, or thought them too dear [expensive]. The Dean, being in Ireland, sent Mrs. Howard a piece of Indian plaid made in that kingdom [Ireland]: which the Queen seeing took from her, and wore it herself, and sent to the Dean for as much as would clothe herself and her children, desiring he would send charge of it. He did the former. It cost thirty-five pounds, but he said he would have nothing except the medals. He was the summer following in England, was treated as usual, and she being then Queen, the Dean was promised a settlement in England, but returned as he went, and, instead of favor or medals, hath been ever since under her Majesty's displeasure [Swift's note].
6. Chartres is a most infamous, vile scoundrel, grown from a foot-boy, or worse, to a prodigious fortune [Swift's note]. Francis Charteris was convicted of rape, and pardoned by the prime minister, Robert Walpole, in 1730.
7. A morning audience held in the bedchamber of a person of distinction before or after rising.
8. I.e., in his bed, rather than meeting a violent death or being hanged.
9. Sir Robert Walpole, Chief Minister of State, treated the Dean, in 1726, with great distinction, invited him to dinner at Chelsea, with the Dean's friends chosen on purpose; appointed an hour to talk with him of Ireland, to which kingdom and people the Dean found him no great friend. . . . The Dean would see him no more [Swift's note].

And in his place my good friend Will;[1]
195   Or had a miter° on his head,   *bishop's hat*
Provided Bolingbroke[2] were dead."

Now Curll his shop from rubbish drains:
Three genuine tomes of Swift's remains.[3]
And then to make them pass the glibber,°   *sell better*
200   Revised by Tibbalds, Moore, and Cibber.[4]
He'll treat me as he does my betters:
Publish my will, my life, my letters,[5]
Revive the libels born to die;
Which Pope must bear, as well as I.

205   Here shift the scene, to represent
How those I love, my death lament.
Poor Pope will grieve a month; and Gay
A week; and Arbuthnot a day.

St. John himself will scarce forbear
210   To bite his pen, and drop a tear.
The rest will give a shrug and cry
"I'm sorry; but we all must die."
Indifference clad in wisdom's guise
All fortitude of mind supplies:
215   For how can stony bowels melt,[6]
In those who never pity felt;
When *we* are lashed, *they* kiss the rod,[7]
Resigning to the will of God.

The fools, my juniors by a year,
220   Are tortured with suspense and fear—
Who wisely thought my age a screen,
When death approached, to stand between:
The screen removed, their hearts are trembling,
They mourn for me without dissembling.

225   My female friends, whose tender hearts
Have better learnt to act their parts,

1. Mr. William Pulteney, from being Mr. Walpole's intimate friend, detesting his Administration, opposed his measures, and joined with my Lord Bolingbroke, to represent his conduct in an excellent paper, called the *Craftsman*, which is still continued [Swift's note].

2. Henry St. John, Lord Viscount Bolingbroke, Secretary of State to Queen Anne of blessed memory. He is reckoned the most universal genius in Europe; Walpole dreading his abilities, treated him most injuriously, working with King George, who forgot his promise of restoring the said Lord, upon the restless importunity of Walpole [Swift's note].

3. Edmund Curll hath been the most infamous bookseller of any age or country: his character in part may be found in Mr. Pope's *Dunciad*. He published three volumes all charged on [i.e., attributed to] the Dean, who never writ three pages of them: he hath used many of the Dean's

friends in almost as vile a manner [Swift's note].

4. Three stupid verse writers in London, the last to the shame of the Court, and the highest disgrace to wit and learning, was made Laureate [Swift's note]. Lewis Theobald (1688–1744), Shakespearean scholar and poet; James Moore Smythe (1702–1734), playwright whom Pope accused of plagiarism; Colley Cibber (1671–1757), actor and playwright. All three men are satirized in Pope's *Dunciad*.

5. Curll is notoriously infamous for publishing the lives, letters, and last Wills and Testaments of the nobility and ministers of State, as well as of all the rogues who are hanged at Tyburn [Swift's note].

6. I.e., how can one feel compassion.

7. Accept chastisement submissively; kissing a monarch's scepter or a state official's staff was a ritual of submission to authority.

Receive the news in doleful dumps,
"The Dean is dead (*and what is trumps?*),
Then Lord have mercy on his soul.
230   (*Ladies, I'll venture for the vole.*[8])
Six deans they say must bear the pall.
(*I wish I knew which king to call.*)"
"Madam, your husband will attend
The funeral of so good a friend."
235   "No madam, 'tis a shocking sight,
And he's engaged tomorrow night!
My Lady Club would take it ill,
If he should fail her at quadrille.
He loved the Dean. (*I lead a heart.*)
240   But dearest friends, they say, must part.
His time was come, he ran his race;
We hope he's in a better place."

      Why do we grieve that friends should die?
No loss more easy to supply.
245   One year is past; a different scene;
No further mention of the Dean;
Who now, alas, no more is missed
Than if he never did exist.
Where's now this fav'rite of Apollo?[9]
250   Departed; and his works must follow:
Must undergo the common fate;
His kind of wit is out of date.
Some country squire to Lintot[1] goes,
Inquires for Swift in verse and prose:
255   Says Lintot, "I have heard the name:
He died a year ago." "The same."
He searcheth all his shop in vain;
"Sir, you may find them in Duck Lane:[2]
I sent them with a load of books
260   Last Monday to the pastry-cook's.[3]
To fancy they could live a year!
I find you're but a stranger here.
The Dean was famous in his time
And had a kind of knack at rhyme:
265   His way of writing now is past;
The town hath got a better taste:
I keep no antiquated stuff;
But, spick and span I have enough.
Pray, do but give me leave to show 'em;

---

8. All the tricks in the highly popular four-handed card game, quadrille.
9. Patron of poets.
1. Bernard Lintot (1675–1736), London publisher of Pope, Gay, and Steele, among others.
2. A place in London where old [i.e., remaindered] books

are sold [Swift's note].
3. Wastepaper from unsold books was used to line baking tins. Cf. Dryden's *Mac Flecknoe* (1682), who notes similar uses for old texts: "Martyrs of pies, and relics of the bum" (line 101).

270   Here's Colley Cibber's birthday poem.[4]
       This ode you never yet have seen
       By Stephen Duck,[5] upon the Queen.
       Then, here's a letter finely penned,
       Against the *Craftsman*[6] and his friend;
275   It clearly shows that all reflection
       On ministers, is disaffection.
       Next, here's Sir Robert's vindication,[7]
       And Mr Henley's last oration:[8]
       The hawkers° have not got 'em yet,   street sellers
280   Your Honor please to buy a set?

       "Here's Woolston's tracts,[9] the twelfth edition;
       'Tis read by every politician:
       The country members,[1] when in town,
       To all their boroughs send them down:
285   You never met a thing so smart;
       The courtiers have them all by heart:
       Those maids of honor (who can read)
       Are taught to use them for their creed.
       The reverend author's good intention
290   Hath been rewarded with a pension:
       He doth an honor to his gown,
       By bravely running priestcraft down:
       He shows, as sure as God's in Gloucester,[2]
       That Jesus was a grand impostor:
295   That all his miracles were cheats,
       Performed as jugglers do their feats;
       The church had never such a writer:
       A shame he hath not got a miter!"

       Suppose me dead; and then suppose
300   A club assembled at the Rose;[3]
       Where from discourse of this and that,
       I grow the subject of their chat:
       And while they toss my name about,

4. The Poet Laureate was required to write an ode for the monarch's birthday each year. Cibber's appointment as Laureate in 1730 was based on politics, not literary merit.
5. Stephen Duck (1705–1756), known as "the thresher poet," was a laborer whose poetry won him Queen Caroline's favor; Swift made fun of him in *On Stephen Duck, the Thresher, and Favorite Poet, A Quibbling Epigram* (1730).
6. From 1726, the principal periodical written in opposition to Robert Walpole's government. Its title was meant to indicate that Walpole was "a man of craft" (i.e., scheming and deceptive).
7. Walpole hires a set of Party scribblers, who do nothing else but write in his defense [Swift's note].
8. John Henley (1692–1756), known as "Orator Henley" for the Oratory he founded where "at set times, he delivereth strange speeches compiled by himself and his associates . . . . He is an absolute dunce, but generally reputed crazy" [Swift's note].
9. Woolston was a clergyman, but for want of bread, hath in several treatises, in the most blasphemous manner, attempted to turn our Savior and his miracles into ridicule. He is much caressed by many great courtiers, and by all the infidels, and his books read generally by the Court ladies [Swift's note]. Swift appears to conflate the identities of two contemporary clergymen: Thomas Woolston (1670–1733), a notorious Deist, and William Woollaston (1660–1724).
1. Members of Parliament from rural boroughs.
2. A proverb derived from the number of monasteries there once were in that county.
3. The Rose Tavern, near Drury Lane Theatre, and therefore popular with playgoers.

With favor some, and some without;
305   One quite indifferent in the cause
My character impartial draws:

"The Dean, if we believe report,
Was never ill received at court;
As for his works in verse and prose,
310   I own myself no judge of those:
Nor can I tell what critics thought 'em;
But this I know, all people bought 'em;
As with a moral view designed
To cure the vices of mankind:
315   His vein, ironically grave,
Exposed the fool, and lashed the knave:
To steal a hint was never known,
But what he writ was all his own.[4]

"He never thought an honor done him,
320   Because a duke was proud to own him:
Would rather slip aside, and choose
To talk with wits in dirty shoes:
Despised the fools with stars and garters,[5]
So often seen caressing Chartres:
325   He never courted men in station,
Nor persons had in admiration;°   *was in awe of*
Of no man's greatness was afraid,
Because he sought for no man's aid.
Though trusted long in great affairs,
330   He gave himself no haughty airs;
Without regarding private ends,
Spent all his credit for his friends,
And only chose the wise and good;
No flatt'rers; no allies in blood;°   *relatives*
335   But succored virtue in distress,
And seldom failed of good success;
As numbers in their hearts must own,
Who, but for him, had been unknown.

"With princes kept a due decorum,
340   But never stood in awe before 'em:
And to her Majesty, God bless her,
Would speak as free as to her dresser,[6]
She thought it his peculiar whim,
Nor took it ill as come from him.
345   He followed David's lesson just,
"In princes never put thy trust."[7]

---

4. Swift is here having fun with the reader, since this line claiming Swift's originality is stolen from Sir John Denham's elegy On Mr. *Abraham Cowley:* "To him no author was unknown / Yet what he wrote was all his own."

5. Worn by Knights of the Garter.
6. Queen Caroline and Lady Suffolk, one of the Ladies of Her Majesty's bedchamber.
7. Psalm 146.3.

And, would you make him truly sour,
Provoke him with a slave in power:
The Irish senate, if you named,
350   With what impatience he declaimed!
Fair LIBERTY was all his cry;
For her he stood prepared to die;
For her he boldly stood alone;
For her he oft exposed his own.
355   Two kingdoms, just as factions led,
Had set a price upon his head;
But not a traitor could be found,
To sell him for six hundred pound.[8]

    "Had he but spared his tongue and pen,
360   He might have rose like other men:
But power was never in his thought,
And wealth he valued not a groat;
Ingratitude he often found,
And pitied those who meant the wound;
365   But kept the tenor° of his mind,   *prevailing course*
To merit well of humankind;
Nor made a sacrifice of those
Who still° were true, to please his foes.   *always*
He labored many a fruitless hour
370   To reconcile his friends in power;
Saw mischief by a faction brewing,
While they pursued each other's ruin.
But finding vain was all his care,
He left the Court in mere° despair.[9]   *total*

375   "And, oh! how short are human schemes!
Here ended all our golden dreams.
What St. John's skill in state affairs,
What Ormonde's valor,[1] Oxford's cares,
To save their sinking country lent,
380   Was all destroyed by one event.
Too soon that precious life was ended,[2]
On which alone our weal° depended.   *well-being*
When up a dangerous faction starts,[3]
With wrath and vengeance in their hearts:

---

8. Two rewards of £300 each were offered in 1713 and 1724 for the revelation of the author of *The Public Spirit of the Whigs* and *The Drapier's Fourth Letter*, respectively, "but in neither kingdoms was the Dean discovered" [Swift's note].
9. Under Queen Anne's Tory ministry, Swift tried to resolve differences between the Chancellor, Simon Harcourt (1661–1727), Lord Bolingbroke, and the Earl of Oxford, but was unsuccessful, and left London shortly before the collapse of their government.

1. James Butler (1665–1745), second Earl of Ormonde, succeeded Marlborough as commander in chief of the allied forces in 1712.
2. In the height of the quarrel between the ministers, the Queen [Anne] died [Swift's note].
3. When Queen Anne died, the Whigs were restored to power, "which they exercised with the utmost rage and revenge" [Swift's note]. Swift initially feared for his own safety, and considered emigrating to the island of Guernsey.

385   By *solemn league and covenant bond*,[4]
       To ruin, slaughter, and confound;
       To turn religion to a fable,
       And make the government a Babel:
       Pervert the law, disgrace the gown,
390   Corrupt the senate, rob the crown;
       To sacrifice old England's glory,
       And make her infamous in story.
       When such a tempest shook the land,
       How could unguarded virtue stand?
395   "With horror, grief, despair the Dean
       Beheld the dire destructive scene:
       His friends in exile, or the Tower,[5]
       Himself within the frown of power;
       Pursued by base, envenomed pens,[6]
400   Far to the land of slaves and fens;°   *Ireland*
       A servile race in folly nursed,
       Who truckle° most, when treated worst.   *cringe obsequiously*

       "By innocence and resolution,
       He bore continual persecution;
405   While numbers to preferment[7] rose;
       Whose merits were, to be his foes.
       When, *ev'n his own familiar° friends*   *close*
       Intent upon their private ends,
       Like renegadoes now he feels,
410   *Against him lifting up their heels.*[8]

       "The Dean did by his pen defeat
       An infamous, destructive cheat,[9]
       Taught fools their interest to know,
       And gave them arms to ward the blow.°   *defend themselves*
415   Envy hath owned it was his doing
       To save that helpless land from ruin,
       While they who at the steerage[1] stood,
       And reaped the profit, sought his blood.

       "To save them from their evil fate,
420   In him was held a crime of state.
       A wicked monster on the bench,[2]

4. Alluding to the establishment of Scottish Presbyterianism in 1643, which Swift (as an Anglican) regretted.
5. The Tower of London, where convicted (or suspected) traitors were held.
6. Upon the Queen's death, the Dean returned to live in Dublin . . . numberless libels were writ against him in England, as a Jacobite; he was insulted in the street, and at nights was forced to be attended by his servants armed [Swift's note].
7. Places at the Court or in the church hierarchy, especially bishoprics.
8. From Psalm 41.9: "Yea, mine own familiar friend, in whom I trusted, which did eat of my bread, hath lifted up his heel against me."

9. One Wood, a Hardware-man from England, had a patent for coining copper halfpence in Ireland, to the sum of £108,000, which in the consequence, must leave the kingdom without gold or silver [Swift's note]. Swift responded with *The Drapier's Letters* (1724–1725).
1. The helm (of the ship of state).
2. One Whitshed was then Chief Justice: he had some years before prosecuted a printer for a pamphlet writ by the Dean, to persuade the people of Ireland to wear their own manufactures. . . . He sat as Judge afterwards on the trial of the printer of the Drapier's Fourth Letter; but the Jury, against all he could say or swear, threw out the Bill [Swift's note].

Whose fury blood could never quench;
As vile and profligate a villain,
As modern Scroggs, or old Tresilian;[3]
425 Who long all justice had discarded,
Nor feared he God, nor man regarded;[4]
Vowed on the Dean his rage to vent,
And make him of his zeal repent;
But heaven his innocence defends,
430 The grateful people stand his friends;
Not strains of law, nor judges' frown,
Nor topics° brought to please the crown,   charges
Nor witness hired, nor jury picked,
Prevail to bring him in convict.

435   "In exile[5] with a steady heart,
He spent his life's declining part;
Where folly, pride, and faction sway,
Remote from St. John, Pope, and Gay.

"His friendship there to few confined,
440 Were always of the middling kind:[6]
No fools of rank, a mongrel breed,
Who fain would pass for lords indeed:
Where titles give no right or power,
And peerage is a withered flower,[7]
445 He would have held it a disgrace,
If such a wretch had known his face.
On rural squires, that kingdom's bane,
He vented oft his wrath in vain:
Biennial squires,[8] to market brought,
450 Who sell their souls and votes for naught;
The nation stripped, go joyful back,
To rob the church, their tenants rack,[9]
Go snacks° with thieves and rapparees,[1]   *divide the spoils*
And keep the peace,[2] to pick up fees:

---

3. Scroggs was Chief Justice under King Charles the Second: his judgment always varied in State trials, according to directions from the [royal] Court. Tresilian was a wicked Judge, hanged above three hundred years ago [Swift's note].
4. Cf. Luke 18.2: "There was in a city a judge, which feared not God, neither regarded man."
5. In Ireland, which he had reason to call a place of exile; to which country nothing could have driven him, but the Queen's death, who had determined to fix him in England [Swift's note].
6. The Dean was not acquainted with one single Lord spiritual or temporal. He only conversed with private gentlemen of the clergy or laity, and but a small number of either [Swift's note]; not entirely true.
7. The peers of Ireland lost a great part of their jurisdiction

by one single Act [of 1720], and tamely submitted to this infamous mark of slavery without the least resentment, or remonstrance [Swift's note].
8. The Parliament (as they call it) in Ireland meet but once in two years; and after giving five times more than they can afford, return home to reimburse themselves by all country jobs and oppressions, of which some few only are here mentioned [Swift's note].
9. I.e., torture by extortionate rent; "rack-rent" was an excessive rent nearly equal to the full value of the land.
1. The highwaymen in Ireland are, since the late wars there, usually called rapparees, which was a name given to those Irish soldiers who in small parties used, at that time, to plunder the Protestants [Swift's note].
2. Act as magistrates.

455   In every job[3] to have a share,
      A jail or barrack[4] to repair;
      And turn the tax for public roads
      Commodious to their own abodes.[5]

      "Perhaps I may allow the Dean
460   Had too much satire in his vein;
      And seemed determined not to starve it,
      Because no age could more deserve it.
      Yet, malice never was his aim;
      He lashed the vice but spared the name.[6]
465   No individual could resent,
      Where thousands equally were meant.
      His satire points at no defect,
      But what all mortals may correct;
      For he abhorred that senseless tribe,
470   Who call it humor when they jibe;
      He spared a hump or crooked nose,
      Whose owners set not up for beaux.
      True, genuine dullness moved his pity,
      Unless it offered to be witty.
475   Those who their ignorance confessed,
      He ne'er offended with a jest;
      But laughed to hear an idiot quote,
      A verse from Horace, learned by rote.

      "He knew an hundred pleasant stories,
480   With all the turns of Whigs and Tories:
      Was cheerful to his dying day,
      And friends would let him have his way.

      "He gave the little wealth he had
      To build a house for fools and mad:[7]
485   And showed by one satiric touch,
      No nation wanted it so much:
      That kingdom he hath left his debtor,
      I wish it soon may have a better."

1731–1732   1739

JOURNAL TO STELLA In 1710, Swift was sent from Dublin to London by his patron, Archbishop King, with an important commission—to petition the Queen's Bounty (via the government and the Court) for the remission of the Irish "first fruits," the British monarch's tax on the revenues of clergymen in the Church of Ireland. Swift saw the campaign to repeal the "first fruits"—and his contribution to its success—as his passport to fame and preferment. Though

3. Implying a business racket.
4. The army in Ireland is lodged in barracks, the building and repairing whereof, and other charges, have cost a prodigious sum to that unhappy kingdom [Swift's note].
5. There were complaints that the new system of public turnpike roads, then being established in England and in Ireland, was manipulated by estate owners so that the roads ran directly to their own properties.
6. Swift is being ironic, since the poem explicitly identifies many targets of his satire.
7. In his will, Swift made a large bequest to build a mental institution (the first in Ireland), St. Patrick's Hospital, which was opened in 1757.

Swift did not yet realize it, these were to be the greatest years of his career, a time when he routinely mixed with the most powerful men of his day, when he was courted for his considerable influence, and when he established himself as the most brilliant and successful of the Tory pamphleteers. He was heavily involved in the intricacies of party politics on his country's behalf and for his own advancement; his prospects for success on both fronts were highly promising. Swift never intended to publish the diary-like letters he wrote to his beloved Esther Johnson and her companion, Rebecca Dingley, during the first three years of his extended sojourn in London from 1710 to 1714. He wrote them, as Virginia Woolf keenly observed in *The Common Reader*, because "the reserved, the powerful, the admired, have the most need of such a refuge." After Esther Johnson's death in 1728, Swift preserved this highly personal "journal" probably both for sentimental reasons and for its historical importance, since it provided a unique insider's view of political affairs and Court intrigues—in addition to social gossip and immediate reactions to important public events—in the final years of Queen Anne's reign. Some of these letters were published in the 1750s and 1760s, in collections of Swift's correspondence and works; the entire sequence first appeared, as *Dr. Swift's Journal to Stella*, in 1784.

from Journal to Stella
from *Letter 10*

[SATURDAY]   London, Nov. 25, 1710

I'll tell you something that's plaguy[1] silly: I had forgot to say on the 23d in my last, where I dined, and because I had done it constantly, I thought it was a great omission, and was going to interline it;[2] but at last the silliness of it made me cry, "Pshaw," and I let it alone. I was today to see the Parliament meet; but only saw a great crowd: and Ford[3] and I went to see the tombs at Westminster,[4] and sauntered so long I was forced to go to an eating house for my dinner. Bromley is chosen speaker,[5] *nemine contradicente:*[6] Do you understand those two words? And Pompey, Colonel Hill's[7] black, designs to stand speaker for the footmen.[8] I am engaged to use my interest for him, and have spoken to Patrick[9] to get him some votes. We are now all impatient for the Queen's speech, what she will say about removing the ministry, &c.[1] I have got a cold, and I don't know how; but got it I have, and am hoarse: I don't know whether it will grow better or worse. What's that to you? I won't answer your letter to-night. I'll keep you a little longer in suspense: I can't send it. Your mother's cakes are very good, and one of them serves me for a breakfast, and so I'll go sleep like a good boy.

26. I have got a cruel cold, and stayed within all this day in my nightgown, and dined on six pennyworth of victuals, and read and writ, and was denied to everybody.[2] Dr. Raymond[3] called often, and I was denied; and at last, when I was weary, I let him

---

1. Annoyingly, exceedingly.
2. Write it in between the lines he had already written.
3. Charles Ford (1682–1741), an Anglo-Irish friend of Swift's living in London, with whom he corresponded (on and off) for nearly 30 years.
4. Royalty and other members of the aristocracy were buried at Westminster Abbey.
5. William Bromley (1664–1732), high churchman and Member of Parliament for Oxford University from 1702, was chosen speaker of the House of Commons on this day.
6. Nobody voting against.
7. John Hill (d. 1735), major general; like his sister Mrs. Masham, Hill was a favorite of Queen Anne.
8. The footmen to Members of Parliament sometimes

held their own unofficial "parliament" and debated the issues of the day while their masters were legislating inside the House.
9. Swift's manservant.
1. Following the trial of the high churchman Dr. Henry Sacheverell (c. 1674–1724) in 1710 for a contentious sermon he had given, there was such strong feeling against the Whig Ministry's apparent oppression of the established Church that the Queen dismissed the Ministry, dissolving Parliament on 21 September 1710. When the new Parliament opened in November, a Tory administration was given control of the government.
2. I.e., visitors were not allowed to see him.
3. Rev. Anthony Raymond (c. 1675–1726), rector of Trim, and neighbor of Swift's.

come up, and asked him, without consequence, "How Patrick denied me, and whether he had the art of it?" So by this means he shall be used to have me denied to him;[4] otherwise he would be a plaguy trouble and hindrance to me: he has sat with me two hours, and drank a pint of ale cost me five pence, and smoked his pipe, and 'tis now past eleven that he is just gone. Well, my eighth is with you now, young women, and your seventh to me is somewhere in a postboy's bag; and so go to your gang of Deans, and Stoytes, and Walls, and lose your money;[5] go, sauce-boxes, and so goodnight and be happy, dear rogues. Oh, but your box was sent to Dr. Hawkshaw by Sterne, and you will have it with Hawkshaw, and spectacles, &c. &c.

27.[6] To-day Mr. Harley[7] met me in the court of requests,[8] and whispered me to dine with him. At dinner I told him what those bishops had done, and the difficulty I was under.[9] He bid me never trouble myself; he would tell the Duke of Ormonde the business was done, and that he need not concern himself about it. So now I am easy, and they may hang themselves for a parcel of insolent ungrateful rascals. I suppose I told you in my last, how they sent an address to the Duke of Ormonde, and a letter to Southwell, to call on me for the papers, after the thing was over, but they had not received my letter; though the Archbishop might, by what I writ to him, have expected it would be done. Well, there's an end of that; and in a little time the Queen will send them notice, &c. And so the methods will be settled; and then I shall think of returning, although the baseness of those bishops makes me love Ireland less than I did.

28. Lord Halifax[1] sent to invite me to dinner, where I stayed till six, and crossed him in all his Whig talk, and made him often come over to me.[2] I know he makes court to the new men, although he affects to talk like a Whig. I had a letter today from the Bishop of Clogher;[3] but I writ to him lately, that I would obey his commands to the Duke of Ormonde. He says I bid him read the *London Shaver*, and that you both swore it was *Shaver*, and not *Shower*.[4] You all lie, and you are puppies, and can't read Presto's hand.[5] The Bishop is out entirely in his conjectures of my share in

4. I.e., Swift let Raymond know that he would not always be admitted on demand.
5. Stella played cards—and often gambled for small stakes—with a circle of friends, including Dean Sterne, Alderman Stoyte, his wife and her sister, and Archdeacon Walls and his wife.
6. Parliament was formally opened by the queen on this day (Swift does not mention it).
7. Swift cultivated friendships with Robert Harley (1661–1724), first Earl of Oxford, and Henry St. John, first Viscount Bolingbroke (1678–1751), as it became clear that they would rule the new Tory Ministry, in the hope, no doubt, of various favors.
8. A court of equity, actually abolished in 1641; it seems the room at Whitehall retained its name long after losing its function.
9. Swift was concerned to receive due recognition for his part in the success of the "first fruits" scheme: Harley had by this time told Swift that the Queen had accepted his proposal, but enjoined him to secrecy until it could be made public. While Harley eventually allowed Swift to report some limited success to Archbishop King, the politician procrastinated on making the matter more widely known. The Queen, meanwhile, appointed a new Governor of Ireland (Ormonde), and the Irish bishops who had commissioned Swift naturally felt it would be

politically expedient to hand Swift's petition over to the Secretary of State for Ireland, Edward Southwell, especially since they still saw Swift as a Whig. When the letter patent was eventually granted, in July 1711 (though dated 17 February 1711), no mention of Swift was made.
1. Charles Montague, Earl of Halifax (1661–1715), a senior Whig statesman; on 2 October 1710, Swift noted in the *Journal* that he had refused to join Halifax in toasting the revival of Whig fortunes: "I told him he was the only Whig in England I loved."
2. I.e., Swift argued against Halifax, and persuaded him to his point of view.
3. St. George Ashe (c. 1658–1718), successively Bishop of Cloyne, of Clogher, and of Derry, and Swift's tutor at Trinity College, Dublin; obviously he was writing to Swift about the "first fruits" question.
4. Stella and Mrs. Dingley have persuaded the bishop that he should read "shaver" for "shower" in Swift's *Description of a City Shower*; the verses first appeared in the *Tatler*, No. 238 (17 October 1710). Swift was extremely proud of this poem; he mentions it in several letters to Stella.
5. After the Duchess of Shrewsbury called him "Dr. Presto" (a pun on "Swift"), Swift adopted this name throughout his *Journal*.

the *Tatlers*.[6]—I have other things to mind, and of much greater importance,[7] else I have little to do to be acquainted with a new ministry, who consider me a little more than Irish bishops do.

29. Now for your saucy good dear letter: let me see, what does it say? Come then. I dined today with Ford, and went home early; he debauched me to his chamber again with a bottle of wine till twelve: so goodnight. I can't write an answer now, you rogues.

30. Today I have been visiting, which I had long neglected; and I dined with Mrs. Barton[8] alone; and sauntered at the coffeehouse till past eight, and have been busy till eleven, and now I'll answer your letter, sauce-box. Well, let me see now again. My wax candle's almost out, but however I'll begin. Well then, don't be so tedious, Mr. Presto; what can you say to MD's letter?[9] Make haste, have done with your preambles—Why, I say I am glad you are so often abroad; your mother thinks it is want of exercise hurts you, and so do I. (She called here tonight, but I was not within, that's by the bye.) Sure you don't deceive me, Stella, when you say you are in better health than you were these three weeks; for Dr. Raymond told me yesterday, that Smyth[1] of the Blind Quay had been telling Mr. Leigh, that he left you extremely ill; and in short, spoke so, that he almost put poor Leigh into tears, and would have made me run distracted; though your letter is dated the 11th instant, and I saw Smyth in the city above a fortnight ago, as I passed by in a coach. Pray, pray, don't write, Stella, until you are mighty, mighty, mighty, mighty well in your eyes, and are sure it won't do you the least hurt. Or come, I'll tell you what; you, mistress Stella, shall write your share at five or six sittings, one sitting a day; and then comes Dingley all together, and then Stella a little crumb towards the end, to let us see she remembers Presto; and then conclude with something handsome and genteel, as your most humblecumdumble, or, &c. O Lord! does Patrick write word of my not coming till *spring*? Insolent man! he know my secrets? No; as my Lord Mayor said, No; if I thought my shirt knew, &c.[2] Faith, I will come as soon as it is any way proper for me to come; but, to say the truth, I am at present a little involved with the present ministry in some certain things (which I tell you as a secret) and soon as ever I can clear my hands, I will stay no longer: for I hope the first-fruit business will be soon over in all its forms. But, to say the truth, the present ministry have a difficult task, and want me, &c. Perhaps they may be just as grateful as others: but, according to the best judgment I have, they are pursuing the true interest of the public; and therefore I am glad to contribute what is in my power. For God's sake, not a word of this to any alive.—Your chancellor?[3] Why, madam, I can tell you he has been dead this fortnight. Faith, I could hardly forbear our little lan-

---

6. The *Tatler*, founded by Swift's sometime friend Richard Steele, ran from 12 April 1709 to 2 January 1711; Swift contributed to several early numbers.

7. At the request of Harley, Swift took control of the *Examiner*, a weekly Tory periodical founded by Bolingbroke in August 1710, between November 1710 and June 1711 (Nos. 14–46).

8. Catherine Barton (1679–1740), niece of Sir Isaac Newton, and a noted beauty who, despite her Whig affiliations and argumentative ability, remained one of Swift's favorites.

9. MD/Md (my dears?) refers to both Esther Johnson and Rebecca Dingley, though Swift is chiefly directing his thoughts to Esther.

1. "Smyth" may be John Smith, one of Swift's booksellers.

2. Patrick is not as close to Swift as his shirt, and even his shirt does not know.

3. Richard Freeman, a Whig, appointed Lord Chancellor of Ireland in 1707, apparently on the basis of his politics, not his abilities.

guage about a nasty dead chancellor, as you may see by the blot.[4] Ploughing? A pox plough them; they'll plough me to nothing. But have you got your money, both the ten pounds? How durst he pay you the second so soon? Pray be good huswives.—Aye, well, and Joe;[5] why, I had a letter lately from Joe, desiring I would take some care of their poor town, who, he says, will lose their liberties. To which I desired Dr. Raymond would return answer; that the town had behaved themselves so ill to me, so little regarded the advice I gave them, and disagreed so much among themselves, that I was resolved never to have more to do with them; but that whatever personal kindness I could do to Joe, should be done. Pray, when you happen to see Joe, tell him this, lest Raymond should have blundered or forgotten.—Poor Mrs. Wesley—Why these poligyes[6] for being abroad?[7] Why should you be at home at all, until Stella is quite well?—So, here is mistress Stella again with her two eggs, &c. My *Shower* admired with you; why, the Bishop of Clogher says, he has seen something of mine of the same sort, better than the *Shower*. I suppose he means *The Morning*;[8] but it is not half so good. I want your judgment of things, and not your country's. How does MD like it? and do they taste it *all*? &c.[9] I am glad Dean Bolton has paid the twenty pounds.[1] Why should not I chide the Bishop of Clogher for writing to the Archbishop of Cashel, without sending the letter first to me?[2] It does not signify a ——; for he has no credit at court. Stuff—they are all puppies. I'll break your head in good earnest, young woman, for your nasty jest about Mrs. Barton. Unlucky sluttikin, what a word is there! Faith, I was thinking yesterday, when I was with her, whether she could break them or no,[3] and it quite spoiled my imagination. Mrs. Walls, does Stella win as she pretends? No indeed, *doctor*; she loses always, and will play so *ventursomely*, how can she win? See here now; an't you an impudent lying slut? Do, open Domville's[4] letter; what does it signify, if you have a mind? Yes, faith, you write smartly with your eyes shut; all was well but the w. See how I can do it; *Madam Stella, your humble servant.*[5] O, but one may look whether one goes crooked or no, and so write on. I'll tell you what you may do; you may write with your eyes half shut, just as when one is going to sleep: I have done so for two or three lines now; 'tis but just seeing enough to go straight.—Now, madam Dingley, I think I bid you tell Mr. Walls, that in case there be occasion, I will serve his friend as far as I can; but I hope there will be none.[6] Yet I believe you will

4. To make this intelligible, it is necessary to observe, that the words "this fortnight" in the preceding sentence, were first written in what he calls their little language, and afterwards scratched out and written plain. It must be confessed this little language, which passed current between Swift and Stella, had occasioned infinite trouble in the revisal of theses papers [Deane Swift' s note]. In 1768, Deane Swift (1706–1783), the son of Swift' s cousin and a favorite relation of Jonathan Swift, published a selection of his famous relation's correspondence with his own annotations, including some of the letters to Esther Johnson and Rebecca Dingley that comprise the *Journal*.
5. Joseph Beaumont (d. 1731), a linen draper from Trim and Swift's business agent.
6. Apologies.
7. Leaving the house.
8. A *Description of the Morning*, which appeared in the *Tatler*, No. 9 (30 April 1709).
9. I.e., do they understand and appreciate it?
1. John Bolton (c. 1656–1724), Dean of Derry.
2. William Palliser (1646–1726), Archbishop of Cashel

since 1694, and a signatory of Swift's commission to petition on behalf of the Irish "first fruits" proposal.
3. This jest is lost, whatever it was, for want of MD's letter [Deane Swift's note].
4. William Domville (born c. 1686), Irishman living in London, and grandson of the attorney general, whom Swift called "perfectly as fine a gentleman as I know" (*Journal*, 27 November 1711).
5. Here he writ with his eyes shut, and the writing is somewhat crooked, although as well in other respects as if his eyes had been open [Deane Swift's note]. Swift had expressed concern about Stella straining her eyes in an earlier letter (7), and suggested that "if you will write, shut your eyes, and write just a line, and no more."
6. Rev. Thomas Wall's friend was Captain John Pratt (born c. 1670), Deputy Vice-Treasurer of Ireland and younger brother of Benjamin Pratt, Provost of Trinity College, Dublin; his place in Parliament was in jeopardy. He later embezzled large sums of Swift's (and Ireland's) cash.

have a new Parliament; but I care not whether you have or no a better.[7] You are mistaken in all your conjectures about the *Tatlers*. I have given him one or two hints, and you have heard me talk about the *Shilling*.[8] Faith, these answering letters are very long ones: you have taken up almost the room of a week in journals; and I'll tell you what, I saw fellows wearing crosses today,[9] and I wondered what was the matter; but just this minute I recollect it is little Presto's birthday;[1] and I was resolved these three days to remember it when it came, but could not. Pray, drink my health today at dinner; do, you rogues. Do you like *Sid Hamet's Rod?*[2] Do you understand it all? Well, now at last I have done with your letter, and so I'll lay me down to sleep, and about fair maids; and I hope merry maids all. * * *

1768

GULLIVER'S TRAVELS *Travels into Several Remote Nations of the World. In Four Parts. By Lemuel Gulliver*—better known as *Gulliver's Travels*—was first published in late October 1726 and enjoyed instant success. One contemporary observer noted that "several thousands sold in a week," and Swift's London friends wrote to him in Dublin to say that everyone was reading and talking about Gulliver (see "Gulliver's Travels and Its Time" on page 2426). Readers continue to be fascinated by Swift's masterpiece: since 1945, more than 500 books and scholarly articles have been devoted to *Gulliver's Travels*. Variously classified as an early novel, an imaginary voyage, a moral and political allegory, and even a children's story, Lemuel Gulliver's four journeys, representing the four directions of the globe, comprise a survey of the human condition: a comic, ironic, and sometimes harrowing answer to the question, "What does it mean to be a human being?"

In the first voyage, the diminutive citizens of Lilliput represent human small-mindedness and petty ambitions. Filled with self-importance, the Lilliputians are cruel, treacherous, malicious, and destructive. The perspective is reversed in the second voyage to Brobdingnag, land of giants, where Gulliver has the stature of a Lilliputian. He is humbled by his own helplessness and, finding the huge bodies of the Brobdingnagians grotesque, he realizes how repulsive the Lilliputians must have found him. When Gulliver gives the wise king an account of the political affairs of England—which manifest hypocrisy, avarice, and hatred—the enlightened monarch concludes that most of the country's inhabitants must be "the most pernicious race of little odious vermin that Nature ever suffered to crawl upon the surface of the earth." In the third voyage (which was written last), Gulliver visits the flying island of Laputa and the metropolis of Lagado, on an adjacent continent, where he encounters the misuse of human reason. In Laputa, those who are supposedly "wise" lack all common sense and practical ability; at Lagado, the Academy of Projectors is staffed by professors who waste both money and intelligence on absurd endeavors. Swift aims his satire at so-called intellectuals—especially the "virtuosi," or amateur scientists of the Royal Society—who live in the world of their own speculations and so fail to use their gifts for the common good. Throughout *Gulliver's Travels* that which is admirable is held up to expose corruption in the reader's world, and that which is deplorable is identified with the institutions and practices associated with contemporary Europe, particularly Britain.

Gulliver's fourth voyage (printed in its entirety below) finds him on the island of the Houyhnhnms, horses endowed with reason, whose highly rational and well-ordered

---

7. The Irish House of Commons was adjourned on 28 August 1710 and reassembled on 9 July 1711.
8. Discussion of John Philips's *The Splendid Shilling* (1701) appeared in the *Tatler*, No. 249 (11 November 1710).
9. For St. Andrew's Day.
1. I.e., his own birthday.
2. Swift's The *Virtues of Sid Hamet the Magician's Rod* (1710), a satire on Sidney Godolphin.

(though emotionally sterile) society is contrasted with the violence, selfishness, and brutality of the Yahoos, irrational beasts who bear a disconcerting resemblance to humans. In his foolish pride, Gulliver believes that he can escape the human condition and live as a stoical Houyhnhnm, even when he returns to his family in England. Of course, Gulliver is neither Houyhnhnm nor Yahoo, but a man. His time in Houyhnhnm-land does not teach him to be more rational or compassionate, but makes him more foolish, derelict in his duties as husband, father, and citizen. Instead of seeking to become a better man, Gulliver strives to become what he is not—with results that are both tragic and farcical. Although the poet Edward Young charged Swift with having "blasphemed a nature little lower than that of the angels" in satirizing the follies of humankind, *Gulliver's Travels* reveals the Dean of Saint Patrick's to be more a humanist than a misanthrope. With brilliantly modulated ironic self-awareness, Swift's painful comedy of exposure to the truth of human frailty demonstrates that there is no room for the distortions of human pride in a world where our practices are so evidently at variance with our principles. Swift advances no program of social reform, but provokes a new recognition—literally, a rethinking—of our own humanity.

from Gulliver's Travels

from Part 3. A Voyage to Laputa

CHAPTER 5

The author permitted to see the grand Academy of Lagado. The Academy largely[1] described. The arts wherein the professors employ themselves.

This Academy is not an entire single building, but a continuation of several houses on both sides of a street, which growing waste,[2] was purchased and applied to that use.

I was received very kindly by the Warden, and went for many days to the Academy. Every room has in it one or more projectors,[3] and I believe I could not be[4] in fewer than five hundred rooms.

The first man I saw was of a meager aspect, with sooty hands and face, his hair and beard long, ragged and singed in several places. His clothes, shirt, and skin were all of the same color. He had been eight years upon a project for extracting sunbeams out of cucumbers,[5] which were to be put into vials hermetically sealed, and let out to warm the air in raw, inclement summers. He told me, he did not doubt in eight years more, that he should be able to supply the Governor's gardens with sunshine at a reasonable rate; but he complained that his stock was low, and entreated me to give him something as an encouragement to ingenuity,[6] especially since this had been a very dear season for cucumbers. I made him a small present, for my Lord[7]

---

1. In general. The academy is a satire of the Royal Society, founded in 1662 for the purpose of scientific experimentation (see Perspectives: The Royal Society and the New Science, page 2039). Though many of its members made major contributions to science, the Society had a reputation for bizarre speculation. Swift had visited the Society in 1710 and here parodies actual experiments recorded in its *Philosophical Transactions*; he is also parodying the description of "Solomon's House," an academy of science in Francis Bacon's *New Atlantis* (1626).

2. Falling into disuse.
3. Those people undertaking the project.
4. Could not have been.
5. Stephen Hales (1677–1761), English botanist and physiologist, had recently investigated sunlight's agency in plant respiration. This and other studies were published in his *Vegetable Staticks* (1726).
6. His investigative powers.
7. The warden of the Academy.

had furnished me with money on purpose, because he knew their practice of begging from all who go to see them.

I went into another chamber, but was ready to hasten back, being almost overcome with a horrible stink. My conductor pressed me forward, conjuring me in a whisper to give no offense, which would be highly resented, and therefore I durst not so much as stop my nose. The projector of this cell was the most ancient student of the Academy. His face and beard were of a pale yellow; his hands and clothes daubed over with filth. When I was presented to him, he gave me a very close embrace (a compliment I could well have excused). His employment from his first coming into the Academy was an operation to reduce human excrement to its original food, by separating the several parts, removing the tincture which it receives from the gall, making the odor exhale, and scumming off the saliva. He had a weekly allowance from the Society of a vessel filled with human ordure,[8] about the bigness of a Bristol barrel.[9]

I saw another at work to calcine[1] ice into gunpowder, who likewise showed me a treatise he had written concerning the malleability of fire,[2] which he intended to publish.

There was a most ingenious architect who had contrived a new method for building houses, by beginning at the roof and working downwards to the foundation, which he justified to me by the like practice of those two prudent insects, the bee and the spider.

There was a man born blind, who had several apprentices in his own condition: their employment was to mix colors for painters, which their master taught them to distinguish by feeling and smelling.[3] It was indeed my misfortune to find them at that time not very perfect in their lessons, and the professor himself happened to be generally mistaken: this artist is much encouraged and esteemed by the whole fraternity.

In another apartment I was highly pleased with a projector, who had found a device of ploughing the ground with hogs, to save the charges of ploughs, cattle, and labor. The method is this; in an acre of ground you bury, at six inches distance, and eight deep, a quantity of acorns, dates, chestnuts, and other mast[4] or vegetables whereof these animals are fondest: then you drive six hundred or more of them into the field, where in a few days they will root up the whole ground in search of their food, and make it fit for sowing, at the same time manuring it with their dung; it is true upon experiment they found the charge and trouble very great, and they had little or no crop. However, it is not doubted that this invention may be capable of great improvement.

I went into another room, where the walls and ceiling were all hung round with cobwebs, except a narrow passage for the artist[5] to go in and out. At my entrance he called aloud to me not to disturb his webs. He lamented the fatal mistake the world had been so long in of using silkworms, while we had such plenty of domestic insects, who infinitely excelled the former, because they understood how to weave as

---

8. Excrement.
9. A medium-size barrel, holding about 37 gallons.
1. Desiccate.
2. Cf. Rabelais, *Gargantua and Pantagruel* (1532–1564), bk. 5, ch. 22: "Others were cutting fire with a knife, and drawing water up in a net."
3. Based on Robert Boyle's account in *Experiments and Observations Upon Colors* (1665), of a blind man who

could distinguish colors.
4. Nuts.
5. Modeled on both the Frenchman M. Bon, who believed silk could be made from cobwebs, and Dr. Wall, who suggested that the excreta of ants fed on plant sap could be used as dye; both suggestions were published in the *Transactions of the Royal Society*.

well as spin. And he proposed farther, that by employing spiders, the charge[6] of dyeing silks would be wholly saved, whereof I was fully convinced when he showed me a vast number of flies most beautifully colored, wherewith he fed his spiders, assuring us, that the webs would take a tincture from them; and as he had them of all hues, he hoped to fit everybody's fancy, as soon as he could find proper food for the flies, of certain gums, oils, and other glutinous matter to give a strength and consistence to the threads.

There was an astronomer who had undertaken to place a sundial upon the great weathercock on the Town House,[7] by adjusting the annual and diurnal motions of the earth and sun, so as to answer and coincide with all accidental turnings of the wind.

I was complaining of a small fit of the colic, upon which my conductor led me into a room, where a great physician resided, who was famous for curing that disease by contrary operations from the same instrument. He had a large pair of bellows with a long slender muzzle of ivory. This he conveyed eight inches up the anus, and drawing in the wind, he affirmed he could make the guts as lank as a dried bladder. But when the disease was more stubborn and violent, he let in the muzzle while the bellows was full of wind, which he discharged into the body of the patient, then withdrew the instrument to replenish it, clapping his thumb strongly against the orifice of the fundament; and this being repeated three or four times, the adventitious wind would rush out, bringing the noxious along with it (like water put into a pump) and the patient recover. I saw him try both experiments upon a dog, but could not discern any effect from the former. After the latter, the animal was ready to burst, and made so violent a discharge, as was very offensive to me and my companions. The dog died on the spot, and we left the doctor endeavoring to recover him by the same operation.[8]

I visited many other apartments, but shall not trouble my reader with all the curiosities I observed, being studious of brevity.

I had hitherto seen only one side of the Academy, the other being appropriated to the advancers of speculative learning, of whom I shall say something when I have mentioned one illustrious person more, who is called among them *the universal artist*.[9] He told us he had been thirty years employing his thoughts for the improvement of human life. He had two large rooms full of wonderful curiosities, and fifty men at work. Some were condensing air into a dry, tangible substance, by extracting the niter,[1] and letting the aqueous or fluid particles percolate; others softening marble for pillows and pincushions; others petrifying the hoofs of a living horse to preserve them from foundering. The artist himself was at that time busy upon two great designs: the first, to sow land with chaff, wherein he affirmed the true seminal virtue to be contained, as he demonstrated by several experiments which I was not skillful enough to comprehend. The other was, by a certain composition of gums, minerals, and vegetables outwardly applied, to prevent the growth of wool upon two young lambs; and he hoped in a reasonable time to propagate the breed of naked sheep all over the kingdom.

We crossed a walk to the other part of the Academy, where, as I have already said, the projectors in speculative learning resided.

---

6. Expense.
7. Town Hall.
8. Robert Hooke (1635–1703) produced artificial respiration in a dog (1667) by blowing air into its windpipe with a pair of bellows.

9. Possibly Robert Boyle (1627–1691), whose many scientific experiments investigated the nature of air, marble, petrifaction, agriculture, and sheep breeding.
1. Air was believed to contain nitrous matter.

The first professor I saw was in a very large room, with forty pupils about him. After salutation, observing me to look earnestly upon a frame, which took up the greatest part of both the length and breadth of the room, he said perhaps I might wonder to see him employed in a project for improving speculative knowledge by practical and mechanical operations. But the world would soon be sensible[2] of its usefulness, and he flattered himself that a more noble exalted thought never sprang in any other man's head. Everyone knew how laborious the usual method is of attaining to arts and sciences; whereas by his contrivance, the most ignorant person at a reasonable charge, and with a little bodily labor, may write books in philosophy, poetry, politics, law, mathematics, and theology, without the least assistance from genius or study. He then led me to the frame, about the sides whereof all his pupils stood in ranks. It was twenty foot square, placed in the middle of the room. The superficies[3] was composed of several bits of wood, about the bigness of a die,[4] but some larger than others. They were all linked together by slender wires. These bits of wood were covered on every square with papers pasted on them, and on these papers were written all the words of their language in their several moods, tenses, and declensions, but without any order. The professor then desired me to observe, for he was going to set his engine[5] at work. The pupils at his command took each of them hold of an iron handle, whereof there were forty fixed round the edges of the frame, and giving them a sudden turn, the whole disposition of the words was entirely changed. He then commanded six and thirty of the lads to read the several lines softly as they appeared upon the frame; and where they found three or four words together that might make part of a sentence, they dictated to the four remaining boys who were scribes. This work was repeated three or four times, and at every turn the engine was so contrived, that the words shifted into new places, as the square bits of wood moved upside down.

Six hours a day the young students were employed in this labor, and the professor showed me several volumes in large folio already collected, of broken sentences, which he intended to piece together, and out of those rich materials to give the world a complete body of all arts and sciences; which however might be still improved, and much expedited, if the public would raise a fund for making and employing five hundred such frames in Lagado, and oblige the managers to contribute in common their several[6] collections.

He assured me, that this invention had employed all his thoughts from his youth, that he had emptied the whole vocabulary into his frame, and made the strictest computation of the general proportion there is in books between the numbers of particles, nouns, and verbs, and other parts of speech.

I made my humblest acknowledgments to this illustrious person for his great communicativeness, and promised if ever I had the good fortune to return to my native country, that I would do him justice, as the sole inventor of this wonderful machine; the form and contrivance of which I desired leave to delineate upon paper as in the figure here annexed. I told him, although it were the custom of our learned in Europe to steal inventions from each other,[7] who had thereby at least this advantage, that it became a controversy which was the right owner, yet I would take such caution, that he should have the honor entire without a rival.

---

2. Aware.
3. Surface.
4. Singular of dice.
5. Machine.
6. Individual.

7. No international patent agreement existed at this time, and the theft of inventions was common as nations competed in developing technology for commercial manufacturing and navigation on the open seas.

We next went to the school of languages, where three professors sat in consultation upon improving that of their own country.[8]

The first project was to shorten discourse by cutting polysyllables into one, and leaving out verbs and participles, because in reality all things imaginable are but nouns.

The other project was a scheme for entirely abolishing all words whatsoever; and this was urged as a great advantage in point of health as well as brevity. For, it is plain, that every word we speak is in some degree a diminution of our lungs by corrosion, and consequently contributes to the shortening of our lives. An expedient was therefore offered, that since words are only names for *things*, it would be more convenient for all men to carry about them such *things* as were necessary to express the particular business they are to discourse on.[9] And this invention would certainly have taken place, to the great ease as well as health of the subject.[1] If the women in conjunction with the vulgar and illiterate had not threatened to raise a rebellion, unless they might be allowed the liberty to speak with their tongues, after the manner of their forefathers; such constant irreconcilable enemies to science are the common people. However, many of the most learned and wise adhere to the new scheme of expressing themselves by *things*, which hath only this inconvenience attending it, that if a man's business be very great, and of various kinds, he must be obliged in proportion to carry a greater bundle of *things* upon his back, unless he can afford one or two strong servants to attend him. I have often beheld two of those sages almost sinking under the weight of their packs, like peddlers among us; who when they met in the streets would lay down their loads, open their sacks, and hold conversation for an hour together; then put up their implements, help each other to resume their burdens, and take their leave.

But for short conversations a man may carry implements in his pockets and under his arms, enough to supply him, and in his house he cannot be at a loss; therefore the room where company meet who practice this art, is full of all *things* ready at hand, requisite to furnish matter for this kind of artificial converse.[2]

Another great advantage proposed by this invention, was that it would serve as a universal language to be understood in all civilized nations, whose goods and utensils are generally of the same kind, or nearly resembling, so that their uses might easily be comprehended. And thus, ambassadors would be qualified to treat with foreign princes or ministers of state, to whose tongues they were utter strangers.

I was at the mathematical school, where the master taught his pupils after a method scarce imaginable to us in Europe. The proposition and demonstration were fairly written on a thin wafer, with ink composed of a cephalic[3] tincture. This the student was to swallow upon a fasting stomach, and for three days following eat nothing but bread and water. As the wafer digested, the tincture mounted to his brain, bearing the proposition along with it. But the success has not hitherto been

8. The first secretary to the Royal Society, Thomas Sprat, in his *History* (1667) of that institution, recommended that such an Academy be founded, as the new style of science writing should strive to describe "so many *things* in an equal number of words." Although Swift burlesques this notion, he himself had published *Proposals for Correcting, Improving and Ascertaining the English Tongue* (1712), in which he suggested that an Academy be established with the aim of preserving culture and "fixing our language for ever."
9. The growth of scientific knowledge about the nature of the material world had encouraged suggestions that language should be made less abstract. In satirizing the projector, Swift alludes to John Locke's theory of language in Book 3 of *An Essay Concerning Human Understanding* (1690), where Locke argues that words stand for things only indirectly.
1. Both the individual practitioner and the people of the nation as a whole.
2. A reference to the Royal Society's attempt to collect one specimen or example of every thing in the world.
3. Of or for the head.

answerable, partly by some error in the *quantum* or composition, and partly by the perverseness of lads, to whom this bolus[4] is so nauseous that they generally steal aside, and discharge it upwards before it can operate; neither have they been yet persuaded to use so long an abstinence as the prescription requires.

CHAPTER 10

The Luggnaggians commended. A particular description of the Struldbruggs, with many conversations between the author and some eminent persons upon that subject.[5]

The Luggnaggians are a polite and generous people, and although they are not without some share of that pride which is peculiar to all Eastern countries, yet they show themselves courteous to strangers, especially such who are countenanced by the Court. I had many acquaintance among persons of the best fashion, and being always attended by my interpreter, the conversation we had was not disagreeable.

One day in much good company, I was asked by a person of quality, whether I had seen any of their Struldbruggs or Immortals. I said I had not, and desired he would explain to me what he meant by such an appellation applied to a mortal creature. He told me, that sometimes, though very rarely, a child happened to be born in a family with a red circular spot in the forehead, directly over the left eyebrow, which was an infallible mark that it should never die. The spot, as he described it, was about the compass of a silver threepence, but in the course of time grew larger, and changed its color; for at twelve years old it became green, so continued till five and twenty, then turned to a deep blue; at five and forty it grew coal black, and as large as an English shilling, but never admitted any farther alteration. He said these births were so rare, that he did not believe there could be above eleven hundred Struldbruggs of both sexes in the whole kingdom, of which he computed about fifty in the metropolis, and among the rest a young girl born about three years ago. That these productions were not peculiar to any family, but a mere effect of change, and the children of the Struldbruggs themselves, were equally mortal with the rest of the people.

I freely own myself to have been struck with inexpressible delight upon hearing this account: and the person who gave it me happening to understand the Balnibarbian language, which I spoke very well, I could not forbear breaking out into expressions perhaps a little too extravagant. I cried out as in a rapture: Happy nation where every child hath at least a chance for being immortal! Happy people who enjoy so many living examples of ancient virtue, and have masters ready to instruct them in the wisdom of all former ages! But, happiest beyond all comparison are those excellent Struldbruggs, who being born exempt from that universal calamity of human nature, have their minds free and disengaged, without the weight and depression of spirits caused by the continual apprehension of death. I discovered my admiration[6] that I had not observed any of these illustrious persons at Court, the black spot on the forehead being so remarkable a distinction, that I could not have easily overlooked it; and it was impossible that his Majesty, a most judicious prince, should not provide himself with a good number of such wise and able counselors. Yet perhaps the virtue of those reverend sages was too strict for the corrupt and

---

4. Mass of chewed food.
5. In order to return to England, Gulliver sails west on the Pacific from Balnibarbi (the country of which Lagado

is the capital) to Japan, stopping en route at the island of "Luggnagg," where he makes the following observations.
6. Expressed my surprise.

libertine manners of a Court. And we often find by experience that young men are too opinionative and volatile to be guided by the sober dictates of their seniors. However, since the King was pleased to allow me access to his royal person, I was resolved upon the very first occasion to deliver my opinion to him on this matter freely, and at large, by the help of my interpreter; and whether he would please to take my advice or no, yet in one thing I was determined, that his Majesty having frequently offered me an establishment in this country, I would with great thankfulness accept the favor, and pass my life here in the conversation of those superior beings the Struldbruggs, if they would please to admit me.

The gentleman to whom I addressed my discourse, because (as I have already observed) he spoke the language of Balnibarbi, said to me with a sort of a smile, which usually ariseth from pity to the ignorant, that he was glad of any occasion to keep me among them, and desired my permission to explain to the company what I had spoke. He did so, and they talked together for some time in their own language, whereof I understood not a syllable, neither could I observe by their countenances what impression my discourse had made on them. After a short silence the same person told me, that his friends and mine (so he thought fit to express himself) were very much pleased with the judicious remarks I had made on the great happiness and advantages of immortal life, and they were desirous to know in a particular manner, what scheme of living I should have formed to myself, if it had fallen to my lot to have been born a Struldbrugg.

I answered, it was easy to be eloquent on so copious and delightful a subject, especially to me who have been often apt to amuse myself with visions of what I should do if I were a king, a general, or a great lord; and upon this very case I had frequently run over the whole system how I should employ myself, and pass the time if I were sure to live for ever.

That, if it had been my good fortune to come into the world a Struldbrugg, as soon as I could discover my own happiness by understanding the difference between life and death, I would first resolve by all arts and methods whatsoever to procure myself riches. In the pursuit of which by thrift and management, I might reasonably expect in about two hundred years, to be the wealthiest man in the kingdom. In the second place, I would from my earliest youth apply myself to the study of arts and sciences, by which I should arrive in time to excel all others in learning. Lastly I would carefully record every action and event of consequence that happened in the public,[7] impartially draw the characters of the several successions of princes, and great ministers of state, with my own observations on every point. I would exactly set down the several changes in customs, language, fashions of dress, diet and diversions. By all which acquirements, I should be a living treasury of knowledge and wisdom, and certainly become the oracle of the nation.

I would never marry after threescore, but live in an hospitable manner, yet still on the saving side. I would entertain myself in forming and directing the minds of hopeful young men, by convincing them from my own remembrance, experience, and observation, fortified by numerous examples, of the usefulness of virtue in public and private life. But, my choice and constant companions should be a set of my own immortal brotherhood, among whom I would elect a dozen from the most ancient down to my own contemporaries. Where any of these wanted[8] fortunes, I would

7. The state (from Latin *res publica*, the "public thing,"   8. Lacked.
from which derives the word *republic*).

provide them with convenient lodges round my own estate, and have some of them always at my table, only mingling a few of the most valuable among you mortals, whom length of time would harden me to lose with little or no reluctance, and treat your posterity after the same manner, just as a man diverts himself with the annual succession of pinks and tulips in his garden, without regretting the loss of those which withered the preceding year.

These Struldbruggs and I would mutually communicate our observations and memorials through the course of time, remark the several gradations by which corruption steals into the world, and oppose it in every step, by giving perpetual warning and instruction to mankind; which, added to the strong influence of our own example, would probably prevent that continual degeneracy of human nature so justly complained of in all ages.

Add to all this, the pleasure of seeing the various revolutions of states and empires, the changes in the lower and upper world,[9] ancient cities in ruins, and obscure villages become the seats of kings. Famous rivers lessening into shallow brooks, the ocean leaving one coast dry, and overwhelming another, the discovery of many countries yet unknown. Barbarity overrunning the politest nations, and the most barbarous becoming civilized. I should then see the discovery of the longitude, the perpetual motion, the universal medicine,[1] and many other great inventions brought to the utmost perfection.

What wonderful discoveries should we make in astronomy, by outliving and confirming our own predictions, by observing the progress and returns of comets, with the changes of motion in the sun, moon, and stars.

I enlarged upon many other topics, which the natural desire of endless life and sublunary[2] happiness could easily furnish me with. When I had ended, and the sum of my discourse had been interpreted as before, to the rest of the company, there was a good deal of talk among them in the language of the country, not without some laughter at my expense. At last the same gentleman who had been my interpreter said, he was desired by the rest to set me right in a few mistakes, which I had fallen into through the common imbecility of human nature, and upon that allowance was less answerable for them. That, this breed of Struldbruggs was peculiar to their country, for there were no such people either in Balnibarbi or Japan, where he had the honor to be ambassador from his Majesty, and found the natives in both those kingdoms very hard to believe[3] that the fact was possible, and it appeared from my astonishment when he first mentioned the matter to me, that I received it as a thing wholly new, and scarcely to be credited. That in the two kingdoms above-mentioned, where during his residence he had conversed very much, he observed long life to be the universal desire and wish of mankind. That whoever had one foot in the grave, was sure to hold back the other as strongly as he could. That the oldest had still hopes of living one day longer, and looked on death as the greatest evil, from which nature always prompted him to retreat; only in this island of Luggnagg, the appetite for living was not so eager, from the continual example of the Struldbruggs before their eyes.

---

9. On the earth and in the heavens.
1. As at Lagado, Gulliver enumerates scientific quests Swift scoffed at: for a method of determining the longitude of a ship at sea, for a perpetual motion machine, for one drug sufficient to cure all ills.
2. Earthly.
3. To convince.

That the system of living contrived by me was unreasonable and unjust, because it supposed a perpetuity of youth, health, and vigor, which no man could be so foolish to hope, however extravagant he may be in his wishes. That the question therefore was not whether a man would choose to be always in the prime of youth, attended with prosperity and health, but how he would pass a perpetual life under all the usual disadvantages which old age brings along with it. For although few men will avow their desires of being immortal upon such hard conditions, yet in the two kingdoms before-mentioned of Balnibarbi and Japan, he observed that every man desired to put off death for some time longer, let it approach ever so late, and he rarely heard of any man who died willingly, except he were incited by the extremity of grief or torture. And he appealed to me whether in those countries I had traveled, as well as my own, I had not observed the same general disposition.

After this preface he gave me a particular account of the Struldbruggs among them. He said they commonly acted like mortals, till about thirty years old, after which by degrees they grew melancholy and dejected, increasing in both till they came to fourscore. This he learned from their own confession; for otherwise there not being above two or three of that species born in an age, they were too few to form a general observation by. When they came to fourscore years, which is reckoned the extremity of living in this country, they had not only all the follies and infirmities of other old men, but many more which arose from the dreadful prospect of never dying. They were not only opinionative, peevish, covetous, morose, vain, talkative, but uncapable of friendship, and dead to all natural affection, which never descended below their grandchildren. Envy and impotent desires are their prevailing passions. But those objects against which their envy seems principally directed, are the vices of the younger sort, and the deaths of the old. By reflecting on the former, they find themselves cut off from all possibility of pleasure; and whenever they see a funeral, they lament and repine that others have gone to an harbor of rest, to which they themselves never can hope to arrive. They have no remembrance of anything but what they learned and observed in their youth and middle age, and even that is very imperfect. And for the truth or particulars of any fact, it is safer to depend on common traditions than upon their best recollections. The least miserable among them appear to be those who turn to dotage, and entirely lose their memories; these meet with more pity and assistance, because they want many bad qualities which abound in others.

If a Struldbrugg happen to marry one of his own kind, the marriage is dissolved of course by the courtesy of the kingdom, as soon as the younger of the two comes to be fourscore. For the law thinks it a reasonable indulgence, that those who are condemned without any fault of their own to a perpetual continuance in the world, should not have their misery doubled by the load of a wife.[4]

As soon as they have completed the term of eighty years, they are looked on as dead in law; their heirs immediately succeed to their estates, only a small pittance is reserved for their support, and the poor ones are maintained at the public charge. After that period they are held incapable of any employment of trust or profit, they cannot purchase lands or take leases, neither are they allowed to be witnesses in any cause, either civil or criminal, not even for the decision of meres[5] and bounds.

---

4. Swift himself never married.   5. Property lines (at issue in property disputes).

At ninety they lose their teeth and hair, they have at that age no distinction of taste, but eat and drink whatever they can get, without relish or appetite. The diseases they were subject to, still continue without increasing or diminishing. In talking they forget the common appellation of things, and the names of persons, even of those who are their nearest friends and relations. For the same reason they never can amuse themselves with reading, because their memory will not serve to carry them from the beginning of a sentence to the end; and by this defect they are deprived of the only entertainment whereof they might otherwise be capable.

The language of this country being always upon the flux, the Struldbruggs of one age do not understand those of another, neither are they able after two hundred years to hold any conversation (farther than by a few general words) with their neighbors the mortals, and thus they lie under the disadvantage of living like foreigners in their own country. This was the account given me of the Struldbruggs, as near as I can remember. I afterwards saw five or six of different ages, the youngest not above two hundred years old, who were brought to me at several times by some of my friends; but although they were told that I was a great traveler, and had seen all the world, they had not the least curiosity to ask me a question; only desired I would give them *slumskudask*, or a token of remembrance, which is a modest way of begging, to avoid the law that strictly forbids it, because they are provided for by the public, although indeed with a very scanty allowance.

They are despised and hated by all sorts of people; when one of them is born, it is reckoned ominous, and their birth is recorded very particularly; so that you may know their age by consulting the registry, which however hath not been kept above a thousand years past, or at least hath been destroyed by time or public disturbances. But the usual way of computing how old they are, is, by asking them what kings or great persons they can remember, and then consulting history, for infallibly the last prince in their mind did not begin his reign after they were fourscore years old.

They were the most mortifying sight I ever beheld, and the women more horrible than the men. Besides the usual deformities in extreme old age, they acquired an additional ghastliness in proportion to their number of years, which is not to be described, and among half a dozen I soon distinguished which was the eldest, although there were not above a century or two between them.

The reader will easily believe, that from what I had heard and seen, my keen appetite for perpetuity of life was much abated. I grew heartily ashamed of the pleasing visions I had formed, and thought no tyrant could invent a death into which I would not run with pleasure from such a life. The king heard of all that had passed between me and my friends upon this occasion, and rallied me very pleasantly, wishing I would send a couple of Struldbruggs to my own country, to arm our people against the fear of death; but this it seems is forbidden by the fundamental laws of the kingdom, or else I should have been well content with the trouble and expense of transporting them.

I could not but agree that the laws of this kingdom, relating to the Struldbruggs, were founded upon the strongest reasons, and such as any other country would be under the necessity of enacting in the like circumstances. Otherwise, as avarice is the necessary consequent of old age, those Immortals would in time become proprietors of the whole nation, and engross the civil power, which, for want of abilities to manage, must end in the ruin of the public.

Part 4. A Voyage to the Country of the Houyhnhnms[1]

CHAPTER 1

The author sets out as Captain of a ship. His men conspire against him, confine him a long time to his cabin, set him on shore in an unknown land. He travels up into the country. The Yahoos,[2] a strange sort of animal, described. The author meets two Houyhnhnms.

I continued at home with my wife and children about five months in a very happy condition, if I could have learned the lesson of knowing when I was well. I left my poor wife big with child, and accepted an advantageous offer made me to be Captain of the *Adventure*,[3] a stout merchantman of 350 tons: for I understood navigation well, and being grown weary of a surgeon's employment at sea, which however I could exercise upon occasion, I took a skillful young man of that calling, one Robert Purefoy,[4] into my ship. We set sail from Portsmouth upon the seventh day of September, 1710; on the fourteenth, we met with Captain Pocock[5] of Bristol, at Teneriffe,[6] who was going to the bay of Campeche, to cut logwood. On the sixteenth, he was parted from us by a storm; I heard since my return, that his ship foundered, and none escaped, but one cabin boy. He was an honest man, and a good sailor, but a little too positive in his own opinions, which was the cause of his destruction, as it hath been of several others. For if he had followed my advice, he might at this time have been safe at home with his family as well as myself.

I had several men died in my ship of calentures,[7] so that I was forced to get recruits out of Barbados, and the Leeward Islands, where I touched by[8] the direction of the merchants who employed me, which I had soon too much cause to repent; for I found afterwards that most of them had been buccaneers. I had fifty hands on board, and my orders were, that I should trade with the Indians in the South Sea, and make what discoveries I could. These rogues whom I had picked up debauched my other men, and they all formed a conspiracy to seize the ship and secure me; which they did one morning, rushing into my cabin, and binding me hand and foot, threatening to throw me overboard, if I offered to stir. I told them, I was their prisoner, and would submit. This they made me swear to do, and then unbound me, only fastening one of my legs with a chain near my bed, and placed a sentry at my door with his piece charged,[9] who was commanded to shoot me dead, if I attempted my liberty. They sent me down victuals and drink, and took the government of the ship to themselves. Their design was to turn pirates, and plunder the Spaniards, which they could not do till they got more men. But first they resolved to sell the goods in the

1. Pronounced "whinnims," to mimic the sound of a horse's whinny, though some scholars have offered more complex interpretations of this name. With characteristic irony, Swift probably chose horses to represent rational creatures because the philosopher John Locke (1632–1704) and Bishop Edward Stillingfleet (1635–1699) had argued extensively about how one might distinguish man as a rational animal from an evidently irrational animal, such as a horse.

2. The name may be derived from similarly titled African or Guianan tribes. The animals represent sinful, fallen humanity, and their juxtaposition with the Houyhnhnms is designed to question belief in the innate rationality of humankind and the superiority of humans over other creatures.

3. The name of two ships of the notorious pirate Captain William Kidd (d. 1701). Kidd, originally commissioned to capture pirates, was also subject to a mutiny.

4. "Pure faith," associating Gulliver with the overzealous Puritans.

5. Probably modeled on the dogmatic Captain Dampier (1652–1715), who had spent three years logcutting around the Campeche Bay, on the Yucatan Peninsula, in the Gulf of Mexico. His violent disagreements with his lieutenant led to a court martial.

6. One of the Canary Islands, off the northwestern coast of Africa.

7. Tropical fevers.

8. Landed according to.

9. Gun loaded.

ship, and then go to Madagascar[1] for recruits, several among them having died since my confinement. They sailed many weeks, and traded with the Indians, but I knew not what course they took, being kept close prisoner in my cabin, and expecting nothing less than to be murdered, as they often threatened me.

Upon the ninth day of May, 1711, one James Welch came down to my cabin; and said he had orders from the Captain to set me ashore. I expostulated with him, but in vain; neither would he so much as tell me who their new captain was. They forced me into the longboat, letting me put on my best suit of clothes, which were good as new, and a small bundle of linen, but no arms except my hanger;[2] and they were so civil as not to search my pockets, into which I conveyed what money I had, with some other little necessaries. They rowed about a league; and then set me down on a strand.[3] I desired them to tell me what country it was. They all swore, they knew no more than myself, but said, that the Captain (as they called him) was resolved, after they had sold the lading,[4] to get rid of me in the first place where they discovered land. They pushed off immediately, advising me to make haste, for fear of being overtaken by the tide, and bade me farewell.

In this desolate condition I advanced forward, and soon got upon firm ground, where I sat down on a bank to rest myself, and consider what I had best to do. When I was a little refreshed, I went up into the country, resolving to deliver myself to the first savages I should meet, and purchase my life from them by some bracelets, glass rings, and other toys,[5] which sailors usually provide themselves with in those voyages, and whereof I had some about me: the land was divided by long rows of trees, not regularly planted, but naturally growing; there was great plenty of grass, and several fields of oats. I walked very circumspectly for fear of being surprised, or suddenly shot with an arrow from behind or on either side. I fell into a beaten road, where I saw many tracks of human feet, and some of cows, but most of horses. At last I beheld several animals in a field, and one or two of the same kind sitting in trees. Their shape was very singular, and deformed, which a little discomposed me, so that I lay down behind a thicket to observe them better. Some of them coming forward near the place where I lay, gave me an opportunity of distinctly marking[6] their form. Their heads and breasts were covered with a thick hair, some frizzled and others lank; they had beards like goats, and a long ridge of hair down their backs, and the foreparts of their legs and feet, but the rest of their bodies were bare, so that I might see their skins, which were of a brown buff color. They had no tails, nor any hair at all on their buttocks, except about the anus; which, I presume, Nature had placed there to defend them as they sat on the ground; for this posture they used, as well as lying down, and often stood on their hind feet. They climbed high trees, as nimbly as a squirrel, for they had strong extended claws before and behind, terminating in sharp points, and hooked. They would often spring, and bound, and leap with prodigious agility. The females were not so large as the males; they had long lank hair on their heads, and only a sort of down on the rest of their bodies, except about the anus, and pudenda.[7] Their dugs[8] hung between their forefeet, and often reached almost to the ground as they walked. The hair of both sexes was of several colors, brown, red, black, and yellow. Upon the whole, I never beheld in all my travels so

1. A popular meeting place for pirates.
2. A short sword, typically hung from the belt.
3. The shore; in this context, apparently a spit extending into the sea.
4. Cargo.

5. Trinkets.
6. Observing.
7. Genitals.
8. Breasts.

disagreeable an animal, nor one against which I naturally conceived so strong an antipathy. So that thinking I had seen enough, full of contempt and aversion, I got up and pursued the beaten road, hoping it might direct me to the cabin of some Indian. I had not gone far when I met one of these creatures full in my way, and coming up directly to me. The ugly monster, when he saw me, distorted several ways every feature of his visage, and stared as at an object he had never seen before; then approaching nearer, lifted up his forepaw, whether out of curiosity or mischief, I could not tell. But I drew my hanger, and gave him a good blow with the flat side of it; for I durst not strike him with the edge, fearing the inhabitants might be provoked against me, if they should come to know, that I had killed or maimed any of their cattle. When the beast felt the smart, he drew back, and roared so loud, that a herd of at least forty came flocking about me from the next field, howling and making odious faces; but I ran to the body of a tree, and leaning my back against it, kept them off, by waving my hanger. Several of this cursed brood getting hold of the branches behind leaped up into the tree, from whence they began to discharge their excrements on my head: however, I escaped pretty well, by sticking close to the stem of the tree, but was almost stifled with the filth, which fell about me on every side.

In the midst of this distress, I observed them all to run away on a sudden as fast as they could, at which I ventured to leave the tree, and pursue the road, wondering what it was that could put them into this flight. But looking on my left hand, I saw a horse walking softly in the field, which my persecutors having sooner discovered, was the cause of their flight. The horse started a little when he came near me, but soon recovering himself, looked full in my face with manifest tokens of wonder: he viewed my hands and feet, walking round me several times. I would have pursued my journey, but he placed himself directly in the way, yet looking with a very mild aspect, never offering the least violence. We stood gazing at each other for some time; at last I took the boldness to reach my hand towards his neck, with a design to stroke it, using the common style and whistle of jockeys when they are going to handle a strange horse. But this animal, seeming to receive my civilities with disdain, shook his head, and bent his brows, softly raising up his left forefoot to remove my hand. Then he neighed three or four times, but in so different a cadence, that I almost began to think he was speaking to himself in some language of his own.

While he and I were thus employed, another horse came up; who applying[9] himself to the first in a very formal manner, they gently struck each other's right hoof before, neighing several times by turns, and varying the sound, which seemed to be almost articulate. They went some paces off, as if it were to confer together, walking side by side, backward and forward, like persons deliberating upon some affair of weight, but often turning their eyes towards me, as it were to watch that I might not escape. I was amazed to see such actions and behavior in brute beasts, and concluded with myself, that if the inhabitants of this country were endued with a proportionable degree of reason, they must needs be the wisest people upon earth. This thought gave me so much comfort, that I resolved to go forward until I could discover some house or village, or meet with any of the natives, leaving the two horses to discourse together as they pleased. But the first, who was a dapple-grey, observing me to steal off, neighed after me in so expressive a tone, that I fancied myself to understand what he meant; whereupon I turned back, and came near him, to expect[1] his farther commands. But concealing my fear as much as I could, for I

---

9. Addressing.   1. Await.

began to be in some pain,[2] how this adventure might terminate; and the reader will easily believe I did not much like my present situation.

The two horses came up close to me, looking with great earnestness upon my face and hands. The grey steed rubbed my hat all round with his right forehoof, and discomposed it so much, that I was forced to adjust it better, by taking it off, and settling it again; whereat both he and his companion (who was a brown bay) appeared to be much surprised; the latter felt the lappet[3] of my coat, and finding it to hang loose about me, they both looked with new signs of wonder. He stroked my right hand, seeming to admire the softness, and color; but he squeezed it so hard between his hoof and his pastern,[4] that I was forced to roar; after which they both touched me with all possible tenderness. They were under great perplexity about my shoes and stockings, which they felt very often, neighing to each other, and using various gestures, not unlike those of a philosopher,[5] when he would attempt to solve some new and difficult phenomenon.

Upon the whole, the behavior of these animals was so orderly and rational, so acute and judicious, that I at last concluded, they must needs be magicians, who had thus metamorphosed themselves upon some design, and seeing a stranger in the way, were resolved to divert themselves with him; or perhaps were really amazed at the sight of a man so very different in habit, feature, and complexion from those who might probably live in so remote a climate.[6] Upon the strength of this reasoning, I ventured to address them in the following manner: Gentlemen, if you be conjurers, as I have good cause to believe, you can understand any language; therefore I make bold to let your Worships know, that I am a poor distressed Englishman, driven by his misfortunes upon your coast, and I entreat one of you, to let me ride upon his back, as if he were a real horse, to some house or village, where I can be relieved. In return of which favor, I will make you a present of this knife and bracelet (taking them out of my pocket). The two creatures stood silent while I spoke, seeming to listen with great attention; and when I had ended, they neighed frequently towards each other, as if they were engaged in serious conversation. I plainly observed that their language expressed the passions[7] very well, and the words might with little pains be resolved into an alphabet more easily than the Chinese.

I could frequently distinguish the word *Yahoo,* which was repeated by each of them several times; and although it were impossible for me to conjecture what it meant, yet while the two horses were busy in conversation, I endeavored to practice this word upon my tongue; and as soon as they were silent, I boldly pronounced *Yahoo* in a loud voice, imitating, at the same time, as near as I could, the neighing of a horse; at which they were both visibly surprised, and the grey repeated the same word twice, as if he meant to teach me the right accent, wherein I spoke after him as well as I could, and found myself perceivably to improve every time, although very far from any degree of perfection. Then the bay tried me with a second word, much harder to be pronounced; but reducing it to the English *orthography*,[8] may be spelled thus, *Houyhnhnm.* I did not succeed in this so well as the former, but after two or three farther trials, I had better fortune; and they both appeared amazed at my capacity.

2. Began to be worried.
3. Lapel.
4. Part of a horse's foot between the fetlock (a projection of the lower leg) and the hoof.

5. Scientist.
6. Region.
7. Emotions.
8. Spelling.

After some farther discourse, which I then conjectured might relate to me, the two friends took their leaves, with the same compliment of striking each other's hoof; and the grey made me signs that I should walk before him; wherein I thought it prudent to comply, till I could find a better director. When I offered to slacken my pace, he would cry *Hhuun, Hhuun;* I guessed his meaning, and gave him to understand, as well as I could, that I was weary, and not able to walk faster; upon which, he would stand a while to let me rest.

CHAPTER 2

The author conducted by a Houyhnhnm to his house. The house described. The author's reception. The food of the Houyhnhnms. The author in distress for want of meat, is at last relieved. His manner of feeding in that country.

Having traveled about three miles, we came to a long kind of building, made of timber stuck in the ground, and wattled across;[9] the roof was low, and covered with straw. I now began to be a little comforted, and took out some toys, which travelers usually carry for presents to the savage Indians of America and other parts, in hopes the people of the house would be thereby encouraged to receive me kindly. The horse made me a sign to go in first; it was a large room with a smooth, clay floor, and a rack[1] and manger extending the whole length on one side. There were three nags,[2] and two mares, not eating, but some of them sitting down upon their hams,[3] which I very much wondered at; but wondered more to see the rest employed in domestic business. The last seemed but ordinary cattle; however, this confirmed my first opinion, that a people who could so far civilize brute animals, must needs excel in wisdom all the nations of the world. The grey came in just after, and thereby prevented any ill treatment, which the others might have given me. He neighed to them several times in a style of authority, and received answers.

Beyond this room there were three others, reaching the length of the house, to which you passed through three doors, opposite to each other, in the manner of a vista;[4] we went through the second room towards the third; here the grey walked in first, beckoning me to attend.[5] I waited in the second room, and got ready my presents, for the master and mistress of the house: they were two knives, three bracelets of false pearl, a small looking glass, and a bead necklace. The horse neighed three or four times, and I waited to hear some answers in a human voice, but I heard no other returns than in the same dialect, only one or two a little shriller than his. I began to think that this house must belong to some person of great note among them, because there appeared so much ceremony before I could gain admittance. But, that a man of quality should be served all by horses, was beyond my comprehension. I feared my brain was disturbed by my sufferings and misfortunes: I roused myself, and looked about me in the room where I was left alone; this was furnished as the first, only after a more elegant manner. I rubbed mine eyes often, but the same objects still occurred. I pinched my arms and sides, to awake myself, hoping I might be in a dream. I then absolutely concluded, that all these appearances could be nothing else but necromancy[6] and magic. But I had no time to pursue these reflections;

---

9. Filled in with twigs and branches.
1. Hayrack for the feed.
2. Ponies.
3. Buttocks.

4. Long, narrow view (usually between rows of trees).
5. Wait.
6. Sorcery.

for the grey horse came to the door, and made me a sign to follow him into the third room, where I saw a very comely mare, together with a colt and foal, sitting on their haunches, upon mats of straw, not unartfully made, and perfectly neat and clean.

The mare, soon after my entrance, rose from her mat, and coming up close, after having nicely[7] observed my hands and face, gave me a most contemptuous look; then turning to the horse, I heard the word *Yahoo* often repeated betwixt them; the meaning of which word I could not then comprehend, although it were the first I had learned to pronounce; but I was soon better informed, to my everlasting mortification: for the horse beckoning to me with his head, and repeating the word *Hhuun*, *Hhuun*, as he did upon the road, which I understood was to attend him, led me out into a kind of court, where was another building at some distance from the house. Here we entered, and I saw three of those detestable creatures, which I first met after my landing, feeding upon roots, and the flesh of some animals, which I afterwards found to be that of asses and dogs, and now and then a cow dead by accident or disease.[8] They were all tied by the neck with strong withes,[9] fastened to a beam; they held their food between the claws of their forefeet, and tore it with their teeth.

The master horse ordered a sorrel nag, one of his servants, to untie the largest of these animals, and take him into the yard. The beast and I were brought close together, and our countenances diligently compared, both by master and servant, who thereupon repeated several times the word *Yahoo*. My horror and astonishment are not to be described, when I observed, in this abominable animal, a perfect human figure; the face of it indeed was flat and broad, the nose depressed, the lips large, and the mouth wide. But these differences are common to all savage nations, where the lineaments of the countenance are distorted by the natives suffering[1] their infants to lie groveling on the earth, or by carrying them on their backs, nuzzling with their face against the mother's shoulders. The forefeet of the Yahoo differed from my hands in nothing else but the length of the nails, the coarseness and brownness of the palms, and the hairiness on the backs. There was the same resemblance between our feet, with the same differences, which I knew very well, though the horses did not, because of my shoes and stockings; the same in every part of our bodies, except as to hairiness and color, which I have already described.

The great difficulty that seemed to stick with the two horses, was, to see the rest of my body so very different from that of a Yahoo, for which I was obliged to my clothes, whereof they had no conception: the sorrel nag offered me a root, which he held (after their manner, as we shall describe in its proper place) between his hoof and pastern; I took it in my hand, and having smelt it, returned it to him as civilly as I could. He brought out of the Yahoo's kennel a piece of ass's flesh, but it smelt so offensively that I turned from it with loathing; he then threw it to the Yahoo, by whom it was greedily devoured. He afterwards showed me a wisp of hay, and a fetlock full of oats; but I shook my head, to signify, that neither of these were food for me. And indeed, I now apprehended, that I must absolutely starve, if I did not get to some of my own species: for as to those filthy Yahoos, although there were few greater lovers of mankind, at that time, than myself; yet I confess I never saw any sensitive[2] being so detestable on all accounts; and the more I came near them, the more hateful they grew, while I stayed in that country. This the master horse

---

7. Closely.
8. The Yahoos eat food listed in Leviticus (11.3, 27, 39–40) as unclean, suggesting that they exemplify the human condition distorted and debased by sin.

9. Leashes.
1. Allowing.
2. "Having sense or perception, but not reason" (Johnson's *Dictionary*).

observed by my behavior, and therefore sent the Yahoo back to his kennel. He then put his forehoof to his mouth, at which I was much surprised, although he did it with ease, and with a motion that appeared perfectly natural, and made other signs to know what I would eat; but I could not return him such an answer as he was able to apprehend; and if he had understood me, I did not see how it was possible to contrive any way for finding myself nourishment. While we were thus engaged, I observed a cow passing by, whereupon I pointed to her, and expressed a desire to let me go and milk her. This had its effect; for he led me back into the house, and ordered a mare-servant to open a room, where a good store of milk lay in earthen and wooden vessels, after a very orderly and cleanly manner. She gave me a large bowl full, of which I drank very heartily, and found myself well refreshed.

About noon I saw coming towards the house a kind of vehicle drawn like a sledge by four Yahoos. There was in it an old steed, who seemed to be of quality; he alighted with his hind feet forward, having by accident got a hurt in his left forefoot. He came to dine with our horse, who received him with great civility. They dined in the best room, and had oats boiled in milk for the second course, which the old horse ate warm, but the rest cold. Their mangers were placed circular in the middle of the room and divided into several partitions, round which they sat on their haunches upon bosses[3] of straw. In the middle was a large rack with angles answering to every partition of the manger. So that each horse and mare ate their own hay, and their own mash of oats and milk, with much decency and regularity. The behavior of the young colt and foal appeared very modest, and that of the master and mistress extremely cheerful and complaisant[4] to their guest. The grey ordered me to stand by him, and much discourse passed between him and his friend concerning me, as I found by the stranger's often looking on me, and the frequent repetition of the word Yahoo.

I happened to wear my gloves, which the master grey observing, seemed perplexed, discovering signs of wonder what I had done to my forefeet; he put his hoof three or four times to them, as if he would signify, that I should reduce them to their former shape, which I presently did, pulling off both my gloves, and putting them into my pocket. This occasioned farther talk, and I saw the company was pleased with my behavior, whereof I soon found the good effects. I was ordered to speak the few words I understood, and while they were at dinner, the master taught me the names for oats, milk, fire, water, and some others; which I could readily pronounce after him, having from my youth a great facility in learning languages.

When dinner was done, the master horse took me aside, and by signs and words made me understand the concern he was in, that I had nothing to eat. Oats in their tongue are called *hlunnh*. This word I pronounced two or three times; for although I had refused them at first, yet upon second thoughts, I considered that I could contrive to make of them a kind of bread, which might be sufficient with milk to keep me alive, till I could make my escape to some other country, and to creatures of my own species. The horse immediately ordered a white mare-servant of his family to bring me a good quantity of oats in a sort of wooden tray. These I heated before the fire as well as I could, and rubbed them till the husks came off, which I made a shift[5] to winnow from the grain; I ground and beat them between two stones, then took water, and made them into a paste or cake, which I toasted at the fire, and ate warm

3. Piles or seats.   5. Attempted.
4. Courteous.

with milk. It was at first a very insipid diet, although common enough in many parts of Europe, but grew tolerable by time; and having been often reduced to hard fare in my life, this was not the first experiment I had made how easily nature is satisfied.[6] And I cannot but observe, that I never had one hour's sickness, while I stayed in this island. 'Tis true, I sometimes made a shift to catch a rabbit, or bird, by springes[7] made of Yahoos' hairs, and I often gathered wholesome herbs, which I boiled, or ate as salads with my bread, and now and then, for a rarity, I made a little butter, and drank the whey. I was at first at a great loss for salt; but custom soon reconciled the want of it; and I am confident that the frequent use of salt among us is an effect of luxury, and was first introduced only as a provocative to drink; except where it is necessary for preserving of flesh in long voyages, or in places remote from great markets. For we observe no animal to be fond of it but man[8] and as to myself, when I left this country, it was a great while before I could endure the taste of it in anything that I ate.

This is enough to say upon the subject of my diet, wherewith other travelers fill their books, as if the readers were personally concerned whether we fared[9] well or ill. However, it was necessary to mention this matter, lest the world should think it impossible that I could find sustenance for three years in such a country, and among such inhabitants.

When it grew towards evening, the master horse ordered a place for me to lodge in; it was but six yards from the house, and separated from the stable of the Yahoos. Here I got some straw, and covering myself with my own clothes, slept very sound. But I was in a short time better accommodated, as the reader shall know hereafter, when I come to treat more particularly about my way of living.

CHAPTER 3

The author studious to learn the language, the Houyhnhnm his master assists in teaching him. The language described. Several Houyhnhnms of quality come out of curiosity to see the author. He gives his master a short account of his voyage.

My principal endeavor was to learn the language, which my master (for so I shall henceforth call him) and his children, and every servant of his house were desirous to teach me. For they looked upon it as a prodigy that a brute animal should discover[1] such marks of a rational creature. I pointed to everything, and inquired the name of it, which I wrote down in my journal book when I was alone, and corrected my bad accent, by desiring those of the family to pronounce it often. In this employment, a sorrel nag, one of the under servants, was very ready to assist me.

In speaking, they pronounce through the nose and throat, and their language approaches nearest to the High Dutch or German, of any I know in Europe; but is much more graceful and significant.[2] The Emperor Charles V made almost the same observation, when he said, that if he were to speak to his horse, it should be in High Dutch.[3]

---

6. A commonplace idea in ancient satire; Swift may here be mocking it.
7. Snares.
8. This is, of course, untrue, but Gulliver's subsequent dislike of salt indicates his dislike of human society in general.

9. A pun on "fare," meaning both food and "to get along."
1. Display.
2. Expressive.
3. I.e., German; Charles V of Spain (1500-1551) was believed to have said that he would address his God in Spanish, his mistress in Italian, and his horse in German.

The curiosity and impatience of my master were so great, that he spent many hours of his leisure to instruct me. He was convinced (as he afterwards told me) that I must be a Yahoo, but my teachableness, civility, and cleanliness astonished him; which were qualities altogether so opposite to those animals. He was most perplexed about my clothes, reasoning sometimes with himself, whether they were a part of my body; for I never pulled them off till the family were asleep, and got them on before they waked in the morning. My master was eager to learn from whence I came, how I acquired those appearances of reason, which I discovered in all my actions, and to know my story from my own mouth, which he hoped he should soon do by the great proficiency I made in learning and pronouncing their words and sentences. To help my memory, I formed all I learned into the English alphabet, and writ the words down with the translations. This last, after some time, I ventured to do in my master's presence. It cost me much trouble to explain to him what I was doing; for the inhabitants have not the least idea of books or literature.

In about ten weeks' time I was able to understand most of his questions, and in three months could give him some tolerable answers. He was extremely curious to know from what part of the country I came, and how I was taught to imitate a rational creature, because the Yahoos (whom he saw I exactly resembled in my head, hands, and face, that were only visible), with some appearance of cunning, and the strongest disposition to mischief, were observed to be the most unteachable of all brutes. I answered, that I came over the sea, from a far place, with many others of my own kind, in a great hollow vessel made of the bodies of trees. That my companions forced me to land on this coast, and then left me to shift for myself. It was with some difficulty, and by the help of many signs, that I brought him to understand me. He replied, that I must needs be mistaken, or that I *said the thing which was not.* (For they have no word in their language to express lying or falsehood.) He knew it was impossible[4] that there could be a country beyond the sea, or that a parcel of brutes could move a wooden vessel whither they pleased upon water. He was sure no Houyhnhnm alive could make such a vessel, or would trust Yahoos to manage it.

The word *Houyhnhnm*, in their tongue, signifies a *horse,* and in its etymology, the *Perfection of Nature.* I told my master, that I was at a loss for expression, but would improve as fast as I could; and hoped in a short time I should be able to tell him wonders: he was pleased to direct his own mare, his colt and foal, and the servants of the family to take all opportunities of instructing me, and every day for two or three hours, he was at the same pains himself: several horses and mares of quality in the neighborhood came often to our house upon the report spread of a wonderful Yahoo, that could speak like a Houyhnhnm, and seemed in his words and actions to discover some glimmerings of reason. These delighted to converse with me; they put many questions, and received such answers as I was able to return. By all which advantages, I made so great a progress, that in five months from my arrival, I understood whatever was spoke, and could express myself tolerably well.

The Houyhnhnms who came to visit my master, out of a design of seeing and talking with me, could hardly believe me to be a right[5] Yahoo, because my body had a different covering from others of my kind. They were astonished to observe me without the usual hair or skin, except on my head, face, and hands; but I discovered that secret to my master, upon an accident, which happened about a fortnight before.

---

4. The Houyhnhnm thus shows himself to be so dependent on reason that he is dogmatic in his ignorance, unable (like rationalists in religion) to accept what he does not know by his own reasoning.
5. True.

I have already told the reader, that every night when the family were gone to bed, it was my custom to strip and cover myself with my clothes: it happened one morning early, that my master sent for me, by the sorrel nag, who was his valet; when he came, I was fast asleep, my clothes fallen off on one side, and my shirt above my waist. I awaked at the noise he made, and observed him to deliver his message in some disorder; after which he went to my master, and in a great fright gave him a very confused account of what he had seen: this I presently discovered; for going as soon as I was dressed, to pay my attendance upon his Honor, he asked me the meaning of what his servant had reported, that I was not the same thing when I slept as I appeared to be at other times; that his valet assured him, some part of me was white, some yellow, at least not so white, and some brown.

I had hitherto concealed the secret of my dress, in order to distinguish myself as much as possible, from that cursed race of Yahoos; but now I found it in vain to do so any longer. Besides, I considered that my clothes and shoes would soon wear out, which already were in a declining condition, and must be supplied by some contrivance from the hides of Yahoos or other brutes; whereby the whole secret would be known: I therefore told my master, that in the country from whence I came, those of my kind always covered their bodies with the hairs of certain animals prepared by art, as well for decency, as to avoid inclemencies of air both hot and cold; of which, as to my own person, I would give him immediate conviction, if he pleased to command me; only desiring his excuse, if I did not expose those parts that Nature taught us to conceal. He said my discourse was all very strange, but especially the last part; for he could not understand why Nature should teach us to conceal what Nature had given. That neither himself nor family were ashamed of any parts of their bodies; but however I might do as I pleased. Whereupon, I first unbuttoned my coat, and pulled it off. I did the same with my waistcoat,[6] I drew off my shoes, stockings, and breeches. I let my shirt down to my waist, and drew up the bottom, fastening it like a girdle about my middle to hide my nakedness.

My master observed the whole performance with great signs of curiosity and admiration. He took up all my clothes in his pastern, one piece after another, and examined them diligently; he then stroked my body very gently, and looked round me several times, after which he said, it was plain I must be a perfect Yahoo; but that I differed very much from the rest of my species, in the softness, and whiteness, and smoothness of my skin, my want of hair in several parts of my body, the shape and shortness of my claws behind and before, and my affectation of walking continually on my two hinder feet. He desired to see no more, and gave me leave to put on my clothes again, for I was shuddering with cold.

I expressed my uneasiness at his giving me so often the appellation of *Yahoo*, an odious animal, for which I had so utter an hatred and contempt; I begged he would forbear applying that word to me, and take the same order in his family, and among his friends whom he suffered to see me. I requested likewise, that the secret of my having a false covering to my body might be known to none but himself, at least as long as my present clothing should last; for, as to what the sorrel nag his valet had observed, his Honor might command him to conceal it.

All this my master very graciously consented to,[7] and thus the secret was kept till my clothes began to wear out, which I was forced to supply by several

---

6. Vest.

7. The Houyhnhnms may have no word for "lying," but they can hide the truth.

contrivances, that shall hereafter be mentioned. In the meantime, he desired I would go on with my utmost diligence to learn their language, because he was more astonished at my capacity for speech and reason, than at the figure of my body, whether it were covered or no; adding, that he waited with some impatience to hear the wonders which I promised to tell him.

From thenceforward he doubled the pains he had been at to instruct me; he brought me into all company, and made them treat me with civility, because, as he told them privately, this would put me into good humor, and make me more diverting.

Every day when I waited on him, beside the trouble he was at in teaching, he would ask me several questions concerning myself, which I answered as well as I could; and by those means he had already received some general ideas, though very imperfect. It would be tedious to relate the several steps, by which I advanced to a more regular conversation: but the first account I gave of myself in any order and length, was to this purpose:

That, I came from a very far country, as I already had attempted to tell him, with about fifty more of my own species; that we traveled upon the seas, in a great hollow vessel made of wood, and larger than his Honor's house. I described the ship to him in the best terms I could, and explained by the help of my handkerchief displayed, how it was driven forward by the wind. That upon a quarrel among us, I was set on shore on this coast, where I walked forward without knowing whither, till he delivered me from the persecution of those execrable Yahoos. He asked me, who made the ship, and how it was possible that the Houyhnhnms of my country would leave it to the management of brutes? My answer was, that I durst proceed no farther in my relation, unless he would give me his word and honor that he would not be offended, and then I would tell him the wonders I had so often promised. He agreed; and I went on by assuring him, that the ship was made by creatures like myself, who in all the countries I had traveled, as well as in my own, were the only governing, rational animals, and that upon my arrival hither, I was as much astonished to see the Houyhnhnms act like rational beings, as he or his friends could be in finding some marks of reason in a creature he was pleased to call a Yahoo, to which I owned my resemblance in every part, but could not account for their degenerate and brutal nature. I said farther, that if good fortune ever restored me to my native country, to relate my travels hither, as I resolved to do, everybody would believe that I *said the thing which was not*; that I invented the story out of my own head; and with all possible respect to himself, his family, and friends, and under his promise of not being offended, our countrymen would hardly think it probable, that a Houyhnhnm should be the presiding creature of a nation, and a Yahoo the brute.

CHAPTER 4

The Houyhnhnms' notion of truth and falsehood. The author's discourse disapproved by his master. The author gives a more particular account of himself, and the accidents of his voyage.

My master heard me with great appearances of uneasiness in his countenance, because *doubting* or *not believing*, are so little known in this country, that the inhabitants cannot tell how to behave themselves under such circumstances. And I remember in frequent discourses with my master concerning the nature of manhood,[8] in other parts of the world, having occasion to talk of *lying*, and *false*

---

8. Human nature.

representation, it was with much difficulty that he comprehended what I meant, although he had otherwise a most acute judgment. For he argued thus: that the use of speech was to make us understand one another, and to receive information of facts; now if any one *said the thing which was not*, these ends were defeated; because I cannot properly be said to understand him, and I am so far from receiving information, that he leaves me worse than in ignorance, for I am led to believe a thing *black* when it is *white*, and *short* when it is *long*. And these were all the notions he had concerning that faculty of *lying*, so perfectly well understood, and so universally practiced among human creatures.

To return from this digression; when I asserted that the Yahoos were the only governing animal in my country, which my master said was altogether past his conception, he desired to know, whether we had Houyhnhnms among us, and what was their employment: I told him, we had great numbers, that in summer they grazed in the fields, and in winter were kept in houses, with hay and oats, where Yahoo servants were employed to rub their skins smooth, comb their manes, pick their feet, serve them with food, and make their beds. I understand you well, said my master; it is now very plain, from all you have spoken, that whatever share of reason the Yahoos pretend to, the Houyhnhnms are your masters;[9] I heartily wish our Yahoos would be so tractable. I begged his Honor would please to excuse me from proceeding any farther, because I was very certain that the account he expected from me would be highly displeasing. But he insisted in commanding me to let him know the best and the worst: I told him, he should be obeyed. I owned, that the Houyhnhnms among us, whom we called *horses*, were the most generous and comely animal we had, that they excelled in strength and swiftness; and when they belonged to persons of quality, employed in traveling, racing, or drawing chariots, they were treated with much kindness and care, till they fell into diseases, or became foundered in the feet;[1] but then they were sold, and used to all kind of drudgery till they died; after which their skins were stripped and sold for what they were worth, and their bodies left to be devoured by dogs and birds of prey.[2] But the common race of horses had not so good fortune, being kept by farmers and carriers and other mean people, who put them to greater labor, and fed them worse. I described as well as I could, our way of riding, the shape and use of a bridle, a saddle, a spur, and a whip, of harness and wheels. I added, that we fastened plates of a certain hard substance called *iron* at the bottom of their feet, to preserve their hoofs from being broken by the stony ways on which we often traveled.

My master, after some expressions of great indignation, wondered how we dared to venture upon a Houyhnhnm's back, for he was sure that the weakest servant in his house would be able to shake off the strongest Yahoo, or by lying down, and rolling upon his back, squeeze the brute to death. I answered, that our horses were trained up from three or four years old to the several uses we intended them for; that if any of them proved intolerably vicious, they were employed for carriages; that they were severely beaten while they were young, for any mischievous tricks; that the males, designed for the common use of riding or draft, were generally *castrated* about two years after their birth, to take down their spirits, and make them more tame and gentle; that they were indeed sensible of rewards and punishments; but his

---

9. Possibly a satire on the English love of horses.
1. Until their feet give in from overwork.
2. Swift mockingly paraphrases the *Iliad* 1.4-6: "The souls of mighty Chiefs untimely slain; / Whose limbs unburied on the naked shore, / Devouring dogs and hungry vultures tore" (Pope's translation).

Honor would please to consider, that they had not the least tincture of reason any more than the Yahoos in this country.

It put me to the pains of many circumlocutions to give my master a right idea of what I spoke; for their language doth not abound in variety of words, because their wants and passions are fewer than among us. But it is impossible to express his noble resentment at our savage treatment of the Houyhnhnm race, particularly after I had explained the manner and use of *castrating* horses among us, to hinder them from propagating their kind, and to render them more servile. He said, if it were possible there could be any country where Yahoos alone were endued with reason, they certainly must be the governing animal, because reason will in time always prevail against brutal strength. But, considering the frame of our bodies, and especially of mine, he thought no creature of equal bulk was so ill-contrived for employing that reason in the common offices of life; whereupon he desired to know whether those among whom I lived, resembled me or the Yahoos of his country. I assured him, that I was as well shaped as most of my age, but the younger and the females were much more soft and tender, and the skins of the latter generally as white as milk. He said, I differed indeed from other Yahoos, being much more cleanly, and not altogether so deformed, but in point of real advantage, he thought I differed for the worse. That my nails were of no use either to my fore or hinder feet; as to my forefeet, he could not properly call them by that name, for he never observed me to walk upon them; that they were too soft to bear the ground; that I generally went with them uncovered, neither was the covering I sometimes wore on them of the same shape, or so strong as that on my feet behind. That I could not walk with any security, for if either of my hinder feet slipped, I must inevitably fall. He then began to find fault with other parts of my body, the flatness of my face, the prominence of my nose, mine eyes placed directly in front, so that I could not look on either side without turning my head, that I was not able to feed myself, without lifting one of my forefeet to my mouth, and therefore Nature had placed those joints to answer that necessity. He knew not what could be the use of those several clefts and divisions in my feet behind; that these were too soft to bear the hardness and sharpness of stones without a covering made from the skin of some other brute; that my whole body wanted a fence against heat and cold, which I was forced to put on and off every day with tediousness and trouble. And lastly, that he observed every animal in this country naturally to abhor the Yahoos, whom the weaker avoided, and the stronger drove from them. So that supposing us to have the gift of reason, he could not see how it were possible to cure that natural antipathy which every creature discovered[3] against us; nor consequently, how we could tame and render them serviceable. However, he would (as he said) debate that matter no farther, because he was more desirous to know my own story, the country where I was born, and the several actions and events of my life before I came hither.

I assured him, how extremely desirous I was that he should be satisfied in every point; but I doubted much, whether it would be possible for me to explain myself on several subjects whereof his Honor could have no conception, because I saw nothing in his country to which I could resemble[4] them. That, however, I would do my best, and strive to express myself by similitudes, humbly desiring his assistance when I wanted proper words; which he was pleased to promise me.

3. Displayed.   4. Compare.

I said, my birth was of honest parents, in an island called England, which was remote from this country, as many days' journey as the strongest of his Honor's servants could travel in the annual course of the sun. That I was bred a surgeon, whose trade it is to cure wounds and hurts in the body, got by accident or violence; that my country was governed by a female man, whom we called a *Queen*. That I left it to get riches,[5] whereby I might maintain myself and family when I should return. That in my last voyage, I was commander of the ship, and had about fifty Yahoos under me, many of which died at sea, and I was forced to supply[6] them by others picked out from several nations. That our ship was twice in danger of being sunk; the first time by a great storm, and the second, by striking against a rock. Here my master interposed, by asking me, how I could persuade strangers out of different countries to venture with me, after the losses I had sustained, and the hazards I had run. I said, they were fellows of desperate fortunes, forced to fly from the places of their birth, on account of their poverty or their crimes. Some were undone by lawsuits; others spent all they had in drinking, whoring, and gaming; others fled for treason; many for murder, theft, poisoning, robbery, perjury, forgery, coining false money, for committing rapes or sodomy, for flying from their colors,[7] or deserting to the enemy, and most of them had broken prison; none of these durst return to their native countries for fear of being hanged, or of starving in a jail; and therefore were under a necessity of seeking a livelihood in other places.

During this discourse, my master was pleased often to interrupt me. I had made use of many circumlocutions in describing to him the nature of the several crimes, for which most of our crew had been forced to fly their country. This labor took up several days' conversation before he was able to comprehend me. He was wholly at a loss to know what could be the use or necessity of practicing those vices. To clear up which I endeavored to give him some ideas of the desire of power and riches, of the terrible effects of lust, intemperance, malice, and envy. All this I was forced to define and describe by putting of cases, and making suppositions. After which, like one whose imagination was struck with something never seen or heard of before, he would lift up his eyes with amazement and indignation. Power, government, war, law, punishment, and a thousand other things had no terms, wherein that language could express them, which made the difficulty almost insuperable to give my master any conception of what I meant. But being of an excellent understanding, much improved by contemplation and converse, he at last arrived at a competent knowledge of what human nature in our parts of the world is capable to perform, and desired I would give him some particular account of that land, which we call Europe, but especially, of my own country.

CHAPTER 5

The author at his master's commands informs him of the state of England. The causes of war among the princes of Europe. The author begins to explain the English Constitution.

The reader may please to observe, that the following extract of many conversations I had with my master, contains a summary of the most material points, which were discoursed at several times for above two years; his Honor often desiring fuller satisfaction[8] as I farther improved in the Houyhnhnm tongue. I laid before him, as well

---

5. Gulliver originally stated that he undertook his second and third voyages out of a desire to travel: he now reads all human motivation in the worst possible light.

6. Replace.
7. Deserting their regiment in the army.
8. Better explanation.

as I could, the whole state of Europe; I discoursed of trade and manufactures, of arts and sciences; and the answers I gave to all the questions he made, as they arose upon several subjects, were a fund of conversation not to be exhausted. But I shall here only set down the substance of what passed between us concerning my own country, reducing it into order as well as I can, without any regard to time or other circumstances, while I strictly adhere to truth. My only concern is, that I shall hardly be able to do justice to my master's arguments and expressions, which must needs suffer by my want of capacity, as well as by a translation into our barbarous English.[9]

In obedience therefore to his Honor's commands, I related to him the Revolution under the Prince of Orange,[1] the long war with France[2] entered into by the said Prince, and renewed by his successor the present Queen, wherein the greatest powers of Christendom were engaged, and which still continued: I computed, at his request, that about a million of Yahoos might have been killed in the whole progress of it, and perhaps a hundred or more cities taken, and five times as many ships burnt or sunk.

He asked me what were the usual causes or motives that made one country go to war with another. I answered they were innumerable, but I should only mention a few of the chief. Sometimes the ambition of princes, who never think they have land or people enough to govern; sometimes the corruption of ministers, who engage their master in a war in order to stifle or divert the clamor of the subjects against their evil administration. Difference in opinions[3] hath cost many millions of lives: for instance, whether *flesh* be *bread*, or *bread* be *flesh*; whether the juice of a certain *berry* be *blood* or *wine*; whether *whistling* be a vice or a virtue; whether it be better to *kiss a post*, or throw it into the fire; what is the best color for a *coat*, whether *black*, *white*, *red*, or *grey*; and whether it should be *long* or *short*, *narrow* or *wide*, *dirty* or *clean*, with many more. Neither are any wars so furious and bloody, or of so long continuance, as those occasioned by difference in opinion, especially if it be in things indifferent.[4]

Sometimes the quarrel between two princes is to decide which of them shall dispossess a third of his dominions, where neither of them pretend to any right. Sometimes one prince quarrels with another, for fear the other should quarrel with him. Sometimes a war is entered upon, because the enemy is too *strong*, and sometimes because he is too *weak*. Sometimes our neighbors *want* the *things* which we *have*, or *have* the *things* which we *want*; and we both fight, till they take ours or give us theirs. It is a very justifiable cause of war to invade a country after the people have been wasted by famine, destroyed by pestilence, or embroiled by factions amongst themselves.[5] It is justifiable to enter into a war against our nearest ally, when one of his towns lies convenient for us, or a territory of land, that would render our dominions round and compact. If a prince send forces into a nation where the people are poor and ignorant, he may lawfully put half of them to death, and make slaves of the rest, in order to civilize and reduce[6] them from their barbarous way of living. It is a

9. Presumably "barbarous," because English both lacks appropriate words to express Houyhnhnm concepts and has concepts (e.g., of lust, malice, envy) for which the other language has no words.

1. The Glorious Revolution of 1688 by which William of Orange, and his wife, Mary Stuart, ascended to the English throne in 1689.

2. The War of the League of Augsburg (1689–1697) and the War of the Spanish Succession (1701–1713), which Swift (as a good Tory) opposed.

3. Religious controversies, over the doctrine of transubstantiation, the place of music (whistling) and images (the post) in church, and the color and style of liturgical vestments.

4. Of no importance either way.

5. Probably a reference to the English Civil War of 1642–1646, 1648.

6. Convert.

very kingly, honorable, and frequent practice, when one prince desires the assistance of another to secure him against an invasion, that the assistant, when he hath driven out the invader, should seize on the dominions himself, and kill, imprison, or banish the prince he came to relieve. Alliance by blood or marriage is a sufficient cause of war between princes, and the nearer the kindred is, the greater is their disposition to quarrel: *poor* nations are *hungry*, and *rich* nations are *proud*, and pride and hunger will ever be at variance. For these reasons, the trade of a *soldier* is held the most honorable of all others: because a *soldier* is a Yahoo hired to kill in cold blood as many of his own species, who have never offended him, as possibly he can.

There is likewise a kind of beggarly princes in Europe, not able to make war by themselves, who hire out their troops to richer nations, for so much a day to each man; of which they keep three fourths to themselves, and it is the best part of their maintenance; such are those in Germany and other northern parts of Europe.[7]

What you have told me (said my master), upon the subject of war, doth indeed discover most admirably the effects of that reason you pretend to: however, it is happy that the *shame* is greater than the *danger*; and that Nature hath left you utterly uncapable of doing much mischief. For your mouths lying flat with your faces, you can hardly bite each other to any purpose, unless by consent. Then as to the claws upon your feet before and behind, they are so short and tender, that one of our Yahoos would drive a dozen of yours before him. And therefore in recounting the numbers of those who have been killed in battle, I cannot but think that you have *said the thing which is not.*

I could not forbear shaking my head and smiling a little at his ignorance. And, being no stranger to the art of war, I gave him a description of cannons, culverins,[8] muskets, carabines,[9] pistols, bullets, powder, swords, bayonets, battles, sieges, retreats, attacks, undermines, countermines,[1] bombardments, seafights; ships sunk with a thousand men, twenty thousand killed on each side; dying groans, limbs flying in the air, smoke, noise, confusion, trampling to death under horses' feet; flight, pursuit, victory; fields strewed with carcasses left for food to dogs, and wolves, and birds of prey; plundering, stripping, ravishing, burning, and destroying. And to set forth the valor of my own dear countrymen, I assured him, that I had seen them blow up a hundred enemies at once in a siege, and as many in a ship, and beheld the dead bodies drop down in pieces from the clouds, to the great diversion of all the spectators.

I was going on to more particulars, when my master commanded me silence. He said, whoever understood the nature of Yahoos might easily believe it possible for so vile an animal to be capable of every action I had named, if their strength and cunning equaled their malice. But as my discourse had increased his abhorrence of the whole species, so he found it gave him a disturbance in his mind, to which he was wholly a stranger before. He thought his ears being used to such abominable words, might by degrees admit them with less detestation. That although he hated the Yahoos of this country, yet he no more blamed them for their odious qualities, than he did a *gnnayh* (a bird of prey) for its cruelty, or a sharp stone for cutting his hoof. But when a creature pretending to reason could be capable of such enormities, he dreaded lest[2] the corruption of that faculty might be worse than brutality itself. He

---

7. George I employed German mercenaries in his defense of Hanover.
8. Large cannons.
9. Short firearms.

1. Digging under fortification walls, and counter-digging by those inside the fort to stop the besiegers.
2. Worried that.

seemed therefore confident, that instead of reason, we were only possessed of some quality fitted to increase our natural vices; as the reflection from a troubled stream returns the image of an ill-shapen body, not only *larger*, but more *distorted*.

He added, that he had heard too much upon the subject of war, both in this, and some former discourses. There was another point which a little perplexed him at present. I had said, that some of our crew left their country on account of being ruined by *law*; that I had already explained the meaning of the word; but he was at a loss how it should come to pass, that the *law* which was intended for *every* man's preservation, should be any man's ruin. Therefore he desired to be farther satisfied what I meant by *law*, and the dispensers thereof, according to the present practice in my own country; because he thought Nature and reason were sufficient guides for a reasonable animal, as we pretended to be, in showing us what we ought to do, and what to avoid.

I assured his Honor, that law was a science wherein I had not much conversed,[3] further than by employing advocates in vain, upon some injustices that had been done me; however, I would give him all the satisfaction I was able.

I said there was a society of men among us, bred up from their youth in the art of proving by words multiplied for the purpose, that white is black, and black is white, according as they are paid.[4] To this society all the rest of the people are slaves. For example, if my neighbor hath a mind to my cow, he hires a lawyer to prove that he ought to have my cow from me. I must then hire another to defend my right, it being against all rules of law that any man should be allowed to speak for himself.[5] Now in this case, I who am the true owner lie under two great disadvantages. First, my lawyer, being practiced almost from his cradle in defending falsehood, is quite out of his element when he would be an advocate for justice, which as an office unnatural, he always attempts with great awkwardness, if not with ill will. The second disadvantage is, that my lawyer must proceed with great caution, or else he will be reprimanded by the judges, and abhorred by his brethren, as one who would lessen the practice[6] of the law. And therefore I have but two methods to preserve my cow. The first is to gain over my adversary's lawyer with a double fee, who will then betray his client by insinuating that he hath justice on his side. The second way is for my lawyer to make my cause appear as unjust as he can, by allowing the cow to belong to my adversary; and this if it be skillfully done will certainly bespeak[7] the favor of the Bench.

Now, your Honor is to know that these judges are persons appointed to decide all controversies of property, as well as for the trial of criminals, and picked out from the most dexterous lawyers who are grown old or lazy, and having been biased all their lives against truth and equity, lie under such a fatal necessity of favoring fraud, perjury, and oppression, that I have known several of them refuse a large bribe from the side where justice lay, rather than injure the *Faculty*[8] by doing anything unbecoming their nature or their office.

---

3. Had not had much instruction.
4. Swift's satirical treatment of lawyers probably stems from his dislike of Lord Chief Justice Whitehead, who tried to force juries to give verdicts against Swift and the printer of two of his political pamphlets.
5. One of Swift's many references to Thomas More's *Utopia* (1516) in this discussion of the ideals of human and Houyhnhnm society. *Utopia* suggests that it is "better for each man to plead for his own cause, and tell the judge the same story he'd otherwise tell his lawyer." Other important sources for *Gulliver* include Lucian's

True History (mid-second century A.D.); Cyrano de Bergerac's *Histoire comique des états et empires de la lune* (1656); William Temple's essay *Of Heroick Virtue* (in *Miscellanea*, pt. 2, 1692); William Dampier's *New Voyage Round the World* (1697); and Lionel Wafer's *A New Voyage and Description of the Isthmus of America* (1699), which includes descriptions of monkeys Swift may have used for the Yahoos.
6. Both profession, and morally questionable dealing.
7. Gain.
8. Legal profession.

It is a maxim among these lawyers, that whatever hath been done before, may legally be done again; and therefore they take special care to record all the decisions formerly made against common justice and the general reason of mankind. These, under the name of *precedents*, they produce as authorities to justify the most iniquitous opinions; and the judges never fail of directing accordingly.

In pleading, they studiously avoid entering into the *merits* of the cause; but are loud, violent, and tedious in dwelling upon all *circumstances* which are not to the purpose. For instance, in the case already mentioned; they never desire to know what claim or title my adversary hath to my cow, but whether the said cow were red or black, her horns long or short, whether the field I graze her in be round or square, whether she were milked at home or abroad, what diseases she is subject to, and the like; after which they consult *precedents*, adjourn the cause from time to time, and in ten, twenty, or thirty years come to an issue.

It is likewise to be observed that this society hath a peculiar cant[9] and jargon of their own, that no other mortal can understand, and wherein all their laws are written, which they take special care to multiply; whereby they have wholly confounded the very essence of truth and falsehood, of right and wrong; so that it will take thirty years to decide whether the field, left me by my ancestors for six generations, belong to me or to a stranger three hundred miles off.

In the trial of persons accused for crimes against the state the method is much more short and commendable: the judge first sends to sound the disposition of those in power, after which he can easily hang or save the criminal, strictly preserving all the forms of law.

Here my master, interposing, said it was a pity, that creatures endowed with such prodigious abilities of mind as these lawyers, by the description I gave of them, must certainly be, were not rather encouraged to be instructors of others in wisdom and knowledge. In answer to which, I assured his Honor, that in all points out of their own trade they were usually the most ignorant and stupid generation among us, the most despicable in common conversation, avowed enemies to all knowledge and learning, and equally disposed to pervert the general reason of mankind in every other subject of discourse, as in that of their own profession.

CHAPTER 6

A continuation of the state of England. The character of a first Minister.[1]

My master was yet wholly at a loss to understand what motives could incite this race of lawyers to perplex, disquiet, and weary themselves by engaging in a confederacy of injustice, merely for the sake of injuring their fellow animals; neither could he comprehend what I meant in saying they did it for *hire*. Whereupon I was at much pains to describe to him the use of *money*, the materials it was made of, and the value of the metals; that when a Yahoo had got a great store of this precious substance, he was able to purchase whatever he had a mind to, the finest clothing, the noblest houses, great tracts of land, the most costly meats and drinks, and have his choice of the most beautiful females. Therefore since *money* alone was able to perform all these feats, our Yahoos thought they could never have enough of it to spend or to save, as they found

---

9. Both insincere and specialist language.
1. Swift's first printer/publisher, Benjamin Motte, prudently added "under Queen Anne" and "in the Courts of

Europe" at the end of these two sentences, respectively, to remove some of the sting from this satire on George I's reign.

themselves inclined from their natural bent either to profusion or avarice. That the rich man enjoyed the fruit of the poor man's labor, and the latter were a thousand to one in proportion to the former.[2] That the bulk of our people was forced to live miserably, by laboring every day for small wages to make a few live plentifully. I enlarged myself[3] much on these and many other particulars to the same purpose: but his Honor was still to seek,[4] for he went upon a supposition that all animals had a title to their share in the productions of the earth, and especially those[5] who presided over the rest. Therefore he desired I would let him know, what these costly meats were, and how any of us happened to want them. Whereupon I enumerated as many sorts as came into my head, with the various methods of dressing them, which could not be done without sending vessels by sea to every part of the world, as well for liquors to drink, as for sauces, and innumerable other conveniencies. I assured him, that this whole globe of earth must be at least three times gone round, before one of our better female Yahoos could get her breakfast, or a cup to put it in.[6] He said, that must needs be a miserable country which cannot furnish food for its own inhabitants. But what he chiefly wondered at was how such vast tracts of ground as I described should be wholly without *fresh water*, and the people put to the necessity of sending over the sea for drink. I replied, that England (the dear place of my nativity) was computed to produce three times the quantity of food more than its inhabitants are able to consume, as well as liquors extracted from grain, or pressed out of the fruit of certain trees, which made excellent drink, and the same proportion in every other convenience of life. But in order to feed the luxury and intemperance of the males, and the vanity of the females, we sent away the greatest part of our necessary things to other countries, from whence in return we brought the materials of diseases, folly, and vice, to spend among ourselves. Hence it follows of necessity, that vast numbers of our people are compelled to seek their livelihood by begging, robbing, stealing, cheating, pimping, forswearing,[7] flattering, suborning,[8] forging, gaming, lying, fawning, hectoring,[9] voting, scribbling, stargazing,[1] poisoning, whoring, canting,[2] libeling, freethinking,[3] and the like occupations: every one of which terms, I was at much pains to make him understand.

That *wine* was not imported among us from foreign countries to supply the want of water or other drinks, but because it was a sort of liquid which made us merry, by putting us out of our senses; diverted all melancholy thoughts, begat wild extravagant imaginations in the brain, raised our hopes, and banished our fears, suspended every office of reason for a time, and deprived us of the use of our limbs, till we fell into a profound sleep; although it must be confessed, that we always awaked sick and dispirited, and that the use of this liquor filled us with diseases, which made our lives uncomfortable and short.[4]

But beside all this, the bulk of our people supported themselves by furnishing the necessities or conveniencies of life to the rich, and to each other. For instance, when I am at home and dressed as I ought to be, I carry on my body the workmanship of an hundred tradesmen; the building and furniture of my house employ as many more, and five times the number to adorn my wife.

---

2. A theme of Thomas More's *Utopia* (1516).
3. Explained myself further.
4. Unable to understand.
5. The ruling species.
6. Coffee, tea, and chocolate were relatively new (and highly fashionable) drinks; chinaware was also imported.
7. Perjury.
8. Inducing through bribery.

9. Bullying.
1. Sensationalist popular astrology of the type Swift mocked when writing as "Isaac Bickerstaff" in 1708.
2. Using jargon, often for deceit.
3. Freethinkers rejected religious authority and dogma in favor of rational inquiry and speculation.
4. Swift, however, was a great wine drinker.

I was going on to tell him of another sort of people, who get their livelihood by attending the sick, having upon some occasions informed his Honor that many of my crew had died of diseases. But here it was with the utmost difficulty that I brought him to apprehend what I meant. He could easily conceive, that a Houyhnhnm grew weak and heavy a few days before his death, or by some accident might hurt a limb. But that Nature, who worketh all things to perfection, should suffer any pains to breed in our bodies, he thought impossible, and desired to know the reason of so unaccountable an evil. I told him, we fed on a thousand things which operated contrary to each other; that we ate when we were not hungry, and drank without the provocation of thirst; that we sat whole nights drinking strong liquors without eating a bit, which disposed us to sloth, inflamed our bodies, and precipitated or prevented digestion. That prostitute female Yahoos acquired a certain malady, which bred rottenness in the bones of those who fell into their embraces; that this and many other diseases were propagated from father to son, so that great numbers come into the world with complicated maladies upon them; that it would be endless to give him a catalog of all diseases incident to human bodies; for they could not be fewer than five or six hundred, spread over every limb, and joint; in short, every part, external and intestine, having diseases appropriated to each. To remedy which, there was a sort of people bred up among us, in the profession or pretense of curing the sick. And because I had some skill in the faculty, I would, in gratitude to his Honor, let him know the whole mystery[5] and method by which they proceed.

Their fundamental is, that all diseases arise from *repletion*, from whence they conclude, that a great *evacuation* of the body is necessary, either through the natural passage, or upwards at the mouth. Their next business is, from herbs, minerals, gums, oils, shells, salts, juices, seaweed, excrements, barks of trees, serpents, toads, frogs, spiders, dead men's flesh and bones, birds, beasts and fishes, to form a composition for smell and taste the most abominable, nauseous, and detestable that they can possibly contrive, which the stomach immediately rejects with loathing; and this they call a *vomit*;[6] or else from the same storehouse, with some other poisonous additions, they command us to take in at the orifice *above* or *below* (just as the physician then happens to be disposed), a medicine equally annoying and disgustful to the bowels, which, relaxing the belly, drives down all before it; and this they call a *purge*, or a *clyster*.[7] For Nature (as the physicians allege) having intended the superior anterior orifice[8] only for the *intromission* of solids and liquids, and the inferior posterior for ejection, these artists ingeniously considering that in all diseases Nature is forced out of her seat; therefore to replace her in it, the body must be treated in a manner directly contrary, by interchanging the use of each orifice, forcing solids and liquids in at the anus, and making evacuations at the mouth.

But, besides real diseases, we are subject to many that are only imaginary, for which the physicians have invented imaginary cures; these have their several names, and so have the drugs that are proper for them, and with these our female Yahoos are always infested.

One great excellency in this tribe is their skill at *prognostics*, wherein they seldom fail; their predictions in real diseases, when they rise to any degree of malignity, generally portending *death*, which is always in their power, when recovery is not: and therefore, upon any unexpected signs of amendment, after they have pronounced their sentence, rather than be accused as false prophets, they know how to approve their sagacity to the world by a seasonable dose.[9]

They are likewise of special use to husbands and wives who are grown weary of their mates, to eldest sons, to great ministers of state, and often to princes.[1]

I had formerly upon occasion discoursed with my master upon the nature of *government* in general, and particularly of our own *excellent Constitution*, deservedly the wonder and envy of the whole world. But having here accidentally mentioned a *Minister of State*, he commanded me some time after to inform him, what species of Yahoo I particularly meant by that appellation.

I told him, that a *First* or *Chief Minister of State*[2] whom I intended to describe, was a creature wholly exempt from joy and grief, love and hatred, pity and anger; at least made use of no other passions but a violent desire of wealth, power, and titles; that he applies his words to all uses, except to the indication of his mind,[3] that he never tells a *truth*, but with an intent that you should take it for a *lie*; nor a *lie*, but with a design that you should take it for a *truth* that those he speaks worst of behind their backs are in the surest way to preferment[4] and whenever he begins to praise you to others or to yourself, you are from that day forlorr.[5] The worst mark you can receive is a *promise*, especially when it is confirmed with an oath; after which every wise man retires, and gives over all hopes.

There are three methods by which a man may rise to be Chief Minister: the first is, by knowing how with prudence to dispose of a wife, a daughter, or a sister; the second, by betraying or undermining his predecessor; and the third is, by a *furious zeal* in public assemblies against the corruptions of the Court. But a wise prince would rather choose to employ those who practice the last of these methods; because such zealots prove always the most obsequious and subservient to the will and passions of their master. That the *Ministers* having all employment[6] at their disposal, preserve themselves in power by bribing the majority of a senate or great council; and at last, by an expedient called an *Act of Indemnity*,[7] (whereof I described the nature to him) they secure themselves from after-reckonings, and retire from the public, laden with the spoils of the nation.

The palace of a *Chief Minister* is a seminary to breed up others in his own trade: the pages, lackeys, and porter, by imitating their master, become *Ministers of State* in their several districts, and learn to excel in the three principal *ingredients*, of *insolence*, *lying*, and *bribery*. Accordingly, they have a *subaltern*[8] court paid to them by persons of the best rank, and sometimes by the force of dexterity and impudence arrive through several gradations to be successors to their lord.

He is usually governed by a decayed wench[9] or favorite footman, who are the tunnels[1] through which all graces[2] are conveyed, and may properly be called, *in the last resort*, the governors of the kingdom.

---

9. Cf. *Verses on the Death of Dr. Swift*, lines 131–132: "He'd rather choose that I should die / Than his prediction prove a lie" (page 2356).
1. The references are to Queen Caroline, Prince Frederick, and Walpole.
2. A satire on Robert Walpole, then the First Minister or "Prime Minister."
3. Real thoughts or intentions.
4. Most likely to receive a government position or promotion.
5. Forsaken, ruined.
6. Government positions.

7. Swift here suggests that corrupt government ministers make themselves secure from any future legal prosecution for their illegal dealings. He refers to the Act of Indemnity and Oblivion of 1660, which pardoned almost all those who had taken part in the English Civil War (1642–1646, 1648), or the subsequent Commonwealth government (1649–1660).
8. Lower-ranking.
9. The government Minister's mistress is "decayed" either in age or in morals.
1. Routes or conduits.
2. Favors.

One day my master, having heard me mention the *nobility* of my country, was pleased to make me a compliment which I could not pretend to deserve: that he was sure I must have been born of some noble family, because I far exceeded in shape, color, and cleanliness, all the Yahoos of his nation, although I seemed to fail in strength and agility, which must be imputed to my different way of living from those other brutes; and besides, I was not only endowed with a faculty of speech, but likewise with some rudiments of reason, to a degree, that with all his acquaintance I passed for a prodigy.

He made me observe, that among the Houyhnhnms, the white, the *sorrel*, and the *iron-grey* were not so exactly shaped as the *bay*, the *dapple-grey*, and the *black*; nor born with equal talents of mind, or a capacity to improve them; and therefore continued always in the condition of servants, without ever aspiring to match[3] out of their own race, which in that country would be reckoned monstrous and unnatural.

I made his Honor my most humble acknowledgments for the good opinion he was pleased to conceive of me; but assured him at the same time, that my birth was of the lower sort, having been born of plain, honest parents, who were just able to give me a tolerable education; that *nobility* among us was altogether a different thing from the idea he had of it; that our young *noblemen* are bred from their childhood in idleness and luxury; that as soon as years will permit, they consume their vigor and contract odious diseases among lewd females; and when their fortunes are almost ruined, they marry some woman of mean birth, disagreeable person, and unsound constitution, merely for the sake of money, whom they hate and despise. That the productions of such marriages are generally scrofulous,[4] rickety,[5] or deformed children, by which means the family seldom continues above three generations, unless the wife take care to provide a healthy father among her neighbors or domestics, in order to improve and continue the breed. That a weak diseased body, a meager countenance, and sallow complexion are the true marks of *noble blood*; and a healthy robust appearance is so disgraceful in a man of quality, that the world concludes his real father to have been a groom, or a coachman. The imperfections of his mind run parallel with those of his body, being a composition of spleen, dullness, ignorance, caprice, sensuality, and pride.

Without the consent of this *illustrious body* no law can be enacted, repealed, or altered, and these nobles have likewise the decision of all our possessions without appeal.[6]

Chapter 7

The author's great love of his native country. His master's observations upon the Constitution and Administration of England, as described by the author, with parallel cases and comparisons. His master's observations upon human nature.

The reader may be disposed to wonder how I could prevail on myself to give so free a representation of my own species, among a race of mortals who were already too apt to conceive the vilest opinion of humankind from that entire congruity betwixt me and their Yahoos. But I must freely confess, that the many virtues of those excellent *quadrupeds*, placed in opposite view to human corruptions, had so far opened mine

---

3. Mate.
4. Tubercular.
5. Feeble, weak-jointed.

6. Swift here refers to the House of Lords, the upper house of Parliament and the highest law court in the land.

eyes and enlarged my understanding, that I began to view the actions and passions of man in a very different light, and to think the honor of my own kind not worth managing[7] which, besides, it was impossible for me to do before a person of so acute a judgment as my master, who daily convinced me of a thousand faults in myself, whereof I had not the least perception before, and which with us would never be numbered even among human infirmities. I had likewise learned from his example an utter detestation of all falsehood or disguise; and *truth* appeared so amiable to me, that I determined upon sacrificing everything to it.

Let me deal so candidly with the reader, as to confess, that there was yet a much stronger motive for the freedom I took in my representation of things. I had not been a year in this country before I contracted such a love and veneration for the inhabitants, that I entered on a firm resolution never to return to humankind, but to pass the rest of my life among these admirable Houyhnhnms in the contemplation and practice of every virtue; where I could have no example or incitement to vice. But it was decreed by Fortune, my perpetual enemy, that so great a felicity should not fall to my share. However, it is now some comfort to reflect, that in what I said of my countrymen, I *extenuated* their faults as much as I durst before so strict an examiner, and upon every article gave as *favorable* a turn as the matter would bear. For, indeed, who is there alive that will not be swayed by his bias and partiality to the place of his birth?

I have related the substance of several conversations I had with my master, during the greatest part of the time I had the honor to be in his service, but have indeed for brevity sake omitted much more than is here set down.

When I had answered all his questions, and his curiosity seemed to be fully satisfied, he sent for me one morning early, and commanding me to sit down at some distance (an honor which he had never before conferred upon me), he said, he had been very seriously considering my whole story, as far as it related both to myself and my country: that he looked upon us as a sort of animals to whose share, by what accident he could not conjecture, some small pittance of *reason* had fallen, whereof we made no other use than by its assistance to aggravate our *natural* corruptions, and to acquire new ones which Nature had not given us. That we disarmed ourselves of the few abilities she had bestowed, had been very successful in multiplying our original wants, and seemed to spend our whole lives in vain endeavors to supply them by our own inventions. That as to myself, it was manifest I had neither the strength or agility of a common Yahoo, that I walked infirmly on my hinder feet, had found out a contrivance to make my claws of no use or defense, and to remove the hair from my chin, which was intended as a shelter from the sun and the weather. Lastly, that I could neither run with speed, nor climb trees like my *brethren* (as he called them) the Yahoos in this country.

That our institutions of *government* and *law* were plainly owing to our gross defects in *reason,* and by consequence, in *virtue;* because *reason* alone is sufficient to govern a *rational* creature; which was therefore a character we had no pretense to challenge,[8] even from the account I had given of my own people, although he manifestly perceived, that in order to favor them I had concealed many particulars, and often *said the thing which was not.*

He was the more confirmed in this opinion, because he observed, that as I agreed in every feature of my body with other Yahoos, except where it was to my real disadvantage in point of strength, speed, and activity, the shortness of my claws,

---

7. Maintaining.   8. We had no right to claim to be rational creatures.

and some other particulars where Nature had no part; so from the representation I had given him of our lives, our manners, and our actions, he found as near a resemblance in the disposition of our minds. He said the Yahoos were known to hate one another more than they did any different species of animals; and the reason usually assigned, was, the odiousness of their own shapes, which all could see in the rest, but not in themselves. He had therefore begun to think it not unwise in us to *cover* our bodies, and, by that invention, conceal many of our deformities from each other, which would else be hardly supportable. But, he now found he had been mistaken, and that the dissensions of those brutes in his country were owing to the same cause with ours, as I had described them. For if (said he) you throw among five Yahoos as much food as would be sufficient for fifty, they will, instead of eating peaceably, fall together by the ears, each single one impatient to *have all to itself*; and therefore a servant was usually employed to stand by while they were feeding abroad, and those kept at home were tied at a distance from each other; that if a cow died of age or accident, before a Houyhnhnm could secure it for his own Yahoos, those in the neighborhood would come in herds to seize it, and then would ensue such a battle as I had described, with terrible wounds made by their claws on both sides, although they seldom were able to kill one another, for want of such convenient instruments of death as we had invented. At other times the like battles have been fought between the Yahoos of several neighborhoods without any visible cause: those of one district watching all opportunities to surprise the next before they are prepared. But if they find their project hath miscarried, they return home, and for want of enemies, engage in what I call a civil war among themselves.

That in some fields of his country there are certain *shining stones* of several colors, whereof the Yahoos are violently fond, and when part of these *stones* are fixed in the earth, as it sometimes happens, they will dig with their claws for whole days to get them out, and carry them away, and hide them by heaps in their kennels; but still looking round with great caution, for fear their comrades should find out their treasure. My master said, he could never discover the reason of this unnatural appetite, or how these *stones* could be of any use to a Yahoo; but now he believed it might proceed from the same principle of *avarice* which I had ascribed to mankind; that he had once, by way of experiment, privately removed a heap of these *stones* from the place where one of his Yahoos had buried it: whereupon, the sordid animal, missing his treasure, by his loud lamenting brought the whole herd to the place, there miserably howled, then fell to biting and tearing the rest, began to pine away, would neither eat, nor sleep, nor work, till he ordered a servant privately to convey the *stones* into the same hole, and hide them as before; which when his Yahoo had found, he presently recovered his spirits and good humor, but took care to remove them to a better hiding place, and hath ever since been a very serviceable brute.

My master farther assured me, which I also observed myself, that in the fields where these *shining stones* abound, the fiercest and most frequent battles are fought, occasioned by perpetual inroads of the neighboring Yahoos.[9]

He said, it was common, when two Yahoos discovered such a *stone* in a field, and were contending which of them should be the proprietor, a third would take the advantage,[1] and carry it away from them both; which my master would needs

---

9. Neighboring Yahoos attempt invasions to steal these stones.

1. Opportunity.

contend to have some resemblance with our *suits at law*; wherein I thought it for our credit not to undeceive him; since the decision he mentioned was much more equitable than many decrees among us: because the plaintiff and defendant there lost nothing beside the *stone* they contended for, whereas our *Courts of Equity*[2] would never have dismissed the cause while either of them had anything left.

My master, continuing his discourse, said, there was nothing that rendered the Yahoos more odious, than their undistinguishing appetite to devour everything that came in their way, whether herbs, roots, berries, the corrupted flesh of animals, or all mingled together; and it was peculiar in their temper, that they were fonder of what they could get by rapine or stealth at a greater distance, than much better food provided for them at home. If their prey held out, they would eat till they were ready to burst, after which Nature had pointed out to them a certain *root* that gave them a general evacuation.

There was also another kind of *root* very *juicy*, but something rare and difficult to be found, which the Yahoos sought for with much eagerness, and would suck it with great delight; and it produced in them the same effects that wine hath upon us. It would make them sometimes hug, and sometimes tear one another; they would howl and grin, and chatter, and reel, and tumble, and then fall asleep in the mud.

I did indeed observe, that the Yahoos were the only animals in this country subject to any diseases; which, however, were much fewer than horses have among us, and contracted not by any ill treatment they meet with, but by the nastiness and greediness of that sordid brute. Neither has their language any more than a general appellation for those maladies, which is borrowed from the name of the beast, and called *hnea-Yahoo*, or the *Yahoo's-evil*, and the cure prescribed is a mixture of *their own dung* and *urine* forcibly put down the Yahoo's throat. This I have since often known to have been taken with success, and do here freely recommend it to my countrymen, for the public good, as an admirable specific against all diseases produced by repletion.[3]

As to learning, government, arts, manufactures, and the like, my master confessed he could find little or no resemblance between the Yahoos of that country and those in ours. For, he only meant to observe what parity there was in our natures. He had heard indeed some curious Houyhnhnms observe, that in most herds there was a sort of ruling Yahoo (as among us there is generally some leading or principal stag in a park), who was always more *deformed* in body, and *mischievous* in *disposition*, than any of the rest. That this *leader* had usually a favorite as *like himself* as he could get, whose employment was to *lick his master's feet and posteriors, and drive the female Yahoos to his kennel*; for which he was now and then rewarded with a piece of ass's flesh. This *favorite* is hated by the whole herd, and therefore to protect himself, keeps always *near the person of his leader*. He usually continues in office till a worse can be found; but the very moment he is discarded, his successor, at the head of all the Yahoos in that district, young and old, male and female, come in a body, and discharge their excrements upon him from head to foot. But how far this might be applicable to our *Courts* and *favorites*, and *Ministers of State*, my master said I could best determine.

I durst make no return to this malicious insinuation, which debased human understanding below the sagacity of a common *hound*, who hath judgment enough to distinguish and follow the cry of the *ablest dog in the pack*, without being ever mistaken.

2. Courts that decide on general (rather than common) principles of law. Swift ironically plays on the name of the court.
3. Overeating.

My master told me, there were some qualities remarkable in the Yahoos, which he had not observed me to mention, or at least very slightly, in the accounts I had given him of humankind: he said, those animals, like other brutes, had their females in common,[4] but in this they differed, that the she-Yahoo would admit the male while she was pregnant, and that the hes[5] would quarrel and fight with the females as fiercely as with each other. Both which practices were such degrees of infamous brutality, that no other sensitive[6] creature ever arrived at.

Another thing he wondered at in the Yahoos, was their strange disposition to nastiness and dirt, whereas there appears to be a natural love of cleanliness in all other animals. As to the two former accusations, I was glad to let them pass without any reply, because I had not a word to offer upon them in defense of my species, which otherwise I certainly had done from my own inclinations. But I could have easily vindicated humankind from the imputation of singularity upon the last article, if there had been any *swine* in that country (as unluckily for me there were not), which although it may be a *sweeter quadruped* than a Yahoo, cannot, I humbly conceive, in justice pretend to more cleanliness; and so his Honor himself must have owned, if he had seen their filthy way of feeding, and their custom of wallowing and sleeping in the mud.

My master likewise mentioned another quality which his servants had discovered in several Yahoos, and to him was wholly unaccountable. He said, a fancy would sometimes take a Yahoo to retire into a corner, to lie down and howl, and groan, and spurn away all that came near him, although he were young and fat, and wanted neither food nor water; nor did the servants imagine what could possibly ail him. And the only remedy they found was to set him to hard work, after which he would infallibly come to himself. To this I was silent out of partiality to my own kind; yet here I could plainly discover the true seeds of *spleen*,[7] which only seizeth on the *lazy*, the *luxurious*, and the *rich*; who, if they were forced to undergo the *same regimen*, I would undertake for[8] the cure.

His Honor had farther observed, that a female Yahoo would often stand behind a bank or a bush, to gaze on the young males passing by, and then appear, and hide, using many antic gestures and grimaces, at which time it was observed, that she had a most *offensive smell*; and when any of the males advanced, would slowly retire, looking often back, and with a counterfeit show of fear, run off into some convenient place where she knew the male would follow her.[9]

At other times if a female stranger came among them, three or four of her own sex would get about her, and stare and chatter, and grin, and smell her all over, and then turn off with gestures that seemed to express contempt and disdain.

Perhaps my master might refine a little in these speculations, which he had drawn from what he observed himself, or had been told him by others; however, I could not reflect without some amazement, and much sorrow, that the rudiments of *lewdness*, *coquetry*, *censure*, and *scandal*, should have place by instinct in womankind.

I expected every moment that my master would accuse the Yahoos of those unnatural appetites in both sexes, so common among us. But Nature it seems hath not

---

4. Implying that English society did the same.
5. The males.
6. Sensible, thinking.
7. Depression.

8. Guarantee.
9. The sort of seduction tactics used by female characters in literary pastoral.

been so expert a schoolmistress; and these politer pleasures are entirely the productions of art and reason, on our side of the globe.

CHAPTER 8

The author relateth several particulars of the Yahoos. The great virtues of the Houyhnhnms. The education and exercise of their youth. Their general Assembly.

As I ought to have understood human nature much better than I supposed it possible for my master to do, so it was easy to apply the character he gave of the Yahoos to myself and my countrymen, and I believed I could yet make farther discoveries from my own observation. I therefore often begged his Honor to let me go among the herds of Yahoos in the neighborhood, to which he always very graciously consented, being perfectly convinced that the hatred I bore those brutes would never suffer me to be corrupted by them; and his Honor ordered one of his servants, a strong sorrel nag, very honest and good-natured, to be my guard, without whose protection I durst not undertake such adventures. For I have already told the reader how much I was pestered by those odious animals upon my first arrival. I afterwards failed very narrowly three or four times of falling into their clutches, when I happened to stray at any distance without my hanger. And I have reason to believe they had some imagination that I was of their own species, which I often assisted myself, by stripping up my sleeves, and showing my naked arms and breast in their sight, when my protector was with me. At which times they would approach as near as they durst, and imitate my actions after the manner of monkeys, but ever with great signs of hatred, as a tame *jackdaw*,[1] with cap and stockings, is always persecuted by the wild ones, when he happens to be got among them.

They are prodigiously nimble from their infancy; however, I once caught a young male of three years old, and endeavored by all marks of tenderness to make it quiet; but the little imp fell a squalling, and scratching, and biting with such violence, that I was forced to let it go, and it was high time, for a whole troop of old ones came about us at the noise, but finding the cub was safe (for away it ran), and my sorrel nag being by, they durst not venture near us. I observed the young animal's flesh to smell very rank, and the stink was somewhat between a *weasel* and a *fox*, but much more disagreeable. I forgot another circumstance (and perhaps I might have the reader's pardon, if it were wholly omitted), that while I held the odious vermin in my hands, it voided its filthy excrements of a yellow liquid substance all over my clothes; but by good fortune there was a small brook hard by, where I washed myself as clean as I could, although I durst not come into my master's presence, until I were sufficiently aired.

By what I could discover, the Yahoos appear to be the most unteachable of all animals, their capacities never reaching higher than to draw or carry burdens. Yet I am of opinion this defect ariseth chiefly from a perverse, restive[2] disposition. For they are cunning, malicious, treacherous, and revengeful. They are strong and hardy, but of a cowardly spirit, and by consequence insolent, abject, and cruel. It is observed, that the *red-haired* of both sexes are more libidinous and mischievous than the rest, whom yet they much exceed in strength and activity.[3]

The Houyhnhnms keep the Yahoos for present[4] use in huts not far from the house; but the rest are sent abroad to certain fields, where they dig up roots, eat several

---

1. Small crow, often kept as a pet.
2. Stubborn.

3. A prejudice dating back to medieval times.
4. Daily.

kinds of herbs, and search about for carrion, or sometimes catch weasels and *luhimuhs* (a sort of wild rat), which they greedily devour. Nature hath taught them to dig deep holes with their nails on the side of a rising ground, wherein they lie by themselves, only the kennels of the females are larger, sufficient to hold two or three cubs.

They swim from their infancy like frogs, and are able to continue long under water, where they often take fish, which the females carry home to their young. And upon this occasion, I hope the reader will pardon my relating an odd adventure.

Being one day abroad with my protector the sorrel nag, and the weather exceeding hot, I entreated him to let me bathe in a river that was near. He consented, and I immediately stripped myself stark naked, and went down softly into the stream. It happened that a young female Yahoo, standing behind a bank, saw the whole proceeding, and inflamed by desire, as the nag and I conjectured, came running with all speed, and leaped into the water within five yards of the place where I bathed. I was never in my life so terribly frighted; the nag was grazing at some distance, not suspecting any harm. She embraced me after a most fulsome manner; I roared as loud as I could, and the nag came galloping towards me, whereupon she quitted her grasp, with the utmost reluctancy, and leaped upon the opposite bank, where she stood gazing and howling all the time I was putting on my clothes.

This was matter of diversion to my master and his family, as well as of mortification to myself. For now I could no longer deny, that I was a real Yahoo in every limb and feature, since the females had a natural propensity to me as one of their own species; neither was the hair of this brute of a red color (which might have been some excuse for an appetite a little irregular) but black as a sloe[5] and her countenance did not make an appearance altogether so hideous as the rest of the kind; for, I think, she could not be above eleven years old.[6]

Having already lived three years in this country, the reader I suppose will expect that I should, like other travelers, give him some account of the manners and customs of its inhabitants, which it was indeed my principal study to learn.

As these noble Houyhnhnms are endowed by Nature with a general disposition to all virtues, and have no conceptions or ideas of what is evil in a rational creature, so their grand maxim is, to cultivate *Reason*, and to be wholly governed by it. Neither is *Reason* among them a point problematical as with us, where men can argue with plausibility on both sides of a question, but strikes you with immediate conviction, as it must needs do where it is not mingled, obscured, or discolored by passion and interest.[7] I remember it was with extreme difficulty that I could bring my master to understand the meaning of the word opinion, or how a point could be disputable, because *Reason* taught us to affirm or deny only where we are certain, and beyond our knowledge we cannot do either.[8] So that controversies, wranglings, disputes, and positiveness[9] in false or dubious propositions are evils unknown among the Houyhnhnms. In the like manner, when I used to explain to him our several systems of *natural philosophy*, he would laugh that a creature pretending to *Reason* should value itself upon the knowledge of other people's conjectures, and in things where that knowledge, if it were certain, could be of no use. Wherein he agreed

5. A wild berry.
6. The disparity in age between Gulliver and the Yahoo may suggest a grotesque parody of Esther Vanhomrigh's pursuit of Swift, she being 21 years his junior.
7. Prejudice based on interest in personal benefit. Both Descartes (*Discourse on Method*) and Locke (*Essay Concerning Human Understanding*) wrote of the intuitive nature of some knowledge.
8. Gulliver's master has clearly expressed "opinion" (i.e., prejudice) himself, however.
9. Assertiveness.

entirely with the sentiments of Socrates, as Plato delivers them[1] which I mention as the highest honor I can do that prince of philosophers. I have often since reflected what destruction such a doctrine would make in the libraries of Europe, and how many paths to fame would be then shut up in the learned world.

Friendship and benevolence are the two principal virtues among the Houyhnhnms, and these not confined to particular objects,[2] but universal to the whole race. For a stranger from the remotest part is equally treated with the nearest neighbor, and wherever he goes, looks upon himself as at home. They preserve *decency* and *civility* in the highest degrees, but are altogether ignorant of *ceremony*.[3] They have no fondness for their colts or foals, but the care they take in educating them proceedeth entirely from the dictates of *Reason*. And I observed my master to show the same affection to his neighbor's issue that he had for his own.[4] They will have it that *Nature* teaches them to love the whole species, and it is *Reason* only that maketh a distinction of persons, where there is a superior degree of virtue.

When the matron Houyhnhnms have produced one of each sex, they no longer accompany with[5] their consorts, except they lose one of their issue by some casualty, which very seldom happens: but in such a case they meet again. Or when the like accident befalls a person,[6] whose wife is past bearing, some other couple bestow him one of their own colts, and then go together a second time, till the mother be pregnant. This caution is necessary to prevent the country from being overburdened with numbers.[7] But the race of inferior Houyhnhnms bred up to be servants is not so strictly limited upon this article; these are allowed to produce three of each sex, to be domestics in the noble families.

In their marriages they are exactly careful to choose such colors as will not make any disagreeable mixture in the breed.[8] *Strength* is chiefly valued in the male, and *comeliness* in the female, not upon the account of *love*, but to preserve the race from degenerating; for where a female happens to excel in *strength*, a consort is chosen with regard to *comeliness*. Courtship, love, presents, jointures,[9] settlements, have no place in their thoughts, or terms whereby to express them in their language. The young couple meet and are joined, merely because it is the determination of their parents and friends: it is what they see done every day, and they look upon it as one of the necessary actions in a reasonable being. But the violation of marriage, or any other unchastity, was never heard of, and the married pair pass their lives with the same friendship, and mutual benevolence that they bear to others of the same species who come in their way; without jealousy, fondness, quarreling, or discontent.

In educating the youth of both sexes, their method is admirable, and highly deserveth our imitation. These are not suffered to taste a grain of *oats*, except upon certain days, till eighteen years old; nor *milk*, but very rarely; and in summer they graze two hours in the morning, and as many in the evening, which their parents likewise observe, but the servants are not allowed above half that time, and a great part of their grass is brought home, which they eat at the most convenient hours, when they can be best spared from work.

---

1. I.e., that ethics (human nature) is worth studying, while the physical world is not, as we can never have certain knowledge of it: "Socrates: I am a friend of learning—the trees and the countryside won't teach me anything, but the people in the city do" *Phaedrus* (230d3–5).
2. To other, particular Houyhnhnms.
3. As are the Utopians.
4. As do men in Plato's *Republic* (461d).
5. Have sex with.

6. A male Houyhnhnm.
7. The Utopians are under no such restriction, knowing (as the Houyhnhnms do not) of other lands to which they can send their excess population.
8. In Plato's *Republic* (458d–461e), eugenic principles also control mating.
9. Marriage settlements for wives, should they survive their husbands.

Temperance, industry, exercise, and *cleanliness,* are the lessons equally enjoined to the young ones of both sexes, and my master thought it monstrous in us to give the females a different kind of education from the males, except in some articles of domestic management,[1] whereby as he truly observed, one half of our natives were good for nothing but bringing children into the world, and to trust the care of their children to such useless animals, he said, was yet a greater instance of brutality.

But the Houyhnhnms train up their youth to strength, speed, and hardiness, by exercising them in running races up and down steep hills, or over hard stony grounds, and when they are all in a sweat, they are ordered to leap over head and ears into a pond or a river. Four times a year the youth of certain districts meet to show their proficiency in running, and leaping, and other feats of strength or agility, where the victor is rewarded with a song made in his or her praise. On this festival the servants drive a herd of Yahoos into the field, laden with hay, and oats, and milk for a repast to the Houyhnhnms; after which, these brutes are immediately driven back again, for fear of being noisome to the assembly.

Every fourth year, at the *vernal equinox,* there is a Representative Council of the whole nation, which meets in a plain about twenty miles from our house, and continueth about five or six days. Here they inquire into the state and condition of the several districts, whether they abound or be deficient in hay or oats, or cows or Yahoos? And wherever there is any want (which is but seldom) it is immediately supplied by unanimous consent and contribution. Here likewise the regulation of children is settled: as for instance, if a Houyhnhnm hath two males, he changeth one of them with another who hath two females: and when a child hath been lost by any casualty, where the mother is past breeding, it is determined what family in the district shall breed another to supply the loss.

CHAPTER 9

A grand debate at the general Assembly of the Houyhnhnms, and how it was determined. The learning of the Houyhnhnms. Their buildings. Their manner of burials. The defectiveness of their language.

One of these grand Assemblies was held in my time, about three months before my departure, whither my master went as the Representative of our district. In this Council was resumed their old debate, and indeed, the only debate that ever happened in their country; whereof my master after his return gave me a very particular account.

The question to be debated, was, whether the Yahoos should be exterminated from the face of the earth. One of the *members* for the affirmative offered several arguments of great strength and weight, alleging, that as the Yahoos were the most filthy, noisome, and deformed animal which Nature ever produced, so they were the most restive and indocible,[2] mischievous, and malicious: they would privately suck the teats of the Houyhnhnms' cows, kill and devour their cats, trample down their oats and grass, if they were not continually watched, and commit a thousand other extravagancies. He took notice of a general tradition, that Yahoos had not been always in their country, but, that many ages ago, two of these brutes appeared together upon a mountain,[3] whether produced by the heat of the sun upon corrupted mud

---

1. In both Plato's *Republic* (451e6–7) and *Utopia,* the sexes receive the same education; Swift also began (but never completed) an essay entitled *Of the Education of Ladies* (c. 1728).

2. Unteachable.
3. Probably Milton's "steep savage Hill," the garden of Eden (*Paradise Lost,* 4,172).

and slime, or from the ooze and froth of the sea, was never known.[4] That these Yahoos engendered, and their brood in a short time grew so numerous as to overrun and infest the whole nation. That the Houyhnhnms, to get rid of this evil, made a general hunting, and at last enclosed the whole herd; and destroying the elder, every Houyhnhnm kept two young ones in a kennel, and brought them to such a degree of tameness, as an animal so savage by nature can be capable of acquiring; using them for draft and carriage. That there seemed to be much truth in this tradition, and that those creatures could not be *ylnhniamshy* (or *aborigines* of the land) because of the violent hatred the Houyhnhnms, as well as all other animals, bore them; which although their evil disposition sufficiently deserved, could never have arrived at so high a degree, if they had been *aborigines*, or else they would have long since been rooted out. That the inhabitants taking a fancy to use the service of the Yahoos, had very imprudently neglected to cultivate the breed of *asses*, which were a comely animal, easily kept, more tame and orderly, without any offensive smell, strong enough for labor, although they yield to the other in agility of body; and if their braying be no agreeable sound, it is far preferable to the horrible howlings of the Yahoos.[5]

Several others declared their sentiments to the same purpose, when my master proposed an expedient to the assembly, whereof he had indeed borrowed the hint from me. He approved of the tradition, mentioned by the Honorable Member who spoke before, and affirmed, that the two Yahoos said to be first seen among them had been driven thither over the sea; that coming to land, and being forsaken by their companions, they retired to the mountains, and degenerating by degrees, became in process of time, much more savage than those of their own species in the country from whence these two originals came. The reason of his assertion was, that he had now in his possession a certain wonderful[6] Yahoo (meaning myself), which most of them had heard of, and many of them had seen. He then related to them, how he first found me: that my body was all covered with an artificial composure of the skins and hairs of other animals; that I spoke in a language of my own, and had thoroughly learned theirs; that I had related to him the accidents which brought me thither; that when he saw me without my covering, I was an exact Yahoo in every part, only of a whiter color, less hairy, and with shorter claws. He added, how I had endeavored to persuade him, that in my own and other countries the Yahoos acted as the governing, rational animal, and held the Houyhnhnms in servitude; that he observed in me all the qualities of a Yahoo, only a little more civilized by some tincture of reason, which however was in a degree as far inferior to the Houyhnhnm race, as the Yahoos of their country were to me;[7] that, among other things, I mentioned a custom we had of *castrating* Houyhnhnms when they were young, in order to render them tame; that the operation was easy and safe; that it was no shame to learn wisdom from brutes, as industry is taught by the ant, and building by the swallow. (For so I translate the word *lyhannh*, although it be a much larger fowl.) That this invention might be practiced upon the younger Yahoos here, which, besides rendering them tractable and fitter for use, would in an age put an end to the whole species without destroying life. That, in the meantime the Houyhnhnms should be

4. Humans are supposed to be of divine origin, but the Yahoos represent such a degraded form of humanity that they (like, it was believed, insects on the Nile's banks) were formed from the action of the sun on mud.
5. The commonplace comparison of humans to asses was one Swift had previously used in *A Tale of a Tub* (1704)

and *The Battle of the Books* (1704).
6. Amazing, unusual.
7. Gulliver falls between the Houyhnhnms and the Yahoos in reason, as he did between the Lilliputians and the Brobdingnagians in size.

exhorted to cultivate the breed of asses, which, as they are in all respects more valuable brutes, so they have this advantage, to be fit for service at five years old, which the others are not till twelve.

This was all my master thought fit to tell me at that time, of what passed in the grand Council. But he was pleased to conceal[8] one particular, which related personally to myself, whereof I soon felt the unhappy effect, as the reader will know in its proper place, and from whence I date all the succeeding misfortunes of my life.

The Houyhnhnms have no letters, and consequently their knowledge is all traditional. But there happening few events of any moment among a people so well united, naturally disposed to every virtue, wholly governed by reason, and cut off from all commerce with other nations, the historical part is easily preserved without burdening their memories. I have already observed, that they are subject to no diseases, and therefore can have no need of physicians. However, they have excellent medicines composed of herbs, to cure accidental bruises and cuts in the pastern or frog of the foot by sharp stones, as well as other maims and hurts in the several parts of the body.

They calculate the year by the revolution of the sun and the moon, but use no subdivisions into weeks. They are well enough acquainted with the motions of those two luminaries, and understand the nature of eclipses; and this is the utmost progress of their astronomy.

In poetry they must be allowed to excel all other mortals; wherein the justness of their similes, and the minuteness, as well as exactness of their descriptions, are indeed inimitable. Their verses abound very much in both of these, and usually contain either some exalted notions of friendship and benevolence, or the praises of those who were victors in races, and other bodily exercises.[9] Their buildings, although very rude and simple, are not inconvenient, but well contrived to defend them from all injuries of cold and heat. They have a kind of tree, which at forty years old loosens in the root, and falls with the first storm; it grows very straight, and being pointed like stakes with a sharp stone (for the Houyhnhnms know not the use of iron), they stick them erect in the ground about ten inches asunder,[1] and then weave in oat-straw, or sometimes wattles betwixt them. The roof is made after the same manner, and so are the doors.

The Houyhnhnms use the hollow part between the pastern and the hoof of their forefeet as we do our hands, and this with greater dexterity than I could at first imagine. I have seen a white mare of our family thread a needle (which I lent her on purpose) with that joint. They milk their cows, reap their oats, and do all the work which requires hands, in the same manner. They have a kind of hard flints, which by grinding against other stones, they form into instruments, that serve instead of wedges, axes, and hammers. With tools made of these flints they likewise cut their hay, and reap their oats, which there groweth naturally in several fields: the Yahoos draw home the sheaves in carriages, and the servants tread them in certain covered huts, to get out the grain, which is kept in stores. They make a rude kind of earthen and wooden vessels, and bake the former in the sun.

If they can avoid casualties, they die only of old age, and are buried in the obscurest places that can be found, their friends and relations expressing neither joy nor grief at their departure; nor does the dying person discover the least regret that

---

8. Another indication that the Houyhnhnms are not completely honest or candid.
9. The type of poetry advocated in Plato's *Republic*

(390d1–3) and practiced in Sparta.
1. Apart.

he is leaving the world, any more than if he were upon returning[2] home from a visit to one of his neighbors;[3] I remember, my master having once made an appointment with a friend and his family to come to his house upon some affair of importance, on the day fixed, the mistress and her two children came very late; she made two excuses, first for her husband, who, as she said, happened that very morning to *lhnuwnh.* The word is strongly expressive in their language, but not easily rendered into English; it signifies, *to retire to his first mother.* Her excuse for not coming sooner, was, that her husband dying late in the morning, she was a good while consulting her servants about a convenient place where his body should be laid; and I observed she behaved herself at our house as cheerfully as the rest; she died about three months after.

They live generally to seventy or seventy-five years, very seldom to fourscore; some weeks before their death they feel a gradual decay, but without pain. During this time they are much visited by their friends, because they cannot go abroad with their usual ease and satisfaction. However, about ten days before their death, which they seldom fail in computing, they return the visits that have been made them by those who are nearest in the neighborhood, being carried in a convenient sledge drawn by Yahoos, which vehicle they use, not only upon this occasion, but when they grow old, upon long journeys, or when they are lamed by an accident. And therefore when the dying Houyhnhnms return those visits, they take a solemn leave of their friends, as if they were going to some remote part of the country, where they designed to pass the rest of their lives.

I know not whether it may be worth observing, that the Houyhnhnms have no word in their language to express anything that is *evil,* except what they borrow from the deformities or ill qualities of the Yahoos. Thus they denote the folly of a servant, an omission of a child, a stone that cuts their feet, a continuance of foul or unseasonable weather, and the like, by adding to each the epithet of *yahoo.* For instance, *hhnm yahoo, whnaholm yahoo, ynlhmnawihlma yahoo,* and an ill-contrived house, *ynholmhnmrohlnw yahoo.*

I could with great pleasure enlarge farther upon the manners and virtues of this excellent people; but intending in a short time to publish a volume by itself expressly upon that subject, I refer the reader thither. And in the meantime, proceed to relate my own sad catastrophe.

CHAPTER 10

The author's economy[4] and happy life among the Houyhnhnms. His great improvement in virtue, by conversing with them. Their conversations. The author hath notice given him by his master that he must depart from the country. He falls into a swoon for grief, but submits. He contrives and finishes a canoe, by the help of a fellow servant, and puts to sea at a venture.[5]

I had settled my little economy to my own heart's content. My master had ordered a room to be made for me after their manner, about six yards from the house, the sides and floors of which I plastered with clay, and covered with rush mats of my own contriving; I had beaten hemp, which there grows wild, and made of it a sort of ticking;[6] this I filled with the feathers of several birds I had taken with springes made of

---

2. About to return.
3. This attitude toward death is characteristic of both the Stoics, and the Utopians.

4. Method of living.
5. Without further planning.
6. Sturdy material used for making mattress covering.

Yahoos' hairs, and were excellent food; I had worked[7] two chairs with my knife, the sorrel nag helping me in the grosser[8] and more laborious part. When my clothes were worn to rags, I made myself others with the skins of rabbits, and of a certain beautiful animal about the same size, called *nnuhnoh*, the skin of which is covered with a fine down. Of these I likewise made very tolerable stockings. I soled my shoes with wood which I cut from a tree, and fitted to the upper leather, and when this was worn out, I supplied it with the skins of Yahoos dried in the sun. I often got honey out of hollow trees, which I mingled with water;[9] or ate it with my bread. No man could more verify the truth of these two maxims, *That nature is very easily satisfied;* and, *That necessity is the mother of invention.* I enjoyed perfect health of body and tranquillity of mind; I did not feel the treachery or inconstancy of a friend, nor the injuries of a secret or open enemy. I had no occasion of bribing, flattering, or pimping, to procure the favor of any great man or of his minion. I wanted no fence[1] against fraud or oppression; here was neither physician to destroy my body, nor lawyer to ruin my fortune; no informer to watch my words and actions, or forge accusations against me for hire; here were no jibers, censurers, backbiters, pickpockets, highwaymen, housebreakers, attorneys, bawds, buffoons, gamesters, politicians, wits, splenetics, tedious talkers, controvertists, ravishers, murderers, robbers, virtuosos;[2] no leaders or followers of party and faction; no encouragers to vice, by seducement or examples; no dungeon, axes, gibbets, whipping posts, or pillories; no cheating shopkeepers or mechanics;[3] no pride, vanity, or affectation; no fops, bullies, drunkards, strolling whores, or poxes;[4] no ranting, lewd, expensive wives; no stupid, proud pendants; no importunate, overbearing, quarrelsome, noisy, roaring, empty, conceited, swearing companions; no scoundrels, raised from the dust upon the merit of their vices, or nobility thrown into it on account of their virtues; no lords, fiddlers, judges, or dancing masters.[5]

I had the favor of being admitted to[6] several Houyhnhnms, who came to visit or dine with my master; where his Honor graciously suffered me to wait in the room, and listen to their discourse. Both he and his company would often descend to ask me questions, and receive my answers. I had also sometimes the honor of attending my master in his visits to others. I never presumed to speak, except in answer to a question, and then I did it with inward regret, because it was a loss of so much time for improving myself; but I was infinitely delighted with the station of a humble auditor in such conversations, where nothing passed but what was useful, expressed in the fewest and most significant words; where (as I have already said) the greatest *decency* was observed, without the least degree of ceremony; where no person spoke without being pleased himself, and pleasing his companions; where there was no interruption, tediousness, heat,[7] or difference of sentiments. They have a notion, that when people are met together, a short silence doth much improve conversation: this I found to be true, for during those little intermissions of talk, new ideas would arise in their minds, which very much enlivened the discourse. Their subjects are generally on friendship and benevolence, or order and economy, sometimes upon the visible operations of Nature, or ancient traditions, upon the bounds and limits of virtue,

---

7. Made.
8. Heavier, larger.
9. Honey-sweetened water was a Utopian drink.
1. Defense.
2. One knowledgeable or interested in apparently trivial "scientific" pursuits.
3. Laborers.

4. Venereal diseases.
5. That necessary tutor for the socially aspiring, the dancing master (usually French), was a particular figure of fun; he usually accompanied himself on the fiddle.
6. Allowed to meet.
7. Heat of argument.

upon the unerring rules of reason, or upon some determinations to be taken at the next great Assembly, and often upon the various excellencies of *poetry*. I may add without vanity, that my presence often gave them sufficient matter for discourse, because it afforded my master an occasion of letting his friends into the history of me and my country, upon which they were all pleased to descant in a manner not very advantageous to humankind; and for that reason I shall not repeat what they said: only I may be allowed to observe, that his Honor, to my great admiration, appeared to understand the nature of Yahoos much better than myself. He went through all our vices and follies, and discovered many which I had never mentioned to him, by only supposing what qualities a Yahoo of their country, with a small proportion of reason, might be capable of exerting; and concluded, with too much probability, how vile as well as miserable such a creature must be.

I freely confess, that all the little knowledge I have of any value, was acquired by the lectures I received from my master, and from hearing the discourses of him and his friends; to which I should be prouder to listen, than to dictate to the greatest and wisest assembly in Europe. I admired the strength, comeliness, and speed of the inhabitants; and such a constellation of virtues in such amiable persons produced in me the highest veneration. At first, indeed, I did not feel that natural awe which the Yahoos and all other animals bear towards them, but it grew upon me by degrees, much sooner than I imagined, and was mingled with a respectful love and gratitude, that they would condescend to distinguish me from the rest of my species.

When I thought of my family, my friends, my countrymen, or human race in general, I considered them as they really were, Yahoos in shape and disposition, perhaps a little more civilized, and qualified with the gift of speech, but making no other use of reason, than to improve and multiply those vices, whereof their brethren in this country had only the share that Nature allotted them. When I happened to behold the reflection of my own form in a lake or a fountain, I turned away my face in horror and detestation of myself,[8] and could better endure the sight of a common Yahoo, than of my own person. By conversing with the Houyhnhnms, and looking upon them with delight, I fell to imitate their gait and gesture, which is now grown into a habit, and my friends often tell me in a blunt way, that *I trot like a horse*; which, however, I take for a great compliment; neither shall I disown, that in speaking I am apt to fall into the voice and manner of the Houyhnhnms, and hear myself ridiculed on that account without the least mortification.

In the midst of all this happiness, when I looked upon myself to be fully settled for life, my master sent for me one morning a little earlier than his usual hour. I observed by his countenance that he was in some perplexity, and at a loss how to begin what he had to speak. After a short silence, he told me, he did not know how I would take what he was going to say; that in the last general Assembly, when the affair of the Yahoos was entered upon, the representatives had taken offense at his keeping a Yahoo (meaning myself) in his family more like a Houyhnhnm, than a brute animal. That he was known frequently to converse with me, as if he could receive some advantage or pleasure in my company; that such a practice was not agreeable to reason or Nature, or a thing ever heard of before among them. The Assembly did therefore *exhort* him, either to employ me like the rest of my species, or command me to swim back to the place from whence I came. That the first of these expedients was utterly rejected by all the Houyhnhnms who had ever seen me

---

8. A mocking reversal both of a common pattern in pastoral love poetry and of the Greek myth of Narcissus.

at his house or their own, for they alleged, that because I had some rudiments of reason, added to the natural pravity[9] of those animals, it was to be feared, I might be able to seduce them into the woody and mountainous parts of the country, and bring them in troops by night to destroy the Houyhnhnms' cattle, as being naturally of the ravenous[1] kind, and averse from labor.

My master added, that he was daily pressed by the Houyhnhnms of the neighborhood to have the Assembly's *exhortation* executed, which he could not put off much longer. He doubted[2] it would be impossible for me to swim to another country, and therefore wished I would contrive some sort of vehicle resembling those I had described to him, that might carry me on the sea, in which work I should have the assistance of his own servants, as well as those of his neighbors. He concluded, that for his own part he could have been content to keep me in his service as long as I lived, because he found I had cured myself of some bad habits and dispositions, by endeavoring, as far as my inferior nature was capable, to imitate the Houyhnhnms.

I should here observe to the reader, that a decree of the general Assembly in this country is expressed by the word *hnhloayn*, which signifies an *exhortation*, as near as I can render it, for they have no conception how a rational creature can be *compelled*, but only advised, or *exhorted*, because no person can disobey reason, without giving up his claim to be a rational creature.

I was struck with the utmost grief and despair at my master's discourse, and being unable to support the agonies I was under, I fell into a swoon at his feet; when I came to myself, he told me, that he concluded I had been dead. (For these people are subject to no such imbecilities of nature.) I answered, in a faint voice, that death would have been too great an happiness; that although I could not blame the Assembly's *exhortation*, or the urgency[3] of his friends, yet in my weak and corrupt judgment, I thought it might consist[4] with reason to have been less rigorous. That I could not swim a league, and probably the nearest land to theirs might be distant above a hundred; that many materials, necessary for making a small vessel to carry me off, were wholly wanting in this country, which, however, I would attempt in obedience and gratitude to his Honor, although I concluded the thing to be impossible, and therefore looked on myself as already devoted to destruction. That the certain prospect of an unnatural death was the least of my evils: for, supposing I should escape with life by some strange adventure, how could I think with temper[5] of passing my days among Yahoos, and relapsing into my old corruptions, for want of examples to lead and keep me within the paths of virtue? That I knew too well upon what solid reasons all the determinations of the wise Houyhnhnms were founded, not to be shaken by arguments of mine, a miserable Yahoo; and therefore after presenting him with my humble thanks for the offer of his servants' assistance in making a vessel, and desiring a reasonable time for so difficult a work, I told him I would endeavor to preserve a wretched being; and, if ever I returned to England, was not without hopes of being useful to my own species, by celebrating the praises of the renowned Houyhnhnms, and proposing their virtues to the imitation of mankind.

My master in a few words made me a very gracious reply, allowed me the space of two *months* to finish my boat; and ordered the sorrel nag, my fellow servant (for so at this distance I may presume to call him) to follow my instructions, because I told my master, that his help would be sufficient, and I knew he had a tenderness for me.

9. Depravity.
1. Rapacious, predatory, or greedy.
2. Feared.
3. Urging.
4. Be consistent.
5. Calmness.

In his company my first business was to go to that part of the coast, where my rebellious crew had ordered me to be set on shore. I got upon a height, and looking on every side into the sea, fancied I saw a small island, towards the northeast: I took out my pocket glass, and could then clearly distinguish it about five leagues off, as I computed; but it appeared to the sorrel nag to be only a blue cloud: for, as he had no conception of any country beside his own, so he could not be as expert in distinguishing remote objects at sea, as we who so much converse[6] in that element.

After I had discovered this island, I considered no farther; but resolved it should, if possible, be the first place of my banishment, leaving the consequence to Fortune.

I returned home, and consulting with the sorrel nag, we went into a copse at some distance, where I with my knife, and he with a sharp flint fastened very artificially, after their manner, to a wooden handle, cut down several oak wattles about the thickness of a walking staff, and some larger pieces. But I shall not trouble the reader with a particular description of my own mechanics; let it suffice to say, that in six weeks' time, with the help of the sorrel nag, who performed the parts that required most labor, I finished a sort of Indian canoe, but much larger, covering it with the skins of Yahoos well stitched together, with hempen threads of my own making. My sail was likewise composed of the skins of the same animal; but I made use of the youngest I could get, the older being too tough and thick, and I likewise provided myself with four paddles. I laid in a stock of boiled flesh, of rabbits and fowls, and took with me two vessels, one filled with milk, and the other with water.

I tried my canoe in a large pond near my master's house, and then corrected in it what was amiss; stopping all the chinks with Yahoos' tallow, till I found it staunch,[7] and able to bear me and my freight. And when it was as complete as I could possibly make it, I had it drawn on a carriage very gently by Yahoos, to the seaside, under the conduct of the sorrel nag, and another servant.

When all was ready, and the day came for my departure, I took leave of my master and lady, and the whole family, mine eyes flowing with tears, and my heart quite sunk with grief. But his Honor, out of curiosity, and perhaps (if I may speak it without vanity) partly out of kindness, was determined to see me in my canoe, and got several of his neighboring friends to accompany him. I was forced to wait above an hour for the tide, and then observing the wind very fortunately bearing towards the island, to which I intended to steer my course, I took a second leave of my master, but as I was going to prostrate myself to kiss his hoof, he did me the honor to raise it gently to my mouth. I am not ignorant how much I have been censured for mentioning this last particular. For my detractors are pleased to think it improbable, that so illustrious a person should descend to give so great a mark of distinction to a creature so inferior as I. Neither have I forgot, how apt some travelers are to boast of extraordinary favors they have received.[8] But if these censurers were better acquainted with the noble and courteous disposition of the Houyhnhnms, they would soon change their opinion.

I paid my respects to the rest of the Houyhnhnms in his Honor's company; then getting into my canoe, I pushed off from shore.

6. Are familiar with.
7. Watertight.

8. Swift heightens the absurdity of Gulliver's action, and draws attention to his later misanthropy.

CHAPTER 11

The author's dangerous voyage. He arrives at New Holland, hoping to settle there. Is wounded with an arrow by one of the natives. Is seized and carried by force into a Portuguese ship. The great civilities of the captain. The author arrives at England.

I began this desperate voyage on February 15, 1715, at 9 o'clock in the morning. The wind was very favorable; however, I made use at first only of my paddles, but considering I should soon be weary, and that the wind might probably chop about,[9] I ventured to set up my little sail; and thus, with the help of the tide, I went at the rate of a league and a half an hour, as near as I could guess. My master and his friends continued[1] on the shore, till I was almost out of sight; and I often heard the sorrel nag (who always loved me) crying out, *Hnuy illa nyha maiah Yahoo,* Take care of thyself, gentle Yahoo.

My design was, if possible, to discover some small island uninhabited, yet sufficient by my labor to furnish me with the necessaries of life, which I would have thought a greater happiness than to be first minister in the politest court of Europe; so horrible was the idea I conceived of returning to live in the society and under the government of Yahoos. For in such a solitude as I desired, I could at least enjoy my own thoughts, and reflect with delight on the virtues of those inimitable Houyhnhnms, without any opportunity of degenerating into the vices and corruptions of my own species.

The reader may remember what I related when my crew conspired against me, and confined me to my cabin. How I continued there several weeks, without knowing what course we took, and when I was put ashore in the longboat, how the sailors told me with oaths, whether true or false, that they knew not in what part of the world we were. However, I did then believe us to be about ten degrees southward of the Cape of Good Hope, or about 45 degrees southern latitude, as I gathered from some general words I overheard among them, being I supposed to the southeast in their intended voyage to Madagascar. And although this were but little better than conjecture, yet I resolved to steer my course eastward, hoping to reach the southwest coast of New Holland, and perhaps some such island as I desired, lying westward of it. The wind was full west, and by six in the evening I computed I had gone eastward at least eighteen leagues, when I spied a very small island about half a league off, which I soon reached. It was nothing but a rock, with one creek, naturally arched by the force of tempests. Here I put in my canoe, and climbing a part of the rock, I could plainly discover[2] land to the east, extending from south to north. I lay all night in my canoe, and repeating my voyage early in the morning, I arrived in seven hours to the southwest point of New Holland.[3] This confirmed me in the opinion I have long entertained, that the maps and charts place this country at least three degrees more to the east than it really is,[4] which thought I communicated many years ago to my worthy friend Mr. Herman Moll, and gave him my reasons for it, although he hath rather chosen to follow other authors.[5]

9. Change direction.
1. Stayed.
2. Discern.
3. New Holland was the name the explorer Abel Tasman originally gave to the western coast of Australia. Gulliver seems to place the land of the Houyhnhnms west of southwestern Australia, in which case the distance he covers to reach New Holland is improbable (1,500 to 2,000 nautical miles in 16 hours). It is possible, however, that Gulliver is meant to have landed on Tasmania, thus putting the Houyhnhnms a short distance west of this island.
4. Dampier claimed that he had found New Holland further west than indicated in Tasman's charts.
5. This geographer's *New and Correct Map of the Whole World* (1719) was probably the basis for Swift's geography in *Gulliver's Travels.*

I saw no inhabitants in the place where I landed, and being unarmed, I was afraid of venturing far into the country. I found some shellfish on the shore, and ate them raw, not daring to kindle a fire, for fear of being discovered by the natives. I continued three days feeding on oysters and limpets,[6] to save my own provisions, and I fortunately found a brook of excellent water, which gave me great relief.

On the fourth day, venturing out early a little too far, I saw twenty or thirty natives upon a height, not above five hundred yards from me. They were stark naked, men, women, and children, round a fire, as I could discover by the smoke. One of them spied me, and gave notice to the rest; five of them advanced towards me, leaving the women and children at the fire. I made what haste I could to the shore, and getting into my canoe, shoved off: the savages observing me retreat, ran after me; and before I could get far enough into the sea, discharged an arrow, which wounded me deeply on the inside of my left knee (I shall carry the mark to my grave). I apprehended the arrow might be poisoned, and paddling out of the reach of their darts (being a calm day) I made a shift to suck the wound, and dress it as well as I could.

I was at a loss what to do, for I durst not return to the same landing place, but stood[7] to the north, and was forced to paddle; for the wind though very gentle was against me, blowing northwest. As I was looking about for a secure landing place, I saw a sail to the north-north-east, which appearing every minute more visible, I was in some doubt, whether I should wait for them or no; but at last my detestation of the Yahoo race prevailed, and turning my canoe, I sailed and paddled together to the south, and got into the same creek from whence I set out in the morning, choosing rather to trust myself among these *barbarians*, than live with European Yahoos. I drew up my canoe as close as I could to the shore, and hid myself behind a stone by the little brook, which, as I have already said, was excellent water.

The ship came within a half a league of this creek, and sent out her longboat with vessels to take in fresh water (for the place it seems was very well known) but I did not observe it till the boat was almost on shore, and it was too late to seek another hiding place. The seamen at their landing observed my canoe, and rummaging it all over, easily conjectured that the owner could not be far off. Four of them well armed searched every cranny and lurking hole, till at last they found me flat on my face behind the stone. They gazed a while in admiration[8] at my strange uncouth dress, my coat made of skins, my wooden-soled shoes, and my furred stockings; from whence, however, they concluded I was not a native of the place, who all go naked. One of the seamen in Portuguese bid me rise, and asked who I was. I understood that language very well, and getting upon my feet, said, I was a poor Yahoo, banished from the Houyhnhnms, and desired they would please to let me depart. They admired to hear me answer them in their own tongue, and saw by my complexion I must be a European; but were at a loss to know what I meant by Yahoos and Houyhnhnms, and at the same time fell a laughing at my strange tone in speaking, which resembled the neighing of a horse. I trembled all the while betwixt fear and hatred: I again desired leave to depart, and was gently moving to my canoe; but they laid hold on me, desiring to know, what country I was of? whence I came? with many other questions. I told them, I was born in England, from whence I came about five years ago, and then their country and ours were at peace. I therefore hoped they would not treat me as an enemy, since I meant them no harm, but was a

6. Small mollusks that attach themselves to rocks.   8. Wonder, amazement.
7. Steered.

poor Yahoo, seeking some desolate place where to pass the remainder of his unfortunate life.

When they began to talk, I thought I never heard or saw anything so unnatural; for it appeared to me as monstrous as if a dog or a cow should speak in England, or a Yahoo in Houyhnhnmland. The honest Portuguese were equally amazed at my strange dress, and the odd manner of delivering my words, which however they understood very well. They spoke to me with great humanity, and said they were sure their captain would carry me *gratis* to Lisbon, from whence I might return to my own country; that two of the seamen would go back to the ship, to inform the captain of what they had seen, and receive his orders; in the meantime, unless I would give my solemn oath not to fly;[9] they would secure me by force. I thought it best to comply with their proposal. They were very curious to know my story, but I gave them very little satisfaction; and they all conjectured, that my misfortunes had impaired my reason. In two hours the boat, which went loaden with vessels of water, returned with the captain's commands to fetch me on board. I fell on my knees to preserve my liberty; but all was in vain, and the men having tied me with cords, heaved me into the boat, from whence I was taken into the ship, and from thence into the captain's cabin.

His name was Pedro de Mendez; he was a very courteous and generous person; he entreated me to give some account of myself, and desired to know what I would eat or drink; said, I should be used as well as himself, and spoke so many obliging things, that I wondered to find such civilities from a Yahoo. However, I remained silent and sullen; I was ready to faint at the very smell of him and his men. At last I desired something to eat out of my own canoe; but he ordered me a chicken and some excellent wine, and then directed that I should be put to bed in a very clean cabin. I would not undress myself, but lay on the bed clothes, and in half an hour stole out, when I thought the crew was at dinner, and getting to the side of the ship was going to leap into the sea, and swim for my life, rather than continue among Yahoos. But one of the seamen prevented me, and having informed the captain, I was chained to my cabin.

After dinner Don Pedro came to me, and desired to know my reason for so desperate an attempt: assured me he only meant to do me all the service he was able, and spoke so very movingly, that at last I descended[1] to treat him like an animal which had some little portion of reason. I gave him a very short relation of my voyage, of the conspiracy against me by my own men, of the country where they set me on shore, and of my three years' residence there. All which he looked upon as if it were a dream or a vision; whereat I took great offense; for I had quite forgot the faculty of lying, so peculiar to Yahoos in all countries where they preside, and consequently the disposition of suspecting truth in others of their own species. I asked him, whether it were the custom of his country to *say the thing that was not?* I assured him I had almost forgot what he meant by falsehood, and if I had lived a thousand years in Houyhnhnmland, I should never have heard a lie from the meanest servant; that I was altogether indifferent whether he believed me or no; but however, in return for his favors, I would give so much allowance to the corruption of his nature, as to answer any objection he would please to make, and then he might easily discover the truth.

9. Attempt to escape.   1. Condescended.

The captain, a wise man, after many endeavors to catch me tripping in some part of my story, at last began to have a better opinion of my veracity.[2] But he added, that since I professed so inviolable an attachment to truth, I must give him my word of honor to bear him company in this voyage without attempting anything against my life, or else he would continue[3] me a prisoner till we arrived at Lisbon. I gave him the promise he required; but at the same time protested that I would suffer the greatest hardships rather than return to live among Yahoos.

Our voyage passed without any considerable accident.[4] In gratitude to the captain I sometimes sat with him at his earnest request, and strove to conceal my antipathy against human kind, although it often broke out, which he suffered to pass without observation. But the greatest part of the day, I confined myself to my cabin, to avoid seeing any of the crew. The captain had often entreated me to strip myself of my savage dress, and offered to lend me the best suit of clothes he had. This I would not be prevailed on to accept, abhorring to cover myself with anything that had been on the back of a Yahoo. I only desired he would lend me two clean shirts, which having been washed since he wore them, I believed would not so much defile me. These I changed every second day, and washed them myself.

We arrived at Lisbon, Nov. 5, 1715. At our landing the captain forced me to cover myself with his cloak, to prevent the rabble from crowding about me. I was conveyed to his own house and at my earnest request, he led me up to the highest room backwards.[5] I conjured[6] him to conceal from all persons what I had told him of the Houyhnhnms, because the least hint of such a story would not only draw numbers of people to see me, but probably put me in danger of being imprisoned, or burnt by the Inquisition.[7] The captain persuaded me to accept a suit of clothes newly made, but I would not suffer the tailor to take my measure; however, Don Pedro being almost of my size, they fitted me well enough. He accoutered[8] me with other necessaries all new, which I aired for twenty-four hours before I would use them.

The captain had no wife, nor above three servants, none of which were suffered to attend at meals, and his whole deportment was so obliging, added to very good *human* understanding, that I really began to tolerate his company. He gained so far upon me, that I ventured to look out of the back window. By degrees I was brought into another room, from whence I peeped into the street, but drew my head back in a fright. In a week's time he seduced me down to the door. I found my terror gradually lessened, but my hatred and contempt seemed to increase. I was at last bold enough to walk the street in his company, but kept my nose well stopped with rue,[9] or sometimes with tobacco.

In ten days Don Pedro, to whom I had given some account of my domestic affairs, put it upon me as a point of honor and conscience, that I ought to return to my native country, and live at home with my wife and children. He told me, there was an English ship in the port just ready to sail, and he would furnish me with all things necessary.

---

2. In the first edition, the sentence continues: "and the rather, because he confessed, he met with a Dutch Skipper, who pretended to have landed with five others of his crew upon a certain island or continent south of New Holland, where they went for fresh water, and observed a horse driving before him several animals exactly resembling those I had described under the name of Yahoos, with some other particulars, which the captain said he had forgot, because he then concluded them all to be lies." In 1735 Swift's Dublin publisher, George Faulkener, omitted these lines, probably because they contradicted Gulliver's later statement that no other European had visited this land.

3. Keep.

4. Incident.

5. At the back of the house.

6. Appealed earnestly to.

7. Either because the Houyhnhnm hierarchy contradicted Genesis, in which man has dominion over the earth, or because Gulliver had been associating with diabolical powers, who could make humans appear to be horses (as Gulliver himself had first believed).

8. Attired.

9. Strong-smelling shrub, used for medicinal purposes.

It would be tedious to repeat his arguments, and my contradictions. He said, it was altogether impossible to find such a solitary island as I had desired to live in; but I might command in my own house, and pass my time in a manner as recluse as I pleased.

I complied at last, finding I could not do better. I left Lisbon the 24th day of November, in an English merchantman, but who was the master I never inquired. Don Pedro accompanied me to the ship, and lent me twenty pounds. He took kind leave of me, and embraced me at parting, which I bore as well as I could. During this last voyage I had no commerce[1] with the master or any of his men, but pretending I was sick kept close in my cabin. On the fifth of December, 1715, we cast anchor in the Downs[2] about nine in the morning, and at three in the afternoon I got safe to my house at Redriff.

My wife and family received me with great surprise and joy, because they concluded me certainly dead; but I must freely confess the sight of them filled me only with hatred, disgust, and contempt, and the more by reflecting on the near alliance I had to them. For, although since my unfortunate exile from the Houyhnhnm country, I had compelled myself to tolerate the sight of Yahoos, and to converse with Don Pedro de Mendez, yet my memory and imaginations were perpetually filled with the virtues and ideas of those exalted Houyhnhnms. And when I began to consider, that by copulating with one of the Yahoo species, I had become a parent of more, it struck me with the utmost shame, confusion, and horror.

As soon as I entered the house, my wife took me in her arms, and kissed me, at which, having not been used to the touch of that odious animal for so many years, I fell in a swoon for almost an hour. At the time I am writing it is five years since my last return to England: during the first year I could not endure my wife or children in my presence, the very smell of them was intolerable, much less could I suffer them to eat in the same room. To this hour they dare not presume to touch my bread, or drink out of the same cup, neither was I ever able to let one of them take me by the hand.[3] The first money I laid out was to buy two young stone-horses,[4] which I keep in a good stable, and next to them the groom is my greatest favorite; for I feel my spirits revived by the smell he contracts in the stable. My horses understand me tolerably well; I converse with them at least four hours every day. They are strangers to bridle or saddle, they live in great amity with me, and friendship to each other.

CHAPTER 12

The author's veracity. His design in publishing this work. His censure of those travelers who swerve from the truth. The author clears himself from any sinister ends in writing. An objection answered. The method of planting Colonies. His native country commended. The right of the Crown to those countries described by the author is justified. The difficulty of conquering them. The author takes his last leave of the reader, proposeth his manner of living for the future, gives good advice, and concludeth.

Thus, gentle reader,[5] I have given thee a faithful history of my travels for sixteen years, and above seven months, wherein I have not been so studious of ornament as of truth. I could perhaps like others have astonished thee with strange improbable tales; but I rather chose to relate plain matter of fact in the simplest manner and style, because my principal design was to inform, and not to amuse thee.

---

1. Interaction.
2. The sea off the North Downs in East Kent.
3. Gulliver's unwillingness to share his bread or cup with his wife or children emphasizes his unchristian behavior.

4. Stallions.
5. Highly ironic, since the "gentle" readers must be Yahoos.

It is easy for us who travel into remote countries, which are seldom visited by Englishmen or other Europeans, to form descriptions of wonderful animals both at sea and land. Whereas a traveler's chief aim should be to make men wiser and better, and to improve their minds by the bad as well as good example of what they deliver concerning foreign places.[6]

I could heartily wish a law were enacted, that every traveler, before he were permitted to publish his voyages, should be obliged to make oath before the Lord High Chancellor that all he intended to print was absolutely true to the best of his knowledge; for then the world would no longer be deceived as it usually is, while some writers, to make their works pass the better upon the public, impose the grossest falsities on the unwary reader. I have perused several books of travels with great delight in my younger days; but having since gone over most parts of the globe, and been able to contradict many fabulous accounts from my own observation, it hath given me a great disgust against this part of reading, and some indignation to see the credulity of mankind so impudently abused. Therefore since my acquaintance were pleased to think my poor endeavors might not be unacceptable to my country, I imposed on myself as a maxim, never to be swerved from, that I would *strictly adhere to truth*; neither indeed can I be ever under the least temptation to vary from it, while I retain in my mind the lectures and example of my noble master, and the other illustrious Houyhnhnms, of whom I had so long the honor to be an humble hearer.

> —*Nec si miserum Fortuna Sinonem*
> *Finxit, vanum etiam mendacemque improba finget.*[7]

I know very well how little reputation is to be got by writings which require neither genius nor learning, nor indeed any other talent, except a good memory or an exact journal. I know likewise, that writers of travels, like dictionary-makers, are sunk into oblivion by the weight and bulk of those who come last, and therefore lie uppermost.[8] And it is highly probable, that such travelers who shall hereafter visit the countries described in this work of mine, may, by detecting my errors (if there be any), and adding many new discoveries of their own, jostle me out of vogue, and stand in my place, making the world forget that ever I was an author. This indeed would be too great a mortification if I wrote for fame; but, as my sole intention was the PUBLIC GOOD.[9] I cannot be altogether disappointed. For who can read of the virtues I have mentioned in the glorious Houyhnhnms, without being ashamed of his own vices, when he considers himself as the reasoning, governing animal of his country? I shall say nothing of those remote nations where Yahoos preside, amongst which the least corrupted are the Brobdingnagians, whose wise maxims in morality and government it would be our happiness to observe. But I forbear descanting further, and rather leave the judicious reader to his own remarks and applications.

I am not a little pleased that this work of mine can possibly meet with no[1] censurers: for what objections can be made against a writer who relates only plain facts that happened in such distant countries, where we have not the least interest with

---

6. More's *Utopia* also argues that accounts of distant travels should provide useful lessons rather than fabulous tales.

7. "Nor, if cruel Fortune has made Sinon miserable, shall he also make him false and deceitful" (Virgil, *Aeneid* 2. 79–80). Swift cleverly employs the words that the Greek Sinon, the most famous liar in antiquity, used in the fraudulent tale he told to fool the Trojans into accepting

his (wooden) horse.

8. The most current dictionary is the one most frequently used.

9. The English buccaneer and navigator William Dampier professes a similar aim in the dedication to his *New Voyage Round the World* (1697).

1. Cannot possibly encounter any.

respect either to trade or negotiations? I have carefully avoided every fault with which common writers of travels are often too justly charged. Besides, I meddle not the least with any *party*, but write without passion, prejudice, or ill-will against any man or number of men whatsoever. I write for the noblest end, to inform and instruct mankind, over whom I may, without breach of modesty, pretend to some superiority from the advantages I received by conversing so long among the most accomplished Houyhnhnms. I write without any view towards profit or praise. I never suffer a word to pass that may look like reflection,[2] or possibly give the least offense even to those who are most ready to take it. So that I hope I may with justice pronounce myself an author perfectly blameless, against whom the tribe of answerers, considerers, observers, reflecters, detecters, remarkers, will never be able to find matter for exercising their talents.[3]

I confess, it was whispered to me, that I was bound in duty as a subject of England, to have given in a memorial to a Secretary of State, at my first coming over; because, whatever lands are discovered by a subject belong to the Crown. But I doubt whether our conquests in the countries I treat of, would be as easy as those of Ferdinando Cortez over the naked Americans.[4] The Lilliputians, I think, are hardly worth the charge of a fleet and army to reduce them, and I question whether it might be prudent or safe to attempt the Brobdingnagians. Or whether an English army would be much at their ease with the Flying Island over their heads.[5] The Houyhnhnms, indeed, appear not to be so well prepared for war, a science to which they are perfect strangers, and especially against missive weapons.[6] However, supposing myself to be a minister of State, I could never give my advice for invading them. Their prudence, unanimity, unacquaintedness with fear, and their love of their country would amply supply all defects in the military art. Imagine twenty thousand of them breaking into the midst of an European army, confounding the ranks, overturning the carriages, battering the warriors' faces into mummy,[7] by terrible yerks[8] from their hinder hoofs. For they would well deserve the character given to Augustus; *Recalcitrat undique tutus.*[9] But instead of proposals for conquering that magnanimous nation, I rather wish they were in a capacity or disposition to send a sufficient number of their inhabitants for civilizing Europe, by teaching us the first principles of honor, justice, truth, temperance, public spirit, fortitude, chastity, friendship, benevolence, and fidelity. The *names* of all which virtues are still retained among us in most languages, and are to be met with in modern as well as ancient authors; which I am able to assert from my own small reading.

But I had another reason which made me less forward[1] to enlarge his Majesty's dominions by my discoveries. To say the truth, I had conceived a few scruples with

2. Criticism.

3. At this time it was common for historical and fictional accounts to be "applied" to contemporary situations or persons; by having Gulliver deny at such length that he is doing this, Swift draws attention to the possibility of making such connections.

4. In the 1520s, Cortés and 400 soldiers rapidly conquered the Aztec empire in Mexico.

5. These sentences refer to Gulliver's other travels: in Lilliput he encountered a miniature people; in Brobdingnag he met with giants; and in Laputa he encountered the Flying Island (able to force inhabitants below to submit either through starving them by blocking out the sun or by crushing them).

6. Anything thrown or shot through the air.

7. Pulp.

8. Kicks.

9. "He kicks back, well protected on every side" (Horace, *Satires* 2.i.20). While Gulliver refers admiringly to the horse's ability to defend itself, Swift recalls the context for Horace's decision to use satire (rather than praise) when writing about Augustus: according to Horace, Augustus would kick out like a horse if he sensed servile flattery, so flattery was pointless. Gulliver's lavish praise of the Houyhnhnms backfires on him, not because the Houyhnhnms disliked it, but because his uncritical identification with them leaves him unable to cope with human society.

1. Eager.

relation to the distributive justice[2] of princes upon those occasions. For instance, a crew of pirates[3] are driven by a storm they know not whither, at length a boy discovers land from the topmast, they go on shore to rob and plunder; they see a harmless people, are entertained with kindness, they give the country a new name, they take formal possession of it for the king, they set up a rotten plank or a stone for a memorial, they murder two or three dozen of the natives, bring away a couple more by force for a sample, return home, and get their pardon. Here commences a new dominion acquired with a title by *divine right*. Ships are sent with the first opportunity, the natives driven out or destroyed, their princes tortured to discover their gold;[4] a free license given to all acts of inhumanity and lust, the earth reeking with the blood of its inhabitants; and this execrable crew of butchers employed in so pious an expedition, is a *modern colony* sent to convert and civilize an idolatrous and barbarous people.

But this description, I confess, doth by no means affect the British nation, who may be an example to the whole world for their wisdom, care, and justice in planting colonies,[5] their liberal endowments for the advancement of religion and learning; their choice of devout and able pastors to propagate Christianity; their caution in stocking their provinces with people of sober lives and conversations from this the mother kingdom,[6] their strict regard to the distribution of justice, in supplying the civil administration through all their colonies with officers of the greatest abilities, utter strangers to corruption; and to crown all, by sending the most vigilant and virtuous governors, who have no other views than the happiness of the people over whom they preside, and the honor of the King their master.

But, as those countries which I have described do not appear to have any desire of being conquered, and enslaved, murdered, or driven out by colonies, nor abound either in gold, silver, sugar, or tobacco; I did humbly conceive they were by no means proper objects of our zeal, our valor, or our interest. However, if those whom it more concerns, think fit to be of another opinion, I am ready to depose, when I shall be lawfully called, that no European did ever visit those countries before me. I mean, if the inhabitants ought to be believed.[7]

But as to the formality of taking possession in my Sovereign's name, it never came once into my thoughts; and if it had, yet as my affairs then stood, I should perhaps in point of prudence and self-preservation, have put it off to a better opportunity.

Having thus answered the *only* objection that can ever be raised against me as a traveler, I here take a final leave of my courteous readers, and return to enjoy my own speculations in my little garden at Redriff, to apply those excellent lessons of virtue which I learned among the Houyhnhnms, to instruct the Yahoos of my own family as far as I shall find them docible[8] animals, to behold my figure often in a glass, and thus if possible habituate myself by time to tolerate the sight of a human creature, to lament the brutality of Houyhnhnms in my own country, but always treat their persons with respect, for the sake of my noble master, his family, his

2. Fairness with regard to the rights of the native people.
3. Referring to the first Spanish colonizers of America.
4. Montezuma was tortured by Cortés and the Incan emperor Atahuallpa by Pizarro (1533).
5. Intended ironically.
6. Felons were commonly given a sentence of mandatory "transportation" to Britain's colonies.
7. The first edition continued: "unless a dispute may arise about the two Yahoos, said to have been seen many Ages ago on a mountain in Houyhnhnm-land, from whence the opinion is, that the race of those brutes hath descended; and these, for anything I know, may have been English, which indeed I was apt to suspect from the lineaments of their posterity's countenances, although very much defaced. But how far that will go to make out a title, I leave to the learned in colony law." Faulkener omitted this passage in the 1735 edition.
8. Teachable.

friends, and the whole Houyhnhnm race, whom these of ours[9] have the honor to resemble in all their lineaments, however their intellectuals[1] came to degenerate.

I began last week to permit my wife to sit at dinner with me, at the farthest end of a long table, and to answer (but with the utmost brevity) the few questions I ask her. Yet the smell of a Yahoo continuing very offensive, I always keep my nose well stopped with rue, lavender, or tobacco leaves. And although it be hard for a man late in life to remove old habits, I am not altogether out of hopes in some time to suffer a neighbor Yahoo in my company, without the apprehensions I am yet under of his teeth or his claws.

My reconcilement to the Yahoo-kind in general might not be so difficult if they would be content with those vices and follies only, which Nature hath entitled them to. I am not in the least provoked at the sight of a lawyer, a pickpocket, a colonel, a fool, a lord, a gamester, a politician, a whoremonger, a physician, an evidence,[2] a suborner,[3] an attorney, a traitor, or the like: this is all according to the due course of things; but when I behold a lump of deformity and diseases both in body and mind, smitten with *pride*, it immediately breaks all the measures of my patience; neither shall I be ever able to comprehend how such an animal and such a vice could tally together. The wise and virtuous Houyhnhnms, who abound in all excellencies that can adorn a rational creature, have no name for this vice in their language, which hath no terms to express anything that is evil, except those whereby they describe the detestable qualities of their Yahoos, among which they were not able to distinguish this of pride, for want of thoroughly understanding human nature, as it showeth itself in other countries, where that animal presides. But I, who had more experience, could plainly observe some rudiments of it among the wild Yahoos.

But the Houyhnhnms, who live under the government of Reason, are no more proud of the good qualities they possess, than I should be for not wanting a leg or an arm, which no man in his wits would boast of, although he must be miserable without them. I dwell the longer upon this subject from the desire I have to make the society of an English Yahoo by any means not insupportable, and therefore I here entreat those who have any tincture of this absurd vice, that they will not presume to appear in my sight.[4]

FINIS

c. 1721–1725   1726

❂ *GULLIVER'S TRAVELS* AND ITS TIME ❂

The following five letters to and from Jonathan Swift were written over a period of nearly eighteen months and span the progress of *Gulliver's Travels* from Swift's corrections of the manuscript to reports on the reactions of London readers. The celebratory letters from his old friends Pope and Gay are valuable in chronicling the reception of *Gulliver,* and the three letters from Swift himself are particularly interesting, revealing a playfulness, warmth, and gift for friendship not ordinarily associated with the common misconception of Swift as darkly misanthropic and sarcastic.

---

9. I.e., horses.
1. Intellects.
2. A (false) witness.

3. One who bribes another to commit a misdeed.
4. Gulliver thus falls into pride, the very vice he rejects.

Jonathan Swift to Alexander Pope

29 Sep[tember] 1725

Sir, * * * I have employed my time (besides ditching)[1] in finishing correcting, amending, and transcribing my *Travels*, in four parts complete newly augmented, and intended for the press when the world shall deserve them, or rather when a printer shall
be found brave enough to venture his ears.[2] I like your schemes of our meeting after
distresses and dispersions, but the chief end I propose to myself in all my labors is to
vex the world rather than divert it; and if I could compass that design[3] without hurt-
ing my own person or fortune, I would be the most indefatigable writer you have ever
seen without reading.[4] I am exceedingly pleased that you have done with translations.
Lord Treasurer Oxford,[5] often lamented that a rascally world should lay you under a
necessity of misemploying your genius for so long a time.[6] But since you will now be so
much better employed, when you think of the world give it one lash the more at my
request. I have ever hated all nations, professions, and communities and all my love is
towards individuals. For instance, I hate the tribe of lawyers, but I love Councilor
Such-a-one, Judge Such-a-one, for so with physicians (I will not speak of my own
trade), soldiers, English, Scotch, French, and the rest. But principally I hate and detest
that animal called man, although I heartily love John, Peter, Thomas, and so forth.
This is the system upon which I have governed myself many years (but do not tell),
and so I shall go on till I have done with them. I have got materials towards a treatise
proving the falsity of that definition *animal rationale* and to show it should be only
rationis capax.[7] Upon this great foundation of misanthropy (though not Timon's manner[8]), the whole building of my *Travels* is erected, and I never will have peace of mind
till all honest men are of my opinion. By consequence you are to embrace it immediately and procure that all who deserve my esteem may do so too. The matter is so clear
that it will admit little dispute. Nay, I will hold a hundred pounds that you and I agree
in the point. * * *

Alexander Pope to Jonathan Swift

November 16, 1726

I have resolved to take time, and in spite of all misfortunes and demurs, which
sickness, lameness, or disability of any kind can throw in my way, to write you (at intervals) a long letter. My two least fingers of one hand hang impediments to the others, like useless dependents, who only take up room, and never are active or assistant
to our wants: I shall never be much the better for 'em.[9] I congratulate you first upon

1. Digging ditches or doing one's daily labor.
2. In earlier times printers could have their ears cut off as
punishment for printing seditious material. Since the legal penalty had lapsed, the idea of venturing one's ears
more generally meant being willing to risk punishment or
make a sacrifice.
3. Achieve that end.
4. Education; Swift ironically deprecates his own learning.
5. Robert Harley (1661–1724), first Earl of Oxford; a
Tory statesman and member of the Scriblenis Club, he
was a mutual friend of Pope and of Swift.

6. Pope spent 12 years (1713–1725) translating Homer's
Iliad and *Odyssey*.
7. Humans are not automatically rational animals, as
Aristotle had said, but rather only *rationis capax*—capable
of reasoning.
8. Timon, a nobleman of Athens who, after losing his
riches and receiving no help from his wealthy friends, lived
a life of solitary misanthropy in a cave outside the city.
9. In September the tendons of Pope's two fingers had
been severed when his hand was cut in a near-fatal coach
accident.

what you call your cousin's wonderful book,[1] which is *publica trita man*,[2] at present, and I prophesy will be in future the admiration of all men. That countenance[3] with which it is received by some statesmen is delightful; I wish I could tell you how every single man looks upon it, to observe which has been my whole diversion this fortnight. I've never been a night in London since you left me[4] till now for this very end, and indeed it has fully answered my expectations.

I find no considerable man very angry at the book: some indeed think it rather too bold and too general a satire, but none that I hear of accuse it of particular reflections.[5] (I mean no persons of consequence, or good judgment; the mob of critics, you know, always are desirous to apply satire to those that they envy for being above them), so that you needed not to have been so secret upon this head. Motte,[6] received the copy (he tells me) he knew not from whence, nor from whom, dropped at his house in the dark from a hackney coach; by computing the time, I found it was after you left England, so for my part, I suspend my judgment.[7] * * *

John Gay to Jonathan Swift

Nov. 17. 1726

About ten days ago a book was published here of the travels of one Gulliver, which hath been the conversation of the whole town ever since. The whole impression,[8] told in a week, and nothing is more diverting than to hear the different opinions people give of it, though all agree in liking it extremely. 'Tis generally said that you are the author, but I am told, the bookseller declares he knows not from what hand it came.[9] From the highest to the lowest it is universally read, from the Cabinet council to the nursery. The politicians to a man agree that it is free from particular reflections, but that the satire on general societies of men is too severe. Not but we now and then meet with people of greater perspicuity, who are in search for particular applications in every leaf; and it is highly probable we shall have keys[1] published to give light into Gulliver's design. Your Lord ———[2] is the person who least approves it, blaming it as a design of evil consequence to depreciate human nature, at which it cannot be wondered that he takes most offense, being himself the most accomplished of his species, and so losing more than any other of that praise which is due both to the dignity and virtue of a man. Your friend, my Lord Harcourt,[3] commends it very much, though he thinks in some places the matter too far carried. The

---

1. The manuscript for *Gulliver's Travels* was submitted to the London publisher Benjamin Motte, by "Richard Sympson," the imaginary cousin of Gulliver.
2. Passed from hand to hand.
3. Both the expression on the face and general composure of temperament.
4. Swift had been visiting friends in London from mid-March to mid-August this year and stayed mainly at Pope's house at Twickenham.
5. Direct satire of contemporary people or affairs.
6. Benjamin Motte (d. 1738), bookseller and printer.
7. Pope had assisted his friend in getting *Gulliver* published anonymously.
8. Print run.
9. Gay had copied out Swift's original letter to the publisher (signing it "Richard Sympson," Gulliver's alleged

cousin), in order to assist Swift in hiding his authorship of *Gulliver* from his publisher, and, thus, from the general public.
1. The publication of "keys," which helped readers unlock the contemporary application of satires, was highly popular at this time; a "key" to Gay's *Beggar's Opera* was published after its success, in 1728. Alexander Pope took advantage of this trend by publishing a pamphlet entitled *A Key to the Lock. Or, A Treatise proving . . . the dangerous Tendency of a late Poem, The Rape of the Lock, To Government and Religion* (1715).
2. Bolingbroke.
3. Simon Harcourt, first Viscount (1667–1727), an old friend of Swift's, one of the few who managed to do well under the new Whig government without losing touch with his old friends.

Duchess Dowager of Marlborough[4] is in raptures at it; she says she can dream of nothing else since she read it; she declares, that she hath now found out that her whole life hath been lost in caressing the worst part of mankind and treating the best as her foes, and that if she knew Gulliver, though he had been the worst enemy she ever had, she would give up all her present acquaintance for his friendship. You may see by this, that you are not much injured by being supposed the author of this piece. If you are, you have disobliged us, and two or three of your best friends, in not giving us the least hint of it while you were with us, and in particular Dr. Arbuthnot, who says it is ten thousand pities he had not known it, he could have added such abundance of things upon every subject.[5] Among lady critics, some have found out that Mr. Gulliver had a particular malice to maids of honor.[6] Those of them who frequent the church say his design is impious, and that it is an insult on Providence, by depreciating the works of the Creator. Notwithstanding, I am told the Princess hath read it with great pleasure. As to other critics, they think the flying island is the least entertaining,[7] and so great an opinion the town have of the impossibility of Gulliver's writing at all below himself, that 'tis agreed that part was not writ by the same hand, though this hath its defenders too. It hath passed Lords and Commons, *nemine contradicente;*[8] and the whole town, men, women, and children are quite full of it.

Perhaps I may all this time be talking to you of a book you have never seen, and which hath not yet reached Ireland; if it hath not, I believe what we have said will be sufficient to recommend it to your reading, and that you order me to send it to you.

But it will be much better to come over yourself, and read it here. ＊ ＊ ＊

Jonathan Swift to Alexander Pope

Dublin, Nov. [27] 1726

I am just come from answering a letter of Mrs. Howard's writ in such mystical terms that I should never have found out the meaning,[9] if a book had not been sent me called *Gulliver's Travels,* of which you say so much in yours.[1] I read the book over, and in the second volume observe several passages which appear to be patched and altered, and the style of a different sort (unless I am much mistaken).[2] Dr. Arbuthnot likes the projectors least; others you tell me, the flying island; some think it wrong to be so hard upon whole bodies or corporations.[3] Yet the general opinion is that reflections on particular persons are most to be blamed, so that in these cases, I think the best method is to let censure and opinion take their course. A Bishop here said, that book was full of improbable lies, and for his part, he hardly believed a word of it; and so much for Gulliver. ＊ ＊ ＊

---

4. Sarah Churchill (1660–1744), a favorite of Queen Anne's.
5. Gay here feigns complete ignorance of *Gulliver's* authorship partly in jest, partly because both men knew that the letters of those hostile to the government were routinely opened and read by officials in the post office.
6. Companions to the queen. Swift's references to the maids of honor in Lilliput and Brobdingnag involved incidents that were indelicate and, by implication, potentially embarrassing to the women of rank at the English Court; see, for example, "A Voyage to Brobdingnag,"

chapter 5, in which the maids of honor use the dimunitive Gulliver to titillate their breasts.
7. "A Voyage to Laputa."
8. Nobody voting against.
9. A letter of 17 November, to which Swift replied in tones of mock-mystification.
1. His letter of 17 November.
2. Fearful of the law, Swift's publisher Benjamin Motte made several alterations to the *Travels.*
3. Professions or groups, all from "A Voyage to Laputa."

"The Prince of Lilliput" to Stella[4]

[11 March 1727]

† **† † *[5]

In *European* characters and *English* thus;

The high and mighty prince EGROEGO[6] born to the most puissant[7] empire of the *East*,

Unto STELLA, the most resplendent glory of the *Western* hemisphere, sendeth health and happiness.

BRIGHTEST PRINCESS,

That invincible hero, the MAN MOUNTAIN,[8] fortunately arriving at our coasts some years ago, delivered us from ruin by conquering the fleets and armies of our enemies, and gave us hopes of a durable peace and happiness. But now the martial people of *Blefuscu*, encouraged from his absence, have renewed the war,[9] to revenge upon us the loss and disgrace they suffered by our valiant champion.

The fame of your superexcellent person and virtue, and the huge esteem which that great general has for you, urged us in this our second distress to sue for[1] your favor. In order to which we have sent our able and trusty Nardac[2] KOORBNILOB,[3] requesting, that if our general does yet tread upon the terrestrial globe, you, in compassion for us, would prevail upon him to take another voyage for our deliverance.

And, lest any apprehensions of famine amongst us, should render Nardac MOUNTAIN averse to the undertaking, we signify to you, that we have stored our folds, our coops, our granaries, and cellars with plenty of provision for a long supply of the wastes to be made by his capacious stomach.

And furthermore, because as we hear you are not so well as we could wish, we beg you would complete our happiness by venturing your most valuable person along with him into our country; where, by the salubrity[4] of our finer air and diet, you will soon recover your health and stomach.[5]

In full assurance of your complying goodness, we have sent you some provision for your voyage, and we shall with impatience wait for your safe arrival in our kingdom. Most illustrious lady, farewell. Prince EGROEGO.

Dated the 11th day of the 6th Moon, in the
2001 year of the *Lilliputian* era.

END OF *GULLIVER'S TRAVELS* AND ITS TIME

A MODEST PROPOSAL   In a letter written to Alexander Pope in August 1729, Swift described the condition of Ireland: "There have been three terrible years' dearth of corn [i.e., wheat], and every place strewn with beggars, but dearths are common in better climates, and our evils lie much deeper. Imagine a nation the two-thirds of whose revenues are spent out of it, and who are not permitted [by Britain] to trade with the other third, and where the pride of

---

4. Esther Johnson (1681–1728), Swift's beloved and most valued friend.
5. Here we have a parcel of characters formed at random, by way of the address in the *Lilliputian* tongue [Swift's note].
6. I.e., O'George (an anagram).
7. Powerful.
8. Gulliver, later also called "that great general."
9. Spain had besieged Gibraltar in February.

1. Ask for.
2. The "highest title of honor" among the Lilliputians; see "A Voyage to Lilliput," chapter 5, in which Gulliver is created a Nardac for his service to the nation.
3. An anagram: Bolinbrook, i.e., the Tory politician.
4. Healthfulness.
5. Appetite. Stella had been in declining health for some time. Swift's playful letter was obviously meant to cheer her.

the women will not suffer them to wear their own manufactures even where they excel what come from abroad." Two months later, Swift published what is today his most famous political essay: A Modest Proposal. Swift had previously written a dozen or more tracts to help free Ireland from its desperate social, economic, and political plight. In A Modest Proposal, however, Swift wielded two favorite weapons from his armory of satirical techniques—irony and parody—with devastating effect. In creating a persona who combines a mixture of calculating rationality and misplaced compassion but does not comprehend the enormity of his plan, Swift aims his satire not only at the political arithmeticians (forerunners of today's social engineers and economic planners) and the exploitative and predatory absentee landlords living in England but at the Irish people as well. Believing Ireland to be its own worst enemy, Swift delineates a program of commercial cannibalism that institutionalizes the country's own self-destructive tendencies. Preserving a nation through the consumption of its children is self-defeating, however demographically logical, because it undermines the understanding of humanity upon which civil society depends. Swift thus highlights the futility of financial improvement unaccompanied by social and moral reform.

A Modest Proposal

FOR PREVENTING THE CHILDREN OF POOR PEOPLE IN IRELAND
FROM BEING A BURDEN TO THEIR PARENTS OR COUNTRY,
AND FOR MAKING THEM BENEFICIAL TO THE PUBLIC

It is a melancholy object to those who walk through this great town,[1] or travel in the country, when they see the streets, the roads, and cabin doors crowded with beggars of the female sex, followed by three, four, or six children, *all in rags,* and importuning every passenger[2] for an alms. These mothers, instead of being able to work for their honest livelihood, are forced to employ all their time in strolling,[3] to beg sustenance for their helpless infants, who, as they grow up, either turn thieves for want of work, or leave their dear native country to fight for the Pretender in Spain,[4] or sell themselves to the Barbados.[5]

I think it is agreed by all parties that this prodigious number of children, in the arms, or on the backs, or at the heels of their mothers, and frequently of their fathers, is in the present deplorable state of the kingdom a very great additional grievance; and therefore whoever could find out a fair, cheap, and easy method of making these children sound, useful members of the commonwealth would deserve so well of the public, as to have his statue set up for a preserver of the nation.

But my intention is very far from being confined to provide only for the children of professed beggars; it is of a much greater extent, and shall take in the whole number of infants at a certain age who are born of parents in effect as little able to support them as those who demand our charity in the streets.

As to my own part, having turned my thoughts for many years upon this important subject, and maturely weighed the several schemes of other projectors,[6] I have always found them grossly mistaken in their computation. It is true a child just dropped from its dam may be supported by her milk for a solar year with little other nourishment, at most not above the value of two shillings, which the mother may

1. Dublin.
2. Passerby.
3. Wandering aimlessly.
4. Catholic Ireland was loyal to the Pretender, James Francis Edward Stuart (1688–1766), son of James II, who was deposed from the English throne in 1688 because of his

Catholicism. Religious ties also made the Irish ideal recruits for France and Spain in their wars against England.
5. The impoverished Irish emigrated to the West Indies in large numbers, buying their passage by selling their labor in advance to the sugar plantations.
6. Devisers of new "projects," usually of doubtful value.

certainly get, or the value in scraps, by her lawful occupation of begging, and it is exactly at one year old that I propose to provide for them, in such a manner as instead of being a charge upon their parents or the parish, or wanting food and raiment for the rest of their lives, they shall, on the contrary, contribute to the feeding and partly to the clothing of many thousands.

There is likewise another great advantage in my scheme, that it will prevent those voluntary abortions, and that horrid practice of women murdering their bastard children, alas, too frequent among us, sacrificing the poor innocent babes, I doubt[7] more to avoid the expense than the shame, which would move tears and pity in the most savage and inhuman breast.

The number of souls in this kingdom being usually reckoned one million and a half, of these I calculate there may be about two hundred thousand couple whose wives are breeders, from which number I subtract thirty thousand couple who are able to maintain their own children, although I apprehend there cannot be so many under the present distresses of the kingdom; but this being granted, there will remain an hundred and seventy thousand breeders. I again subtract fifty thousand for those women who miscarry, or whose children die by accident or disease within the year.[8] There only remain a hundred and twenty thousand children of poor parents annually born: the question therefore is how this number shall be reared and provided for, which, as I have already said, under the present situation of affairs, is utterly impossible by all the methods hitherto proposed: for we can neither employ them in handicraft, or agriculture; we neither build houses (I mean in the country) nor cultivate land;[9] they can very seldom pick up a livelihood by stealing till they arrive at six years old, except where they are of towardly parts,[1] although, I confess they learn the rudiments much earlier, during which time they can however be properly looked upon only as *probationers*, as I have been informed by a principal gentleman in the County of Cavan, who protested to me, that he never knew above one or two instances under the age of six, even in a part of the kingdom so renowned for the quickest proficiency in that art.

I am assured by our merchants that a boy or a girl, before twelve years old, is no salable commodity, and even when they come to this age, they will not yield above three pounds, or three pounds and half-a-crown at most on the Exchange,[2] which cannot turn to account[3] either to the parents or kingdom, the charge of nutriment and rags having been at least four times that value.

I shall now therefore humbly propose my own thoughts, which I hope will not be liable to the least objection.

I have been assured by a very knowing American[4] of my acquaintance in London, that a young healthy child well nursed is at a year old a most delicious, nourishing, and wholesome food, whether stewed, roasted, baked, or boiled, and I make no doubt that it will equally serve in a fricassee or ragout.[5]

I do therefore humbly offer it to public consideration, that of the hundred and twenty thousand children already computed, twenty thousand may be reserved for

---

7. Believe.
8. It is telling that Swift here projects an infant mortality rate of approximately 30 percent in a child's first year.
9. The vast estates of English absentee landlords, and British retention of Irish land for grazing sheep, rather than agriculture, contributed to Ireland's poverty.
1. Precocious.
2. At the market.

3. Be of value.
4. Some of the British believed that the harsh living conditions in America made the colonists adopt "savage" practices.
5. A fricassee is meat stewed in gravy, a ragout is a highly seasoned French stew; such foreign dishes were becoming increasingly popular with fashionable Britons.

breed, whereof only one fourth part to be males, which is more than we allow to sheep, black cattle, or swine, and my reason is that these children are seldom the fruits of marriage, a circumstance not much regarded by our savages, therefore one male will be sufficient to serve four females. That the remaining hundred thousand may at a year old be offered in sale to the persons of quality and fortune through the kingdom, always advising the mother to let them suck plentifully in the last month, so as to render them plump, and fat for a good table. A child will make two dishes at an entertainment for friends, and when the family dines alone, the fore or hind quarter will make a reasonable dish, and seasoned with a little pepper or salt will be very good boiled on the fourth day, especially in winter.

I have reckoned upon a medium, that a child just born will weigh 12 pounds, and in a solar year if tolerably nursed increaseth to 28 pounds.

I grant this food will be somewhat dear,[6] and therefore very proper for landlords, who, as they have already devoured most of the parents, seem to have the best title to the children.

Infants' flesh will be in season throughout the year, but more plentiful in March, and a little before and after, for we are told by a grave author,[7] an eminent French physician, that fish being a prolific diet,[8] there are more children born in Roman Catholic countries about nine months after Lent than at any other season; therefore reckoning a year after Lent, the markets will be more glutted than usual, because the number of Popish infants is at least three to one in this kingdom, and therefore it will have one other collateral advantage by lessening the number of Papists among us.

I have already computed the charge of nursing a beggar's child (in which list I reckon all cottagers,[9] laborers, and four-fifths of the farmers) to be about two shillings *per annum*, rags included, and I believe no gentleman would repine to give ten shillings for the carcass of a good fat child, which, as I have said, will make four dishes of excellent nutritive meat, when he hath only some particular friend or his own family to dine with him. Thus the Squire will learn to be a good landlord and grow popular among his tenants, the mother will have eight shillings net profit, and be fit for work till she produces another child.

Those who are more thrifty (as I must confess the times require) may flay the carcass, the skin of which, artificially[1] dressed, will make admirable gloves for ladies and summer boots for fine gentlemen.

As to our City of Dublin, shambles[2] may be appointed for this purpose in the most convenient parts of it, and butchers we may be assured will not be wanting, although I rather recommend buying the children alive and dressing them hot from the knife,[3] as we do roasting pigs.

A very worthy person, a true lover of his country, and whose virtues I highly esteem, was lately pleased, in discoursing on this matter, to offer a refinement upon my scheme. He said that many gentlemen of this kingdom, having of late destroyed their deer, he conceived that the want of venison might be well supplied by the bodies of young lads and maidens, not exceeding fourteen years of age nor under twelve, so great a number of both sexes in every country being now ready to starve for want of work and service;[4] and these to be disposed of by their parents if alive, or

---

6. Both expensive and, of course, beloved.
7. The satirist François Rabelais, in *Gargantua and Pantagruel* (1532–1564), Book 5, ch. 29.
8. One increasing fertility.
9. Tenant farmers.

1. Skillfully.
2. Places where meat is slaughtered and sold.
3. Skinning and gutting them immediately after killing.
4. Positions as servants.

otherwise by their nearest relations. But with due deference to so excellent a friend and so deserving a patriot, I cannot be altogether in his sentiments; for as to the males, my American acquaintance assured me from frequent experience that their flesh was generally tough and lean, like that of our schoolboys, by continual exercise, and their taste disagreeable, and to fatten them would not answer the charge. Then as to the females, it would, I think with humble submission, be a loss to the public, because they soon would become breeders themselves; and besides, it is not improbable that some scrupulous people might be apt to censure such a practice (although indeed very unjustly) as a little bordering upon cruelty which, I confess, hath always been with me the strongest objection against any project, however so well intended.

But in order to justify my friend, he confessed that this expedient was put into his head by the famous Psalmanazar,[5] a native of the island Formosa, who came from thence to London above twenty years ago, and in conversation told my friend that in his country when any young person happened to be put to death, the executioner sold the carcass to persons of quality as a prime dainty, and that, in his time, the body of a plump girl of fifteen, who was crucified for an attempt to poison the emperor, was sold to his Imperial Majesty's Prime Minister of State[6] and other great Mandarins of the Court, in joints from the gibbet,[7] at four hundred crowns. Neither indeed can I deny that if the same use were made of several plump young girls in this town, who, without one single groat[8] to their fortunes, cannot stir abroad without a chair,[9] and appear at the playhouse and assemblies[1] in foreign fineries which they never will pay for, the kingdom would not be the worse.

Some persons of a desponding spirit are in great concern about that vast number of poor people who are aged, diseased, or maimed, and I have been desired to employ my thoughts what course may be taken to ease the nation of so grievous an encumbrance. But I am not in the least pain upon that matter, because it is very well known that they are every day dying, and rotting, by cold, and famine, and filth, and vermin, as fast as can be reasonably expected. And as to the younger laborers they are now in almost as hopeful a condition. They cannot get work, and consequently pine away for want of nourishment, to a degree that if at any time they are accidentally hired to common labor, they have not strength to perform it; and thus the country and themselves are in a fair way of being soon delivered from the evils to come.

I have too long digressed, and therefore shall return to my subject. I think the advantages by the proposal which I have made are obvious and many, as well as of the highest importance.

For first, as I have already observed, it would greatly lessen the number of Papists, with whom we are yearly overrun, being the principal breeders of the nation as well as our most dangerous enemies, and who stay at home on purpose with a design to deliver the kingdom to the Pretender, hoping to take their advantage by the absence of so many good Protestants, who have chosen rather to leave their country than stay at home, and pay tithes against their conscience, to an Episcopal curate.[2]

---

5. George Psalmanazar, a Frenchman who pretended to be from Formosa (now Taiwan), wrote a book about its customs, the *Historical and Geographical Description of Formosa* (1704), which was quickly exposed as fraudulent.
6. A reference to Robert Walpole.
7. Gallows.

8. Silver coin (issued 1351–1662) equal to four pennies.
9. A sedan chair, carried by two men.
1. Social gatherings.
2. The tithes, or ecclesiastical taxes, that supported the Church were avoided by the many "good" Protestants who absented themselves from Ireland on the grounds—spurious, Swift implies—of "conscience."

Secondly, the poorer tenants will have something valuable of their own, which by law may be made liable to distress,[3] and help to pay their landlords rent, their corn and cattle being already seized, and *money a thing unknown*.

Thirdly, whereas the maintenance of a hundred thousand children from two years old and upwards cannot be computed at less than ten shillings a piece *per annum*, the nation's stock will be thereby increased fifty thousand pounds *per annum*, besides the profit of a new dish introduced to the tables of all gentlemen of fortune in the kingdom who have any refinement in taste, and the money will circulate among ourselves, the goods being entirely of our own growth and manufacture.

Fourthly, the constant breeders, besides the gain of eight shillings sterling *per annum* by the sale of their children, will be rid of the charge of maintaining them after the first year.

Fifthly, this food would likewise bring great custom to taverns, where the vintners will certainly be so prudent as to procure the best receipts[4] for dressing it to perfection, and consequently have their houses frequented by all the fine gentlemen, who justly value themselves upon their knowledge in good eating; and a skillful cook who understands how to oblige his guests will contrive to make it as expensive as they please.

Sixthly, this would be a great inducement to marriage, which all wise nations have either encouraged by rewards or enforced by laws and penalties. It would increase the care and tenderness of mothers toward their children, when they were sure of a settlement for life to the poor babes, provided in some sort by the public to their annual profit instead of expense. We should see an honest emulation[5] among the married women, which of them could bring the fattest child to the market; men would become as fond of their wives, during the time of their pregnancy, as they are now of their mares in foal, their cows in calf, or sows when they are ready to farrow,[6] nor offer to beat or kick them (as it is too frequent a practice) for fear of a miscarriage.

Many other advantages might be enumerated: for instance, the addition of some thousand carcasses in our exportation of barreled beef;[7] the propagation of swine's flesh, and improvement in the art of making good bacon, so much wanted among us by the great destruction of pigs, too frequent at our tables, which are no way comparable in taste or magnificence to a well-grown, fat yearling child, which roasted whole will make a considerable figure at a Lord Mayor's feast or any other public entertainment. But this and many others I omit, being studious of brevity.

Supposing that one thousand families in this city would be constant customers for infants' flesh, besides others who might have it at merry-meetings, particularly weddings and christenings, I compute that Dublin would take off annually about twenty thousand carcasses, and the rest of the kingdom (where probably they will be sold somewhat cheaper) the remaining eighty thousand.

I can think of no one objection that will possibly be raised against this proposal, unless it should be urged that the number of people will be thereby much lessened in the kingdom. This I freely own, and was indeed one principal design in offering it to the world. I desire the reader will observe that I calculate my remedy *for this one individual Kingdom of Ireland, and for no other that ever was, is, or, I think, ever can be upon earth*. Therefore let no man talk to me of other expedients:[8] *Of taxing our absentees at*

---

3. Seizure for debt.
4. Recipes.
5. Competition.
6. Give birth.
7. Pickled beef.

8. The kind of proposals Swift himself had made in earnest for remedying the poverty of Ireland; his *Proposal for the Universal Use of Irish Manufacture in Cloaths and Furniture . . . Utterly Rejecting and Renouncing Everything Wearable that Comes from England* (1720) is a typical example.

five shillings a pound; of using neither clothes nor household furniture, except what is of our own growth and manufacture; of utterly rejecting the materials and instruments that promote foreign luxury; of curing the expensiveness of pride, vanity, idleness, and gaming in our women; of introducing a vein of parsimony, prudence, and temperance; of learning to love our country, wherein we differ even from LAPLANDERS, *and the inhabitants of* TOPINAMBOO;[9] *of quitting our animosities and factions, nor act any longer like the Jews, who were murdering one another at the very moment their city was taken;[1] of being a little cautious not to sell our country and consciences for nothing; of teaching landlords to have at least one degree of mercy toward their tenants. Lastly, of putting a spirit of honesty, industry, and skill into our shopkeepers, who, if a resolution could now be taken to buy our native goods, would immediately unite to cheat and exact upon us in the price, the measure, and the goodness, nor could ever yet be brought to make one fair proposal of just dealing, though often and earnestly invited to it.*

Therefore I repeat, let no man talk to me of these and the like expedients till he hath at least some glimpse of hope that there will ever be some hearty and sincere attempt to put them in practice.

But as to myself, having been wearied out for many years with offering vain, idle, visionary thoughts, and at length utterly despairing of success, I fortunately fell upon this proposal, which as it is wholly new, so it hath something solid and real, of no expense and little trouble, full in our own power, and whereby we can incur no danger in *disobliging* ENGLAND. For this kind of commodity will not bear exportation, the flesh being of too tender a consistence, to admit a long continuance in salt, *although perhaps I could name a country[2] which would be glad to eat up our whole nation without it.*

After all I am not so violently bent upon my own opinion as to reject any offer proposed by wise men, which shall be found equally innocent, cheap, easy, and effectual. But before something of that kind shall be advanced in contradiction to my scheme and offering a better, I desire the author or authors will be pleased maturely to consider two points. First, as things now stand, how they will be able to find food and raiment for an hundred thousand useless mouths and backs. And secondly, there being a round million of creatures in human figure throughout this kingdom whose whole subsistence put into a common stock would leave them in debt two millions of pounds sterling; adding those who are beggars by profession to the bulk of farmers, cottagers, and laborers with their wives and children, who are beggars in effect; I desire those politicians who dislike my overture, and may perhaps be so bold to attempt an answer, that they will first ask the parents of these mortals whether they would not at this day think it a great happiness to have been sold for food at a year old, in the manner I prescribe, and thereby have avoided such a perpetual scene of misfortunes as they have since gone through, by the oppression of landlords, the impossibility of paying rent without money or trade, the want of common sustenance, with neither house nor clothes to cover them from the inclemencies of the weather, and the most inevitable prospect of entailing[3] the like or greater miseries upon their breed forever.

I profess in the sincerity of my heart that I have not the least personal interest in endeavoring to promote this necessary work, having no other motive than the *public good of my country, by advancing our trade, providing for infants, relieving the poor, and*

---

9. The inhabitants of the most hostile environments— the frozen north or the Brazilian jungle—love their countries more than the Irish.

1. According to one historian, when Jerusalem was besieged and captured by the Emperor Titus in 70 C.E., factional fighting inside the city contributed to its destruction.

2. England.

3. Bequeathing.

giving some pleasure to the rich. I have no children by which I can propose to get a single penny; the youngest being nine years old, and my wife past child-bearing.
1729   1729

❖ *A MODEST PROPOSAL* AND ITS TIME ❖
William Petty: from *Political Arithmetic*[1]

from Chapter 4. How to enable the people of England and Ireland to spend 5 millions worth of commodities more than now; and how to raise the present value of the lands and goods of Ireland from 2 to 3.

This is to be done: 1. By bringing one million of the present 1,300 thousand of the people out of Ireland into England, though at the expense of a million of money. 2. That the remaining three hundred thousand left behind be all herdsmen and dairy women, servants to the owners of the lands and stock transplanted into England, all aged between 16 and 60 years, and to quit all other trades, but that of cattle, and to import nothing but salt and tobacco. Neglecting all housing, but what is fittest for these 300 thousand people, and this trade, though to the loss of 2 millions-worth of houses. Now if a million of people be worth 70 pounds per head one with another, the whole are worth 70 millions; then the said people, reckoned as money at 5 percent interest, will yield 3 millions and a half per annum. 3. And if Ireland send into England 1 million and a half worth of effects (receiving nothing back), then England will be enriched from Ireland, and otherwise, 5 millions per annum more than now, which, at 20 year's purchase, is worth one hundred millions of pounds sterling, as was propounded. * * *

POSTSCRIPT

If in this jealous age this essay should be taxed of an evil design to waste and dispeople Ireland, we say that the author of it intends not to be *Felo de se*,[2] and propound something quite contrary, by saying it is naturally possible in about 25 years to double the inhabitants of Great Britain and Ireland and make the people full as many as the territory of those kingdoms can with tolerable labor afford a competent livelihood unto, which I prove thus, (viz.)

1. The sixth part of the people are teeming women[3] of between 18 and 44 years old.
2. It is found by observation that but 1/3 part or between 30 and 40 of the teeming women are married.
3. That a teeming woman, at a medium, bears a child every two years and a half.
4. That in mankind at London, there are 14 males for 13 females, and because males are prolific[4] 40 years, and females but 25, there are in effect 560 males for 325 females.

1. William Petty (1623–1687) represents the type of Englishman Swift had in mind in his implicit criticism of English rapaciousness in Ireland in A Modest Proposal. Petty, the son of a London clothier and weaver, was an extraordinary scholar and anatomist, and a charter member of the Royal Society. Appointed physician-general to the parliamentary army in Ireland in 1652, he obtained considerable property holdings in Ireland through his additional task of surveying lands forfeited by Roman Catholics. His newfound fortune enabled him to devote his attention to his economic writings and to the Royal Society in London, though he was less than solicitous of his tenants in Ireland.

Swift's friendship with Petty's children, Lord Shelburne and Lady Kerry, did not prevent him parodying Petty's *Political Arithmetic* (1691) in *A Modest Proposal*. Petty's suggestion that Ireland be turned into one huge farm to supply England by removing all the Irish was only one of many "political arithmetic" projects published during the Restoration and 18th century, reflecting English interest in "scientific" programs for social "improvement."
2. Suicidal; literally, "felon of (one)self."
3. Women capable of breeding.
4. Capable of procreation.

5. That out of the mass of mankind there dies one out of 30 per annum.
6. That at Paris, where the christenings and the births are the same in number, the christenings are above 18,000 per annum, and consequently the births at London, which far exceed the christenings there, cannot be less than 19,000 where the burials are above 23,000.

As for Example

Of 600 people, the sixth part (viz. 100) are teeming women, which (if they were all married) might bear 40 children per annum (viz.) 20 more than do die out of 600, at the rate of one out of 30; and consequently in 16 years the increase will be 320, making the whole 920. And by the same reason, in the next 9 years, the said 920 will be 280 more, in all 1,200, viz. double of the original number of 600.

Upon these principles, if there be about 19,000 births per annum at London, the number of the married teeming women must be above 38,000; and of the whole stock of the teeming women must be above 114,000, and of the whole people six times as many viz. 684,000; which agrees well enough with 696,000, which they have been elsewhere computed to be.

To conclude it is naturally possible, that all teeming women may be married, since there are in effect 560 males to 325 females; and since Great Britain and Ireland can with moderate labor, food, and other necessaries to near double the present people or to about 20 millions of heads, as shall when occasion requires it, be demonstrated. * * *

1691

END OF *A MODEST PROPOSAL* AND ITS TIME

Alexander Pope
1688–1744

William Hoare, *Sketch of Alexander Pope*.

"The life of a wit is a warfare upon earth; and the present spirit of the learned world is such, that to serve it . . . one must have the constancy of a martyr, and a resolution to suffer for its sake." Though still in his twenties when he wrote these words, Alexander Pope knew from painful experience their bitter truth. As a Roman Catholic, he could not vote, inherit or purchase land, attend a "public" school or a university, live within ten miles of London, hold public office, or openly practice his religion. He was obliged to pay double taxes. Such civil disenfranchisement barred him from receiving the literary patronage most talented writers depended upon for their livelihood. No wonder Pope wrote of "certain laws, by suff'rers thought unjust," by which he was "denied all posts of profit or of trust" (*Imitations of Horace*, Epistle 2.2.60–61). Despite whatever patriotism or loyalty to their country they may have felt, Catholics were widely regarded as alien and seditious. Pope's resentment of this attitude is evident in the *Epistle to Bathurst* (1733) when he calls the London Monument, which bears an inscription blaming the Great Fire of 1666 on a Papist conspiracy to destroy the capital, "a tall bully" who "lies."

Religion was not Pope's greatest impediment to success, however. When he was twelve, he contracted tuberculosis of the spine (Pott's disease), a condition that stunted his growth and left him humpbacked and deformed. At four feet six inches, he could not sit at an ordinary table with other adults unless his seat was raised. His constitution was so weakened that he frequently suffered from migraine headaches, asthma, nausea, and fevers. For much of his life, he could not hold his body upright without the help of stays, and he was unable to bathe, dress or undress, rise or go to bed by himself. Pope summarized his condition most succinctly in *An Epistle to Dr. Arbuthnot* (1735), when he wrote of "this long disease, my life."

Pope was born in London in 1688, the only child of his parents' marriage. Pope's *Epistle to Dr. Arbuthnot* includes a tribute to his father's equanimity and goodness; his mother is praised as "a noble wife." At the age of nine, Pope was sent to a school for Catholic boys but was expelled in his first year for writing a satire on his schoolmaster—a sign of things to come. When he was twelve, his family moved from the environs of London to Binfield, in the royal forest of Windsor; the effect of Windsor's "green retreats" on Pope's youthful imagination is apparent in the *Pastorals* (1709) and in *Windsor-Forest* (1713). At Binfield, he began to teach himself Greek and Latin with great determination, though the rigors of his studies made his sickness worse. Refusing to yield to his infirmity, he began, at fifteen, to journey into London to learn French and Italian. Pope spoke of these adolescent years as his "great reading period" when he "went through all the best critics, almost all the English, French, and Latin poets of any name . . . [and] Homer and some other of the Greek poets in the original." During this time Pope met his great friend John Caryll, at whose request he would write *The Rape of the Lock*, and Martha Blount, who was to become his lifelong intimate companion and to whom he addressed *Of the Characters of Women: An Epistle to a Lady* (1735).

Pope claimed that "as yet a child . . . I lisp'd in numbers [i.e., meter]." Certainly he was a precocious poet and his early efforts were encouraged by many, including the playwrights William Wycherley and William Congreve, to whom Pope dedicated his *Iliad* (1715–1720). If Pope had encouraging friends, he soon had detracting enemies as well. His first publication, the *Pastorals* (1709), occasioned a rivalry between Pope's Tory supporters and the Whig partisans of Ambrose Philips, whose *Pastorals* appeared in the same volume. Pope's next important poem, *An Essay on Criticism* (1711), brought a barrage of vituperative abuse from the critic John Dennis, who called Pope "a hunch-backed toad" and argued that his deformity was merely the outward sign of mental and moral ugliness. Undaunted, Pope continued to publish: the *Messiah* (1712), *The Rape of the Lock* (1712, substantially enlarged in 1714), *Windsor-Forest* (1713), and *The Temple of Fame* (1715). With the publication of his *Works* (1717), Pope had proved himself master of a dazzling repertoire of poetic modes: pastoral and georgic, didactic, eclogue, mock-epic, allegorical dream-vision, heroic, and elegiac. No other living poet could display such dazzling versatility and comprehensive control.

There was still another area, however, in which Pope was proving the breathtaking range of his poetic gifts. Between 1713 and 1726, Pope devoted much of his creative energy to translating Homer's epics, the *Iliad* and the *Odyssey*, into heroic couplets. "Pope's Homer" not only won for him financial independence so that he could "live and thrive, / Indebted to no Prince or Peer alive" (*Imitations of Horace, Epistle 2.2*), it also confirmed his reputation as the presiding poetic genius of his time. While he was working on the *Odyssey*, Pope produced a six-volume edition of Shakespeare's works (1725), which, though it contained some valuable insights, was very much an amateur effort. When Lewis Theobald, the leading Shakespeare scholar of the time, rather pedantically highlighted Pope's many editorial shortcomings in *Shakespeare Restored, or, a Specimen of the Many Errors Committed . . . by Mr. Pope* (1726), Pope's revenge was not far off: two years later, he published *The Dunciad*, a savagely satirical assault on Pope's critics and the bankrupt cultural values they embodied.

In the seventeen years between Dennis's attack and the publication of *The Dunciad*, Pope's appearance, talent, and character had been assailed in print more than fifty times. His enemies accused him of being obscene, seditious, duplicitous, venal, vain, blasphemous, libelous, ignorant, and a bad poet. Theobald's rebuke was the last straw, perhaps because it was the most justified. Pope's style of comic social criticism owed much to his membership in the Scriblerus Club with John Gay, Jonathan Swift, Dr. John Arbuthnot, Thomas Parnell, and Robert Harley, Earl of Oxford. The Scriblerians originally planned to produce a series entitled *The Works of the Unlearned*; although the group regularly met only for a short while in 1714, its members remained in contact. In addition to *The Dunciad*, the fruit of their exchanges may be seen in Swift's *Gulliver's Travels* (1726), Gay's *The Beggar's Opera* (1728), Pope's *Peri Bathous: Or, the Art of Sinking in Poetry* (1728), and Arbuthnot's and Pope's *Memoirs of the Extraordinary Life, Works, and Discoveries of Martinus Scriblerus* (1741).

An *Essay on Man* (1733–1734) showcased Pope's talent for philosophical poetry. This work and four *Moral Essays* (1731–1735) were originally intended to form part of a long poetic sequence on the nature of humankind that Pope had hoped would be his greatest work, though the project was abandoned. Between 1733 and 1738, Pope published more than a dozen *Imitations of Horace*. In these loose adaptations of Horace's epistles and satires, Pope invested his modern social criticism with the classical authority of a revered Roman poet. The *Moral Essays*, or "Epistles to Several Persons" as Pope called them, also show Pope assuming the mantle of Horace by using the familiar epistle as a vehicle for social commentary. Pope's Horatian poems are his most mature, elegant, and self-assured works.

In 1737, he published an authorized version of his letters, which he doctored to improve his reputation. His last years were a time of retirement at his villa at Twickenham, famous for its grotto of "Friendship and Liberty" and for the five-acre landscape garden Pope had designed. In *The New Dunciad* (1742), Pope shifted his attack from hack writers and low culture to all forms of hypocrisy and pretense. It was his final triumph. He worked with William Warburton on a new edition of his *Works* (1751), even as his many illnesses became still more overwhelming. Though he was a self-confessed "fool to Fame" (*Arbuthnot*), he told those gathered around his deathbed: "There is nothing that is meritorious but virtue and friendship." He was, as his enemies claimed, bellicose, self-indulgent, and self-aggrandizing. He was morally and physically courageous and had a great gift for friendship. Although it is no longer fashionable to call the first half of the eighteenth century the "Age of Pope," many of his contemporaries saw him as the predominant literary genius of his time. Today, most literary historians agree that the greatest English poet between John Milton and William Wordsworth was Alexander Pope.

For additional resources on Pope, go to *The Longman Anthology of British Literature* Web site at www.myliteraturekit.com.

AN ESSAY ON CRITICISM   Pope was only twenty-one years old when he wrote *An Essay on Criticism*, which was published anonymously in 1711. This aesthetic manifesto in heroic couplets is written in the tradition of Horace's *Ars Poetica* (c. 19 B.C.E.), Boileau's *Art poétique* (1674), and other verse essays delineating poetic principles and practices. Pope's chief contributions to the genre are his ringing epigrams and the playful ease with which he satirizes contemporary critics who lack genuine poetic understanding. *The Essay on Criticism* is divided into three parts: the first examines the rules of taste, their relationship to Nature, and the authority of classical authors. The second (lines 201–559) considers the impediments preventing the attainment of the classical ideals outlined in part one. In the third part, Pope proposes an aesthetic and moral reformation to restore wit, sense, and taste to their former glory. While acknowledging the importance of precepts, Pope asserts the primacy of poetic genius and the power of imagination.

An Essay on Criticism

'Tis hard to say, if greater want of skill
Appear in writing or in judging ill;
But, of the two, less dang'rous is th' offense
To tire our patience, than mislead our sense:°   *judgment*
5 Some few in that, but numbers err in this,
Ten censure wrong for one who writes amiss;
A fool might once himself alone expose;
Now one in verse makes many more in prose.[1]
  'Tis with our judgments as our watches, none
10 Go just alike, yet each believes his own.
In poets as true genius is but rare,
True taste as seldom is the critic's share;
Both must alike from Heav'n derive their light,
These born to judge, as well as those to write.
15 Let such teach others who themselves excel,
And censure freely who have written well.
Authors are partial to their wit,[2] 'tis true,
But are not critics to their judgment too?
  Yet if we look more closely, we shall find
20 Most have the seeds of judgment in their mind;
Nature affords at least a glimm'ring light;
The lines, though touched but faintly, are drawn right.
But as the slightest sketch, if justly traced, ⎤
Is by ill coloring but the more disgraced,   ⎬
25 So by false learning is good sense defaced. ⎦
Some are bewildered in the maze of schools,[3]
And some made coxcombs[4] Nature meant but fools.
In search of wit these lose their common sense,
And then turn critics in their own defense:
30 Each burns alike, who can, or cannot write,
Or° with a rival's or an eunuch's spite.[5]   *either*
All fools have still° an itching to deride,[6]   *continually*
And fain° would be upon the laughing side.   *gladly*
If Mævius scribble in Apollo's spite,[7]
35 There are, who judge still worse than he can write.
  Some have at first for wits,° then poets passed,   *intellectuals*
Turned critics next, and proved plain fools at last.
Some neither can for wits nor critics pass,
As heavy mules are neither horse nor ass.
40 Those half-learned witlings, num'rous in our isle,
As half-formed insects on the banks of Nile;
Unfinished things, one knows not what to call,

1. I.e., many bad critics respond to one bad poet.
2. Both their writings and their (fancied) ability to write
well.
3. Schools of criticism.
4. Conceited show-offs.

5. I.e., they either seek to compete, or, knowing them
selves incapable, criticize out of envy.
6. The fool's perpetual itching suggests disease.
7. Maevius, a third-rate Roman poet, is set against
Apollo, patron of good poetry.

Their generation's so equivocal:[8]
To tell° 'em, would a hundred tongues require,   count
45   Or one vain wit's, that might a hundred tire.
    But you who seek to give and merit° fame,   deserve
And justly bear a critic's noble name,
Be sure yourself and your own reach° to know,   ability
How far your genius, taste, and learning go;
50   Launch not beyond your depth, but be discrete,
And mark° that point where sense and dullness meet.   note
    Nature to all things fixed the limits fit,
And wisely curbed proud man's pretending° wit.   aspiring
As on the land while here the ocean gains,
55   In other parts it leaves wide sandy plains;
Thus in the soul while memory prevails,
The solid pow'r of understanding fails;
Where beams of warm imagination play,
The memory's soft figures melt away.
60   One science only will one genius fit;[9]
So vast is art, so narrow human wit:°   understanding
Not only bounded to peculiar° arts,   particular
But oft in those confined to single parts.
Like kings we lose the conquests gained before,
65   By vain ambition still to make them more;
Each might his sev'ral province well command,
Would all but stoop to what they understand.
    First follow Nature, and your judgment frame
By her just standard, which is still° the same: always
70   Unerring Nature, still divinely bright,
One clear, unchanged, and universal light,
Life, force, and beauty, must to all impart,
At once the source, and end, and test of art.
Art from that fund each just supply provides,
75   Works without show,[1] and without pomp presides:
In some fair body thus th' informing soul[2]
With spirits feeds, with vigor fills the whole,
Each motion guides, and ev'ry nerve sustains;
Itself unseen, but in th' effects remains.
80   Some, to whom Heav'n in wit has been profuse,
Want° as much more, to turn it to its use;   need
For wit and judgment often are at strife,
Though meant each other's aid, like man and wife.
'Tis more to guide than spur the Muse's steed;[3]
85   Restrain his fury, than provoke his speed;

8. Like the generation of insects on the banks of the Nile, thought to occur spontaneously, through the action of sun on mud.
9. The artist can hope to succeed in one subject area or object of study.

1. The suggestion that art should mask its presence came from Horace.
2. The force that animates.
3. Pegasus, the winged horse.

The winged courser,° like a gen'rous horse,   *swift horse*
Shows most true mettle° when you check his course.   *spirit*
　　Those Rules of old discovered, not devised,
Are Nature still, but Nature methodized;
90 Nature, like liberty, is but restrained
By the same laws which first herself ordained.
　　Hear how learn'd Greece her useful rules indites,°   *composes*
When to repress, and when indulge our flights:
High on Parnassus'[4] top her sons she showed,
95 And pointed out° those arduous paths they trod;   *appointed*
Held from afar, aloft, th' immortal prize,
And urged the rest by equal steps to rise.
Just precepts thus from great examples giv'n,
She drew from them what they derived from Heav'n.
100 The gen'rous critic fanne'd the poet's fire,
And taught the world, with reason to admire.
Then criticism the Muses' handmaid proved,
To dress her charms,[5] and make her more belov'd;
But following wits from that intention strayed;
105 Who could not win the mistress, wooed the maid;
Against the poets their own arms they turned,
Sure to hate most the men from whom they learned.
So modern 'pothecaries,° taught the art   *druggists*
By doctor's bills° to play the doctor's part,   *prescriptions*
110 Bold in the practice of mistaken° rules,   *misunderstood*
Prescribe, apply, and call their masters fools.
Some on the leaves of ancient authors prey,[6]
Nor time nor moths e'er spoiled so much as they.
Some drily plain, without invention's° aid,   *imagination's*
115 Write dull receipts° how poems may be made.   *recipes*
These leave the sense, their learning to display,
And those explain the meaning quite away.
　　You then whose judgment the right course would steer,
Know well each Ancient's proper character;[7]
120 His fable,° subject, scope° in every page;   *plot / intention*
Religion, country, genius of his age:
Without all these at once before your eyes,
Cavil° you may, but never criticize.   *quibble*
Be Homer's works your study, and delight,
125 Read them by day, and meditate by night;
Thence form your judgment, thence your maxims bring,
And trace the Muses upward to their spring.
Still with itself compared, his text peruse;
And let your comment be the Mantuan Muse.[8]

---

4. Mount Parnassus in Greece was sacred to the Muses.
5. Both dress and address: i.e., both interpret and adjust.
6. Textual commentators, depicted as literal book worms
in continuation of the earlier insect metaphor.

7. An interest in the historical method in criticism was
on the rise.
8. Virgil (born near Mantua) and his *Aeneid*, which took
Homer's epics as models, and was the best commentary
on them.

130	When first young Maro° in his boundless mind	*Virgil*
	A work t' outlast immortal Rome designed,	
	Perhaps he seemed° above the critic's law,	*thought himself*
	And but from Nature's fountains scorned to draw:	
	But when t' examine ev'ry part he came,	
135	Nature and Homer were, he found, the same.	
	Convinced, amazed, he checks the bold design,⎫	
	And rules as strict his labored work confine, ⎬	
	As if the Stagyrite⁹ o'erlooked each line. ⎭	
	Learn hence for ancient rules a just esteem;	
140	To copy nature is to copy them.	
	Some beauties yet no precepts can declare,¹	
	For there's a happiness° as well as care.	*luck*
	Music resembles poetry, in each ⎫	
	Are nameless graces which no methods teach, ⎬	
145	And which a master-hand alone can reach. ⎭	
	If, where the rules not far enough extend	
	(Since rules were made but to promote their end),	
	Some lucky license° answers to the full	*deviation*
	Th' intent proposed, that license is a rule.	
150	Thus Pegasus, a nearer way to take,	
	May boldly deviate from the common track.	
	Great wits sometimes may gloriously offend,	
	And rise to faults true critics dare not mend.	
	From vulgar bounds with brave disorder part,	
155	And snatch a grace beyond the reach of Art,	
	Which, without passing through the judgment, gains	
	The heart, and all its end at once attains.	
	In prospects,² thus, some objects please our eyes,⎫	
	Which out of Nature's common order rise, ⎬	
160	The shapeless rock, or hanging precipice. ⎭	
	But though the Ancients thus their rules invade,	
	(As kings dispense with laws themselves have made),	
	Moderns, beware! Or if you must offend	
	Against the precept, ne'er transgress its end;	
165	Let it be seldom, and compelled by need;	
	And have, at least, their precedent to plead.	
	The critic else proceeds without remorse,	
	Seizes your fame, and puts his laws in force.	
	I know there are, to whose presumptuous thoughts	
170	Those freer beauties, ev'n in them, seem faults.³	
	Some figures⁴ monstrous and misshaped appear,	
	Considered singly, or beheld too near,	

---

9. Aristotle, whose *Poetics* provided the basis for later rules on poetry and epic writing.
1. Pope's belief that true poetic genius consisted not of rigid adherence to rules, but of "brave disorder" and "grace beyond the reach of art" had earlier been expressed in the treatise *On the Sublime*, attributed to the Greek rhetorician Longinus (210?–273).

2. Views of an extensive landscape.
3. I.e., there are those critics to whom even the Ancients' occasional "glorious offense" is unforgivable.
4. Both figures in the landscape and rhetorical figures or literary style.

Which, but proportioned to their light, or place,
Due distance reconciles to form and grace.
175   A prudent chief not always must display
His pow'rs in equal ranks, and fair array,
But with th' occasion and the place comply,
Conceal his force, nay seem sometimes to fly.
Those oft are stratagems which errors seem,
180   Nor is it Homer nods, but we that dream.
        Still green with bays[5] each ancient altar[6] stands,
Above the reach of sacrilegious hands;
Secure from flames, from envy's fiercer rage,
Destructive war, and all-involving age.
185   See, from each clime the learn'd their incense bring!
Hear, in all tongues consenting pæans° ring!   *songs of praise*
In praise so just let ev'ry voice be joined,
And fill the gen'ral chorus of mankind.
Hail bards triumphant! born in happier days;
190   Immortal heirs of universal praise!
Whose honors with increase of ages grow,
As streams roll down, enlarging as they flow!
Nations unborn your mighty names shall sound,
And worlds applaud that must not yet be found!
195   Oh may some spark of your celestial fire
The last, the meanest of your sons inspire[7]
(That on weak wings, from far, pursues your flights;
Glows while he reads, but trembles as he writes)
To teach vain wits° a science little known,   *would-be critics*
200   T' admire superior sense, and doubt their own!

        Of all the causes which conspire to blind
Man's erring judgment, and misguide the mind,
What the weak head with strongest bias[8] rules,
Is pride, the never-failing vice of fools.
205   Whatever Nature has in worth denied,
She gives in large recruits° of needful° pride;   *supplies / needed*
For as in bodies, thus in souls, we find
What wants° in blood and spirits, swelled with wind: *is needed*
Pride, where wit fails, steps in to our defense,
210   And fills up all the mighty void of sense.
If once right reason drives that cloud away,
Truth breaks upon us with resistless day.
Trust not yourself; but your defects to know,
Make use of ev'ry friend—and ev'ry foe.
215   A little learning is a dang'rous thing;
Drink deep, or taste not the Pierian spring:[9]

---

5. Laurels, used to crown both poets and military heroes.
6. The works of each ancient author.
7. Pope himself, who follows tradition in writing about writing.

8. Not only prejudice but a kind of bowling ball. (In bowls, the bias ball is one weighted to roll obliquely.)
9. Hippocrene, the stream associated with the Muses.

There shallow draughts[1] intoxicate the brain,
And drinking largely sobers us again.
Fired at first sight with what the Muse imparts,
220   In fearless youth we tempt° the heights of arts,   *attempt*
While from the bounded° level of our mind,   *limited*
Short views we take, nor see the lengths behind;
But, more advanced, behold with strange surprise
New distant scenes of endless science[2] rise!
225   So pleased at first the tow'ring Alps we try,
Mount o'er the vales, and seem to tread the sky;
Th' eternal snows appear already past,
And the first clouds and mountains seem the last:
But, those attained, we tremble to survey
230   The growing labors of the lengthened way,
Th' increasing prospect tires our wand'ring eyes,
Hills peep o'er hills, and Alps on Alps arise!
    A perfect judge will read each work of wit
With the same spirit that its author writ,
235   Survey the whole, nor seek slight faults to find,
Where Nature moves, and rapture warms the mind;
Nor lose, for that malignant dull delight,
The gen'rous pleasure to be charmed with wit.
But in such lays° as neither ebb, nor flow,   *poems*
240   Correctly cold, and regularly low,
That shunning faults, one quiet tenor° keep,   *tone*
We cannot blame indeed—but we may sleep.
In wit, as Nature, what affects our hearts
Is not th' exactness of peculiar° parts;   *particular*
245   'Tis not a lip, or eye, we beauty call,
But the joint force and full result of all.
Thus when we view some well-proportioned dome[3]
(The world's just wonder, and ev'n thine O Rome!),
No single parts unequally surprise,
250   All comes united to th' admiring eyes;
No monstrous height, or breadth, or length appear;
The whole at once is bold, and regular.°   *well-proportioned*
    Whoever thinks a faultless piece to see,
Thinks what ne'er was, nor is, nor e'er shall be.
255   In ev'ry work regard the writer's end,
Since none can compass° more than they intend;   *encompass*
And if the means be just, the conduct° true,   *execution*
Applause, in spite of trivial faults, is due.
As men of breeding,[4] sometimes men of wit,
260   T' avoid great errors must the less commit,
Neglect the rules each verbal critic lays,[5]

1. I.e., small amounts.
2. Knowledge, subjects requiring study.
3. Any large and stately building, but those of a classical design are particularly implied.

4. Good breeding (in both birth and upbringing).
5. Lays down. A verbal critic is one concerned with linguistic detail rather than literary whole.

For not to know some trifles is a praise.
Most critics, fond of some subservient art,
Still make the whole depend upon a part:
265   They talk of principles, but notions° prize,   *prejudices*
And all to one loved folly sacrifice.
    Once on a time, La Mancha's knight,[6] they say,
A certain bard encount'ring on the way,
Discoursed in terms as just, with looks as sage,
270   As e'er could Dennis,[7] of the Grecian stage;
Concluding all were desp'rate sots and fools,
Who durst depart from Aristotle's rules.
Our author, happy in a judge so nice,
Produced his play, and begged the knight's advice;
275   Made him observe the subject, and the plot,
The manners, passions, unities;[8] what not?
All which, exact to rule, were brought about,
Were but a combat in the lists[9] left out.
"What! leave the combat out?" exclaims the knight;
280   Yes, or we must renounce the Stagyrite.°   *Aristotle*
"Not so, by Heav'n" (he answers in a rage)
"Knights, squires, and steeds must enter on the stage."
So vast a throng the stage can ne'er contain.
"Then build a new, or act it in a plain."
285   Thus critics, of less judgment than caprice,
Curious,° not knowing, not exact, but nice,°   *picky / fussy*
Form short ideas, and offend in arts
(As most in manners) by a love to parts.[1]
    Some to conceit[2] alone their taste confine,
290   And glitt'ring thoughts struck out at ev'ry line;
Pleased with a work where nothing's just or fit:
One glaring chaos and wild heap of wit.
Poets, like painters, thus unskilled to trace
The naked Nature and the living grace,
295   With gold and jewels cover ev'ry part,
And hide with ornaments their want° of art.   *lack*
True wit is Nature to advantage dressed,
What oft was thought, but ne'er so well expressed;
Something, whose truth convinced at sight we find,
300   That gives us back the image of our mind.
As shades° more sweetly recommend the light,   *shadows*
So modest plainness sets off sprightly wit.
For works may have more wit than does 'em good,
As bodies perish through excess of blood.[3]

---

6. Don Quixote, Cervantes's foolish knight errant. This episode comes from Part 2 of *Don Quixote* (1615), bk. 3, ch. 10.
7. John Dennis (1657–1734), an eminent critic, but not one in Pope's favor.
8. The three unities of plot (one story), time (one 24-hour day), and place (one location) were thought to have been the Greek playwrights' structuring principles, recommended by Aristotle.
9. The field of combat in medieval jousting tournaments.
1. Individual talents.
2. Extravagant use of metaphor.
3. Apoplexy, it was thought, was caused by such an excess.

305   Others for language all their care express,
         And value books, as women men, for dress:
         Their praise is still—the style is excellent:
         The sense they humbly take upon content.°   *trust*
         Words are like leaves; and where they most abound,
310   Much fruit of sense beneath is rarely found.
         False eloquence, like the prismatic glass,
         Its gaudy colors spreads on ev'ry place;
         The face of Nature we no more survey,°   *observe*
         All glares alike, without distinction gay.
315   But true expression, like th' unchanging sun, ⎤
         Clears and improves whate'er it shines upon, ⎬
         It gilds all objects, but it alters none.   ⎦
         Expression is the dress of thought,⁴ and still
         Appears more decent,° as more suitable;   *correct*
320   A vile conceit° in pompous words expressed,   *idea*
         Is like a clown° in regal purple dressed: *peasant*
         For different styles with different subjects sort,°   *belong*
         As several garbs with country, town, and court.⁵
         Some by old words to fame have made pretense,⁶
325   Ancients in phrase, mere Moderns in their sense:
         Such labored nothings, in so strange a style,
         Amaze th' unlearn'd, and make the learned smile.
         Unlucky, as Fungoso in the play,⁷   ⎤
         These sparks⁸ with awkward vanity display ⎬
330   What the fine gentleman wore yesterday;   ⎦
         And but so mimic ancient wits at best,
         As apes our grandsires in their doublets⁹ dressed.
         In words, as fashions, the same rule will hold;
         Alike fantastic, if too new, or old:
335   Be not the first by whom the new are tried,
         Nor yet the last to lay the old aside.
               But most by numbers¹ judge a poet's song,
         And smooth or rough, with them, is right or wrong;
         In the bright Muse though thousand charms conspire,°   *work together*
340   Her voice is all these tuneful fools admire;
         Who haunt Parnassus but to please their ear, ⎤
         Not mend their minds; as some to church repair, ⎬
         Not for the doctrine, but the music there.   ⎦
         These equal syllables alone require,
345   Though oft the ear the open vowels tire,²

4. It was generally held that a person's appearance reflected his or her inner self.
5. As various styles of dress suit country, mercantile, and courtly life.
6. Made a claim. Deliberately archaic language was used by Spenser, and by a number of his 18th-century imitators.
7. In Ben Jonson's *Every Man Out of his Humor* (1599), this student lagged behind the fashions.

8. Hot-blooded young men, aspiring to fame and romantic conquest.
9. Close-fitting garment for the upper body.
1. Meter of verse, patterns of sound.
2. This line, like the couplets that follow, illustrates the fault it criticizes.

While expletives their feeble aid do join,
And ten low words oft creep in one dull line,
While they ring round the same unvaried chimes,
With sure returns of still expected rhymes.
350 Where-e'er you find "the cooling western breeze,"
In the next line, it "whispers through the trees";
If crystal streams "with pleasing murmurs creep,"
The reader's threatened (not in vain) with "sleep."
Then, at the last, and only couplet fraught
355 With some unmeaning thing they call a thought,
A needless Alexandrine³ ends the song,
That, like a wounded snake, drags its slow length along.
Leave such to tune their own dull rhymes, and know
What's roundly smooth, or languishingly slow;
360 And raise the easy vigor of a line,
Where Denham's strength, and Waller's sweetness join.⁴
True ease in writing comes from art, not chance,
As those move easiest who have learned to dance.
'Tis not enough no harshness gives offense,
365 The sound must seem an echo to the sense.⁵
Soft is the strain when Zephyr° gently blows,   the west wind
And the smooth stream in smoother numbers flows;
But when loud surges lash the sounding shore,
The hoarse, rough verse should like the torrent roar.
370 When Ajax⁶ strives, some rock's vast weight to throw,
The line too labors, and the words move slow;
Not so, when swift Camilla⁷ scours the plain,
Flies o'er th' unbending corn, and skims along the main.°   sea
Hear how Timotheus'⁸ varied lays surprise,
375 And bid alternate passions fall and rise!
While at each change the son of Lybian Jove⁹
Now burns with glory, and then melts with love;
Now his fierce eyes with sparkling fury glow,
Now sighs steal out, and tears begin to flow:
380 Persians and Greeks like turns of nature¹ found,
And the world's victor stood subdued by sound!
The pow'r of music all our hearts allow,°   admit to
And what Timotheus was, is Dryden now.
    Avoid extremes; and shun the fault of such,
385 Who still are pleased too little, or too much.

---

3. The 12 syllables and six stresses of an Alexandrine are illustrated in the next line.
4. Pope follows Dryden in his stylistic characterization of John Denham (1615–1669) and Edmund Waller (1606–1687), two poets greatly respected by writers of the early 18th century, especially for their work in heroic couplets.
5. The nine lines that follow exemplify the rule laid down here.

6. The fabulously strong Greek hero in Homer's *Iliad*.
7. An Amazon warrior in Virgil's *Aeneid*.
8. Musician to Alexander the Great, as portrayed in Dryden's *Alexander's Feast* (1697).
9. Alexander the Great.
1. Similar changes of emotion.

At ev'ry trifle scorn to take offense,
That always shows great pride, or little sense;
Those heads, as stomachs, are not sure the best,
Which nauseate° all, and nothing can digest.   *feel sick at*
390   Yet let not each gay turn° thy rapture move,   *phrase*
For fools admire,[2] but men of sense approve.
As things seem large which we through mists descry,°   *see*
Dullness is ever apt to magnify.
    Some foreign writers, some our own despise;
395   The Ancients only, or the Moderns prize.
(Thus wit, like faith, by each man is applied
To one small sect, and all are damned beside.)
Meanly they seek the blessing to confine,
And force that sun but on a part to shine;
400   Which not alone the southern wit sublimes,°   *exalts*
But ripens spirits in cold northern climes;
Which from the first has shone on ages past,
Enlights the present, and shall warm the last
(Though each may feel increases and decays,
405   And see now clearer and now darker days):
Regard not then if wit be old or new,
But blame the false, and value still the true.
    Some ne'er advance a judgment of their own,
But catch the spreading notion° of the Town;[3]   *fashion*
410   They reason and conclude by precedent,
And own° stale nonsense which they ne'er invent.   *express*
Some judge of authors' names, not works, and then
Nor° praise nor blame the writings, but the men.   *neither*
Of all this servile herd, the worst is he
415   That in proud dullness joins with Quality.[4]
A constant critic at the great man's board,[5]
To fetch and carry nonsense for my Lord.
What woeful stuff this madrigal would be,
In some starved Hackney sonneteer,[6] or me!
420   But let a Lord once own[7] the happy lines,
How the wit brightens! How the style refines!
Before his sacred name flies ev'ry fault,
And each exalted stanza teems with thought!
    The vulgar thus through imitation err;
425   As oft the learn'd by being singular;
So much they scorn the crowd, that if the throng
By chance go right, they purposely go wrong:
So schismatics[8] the plain believers quit,

2. Wonder at the poetry, while "men of sense" deliberate before reaching favorable judgment.
3. The term was commonly used for fashionable London society.
4. The nobility, people of quality.
5. Dining table; i.e., he always eats there.
6. Like the horses from Hackney, in Middlesex, this

poet's services are readily for hire. The designation "sonneteer" indicates one who writes poor poetry. Pope, who made a point of refusing to sell his services, includes himself here perhaps because of his youth when the *Essay* was written.
7. Own up to, admit that they are his.
8. Religious sectarians.

And are but damned for having too much wit.
430　　　Some praise at morning what they blame at night;
But always think the last° opinion right.　　　　　　　　　　　　　*latest*
A Muse by these is like a mistress used;
This hour she's idolized, the next abused;
While their weak heads, like towns unfortified,
435　　'Twixt sense and nonsense daily change their side.
Ask them the cause; they're wiser still, they say;
And still tomorrow's wiser than today.
We think our fathers fools, so wise we grow;
Our wiser sons, no doubt, will think us so.
440　　Once school divines[9] this zealous isle o'erspread;
Who knew most sentences,[1] was deepest read;
Faith, gospel, all, seemed made to be disputed,
And none had sense enough to be confuted:°　　　　　　　　　*disproved*
Scotists and Thomists,[2] now, in peace remain,
445　　Amidst their kindred cobwebs in Duck Lane.[3]
If faith itself has diff'rent dresses worn,
What wonder modes in wit should take their turn?
Oft, leaving what is natural and fit,
The current folly proves the ready wit;[4]
450　　And authors think their reputation safe,
Which lives as long as fools are pleased to laugh.
　　　Some, valuing those of their own side[5] or mind,
Still make themselves the measure of mankind;
Fondly we think we honor merit then,
455　　When we but praise ourselves in other men.
Parties in wit attend on those of state,
And public faction doubles private hate.
Pride, malice, folly against Dryden rose,
In various shapes of parsons, critics, beaus;[6]
460　　But sense survived, when merry jests were past;
For rising merit will buoy up at last.
Might he return, and bless once more our eyes,
New Blackmores and new Milbourns must arise;
Nay, should great Homer lift his awful head,
465　　Zoilus[7] again would start up from the dead.
Envy will merit, as its shade,° pursue;　　　　　　　　　　　　*shadow*

9. Theologians who followed the highly formal Scholastic method.
1. The *sententiae*, or sayings of the Church Fathers, presented and explained for the student in works like Peter Lombard's *Book of Sentences* (1148–1151).
2. The schools of medieval philosophy formed by followers of Duns Scotus and Thomas Aquinas.
3. A street in London where old and secondhand books were sold.
4. Current folly allows ready wit to show itself.
5. Political persuasion.
6. The parsons: Jeremy Collier, A *Short View of the*

Profaneness and Immorality of the English Stage (1698); Luke Milbourne, *Notes on Dryden's Virgil* (1698). The critics: Thomas Shadwell (1642?–1692); Elkanah Settle (1648–1724); Gerard Langbaine (1656–1692), *An Account of the English Dramatic Poets*; Richard Blackmore (1654–1729). Among the beaus: George Villiers, Second Duke of Buckingham, who coauthored *The Rehearsal* (1671); John Wilmot, Second Earl of Rochester, *An Allusion to Horace: the 10th Satyr of the 1st Book* (1680).
7. A critic of Homer's, of the 4th century B.C.E.

But like a shadow, proves the substance true;
For envied wit, like Sol° eclipsed, makes known   *the sun*
Th' opposing body's grossness,° not its own.   *ponderousness*
470 When first that sun too pow'rful beams displays,
It draws up vapors which obscure its rays;
But ev'n those clouds at last adorn its way,
Reflect new glories, and augment the day.
     Be thou the first true merit to befriend;
475 His praise is lost, who stays till all commend.
Short is the date,° alas, of modern rhymes,   *life*
And 'tis but just to let them live betimes.°   *awhile*
No longer now that golden age appears,
When patriarch wits survived a thousand years:
480 Now length of fame (our second life) is lost,
And bare threescore is all ev'n that can boast;
Our sons their fathers' failing language see,
And such as Chaucer[8] is, shall Dryden be.
So when the faithful pencil has designed
485 Some bright idea of the master's mind,
Where a new world leaps out at his command,
And ready Nature waits upon his hand;
When the ripe colors soften and unite,
And sweetly melt into just shade and light;
490 When mellowing years their full perfection give,
And each bold figure just begins to live;
The treach'rous colors the fair art betray,
And all the bright creation fades away!
     Unhappy wit, like most mistaken° things,   *misunderstood*
495 Atones not for that envy which it brings.
In youth alone its empty praise we boast,
But soon the short-lived vanity is lost!
Like some fair flow'r the early spring supplies,
That gaily blooms, but ev'n in blooming dies.
500 What is this wit, which must our cares employ?
The owner's wife, that other men enjoy;
Then most our trouble still when most admired,
And still the more we give, the more required;
Whose fame with pains we guard, but lose with ease,
505 Sure some to vex, but never all to please;
'Tis what the vicious° fear, the virtuous shun;   *wicked*
By fools 'tis hated, and by knaves undone!
     If wit so much from ign'rance undergo,
Ah, let not learning too commence° its foe!   *start to be*
510 Of old, those met rewards who could excel,
And such were praised who but endeavored well:
Though triumphs were to gen'rals only due,

---

8. Chaucer was admired but seen as quaint and arcane, his language unintelligible. It was common at this time to complain of the transience of the English language.

Crowns were reserved to grace the soldiers too.[9]
Now, they who reached Parnassus' lofty crown,
515   Employ their plans to spurn some others down;
And while self-love each jealous writer rules,
Contending wits become the sport of fools:
But still the worst with most regret commend,
For each ill author is as bad a friend.
520   To what base ends, and by what abject ways,
Are mortals urged through sacred° lust of praise!   *accursed*
Ah, ne'er so dire a thirst of glory boast,
Nor in the critic let the man be lost!
Good nature and good sense must ever join;
525   To err is human; to forgive, divine.
    But if in noble minds some dregs remain,
Not yet purged off, of spleen° and sour disdain,   *bad temper*
Discharge that rage on more provoking crimes,
Nor fear a dearth in these flagitious° times.   *corrupt*
530   No pardon vile obscenity should find,
Though wit and art conspire to move your mind;
But dullness with obscenity must prove
As shameful sure as impotence in love.
In the fat age of pleasure, wealth, and ease
535   Sprung the rank weed, and thrived with large increase;
When love was all an easy monarch's[1] care,
Seldom at council, never in a war:[2]
Jilts ruled the state, and statesmen farces writ;[3]
Nay, wits had pensions,° and young lords had wit: *government salaries*
540   The fair sat panting at a courtier's play,
And not a mask[4] went unimproved away:
The modest fan was lifted up no more,
And virgins smiled at what they blushed before.
The following license of a foreign reign[5]
545   Did all the dregs of bold Socinus[6] drain;
Then unbelieving priests reformed the nation,
And taught more pleasant methods of salvation;
Where Heav'n's free subjects might their rights dispute,
Lest God himself should seem too absolute.
550   Pulpits their sacred satire learned to spare,
And Vice admired° to find a flatt'rer there!   *was surprised*

9. Soldiers who had distinguished themselves in the field received crowns. Unlike those soldiers rewarded for assisting one another, the poets in the following lines achieve their crowns, then turn on their fellow writers.
1. Charles II (1630–1685). Ease was a much prized social grace in the late 17th and early 18th centuries.
2. Charles had commanded an army defeated at the Battle of Worcester in 1651.
3. "Jilts" were whores, a reference to Charles's mistresses. The statesmen were the Duke of Buckingham, *The Rehearsal* (1671); Sir Charles Sedley, *The Mulberry*

Garden (1668); Sir George Etherege (1634–1691), *The Man of Mode* and other plays.
4. At Restoration playhouses, masks were initially a fashion among noblewomen in the audience; but their capacity for concealing identity made them a popular device among prostitutes too.
5. That of William III (1650–1702), from the Netherlands, who introduced policies of increased religious toleration.
6. Laelius Socinus (1525–1562) and Faustus Socinus (1539–1604), two Italian theologians who sponsored various heresies, including denying the divinity of Christ.

Encouraged thus, wit's titans[7] braved the skies,
And the press groaned with licensed blasphemies.[8]
These monsters, critics! with your darts engage,
555   Here point your thunder, and exhaust your rage!
Yet shun their fault, who, scandalously nice,°   *fastidious*
Will needs mistake an author into vice;
All seems infected that th' infected spy,°   *see*
As all looks yellow to the jaundiced eye.

560   Learn then what morals critics ought to show,
For 'tis but half a judge's task, to know.
'Tis not enough, taste, judgment, learning, join;
In all you speak, let truth and candor shine;
That not alone what to your sense is due,
565   All may allow; but seek your friendship too.
Be silent always when you doubt your sense;
And speak, though sure, with seeming diffidence:
Some positive, persisting fops we know,
Who, if once wrong, will needs be always so;
570   But you, with pleasure own your errors past,
And make each day a critic on° the last.   *assessment of*
'Tis not enough your counsel still be true;
Blunt truths more mischief than nice° falsehoods do;   *delicate*
Men must be taught as if you taught them not,
575   And things unknown proposed as things forgot.
Without good breeding, truth is disapproved;
That only makes superior sense belov'd.
Be niggards of advice on no pretense;[9]
For the worse avarice is that of sense.
580   With mean complacence ne'er betray your trust,[1]
Nor be so civil as to prove unjust.
Fear not the anger of the wise to raise;
Those best can bear reproof, who merit praise.
'Twere well might critics still this freedom take;
585   But Appius[2] reddens at each word you speak,
And stares, tremendous,[3] with a threat'ning eye,
Like some fierce tyrant in old tapestry.
Fear most to tax an honorable fool,
Whose right it is, uncensured to be dull;
590   Such without wit are poets when they please,
As without learning they can take degrees.[4]
Leave dang'rous truths to unsuccessful satires,

7. This reference compares the deistic writers to the classical giants, the Titans, who attempted to conquer heaven, and were severely punished as a result.
8. The Licensing Act lapsed in 1663, allowing books to be published that Pope and others found blasphemous.
9. Do not withhold your advice however good your reasons.
1. Do not avoid your duty to give judgment by being unnecessarily servile or polite.

2. Dennis; the hero of his tragedy, *Appius and Virginia* (1705), was also sensitive to criticism.
3. Staring, and use of the adjective "tremendous," were both characteristic of Dennis.
4. Privy Councilors, bishops, and peers could obtain academic degrees without fulfilling normal examination or residence requirements.

And flattery to fulsome dedicators,
Whom, when they praise, the world believes no more,
595 Than when they promise to give scribbling o'er.
'Tis best sometimes your censure to restrain,
And charitably let the dull be vain:
Your silence there is better than your spite,
For who can rail so long as they can write?
600 Still humming on, their drowsy course they keep,
And lashed so long, like tops,° are lashed asleep.   *spinning tops*
False steps but help them to renew the race,
As, after stumbling, jades° will mend their pace.   *ruined horses*
What crowds of these, impenitently bold,
605 In sounds and jingling syllables grown old,
Still run on poets, in a raging vein,
Ev'n to the dregs and squeezings of the brain,
Strain out the last dull droppings of their sense,
And rhyme with all the rage of impotence.
610   Such shameless bards we have; and yet 'tis true,
There are as mad, abandoned critics too.
The bookful blockhead, ignorantly read,
With loads of learned lumber in his head,
With his own tongue still edifies his ears,
615 And always list'ning to himself appears.
All books he reads, and all he reads assails,
From Dryden's *Fables* down to Durfey's *Tales*.[5]
With him, most authors steal their works, or buy;
Garth did not write his own *Dispensary*.[6]
620 Name a new play, and he's the poet's friend,
Nay showed his faults—but when would poets mend?
No place so sacred from such fops is barred,
Nor is Paul's church more safe than Paul's churchyard:[7]
Nay, fly to altars; there they'll talk you dead:
625 For fools rush in where angels fear to tread.
Distrustful sense with modest caution speaks, ⎫
It still looks home, and short excursions makes; ⎬
But rattling nonsense in full volleys breaks, ⎭
And never shocked, and never turned aside,
630 Bursts out, resistless, with a thund'ring tide.
   But where's the man, who counsel can bestow,
Still pleased to teach, and yet not proud to know?°   *of knowing*
Unbiased, or° by favor, or by spite;   *either*
Not dully prepossessed, nor blindly right;
635 Though learn'd, well-bred; and though well-bred, sincere;
Modestly bold, and humanly severe?

5. Dryden, *Fables Ancient and Modern* (1700); Thomas D'Urfey, *Tales Tragical and Comical* (1704). D'Urfey, a popular playwright and singer, is best known for the ballad collection *Pills to Purge Melancholy*, to which his name was attached.

6. The report that Pope's friend Samuel Garth had plagiarized his popular mock-heroic work, *The Dispensary* (1699) was, according to William Warburton, "a common slander at that time."

7. Booksellers kept stalls in St. Paul's churchyard.

Who to a friend his faults can freely show,
And gladly praise the merit of a foe?
Blessed with a taste exact, yet unconfined;
640 A knowledge both of books and humankind;
Gen'rous converse;[8] a soul exempt from pride;
And love to praise, with reason on his side?
     Such once were critics; such the happy few,
Athens and Rome in better ages knew.
645 The mighty Stagyrite° first left the shore,   *Aristotle*
Spread all his sails, and durst the deeps explore;
He steered securely, and discovered far,
Led by the light of the Mæonian star.°   *Homer*
Poets, a race long unconfined and free,
650 Still fond and proud of savage liberty,
Received his laws;[9] and stood convinced 'twas fit
Who conquered Nature,[1] should preside o'er wit.
     Horace still charms with graceful negligence,
And without method talks us into sense,
655 Will, like a friend, familiarly convey
The truest notions in the easiest way.
He, who supreme in judgment, as in wit,
Might boldly censure, as he boldly writ,
Yet judged with coolness, though he sung with fire;
660 His precepts teach but what his works inspire.
Our critics take a contrary extreme;
They judge with fury, but they write with phlegm.[2]
Nor suffers Horace more in wrong translations
By wits, than critics in as wrong quotations.
665   See Dionysius[3] Homer's thoughts refine,
And call new beauties forth from ev'ry line!
     Fancy and art in gay Petronius[4] please,
The scholar's learning, with the courtier's ease.
     In grave Quintilian's copious work,[5] we find
670 The justest rules, and clearest method joined.
Thus useful arms in magazines° we place,   *storehouses*
All ranged in order, and disposed with grace,
But less to please the eye, than arm the hand,
Still fit for use, and ready at command.
675   Thee, bold Longinus![6] all the Nine° inspire,   *the Muses*
And bless their critic with a poet's fire.

8. Good conversation and gracious behavior.
9. Aristotle's *Poetics* set rules for poetic composition.
1. Aristotle was also noted for his study of the physical world.
2. Under the humoral understanding of the body, an excess of phlegm caused disease, and so the term came to mean coolness, dullness, or apathy.
3. Dionysius of Halicarnassus, a Roman critic contemporary with Horace.
4. Petronius Arbiter (d. 66 C.E.) judged questions of taste in Nero's court.
5. Quintilian (c. 35–c. 99 C.E.) was a Latin rhetorician, whose *Institutio Oratoria* Pope knew well.
6. Longinus (210?–273 C.E.) was a Greek rhetorician, to whom was attributed the enormously influential treatise *On the Sublime*.

An ardent judge, who, zealous in his trust,
With warmth gives sentence, yet is always just;
Whose own example strengthens all his laws,
680   And is himself that great sublime he draws.
        Thus long succeeding critics justly reigned,
License repressed, and useful laws ordained.
Learning and Rome alike in empire grew;
And arts still followed where her eagles⁷ flew;
685   From the same foes, at last, both felt their doom,
And the same age saw learning fall, and Rome.
With tyranny, then superstition joined,
As that the body, this enslaved the mind;
Much was believed, but little understood,
690   And to be dull was construed to be good;
A second deluge learning thus o'errun,
And the monks finished what the Goths begun.
        At length, Erasmus, that great, injured name
(The glory of the priesthood, and the shame!),⁸
695   Stemmed the wild torrent of a barb'rous age,
And drove those holy vandals off the stage.
        But see! each Muse, in Leo's⁹ golden days,
Starts from her trance, and trims her withered bays!
Rome's ancient Genius,° o'er its ruins spread,   *guardian spirit*
700   Shakes off the dust, and rears his rev'rend head.
Then Sculpture and her sister Arts revive;
Stones leaped to form, and rocks began to live;
With sweeter notes each rising temple rung;
A Raphael painted, and a Vida sung!¹
705   Immortal Vida! on whose honored brow
The poet's bays and critic's ivy² grow:
Cremona now shall ever boast thy name,
As next in place to Mantua, next in fame!³
        But soon by impious arms from Latium⁴ chased,
710   Their ancient bounds the banished Muses passed;
Thence arts o'er all the northern world advance;
But critic learning flourished most in France:
The rules, a nation born to serve,⁵ obeys;
And Boileau⁶ still in right of Horace sways.
715   But we, brave Britons, foreign laws despised,
And kept° unconquered, and uncivilized;   *remained*
Fierce for the liberties of wit, and bold,

---

7. The emblem of the Roman empire.
8. Erasmus (c. 1466–1536), the Dutch humanist who influenced the course of the Reformation; the "glory of the priesthood" because of his learning, Erasmus was its "shame" both because he criticized priests, and because he was persecuted for his outspokenness.
9. Pope Leo X (1475–1521), patron of letters and arts.
1. Raphael (1483–1520) was considered the greatest of painters; Girolamo Vida (c. 1485–1566), Italian poet.

2. Ivy was associated with poets (and with Bacchus), but also with learning.
3. Cremona and Mantua were the birthplaces of Vida and Virgil, respectively.
4. Italy; Rome was conquered by the Holy Roman Empire in 1527.
5. A reference to the despotic reign of Louis XIV.
6. Nicolas Boileau-Despréaux (1636–1711), poet and critic wrote much that was admired in England.

We still defied the Romans, as of old.
Yet some there were, among the sounder few
720   Of those who less presumed, and better knew,
Who durst° assert the juster ancient cause,   *dared to*
And here restored wit's fundamental laws.
Such was the Muse, whose rules and practice tell,
"Nature's chief masterpiece is writing well."[7]
725   Such was Roscommon,[8]—not more learn'd than good,
With manners gen'rous as his noble blood;
To him the wit of Greece and Rome was known,
And ev'ry author's merit, but his own.
Such late was Walsh[9]—the Muse's judge and friend,
730   Who justly knew° to blame or to commend;   *knew when*
To failings mild, but zealous for desert;
The clearest head, and the sincerest heart.
This humble praise, lamented shade!° receive,   *spirit*
This praise at least a grateful Muse may give:
735   The Muse, whose early voice you taught to sing,
Prescribed her heights, and pruned° her tender wing,   *groomed*
(Her guide now lost) no more attempts to rise,
But in low numbers° short excursions tries: *lowly verses*
Content, if hence th' unlearn'd their wants° may view,   *lacks*
740   The learn'd reflect on what before they knew:
Careless of censure, nor too fond of fame;
Still pleas'd to praise, yet not afraid to blame;
Averse alike to flatter, or offend;
Not free from faults, nor yet too vain to mend.
c. 1709   1711

WINDSOR-FOREST "Mr. Pope has published a fine poem called Windsor Forest," wrote Jonathan Swift to his beloved Stella; "read it," he urged her in a letter sent just two days after the poem went on sale. Pope wrote *Windsor-Forest* in two distinct stages: the first part (lines 1–290) was composed in 1704–1705, but the remaining lines celebrating the imminent Peace of Utrecht (1713) that formally ended the long War of Spanish Succession were penned in late 1712 and early 1713. The Peace—a great triumph for the ruling Tory party and the last Stuart monarch, Queen Anne—recognized Great Britain as the world's leading naval power and greatly augmented its colonial and commercial empire at the expense of Spain and France. It would be wrong, however, to imagine that *Windsor-Forest* is half pastoral idyll and half Tory political propaganda; it is, rather, a thoroughgoing synthesis of the topographical, the moral, and the political. Pope's sources for *Windsor-Forest* include Virgil's *Eclogues* and *Georgics*, Ovid's *Metamorphoses*, the Bible, Spenser's *Faerie Queene*, Milton's *Paradise Lost*, Edmund Waller's *On St. James's Park* (1661), and Thomas Otway's *Windsor Castle* (1685). It is, however, Pope's comment on "the distinguishing excellence" of John Denham's *Cooper's Hill* (1642) that best explains Pope's own imaginative procedure in *Windsor-Forest*: "the descriptions of places, and

---

7. This line is quoted from the then well-known *Essay on Poetry* (1682) by John Sheffield (1648–1721), third Earl of Mulgrave and later first Duke of Buckingham and Normady.

8. Wentworth Dillon (c. 1630–1685), fourth Earl of Roscommon; poet, critic, didactic writer.
9. William Walsh (1663–1708), friend and mentor of Pope.

images raised by the poet, are still [i.e., continually] tending to some hint, or leading into some reflection, upon moral life or political institution" (*Iliad* 16.466n). Windsor was the ideal setting for a political poem in which landscape evoked England's proud heritage: from William the Conqueror, who first established a royal residence at Windsor, to "great ANNA" (line 327), who made Windsor Castle her chief residence and frequently rode and hunted in the forest, this was a place suffused with English history. From this enclave of natural beauty and political tradition—the home of monarchs and the haven of Muses—Pope's myth-making genius created a triumphant vision of peace and prosperity, the dawning of a Golden Age.

Windsor-Forest
To the Right Honorable George Lord Lansdowne[1]

> *Non injussa cano: te nostræ, Vare, myricæ*
> *Te nemus omne canet; nec Phœbo gratior ulla est*
> *Quam sibi quæ Vari præscripsit Pagina nomen.*[2]

Thy forests, Windsor! and thy green retreats,
At once the monarch's and the Muse's seats,[3]
Invite my lays.° Be present, sylvan maids![4]   *prompt my poetry*
Unlock your springs, and open all your shades.
5   Granville commands: Your aid O Muses bring!
What Muse for Granville can refuse to sing?
  The groves of Eden, vanished now so long,
Live in description, and look green in song:[5]
These, were my breast inspired with equal flame,
10   Like them in beauty, should be like in fame.
Here hills and vales, the woodland and the plain,
Here earth and water seem to strive again,
Not chaos-like together crushed and bruised,
But as the world, harmoniously confused:
15   Where order in variety we see,
And where, though all things differ, all agree.
Here waving groves a checkered scene display,
And part admit and part exclude the day;
As some coy nymph her lover's warm address
20   Nor° quite indulges, nor can quite repress.   *neither*
There, interspersed in lawns° and opening glades,   *clearings*
Thin trees arise that shun each other's shades.
Here in full light the russet plains extend;
There wrapped in clouds the blueish hills ascend:

1. George Granville (1667–1735), Baron Lansdowne, was himself a poet and playwright. A Tory politician close to Queen Anne, he became Secretary of War in 1710 and so was partly responsible for both British victory and the peace that followed. Lord Lansdowne greatly admired Pope's poetry and encouraged him to publish a poem on the Peace.
2. Adapted from Virgil's sixth *Eclogue*, lines 9–12, in which the poet dedicates his pastoral poem to his friend Varus (like Lansdowne, a prominent military figure): "I do not sing without purpose: our tamarisks, Varus, every grove will sing of you; nor is any page more pleasing to

Apollo than one that begins with the name of Varus."
3. Windsor Forest, seat (country home) of Britain's monarchs since Norman times (and even fabled to be the site of the legendary King Arthur's court), in Pope's view was also home to the Muses because the poets Sir John Denham and Abraham Cowley had lived in the vicinity.
4. Dryads and naiads, spirits of the trees and water.
5. The ancient biblical description of the Garden of Eden was made "green in song" by Milton's (relatively) recent *Paradise Lost*.

25   Ev'n the wild heath displays her purple dyes,[6]
       And 'midst the desert° fruitful fields arise,   *uncultivated land*
       That crowned with tufted trees[7] and springing corn,
       Like verdant isles the sable waste adorn.
       Let India boast her plants, nor envy we
30   The weeping amber or the balmy tree,
       While by our oaks the precious loads are borne,[8]
       And realms commanded which those trees adorn.
       Not proud Olympus[9] yields a nobler sight,
       Though gods assembled grace his tow'ring height,
35   Than what more humble mountains offer here,
       Where, in their blessings, all those gods appear.
       See Pan with flocks, and fruits Pomona crowned,
       Here blushing Flora[1] paints th' enameled ground,[2]
       Here Ceres' gifts° in waving prospect stand,   *grain crops*
40   And nodding tempt the joyful reaper's hand,
       Rich Industry sits smiling on the plains,
       And Peace and Plenty tell, a STUART reigns.[3]
          Not thus the land appeared in ages past,[4]
       A dreary desert and a gloomy waste,
45   To savage beasts and savage laws a prey,[5]
       And kings more furious and severe than they:
       Who claimed the skies, dispeopled° air and floods,   *depopulated*
       The lonely lords of empty wilds and woods.
       Cities laid waste, they stormed the dens and caves
50   (For wiser brutes were backward° to be slaves).   *unwilling*
       What could be free, when lawless beasts obeyed,
       And ev'n the elements a tyrant swayed?[6]
       In vain kind seasons swelled the teeming grain,
       Soft show'rs distilled, and suns grew warm in vain;
55   The swain with tears his frustrate labor yields,
       And famished dies amidst his ripened fields.[7]
       What wonder then, a beast or subject slain
       Were equal crimes in a despotic reign?
       Both doomed alike for sportive tyrants bled,
60   But while the subject starved, the beast was fed.
       Proud Nimrod[8] first the bloody chase began,

6. Heather's purple blooms cover open moorland in late summer.
7. A cluster of trees; Pope borrowed the phrase from Milton's *L'Allegro* (1632).
8. British ships made of oak allowed Britain both to conquer distant countries and to carry goods from them.
9. The mountain home of the Greek gods.
1. Three deities of natural abundance: Pan presides over shepherds and sheep; Pomona over fruits; Flora over flowers.
2. The enameling of metal to allow for overlayers of intricate painted designs was commonly used as a metaphor for nature.
3. Queen Anne (r. 1702–1714), last of the Stuart monarchs.

4. Pope's history of the landscape (lines 43–86) begins with William the Conqueror's creation of the New Forest as a hunting ground reserved for royalty, and chronicles the disastrous impact of this appropriation on his successors and their subjects.
5. The Forest Laws had imposed harsh penalties on those caught stealing the king's game.
6. By controlling the animals, the "tyrant" effectually controlled their "elements" (environments).
7. The farmer dies "famished" because he has been forced to cultivate food for game animals, not humans.
8. In Genesis 10.9, Nimrod is described as a mighty hunter, but he was also seen as a tyrant; he founded the kingdoms of Babylon and Assyria.

A mighty hunter, and his prey was man.
Our haughty Norman boasts that barb'rous name,
And makes his trembling slaves the royal game.
65 The fields are ravished from th' industrious swains,
From men their cities, and from gods their fanes:⁹
The leveled towns with weeds lie covered o'er,
The hollow winds through naked temples roar;
Round broken columns clasping ivy twined;
70 O'er heaps of ruins stalked the stately hind;°   *female deer*
The fox obscene° to gaping tombs retires,   *loathsome*
And savage howlings fill the sacred quires.¹
Awed by his nobles, by his commons° cursed,   *commoners*
Th' oppressor ruled tyrannic where he durst,
75 Stretched o'er the poor, and church, his iron rod,
And treats alike his vassals and his God.
Whom ev'n the Saxon spared, and bloody Dane,
The wanton victims of his sport remain.
But see, the man who spacious regions gave
80 A waste for beasts, himself denied a grave!²
Stretched on the lawn his second hope³ survey,
At once the chaser, and at once the prey.
Lo Rufus, tugging at the deadly dart,
Bleeds in the forest, like a wounded hart.⁴
85 Succeeding monarchs heard the subjects' cries,
Nor saw displeased the peaceful cottage rise.
Then gath'ring flocks on unknown° mountains fed,   *unfamiliar*
O'er sandy wilds were yellow harvests spread,
The forests wondered at th' unusual grain,
90 And secret transports touched the conscious swain.⁵
Fair Liberty, Britannia's goddess, rears
Her cheerful head, and leads the golden years.
      Ye vig'rous swains! while youth ferments your blood,⁶
And purer spirits swell the sprightly flood,
95 Now range the hills, the gameful woods beset,
Wind° the shrill horn, or spread the waving net.   *blow*
When milder autumn summer's heat succeeds,
And in the new-shorn field the partridge feeds,
Before his lord the ready spaniel bounds;

9. Temples; to create the New Forest, William I destroyed many villages and churches. He was sharply criticized for demolishing God's houses to make dens for wild beasts.
1. Choir stalls; Pope deliberately uses archaic spelling. His description of "quires," "broken columns," and "temples" also suggests grander buildings than the parish churches of this time, calling to mind the destruction of the abbeys during the Reformation.
2. Reportedly, at William I's funeral, a knight had tried to prevent the king's burial in land he claimed to own. Pope suggests that this incident and thhe several royal deaths

related to hunting in the forest (depicted in the following four lines) were divine vengeance.
3. Richard, second son of William the Conqueror [Pope's note].
4. William Rufus was accidentally killed by a companion's arrow while out hunting; a hart is a male deer.
5. Joy moves the peasant, well aware of what he has gained; this is a fairly new use of "conscious" in this sense.
6. The blood is quickened by the animal spirits supposed to move in it.

100 Panting with hope, he tries the furrowed grounds;
    But when the tainted[7] gales the game betray,
    Couched close[8] he lies, and meditates the prey:
    Secure they trust th' unfaithful field, beset,
    Till hov'ring o'er 'em sweeps the swelling net.
105 Thus (if small things we may with great compare)
    When Albion° sends her eager sons to war,   England
    Some thoughtless town, with ease and plenty blessed,
    Near, and more near, the closing lines invest;°   surround
    Sudden they seize the' amazed, defenseless prize,
110 And high in air Britannia's standard flies.
        See! from the brake° the whirring pheasant springs,   bushes
    And mounts exulting on triumphant wings;
    Short is his joy! He feels the fiery wound,
    Flutters in blood, and panting beats the ground.
115 Ah! what avail his glossy, varying dyes,
    His purple crest, and scarlet-circled eyes,
    The vivid green his shining plumes unfold,
    His painted wings, and breast that flames with gold?
        Nor yet, when moist Arcturus[9] clouds the Sky,
120 The woods and fields their pleasing toils deny.
    To plains with well-breathed beagles we repair,
    And trace the mazes of the circling hare.
    (Beasts, urged by us, their fellow beasts pursue,
    And learn of Man each other to undo.)
125 With slaught'ring guns th' unwearied fowler roves,
    When frosts have whitened all the naked groves;
    Where doves in flocks the leafless trees o'ershade,
    And lonely woodcocks haunt the wat'ry glade.
    He lifts the tube, and levels with his eye;
130 Straight° a short thunder breaks the frozen sky.   immediately
    Oft, as in airy rings they skim the heath,
    The clam'rous lapwings feel the leaden death:
    Oft as the mounting larks their notes prepare,
    They fall, and leave their little lives in air.
135   In genial spring, beneath the quiv'ring shade
    Where cooling vapors breathe along the mead,
    The patient fisher takes his silent stand
    Intent, his angle trembling in his hand;
    With looks unmoved, he hopes the scaly breed,
140 And eyes the dancing cork and bending reed.
    Our plenteous streams a various race supply;
    The bright-eyed perch with fins of Tyrian° dye,   purple
    The silver eel, in shining volumes° rolled,   coils
    The yellow carp, in scales bedropped with gold,

---

7. With the animal's scent.
8. Crouching near the ground.
9. One of the stars in the Great Bear constellation; in

antiquity, its rise with the sun in September was associated with bad weather.

145   Swift trouts, diversified with crimson stains,
    And pikes, the tyrants of the wat'ry plains.
       Now Cancer glows with Phœbus' fiery car;[1]
    The youth rush eager to the sylvan war;
    Swarm o'er the lawns, the forest walks surround,
150   Rouse° the fleet hart, and cheer the opening° hound.   *flush out / baying*
    Th' impatient courser° pants in ev'ry vein,   *fast horse*
    And pawing, seems to beat the distant plain;
    Hills, vales, and floods appear already crossed,
    And ere he starts, a thousand steps are lost.
155   See! the bold youth strain up the threatening steep,
    Rush through the thickets, down the valleys sweep,
    Hang o'er their coursers' heads with eager speed,
    And earth rolls back beneath the flying steed.
    Let old Arcadia boast her spacious plain,
160   Th' immortal huntress, and her virgin train;
    Nor envy, Windsor! since thy shades have seen
    As bright a goddess, and as chaste a queen;[2]
    Whose care, like hers, protects the sylvan reign,
    The earth's fair light, and empress of the main.[3]
165   Here too, 'tis sung, of old Diana strayed,
    And Cynthus' top[4] forsook for Windsor shade;
    Here was she seen o'er airy wastes to rove,
    Seek the clear spring, or haunt the pathless grove;
    Here armed with silver bows, in early dawn,
170   Her buskined° virgins traced the dewy lawn.   *boot-wearing*
       Above the rest a rural nymph was famed,
    Thy offspring, Thames! the fair Lodona named.
    (Lodona's fate, in long oblivion cast,
    The Muse shall sing, and what she sings shall last.)
175   Scarce could the goddess from her nymph be known,
    But by the crescent° and the golden zone,°   *moon / belt*
    She scorned the praise of beauty, and the care;
    A belt her waist, a fillet° binds her hair;   *headband*
    A painted quiver on her shoulder sounds,
180   And with her dart the flying deer she wounds.
    It chanced, as eager of the chase the maid
    Beyond the forest's verdant limits strayed,
    Pan saw and loved, and furious with desire
    Pursued her flight; her flight increased his fire.
185   Not half so swift the trembling doves can fly,
    When the fierce eagle cleaves the liquid° sky;   *transparent*
    Not half so swiftly the fierce eagle moves,

---

1. The sun (Phoebus's "car": chariot) enters the constellation of Cancer, the crab, on 22 June.
2. Queen Anne is here being compared both to the "immortal huntress," Diana, and to Anne's illustrious forebear, the "virgin queen" Elizabeth I.

3. Like Diana, the moon goddess who governed the tides, Britannia ruled the seas.
4. The mountain on which Diana was said to have been born.

When through the clouds he drives the trembling doves;
As from the god she flew with furious pace,
190   Or as the god, more furious, urged the chase.
Now fainting, sinking, pale, the nymph appears;
Now close behind his sounding steps she hears;
And now his shadow reached her as she run
(His shadow lengthened by the setting sun);
195   And now his shorter breath with sultry air
Pants on her neck, and fans her parting hair.
In vain on Father Thames she calls for aid,
Nor could Diana help her injured maid.
Faint, breathless, thus she prayed, nor prayed in vain:
200   "Ah Cynthia! ah—though banished from thy train,
Let me, O let me, to the shades repair,
My native shades—there weep, and murmur there."
She said, and melting as in tears she lay,
In a soft, silver stream dissolved away.
205   The silver stream her virgin coldness keeps,
Forever murmurs, and forever weeps;
Still bears the name the hapless virgin bore,[5]
And bathes the forest where she ranged before.
In her chaste current oft the goddess laves,°   bathes
210   And with celestial tears augments the waves.
Oft in her glass the musing shepherd spies
The headlong mountains and the downward skies,
The wat'ry landscape of the pendant[6] woods,
And absent° trees that tremble in the floods;   illusory
215   In the clear azure gleam the flocks are seen,
And floating forests paint the waves with green.
Through the fair scene roll slow the ling'ring streams,
Then foaming pour along, and rush into the Thames.
        Thou too, great father° of the British floods!   the Thames
220   With joyful pride survey'st our lofty woods,
Where tow'ring oaks their growing honors rear,
And future navies on thy shores appear.
Not Neptune's self from all his streams receives
A wealthier tribute, than to thine he gives.
225   No seas so rich, so gay no banks appear,
No lake so gentle, and no spring so clear.
Nor Po so swells the fabling poet's lays,[7]
While led along the skies his shining current strays,
Than thine, which visits Windsor's famed abodes,
230   To grace the mansion of our earthly gods.
Nor all his stars above a luster show,

5. I.e., Loddon, a river that runs through Windsor Forest
and into the Thames.
6. Hanging; the woods both hang over the stream, and, in
the stream's reflection, appear to stand upside down.

7. Both Virgil and Ovid compared the Po, a river in Italy,
to the winding constellation Eridanus, named for a river
in Greek mythology.

Like the bright beauties on thy banks below;
Where Jove, subdued by mortal passion still,
Might change Olympus for a nobler hill.
235   Happy the man whom this bright court approves,
His sov'reign favors, and his country loves;
Happy next him who to these shades retires,
Whom Nature charms, and whom the Muse inspires,
Whom humbler joys of home-felt quiet please,
240   Successive study, exercise, and ease.
He gathers health from herbs the forest yields,
And of their fragrant physic° spoils° the fields: *medicines / robs*
With chemic art[8] exalts° the min'ral pow'rs,   *refines*
And draws° the aromatic souls of flow'rs.   *extracts*
245   Now marks the course of rolling orbs on high;
O'er figured worlds[9] now travels with his eye.
Of ancient writ unlocks the learned store,
Consults the dead, and lives past ages o'er.
Or wand'ring thoughtful in the silent wood,
250   Attends the duties of the wise and good,
T' observe a mean,[1] be to himself a friend,
To follow Nature, and regard his end.
Or looks on Heav'n with more than mortal eyes,
Bids his free soul expatiate in the skies,
255   Amid her kindred stars familiar roam,
Survey the region, and confess her home!
Such was the life great Scipio[2] once admired,
Thus Atticus,[3] and Trumbull[4] thus retired.
    Ye sacred Nine![5] that all my soul possess,
260   Whose raptures fire me, and whose visions bless,
Bear me, oh bear me to sequestered scenes,
The bow'ry mazes and surrounding greens;
To Thames's banks which fragrant breezes fill,
Or where ye Muses sport on Cooper's Hill.
265   (On Cooper's Hill eternal wreaths shall grow,[6]
While lasts the mountain, or while Thames shall flow.)
I seem through consecrated walks to rove,
I hear soft music die along the grove;
Led by the sound I roam from shade to shade,
270   By god-like poets venerable made:
Here his first lays majestic Denham sung;[7]

---

8. The skills of the chemist.
9. The earth, or possibly the zodiac, portrayed on a globe.
1. To maintain a steady, balanced course through life; according to Aristotle, wisdom lay in following the "golden mean," or middle way.
2. Scipio Africanus, the Roman general who defeated Hannibal and the Carthaginians in 202 B.C.E. but declined political office, choosing eventually to retire to the country.
3. Titus Pomponius (109–32 B.C.E.), despite his friendship and correspondence with Cicero, refused to become involved in politics; he was called Atticus because he

spent much time studying in Athens, which lies in the region of Attica.
4. Sir William Trumbull (1639–1716), Pope's elderly friend.
5. The Nine Muses, daughters of Mnemosyne (goddess of memory) and Zeus, each of whom presided over a different art or science.
6. Because commemorated in Sir John Denham's poem *Cooper's Hill* (1642).
7. Denham, described as "majestic" because of the (then unusual) style of the couplets in *Cooper's Hill*, lived near Windsor before the Civil Wars.

There the last numbers flowed from Cowley's tongue.[8]
O early lost![9] what tears the river shed
When the sad pomp along his banks was led?
275   His drooping swans on ev'ry note expire,
And on his willows[1] hung each Muse's lyre.
    Since Fate relentless stopped their heav'nly voice,
No more the forests ring, or groves rejoice;
Who now shall charm the shades where Cowley strung
280   His living harp, and lofty Denham sung?
But hark! the groves rejoice, the forest rings!
Are these revived? Or is it Granville sings?
    'Tis yours, my Lord, to bless our soft retreats,
And call the Muses to their ancient seats,
285   To paint anew the flow'ry sylvan scenes,
To crown the forests with immortal greens,
Make Windsor hills in lofty numbers rise,
And lift her turrets nearer to the skies;
To sing those honors you deserve to wear,
290   And add new luster to her silver star.[2]
    Here noble Surrey[3] felt the sacred rage,
Surrey, the Granville of a former age:
Matchless his pen, victorious was his lance;
Bold in the lists, and graceful in the dance:
295   In the same shades the Cupids tuned his lyre,
To the same notes of love, and soft desire:
Fair Geraldine,[4] bright object of his vow,
Then filled the groves, as heav'nly Myra[5] now.
    Oh wouldst thou sing what heroes Windsor bore,
300   What kings first breathed upon her winding shore,[6]
Or raise old warriors whose adored remains
In weeping vaults[7] her hallowed earth contains!
With Edward's[8] acts adorn the shining page,[9]
Stretch his long triumphs down through ev'ry age,
305   Draw monarchs chained, and Cressi's glorious Field,[1]
The lilies[2] blazing on the regal shield.
Then, from her roofs when Verrio's colors fall,
And leave inanimate the naked wall;[3]

---

8. Mr. [Abraham] Cowley died at Chertsey, on the borders of the Forest, and was from thence conveyed to
Westminster [Pope's note], where he was buried in state.
9. Cowley died at age 49.
1. Emblems of sorrow.
2. The star worn by members inducted into the highly
prestigious Order of the Garter, founded by Edward III in
Windsor Castle's Chapel of St. George.
3. Henry Howard, Earl of Surrey, one of the first refiners
of the English poetry; famous in the time of Henry VIII
for his sonnets, the scene of many of which is laid at
Windsor [Pope's note].
4. Lady Elizabeth Fitzgerald (1528?–1589) to whom Surrey
was thought to have directed his love poems.
5. The poetical name Granville used for his female addressee.

6. Suggesting the etymological meaning of "Windsor."
7. Because of the seepage of water through the walls; similar natural phenomena explain the conceits in lines 307
and 313.
8. Edward III born here [Pope's note].
9. Pope her urges Granville to describe in verse the conquest of France, in the mid-fourteenth-century, by Edward III and his son Edward the Black Prince; the artist
Antonio Verrio (1639–1707) had commemorated their
victories in ceiling paintings at Windsor Castle.
1. The village in northern France where Edward III defeated the French.
2. Emblem of France, but added to the English crest of
arms.
3. In ceiling paintings at Windsor had already begun to
disintegrate.

Still in thy song should vanquished France appear,
310   And bleed forever under Britain's spear.
       Let softer strains ill-fated Henry[4] mourn,
And palms eternal flourish round his urn.
Here o'er the martyr king the marble weeps,
And fast beside him, once-feared Edward[5] sleeps:
315   Whom not th' extended Albion could contain,
From old Belerium[6] to the German main,
The grave unites; where ev'n the great find rest,
And blended lie th' oppressor and th' oppressed!
       Make sacred Charles's tomb forever known,[7]
320   (Obscure the place, and uninscribed the stone).
Oh fact accursed!° What tears has Albion shed,   *evil deed*
Heav'ns! what new wounds, and how her old have bled?
She saw her sons with purple deaths[8] expire,
Her sacred domes° involved in rolling fire,   *stately buildings*
325   A dreadful series of intestine wars,[9]
Inglorious triumphs, and dishonest° scars.   *shameful*
At length great ANNA° said—"Let Discord cease!"   *Queen Anne*
She said, the world obeyed, and all was peace!
       In that blessed moment, from his oozy bed
330   Old Father Thames advanced his rev'rend head.
His tresses dropped with dews, and o'er the stream
His shining horns[1] diffused a golden gleam:
Graved on his urn appeared the moon, that guides
His swelling waters, and alternate tides;
335   The figured streams in waves of silver rolled,
And on their banks Augusta[2] rose in gold.[3]
Around his throne the sea-born brothers[4] stood,
That swell with tributary urns his flood.
First the famed authors of his ancient name,
340   The winding Isis and the fruitful Thame:[5]
The Kennet swift, for silver eels renowned;
The Loddon slow, with verdant alders crowned:
Cole, whose dark streams his flow'ry islands lave;
And chalky Wey, that rolls a milky wave:

4. Henry VI, murdered in 1471, was looked upon by some in northern Britain (where he lived for some time as a fugitive) as a saint; the "palms" in the following line are emblems of martyrdom.
5. Edward IV, responsible for Henry VI's murder, was buried in St. George's chapel, Windsor, where Henry was later re-interred.
6. Land's End in Cornwall, the southwestern-most point in England.
7. Charles I, executed by the Puritans in 1649 and consequently considered by many a Christian and political martyr, was buried in St. George's Chapel without any service; his tomb remained unidentified until 1813.
8. Death from the Great Plague in 1665; this event, like the fire of London (1666) and the 1688 Revolution alluded to in the following lines, was viewed by many as a

result of God's wrath, possibly (as Pope here implies) visited on the nation as a result of the murder of Charles I.
9. The Civil Wars during the reigns of Charles I, Cromwell (in Ireland), James II, and William III (in Ireland).
1. River gods often had bulls' horns, representing their strength, noisiness, and importance for agriculture.
2. The name given to London by the Romans.
3. A reference to Dryden's description of London's rebuilding after the Great Fire (in brick and white Portland stone) in *Annus Mirabilis* (1667), to which work the rest of this poem is indebted.
4. According to myth, all rivers were children of the sea gods (Oceanus and Thethys).
5. The Thames was seen as the son of the Thame and the Isis rivers.

345   The blue, transparent Vandalis° appears;   *the Wandle*
         The gulfy Lee his sedgy tresses rears:
         And sullen Mole, that hides his diving flood;
         And silent Darent, stained with Danish blood.⁶
            High in the midst, upon his urn reclined,
350   (His sea-green mantle waving with the wind)
         The god appeared; he turned his azure eyes
         Where Windsor domes and pompous turrets rise,
         Then bowed and spoke; the winds forget to roar,
         And the hushed waves glide softly to the shore.
355   Hail sacred peace!⁷ hail long-expected days,
         Which Thames's glory to the stars shall raise!
         Though Tiber's streams immortal Rome behold,
         Though foaming Hermus⁸ swells with Tides of gold,
         From Heav'n itself though sev'nfold Nilus⁹ flows,
360   And harvests on a hundred realms bestows;
         These now no more shall be the Muse's themes,
         Lost in my fame, as in the sea their streams.
         Let Volga's banks¹ with iron squadrons° shine,   *cavalry*
         And groves of lances glitter on the Rhine,
365   Let barb'rous Ganges² arm a servile train;
         Be mine the blessings of a peaceful reign.
         No more shall my sons dye with British blood
         Red Iber's³ sands, or Ister's⁴ foaming flood;
         Safe on my shore each unmolested swain
370   Shall tend the flocks, or reap the bearded grain;
         The shady empire shall retain no trace
         Of war or blood, but in the sylvan chase,
         The trumpets sleep, while cheerful horns are blown,
         And arms employed on birds and beasts alone.
375   Behold! th' ascending villas⁵ on my side
         Project long shadows o'er the crystal tide.
         Behold! Augusta's glitt'ring spires increase,
         And temples⁶ rise, the beauteous works of peace.
         I see, I see where two fair cities⁷ bend
380   Their ample bow,° a new Whitehall ascend!⁸   *riverbend*
         There mighty nations shall inquire their doom,⁹

6. The Danes were defeated at Otford, on the Darent, in 1016.

7. The War of the Spanish Succession had begun in 1701; peace treaties were signed in London in 1711, and in Utrecht in 1713.

8. An Italian river distinguished by Virgil.

9. Because of its delta, Ovid called the Nile *septemfluus*.

1. Charles XII of Sweden was defeated by the Russians in 1709 (nowhere near the Volga).

2. Alluding to the Mogul Emperor Aurangzeb's recent wars in India.

3. The Ebro in Spain, where the Allies had gained victory in 1710.

4. The Danube, where Marlborough achieved his famous victory at Blenheim in 1704.

5. Many new private country homes were being built along the Thames upriver from London at this time.

6. The fifty new churches [Pope's note], built on the Queen's orders to meet the requirements of a growing London.

7. London and Westminster, separated by the Thames, were still distinct cities at this time.

8. There were plans to rebuild the palace of Whitehall, which had largely burned down in the fires of 1691 and 1697.

9. Fate or destiny. In lines 381–422 Pope makes extensive use of Isaiah 60, which forecasts Zion's future glory.

The world's great oracle in times to come;
There kings shall sue, and suppliant states be seen
Once more to bend before a British QUEEN.

385   Thy trees, fair Windsor! now shall leave their woods,
And half thy forests rush into my floods,
Bear Britain's thunder, and her cross[1] display,
To the bright regions of the rising day;
Tempt° icy seas, where scarce the waters roll,   *attempt*
390   Where clearer flames glow round the frozen pole;
Or under southern skies exalt° their sails,   *raise*
Led by new stars, and born by spicy gales!
For me the balm[2] shall bleed, and amber flow,
The coral redden, and the ruby glow,
395   The pearly shell its lucid globe infold,
And Phœbus warm the ripening ore to gold.[3]
The time shall come, when free as seas or wind
Unbounded Thames[4] shall flow for all mankind,
Whole nations enter with each swelling tide,
400   And seas but join the regions they divide;
Earth's distant ends our glory shall behold,
And the new world launch forth to seek the old.
Then ships of uncouth form shall stem the tide,
And feathered people crowd my wealthy side,[5]
405   While naked youth and painted chiefs admire
Our speech, our color, and our strange attire!
Oh stretch thy reign, fair Peace! from shore to shore,
Till conquest cease, and slav'ry be no more:
Till the freed[6] Indians in their native groves
410   Reap their own fruits and woo their sable loves,
Peru once more a race of kings behold,
And other Mexicos be roofed with gold.
Exiled by thee from earth to deepest hell,
In brazen bonds shall barb'rous Discord dwell:
415   Gigantic Pride, pale Terror, gloomy Care,
And mad Ambition shall attend her there.
There purple Vengeance bathed in gore retires,
Her weapons blunted, and extinct her fires:
There hateful Envy her own snakes shall feel,
420   And Persecution mourn her broken wheel:[7]
There Faction roar, Rebellion bite her chain,

---

1. St. George's cross which, with the cross of St. Andrew, made the new Union flag of Great Britain; Pope may also allude to recent British missionary work overseas.
2. Tree sap, often having soothing or healing properties.
3. Phoebus Apollo, god of the sun and patron of poets, was commonly believed to ripen metal into gold with his rays.
4. A wish that London may be made a FREE PORT [Pope's note]; many merchants proposed that customs duties should
be abolished to make Britain more open to international trade.
5. Four Iroquois Indian chiefs visited England in 1710, causing a sensation.
6. From Spanish oppression.
7. An instrument of torture.

And gasping Furies thirst for blood in vain.
    Here cease thy flight, nor with unhallowed lays
Touch the fair fame of Albion's golden days.
425   The thoughts of gods let Granville's verse recite,
And bring the scenes of opening fate to light.
My humble Muse, in unambitious strains,
Paints the green forests and the flow'ry plains,
Where Peace descending bids her olives spring,
430   And scatters blessings from her dove-like wing.
Ev'n I more sweetly pass my careless days,
Pleased in the silent shade with empty praise;
Enough for me, that to the list'ning swains
First in these fields I sung the sylvan strains.

1704–1713   1713

THE RAPE OF THE LOCK   "New things are made familiar, and familiar things are made new," wrote Samuel Johnson about the most accomplished poem of Pope's younger years. "The whole detail of a female day is brought before us invested with so much art of decoration that, though nothing is disguised, everything is striking."

Only a poet with formidable imaginative powers could have made a great mock-heroic poem out of such unpromising materials. When Robert, Lord Petre, cut a love-lock from the head of Arabella Fermor without her permission, the two young people, both in their early twenties, quarreled bitterly. Their families, leading members of the Roman Catholic gentry once on the friendliest terms, became seriously estranged. Pope's friend John Caryll, who saw himself as a mediator among the group, asked him "to write a poem to make a jest of it, and laugh them together."

Pope's first effort was a poem in two cantos, The Rape of the Locke, printed in 1712 with some of his other pieces and the work of other poets. Two years later, Pope separately published The Rape of the Lock, enlarged to five cantos by the addition of the "machinery" of the sylphs and gnomes, and by the game of Ombre. The poem reached its final form in 1717 when Pope added the moralizing declamation of Clarissa (5.7–35), a parody of the speech of Sarpedon to Glaucus in the Iliad. The mock-epic tenor of the five-canto poem was clearly influenced by Pope's translation of the Iliad, his main project while most of The Rape of the Lock was being composed. Other influences were Homer's Odyssey, Virgil's Aeneid, Milton's Paradise Lost, and Boileau's Le Lutrin (1674, 1683), a mock-heroic satire on clerical infighting over the placement of a lectern. Yoking together the mundanely trivial and the mythically heroic as he follows the course of Belinda's day, Pope produced a vivid, yet affectionate, mockery of the fashions and sexual mores common in his own social circle.

The arming of the champion for war became the application of Belinda's (i.e., Arabella's) make-up for the battle of the sexes; the larger-than-life gods of classical mythology became miniature cartoon-like sylphs; Aeneas's voyage up the Tiber became Belinda's progress up the Thames; the depiction of Achilles's shield became the description of Belinda's petticoat; the test of single combat became the game of cards; the hero's journey to the underworld became the gnome's adventure in the Cave of Spleen; and the rape of Helen that started the Trojan War became the "rape" (stealing) of Belinda's hair that began an unpleasant social squabble. All the trappings of classical epic are here: the divine messenger appearing to the hero in a dream, the sacrifice to the gods, the inspirational speech to the troops before battle, the epic feast, the violent melee, and the final triumphant apotheosis. Throughout the poem, the enormous distance between the trivial matter and the heroic manner produces brilliantly comic results.

The Rape of the Lock
An Heroi-Comical Poem in Five Cantos

Nolueram, Belinda, *tuos violare capillos,*
Sed juvat hoc precibus me tribuisse tuis.

Martial[1]

To Mrs. Arabella Fermor

Madam,

It will be in vain to deny that I have some regard for this piece, since I dedicate it to you. Yet you may bear me witness, it was intended only to divert a few young ladies, who have good sense and good humor enough, to laugh not only at their sex's little unguarded follies, but at their own.[2] But as it was communicated with the air of a secret, it soon found its way into the world. An imperfect copy having been offered to a bookseller, you had the good nature for my sake to consent to the publication of one more correct; this I was forced to before I had executed half my design, for the *machinery* was entirely wanting to complete it.

The *machinery*, Madam, is a term invented by the critics, to signify that part which the deities, angels, or demons, are made to act in a poem; for the ancient poets are in one respect like many modern ladies: let an action be never so trivial in itself, they always make it appear of the utmost importance. These machines I determined to raise on a very new and odd foundation, the Rosicrucian[3] doctrine of spirits.

I know how disagreeable it is to make use of hard words before a lady; but 'tis so much the concern of a poet to have his works understood, and particularly by your sex, that you must give me leave to explain two or three difficult terms.

The Rosicrucians are a people I must bring you acquainted with. The best account I know of them is in a French book called *Le Comte de Gabalis*,[4] which both in its title and size is so like a novel that many of the fair sex have read it for one by mistake. According to these gentlemen, the four elements are inhabited by spirits, which they call Sylphs, Gnomes, Nymphs, and Salamanders.[5] The Gnomes, or Demons of Earth, delight in mischief; but the Sylphs, whose habitation is in the air, are the best-conditioned[6] creatures imaginable. For they say any mortals may enjoy the most intimate familiarities with these gentle spirits, upon a condition very easy to all true adepts: an inviolate preservation of chastity.

As to the following cantos, all the passages of them are as fabulous[7] as the vision at the beginning, or the transformation at the end (except the loss of your hair, which I always mention with reverence). The human persons are as fictitious as the airy ones; and the character of Belinda, as it is now managed, resembles you in nothing but in beauty.

If this poem had as many graces as there are in your person, or in your mind, yet I could never hope it should pass through the world half so uncensured as you have

---

1. "I did not wish, [Belinda,] to violate your locks, but I rejoice to have yielded this to your wishes" (Martial, *Epigrams* 12.84). Pope has substituted "Belinda" for Martial's "Polytimus."
2. I.e., at their own individual follies as well.
3. A secret society of the 17th and 18th centuries, devoted to the study of ancient religious, philosophical, and mystical doctrines.

4. Written in 1670 by the Abbé de Monfaucon de Villars, its approach to Rosicrucian philosophy was lighthearted. It was printed in duodecimo, a small "pocketbook" size common to many inexpensive novels.
5. Elemental spirits living in fire.
6. Best natured, having the best character.
7. Fictional.

done. But let its fortune be what it will, mine is happy enough, to have given me this occasion of assuring you that I am, with the truest esteem,

Madam,

Your most obedient, humble servant,

A. Pope

CANTO 1

What dire offense from am'rous causes springs,
What mighty contests rise from trivial things,
I sing[1]—This verse to Caryll, Muse! is due;
This, ev'n Belinda may vouchsafe to view:
5 Slight is the subject, but not so the praise,
If she inspire, and he approve my lays.°   *verses*
     Say what strange motive, Goddess!° could compel   *his Muse*
A well-bred lord t' assault a gentle belle?
Oh say what stranger cause, yet unexplored,
10 Could make a gentle belle reject a lord?
In tasks so bold, can little men engage,
And in soft bosoms dwells such mighty rage?
     Sol through white curtains shot a tim'rous ray,
And op'd those eyes that must eclipse the day;
15 Now lapdogs[2] give themselves the rousing shake,
And sleepless lovers, just at twelve, awake:
Thrice rung the bell, the slipper knocked the ground,[3]
And the pressed watch returned a silver sound.[4]
Belinda still her downy pillow pressed,
20 Her guardian Sylph prolonged the balmy rest.
'Twas he had summoned to her silent bed
The morning dream that hovered o'er her head.
A youth more glitt'ring than a birth-night beau[5]
(That ev'n in slumber caused her cheek to glow)
25 Seemed to her ear his winning lips to lay,
And thus in whispers said, or seemed to say:[6]
     "Fairest of mortals, thou distinguished care
Of thousand bright inhabitants of air!
If e'er one vision touched thy infant thought,
30 Of all the nurse and all the priest have taught,[7]
Of airy elves by moonlight shadows seen,
The silver token, and the circled green,[8]

---

1. Pope begins with the ancient epic formula of "proposition" of the work as a whole, and "invocation" of the gods' assistance, continuing with the traditional epic questions.
2. Small dogs imported from Asia were highly fashionable ladies' pets at this time.
3. Belinda rings the bell and then finally bangs her slipper on the floor to call her maid.
4. The popular "pressed watch" chimed the hour and quarter hours when its stem was pressed, saving its owner

from striking a match to see the time.
5. On a royal birthday, courtiers' clothes were particularly extravagant.
6. His whispering recalls the serpent's temptation of Eve in Milton's *Paradise Lost*.
7. The nurse and priest were seen as two standard sources of superstition.
8. Withered circles in the grass and silver coins were supposed to be signs of fairies' presence.

Or virgins visited by angel pow'rs,[9]
With golden crowns and wreaths of heav'nly flow'rs,
35 Hear and believe! thy own importance know,
Nor bound thy narrow views to things below.
Some secret truths from learned pride concealed,
To maids alone and children are revealed:
What though no credit doubting wits may give?[1]
40 The fair and innocent shall still believe.
Know then, unnumbered spirits round thee fly,
The light militia of the lower sky;
These, though unseen, are ever on the wing,
Hang o'er the box, and hover round the ring.[2]
45 Think what an equipage[3] thou hast in air,
And view with scorn two pages and a chair.[4]
As now your own, our beings were of old,
And once enclosed in woman's beauteous mold;
Thence, by a soft transition, we repair
50 From earthly vehicles[5] to these of air.
Think not, when woman's transient breath is fled,
That all her vanities at once are dead:
Succeeding vanities she still regards,
And though she plays no more, o'erlooks the cards.
55 Her joy in gilded chariots, when alive,
And love of Ombre,[6] after death survive.
For when the fair in all their pride expire,
To their first elements[7] their souls retire:
The sprites of fiery termagants° in flame   *scolding women*
60 Mount up, and take a salamander's name.
Soft yielding minds to water glide away,
And sip with Nymphs, their elemental tea.
The graver prude sinks downward to a Gnome,
In search of mischief still on earth to roam.
65 The light coquettes in Sylphs aloft repair,
And sport and flutter in the fields of air.
    "Know farther yet; whoever fair and chaste
Rejects mankind, is by some Sylph embraced:
For spirits, freed from mortal laws, with ease
70 Assume what sexes and what shapes they please.[8]
What guards the purity of melting maids,[9]

---

9. Belinda is reminded of the many virgin saints, and particularly the Annunciation to the Virgin Mary.
1. Religious skepticism was on the increase.
2. The theater box and the equally fashionable drive round Hyde Park.
3. Carriage, horses, and attendants.
4. A sedan chair, carried by two chairmen.
5. Both the carriage and the physical body.
6. Ombre (pronounced *Omber*) was an elaborate card game, introduced into England in the 17th century and considered highly fashionable in the early 18th century.

Given the general tenor of the poem, Pope may also be punning on the origin of the word "Ombre," from the Spanish *hombre*, meaning "man."
7. The four elements of fire, water, earth, and air were thought to make up all things; so an individual's character was determined by whichever element dominated his or her soul.
8. Cf. *Paradise Lost*: "For spirits when they please / Can either sex assume, or both" (1.423–24).
9. I.e., the chastity of weakening virgins.

In courtly balls, and midnight masquerades,
Safe from the treach'rous friend, the daring spark,[1]
The glance by day, the whisper in the dark;
75 When kind occasion prompts their warm desires,
When music softens, and when dancing fires?
'Tis but their Sylph, the wise celestials know,
Though honor is the word with men below.
    "Some nymphs there are, too conscious of their face,
80 For life predestined to the Gnomes' embrace.
These swell their prospects and exalt their pride,
When offers are disdained, and love denied.
Then gay ideas crowd the vacant brain;
While peers° and dukes, and all their sweeping train,   *aristocrats*
85 And garters, stars, and coronets[2] appear,
And in soft sounds, 'your Grace'[3] salutes their ear.
'Tis these that early taint the female soul,
Instruct the eyes of young coquettes to roll,
Teach infant cheeks a bidden° blush to know,   *deliberate*
90 And little hearts to flutter at a beau.
    "Oft when the world imagine women stray,
The Sylphs through mystic mazes guide their way,
Through all the giddy circle they pursue,
And old impertinence° expel by new.   *frivolity*
95 What tender maid but must a victim fall
To one man's treat, but for another's ball?
When Florio speaks, what virgin could withstand,
If gentle Damon did not squeeze her hand?
With varying vanities, from ev'ry part,
100 They shift the moving toy shop[4] of their heart;
Where wigs with wigs, with sword knots sword knots strive,[5]
Beaus banish beaus, and coaches coaches drive.[6]
This erring mortals levity may call;
Oh blind to truth! the Sylphs contrive it all.
105   "Of these am I, who thy protection claim,
A watchful sprite, and Ariel is my name.
Late, as I ranged the crystal wilds of air,
In the clear mirror of thy ruling star
I saw, alas! some dread event impend,
110 Ere to the main° this morning sun descend.   *sea*
But heaven reveals not what, or how, or where:
Warned by thy Sylph, O pious maid, beware!
This to disclose is all thy guardian can.
Beware of all, but most beware of Man!"
115   He said; when Shock,[7] who thought she slept too long,

1. A bold, brash, and showy young man.
2. Emblems of noble rank.
3. Form of address for a duke or a duchess.
4. Where toys and trinkets are sold; "moving" here means
easily changed, unstable.
5. Most men wore wigs in public; formally dressed men

tied ribbons to the hilt of their swords.
6. In word order and versification, these two lines mimic
both Homer's and Ovid's description of heroic combat.
7. The shock or shough, a long-haired Icelandic poodle,
fashionable as a lapdog.

Leaped up, and waked his mistress with his tongue.
'Twas then, Belinda! if report say true,
Thy eyes first opened on a *billet-doux;*°   *love letter*
Wounds, charms, and ardors were no sooner read,
120   But all the vision vanished from thy head.
    And now, unveiled, the toilet° stands displayed,   *dressing table*
Each silver vase in mystic order laid.
First, robed in white, the nymph intent adores
With head uncovered, the cosmetic pow'rs.
125   A heav'nly image[8] in the glass appears;
To that she bends, to that her eyes she rears;°   *raises*
Th' inferior priestess,[9] at her altar's side,
Trembling, begins the sacred rites of pride.
Unnumbered treasures ope at once, and here
130   The various off'rings of the world appear;
From each she nicely culls with curious° toil,   *careful*
And decks the goddess with the glitt'ring spoil.
This casket India's glowing gems unlocks,
And all Arabia breathes from yonder box.
135   The tortoise here and elephant unite,
Transformed to combs, the speckled and the white.[1]
Here files of pins extend their shining rows,
Puffs, powders, patches, Bibles,[2] *billet-doux.*
Now awful° Beauty puts on all its arms;   *awe-inspiring*
140   The fair each moment rises in her charms,
Repairs her smiles, awakens ev'ry grace,
And calls forth all the wonders of her face;
Sees by degrees a purer blush[3] arise,
And keener lightnings[4] quicken in her eyes.
145   The busy Sylphs surround their darling care;
These set the head, and those divide the hair,
Some fold the sleeve, whilst others plait the gown;
And Betty's praised for labors not her own.

CANTO 2

Not with more glories, in th' ethereal plain,°   *sky*
The sun first rises o'er the purpled main,
Than, issuing forth, the rival of his beams
Launched on the bosom of the silver Thames.[5]
5   Fair nymphs and well-dressed youths around her shone,
But ev'ry eye was fixed on her alone.
On her white breast a sparkling cross she wore,
Which Jews might kiss, and infidels adore.[6]

---

8. I.e., Belinda herself.
9. Belinda's maid, Betty.
1. Tortoise-shell and ivory.
2. Patches were small pieces of black silk, pasted onto the face to make the skin appear whiter. It was fashionable to own Bibles in very small format.
3. The even, artificial blush of rouge.

4. Caused by drops of belladonna (deadly nightshade), which dilates the pupils.
5. Belinda takes a boat from London to Hampton Court, avoiding the dirt and squalor of the streets; her voyage compares with Aeneas's up the Tiber (*Aeneid* 7), or, alternatively, Cleopatra's up the Nile (*Antony and Cleopatra* 2.2).
6. Kissing the cross was the sign of religious conversion.

Her lively looks a sprightly mind disclose,
10   Quick as her eyes, and as unfixed as those:
Favors to none, to all she smiles extends,
Oft she rejects, but never once offends.
Bright as the sun, her eyes the gazers strike,
And, like the sun, they shine on all alike.
15   Yet graceful ease, and sweetness void of pride,
Might hide her faults, if belles had faults to hide:
If to her share some female errors fall,
Look on her face, and you'll forget 'em all.
    This nymph, to the destruction of mankind,
20   Nourished two locks, which graceful hung behind
In equal curls, and well conspired to deck
With shining ringlets the smooth iv'ry neck.
Love in these labyrinths his slaves detains,
And mighty hearts are held in slender chains.
25   With hairy springes° we the birds betray,   *noose traps*
Slight lines° of hair surprise the finny prey,   *fishing lines*
Fair tresses man's imperial race ensnare,
And beauty draws us with a single hair.
    Th' advent'rous Baron[7] the bright locks admired;
30   He saw, he wished, and to the prize aspired:
Resolved to win, he meditates the way,
By force to ravish, or by fraud betray;
For when success a lover's toil attends,
Few ask, if fraud or force attained his ends.
35   For this, ere Phoebus rose, he had implored
Propitious Heav'n, and ev'ry pow'r adored,°   *worshipped*
But chiefly Love—to Love an altar built,
Of twelve vast French romances, neatly gilt.[8]
There lay three garters, half a pair of gloves;
40   And all the trophies of his former loves.
With tender *billet-doux* he lights the pyre,
And breathes three am'rous sighs to raise the fire.
Then prostrate falls, and begs with ardent eyes
Soon to obtain, and long possess the prize:
45   The pow'rs gave ear, and granted half his pray'r,
The rest the winds dispersed in empty air.[9]
    But now secure the painted vessel glides,
The sunbeams trembling on the floating tides,
While melting music steals upon the sky,
50   And softened sounds along the waters die.
Smooth flow the waves, the zephyrs° gently play,   *breezes*

---

7. Robert, Lord Petre (1690–1713), responsible for the original incident.
8. Long love stories, here attractively bound with embossed gold lettering.

9. Cf. *The Aeneid* 2.794–95, which Dryden translated: "Apollo heard, and granting half his pray'r, / Shuffled in winds the rest, and tossed in empty air."

Belinda smiled, and all the world was gay.
All but the Sylph—with careful° thoughts oppressed,   *worried*
Th' impending woe sat heavy on his breast.
He summons strait his denizens[1] of air;
The lucid squadrons round the sails repair:
Soft o'er the shrouds° aerial whispers breathe,   *ropes*
That seemed but zephyrs to the train beneath.
Some to the sun their insect-wings unfold,
Waft on the breeze, or sink in clouds of gold.
Transparent forms, too fine for mortal sight,
Their fluid bodies half dissolved in light,
Loose to the wind their airy garments flew,
Thin glitt'ring textures of the filmy dew,
Dipped in the richest tincture of the skies,
Where light disports in ever-mingling dyes,
While ev'ry beam new transient colors flings,
Colors that change whene'er they wave their wings.
Amid the circle, on the gilded mast,
Superior by the head, was Ariel placed;[2]
His purple pinions opening to the sun,
He raised his azure wand, and thus begun:
    "Ye Sylphs and Sylphids,° to your chief give ear,   *female Sylphs*
Fays, Fairies, Genii, Elves, and Demons hear!
Ye know the spheres and various tasks assigned
By laws eternal to th' aerial kind.
Some in the fields of purest ether[3] play,
And bask and whiten in the blaze of day.
Some guide the course of wandering orbs° on high,   *comets*
Or roll the planets through the boundless sky.
Some, less refined, beneath the moon's pale light
Pursue the stars that shoot athwart the night;
Or suck the mists in grosser° air below,   *heavier*
Or dip their pinions in the painted bow,°   *rainbow*
Or brew fierce tempests on the wintry main,
Or o'er the glebe° distill the kindly rain.   *farmland*
Others on earth o'er human race preside,
Watch all their ways, and all their actions guide:
Of these the chief the care of nations own,
And guard with arms divine the British throne.
    "Our humbler province is to tend the fair;
Not a less pleasing, though less glorious care.
To save the powder from too rude° a gale,   *rough*
Nor let th' imprisoned essences° exhale,   *perfumes*
To draw fresh colors from the vernal flow'rs,
To steal from rainbows ere they drop in show'rs
A brighter wash;[4] to curl their waving hairs,

Line numbers: 55, 60, 65, 70, 75, 80, 85, 90, 95

---

1. Naturalized foreigners.
2. Heroes of epics were typically taller than their men.
3. Air beyond the moon.
4. A cosmetic rinse.

Assist their blushes, and inspire their airs;
Nay oft, in dreams, invention we bestow,
100   To change a flounce, or add a furbelow.°   *fringe*
    "This day, black omens threat the brightest fair
That e'er deserved a watchful spirit's care;
Some dire disaster, or° by force or sleight;°   *either / trick*
But what, or where, the fates have wrapped in night.
105   Whether the nymph shall break Diana's law,°   *virginity*
Or some frail china jar receive a flaw,
Or stain her honor, or her new brocade,
Forget her pray'rs, or miss a masquerade,
Or lose her heart, or necklace, at a ball;
110   Or whether Heav'n has doomed that Shock must fall.
Haste then ye spirits! to your charge° repair;   *duty*
The flutt'ring fan be Zephyretta's care;
The drops° to thee, Brillante, we consign;   *earrings*
And Momentilla, let the watch be thine;
115   Do thou, Crispissa,[5] tend her fav'rite lock;
Ariel himself shall be the guard of Shock.
    "To fifty chosen Sylphs, of special note,
We trust th' important charge, the petticoat:
Oft have we known that sev'nfold fence[6] to fail,
120   Though stiff with hoops, and armed with ribs of whale.
Form a strong line about the silver bound,
And guard the wide circumference around.
    "Whatever spirit, careless of his charge,
His post neglects, or leaves the fair at large,
125   Shall feel sharp vengeance soon o'ertake his sins,
Be stopped in vials, or transfixed with pins;
Or plunged in lakes of bitter washes lie,
Or wedged whole ages in a bodkin's[7] eye:
Gums and pomatums° shall his flight restrain,   *ointments*
130   While clogged he beats his silken wings in vain;
Or alum styptics[8] with contracting power
Shrink his thin essence like a rivelled° flower: *shriveled*
Or as Ixion[9] fixed, the wretch shall feel
The giddy motion of the whirling mill,[1]
135   In fumes of burning chocolate shall glow,
And tremble at the sea that froths below!"
    He spoke; the spirits from the sails descend;
Some, orb in orb, around the nymph extend,

---

5. The Latin *crispere* means to curl.
6. Serving Belinda like the epic warrior's shield, her petticoat has seven layers bound together with a silver band
(cf. *Iliad* 18 or *Aeneid* 8).
7. Blunt, thick needle; the Sylph, like the camel in Matthew
19.24 and Mark 10.25, has difficulty getting through. Pope
later plays on the various meanings of "bodkin," which also

include a hair ornament and a dagger.
8. Astringents that stopped bleeding.
9. Having tried the chastity of Hera, Ixion was punished
by being tied to a continually revolving wheel of fire.
1. For beating chocolate, a new and highly fashionable
drink.

Some thrid° the mazy ringlets of her hair,   *slid through*
140 Some hang upon the pendants of her ear;
With beating hearts the dire event they wait,
Anxious, and trembling for the birth of Fate.

CANTO 3

Close by those meads forever crowned with flow'rs,
Where Thames with pride surveys his rising tow'rs,
There stands a structure of majestic frame,
Which from the neighb'ring Hampton takes its name.[2]
5 Here Britain's statesmen oft the fall foredoom
Of foreign tyrants, and of nymphs at home;
Here thou, great Anna! whom three realms obey,[3]
Dost sometimes counsel take—and sometimes tea.
    Hither the heroes and the nymphs resort,
10 To taste awhile the pleasures of a court;
In various talk th' instructive hours they passed,
Who gave the ball, or paid the visit last:
One speaks the glory of the British Queen,
And one describes a charming Indian screen;
15 A third interprets motions, looks, and eyes;
At ev'ry word a reputation dies.
Snuff, or the fan, supply each pause of chat,
With singing, laughing, ogling, and all that.
    Meanwhile declining from the noon of day,
20 The sun obliquely shoots his burning ray;
The hungry judges soon the sentence sign,
And wretches hang that jurymen may dine;
The merchant from th' Exchange° returns in peace,   *market*
And the long labors of the toilet cease.
25 Belinda now, whom thirst of fame invites,
Burns to encounter two advent'rous knights,
At Ombre[4] singly to decide their doom;
And swells her breast with conquests yet to come.
Straight the three bands prepare in arms to join,
30 Each band the number of the Sacred Nine.[5]
Soon as she spreads her hand, th' aerial guard
Descend, and sit on each important card:
First Ariel perch'd upon a Matador,[6]
Then each, according to the rank they bore;

2. Hampton Court, about 15 miles upriver from London, was built in the 16th century by Cardinal Wolsey; by Queen Anne's day it was associated with wits as well as with statesmen.
3. The English Crown still maintained its ancient claim to rule France as well as Great Britain and Ireland.
4. A card game played with 40 cards, similar to modern bridge: three players hold nine cards each and bid for tricks, with the highest bidder becoming the "ombre" (man) and choosing trumps.
5. Pope links the nine Muses to the nine cards each player holds.
6. The Matadors are the three cards of highest value; Belinda holds all three: when trumps are black, they are the Spadillio (ace of spades), Manillio (deuce of spades), and Basto (ace of clubs).

35   For Sylphs, yet mindful of their ancient race,
        Are, as when women, wondrous fond of place.°   rank
            Behold, four kings in majesty revered,
        With hoary whiskers[7] and a forky beard:
        And four fair queens whose hands sustain° a flow'r,   hold
40   Th' expressive emblem of their softer pow'r;
        Four knaves in garbs succinct,° a trusty band,   girded up
        Caps on their heads, and halberds in their hand;
        And particolored troops, a shining train,
        Draw forth to combat on the velvet plain.[8]
45   The skillful nymph reviews her force with care;
        "Let spades be trumps!" she said, and trumps they were.[9]
            Now move to war her sable Matadors,
        In show like leaders of the swarthy moors.
        Spadillio first, unconquerable lord!
50   Led off two captive trumps, and swept the board.
        As many more Manillio forced to yield,
        And marched a victor from the verdant field.
        Him Basto followed, but his fate more hard
        Gained but one trump and one plebeian card.
55   With his broad saber next, a chief in years,
        The hoary majesty of spades appears;
        Puts forth one manly leg, to sight revealed,
        The rest his many-colored robe concealed.
        The rebel knave, who dares his prince engage,
60   Proves the just victim of his royal rage.
        Ev'n mighty Pam[1] that kings and queens o'erthrew,
        And mowed down armies in the fights of Lu,
        Sad chance of war! now, destitute of aid,
        Falls undistinguished by the victor spade!
65   Thus far both armies to Belinda yield;
        Now to the Baron fate inclines the field.
        His warlike Amazon her host invades,
        Th' imperial consort of the crown of spades.
        The club's black tyrant first her victim died,
70   Spite of his haughty mien and barb'rous pride:
        What boots the regal circle on his head,
        His giant limbs in state unwieldy spread;
        That long behind he trails his pompous robe,
        And of all monarchs only grasps the globe?
75   The Baron now his diamonds pours apace;
        Th' embroidered king who shows but half his face,

7. Gray mustache. The royal figures on the cards now conduct a mock-epic review of their forces, and the whole game is described as an epic battle, with the characters appearing as on the cards.
8. The green velvet card table.

9. Cf. Genesis 1.3: "Then God said, 'Let there be light'; and there was light."
1. The knave or jack of clubs, which took precedence over all trumps in the game of Lu, or Loo.

And his refulgent queen, with pow'rs combined,
Of broken troops an easy conquest find.
Clubs, diamonds, hearts, in wild disorder seen,
80   With throngs promiscuous strew the level green.
Thus when dispersed a routed army runs,
Of Asia's troops and Afric's sable sons,
With like confusion different nations fly,
Of various habit and of various dye,
85   The pierced battalions disunited fall,
In heaps on heaps; one fate o'erwhelms them all.
      The knave of diamonds tries his wily arts,
And wins (oh shameful chance!) the queen of hearts.
At this, the blood the virgin's cheek forsook,
90   A livid paleness spreads o'er all her look;
She sees, and trembles at th' approaching ill,
Just in the jaws of ruin, and codille.[2]
And now (as oft in some distempered state)
On one nice trick[3] depends the gen'ral fate.
95   An ace of hearts steps forth: the king[4] unseen
Lurked in her hand, and mourned his captive queen.
He springs to vengeance with an eager pace,
And falls like thunder on the prostrate ace.
The nymph exulting fills with shouts the sky,
100   The walls, the woods, and long canals reply.
      Oh thoughtless mortals! ever blind to fate,
Too soon dejected, and too soon elate!
Sudden these honors shall be snatched away,
And cursed forever this victorious day.
105   For lo! the board with cups and spoons is crowned,
The berries crackle, and the mill turns round.[5]
On shining altars of Japan[6] they raise
The silver lamp; the fiery spirits blaze.
From silver spouts the grateful° liquors glide,   *pleasing*
110   While China's earth receives the smoking tide.
At once they gratify their scent and taste,
While frequent cups prolong the rich repast.
Straight° hover round the fair her airy band;   *immediately*
Some, as she sipped, the fuming liquor fanned,
115   Some o'er her lap their careful plumes displayed,
Trembling, and conscious of the rich brocade.
Coffee (which makes the politician wise,
And see through all things with his half-shut eyes)
Sent up in vapors[7] to the Baron's brain

---

2. Literally "elbow": the defeat suffered by the ombre if
another player wins more tricks.
3. "Trick" applies in both its technical and general senses
as Belinda makes this careful maneuver.
4. The king of hearts.

5. Grinding coffee beans.
6. Lacquered tables ("Japan" was a type of varnish originating in that country).
7. Both steam and vain imaginations.

120 New stratagems, the radiant lock to gain.
Ah cease rash youth! desist e'er 'tis too late;
Fear the just gods, and think of Scylla's fate![8]
Changed to a bird, and sent to flit in air,
She dearly pays for Nisus' injured hair!
125   But when to mischief mortals bend their will,
How soon they find fit instruments of ill!
Just then, Clarissa drew with tempting grace
A two-edged weapon from her shining case;
So ladies in romance assist their knight,
130 Present the spear, and arm him for the fight.
He takes the gift with rev'rence, and extends
The little engine° on his fingers' ends;   *instrument*
This just behind Belinda's neck he spread,
As o'er the fragrant steams she bends her head:
135 Swift to the lock a thousand sprites repair,
A thousand wings, by turns, blow back the hair,
And thrice they twitched the diamond in her ear,
Thrice she looked back, and thrice the foe drew near.
Just in that instant, anxious Ariel sought
140 The close recesses of the virgin's thought;
As, on the nosegay in her breast reclined,
He watched th' ideas rising in her mind,
Sudden he viewed, in spite of all her art,
An earthly lover lurking at her heart.
145 Amazed, confused, he found his pow'r expired,
Resigned to fate, and with a sigh retired.
     The peer now spreads the glitt'ring forfex° wide,   *scissors*
T' enclose the lock; now joins it, to divide.
Ev'n then, before the fatal engine closed,
150 A wretched Sylph too fondly interposed;
Fate urged the shears, and cut the Sylph in twain
(But airy substance soon unites again)[9]
The meeting points the sacred hair dissever
From the fair head, forever and forever!
155   Then flashed the living lightning from her eyes,
And screams of horror rend th' affrighted skies.
Not louder shrieks to pitying Heav'n are cast,
When husbands or when lapdogs breathe their last;
Or when rich china vessels, fall'n from high,
160 In glitt'ring dust and painted fragments lie!
     Let wreaths of triumph now my temples twine.
(The victor cried) The glorious prize is mine!
While fish in streams, or birds delight in air,
Or in a coach and six[1] the British fair,

8. Scylla plucked purple hair from the head of her father, King Nisus, to offer to her lover, Minos, so destroying her father's power. Minos rejected her impiety, and Scylla was transformed into a bird.
9. *Milton* lib. 6 [Pope's note], citing *Paradise Lost* 6.329–31:

"The girding sword with discontinuous wound / Passed through him, but the ethereal substance closed / Not long divisible. . . ."
1. A carriage drawn by six horses; a symbol of wealth and prestige.

165 As long as *Atalantis*[2] shall be read,
Or the small pillow grace a lady's bed,[3]
While visits shall be paid on solemn days,
When num'rous wax-lights[4] in bright order blaze,
While nymphs take treats, or assignations give,
170 So long my honor, name, and praise shall live!
    What time would spare, from steel receives its date,°   end
And monuments, like men, submit to fate!
Steel could the labor of the gods destroy,
And strike to dust th' imperial tow'rs of Troy;[5]
175 Steel could the works of mortal pride confound,
And hew triumphal arches to the ground.
What wonder then, fair nymph! thy hairs should feel
The conqu'ring force of unresisted steel?

CANTO 4

But anxious cares the pensive nymph oppressed,
And secret passions labored in her breast.
Not youthful kings in battle seized alive,
Not scornful virgins who their charms survive,
5 Not ardent lovers robbed of all their bliss,
Not ancient ladies when refused a kiss,
Not tyrants fierce that unrepenting die,
Not Cynthia when her manteau's° pinned awry,   gown's
E'er felt such rage, resentment, and despair,
10 As thou, sad virgin! for thy ravished hair.
    For, that sad moment, when the Sylphs withdrew,
And Ariel weeping from Belinda flew,
Umbriel, a dusky melancholy sprite
As ever sullied the fair face of light,
15 Down to the central earth, his proper scene,
Repaired to search the gloomy Cave of Spleen.[6]
    Swift on his sooty pinions flits the Gnome,
And in a vapor[7] reached the dismal dome.
No cheerful breeze this sullen region knows,
20 The dreaded east[8] is all the wind that blows.
Here, in a grotto, sheltered close from air,
And screened in shades° from day's detested glare,   shadows
She sighs forever on her pensive bed,

2. The scandalous *Atalantis: Secret Memoirs and Manners of Several Persons of Quality* (1709), by Mary Delarivière Manley (1672–1724).
3. Said to be a place where ladies hid romance novels and other contraband.
4. Candles made of wax, rather than the cheaper tallow. Evening social visits were an essential part of the fashionable woman's routine.
5. Even Troy, fabled to have been built by Apollo and Poseidon, was destroyed by arms.
6. Named after the bodily organ, "spleen" was the current term for the fashionable affliction of melancholy or ill-humor. Umbriel's descent into the womblike Cave of Spleen suggests the epic commonplace of the journey to the underworld.
7. "The spleen" was also called "the vapors."
8. The east wind was supposed to induce fits of spleen.

Pain at her side, and Megrim° at her head.   *migraine*
25   Two handmaids wait the throne: alike in place,
But diff'ring far in figure and in face.
Here stood Ill-Nature like an ancient maid,
Her wrinkled form in black and white arrayed;
With store of pray'rs, for mornings, nights, and noons,
30   Her hand is filled; her bosom with lampoons.
         There Affectation with a sickly mien
Shows in her cheek the roses of eighteen,
Practiced to lisp, and hang the head aside,
Faints into airs, and languishes with pride;
35   On the rich quilt sinks with becoming woe,
Wrapped in a gown, for sickness and for show.
The fair ones feel such maladies as these,
When each new nightdress gives a new disease.
         A constant vapor o'er the palace flies,
40   Strange phantoms rising as the mists arise;
Dreadful, as hermit's dreams in haunted shades,
Or bright as visions of expiring maids.⁹
Now glaring fiends, and snakes on rolling spires,°   *coils*
Pale specters, gaping tombs, and purple fires;
45   Now lakes of liquid gold, Elysian scenes,¹
And crystal domes, and angels in machines.
         Unnumbered throngs on every side are seen,
Of bodies changed to various forms by Spleen.²
Here living teapots stand, one arm held out,
50   One bent; the handle this, and that the spout:
A pipkin³ there like Homer's tripod walks;
Here sighs a jar, and there a goose-pie⁴ talks;
Men prove with child, as pow'rful fancy works,
And maids, turned bottles, call aloud for corks.
55   Safe passed the Gnome through this fantastic band,
A branch of healing spleenwort⁵ in his hand.
Then thus addressed the pow'r: "Hail, wayward Queen!
Who rule the sex to fifty from fifteen,
Parent of vapors and of female wit,
60   Who give th' hysteric or poetic fit,
On various tempers act by various ways,
Make some take physic,° others scribble plays;⁶   *medicine*
Who cause the proud their visits to delay,
And send the godly in a pet° to pray.   *ill-humor*
65   A nymph there is that all thy pow'r disdains,

---

9. Religious visions of hell and heaven.
1. Elysium was the classical paradise, but this also recalls contemporary theater, which made much of scenic spectacle and the use of machinery.
2. Hallucinations similar to those described in the following lines were common to those afflicted with spleen.
3. Small pot or pan. Hephaistos's "walking" tripods are

described in the *Iliad* 18.439ff.
4. Alludes to a real fact, a Lady of distinction imagined herself in this condition [Pope's note].
5. Pope changes the golden bough that protected Aeneas on his trip through the underworld into an herb that was supposed to be good for the spleen.
6. Melancholy was associated with artistic creativity.

And thousands more in equal mirth maintains.
But oh! if e'er thy Gnome could spoil a grace,
Or raise a pimple on a beauteous face,
Like citron-waters° matrons' cheeks inflame,   *flavored brandy*
70 Or change complexions at a losing game;
If e'er with airy horns[7] I planted heads,
Or rumpled petticoats, or tumbled beds,
Or caused suspicion when no soul was rude,
Or discomposed the head-dress of a prude,
75 Or e'er to costive° lapdog gave disease,   *constipated*
Which not the tears of brightest eyes could ease:
Hear me, and touch Belinda with chagrin;
That single act gives half the world the spleen."
        The goddess with a discontented air
80 Seems to reject him, though she grants his pray'r.
A wondrous bag with both her hands she binds,
Like that where once Ulysses held the winds;[8]
There she collects the force of female lungs,
Sighs, sobs, and passions, and the war of tongues.
85 A vial next she fills with fainting fears,
Soft sorrows, melting griefs, and flowing tears.
The Gnome rejoicing bears her gifts away,
Spreads his black wings, and slowly mounts to day.
        Sunk in Thalestris'[9] arms the nymph he found,
90 Her eyes dejected and her hair unbound.
Full o'er their heads the swelling bag he rent,
And all the furies issued at the vent.
Belinda burns with more than mortal ire,
And fierce Thalestris fans the rising fire.
95 "O wretched maid!" she spread her hands, and cried
(While Hampton's echoes "Wretched maid!" replied),
"Was it for this you took such constant care
The bodkin, comb, and essence to prepare?
For this your locks in paper durance° bound,   *curling papers*
100 For this with tort'ring irons wreathed around?
For this with fillets[1] strained your tender head,
And bravely bore the double loads of lead?°   *wire supports*
Gods! shall the ravisher display your hair,
While the fops envy, and the ladies stare!
105 Honor forbid! at whose unrivaled shrine
Ease, pleasure, virtue, all, our sex resign.
Methinks already I your tears survey,
Already hear the horrid things they say,
Already see you a degraded toast,[2]

---

7. A sign that a husband had been cuckolded.
8. Given to him by the wind god Aeolus (*Odyssey* 10.19ff.).
9. A queen of the Amazons; here Mrs. Morley, Arabella's second cousin.
1. Headbands, with reference to priestesses in the *Aeneid*.

2. A woman whose toast is often drunk, and who by implication is all too well known to her (male) toasters: (cf. Canto 5.10, and Fielding's *Tom Jones*, where Sophia is not pleased by reports that she has been Tom's toast, bk. 13, ch. 11).

110 And all your honor in a whisper lost!
How shall I, then, your helpless fame defend?
'Twill then be infamy to seem your friend!
And shall this prize, th' inestimable prize,
Exposed through crystal to the gazing eyes,
115 And heightened by the diamond's circling rays,
On that rapacious hand forever blaze?[3]
Sooner shall grass in Hyde Park Circus grow,[4]
And wits take lodgings in the sound of Bow;[5]
Sooner let earth, air, sea, to chaos fall,
120 Men, monkeys, lapdogs, parrots, perish all!"
    She said; then raging to Sir Plume[6] repairs,
And bids her beau demand the precious hairs
(Sir Plume, of amber snuffbox justly vain,
And the nice conduct of a clouded cane[7]),
125 With earnest eyes, and round unthinking face,
He first the snuffbox opened, then the case,
And thus broke out—"My Lord, why, what the devil?
Z—ds![8] damn the lock! 'fore Gad, you must be civil!
Plague on't! 'tis past a jest—nay prithee, Pox!
130 Give her the hair"—he spoke, and rapped his box.
    "It grieves me much" (replied the Peer again)
"Who speaks so well should ever speak in vain.
But by this lock, this sacred lock I swear
(Which never more shall join its parted hair,
135 Which never more its honors shall renew,
Clipped from the lovely head where late it grew)
That while my nostrils draw the vital air,
This hand, which won it shall forever wear."
He spoke, and speaking, in proud triumph spread
140 The long-contended honors[9] of her head.
    But Umbriel, hateful Gnome! forbears not so;
He breaks the vial whence the sorrows flow.
Then see! the nymph in beauteous grief appears,
Her eyes half-languishing, half-drowned in tears;
145 On her heaved bosom hung her drooping head,
Which, with a sigh, she raised; and thus she said:
    "Forever cursed be this detested day,[1]
Which snatched my best, my fav'rite curl away!
Happy! ah, ten times happy, had I been,
150 If Hampton Court these eyes had never seen!
Yet am not I the first mistaken maid,

---

3. I.e., mounted in a ring.
4. The fashion for driving coaches around Hyde Park prevented grass from growing there.
5. A commercial area round St. Mary-le-Bow, and not at all fashionable.
6. Sir George Browne, cousin of Arabella's mother.

7. Skilled use of a cane with a head of dark polished stone.
8. Zounds, a corruption of "God's wounds," a mild oath.
9. Her beautiful hair.
1. Echoing Achilles' lament for his slain friend Patroclus (Iliad 18.107ff.).

By love of courts to num'rous ills betrayed.
Oh, had I rather unadmired remained
In some lone isle, or distant northern land;
155   Where the gilt chariot never marks the way,
Where none learn Ombre, none e'er taste bohea!°   tea
There kept my charms concealed from mortal eye,
Like roses that in deserts bloom and die.
What moved my mind with youthful lords to roam?
160   Oh, had I stayed, and said my pray'rs at home!
'Twas this the morning omens seemed to tell:
Thrice from my trembling hand the patch box fell;
The tott'ring china shook without a wind;
Nay, Poll° sat mute, and Shock was most unkind!   her parrot
165   A Sylph too warned me of the threats of fate,
In mystic visions, now believed too late!
See the poor remnants of these slighted hairs!
My hands shall rend what ev'n thy rapine spares:
These, in two sable ringlets taught to break,°   divide
170   Once gave new beauties to the snowy neck;
The sister lock now sits uncouth, alone,
And in its fellow's fate foresees its own;
Uncurled it hangs, the fatal shears demands;
And tempts once more thy sacrilegious hands.
175   Oh hadst thou, cruel! been content to seize
Hairs less in sight, or any hairs but these!"

CANTO 5

She said: the pitying audience melt in tears,
But Fate and Jove had stopped the Baron's ears.
In vain Thalestris with reproach assails,
For who can move when fair Belinda fails?
5   Not half so fixed the Trojan[2] could remain,
While Anna begged and Dido raged in vain.
Then grave Clarissa[3] graceful waved her fan;
Silence ensued, and thus the nymph began:
    "Say, why are beauties praised and honored most,
10   The wise man's passion, and the vain man's toast?
Why decked with all that land and sea afford,
Why angels called, and angel-like adored?
Why round our coaches crowd the white-gloved beaus,
Why bows the side box from its inmost rows?[4]
15   How vain are all these glories, all our pains,

---

2. Aeneas, fixed on his decision to leave Carthage and abandon Dido despite her pleas and those of her sister Anna (*Aeneid* 4.269–449).
3. A new character introduced . . . to open more clearly the moral of the poem, in a parody of the speech of Sarpedon to Glaucus in Homer [Pope's note in the 1717 edition]. For Pope's translation of Sarpedon's speech (*Iliad* 12), see pages 2491–92.
4. At the theater, gentlemen sat in the side boxes, ladies in the front boxes facing the stage.

Unless good sense preserve what beauty gains:
That men may say, when we the front box grace,
'Behold the first in virtue as in face!'
Oh! if to dance all night, and dress all day,
20   Charmed the smallpox,[5] or chased old age away,
Who would not scorn what housewife's cares produce,
Or who would learn one earthly thing of use?
To patch, nay ogle, might become a saint,
Nor could it sure be such a sin to paint.
25   But since, alas! frail beauty must decay,
Curled or uncurled, since locks will turn to grey,
Since painted or not painted, all shall fade,
And she who scorns a man must die a maid;
What then remains, but well our pow'r to use,
30   And keep good humor still whate'er we lose?
And trust me, dear! good humor can prevail,
When airs, and flights, and screams, and scolding fail.
Beauties in vain their pretty eyes may roll;
Charms strike the sight, but merit wins the soul."
35   So spoke the dame, but no applause ensued;
Belinda frowned, Thalestris called her prude.
"To arms, to arms!" the fierce virago[6] cries,
And swift as lightning to the combat flies.
All side in parties, and begin th' attack;
40   Fans clap, silks rustle, and tough whalebones crack;
Heroes' and heroines' shouts confus'dly rise,
And bass and treble voices strike the skies.
No common weapons in their hands are found,
Like gods they fight, nor dread a mortal wound.
45   So when bold Homer makes the gods engage,
And heav'nly breasts with human passions rage;
'Gainst Pallas,° Mars; Latona,[7] Hermes arms;   *Athena*
And all Olympus rings with loud alarms:
Jove's thunder roars, heav'n trembles all around;
50   Blue Neptune storms, the bellowing deeps resound;
Earth shakes her nodding tow'rs, the ground gives way,
And the pale ghosts start at the flash of day!
        Triumphant Umbriel on a sconce's[8] height
Clapped his glad wings, and sat to view the fight;
55   Propped on their bodkin spears, the sprites survey
The growing combat, or assist the fray.
        While through the press enraged Thalestris flies,
And scatters deaths around from both her eyes,
A beau and witling° perished in the throng;   *little wit*

---

5. A common disease, which frequently left permanent
facial scars.
6. Woman who behaves like a man.

7. Mother of Diana and Apollo.
8. Candlestick attached to the wall.

60   One died in metaphor, and one in song.
      "O cruel nymph! a living death I bear,"
      Cried Dapperwit, and sunk beside his chair.
      A mournful glance Sir Fopling upwards cast,
      "Those eyes are made so killing"⁹—was his last.
65   Thus on Meander's flow'ry margin lies
      Th' expiring swan, and as he sings he dies.¹
           When bold Sir Plume had drawn Clarissa down,
      Chloe stepped in, and killed him with a frown;
      She smiled to see the doughty hero slain,
70   But at her smile, the beau revived again.
           Now Jove suspends his golden scales in air,²
      Weighs the men's wits against the lady's hair;
      The doubtful beam long nods from side to side;
      At length the wits mount up, the hairs subside.
75   See, fierce Belinda on the Baron flies,
      With more than usual lightning in her eyes;
      Nor feared the chief th' unequal fight to try,
      Who sought no more than on his foe to die.³
      But this bold lord, with manly strength indued,
80   She with one finger and a thumb subdued:
      Just where the breath of life his nostrils drew,
      A charge of snuff the wily virgin threw;
      The Gnomes direct, to ev'ry atom just,
      The pungent grains of titillating dust.
85   Sudden, with starting tears each eye o'erflows,
      And the high dome re-echoes to his nose.⁴
           "Now meet thy fate," incensed Belinda cried,
      And drew a deadly bodkin⁵ from her side.
      (The same, his ancient personage to deck,
90   Her great great grandsire wore about his neck
      In three seal rings; which after, melted down,
      Formed a vast buckle for his widow's gown:
      Her infant grandame's° whistle next it grew,   *grandmother's*
      The bells she jingled, and the whistle blew;
95   Then in a bodkin graced her mother's hairs,
      Which long she wore, and now Belinda wears.)
           "Boast not my fall," he cried, "insulting foe!
      Thou by some other shalt be laid as low.
      Nor think, to die dejects my lofty mind;
100   All that I dread is leaving you behind!
      Rather than so, ah let me still survive,
      And burn in Cupid's flames—but burn alive."

9. A line from Giovanni Bononcini's opera, *Camilla* (1696), which at this time was popular in London.
1. Meander: A river in Asia Minor. Swans were popularly believed to sing only on their death. This simile refers to Ovid's *Heroides* 7, a lament from Dido to Aeneas.

2. To determine victory in battle; a convention found in both Homer and Virgil.
3. A standard metaphor for sexual climax.
4. Cf. his boast, 4.133–38.
5. A decorative pin, shaped like a dagger.

"Restore the lock!" she cries; and all around
"Restore the lock!" the vaulted roofs rebound.
105   Not fierce Othello in so loud a strain
Roared for the handkerchief that caused his pain.
But see how oft ambitious aims are crossed,
And chiefs contend till all the prize is lost!
The lock, obtained with guilt, and kept with pain,
110   In ev'ry place is sought, but sought in vain:
With such a prize no mortal must be blessed,
So Heav'n decrees! with Heav'n who can contest?
Some thought it mounted to the lunar sphere,[6]
Since all things lost on earth are treasured there.
115   There heroes' wits are kept in ponderous vases,
And beaus' in snuff-boxes and tweezer cases.
There broken vows and deathbed alms are found,
And lovers' hearts with ends of riband bound;
The courtier's promises, and sick man's pray'rs,
120   The smiles of harlots, and the tears of heirs,
Cages for gnats, and chains to yoke a flea;
Dried butterflies, and tomes of casuistry.[7]
But trust the Muse—she saw it upward rise,
Though marked by none but quick poetic eyes:
125   (So Rome's great founder to the heav'ns withdrew,
To Proculus alone confessed in view.[8])
A sudden star, it shot through liquid air,
And drew behind a radiant trail of hair.
Not Berenice's locks first rose so bright,[9]
130   The heav'ns bespangling with disheveled light.
The Sylphs behold it kindling as it flies,
And pleased pursue its progress through the skies.
This the beau monde shall from the Mall[1] survey,
And hail with music its propitious ray.
135   This, the blessed lover shall for Venus° take,   *the planet*
And send up vows from Rosamonda's lake.[2]
This Partridge[3] soon shall view in cloudless skies,
When next he looks through Galileo's eyes;[4]
And hence th' egregious wizard shall foredoom
140   The fate of Louis, and the fall of Rome.
Then cease, bright nymph! to mourn thy ravished hair,

---

6. Cf. Ariosto's *Orlando Furioso* (1516–1532), in which Orlando's lost wits are sought on the moon. See also *Paradise Lost* 3.444ff.
7. Subtle reasoning (often used of arguments justifying immoral conduct).
8. When Romulus was killed mysteriously, Proculus soothed popular grief by asserting that he had been taken up to heaven.
9. The Egyptian queen Berenice made an offering of her hair after her husband returned victorious from the wars;

when it disappeared from the temple, the court astronomer claimed it had been made into a new constellation.
1. A fashionable walk in St. James's Park.
2. Where lovers met in St. James's Park.
3. John Partridge was a ridiculous star-gazer, who in his almanacs every year, never failed to predict the downfall of the Pope, and the King of France, then at war with the English [Pope's note].
4. I.e., a telescope.

Which adds new glory to the shining sphere!
Not all the tresses that fair head can boast
Shall draw such envy as the lock you lost.
145   For, after all the murders of your eye,
When, after millions slain, yourself shall die;
When those fair suns⁵ shall set, as set they must,
And all those tresses shall be laid in dust;
This lock, the Muse shall consecrate to fame,
150   And 'midst the stars inscribe Belinda's name!

1711–1717   1712; 1714; 1717

from The Iliad
from *Book 12*
[SARPEDON'S SPEECH]¹

Resolved alike, divine Sarpedon² glows
With gen'rous rage that drives him on the foes.
He views the tow'rs,³ and meditates° their fall,   *plans*
To sure destruction dooms th' aspiring° wall;   *high*
5   Then casting on his friend an ardent look,
Fired with the thirst of glory, thus he spoke.
    "Why boast we, Glaucus! our extended reign,
Where Xanthus' streams⁴ enrich the Lycian plain,
Our num'rous herds that range the fruitful field,
10   And hills where vines their purple harvest yield,
Our foaming bowls with purer nectar⁵ crowned,
Our feasts enhanced with music's sprightly° sound?   *lively*
Why on those shores are we with joy surveyed,°   *observed*
Admired as heroes, and as gods obeyed?
15   Unless great acts superior merit prove,
And vindicate the bounteous pow'rs above.⁶
'Tis ours,⁷ the dignity they give, to grace;
The first in valor, as the first in place.
That when with wond'ring eyes our martial bands
20   Behold our deeds transcending our commands,
'Such,' they may cry, 'deserve the sov'reign state,°   *role*
Whom those that envy, dare not imitate!'

---

5. I.e., her eyes.
1. Pope spent nearly seven years (1713–1720) translating Homer's *Iliad* and writing critical notes to accompany his text. His work was an outstanding commercial and literary success; it earned him about £5000, more than a hundred times the earnings of a skilled craftsman or shop owner, and it later garnered Samuel Johnson's praise as "the noblest version [translation] of poetry which the world has ever seen." The speech of Sarpedon, a king fighting for the Trojans against the Greeks, was the first passage from Pope's *Iliad* that made its way into print, as part of *Pastorals* (1709), his first published collection; he later drew upon it deftly in his mock epic *The Rape of the Lock*, where in Canto 5, Clarissa's injunction to her fellow fashionistas echoes and

parodies Sarpedon's speech (and Pope's own translation) almost line for line (5.9–34; see pages 2487–88).
2. Sarpedon, king of the Lycians, was the son of the supreme deity Zeus and the mortal Laodemia. Here, he exhorts his lieutenant Glaucus to bravery as they lead the Lycians into battle.
3. The high ramparts that the Greeks have built outside the walls of Troy.
4. The Xanthus is the principal river flowing through Lycia, a mountainous country in southwestern Asia Minor.
5. Perhaps mead (made from fermented honey).
6. I.e., the gods' blessings on us.
7. I.e., our obligation (to prove worthy of this bounty).

dark

Could all our care elude the gloomy° grave,
Which claims no less the fearful than the brave,
25 For lust of fame I should not vainly dare
In fighting fields, nor urge thy soul to war.
But since, alas! Ignoble age must come,
Disease, and death's inexorable doom;
The life which others pay, let us bestow,
30 And give to fame what we to nature owe;
Brave though we fall, and honored if we live,
Or° let us glory gain, or glory give!"[8]   *either*
    He said; his words the list'ning chief inspire
With equal warmth, and rouse the warrior's fire;
35 The troops pursue their leaders with delight,
Rush to the foe, and claim the promised fight.

c. 1707   1709

ELOISA TO ABELARD   Peter Abelard (1079–1142), a great French philosopher and theologian, was tutor to the young Heloise (Eloisa). They fell in love, had a son, and secretly married. When the affair became known, Heloise was forced to enter a convent and Abelard was castrated by a gang of thugs hired by Heloise's enraged uncle. Abelard became a Benedictine monk, founding the monastery of the Paraclete, or Holy Spirit. After many years of living respectable and successful lives devoted to God, the two former lovers exchanged a series of epistles in Latin. These austere letters were made more romantic and psychologically complex when they were loosely translated into French in the later seventeenth century. In 1713 Pope's friend John Hughes translated the silently "improved" French version into English; this became the source for Pope's poem, which he chose to conclude his 1717 *Works*. Modeled upon Ovid's *Heroides*, *Eloisa to Abelard* is a "heroic epistle," a dramatic expression of a lover's feelings in a verse letter addressed to an absent loved one. Alternately erotic and pious, gothic and tender, Pope's intensely passionate and penetratingly psychological portrait of Eloisa's conflicting feelings was one of his most widely admired works, particularly among eighteenth-century women readers.

Eloisa to Abelard
The Argument

Abelard and Eloisa flourished in the twelfth century; they were two of the most distinguished persons of their age in learning and beauty, but for nothing more famous than for their unfortunate passion. After a long course of calamities, they retired each to a several[1] convent, and consecrated the remainder of their days to religion. It was many years after this separation that a letter of Abelard's to a friend which contained the history of his misfortune fell into the hands of Eloisa. This, awakening all her tenderness, occasioned those celebrated letters (out of which the following is partly extracted) which give so lively a picture of the struggles of grace and nature, virtue and passion.

---

8. There is not a more forcible argument than this, to make all men condemn dangers, and seek glory by brave actions. Immortality with eternal youth is certainly preferable to glory purchased with the loss of life; but glory is certainly better than an ignominious life, which at last, though perhaps late, must end . . . This is incontestable, and whoever weighs his actions in these scales, can never hesitate in his choice; but what is most remarkable is that Homer does not put this in the mouth of an ordinary person, but ascribes it to the son of Jupiter [Pope's note].
1. Separate.

In these deep solitudes and awful° cells,   *awe-inspiring*
Where heav'nly-pensive contemplation dwells,
And ever-musing melancholy reigns;
What means this tumult in a vestal's² veins?
5   Why rove my thoughts beyond this last retreat?
Why feels my heart its long-forgotten heat?
Yet, yet³ I love!—From Abelard it came,
And Eloisa yet must kiss the name.
    Dear fatal name! rest ever unrevealed,
10   Nor pass these lips in holy silence sealed.
Hide it, my heart, within that close disguise,
Where, mixed with God's, his loved idea° lies.   *image*
Oh write it not, my hand—the name appears
Already written—wash it out, my tears!
15   In vain lost Eloisa weeps and prays,
Her heart still dictates, and her hand obeys.
    Relentless walls! whose darksome round contains
Repentant sighs, and voluntary pains;
Ye rugged rocks! which holy knees have worn;
20   Ye grots° and caverns shagged with horrid° thorn!   *grottos / bristling*
Shrines! where their vigils pale-eyed virgins keep,
And pitying saints, whose statues learn to weep!⁴
Though cold like you, unmoved, and silent grown,
I have not yet forgot myself to stone.⁵
25   Heav'n claims me all in vain, while he has part,
Still rebel nature holds out half my heart;
Nor pray'rs nor fast its stubborn pulse restrain,
Nor tears, for ages, taught to flow in vain.
    Soon as thy letters trembling I unclose,
30   That well-known name awakens all my woes.
Oh name forever sad! forever dear!
Still breathed in sighs, still ushered with a tear.
I tremble too wheree'er my own I find,
Some dire misfortune follows close behind.
35   Line after line my gushing eyes o'erflow,
Led through a sad variety of woe:
Now warm in love, now with'ring in thy bloom,
Lost in a convent's° solitary gloom!   *monastery's*
There stern religion quenched th' unwilling flame,
40   There died the best of passions, love and fame.
    Yet write, or write me all, that I may join
Griefs to thy griefs, and echo sighs to thine.
Nor foes nor fortune take this pow'r away.
And is my Abelard less kind than they?

---

2. Virgin bound to the service of the Roman goddess Vesta. As a nun Eloisa, like the vestals, was now sequestered for service to the divine.
3. In the sense of both "but" and "still."
4. Through condensation that ran down the statues.

5. This metaphor comes from Hughes's translation of the *Letters of Abelard and Heloise*: "O Vows! O Convent! I have not lost my humanity under your inexorable discipline! You have not made me marble by changing my habit" (129). See also Milton, *Il Penseroso*, line 42.

45   Tears still are mine, and those I need not spare,
      Love but demands what else were shed in pray'r;
      No happier task these faded eyes pursue,
      To read and weep is all they now can do.
          Then share thy pain, allow that sad relief;
50   Ah more than share it! give me all thy grief.
      Heav'n first taught letters for some wretch's aid,
      Some banished lover, or some captive maid;
      They live, they speak, they breathe what love inspires,
      Warm from the soul, and faithful to its fires,
55   The virgin's wish without her fears impart,
      Excuse[6] the blush, and pour out all the heart,
      Speed the soft intercourse from soul to soul,
      And waft a sigh from Indus[7] to the Pole.
          Thou know'st how guiltless first I met thy flame,
60   When love approached me under friendship's name;
      My fancy formed thee of angelic kind,
      Some emanation of th' all-beauteous Mind.°   God
      Those smiling eyes, attemp'ring° ev'ry ray,   softening
      Shone sweetly lambent° with celestial day: radiant
65   Guiltless I gazed; Heav'n listened while you sung;
      And truths divine came mended from that tongue.[8]
      From lips like those what precept failed to move?
      Too soon they taught me 'twas no sin to love.
      Back through the paths of pleasing sense I ran,
70   Nor wished an angel whom I loved a man.[9]
      Dim and remote the joys of saints I see,
      Nor envy them, that Heav'n I lose for thee.
          How oft, when pressed to marriage, have I said,
      Curse on all laws but those which love has made?
75   Love, free as air, at sight of human ties,
      Spreads his light wings, and in a moment flies.
      Let wealth, let honor, wait the wedded dame,
      August her deed, and sacred be her fame;
      Before true passion all those views remove,°   disperse
80   Fame, wealth, and honor! what are you to love?
      The jealous god,° when we profane his fires,   Cupid
      Those restless passions in revenge inspires;
      And bids them make mistaken mortals groan,
      Who seek in love for ought but love alone.
85   Should at my feet the world's great master fall,
      Himself, his throne, his world, I'd scorn 'em all:
      Not Caesar's empress would I deign to prove;
      No, make me mistress to the man I love;
      If there be yet another name more free,

6. Release from the need for.
7. A southern constellation far distant from the northern Polestar.
8. He was her preceptor in philosophy and divinity

[Pope's note].
9. Having thought you an angel, I now return to my senses, and happily accept you as human.

90 More fond° than mistress, make me that to thee!   *beloved*
Oh happy state! when souls each other draw,
When love is liberty, and nature, law:
All then is full, possessing, and possessed,
No craving void left aching in the breast:
95 Ev'n thought meets thought ere from the lips it part,
And each warm wish springs mutual from the heart.
This sure is bliss (if bliss on earth there be)
And once the lot of Abelard and me.
        Alas how changed! what sudden horrors rise!
100 A naked lover bound and bleeding lies!
Where, where was Eloise? her voice, her hand,
Her poniard, had opposed the dire command.
Barbarian stay! that bloody stroke restrain;
The crime was common, common be the pain.[1]
105 I can no more; by shame, by rage suppressed,
Let tears and burning blushes speak the rest.
        Canst thou forget that sad, that solemn day,
When victims at yon altar's foot we lay?
Canst thou forget what tears that moment fell,
110 When, warm in youth, I bade the world farewell?
As with cold lips I kissed the sacred veil,
The shrines all trembled, and the lamps grew pale:
Heav'n scarce believed the conquest it surveyed,
And saints with wonder heard the vows I made.
115 Yet then, to those dread altars as I drew,
Not on the Cross my eyes were fixed, but you;
Not grace, or zeal, love only was my call,
And if I lose thy love, I lose my all.
Come! with thy looks, thy words, relieve my woe;
120 Those still at least are left thee to bestow.
Still on that breast enamored let me lie,
Still drink delicious poison from thy eye,
Pant on thy lip, and to thy heart be pressed;
Give all thou canst—and let me dream the rest.
125 Ah no! instruct me other joys to prize,
With other beauties charm my partial° eyes,   *fondly biased*
Full in my view set all the bright abode,
And make my soul quit Abelard for God.
        Ah think at least thy flock deserves thy care,
130 Plants of thy hand, and children of thy pray'r.
From the false world in early youth they fled,
By thee to mountains, wilds, and deserts led.
You raised these hallowed walls;[2] the desert smiled,
And paradise was opened in the wild.
135 No weeping orphan saw his father's stores
Our shrines irradiate, or emblaze the floors;[3]

1. The crime was shared, so also should have been the   3. "Irradiate" and "emblaze," meaning "adorn gloriously,"
penalty.   both come from Milton.
2. He founded the monastery [Pope's note].

No silver saints, by dying misers giv'n,
Here bribed the rage of ill-requited Heav'n:
But such plain roofs as piety could raise,
140   And only vocal with the Maker's[4] praise.
In these lone walls (their days eternal bound)
These moss-grown domes° with spiry turrets crowned,   *buildings*
Where awful arches make a noon-day night,
And the dim windows shed a solemn light;
145   Thy eyes diffused a reconciling ray,
And gleams of glory brightened all the day.
But now no face divine contentment wears,
'Tis all blank sadness, or continual tears.
See how the force of others' pray'rs I try
150   (Oh pious fraud of am'rous charity!),
But why should I on others' pray'rs depend?
Come thou, my father, brother,[5] husband, friend!
Ah let thy handmaid, sister, daughter move,
And, all those tender names in one, thy love!
155   The darksome pines that o'er yon rocks reclined
Wave high, and murmur to the hollow wind,
The wand'ring streams that shine between the hills,
The grots that echo to the tinkling rills,
The dying gales that pant upon the trees,
160   The lakes that quiver to the curling breeze;
No more these scenes my meditation aid,
Or lull to rest the visionary maid:[6]
But o'er the twilight groves, and dusky caves,
Long-sounding isles, and intermingled graves,
165   Black melancholy sits, and round her throws
A death-like silence, and a dread repose:
Her gloomy presence saddens all the scene,
Shades ev'ry flow'r, and darkens ev'ry green,
Deepens the murmur of the falling floods,
170   And breathes a browner horror on the woods.
    Yet here for ever, ever must I stay;
Sad proof how well a lover can obey!
Death, only death, can break the lasting chain;
And here ev'n then, shall my cold dust remain,
175   Here all its frailties, all its flames resign,
And wait, till 'tis no sin to mix with thine.
    Ah wretch! believed the spouse of God in vain,
Confessed within the slave of love and man.
Assist me Heav'n! but whence arose that pray'r?
180   Sprung it from piety, or from despair?
Ev'n here, where frozen chastity retires,

---

4. The satirical tone of the previous lines prompts us to ask whether the "Maker" is God or Abelard.
5. "Father" and "brother" in the ecclesiastical, as well as

emotional, sense. This also applies for "handmaid," "sister," and "daughter" in the following line.
6. One prone to visions.

Love finds an altar for forbidden fires.
I ought to grieve, but cannot what I ought;
I mourn the lover, not lament the fault;
185   I view my crime, but kindle at the view,
Repent old pleasures, and solicit new:
Now turned to Heav'n, I weep my past offense,
Now think of thee, and curse my innocence.[7]
Of all affliction taught a lover yet,
190   'Tis sure the hardest science° to forget!   *knowledge*
How shall I lose the sin, yet keep the sense,
And love th' offender, yet detest th' offense?
How the dear object from the crime remove,
Or how distinguish penitence from love?
195   Unequal task! a passion to resign,
For hearts so touched, so pierced, so lost as mine.
E'er such a soul regains its peaceful state,
How often must it love, how often hate!
How often, hope, despair, resent, regret,
200   Conceal, disdain—do all things but forget.
But let Heav'n seize it, all at once 'tis fired,
Not° touched, but rapt; not wakened, but inspired!   *not only*
Oh come! oh teach me nature to subdue,
Renounce my love, my life, my self—and you.
205   Fill my fond heart with God alone, for he
Alone can rival, can succeed to thee.
     How happy is the blameless vestal's lot!
The world forgetting, by the world forgot.
Eternal sunshine of the spotless mind!
210   Each pray'r accepted, and each wish resigned;
Labor and rest, that equal periods keep;
"Obedient slumbers that can wake and weep;"[8]
Desires composed, affections ever even,
Tears that delight, and sighs that waft to Heav'n.
215   Grace shines around her with serenest beams,
And whisp'ring angels prompt her golden dreams.
For her the Spouse° prepares the bridal ring,   *Christ*
For her white virgins hymenaeals° sing;   *wedding songs*
For her th' unfading rose of Eden blooms,
220   And wings of seraphs shed divine perfumes;
To sounds of heav'nly harps, she dies away,
And melts in visions of eternal day.
     Far other dreams my erring soul employ,
Far other raptures, of unholy joy:
225   When at the close of each sad, sorrowing day,

7. Cf. *Letters of Abelard and Heloise:* "Among those who are wedded to God I serve a man. . . . I am here, I confess, a sinner, but one who far from weeping for her sins, weeps only for her lover. . . . Every object brings to my mind what I ought to forget. . . . Even into the holy places before the altar I carry with me the memory of our guilty loves" (trans. Hughes, 120–24).
8. Line 16 from *Description of a Religious House*, by Richard Crashaw (1612–1649).

Fancy restores what vengeance snatched away,
Then conscience sleeps, and leaving nature free,
All my loose soul unbounded springs to thee.
O cursed, dear horrors of all-conscious° night!   *all-knowing*
230   How glowing guilt exalts the keen delight!
Provoking demons all restraint remove,
And stir within me ev'ry source of love.
I hear thee, view thee, gaze o'er all thy charms,
And round thy phantom glue my clasping arms.
235   I wake—no more I hear, no more I view,
The phantom flies me, as unkind as you.
I call aloud; it hears not what I say;
I stretch my empty arms; it glides away:
To dream once more I close my willing eyes;
240   Ye soft illusions, dear deceits, arise!
Alas no more!—methinks we wand'ring go
Through dreary wastes, and weep each other's woe;
Where round some mold'ring tow'r pale ivy creeps,
And low-browed rocks hang nodding o'er the deeps.
245   Sudden you mount! you beckon from the skies;
Clouds interpose, waves roar, and winds arise.
I shriek, start up, the same sad prospect find,
And wake to all the griefs I left behind.
      For thee the fates, severely kind, ordain
250   A cool suspense from pleasure and from pain;
Thy life a long, dead calm of fixed repose;
No pulse that riots, and no blood that glows.
Still as the sea, ere winds were taught to blow,
Or moving spirit bade the waters flow;
255   Soft as the slumbers of a saint forgiv'n,
And mild as opening gleams of promised Heav'n.
      Come Abelard! for what hast thou to dread?
The torch of Venus burns not for the dead;
Cut from the root my perished joys I see,
260   And love's warm tide forever stopped in thee.
Nature stands checked; religion disapproves;
Ev'n thou art cold—yet Eloisa loves.
Ah hopeless, lasting flames! like those that burn
To light the dead, and warm th' unfruitful urn.[9]
265   What scenes appear where'er I turn my view,
The dear ideas, where I fly, pursue,
Rise in the grove, before the altar rise,
Stain all my soul, and wanton in my eyes!
I waste the matin[1] lamp in sighs for thee,
270   Thy image steals between my God and me,
Thy voice I seem in ev'ry hymn to hear,
With ev'ry bead I drop too soft a tear.[2]

9. The Romans attempted to supply tombs with inextinguishable fires.

1. Morning; Matins are the psalms sung at dawn.
2. Tears of love, not repentance.

When from the censer clouds of fragrance roll,
And swelling organs lift the rising soul;
275   One thought of thee puts all the pomp to flight,
Priests, tapers, temples, swim before my sight:
In seas of flame my plunging soul is drowned,
While altars blaze, and angels tremble round.
        While prostrate here in humble grief I lie,
280   Kind, virtuous drops just gath'ring in my eye,
While praying, trembling, in the dust I roll,
And dawning grace is opening on my soul.
Come, if thou dar'st, all charming as thou art!
Oppose thyself to Heav'n; dispute° my heart;   *compete for*
285   Come, with one glance of those deluding eyes,
Blot out each bright idea of the skies.
Take back that grace, those sorrows, and those tears,
Take back my fruitless penitence and pray'rs,
Snatch me, just mounting, from the blest abode,
290   Assist the fiends and tear me from my God!
        No, fly me, fly me! far as pole from pole;
Rise Alps between us! and whole oceans roll!
Ah come not, write not, think not once of me,
Nor share one pang of all I felt for thee.
295   Thy oaths I quit,° thy memory resign,   *absolve*
Forget, renounce me, hate whate'er was mine.
Fair eyes, and tempting looks (which yet I view!)
Long loved, adored ideas! all adieu!
O grace serene! oh virtue heav'nly fair!
300   Divine oblivion of low-thoughted care!
Fresh blooming hope, gay daughter of the sky!
And faith, our early immortality![3]
Enter each mild, each amicable guest;
Receive, and wrap me in eternal rest!
305   See in her cell sad Eloisa spread,
Propped on some tomb, a neighbor of the dead!
In each low wind methinks a spirit calls,
And more than echoes talk along the walls.
Here, as I watched the dying lamps around,
310   From yonder shrine I heard a hollow sound.
"Come, sister come!" (it said, or seemed to say)
"Thy place is here, sad sister come away!
Once like thy self, I trembled, wept, and prayed,
Love's victim then, though now a sainted maid:
315   But all is calm in this eternal sleep;
Here grief forgets to groan, and love to weep,
Ev'n superstition loses ev'ry fear:
For God, not man, absolves our frailties here."
        I come, ye ghosts! prepare your roseate bow'rs,
320   Celestial palms, and ever-blooming flow'rs.

3. Faith seen as a foretaste of immortality.

Thither, where sinners may have rest, I go,
Where flames refined in breasts seraphic glow.
Thou, Abelard! the last sad office pay,
And smooth my passage to the realms of day:
325   See my lips tremble, and my eyeballs roll,
Suck my last breath, and catch my flying soul!
Ah no—in sacred vestments may'st thou stand,
The hallowed taper trembling in thy hand,
Present the cross before my lifted eye,
330   Teach me at once, and learn of° me to die.   from
Ah then, thy once-loved Eloisa see!
It will be then no crime to gaze on me.
See from my cheek the transient roses fly!
See the last sparkle languish in my eye!
335   Till ev'ry motion, pulse, and breath, be o'er;
And ev'n my Abelard beloved no more.
O death all-eloquent! you only prove
What dust we dote on, when 'tis man we love.
      Then too, when fate shall thy fair frame destroy
340   (That cause of all my guilt, and all my joy),
In trance ecstatic may thy pangs be drowned,
Bright clouds descend, and angels watch thee round,
From opening skies may streaming glories shine,
And saints embrace thee with a love like mine.
345   May one kind grave unite each hapless name,[4]
And graft my love immortal on thy fame.
Then, ages hence, when all my woes are o'er,
When this rebellious heart shall beat no more;
If ever chance two wand'ring lovers brings
350   To Paraclete's white walls, and silver springs,
O'er the pale marble shall they join their heads,
And drink the falling tears each other sheds,
Then sadly say, with mutual pity moved,
Oh may we never love as these have loved!
355   From the full choir when loud Hosannas rise,
And swell the pomp of dreadful sacrifice,[5]
Amid that scene, if some relenting eye
Glance on the stone where our cold relics lie,
Devotion's self shall steal a thought from Heav'n,
360   One human tear shall drop, and be forgiv'n.
And sure if fate some future bard[6] shall join
In sad similitude of griefs to mine,
Condemned whole years in absence to deplore,
And image charms he must behold no more,

4. Abelard and Eloisa were interred in the same grave, or in monuments adjoining, in the Monastery of the Paraclete [Pope's note].
5. The Mass, in which Christ's saving sacrifice is ritually reenacted.

6. Pope himself; he probably refers to Lady Mary Wortley Montagu, then traveling in the Middle East; he and she later quarreled and became estranged.

365   Such if there be, who loves so long, so well;
      Let him our sad, our tender story tell;
      The well-sung woes will soothe my pensive ghost;
      He best can paint 'em, who shall feel 'em most.

c. 1716   1717

from An Essay on Man
In Four Epistles to Henry St. John, Lord Bolingbroke[1]

TO THE READER

As the epistolary way of writing hath prevailed much of late, we have ventured to publish this piece composed some time since, and whose author chose this manner, notwithstanding his subject was high and of dignity, because of its being mixed with argument, which of its nature approacheth to prose. This,[2] which we first give the reader, treats of the Nature and State of MAN, with respect to the UNIVERSAL SYSTEM;[3] and the rest will treat of him with respect to his OWN SYSTEM, as an Individual, and as a Member of Society; under one or other of which heads all ethics are included.

As he imitates no man, so he would be thought to vie with no man in these Epistles, particular with the noted author of two lately published;[4] but this he may most surely say: that the matter of them is such, as is of importance to all in general, and of offense to none in particular.

THE DESIGN

Having proposed to write some pieces on human life and manners, such as (to use my lord Bacon's expression) *come home to men's business and bosoms*,[5] I thought it more satisfactory to begin with considering Man in the abstract, his Nature and his State: since, to prove any moral duty, to enforce any moral precept, or to examine the perfection or imperfection of any creature whatsoever, it is necessary first to know what condition and relation it is placed in, and what is the proper end and purpose of its being.

The science[6] of human nature is, like all other sciences, reduced to a few clear points: there are not many certain truths in this world. It is therefore in the anatomy of the mind as in that of the body: more good will accrue to mankind by attending to the large, open, and perceptible parts, than by studying too much such finer nerves and vessels, the conformations and uses of which will forever escape our observation. The disputes are all upon these last, and, I will venture to say, they

1. "I believe," wrote Pope to his friend John Caryll, "that there is not in the whole course of the Scripture any precept so often and so strongly inculcated, as the trust and eternal dependence we ought to repose in that Supreme Being who is our constant preserver and benefactor." This is the theme of Pope's didactic and exhortatory *Essay on Man*, whose four epistles were published anonymously over 11 months in 1733–1734. For Pope, "to reason right is to submit" (line 164), not least because humankind occupies a middle ground—between angels and beasts—in a divinely ordered universe. Pope had intended the *Essay on Man* and the four *Moral Essays* (1731–1735) to be the first and last parts of a great poetic sequence on the nature of humankind, though he never completed the project. The *Essay* is addressed to Henry

St. John, first Viscount Bolingbroke (1678–1751), a leading Tory statesman and political writer whom Pope described as "my guide, philosopher, and friend."
2. I.e., the first Epistle.
3. I.e., within the cosmic order, ordained by God.
4. I.e., Pope himself, whose *Epistle to Bathurst* (1733) and the first *Imitation of Horace* (1733) had recently been published. The *Essay on Man* was published anonymously; Pope uses his little address to the reader both to advertise his own work and to confuse his enemies about the identity of the poem's author.
5. From Bacon's Dedicatory Epistle in the collected edition of the *Essays* (1625).
6. Knowledge.

have less sharpened the wits than the hearts of men against each other, and have diminished the practice, more than advanced the theory, of morality. If I could flatter myself that this Essay has any merit, it is in steering betwixt the extremes of doctrines seemingly opposite, in passing over terms utterly unintelligible, and in forming a temperate yet not inconsistent, and a short yet not imperfect system of ethics.

This I might have done in prose; but I chose verse, and even rhyme, for two reasons. The one will appear obvious; that principles, maxims, or precepts so written, both strike the reader more strongly at first, and are more easily retained by him afterwards. The other may seem odd, but is true: I found I could express them more shortly this way than in prose itself; and nothing is more certain, than that much of the force as well as grace of arguments or instructions, depends on their conciseness. I was unable to treat this part of my subject in more detail, without becoming dry and tedious; or more poetically, without sacrificing perspicuity to ornament, without wandering from the precision, or breaking the chain of reasoning. If any man can unite all these without diminution of any of them, I freely confess he will compass a thing above my capacity.

What is now published, is only to be considered as a general map of MAN, marking out no more than the greater parts, their extent, their limits, and their connection, but leaving the particular to be more fully delineated in the charts which are to follow. Consequently, these Epistles in their progress (if I have health and leisure to make any progress) will be less dry and more susceptible of poetical ornament. I am here only opening the fountains, and clearing the passage. To deduce the rivers, to follow them in their course, and to observe their effects, may be a task more agreeable.

Epistle 1

	Awake, my ST. JOHN! leave all meaner° things	base
	To low ambition, and the pride of kings.	
	Let us (since life can little more supply	
	Than just to look about us and to die)	
5	Expatiate free[7] o'er all this scene of man;	
	A mighty maze! but not without a plan;	
	A wild, where weeds and flow'rs promiscuous° shoot,	randomly mixed
	Or garden, tempting with forbidden fruit.	
	Together let us beat[8] this ample field,	
10	Try what the open, what the covert yield;	
	The latent tracts, the giddy heights explore	
	Of all who blindly creep, or sightless soar;[9]	
	Eye nature's walks,° shoot folly as it flies,	behaviors
	And catch the manners living as they rise;	
15	Laugh where we must, be candid° where we can;	generous
	But vindicate the ways of God to Man.[1]	

1. Say first, of God above, or Man below,
What can we reason, but from what we know?
Of Man what see we, but his station here,

---

7. Wander or speak unrestrainedly.
8. "Beat," "open," "covert" are all hunting terms: Pope imagines himself and Boling broke to be searching out game by walking back and forth across open and wooded land.
9. The line envisions a middle way appropriate to man between ignorance and presumption.

1. An echo of Milton's invocation and aspiration at the start of Paradise Lost: "That to the highth of this great argument / I may assert eternal providence, / And justify the ways of God to men" (1.24–26). Pope's mention of the "garden, tempting with forbidden fruit" (line 8) also calls to mind the opening lines of Milton's epic.

20 From which to reason, or to which refer?
Through worlds unnumbered though the God be known,
'Tis ours to trace him only in our own.
He, who through vast immensity can pierce,
See worlds on worlds compose one universe,
25 Observe how system into system runs,
What other planets circle other suns,
What varied being° peoples° ev'ry star,   *forms of existence / populate*
May tell why Heav'n has made us as we are.
But of this frame the bearings, and the ties,
30 The strong connections, nice° dependencies,   *intricate*
Gradations just,² has thy° pervading soul   *the reader's*
Looked through? or can a part contain the whole?
Is the great chain,³ that draws all to agree,
And drawn supports, upheld by God, or thee?

35   2. Presumptuous Man! the reason wouldst thou find,
Why formed so weak, so little, and so blind!
First, if thou canst, the harder reason guess,
Why formed no weaker, blinder, and no less!
Ask of thy mother earth, why oaks are made
40 Taller or stronger than the weeds they shade?
Or ask of yonder argent fields above,
Why Jove's satellites⁴ are less than Jove?
Of systems possible, if 'tis confessed
That wisdom infinite must form the best,
45 Where all must full or not coherent be,⁵
And all that rises, rise in due degree;
Then, in the scale of reas'ning life, 'tis plain
There must be, somewhere, such a rank as Man;
And all the question (wrangle e'er so long)
50 Is only this, if God has placed him wrong?
Respecting Man, whatever wrong we call,
May, must be right, as relative to all.
In human works, though labored on with pain,
A thousand movements scarce one purpose gain;
55 In God's, one single can its end produce;
Yet serves to second too some other use.
So Man, who here seems principal alone,
Perhaps acts second to some sphere unknown,
Touches some wheel, or verges to some goal;
60 'Tis but a part we see, and not a whole.
When the proud steed shall know why Man restrains
His fiery course, or drives him o'er the plains;
When the dull ox, why now he breaks the clod,

---

2. "Connections," "dependencies," and "gradations" were
key terms of the new sciences.
3. The Great Chain of Being linked all levels of creation,
at the same time maintaining a fixed hierarchy.

4. Jupiter's moons. "Satellites" here has four syllables.
5. The Great Chain of Being could not be broken at any
point.

Is now a victim, and now Egypt's god:[6]
65   Then shall Man's pride and dullness comprehend
His actions', passions', being's, use and end;
Why doing, suff'ring, checked, impelled; and why
This hour a slave, the next a deity.
    Then say not Man's imperfect, Heav'n in fault;
70   Say rather, Man's as perfect as he ought;
His knowledge measured to his state and place,
His time a moment, and a point his space.
If to be perfect in a certain sphere,°   *area of influence*
What matter, soon or late, or here or there?
75   The blessed today is as completely so,
As who began a thousand years ago.

    3. Heav'n from all creatures hides the book of fate,
All but the page prescribed, their present state;
From brutes what men, from men what spirits° know: *angels*
80   Or who could suffer being here below?
The lamb thy riot° dooms to bleed today,   *extravagance*
Had he thy reason, would he skip and play?
Pleased to the last, he crops the flow'ry food,
And licks the hand just raised to shed his blood.
85   O blindness to the future! kindly giv'n,
That each may fill the circle marked by Heav'n;
Who sees with equal eye, as God of all,
A hero perish, or a sparrow fall,
Atoms or systems° into ruin hurled,   *solar systems*
90   And now a bubble burst, and now a world.
Hope humbly then; with trembling pinions° soar;   *wings*
Wait the great teacher Death, and God adore!
What future bliss, he gives not thee to know,
But gives that hope to be thy blessing now.
95   Hope springs eternal in the human breast:
Man never *is*, but always *to be* blessed:
The soul, uneasy and confined from home,
Rests and expatiates in a life to come.
    Lo! the poor Indian, whose untutored mind
100   Sees God in clouds, or hears him in the wind;
His soul proud science never taught to stray
Far as the solar walk, or Milky Way;
Yet simple nature to his hope has giv'n,
Behind the cloud-topped hill, an humbler Heav'n;
105   Some safer world in depth of woods embraced,
Some happier island in the wat'ry waste,
Where slaves once more their native land behold,
No fiends torment, no Christians thirst for gold![7]

---

6. Apis, sacred bull of Memphis.   7. The Christian is meant to "thirst for God" (Psalm 42.2).

To be, contents his natural desire,
110 He asks no angel's wings, no seraph's fire;[8]
But thinks, admitted to that equal sky,
His faithful dog shall bear him company.

    4. Go, wiser thou! and in thy scale of sense
Weigh thy opinion against Providence;
115 Call imperfection what thou fancy'st such,
Say, here he gives too little, there too much;
Destroy all creatures for thy sport or gust,°   appetite
Yet cry, If Man's unhappy, God's unjust;
If Man alone engross° not Heav'n's high care,   monopolize
120 Alone made perfect here, immortal there:
Snatch from his hand the balance and the rod,
Rejudge his justice, be the God of God!
    In pride, in reas'ning pride, our error lies;
All quit their sphere, and rush into the skies.
125 Pride still is aiming at the blessed abodes,
Men would be angels, angels would be gods.
Aspiring to be gods, if angels fell,
Aspiring to be angels, men rebel;
And who but wishes to invert the laws
130 Of ORDER, sins against th' Eternal Cause.

    5. Ask for what end the heav'nly bodies shine,
Earth for whose use? Pride answers, "'Tis for mine:
For me kind Nature wakes her genial° pow'r,   generating
Suckles each herb, and spreads out ev'ry flow'r;
135 Annual for me, the grape, the rose renew
The juice nectareous, and the balmy dew;
For me, the mine a thousand treasures brings;
For me, health gushes from a thousand springs;
Seas roll to waft me, suns to light me rise;
140 My foot-stool earth, my canopy the skies."[9]
    But errs not Nature from this gracious end,
From burning suns when livid deaths descend,
When earthquakes swallow, or when tempests sweep
Towns to one grave, whole nations to the deep?
145 "No" ('tis replied) "the first Almighty cause[1]
Acts not by partial, but by gen'ral laws;
Th' exceptions few; some change since all began,
And what created perfect?"—Why then Man?
If the great end be human happiness,
150 Then Nature deviates; and can Man do less?
As much that end a constant course requires
Of show'rs and sunshine, as of Man's desires;
As much eternal springs and cloudless skies,

8. Seraphs were traditionally thought of as aflame, incandescent.
9. The line envisions the universe as throne, with footrest below and brightly ornamented fabrics hanging above.
1. God the Creator.

As men forever temp'rate, calm, and wise.
155 If plagues or earthquakes break not Heav'n's design,
Why then a Borgia, or a Catiline?[2]
Who knows but he, whose hand the light'ning forms,
Who heaves old ocean, and who wings the storms,
Pours fierce ambition in a Caesar's mind,
160 Or turns young Ammon[3] loose to scourge mankind?
From pride, from pride, our very reas'ning springs;
Account for moral, as for nat'ral things:
Why charge we Heav'n in those, in these acquit?
In both, to reason right is to submit.
165   Better for us, perhaps, it might appear,
Were there all harmony, all virtue here;
That never air or ocean felt the wind;
That never passion discomposed the mind:
But all subsists by elemental strife;
170 And passions are the elements of life.
The gen'ral ORDER, since the whole began,
Is kept in Nature, and is kept in Man.

    6. What would this Man? Now upward will he soar,
And little less than angel, would be more;
175 Now looking downwards, just as grieved appears
To want the strength of bulls, the fur of bears.
Made for his use all creatures if he call,
Say what their use, had he the pow'rs of all?
Nature to these, without profusion kind,
180 The proper organs, proper pow'rs assigned;
Each seeming want compensated of course,[4]
Here with degrees of swiftness, there of force;
All in exact proportion to the state;
Nothing to add, and nothing to abate.
185 Each beast, each insect, happy in its own;
Is Heav'n unkind to Man, and Man alone?
Shall he alone, whom rational we call,
Be pleased with nothing, if not blessed with all?
    The bliss of Man (could pride that blessing find)
190 Is not to act or think beyond mankind;
No pow'rs of body or of soul to share,
But what his nature and his state can bear.
Why has not Man a microscopic eye?
For this plain reason, Man is not a fly.
195 Say what the use, were finer optics giv'n,
T' inspect a mite, not comprehend the Heav'n?[5]

---

2. Cesare Borgia (1476–1507), an Italian duke from a notoriously ruthless family. Lucius Sergius Catiline (d. 62 B.C.E.)
plotted unsuccessfully against the Roman state.
3. Alexander the Great, King of Macedonia (336–323
B.C.E.) and conqueror of Asia Minor, Syria, Egypt,

Babylonia, and Persia.
4. As is fitting, in the normal course of events.
5. It was commonly believed that man alone of all the
animals was able to look up to heaven.

Or touch, if tremblingly alive all o'er,
To smart and agonize at ev'ry pore?
Or quick effluvia darting through the brain,[6]
200   Die of a rose in aromatic pain?
If Nature thundered in his op'ning ears,
And stunned him with the music of the spheres,
How would he wish that Heav'n had left him still
The whisp'ring zephyr,° and the purling rill?   *breeze*
205   Who finds not Providence all good and wise,
Alike in what it gives, and what denies?

    7. Far as creation's ample range extends,
The scale of sensual, mental pow'rs ascends:
Mark how it mounts, to Man's imperial race,
210   From the green myriads in the peopled grass:
What modes of sight betwixt each wide extreme,
The mole's dim curtain, and the lynx's beam:
Of smell, the headlong lioness[7] between,
And hound sagacious on the tainted[8] green:
215   Of hearing, from the life that fills the flood,
To that which warbles through the vernal wood:
The spider's touch, how exquisitely fine!
Feels at each thread, and lives along the line:
In the nice° bee what sense so subtly true   *super-sensitive*
220   From pois'nous herbs extracts the healing dew:[9]
How instinct varies in the grov'ling swine,
Compared, half-reas'ning elephant, with thine:
'Twixt that, and reason, what a nice barrier;°   *fine distinction*
Forever sep'rate, yet forever near!
225   Remembrance and reflection how allied;
What thin partitions sense from thought divide:
And middle natures, how they long to join,
Yet never pass th' insuperable line!
Without this just gradation, could they be
230   Subjected these to those, or all to thee?
The pow'rs of all subdued by thee alone,
Is not thy reason all these pow'rs in one?

    8. See, through this air, this ocean, and this earth,
All matter quick,° and bursting into birth.   *living*
235   Above, how high progressive life may go!
Around, how wide! how deep extend below!
Vast chain of being, which from God began,
Natures ethereal, human, angel, Man,

6. Epicurus (c. 340–c. 270 B.C.E.) and others believed that sensations reached the brain from the pores via streams of invisible particles.
7. Lions were, according to Pope, believed to hunt "by the ear, and not by the nostril."
8. Sagacious: of acute perception; tainted: i.e., with the smell of the hunted animal.
9. Honey had been thought to fall on flowers as dew and was used for medicinal purposes.

Beast, bird, fish, insect! what no eye can see,
240 No glass° can reach! from infinite to thee,   *magnifying lens*
From thee to nothing!—On superior pow'rs
Were we to press, inferior might on ours:
Or in the full creation leave a void,
Where, one step broken, the great scale's destroyed:
245 From Nature's chain whatever link you strike,
Tenth or ten thousandth, breaks the chain alike.
    And if each system in gradation roll,
Alike essential to th' amazing whole;
The least confusion but in one, not all
250 That system only, but the whole must fall.
Let earth unbalanced from her orbit fly,[1]
Planets and suns run lawless through the sky,
Let ruling angels from their spheres be hurled,[2]
Being on being wrecked, and world on world,
255 Heav'n's whole foundations to their center nod,
And Nature tremble to the throne of God:
All this dread ORDER break—for whom? for thee?
Vile worm!—oh, madness, pride, impiety!

    9. What if the foot, ordained the dust to tread,
260 Or hand to toil, aspired to be the head?
What if the head, the eye, or ear repined°   *complained*
To serve° mere engines° to the ruling mind?   *serve as / implements*
Just as absurd for any part to claim
To be another, in this gen'ral frame:
265 Just as absurd, to mourn the tasks or pains,
The great directing MIND of ALL ordains.
    All are but parts of one stupendous whole,
Whose body Nature is, and God the soul;
That, changed through all, and yet in all the same,
270 Great in the earth, as in th' ethereal frame,
Warms in the sun, refreshes in the breeze,
Glows in the stars, and blossoms in the trees,
Lives through all life, extends through all extent,
Spreads undivided, operates unspent,
275 Breathes in our soul, informs° our mortal part,   *permeates*
As full, as perfect, in a hair as heart;
As full, as perfect, in vile Man that mourns,
As the rapt seraph that adores and burns;
To him no high, no low, no great, no small;
280 He fills, he bounds, connects, and equals all.

    10. Cease then, nor ORDER imperfection name:[3]
Our proper bliss depends on what we blame.

---

1. Echoes *Paradise Lost*, where God, creating the universe, "spun out the air / and Earth, self-balanced, on her center hung" (7.241–2).

2. A portent of the world's imminent end, according to Thomas Aquinas (c. 1225–1274).

3. I.e., do not label order imperfection.

Know thy own point: this kind, this due degree
Of blindness, weakness, Heav'n bestows on thee.
285   Submit—In this, or any other sphere,
Secure to be as blessed as thou canst bear:
Safe in the hand of one disposing pow'r,
Or° in the natal, or the mortal hour.   *either*
All Nature is but art, unknown to thee;
290   All chance, direction, which thou canst not see;
All discord, harmony, not understood;[4]
All partial evil, universal good:[5]
And, spite of pride, in erring reason's spite,
One truth is clear, "Whatever IS, is RIGHT."

from *Epistle 2*

1. Know then thyself, presume not God to scan;
The proper study of mankind is Man.
Placed on this isthmus of a middle state,
A being darkly wise, and rudely great:
5   With too much knowledge for the skeptic side,
With too much weakness for the Stoic's pride,
He hangs between; in doubt to act, or rest,
In doubt to deem himself a God or beast,
In doubt his mind or body to prefer,
10   Born but to die, and reas'ning but to err;
Alike in ignorance, his reason such,
Whether he thinks too little, or too much.
Chaos of thought and passion, all confused;
Still by himself abused, or disabused;[6]
15   Created half to rise, and half to fall,
Great lord of all things, yet a prey to all;
Sole judge of truth, in endless error hurled:
The glory, jest, and riddle of the world!

1733

AN EPISTLE FROM MR. POPE, TO DR. ARBUTHNOT   The *Epistle to Dr. Arbuthnot,* perhaps the most relaxed and engaging of all Pope's verse letters, is addressed to John Arbuthnot (1667–1735), who was physician to Queen Anne, a close friend of Pope and Swift, a valued member of the Scriblerus Club, and principal author of the *Memoirs of the Extraordinary Life, Works, and Discoveries of Martinus Scriblerus,* published with Pope's *Works* in 1741. Samuel Johnson described Arbuthnot as "the most universal genius," for he was a fine satirist, a skillful physician, an amateur mathematician, and a capable poet. Pope's epistle is an apology both for himself and for the satirist's art, written against those who had attacked his "person, morals, and family." He asserts the social role of the poet, includes moving autobiographical passages, and

---

4. Here, as earlier in the poem, Pope invokes the Horatian principle of *concordia discors* (Horace, *Epistles,* 1.12.19), a harmony of opposites.
5. In a letter to his friend John Caryll, Pope wrote that

"true piety would make us know, that all misfortunes may as well be blessings."
6. Corrected; undeceived.

powerfully assails his enemies. This Horatian epistle, to the friend whose satires had delighted Pope and whose care had helped preserve and prolong Pope's own frail health, was published just seven weeks before the doctor died.

An Epistle from Mr. Pope, to Dr. Arbuthnot

Neque sermonibus vulgi dederis te, ned in Praemiis humanis spem posueris rerum tuarum: suis te oportet illecebris ipsa virtus trahat ad verum decus. Quid de te alii loquantur, ipsi vedeant, sed loquentur tamen.[1]

Advertisement

This paper is a sort of bill of complaint, begun many years since, and drawn up by snatches, as the several occasions offered. I had no thoughts of publishing it, till it pleased some persons of rank and fortune (the authors of *Verses to the Imitator of Horace*, and of an *Epistle to a Doctor of Divinity from a Nobleman at Hampton Court*)[2] to attack in a very extraordinary manner, not only my writings (of which being public the public judge) but my person, morals, and family, whereof to those who know me not, a truer information may be requisite. Being divided between the necessity to say something of myself, and my own laziness to undertake so awkward a task, I thought it the shortest way to put the last hand to this epistle. If it have anything pleasing, it will be that by which I am most desirous to please, the truth and the sentiment; and if anything offensive, it will be only to those I am least sorry to offend, the vicious or the ungenerous.

Many will know their own pictures in it, there being not a circumstance but what is true; but I have, for the most part, spared their names; and they may escape being laughed at, if they please.

I would have some of them know, it was owing to the request of the learned and candid friend to whom it is inscribed, that I make not as free use of theirs as they have done of mine. However I shall have this advantage, and honor, on my side, that whereas by their proceeding, any abuse may be directed at any man, no injury can possibly be done by mine, since a nameless character can never be found out, but by its *truth* and *likeness*.[3]

> Shut, shut the door, good John![4] fatigued I said,
> Tie up the knocker, say I'm sick, I'm dead.
> The Dog-star rages![5] Nay 'tis past a doubt,
> All Bedlam, or Parnassus,[6] is let out:
> 5   Fire in each eye, and papers in each hand,
> They rave, recite, and madden[7] round the land.
>   What walls can guard me, or what shades can hide?

---

1. "You will not give yourself up to the flattery of the vulgar, nor hope for success in your affairs from mortal hands; virtue herself will lead to true honor; see that you follow her guidance. What others see fit to say of you let them say" (Cicero, *De Re Publica*, 6.23).
2. Lady Mary Wortley Montagu (1689–1762) and John Hervey (1696–1743), Baron Hervey of Ickworth.
3. I.e., its similarity to the original.

4. Pope's servant, John Serle.
5. Sirius, which appears in the heat of summer; Pope was finishing the poem in August 1734. The late summer was also the time for reciting poetry in classical Rome.
6. Bedlam (Bethlehem Hospital) was a London "lunatic" asylum; Parnassus was the mountain of the Muses.
7. A word Pope invented.

They pierce my thickets, through my grot[8] they glide,
By land, by water,[9] they renew the charge,

10   They stop the chariot, and they board the barge.
No place is sacred, not the church is free,
Ev'n Sunday shines no Sabbath-day to me:
Then from the Mint[1] walks forth the man of rhyme,
Happy! to catch me, just at dinner time.

15   Is there a parson, much bemused in beer,[2]
A maudlin poetess, a rhyming peer,
A clerk, foredoomed his father's soul to cross,
Who pens a stanza when he should engross?°   copy documents
Is there, who locked from ink and paper, scrawls

20   With desp'rate charcoal round his darkened walls?
All fly to Twit'nam,° and in humble strain   Twickenham
Apply to me, to keep them mad or vain.
Arthur,[3] whose giddy son neglects the laws,
Imputes to me and my damned works the cause:

25   Poor Cornus° sees his frantic wife elope,   cuckold
And curses wit, and poetry, and Pope.[4]
        Friend to my life! (which did not you prolong,
The world had wanted many an idle song)
What drop or nostrum° can this plague remove?   medicines

30   Or which must end me, a fool's wrath or love?
A dire dilemma! Either way I'm sped,°   hurried toward death
If foes, they write, if friends, they read me dead.
Seized and tied down to judge, how wretched I!
Who can't be silent, and who will not lie;

35   To laugh were want of goodness and of grace,
And to be grave exceeds all pow'r of face.
I sit with sad civility, I read
With honest anguish, and an aching head;
And drop at last, but in unwilling ears,

40   This saving counsel, "Keep your piece nine years."[5]
        Nine years! cries he, who high in Drury Lane[6]
Lulled by soft zephyrs° through the broken pane,   breezes
Rhymes 'ere he wakes, and prints before term ends,[7]
Obliged by hunger, and request of friends:[8]

45   "The piece you think is incorrect? why take it,
I'm all submission, what you'd have it, make it."
        Three things another's modest wishes bound,°   encompass

8. Pope's artificial grotto or cavern, his retreat, at Twickenham.
9. Pope's house at Twickenham was on the river Thames, and could be reached by boat from London.
1. Debtors were safe from the law in Southwark, London; on Sunday there were no arrests anywhere.
2. Laurence Eusden (1688–1730), poet laureate and parson given to drink.
3. Arthur Moore; his son James Moore-Smythe had plagiarized from Pope.

4. Both the Pope and the author: as a nation, the British were preoccupied with the threat of Roman Catholicism without (from France and Spain) and within (from Catholics like Pope).
5. Horace's advice to a poet eager to publish (Ars Poetica 386–89).
6. A writer living in a garret in this bad neighborhood.
7. Law court terms were the preferred publishing seasons.
8. It is the second reason, rather than the first, that the aspiring poet gives in his prefaces.

My friendship, and a prologue,[9] and ten pound.
50   Pitholeon[1] sends to me: "You know his Grace,
I want a patron; ask him for a place."°   *paid position*
Pitholeon libelled me—"but here's a letter
Informs you, sir, 'twas when he knew no better.
Dare you refuse him? Curll[2] invites to dine,
He'll write a *Journal*, or he'll turn divine."[3]
55   Bless me! a packet.—"'Tis a stranger sues,
A virgin tragedy, an orphan Muse."
If I dislike it, "Furies, death and rage!"
If I approve, "Commend it to the stage."
There (thank my stars) my whole commission ends,
60   The play'rs and I are, luckily, no friends.
Fired that the house° reject him, "'Sdeath I'll print it,   *theater*
And shame the fools—your int'rest, sir, with Lintot."[4]
Lintot, dull rogue! will think your price too much.
"Not sir, if you revise it, and retouch."
65   All my demurs but double his attacks,
At last he whispers, "Do, and we go snacks."[5]
Glad of a quarrel, straight° I clap the door,   *immediately*
Sir, let me see your works and you no more.
'Tis sung, when Midas' ears began to spring[6]
70   (Midas, a sacred person and a king),
His very minister who spied them first,
(Some say his Queen) was forced to speak, or burst.
And is not mine, my friend, a sorer case,
When every coxcomb° perks° them in my face?   *fool / shoves*
75   "Good friend forbear! you deal in dang'rous things,
I'd never name Queens, Ministers, or Kings;
Keep close to ears,° and those let asses prick,[7]   *whisper it*
'Tis nothing"—Nothing? if they bite and kick?
Out with it, *Dunciad!* let the secret pass,
80   That secret to each fool, that he's an ass:
The truth once told (and wherefore should we lie?),
The Queen of Midas slept, and so may I.
You think this cruel? take it for a rule,
No creature smarts so little as a fool.
85   Let peals of laughter, Codrus![8] 'round thee break,
Thou unconcerned canst hear the mighty crack:[9]

9. To a play of his: a good way to show the public who
your friends were.
1. The name taken from a foolish Poet at Rhodes [Pope's
note].
2. Edmund Curll (1675–1747), a publisher notorious for
commissioning hacks to write libelous journals, full of
"news and scandal."
3. Pope may have meant Leonard Welsted (1688–1747)
who was planning a religious work.
4. Bernard Lintot (1675–1736), who published for Pope.
5. Share the profits.
6. King Midas grew ass's ears when he preferred Pan to

Apollo in their music contest. One of those closest to
him whispered the story to the earth, and it was in turn
told by the reeds. Pope is also referring to that contemporary artistic dunce, King George II, his wife Queen Caroline, and first minister Robert Walpole.
7. Presumably, their ears, as well as the poet.
8. A poet, perhaps fictional, ridiculed by Virgil and Juvenal.
9. "Mighty crack" was a phrase used by Addison to describe the collapse of the world; Pope showed how inadequate he thought it both in *Peri Bathous* and here, where
it signals the failure of a play.

Pit, box, and gall'ry in convulsions hurled,
Thou stand'st unshook amidst a bursting world.
Who shames a scribbler? break one cobweb through,
90   He spins the slight, self-pleasing thread anew;
Destroy his fib, or sophistry, in vain,
The creature's at his dirty work again,
Throned in the center of his thin designs,
Proud of a vast extent of flimsy lines!
95   Whom have I hurt? has poet yet, or peer,
Lost the arched eyebrow, or Parnassian sneer?
And has not Colley[1] still his lord, and whore?
His butchers Henley, his Freemasons Moore?[2]
Does not one table Bavius[3] still admit?
100   Still to one bishop Philips[4] seem a wit?
Still Sappho[5]—"Hold! for God's sake—you'll offend;
No names—be calm—learn prudence of a friend:
I too could write, and I am twice as tall;
But foes like these!"—One flatt'rer's worse than all;
105   Of all mad creatures, if the learn'd are right,
It is the slaver kills, and not the bite.
A fool quite angry is quite innocent.
Alas! 'tis ten times worse when they *repent.*

One dedicates, in high heroic prose,
110   And ridicules beyond a hundred foes;
One from all Grub Street[6] will my fame defend,
And, more abusive, calls himself my friend.
This prints my letters,[7] that expects a bribe,
And others roar aloud, "Subscribe, subscribe."
115   There are, who to my person pay their court,
I cough like Horace, and though lean, am short,
Ammon's great son[8] one shoulder had too high,
Such Ovid's nose, and "Sir! you have an eye—"
Go on, obliging creatures, make me see
120   All that disgraced my betters, met in me.
Say for my comfort, languishing in bed,
"Just so immortal Maro° held his head:"   *Virgil*
And when I die, be sure you let me know
Great Homer died three thousand years ago.

---

1. Colley Cibber (1671–1757), actor, playwright, Poet Laureate; he replaced Lewis Theobald as the "hero" of *The Dunciad,* from which Pope here quotes the phrase "Parnassian sneer."
2. John "Orator" Henley (1692–1759), a popular and unusual preacher, had set up an "oratory" in Newport Market, one of London's principal meat markets, causing enemies to claim that his audiences consisted only of ignorant butchers. James Moore-Smythe was a Freemason.
3. A bad poet who had attacked Virgil and Horace.

4. Ambrose Philips (c. 1675–1749), poet and secretary to the Bishop of Armagh.
5. Lady Mary Wortley Montagu, whom Pope had attacked previously under the name of this Greek lyric poet; by Arbuthnot's interjection, Pope seems to be implying that she was under Walpole's protection.
6. Home of literary hacks.
7. Forged or stolen (as Curll had in 1726).
8. Alexander the Great.

125   Why did I write? what sin to me unknown
Dipped me in ink, my parents', or my own?
As yet a child, nor yet a fool to fame,
I lisped in numbers,° for the numbers came.   *verse, meter*
I left no calling for this idle trade,
130   No duty broke, no father disobeyed.
The Muse but served to ease some friend, not wife,
To help me through this long disease, my life,
To second, Arbuthnot! thy art and care,
And teach the being you preserved to bear.

135   But why then publish? Granville⁹ the polite,
And knowing Walsh, would tell me I could write;
Well-natured Garth inflamed with early praise,
And Congreve loved, and Swift endured my lays;
The courtly Talbot, Somers, Sheffield read,
140   Ev'n mitered Rochester would nod the head,
And St. John's self (great Dryden's friends before)
With open arms received one poet more.
Happy my studies, when by these approved!
Happier their author, when by these beloved!
145   From these the world will judge of men and books,
Not from the Burnets, Oldmixons, and Cookes.¹
Soft were my numbers; who could take offense
While pure description held the place of sense?
Like gentle Fanny's² was my flow'ry theme,
150   A painted mistress, or a purling stream.
Yet then did Gildon³ draw his venal quill;
I wished the man a dinner, and sat still.
Yet then did Dennis rave in furious fret;⁴
I never answered, I was not in debt.
155   If want provoked, or madness made them print,
I waged no war with Bedlam or the Mint.
Did some more sober critic come abroad?
If wrong, I smiled; if right, I kissed the rod.⁵
Pains, reading, study are their just pretense,
160   And all they want is spirit, taste, and sense.
Commas and points they set exactly right,
And 'twere a sin to rob them of their mite.

---

9. Pope associates himself (and Dryden) with a number of important figures, friends, and patrons: George Granville, Baron Lansdowne (1666–1735); William Walsh (1663–1708); Sir Samuel Garth (1661–1719); William Congreve; Jonathan Swift; Charles Talbot, Duke of Shrewsbury (1660–1718); John Lord Somers (1651–1721); Francis Atterbury, Bishop of Rochester (1662–1732); Henry St. John, Viscount Bolingbroke (1678–1751).
1. Thomas Burnet, John Oldmixon, and Thomas Cooke: "authors of secret and scandalous history" [Pope's note]; Pope is comparing the greatness of his friends with the small-mindedness of those who attacked him.

2. Lord Hervey, court Vice Chamberlain, whom Pope thought effeminate, and later satirizes as Sporus (lines 305ff.).
3. Charles Gildon (1665–1724) had attacked *The Rape of the Lock*. Pope insinuates that Gildon writes to keep poverty at bay.
4. John Dennis (1657–1734), had similarly attacked Pope; both Gildon and Dennis, Pope thought, had acted at the instigation of Addison.
5. Accepted their criticism; kissing a monarch's scepter or a state official's staff was a ritual of submission to authority.

Yet ne'er one spring of laurel graced these ribalds,[6]
From slashing Bentley down to piddling Tibalds:[7]
165   Each wight, who reads not, and but scans and spells,
Each word-catcher, that lives on syllables,
Ev'n such small critics some regard may claim,
Preserved in Milton's or in Shakespeare's name.
Pretty! in amber to observe the forms
170   Of hairs, or straws, or dirt, or grubs, or worms!
These things, we know, are neither rich nor rare,
But wonder how the devil they got there?
     Were others angry? I excused them too;
Well might they rage, I gave them but their due.
175   A man's true merit 'tis not hard to find,
But each man's secret standard in his mind,
That casting-weight[8] pride adds to emptiness,
This, who can gratify? for who can *guess?*
The Bard[9] whom pilfered pastorals renown,
180   Who turns a Persian tale for half a crown,[1]
Just writes to make his barrenness appear,
And strains from hard-bound brains eight lines a year:
He, who still wanting though he lives on theft,
Steals much, spends little, yet has nothing left:
185   And he, who now to sense, now nonsense leaning,
Means not, but blunders round about a meaning:
And he, whose fustian's° so sublimely bad,   *bombastic style*
It is not poetry, but prose run mad:
All these, my modest satire bade translate,
190   And owned, that nine such poets made a Tate.[2]
How did they fume, and stamp, and roar, and chafe?
And swear, not Addison himself was safe.
     Peace to all such! but were there one[3] whose fires
True genius kindles, and fair fame inspires;
195   Blessed with each talent and each art to please,
And born to write, converse, and live with ease:
Should such a man, too fond to rule° alone,   *of ruling*
Bear, like the Turk, no brother near the throne,[4]
View him with scornful, yet with jealous eyes,
200   And hate for arts that caused himself to rise;
Damn with faint praise,[5] assent with civil leer,
And without sneering, teach the rest to sneer;

6. Laurel: the poet's crown; ribalds: foolish jesters.
7. Richard Bentley (1662–1742), a classical scholar of great learning and bad temper, earned ridicule for his "corrected" edition of *Paradise Lost* (1732), while Lewis Theobald (1688–1744), sometime "hero" of *The Dunciad*, criticized Pope's edition of Shakespeare in his *Shakespeare Restored* (1726).
8. The weight that tips the balance.
9. Ambrose Philips wrote pastoral poems in imitation of Spenser and translated a book of *Persian Tales*. The fact that, in 1709, his pastorals were published in the same volume as Pope's occasioned a rivalry between the two poets.
1. A standard prostitute's charge.
2. Nahum Tate (1652–1715), playwright and poet.
3. Joseph Addison (1672–1719), here portrayed as Atticus, friend of Cicero. Pope respected Addison's abilities as a writer, but did not like him or his politics.
4. Turkish rulers killed close relatives who might be potential rivals.
5. Cf. William Wycherley's prologue to *The Plain Dealer* (1677): "And, with faint praises, one another damn."

Willing to wound, and yet afraid to strike,
Just hint a fault, and hesitate dislike;
205 Alike reserved to blame, or to commend,
A tim'rous foe, and a suspicious friend;
Dreading ev'n fools, by flatterers besieged,
And so obliging, that he ne'er obliged;
Like Cato, give his little Senate laws,⁶
210 And sit attentive to his own applause;
While wits and templars° ev'ry sentence raise,   *young lawyers*
And wonder with a foolish face of praise—
Who but must laugh, if such a man there be?
Who would not weep, if Atticus were he!
215   What though my name stood rubric on the walls?
Or plastered posts, with claps in capitals?⁷
Or smoking forth, a hundred hawkers'⁸ load,
On wings of winds came flying all abroad?
I sought no homage from the race that write;
220 I kept, like Asian monarchs, from their sight:
Poems I heeded (now berhymed so long)
No more than thou, great George! a birthday song.⁹
I ne'er with wits or witlings passed my days,
To spread about the itch of verse and praise;
225 Nor like a puppy, daggled° through the town,   *wandered*
To fetch and carry sing-song up and down;
Nor at rehearsals sweat, and mouthed, and cried,
With handkerchief and orange¹ at my side;
But sick of fops, and poetry, and prate,
230 To Bufo left the whole Castalian state.²
Proud, as Apollo on his forked hill,
Sat full-blown Bufo, puffed by every quill;
Fed with soft dedication all day long,
Horace and he went hand in hand in song.³
235 His library (where busts of poets dead
And a true Pindar stood without a head)⁴
Received of wits an undistinguished race,
Who first his judgment asked, and then a place:
Much they extolled his pictures, much his seat,°   *estate*
240 And flattered ev'ry day, and some days eat:
Till grown more frugal in his riper days,
He paid some bards with port, and some with praise,

---

6. Pope's prologue to Addison's play *Cato* (1713) included a version of this line. Now Pope turns the tables: the noble Roman senator becomes the petty Addison, and the senate, his coffeehouse clique.
7. Red lettering, or rubric, was often used by Lintot, Pope's publisher; "claps" were placards, pasted up around the city by booksellers.
8. Hawking by street criers was another way to publicize new works.
9. The Poet Laureate's official ode to the king.
1. Sold in the theaters for eating or throwing.

2. Poetry is the "Castalian State," named for the spring sacred to the Muses on Parnassus (the "forked hill"); it is left to "Bufo," a patron whose name derives from the Latin for toad, and who was probably George Bubb Dodington (1691–1762).
3. Dodington, a patron of literature, had been accorded the place of Maecenas, patron of Virgil and Horace, in a recent translation from Horace's *Odes*.
4. In *Peri Bathous* (1728), Pope ridiculed those antiquaries who exhibited headless statues, claiming they were busts of great poets.

To some a dry rehearsal was assigned,
And others (harder still) he paid in kind.[5]
245 Dryden alone (what wonder?) came not nigh,
Dryden alone escaped this judging eye:
But still the great have kindness in reserve,
He helped to bury whom he helped to starve.[6]
         May some choice patron bless each gray goose quill!
250 May ev'ry Bavius have his Bufo still!
So when a statesman wants a day's defense,
Or envy holds a whole week's war with sense,
Or simple pride for flatt'ry makes demands,
May dunce by dunce be whistled off my hands!
255 Blessed be the great! for those they take away,
And those they left me; for they left me Gay;[7]
Left me to see neglected genius bloom,
Neglected die, and tell it on his tomb:
Of all thy blameless life the sole return
260 My verse, and Queensb'ry[8] weeping o'er thy urn!
         Oh let me live my own, and die so too!
("To live and die is all I have to do")[9]
Maintain a poet's dignity and ease,
And see what friends, and read what books I please:
265 Above a patron, though I condescend
Sometimes to call a minister my friend.
I was not born for courts or great affairs;
I pay my debts, believe, and say my pray'rs;
Can sleep without a poem in my head,
270 Nor know, if Dennis be alive or dead.
         Why am I asked what next shall see the light?
Heav'ns! was I born for nothing but to write?
Has life no joys for me? or (to be grave)
Have I no friend to serve, no soul to save?
275 "I found him close with Swift"—"Indeed? no doubt"
(Cries prating Balbus[1]) "something will come out."
'Tis all in vain, deny it as I will.
"No, such a genius never can lie still"
And then for mine obligingly mistakes
280 The first lampoon Sir Will or Bubo[2] makes.
Poor guiltless I! and can I choose but smile,
When ev'ry coxcomb knows me by my *style?*
         Cursed be the verse, how well so'er it flow,
That tends to make one worthy man my foe,
285 Give virtue scandal, innocence a fear,

---

5. I.e., he read or gave them his own poetry.
6. Mr. Dryden, after having lived in exigencies, had a magnificent funeral bestowed upon him by the contributions of several persons of quality [Pope's note].
7. John Gay, poet, playwright, and friend of Pope; it was apparently his failure to win patronage that prompted him to write *The Beggar's Opera* (1728).

8. The Duke and Duchess of Queensberry were Gay's patrons.
9. Slightly adapted from *Of Prudence* (1668) by Sir John Denham.
1. A Roman lawyer.
2. Sir William Yonge (d. 1755) and Dodington.

Or from the soft-eyed virgin steal a tear!
But he who hurts a harmless neighbor's peace,
Insults fall'n worth, or beauty in distress,
Who loves a lie, lame slander helps about,
290   Who writes a libel, or who copies out:
That fop, whose pride affects a patron's name,
Yet absent, wounds an author's honest fame:
Who can your merits selfishly approve,
And show the sense of it without the love;
295   Who has the vanity to call you friend,
Yet wants the honor injured to defend![3]
Who tells whate'er you think, whate'er you say,
And if he lie not must at least betray:
Who to the Dean, and silver bell can swear,
300   And sees at Cannons what was never there;[4]
Who reads but with a lust to misapply,
Make satire a lampoon, and fiction lie.
A lash like mine no honest man shall dread,
But all such babbling blockheads in his stead.
305   Let Sporus[5] tremble—"What? that thing of silk,
Sporus, that mere white curd of ass's mik?
Satire or sense alas! can Sporus feel?
Who breaks a butterfly upon a wheel?"[6]
Yet let me flap this bug with gilded wings,
310   This painted child of dirt, that stinks and stings,
Whose buzz the witty and the fair annoys,
Yet wit ne'er tastes, and beauty ne'er enjoys:
So well-bred spaniels civilly delight
In mumbling of the game they dare not bite.
315   Eternal smiles his emptiness betray,
As shallow streams run dimpling all the way.
Whether in florid impotence he speaks,
And, as the prompter breathes, the puppet squeaks,
Or at the ear of Eve,[7] familiar toad,
320   Half froth, half venom, spits himself abroad.
In puns, or politicks, or tales, or lies,
Or spite, or smut, or rhymes, or blasphemies.
His wit all see-saw, between *that* and *this*,
Now high, now low, now master up, now miss,
325   And he himself one vile antithesis.
Amphibious thing! that acting either part,
The trifling head, or the corrupted heart,
Fop at the toilet,[8] flatt'rer at the board,°   *dining table*

---

3. I.e., lacks the honor to defend you when you are injured.
4. I.e., who misapplies satirical references in Pope's *Epistle
to Burlington*. Pope was upset by the willful misreading of
"Timon's villa" in the poem as Cannons, estate of the
Duke of Chandos.
5. A boy, Nero's favorite sexual partner; here, Lord Hervey,

confidant of Queen Caroline.
6. The rack, an instrument of torture.
7. In the fourth book of Milton [i.e., *Paradise Lost*, IV.
800] the devil is represented in this posture [Pope's note].
"Eve" is Queen Caroline, with whom Hervey is both familiar and a familiar (a witch's pet).
8. Dressing table.

Now trips a lady, and now struts a lord.
330   Eve's tempter thus the rabbins° have expressed,   *Jewish scholars*
A cherub's face, a reptile all the rest,
Beauty that shocks you, parts that none will trust,
Wit that can creep, and pride that licks the dust.
     Not fortune's worshipper, nor fashion's fool,
335   Not lucre's madman, nor ambition's tool,
Not proud, nor servile; be one poet's praise,
That, if he pleased, he pleased by manly ways;
That flatt'ry, ev'n to kings, he held a shame,
And thought a lie in verse or prose the same.
340   That not in fancy's maze he wandered long,
But stooped° to truth, and moralized his song: *pounced upon*
That not for fame, but virtue's better end,
He stood° the furious foe, the timid friend,   *withstood*
The damning critic, half approving wit,
345   The coxcomb hit, or fearing to be hit;
Laughed at the loss of friends he never had,
The dull, the proud, the wicked, and the mad;
The distant threats of vengeance on his head,
The blow unfelt, the tear he never shed;[9]
350   The tale revived, the lie so oft o'erthrown,
Th' imputed trash, and dullness not his own;
The morals blackened when the writings scape,
The libeled person, and the pictured shape;[1]
Abuse, on all he loved, or loved him, spread,
355   A friend in exile, or a father, dead;
The whisper, that to greatness still too near,
Perhaps, yet vibrates on his sovereign's ear—
Welcome for thee, fair virtue! all the past:
For thee, fair virtue! welcome ev'n the last!
360   "But why insult the poor, affront the great?"
A knave's a knave, to me, in ev'ry state:
Alike my scorn, if he succeed or fail,
Sporus at court, or Japhet[2] in a jail,
A hireling scribbler, or a hireling peer,
365   Knight of the post[3] corrupt, or of the shire;
If on a pillory, or near a throne,
He gain his prince's ear, or lose his own.
     Yet soft by nature, more a dupe than wit,
Sappho[4] can tell you how this man was bit:°   *deceived*
370   This dreaded sat'rist Dennis will confess
Foe to his pride, but friend to his distress:[5]

---

9. A *Pop upon Pope* (1728) attempted to humiliate Pope by pretending he had been whipped.
1. Pope was frequently vilified in print by his enemies; his deformity and Roman Catholicism were often mocked— he was even caricatured as a hunchbacked ape wearing the papal crown.
2. Japhet Crook, a forger.
3. A person who supported himself by giving false evidence.
4. Lady Mary Wortley Montagu hurt Pope, who had been very close to her, by switching loyalties to Hervey.
5. In Dennis's old age, Pope had publicly supported his work.

So humble, he has knocked at Tibald's door,
Has drunk with Cibber, nay has rhymed for Moore.[6]
Full ten years slandered, did he once reply?
375   Three thousand suns went down on Welsted's lie.[7]
To please a mistress one aspersed his life;
He lashed him not, but let her be his wife:
Let Budgell[8] charge low Grub Street on his quill,
And write whate'er he pleased, except his will;
380   Let the two Curlls,[9] of Town and Court, abuse
His father, mother, body, soul, and Muse.
Yet why? that father held it for a rule,
It was a sin to call our neighbor fool:
That harmless mother thought no wife a whore:
385   Hear this, and spare his family, James Moore!
Unspotted names! and memorable long,
If there be force in virtue, or in song.
    Of gentle blood (part shed in honor's cause,
While yet in Britain honor had applause)
390   Each parent sprung—"What fortune, pray?"—Their own,
And better got, than Bestia's[1] from the throne.
Born to no pride, inheriting no strife,
Nor marrying discord in a noble wife,
Stranger to civil and religious rage,
395   The good man walked innoxious through his age.
No courts he saw, no suits would ever try,
Nor dared an oath,[2] nor hazarded a lie.
Unlearned, he knew no schoolman's subtle art,
No language, but the language of the heart.
400   By nature honest, by experience wise,
Healthy by temp'rance, and by exercise;
His life, though long, to sickness passed unknown,
His death was instant, and without a groan.
O grant me thus to live, and thus to die!
405   Who spring from kings shall know less joy than I.
    O Friend!° may each domestic bliss be thine!   Arbuthnot
Be no unpleasing melancholy mine:
Me, let the tender office long engage,
To rock the cradle of reposing age,
410   With lenient arts extend a mother's breath,[3]
Make languor smile, and smooth the bed of death,

---

6. Or rather, James Moore-Smythe plagiarized from him.
7. Leonard Welsted (1688–1747) had sharply criticized Pope's works and character, and accused him of having "occasioned a lady's death" [Pope's note].
8. Eustace Budgell (1686–1737), a writer who blamed Pope for an accusation, published in the *Grub-Street Journal*, that Budgell had forged the will of Dr. Matthew Tindal to make himself inheritor.
9. Pope both derides the London publisher Edmund Curll, and deploys his name as a derogatory epithet for the courtier Hervey. Curll is attacked also in *The Dunciad* and in Swift's *Verses on the Death of Dr. Swift*.
1. A Roman consul who accepted bribes for peace, suggesting the Duke of Marlborough's rewards from Queen Anne.
2. Pope's father refused to take oaths against the Pope, which would have helped him avoid anti-Catholic measures.
3. Pope's mother died two years before the poem was published, but he retained these lines, written in 1731.

Explore the thought, explain the asking eye,
And keep a while one parent from the sky!
On cares like these if length of days attend,
415   May Heav'n, to bless those days, preserve my friend,
Preserve him social, cheerful, and serene,
And just as rich as when he served a Queen!⁴
Whether that blessing be denied or giv'n,
Thus far was right, the rest belongs to Heav'n.

1731–34   1735

AN EPISTLE TO A LADY: OF THE CHARACTERS OF WOMEN   For years Pope planned to write a magnum opus, a "system of ethics in the Horatian way." Though this ambitious project was never completed, some of its parts were written, including a set of four verse letters that were intended to conclude the work. Pope himself called the poems *Epistles to Several Persons*; a later editor dubbed them *Moral Essays*. Each work is a familiar letter addressed to someone Pope knew well and admired. *Epistle to a Lady*, the last written of the poems but second in the published sequence, is addressed (without ever explicitly identifying her) to Martha Blount (1690–1783), with whom Pope sustained a friendship so abiding and intense that contemporary gossips construed the pair as lovers and even secret spouses. About the depth of the relationship (though not the circumstances) rumor was right; nearing death, Pope bought Blount a house and bequeathed to her the use of his estate for the remainder of her life. In his verse epistle, he treats her first as muse and finally as paragon. But in between, he mocks "most women" in a gallery of portraiture marked by scorn, misogyny, and a recurrent, oddly angled empathy. "Contrarieties" is the key term in Pope's own footnote-explication of this poem; its application extends across his *oeuvre*. Alongside *The Rape of the Lock*, *Eloisa to Abelard*, and Pope's many shorter poems on women, *Epistle to a Lady* forms part of one of the most complex constellations in eighteenth-century poetry: luminous and laden with contradiction; by turns bounteous and belittling, baleful and brilliant.

Epistle 2. To a Lady:
Of the Characters of Women¹

Nothing so true as what you once let fall,
"Most women have no characters at all."
Matter too soft a lasting mark to bear,
And best distinguished by black, brown, or fair.
5   How many pictures of one nymph we view,
All how unlike each other, all how true!
Arcadia's Countess, here, in ermined pride,
Is there Pastora by a fountain side.²
Here Fannia,³ leering on her own good man,

4. Arbuthnot had been physician to Queen Anne.
1. The present text is modernized from the 1744 edition of the *Epistles*, which was based on a revision Pope prepared during the last months of his life, in which he included three "characters"—Atossa, Chloe, and Philomedé—omitted from earlier print versions of the poem.
2. Throughout the poem, Pope invokes names of women

from history, myth, and legend, deploying them as types or templates of the modern women he undertakes to describe and deride. Here he alludes in part to Sir Philip Sidney's romance *The Countess of Pembroke's Arcadia* (1590), named for Sidney's elegant ("ermined") sister, and in part to a later countess who posed for pastoral portraits.
3. An ancient Roman adulteress.

10   And there, a naked Leda with a swan.[4]
       Let then the fair one beautifully cry,
       In Magdalene's loose hair and lifted eye,[5]
       Or dressed in smiles of sweet Cecilia[6] shine,
       With simp'ring angels, psalms, and harps divine.
15   Whether the charmer sinner it, or saint it,
       If folly grows romantic,° I must paint it.   *extravagant*
           Come then, the colors and the ground prepare!
       Dip in the rainbow, trick her off in air,[7]
       Choose a firm cloud, before it fall, and in it,
20   Catch, ere she change, the Cynthia[8] of this minute.[9]
           Rufa,[1] whose eye quick-glancing o'er the park,
       Attracts each light gay meteor of a spark,[2]
       Agrees as ill with Rufa studying Locke,[3]
       As Sappho's[4] diamonds with her dirty smock,
25   Or Sappho at her toilet's greasy task,
       With Sappho fragrant in an evening mask:
       So morning insects that in muck begun,
       Shine, buzz, and fly-blow° in the setting sun.   *infect*
           How soft is Silia![5] fearful to offend,
30   The frail one's advocate, the weak one's friend.
       To her Calista proved her conduct nice,°   *refined*
       And good Simplicius asks of her advice.
       Sudden, she storms! she raves! You tip the wink,
       But spare your censure; Silia does not drink.
35   All eyes may see from what the change arose,
       All eyes may see—a pimple on her nose.
           Papillia,[6] wedded to her am'rous spark,
       Sighs for the shades: "How charming is a park!"
       A park is purchased, but the fair he sees
40   All bathed in tears: "Oh odious, odious trees!"
           Ladies like variegated tulips show;
       'Tis to their changes half their charms we owe.
       Their happy spots the nice admirer take,
       Fine by defect, and delicately weak.
45   'Twas thus Calypso[7] once each heart alarmed,[8]

4. In Greek myth, Zeus, taking the form of a swan, rapes Leda; Pope here depicts the woman as wanton and complicit.
5. Mary Magdalene is the repentant prostitute who followed Christ; she is traditionally identified with the nameless woman in the New Testament who "washed [Christ's] feet with [her] tears, and did wipe them" with her hair (Luke 7.38).
6. Patron saint of religious music.
7. Pope addresses the couplet as though to a portrait-painter: prepare the first layer of paint on the canvas (the "ground"); dip the brush; portray the subject.
8. Goddess of the moon in all its shifting phases.
9. In a note at this point, Pope summarizes the poem's main purpose as providing "instances of contrarieties, given even from such characters as are most strongly marked and seemingly therefore most consistent." He begins, in the next lines (21–28), with the contradictions displayed by "the *Affected.*"

1. "Red-haired" (Latin): a trait the 18th century linked with lustfulness.
2. "A lively, showy . . . man" (Johnson's *Dictionary*).
3. John Locke (1632–1704), author of *An Essay Concerning Human Understanding* (1692).
4. Pope alludes partly to the ancient Greek poet of lesbian love, and partly to his former friend Lady Mary Wortley Montagu (see pages 2543–54), who remarked in a letter that readers "generally suppose Pope means me, whenever he mentions that name."
5. "Contrarieties in the *Soft-natured*" (Pope's note, summarizing lines 29–40).
6. "Butterfly" (Latin).
7. The nymph who held Odysseus in thrall, a prisoner on her island, for seven years.
8. "Contrarieties in the *Cunning* and the *Artful*" (Pope's note, summarizing lines 45–52).

Awed without virtue, without beauty charmed;
Her tongue bewitched as oddly as her eyes;
Less wit than mimic, more a wit than wise.
Strange graces still, and stranger flights she had,
50 Was just not ugly, and was just not mad;
Yet ne'er so sure our passion to create,
As when she touched the brink of all we hate.
      Narcissa's⁹ nature, tolerably mild,
To make a wash° would hardly stew a child,   *liquid makeup*
55 Has ev'n been proved to grant a lover's prayer,
And paid a tradesman once to make him stare,
Gave alms at Easter, in a Christian trim,°   *fashion*
And made a widow happy, for a whim.
Why then declare good nature is her scorn,
60 When 'tis by that alone she can be borne?
Why pique all mortals, yet affect a name?
A fool to pleasure, yet a slave to fame:
Now deep in Taylor and the Book of Martyrs,¹
Now drinking citron° with his Grace and Chartres.²   *lemon-flavored brandy*
65 Now conscience chills her, and now passion burns;
And atheism and religion take their turns;
A very heathen in the carnal part,
Yet still a sad, good Christian at her heart.
      See sin in state, majestically drunk,
70 Proud as a peeress, prouder as a punk;°   *prostitute*
Chaste to her husband, free to all beside,
A teeming mistress, but a barren bride.
What then? Let blood and body bear the fault,
Her head's untouched, that noble seat of thought;
75 Such this day's doctrine—in another fit
She sins with poets through pure love of wit.
What has not fired her bosom or her brain?
Caesar and Tall-boy, Charles and Charlemagne.³
As Helluo,⁴ late dictator of the feast,
80 The nose of hautgout,⁵ and the tip° of taste,   *paragon*
Criticked your wine, and analyzed your meat,
Yet on plain pudding deigned at home to eat;
So Philomedé,⁶ lect'ring all mankind
On the soft passion, and the taste refined,
85 Th' address, the delicacy—stoops at once,
And makes her hearty meal upon a dunce.

9. "[Contrarieties] in the *Whimsical*" (Pope's note, summarizing lines 53–68). Narcissa is named for Narcissus, who in Greek myth looked on smooth water, fell in love with the reflection of his own face, and dwindled to nothing under a spell of self-regard.
1. Books of piety: Jeremy Taylor's *Holy Living* (1650) and *Holy Dying* (1651); John Foxe's *Acts and Monuments* (1563), known as *Foxe's Book of Martyrs* because it chronicled the sufferings of English protestants oppressed and executed under Catholic rule.
2. Rakes of notoriety: Philip, Duke of Wharton, and Francis Charteris.
3. The line mingles high and low: the emperors Caesar and Charlemagne; "Tall-boy," the foolish lover from a popular stage comedy, and "Charles," the name applied generically to footmen (as "Betty" was to maids).
4. "Glutton" (Latin).
5. I.e., the savorer (or sniffer-out) of strong flavors.
6. "Laughter-loving" (Greek); Homer's epithet for Aphrodite, goddess of love.

Flavia's a wit,[7] has too much sense to pray,
To toast our wants and wishes is her way;
Nor asks of God, but of her stars to give
90   The mighty blessing, "while we live, to live."
Then all for death, that opiate of the soul!
Lucretia's dagger, Rosamonda's bowl.[8]
Say, what can cause such impotence of mind?
A spark too fickle, or a spouse too kind.
95   Wise wretch! With pleasures too refined to please,
With too much spirit to be e'er at ease,
With too much quickness ever to be taught,
With too much thinking to have common thought:
You purchase pain with all that joy can give,
100   And die of nothing but a rage to live.
        Turn then from wits, and look on Simo's mate,[9]
No ass so meek, no ass so obstinate;
Or her, that owns her faults, but never mends,
Because she's honest, and the best of friends;
105   Or her, whose life the church and scandal share,
Forever in a passion, or a prayer;
Or her, who laughs at hell, but (like her Grace)
Cries, "Ah! How charming, if there's no such place!"
Or who in sweet vicissitude appears
110   Of mirth and opium, ratafie° and tears,   *cherry brandy*
The daily anodyne, and nightly draught,
To kill those foes to fair ones, time and thought.
Woman and fool are two hard things to hit,
For true no-meaning puzzles more than wit.
115   But what are these to great Atossa's mind?[1]
Scarce once herself, by turns all womankind!
Who, with herself, or others, from her birth
Finds all her life one warfare upon earth;
Shines, in exposing knaves, and painting fools,
120   Yet is whate'er she hates and ridicules.
No thought advances, but her eddy brain
Whisks it about, and down it goes again.
Full sixty years the world has been her trade,
The wisest fool much time has ever made.
125   From loveless youth to unrespected age,
No passion gratified except her rage.
So much the Fury still outran the wit,
The pleasure missed her, and the scandal hit.
Who breaks with her provokes revenge from hell,
130   But he's a bolder man who dares be well;

7. "[Contrarieties] in the *Witty* and *Refined*" (Pope's note, summarizing lines 87–100).
8. The Roman wife Lucretia killed herself after suffering rape; according to legend, Rosamunda Clifford, mistress to Henry II, was forced by his wife to drink poison.
9. In *Andria*, an ancient Roman comedy, Simo is a meddling old man.

1. Atossa was the daughter of Cyrus the Great, king of Persia. Under her name, Pope here portrays the volatile Katherine, Duchess of Buckinghamshire, illegitimate daughter of James II. She and Pope sustained an agitated, on-and-off friendship; he omitted this portrait from early editions of the poem, and included it only after her death.

Her every turn with violence pursued,
Nor more a storm her hate than gratitude.
To that each passion turns, or soon or late;
Love, if it makes her yield, must make her hate;
135 Superiors? death! And equals? what a curse!
But an inferior not dependent? worse.
Offend her, and she knows not to forgive;
Oblige her, and she'll hate you while you live;
But die, and she'll adore you—then the bust
140 And temple rise—then fall again to dust.
Last night, her lord was all that's good and great,
A knave this morning, and his will a cheat.
Strange! By the means defeated of the ends,
By spirit robbed of power, by warmth of friends,
145 By wealth of followers! without one distress
Sick of herself through very selfishness!
Atossa, cursed with every granted prayer,
Childless with all her children, wants an heir.
To heirs unknown descends th' unguarded store
150 Or wanders, Heav'n-directed, to the poor.
　　Pictures like these, dear madam, to design,
Asks no firm hand, and no unerring line;
Some wandering touches, some reflected light,
Some flying stroke alone can hit 'em right:
155 For how should equal colors do the knack?
Chameleons who can paint in white and black?
　　"Yet Chloe sure was formed without a spot—"
Nature in her then erred not, but forgot.
"With every pleasing, every prudent part,
160 Say, what can Chloe want?"—She wants a heart.
She speaks, behaves, and acts just as she ought;
But never, never, reached one gen'rous thought.
Virtue she finds too painful an endeavor,
Content to dwell in decencies forever.
165 So very reasonable, so unmoved,
As never yet to love, or to be loved.
She, while her lover pants upon her breast,
Can mark° the figures on an Indian chest;   notice
And when she sees her friend in deep despair,
170 Observes how much a chintz exceeds mohair.[2]
Forbid it Heav'n, a favor or a debt
She e'er should cancel—but she may forget.
Safe is your secret still in Chloe's ear;
But none of Chloe's shall you ever hear.
175 Of all her dears she never slandered one,
But cares not if a thousand are undone.
Would Chloe know if you're alive or dead?
She bids her footman put it in her head.

2. Chloe contrasts two fabrics: chintz, a brightly colored cotton; and mohair, woven either from goat's wool, or from silk.

Chloe is prudent—would you too be wise?
180 Then never break your heart when Chloe dies.
         One certain portrait may (I grant) be seen,
Which Heav'n has varnished out, and made a Queen:[3]
The same forever! and described by all
With truth and goodness, as with crown and ball.
185 Poets heap virtues, painters gems at will,
And show their zeal, and hide their want of skill.
'Tis well—but, artists! who can paint or write,
To draw the naked is your true delight.
That robe of quality so struts and swells,
190 None see what parts or nature it conceals.
Th' exactest traits of body or of mind
We owe to models of an humble kind.
If Queensbury[4] to strip there's no compelling,
'Tis from a handmaid we must take a Helen.[5]
195 From peer and bishop 'tis no easy thing
To draw the man who loves his God, or king.
Alas! I copy (or my draught would fail)
From honest Mah'met,[6] or plain Parson Hale.[7]
         But grant, in public men sometimes are shown,
200 A woman's seen in private life alone.
Our bolder talents in full light displayed,
Your virtues open fairest in the shade.
Bred to disguise, in public 'tis you hide;
There, none distinguish 'twixt your shame or pride,
205 Weakness or delicacy; all so nice,
That each may seem a virtue, or a vice.[8]
         In men, we various ruling passions find,
In women, two almost divide the kind;
Those, only fixed, they first or last obey:
210 The love of pleasure, and the love of sway.
         That,[9] Nature gives; and where the lesson taught
Is but to please, can pleasure seem a fault?
Experience, this;[1] by man's oppression cursed,
They seek the second not to lose the first.
215 Men, some to business, some to pleasure take,
But ev'ry woman is at heart a rake:
Men, some to quiet, some to public strife;
But ev'ry lady would be queen for life.
         Yet mark the fate of a whole sex of queens!
220 Pow'r all their end, but beauty all the means.
In youth they conquer, with so wild a rage,

---

3. Queen Caroline (1683–1737), who secured Pope's enmity by her unstinting support of Robert Walpole.
4. Catherine Hyde, Duchess of Queensberry (1700–1777), one of the century's most celebrated beauties.
5. Helen of Troy, the mythical beauty whose adultery brought about the Trojan War.
6. A Turkish servant to George I.
7. Dr. Stephen Hales (1677–1761), scientist, inventor,

and curate; Pope's trusted friend, and a witness to his will.
8. In a note, Pope introduces the poem's next section this way: "The former part having shown that the *particular characters* of women are more various than those of men, it is nevertheless observed, that the *general* characteristic of the sex, as to the *ruling passion,* is more uniform."
9. I.e., love of pleasure.
1. I.e., love of power ("sway").

As leaves them scarce a subject in their age.
For foreign glory, foreign joy, they roam;
No thought of peace and happiness at home.
225 But wisdom's triumph is well-timed retreat,
As hard a science to the fair as great!
Beauties, like tyrants, old and friendless grown,
Yet hate repose, and dread to be alone,
Worn out in public, weary ev'ry eye,
230 Nor leave one sigh behind them when they die.
　　Pleasures the sex, as children birds, pursue,
Still out of reach, yet never out of view;
Sure, if they catch, to spoil the toy at most,
To covet flying, and regret when lost.
235 At last, to follies youth could scarce defend,
It grows their age's prudence to pretend;
Ashamed to own° they gave delight before,   *admit*
Reduced to feign it, when they give no more:
As hags° hold sabbaths, less for joy than spite,   *witches*
240 So these their merry, miserable night;
Still round and round the ghosts of beauty glide,
And haunt the places where their honor died.
　　See how the world its veterans rewards!
A youth of frolics, an old age of cards,
245 Fair to no purpose, artful to no end,
Young without lovers, old without a friend,
A fop their passion, but their prize a sot,
Alive, ridiculous, and dead, forgot!
　　Ah! Friend! To dazzle let the vain design,
250 To raise the thought, and touch the heart, be thine!
That charm shall grow, while what fatigues the Ring[2]
Flaunts and goes down, an unregarded thing.
So when the sun's broad beam has tired the sight,
All mild ascends the moon's more sober light;
255 Serene in virgin modesty she shines,
And unobserved the glaring orb declines.
　　Oh! blessed with temper, whose unclouded ray
Can make tomorrow cheerful as today;
She, who can love a sister's charms, or hear
260 Sighs for a daughter[3] with unwounded ear;
She, who ne'er answers till a husband cools,
Or, if she rules him, never shows the rules;
Charms by accepting, by submitting sways,
Yet has her humor most, when she obeys;
265 Let fops or fortune fly which way they will;
Disdains all loss of tickets,° or codille;[4]   *lottery tickets*

2. Members of London high society, who enjoyed displaying themselves and their elegant carriages on a circular
road called the Ring, located in fashionable Hyde Park.
3. In earlier editions the noun was "sister." Martha Blount's
sister Teresa was regarded as the more attractive of the
two; Pope, who may at one point have fallen in love with
her, changed the word to suppress speculation about his
own opinion and desires.
4. A term in the fashionable card game Ombre, played
triumphantly by Belinda in *Rape of the Lock* (3.19–100).

Spleen, vapors, or smallpox, above them all,
And mistress of herself, though China fall.[5]
    And yet, believe me, good as well as ill,
270   Woman's at best a contradiction still.[6]
Heav'n, when it strives to polish all it can
Its last best work,[7] but forms a softer man;
Picks from each sex, to make the fav'rite blessed,
Your love of pleasure, our desire of rest,
275   Blends, in exception to all gen'ral rules,
Your taste of follies, without scorn of fools,
Reserve with frankness, art with truth allied,
Courage with softness, modesty with pride,
Fixed principles, with fancy ever new;
280   Shakes all together, and produces—you.
    Be this a woman's fame: with this unblessed,
Toasts[8] live a scorn, and queens may die a jest.
This Phoebus[9] promised (I forget the year)
When those blue eyes first opened on the sphere;
285   Ascendant Phoebus watched that hour with care,
Averted half your parents' simple prayer,
And gave you beauty, but denied the pelf[1]
That buys your sex a tyrant o'er itself.
The gen'rous god, who wit and gold refines,
290   And ripens spirits as he ripens mines,
Kept dross for duchesses, the world shall know it,
To give you sense, good humor, and a poet.

1733–1735   1735; 1740

⌒∞⌒

RESPONSE
Mary Leapor: An Essay on Woman[1]

WOMAN—a pleasing but a short-lived flow'r,
Too soft for business and too weak for pow'r:[2]
A wife in bondage, or neglected maid;
Despised, if ugly; if she's fair, betrayed.
5   'Tis wealth alone inspires ev'ry grace,
And calls the raptures to her plenteous face.

5. More echoes of the *Rape*: the Cave of Spleen in Canto 4 (*spleen* and *vapors* both denote depression); the frailty of China (vases) at 3.157–60.
6. In a note, Pope introduces the poem's closing section this way: "The picture of an estimable woman, with the best kinds of contrarieties."
7. As Eve was the final being created in Eden.
8. Women celebrated for their beauty, hence widely "toasted" by drinking admirers.
9. Apollo, Greek god of the sun (hence linked here with the dawn of life), prophesy, and poetry.
1. Wealth (here, the dowry that would "buy" a husband).
1. During her short, surprising life, Mary Leapor labored as a kitchen maid, wrote poetry for pleasure, and read Pope assiduously, absorbing his methods, reworking his tones and topics, and responding to his thought throughout her own varied output. In *An Essay on Woman*, Leapor pointedly reverses the gendered title of Pope's ambitious *Essay on Man*, and takes it as rubric for her own rumination on his arguments in *An Epistle to a Lady*. Where Pope finds fault with "the characters of women," Leapor focuses instead on the misperceptions of them, by men who (seeking wealth, seeking marriage) at once subordinate and undervalue them, and by those women who themselves misguidedly collude in such debilitating constructs. Assaying these dark matters, Leapor strikes a characteristic balance between precariousness and playfulness, acerbity and sorrow. For more of Leapor's poetry, see pages 2192–201.
2. Compare Pope's *Epistle to a Lady*, lines 1–4.

What numbers for those charming features pine,
If blooming acres round her temples twine?[3]
Her lip the strawberry, and her eyes more bright
10   Than sparkling Venus in a frosty night.
Pale lilies fade and, when the fair appears,
Snow turns a negro[4] and dissolves in tears.
And where the charmer treads her magic toe,
On English ground Arabian odors grow;
15   Till mighty Hymen° lifts his sceptred rod,   *god of marriage*
And sinks her glories with a fatal nod,
Dissolves her triumphs, sweeps her charms away,
And turns the goddess to her native clay.

But, Artemisia,[5] let your servant sing
20   What small advantage wealth and beauties bring.
Who would be wise, that knew Pamphilia's fate?[6]
Or who be fair, and joined to Sylvia's mate?
Sylvia, whose cheeks are fresh as early day,
As evening mild, and sweet as spicy May:
25   And yet that face her partial husband tires,
And those bright eyes, that all the world admires.
Pamphilia's wit who does not strive to shun,
Like death's infection or a dog-day's sun?
The damsels view her with malignant eyes:
30   The men are vexed to find a nymph so wise:
And wisdom only serves to make her know
The keen sensation of superior woe.
The secret whisper and the list'ning ear,
The scornful eyebrow and the hated sneer,
35   The giddy censures of her babbling kind,
With thousand ills that grate a gentle mind,
By her are tasted in the first degree,
Though overlooked by Simplicus and me.[7]
Does thirst of gold a virgin's heart inspire,
40   Instilled by Nature or a careful sire?
Then let her quit extravagance and play,
The brisk companion and expensive tea,
To feast with Cordia in her filthy sty
On stewed potatoes or on mouldy pie;[8]

---

3. I.e., if her dowry includes valuable land.
4. I.e., seems black by comparison.
5. The name of an ancient ruler celebrated as a patron of literature; Leapor applies it to her friend and patron Bridget Freemantle.
6. The lines about Pamphilia suggest that she may serve here as Leapor's alter ego (the historical Pamphilia was an ancient woman author). But in a letter Leapor wrote to Bridget Freemantle about the poem, replying to what she deemed her patron's "agreeable raillery [i.e., teasing]," Leapor protested that "notwithstanding your compliment,

of seeing my picture in Pamphilia, I must affirm it is not so." The other pastoral names (Sylvia, Simplicus, etc.) conjure up acquaintances real or imaginary.
7. Compare the briefly mentioned Simplicius in Pope's *Epistle* (1.32).
8. In her letter about the poem, Leapor elaborates on these grim foodstuffs: "You are not to suppose a woman of [Cordia's] character would admit of two dishes upon her table at once. No: they are separate meals, and the potatoes are not introduced as sauce to the pie."

45   Whose eager eyes stare ghastly at the poor,
      And fright the beggars from her hated door;
      In greasy clouts° she wraps her smokey chin,   *rags*
      And holds that pride's a never-pardoned sin.
          If this be wealth, no matter where it falls;
50   But save, ye Muses, save your Mira's walls:⁹
      Still give me pleasing indolence and ease,
      A fire to warm me and a friend to please.
          Since, whether sunk in avarice or pride,
      A wanton virgin or a starving bride;
55   Or° wondering crowds attend her charming tongue,   *whether*
      Or, deemed an idiot, ever speaks the wrong;
      Though Nature armed us for the growing ill
      With fraudful cunning and a headstrong will;
      Yet, with ten thousand follies to her charge,
60   Unhappy woman's but a slave at large.

                                                                      1751

THE DUNCIAD   Pope spent strikingly long stretches of his career making and remaking epics: *The Rape of the Lock* (1711–1717); translations of Homer's *Iliad* (1713–1720) and *Odyssey* (1720–1726). Of all such enterprises, his last ran longest. *The Dunciad* absorbed him, on and off, for fifteen years (1728–1743). It centers on a conflict that had mattered to him throughout his working life: the culture wars, transacted with furious conviction on both sides, between the Ancients and the Moderns. The Ancients were readers and writers for whom the classical cultures of Greece and Rome formed the proper foundation for civic virtue, social conduct, and literary greatness. The Moderns were an amalgam of prolific innovators deliberately divorcing themselves from old ways: the practitioners of new techniques in scholarship and the sciences; the pursuers of new profits in commerce and politics; and above all, the denizens of the new print industry known as Grub Street, hack authors who, writing badly, rapidly, and plentifully, threatened (in Pope's view) to glut the world with worthlessness. These are the "dunces" from whom the epic takes its name. In its design, Pope achieved satiric leverage worthy of a catapult: a mock epic (in which the ancient literary model mocks modern literary practice), centered, as the first line promises, on a "Mother, and her son" in whom Pope contrives to encapsulate the imminent end of civilization. The mother is the Goddess Dulness ("stupidity," "sluggishness") who seeks to recover her dominion over mortal minds; her son is the real-life dunce whom she has selected as the avatar best suited to restore her rule; and the entire scheme reenacts, with savage indignation, some of the central stories of god and mortal, parent and child (*Iliad, Aeneid*, Genesis, the New Testament, *Paradise Lost*) in classical and Christian culture. In the epic's first three versions (beginning with *The Dunciad*, 1728), Dulness's choice for chief dunce had been a scholar, Lewis Theobald, whose infuriating (but accurate) critique of Pope's *Shakespeare* had prompted the poet to mock him as a pedant; the satire swelled in the second version (*The Dunciad Variorum*, 1729), which added an enormous, parodic scholarly apparatus of half-deranged prefaces, footnotes, and appendices; and in the third (*The New Dunciad*, 1742), a wholly new poem in which Pope shifted his satiric aim from Grub Street to a wider range of intellectual pursuits (the New Science) and cultural practices (the Grand Tour). In the epic's final incarnation—*The Dunciad in Four Books* (1743), excerpted here—Dulness and Pope select a different

---

9. "Mira" (derived from "Mary") was Leapor's pen name. Her letter glosses the line: "Now to the Muses: I don't call them to fortify my walls against wealth itself, but against wealth in such a shape as we had then described; and you are to not think, that poets, who love ease and pleasure, and the most gay delights of life, should hate the only means of obtaining it."

dunce: Colley Cibber (1671–1757), actor, playwright, shamelessly self-satisfied autobiographer, and clumsy versifier, whose appointment as Poet Laureate (1730), payback for his loyalty to Robert Walpole and the Whig regime, had outraged Pope and many of his cohort in the wit-rich, power-destitute anti-Walpolean Opposition. Royally rewarded for political pandering and bad writing, Cibber becomes in Pope's portrait the distillation of all duncery, the embodiment and instrument of Dulness's imminent, inexorable victory.

from The Dunciad in Four Books
Book the First

The mighty Mother, and her son[1] who brings
The Smithfield Muses to the ear of kings,[2]
I sing. Say you, her instruments the great!
Called to this work by Dulness, Jove, and Fate;
5 You by whose care, in vain decried and cursed,
Still Dunce the Second reigns like Dunce the First;[3]
Say how the Goddess bade Britannia sleep,
And poured her spirit o'er the land and deep.[4]
  In eldest time, ere mortals writ or read,
10 Ere Pallas issued from the Thund'rer's head,[5]
Dulness o'er all possessed her ancient right,
Daughter of Chaos and eternal Night:
Fate in their dotage° this fair idiot gave,   *old age*
Gross as her sire, and as her mother grave,
15 Laborious, heavy, busy, bold, and blind,
She ruled, in native anarchy, the mind.
  Still her old empire to restore she tries,
For, born a Goddess, Dulness never dies.
  O thou! Whatever title please thine ear,
20 Dean, Drapier, Bickerstaff, or Gulliver![6]
Whether thou choose Cervantes' serious air,
Or laugh and shake in Rab'lais' easy chair,[7]
Or praise the court, or magnify mankind,[8]

1. The Goddess Dulness, and Colley Cibber, whose roles in the poem are spelled out in Pope's first footnote: "The reader ought here to be cautioned, that the *Mother,* and not the *Son,* is the principal agent of this poem . . . the main action of the poem being by no means the coronation of the Laureate, which is performed in the very first book, but the restoration of the empire of Dulness in Britain, which is not accomplished till the last."

2. Smithfield was London's major meat market, and the site also of (as Pope's note puts it) crowd-pleasing "shows . . . and dramatical entertainments, formerly agreeable only to the taste of the rabble, [which] were by the Hero of this poem and others of equal genius" exported to the upscale theaters of the West End, to become "the reigning pleasures of the court and town. This happened in the reigns of King George I, and II."

3. I.e., one mediocre Poet Laureate (Cibber) succeeds another: Laurence Eusden (1688–1730). The line launches the poem's pervasive motif of royal succession as the means by which Dulness hopes to secure eternal dominion over Britain.

4. The line echoes, as will many that follow, both the biblical and the Miltonic accounts of Creation: "and darkness was on the face of the deep. And the Spirit of God moved upon the face of the waters" (Genesis 1.2).

5. In Greek mythology, Pallas Athena, goddess of wisdom (and hence, throughout the *Dunciad,* Dulness's contrasting counterpart) leapt forth fully formed from the head of her father Zeus, thunder-bearer and ruler of the gods.

6. All alternate labels for Pope's cherished friend Jonathan Swift, to whom the *Dunciad* is dedicated; he was Dean of St. Paul's, and wrote satire under many "titles," assuming the guise of a cloth-dealer (*The Drapier's Letters,* 1724), an astrologer (the Bickerstaff papers, 1708), and a mariner (*Gulliver's Travels,* 1726).

7. Miguel de Cervantes's *Don Quixote* (1605–1615) and Francois Rabelais's *Gargantua and Pantagruel* (1532–1552) were perhaps the preeminent precedents for Swift's own satire.

8. As Swift does in his portrayal of Brobdingnag, his fictive country of giants, in Book 2 of *Gulliver's Travels.*

25
Or thy grieved country's[9] copper chains unbind;
From thy Boeotia though her pow'r retires,
Mourn not, my Swift, at ought our realm acquires,[1]
Here pleased behold her mighty wings outspread
To hatch a new Saturnian age of lead.[2]
30
      Close to those walls where Folly holds her throne,
And laughs to think Monroe would take her down,[3]
Where o'er the gates, by his famed by father's hand
Great Cibber's brazen, brainless brothers stand;[4]
One cell there is, concealed from vulgar eye,
The Cave of Poverty and Poetry.[5]
35
Keen, hollow winds howl through the bleak recess,
Emblem of music caused by emptiness.
Hence bards, like Proteus long in vain tied down,
Escape in monsters, and amaze the town.[6]
Hence miscellanies spring, the weekly boast
40
Of Curll's[7] chaste press, and Lintot's rubric post:[8]
Hence hymning Tyburn's elegiac lines,[9]
Hence *Journals, Medleys, Merc'ries, Magazines:*[1]
Sepulchral lies, our holy walls to grace,[2]
And New Year Odes,[3] and all the Grub Street race.

---

9. I.e., Ireland; in *The Drapier's Letters*, Swift waged successful satiric combat against a profit-driven British scheme to establish a potentially ruinous currency of copper coinage in Ireland.

1. Because Dulness rules so thoroughly over England ("our realm"), Pope teasingly infers that she must have entirely withdrawn her "pow'r" from Swift's Ireland; Boeotia, in ancient Greece, was reputedly a province full of fools.

2. Milton, in his account of Creation, addresses the Holy Spirit who "with mighty wings outspread / Dove-like sat'st brooding on the vast abyss / And mad'st it pregnant" (*Paradise Lost* 1.20–22). The god Saturn, in Roman mythology, ruled over a glorious Age of Gold, but his name (as Pope points out in a footnote) became associated by alchemists with the far less luminous substance lead—which will serve as one of Dulness's emblems throughout the poem.

3. I.e, the walls of Bethlehem ("Bedlam"), London's lunatic asylum, whose chief physician James Monro strives to end the reign of Folly (madness) over his patients' minds.

4. The sculptor Caius Cibber (1630–1700), Colley's father, created the paired statues of Melancholy and Raving Madness that stood on either side of Bedlam's gates.

5. The line ushers in Pope's mythic refiguring of Grub Street, a London neighborhood overflowing with impoverished and (by Pope's reckoning) mediocre writers. It was located near Bedlam, and Pope's note makes a point of that proximity: "there cannot be a plainer indication of madness than in men's persisting to starve themselves and offend the public by scribbling . . . when they might have benefited themselves and others in profitable and honest employments. The qualities and productions of [Grub Street's inhabitants] are afterwards described in this first book."

6. The mythic Proteus could transform himself into many shapes (boar, snake, bull, fire) in order to elude capture. A footnote elaborates the comparison: "by Proteus must certainly be meant a hackneyed town scribbler; and by his transformations, the various disguises such a one assumes, to elude the pursuit of his irreconcilable enemy, the bailiff" [i.e., the officer in charge of arrests for debt and other crimes]. In the short list that follows (lines 38–44), Pope enumerates the "monsters"—new modes of cheap, popular publication—into which the Grub-Street Proteuses rapidly and repeatedly transform themselves in hopes of making money.

7. The bookseller Edmund Curll (d. 1747) published many unchaste pieces of prose and verse, as well as several attacks on Pope.

8. Bernard Lintot (1675–1736) published many of Pope's works; he made profitable use of "rubric posts," red-lettered title pages displayed as advertisements for his newly published wares.

9. Tyburn was the site of executions; ballads and memoirs concerning the criminals hanged there were popular forms of cheap reading matter.

1. Oft-used titles for periodicals, conjuring speed (*Mercury*: the swift-moving messenger god) and copious storage (*magazine*: a warehouse or stockpile). Pope's footnote elaborates on the magazines' content, in which "Dulness appears in a thousand shapes. These were thrown out weekly and monthly by every miserable scribbler; or picked up piecemeal and stolen from anybody."

2. A just satire on the flatteries and falsehoods admitted to be inscribed on the walls of churches, in epitaphs [Pope's note].

3. Made by the Poet Laureate . . . to be sung at court on every New Year's Day, the words of which are happily drowned in the voices and instruments [Pope's note].

45   In clouded majesty here Dulness shone;
      Four guardian Virtues, round, support her throne:
      Fierce champion Fortitude, that knows no fears
      Of hisses, blows, or want, or loss of ears:[4]
      Calm Temperance, whose blessings those partake
50   Who hunger and who thirst for scribbling sake:
      Prudence, whose glass° presents th' approaching jail.   *mirror*
      Poetic Justice, with her lifted scale,
      Where, in nice° balance, truth with gold she weighs,   *careful*
      And solid pudding against empty praise.[5]
55   Here she beholds the Chaos dark and deep,
      Where nameless somethings in their causes sleep,[6]
      'Till genial Jacob, or a warm third day,
      Call forth each mass, a poem, or a play:[7]
      How hints, like spawn, scarce quick° in embryo lie,   *barely alive*
60   How newborn nonsense first is taught to cry,
      Maggots half formed, in rhyme exactly meet,
      And learn to crawl upon poetic feet.[8]
      Here one poor word an hundred clenches° makes,   *puns*
      And ductile° dullness new meanders takes;   *flexible*
65   There motley[9] images her fancy strike,
      Figures ill paired, and similes unlike.
      She sees a mob of metaphors advance,
      Pleased with the madness of the mazy dance:
      How tragedy and comedy embrace;
70   How farce and epic get a jumbled race;
      How Time himself stands still at her command,
      Realms shift their place, and ocean turns to land.
      Here gay description Egypt glads° with show'rs,   *gladdens, bestows*
      Or gives to Zembla[1] fruits, to Barca[2] flow'rs;
75   Glitt'ring with ice here hoary hills are seen,
      There painted valleys of eternal green,
      In cold December fragrant chaplets° blow,   *flower wreaths*
      And heavy harvests nod beneath the snow.
          All these, and more, the cloud-compelling Queen
80   Beholds through fogs, that magnify the scene:
      She, tinseled o'er in robes of varying hues,

4. The cutting-off of ears was a punishment occasionally meted out (in the seventeenth century) to writers found guilty of libel against government or religion.
5. "Poetic Justice," which ordinarily refers to the morally satisfying resolution of plot, becomes here a figure for the Grub Street hack's painstaking adjudication between the claims of unprofitable truth and less honorably secured payment (money, food).
6. The lines evoke the chaos out of which, in Genesis and in *Paradise Lost*, God creates the universe.
7. Each shapeless "mass" is transformed into a viable piece of writing by the sunlike influence of either a prestigious publisher (Jacob Tonson [c. 1655–1736], whose good will toward any poem ensured its emergence from obscurity into print) or a warmly receptive audience: a

playwright received payment only when the play ran for at least three nights.
8. Tradition held that maggots were spawned by the action of sunlight upon dead flesh; the word also connoted "notion" or "idea." Here the creatures combine in rhyme and move by means of "poetic feet" (the rhythmic units of verse meter)—an image rendered all the weirder because maggots have no feet at all.
9. Random, confusedly mixed; in the lines that follow (66–78), Pope catalogs the incoherent combinations (of figures, genres, ideas, and details) perpetrated by Grub Street dunces in their frantic pursuit of publication.
1. A cluster of islands in the Arctic Ocean.
2. A city in North Africa.

With self-applause her wild Creation views;
Sees momentary monsters rise and fall,
And with her own fools'-colors gilds them all.
85   'Twas on the day, when * *³ rich and grave,
Like Cimon,⁴ triumphed both on land and wave:
(Pomps, without guilt, of bloodless swords and maces,
Glad chains, warm furs, broad banners, and broad faces)⁵
Now night descending, the proud scene was o'er,
90   But lived, in Settle's⁶ numbers,° one day more.   *verses*
Now may'rs and shrieves° all hushed and satiate lay,   *sheriffs*
Yet eat, in dreams, the custard⁷ of the day;
While pensive poets painful vigils keep,
Sleepless themselves, to give their readers sleep.
95   Much to the mindful Queen the feast recalls
What City swans⁸ once sung within the walls;
Much she revolves° their arts, their ancient praise,   *contemplates*
And sure succession down from Heywood's⁹ days.
She saw, with joy, the line immortal run,
100   Each sire impressed and glaring in his son:
So watchful bruin forms, with plastic care,
Each growing lump, and brings it to a bear.¹
She saw old Prynne² in restless Daniel³ shine,
And Eusden⁴ eke out Blackmore's⁵ endless line;
105   She saw slow Philips⁶ creep like Tate's poor page,⁷
And all the mighty mad in Dennis rage.⁸
In each she marks her image full expressed,⁹

---

3. In earlier versions, this blank read "Thorold"; George Thorold was at one time Lord Mayor of London. Pope sets Book 1 on Lord Mayor's Day, and parodies both mayoral and royal processionals, ceremonies, and celebrations conducted in the City of London, whose commerce-driven culture and politics the *Dunciad* deplores.
4. Athenian general, admiral (hence "wave"), and statesman (c. 510–c.450 B.C.E.).
5. Pope describes the adornments and appearance of the City dignitaries who march in the Lord Mayor's procession.
6. [Elkanah] Settle [1648–1724] was poet to the City of London. His office was to compose yearly panegyrics upon the Lord Mayor's [Day], and verses to be spoken in the pageants: but that part of the shows being at length frugally abolished, the employment of the City Poet ceased; so that upon Settle's demise there was no successor to that place [Pope's note].
7. A favorite foodstuff at City feasts.
8. Poets who dwelt in the City and "sang" (like dying swans) its values; in the lines that follow (98–106) Pope traces a parodic genealogy, an "immortal line" that runs in "sure succession" from dunce to dunce.
9. Thomas Heywood (d. 1641), a playwright who wrote scripts for City pageants.
1. Animal folklore held that the mother bear ("bruin") gave birth to a shapeless "lump" of flesh and fur, which she licked, with "plastic" (i.e., sculpting) power, into the form of a living cub.
2. William Prynne (1600–1669), Puritan pamphleteer, was imprisoned (and ear-deprived) for the criticisms of

Charles I and Queen Henrietta Maria that he published in *Histrio-Mastix* (1633).
3. Daniel Defoe (c. 1660–1731), prolific (hence "restless") author and controversialist, was pilloried for his satire of church and state in *The Shortest Way with the Dissenters* (1702).
4. Laurence Eusden (1688–1730), Cibber's immediate predecessor as Poet Laureate.
5. Sir Richard Blackmore (1654–1729), physician and writer of widely mocked, very lengthy epics; "endless line" here suggests lineage (the limitless succession of dunce-heirs) as well as tedium.
6. Ambrose Phillips (ca. 1674–1749), poet, playwright, and sometime rival of Pope, who derided Phillips, in *Peri-Bathous*, as a literary tortoise, "slow and chill."
7. Nahum Tate [1652–1715] was Poet Laureate, a cold writer, of no invention [Pope's note].
8. John Dennis (1658–1734), acute and at times caustic critic, with whom Pope had sustained a furious, ongoing literary quarrel since early in his own career. In an anonymous pamphlet (1713), Pope had insisted (satirically) that Dennis was actually mad; in a footnote to the present line he ironically modifies the claim: "This is by no means to be understood literally . . . No—it is spoken of that *excellent* and *divine madness* [i.e., mystical inspiration] so often mentioned by Plato; that poetical rage and enthusiasm, with which Mr. D. hath, in his time, been highly possessed."
9. As does Milton's God, who sees in Christ "the radiant image of his glory" (*Paradise Lost* 3.63).

But chief in BAYS'S[1] monster-breeding breast;
Bays, formed by Nature stage and town to bless,
110 And act, and be, a coxcomb° with success.   *preening fool*
Dulness with transport° eyes the lively dunce,   *ecstasy*
Rememb'ring she herself was pertness° once.   *impudence*
Now (shame to fortune!) an ill run at play°   *bad luck at dice*
Blanked his bold visage, and a thin third day:[2]
115 Swearing[3] and supperless the hero sate,°   *sat*
Blasphemed his gods, the dice, and damned his fate.
Then gnawed his pen, then dashed it on the ground,
Sinking from thought to thought, a vast profound![4]
Plunged for his sense, but found no bottom there,
120 Yet wrote, and floundered on, in mere despair.
Round him much embryo, much abortion lay,
Much future ode, and abdicated play;
Nonsense precipitate,[5] like running lead,
That slipped through cracks and zig-zags of the head;
125 All that on Folly Frenzy could beget,
Fruits of dull heat, and sooterkins of wit.[6]
Next, o'er his books his eyes began to roll,
In pleasing memory of all he stole,[7]
How here he sipped, how there he plundered snug,°   *deftly and undetected*
130 And sucked all o'er, like an industrious bug.
Here lay poor Fletcher's half-eat° scenes,[8] and here   *eaten*
The frippery° of crucified Moliere;[9]   *old clothes*
There hapless Shakespeare, yet of Tibbald sore,[1]
Wished he had blotted for himself before.[2]
135 The rest on outside merit[3] but presume,

1. I.e., Cibber's, sardonically renamed here for the wreath of bay leaves awarded to the Laureate.
2. I.e., a poor turnout for the third, payment-clinching performance of his new play (see above, line 58 and note).
3. A habit for which Cibber was notorious.
4. The line echoes both Rochester, who describes the mind, deluded as to its own powers of reason, "Stumbling from thought to thought" before falling "headlong down / Into doubt's boundless sea" ("A Satyr against Reason and Mankind" ll. 18–19); and Milton, whose angel Raphael describes the chaos before creation as "the vast profound" (*Paradise Lost* 7.229).
5. The adjective denotes both speed and downward motion, like the leaden creations (liquid but molten) that seep, in this couplet, from Bays's cracked skull.
6. The line sustains the imagery of miscarriage and monstrous birth: in Aristotelian medicine, "dull heat" (faint passion) produced pallid progeny; folkloric "sooterkins" ("little soot-balls") were mouse-like creatures conceived by women unwary enough to warm themselves by means of small stoves tucked under their skirts.
7. In the ensuing lines, Cibber fondly recalls his plagiarisms.
8. John Fletcher (1579–1625), Jacobean playwright whose faded popularity enables Bays to plagiarize with impunity: "A great number of [Fletcher's scenes were] taken out to patch up [Cibber's] plays" [Pope's note].

9. Stage name of the French playwright Jean-Baptiste Poquelin (1622–1673); Cibber had reworked Molière's celebrated *Tartuffe* into *The Non-Juror* (1718), an anti-Catholic comedy peppered with specific (albeit indirect) attacks on Pope.
1. Lewis Theobald (1688–1744), a textual scholar and editor who had enraged Pope by criticizing his edition of Shakespeare's works (1725), and who had preceded Cibber as chief dunce and target in all previous versions of the *Dunciad* (1728, 1729, 1742) until, in 1743, the Poet Laureate took his place.
2. "It was a ridiculous praise which the players gave to Shakespeare [in the First Folio of his works] 'that he had never blotted [cancelled, crossed out] a line.' Ben Jonson honestly wished he had blotted a thousand, and Shakespeare would certainly have wished the same, if he had lived to see those alterations in his works, which, not the actors only (and especially the daring Hero of this poem) have made on the stage but the presumptuous critics of our days in their *editions*" [Pope's note]. Cibber had successfully starred in his own radical revision of Shakespeare's *Richard III*; Theobald was of course preeminent among Pope's "presumptuous critics."
3. I.e., external beauty: bound volumes whose elegance belies the ineptitude of the writing they contain; Pope catalogs some of their occupants in the ensuing lines (140–42).

Or serve (like other fools) to fill a room;
Such with their shelves as due proportion hold,
Or their fond parents dressed in red and gold;[4]
Or where the pictures for the page atone,°   *compensate*
140   And Quarles[5] is saved by beauties not his own.
Here swells the shelf with Ogilby the great;[6]
There, stamped with arms, Newcastle[7] shines complete:
Here all his° suff'ring brotherhood retire,   *Cibber's*
And 'scape the martyrdom of jakes° and fire;[8]   *outhouse*
145   A Gothic library! of Greece and Rome
Well purged,[9] and worthy° Settle, Banks, and Broome.[1]   *worthy of*
    But, high above, more solid learning shone,
The classics of an age that heard of none;
There Caxton slept, with Wynkin at his side,[2]
150   One clasped in wood, and one in strong cow-hide;[3]
There, saved by spice,[4] like mummies, many a year,
Dry bodies of divinity° appear: *theology*
De Lyra[5] there a dreadful front extends,
And here the groaning shelves Philemon[6] bends.
155   Of these twelve volumes, twelve of amplest size,
Redeemed from tapers and defrauded pies,[7]
Inspired he seizes: these an altar raise:
An hecatomb° of pure, unsullied lays°   *sacrifice / songs*
That altar crowns:[8] a folio commonplace[9]
160   Founds the whole pile, of all his works the base:
Quartos, octavos shape the less'ning pyre,
A twisted Birthday Ode[1] completes the spire.
    Then he: "Great tamer of all human art!
First in my care, and ever at my heart;

---

4. I.e., the books, like the children of "fond parents," are overdressed.

5. Frances Quarles (1592–1644), religious poet, whose widely published *Emblems* combined poetic and pictorial depictions of moral allegories.

6. John Ogilby (1600–1676), writer and publisher, had produced a sumptuously illustrated translation of Homer's *Iliad* (1660).

7. Margaret Cavendish, Duchess of Newcastle (1623–1673), prolific writer now much studied, whose poetry, plays, fiction, and treatises (scientific and proto-feminist), now much studied, were regarded in the eighteenth century as merely plentiful and eccentric (see pages 2058–73).

8. The customary fates of worthless print; compare Dryden, who describes the literary detritus of his age, recycled as wrapping- and toilet-paper, as "Martyrs of pies, and relics of the bum [buttocks]" (*Mac Flecknoe* line 101).

9. Cibber's book collection, like the Gothic age, is devoid of classical literature (and values).

1. John Banks (1652–1706) and Richard Brome (c. 1590–1692), tragic and comic playwrights respectively, here linked with Pope's recurrent target Elkanah Settle, City Poet.

2. William Caxton (1422?–1491), the first English printer, and Wynkin de Worde (d. 1535), his assistant and successor, produced English adaptations of French retellings of classical tales out of Virgil and Homer; Pope saw these as useless distortions of the originals.

3. Common materials in medieval bookbindings.

4. Fragrant spices acted as a repellent against bookworms.

5. Nicholas de Lyra (d. 1340), biblical commentator.

6. Philemon Holland (1552–1637), prolific translator of ancient Roman texts.

7. More "martyrdom" (see line 144): pages from unwanted books were used to light candles and line pie tins.

8. Atop the old volumes, Bays places plentiful copies of his own poetry, "unsullied" (un-dirtied) because no one's buying or reading them.

9. The folio was the largest format for books, the "commonplace" the most derivative genre: it collected (into one "common place") quotations from other writers. Pope implies that Cibber, destitute of his own ideas, needs to draw on a large collection.

1. Another recurrent duty of the Laureate: to write odes celebrating the birthdays of members of the royal family.

165 Dulness! Whose good old cause[2] I yet defend,
    With whom my Muse began, with whom shall end:
    E'er since Sir Fopling's periwig was praise,[3]
    To the last honors of the butt and bays.[4]
    O thou! Of bus'ness the directing soul!
170 To this our head, like bias to the bowl,[5]
    Which, as more pond'rous, made its aim more true,
    Obliquely waddling to the mark in view.
    O! ever gracious to perplexed mankind,
    Still spread a healing mist before the mind;
175 And lest we err by wit's wild dancing light,
    Secure us kindly in our native night:
    Or, if to wit a coxcomb make pretense,
    Guard the sure barrier between that and sense;
    Or quite unravel all the reas'ning thread,
180 And hang some curious cobweb in its stead!
    As, forced from wind-guns, lead itself can fly,
    And pond'rous slugs cut swiftly through the sky;
    As clocks to weight their nimble motion owe,
    The wheels above urged by the load below;
185 Me emptiness and dullness could inspire,
    And were my elasticity[6] and fire.
    Some daemon stole my pen (forgive th' offense)
    And once betrayed me into common sense:[7]
    Else all my prose and verse were much the same;
190 This, prose on stilts; that, poetry fall'n lame.
    Did on the stage my fops appear confined?°   *too moderate*
    My life gave ampler lessons to mankind.
    Did the dead letter[8] unsuccessful prove?
    The brisk example never failed to move.
195 Yet sure had Heav'n decreed to save the state,
    Heav'n had decreed those works a longer date.[9]
    Could Troy be saved by any single hand,
    This grey-goose weapon° must have made her stand.   *goose-quill pen*
    What can I now?[1] My Fletcher cast aside,

---

2. The phrase was conventionally (and ironically) applied to the antiroyalist faction in the English Civil Wars; Tories like Pope regarded Whigs like Cibber as direct political descendants of those earlier rebels. Cibber's prayer extends the "oldness" backward: The first period of Dulness's dominion began long before the rise of sense and learning.

3. Cibber first attained fame as an actor in a role he wrote for himself: the lavishly bewigged fop in *Love's Last Shift; or, The Fool in Fashion* (1696). From Pope's sardonic note: "The first visible cause of the passion of the Town for our Hero was a fair flaxen full-bottomed periwig . . . This remarkable periwig usually made its entrance upon the stage in a sedan, brought in by two chairmen, with infinite approbation of the audience."

4. Emblems of the Laureate: a regular royal allotment of wine (butt); a wreath of laurel (bay) leaves.

5. In the game of bowls, the asymmetrical weighting ("bias") of each ball affects the direction in which it rolls. Pope echoes Dryden, describing Shadwell's special gifts, in *Mac Flecknoe*: "This is the boasted bias of thy mind, / By which one way, to dullness, 'tis inclined" (lines 189–90).

6. I.e., the power of gases to expand: a flatulent mode of "inspiration."

7. Another echo of *Mac Flecknoe*: "The rest to some faint meaning make pretense, / But Sh[adwell] never deviates into sense" (lines 19–20).

8. I.e., Bays's inert writing.

9. Bays's grandiose lament on the ephemerality of his work echoes (and inverts) the despair of the Trojan Anchises at the fall of Troy: "if the gods had wished me longer life, they would have saved the city" (*Aeneid* 2.641–2).

1. I.e., "what should I do now?" In the ensuing lines (199–216), Bays weighs alternate courses of action.

200 Take up the Bible, once my better guide?[2]
Or tread the path by vent'rous heroes trod,
This box my thunder, this right hand my god?[3]
Or chaired at White's amidst the doctors sit,[4]
Teach oaths to gamesters, and to nobles wit?
205 Or bidst thou° rather party to embrace?[5]   *i.e., Dulness*
(A friend to party thou, and all her race;
'Tis the same rope at different ends they twist;
To Dulness, Ridpath[6] is as dear as Mist.[7])
Shall I like Curtius, desp'rate in my zeal,
210 O'er head and ears plunge for the commonweal?
Or rob Rome's ancient geese of all their glories,
And cackling save the monarchy of Tories?[8]
Hold—to the Minister[9] I more incline;
To serve his cause, O Queen![1] is serving thine;
215 Now, see! thy very Gazetteers[2] give o'er,°   *surrender*
Ev'n Ralph is lost,[3] and Henley writes no more![4]
What then remains? Ourself.[5] Still, still remain
Cibberian forehead, and Cibberian brain;[6]
This brazen brightness, to the squire so dear;
220 This polished hardness, that reflects the peer;
This arch absurd,° that wit and fool delights;   *absurdity*
This mess,° tossed up of Hockley-Hole[7] and White's,   *hodgepodge*
Where dukes and butchers join to wreath my crown,
At once the bear and fiddle[8] of the town.
225   "O born in sin, and forth in folly brought![9]

2. I.e., give up playwriting for piety (Cibber notes in his *Apology* that his father hoped he would become a clergyman).
3. Bays, like Cibber an ardent gambler, pictures himself both as ancient hero (Virgil's Mezentius, who chose to trust the spear in his "right hand" rather than the gods [*Aeneid* 10.773]) and as divinity: Jupiter, who wields the thunder as Bays will wield the noisy dice-box.
4. White's: a fashionable gambling club (Cibber was a member); doctors: slang for dice.
5. Bays considers engaging himself as author in the political controversies between Whigs and Tories, whom Dulness cherishes for the plenitude and mediocrity of their propaganda.
6. George Ridpath (d. 1726), Whig journalist.
7. Nathaniel Mist (d. 1737), Tory publisher.
8. Bays, deliberating whether to remain loyal to the Whigs or to sell out to the Tories, invokes Roman precedents: Marcus Curtius, who according to legend "plunged" into a pit in order to restore the Roman Forum; and the geese of Rome, whose cackling one night awoke the Romans in time to preserve the city from an enemy's surprise attack. Pope's juxtaposition of "commonweal" and "monarchy" recalls the key terms and tensions of the Civil Wars.
9. I.e., Robert Walpole (1676–1745), Whig prime minister, who had secured Cibber's loyalty (and compounded Pope's disgust) by orchestrating his appointment as Poet Laureate.
1. I.e., Dulness, and (by association) Queen Caroline (1683–1737), wife to George II and Walpole's closest ally within the Hanoverian royal family.

2. The *Daily Gazetteer*, which had served as Walpole's chief venue for propaganda, had become notably more neutral after his resignation in 1742.
3. James Ralph (d. 1762), political writer, had in truth been "lost" to Walpole for a long while; his antiministerial journalism became increasingly vociferous and effectual throughout the late 1730s and early 1740s.
4. John ("Orator") Henley (1692–1756), a preacher who had frequently served Walpole by attacking Pope, had terminated his pro-ministerial periodical *Hyp Doctor* in 1741.
5. Bays echoes the protagonist of Seneca's *Medea*, who on learning that she's been abandoned by her husband and her friends, insists "Medea superest": Medea remains (5.166).
6. Pope, in a mock-scholarly textual note, insists that the adjective originally read "Cerberian," after Cerberus, the three-headed canine guardian of Hades: "The *Dog* was the ancient . . . symbol of Impudence." In the ensuing lines, Bays catalogs the varied ways in which his "Cibberian brain" appeals to admirers from several social strata.
7. A London location (like Smithfield in line 2) for bear-baiting and other "low" entertainments, here contrasted with White's (Cibber's gleaming gambling club).
8. Fiddle-playing often served as an overture to bear-baiting; the word could also mean "butt of a joke" (as Cibber is throughout Pope's poem).
9. Bays now addresses his own neglected publications, heaped into a pyre and ready for burning.

Works damned, or to be damned (your father's fault),
Go, purified by flame, ascend the sky,
My better and more Christian progeny!
Unstained, unstitched, and yet in maiden sheets;[1]
230 While all your smutty sisters walk the streets.[2]
Ye shall not beg, like gratis-given Bland,[3]
Sent with a pass, and vagrant through the land;
Not sail, with Ward,[4] to ape-and-monkey climes,
Where vile mundungus° trucks° for viler rhymes;   *cheap tobacco* / *is traded*
235 Not sulfur-tipped emblaze an ale-house fire;
Not wrap up oranges, to pelt your sire![5]
O! pass more innocent, in infant state,
To the mild limbo[6] of our father Tate:[7]
Or peaceably forgot, at once be blessed
240 In Shadwell's bosom, with eternal rest![8]
Soon to that mass of nonsense to return,
Where things destroyed are swept to things unborn."
      With that, a tear (portentous sign of grace!)
Stole from the master of the sev'nfold face:[9]
245 And thrice he lifted high the birthday brand,[1]
And thrice he dropped it from his quiv'ring hand;
Then lights the structure, with averted eyes:
The rolling smokes involve° the sacrifice.   *engulf*
The op'ning clouds disclose each work[2] by turns,
250 Now flames the Cid, and now Perolla burns;
Great Caesar roars, and hisses in the fires;
King John in silence modestly expires:
No merit now the dear Nonjuror claims,
Moliere's old stubble in a moment flames.
255 Tears gushed again, as from pale Priam's eyes,
When the last blaze sent Ilion° to the skies.[3]   *Troy*
      Roused by the light, old Dulness heaved the head;

---

1. I.e., just as they emerged from the press: pure of the processes (stitching and binding) that would prepare them for sale.
2. Two of Cibber's actual children, the actors Theophilus Cibber and Charlotte Charke, had attained a complex notoriety for outrageous sexual and/or theatrical activities.
3. Henry Bland (d. 1746), Whig propagandist, here pictured as a beggar in the wake of Walpole's fall.
4. Edward Ward (1667–1731), satirist, travel-writer and tavern-keeper; he had "sailed" to tropical territories in two senses: he had written A Trip to Jamaica (1697), and his books sold well (so Pope's note scornfully insists) in the Caribbean colonial plantations.
5. Still more martyrdom: if Bays does not burn them now, he fears that his sheets will serve to light fires, or to wrap oranges for sale at the playhouse, where the fruit might well be used to "pelt" bad actors (himself included).
6. I.e., the afterlife allotted to sinless infants.

7. See above, line 105 and note.
8. Thomas Shadwell (c. 1640–1692), playwright, Poet Laureate, and principal target of Dryden's satire in Mac Flecknoe (1682).
9. "Sevenfold" because Cibber, as actor, has played many parts.
1. Torch (here, the "twisted Birthday Ode" that Bays uses as igniter).
2. Pope proceeds to list some of Cibber's plays: Ximena (1719), adapted from Pierre Corneille's Le Cid; Perolla and Izadora (1706); Caesar in Egypt (1725); and Papal Tyranny in the Reign of King John, adapted from Shakespeare's King John but "silent" (in 1743) because as yet unperformed; The Non-Juror (1717), adapted from Molière's Tartuffe (see above, line 132 and note).
3. Priam, last king of Troy, wept to witness the fire that destroyed his city.

Then snatched a sheet of *Thulè*[4] from her bed,
Sudden she flies, and whelms it o'er the pyre;
260   Down sink the flames, and with a hiss expire.
    Her ample presence fills up all the place;
A veil of fogs dilates her awful° face: *awesome*
Great in her charms! as when on shrieves and may'rs
She looks, and breathes herself into their airs.°   *pretensions*
265   She bids him wait° her to her sacred dome: *accompany*
Well pleased he entered, and confessed his home.
So spirits ending their terrestrial race,
Ascend and recognize their native place.
This the Great Mother dearer held than all
270   The clubs of quidnuncs,[5] or her own Guildhall.[6]
Her stood her opium,[7] here she nursed her owls,[8]
And here she planned th' imperial seat[9] of fools.
    Here to her chosen all her works she shows;
Prose swelled to verse, verse loit'ring into prose:
275   How random thoughts now meaning chance to find,
Now leave all memory of sense behind:
How prologues into prefaces decay,
And these to notes are frittered quite away.
How index-learning turns no student pale,[1]
280   Yet holds the eel of science by the tail.[2]
How, with less reading than makes felons 'scape,[3]
Less human genius than God gives an ape,
Small thanks to France, and none to Rome or Greece,
A past, vamped,° future, old, revived, new piece,   *patched up*
285   'Twixt Plautus,[4] Fletcher, Shakespeare, and Corneille,[5]
Can make a Cibber, Tibbald, or Ozell.[6]
The Goddess then, o'er his anointed head,
With mystic words, the sacred opium shed.
And lo! her bird (a monster of a fowl!
290   Something betwixt a Heidegger[7] and owl),
Perched on his crown. "All hail! And hail again,
My son! The promised land expects thy reign.

---

4. An unfinished poem by Ambrose Phillips, whom Pope at career's outset regarded as a rival; his note makes explicit what his couplet implies: "the coldness and heaviness of [Phillips's] writing."
5. The Latin phrase *quid nunc*—what now? what news?—had become a label for news addicts, who compulsively asked each other the question.
6. The center of City politics and ceremonies.
7. The drug was used by impoverished writers (among others) to allay hunger, subdue pain, and induce stupefaction.
8. The bird associated with Athena, goddess of wisdom, is here linked ironically (as a creature of the night) with her divine opposite, Dulness, and with the dominion of the night.
9. I.e., the site of the future emperor's (Bays's) palace, throne, and court.

1. Because the index shortens labor, it allows its users (the textual scholars Pope here mocks, for whom indexes were a necessary tool of research) more time for sleep.
2. The metaphor figures "science" (knowledge) as elusive, and the index-learners as grabbing it by the wrong end.
3. Under British law, proof of even limited literacy in Latin sometimes exempted criminals from punishment.
4. Roman comic playwright (c. 254–184 B.C.E.).
5. French tragic playwright (1606–1684).
6. John Ozell (d. 1743), translator, whose critical attack on plays by Pope's friend William Wycherley prompted the poet to satiric countermeasures.
7. Johann Jakob Heidegger, Swiss-born London impresario, famed for his extraordinary ugliness.

Know, Eusden thirsts no more for sack[8] or praise,
He sleeps[9] among the dull of ancient days,

295 Safe, where no critics damn, no duns molest,
Where wretched Withers,[1] Ward, and Gildon[2] rest,
And high-born Howard,[3] more majestic sire,
With Fool of Quality[4] completes the quire.[5]
Thou Cibber! thou his[6] laurel shall support,

300 Folly, my son, has still a friend at court.
Lift up your gates, ye princes, see him° come!   *Cibber*
Sound, sound ye viols, be the catcall dumb![7]
Bring, bring the madding° bay, the drunken vine;   *maddening*
The creeping, dirty, courtly ivy join![8]

305 And thou! his aide de camp,[9] lead out my sons,
Light-armed with points, antitheses, and puns.[1]
Let bawdry, Billingsgate,[2] two sisters dear,
Support his front, and oaths bring up the rear:
And under his, and under Archer's[3] wing,

310 Gaming and Grub Street skulk behind the King.
    "O! when shall rise a monarch, all our own,
And I, a nursing mother, rock the throne;
'Twixt prince and people close the curtain draw,
Shade him from light, and cover him from law!

315 Fatten the courtier, starve the learned band,
And suckle armies, and dry-nurse the land:[4]
'Till senates nod to lullabies divine,
And all be sleep, as at an ode of thine?"

    She ceased. Then swells the Chapel Royal throat:[5]

320 "God save King Cibber!" mounts in ev'ry note.
Familiar White's "God save King Colley!" cries;
"God save King Colley!" Drury-lane replies:

---

8. White wine; Cibber's laureate-predecessor Laurence Eusden had been reputed a heavy drinker.

9. I.e., Eusden is now (like the other dunce-forebears listed in lines, 296–98) dead.

1. George Withers (1588–1667), poet and satirist, derided by Jonson, Dryden, Swift, and others as a hack who had pandered to popular taste.

2. Charles Gildon (1665–1724), prolific writer for the popular press.

3. Edward Howard (1624–1712), playwright and poet, energetically mocked by Restoration wits.

4. John Hervey (1696–1743), high-ranking courtier, ardent adherent to Walpole and Caroline, and caustic insulter of Pope, who retaliated with his portrait of Hervey as Lord Sporus in *Epistle to Dr. Arbuthnot* (lines 305–33); Hervey's death in 1743 enabled Pope to include him, just in time, as capper to this list of departed dunces.

5. A pun, envisioning the choir of dead dunces as also a quire—an unbound (hence unsold, unread) cluster of printed pages.

6. I.e., Eusden's, though the pronouns here and in the ensuing lines (300–309) are famously and perhaps pointedly ambiguous; laurel: the wreath of bay leaves worn by laureates.

7. The line conjures a theater, where musicians played violins, and restive audience members blew high-pitched whistles ("catcalls") to express their disgust.

8. Though ivy (unlike bay leaf and vine) forms no part of the laureate's traditional wreath, Pope in an appendix defended its inclusion here as "emblematical of the three virtues of a court poet in particular: it is *creeping*, *dirty*, and *dangling*."

9. Lord Hervey. Aide de camp: a general's (here, Cibber's) assistant officer.

1. Hervey's favored forms of wordplay; points: surprising turns of thought and phrase; antitheses: quick, provocative juxtapositions (compare *Arbuthnot*, lines 323–25).

2. The obscene speech associated with the women who sold fish at Billingsgate market.

3. Thomas Archer (1668–1743), a high-placed architect whose prerogatives included furnishing the royal apartments toward which Cibber and his entourage are headed, as well as the royally sanctioned gambling privileges touched on in the next line.

4. Dulness envisions herself as prodigiously nurturing: queen-mother to a dunce-monarch, wet nurse to the army, dry nurse (nanny) to the nation.

5. I.e., the choir of the chapel where the royal family worshipped.

To Needham's[6] quick the voice triumphal rode,
But pious Needham dropped the name of God;
325   Back to the Devil[7] the last echoes roll,
And "Coll!"[8] each butcher roars at Hockley-Hole.[9]
    So when Jove's block° descended from on high   *log*
(As sings thy great forefather Ogilby[1])
Loud thunder to its bottom shook the bog,
330   And the hoarse nation croaked, "God save King Log!"[2]

from *Book the Fourth*[1]

    O Muse! relate (for you can tell alone,
620   Wits have short memories, and dunces none)
Relate, who first, who last resigned to rest;
Whose heads she partly, whose completely blessed;
What charms could faction, what ambition lull,
The venal quiet, and entrance the dull;
625   Till drowned was sense, and shame, and right, and wrong—
O sing, and hush the nations with thy song!

* *

In vain, in vain—the all-composing hour
Resistless falls: the Muse obeys the Pow'r.
She comes! She comes! the fabled throne behold
630   Of Night primeval, and of Chaos old!
Before her, Fancy's gilded clouds decay,
And all its varying rainbows die away.
Wit shoots in vain its momentary fires,
The meteor drops, and in a flash expires.
635   As one by one, at dread Medea's strain,[2]
The sick'ning stars fade off th' ethereal plain;
As Argus' eyes by Hermes' wand oppressed,[3]
Close one by one to everlasting rest;
Thus at her felt approach, and secret might,
640   Art after art goes out, and all is night.
See skulking Truth to her old cavern fled,
Mountains of casuistry° heaped o'er her head!   *false reasoning*
Philosophy, that leaned on Heav'n before,

---

6. A famous brothel near the royal palace, run by Elizabeth Needham (d. 1731).
7. The Devil Tavern in Fleet Street, where these odes are usually rehearsed before they are performed at court [Pope's note].
8. The word was slang for "fool," "dupe."
9. See line 222 and note; the acclamation has traveled from the aristocratic precincts of the Town back to the shabbier terrain of the City, where both Bays and the *Dunciad* began.
1. See line 141 and note.
2. Pope echoes Ogilby's verse retelling of an Aesop's fable: when the frogs petitioned Jupiter ("Jove") to provide them with a king, he contemptuously sent down a block of wood: "Then all the bog / Proclaim their king, and cry, 'Jove save King Log.' " This story of an "alien" (and inert) monarch, confirmed not by heredity but by popular

acclamation, resonates with the period's impassioned party politics: the Tory and Jacobite resentment of Whig policies (here embodied by Cibber, the City, and the dunces) that successfully supplanted the hereditary Stuart succession with the more distant Hanoverian line.
1. Throughtout Book 4, the *Dunciad*'s hero does nothing; in these, the poem's closing lines, Dulness's infectious yawn spreads sleep everywhere and ushers in apocalypse, silencing even Pope's own muse, and returning the world to the primeval darkness and chaos that preceded Creation.
2. In Seneca's tragedy *Medea*, the title character, a sorceress, attempts to avenge herself upon her unfaithful lover by summoning constellations down from the sky and making the sun stand still.
3. Argus's hundred eyes enabled him to guard Io against Jupiter's advances—but Jupiter sent Mercury (Hermes) to lull Argus asleep, then kill him.

645

Shrinks to her second cause,[4] and is no more.
Physic of Metaphysic begs defense,
And Metaphysic calls for aid on Sense![5]
See Mystery to Mathematics fly![6]
In vain! they[7] gaze, turn giddy, rave, and die.
Religion blushing veils her sacred fires,

650
And unawares Morality expires.
Nor public fame, nor private, dares to shine;
Nor human spark is left, nor glimpse divine!
Lo! thy dread empire, CHAOS! is restored;
Light dies before thy uncreating word:[8]

655
Thy hand, great Anarch![9] lets the curtain fall;
And Universal Darkness buries All.

Lady Mary Wortley Montagu
1689–1762

In learning, literature, and travel, Lady Mary Wortley Montagu outdistanced almost all of her contemporaries. Born Mary Pierrepont, she acquired her title at age one (when her father became an earl), lost her mother at age three, and immersed herself throughout her youth in the Roman classics, fervently pursuing a plan of self-education at odds with the conventional domesticating agenda (dancing, drawing, social graces) laid out for young women of her rank. For a time in her teens she aspired to implement the idea set forth by the feminist Mary Astell, of founding a convent consecrated to women's learning. In 1712 she married, against her father's wishes, a Whig Member of Parliament named Edward Wortley Montagu, after conducting with him a wary, carefully reasoned courtship mostly by means of letters. When he was appointed Ambassador to Turkey four years later, she accompanied him, and was fascinated by what she saw: by the Turkish practice of inoculating against smallpox, which (having survived the disease herself) she successfully championed in England at her return; by the gaps and continuities between British and Turkish culture, on which she reported eloquently in missives home. Her *Turkish Embassy Letters*, which she compiled from her writings during this sojourn for publication after her death, remain the foundation of her fame.

Her life as a writer yielded other riches, just now beginning to be explored. She wrote essays, including a *Spectator* for Addison and Steele and a later periodical series of her own (1737–1738). She produced short fiction and a comedy but worked more steadily at verse, collaborating with Alexander Pope on some poems and combating him in others, after their friendship had disintegrated into a round of bitter, witty recriminations. Most plentifully she wrote letters, sharp and searching, adroitly tailored to please her wide array of correspondents.

Montagu's spate of accomplishment made her alert to the constrictions of gender. "There is hardly a character in the world," she wrote at age twenty, "more liable to universal ridicule than that of a Learned Woman." Women, she counseled, should know much but hide their

---

4. Science ("Philosophy") now resorts to mechanical rather than religious explanations for the way things are.
5. Natural science seeks support from theoretical speculations, which in turn have come to rely on empirical investigation.
6. Divine revelation is under threat from "certain defenders of religion [who have] attempted to show that the mysteries of religion may be mathematically demonstrated"

[Pope's note].
7. I.e., all the modes of thought and endeavor personified in the preceding six lines.
8. Reversing the sequence of the world's creation (Genesis 1.1–10), and restoring the chaos that preceded it.
9. A ruler with no legitimate political authority; one who promotes disorder and confusion.

knowledge, lest they lose out on the comforts of love, marriage, and social ease. Deeply attentive to the burdens imposed on women and the tactics available to them, Montagu's idiosyncratic feminism earned esteem from her predecessor Astell, and from many who came after.

Idiosyncrasy exacted costs, in the form of that "ridicule" she had early anticipated, and in the breakdown of important relationships. Her marriage failed, as did a passionate love affair (again largely epistolary) with the bisexual Italian writer Francesco Algarotti. Montagu lived her last twenty-five years mostly in Italy. In retrospect, her self-removal looks like part of a lifelong strategy. Montagu had always held it crucial to keep some distance from her culture's assumptions in order to see them clearly, to critique them, to change or expunge their operations in herself and in the world. The title she chose for her periodical series, *The Nonsense of Common Sense,* encapsulates her lifelong conviction. By the eccentricity of her self-education, the remoteness of her travels and her residences, the originality of her thought and conduct, the amused acerbity of her style, Montagu kept her distance and found her voice.

from The Turkish Embassy Letters[1]
To Lady ———[2]
[ON THE TURKISH BATHS]

Adrianople, 1 April 1717

I am now got into a new world where everything I see appears to me a change of scene, and I write to your Ladyship with some content of mind, hoping at least that you will find the charm of novelty in my letters and no longer reproach me that I tell you nothing extraordinary. I won't trouble you with a relation of our tedious journey, but I must not omit what I saw remarkable at Sophia, one of the most beautiful towns in the Turkish Empire and famous for its hot baths that are resorted to both for diversion and health. I stopped here one day on purpose to see them. Designing to go incognito, I hired a Turkish coach. These *voitures* are not at all like ours, but much more convenient for the country, the heat being so great that glasses[3] would be very troublesome. They are made a good deal in the manner of the Dutch coaches, having wooden lattices painted and gilded, the inside being painted with baskets and nosegays of flowers, intermixed commonly with little poetical mottoes. They are covered all over with scarlet cloth, lined with silk and very often richly embroidered and fringed. This covering entirely hides the persons in them, but may be thrown back at pleasure and the ladies peep through the lattices. They hold four people very conveniently, seated on cushions, but not raised.

In one of these covered wagons I went to the bagnio[4] about ten o'clock. It was already full of women. It is built of stone in the shape of a dome with no windows but in the roof, which gives light enough. There was five of these domes joined together, the outmost being less than the rest and serving only as a hall where the porteress stood at the door. Ladies of quality generally give this woman the value of

1. The text of the *Turkish Embassy Letters* comes not from the actual letters Montagu sent while on her travels but from two manuscript books in which she combined portions of her letters and travel journals with new prose to produce a hybrid account of the trip, which she intended for posthumous publication. In 1724 Montagu lent the volumes to Mary Astell, who inscribed into the second a preface addressed to future readers: ". . . I confess I am malicious enough to desire that the world should see to how much better purpose the *ladies* travel than their *lords,* and that whilst it is surfeited with male travels [i.e.,

travel-books], all in the same tone and stuffed with the same trifles, a *lady* has the skill to strike out a new path and to embellish a worn out subject with variety of fresh and elegant entertainment . . . Let us freely own the superiority of this sublime genius as I do in sincerity of my soul, pleased that a *woman* triumphs, and proud to follow in her train."
2. In the manuscript, Montagu supplies no name for this person, who may be a fictive "recipient."
3. Glass windows (which the Turkish coaches lacked).
4. The bath.

a crown or ten shillings, and I did not forget that ceremony. The next room is a very large one, paved with marble, and all round it raised two sofas of marble, one above another. There were four fountains of cold water in this room, falling first into marble basins and then running on the floor in little channels made for that purpose, which carried the streams into the next room, something less than this, with the same sort of marble sofas, but so hot with steams of sulphur proceeding from the baths joining to it, 'twas impossible to stay there with one's clothes on. The two other domes were the hot baths, one of which had cocks of cold water turning into it to temper it to what degree of warmth the bathers have a mind to.

I was in my traveling habit, which is a riding dress, and certainly appeared very extraordinary to them, yet there was not one of 'em that showed the least surprise or impertinent curiosity, but received me with all the obliging civility possible. I know of no European court where the ladies would have behaved themselves in so polite a manner to a stranger.

I believe in the whole there were two hundred women, and yet none of those disdainful smiles or satiric whispers that never fail in our asemblies when anybody appears that is not dressed exactly in fashion. They repeated over and over to me, *uzelle, pek uzelle*, which is nothing but "charming, very charming." The first sofas were covered with cushioned and rich carpets, on which sat the ladies, and on the second their slaves behind 'em, but without any distinction of rank by their dress, all being in the state of nature, that is, in plain English, stark naked, without any beauty or defect concealed, yet there was not the least wanton smile or immodest gesture amongst 'em. They walked and moved with the same majestic grace which Milton describes of our "general mother."[5] There were many amongst them as exactly proportioned as ever any goddess was drawn by the pencil of Guido or Titian,[6] and most of their skins shiningly white, only adorned by their beautiful hair divided into many tresses hanging on their shoulders, braided either with pearl or riband,[7] perfectly representing the figures of the Graces.[8] I was here convinced of the truth of a reflection that I had often made, that if 'twas the fashion to go naked, the face would be hardly observed. I perceived that the ladies with the finest skins and most delicate shapes had the greatest share of my admiration, though their faces were sometimes less beautiful than those of their companions. To tell you the truth, I had wickedness enough to wish secretly that Mr. Gervase could have been there invisible.[9] I fancy it would have very much improved his art to see so many fine women naked in different postures, some in conversation, some working, others drinking coffee or sherbet, and many negligently lying on their cushions while their slaves (generally pretty girls of seventeen or eighteen) were employed in braiding their hair in several pretty manners. In short, 'tis the women's coffee-house, where all the news of the town is told, scandal invented, etc. They generally take this diversion once a week, and stay there at least four or five hours without getting cold by immediate coming out of the hot bath into the cool room, which was very surprising to me. The lady that seemed the most considerable among them entreated me to sit by

---

5. Eve (*Paradise Lost* 4.304–18).
6. Artists of the Italian Renaissance.
7. Ribbon.
8. Resembling the three sister divinities who (in Greek mythology) embody and endow grace and beauty.
9. Charles Jervas (c. 1675–1739), a successful portraitist who had once painted Montagu as a shepherdess. The French

painter Jean Auguste Dominique Ingres (1780–1867) later took up the hint implicit in Montagu's "fancy" here. Having transcribed portions of this letter from a French edition (1805), he made use of Montagu's descriptions in his painting *Le Bain Turc* (The Turkish Bath, 1862).

her and would fain have undressed me for the bath. I excused myself with some difficulty, they being all so earnest in persuading me. I was at last forced to open my skirt and show them my stays,[1] which satisfied them very well, for I saw they believed I was so locked up in that machine that it was not in my own power to open it, which contrivance they attributed to my husband. I was charmed with their civility and beauty, and should have been very glad to pass more time with them, but Mr. W[2] resolving to pursue his journey the next morning early, I was in haste to see the ruins of Justinian's church,[3] which did not afford me so agreeable a prospect as I had left, being little more than a heap of stones.

Adieu, Madam. I am sure I have now entertained you with an account of such a sight as you never saw in your life and that no book of travels could inform you of. 'Tis no less than death for a man to be found in one of those places.

To Lady Mar[1]
[ON TURKISH DRESS]

Adrianople, 1 April 1717

I wish to God (dear Sister) that you was as regular in letting me have the pleasure of knowing what passes on your side of the globe as I am careful in endeavoring to amuse you by the account of all I see that I think you care to hear of. You content yourself with telling me over and over that the town is very dull. It may possibly be dull to you when every day does not present you with something new, but for me that am in arrear at least two months' news, all that seems very stale with you would be fresh and sweet here; pray let me into more particulars. I will try to awaken your gratitude by giving you a full and true relation of the novelties of this place, none of which would surprise you more than a sight of my person as I am now in my Turkish habit, though I believe you would be of my opinion that 'tis admirably becoming. I intend to send you my picture; in the meantime accept of it here.

The first piece of my dress is a pair of drawers, very full, that reach to my shoes and conceal the legs more modestly than your petticoats. They are of a thin rose-color damask brocaded with silver flowers, my shoes of white kid leather embroidered with gold. Over this hangs my smock of a fine white silk gauze edged with embroidery. This smock has wide sleeves hanging half way down the arm and is closed at the neck with a diamond button, but the shape and color of the bosom very well to be distinguished through it. The *antery* is a waistcoat[2] made close to the shape, of white and gold damask, with very long sleeves falling back and fringed with deep gold fringe, and should have diamond or pearl buttons. My caftan, of the same stuff with my drawers, is a robe exactly fitted to my shape and reaching to my feet, with very long straight falling sleeves. Over this is the girdle of about four fingers broad, which all that can afford have entirely of diamonds or other precious stones. Those that will not be at that expense have it of exquisite embroidery on satin, but it must be fastened before with a clasp of diamonds. The *curdée* is a loose robe they throw off or put on according to the weather, being of a rich brocade (mine is green and gold) either lined with ermine or sables; the sleeves reach very

---

1. A tightly laced undergarment, stiffened with whale-bone, extending from breast to thigh.
2. Her husband, Edward Wortley Montagu.
3. The Church of St. Sofia, built during the reign of the

Byzantine Emperor Justinian (483–565).
1. Montagu's sister Frances (1690–1761), who had married the Earl of Mar.
2. A vest.

little below the shoulders. The headdress is composed of a cap called *talpock*, which is in winter of fine velvet embroidered with pearls or diamonds and in summer of a light shining silver stuff. This is fixed on one side of the head, hanging a little way down with a gold tassel and bound on either with a circle of diamonds (as I have seen several) or a rich embroidered handkerchief. On the other side of the head the hair is laid flat, and here the ladies are at liberty to show their fancies, some putting flowers, others a plume of heron's feathers, and, in short, what they please, but the most general fashion is a large bouquet of jewels made like natural flowers, that is, the buds of pearl, the roses of different colored rubies, the jasmines of diamonds, jonquils of topazes, etc., so well set and enameled 'tis hard to imagine anything of that kind so beautiful. The hair hangs at its full length behind, divided into tresses braided with pearl or riband, which is always in great quantity.

I never saw in my life so many fine heads of hair. I have counted 110 of these tresses of one lady's, all natural; but it must be owned that every beauty is more common here than with us. 'Tis surprising to see a young woman that is not very handsome. They have naturally the most beautiful complexions in the world and generally large black eyes. I can assure you with great truth that the Court of England (though I believe it the fairest in Christendom) cannot show so many beauties as are under our protection here. They generally shape their eyebrows, and the Greeks and Turks have a custom of putting round their eyes on the inside a black tincture that, at a distance or by candlelight, adds very much to the blackness of them. I fancy many of our ladies would be overjoyed to know this secret, but 'tis too visible by day. They dye their nails rose color; I own I cannot enough accustom myself to this fashion to find any beauty in it.

As to their morality or good conduct, I can say like Arlequin, 'tis just as 'tis with you,[3] and the Turkish ladies don't commit one sin the less for not being Christians. Now I am a little acquainted with their ways, I cannot forbear admiring either the exemplary discretion or extreme stupidity of all the writers that have given accounts of 'em.[4] 'Tis very easy to see they have more liberty than we have, no woman of what rank soever being permitted to go in the streets without two muslins, one that covers her face all but her eyes and another that hides the whole dress of her head and hangs half way down her back; and their shapes are wholly concealed by a thing they call a *ferigée*, which no woman of any sort appears without. This has straight sleeves that reaches to their fingers' ends and it laps all round 'em, not unlike a riding hood. In winter 'tis of cloth, and in summer, plain stuff or silk. You may guess how effectually this disguises them, that there is no distinguishing the great lady from her slave, and 'tis impossible for the most jealous husband to know his wife when he meets her, and no man dare either touch or follow a woman in the street.

This perpetual masquerade gives them entire liberty of following their inclinations without danger of discovery. The most usual method of intrigue is to send an appointment to the lover to meet the lady at a Jew's shop,[5] which are as notoriously convenient as our Indian houses,[6] and yet even those that don't make that use of

---

3. A paraphrase (and misattribution) of a line from Aphra Behn's comedy *The Emperor of the Moon* (1687): the prankster Harlequin, pretending to be an ambassador from the moon, describes the corrupt social customs of his world to a gullible listener, who repeatedly exclaims that morality there is "just as 'tis here" (3.2).

4. Many (though not all) writers on Turkey had emphasized the strict confinement and chastity of the women there.
5. Jewish women sometimes helped arrange these assignations; being permitted to enter the harems, they could transmit secret messages.
6. London shops selling goods imported from India.

'em do not scruple to go to buy pennorths and tumble over[7] rich goods, which are chiefly to be found amongst that sort of people.[8] The great ladies seldom let their gallants[9] know who they are, and 'tis so difficult to find it out that they can very seldom guess at her name they have corresponded with above half a year together. You may easily imagine the number of faithful wives very small in a country where they have nothing to fear from their lovers' indiscretion, since we see so many that have the courage to expose themselves to that in this world and all the threatened punishment of the next, which is never preached to the Turkish damsels. Neither have they much to apprehend from the resentment of their husbands, those ladies that are rich having all their money in their own hands, which they take with 'em upon a divorce with an addition which he is obliged to give 'em. Upon the whole, I look upon the Turkish women as the only free people in the Empire. The very *Divan*[1] pays a respect to 'em, and the *Grand Signor* himself, when a *Bassa*[2] is executed, never violates the privileges of the harem (or women's apartment), which remains unsearched entire to the widow. They are queens of their slaves, which the husband has no permission so much as to look upon, except it be an old woman or two that his lady chooses. 'Tis true their law permits them four wives, but there is no instance of a man of quality that makes use of this liberty, or of a woman of rank that would suffer it. When a husband happens to be inconstant (as those things will happen) he keeps his mistress in a house apart and visits her as privately as he can, just as 'tis with you. Amongst all the great men here I only know the *Tefterdar* (i.e. treasurer) that keeps a number of she slaves for his own use (that is, on his own side of the house, for a slave once given to serve a lady is entirely at her disposal) and he is spoke of as a libertine, or what we should call a rake, and his wife won't see him, though she continues to live in his house.

Thus you see, dear Sister, the manners of mankind do not differ so widely as our voyage writers would make us believe. Perhaps it would be more entertaining to add a few surprising customs of my own invention, but nothing seems to me so agreeable as truth, and I believe nothing so acceptable to you. I conclude with repeating the great truth of my being, dear Sister, etc.

Letter to Lady Bute[1]
[ON HER GRANDDAUGHTER]

28 January 1753

Dear Child,

You have given me a great deal of satisfaction by your account of your eldest daughter. I am particularly pleased to hear she is a good arithmetician; it is the best proof of understanding. The knowledge of numbers is one of the chief distinctions between us and brutes. If there is anything in blood, you may reasonably expect your children should be endowed with an uncommon share of good sense. Mr. Wortley's[2] family and mine have both produced some of the greatest men that have been born

---

7. Penny-worths: good bargains; tumble over: browse through.
8. Jews.
9. Lovers.
1. A governmental official.
2. *Bassa:* a high official.

1. Montagu's only daughter, Mary (1718–1794), had in 1736 married John Stuart, third Earl of Bute. At the time this letter was written, Montagu had been long separated from her husband and was living in Italy.
2. Her estranged husband, Edward Wortley Montagu.

in England. I mean Admiral Sandwich,[3] and my great grandfather who was distinguished by the name of Wise William.[4] I have heard Lord Bute's father mentioned as an extraordinary genius (though he had not many opportunities of showing it), and his uncle the present Duke of Argyll has one of the best heads I ever knew.

I will therefore speak to you as supposing Lady Mary not only capable but desirous of learning. In that case, by all means let her be indulged in it. You will tell me, I did not make it a part of your education. Your prospect was very different from hers, as you had no defect either in mind or person to hinder, and much in your circumstances to attract, the highest offers. It seemed your business to learn how to live in the world, as it is hers to know how to be easy out of it. It is the common error of builders and parents to follow some plan they think beautiful (and perhaps is so) without considering that nothing is beautiful that is misplaced. Hence we see so many edifices raised that the raisers can never inhabit, being too large for their fortunes. Vistas are laid open over barren heaths, and apartments contrived for a coolness very agreeable in Italy but killing in the north of Britain. Thus every woman endeavors to breed her daughter a fine lady, qualifying her for a station in which she will never appear, and at the same time incapacitating her for that retirement to which she is destined. Learning (if she has a real taste for it) will not only make her contented but happy in it. No entertainment is so cheap as reading, nor any pleasure so lasting. She will not want new fashions nor regret the loss of expensive diversions or variety of company if she can be amused with an author in her closet. To render this amusement extensive, she should be permitted to learn the languages. I have heard it lamented that boys lose so many years in mere learning of words. This is no objection to a girl, whose time is not so precious. She cannot advance herself in any profession, and has therefore more hours to spare; and as you say her memory is good, she will be very agreeably employed this way.

There are two cautions to be given on this subject: first, not to think herself learned when she can read Latin or even Greek. Languages are more properly to be called vehicles of learning than learning itself, as may be observed in many schoolmasters, who though perhaps critics in grammar are the most ignorant fellows upon earth. True knowledge consists in knowing things, not words. I would wish her no farther a linguist than to enable her to read books in their originals, that are often corrupted and always injured by translations. Two hours' application every morning will bring this about much sooner than you can imagine, and she will have leisure enough beside to run over the English poetry, which is a more important part of a woman's education than it is generally supposed. Many a young damsel has been ruined by a fine copy of verses, which she would have laughed at if she had known it had been stolen from Mr. Waller.[5] I remember when I was a girl I saved one of my companions from destruction, who communicated to me an epistle she was quite charmed with. As she had a natural good taste, she observed the lines were not so smooth as Prior's[6] or Pope's, but had more thought and spirit than any of theirs. She was wonderfully delighted with such a demonstration of her lover's sense and passion, and not a little pleased with her own charms, that had force enough to inspire such elegancies. In the midst of this triumph, I showed her they were taken from

---

3. Edward Montagu (1625–1672), first Earl of Sandwich (and Samuel Pepys's patron), was Wortley's grandfather.
4. The Hon. William Pierrepont (1608–1678) was a prominent politician.

5. Edmund Waller (1606–1687), love poet frequently quoted (or plagiarized) by amorous wooers.
6. Matthew Prior (1664–1721), like Alexander Pope a celebrated poet.

Randolph's poems,[7] and the unfortunate transcriber was dismissed with the scorn he deserved. To say truth, the poor plagiary was very unlucky to fall into my hands; that author, being no longer in fashion, would have escaped anyone of less universal reading than myself. You should encourage your daughter to talk over with you what she reads, and as you are very capable of distinguishing, take care she does not mistake pert folly for wit and humor, or rhyme for poetry, which are the common errors of young people, and have a train of ill consequences.

The second caution to be given her (and which is most absolutely necessary) is to conceal whatever learning she attains, with as much solicitude as she would hide crookedness or lameness. The parade of it can only serve to draw on her the envy, and consequently the most inveterate hatred, of all he and she fools, which will certainly be at least three parts in four of all her acquaintance. The use of knowledge in our sex (beside the amusement of solitude) is to moderate the passions and learn to be contented with a small expense, which are the certain effects of a studious life and, it may be, preferable even to that fame which men have engrossed to themselves and will not suffer us to share. You will tell me I have not observed this rule myself, but you are mistaken; it is only inevitable accident that has given me any reputation that way. I have always carefully avoided it, and ever thought it a misfortune.

The explanation of this paragraph would occasion a long digression, which I will not trouble you with, it being my present design only to say what I think useful for the instruction of my granddaughter, which I have much at heart. If she has the same inclination (I should say passion) for learning that I was born with, history, geography, and philosophy will furnish her with materials to pass away cheerfully a longer life than is allotted to mortals. I believe there are few heads capable of making Sir I. Newton's[8] calculations, but the result of them is not difficult to be understood by a moderate capacity. Do not fear this should make her affect the character of Lady ——, or Lady ——, or Mrs.——.[9] Those women are ridiculous, not because they have learning but because they have it not. One thinks herself a complete historian after reading Eachard's *Roman History*,[1] another a profound philosopher having got by heart some of Pope's unintelligible essays,[2] and a third an able divine on the strength of Whitfield's sermons.[3] Thus you hear them screaming politics and controversy. It is a saying of Thucydides, ignorance is bold, and knowledge reserved.[4] Indeed it is impossible to be far advanced in it without being more humbled by a conviction of human ignorance than elated by learning.

At the same time I recommend books, I neither exclude work nor drawing. I think it as scandalous for a woman not to know how to use a needle, as for a man not to know how to use a sword. I was once extreme fond of my pencil, and it was a great mortification to me when my father turned off[5] my master, having made a considerable progress for the short time I learnt. My over eagerness in the pursuit of it had brought a weakness on my eyes that made it necessary to leave it off, and all the advantage I got was the improvement of my hand. I see by hers that practice will make her a ready writer. She may attain it by serving you for a secretary when your

7. The minor writer Thomas Randolph (1605–1635), whose collected *Poems* were published in 1638.
8. Isaac Newton, mathematician and scientist, author of *Principia Mathematica* (1687).
9. The names, which Montagu omitted in her manuscript, have not been recovered.
1. Lawrence Echard, *The Roman History* (1695–1698).
2. Probably his *Essay on Man* (1733–1734) in four epistles,

published long after the friendship between him and Montagu had ended.
3. George Whitfield (1714–1770), Methodist preacher.
4. Thucydides (c. 460–c. 399 B.C.E.), Greek historian of the Peloponnesian War; Montagu paraphrases his assertion that "boldness means ignorance and reflection brings hesitation" (*History* 2.40.3).
5. Dismissed.

health or affairs make it troublesome to you to write yourself, and custom will make it an agreeable amusement to her. She cannot have too many for that station of life which will probably be her fate. The ultimate end of your education was to make you a good wife (and I have the comfort to hear that you are one); hers ought to be, to make her happy in a virgin state. I will not say it is happier, but it is undoubtedly safer than any marriage. In a lottery where there is (at the lowest computation) ten thousand blanks to a prize, it is the most prudent choice not to venture.

I have always been so thoroughly persuaded of this truth that, notwithstanding the flattering views I had for you (as I never intended you a sacrifice to my vanity), I thought I owed you the justice to lay before you all the hazards attending matrimony. You may recollect I did so in the strongest manner. Perhaps you may have more success in the instructing your daughter. She has so much company at home she will not need seeking it abroad, and will more readily take the notions you think fit to give her. As you were alone in my family, it would have been thought a great cruelty to suffer you no companions of your own age, especially having so many near relations, and I do not wonder their opinions influenced yours. I was not sorry to see you not determined on a single life, knowing it was not your father's intention, and contented myself with endeavoring to make your home so easy that you might not be in haste to leave it.

I am afraid you will think this a very long and insignificant letter. I hope the kindness of the design will excuse it, being willing to give you every proof in my power that I am your most affectionate Mother,

M. Wortley.

Epistle from Mrs. Yonge to Her Husband[1]

Think not this paper comes with vain pretense
To move your pity, or to mourn th' offense.
Too well I know that hard obdurate heart;
No soft'ning mercy there will take my part,
5   Nor can a woman's arguments prevail,
When even your patron's wise example fails,[2]
But this last privilege I still retain,
Th' oppressed and injured always may complain.
    Too, too severely laws of honor bind
10   The weak submissive sex of womankind.
If sighs have gained or force compelled our hand,
Deceived by art, or urged by stern command,
Whatever motive binds the fatal tie,
The judging world expects our constancy.
15   Just Heaven! (for sure in heaven does justice reign
Though tricks below that sacred name profane)

1. In 1724 the heiress Mary Yonge became embroiled in a highly publicized divorce from her notorious, womanizing husband William, who accused her (accurately) of adultery committed during the couple's separation. Public sympathy was on her side, but the king approved a divorce that allowed her husband to retain most of her fortune. Montagu's poem remained in manuscript throughout her life.

2. I.e., Robert Walpole's. William Yonge was a devoted adherent of the powerful minister, who carried on open adulteries himself but also (unlike Yonge) permitted them to his wife.

To you appealing I submit my cause
Nor fear a judgment from impartial laws.
All bargains but conditional are made;
20   The purchase void, the creditor unpaid,
Defrauded servants are from service free;
A wounded slave regains his liberty.
For wives ill used no remedy remains,
To daily racks condemned, and to eternal chains.
25   From whence is this unjust distinction grown?
Are we not formed with passions like your own?
Nature with equal fire our souls endued,
Our minds as haughty, and as warm our blood;
O're the wide world your pleasures you pursue, ⎤
30   The change is justified by something new;   ⎬
But we must sigh in silence—and be true.   ⎦
Our sex's weakness you expose and blame
(Of every prattling fop the common theme),
Yet from this weakness you suppose is due
35   Sublimer virtue than your Cato[3] knew.
Had Heaven designed us trials so severe,
It would have formed our tempers then to bear.
        And I have borne (O what have I not borne!)
The pang of jealousy, th' insults of scorn.
40   Wearied at length, I from your sight remove,
And place my future hopes in secret love.
In the gay bloom of glowing youth retired,
I quit the woman's joy to be admired,
With that small pension your hard heart allows,
45   Renounce your fortune, and release your vows.
To custom (though unjust) so much is due;
I hide my frailty from the public view.
My conscience clear, yet sensible of shame,
My life I hazard, to preserve my fame.
50   And I prefer this low inglorious state,   ⎤
To vile dependence on the thing I hate—   ⎬
But you pursue me to this last retreat.   ⎦
Dragged into light, my tender crime is shown
And every circumstance of fondness known.
55   Beneath the shelter of the law you stand,
And urge my ruin with a cruel hand.
While to my fault thus rigidly severe,
Tamely submissive to the man you fear.
        This wretched outcast, this abandoned wife,
60   Has yet this joy to sweeten shameful life,
By your mean conduct, infamously loose,

---

3. Marcus Porcius Cato of Utica (95–46 B.C.E.), champion of the Roman Republic, whose name had become a byword for
integrity.

You are at once my accuser, and excuse.
Let me be damned by the censorious prude
(Stupidly dull, or spiritually lewd),
65 My hapless case will surely pity find
From every just and reasonable mind,
When to the final sentence I submit;
The lips condemn me, but their souls acquit.
No more my husband, to your pleasures go,
70 The sweets of your recovered freedom know;
Go; court the brittle friendship of the great,
Smile at his board, or at his levée⁴ wait
And when dismissed, to Madam's toilet° fly,   *dressing room*
More than her chambermaids, or glasses,° lie,   *mirrors*
75 Tell her how young she looks, how heavenly fair,
Admire the lilies and the roses there;
Your high ambition may be gratified,
Some cousin of her own be made your bride,
And you the father of a glorious race
80 Endowed with Ch——l's strength and Low—r's face.⁵

1724   1972

The Lover: A Ballad

1

At length, by so much importunity pressed,
Take (Molly¹) at once the inside of my breast;
This stupid indifference so often you blame
Is not owing to nature, to fear, or to shame;
5 I am not as cold as a virgin in lead,
Nor is Sunday's sermon so strong in my head;
I know but too well how time flies along,
That we live but few years and yet fewer are young.

2

But I hate to be cheated, and never will buy
10 Long years of repentance for moments of joy.
Oh was there a man (but where shall I find
Good sense, and good nature so equally joined?)
Would value his pleasure, contribute to mine,
Not meanly would boast, nor lewdly design,
15 Not over severe, yet not stupidly vain,
For I would have the power though not give the pain.

---

4. Social assemblies at the homes of the "great," often crowded with petitioners, opportunists, and sycophants.
5. The line implies that the adulterous William Yonge will himself be supplanted in his next wife's bed by fellow-libertines: Charles Churchill (c. 1679–1745) and Antony Lowther (d. 1741).
1. Probably Maria ("Molly") Skerrett (1702–1738), Montagu's friend and Robert Walpole's mistress.

3

No pedant yet learned, not rakehelly gay
Or laughing because he has nothing to say,
To all my whole sex obliging and free,
20   Yet never be fond of any but me.
In public preserve the decorums are just
And show in his eyes he is true to his trust,
Then rarely approach, and respectfully bow,
Yet not fulsomely pert, nor yet foppishly low.

4

25   But when the long hours of public are past
And we meet with champagne and a chicken at last,
May every fond pleasure that hour endear,
Be banished afar both discretion and fear,
Forgetting or scorning the airs of the crowd
30   He may cease to be formal, and I to be proud,
Till lost in the joy, we confess that we live
And he may be rude, and yet I may forgive.

5

And that my delight may be solidly fixed
Let the friend and the lover be handsomely mixed,
35   In whose tender bosom my soul might confide,
Whose kindness can soothe me, whose counsel could guide;
From such a dear lover as here I describe
No danger should fright me, no millions should bribe,
But till this astonishing creature I know
40   As I long have lived chaste I will keep myself so.

6

I never will share with the wanton coquette,
Or be caught by a vain affectation of wit.
The toasters and songsters may try all their art
But never shall enter the pass of my heart;
45   I loathe the lewd rake, the dressed fopling despise,
Before such pursuers the nice virgin flies;
And as Ovid has sweetly in parables told
We harden like trees, and like rivers are cold.[2]

c. 1721–1725   1747

---

2. In his *Metamorphoses*, Ovid tells stories of virgins who are transformed into a laurel tree (Daphne) or a fountain (Arethusa), rather than succumb to the importunities of a pursuing god (1.452–567; 5.572–641).

John Gay
1685–1732

John Gay was born to hardworking, pious tradespeople in Barnstaple, a busy port town in southwestern England. Educated well but orphaned early, he moved at age eighteen to London, where he tried trade for a time, gave it up for literature, and made himself a master of the mock, at a moment when the mock mattered most.

In the early eighteenth century, the "mock" was not just a gesture of derision but an intricate art form, in which scenes of contemporary life, appropriated from streets, stables, salons, and other ordinary sites, were represented in grand styles first crafted for the actions of ancient heroes. In his mock-pastoral *Description of a City Shower* (1709), for example, Swift depicted the muddy chaos of an urban rainstorm in the language Virgil had devised to render the rural delights of a Golden Age; in his mock-epic *Rape of the Lock* (1712), Pope portrayed the trivial agitations of London beaux and belles in formulations absorbed from Homer. Befriended by Pope and Swift, Gay became perhaps the most supple and assiduous practitioner in their mock-heroic vein. In his early successes, he showed himself adept at devising new combinations of mode and topic, new ways of savoring both high styles and low subjects even while making fun of them. In *The Shepherd's Week* (1714), he took on both Virgil's idealism and also the ungainly "realism" attempted by some of that Roman poet's eighteenth-century imitators. He endowed his shepherds with preposterously "rustic" names (Bumkinet, Hobnelia, Bowzybeus) and a ludicrously hybrid language, alternately high-flying and homespun. But he gave them also a grace and good nature that survive the mock. The poem's closing image of a drunken swain sleeping out the sunset ("ruddy, like his face, the sun descends") reads like the poet's own benediction. In his next big work, *Trivia, or the Art of Walking the Streets of London* (1716), Gay's grandiloquent Virgilian instruction makes city walking seem not just a "trivial" chore but an "art," comic, challenging, alternately appalling and attractive.

Gay built his life as he made his art, by improvising. He earned money by his plays and poems; he lost money in that evanescent investment scheme the South Sea Bubble; he served as Commissioner of Lotteries, and as secretary, steward, and companion to several members of the nobility; and he sought for years to secure steady patronage at court, by means of flattering verse and ingratiating conduct. His frustration peaked when he published a virtuosic set of *Fables* (1727) for the four-year-old Prince William and received as reward a royal appointment as attendant to the prince's two-year-old sister. The aristocrats he courted valued him for his compliant temper and beguiling company, but they patronized him in both senses of the word.

Gay refused the royal appointment, staking his hopes instead on his new project for the stage, *The Beggar's Opera* (1728). The initial notion for the piece had come from Swift, who suggested a "Newgate pastoral"—that is, a mixture in which the "whores and thieves" who inhabited Newgate prison and its neighborhood would supplant the nymphs and shepherds frolicking on Arcadian hillsides. Swift's hint is an ordinary mock recipe: two worlds collide, one real, one fictitious. Gay built from it an intricate hall of mirrors, where many more worlds met. For his thieves he drew on two real-life models, recently executed: Jonathan Wild and Jack Sheppard. Wild had run a large criminal organization that profited him two ways: he collected money from the resale of goods stolen by his subordinates; and he collected rewards from the government for turning in his associates and rivals whenever they became too troublesome. Sheppard had acquired fame as Wild's most high-spirited and elusive prey; a brilliant thief in his own right, he had often managed to escape the prisons and predicaments into which Wild had betrayed him. In *The Beggar's Opera*, Gay resurrects the two late criminals as Mr. Peachum, who like Wild manages a lucrative double life, and Captain Macheath, who like Sheppard proves susceptible of capture and gifted at escape. Here the worlds begin to multiply. Developing a comparison then current in the political press, Gay made his criminals conjure up the most powerful politician alive: Robert Walpole, the Whig prime minister who ran his political machine (so the *Opera* insists) with the efficiency of Peachum and the self-indulgence of Macheath.

The Beggar's Opera mixed low with high in form as well as content. Like "Newgate pastoral," the phrase "beggar's opera" fuses opposites. Italian opera was the most expensive, exotic, and fashionable entertainment in London. Gay's theatrical game was to replay opera's intricacies using beggars' means. He supplanted the elaborate arias of foreign composers with the simpler tunes of British street songs; he replaced the original words to those tunes with new lyrics that voiced his characters' strong emotions; he even re-enacted a recent, much-publicized rivalry between two high-paid prima donnas, at war for the allegiance of their audience, in the contest he stages between Peachum's daughter Polly and the jailer's daughter Lucy Lockit for the devotion of fickle Captain Macheath. On Gay's stage, worlds converge with a density even Swift could not have foreseen. Opera house and street corner; Whitehall and Newgate; art and commerce; politics, business, and crime: all of these turn out to operate on the same principles of self-interest.

Reading the new piece before its premiere, Gay's well-wishers hedged their bets as to its success. "It would either take greatly," the playwright William Congreve predicted, "or be damned confoundedly." In the event, it did both. The triumph of the opening night is the stuff of theatrical legend, but it provoked a counter-chorus of condemnation from critics who saw the play as endangering opera, glorifying thieves, traducing government. Amid the debate, the play enjoyed a long run, entrancing an audience made up of the very people it mocked (including Walpole himself, who reportedly conducted an extra chorus of the play's most satiric song, "When you censure the age"). *The Beggar's Opera* offered theatergoers simple pleasures (deft performances, comic reversals, well-loved tunes) and intricate ones too: the often ironic play of Gay's new lyrics against the original words that the auditors had already in their heads; the debunking of love and marriage in sharp dialogue and the glorifying of it in sentimental song; the volatile charisma of the mock-hero Macheath, who for many observers came to seem utterly heroic by evening's end; the arresting alchemy by which Gay transmuted (as the Romantic essayist William Hazlitt later expressed it) "this motley group" of "highwaymen, turnkeys, their mistresses, wives, or daughters . . . into a set of fine gentlemen and ladies, satirists and philosophers." In his painting of the opening night (Color Plate 26), William Hogarth suggests how these transformations came to include the spectators as well. Occupying the sides of the stage, an audience of aristocrats, politicians, and theater people (Gay himself among them) observe the play in progress; they are encompassed by the same prison walls wherein Macheath and his pursuers play out their intricate transactions, in which everything and everyone—goods, votes, spouses—had become commodities, items of exchange, reckoned in account books as profit and as loss.

The Beggar's Opera brought Gay prosperity and celebrity but not security. Walpole evicted him from his subsidized lodgings and banned production of the *Opera*'s much-anticipated sequel *Polly*. When Gay died less than five years after his fabled first night, however, he was buried with elaborate ceremony in the Poet's Corner of Westminster Abbey. Friends commended the appropriateness of the site but marveled at the incongruity of the pomp. Incongruity, though, had been Gay's stock in trade, and nowhere more so than in his greatest hit. Its long run continues in theaters around the world. It spawned numberless short-lived imitations in its own time and a more durable descendant in the twentieth century: *Die Dreigroschenoper* (*The Threepenny Opera*, 1928), in which Bertolt Brecht and Kurt Weill adapted Gay's characters, plot, and critique of commerce to produce their own dark and gleeful Marxist assault on contemporary capitalism. By routes less direct, Gay's work has infused both the modern musical theater (which continues to combine operatic and popular modes) and pop culture in general—where, for example, Brecht and Weill's sardonic *Ballad of Mack the Knife* became a pop hit of the early 1960s. *The Beggar's Opera* grabbed attention first—and sustains it still—for the ironic dexterity with which it mixed things up, in full mock mode.

Beggar's Opera

Nos hæc novimus esse nihil.[1]

Dramatis Personæ[2]

Men

PEACHUM
LOCKIT
MACHEATH
FILCH
JEMMY TWITCHER
CROOK-FINGERED JACK
WAT DREARY
ROBIN OF BAGSHOT   *Macheath's Gang*
NIMMING NED
HARRY PADDINGTON
MATT OF THE MINT
BEN BUDGE
BEGGAR
PLAYER
DRAWER, HARPER, JAILER, OTHER MEMBERS OF THE GANG, CONSTABLES, TURNKEYS, PRISONERS, RABBLE

Women

MRS. PEACHUM
POLLY PEACHUM
LUCY LOCKIT
DIANA TRAPES
MRS. COAXER
DOLLY TRULL
MRS. VIXEN
BETTY DOXY
JENNY DIVER   *Women of the Town*
MRS. SLAMMEKIN
SUKY TAWDRY
MOLLY BRAZEN
FOUR WOMEN WITH CHILDREN

---

1. We know these things to be nothing (Martial, *Epigrams* 13.2.8).
2. Many of these names reflect the characters' low-life habits: to "peach" is to inform on, to "filch" is to steal, "twitchers" are pickpockets, "nimmers" are thieves, and "trulls" and "doxies" are prostitutes.

INTRODUCTION

[Beggar, Player]

BEGGAR: If poverty be a title[3] to poetry, I am sure nobody can dispute mine. I own myself of the Company of Beggars; and I make one at their weekly festivals at St. Giles's.[4] I have a small yearly salary for my catches,[5] and am welcome to a dinner there whenever I please, which is more than most poets can say.

PLAYER: As we live by the Muses, 'tis but gratitude in us to encourage poetical merit wherever we find it. The Muses, contrary to all other ladies, pay no distinction to dress, and never partially[6] mistake the pertness of embroidery for wit, nor the modesty of want for dullness. Be the author who he will, we push his play as far as it will go. So (though you are in want) I wish you success heartily.

BEGGAR: This piece I own was originally writ for the celebrating the marriage of James Chanter and Moll Lay, two most excellent ballad singers. I have introduced the similes that are in all your celebrated operas: the swallow, the moth, the bee, the ship, the flower, etc. Besides, I have a prison scene, which the ladies always reckon charmingly pathetic. As to the parts, I have observed such a nice impartiality to our two ladies, that it is impossible for either of them to take offense.[7] I hope I may be forgiven, that I have not made my opera throughout unnatural, like those in vogue; for I have no recitative.[8] Excepting this, as I have consented to have neither prologue nor epilogue, it must be allowed an opera in all its forms. The piece indeed hath been heretofore frequently represented by ourselves in our great room at St. Giles's, so that I cannot too often acknowledge your charity in bringing it now on the stage.

PLAYER: But I see 'tis time for us to withdraw; the actors are preparing to begin. Play away the overture.

[Exeunt.]

ACT 1

Scene 1. Peachum's House

[Peachum sitting at a table with a large book of accounts before him.]

Air 1. An old woman clothed in gray[9]

Through all the employments of life
Each neighbor abuses his brother;
Whore and rogue they call husband and wife:
All professions be-rogue one another.
The priest calls the lawyer a cheat,
The lawyer be-knaves the divine;

---

3. Deed of ownership.
4. An almshouse near the parish of St. Giles, patron saint of lepers and beggars.
5. Rounds, songs for two or more voices in which each voice starts the same melody at a different time. The form was very popular; enthusiasts assembled in "catch clubs" for whole evenings of singing.
6. In a prejudiced way.

7. The Beggar alludes to recent rivalries between leading ladies in Italian operas.
8. In Italian opera, arias are interspersed with sung speech ("recitative"); this English opera will avoid the second, "unnatural" convention.
9. I.e., this air is to be sung to the familiar ballad tune, "An Old Woman Clothed in Gray."

And the statesman, because he's so great,[1]
Thinks his trade as honest as mine.

A lawyer is an honest employment; so is mine. Like me too he acts in a double capacity, both against rogues and for 'em; for 'tis but fitting that we should protect and encourage cheats, since we live by them.

Scene 2

[Peachum, Filch]

FILCH: Sir, Black Moll hath sent word her trial comes on in the afternoon, and she hopes you will order matters so as to bring her off.

PEACHUM: Why, she may plead her belly at worst;[2] to my knowledge she hath taken care of that security. But as the wench is very active and industrious, you may satisfy her that I'll soften the evidence.

FILCH: Tom Gagg, Sir, is found guilty.

PEACHUM: A lazy dog! When I took him the time before, I told him what he would come to if he did not mend his hand. This is death without reprieve. I may venture to book him.[3] [Writes.] For Tom Gagg, forty pounds. Let Betty Sly know that I'll save her from transportation,[4] for I can get more by her staying in England.

FILCH: Betty hath brought more goods into our lock[5] to-year than any five of the gang; and in truth, 'tis a pity to lose so good a customer.

PEACHUM: If none of the gang take her off,[6] she may, in the common course of business, live a twelve-month longer. I love to let women 'scape. A good sportsman always lets the hen partridges fly, because the breed of the game depends upon them. Besides, here the law allows us no reward; there is nothing to be got by the death of women—except our wives.[7]

FILCH: Without dispute, she is a fine woman! 'Twas to her I was obliged for my education, and (to say a bold word) she hath trained up more young fellows to the business than the gaming-table.

PEACHUM: Truly, Filch, thy observation is right. We and the surgeons[8] are more beholden to women than all the professions besides.

Air 2. The bonny gray-eyed morn

FILCH: *'Tis woman that seduces all mankind,*
        By her we first were taught the wheedling arts:
    Her very eyes can cheat; when most she's kind,
        She tricks us of our money with our hearts.
    For her, like wolves by night we roam for prey,
        And practice ev'ry fraud to bribe her charms;
    For suits of love, like law, are won by pay,
        And beauty must be fee'd into our arms.

PEACHUM: But make haste to Newgate,[9] boy, and let my friends know what I intend; for I love to make them easy one way or other.

---

1. The word "great" was often attached to the Whig Prime Minister Robert Walpole, whom Gay's Tory party opposed vigorously in the 1720s and 1730s.
2. A pregnant woman could not be hanged.
3. I.e., enter in the books the reward for "peaching" him.
4. Convicted criminals were sometimes transported to the colonies.
5. A holding-place for stolen goods.
6. Turn her in (or kill her).
7. Husbands inherited their wives' property.
8. Who treat venereal diseases.
9. London's main prison.

FILCH: When a gentleman is long kept in suspense, penitence may break his spirit ever after. Besides, certainty gives a man a good air upon his trial, and makes him risk another without fear or scruple. But I'll away, for 'tis a pleasure to be the messenger of comfort to friends in affliction.

Scene 3

[Peachum]

But 'tis now high time to look about me for a decent execution against next Sessions.[1] I hate a lazy rogue, by whom one can get nothing 'til he is hanged. A register of the gang, [*reading*] "Crook-Fingered Jack." A year and a half in the service. Let me see how much the stock owes to his industry: one, two, three, four, five gold watches, and seven silver ones. A mighty clean-handed fellow! Sixteen snuff-boxes, five of them of true gold. Six dozen of handkerchiefs, four silver-hilted swords, half a dozen of shirts, three tie-periwigs, and a piece of broad cloth. Considering these are only the fruits of his leisure hours, I don't know a prettier fellow, for no man alive hath a more engaging presence of mind upon the road. "Wat Dreary, alias Brown Will." An irregular dog, who hath an underhand way of disposing of his goods. I'll try him[2] only for a Sessions or two longer upon his good behavior. "Harry Paddington." A poor petty-larceny rascal, without the least genius; that fellow, though he were to live these six months, will never come to the gallows with any credit. "Slippery Sam": he goes off the next Sessions, for the villain hath the impudence to have views of following his trade as a tailor, which he calls an honest employment. "Matt of the Mint": lifted[3] not above a month ago, a promising sturdy fellow, and diligent in his way; somewhat too bold and hasty, and may raise good contributions on[4] the public, if he does not cut himself short by murder. "Tom Tipple." A guzzling soaking sot, who is always too drunk to stand himself, or to make others stand. A cart is absolutely necessary for him.[5] "Robin of Bagshot, alias Gorgon, alias Bluff Bob, alias Carbuncle, alias Bob Booty."[6]

Scene 4

[Peachum, Mrs. Peachum]

MRS. PEACHUM: What of Bob Booty, husband? I hope nothing bad hath betided him. You know, my dear, he's a favorite customer of mine. 'Twas he made me a present of this ring.

PEACHUM: I have set his name down in the blacklist, that's all, my dear; he spends his life among women, and as soon as his money is gone, one or other of the ladies will hang him for the reward, and there's forty pound lost to us forever.

MRS. PEACHUM: You know, my dear, I never meddle in matters of death; I always leave those affairs to you. Women indeed are bitter bad judges in these cases, for they are so partial to the brave that they think every man handsome who is going to the camp[7] or the gallows.

---

1. For the next sitting of the criminal court.
2. Keep him on.
3. Enlisted.
4. From.
5. Condemned prisoners were carried in carts to the place of execution.
6. All these names point towards (and mock) prime minister Robert Walpole.
7. I.e., to war.

Air 3. Cold and raw

If any wench Venus's girdle wear,
  Though she be never so ugly;
Lilies and roses will quickly appear,
  And her face look wond'rous smugly.
Beneath the left ear so fit but a cord,
  (A rope so charming a zone⁸ is!)
The youth in his cart hath the air of a lord,
  And we cry, "There dies an Adonis!"

But really, husband, you should not be too hardhearted, for you never had a finer, braver set of men than at present. We have not had a murder among them all, these seven months. And truly, my dear, that is a great blessing.

PEACHUM: What a dickens is the woman always a-whimpering about murder for? No gentleman is ever looked upon the worse for killing a man in his own defense; and if business cannot be carried on without it, what would you have a gentleman do?

MRS. PEACHUM: If I am in the wrong, my dear, you must excuse me, for nobody can help the frailty of an overscrupulous conscience.

PEACHUM: Murder is as fashionable a crime as a man can be guilty of. How many fine gentlemen have we in Newgate every year, purely upon that article! If they have wherewithal to persuade the jury to bring it in⁹ manslaughter, what are they the worse for it? So, my dear, have done upon this subject. Was Captain Macheath here this morning, for the banknotes¹ he left with you last week?

MRS. PEACHUM: Yes, my dear; and though the bank hath stopped payment, he was so cheerful and so agreeable! Sure there is not a finer gentleman upon the road than the Captain! If he comes from Bagshot² at any reasonable hour he hath promised to make one this evening with Polly and me, and Bob Booty, at a party of quadrille.³ Pray, my dear, is the Captain rich?

PEACHUM: The Captain keeps too good company ever to grow rich. Marybone and the chocolate-houses⁴ are his undoing. The man that proposes to get money by play should have the education of a fine gentleman, and be trained up to it from his youth.

MRS. PEACHUM: Really, I am sorry upon Polly's account the Captain hath not more discretion. What business hath he to keep company with lords and gentlemen? He should leave them to prey upon one another.

PEACHUM: Upon Polly's account! What a plague does the woman mean? Upon Polly's account!

MRS. PEACHUM: Captain Macheath is very fond of the girl.

PEACHUM: And what then?

MRS. PEACHUM: If I have any skill in the ways of women, I am sure Polly thinks him a very pretty man.

PEACHUM: And what then? You would not be so mad to have the wench marry him! Gamesters and highwaymen are generally very good to their whores, but they are very devils to their wives.

---

8. Belt.
9. Reduce it to.
1. Bankers' checks, payable to bearer.
2. Bagshot Heath, west of London, where many highway-

men plied their trade.
3. A fashionable card game for four.
4. Both were popular sites for gambling.

MRS. PEACHUM: But if Polly should be in love, how should we help her, or how can she help herself? Poor girl, I am in the utmost concern about her.

Air 4. Why is your faithful slave disdained?

> *If love the virgin's heart invade,*
> *How, like a moth, the simple maid*
> *Still[5] plays about the flame!*
> *If soon she be not made a wife,*
> *Her honor's singed, and then for life,*
> *She's—what I dare not name.*

PEACHUM: Look ye, wife. A handsome wench in our way of business is as profitable as at the bar of a Temple[6] coffee-house, who looks upon it as her livelihood to grant every liberty but one. You see I would indulge the girl as far as prudently we can—in anything but marriage! After that, my dear, how shall we be safe? Are we not then in her husband's power? For a husband hath the absolute power over all a wife's secrets but her own. If the girl had the discretion of a court lady, who can have a dozen young fellows at her ear without complying with one, I should not matter it; but Polly is tinder, and a spark will at once set her on a flame. Married! If the wench does not know her own profit, sure she knows her own pleasure better than to make herself a property! My daughter to me should be, like a court lady to a minister of state, a key to the whole gang. Married! If the affair is not already done, I'll terrify her from it, by the example of our neighbors.

MRS. PEACHUM: Mayhap, my dear, you may injure the girl. She loves to imitate the fine ladies, and she may only allow the Captain liberties in the view of interest.[7]

PEACHUM: But 'tis your duty, my dear, to warn the girl against her ruin, and to instruct her how to make the most of her beauty. I'll go to her this moment, and sift[8] her. In the meantime, wife, rip out the coronets and marks[9] of these dozen of cambric[1] handkerchiefs, for I can dispose of them this afternoon to a chap[2] in the City.

Scene 5

[Mrs. Peachum]

Never was a man more out of the way in an argument than my husband! Why must our Polly, forsooth, differ from her sex, and love only her husband? And why must Polly's marriage, contrary to all observation, make her the less followed by other men? All men are thieves in love, and like a woman the better for being another's property.

Air 5. Of all the simple things we do

> *A maid is like the golden ore*
> *Which hath guineas intrinsical in't,*
> *Whose worth is never known before*
> *It is tried and impressed[3] in the mint.*

---

5. Constantly.
6. A law school, whose students frequented the nearby gathering places.
7. Self-interest; profit.
8. Question.

9. The embroidered monograms by which the wealthy designated their property.
1. Fine white linen.
2. Dealer.
3. Smelted and stamped.

A wife's like a guinea in gold,
Stamped with the name of her spouse;
   Now here, now there, is bought, or is sold,
And is current in every house.

Scene 6

[Mrs. Peachum, Filch]

MRS. PEACHUM: Come hither, Filch. I am as fond of this child, as though my mind misgave me⁴ he were my own. He hath as fine a hand at picking a pocket as a woman, and is as nimble-fingered as a juggler. If an unlucky session does not cut the rope of thy life, I pronounce, boy, thou wilt be a great man⁵ in history. Where was your post last night, my boy?

FILCH: I plied at the opera, madam; and considering 'twas neither dark nor rainy, so that there was no great hurry in getting chairs and coaches, made a tolerable hand on't. These seven handkerchiefs, madam.

MRS. PEACHUM: Colored ones, I see. They are of sure sale from our warehouse at Redriff among the seamen.

FILCH: And this snuffbox.

MRS. PEACHUM: Set in gold! A pretty encouragement this to a young beginner!

FILCH: I had a fair tug at a charming gold watch. Pox take the tailors for making the fobs⁶ so deep and narrow! It stuck by the way, and I was forced to make my escape under a coach. Really, madam, I fear I shall be cut off in the flower of my youth, so that every now and then (since I was pumped⁷) I have thoughts of taking up⁸ and going to sea.

MRS. PEACHUM: You should go to Hockley in the Hole,⁹ and to Marybone, child, to learn valor. These are the schools that have bred so many brave men. I thought, boy, by this time, thou hadst lost fear as well as shame. Poor lad! How little does he know as yet of the Old Bailey!¹ For the first fact² I'll insure thee from being hanged; and going to sea, Filch, will come time enough upon a sentence of transportation. But now, since you have nothing better to do, ev'n go to your book, and learn your catechism;³ for really a man makes but an ill figure in the Ordinary's Paper,⁴ who cannot give a satisfactory answer to his questions. But, hark you, my lad. Don't tell me a lie, for you know I hate a liar. Do you know of anything that hath passed between Captain Macheath and our Polly?

FILCH: I beg you, Madam, don't ask me; for I must either tell a lie to you or to Miss Polly; for I promised her I would not tell.

MRS. PEACHUM: But when the honor of our family is concerned—

FILCH: I shall lead a sad life with Miss Polly, if ever she come to know that I told you. Besides, I would not willingly forfeit my own honor by betraying anybody.

MRS. PEACHUM: Yonder comes my husband and Polly. Come, Filch, you shall go with me into my own room, and tell me the whole story. I'll give thee a glass of a most delicious cordial that I keep for my own drinking.

---

4. Suspected.
5. Another jab at Walpole's covert criminality.
6. Watch-pockets.
7. Half-drowned under a pump (a common punishment for pickpockets).
8. Reforming.
9. An area known for bear-baiting, dogfights, and other sporting contests.
1. London's central criminal court.

2. Crime.
3. In keeping with the legal provision called "benefit of clergy," first offenders who could answer questions from the Christian catechism might have their sentences commuted from execution to transportation.
4. The Ordinary (prison chaplain) determined whether prisoners qualified for "benefit of clergy"—and also published accounts of how condemned prisoners conducted themselves in the hours leading up to execution.

Scene 7

[*Peachum, Polly*]

POLLY: I know as well as any of the fine ladies how to make the most of my self and of my man too. A woman knows how to be mercenary, though she hath never been in a court or at an assembly.[5] We have it in our natures, Papa. If I allow Captain Macheath some trifling liberties, I have this watch and other visible marks of his favor to show for it. A girl who cannot grant some things, and refuse what is most material, will make but a poor hand of her beauty, and soon be thrown upon the common.

Air 6. What shall I do to show how much I love her?

Virgins are like the fair flower in its luster,
　　Which in the garden enamels the ground;
Near it the bees in play flutter and cluster,
　　And gaudy butterflies frolic around.
But, when once plucked, 'tis no longer alluring,
　　To Covent Garden[6] *'tis sent (as yet sweet),*
There fades, and shrinks, and grows past all enduring,
　　Rots, stinks, and dies, and is trod under feet.

PEACHUM: You know, Polly, I am not against your toying and trifling with a customer in the way of business, or to get out a secret, or so. But if I find out that you have played the fool and are married, you jade you, I'll cut your throat, hussy. Now you know my mind.

Scene 8

[*Peachum, Polly, Mrs. Peachum*]

Air 7. Oh London is a fine town

[*Mrs. Peachum, in a very great passion*]

Our Polly is a sad slut! nor heeds what we have taught her.
I wonder any man alive will ever rear a daughter!
For she must have both hoods and gowns, and hoops to swell her pride,
With scarves and stays,[7] *and gloves and lace; and she will have men beside;*
And when she's dressed with care and cost, all tempting, fine and gay,
As men should serve a cowcumber,[8] *she flings herself away.*
　　Our Polly is a sad slut, etc.

You baggage! You hussy! You inconsiderate jade! Had you been hanged, it would not have vexed me, for that might have been your misfortune; but to do such a mad thing by choice! The wench is married, husband.
PEACHUM: Married! The Captain is a bold man, and will risk anything for money; to be sure he believes her a fortune. Do you think your mother and I should have lived comfortably so long together, if ever we had been married? Baggage!

---

5. A fashionable social gathering.
6. A London market for flowers, fruits, and vegetables; also a haunt of prostitutes.

7. Corsets.
8. I.e., as though she were throwing away a (worthless) cucumber.

MRS. PEACHUM: I knew she was always a proud slut; and now the wench hath played the fool and married, because forsooth she would do like the gentry. Can you support the expense of a husband, hussy, in gaming, drinking, and whoring? Have you money enough to carry on the daily quarrels of man and wife about who shall squander most? There are not many husbands and wives who can bear the charges[9] of plaguing one another in a handsome way. If you must be married, could you introduce nobody into our family but a highwayman? Why, thou foolish jade, thou wilt be as ill used, and as much neglected, as if thou hadst married a lord!

PEACHUM: Let not your anger, my dear, break through the rules of decency, for the Captain looks upon himself in the military capacity, as a gentleman by his profession. Besides what he hath already, I know he is in a fair way of getting, or of dying;[1] and both these ways, let me tell you, are most excellent chances for a wife. Tell me, hussy, are you ruined or no?

MRS. PEACHUM: With Polly's fortune, she might very well have gone off to a person of distinction. Yes, that you might, you pouting slut!

PEACHUM: What, is the wench dumb? Speak, or I'll make you plead by squeezing out an answer from you.[2] Are you really bound wife to him, or are you only upon liking?

[*Pinches her.*]

POLLY [*Screaming*]: Oh!

MRS. PEACHUM: How the mother is to be pitied who hath handsome daughters! Locks, bolts, bars, and lectures of morality are nothing to them. They break through them all. They have as much pleasure in cheating a father and mother as in cheating at cards.

PEACHUM: Why, Polly, I shall soon know if your are married, by Macheath's keeping from[3] our house.

Air 8. Grim king of the ghosts

POLLY: *Can love be controlled by advice?*
    Will Cupid our mothers obey?
Though my heart were as frozen as ice,
    At his flame 'twould have melted away.

When he kissed me so closely he pressed,
    'Twas so sweet that I must have complied;
So I thought it both safest and best
    To marry, for fear you should chide.

MRS. PEACHUM: Then all the hopes of our family are gone forever and ever!

PEACHUM: And Macheath may hang his father and mother-in-law, in hope to get into their daughter's fortune.

POLLY: I did not marry him (as 'tis the fashion) coolly and deliberately for honor and money. But, I love him.

MRS. PEACHUM: Love him! Worse and worse! I thought the girl had been better bred. Oh husband, husband! Her folly makes me mad! My head swims! I'm distracted! I can't support myself—Oh!

9. Expense.
1. He is likely to grow richer, or to die on the gallows.
2. Confessions were sometimes extracted by pressing the prisoner with weights.
3. Avoiding.

[*Faints.*]

PEACHUM: See, wench, to what a condition you have reduced your poor mother! A glass of cordial, this instant. How the poor woman takes it to heart!

[*Polly goes out, and returns with it.*]

Ah, hussy, now this is the only comfort your mother has left!

POLLY: Give her another glass, Sir; my mama drinks double the quantity whenever she is out of order. This, you see, fetches[4] her.

MRS. PEACHUM: The girl shows such a readiness, and so much concern, that I could almost find in my heart to forgive her.

Air 9. Oh Jenny, Oh Jenny, where hast thou been.

> *Oh Polly, you might have toyed and kissed.*
> *By keeping men off, you keep them on.*
> POLLY: *But he so teased me,*
> *And he so pleased me,*
> *What I did, you must have done.*

MRS. PEACHUM: Not with a highwayman, you sorry slut!

PEACHUM: A word with you, wife. 'Tis no new thing for a wench to take man without consent of parents. You know 'tis the frailty of woman, my dear.

MRS. PEACHUM: Yes, indeed, the sex is frail. But the first time a woman is frail, she should be somewhat nice[5] methinks, for then or never is the time to make her fortune. After that, she hath nothing to do but guard herself from being found out, and she may do what she pleases.

PEACHUM: Make yourself a little easy; I have a thought shall soon set all matters again to rights. Why so melancholy, Polly? Since what is done cannot be undone, we must all endeavor to make the best of it.

MRS. PEACHUM: Well, Polly, as far as one woman can forgive another, I forgive thee. Your father is too fond of you, hussy.

POLLY: Then all my sorrows are at an end.

MRS. PEACHUM: A mighty likely speech in troth, for a wench who is just married!

Air 10. Thomas, I cannot

> POLLY: *I, like a ship in storms, was tossed;*
> *Yet afraid to put in to land;*
> *For seized in the port the vessel's lost,*
> *Whose treasure is contraband.*
> *The waves are laid,[6]*
> *My duty's paid.*
> *O joy beyond expression!*
> *Thus, safe ashore,*
> *I ask no more,*
> *My all is in my possession.*

PEACHUM: I hear customers in t'other room. Go, talk with 'em, Polly; but come to us again, as soon as they are gone. But, hark ye, child, if 'tis the gentleman who

---

4. Revives.   6. Calmed.
5. Careful, fastidious.

was here yesterday about the repeating watch,[7] say you believe we can't get intelligence of it till tomorrow. For I lent it to Suky Straddle, to make a figure with it tonight at a tavern in Drury Lane.[8] If t'other gentleman calls for the silver-hilted sword, you know beetle-browed Jemmy hath it on, and he doth not come from Tunbridge till Tuesday night, so that it cannot be had till then.

Scene 9

[Peachum, Mrs. Peachum]

PEACHUM: Dear wife, be a little pacified. Don't let your passion run away with your senses. Polly, I grant you, hath done a rash thing.

MRS. PEACHUM: If she had had only an intrigue with the fellow, why the very best families have excused and huddled up a frailty of that sort. 'Tis marriage, husband, that makes it a blemish.

PEACHUM: But money, wife, is the true fuller's earth[9] for reputations; there is not a spot or a stain but what it can take out. A rich rogue nowadays is fit company for any gentleman; and the world, my dear, hath not such a contempt for roguery as you imagine. I tell you, wife, I can make this match turn to our advantage.

MRS. PEACHUM: I am very sensible,[1] husband, that Captain Macheath is worth money, but I am in doubt whether he hath not two or three wives already, and then if he should die in a Session or two, Polly's dower would come into dispute.

PEACHUM: That, indeed, is a point which ought to be considered.

Air 11. A soldier and a sailor

A fox may steal your hens, sir,
A whore your health and pence, sir,
Your daughter rob your chest, sir,
Your wife may steal your rest, sir,
   A thief your goods and plate.[2]
But this is all but picking,
With rest, pence, chest and chicken;
It ever was decreed, sir,
If lawyer's hand is fee'd, sir,
   He steals your whole estate.

The lawyers are bitter enemies to those in our way.[3] They don't care that anybody should get a clandestine livelihood but themselves.

Scene 10

[Mrs. Peachum, Peachum, Polly]

POLLY: 'Twas only Nimming Ned. He brought in a damask window curtain, a hoop petticoat, a pair of silver candlesticks, a periwig, and one silk stocking, from the fire that happened last night.

---

7. An especially valuable timepiece: it announced the current hour and quarter-hour by a series of bells that rang at the push of a button.
8. Another haunt of prostitutes; also the location of the rival playhouse (which had rejected the opportunity to produce Gay's *Opera*).
9. A mineral used as a cleaning solvent.
1. Well aware.
2. Utensils plated with silver or gold.
3. Line of work.

PEACHUM: There is not a fellow that is cleverer in his way, and saves more goods out of the fire, than Ned. But now, Polly, to your affair, for matters must not be left as they are. You are married then, it seems?

POLLY: Yes, Sir.

PEACHUM: And how do you propose to live, child?

POLLY: Like other women, Sir, upon the industry of my husband.

MRS. PEACHUM: What, is the wench turned fool? A highwayman's wife, like a soldier's, hath as little of his pay, as of his company.

PEACHUM: And had not you the common views of a gentlewoman in your marriage, Polly?

POLLY: I don't know what you mean, Sir.

PEACHUM: Of a jointure,⁴ and of being a widow.

POLLY: But I love him, Sir: how then could I have thoughts of parting with him?

PEACHUM: Parting with him! Why, that is the whole scheme and intention of all marriage articles. The comfortable estate of widowhood is the only hope that keeps up a wife's spirits. Where is the woman who would scruple to be a wife, if she had it in her power to be a widow whenever she pleased? If you have any views of this sort, Polly, I shall think the match not so very unreasonable.

POLLY: How I dread to hear your advice! Yet I must beg you to explain yourself.

PEACHUM: Secure what he hath got, have him peached the next Sessions, and then at once you are made a rich widow.

POLLY: What, murder the man I love! The blood runs cold at my heart with the very thought of it.

PEACHUM: Fie, Polly! What hath murder to do in the affair? Since the thing sooner or later must happen, I dare say the Captain himself would like that we should get the reward for his death sooner than a stranger. Why, Polly, the Captain knows, that as 'tis his employment to rob, so 'tis ours to take robbers; every man in his business. So that there is no malice in the case.

MRS. PEACHUM: Ay, husband, now you have nicked the matter. To have him peached is the only thing could ever make me forgive her.

Air 12. Now ponder well, ye parents dear

POLLY:
Oh, ponder well! be not severe;
So save a wretched wife!
For on the rope that hangs my dear
Depends poor Polly's life.

MRS. PEACHUM: But your duty to your parents, hussy, obliges you to hang him. What would many a wife give for such an opportunity!

POLLY: What is a jointure, what is widowhood to me? I know my heart. I cannot survive him.

Air 13. Le printemps rappelle aux armes⁵

The turtle⁶ thus with plaintive crying,
Her lover dying,

---

4. "Estate settled on a wife to be enjoyed after her husband's decease" (Johnson's *Dictionary*).

5. Spring calls to arms.
6. Turtledove (emblem of conjugal fidelity).

The turtle thus with plaintive crying,
      Laments her dove.
Down she drops quite spent with sighing,
      Paired in death, as paired in love.

Thus, Sir, it will happen to your poor Polly.

MRS. PEACHUM: What, is the fool in love in earnest then? I hate thee for being particular.[7] Why, wench, thou art a shame to thy very sex.

POLLY: But hear me, Mother. If you ever loved—

MRS. PEACHUM: Those cursed playbooks she reads have been her ruin. One word more, hussy, and I shall knock your brains out, if you have any.

PEACHUM: Keep out of the way, Polly, for fear of mischief, and consider of what is proposed to you.

MRS. PEACHUM: Away, hussy. Hang your husband, and be dutiful.

Scene 11

[Mrs. Peachum, Peachum]

[Polly listening.]

MRS. PEACHUM: The thing, husband, must and shall be done. For the sake of intelligence[8] we must take other measures, and have him peached the next session without her consent. If she will not know her duty, we know ours.

PEACHUM: But really, my dear, it grieves one's heart to take off a great man. When I consider his personal bravery, his fine stratagem, how much we have already got by him, and how much more we may get, methinks I can't find in my heart to have a hand in his death. I wish you could have made Polly undertake it.

MRS. PEACHUM: But in a case of necessity—our own lives are in danger.

PEACHUM: Then, indeed, we must comply with the customs of the world, and make gratitude give way to interest. He shall be taken off.

MRS. PEACHUM: I'll undertake to manage Polly.

PEACHUM: And I'll prepare matters for the Old Bailey.

Scene 12

[Polly]

Now I'm a wretch, indeed. Methinks I see him already in the cart, sweeter and more lovely than the nosegay[9] in his hand! I hear the crowd extolling his resolution and intrepidity! What volleys of sighs are sent from the windows of Holborn,[1] that so comely a youth should be brought to disgrace! I see him at the tree![2] The whole circle are in tears! Even butchers weep! Jack Ketch[3] himself hesitates to perform his duty, and would be glad to lose his fee, by a reprieve. What then will become of Polly! As yet I may inform him of their design, and aid him in his escape. It shall be so. But then he flies, absents himself, and I bar myself from his dear, dear conversation! That too will distract me.[4] If he keep out of the way, my papa and mama may in time relent, and we may be happy. If he stays, he is hanged, and then

---

7. Partial (i.e., to one man over another).
8. "Account of things distant or secret" (Johnson's *Dictionary*).
9. Bouquet (often carried by condemned prisoners).
1. The road from Newgate to Tyburn, along which criminals were carted to execution.

2. The gallows ("Tyburn tree").
3. England's most famous hangman (d. 1686); thereafter, any hangman.
4. Drive me mad.

he is lost forever! He intended to lie concealed in my room, till the dusk of the evening. If they are abroad, I'll this instant let him out, lest some accident should prevent him. [*Exit, and returns.*]

Scene 13

[*Polly, Macheath*]

Air 14. Pretty parrot, say—

MACHEATH: *Pretty Polly, say,*
                              When I was away,
              Did your fancy never stray
                        To some newer lover?
POLLY: *Without disguise,*
                              Heaving sighs,
                              Doting eyes,
              My constant heart discover[5]
                        Fondly let me loll!
MACHEATH: *O pretty, pretty Poll.*

POLLY: And are *you* as fond as ever, my dear?
MACHEATH: Suspect my honor, my courage, suspect anything but my love. May my pistols miss fire, and my mare slip her shoulder while I am pursued, if I ever forsake thee!
POLLY: Nay, my dear, I have no reason to doubt you, for I find in the romance you lent me, none of the great heroes were ever false in love.

Air 15. Pray, fair one, be kind

MACHEATH: *My heart was so free,*
                        It roved like the bee,
              Till Polly my passion requited;
                        I sipped each flower,
                        I changed ev'ry hour,
              But here ev'ry flower is united.

POLLY: Were you sentenced to transportation, sure, my dear, you could not leave me behind you—could you?
MACHEATH: Is there any power, any force that could tear me from thee? You might sooner tear a pension out of the hands of a courtier, a fee from a lawyer, a pretty woman from a looking glass, or any woman from quadrille. But to tear me from thee is impossible!

Air 16. Over the hills and far away

Were I laid on Greenland's coast,
And in my arms embraced my lass,
Warm amidst eternal frost,
Too soon the half year's night[6] *would pass.*

---

5. Reveal.   6. The long dark winter of the polar regions.

POLLY: *Were I sold on Indian soil,*
                         Soon as the burning day was closed,
                         I could mock the sultry toil,
                         When on my charmer's breast reposed.
MACHEATH: *And I would love you all the day,*
POLLY: *Every night would kiss and play,*
MACHEATH: *If with me you'd fondly stray*
POLLY: *Over the hills and far away.*

POLLY: Yes, I would go with thee. But oh! How shall I speak it? I must be torn from thee. We must part.

MACHEATH: How! Part!

POLLY: We must, we must. My papa and mama are set against thy life. They now, even now are in search after thee. They are preparing evidence against thee. Thy life depends upon a moment.

Air 17. Gin thou wert mine awn thing

O what pain it is to part!
Can I leave thee, can I leave thee?
O what pain it is to part!
Can thy Polly ever leave thee?
But lest death my love should thwart,
And bring thee to the fatal cart,
Thus I tear thee from my bleeding heart!
    Fly hence, and let me leave thee.

One kiss and then—one kiss—begone—farewell.

MACHEATH: My hand, my heart, my dear, is so riveted to thine, that I cannot unloose my hold.

POLLY: But my papa may intercept thee, and then I should lose the very glimmering of hope. A few weeks, perhaps, may reconcile us all. Shall thy Polly hear from thee?

MACHEATH: Must I then go?

POLLY: And will not absence change your love?

MACHEATH: If you doubt it, let me stay—and be hanged.

POLLY: Oh how I fear! How I tremble! Go—but when safety will give you leave, you will be sure to see me again; for till then Polly is wretched.

Air 18. Oh the broom

[*Parting, and looking back at each other with fondness; he at one door, she at the other.*]

MACHEATH: *The miser thus a shilling sees,*
                     Which he's obliged to pay,
                     With sighs resigns it by degrees,
                     And fears 'tis gone for aye.[7]

---

7. Forever.

POLLY: *The boy, thus, when his sparrow's flown,*
           The bird in silence eyes;
           But soon as out of sight 'tis gone,
           Whines, whimpers, sobs and cries.

ACT 2

Scene 1. A tavern near Newgate.

[*Jemmy Twitcher, Crook-Fingered Jack, Wat Dreary, Robin of Bagshot, Nimming Ned, Henry Paddington, Matt of the Mint, Ben Budge, and the rest of the gang, at the table, with wine, brandy, and tobacco.*]

BEN: But prithee, Matt, what is become of thy brother Tom? I have not seen him since my return from transportation.

MATT: Poor brother Tom had an accident this time twelvemonth, and so clever a made fellow he was, that I could not save him from those fleaing[8] rascals the surgeons; and now, poor man, he is among the otamys[9] at Surgeon's Hall.

BEN: So it seems his time was come.

JEMMY: But the present time is ours, and nobody alive hath more. Why are the laws leveled at us? Are we more dishonest than the rest of mankind? What we win, gentlemen, is our own by the law of arms, and the right of conquest.

JACK: Where shall we find such another set of practical philosophers, who to a man are above the fear of death?

WAT: Sound men, and true!

ROBIN: Of tried courage, and indefatigable industry!

NED: Who is there here that would not die for his friend?

HARRY: Who is there here that would betray him for his interest?

MATT: Show me a gang of courtiers that can say as much.

BEN: We are for a just partition of the world, for every man hath a right to enjoy life.

MATT: We retrench[1] the superfluities of mankind. The world is avaricious, and I hate avarice. A covetous fellow, like a jackdaw,[2] steals what he was never made to enjoy, for the sake of hiding it. These are the robbers of mankind, for money was made for the free-hearted and generous, and where is the injury of taking from another, what he hath not the heart to make use of?

JEMMY: Our several stations for the day are fixed. Good luck attend us all. Fill the glasses.

Air 19. Fill ev'ry glass

MATT: *Fill ev'ry glass, for wine inspires us,*
               And fires us
           With courage, love and joy.
           Women and wine should life employ.

---

8. Flaying, robbing.
9. Skeletons (from "anatomies"). The corpses of executed criminals were often used for medical instruction.

1. Reduce, limit.
2. A bird regarded in animal lore as an inveterate thief.

Is there ought else on earth desirous?
CHORUS: *Fill ev'ry glass, etc.*

Scene 2

[*To them enter Macheath*]

MACHEATH: Gentlemen, well met. My heart hath been with you this hour; but an unexpected affair hath detained me. No ceremony, I beg you.

MATT: We were just breaking up to go upon duty. Am I to have the honor of taking the air with you, Sir, this evening upon the heath? I drink a dram now and then with the stagecoachmen in the way of friendship and intelligence; and I know that about this time there will be passengers upon the western road,³ who are worth speaking with.

MACHEATH: I was to have been of that party—but—

MATT: But what, Sir?

MACHEATH: Is there any man who suspects my courage?

MATT: We have all been witnesses of it.

MACHEATH: My honor and truth to the gang?

MATT: I'll be answerable for it.

MACHEATH: In the division of our booty, have I ever shown the least marks of avarice or injustice?

MATT: By these questions something seems to have ruffled you. Are any of us suspected?

MACHEATH: I have a fixed confidence, gentlemen, in you all, as men of honor, and as such I value and respect you. Peachum is a man that is useful to us.

MATT: Is he about to play us any foul play? I'll shoot him through the head.

MACHEATH: I beg you, gentlemen, act with conduct and discretion. A pistol is your last resort.

MATT: He knows nothing of this meeting.

MACHEATH: Business cannot go on without him. He is a man who knows the world, and is a necessary agent to us. We have had a slight difference, and till it is accommodated I shall be obliged to keep out of his way. Any private dispute of mine shall be of no ill consequence to my friends. You must continue to act under his direction, for the moment we break loose from him, our gang is ruined.

MATT: As a bawd⁴ to a whore, I grant you, he is to us of great convenience.

MACHEATH: Make him believe I have quitted the gang, which I can never do but with life.⁵ At our private quarters I will continue to meet you. A week or so will probably reconcile us.

MATT: Your instructions shall be observed. 'Tis now high time for us to repair to our several duties; so till the evening at our quarters in Moorfields,⁶ we bid you farewell.

MACHEATH: I shall wish myself with you. Success attend you.
    [*Sits down melancholy at the table.*]

---

3. Through Bagshot Heath, west of London.
4. Pimp.

5. I.e., by dying.
6. Just outside the old City wall.

Air 20. March in Rinaldo,[7] *with drums and trumpets*

MATT: Let us take the road.
      Hark! I hear the sound of coaches!
      The hour of attack approaches,
  To your arms, brave boys, and load.
      See the ball I hold!
      Let the chemists[8] toil like asses,
      Our fire their fire surpasses,
      And turns all our lead to gold.

[*The gang, ranged in the front of the stage, load their pistols, and stick them under their girdles;*[9] *then go off singing the first part in chorus.*]

Scene 3

[*Macheath, Drawer*[1]]

MACHEATH: What a fool is a fond wench! Polly is most confoundedly bit.[2] I love the sex. And a man who loves money might as well be contented with one guinea, as I with one woman. The town perhaps hath been as much obliged to me, for recruiting it with free-hearted ladies, as to any recruiting officer in the army. If it were not for us and the other gentlemen of the sword, Drury Lane would be uninhabited.

Air 21. Would you have a young virgin

If the heart of a man is depressed with cares,
The mist is dispelled when a woman appears;
Like the notes of a fiddle, she sweetly, sweetly
Raises the spirits, and charms our ears,
   Roses and lilies her cheeks disclose,
   But her ripe lips are more sweet than those.
     Press her,
     Caress her
     With blisses,
     Her kisses
Dissolve us in pleasure, and soft repose.

I must have women. There is nothing unbends[3] the mind like them. Money is not so strong a cordial for the time. Drawer! [*Enter Drawer.*] Is the porter gone for all the ladies, according to my directions?

DRAWER: I expect him back every minute. But you know, Sir, you sent him as far as Hockley in the Hole, for three of the ladies, for one in Vinegar Yard, and for the rest of them somewhere about Lewkner's Lane.[4] Sure some of them are below, for I hear the bar bell. As they come I will show them up. Coming, coming!

---

7. A heroic Italian opera (1711) by George Frideric Handel (1685–1759).
8. Alchemists, who strove to turn base metals into gold.
9. Belts.
1. Bartender.

2. Enamored.
3. Relaxes.
4. Both the Yard and the Lane were places of prostitution.

Scene 4

[*Macheath, Mrs. Coaxer, Dolly Trull, Mrs. Vixen, Betty Doxy, Jenny Diver, Mrs. Slammekin, Suky Tawdry, and Molly Brazen*]

MACHEATH: Dear Mrs. Coaxer, you are welcome. You look charmingly today. I hope you don't want the repairs of quality, and lay on paint.[5] —Dolly Trull! Kiss me, you slut; are you as amorous as ever, hussy? You are always so taken up with stealing hearts that you don't allow yourself time to steal anything else. Ah, Dolly, thou wilt ever be a coquette!—Mrs. Vixen, I'm yours; I always loved a woman of wit and spirit; they make charming mistresses, but plaguy wives.—Betty Doxy! Come hither, hussy. Do you drink as hard as ever? You had better stick to good wholesome beer; for in troth, Betty, strong waters[6] will in time ruin your constitution. You should leave those to your betters.—What! and my pretty Jenny Diver too! As prim and demure as ever! There is not any prude, though ever so high bred, hath a more sanctified look, with a more mischievous heart. Ah! Thou art a dear artful hypocrite.—Mrs. Slammekin! As careless and genteel as ever! All you fine ladies, who know your own beauty, affect an undress.—But see, here's Suky Tawdry come to contradict what I was saying. Everything she gets one way she lays out upon her back. Why, Suky, you must keep at least a dozen tallymen.[7]—Molly Brazen! [*She kisses him.*] That's well done. I love a free-hearted wench. Thou hast a most agreeable assurance, girl, and art as willing as a turtle.—But hark! I hear music. The harper is at the door. "If music be the food of love, play on."[8] Ere you seat yourselves, ladies, what think you of a dance? Come in. [*Enter Harper.*] Play the French tune that Mrs. Slammekin was so fond of.

[*A dance a la ronde[9] in the French manner; near the end of it this song and chorus:*]

Air 22. Cotillon

Youth's the season made for joys,
　　Love is then our duty,
She alone who that employs,
　　Well deserves her beauty.
　　　　Let's be gay,
　　　　While we may,
　　　　Beauty's a flower despised in decay.
Youth's the season, etc.

Let us drink and sport today,
　　Ours is not tomorrow.
Love with youth flies swift away,
　　Age is nought but sorrow.
　　　　Dance and sing,
　　　　Time's on the wing,
　　　　Life never knows the return of spring.

---

5. I hope you do not need to paint your face as high-class women do.
6. Hard liquor.

7. Merchants who provided clothes on credit.
8. The opening line of Shakespeare's *Twelfth Night*.
9. In a circle.

CHORUS: *Let us drink, etc.*

MACHEATH: Now, pray ladies, take your places. Here fellow. [*Pays the Harper.*] Bid the drawer bring us more wine. [*Exit Harper.*] If any of the ladies choose gin, I hope they will be so free to call for it.

JENNY: You look as if you meant me. Wine is strong enough for me. Indeed, Sir, I never drink strong waters but when I have the cholic.[1]

MACHEATH: Just the excuse of the fine ladies! Why, a lady of quality is never without the cholic. I hope, Mrs. Coaxer, you have had good success of late in your visits among the mercers.[2]

COAXER: We have so many interlopers—yet with industry, one may still have a little picking. I carried a silver flowered lutestring, and a piece of black padesoy[3] to Mr. Peachum's lock but last week.

VIXEN: There's Molly Brazen hath the ogle of a rattlesnake. She riveted a linen draper's eye so fast upon her, that he was nicked[4] of three pieces of cambric before he could look off.

BRAZEN: Oh, dear Madam! But sure nothing can come up to your handling of laces! And then you have such a sweet deluding tongue! To cheat a man is nothing; but the woman must have fine parts indeed who cheats a woman!

VIXEN: Lace, Madam, lies in a small compass, and is of easy conveyance. But you are apt, Madam, to think too well of your friends.

COAXER: If any woman hath more art than another, to be sure, 'tis Jenny Diver. Though her fellow be never so agreeable, she can pick his pocket as coolly, as if money were her only pleasure. Now that is a command of the passions uncommon in a woman!

JENNY: I never go to the tavern with a man, but in the view of business. I have other hours, and other sort of men, for my pleasure. But had I your address,[5] Madam—

MACHEATH: Have done with your compliments, ladies, and drink about. You are not so fond of me, Jenny, as you use to be.

JENNY: 'Tis not convenient, Sir, to show my fondness among so many rivals. 'Tis your own choice, and not the warmth of my inclination, that will determine you.[6]

Air 23. All in a misty morning

Before the barn-door crowing,
   The cock by hens attended,
His eyes around him throwing,
   Stands for a while suspended.
Then one he singles from the crew,
   And cheers the happy hen;
With how do you do, and how do you do,
   And how do you do again.

MACHEATH: Ah, Jenny! Thou art a dear slut.

TRULL: Pray, Madam, were you ever in keeping?[7]

1. Stomach pains.
2. Fabric dealers.
3. Expensive silk fabrics.
4. Robbed.

5. Elegant manner.
6. Clinch your decision.
7. I.e., the kept mistress of a wealthy man.

TAWDRY: I hope, Madam, I ha'nt been so long upon the town, but I have met with some good fortune as well as my neighbors.

TRULL: Pardon me, Madam, I meant no harm by the question; 'twas only in the way of conversation.

TAWDRY: Indeed, Madam, if I had not been a fool, I might have lived very handsomely with my last friend. But upon his missing five guineas, he turned me off. Now I never suspected he had counted them.

SLAMMEKIN: Who do you look upon, Madam, as your best sort of keepers?

TRULL: That, Madam, is thereafter as they be.[8]

SLAMMEKIN: I, Madam, was once kept by a Jew; and bating[9] their religion, to women they are a good sort of people.

TAWDRY: Now for my part, I own I like an old fellow; for we always make them pay for what they can't do.

VIXEN: A spruce[1] prentice, let me tell you, ladies, is no ill thing; they bleed[2] freely. I have sent at least two or three dozen of them in my time to the plantations.[3]

JENNY: But to be sure, Sir, with so much good fortune as you have had upon the road, you must be grown immensely rich.

MACHEATH: The road, indeed, hath done me justice, but the gaming table hath been my ruin.

Air 24. When once I lay with another man's wife

JENNY: *The gamesters and lawyers are jugglers[4] alike,*
  If they meddle your all is in danger.
  Like gypsies, if once they can finger a souse,[5]
  Your pockets they pick, and they pilfer your house,
  And give your estate to a stranger.

A man of courage should never put anything to the risk but his life. These are the tools of a man of honor. Cards and dice are only fit for cowardly cheats, who prey upon their friends. [*She takes up his pistol. Tawdry takes up the other.*]

TAWDRY: This, Sir, is fitter for your hand. Besides your loss of money, 'tis a loss to the ladies. Gaming takes you off from women. How fond could I be of you! But before company, 'tis ill bred.

MACHEATH: Wanton hussies!

JENNY: I must and will have a kiss to give my wine a zest.

[*They take him about the neck, and make signs to Peachum and the constables, who rush in upon him.*]

Scene 5

[*To them, Peachum and constables*]

PEACHUM: I seize you, Sir, as my prisoner.

MACHEATH: Was this well done, Jenny? Women are decoy ducks; who can trust them! Beasts, jades, jilts, harpies, Furies, whores!

---

8. That depends on how they treat me.
9. Apart from.
1. Lively.
2. Spend.

3. I.e., incited them to steal and thereby caused them to be transported to the colonies.
4. Sleight-of-hand artists; tricksters.
5. Get their hands on a sou (French penny).

PEACHUM: Your case, Mr. Macheath, is not particular. The greatest heroes have
been ruined by women. But to do them justice, I must own they are a pretty sort
of creatures, if we could trust them. You must now, Sir, take your leave of the
ladies, and if they have a mind to make you a visit, they will be sure to find you at
home. The gentleman, ladies, lodges in Newgate. Constables, wait upon the
Captain to his lodgings.

Air 25. When first I laid siege to my Chloris

MACHEATH: *At the tree I shall suffer with pleasure,*
          At the tree I shall suffer with pleasure,
              Let me go where I will,
              In all kinds of ill,
          I shall find no such Furies as these are.

PEACHUM: Ladies, I'll take care the reckoning shall be discharged.[6]
[*Exit Macheath, guarded, with Peachum and constables.*]

Scene 6

[*The women remain.*]

VIXEN: Look ye, Mrs. Jenny, though Mr. Peachum may have made a private bargain with you and Suky Tawdry for betraying the Captain, as we were all assisting, we ought all to share alike.
COAXER: I think Mr. Peachum, after so long an acquaintance, might have trusted
me as well as Jenny Diver.
SLAMMEKIN: I am sure at least three men of his hanging, and in a year's time too
(if he did me justice), should be set down to my account.[7]
TRULL: Mrs. Slammekin, that is not fair. For you know one of them was taken in
bed with me.
JENNY: As far as a bowl of punch or a treat, I believe Mrs. Suky will join with me.
As for anything else, ladies, you cannot in conscience expect it.
SLAMMEKIN: Dear Madam—
TRULL: I would not for the world—
SLAMMEKIN: 'Tis impossible for me—
TRULL: As I hope to be saved, Madam—
SLAMMEKIN: Nay, then I must stay here all night—
TRULL: Since you command me.

[*Exit with great ceremony.*]

Scene 7. Newgate

[*Lockit, Turnkeys,[8] Macheath, Constables*]

LOCKIT: Noble Captain, you are welcome. You have not been a lodger of mine
this year and half. You know the custom, Sir. Garnish,[9] Captain, garnish. Hand
me down those fetters there.

---

6. The bill will be paid.
7. I.e., I deserve the credit for at least three men whom
Peachum has had hanged.

8. Prison guards.
9. Pay the bribe that will secure better treatment and
accommodations.

MACHEATH: Those, Mr. Lockit, seem to be the heaviest of the whole set. With your leave, I should like the further pair better.

LOCKIT: Look ye, Captain, we know what is fittest for our prisoners. When a gentleman uses me with civility, I always do the best I can to please him. Hand them down I say. We have them of all prices, from one guinea to ten, and 'tis fitting every gentleman should please himself.

MACHEATH: I understand you, Sir. [*Gives money.*] The fees here are so many, and so exorbitant, that few fortunes can bear the expense of getting off[1] handsomely, or of dying like a gentleman.

LOCKIT: Those, I see, will fit the Captain better. Take down the further pair. Do but examine them, Sir. Never was better work. How genteelly they are made! They will sit as easy as a glove, and the nicest[2] man in England might not be ashamed to wear them. [*He puts on the chains.*] If I had the best gentleman in the land in my custody I could not equip him more handsomely. And so, Sir, I now leave you to your private meditations.

Scene 8

[*Macheath*]

Air 26. Courtiers, courtiers think it no harm

Man may escape from rope and gun;
Nay, some have outlived the doctor's pill;
Who takes a woman must be undone,
  That basilisk[3] is sure to kill.
The fly that sips treacle is lost in the sweets,
So he that tastes woman, woman, woman,
  He that tastes woman, ruin meets.

To what a woeful plight have I brought myself! Here must I (all day long, till I am hanged) be confined to hear the reproaches of a wench who lays her ruin at my door. I am in the custody of her father, and to be sure, if he knows of the matter, I shall have a fine time on't betwixt this[4] and my execution. But I promised the wench marriage. What signifies a promise to a woman? Does not man in marriage itself promise a hundred things that he never means to perform? Do all we can, women will believe us; for they look upon a promise as an excuse for following their own inclinations. But here comes Lucy, and I cannot get from her. Would I were deaf!

Scene 9

[*Macheath, Lucy*]

LUCY: You base man you. How can you look me in the face after what hath passed between us? See here, perfidious wretch, how I am forced to bear about the load of infamy[5] you have laid upon me. Oh, Macheath! Thou hast robbed me of my quiet! To see thee tortured would give me pleasure.

---

1. Escaping punishment.
2. Most discerning.
3. A mythical serpent which killed by its breath or its

glance.
4. I.e., this moment.
5. I.e., my (visible) pregnancy.

Air 27. A lovely lass to a friar came

Thus when a good housewife sees a rat
In her trap in the morning taken,
With pleasure her heart goes pit a pat,
In revenge for her loss of bacon.
Then she throws him
To the dog or cat,
To be worried, crushed, and shaken.

MACHEATH: Have you no bowels,[6] no tenderness, my dear Lucy, to see a husband in these circumstances?

LUCY: A husband!

MACHEATH: In every respect but the form, and that, my dear, may be said over us at any time. Friends should not insist upon ceremonies. From a man of honor, his word is as good as his bond.

LUCY: 'Tis the pleasure of all you fine men to insult the women you have ruined.

Air 28. 'Twas when the sea was roaring

How cruel are the traitors,
Who lie and swear in jest,
To cheat unguarded creatures
Of virtue, fame, and rest!
Whoever steals a shilling,
Through shame the guilt conceals:
In love the perjured villain
With boasts the theft reveals.

MACHEATH: The very first opportunity, my dear (have but patience), you shall be my wife in whatever manner you please.

LUCY: Insinuating monster! And so you think I know nothing of the affair of Miss Polly Peachum. I could tear thy eyes out!

MACHEATH: Sure Lucy, you can't be such a fool as to be jealous of Polly!

LUCY: Are you not married to her, you brute you?

MACHEATH: Married! Very good. The wench gives it out only to vex thee, and to ruin me in thy good opinion. 'Tis true, I go to the house; I chat with the girl, I kiss her, I say a thousand things to her (as all gentlemen do) that mean nothing, to divert myself. And now the silly jade hath set it about that I am married to her, to let me know what she would be at. Indeed, my dear Lucy, these violent passions may be of ill consequence to a woman in your condition.

LUCY: Come, come, Captain, for all your assurance, you know that Miss Polly hath put it out of your power to do me the justice you promised me.

MACHEATH: A jealous woman believes everything her passion suggests. To convince you of my sincerity, if we can find the Ordinary,[7] I shall have no scruples of making you my wife; and I know the consequence of having two at a time.

LUCY: That you are only to be hanged, and so get rid of them both.

MACHEATH: I am ready, my dear Lucy, to give you satisfaction—if you think there is any in marriage. What can a man of honor say more?

6. Compassion.   7. Prison chaplain.

LUCY: So then, it seems you are not married to Miss Polly.

MACHEATH: You know, Lucy, the girl is prodigiously conceited. No man can say a civil thing to her, but (like other fine ladies) her vanity makes her think he's her own forever and ever.

Air 29. The sun had loosed his weary teams

The first time at the looking glass
The mother sets her daughter,
The image strikes the smiling lass
With self-love ever after.
Each time she looks, she, fonder grown,
Thinks every charm grows stronger.
But alas, vain maid, all eyes but your own
Can see you are not younger.

When women consider their own beauties, they are all alike unreasonable in their demands, for they expect their lovers should like them as long as they like themselves.

LUCY: Yonder is my father—perhaps this way we may light upon the Ordinary, who shall try if[8] you will be as good as your word. For I long to be made an honest woman.

Scene 10

[Peachum, Lockit with an account book]

LOCKIT: In this last affair, Brother Peachum, we are agreed. You have consented to go halves in Macheath.

PEACHUM: We shall never fall out about an execution. But as to that article, pray how stands our last year's account?

LOCKIT: If you will run your eye over it, you'll find 'tis fair and clearly stated.

PEACHUM: This long arrear[9] of the government is very hard upon us! Can it be expected that we should hang our acquaintance for nothing, when our betters will hardly save theirs without being paid for it? Unless the people in employment pay better, I promise them for the future, I shall let other rogues live besides their own.

LOCKIT: Perhaps, Brother, they are afraid these matters may be carried too far. We are treated too by them with contempt, as if our profession were not reputable.

PEACHUM: In one respect, indeed, our employment may be reckoned dishonest, because, like great statesmen, we encourage those who betray their friends.

LOCKIT: Such language, Brother, anywhere else, might turn to your prejudice.[1] Learn to be more guarded, I beg you.

Air 30. How happy are we

When you censure the age,
Be cautious and sage,
Lest the courtiers offended should be:

8. Test whether.   1. Be used against you.
9. Delay in debt payment.

> *If you mention vice or bribe,*
> *'Tis so pat[2] to all the tribe,*
> *Each cries, "That was leveled at me!"*

PEACHUM: Here's poor Ned Clincher's name, I see. Sure, Brother Lockit, there was a little unfair proceeding in Ned's case, for he told me in the condemned hold[3] that for value received, you had promised him a Session or two longer without molestation.

LOCKIT: Mr. Peachum, this is the first time my honor was ever called in question.

PEACHUM: Business is at an end if once we act dishonorably.

LOCKIT: Who accuses me?

PEACHUM: You are warm,[4] Brother.

LOCKIT: He that attacks my honor, attacks my livelihood. And this usage, Sir, is not to be borne.

PEACHUM: Since you provoke me to speak, I must tell you, too, that Mrs. Coaxer charges you with defrauding her of her information money[5] for the apprehending of curl-pated Hugh. Indeed, indeed, Brother, we must punctually pay our spies, or we shall have no information.

LOCKIT: Is this language to me, Sirrah, who have saved you from the gallows, Sirrah!
   [*Collaring each other.*]

PEACHUM: If I am hanged, it shall be for ridding the world of an arrant rascal.

LOCKIT: This hand shall do the office of the halter[6] you deserve, and throttle you—you dog!

PEACHUM: Brother, Brother, we are both in the wrong. We shall be both losers in the dispute—for you know we have it in our power to hang each other. You should not be so passionate.

LOCKIT: Nor you so provoking.

PEACHUM: 'Tis our mutual interest; 'tis for the interest of the world we should agree. If I said anything, Brother, to the prejudice of your character, I ask pardon.

LOCKIT: Brother Peachum, I can forgive as well as resent. Give me your hand. Suspicion does not become a friend.

PEACHUM: I only meant to give you occasion to justify yourself. But I must now step home, for I expect the gentleman about this snuffbox that Filch nimmed two nights ago in the park. I appointed him at this hour.

Scene 11

[*Lockit, Lucy*]

LOCKIT: Whence come you, hussy?

LUCY: My tears might answer that question.

LOCKIT: You have then been whimpering and fondling, like a spaniel, over the fellow that hath abused you.

LUCY: One can't help love; one can't cure it. 'Tis not in my power to obey you, and hate him.

LOCKIT: Learn to bear your husband's death like a reasonable woman. 'Tis not the fashion, nowadays, so much as to affect sorrow upon these occasions. No woman

2. Applicable.
3. I.e., on death row.
4. Angry.

5. Payment for informing on a fellow criminal.
6. Noose.

would ever marry, if she had not the chance of mortality for a release. Act like a woman of spirit, hussy, and thank your father for what he is doing.

Air 31. Of a noble race was Shenkin

LUCY: *Is then his fate decreed, Sir?*
          Such a man can I think of quitting?
          When first we met, so moves me yet,
          Oh, see how my heart is splitting!

LOCKIT: Look ye, Lucy: there is no saving him. So I think you must ev'n do like other widows: buy yourself weeds,[7] and be cheerful.

Air 32.

You'll think ere many days ensue
  This sentence not severe;
I hang your husband, child, 'tis true,
  But with him hang your care.
    Twang dang dillo dee.

Like a good wife, go moan over your dying husband. That, child, is your duty. Consider, girl, you can't have the man and the money too—so make yourself as easy as you can, by getting all you can from him.

Scene 12

[Lucy, Macheath]

LUCY: Though the Ordinary was out of the way today, I hope, my dear, you will, upon the first opportunity, quiet my scruples. Oh, Sir! My father's hard heart is not to be softened, and I am in the utmost despair.

MACHEATH: But if I could raise a small sum—would not twenty guineas, think you, move him? Of all the arguments in the way of business, the perquisite[8] is the most prevailing. Your father's perquisites for the escape of prisoners must amount to a considerable sum in the year. Money well timed, and properly applied, will do anything.

Air 33. London ladies

If you at an office solicit your due,[9]
  And would not have matters neglected,
You must quicken the clerk with the perquisite too,
  To do what his duty directed.
Or would you the frowns of a lady prevent,
  She too has this palpable failing,
The perquisite softens her into consent;
  That reason with all is prevailing.

LUCY: What love or money can do shall be done, for all my comfort depends upon your safety.

---

7. Mourning clothes.   9. Seek the service to which you're entitled.
8. Tip; bribe.

Scene 13

[Lucy, Macheath, Polly]

POLLY: Where is my dear husband? Was a rope ever intended for this neck! Oh, let me throw my arms about it, and throttle thee with love! Why dost thou turn away from me? 'Tis thy Polly! 'Tis thy wife!

MACHEATH: Was ever such an unfortunate rascal as I am!

LUCY: Was there ever such another villain!

POLLY: Oh, Macheath! Was it for this we parted? Taken! Imprisoned! Tried! Hanged! Cruel reflection! I'll stay with thee till death. No force shall tear thy dear wife from thee now. What means my love? Not one kind word! Not one kind look! Think what thy Polly suffers to see thee in this condition.

Air 34. All in the downs

Thus when the swallow, seeking prey,
    Within the sash[1] is closely pent,
His comfort, with bemoaning lay,[2]
    Without sits pining for th' event.[3]
Her chatt'ring lovers all around her skim;
She heeds them not (poor bird!); her soul's with him.

MACHEATH [*aside*]: I must disown her. The wench is distracted.

LUCY: Am I then bilked of my virtue? Can I have no reparation? Sure, men were born to lie, and women to believe them! Oh, villain! Villain!

POLLY: Am I not thy wife? Thy neglect of me, thy aversion to me too severely proves it. Look on me. Tell me: am I not thy wife?

LUCY: Perfidious wretch!

POLLY: Barbarous husband!

LUCY: Hadst thou been hanged five months ago, I had been happy.

POLLY: And I too. If you had been kind to me till death, it would not have vexed me. And that's no very unreasonable request (though from a wife) to a man who hath not above seven or eight days to live.

LUCY: Art thou then married to another? Hast thou two wives, monster?

MACHEATH: If women's tongues can cease for an answer, hear me.

LUCY: I won't. Flesh and blood can't bear my usage.

POLLY: Shall I not claim my own? Justice bids me speak.

Air 35. Have you heard of a frolicsome ditty

MACHEATH:
    How happy could I be with either,
      Were t'other dear charmer away!
    But while you thus tease me together,
      To neither a word will I say;
      But tol de rol, etc.

1. Window frame.   3. Outcome.
2. Plaintive song.

POLLY: Sure, my dear, there ought to be some preference shown to a wife! At least she may claim the appearance of it. He must be distracted with his misfortunes, or he could not use me thus!

LUCY: Oh, villain, villain! Thou hast deceived me. I could even inform against thee with pleasure. Not a prude wishes more heartily to have facts against her intimate acquaintance, than I now wish to have facts against thee. I would have her satisfaction, and they should all out.

Air 36. Irish trot

POLLY: *I'm bubbled.*[4]

LUCY: *I'm bubbled.*

POLLY: *Oh how I am troubled!*

LUCY: *Bamboozled, and bit!*

POLLY: *My distresses are doubled.*

LUCY: *When you come to the tree, should the hangman refuse,*
        These fingers, with pleasure, could fasten the noose.

POLLY: *I'm bubbled, etc.*

MACHEATH: Be pacified, my dear Lucy. This is all a fetch[5] of Polly's, to make me desperate with[6] you in case I get off. If I am hanged, she would fain[7] the credit of being thought my widow. Really, Polly, this is no time for a dispute of this sort; for whenever you are talking of marriage, I am thinking of hanging.

POLLY: And hast thou the heart to persist in disowning me?

MACHEATH: And hast thou the heart to persist in persuading me that I am married? Why, Polly, dost thou seek to aggravate my misfortunes?

LUCY: Really, Miss Peachum, you but expose yourself. Besides, 'tis barbarous in you to worry a gentleman in his circumstances.

Air 37.

POLLY: *Cease your funning;*
                  Force or cunning
          Never shall my heart trapan.[8]
                  All these sallies
                  Are but malice
          To seduce my constant man.
                  'Tis most certain,
                  By their flirting
          Women oft have envy shown;
                  Pleased to ruin
                  Others wooing;
          Never happy in their own!

POLLY: Decency, Madam, methinks might teach you to behave yourself with some reserve with the husband, while his wife is present.

MACHEATH: But seriously, Polly, this is carrying the joke a little too far.

---

4. Cheated, fooled.
5. Trick.
6. I.e., to ruin my hopes of having.

7. Would like.
8. Ensnare.

LUCY: If you are determined, Madam, to raise a disturbance in the prison, I shall be obliged to send for the turnkey to show you the door. I am sorry, Madam, you force me to be so ill-bred.

POLLY: Give me leave to tell you, Madam, these forward airs don't become you in the least, madam. And my duty, Madam, obliges me to stay with my husband, Madam.

Air 38. Good morrow, gossip⁹ Joan

LUCY: *Why how now, Madam Flirt?*
           If you thus must chatter;
         And are for flinging dirt,
             Let's try who best can spatter;
               Madam Flirt!

POLLY: *Why how now, saucy jade;*
             Sure the wench is tipsy!
[To him.] *How can you see me made*
           The scoff of such a gypsy?
[To her]   *Saucy jade!*

Scene 14

[Lucy, Macheath, Polly, Peachum]

PEACHUM: Where's my wench? Ah, hussy! Hussy! Come you home, you slut; and when your fellow is hanged, hang yourself, to make your family some amends.

POLLY: Dear, dear father, do not tear me from him. I must speak; I have more to say to him. Oh! Twist thy fetters about me, that he may not haul me from thee!

PEACHUM: Sure all women are alike! If ever they commit the folly, they are sure to commit another by exposing themselves. Away—not a word more. You are my prisoner now, hussy.

Air 39. Irish howl

POLLY: *No power on earth can e'er divide*
         The knot that sacred love hath tied.
         When parents draw against our mind,
         The true-love's knot they faster bind.
             Oh, oh ray, oh Amborah—oh, oh, etc.

[Holding Macheath, Peachum pulling her.]

Scene 15

[Lucy, Macheath]

MACHEATH: I am naturally compassionate, wife, so that I could not use the wench as she deserved, which made you at first suspect there was something in what she said.

---

9. My friend.

LUCY: Indeed, my dear, I was strangely puzzled.

MACHEATH: If that had been the case, her father would never have brought me into this circumstance. No, Lucy, I had rather die than be false to thee.

LUCY: How happy am I, if you say this from your heart! For I love thee so, that I could sooner bear to see thee hanged than in the arms of another.

MACHEATH: But couldst thou bear to see me hanged?

LUCY: Oh, Macheath, I can never live to see that day.

MACHEATH: You see, Lucy, in the account of love you are in my debt, and you must now be convinced, that I rather choose to die than be another's. Make me, if possible, love thee more, and let me owe my life to thee. If you refuse to assist me, Peachum and your father will immediately put me beyond all means of escape.

LUCY: My father, I know, hath been drinking hard with the prisoners, and I fancy he is now taking his nap in his own room. If I can procure the keys, shall I go off with thee, my dear?

MACHEATH: If we are together, 'twill be impossible to lie concealed. As soon as the search begins to be a little cool, I will send to thee. Till then my heart is thy prisoner.

LUCY: Come then, my dear husband, owe thy life to me, and though you love me not, be grateful. But that Polly runs in my head strangely.

MACHEATH: A moment of time may make us unhappy forever.

Air 40. The lass of Patie's mill

LUCY: *I like the fox shall grieve,*
        Whose mate hath left her side.
    Whom hounds, from morn to eve,
        Chase o'er the country wide.
    Where can my lover hide?
        Where cheat the weary pack?
    If love be not his guide,
        He never will come back!

ACT 3

Scene 1. Newgate

[Lockit, Lucy]

LOCKIT: To be sure, wench, you must have been aiding and abetting to help him to this escape.

LUCY: Sir, here hath been Peachum and his daughter Polly, and to be sure they know the ways of Newgate as well as if they had been born and bred in the place all their lives. Why must all your suspicion light upon me?

LOCKIT: Lucy, Lucy, I will have none of these shuffling answers.

LUCY: Well then, if I know anything of him I wish I may be burnt!

LOCKIT: Keep your temper, Lucy, or I shall pronounce you guilty.

LUCY: Keep yours, Sir. I do wish I may be burnt. I do. And what can I say more to convince you?

LOCKIT: Did he tip handsomely? How much did he come down with? Come hussy, don't cheat your father, and I shall not be angry with you. Perhaps you have made a better bargain with him than I could have done. How much, my good girl?

LUCY: You know, Sir, I am fond of him, and would have given money to have kept him with me.

LOCKIT: Ah, Lucy! Thy education might have put thee more upon thy guard; for a girl in the bar of an alehouse is always besieged.

LUCY: Dear Sir, mention not my education—for 'twas to that I owe my ruin.

Air 41. If love's a sweet passion

When young at the bar you first taught me to score,[1]
And bid me be free of my lips, and no more,
I was kissed by the parson, the squire, and the sot;
When the guest was departed, the kiss was forgot.
But his kiss was so sweet, and so closely he pressed,
That I languished and pined till I granted the rest.

If you can forgive me, Sir, I will make a fair confession, for to be sure he hath been a most barbarous villain to me.

LOCKIT: And so you have let him escape, hussy? Have you?

LUCY: When a woman loves, a kind look, a tender word can persuade her to anything. And I could ask no other bribe.

LOCKIT: Thou wilt always be a vulgar[2] slut, Lucy. If you would not be looked upon as a fool, you should never do anything but upon the foot[3] of interest. Those that act otherwise are their own bubbles.[4]

LUCY: But love; Sir, is a misfortune that may happen to the most discreet woman, and in love we are all fools alike. Notwithstanding all he swore, I am now fully convinced that Polly Peachum is actually his wife. Did I let him escape (fool that I was!) to go to her? Polly will wheedle herself into his money, and then Peachum will hang him, and cheat us both.

LOCKIT: So I am to be ruined, because, forsooth, you must be in love! A very pretty excuse!

LUCY: I could murder that impudent happy strumpet. I gave him his life, and that creature enjoys the sweets of it. Ungrateful Macheath!

Air 42. South Sea Ballad

My love is all madness and folly,
*   Alone I lie,*
*   Toss, tumble, and cry,*
What a happy creature is Polly!
Was e'er such a wretch as I!
With rage I redden like scarlet,
That my dear inconstant varlet,
*   Stark blind to my charms,*
*   Is lost in the arms*
Of that jilt, that inveigling harlot!
*   Stark blind to my charms,*
*   Is lost in the arms*

---

1. To keep track of the debts incurred by customers.
2. Common.
3. Basis.
4. I.e., cheat themselves.

> *Of that jilt, that inveigling harlot!*
> *This, this my resentment alarms.*

LOCKIT: And so, after all this mischief, I must stay here to be entertained with your caterwauling, Mistress Puss! Out of my sight, wanton strumpet! You shall fast and mortify yourself into reason, with now and then a little handsome discipline[5] to bring you to your senses. Go.

Scene 2

[*Lockit*]

Peachum then intends to outwit me in this affair, but I'll be even with him. The dog is leaky in his liquor,[6] so I'll ply him that way, get the secret from him, and turn this affair to my own advantage. Lions, wolves, and vultures don't live together in herds, droves, or flocks. Of all animals of prey, man is the only sociable one. Every one of us preys upon his neighbor, and yet we herd together. Peachum is my companion, my friend. According to the custom of the world, indeed, he may quote thousands of precedents for cheating me. And shall not I make use of the privilege of friendship to make him a return?

Air 43. Packington's Pound

> *Thus gamesters united in friendship are found,*
> *Though they know that their industry all is a cheat;*
> *They flock to their prey at the dice-box's sound,*
> *And join to promote one another's deceit.*
> > *But if by mishap*
> > *They fail of a chap,[7]*
> *To keep in their hands, they each other entrap.*
> *Like pikes, lank with hunger, who miss of their ends,[8]*
> *They bite their companions, and prey on their friends.*

Now, Peachum, you and I, like honest tradesmen, are to have a fair trial which of us two can over-reach the other. Lucy! [*Enter Lucy.*] Are there any of Peachum's people now in the house?

LUCY: Filch, Sir, is drinking a quartern[9] of strong waters in the next room with Black Moll.

LOCKIT: Bid him come to me.

Scene 3

[*Lockit, Filch*]

LOCKIT: Why, boy, thou lookest as if thou wert half starved, like a shotten herring.[1]

FILCH: One had need have the constitution of a horse to go through the business. Since the favorite child-getter[2] was disabled by a mishap, I have picked up a little

---

5. Beating.
6. Talkative when drunk.
7. Can't drum up someone to dupe.
8. I.e., fail to catch their prey.

9. Quarter-pint.
1. A herring that has spawned.
2. Begetter (i.e., Macheath).

money by helping the ladies to a pregnancy against their being called down to sentence.[3] But if a man cannot get an honest livelihood any easier way, I am sure 'tis what I can't undertake for another session.

LOCKIT: Truly, if that great man should tip off,[4] 'twould be an irreparable loss. The vigor and prowess of a knight-errant never saved half the ladies in distress that he hath done. But, boy, can'st thou tell me where thy master is to be found?

FILCH: At his lock,[5] Sir, at the Crooked Billet.

LOCKIT: Very well. I have nothing more with you.

[Exit Filch.]

I'll go to him there, for I have many important affairs to settle with him; and in the way of those transactions, I'll artfully get into his secret. So that Macheath shall not remain a day longer out of my clutches.

Scene 4. A Gaming House

[Macheath in a fine tarnished[6] coat, Ben Budge, Matt of the Mint]

MACHEATH: I am sorry, gentlemen, the road was so barren of money. When my friends are in difficulties, I am always glad that my fortune can be serviceable to them. [Gives them money.] You see, gentlemen, I am not a mere court friend, who professes everything and will do nothing.

Air 44. Lillibullero

The modes of the court so common are grown,
    That a true friend can hardly be met;
Friendship for interest is but a loan,
    Which they let out for what they can get.
        'Tis true, you find
        Some friends so kind,
Who will give you good counsel themselves to defend.
        In sorrowful ditty,
        They promise, they pity,
But shift you for money,[7] from friend to friend.

But we, gentlemen, have still honor enough to break through the corruptions of the world. And while I can serve you, you may command me.

BEN: It grieves my heart that so generous a man should be involved in such difficulties as oblige him to live with such ill company, and herd with gamesters.

MATT: See the partiality of mankind! One man may steal a horse, better than another look over a hedge.[8] Of all mechanics,[9] of all servile handicraftsmen, a gamester is the vilest. But yet, as many of the quality[1] are of the profession, he is admitted amongst the politest company. I wonder we are not more respected.

---

3. I.e., to safeguard them from hanging (because pregnant women could not be condemned to execution).
4. Die.
5. A cant word signifying a warehouse where stolen goods are deposited [Gay's note].
6. Discolored.

7. Put you off.
8. I.e., one man is permitted to steal a horse, though another is not permitted even to look at one (proverbial).
9. Manual workers.
1. Gentry; people of high standing.

MACHEATH: There will be deep play[2] tonight at Marybone, and consequently money may be picked up upon the road. Meet me there, and I'll give you the hint who is worth setting.[3]

MATT: The fellow with a brown coat with a narrow gold binding, I am told, is never without money.

MACHEATH: What do you mean, Matt? Sure you will not think of meddling with him! He's a good honest kind of a fellow, and one of us.

BEN: To be sure, Sir, we will put ourselves under your direction.

MACHEATH: Have an eye upon the money-lenders. A rouleau[4] or two would prove a pretty sort of an expedition. I hate extortion.

MATT: Those rouleaus are very pretty things. I hate your bank bills. There is such a hazard in putting them off.[5]

MACHEATH: There is a certain man of distinction, who in his time hath nicked me out of a great deal of the ready.[6] He is in my cash,[7] Ben. I'll point him out to you this evening, and you shall draw upon him for the debt. The company are met; I hear the dice-box in the other room. So, gentlemen, your servant. You'll meet me at Marybone.

Scene 5. Peachum's Lock

[A table with wine, brandy, pipes and tobacco. Peachum, Lockit]

LOCKIT: The Coronation account,[8] Brother Peachum, is of so intricate a nature, that I believe it will never be settled.

PEACHUM: It consists indeed of a great variety of articles. It was worth to our people, in fees of different kinds, above ten installments.[9] This is part of the account, Brother, that lies open before us.

LOCKIT: A lady's tail[1] of rich brocade—that, I see, is disposed of.

PEACHUM: To Mrs. Diana Trapes, the tallywoman;[2] and she will make a good hand[3] on't in shoes and slippers, to trick out young ladies, upon their going into keeping.

LOCKIT: But I don't see any article of the jewels.

PEACHUM: Those are so well known, that they must be sent abroad. You'll find them entered under the article of exportation. As for the snuffboxes, watches, swords, etc., I thought it best to enter them under their several heads.

LOCKIT: Seven and twenty women's pockets[4] complete, with the several things therein contained, all sealed, numbered, and entered.

PEACHUM: But, Brother, it is impossible for us now to enter upon this affair. We should have the whole day before us. Besides, the account of the last half year's plate is in a book by itself, which lies at the other office.

LOCKIT: Bring us then more liquor. Today shall be for pleasure, tomorrow for business. Ah, Brother, those daughters of ours are two slippery hussies. Keep a watchful eye upon Polly, and Macheath in a day or two shall be our own again.

---

2. Gambling for high stakes.
3. Setting upon; robbing.
4. A packet of gold coins.
5. Getting rid of them; passing them off.
6. I.e., ready money; cash.
7. Debt.
8. A manuscript inventory of items stolen during the coronation of George II. Peachum "keeps books" like an ordinary businessman.

9. I.e., the thieves have found a single coronation more than ten times as profitable as the annual installment of the new Lord Mayor.
1. Train (of a woman's dress).
2. One who provides goods on credit.
3. Profit.
4. A pocket was a detachable bag worn outside a woman's dress.

Air 45. Down in the north country

LOCKIT: *What gudgeons⁵ are we men!*
Ev'ry woman's easy prey.
Though we have felt the hook, again
We bite and they betray.

The bird that hath been trapped,
When he hears his calling mate,
To her he flies, again he's clapped
Within the wiry grate.

PEACHUM: But what signifies catching the bird, if your daughter Lucy will set open the door of the cage?

LOCKIT: If men were answerable for the follies and frailties of their wives and daughters, no friends could keep a good correspondence together for two days. This is unkind of you, Brother; for among good friends, what they say or do goes for nothing.

[*Enter a servant.*]

SERVANT: Sir, here's Mrs. Diana Trapes wants to speak with you.

PEACHUM: Shall we admit her, Brother Lockit?

LOCKIT: By all means. She's a good customer, and a fine-spoken woman. And a woman who drinks and talks so freely will enliven the conversation.

PEACHUM: Desire her to walk in.

[*Exit servant.*]

Scene 6

Peachum, Lockit, Mrs. Trapes.

PEACHUM: Dear Mrs. Di, your servant. One may know by your kiss that your gin is excellent.

TRAPES: I was always very curious⁶ in my liquors.

LOCKIT: There is no perfumed breath like it. I have been long acquainted with the flavor of those lips, han't I, Mrs. Di?

TRAPES: Fill it up. I take as large draughts of liquor as I did of love. I hate a flincher⁷ in either.

Air 46. A shepherd kept sheep

In the days of my youth I could bill like a dove, fa, la, la, etc.
Like a sparrow at all times was ready for love, fa, la, la, etc.
The life of all mortals in kissing should pass,
Lip to lip while we're young—then the lip to the glass, fa, la, la, etc.

But now, Mr. Peachum, to our business. If you have blacks⁸ of any kind, brought in of late: mantoes,⁹ velvet scarves, petticoats—let it be what it will—I am your chap,¹ for all my ladies are very fond of mourning.

---

5. "A small fish . . . easily caught, and therefore made a proverbial name for a man easily cheated" (Johnson's *Dictionary*).
6. Choosy.

7. One who resists or refrains.
8. Black clothing.
9. Loose robes (French: *manteaux*).
1. Customer.

PEACHUM: Why, look ye, Mrs. Di, you deal so hard with us that we can afford to give the gentlemen, who venture their lives for the goods, little or nothing.

TRAPES: The hard times oblige me to go very near[2] in my dealing. To be sure, of late years I have been a great sufferer by the Parliament. Three thousand pounds would hardly make me amends. The Act for destroying the Mint[3] was a severe cut upon our business. Till then, if a customer[4] stepped out of the way, we knew where to have her. No doubt you know Mrs. Coaxer; there's a wench now (till today) with a good suit of clothes of mine upon her back, and I could never set eyes upon her for three months together. Since the Act too against imprisonment for small sums,[5] my loss there too hath been very considerable, and it must be so, when a lady can borrow a handsome petticoat, or a clean gown, and I not have the least hank[6] upon her! And, o' my conscience, nowadays most ladies take a delight in cheating, when they can do it with safety.

PEACHUM: Madam, you had a handsome gold watch of us t'other day for seven guineas. Considering we must have our profit, to a gentleman upon the road, a gold watch will be scarce worth the taking.

TRAPES: Consider, Mr. Peachum, that watch was remarkable, and not of very safe sale. If you have any black velvet scarves, they are a handsome winter-wear; and take with most gentlemen who deal with my customers. 'Tis I that put the ladies upon a good foot. 'Tis not youth or beauty that fixes their price. The gentlemen always pay according to their dress, from half a crown to two guineas; and yet those hussies make[7] nothing of bilking of me. Then too, allowing for accidents—I have eleven fine customers now down under the surgeon's hands[8]—what with fees and other expenses, there are great goings-out, and no comings-in, and not a farthing to pay for at least a month's clothing. We run great risks—great risks indeed.

PEACHUM: As I remember, you said something just now of Mrs. Coaxer.

TRAPES: Yes, Sir. To be sure I stripped her of a suit of my own clothes about two hours ago; and have left her as she should be, in her shift, with a lover of hers at my house. She called him upstairs, as he was going to Marybone in a hackney coach. And I hope, for her own sake and mine, she will persuade the Captain to redeem[9] her, for the Captain is very generous to the ladies.

LOCKIT: What Captain?

TRAPES: He thought I did not know him. An intimate acquaintance of yours, Mr. Peachum. Only Captain Macheath—as fine as a lord.

PEACHUM: Tomorrow, dear Mrs. Di, you shall set your own price upon any of the goods you like. We have at least half a dozen velvet scarves, and all at your service. Will you give me leave to make you a present of this suit of nightclothes for your own wearing? But are you sure it is Captain Macheath?

TRAPES: Though he thinks I have forgot him, nobody knows him better. I have taken a great deal of the Captain's money in my time at second hand, for he always loved to have his ladies well dressed.

PEACHUM: Mr. Lockit and I have a little business with the Captain—you understand me—and we will satisfy you for Mrs. Coaxer's debt.

---

2. To pay as little as possible.
3. The Mint was a safe haven for debtors, and hence a gathering place for disreputable characters. The Act (10 October 1723) made it much harder to feign bankruptcy, and thereby to take safe refuge in the Mint.
4. Prostitute.
5. "An Act to Prevent Frivolous and Vexatious Arrests"

(24 June 1726); in a Superior Court matter, "small sums" meant 10 pounds; in an Inferior, 40 shillings.
6. Hold.
7. Think.
8. For treatment of venereal disease.
9. I.e., will help her to buy back (as at a pawn shop) her "suit of . . . clothes."

LOCKIT: Depend upon it: we will deal like men of honor.

TRAPES: I don't inquire after your affairs; so whatever happens, I wash my hands on't. It hath always been my maxim that one friend should assist another. But if you please, I'll take one of the scarves home with me. 'Tis always good to have something in hand.

Scene 7. Newgate

[Lucy]

LUCY: Jealousy, rage, love, and fear are at once tearing me to pieces. How I am weather-beaten and shattered with distresses!

Air 47. One evening, having lost my way

> *I'm like a skiff on the ocean tossed,*
> *Now high, now low, with each billow born,*
> *With her rudder broke, and her anchor lost,*
> *Deserted and all forlorn.*
> *While thus I lie rolling and tossing all night,*
> *That Polly lies sporting on seas of delight!*
> *Revenge, revenge, revenge,*
> *Shall appease my restless sprite.*

I have the ratsbane[1] ready. I run no risk, for I can lay her death upon the gin, and so many die of that naturally that I shall never be called in question. But, say I were to be hanged, I never could be hanged for anything that would give me greater comfort than the poisoning that slut.

[Enter Filch.]

FILCH: Madam, here's our Miss Polly come to wait upon you.

LUCY: Show her in.

Scene 8

[Lucy, Polly]

LUCY: Dear madam, your servant. I hope you will pardon my passion, when I was so happy to see you last. I was so overrun with the spleen[2] that I was perfectly out of myself. And really, when one hath the spleen, everything is to be excused by a friend.

Air 48. Now Roger, I'll tell thee, because thou'rt my son

> *When a wife's in her pout,*
> *(As she's sometimes, no doubt!)*
> *The good husband as meek as a lamb,*
> *Her vapors to still,*
> *First grants her her will,*
> *And the quieting draught is a dram.[3]*
> *Poor man! And the quieting draught is a dram.*

---

1. Rat poison.
2. Generally, ill temper; more specifically, a fashionable disease resembling hypochondria, also known as "the vapors."
3. A shot of alcohol.

I wish all our quarrels might have so comfortable a reconciliation.

POLLY: I have no excuse for my own behavior, Madam, but my misfortunes. And really, Madam, I suffer too upon your account.

LUCY: But, Miss Polly, in the way of friendship, will you give me leave to propose a glass of cordial to you?

POLLY: Strong waters are apt to give me the headache. I hope, Madam, you will excuse me.

LUCY: Not the greatest lady in the land could have better in her closet, for her own private drinking. You seem mighty low in spirits, my dear.

POLLY: I am sorry, Madam, my health will not allow me to accept of your offer. I should not have left you in the rude manner I did when we met last, Madam, had not my papa hauled me away so unexpectedly. I was indeed somewhat provoked, and perhaps might use some expressions that were disrespectful. But really, Madam, the Captain treated me with so much contempt and cruelty that I deserved your pity rather than your resentment.

LUCY: But since his escape, no doubt all matters are made up again. Ah Polly! Polly! 'Tis I am the unhappy wife; and he loves you as if you were only his mistress.

POLLY: Sure, Madam, you cannot think me so happy as to be the object of your jealousy. A man is always afraid of a woman who loves him too well—so that I must expect to be neglected and avoided.

LUCY: Then our cases, my dear Polly, are exactly alike. Both of us indeed have been too fond.

Air 49. Oh, Bessy Bell

POLLY: *A curse attends that woman's love,*
    Who always would be pleasing.

LUCY: *The pertness of the billing dove,*
    Like tickling, is but teasing.

POLLY: *What then in love can woman do?*

LUCY: *If we grow fond they shun us.*

POLLY: *And when we fly them, they pursue.*

LUCY: *But leave us when they've won us.*

LUCY: Love is so very whimsical in both sexes that it is impossible to be lasting. But my heart is particular,[4] and contradicts my own observation.

POLLY: But really, Mistress Lucy, by his last behavior, I think I ought to envy you. When I was forced from him, he did not show the least tenderness. But perhaps he hath a heart not capable of it.

Air 50. Would fate to me Belinda give

Among the men, coquettes we find,
Who court by turns all womankind;
And we grant all their hearts desired,
When they are flattered, and admired.

---

4. In two senses: (1) preoccupied with one person (Macheath), and therefore (2) idiosyncratic—an exception to the rule she has just pronounced.

The coquettes of both sexes are self-lovers, and that is a love no other whatever can dispossess. I fear, my dear Lucy, our husband is one of those.

LUCY: Away with these melancholy reflections. Indeed, my dear Polly, we are both of us a cup too low.[5] Let me prevail upon you to accept of my offer.

Air 51. Come, sweet lass

> Come, sweet lass,
> Lets banish sorrow
> Till tomorrow;
> Come, sweet lass,
> Let's take a chirping[6] glass.
> Wine can clear
> The vapors of despair;
> And make us light as air;
> Then drink, and banish care.

I can't bear, child, to see you in such low spirits. And I must persuade you to what I know will do you good. [*Aside.*] I shall now soon be even with the hypocritical strumpet.

Scene 9

[Polly]

POLLY: All this wheedling of Lucy cannot be for nothing. At this time too! When I know she hates me! The dissembling of a woman is always the forerunner of mischief. By pouring strong waters down my throat, she thinks to pump some secrets out of me. I'll be upon my guard, and won't taste a drop of her liquor, I'm resolved.

Scene 10

[Lucy, with strong waters; Polly]

LUCY: Come, Miss Polly.

POLLY: Indeed, child, you have given yourself trouble to no purpose. You must, my dear, excuse me.

LUCY: Really, Miss Polly, you are so squeamishly affected about taking a cup of strong waters as a lady before company. I vow, Polly, I shall take it monstrously ill if you refuse me. Brandy and men (though women love them never so well)[7] are always taken by us with some reluctance—unless 'tis in private.

POLLY: I protest, Madam, it goes against me. What do I see! Macheath again in custody! Now every glimmering of happiness is lost.

[*Drops the glass of liquor on the ground.*]

LUCY: Since things are thus, I'm glad the wench hath escaped; for by this event, 'tis plain, she was not happy enough to deserve to be poisoned.

---

5. I.e., we both need a drink.
6. Cheering.

7. However much women may love them.

Scene 11

[Lockit, Macheath, Peachum, Lucy, Polly]

LOCKIT: Set your heart to rest, Captain. You have neither the chance of love or money for another escape, for you are ordered to be called down upon your trial immediately.

PEACHUM: Away, hussies! This is not a time for a man to be hampered with his wives. You see, the gentleman is in chains already.

LUCY: Oh, husband, husband, my heart longed to see thee. But to see thee thus distracts me!

POLLY: Will not my dear husband look upon his Polly? Why hadst thou not flown to me for protection? With me thou hadst been safe.

Air 52. The last time I went o'er the moor

POLLY: *Hither, dear husband, turn your eyes.*
LUCY: *Bestow one glance to cheer me.*
POLLY: *Think with that look, thy Polly dies.*
LUCY: *Oh, shun me not—but hear me.*
POLLY: *'Tis Polly sues.*
LUCY: *'Tis Lucy speaks.*
POLLY: *Is thus true love requited?*
LUCY: *My heart is bursting.*
POLLY: *Mine too breaks.*
LUCY: *Must I—*
POLLY: *Must I be slighted?*

MACHEATH: What would you have me say, ladies? You see this affair will soon be at an end, without my disobliging either of you.

PEACHUM: But the settling this point, Captain, might prevent a lawsuit between your two widows.

Air 53. Tom Tinker's my true love

MACHEATH: *Which way shall I turn me? How can I decide?*
    Wives, the day of our death, are as fond as a bride.
    One wife is too much for most husbands to hear,
    But two at a time there's no mortal can bear.
    This way, and that way, and which way I will,
    What would comfort the one, t'other wife would take ill.

POLLY: But if his own misfortunes have made him insensible to mine, a father sure will be more compassionate. Dear, dear Sir, sink[8] the material evidence, and bring him off at his trial—Polly upon her knees begs it of you.[9]

Air 54. I am a poor shepherd undone

When my hero in court appears,
    And stands arraigned for his life;

---

8. Suppress.   9. This is the moment Hogarth painted; see Color plate 26.

> Then think of poor Polly's tears;
>   For Ah! Poor Polly's his wife.
> Like the sailor he holds up his hand,
>   Distressed on the dashing wave.
> To die a dry death at land,
>   Is as bad as a watery grave.
> And alas, poor Polly!
> Alack, and well-a-day!
> Before I was in love,
>   Oh! Every month was May.

LUCY: If Peachum's heart is hardened, sure you, Sir, will have more compassion on a daughter. I know the evidence is in your power. How then can you be a tyrant to me?
[Kneeling.]

Air 55. Ianthe the lovely

> When he holds up his hand arraigned for his life,
> Oh, think of your daughter, and think I'm his wife!
> What are cannons, or bombs, or clashing of swords?
> For death is more certain by witnesses' words.
> Then nail up their lips; that dread thunder allay;
> And each month of my life will hereafter be May.

LOCKIT: Macheath's time is come, Lucy. We know our own affairs; therefore let us have no more whimpering or whining.

Air 56. A cobbler there was

> Ourselves, like the great, to secure a retreat,
> When matters require it, must give up our gang:
>   And good reason why,
>   Or, instead of the fry,[1]
>   Ev'n Peachum and I,
> Like poor petty rascals, might hang, hang;
> Like poor petty rascals, might hang.

PEACHUM: Set your heart at rest, Polly. Your husband is to die today. Therefore, if you are not already provided, 'tis high time to look about for another. There's comfort for you, you slut.
LOCKIT: We are ready, Sir, to conduct you to the Old Bailey.

Air 57. Bonny Dundee

MACHEATH: *The charge is prepared; the lawyers are met,*
The judges all ranged; (a terrible show!).
I go undismayed, for death is a debt,
A debt on demand, so take what I owe.

---

1. Small fish.

Then farewell, my love. Dear charmers, adieu.
Contented I die. 'Tis the better for you.
Here ends all dispute the rest of our lives.
For this way at once I please all my wives.

Now, gentlemen, I am ready to attend you.

Scene 12

[*Lucy, Polly, Filch*]

POLLY: Follow them, Filch, to the court. And when the trial is over, bring me a particular account of his behavior, and of everything that happened. You'll find me here with Miss Lucy. [*Exit Filch.*] But why is all this music?

LUCY: The prisoners, whose trials are put off till next session, are diverting themselves.

POLLY: Sure, there is nothing so charming as music! I'm fond of it to distraction! But alas! Now all mirth seems an insult upon my affliction. Let us retire, my dear Lucy, and indulge our sorrows. The noisy crew, you see, are coming upon us.

[*Exeunt.*]

[*A dance of prisoners in chains.*]

Scene 13. The Condemned Hold

[*Macheath, in a melancholy posture.*]

Air 58. Happy groves

O cruel, cruel, cruel case!
Must I suffer this disgrace?

Air 59. Of all the girls that are so smart

Of all the friends in time of grief,
When threatning death looks grimmer,
Not one so sure can bring relief,
As this best friend, a brimmer.[2]

[*Drinks.*]

Air 60. Britons strike home

Since I must swing, I scorn, I scorn to wince or whine.

[*Rises.*]

Air 61. Chevy Chase

But now again my spirits sink;
I'll raise them high with wine.

[*Drinks a glass of wine.*]

2. A cup filled to the brim.

Air 62. To old Sir Simon the King

But valor the stronger grows,
The stronger liquor we're drinking.
And how can we feel our woes,
When we've lost the trouble of thinking?

[*Drinks.*]

Air 63. Joy to great Cæsar

If thus—a man can die
Much bolder with brandy.

[*Pours out a bumper of brandy.*]

Air 64. There was an old woman

So I drink off this bumper. And now I can stand the test.
And my comrades shall see, that I die as brave as the best.

[*Drinks.*]

Air 65. Did you ever hear of a gallant sailor

But can I leave my pretty hussies,
Without one tear, or tender sigh?

Air 66. Why are mine eyes still flowing

Their eyes, their lips, their busses[3]
Recall my love. Ah, must I die?

Air 67. Greensleeves

Since laws were made for ev'ry degree,
   To curb vice in others, as well as me,
   I wonder we han't better company,
      Upon Tyburn tree!
   But gold from law can take out the sting;
   And if rich men like us were to swing,
   'Twou'd thin the land, such numbers to string
      Upon Tyburn tree!

[*Enter a Jailer.*]

JAILER: Some friends of yours, Captain, desire to be admitted. I leave you
   together.

---

3. Kisses.

Scene 14

[Macheath, Ben Budge, Matt of the Mint]

MACHEATH: For my having broke[4] prison, you see, gentlemen, I am ordered immediate execution. The sheriff's officers, I believe, are now at the door. That Jemmy Twitcher should peach me, I own surprised me! 'Tis a plain proof that the world is all alike, and that even our gang can no more trust one another than other people. Therefore, I beg you, gentlemen, look well to yourselves, for in all probability you may live some months longer.

MATT: We are heartily sorry, Captain, for your misfortune. But 'tis what we must all come to.

MACHEATH: Peachum and Lockit, you know, are infamous scoundrels. Their lives are as much in your power, as yours are in theirs. Remember your dying friend. 'Tis my last request. Bring those villains to the gallows before you, and I am satisfied.

MATT: We'll do't.

JAILER: Miss Polly and Miss Lucy entreat a word with you.

MACHEATH: Gentlemen, adieu.

Scene 15

[Lucy, Macheath, Polly]

MACHEATH: My dear Lucy—my dear Polly—whatsoever hath passed between us is now at an end. If you are fond of marrying again, the best advice I can give you is to ship yourselves off for the West Indies, where you'll have a fair chance of getting a husband apiece; or by good luck, two or three, as you like best.

POLLY: How can I support this sight!

LUCY: There is nothing moves one so much as a great man in distress.

Air 68. All you that must take a leap

LUCY: *Would I might be hanged!*

POLLY: *And I would so too!*

LUCY: *To be hanged with you.*

POLLY: *My dear, with you.*

MACHEATH: *Oh, leave me to thought! I fear! I doubt!*
           I tremble! I droop!—See, my courage is out. [*Turns up the empty bottle.*]

POLLY: *No token of love?*

MACHEATH: *See, my courage is out.*   [*Turns up the empty pot.*]

LUCY: *No token of love?*

POLLY: *Adieu!*

LUCY: *Farewell!*

MACHEATH: *But hark! I hear the toll of the bell.*

CHORUS: *Tol de rol lol, etc.*

     [*Enter the Jailer.*]

JAILER: Four women more, Captain, with a child apiece! See, here they come.
     [*Enter women and children.*]

4. Escaped.

MACHEATH: What—four wives more! This is too much. Here—tell the sheriff's officers I am ready.

[*Exit Macheath guarded.*]

Scene 16

[*To them, enter Player and Beggar.*]

PLAYER: But, honest friend, I hope you don't intend that Macheath shall be really executed.

BEGGAR: Most certainly, Sir. To make the piece perfect, I was for doing strict poetical justice. Macheath is to be hanged; and for the other personages of the drama, the audience must have supposed they were all either hanged or transported.

PLAYER: Why then, friend, this is a downright deep tragedy. The catastrophe is manifestly wrong, for an opera must end happily.

BEGGAR: Your objection, Sir, is very just, and is easily removed. For you must allow, that in this kind of drama, 'tis no matter how absurdly things are brought about. So—you rabble there—run and cry a reprieve. Let the prisoner be brought back to his wives in triumph.

PLAYER: All this we must do, to comply with the taste of the town.[5]

BEGGAR: Through the whole piece you may observe such a similitude of manners in high and low life, that it is difficult to determine whether (in the fashionable vices) the fine gentlemen imitate the gentlemen of the road, or the gentlemen of the road the fine gentlemen. Had the play remained as I at first intended, it would have carried a most excellent moral. 'Twould have shown that the lower sort of people have their vices in a degree as well as the rich—and that they are punished for them.

Scene 17

[*To them, Macheath with rabble, etc.*]

MACHEATH: So, it seems, I am not left to my choice, but must have a wife at last. Look ye, my dears, we will have no controversy now. Let us give this day to mirth, and I am sure she who thinks herself my wife will testify her joy by a dance.

ALL: Come, a dance, a dance.

MACHEATH: Ladies, I hope you will give me leave to present a partner to each of you. And (if I may without offense) for this time, I take Polly for mine. [*To Polly.*] And for life, you slut—for we were really married. As for the rest—but at present keep your own secret.

A Dance

Air 69. Lumps of pudding

Thus I stand like the Turk, with his doxies around;[6]
From all sides their glances his passion confound;
For black, brown, and fair, his inconstancy burns,

---

5. Fashionable London society.   6. Like a sultan in a harem.

And the different beauties subdue him by turns:
Each calls forth her charms, to provoke his desires:
Though willing to all, with but one he retires.
But think of this maxim, and put off your sorrow,
The wretch of today may be happy tomorrow.

CHORUS: *But think of this maxim, etc.*

FINIS.

1727   1728

For companion readings on *The Beggar's Opera* and its time, including texts by D'Urfey, Defoe, Fielding, and others, go to *The Longman Anthology of British Literature* Web site at www.myliteraturekit.com.

William Hogarth
1697–1764

"I had naturally a good eye," William Hogarth remembered near his life's end. "Shows of all sorts gave me uncommon pleasure when an infant." The "shows" (spectacles) that filled his eye in the turbulent London neighborhood of Smithfield where he grew up suffused his art for life: the antics of actors and the raucousness of audiences at Bartholomew Fair; the chicanery and pathos of prostitutes and thieves; the casual injustice of constables and magistrates. Above all, he watched his father fail. Richard Hogarth, a classical scholar, spent four years as a prisoner for debt, when his coffeehouse (catering to learned men and specializing in Latin conversation) failed to cover its own expenses. The debtor's family was effectually imprisoned too, and Hogarth, in his early teens during the ordeal, never forgot. "The emphasis throughout his work" (notes his biographer Ronald Paulson) "is on prisons, real and metaphorical. Even when he is not dealing with people who are in a prison . . . he portrays rooms that are more like prison cells than boudoirs or parlors."

At age seventeen, Hogarth was apprenticed to a silver engraver, ornamenting platters, rings, tableware, and the like. Finding the work dull, he switched to copper engraving, the technique by which book illustrators and printmakers created and reproduced their pictures. Late in his twenties he commenced his career as painter. His first great successes combined both craft and art. Hogarth produced the series of six pictures that make up *A Harlot's Progress* first as a set of paintings in oil, then as a sequence of copper engravings aimed at wider distribution. If *A Harlot's Progress* launched his popularity, *A Rake's Progress* (engraved in 1735 from canvases painted the year before) clinched his reputation as Britain's most masterly, mocking delineator of contemporary vice and folly. Though he continued for a while to nurture conventional ambitions as a painter of portraits and historical subjects catering to aristocratic tastes, Hogarth came gradually to recognize the originality, force, and commercial viability of his satrical engravings. As he later expressed it (in his own idiosyncratic syntax), he had discovered a style pitched between "the sublime and the grotesque," and had devised "a more new way of proceeding, viz. painting and engraving modern moral subjects, a field unbroke up in any country or any age. . . . Provided I could strike the passions, and by small sums from many, by means of prints which I could engrave from my pictures myself, I could secure my property to myself." Hogarth managed to "strike the passions" both ways: by depicting them vividly in the countenance of his characters, and by igniting them in his audience. He also managed, better than any predecessor, to "secure his property to himself." He petitioned Parliament to pass the Engraver's Copyright Act (often called "Hogarth's Act"), which protected printmakers from the then rampant piratical reproduction of their work, and which thereby (in Hogarth's proud words) "made prints a considerable article and trade in this country, there being more business of that kind done in this town than in Paris or anywhere else." The engravings of A Rake's Progress were first published, pointedly, the day after Hogarth's Act became the law of the land.

Early in his career, Hogarth had been praised as a "Shakespeare in painting," and admirers noted repeatedly the literary force of his graphic art; only he, wrote one, could "teach pictures to speak and to think." Hogarth had appropriated the very idea of an instructive moral "progress" from John Bunyan's phenomenally popular religious narrative Pilgrim's Progress, but he made the journey at once darker and more satiric. Bunyan's Mr. Christian progresses through Vanity Fair and other dangers toward the Celestial City; Hogarth's protagonists remain mired within the Vanity Fair of contemporary London; their "progress" takes them downward to degradation and death. His art also helped shape a newer form of narrative, the novel. Like the novel, Hogarth's sequences abound in suggestive subplots, telling asides, and startling revelations, played out in the tiniest details carefully placed. Novelists as different from one another as Samuel Richardson, Henry Fielding, and Laurence Sterne valued him as a friend, sought him as a collaborator, and embraced him as a past master in their own moral and narrative mode. "I almost dare affirm," wrote Fielding, "that those two works of his, which he calls The Rake's and The Harlot's Progress, are calculated more to serve the cause of virtue, and for the preservation of mankind, than all the folios of morality which have ever been written."

For color reproductions of two Hogarth paintings, see Color Plates 26 and 27.

A Rake's Progress

Plate 1   Tom Rakewell's father (depicted in the portrait above the mantle) has recently died. The old man was miserly: he wore a coat and fur hat indoors so as not to incur the costs of a fire; he saved broken junk (in the open chest); he nearly starved his housecat (lower left). The young man is profligate: he has torn open doors and cabinets in search of sequestered wealth; he is being measured for new and ostentatious clothes; he is trying to pay off the raging mother of Sarah Young, the weeping woman (at right) whom he has made pregnant.

Plate 2   Nearly unrecognizable in his new elegance, Rakewell (the tallest figure in the picture) surrounds himself with instructors and tradespeople eager to sell their services. In the foreground (from left to right) are a composer, a fencing master, a dance teacher (with fiddle), a hired killer (in black; the note in Tom's hand, from "William Stab," vouches for the assassin as "a man of honor"); a huntsman (with horn); and a jockey, whose trophy cup bears the suggestive name of the winning horse: "Silly Tom." The two moping Englishmen at the back may be miffed to find themselves supplanted by the fashionable foreigners in front of them. The painting above the mantle depicts the Judgment of Paris, that indolent princeling whose unrestrained desires precipitated the catastrophe of the Trojan War.

Plate 3 Rakewell (sprawled at left) has bought himself an orgy. All the Roman portraits in the upper-right corner have been defaced, except that of the emperor Nero, who looks out over the havoc like some patron saint of vandalism (his reputed incendarism is re-enacted by the woman standing at the back near the shattered mirror, holding a candle flame to the map of the world). One prostitute caresses Tom while conveying away his watch; in the foreground opposite, a woman disrobes in preparation for an obscene dance that will likely involve the reflective platter and large candle held by the cross-eyed lackey in the doorway. Admonitions to the orgiasts lie at hand, in the form of the chicken's carcass (lower-right corner), stripped and forked; and in the person of the ballad singer, tattered, pregnant, and ignored, whose song bears the telling title "Black Joke."

Plate 4 Carried in his sedan chair to a night of gaming at White's Chocolate House and gambling club (rear left), Tom is stopped by a bailiff who serves him with a notice of arrest for debt. He receives aid not from the revellers in the distance but from Sarah Young, the abandoned lover whose mother he tried to buy off in Plate 1. Reversing that gesture, she seeks to secure his release by offering the money she has earned by making ribbons and caps (sample wares hang at her side). On a ladder a lamplighter, distracted by the goings-on, carelessly (and emblematically) spills his flammable fluid onto Rakewell's head. Hogarth reworked this picture more often than any other in the series. In this late version, a lightning bolt aims pointedly at the gambling house, upper left, while at the lower right, a group of urchins in the open air has made an early start at playing comparably dangerous games.

Plate 5 Intent on wealth, not the love Sarah offers, Rakewell weds an old woman in a dim, disintegrating church where light and faith are in scant supply. On the left, the Poor's Box," receptacle of charity, has long been shut (a cobweb covers its lid); on the right wall, the table of commandments is cracked. The one-eyed bride appears to wink at the grim parson; Rakewell proffers her the ring while eying her maid. On the floor, a canine couple parodies the human ceremony; in the back, a woman with churchkeys flailing tries to prevent the intrusion of Sarah Young, holding the child Rakewell has sired. Sarah's mother does vigorous but unavailing battle.

Plate 6   During a night of gambling, Rakewell has evidently lost the fortune he acquired by his calculating marriage. Wigless, frantic, he falls to one knee and curses his lot; his rage is replicated (as were his nuptials) by a dog on the floor to his right. The croupier at rear center, carrying the candles, echoes the "world-burning" woman in Plate 3. This time, though, the building is actually on fire. The lantern-bearing watchman at left has come to give warning. Most of the gamblers are too immersed in their own operations to notice either Rakewell's anguish or their own danger.

Plate 7 In the wake of his losses, Rakewell has at last been imprisoned for debt, unable to pay the "garnish" (or customary bribe) that the jailer behind him expects, or even the cost of a beer. The note on the table—"I have read your play and find it will not do"—rejects his last poor, literary attempt at solvency. His wife rails, Sarah faints, his daughter tugs at Sarah's skirts, and his cellmates embody futilities even more preposterous than his own playwriting. The impoverished man at left has devised "a new scheme for paying the debts of the nation." The man seated at the stove is an alchemist, vainly trying to transmute base metals into gold; before his imprisonment, he also built himself a pair of wings (upper left), but they, like Rakewell's upward aspirations, have produced only debt and confinement, not flight and freedom.

Plate 8 Rakewell has been moved from debtor's prison to Bethlehem Royal Hospital (better known as Bedlam), London's asylum for the insane. Grinning outright for the first time in the series, Tom claws at his head while guards restrain him. Sarah Young, weeping, has come to give him comfort. The other two women are here to amuse themselves (at the cost of two pence per visit, Bedlam had become one of London's most popular entertainments). Some inmates display lunatic religious zeal; others have gone mad in pursuit of science. The man drawing the world on the wall seeks a solution to the longitude, the navigational problem that had obsessed Britons for many decades. Behind the open door of the central cell, a naked madman sits and thinks he's king. In this final revision of the plate (1763), Hogarth has superimposed upon the longitudinist's globe an emblem of Britannia, as though empire and madhouse were now one.

⇒⊶ PERSPECTIVES ⊷⇐
Mind and God

Nature, and Nature's Laws lay hid in Night.
God said, *Let Newton be!* and All was *Light*.

So wrote Alexander Pope, capturing in a couplet the awe with which many of his contemporaries regarded the accomplishments of Isaac Newton. The lines, intended for Newton's tomb, compass his whole career. Pope's last word evokes one of the scientist's early breakthroughs: the discovery that sunlight, for all its seeming "whiteness," teemed with colors, whose operations could be mathematically described. Later, in his masterwork *Naturalis Philosophiae Principia Mathematica* (The Mathematical Principles of Natural Philosophy, 1687), Newton had expounded "Nature's Laws" on a scale and with a precision heretofore unmatched, pinpointing, in compact mathematical formulas, the laws governing gravity and motion, both on earth and throughout the heavens. In Pope's replaying of Genesis, Newton himself becomes a principle, not merely the interpreter of Creation but virtually synonomous with it: God's luminous word, from which revelation follows. For numberless admirers, the name of Newton figured forth not only the intricate simplicities of "Nature's Laws," but also the astonishing, hitherto unsuspected capacity of the human mind to shed light upon the works of God.

The human mind itself promptly became the object of new investigation, Newtonian in its ambitions and its methods. Two years after the *Principia* appeared, John Locke published his *Essay Concerning Human Understanding* (1689), a work comparably influential, in which he sought answers to key questions of epistemology: what do we know? and by what means do we come to know it? Locke, like Newton, brought luster to the scientific approach championed by the Royal Society (of which both men were members): empiricism, the conviction that truth could be attained solely through experiment and experience. The intimate interplay of those two crucial elements is nicely registered in Albert Einstein's account of the way that Newton did his work: "The conceptions which he used to reduce the material of experience to order seemed to flow spontaneously from experience itself, from the beautiful experiments which he ranged in order like playthings and describes with an affectionate wealth of detail." Locke imported empiricism from the physical sciences into the realms of philosophy and psychology. Striving to found a science of mind, to make sense of the running encounter between the material world and human perception, Locke and his successors found in experience both a method for investigating epistemological problems and the core of their solution: for these thinkers, experience is how we know, it is what we know, and it is how we can learn more about the processes of our knowing. The human mind is intrinsically (though not methodically) empiricist in its ways of gathering its "wealth of detail" about the world.

Under the mind's new scrutinies, God's place and primacy fell open to new questions. Empiricism itself was seen to cut two ways. On the one hand, as Newton and the vast majority of his followers delightedly proclaimed, experimental observation was revealing a universal architecture so exquisite as to prove both the existence and the matchless artistry of God the architect; this route from reason to religious faith became known as the "argument from design." On the other hand, discovery was beginning to conjure up alternative possibilities unsettling to faith: of a God not wholly supreme but subject to nature's inexorable laws; or of laws so efficiently self-sustaining that they needed no God to enforce them. In some of its modes, empiricism itself could be seen to imperil faith, since direct experience or demonstration of the divine proved elusive in a science that limited itself to the observation of material, mechanical causes and effects. For Newton, Locke, and countless other inquirers, empiricism promised to explain the ways of God; but they had begun a process which, in other hands, might threaten to explain God away.

The clash between science and theology gathered force in the mid-nineteenth century, when discoveries in geology (the age of the Earth) and biology (evolution) rendered Scripture strongly suspect. But contention between faith and science was manifest much earlier. At the start of the nineteenth century, William Blake briefly sketched the lines of struggle in his private notebook. "Newton's particles of light," he wrote,

> Are sands upon the Red sea shore,
> Where Israel's tents do shine so bright.

Against the arrogance of inquiry, Blake insists upon humility and awe; biblical revelation trumps all the small advancements of human knowledge. Pope had gestured in this direction some seven decades earlier. He suggested, in his *Essay on Man*, that for "superior beings" (angels, God), the sight of Newton unfolding "all Nature's law" might provide the same kind of amazement and amusement that we mortals derive from the antics of a performing ape—a creature who knows more than we might expect, but far less than we ourselves. So great (Pope argues) is the difference between human and divine capacities. Throughout the eighteenth century, in works suffused by the concepts of Newton and of Locke, the relations between mind and God were brilliantly explicated and newly contested, as poets and philosophers undertook, from varying vantages and factions, to sing God's praise, to parse his ways, to work toward him by reason or (in rare instances) to reason him out of existence altogether.

Isaac Newton
1642–1727

Albert Einstein summed up Newton's abilities as follows: "In one person, he combined the experimenter, the theorist, the mechanic, and, not least, the artist in exposition." Einstein praises magnificently, and omits much. Newton also combined in his one person a supreme mathematician, an obsessive alchemist, a forceful administrator, and (perhaps most important, in his own view) an ardent theologian, eager to discover and expound the place of God in his creation. His voluminous, unorthodox writings on the subject remained unpublished in his lifetime. By denying the full divinity of Christ, Newton accorded God *more* authority than did conventional Anglicanism. His views, if known, would have toppled him from the public eminences he enjoyed: as Lucasian Professor of Mathematics at Cambridge, as Master of the Mint in London, as President of the Royal Society. Still, Newton's first admirers found in his scientific work exhilarating support for a more mainstream theology: the strongest foundation yet for the argument from design. It was the business of natural philosophy, Newton repeatedly insisted, "to deduce causes from effects, until we come to the First Cause, which is certainly not mechanical." Newton's own scientific revelations gave rise to a passionate interest in "natural religion"—a faith in God's existence and benevolence, grounded in the orderliness and beauty of the natural world. One of that faith's adherents was the ambitious young classicist and clergyman Richard Bentley (1662–1742), who, having been commissioned to deliver a series of lectures defending Christianity against atheism, found in Newton's recently published *Principia* abundant new evidence for his own arguments about the divine "origin and frame of the universe." While preparing his lectures for the press, Bentley sent Newton a set of questions, in order to make sure that he was correctly understanding and deploying the *Principia*. Newton's four replies (the first is excerpted here) map the convergence that interests him most, between the discoveries of science and the majesty of God.

from **Letter to Richard Bentley**

10 December 1692

Sir,

When I wrote my treatise about our system, I had an eye upon such principles as might work with considering men for the belief of a Deity, and nothing can rejoice me more than to find it useful for that purpose. But if I have done the public any service this way, 'tis due to nothing but industry and a patient thought.

As to your first query, it seems to me, that if the matter of our sun and planets and all the matter in the universe was evenly scattered throughout all the heavens, and every particle had an innate gravity towards all the rest,[1] and the whole space throughout which this matter was scattered was but finite, the matter on the outside of this space would by its gravity tend towards all the matter on the inside, and by consequence fall down to the middle of the whole space, and there compose one great spherical mass. But if the matter was evenly diffused through an infinite space, it would never convene into one mass, but some of it convene into one mass and some into another so as to make an infinite number of great masses scattered at great distances from one to another throughout all that infinite space. And thus might the sun and fixed stars be formed, supposing the matter were of a lucid[2] nature. But how the matter should divide itself into two sorts, and that part of it which is fit to compose a shining body should fall down into one mass and make a sun, and the rest which is fit to compose an opaque body should coalesce not into one great body like the shining matter but into many little ones; or, if the sun was at first an opaque body like the planets, or the planets lucid bodies like the sun, how he alone should be changed into a shining body whilst all they continue opaque, or all they be changed into opaque ones whilst he remains unchanged, I do not think explicable by mere natural causes but am forced to ascribe it to the counsel[3] and contrivance of a voluntary agent. The same power, whether natural or supernatural, which placed the sun in the center of the orbs[4] of the six primary planets, placed Saturn in the center of the orbs of his five secondary planets,[5] and Jupiter in the center of the orbs of his four secondary ones, and the Earth in the center of the moon's orb; and therefore, had this cause been a blind one without contrivance and design, the sun would have been a body of the same kind with Saturn, Jupiter and the Earth; that is without light and heat. Why there is one body in our system qualified to give light and heat to all the rest I know no reason but because the author of the system thought it convenient, and why there is but one body of this kind I know no reason but because one was sufficient to warm and enlighten all the rest. For the Cartesian hypothesis[6] of suns losing their light and then turning into comets and comets into planets can have no place in my system and is plainly erroneous, because it's certain that comets as often as they appear to us descend into the system of our planets lower than the orb of Jupiter and sometimes lower than the orbs of Venus and Mercury, and yet never stay here but always return from the sun with the same degrees of motion by which they approached him.

---

1. Newton did not endorse this premise. "You sometimes speak," he wrote Bentley in his second letter, "of gravity as essential and inherent to matter: pray do not ascribe that notion to me, for the cause of gravity is what I do not pretend to know."
2. Light-producing.
3. Deliberate design.

4. Orbits.
5. I.e., Saturn's moons; Newton states the numbers of planets and their moons then known.
6. A theory put forth by the French mathematician and philosopher René Descartes (1596–1650) in his highly influential treatises on physics, which Newton's *Principia* had challenged.

To your second query I answer that the motions which the planets now have could not spring from any natural cause alone but were impressed by an intelligent agent. For since comets descend into the region of our planets and here move all manner of ways, going sometimes the same way with the planets, sometimes the contrary way, and sometimes in cross ways in planes inclined to the plane of the ecliptic at all kinds of angles, it's plain that there is no natural cause which could determine all the planets both primary and secondary to move the same way and in the same plane without any considerable variation.[7] This must have been the effect of counsel. Nor is there any natural cause which could give the planets those just degrees of velocity in proportion to their distances from the sun and other central bodies about which they move and to the quantity of matter contained in those bodies, which were requisite to make them move in concentric orbs about those bodies. Had the planets been as swift as comets in proportion to their distances from the sun (as they would have been, had their motions been caused by their gravity, whereby the matter at the first formation of the planets might fall from the remotest regions towards the sun), they would not move in concentric orbs but in such eccentric ones as the comets move in. Were all the planets as swift as Mercury or as slow as Saturn or his satellites, or were their several velocities otherwise much greater or less than they are (as they might have been had they arose from any other cause than their gravity), or had their distances from the centers about which they move been greater or less than they are with the same velocities; or had the quantity of matter in the sun or in Saturn, Jupiter, and the Earth and by consequence their gravitating power been greater or less than it is, the primary planets could not have revolved about the sun nor the secondary ones about Saturn, Jupiter and the Earth in concentric circles as they do, but would have moved in hyperbolas or parabolas or in ellipses very eccentric. To make this system therefore, with all its motions, required a cause which understood and compared together the quantities of matter in the several bodies of the sun and planets and the gravitating powers resulting from thence, the several distances of the primary planets from the sun and secondary ones from Saturn, Jupiter, and the Earth, and the velocities with which these planets could revolve at those distances about those quantities of matter in the central bodies. And to compare and adjust all these things together in so great a variety of bodies argues that cause to be not blind and fortuitous, but very well skilled in mechanics and geometry.

To your third query I answer that it may be represented that the sun may, by heating those planets most which are nearest to him, cause them to be better concocted[8] and more condensed by concoction. But when I consider that our Earth is much more heated in its bowels below the upper crust by subterraneous fermentations of mineral bodies than by the sun, I see not why the interior parts of Jupiter and Saturn might not be as much heated, concocted, and coagulated by those fermentations as our Earth is, and therefore this various density should have some other cause than the various

---

7. Newton oversimplifies: the planes of the planets actually incline to each other by as much as five degrees. Newton's arguments in this letter, suggests his biographer Richard Westfall, "reveal above all a determination to find God in nature," even to impose God upon nature. All the phenomena that Newton here attributes to the intervention of divine "counsel" and "skill" were explained scientifically over the course of the next century by physicists applying and extending Newton's own system, so that (as the most brilliant of the extenders, Pierre Simon Laplace, is said to have remarked to Napoleon) the hypothesis of divine intervention was no longer necessary.

8. Purified by heat (and hence made denser by the absence of the extraneous matter that the heat has annihilated).

distances of the planets from the sun; and I am confirmed in this opinion by considering that the planets of Jupiter and Saturn, as they are rarer[9] than the rest, so they are vastly greater and contain a far greater quantity of matter and have many satellites about them, which qualifications surely arose not from their being placed at so great a distance from the sun, but were rather the cause why the Creator placed them at that great distance. For by their gravitating powers they disturb one another's motions very sensibly, as I find by some late observations of Mr. Flamsteed,[1] and had they been placed much nearer to the sun and to one another they would by the same powers have caused a considerable disturbance in the whole system. * * *

Lastly, I see nothing extraordinary in the inclination of the Earth's axis for proving a Deity unless you will urge it as a contrivance for winter and summer and for making the Earth habitable towards the poles, and that the diurnal rotations of the sun and planets, as they could hardly arise from any cause purely mechanical, so by being determined all the same way with the annual and menstrual[2] motions they seem to make up that harmony in the system which (as I explained above) was the effect of choice rather than of chance.

There is yet another argument for a Deity which I take to be a very strong one, but till the principles on which 'tis grounded be better received I think it more advisable to let it sleep. I am

Your most humble servant to command

Is. NEWTON

John Locke
1632–1704

In the preface to his *Essay Concerning Human Understanding*, Locke depicts "the incomparable Mr. Newton" as one of the "master builders" of the new science, and himself as a mere "underlaborer," busy "clearing the ground a little, and removing some of the rubbish that lies in the way to knowledge." The eighteenth century, though, tended to venerate the two thinkers equally, Newton as master explicator of the cosmos, Locke as master inquirer into the mind. Starting from the claim that "simple ideas," acquired early, constituted the building blocks of thought, Locke constructed a system of the mind of comparable intricacy with Newton's universe, but of greater idiosyncrasy (since the content of consciousness differed from person to person, and indeed determined individual identity). Part of Locke's appeal lay in the comparative accessibility of his empiricism. His experiments, unlike Newton's, required neither telescope nor prism, calculus nor genius: readers could perform them (as Locke repeatedly suggested) in the laboratories of their minds, using their own perceptions and memories as raw material. More than any other text, Locke's *Essay* spurred that fascination with the first person which suffuses so much eighteenth-century writing: autobiographies, essays, diaries, travel

---

9. Less dense.
1. John Flamsteed (1646–1719), astronomer and director of the Royal Greenwich Observatory, had recently supplied Newton with these data; the two men later quarrelled bitterly over Flamsteed's reluctance to make available the immense, precise, and urgently needed records of his celestial observations.
2. Monthly.

journals, philosophic treatises, novels. Locke described the workings of the mind so persuasively that in effect he changed them too, prompting an analytic self-consciousness that had not obtained in the same kind and to the same degree before his book appeared.

from An Essay Concerning Human Understanding
[ON IDEAS[1]]

Every man being conscious to himself that he thinks, and that which his mind is employed about whilst thinking being the *ideas* that are there, 'tis past doubt, that men have in their minds several *ideas*, such as are those expressed by the words *whiteness, hardness, sweetness, thinking, motion, man, elephant, army, drunkenness,* and others. It is in the first place then to be inquired, how he comes by them? I know it is a received doctrine, that men have native *ideas* and original characters[2] stamped upon their minds, in their very first being. This opinion I have at large examined already, and I suppose what I have said in the foregoing book[3] will be much more easily admitted, when I have shown whence the understanding may get all the *ideas* it has, and by what ways and degrees they may come into the mind; for which I shall appeal to everyone's own observation and experience.

Let us then suppose the mind to be, as we say, white paper, void of all characters, without any *ideas*. How comes it to be furnished? Whence comes it by that vast store, which the busy and boundless fancy of man has painted on it, with an almost endless variety? Whence has it all the materials of reason and knowledge? To this I answer, in one word, from *experience*. In that, all our knowledge is founded, and from that it ultimately derives itself. Our observation employed either about *external, sensible objects, or about the internal operations of our minds, perceived and reflected on by ourselves, is that which supplies our understandings with all the materials of thinking*. These two are the fountains of knowledge, from whence all the *ideas* we have, or can naturally have, do spring.

First, *our senses*, conversant about particular sensible objects, do *convey into the mind*, several distinct *perceptions* of things, according to those various ways, wherein those objects do affect them; and thus we come by those *ideas* we have of *yellow, white, heat, cold, soft, hard, bitter, sweet,* and all those which we call sensible qualities, which when I say the senses convey into the mind, I mean, they from external objects convey into the mind what produces there those *perceptions*. This great source of most of the *ideas* we have, depending wholly upon our senses and derived by them to the understanding, I call SENSATION.

Secondly, the other fountain from which experience furnisheth the understanding with *ideas* is the *perception of the operations of our own minds* within us, as it is employed about the *ideas* it has got; which operations, when the soul comes to reflect on, and consider, do furnish the understanding with another set of *ideas*, which could not be had from things without; and such are *perception, thinking, doubting, believing, reasoning, knowing, willing,* and all the different actings of our own minds; which we being conscious of, and observing in ourselves, do from these receive into our understandings, as distinct *ideas*, as we do from bodies affecting our senses. This source of *ideas* every man has wholly in himself. And though it be not sense, as having nothing

---

1. All selections are from Book 2, "Of Ideas"; chapter and section numbers follow each section, in brackets. Most of Locke's italics have been retained.

2. Inscriptions.
3. In which Locke denied the existence of "innate principles," received by the soul "in its very first being" (1.2.1).

to do with external objects, yet it is very like it, and might properly enough be called internal sense. But as I call the other *sensation*, so I call this REFLECTION, the *ideas* it affords being such only, as the mind gets by reflecting on its own operations within itself. By REFLECTION then, in the following part of this discourse, I would be understood to mean, that notice which the mind takes of its own operations, and the manner of them, by reason whereof there come to be *ideas* of these operations in the understanding. These two, I say, *viz.* external, material things, as the objects of SENSATION, and the operations of our own minds within, as the objects of REFLECTION, are, to me, the only originals,[4] from whence all our *ideas* take their beginnings. The term *operations* here I use in a large sense, as comprehending not barely the actions of the mind about its *ideas*, but some sort of passions arising sometimes from them, such as is the satisfaction or uneasiness arising from any thought.

The understanding seems to me not to have the least glimmering of any *ideas*, which it doth not receive from one of these two. *External objects furnish the mind with the ideas of sensible qualities*, which are all those different perceptions they produce in us; and the *mind furnishes the understanding with* ideas *of its own operations*.

These, when we have taken a full survey of them, and their several modes, combinations, and relations, we shall find to contain all our whole stock of *ideas*; and that we have nothing in our minds which did not come in one of these two ways. Let anyone examine his own thoughts, and thoroughly search into his understanding, and then let him tell me, whether all the original *ideas* he has there are any other than of the objects of his *senses*, or of the operations of his mind, considered as objects of his *reflection*; and how great a mass of knowledge soever he imagines to be lodged there, he will, upon taking a strict view, see that he has *not any idea in his mind, but what one of these two have imprinted*; though, perhaps, with infinite variety compounded and enlarged by the understanding, as we shall see hereafter.

He that attentively considers the state of a *child*, at his first coming into the world, will have little reason to think him stored with plenty of *ideas*, that are to be the matter of his future knowledge. 'Tis by degrees he comes to be furnished with them. And though the *ideas* of obvious and familiar qualities imprint themselves before the memory begins to keep a register of time and order, yet 'tis often so late, before some unusual qualities come in the way, that there are few men that cannot recollect the beginning of their acquaintance with them; and if it were worthwhile, no doubt a child might be so ordered as to have but a very few, even of the ordinary *ideas*, till he were grown up to a man. But all that are born into the world being surrounded with bodies that perpetually and diversely affect them, variety of *ideas*, whether care be taken about it or no, are imprinted on the minds of children. *Light* and *colors* are busy at hand everywhere, when the eye is but open; *sounds* and some *tangible qualities* fail not to solicit their proper senses, and force an entrance to the mind; but yet, I think, it will be granted easily, that if a child were kept in a place where he never saw any other but black and white till he were a man, he would have no more *ideas* of scarlet or green, than he that from his childhood never tasted an oyster, or a pineapple, has of those particular relishes.

Men then come to be furnished with fewer or more simple *ideas* from without, according as the *objects* they converse with[5] afford greater or less variety; and from the operation of their minds within, according as they more or less *reflect* on them.

---

4. Origins.   5. Encounter.

For, though he that contemplates the operations of his mind cannot but have plain and clear *ideas* of them; yet unless he turn his thoughts that way, and considers them *attentively*, he will no more have clear and distinct *ideas* of all the *operations of his mind*, and all that may be observed therein, than he will have all the particular *ideas* of any landscape, or of the parts and motions of a clock, who will not turn his eyes to it, and with attention heed all the parts of it. The picture or clock may be so placed that they may come in his way every day; but yet he will have but a confused *idea* of all the parts they are made up of, till he *applies himself with attention*, to consider them each in particular. [1.1–7]

* * *

But to return to the matter in hand, the *ideas* we have of substances, and the ways we come by them; I say *our specific* ideas *of substances* are nothing else but *a collection of a certain number of simple ideas, considered as united in one thing*. These *ideas* of substances, though they are commonly called simple apprehensions, and the names of them simple terms, yet in effect, are complex and compounded. Thus the *idea* which an *Englishman* signifies by the name *swan* is white color, long neck, red beak, black legs, and whole feet, and all these of a certain size, with a power of swimming in the water, and making a certain kind of noise, and, perhaps, to a man who has long observed those kind of birds, some other properties, which all terminate in sensible simple *ideas*, all united in one common subject.

Besides the complex *ideas* we have of material sensible substances, of which I have last spoken, by the simple *ideas* we have taken from those operations of our own minds, which we experiment[6] daily in ourselves, as thinking, understanding, willing, knowing, and power of beginning motion, etc. co-existing in some substance, we are able to frame *the complex* idea *of an immaterial spirit*. And thus by putting together the *ideas* of thinking, perceiving, liberty, and power of moving themselves and other things, we have as clear a perception and notion of immaterial substances, as we have of material. For putting together the *ideas* of thinking and willing, or the power of moving or quieting corporeal motion, joined to substance, of which we have no distinct *idea*, we have the *idea* of an immaterial spirit; and by putting together the *ideas* of coherent solid parts, and a power of being moved, joined with substance, of which likewise we have no positive *idea*, we have the *idea* of matter. The one is as clear and distinct an *idea*, as the other: the *idea* of thinking, and moving a body, being as clear and distinct *ideas*, as the *ideas* of extension, solidity, and being moved. [23.14–15]

* * *

If we examine the *idea* we have of the incomprehensible Supreme Being, we shall find that we come by it the same way; and that the complex *ideas* we have both of God, and separate spirits, are made up of the simple *ideas* we receive from *reflection*; *v.g.* having, from what we experiment in ourselves, got the *ideas* of existence and duration; of knowledge and power; of pleasure and happiness; and of several other qualities and powers, which it is better to have than to be without; when we would frame an *idea* the most suitable we can to the Supreme Being, we enlarge every one of these with our *idea* of infinity; and so putting them together, make our complex *idea of God*. For that the mind has such a power of enlarging some of its *ideas*, received from sensation and reflection, has been already showed. [23.33]

---

6. Experience.

[ON IDENTITY]

Personal identity consists, not in the identity of substance, but, as I have said, in the identity of *consciousness*, wherein, if Socrates and the present Mayor of Queenborough agree, they are the same person. If the same Socrates waking and sleeping do not partake of the same *consciousness*, Socrates waking and sleeping is not the same person. And to punish Socrates waking, for what sleeping Socrates thought, and waking Socrates was never conscious of, would be no more of right, than to punish one twin for what his brother-twin did, whereof he knew nothing, because their outsides were so like that they could not be distinguished; for such twins have been seen.

But yet possibly it will still be objected, suppose I wholly lose the memory of some parts of my life, beyond a possibility of retrieving them, so that perhaps I shall never be conscious of them again; yet am I not the same person that did those actions, had those thoughts, that I was once conscious of, though I have now forgot them? To which I answer, that we must here take notice what the word *I* is applied to, which in this case is the man only. And the same man being presumed to be the same person, *I* is easily here supposed to stand also for the same person. But if it be possible for the same man to have distinct incommunicable consciousness at different times, it is past doubt the same man would at different times make different persons; which, we see, is the sense of mankind in the solemnest declaration of their opinions, human laws not punishing the *mad man* for the *sober man's* actions, nor the *sober man* for what the *mad man* did, thereby making them two persons; which is somewhat explained by our way of speaking in *English*, when we say such an one *is not himself*, or is *besides himself*; in which phrases it is insinuated, as if those who now, or, at least, first used them, thought, that *self* was changed, the *self* same person was no longer in that man.

But yet 'tis hard to conceive that Socrates the same individual man should be two persons. To help us a little in this, we must consider what is meant by *Socrates*, or the same individual *man*.

First, it must be either the same individual, immaterial, thinking substance: in short, the same numerical soul, and nothing else.

Secondly, or the same animal,[7] without any regard to an immaterial soul.

Thirdly, or the same immaterial spirit united to the same animal.

Now take which of these suppositions you please, it is impossible to make personal identity to consist in anything but consciousness, or reach any farther than that does.

For by the first of them, it must be allowed possible that a man born of different women, and in distant times, may be the same man. A way of speaking, which whoever admits, must allow it possible for the same man to be two distinct persons, as any two that have lived in different ages without the knowledge of one another's thoughts.

By the second and third, Socrates in this life, and after it, cannot be the same man any way, but by the same consciousness; and so making *human identity* to consist in the same thing wherein we place *personal identity*, there will be no difficulty to allow the same man to be the same person. But then they who place *human identity* in consciousness only, and not in something else, must consider how they will make the

---

7. Physical, living body.

infant Socrates the same man with Socrates after the resurrection. But whatsoever to some men makes a *man*, and consequently the same individual man, wherein perhaps few are agreed, personal identity can by us be placed in nothing but consciousness (which is that alone which makes what we call *self*) without involving us in great absurdities.

But is not a man drunk and sober the same person? Why else is he punished for the fact[8] he commits when drunk, though he be never afterwards conscious of it? Just as much the same person, as a man that walks, and does other things in his sleep, is the same person, and is answerable for any mischief he shall do in it. Human laws punish both with a justice suitable to their way of knowledge: because in these cases, they cannot distinguish certainly what is real, what counterfeit; and so the ignorance in drunkeness or sleep is not admitted as a plea. For though punishment be annexed to personality, and personality to consciousness, and the drunkard perhaps be not conscious of what he did, yet human judicatures justly punish him; because the fact is proved against him, but what of consciousness cannot be proved for him. But in the great day,[9] wherein the secrets of all hearts shall be laid open, it may be reasonable to think, no one shall be made to answer for what he knows nothing of; but shall receive his doom, his conscience accusing or excusing him. [27.19–22]

1671–1689   1690

★→ ⚜ ←★

Isaac Watts
1674–1748

"As his mind was capacious, his curiosity excursive, and his industry continual," wrote Samuel Johnson in praise of the dissenting minister Isaac Watts, "his writings are very numerous." Watts produced books of poetry, logic, theology, philosophy, and science, but the writings that have mattered most are the hymns and psalm translations (about seven hundred in all) that he began composing in his early twenties. In his philosophical writings, Watts worked hard to absorb the innovations of Newton's physics and Locke's psychology; in his hymns, an older structure of piety prevails. One of empiricism's chief effects was to entangle truth with time, to make knowledge a consequence of *process* (a series of experiments, a sequence of ideas). In Watts's hymns, truth is eternal; the mind's chief tasks are to register God's greatness and to praise it aright. The singing of hymns, and of psalms awkwardly translated from the Hebrew, had been a practice of long standing in Protestant congregations. Watts brought to these forms a new clarity and grace, in verses he carefully crafted, week after week, for the immediate use and pleasure of his congregants. He sought (he once explained) to achieve an "ease of numbers [i.e., meter] and smoothness of sound, and . . . to make the sense plain and obvious." In print, the simplicity of his style gradually won a wider attention, extending far beyond local circles of dissent. As the religious historian and poet Donald Davie has pointed out, Watts's hymns and psalms probably touched more minds (and certainly resounded in more throats) over the course of the eighteenth century than any of the texts we now deem greater hits: *Gulliver's Travels*, Johnson's *Dictionary*, Thomson's *Seasons*. In his lifetime and for more than a century after, Watts was reckoned the English, Christian successor to that ancient king of Israel traditionally

---

8. Deed.   9. I.e., Judgment Day.

credited with creating the Psalms. "Were David to speak English," Watts's brother once remarked to him, "he would choose to make use of your style."

A Prospect of Heaven Makes Death Easy[1]

There is a land of pure delight
    Where saints immortal reign;
Infinite day excludes the night,
    And pleasures banish pain.

5   There everlasting spring abides,
    And never-withering flowers:
Death like a narrow sea divides
    This heav'nly land from ours.

Sweet fields beyond the swelling flood
10   Stand dressed in living green:
So to the Jews old Canaan stood,
    While Jordan rolled between.[2]

But timorous mortals start° and shrink   *tremble*
    To cross this narrow sea,
15   And linger shivering on the brink,
    And fear to launch away.

O! could we make our doubts remove,°   *withdraw*
    Those gloomy doubts that rise,
And see the Canaan that we love,
20   With unbeclouded eyes:

Could we but climb where Moses stood,[3]
    And view the landskip° o'er,   *landscape*
Not Jordan's stream, nor death's cold flood
    Should fright us from the shore.

1707

The Hurry of the Spirits, in a Fever and Nervous Disorders[1]

My frame of nature is a ruffled sea,
And my disease the tempest. Nature feels
A strange commotion to her inmost center;
The throne of reason shakes. "Be still, my thoughts;
5   Peace and be still." In vain my reason gives

---

1. From *Hymns and Spiritual Songs* (1707).
2. In Joshua 3, the children of Israel, at the end of their 40-year journey in the desert, see the promised land of Canaan across the River Jordan.
3. Having led the Israelites to the end of their desert journey, Moses on his last day of life climbed the mountain of

Nebo, and surveyed the entire promised land (Deuteronomy 34.1–4).
1. Not a hymn but an autobiographical poem, the first in a sequence entitled *Thoughts and Meditations in a Long Sickness, 1712 and 1713*, published decades later in Watts's *Reliquiae Juveniles* (writings in youth).

The peaceful word, my spirit strives in vain
To calm the tumult and command my thoughts.
This flesh, this circling blood, these brutal powers
Made to obey, turn rebels to the mind,
10   Nor hear its laws. The engine° rules the man.   body
Unhappy change! When nature's meaner springs,
Fired to impetuous ferments, break all order;
When little restless atoms rise and reign
Tyrants in sovereign uproar, and impose
15   Ideas on the mind; confused ideas
Of non-existents and impossibles,
Who can describe them? Fragments of old dreams,
Borrowed from midnight, torn from fairy fields
And fairy skies, and regions of the dead,
20   Abrupt, ill-sorted. O 'tis all confusion!
If I but close my eyes, strange images
In thousand forms and thousand colors rise,
Stars, rainbows, moons, green dragons, bears and ghosts,
An endless medley rush upon the stage
25   And dance and riot wild in reason's court
Above control. I'm in a raging storm,
Where seas and skies are blended, while my soul
Like some light worthless chip of floating cork
Is tossed from wave to wave: now overwhelmed
30   With breaking floods, I drown, and seem to lose
All being; now high-mounted on the ridge
Of tall foaming surge, I'm all at once
Caught up into the storm, and ride the wind,
The whistling wind; unmanageable steed,
35   And feeble rider! Hurried many a league
Over the rising hills of roaring brine,
Through airy wilds unknown, with dreadful speed
And infinite surprise, till some few minutes
Have spent the blast, and then perhaps I drop
40   Near to the peaceful coast. Some friendly billow
Lodges me on the beach, and I find rest.
Short rest I find; for the next rolling wave
Snatches me back again; then ebbing far
Sets me adrift, and I am borne off to sea,
45   Helpless, amidst the bluster of the winds,
Beyond the ken of shore.

      Ah, when will these tumultuous scenes be gone?
When shall this weary spirit, tossed with tempests,
Harassed and broken, reach the ports of rest,
50   And hold it firm? When shall this wayward flesh
With all th' irregular springs of vital movement
Ungovernable, return to sacred order,
And pay their duties to the ruling mind?

Against Idleness and Mischief[1]

How doth the little busy bee
    Improve each shining hour,
And gather honey all the day
    From every opening flower!

5   How skillfully she builds her cell!
      How neat she spreads the wax!
And labors hard to store it well
    With the sweet food she makes.

In works of labor, or of skill,
10   I would be busy too;
For Satan finds some mischief still°   *always*
    For idle hands to do.

In books, or work, or healthful play,
    Let my first years be passed.
15   That I may give for every day
    Some good account at last.

1715

Man Frail, and God Eternal[1]

Our God, our help in ages past,
    Our hope for years to come,
Our shelter from the stormy blast,
    And our eternal home.

5   Under the shadow of thy throne
      Thy saints have dwelt secure.
Sufficient is thine arm alone,
    And our defense is sure.

Before the hills in order stood,
10   Or earth received her frame,
From everlasting thou art God,
    To endless years the same.

Thy word commands our flesh to dust,
    Return, ye sons of men.
15   All nations rose from earth at first,
    And turn to earth again.

1. From *Divine Songs Attempted in Easy Language, for the Use of Children*. The poems in this durable little collection were memorized by numberless children in the 18th and 19th centuries, including Lewis Caroll's Alice. Wandering through Wonderland, she is commanded by its inhabitants (as she doubtless was in school) to recite these verses, and discovers to her dismay that the lines come out all wrong.

1. An imitation of Psalm 90, lines 1–6. This and the next poem are from *The Psalms of David Imitated in the Language of the New Testament, and Applied to the Christian State and Worship*. As the title indicates, Watts intended not merely to translate the Psalms, but to recast them. In his preface, he declares himself "the first who hath brought down the royal author [King David] into the common affairs of the Christian life, and let the psalmist of Israel into the Church of Christ, without anything of a Jew about him."

A thousand ages in thy sight
   Are like an evening gone;
Short as the watch that ends the night,
20   Before the rising sun.

The busy tribes of flesh and blood
   With all their lives and cares
Are carried downwards by thy flood,
   And lost in following years.

25 Time, like an ever-rolling stream
   Bears all its sons away.
They fly forgotten, as a dream
   Dies at the opening day.

Like flowery fields the nations stand
30   Pleased with the morning light.
The flowers beneath the mower's hand
   Lie withering ere 'tis night.

Our God, our help in ages past,
   Our hope for years to come,
35 Be thou our guard while troubles last,
   And our eternal home.

1719

Miracles Attending Israel's Journey[1]

When Israel, freed from Pharaoh's hand,
Left the proud tyrant and his land,
The tribes with cheerful homage own[2]
Their king, and Judah[3] was his throne.

5   Across the deep[4] their journey lay;
The deep divides to make them way.
Jordan beheld their march, and fled
With backward current to his head.[5]

The mountains shook like frighted sheep.
10   Like lambs the little hillocks leap.[6]

1. An imitation of Psalm 114. In 1712, Watts sent a version of this poem to the *Spectator*, where it appeared (No. 461, Tuesday, 19 August 1712) along with a letter from the poet explaining a discovery he had made while translating: "As I was describing the journey of Israel from Egypt, and added the Divine Presence amongst them, I perceived a beauty in the Psalm which was entirely new to me, and which I was going to lose; and that is, that the poet utterly conceals the presence of God in the beginning of it. . . . The reason now seems evident, and this conduct necessary. For if God had appeared before [i.e., at the start of the poem], there could be no wonder why the mountains should leap and the sea retire; therefore that this convulsion of nature may be brought in with due surprise, his name is not mentioned till afterward, and then with a very agreeable turn of thought God is introduced at once in all his majesty."
2. Acknowledged (God as their king).
3. A portion of the land promised by God to the Israelites; here the name is used to designate the entire promised land.
4. The Red Sea, whose miraculous parting made possible the Israelites' escape from Egypt (Exodus 14.21–31).
5. Alludes to a second, similar miracle later in the journey: God makes the waters of the river Jordan "stand upon an heap," so that the Israelites can pass "clean over" dry ground, into the promised land (Joshua 3.14–17).
6. Lines 9–10 may refer (in the original Psalm) to the hills and mountains of the promised land, the dwelling places of local gods who tremble at Israel's advent.

Not Sinai[7] on her base could stand,
Conscious of sovereign power at hand.

What power could make the deep divide?
Make Jordan backward roll his tide?
15   Why did ye leap, ye little hills?
And whence the fright that Sinai feels?

Let every mountain, every flood,
Retire, and know th'approaching God,
The king of Israel. See him here.
20   Tremble thou earth, adore, and fear.

He thunders, and all nature mourns.
The rock to standing pool he turns.
Flints spring with fountains at his word,[8]
And fires and seas confess the Lord.

1719

Joseph Addison
1672–1719

The ideas of Newton and Locke became widely known not through their own writings (which were voluminous and often dense), but through various popularizations: lectures, demonstrations, explanatory handbooks, the popular press. One of the chief disseminators was the *Spectator*, the phenomenally successful series of daily essays composed by Joseph Addison and Richard Steele (for more on the *Spectator*, see page 2326). Addison in particular undertook to inculcate the ideas of Newton and Locke, sometimes directly by quotation and commentary, but more often indirectly, by absorption and a kind of tacit transmission. "The working of my own mind," Mr. Spectator announces early on, "is the general entertainment of my life," and he recommends this notably Lockean "entertainment" to his readers too; his own name honors Locke's reckoning of sight as the mind's chief instrument for the gathering of ideas. In the following extract, Addison pays comparably implicit homage to Newton, in an ode that quickly became one of the touchstones of eighteenth-century devotion. Though Addison places his poem in a tradition that combines Aristotle with the Psalms, Newton is powerfully present too, in the depiction of a heaven whose silent motions proclaim to human reason the perfection of God's design.

from Spectator No. 465
Saturday, 23 August 1712[1]

* * * The last method which I shall mention for the giving life to a man's faith is frequent retirement from the world, accompanied with religious meditation. When a

---

7. The sacred mountain on which Moses received from the Lord the Ten Commandments. At the Lord's approach, "the whole mount quaked greatly" (Exodus 19.18).
8. In the Book of Numbers (20.8–11), God miraculously produces water from rock in order to sustain the Israelites during their journey.

1. Addison often set Saturdays aside for particularly serious topics, as a way of preparing his readers for the religious solemnities of Sunday (the only day on which the *Spectator* did not appear). He devotes the present paper to "the proper means of strengthening and confirming" Christian faith.

man thinks of any thing in the darkness of the night, whatever deep impressions it may make in his mind, they are apt to vanish as soon as the day breaks about him. The light and noise of the day, which are perpetually soliciting his senses and calling off his attention, wear out of his mind the thoughts that imprinted themselves in it with so much strength during the silence and darkness of the night. A man finds the same difference as to himself in a crowd and in a solitude; the mind is stunned and dazzled amidst that variety of objects which press upon her in a great city: she cannot apply herself to the consideration of those things which are of the utmost concern to her. The cares or pleasures of the world strike in with every thought, and a multitude of vicious examples give a kind of justification to our folly. In our retirements everything disposes us to be serious. In courts and cities we are entertained with the works of men, in the country with those of God. One is the province of art, the other of nature. Faith and devotion naturally grow in the mind of every reasonable man, who sees the impressions of divine power and wisdom in every object on which he casts his eye. The Supreme Being has made the best arguments for his own existence, in the formation of the heavens and the earth, and these are arguments which a man of sense cannot forbear attending to, who is out of the noise and hurry of human affairs. Aristotle says,[2] that should a man live under ground, and there converse with works of art and mechanism, and should afterwards be brought up into the open day, and see the several glories of the heaven and earth, he would immediately pronounce them the works of such a being as we define God to be. The Psalmist has very beautiful strokes of poetry to this purpose, in that exalted strain, "The heavens declare the glory of God: and the firmament showeth his handiwork. One day telleth another: and one night certifieth another. There is neither speech nor language: but their voices are heard among them. Their sound is gone out into all lands: and their words into the ends of the world."[3] As such a bold and sublime manner of thinking furnishes very noble matter for an ode, the reader may see it wrought into the following one.[4]

1

The spacious firmament on high,
With all the blue ethereal sky,
And spangled heav'ns, a shining frame,
Their great original proclaim:
5 Th' unwearied sun, from day to day,
Does his Creator's power display,
And publishes to every land
The works of an almighty hand.

2

Soon as the evening shades prevail,
10 The moon takes up the wondrous tale,
And nightly to the list'ning earth
Repeats the story of her birth:
Whilst all the stars that round her burn,

2. Addison paraphrases lines quoted by Cicero from *De Philosophia*, a work of Aristotle's long lost.
3. Psalm 19.1–4.

4. Addison may have published this ode partly as a response to Watts's imitation of Psalm 114, which had appeared in the *Spectator* just four days earlier (see page 2626).

And all the planets, in their turn,
15   Confirm the tidings as they roll,
And spread the truth from pole to pole.

3

What though, in solemn silence, all
Move round the dark terrestrial ball?
What though nor real voice nor sound
20   Amid their radiant orbs be found?
In reason's ear they all rejoice,
And utter forth a glorious voice,
For ever singing, as they shine,
"The hand that made us is divine."

George Berkeley
1685–1753

For Locke, "ideas" are formed in the mind out of its ongoing encounter with the very real world outside it, where swans swim and elephants plod. For George Berkeley—clergyman, poet, traveler, and philosopher—ideas are all there is. *Esse est percipi*, he argues throughout his philosophical writings: to be is to be perceived. "All those bodies which compose the mighty frame of the world, have not any subsistence without a mind"—a mind engaged in the act of perceiving them. What, then, accounts for the apparent independence and continuity of real objects (trees, to take one of Berkeley's recurrent examples), which seem to remain in place even when no mortal observes them? Berkeley's answer: one mind *is* perpetually engaged in perceiving them. The mind of God creates the ideas, sustains them, renders them consistent with themselves and independent of our intermittent human perceptions. In Berkeley's argument, this divine activity both constitutes proof of God's existence (since such an "infinite mind" is necessary to explain why the world appears to us as it does), and lies at the core of God's benevolence. Berkeley expounded his theory of "immaterialism" in his *Essay Towards a New Theory of Vision* (1709) and *Treatise Concerning the Principles of Human Knowledge* (1710), before recasting it in the more compact, accessible, and popular format of *Three Dialogues Between Hylas and Philonous*. Philonous ("Lover of mind") voices Berkeley's views, while Hylas ("Wooden") expresses the bemused incredulity with which Berkeley's readers continued to greet the philosopher's radical unmaking and reweaving of the fabric of everyday life. Scoffers tended to overlook the solution Berkeley was proffering to an abiding theological problem. Newton's cosmology had given rise (despite his own piety) to the unsettling image of the Clockmaker God, who having made the universe a perfectly efficient mechanism, could now let it run without further intervention. Newton addressed this problem in part by insisting that God had to intervene at intervals in order to adjust his system. Berkeley's God, by contrast, is no clockmaker at all; having authored the world in the beginning, he continues to make it anew at every moment by the creative act of his continual perception.

from Three Dialogues Between Hylas and Philonous

HYLAS: But do you in earnest think, the real existence of sensible things consists in their being actually perceived? If so, how comes it that all mankind distinguish between them? Ask the first man you meet, and he shall tell you, *to be perceived* is one thing, and *to exist* is another.

PHILONOUS: I am content, Hylas, to appeal to the common sense of the world for the truth of my notion. Ask the gardener why he thinks yonder cherry tree exists in the garden, and he shall tell you, because he sees and feels it; in a word, because he perceives it by his senses. Ask him why he thinks an orange tree not to be there, and he shall tell you, because he does not perceive it. What he perceives by sense, that he terms a real being, and saith it *is*, or *exists*; but that which is not perceivable, the same, he saith, hath no being.

HYLAS: Yes, Philonous, I grant the existence of a sensible thing consists in being perceivable, but not in being actually perceived.

PHILONOUS: And what is perceivable but an idea? And can an idea exist without being actually perceived? These are points long since agreed between us.

HYLAS: But be your opinion never so true, yet surely you will not deny it is shocking, and contrary to the common sense of men. Ask the fellow whether yonder tree hath an existence out of his mind: what answer think you he would make?

PHILONOUS: The same that I should myself, to wit, that it doth exist out of his mind. But then to a Christian it cannot surely be shocking to say, the real tree existing without his mind is truly known and comprehended by (that is, *exists in*) the infinite mind of God. Probably he may not at first glance be aware of the direct and immediate proof there is of this, inasmuch as the very being of a tree, or any other sensible thing, implies a mind wherein it is. But the point itself he cannot deny. The question between the materialists[1] and me is not whether things have a real existence out of the mind of this or that person, but whether they have an absolute existence, distinct from being perceived by God, and exterior to all minds. This indeed some heathens and philosophers have affirmed, but whoever entertains notions of the Deity suitable to the Holy Scriptures will be of another opinion.

HYLAS: But according to your notions, what difference is there between real things, and chimeras formed by the imagination, or the visions of a dream, since they are all equally in the mind?

PHILONOUS: The ideas formed by the imagination are faint and indistinct; they have besides an entire dependence on the will. But the ideas perceived by sense, that is, real things, are more vivid and clear, and being imprinted on the mind by a spirit distinct from us, have not a like dependence on our will. There is therefore no danger of confounding these with the foregoing: and there is as little of confounding them with the visions of a dream, which are dim, irregular, and confused. And though they should happen to be never so lively and natural, yet by their not being connected, and of a piece with the preceding and subsequent transactions of our lives, they might easily be distinguished from realities. In short, by whatever method you distinguish *things* from *chimeras* on your own scheme, the same, it is evident, will hold also upon mine. For it must be, I presume, by some perceived difference, and I am not for depriving you of any one thing that you perceive.

HYLAS: But still, Philonous, you hold, there is nothing in the world but spirits and ideas. And this, you must needs acknowledge, sounds very oddly.

PHILONOUS: I own the word *idea*, not being commonly used for *thing*, sounds something out of the way. My reason for using it was, because a necessary relation

---

1. Those who assert the existence of matter, independent of perception.

to the mind is understood to be implied by that term; and it is now commonly used by philosophers to denote the immediate objects of the understanding. But however oddly the proposition may sound in words, yet it includes nothing so very strange or shocking in its sense, which in effect amounts to no more than this, to wit, that there are only things perceiving, and things perceived; or that every unthinking being is necessarily, and from the very nature of its existence, perceived by some mind; if not by any finite created mind, yet certainly by the infinite mind of God, in whom "we live, and move, and have our being."[2] Is this as strange as to say, the sensible qualities are not on the objects, or that we cannot be sure of the existence of things, or know anything of their real natures, though we both see and feel them, and perceive them by all our senses?

HYLAS: And in consequence of this, must we not think there are no such things as physical or corporeal causes but that a spirit is the immediate cause of all the phenomena in nature? Can there be anything more extravagant than this?

PHILONOUS: Yes, it is infinitely more extravagant to say, a thing which is inert, operates on the mind, and which is unperceiving, is the cause of our perceptions. Besides, that which to you, I know not for what reason, seems so extravagant, is no more than the Holy Scriptures assert in a hundred places. In them God is represented as the sole and immediate author of all those effects which some heathens and philosophers are wont to ascribe to nature, matter, fate, or the like unthinking principle. This is so much the constant language of Scripture, that it were needless to confirm it by citations. * * *

1713

David Hume
1711–1776

As he lay dying at home in his native city of Edinburgh, David Hume entertained a visitor by conjuring up, with characteristic cheerfulness, a scenario in the afterlife. He imagined himself begging the fatal ferryman Charon for a little more time: "Have a little patience, good Charon, I have been endeavoring to open the eyes of the public. If I live a few years longer, I may have the satisfaction of seeing the downfall of some of the prevailing systems of superstition." The "prevailing system" which Hume had become most notorious for attacking was the Christian religion, whose favorite tenets—providence, miracles, the argument from design, the afterlife itself—he had called into question, with increasing audacity, over the course of his work. But he had also done much damage to newer systems of thought, notably Locke's. Locke had regarded personal identity as coherent and continuous, the consequence of lifelong experiences and ideas accumulated in the memory. Hume, in his early, massive *Treatise of Human Nature* (1739–1740), waived all this away as an arrant fiction—though perhaps a necessary one, since empiricism properly pursued reveals so radical an incoherence in mortal minds that empiricists themselves must intermittently abandon philosophy in order to go about their daily lives. Like many of his empiric predecessors, Hume argued that knowledge of the real world "must be founded entirely on experience"; more than any predecessor he was willing to entertain (and to entertain with) the doubts and demolitions arising from that premise. In his own lifetime, his skepticism did not prove as contagious as he had

2. Acts 17.28.

hoped. The *Treatise*, he recalled wryly, "fell *deadborn from the press*, without reaching such distinction as even to excite a murmur among the zealots." Though his attempt to recast his chief arguments more succinctly in *An Enquiry Concerning Human Understanding* (1748) prompted a somewhat livelier response, he eventually made his fortune not as a philosopher but as author of the highly successful *History of England* (1754–1763). He faced the general indifference or hostility to his arguments as blithely as he later greeted death, continually refining his views and revising his prose. He knew himself out of sync with his times. When, in his fantasy, he forecasts to Charon the imminent downfall of superstition, the ferryman responds, "You loitering rogue, that will not happen these many hundred years. Do you fancy I will grant you a lease for so long a term? Get into the boat this instant, you lazy loitering rogue."More than two hundred years later, the artful mischief of Hume's work has secured him some such lease. His writings, lucid and elusive, forthright and sly, demand (and receive) continual reassessment; his skepticism has proven more powerful than his contemporaries suspected, and he figures as perhaps the wittiest and most self-possessed philosophical troublemaker since Socrates.

from A Treatise of Human Nature
[THE MIND AS THEATER[1]]

There are some philosophers,[2] who imagine we are every moment intimately conscious of what we call our *self*; that we feel its existence and its continuance in existence; and are certain, beyond the evidence of a demonstration, both of its perfect identity and simplicity. The strongest sensation, the most violent passion, say they, instead of distracting us from this view, only fix it the more intensely, and make us consider their influence on *self* either by their pain or pleasure. To attempt a farther proof of this were to weaken its evidence; since no proof can be derived from any fact, of which we are so intimately conscious; nor is there anything of which we can be certain, if we doubt of this.

Unluckily all these positive assertions are contrary to that very experience which is pleaded for them, nor have we any idea of *self*, after the manner it is here explained. For from what impression could this idea be derived? This question 'tis impossible to answer without a manifest contradiction and absurdity; and yet 'tis a question, which must necessarily be answered, if we would have the idea of self pass for clear and intelligible. It must be some one impression, that gives rise to every real idea. But self or person is not any one impression, but that to which our several impressions and ideas are supposed to have a reference. If any impression gives rise to the idea of self, that impression must continue invariably the same through the whole course of our lives, since self is supposed to exist after that manner. But there is no impression constant and invariable. Pain and pleasure, grief and joy, passions and sensations succeed each other, and never all exist at the same time. It cannot, therefore, be from any of these impressions, or from any other, that the idea of self is derived; and consequently there is no such idea.

But farther, what must become of all our particular perceptions upon this hypothesis? All these are different, and distinguishable, and separable from each other, and may be separately considered, and may exist separately, and have no need of anything to support their existence. After what manner, therefore, do they belong to self; and

---

1. From Book 1, section 6, "Of Personal Identity."
2. Notably Joseph Butler, an Anglican bishop who argued in *The Analogy of Religion* (1736) that the existence of the

self is a truth of which every person is continually (and correctly) certain.

how are they connected with it? For my part, when I enter most intimately into what I call *myself,* I always stumble on some particular perception or other, of heat or cold, light or shade, love or hatred, pain or pleasure. I never can catch *myself* at any time without a perception, and never can observe anything but the perception. When my perceptions are removed for any time, as by sound sleep, so long am I insensible of *myself,* and may truly be said not to exist. And were all my perceptions removed by death, and could I neither think, nor feel, nor see, nor love, nor hate after the dissolution of my body, I should be entirely annihilated, nor do I conceive what is farther requisite to make me a perfect nonentity. If anyone upon serious and unprejudiced reflection, thinks he has a different notion of *himself,* I must confess I can reason no longer with him. All I can allow him is, that he may be in the right as well as I, and that we are essentially different in this particular. He may, perhaps, perceive something simple and continued, which he calls *himself;* though I am certain there is no such principle in me.

But setting aside some metaphysicians of this kind, I may venture to affirm of the rest of mankind, that they are nothing but a bundle or collection of different perceptions, which succeed each other with an inconceivable rapidity, and are in a perpetual flux and movement. Our eyes cannot turn in their sockets without varying our perceptions. Our thought is still more variable than our sight; and all our other senses and faculties contribute to this change; nor is there any single power of the soul which remains unalterably the same, perhaps for one moment. The mind is a kind of theater, where several perceptions successively make their appearance: pass, re-pass, glide away, and mingle in an infinite variety of postures and situations. There is properly no *simplicity* in it at one time, nor *identity* in different; whatever natural propension we may have to imagine that simplicity and identity. The comparison of the theater must not mislead us. They are the successive perceptions only, that constitute the mind; nor have we the most distant notion of the place where these scenes are represented, or of the materials, of which it is composed. * * *

[PHILOSOPHY AND COMMON LIFE³]

But what have I here said, that reflections very refined and metaphysical have little or no influence upon us? This opinion I can scarce forbear retracting, and condemning from my present feeling and experience. The *intense* view of these manifold contradictions and imperfections in human reason has so wrought upon me, and heated my brain, that I am ready to reject all belief and reasoning, and can look upon no opinion even as more probable or likely than another. Where am I, or what? From what causes do I derive my existence, and to what condition shall I return? Whose favor shall I court, and whose anger must I dread? What beings surround me? and on whom have I any influence, or who have any influence on me? I am confounded with all these questions, and begin to fancy myself in the most deplorable condition imaginable, environed with the deepest darkness, and utterly deprived of the use of every member and faculty.

Most fortunately it happens, that since reason is incapable of dispelling these clouds, nature herself suffices to that purpose, and cures me of this philosophical

3. From Book 1, Section 7: "Conclusion of This Book." The first book of the *Treatise* serves as a long prelude to the whole; in concluding it, Hume considers the "manifest contradictions" between the assumptions on which ordinary people lead their lives, and the volatile questions raised by "refined reasoning" (rigorous philosophic inquiry). Pinpointing these contradictions in himself, he contemplates the precariousness of his enterprise, and the intricacy of his motives for undertaking it.

melancholy and delirium, either by relaxing this bent of mind, or by some avocation and lively impression of my senses, which obliterate all these chimeras. I dine, I play a game of backgammon, I converse, and am merry with my friends; and when after three or four hour's amusement, I would return to these speculations, they appear so cold, and strained, and ridiculous, that I cannot find in my heart to enter into them any farther.

Here then I find myself absolutely and necessarily determined to live, and talk, and act like other people in the common affairs of life. But notwithstanding that my natural propensity, and the course of my animal spirits and passions, reduce me to this indolent belief in the general maxims of the world, I still feel such remains of my former disposition, that I am ready to throw all my books and papers into the fire, and resolve never more to renounce the pleasures of life for the sake of reasoning and philosophy. For these are my sentiments in that splenetic[4] humor, which governs me at present. I may, nay I must yield to the current of nature, in submitting to my senses and understanding; and in this blind submission I show most perfectly my skeptical disposition and principles. But does it follow, that I must strive against the current of nature, which leads me to indolence and pleasure; that I must seclude myself, in some measure, from the commerce and society of men, which is so agreeable; and that I must torture my brain with subtleties and sophistries, at the very time that I cannot satisfy myself concerning the reasonableness of so painful an application, nor have any tolerable prospect of arriving by its means at truth and certainty? Under what obligation do I lie of making such an abuse of time? And to what end can it serve either for the service of mankind, or for my own private interest? No: if I must be a fool, as well as those who reason or believe anything *certainly* are, my follies shall at least be natural and agreeable. Where I strive against my inclination, I shall have a good reason for my resistance; and will no more be led a wandering into such dreary solitudes, and rough passages, as I have hitherto met with.

There are the sentiments of my spleen[5] and indolence; and indeed I must confess, that philosophy has nothing to oppose to them, and expects a victory more from the returns of a serious good-humored disposition, than from the force of reason and conviction. In all the incidents of life we ought still to preserve our skepticism. If we believe, that fire warms, or water refreshes, 'tis only because it costs us too much pains to think otherwise. Nay if we are philosophers, it ought only to be upon skeptical principles, and from an inclination, which we feel to the employing ourselves after that manner. Where reason is lively, and mixes itself with some propensity, it ought to be assented to. Where it does not, it never can have any title to operate upon us.

At the time, therefore, that I am tired with amusement and company, and have indulged a *reverie* in my chamber, or in a solitary walk by a riverside, I feel my mind all collected within itself, and am naturally *inclined* to carry my view into all those subjects, about which I have met with so many disputes in the course of my reading and conversation.[6] I cannot forbear having a curiosity to be acquainted with the principles of moral good and evil, the nature and foundation of government, and the cause of those several passions and inclinations, which actuate and govern me. I am uneasy to think I approve of one object, and disapprove of another; call one thing beautiful, and another deformed; decide concerning truth and falsehood, reason and folly, without

---

4. Depressive, irritable.
5. Despondency.

6. In the list that follows, Hume names many of the topics he will take up later in the *Treatise*.

knowing upon what principles I proceed. I am concerned for the condition of the learned world, which lies under such a deplorable ignorance in all these particulars. I feel an ambition to arise in me of contributing to the instruction of mankind, and of acquiring a name by my inventions and discoveries. These sentiments spring up naturally in my present disposition; and should I endeavor to banish them, by attaching myself to any other business or diversion, I *feel* I should be a loser in point of pleasure; and this is the origin of my philosophy.

1734–1737   1739–1740

from An Enquiry Concerning Human Understanding[1]
from *Section 10: Of Miracles*

A miracle is a violation of the laws of nature; and as a firm and unalterable experience has established these laws, the proof against a miracle, from the very nature of the fact, is as entire as any argument from experience can possibly be imagined. Why is it more than probable that all men must die; that lead cannot, of itself, remain suspended in the air; that fire consumes wood, and is extinguished by water; unless it be, that these events are found agreeable to the laws of nature, and there is required a violation of these laws, or in other words, a miracle to prevent them? Nothing is esteemed a miracle, if it ever happen in the common course of nature. It is no miracle that a man, seemingly in good health, should die on a sudden; because such a kind of death, though more unusual than any other, has yet been frequently observed to happen. But it is a miracle that a dead man should come to life; because that has never been observed in any age or country. There must, therefore, be a uniform experience against every miraculous event, otherwise the event would not merit that appellation. And as a uniform experience amounts to a proof, there is here a direct and full *proof,* from the nature of the fact, against the existence of any miracle; nor can such a proof be destroyed, or the miracle rendered credible, but by an opposite proof, which is superior.

The plain consequence is (and it is a general maxim worthy of our attention), "That no testimony is sufficient to establish a miracle, unless the testimony be of such a kind, that its falsehood would be more miraculous than the fact which it endeavors to establish; and even in that case there is a mutual destruction of arguments, and the superior only gives us an assurance suitable to that degree of force which remains after deducting the inferior." When anyone tells me, that he saw a dead man restored to life, I immediately consider with myself, whether it be more probable, that this person should either deceive or be deceived, or that the fact, which he relates, should really have happened. I weigh the one miracle against the other; and according to the superiority which I discover, I pronounce my decision, and always reject the greater miracle. If the falsehood of his testimony would be more miraculous than the event which he relates, then, and not till then, can he pretend to command my belief or opinion.

In the foregoing reasoning we have supposed, that the testimony, upon which a miracle is founded, may possibly amount to an entire proof, and that the falsehood of

---

that testimony would be a real prodigy. But it is easy to show that we have been a great deal too liberal in our concession, and that there never was a miraculous event established on so full an evidence.

For *first*, there is not to be found, in all history, any miracle attested by a sufficient number of men, of such unquestioned good sense, education, and learning, as to secure us against all delusion in themselves; of such undoubted integrity, as to place them beyond all suspicion of any design to deceive others; of such credit and reputation in the eyes of mankind, as to have a great deal to lose in case of their being detected in any falsehood; and at the same time, attesting facts performed in such a public manner and in so celebrated a part of the world, as to render the detection unavoidable. All which circumstances are requisite to give us a full assurance in the testimony of men.

Secondly. We may observe in human nature a principle which, if strictly examined, will be found to diminish extremely the assurance which we might, from human testimony, have, in any kind of prodigy. The maxim by which we commonly conduct ourselves in our reasonings is that the objects of which we have no experience resemble those of which we have; that what we have found to be most usual is always most probable; and that where there is an opposition of arguments, we ought to give the preference to such as are founded on the greatest number of past observations. But though, in proceeding by this rule, we readily reject any fact which is unusual and incredible in an ordinary degree; yet in advancing farther, the mind observes not always the same rule; but when anything is affirmed utterly absurd and miraculous, it rather the more readily admits of such a fact, upon account of that very circumstance which ought to destroy all its authority. The passion of *surprise* and *wonder*, arising from miracles, being an agreeable emotion, gives a sensible tendency towards the belief of those events from which it is derived. And this goes so far, that even those who cannot enjoy this pleasure immediately, nor can believe those miraculous events, of which they are informed, yet love to partake of the satisfaction at second-hand or by rebound, and place a pride and delight in exciting the admiration of others.

With what greediness are the miraculous accounts of travelers received, their descriptions of sea and land monsters, their relations of wonderful adventures, strange men, and uncouth manners? But if the spirit of religion join itself to the love of wonder, there is an end of common sense; and human testimony, in these circumstances, loses all pretensions to authority. A religionist may be an enthusiast,[2] and imagine he sees what has no reality. He may know his narrative to be false, and yet persevere in it, with the best intentions in the world, for the sake of promoting so holy a cause; or even where this delusion has not place, vanity, excited by so strong a temptation, operates on him more powerfully than on the rest of mankind in any other circumstances; and self-interest with equal force. His auditors may not have, and commonly have not, sufficient judgment to canvass his evidence. What judgment they have, they renounce by principle, in these sublime and mysterious subjects; or if they were ever so willing to employ it, passion and a heated imagination disturb the regularity of its operations. Their credulity increases his impudence; and his impudence overpowers their credulity. * * *

Thirdly. It forms a strong presumption against all supernatural and miraculous relations, that they are observed chiefly to abound among ignorant and barbarous

---

2. Fanatic.

nations; or if a civilized people has ever given admission to any of them, that people will be found to have received them from ignorant and barbarous ancestors, who transmitted them with that inviolable sanction and authority, which always attend received opinions. When we peruse the first histories of all nations, we are apt to imagine ourselves transported into some new world, where the whole frame of nature is disjointed, and every element performs its operations in a different manner from what it does at present. Battles, revolutions, pestilence, famine, and death are never the effect of those natural causes which we experience. Prodigies, omens, oracles, judgments, quite obscure the few natural events that are intermingled with them. But as the former grow thinner every page, in proportion as we advance nearer the enlightened ages, we soon learn that there is nothing mysterious or supernatural in the case, but that all proceeds from the usual propensity of mankind towards the marvelous, and that, though this inclination may at intervals receive a check from sense and learning, it can never be thoroughly extirpated from human nature. * * *

Upon the whole, then, it appears that no testimony for any kind of miracle has ever amounted to a probability, much less to a proof; and that, even supposing it amounted to a proof, it would be opposed by another proof; derived from the very nature of the fact, which it would endeavor to establish. It is experience only which gives authority to human testimony; and it is the same experience which assures us of the laws of nature. When, therefore, these two kinds of experience are contrary, we have nothing to do but subtract the one from the other, and embrace an opinion, either on one side or the other, with that assurance which arises from the remainder. But according to the principle here explained, this subtraction, with regard to all popular religions, amounts to an entire annihilation; and therefore we may establish it as a maxim, that no human testimony can have such force as to prove a miracle, and make it a just foundation for any such system of religion. * * *

What we have said of miracles may be applied, without any variation, to prophecies; and indeed, all prophecies are real miracles, and as such only can be admitted as proofs of any revelation. If it did not exceed the capacity of human nature to foretell future events, it would be absurd to employ any prophecy as an argument for a divine mission or authority from heaven. So that, upon the whole, we may conclude, that the *Christian religion* not only was at first attended with miracles, but even at this day cannot be believed by any reasonable person without one. Mere reason is insufficient to convince us of its veracity. And whoever is moved by *faith* to assent to it, is conscious of a continued miracle in his own person, which subverts all the principles of his understanding, and gives him a determination to believe what is most contrary to custom and experience.

c. 1736   1748

Christopher Smart
1722–1771

"Newton . . . is more of error than of the truth, but I am of the Word of God," wrote Christopher Smart in his astonishing poem *Jubilate Agno* ("Rejoice in the Lamb"). For Smart, as for a growing number of Christians in the century's second half, the Newtonian "error" consisted in a commitment to materialist science, to an empiricism that investigated the physical world and sought its seeming system, rather than submitting to faith in a God who worked by will and sometimes by miracle, free of any fixed laws of nature. Smart composed *Jubilate Agno* in his late thirties, while confined in a madhouse; after a brilliant career as a classical scholar at Cambridge, and an auspicious start in London as a literary adventurer (poet, editor, translator, essayist), he suffered a derangement whose chief symptom was his compulsion to pray spontaneously in public places (he was too much "of the Word of God" to be socially acceptable). Released from the asylum after five years, Smart recast much material from the *Jubilate Agno* in his *Song of David* (1763); following Watts's precedent, he published a translation of the Psalms (1767) and (while imprisoned for debt at the very end of his life) a book of *Hymns for the Amusement of Children* (1771). *Jubilate Agno* remained in manuscript and unknown for a century and a half after the poet's death. Smart called it "my Magnificat," *magnificat* being the title of the liturgical hymn first uttered by the Virgin Mary upon learning that she would conceive a son: "My Soul doth magnify the Lord" (Luke 1.46–55). Structured like a responsive prayer, Smart's poem moves rapidly across a wide range of reference, from the scriptural and mystical to the local and the homely ("God be gracious to Baumgarden"—a London bassoon player). But Smart returns repeatedly to a preoccupation touched on in the poem's title: to the animal world as emblem and embodiment of God's grace and greatness (in Smart's time natural history was among the branches of knowledge least touched by the new science, and most inflected by faith and folklore). In the excerpts that follow, Smart punningly pinpoints the animal essences of languages ancient and modern, then depicts the feline who kept him company during his years of confinement, singing Jeoffry's praises with such exuberance as to make *magnificat* seem a latent, sacred, and affectionate pun.

from Jubilate Agno
[ANIMALS IN LANGUAGE[1]]

625   For the power of some animal is predominant in every language.
    For the power and spirit of a CAT is in the Greek.
    For the sound of a cat is in the most useful preposition κατ' ευχην.[2]
    For the pleasantry of a cat at pranks is in the language ten thousand times over.[3]
    For JACK UPON PRANCK is in the performance of πε ρι together or separate.[4]
630   For Clapperclaw[5] is in the grappling of the words upon one another in all the modes of versification.
    For the sleekness of a Cat is in his αγλαιηφι.[6]
    For the Greek is thrown from heaven and falls upon its feet.[7]
    For the Greek when distracted from the line is sooner restored to rank and rallied into some form than any other.
    For the purring of a Cat is his τρυζει.[8]
635   For his cry is in ουαι[9] which I am sorry for.

1. These selections come from Fragment B of Smart's manuscript. Some pages of Smart's manuscript contain long sequences of lines beginning "Let"; other pages contain lines beginning "For," with clear enough indications that the "Let" and "For" lines were meant to be dovetailed and read alternately, in the form of responsive prayer. For the two excerpts printed here, though, lines beginning "Let" have not been found—and may never have been written.
2. *Kat euchen:* "according to prayer" (Greek).

3. The syllable *kat* appears in many Greek word forms.
4. Greek *perikato* means "upside down" (as, probably, does "Jack Upon Pranck").
5. To claw, scratch.
6. *Aglaiefi:* "beauty."
7. Perhaps an allusion to the Greek poetic term *catalexis*, the shortening or omission of a "foot" from a line of verse; the prefix *cata-* means "down."
8. *Truzei:* "murmur."
9. *Ouai:* exclamation of lament ("ah!").

For the Mouse (*Mus*) prevails in the Latin.[1]
For *Edi-mus,bibi-mus,vivi-mus—ore-mus*.[2]
For the Mouse is a creature of great personal valor.
For—this is a true case—Cat takes female mouse from the company of
    male—male mouse will not depart, but stands threat'ning and daring.
640 For this is as much as to challenge, if you will let her go, I will engage you,
    as prodigious a creature as you are.
For the Mouse is of an hospitable disposition.
For bravery and hospitality were said and done by the Romans rather than
    others.
For two creatures the Bull and the Dog prevail in the English.
For all the words ending in -ble are in the creature. Invisi-ble,
    Incomprehensi-ble, ineffa-ble, A-ble.
645 For the Greek and Latin are not dead languages, but taken up and accepted
    for the sake of him that spoke them.
For can is (*canis*[3]) is cause and effect a dog.
For the English is concise and strong. Dog and Bull again.
For Newton's notion of colors is αλογος,[4] unphilosophical.

[MY CAT JEOFFRY]

695 For I will consider my Cat Jeoffry.
For he is the servant of the Living God duly and daily serving him.
For at the first glance of the glory of God in the East he worships in his
    way.
For is this done by wreathing his body seven times round with elegant
    quickness.
For then he leaps up to catch the musk, which is the blessing of God upon
    his prayer.
700 For he rolls upon prank to work it in.
For having done duty and received blessing he begins to consider himself.
For this he performs in ten degrees.
For first he looks upon his fore-paws to see if they are clean.
For secondly he kicks up behind to clear away there.
705 For thirdly he works it upon stretch with the fore-paws extended.
For fourthly he sharpens his paws by wood.
For fifthly he washes himself.
For sixthly he rolls upon wash.
For seventhly he fleas himself, that he may not be interrupted upon the
    beat.
710 For eighthly he rubs himself against a post.
For ninthly he looks up for his instructions.
For tenthly he goes in quest of food.
For having considered God and himself he will consider his neighbor.
For if he meets another cat he will kiss her in kindness.
715 For when he takes his prey he plays with it to give it chance.
For one mouse in seven escapes by his dallying.

---

1. Partly because (as Smart illustrates in line 637), the
syllable *mus* means "mouse" and is also the suffix for first
person plural present-tense conjugations.

2. "We eat, we drink, we live—let us pray."
3. Dog (Latin).
4. *Alogos*: literally, "without the Word."

For when his day's work is done his business more properly begins.

For he keeps the Lord's watch in the night against the adversary.

For he counteracts the powers of darkness by his electrical skin and glaring
    eyes.

720   For he counteracts the Devil, who is death, by brisking about the life.

For in his morning orisons he loves the sun and the sun loves him.

For he is of the tribe of Tiger.

For the Cherub Cat is a term of the Angel Tiger.

For he has the subtlety and hissing of a serpent, which in goodness he
    suppresses.

725   For he will not do destruction, if he is well-fed, neither will he spit without
    provocation.

For he purrs in thankfulness, when God tells him he's a good Cat.

For he is an instrument for the children to learn benevolence upon.

For every house is incomplete without him and a blessing is lacking in the
    spirit.

For the Lord commanded Moses concerning the cats at the departure of the
    Children of Israel from Egypt.[5]

730   For every family had one cat at least in the bag.

For the English Cats are the best in Europe.

For he is the cleanest in the use of his fore-paws of any quadrupede.

For the dexterity of his defense is an instance of the love of God to him
    exceedingly.

For he is the quickest to his mark of any creature.

735   For he is tenacious of his point.

For he is a mixture of gravity and waggery.

For he knows that God is his Savior.

For there is nothing sweeter than his peace when at rest.

For there is nothing brisker than his life when in motion.

740   For he is of the Lord's poor and so indeed is he called by benevolence per-
    petually—Poor Jeoffry! poor Jeoffry! the rat has bit thy throat.

For I bless the name of the Lord Jesus that Jeoffry is better.

For the divine spirit comes about his body to sustain it in complete cat.

For his tongue is exceeding pure so that it has in purity what it wants in
    music.

For he is docile and can learn certain things.

745   For he can set up with gravity which is patience upon approbation.

For he can fetch and carry, which is patience in employment.

For he can jump over a stick which is patience upon proof positive.

For he can spraggle° upon waggle at the word of command.   *sprawl*

For he can jump from an eminence into his master's bosom.

750   For he can catch the cork and toss it again.

For he is hated by the hypocrite and miser.

For the former is afraid of detection.

---

5. "Take your flocks and your herds," says the Egyptian Pharaoh when demanding the Israelites' departure (Exodus 12.32); Smart adds the Lord and the cats.

For the latter refuses the charge.
For he camels his back to bear the first notion of business.
755   For he is good to think on, if a man would express himself neatly.
For he made a great figure in Egypt for his signal services.
For he killed the Ichneumon-rat° very pernicious by land.   *mongoose*
For his ears are so acute that they sting again.
For from this proceeds the passing quickness of his attention.
760   For by stroking of him I have found out electricity.
For I perceived God's light about him both wax and fire.
For the Electrical fire is the spiritual substance, which God sends from
    heaven to sustain the bodies both of man and beast.
For God has blessed him in the variety of his movements.
For, though he cannot fly, he is an excellent clamberer.
765   For his motions upon the face of the earth are more than any other quadru-
    pede.
For he can tread to all the measures upon the music.
For he can swim for life.
For he can creep.

c. 1758–1763   1939

William Cowper
1731–1800

Like Christopher Smart, William Cowper suffered madness, loved animals, wrote hymns, and invented capacious new structures for religious verse. But where Smart wrote to celebrate his sure salvation, Cowper wrote out of the certainty that he was damned—unworthy of redemption and predestined for hellfire. The conviction first took hold in 1763, when a paralyzing panic cut him off from impending attachments (to a new job he was about to secure, a beloved woman he was soon to marry) and prompted several attempts at suicide. The course of recovery took him first to an asylum, then through a conversion to Calvinism, then to the household of Mary Unwin, who loved and looked after him for the next four decades, and finally into partnership with Unwin's neighbor, the austere hymn-writer John Newton, with whom Cowper collaborated for years on a new collection of religious song, the *Olney Hymns* (it included, along with several of Cowper's still-sung texts, Newton's perdurable *Amazing Grace*). A second, sharper attack of madness, ten years after the first, deepened Cowper's conviction of his doom but also ushered in years of plentiful poetic composition. Seizing any small occasion (a fish dinner, the death of a pet bird) to produce a short, often comic piece of verse, Cowper wrote poems to hold terror at bay. As his output increased, his ambition did too. *The Task*, a massive mock-epic grounded in the comforts of Cowper's rural retirement (sofa, garden, seasons) but ranging satirically over the whole wide world, surprised even its author by its scope and popularity. Spurred by its success, Cowper undertook to translate Homer's epics, hoping to surpass Pope's attempts earlier in the century. In a passage near the midpoint of *The Task* (printed here), Newton appears briefly as the embodiment of Cowper's deepest hope, that the mind might merge with God through a science immersed in faith—"philosophy baptized." In his last, autobiographical poem, *The Cast-away*, Cowper draws a darker picture, of a mind sundered from its maker by distance and despair.

Light Shining out of Darkness[1]

God moves in a mysterious way,
    His wonders to perform;
He plants his footsteps in the sea,
    And rides upon the storm.

5   Deep in unfathomable mines
        Of never-failing skill,
He treasures up his bright designs,
    And works his sov'reign will.

Ye fearful saints[2] fresh courage take,
10   The clouds ye so much dread
Are big with mercy, and shall break
    In blessings on your head.

Judge not the Lord by feeble sense,
    But trust him for his grace;
15   Behind a frowning providence,
    He hides a smiling face.

His purposes will ripen fast,
    Unfolding every hour;
The bud may have a bitter taste,
20   But sweet will be the flower.

Blind unbelief is sure to err,
    And scan his work in vain;
God is his own interpreter,
    And he will make it plain.

c. 1773   1774

from The Task
["PHILOSOPHY BAPTIZED"[1]]

God never meant that man should scale the heav'ns
By strides of human wisdom. In his works
Though wond'rous, he commands us in his word
To seek *him* rather, where his mercy shines.
225   The mind indeed enlightened from above
Views him in all. Ascribes to the grand cause
The grand effect. Acknowledges with joy
His manner, and with rapture tastes his style.
But never yet did philosophic° tube   *scientific*
230   That brings the planets home into the eye
Of observation, and discovers, else°   *otherwise*
Not visible, his family of worlds,

---

1. Written and first published during the period of Cowper's collaboration with John Newton; later included in their *Olney Hymns* (1779).
2. Cowper addresses those who (according to Calvinist theology) are predestined for salvation.
1. From Book 3, "The Garden" (for more of *The Task*, see pages 2662–65).

Discover him that rules them; such a veil
Hangs over mortal eyes, blind from the birth
235 And dark in things divine. Full often too
Our wayward intellect, the more we learn
Of nature, overlooks her author more,
From instrumental causes proud to draw
Conclusions retrograde and mad mistake.
240 But if his word once teach us, shoot a ray
Through all the heart's dark chambers, and reveal
Truths undiscerned but by that holy light,
Then all is plain. Philosophy baptized
In the pure fountain of eternal love
245 Has eyes indeed; and viewing all she sees
As meant to indicate a God to man,
Gives *him* his praise, and forfeits not her own.
Learning has borne such fruit in other days
On all her branches. Piety has found
250 Friends in the friends of science, and true prayer
Has flowed from lips wet with Castalian dews.[2]
Such was thy wisdom, Newton, childlike sage!
Sagacious reader of the works of God,
And in his word sagacious. * * *

1783–1785   1785

The Cast-away[1]

Obscurest night involved° the sky,   *encompassed*
   Th' Atlantic billows roared,
When such a destined° wretch as I   *doomed*
   Washed headlong from on board
5 Of friends, of hope, of all bereft,
His floating home for ever left.

No braver chief[2] could Albion° boast   *Britain*
   Than he with whom he went,
Nor ever ship left Albion's coast
10   With warmer wishes sent.
He loved them both, but both in vain,
Nor him beheld, nor her again.

Not long beneath the whelming brine
   Expert to swim, he lay,
15 Nor soon he felt his strength decline

2. I.e., from poets (who have drunk of the inspirational
Castalian spring on the mountain of the Muses).
1. Cowper based this poem on a mariner's account, in a
popular travel book, of having watched helplessly as a
shipmate was hurled overboard during a storm: "We were
the more grieved at his unhappy fate, as we . . . conceived
from the manner in which he swam that he might continue sensible, for a considerable time longer, of the horror attending his irretrievable situation." Cowper collates
the doomed man's situation with his own, which he conceived as also "irretrievable"; the poem, left in manuscript
at his death, is his last surviving original poem in English.
2. George Anson, commander of the naval squadron in
which the sailor was lost.

Or courage die away;
But waged with Death a lasting strife
Supported by despair of life.

He shouted, nor his friends had failed
20   To check the vessel's course,
But so the furious blast prevailed
            That, pitiless perforce,
They left their outcast mate behind,
And scudded still before the wind.

25   Some succor yet they could afford,
            And, such as storms allow,
The cask, the coop, the floated cord
            Delayed not to bestow;
But he, they knew, nor ship nor shore,
30   Whate'er they gave, should visit more.

Nor, cruel as it seemed, could he
            Their haste, himself, condemn,
Aware that flight, in such a sea,
            Alone could rescue them;
35   Yet bitter felt it still to die
Deserted, and his friends so nigh.

He long survives who lives an hour
            In ocean, self-upheld,
And so long he, with unspent power,
40   His destiny repelled,
And ever, as the minutes flew,
Entreated help, or cried, Adieu!

At length, his transient respite past,
            His comrades, who before
45   Had heard his voice in every blast,
            Could catch the sound no more;
For then, by toil subdued, he drank
The stifling wave, and then he sank.

No poet wept him: but the page
50   Of narrative[3] sincere
That tells his name, his worth,° his age,   rank
            Is wet with Anson's tear,
And tears by bards or heroes shed
Alike immortalize the dead.

55   I therefore purpose not or dream,
            Descanting on his fate,
To give the melancholy theme
            A more enduring date,

3. The log book of the ship from which he fell.

But misery still delights to trace
60   Its semblance in another's case.

No voice divine the storm allayed,
   No light propitious shone,
When, snatched from all effectual aid,
   We perished, each, alone;
65   But I beneath a rougher sea,
And whelmed in deeper gulphs than he.

1799   1804

END OF PERSPECTIVES: MIND AND GOD

James Thomson
1700–1748

"Nature delights me in every form," James Thomson declared in a letter at age twenty-five. "I am just now painting her in her most lugubrious dress; for my own amusement describing winter as it presents itself." Though he may not have known it yet, he was "just now" embarking on his life's central work. In his long poem *The Seasons* (of which this piece on winter was the earliest installment), Thomson sought to develop a poetic structure capacious enough to compass the varied forms of nature in which he took so much delight.

Thomson wrote his letter in London, where he had recently arrived, to a friend in his native Scotland, where he would never return. The winters he remembered were those of the terrain where he had spent his first fifteen years, in a village near the border with England. When Thomson was seven, geographical proximity became political reality. The Act of Union, energetically endorsed by the poet's Whig neighbors, linked Scotland with England and Wales to form the new entity of Great Britain; that event resonates throughout the poet's life and work, in his depictions of nature (which remain centered in Scotland even as they span the globe), in his passionate advocacy of the politics he'd absorbed in youth, in his celebration of the incipient British empire.

Born to a Presbyterian minister praised for his "diligence," and to a mother noted for her "imagination," "warmth," and enthusiastic piety, Thomson felt toward both parents a lifelong affection. In deference to their wishes, and despite an early inclination to poetry, he initially planned to follow his father into the ministry. But Edinburgh, where he went at age fifteen to study divinity, abounded in literary aspirants, endeavors, publications, and societies. During his ten years there, Thomson gradually found that the attractions of poetry outflanked those of professional piety. Like many ambitious Scotsmen of the time, Thomson headed for London, along the route the Union had made smooth. There, aided and encouraged by new literary friends (Pope and Gay among them), he launched the poem of nature that he describes in his letter home. *Winter* (1726) was followed by *Summer* and *Spring* (both 1727); *The Seasons* (1730) brought the cycle to completion, with the new piece on *Autumn* added to the three earlier sections, now much expanded and revised. The work struck readers and reviewers as something altogether new, and quickly established the poet's fame. The following years produced another long poem, equally ambitious but less successful (*Liberty*, 1735–1736), a series of verse tragedies, and a plenitude of distractions. Thomson engaged exuberantly in politics and in the pleasures of food and drink, cherished his friends, and fell in love with women who did not love him back. The years also brought recurrent returns of *The Seasons*: the poem reappeared, in a greatly enlarged and altered edition, in 1744, and in yet another incarnation two years later. In *The Castle of Indolence* (1748), Thomson produced an allegory, by turns serious and comic, on that very propensity toward imaginative idleness that had both generated his poetry and prevented his producing more. The poem, deeply autobiographical, proved valedictory as well. Four months after its publication the poet died, mourned by his many friends as "our old, tried, amiable, open, and honest-hearted Thomson," and by a wider world of readers as the writer who had newly transmuted nature into language, in the century's single most popular poem.

The Seasons often gave rise to a measure of puzzlement commingled with its popularity. Thomson had set so much going in the poem that familiar conventions of artistic order and containment seemed overthrown. "The great defect of *The Seasons*," Samuel Johnson opined, "is its want of method"—its lack of a self-evident logical structure. Still, reader after reader (including Johnson) discovered that this seeming defect correlated mysteriously with the poem's many pleasures: its comprehensiveness, its range of tones and modes, its contagious "enthusiasm," whereby (in Johnson's account) "our thoughts expand with [Thomson's] imagery and kindle with his sentiments." Expansiveness had marked the poem's making as well as its impact. During two decades of creation and revision, Thomson kept nature at the center of his scrutiny, but made it the repository for his many preoccupations: Whig politics, imperial expansion, ancient history, Christian faith, modern science. The poem links and navigates all these topics not so much by "method" as by the restless motion of the maker's mind. In this innovative arrangement, the physical world becomes a medium of meditation, a mirror of mind and culture, the meeting place where human inquiry most fully encounters divine display, in order to discern and to wonder at the ways of both self and God. Like his idol Isaac Newton, whose discoveries pervade the poem, Thomson was reading and representing God's Book of Nature in new, immensely influential terms. "Enthusiasm" itself means immersion "in the God," possession by the divine. Thomson makes good on the term when he declares at the poem's close that the seasons "are but the varied God," phenomena that mortals must inhabit and observe with deep discernment, proper awe. Thomson's own enthusiasm proved contagious across boundaries of space, time, and medium. His poem was translated and ardently imitated in most of the languages of Europe; the composer Franz Joseph Haydn set its sentiments to music, and draughtsmen depicted its scenes so often that it remained for a hundred years the most illustrated work in English. For writers of many nations and several generations, *The Seasons* served as almost inexhaustible sourcebook, as supplementary Scripture.

from Winter. A Poem[1]
[Autumn Evening and Night]

> See! Winter comes, to rule the varied year,
> Sullen and sad; with all his rising train,
> Vapors, and clouds, and storms. Be these my theme,
> These, that exalt the soul to solemn thought,
> 5   And heavenly musing. Welcome kindred glooms!
> Wished, wintery horrors, hail! With frequent foot,
> Pleased have I, in my cheerful morn of life,
> When nursed by careless solitude I lived,

---

1. This was the earliest version Thomson published; for some of his subsequent revisions, see the selection from *Autumn* on pages 2650–55.

And sung of Nature with unceasing joy,
10 Pleased have I wandered through your rough domains;
Trod the pure, virgin-snows, myself as pure;
Heard the winds roar, and the big torrent burst;
Or seen the deep-fermenting tempest brewed
In the red evening sky. Thus passed the time
15 Till, through the opening chambers of the south,[2]
Looked out the joyous Spring, looked out, and smiled.

Thee too, inspirer of the toiling swain!
Fair Autumn, yellow robed! I'll sing of thee,
Of thy last, tempered days and sunny calms;
20 When all the golden hours are on the wing,
Attending thy retreat, and round thy wain,°   *chariot*
Slow-rolling, onward to the southern sky.

Behold![3] the well-poised hornet, hovering, hangs
With quivering pinions in the genial blaze;
25 Flies off in airy circles; then returns
And hums and dances to the beating ray.
Nor shall the man that, musing, walks alone,
And, heedless, strays within his radiant lists,°   *boundaries*
Go unchastised away. Sometimes a fleece
30 Of clouds, wide-scattering, with a lucid[4] veil,
Soft, shadow o'er th' unruffled face of heaven;
And, through their dewy sluices,° shed the sun,   *floodgates*
With tempered influence down. Then is the time,
For those, whom Wisdom, and whom Nature charm,
35 To steal themselves from the degenerate crowd,
And soar above this little scene of things:
To tread low-thoughted Vice beneath their feet:
To lay their passions in a gentle calm,
And woo lone Quiet, in her silent walks.

40 Now solitary, and in pensive guise,
Oft let me wander o'er the russet mead,°   *meadow*
Or through the pining grove, where scarce is heard
One dying strain, to cheer the woodman's toil.
Sad Philomel,[5] perchance, pours forth her plaint
45 Far through the withering copse.° Meanwhile the leaves,   *woods*
That late the forest clad with lively green,
Nipped by the drizzly night, and sallow-hued,
Fall wavering through the air; or shower amain,°   *fiercely*
Urged by the breeze, that sobs amid the boughs.
50 Then listening hares forsake the rustling woods,
And, starting at the frequent noise, escape

2. The southern sky, "opening" as clouds dissipate.
3. In *The Seasons*, Thomson transferred this passage (lines 23–79), extensively revised, to *Autumn* (lines 955–1036; see pages 2650–52).

4. The adjective meant both "shining" and "transparent."
5. The nightingale. In Greek myth, the Athenian princess Philomela, raped by her brother-in-law Tereus, is transformed into a bird and nightly laments her fate.

To the rough stubble, and the rushy fen.°   *marsh*
Then woodcocks o'er the fluctuating main
That glimmers to the glimpses of the moon
55   Stretch their long voyage to the woodland glade;
Where, wheeling with uncertain flight, they mock
The nimble fowler's° aim. Now Nature droops;   *bird hunter's*
Languish the living herbs, with pale decay:
And all the various family of flowers
60   Their sunny robes resign. The falling fruits,
Through the still night, forsake the parent bough
That in the first gray glances of the dawn,
Looks wild, and wonders at the wintry waste.

      The year, yet pleasing, but declining fast,
65   Soft, o'er the secret soul, in gentle gales,
A philosophic melancholy breathes,
And bears the swelling thought aloft to heaven.
Then forming fancy rouses to conceive,
What never mingled with the vulgar's° dream: *common people's*
70   Then wake the tender pang, the pitying tear,
The sigh for suffering worth, the wish preferred°   *offered up*
For humankind, the joy to see them blessed,
And all the social offspring of the heart!

      Oh! bear me then to high embowering shades;
75   To twilight groves and visionary vales;
To weeping grottos and to hoary caves;
Where angel forms are seen, and voices heard,
Sighed in low whispers that abstract the soul
From outward sense far into worlds remote.

80   Now,[6] when the western sun withdraws the day,
And humid evening, gliding o'er the sky,
In her chill progress checks the straggling beams,
And robs them of their gathered, vapory prey,
Where marshes stagnate, and where rivers wind,
85   Cluster the rolling fogs, and swim along
The dusky-mantled lawn:° then slow descend,   *open ground*
Once more to mingle with their watery friends.
The vivid stars shine out, in radiant files;
And boundless ether[7] glows; till the fair moon
90   Shows her broad visage, in the crimsoned east;
Now, stooping, seems to kiss the passing cloud:
Now, o'er the pure cerulean,[8] rides sublime.
Wide the pale deluge floats, with silver waves,
O'er the skied° mountain, to the low-laid vale;   *sky-high*

6. In *The Seasons*, this passage (lines 80–103) appeared, revised, in *Autumn* (lines 1082–1102; see pages 2653–54). 7. "An element more fine and subtle than air" (Johnson's *Dictionary*); it was assumed to fill the highest regions above the earth. 8. Deep blue (of the evening sky).

95   From the white rocks, with dim reflection, gleams,
       And faintly glitters through the waving shades.

           All night, abundant dews, unnoted, fall,
       And, at return of morning, silver o'er
       The face of Mother Earth; from every branch
100   Depending,° tremble the translucent gems,   *hanging*
       And, quivering, seem to fall away, yet cling,
       And sparkle in the sun, whose rising eye,
       With fogs bedimmed, portends a beauteous day.

                              * * *

                          [WINTER NIGHT]
           Now, all amid the rigors of the year,
       In the wild depth of winter, while without
255   The ceaseless winds blow keen, be my retreat
       A rural, sheltered, solitary scene;
       Where ruddy fire and beaming tapers join
       To chase the cheerless gloom. There let me sit,
       And hold high converse with the mighty dead—
260   Sages of ancient time, as gods revered,
       As gods beneficent, who blessed mankind
       With arts and arms, and humanized a world.
       Roused at th' inspiring thought, I throw aside
       The long-lived volume[9] and, deep-musing, hail
265   The sacred shades that slowly rising pass
       Before my wondering eyes. First Socrates,[1]
       Truth's early champion, martyr for his God;
       Solon[2] the next, who built his commonweal
       On equity's firm base. Lycurgus[3] then,
270   Severely good; and him of rugged Rome,
       Numa,[4] who softened her rapacious sons.
       Cimon sweet-souled, and Aristides[5] just.
       Unconquered Cato,[6] virtuous in extreme;
       With that attempered hero,[7] mild and firm,
275   Who wept the brother while the tyrant bled.
       Scipio[8] the humane warrior, gently brave,
       Fair learning's friend, who early sought the shade,

---

9. Plutarch's *Lives*: biographies of eminent Greeks and Romans—composed by the Greek historian and philosopher (c. 46–120 C.E.).
1. Socrates (469–399 B.C.E.), Athenian philospher, condemned to death for his teachings.
2. Solon (639–558 B.C.E.), Athenian statesman who introduced a newly humane system of laws.
3. Legendary Spartan lawgiver.
4. Rome's legendary second king, deemed a better ruler than the founder Romulus because his long reign was peaceful and enlightened.
5. Cimon (c. 510–449 B.C.E.) and Aristeides (d. 468 B.C.E.), military leaders and statesmen noted for their victorious strategies in the Persian Wars and for their rectitude in government.
6. Marcus Porcius Cato (96–46 B.C.E.), Roman champion of republican government; he chose to commit suicide rather than surrender himself to Julius Caesar, whose imperial ambitions he had resisted in the Roman civil wars.
7. Timoleon, a Corinthian who, alarmed at the tyrannical aspirations of his brother Timophanes, conspired in his assassination (365 B.C.E.), during which he wept for the kin he had helped to kill.
8. Scipio Africanus (236–183 B.C.E.), charismatic Roman general, conqueror of Spain and defeater of Hannibal.

To dwell, with innocence, and truth, retired.
And, equal to the best, the Theban,[9] he
280   Who, single, raised his country into fame.
Thousands behind, the boast of Greece and Rome,
Whom virtue owns, the tribute of a verse
Demand, but who can count the stars of heaven?
Who sing their influence on this lower world?
285   But see who yonder comes! nor comes alone,
With sober state, and of majestic mien,
The Sister-Muses in his train. 'Tis he!
Maro![1] the best of poets, and of men!
Great Homer too appears, of daring wing!
290   Parent of song! and equal by this side,
The British Muse,[2] joined hand in hand, they walk,
Darkling,[3] nor miss their way to fame's ascent.

Society divine! Immortal minds!
Still visit thus my nights, for you reserved,
295   And mount my soaring soul to deeds like yours.
Silence! thou lonely power! the door be thine:
See, on the hallowed hour, that none intrude,
Save Lycidas,[4] the friend, with sense refined,
Learning digested well, exalted faith,
300   Unstudied wit, and humor ever gay.
1725–1726   1726

from **The Seasons**
from *Autumn*

[NIGHTFALL AND NIGHT[1]]

950   But see the fading many-colored woods,
Shade deepening over shade, the country round
Imbrown; a crowded umbrage,° dusk and dun,   *shade*
Of every hue from wan declining green
To sooty dark. These now the lonesome Muse,
955   Low-whispering, lead into their leaf-strewn walks,
And give the season in its latest view.[2]
Meantime,[3] light shadowing all, a sober calm
Fleeces unbound ether; whose least wave
Stands tremulous, uncertain where to turn

---

9. Either Pelopidas (c. 410–364 B.C.E.) or Epaminondas (d. 362 B.C.E.), military tacticians who led Thebes to victory over Sparta.
1. Virgil (Publius Virgilius Maro, 70–19 B.C.E.), Roman poet, author of the *Aeneid*.
2. John Milton.
3. In the dark (Milton was blind, and Homer was traditionally thought to have been so).
4. Thomson takes the name (and its connotation of learned companion) from Milton's pastoral elegy (1638) lamenting the death of his college friend Edward King.

1. The original version of *Winter* begins with the description of an evening in late autumn; later, Thomson revised this description and transferred it to the section on autumn, which made its first appearance in *The Seasons* (1730). Thomson repeatedly revised the poem in the years that followed; the text here is taken from the last edition he produced (1746).
2. The colors display the very end of autumn.
3. For Thomson's earlier version of this passage (lines 955–1036), see *Winter*, lines 23–79, pages 2647–48.

960   The gentle current; while, illumined wide,
The dewy-skirted clouds imbibe the sun,
And through their lucid veil his softened force
Shed o'er the peaceful world. Then is the time
For those whom Wisdom and whom Nature charm
965   To steal themselves from the degenerate° crowd,   *unworthy*
And soar above this little scene of things—
To tread low-thoughted Vice beneath their feet,
To soothe the throbbing passions into peace,
And woo lone Quiet in her silent walks.
970   Thus solitary, and in pensive guise,
Oft let me wander o'er the russet mead,
And through the saddened grove, where scarce is heard
One dying strain to cheer the woodman's toil.
Haply some widowed songster pours his plaint
975   Far in faint warblings through the tawny copse;
While congregated thrushes, linnets, larks,
And each wild throat whose artless strains so late
Swelled all the music of the swarming shades,
Robbed of their tuneful souls, now shivering sit
980   On the dead tree, a dull despondent flock,
With not a brightness waving o'er their plumes,
And naught save chattering discord in their note.
Oh, let not, aimed from some inhuman eye,
The gun the music of the coming year
985   Destroy, and harmless, unsuspecting harm,
Lay the weak tribes, a miserable prey!
In mingled murder fluttering on the ground!
      The pale descending year, yet pleasing still,
A gentler mood inspires; for now the leaf
990   Incessant rustles from the mournful grove,
Oft startling such as, studious, walk below,
And slowly circles through the waving air.
But should a quicker breeze amid the boughs
Sob, o'er the sky the leafy deluge streams;
995   Till choked, and matted with the dreary shower,
The forest-walks, at every rising gale,
Roll wide the withered waste, and whistle bleak.
Fled is the blasted verdure of the fields;
And, shrunk into their beds, the flowery race
1000   Their sunny robes resign. Even what remained
Of bolder fruits falls from the naked tree;
And woods, fields, gardens, orchards, all around
The desolated prospect thrills the soul.
      He comes! he comes! in every breeze the power
1005   Of Philosophic Melancholy comes!
His near approach the sudden-starting tear,
The glowing cheek, the mild dejected air,
The softened feature, and the beating heart,

Pierced deep with many a virtuous pang, declare.
1010   O'er all the soul his sacred influence breathes;
Inflames imagination; through the breast
Infuses every tenderness; and far
Beyond dim earth exalts the swelling thought.
Ten thousand thousand fleet° ideas, such   *rapid*
1015   As never mingled with the vulgar dream,
Crowd fast into the mind's creative eye.
As fast the correspondent passions rise,
As varied, and as high—devotion raised
To rapture, and divine astonishment;
1020   The love of nature unconfined, and, chief,
Of human race; the large ambitious wish,
To make them blest; the sigh for suffering worth,
Lost in obscurity; the noble scorn,
Of tyrant pride; the fearless great resolve;
1025   The wonder which the dying patriot draws,
Inspiring glory through remotest time;
The awakened throb for virtue, and for fame;
The sympathies of love, and friendship dear;
With all the social offspring of the heart.
1030   Oh! bear me then to vast embowering shades,
To twilight groves, and visionary vales!4
To weeping grottoes, and prophetic glooms!
Where angel forms athwart the solemn dusk,
Tremendous sweep, or seem to sweep along;
1035   And voices more than human, through the void
Deep-sounding, seize the enthusiastic ear.
Or is this gloom too much?5 Then lead, ye powers,
That o'er the garden and the rural seat
Preside, which shining through the cheerful land
1040   In countless numbers blest Britannia sees;
O lead me to the wide-extended walks,
The fair majestic paradise of Stowe!6
Not Persian Cyrus,7 on Ionia's shore,
E'er saw such sylvan scenes; such various art
1045   By genius fired, such ardent genius tamed
By cool judicious art; that, in the strife,
All-beauteous Nature fears to be outdone.
And there, O Pitt,8 thy country's early boast,
There let me sit beneath the sheltered slopes,

---

4. Valleys where I may see visions.
5. Thomson added lines 1036–1081 in his revision of 1744.
6. Stowe, the Buckinghamshire estate of Sir Richard Temple, Viscount Cobham (1669–1749), had been laid out and reworked by a long series of distinguished architects and landscapers; the garden was among the most celebrated of the 18th century.

7. Cyrus the Younger (d. 401 B.C.E.), a Persian prince, designed and planted a famous garden at Sardis (on "Ionia's shore," the coast of Asia Minor).
8. The statesman and orator William Pitt (1708–1778) was esteemed by Thomson and Cobham as a leading voice among those Whigs opposed to the still-dominant party faction led by Robert Walpole; Pitt later became Secretary of State and Prime Minister.

<table>
<tr><td>1050</td><td>Or in that Temple[9] where, in future times,</td></tr>
</table>

1050   Or in that Temple[9] where, in future times,
        Thou well shalt merit a distinguished name;
        And, with thy converse blest, catch the last smiles
        Of Autumn beaming o'er the yellow woods.
        While there with thee the enchanted round I walk,
1055   The regulated wild, gay Fancy° then   *imagination*
        Will tread in thought the groves of Attic land;[1]
        Will from thy standard taste refine her own,[2]
        Correct her pencil to the purest truth
        Of Nature, or, the unimpassioned shades
1060   Forsaking, raise it to the human mind.
        O if hereafter she, with juster hand,
        Shall draw the tragic scene, instruct her thou,
        To mark the varied movements of the heart,
        What every decent[3] character requires,
1065   And every passion speaks. O through her strain°   *song, style*
        Breathe thy pathetic eloquence! that molds
        Th' attentive senate, charms, persuades, exalts,
        Of honest zeal th' indignant lightning throws,
        And shakes corruption on her venal throne.
1070   While thus we talk, and through Elysian vales[4]
        Delighted rove, perhaps a sigh escapes.
        What pity, Cobham, thou thy verdant files
        Of ordered trees shouldst here inglorious range,
        Instead of squadrons flaming o'er the field,
1075   And long-embattled hosts![5] When the proud foe,
        The faithless vain disturber of mankind,
        Insulting Gaul, has roused the world to war;
        When keen, once more, within their bounds to press[6]
        Those polished robbers, those ambitious slaves,
1080   The British youth would hail thy wise command,
        They tempered ardor and thy veteran skill.[7]

        The western sun withdraws the shortened day;[8]
        And humid evening, gliding o'er the sky,
        In her chill progress, to the ground condensed
1085   The vapors throws. Where creeping waters ooze,
        Where marshes stagnate, and where rivers wind,
        Cluster the rolling fogs, and swim along

9. The Temple of Virtue in Stowe Gardens [Thomson's note]; this monument to ancient heroes was one of the gardens' most celebrated buildings.
1. Ancient Greece (Attica was the countryside surrounding Athens).
2. Influenced by your standard of taste, Fancy will refine hers.
3. Appropriate (Thomson, who wrote several tragedies, here asks Pitt for guidance in suiting his language to his characters and their emotions).
4. The Elysian Fields at Stowe (named for Elysium, Greek myth's paradise for heroes) were the most wild and natural area of the gardens.

5. Cobham left the Walpole government in 1733; thereafter he worked on his gardens and formed a group of opposition Whigs known as "Cobham's Cubs." Here Thomson wishes that Cobham, an accomplished soldier, might deploy his gifts as military leader rather than as shaper of landscapes.
6. I.e., contain within their own borders.
7. Thomson here imagines how effective Cobham would be as a leader in the War of the Austrian Succession (1740–1748), England's current conflict with France ("insulting Gaul," "polished robbers," "ambitious slaves").
8. Compare the earlier version of these lines in *Winter* (lines 80–96 on pages 2648–49).

The dusky-mantled lawn. Meanwhile the moon,
Full-orbed and breaking through the scattered clouds,
1090   Shows her broad visage in the crimsoned east.
Turned to the sun direct, her spotted disk
(Where mountains rise, umbrageous dales descend,
And oceans roll, as optic tube° descries)   *telescope*
A smaller earth, gives all his blaze again,
1095   Void of its flame, and sheds a softer day.
Now through the passing cloud she seems to stoop,
Now up the pure cerulean rides sublime.
Wide the pale deluge floats, and streaming mild
O'er the skied° mountain to the shadowy vale,   *sky-high*
1100   While rocks and floods reflect the quivering gleam,
The whole air whitens with a boundless tide
Of silver radiance, trembling round the world.
    But when, half-blotted from the sky, her light,
Fainting, permits the starry fires to burn,
1105   With keener luster through the depth of heaven;
Or quite extinct her deadened orb appears,
And scarce appears, of sickly beamless white;
Oft in this season, silent from the north
A blaze of meteors shoots⁹—ensweeping first
1110   The lower skies, they all at once converge
High to the crown of heaven, and all at once
Relapsing quick as quickly reascend,
And mix, and thwart,° extinguish, and renew,   *cross*
All ether coursing in a maze of light.
1115   From look to look, contagious through the crowd,
The panic runs, and into wondrous shapes
Th' appearance throws—armies in meet array,
Thronged with aërial spears, and steeds of fire;
Till the long lines of full-extended war
1120   In bleeding fight commixed, the sanguine flood
Rolls a broad slaughter o'er the plains of heaven.
As thus they scan the visionary scene,
On all sides swells the superstitious din,
Incontinent;° and busy frenzy talks   *unrestrained*
1125   Of blood and battle; cities overturned,
And late at night in swallowing earthquake sunk,
Or hideous wrapped in fierce ascending flame;
Of sallow famine, inundation, storm;
Of pestilence, and every great distress;
1130   Empires subversed, when ruling fate has struck
The unalterable hour: even Nature's self
Is deemed to totter on the brink of time.
Not so the man of philosophic eye,
And inspect sage;° the waving brightness he   *wise insight*

9. The aurora borealis, or northern lights.

1135   Curious surveys, inquisitive to know
        The causes, and materials, yet unfixed,[1]
        Of this appearance beautiful, and new. * * *
1726–1746   1746

Rule, Britannia[1]

When Britain first, at Heaven's command,
    Arose from out the azure main;°   sea
This was the charter of the land,
And guardian angels sung this strain:
5   "Rule, Britannia, rule the waves;
        "Britons never will be slaves."

The nations, not so blest as thee,
    Must, in their turns, to tyrants fall:
While thou shalt flourish great and free,
10   The dread and envy of them all.
            "Rule," etc.

Still more majestic shalt thou rise,
    More dreadful, from each foreign stroke:
As the loud blast that tears the skies,
15   Serves but to root thy native oak.
            "Rule," etc.

Thee haughty tyrants ne'er shall tame:
    All their attempts to bend thee down
Will but arouse thy generous flame;
20   But work their woe, and thy renown.
            "Rule," etc.

To thee belongs the rural reign;
    Thy cities shall with commerce shine:
All thine shall be the subject main,
25   And every shore it circles thine.
            "Rule," etc.

The Muses, still[2] with freedom found,
    Shall to thy happy coast repair:
Blest isle! with matchless beauty crowned,
30   And manly hearts to guard the fair.

---

1. Unaccounted for (by science).

1. Thomson wrote several longer poems of impassioned patriotism (*Britannia*, 1729; *Liberty*, 1735–1736), but his convictions found their most enduring expression in this short piece, first performed as the climactic song of *Alfred*, a patriotic masque on the subject of the Saxon king (848–899). Defeated by the Danes, the monarch receives comfort from a "venerable bard," who expresses with uncanny prescience the 18th-century appetite for naval conquest and expanding empire. The masque was created by Thomson in collaboration with his fellow Scots expatriate

David Mallet (?1705–1765) and the composer Thomas Arne (1710–1778), as part of an entertainment commissioned by Frederick, Prince of Wales, to celebrate his daughter's third birthday and the anniversary of his German grandfather's accession to the English throne. Thomson's ode outlasted its occasion, gradually acquiring the status of an alternate national anthem (just behind *God Save the King*). While the Empire endured, Thomson's song proffered for many Britons a stirring account of their national origins, essence, and destiny.

2. The word meant both "always" and "as yet."

"Rule, Britannia, rule the waves;
"Britons never will be slaves."

1740   1740

❈ "THE SEASONS" AND ITS TIME ❈
Poems of Nightfall and Night

The aubade, or dawn-song, was a favorite form in the Middle Ages and the Renaissance: poets from Chaucer to Donne portrayed lovers entwined abed, lamenting the intrusive rising of the sun. In eighteenth-century England, poets were more preoccupied with the night piece, as a medium not for amorous pairings but for meditative solitude. In a culture marked by the intensified noise, density, and busyness of the cities, privacy was an experience newly construed and prized; in the scene of nightfall (particularly *country* nightfall), poets found an ideal setting for its enactment. William Collins, in his most famous ode, addresses the Evening as a "maid composed," a "nymph reserved," whose quietude facilitates his solitary thought; in his poem on the death of his friend James Thomson, Collins renders his sense of loss by images of encroaching dark. The other selections here come from larger works—Edward Young's *Night Thoughts* and William Cowper's *The Task*—which participate in the tradition that Thomson's *Seasons* had commenced: copious blank-verse description and meditation, produced, expanded, and revised over the course of years, mingling widely various materials and modes in a new, purportedly improvisatory way. "The method pursued," Young explained of his long poem, "was rather *imposed*, by what spontaneously arose in the author's mind on that occasion, than *meditated* or *designed*"; Cowper, more simply, attributed the expansion of *The Task* to the unexpected directions dictated by his own "train of thought." Drawing on darkness as resource and backdrop, Thomson, Young, and Cowper were working toward a new mode: the epic of the solitary mind in action. From them the lines of influence run long and clear, through the Gothic fiction of the late eighteenth century, through Wordsworth's meditative excursions, into the stream of consciousness in Joyce's *Ulysses* and the nocturnal dreamspeak of *Finnegans Wake*.

Edward Young[1]
from *The Complaint*
or *Night Thoughts on Life, Death, and Immortality*

Tired Nature's sweet restorer, balmy Sleep!
He, like the world, his ready visit pays
Where Fortune smiles; the wretched he forsakes:
Swift on his downy pinion° flies from woe,   *wing*
5   And lights on lids unsullied with a tear.

---

1. After a frustrating London career as poet and playwright in frantic pursuit of political advancement, Edward Young (1683–1765) took holy orders, withdrew to a small village, and at age 59 commenced a set of poems that brought him sudden, staggering success. In *The Complaint*, a sequence of nine night pieces (and more than 9,000 lines) published serially over the course of three years, Young mixed morbid melancholy, Gothic dread, and Christian solace. The combination appealed powerfully to a vast number and variety of readers, in Britain and on the Continent. In its meditative blank verse and its capacious, fluid form, *Night Thoughts* was plainly influenced by Thomson's *Seasons*; well into the 19th century, the two works were often packaged (along with *Paradise Lost*) in a single, highly saleable volume. Both poems pervaded the century's consciousness, and later figured as principal forebears of Romantic thought and writing. This excerpt is from *Night 1*.

From short (as usual) and disturbed repose,
I wake. How happy they, who wake no more!
Yet that were vain, if dreams infest the grave.
I wake, emerging from a sea of dreams
10   Tumultuous; where my wrecked, desponding thought
From wave to wave of fancied misery,
At random drove, her helm of reason lost.
Though now restored, 'tis only change of pain,
(A bitter change!) severer for severe.
15   The day too short for my distress! and Night,
Even in the zenith of her dark domain,
Is sunshine, to the color of my fate.
    Night, sable goddess! from her ebon° throne,   *black*
In rayless majesty, now stretches forth
20   Her leaden scepter o'er a slumb'ring world.
Silence, how dead! and darkness, how profound!
Nor eye, nor list'ning ear an object finds;
Creation sleeps. 'Tis as° the general pulse   *as if*
Of life stood still, and Nature made a pause;
25   An awful pause! prophetic of her end.
And let her prophecy be soon fulfilled;
Fate! drop the curtain; I can lose no more.
    Silence, and Darkness! Solemn sisters! Twins
From ancient Night, who nurse the tender thought
30   To reason, and on reason build resolve
(That column of true majesty in man),
Assist me: I will thank you in the grave;
The grave, your kingdom. There this frame shall fall
A victim sacred to your dreary shrine.
35   But what are ye? Thou,[2] who didst put to flight
Primeval Silence, when the morning stars,
Exulting, shouted o'er the rising ball;
O Thou! whose word from solid darkness struck
That spark, the sun; strike wisdom from my soul;
40   My soul, which flies to Thee, her trust, her treasure,
As misers to their gold, while others rest.
    Through this opaque of nature, and of soul,
This double night, transmit one pitying ray,
To lighten, and to cheer. O lead my mind,
45   (A mind that fain would wander from its woe)
Lead it through various scenes of life and death;
And from each scene the noblest truths inspire.
Nor less inspire my conduct than my song;
Teach my best reason reason; my best will
50   Teach rectitude; and fix my firm resolve
Wisdom to wed, and pay her long arrear:°   *old debt*

---

2. Young here shifts addressees, from the plural "ye" (Silence and Darkness) to the singular "Thou" (God, imagined at the moment of Creation).

Nor let the phial of thy vengeance, poured
On this devoted head, be poured in vain.
    The bell strikes one. We take no note of time
55 But from its loss. To give it then a tongue,
Is wise in man. As if an angel spoke,
I feel the solemn sound. If heard aright,
It is the knell of my departed hours:
Where are they? With the years beyond the flood.
60 It is the signal that demands dispatch;
How much is to be done? my hopes and fears
Start up alarmed, and o'er life's narrow verge
Look down—on what? A fathomless abyss;
A dread eternity! how surely mine!
65 And can eternity belong to me,
Poor pensioner on the bounties of an hour?
    How poor, how rich, how abject, how august,
How complicate, how wonderful, is man?
How passing wonder He, who made him such?
70 Who centered in our make such strange extremes?
From different natures marvelously mixed,
Connection exquisite of distant worlds!
Distinguished link in being's endless chain!
Midway from nothing to the deity!
75 A beam ethereal sullied and absorbed!
Though sullied and dishonored, still divine!
Dim miniature of greatness absolute!
An heir of glory! a frail child of dust!
Helpless immortal! Insect infinite!
80 A worm! a God! I tremble at myself,
And in myself am lost! At home a stranger,
Thought wanders up and down, surprised, aghast,
And wondering at her own. How reason reels!
O what a miracle to man is man,
85 Triumphantly distressed! what joy, what dread!
Alternately transported and alarmed!
What can preserve my life? or what destroy?
An angel's arm can't snatch me from the grave;
Legions of angels can't confine me there.
90   'Tis past conjecture; all things rise in proof:
While o'er my limbs sleep's soft dominion spread,
What, though my soul fantastic measures trod
O'er fairy fields; or mourned along the gloom
Of pathless woods; or down the craggy steep
95 Hurled headlong, swam with pain the mantled pool;
Or scaled the cliff; or danced on hollow winds,
With antic shapes, wild natives of the brain?
Her ceaseless flight, though devious, speaks her nature
Of subtler essence than the trodden clod;
100 Active, aërial, towering, unconfined,

Unfettered with her gross companion's fall.
Even silent night proclaims my soul immortal:
Even silent night proclaims eternal day.
For human weal, Heaven husbands all events,
105   Dull sleep instructs, nor sport vain dreams in vain.
1742   1742, 1750

William Collins[1]
Ode to Evening

If aught of oaten stop,[2] or pastoral song,
May hope, chaste Eve, to soothe thy modest ear,
   Like thy own solemn springs,
   Thy springs, and dying gales,
5   O nymph reserved, while now the bright-haired sun
Sits in yon western tent, whose cloudy skirts,
   With brede° ethereal wove,   braid
   O'erhang his wavy bed:
Now air is hushed, save where the weak-eyed bat,
10   With short shrill shriek flits by on leathern wing,
   Or where the beetle winds°   blows
   His small but sullen horn,
As oft he rises 'midst the twilight path,
Against the pilgrim borne in heedless hum:
15   Now teach me, maid composed,
   To breathe some softened strain,°   song
Whose numbers° stealing through thy darkening vale,   verses
May not unseemly with its stillness suit,
   As musing slow, I hail
20   Thy genial loved return!
For when thy folding star arising shows
His paly circlet, at his warning lamp
   The fragrant Hours, and elves
   Who slept in flowers the day,
25   And many a nymph who wreathes her brows with sedge,
And sheds the freshening dew, and lovelier still,
   The pensive Pleasures sweet
   Prepare thy shadowy car.°   chariot

1. As a student at Oxford, William Collins (1721–1759) secured some distinction, published a few poems, and promptly left for London and the life (as his friend Samuel Johnson described it) of "a literary adventurer." While amusing himself at the city's pleasure gardens and playhouses, amid a spritely circle of actors and writers, Collins planned a number of books. He published only one, a small collection entitled *Odes on Several Descriptive and Allegorical Subjects* (1747); its failure to attract notice prompted him to burn the many copies that had gone unsold. In his late twenties, the poet fell prey to a manic depression verging on madness, which disabled him the rest of his life. His odes, neglected in his time, appealed strongly to tastes that came into vogue just after his death: for sentiment and the sublime, for the expression of overpowering emotions, of disruptive experiences, and of visionary intensities beyond the familiar, civic, human scale.
2. If any music played on an oat-reed pipe (Collins uses the pastoral-archaic idiom associated with Spenser and Milton).

Then lead, calm vot'ress,[3] where some sheety lake

30   Cheers the lone heath, or some time-hallowed pile,°   *building*
  Or upland fallows[4] gray
  Reflect its last cool gleam.
But when chill blustering winds, or driving rain,
Forbid my willing feet, be mine the hut,

35   That from the mountain's side,
  Views wilds, and swelling floods,
And hamlets brown, and dim-discovered spires,
And hears their simple bell, and marks o'er all
  Thy dewy fingers draw

40   The gradual dusky veil.
While Spring shall pour his showers, as oft he wont,[5]
And bathe thy breathing tresses, meekest Eve!
  While Summer loves to sport,
  Beneath thy lingering light;

45   While sallow Autumn fills thy lap with leaves;
Or Winter, yelling through the troublous air,
  Affrights thy shrinking train,
  And rudely rends thy robes;
So long, sure-found beneath the sylvan shed,

50   Shall Fancy, Friendship, Science, rose-lipped Health,
  Thy gentlest influence own,
  And hymn thy favorite name!

1746   1746, 1748

William Collins
Ode Occasioned by the Death of Mr. Thomson

The scene of the following stanzas is supposed to lie on the Thames near Richmond.[1]

> *Haec tibi semper erunt, et cum solennia vota*
> *reddemus Nymphis, et cum lustrabimus agros.*
>
> —— ——*Amavit nos quoque Daphnis.*[2]

---

3. "A woman devoted to . . . worship" (Johnson's *Dictionary*).
4. Fields ploughed but unplanted.
5. Is accustomed to do.
1. A scenic riverside village nine miles from London's center; Thomson had lived there in his last years, and was buried in the parish churchyard. Collins, who had dwelt there too, in close friendship with Thomson, here invokes the local geography quite specifically. His ode compasses two motions: in space, as the speaker moves past Richmond up the river; in time, as day modulates into night. Collins's poem was praised by a contemporary for the "dirge-like melancholy it breathes, and the warmth of

affection that seems to have dictated it"; it has long enjoyed a print intimacy with the poet whom it eulogizes. Thomson's editors have often presented it as a preface to his works; his biographers have reprinted it as a coda to his life, a summation of his worth.
2. "These rites shall be thine forever, both when we pay our yearly vows to the Nymphs, and when we purify our fields . . . Daphnis loved us too" (Virgil, *Eclogues* 5.74–75, 52). In the pastoral tradition, the legendary Daphnis is credited as the first shepherd to have made music, the inventor of bucolic song; in Virgil's lines, one of Daphnis's followers mourns his master's "cruel death" and promises perpetual homage.

1

In yonder grave a Druid[3] lies,
    Where slowly winds the stealing wave!
The year's best sweets shall duteous rise
    To deck its poet's sylvan grave!

2

5   In you deep bed of whispering reeds
    His airy harp[4] shall now be laid,
That he, whose heart in sorrow bleeds,
    May love through life the soothing shade.

3

Then maids and youths shall linger here,
10   And, while its sounds at distance swell,
Shall sadly seem in Pity's ear
    To hear the woodland pilgrim's[5] knell.

4

Remembrance oft shall haunt the shore
    When Thames in summer wreaths is dressed,
15   And oft suspend the dashing oar
    To bid his gentle spirit rest!

5

And oft as Ease and Health retire
    To breezy lawn or forest deep,
The friend shall view yon whitening spire,[6]
20   And mid the varied landscape weep.

6

But thou, who own'st that earthy bed,
    Ah! what will every dirge avail?
Or tears, which Love and Pity shed
    That mourn beneath the gliding sail![7]

7

25   Yet lives there one, whose heedless eye
    Shall scorn thy pale shrine glimmering near?
With him, sweet bard, may Fancy die,
    And Joy desert the blooming year.

---

3. The Druids were the priest-magicians of ancient Britain. In the 18th century they were thought to have possessed extraordinary intimacy with, and power over, the forces of nature.
4. "The harp of Aeolus" [Collins's note], an instrument whose strings make sounds when the breezes play upon them (Aeolus was the mythological Greek monarch of the winds). Thomson, the first to invoke this instrument in English verse, had made it a figure for poetic responsiveness to inspiration; many poets since have taken up the trope.
5. I.e., Thomson's, whose love of forest walks Collins here recalls.
6. Of the parish church where Thomson was buried.
7. Of the boat moving down the Thames (see line 15).

8

But thou, lorn stream,[8] whose sullen tide
30   No sedge-crowned Sisters now attend,
Now waft me from the green hill's side,
      Whose cold turf hides the buried friend!

9

And see, the fairy valleys fade,
      Dun Night has veiled the solemn view![9]
35 —Yet once again, dear parted shade,
      Meek Nature's child, again adieu!

10

The genial meads,° assigned to bless   meadows
      Thy life, shall mourn thy early doom,
Their hinds° and shepherd-girls shall dress   shepherds
40   With simple hands thy rural tomb.

11

Long, long, thy stone and pointed clay[1]
      Shall melt the musing Briton's eyes:
"O! vales and wild woods," shall he say,
      "In yonder grave your Druid lies!"
1748–1749   1749

William Cowper
from The Task[1]

from BOOK 4. THE WINTER EVENING

[READING THE NEWSPAPER]

Now stir the fire, and close the shutters fast,
Let fall the curtains, wheel the sofa round,
And while the bubbling and loud-hissing urn
Throws up a steamy column, and the cups°   of tea
40 That cheer but not inebriate, wait on each,
So let us welcome peaceful evening in.

8. The Thames, forlorn because it is no longer inhabited by the leaf-adorned river nymphs ("sedge-crowned Sisters") who dwelt there during Thomson's lifetime.
9. Collins echoes Thomson's *Autumn* lines 950–952 (see page 2650).
1. I.e., the poet's churchyard monument.
1. For William Cowper, see page 2641. As preface to *The Task*, Cowper offered the following brief "history": "A lady, fond of blank verse, demanded a poem of that kind from the author, and gave him the SOFA for a subject. He obeyed; and having much leisure, connected another subject with it; and pursuing the train of thought to which his situation and turn of mind led him, brought forth at length, instead of the trifle which he at first intended, a serious affair—a volume." The modulation from triviality to seriousness (and back again) is intrinsic not only to the history of the poem but to its substance too. In six epic "Books" bearing markedly domestic titles (*The Sofa, The Time-Piece, The Garden, The Winter Evening, The Winter Morning Walk, The Winter Walk at Noon*), Cowper savors rural pleasures and satirizes the life of cities. Mingling grand diction with cozy fact ("I sing the Sofa," the poem begins), Cowper revels in their seeming disparity, as a resource both for comic self-deprecation and for earnest affirmation. These domestic delights, *The Task* implies, deserve this scale of celebration.

Not such his ev'ning, who with shining face
Sweats in the crowded theater, and squeezed
And bored with elbow-points through both his sides,
45 Out-scolds the ranting actor on the stage.
Nor his, who patient stands till his feet throb,
And his head thumps, to feed upon the breath
Of patriots[2] bursting with heroic rage,
Or placemen,[3] all tranquillity and smiles.
50 This folio of four pages,° happy work!   *the newspaper*
Which not ev'n critics criticize, that holds
Inquisitive attention while I read,
Fast bound in chains of silence, which the fair,[4]
Though eloquent themselves, yet fear to break,
55 What is it, but a map of busy life,
Its fluctuations and its vast concerns?
Here runs the mountainous and craggy ridge
That tempts ambition. On the summit, see,
The seals of office glitter in his eyes;
60 He climbs, he pants, he grasps them. At his heels,
Close at his heels a demagogue ascends,
And with a dext'rous jerk soon twists him down
And wins them, but to lose them in his turn.
Here rills of oily eloquence in soft
65 Meanders lubricate the course they take;
The modest speaker is ashamed and grieved
T' engross a moment's notice, and yet begs,
Begs a propitious ear for his poor thoughts,
However trivial all that he conceives.
70 Sweet bashfulness! it claims, at last, this praise:
The dearth of information and good sense
That it foretells us, always comes to pass.
Cataracts of declamation thunder here,
There forests of no-meaning spread the page
75 In which all comprehension wanders lost;
While fields of pleasantry amuse us there,
With merry descants° on a nation's woes.   *commentaries*
The rest[5] appears a wilderness of strange
But gay confusion: roses for the cheeks,
80 And lilies for the brows of faded age,
Teeth for the toothless, ringlets for the bald,
Heaven, earth, and ocean plundered of their sweets,
Nectareous essences, Olympian dews,
Sermons and city feasts and favorite airs,[6]
85 Aetherial journies,[7] submarine exploits,[8]

2. Political zealots.
3. Office-holders, bureaucrats.
4. The women of the house.
5. I.e., the newspaper's advertisements.
6. Popular melodies (sold as sheet music).

7. In hot-air balloons; the first flight had taken place in 1783.
8. In diving bells, which had been in use for more than a century.

And Katterfelto[9] with his hair on end
At his own wonders, wond'ring for his bread.
   'Tis pleasant through the loop-holes of retreat
To peep at such a world. To see the stir
90   Of the great Babel[1] and not feel the crowd.
To hear the roar she sends through all her gates
At a safe distance, where the dying sound
Falls a soft murmur on th' uninjured ear.
   Thus sitting and surveying thus at ease
95   The globe and its concerns, I seem advanced
To some secure and more than mortal height,
That lib'rates and exempts me from them all.
It turns submitted to my view, turns round
With all its generations; I behold
100   The tumult and am still. The sound of war
Has lost its terrors ere it reaches me;
Grieves but alarms me not. I mourn the pride
And avarice that make man a wolf to man,
Hear the faint echo of those brazen throats
105   By which he speaks the language of his heart,
And sigh, but never tremble at the sound.
He travels and expatiates, as the bee
From flow'r to flow'r, so he from land to land;
The manners, customs, policy of all
110   Pay contribution to the store he gleans,
He sucks intelligence in every clime,
And spreads the honey of his deep research
At his return, a rich repast for me.
He travels and I too. I tread his deck,
115   Ascend his topmast, through his peering eyes
Discover countries, with a kindred heart
Suffer his woes, and share in his escapes,
While fancy, like the finger of a clock,
Runs the great circuit, and is still at home.

[THE INVOCATION]

Come Ev'ning once again,[2] season of peace
Return sweet Ev'ning, and continue long!
245   Methinks I see thee in the streaky west,
With matron-step slow-moving, while the night
Treads on thy sweeping train; one hand employed
In letting fall the curtain of repose

---

9. Gustave Katterfelto, a magician whose performances were advertised under the rubric "Wonders, Wonders, Wonders."
1. The biblical Tower of Babel (Genesis 11.1–9), whose construction God prevented by making the builders speak different languages ("babble"); Cowper here uses the word for its long-established association with "Babylon," meaning any great city.
2. Cowper's invocation in the ensuing lines echoes both Milton's *Paradise Lost* (4.568–609) and Collins's *Ode to Evening* (page 2659).

On bird and beast, the other charged for man
250   With sweet oblivion of the cares of day;
Not sumptuously adorned, nor needing aid
Like homely featured Night, of clust'ring gems,
A star or two just twinkling on thy brow
Suffices thee; save that the moon is thine
255   No less than hers, not worn indeed on high
With ostentatious pageantry, but set
With modest grandeur in thy purple zone,°   *belt*
Resplendent less, but of an ampler round.
Come then, and thou shalt find thy vot'ry° calm   *worshipper*
260   Or make me so. Composure is thy gift.
And whether I devote thy gentle hours
To books, to music, or the poet's toil,
To weaving nets for bird-alluring fruit;
Or twining silken threads round ivory reels.
265   When they° command whom man was born to please,   *women*
I slight thee not, but make thee welcome still.
1783–1785   1785

END OF "THE SEASONS" AND ITS TIME

Thomas Gray
1716–1771

Toward the end of his most famous poem, *Elegy Written in a Country Churchyard*, Thomas Gray commends the quietude with which the villagers have led their ordinary lives:

Along the cool sequestered vale of life
They kept the noiseless tenor of their way.

Tenor here means "course," and the line incorporates a notable revision: Gray had originally written "silent tenor," and then written the new adjective "noiseless" above the old, without crossing out "silent." In retrospect, this manuscript moment of alternate possibilities looks emblematic. Sickly, shy, and melancholic, Gray was often drawn toward silence but never settled there. Words—in ancient literature and in modern history, in talk and correspondence with his friends, in the varied idioms of his own compelling poems—exerted too strong a fascination. The fascination started early. At age nine, having weathered a bleak childhood in the troubled London household of his irascible father and doting mother, he entered the privileged precincts of Eton College, where his uncles worked and where he hit upon the satisfactions that would fill his life: passionate reading (in the classics first and foremost) and passionate friendships, with three schoolmates in particular: Richard West, Thomas Ashton, and Horace Walpole, son of the notorious prime minister Robert Walpole. Dubbing themselves the Quadruple Alliance, the four friends piqued themselves on a collective erudition, refinement, and wit that set them off from their contemporaries. The links among them mattered enormously in Gray's life of writing: West inspired his poems; Walpole sponsored their publication; and all Gray's friendships, at Eton and beyond, drew from Gray a steady flow of virtuosic letters, in which the voice of the "Alliance," at once antic and vulnerable, never abated. "His letters," remarked Walpole (whose own letters have evoked similar praise), "were the best I ever saw, and had more novelty and wit." Gray's affections took form and motion partly from their containment. He was homosexual; yet there is no evidence that he ever physically consummated the great passions of his life—for Walpole, for West, and, in his last years, for the young Swiss scion Charles-Victor de Bonstatten.

After nine years at Eton, Gray was admitted to Cambridge. He found university life far less pleasing, with its drudgeries, pressures, and solitudes, but Cambridge ultimately afforded him a few new friendships and a permanent sanctuary. After a Grand Tour of Europe, undertaken in Walpole's company (the two men quarreled en route, after which they were estranged for five years), Gray returned to the university, ostensibly to learn law, but in fact to pursue his own private program of study. He read widely, copiously, and systematically in many subjects (botany, zoology, and music, as well as literature and history), making himself one of the most learned scholars alive, and eventually becoming (in 1768) Regius Professor of Modern History. He never delivered a lecture, and continued to spend much of his time alone reading, but thoroughgoing privacy had long ceased to be an option. In his late thirties, Gray had stumbled, reluctantly, into enormous poetic fame. He had written Latin verse when young; in 1742, the year his beloved West died of tuberculosis, he commenced English poetry in earnest. Some of his labor's early fruits bespeak an insistent sense of loss: a sonnet on West's death (never printed during the poet's lifetime); the *Ode on a Distant Prospect of Eton College*, in which the distance is one of time as well as space; and the *Elegy*, whose completion took five years or more and whose publication in 1751 (a "distress" the poet had hoped to avoid) brought upon Gray an instantaneous, massive, and baffling celebrity. As if in recoil, he veered onto an alternate poetic path, carefully crafting over the ensuing years a set of intricate Pindaric odes, including *The Bard* and *The Progress of Poesy*; the two poems were printed, on Walpole's own press, in 1757. They provoked both admiration, as a new embodiment of poetic sublimity, and derision, as gratuitously labored, showily obscure. In the years following their murky reception, Gray wrote only a few poems and published none. He pursued other studies (including Norse literature); fell in love one final time; and died abruptly, mourned deeply by his friends and widely by a public whose thoughts and feelings about death itself he had done much to shape. In one early version of the *Elegy* the line about silence appears as an admonition addressed by the poet to himself: "Pursue the silent tenor of thy doom." In his letters (published posthumously) and in his poems, Gray worked for that doom a delicate but decisive reversal.

Sonnet on the Death of Mr. Richard West[1]

> In vain to me the smiling mornings shine,
> And redd'ning Phoebus lifts his golden fire:
> The birds in vain their amorous descant join,
> Or cheerful fields resume their green attire:
> 5   These ears, alas! for other notes repine,
> A different object do these eyes require.
> My lonely anguish melts no heart but mine;
> And in my breast the imperfect joys expire.
> Yet morning smiles the busy race to cheer,
> 10   And new-born pleasure brings to happier men;
> The fields to all their wonted tribute bear;
> To warm their little loves the birds complain.

---

1. West had died of tuberculosis on 1 June 1742, at age 25. Gray composed this sonnet the following August, and in the same month wrote the ode that follows.

I fruitless mourn to him that cannot hear,
And weep the more because I weep in vain.

1742   1775

Ode on a Distant Prospect of Eton College[1]

Ye distant spires, ye antique towers,
That crown the wat'ry glade,
Where grateful Science° still adores   knowledge
Her Henry's holy shade;[2]
5 And ye, that from the stately brow
Of Windsor's heights[3] th' expanse below
Of grove, of lawn, of mead survey,
Whose turf, whose shade, whose flowers among
Wanders the hoary Thames along
10 His silver-winding way.

   Ah happy hills, ah, pleasing shade,
Ah, fields beloved in vain,
Where once my careless childhood strayed,
A stranger yet to pain!
15 I feel the gales, that from ye blow,
A momentary bliss bestow,
As waving fresh their gladsome wing,
My weary soul they seem to soothe,
And, redolent of joy and youth,
20 To breathe a second spring.

   Say, Father Thames, for thou hast seen
Full many a sprightly race
Disporting on thy margent° green   margin
The paths of pleasure trace,
25 Who foremost now delight to cleave
With pliant arm thy glassy wave?
The captive linnet which enthrall?
What idle progeny succeed
To chase the rolling circle's speed,[4]
30 Or urge the flying ball?

   While some on earnest business bent
Their murm'ring labors ply
'Gainst graver hours, that bring constraint
To sweeten liberty:
35 Some bold adventurers disdain
The limits of their little reign,

1. One of England's oldest and most eminent schools for
boys (founded 1440); Gray had attended from 1725 to
1734.
2. The ghost ("shade") of Henry VI (1421–1471), the

school's founder.
3. The college is located within the borough of Windsor,
on the river Thames.
4. A children's game involving a hoop.

And unknown regions dare descry:
Still as they run they look behind,
They hear a voice in every wind,
40   And snatch a fearful joy.

Gay hope is theirs by fancy fed,
Less pleasing when possessed;
The tear forgot as soon as shed,
The sunshine of the breast:
45   Theirs buxom° health of rosy hue,   *lively*
Wild wit, invention ever-new,
And lively cheer of vigor born;
The thoughtless day, the easy night,
The spirits pure, the slumbers light,
50   That fly th' approach of morn.

Alas, regardless of their doom,
The little victims play!
No sense have they of ills to come,
Nor care beyond today:
55   Yet see how all around 'em wait
The ministers of human fate,
And black Misfortune's baleful train!°   *attendants*
Ah, shew them where in ambush stand
To seize their prey the murth'rous° band!   *murderous*
60   Ah, tell them, they are men!

These shall the fury Passions tear,
The vultures of the mind,
Disdainful Anger, pallid Fear,
And Shame that skulks behind;
65   Or pining Love shall waste their youth,
Or Jealousy with rankling tooth,
That inly gnaws the secret heart,
And Envy wan, and faded Care,
Grim-visaged comfortless Despair,
70   And Sorrow's piercing dart.

Ambition this shall tempt to rise,
Then whirl the wretch from high,
To bitter Scorn a sacrifice,
And grinning Infamy.
75   The stings of Falsehood those shall try,
And hard Unkindness' altered eye,
That mocks the tear it forced to flow;
And keen Remorse with blood defiled,
And moody Madness laughing wild
80   Amid severest woe.

Lo, in the vale of years beneath
A grisly troop are seen,

The painful family of Death,
More hideous than their Queen:
85   This racks the joints, this fires the veins,
That every laboring sinew strains,
Those in the deeper vitals rage:
Lo, Poverty, to fill the band,
That numbs the soul with icy hand,
90   And slow-consuming Age.

To each his suff'rings: all are men,
Condemned alike to groan;
The tender for another's pain;
Th' unfeeling for his own.
95   Yet ah! why should they know their fate?
Since sorrow never comes too late,
And happiness too swiftly flies.
Thought would destroy their paradise.
No more; where ignorance is bliss,
100   'Tis folly to be wise.
1742   1747

Ode on the Death of a Favorite Cat, Drowned in a Tub of Gold Fishes[1]

'Twas on a lofty vase's side,
Where China's gayest art had dyed
    The azure flowers, that blow;°   *blossom*
Demurest of the tabby kind,
5   The pensive Selima reclined,
    Gazed on the lake below.

Her conscious tail her joy declared;
The fair round face, the snowy beard,
    The velvet of her paws,
10   Her coat, that with the tortoise vies,
Her ears of jet, and emerald eyes,
    She saw; and purred applause.

Still had she gazed; but 'midst the tide
Two angel forms were seen to glide,
15   The genii° of the stream: *protective deities*
Their scaly armor's Tyrian hue[2]
Through richest purple to the view
    Betrayed a golden gleam.

1. The cat had belonged to Walpole, who asked Gray to write her an epitaph. Gray sent something more substantial: "There's a poem for you; it is rather too long for an epitaph." Walpole admired the ode so much that he saw to its publication and had the first stanza inscribed on the "tub" itself—actually a china vase, which Walpole enshrined on a pedestal and displayed at his home, Strawberry Hill, where it still stands.
2. A deep purple dye made from mollusks, prized by the ancients as a mark of luxury.

The hapless nymph with wonder saw:
20   A whisker first and then a claw,
    With many an ardent wish,
She stretched in vain to reach the prize.
What female heart can gold despise?
    What cat's averse to fish?

25   Presumptuous maid! with looks intent
Again she stretched, again she bent,
    Nor knew the gulf between.
(Malignant Fate sat by and smiled)
The slippery verge her feet beguiled,
30   She tumbled headlong in.

Eight times emerging from the flood
She mewed to ev'ry wat'ry God,
    Some speedy aid to send.
No dolphin came,[3] no Nereid° stirred: *water-nymph*
35   Nor cruel Tom, nor Susan heard.
    A favorite has no friend!

From hence, ye beauties, undeceived,
Know, one false step is ne'er retrieved,
    And be with caution bold.
40   Not all that tempts your wandering eyes
And heedless hearts, is lawful prize;
    Nor all that glisters,° gold.   *glitters*
1747   1748

Elegy Written in a Country Churchyard

The curfew tolls the knell of parting day,
The lowing herd wind slowly o'er the lea,
The plowman homeward plods his weary way,
And leaves the world to darkness and to me.

5   Now fades the glimmering landscape on the sight,
And all the air a solemn stillness holds,
Save where the beetle wheels his droning flight,
And drowsy tinklings lull the distant folds;

Save that from yonder ivy-mantled tower
10   The moping owl does to the moon complain
Of such as, wand'ring near her secret bower,
Molest her ancient solitary reign.

Beneath those rugged elms, that yew-tree's shade,
Where heaves the turf in many a mouldering heap,
15   Each in his narrow cell for ever laid,
The rude forefathers of the hamlet sleep.

3. As did the dolphin who, in Greek mythology, rescued the drowning poet Arion.

The breezy call of incense-breathing morn,
The swallow twitt'ring from the straw-built shed,
The cock's shrill clarion, or the echoing horn,
20   No more shall rouse them from their lowly bed.

For them no more the blazing hearth shall burn,
Or busy housewife ply her evening care:
No children run to lisp their sire's return,
Or climb his knees the envied kiss to share.

25   Oft did the harvest to their sickle yield,
Their furrow oft the stubborn glebe° has broke;   *clod of earth*
How jocund did they drive their team afield!
How bowed the woods beneath their sturdy stroke!

Let not Ambition mock their useful toil,
30   Their homely joys, and destiny obscure;
Nor Grandeur hear, with a disdainful smile,
The short and simple annals of the poor.

The boast of heraldry, the pomp of power,
And all that beauty, all that wealth e'er gave,
35   Awaits alike th' inevitable hour.
The paths of glory lead but to the grave.

Nor you, ye Proud, impute to these the fault,
If Mem'ry o'er their tomb no trophies raise,
Where through the long-drawn aisle and fretted vault
40   The pealing anthem swells the note of praise.

Can storied urn or animated bust
Back to its mansion call the fleeting breath?
Can Honor's voice provoke the silent dust,
Or Flatt'ry soothe the dull cold ear of Death?

45   Perhaps in this neglected spot is laid
Some heart once pregnant with celestial fire;
Hands that the rod of empire might have swayed,
Or waked to ecstasy the living lyre.

But Knowledge to their eyes her ample page
50   Rich with the spoils of time did ne'er unroll;
Chill Penury repressed their noble rage,
And froze the genial current of the soul.

Full many a gem of purest ray serene,
The dark unfathomed caves of ocean bear:
55   Full many a flower is born to blush unseen,
And waste its sweetness on the desert air.

Some village-Hampden¹ that with dauntless breast
The little tyrant of his fields withstood;

1. John Hampden (1594–1643), parliamentary statesman and general in the Civil Wars, famed for his firm defiance of Charles I.

60
Some mute inglorious Milton here may rest,
Some Cromwell guiltless of his country's blood.

Th' applause of listening senates to command,
The threats of pain and ruin to despise,
To scatter plenty o'er a smiling land,
And read their history in a nation's eyes,

65
Their lot forbade: nor circumscribed alone
Their growing virtues, but their crimes confined;
Forbade to wade through slaughter to a throne,
And shut the gates of mercy on mankind,

70
The struggling pangs of conscious truth to hide,
To quench the blushes of ingenuous shame,
Or heap the shrine of Luxury and Pride
With incense kindled at the Muse's flame.[2]

Far from the madding crowd's ignoble strife,
Their sober wishes never learned to stray;
75
Along the cool sequestered vale of life
They kept the noiseless tenor of their way.

Yet ev'n these bones from insult to protect
Some frail memorial still erected nigh,
With uncouth rhymes and shapeless sculpture decked,
80
Implores the passing tribute of a sigh.

Their name, their years, spelt by th' unlettered muse,
The place of fame and elegy supply:
And many a holy text around she strews,
That teach the rustic moralist to die.

85
For who to dumb Forgetfulness a prey,
This pleasing anxious being e'er resigned,
Left the warm precincts of the cheerful day,
Nor cast one longing ling'ring look behind?

On some fond breast the parting soul relies,
90
Some pious drops the closing eye requires;
Ev'n from the tomb the voice of nature cries,
Ev'n in our ashes live their wonted fires.

2. According to Gray's friend William Mason, the poem originally concluded at this juncture with the following four stanzas, preserved in a manuscript at Eton College:

The thoughtless world to majesty may bow
Exalt the brave, and idolize success,
But more to innocence their safety owe
Than power and genius e'er conspired to bless.

And thou, who mindful of the unhonored dead
Dost in these notes their artless tale relate
By night and lonely contemplation led
To linger in the gloomy walks of fate,

Hark how the sacred calm, that broods around
Bids ev'ry fierce tumultuous passion cease
In still small accents whisp'ring from the ground
A grateful earnest of eternal peace.

No more with reason and thyself at strife;
Give anxious cares and endless wishes room
But through the cool sequestered vale of life
Pursue the silent tenor of thy doom.

For thee, who mindful of th' unhonored dead
Dost in these lines their artless tale relate;
95 If chance, by lonely Contemplation led,
Some kindred spirit shall inquire thy fate,

Haply some hoary-headed swain may say,
"Oft have we seen him at the peep of dawn
Brushing with hasty steps the dews away
100 To meet the sun upon the upland lawn.

"There at the foot of yonder nodding beech
That wreathes its old fantastic roots so high,
His listless length at noontide would he stretch,
And pore upon the brook that babbles by.

105 "Hard by yon wood, now smiling as in scorn,
Mutt'ring his wayward fancies he would rove,
Now drooping, woeful wan, like one forlorn,
Or crazed with care, or crossed in hopeless love.

"One morn I missed him on the 'customed hill,
110 Along the heath and near his favorite tree;
Another came; nor yet beside the rill,
Nor up the lawn, nor at the wood was he;

"The next with dirges due in sad array
Slow through the church-way path we saw him borne.
115 Approach and read (for thou can'st read) the lay,
Graved on the stone beneath yon aged thorn."

The Epitaph

Here rests his head upon the lap of earth
A youth to fortune and to fame unknown.
Fair Science frowned not on his humble birth,
120 *And Melancholy marked him for her own.*

Large was his bounty, and his soul sincere,
Heaven did a recompense as largely send:
He gave to Mis'ry all he had, a tear,
He gained from Heav'n ('twas all he wished) a friend.

125 *No farther seek his merits to disclose,*
Or draw his frailties from their dread abode,
(There they alike in trembling hope repose)
The bosom of his Father and his God.

1746–1750   1751

Samuel Johnson
1709–1784

James Barry, *Samuel Johnson.*

Samuel Johnson was born among books—his father sold them, not very successfully, at the family's combined home and shop in the market town of Lichfield. The son went on to create some of the most celebrated books of his age: an entire *Dictionary*, an edition of Shakespeare, a travel book, philosophical fictions, two eminent series of essays, a thick cluster of biographies. Despite his output, Johnson suffered from a chronic sense that he was underusing his talent, and throughout his *oeuvre* he wrote about "human unsuccess" (in W. H. Auden's phrase) with an empathy and acuity that few have matched before or since.

Johnson's struggles began early. An infection in infancy, followed by an attack of scrofula at age two, left his face scarred and his sight and hearing permanently impaired; by the age of eight a nervous disorder, probably Tourette's syndrome, brought on the compulsive gesticulations and intermittent muttering that would afflict him throughout his life, making him appear bizarre or even repellent at first encounter—until (as many testified) the stunning moment when he would begin to speak. His impressiveness had begun early, too. In childhood, the speed with which he acquired knowledge and the force with which he retained it astonished classmates and teachers, and also his parents, whose desire to show off his attainments often made him miserable. Johnson found more congenial mentors in his cousin, the rakish but learned young clergyman Cornelius Ford, at whose home he spent about half a year at age sixteen, and in Gilbert Walmesley, a middle-aged Lichfield lawyer, who welcomed Johnson often to his ample table and to the intelligent, disputatious company there assembled. Under Ford's and Walmesley's influence, Johnson undertook an intense but improvisatory program of reading, mostly in his father's shop. He read with a ferocious concentration that locked the texts into lifelong memory. "In this irregular manner," he later recalled, "I had looked into a great many books, which were not commonly known at the university, where they seldom read any books but what are put into their hands by their tutors; so that when I came to Oxford, Dr. Adams, now master of Pembroke College, told me, I was the best qualified for the university that he had ever known come there."

Despite such qualifications, Johnson's time at Oxford ushered in not triumph but frustration, and an oppressive sense of failure. Though he continued to be admired for his reading, and began to be noted for his writing, Johnson left the university after only thirteen months, "miserably poor" and unable to pay the fees, unbearably depressed and incapable of envisioning a viable future. After a melancholy year at home, during which his father died in debt, Johnson tried his hand at a variety of jobs beneath his earlier expectations: as assistant at a grammar school (he applied for three such positions, secured one, and left it in disgust after six months), and as occasional contributor to *The Birmingham Journal.* At Birmingham, he befriended the merchant Harry Porter and his wife Elizabeth ("Tetty"); she saw past his awkwardness at their first encounter, remarking to her daughter, "This is the most sensible man that I ever saw in my life." In 1735, ten months after her husband's death, she and Johnson married, despite wariness in both families at their difference in age (she was twenty years his senior). The new husband and wife tried to start a country boarding school, but it attracted only a handful of students. Early in 1737, Johnson decided to try something new: the life of a freelance writer in London.

The generic term for such a life was "Grub Street": it identified both an actual London street where some writers lived and plied their trade, and also the painful state of mind in which almost all of them did so, eking out precarious incomes from whatever assignments they could drum up. From the first, Johnson fared a little better than most. He attached himself immediately to Edward Cave, founder of the flourishing *Gentleman's Magazine*, in which Johnson's writing appeared plentifully over the next decade: essays, poems, short biographies, reviews, and voluminous, ingeniously fictionalized reports of debates in Parliament (authentic transcriptions were prohibited by law). The work provided some security but no prosperity: Johnson and his wife lived in poverty for many years. The struggle fueled articulate rage: in his poem *London* (1738), Johnson inveighed against the corruption of Robert Walpole's government and the cruelties of the city. Among his Grub Street colleagues he found a friend who, far more than himself, had made a sense of injury the basis of both life and art. The poet Richard Savage, generous, brilliant, and unstable, believed himself the abandoned offspring of a wealthy countess, and squandered much of his short life in the vain pursuit of recognition and redress. In *The Life of Richard Savage* (1744), published soon after his friend's early death, Johnson for the first time orchestrated many of the elements that would make his own work great: a commitment to biographical precision rather than routine panegyric; an analysis of expectation, self-delusion, and disappointment; a deep sympathy combined with nuanced judgment.

Savage was a memoir of Grub Street, but not yet for Johnson a valedictory. For two more years he continued his life of anonymous publication, narrow income, and declining spirits— "lost," as a friend lamented, "both to himself and the world." Then a new project found him. In 1746, the bookseller Robert Dodsley, struck by the erudition evident in Johnson's unsigned pieces, persuaded him to create a new dictionary of English, and assembled a consortium of publishers to finance (and profit from) the enormous undertaking. Johnson and his wife promptly moved from cramped and squalid quarters to a three-story house complete with a well-lit garret. There, with the help of six part-time assistants, Johnson made his lexicon, compiling word lists, tracking shifts and gradations of meaning, devising definitions, and illustrating them with quotations culled from the authors he most admired. The writer who (as Adam Smith later testified) "knew more books than any man alive" now decanted them discriminatingly into the two folio volumes of his *Dictionary* (1755), so as to make the work not only a standard reference for the language but also a compendium of its literature and its learning. The task took Johnson longer than he had anticipated—seven years, not three—but during this span he had busied himself in other ways as well: publishing *The Vanity of Human Wishes* (1749), a long poem on the pain of disillusion; witnessing the long-postponed production of his tragedy *Irene* (which brought him welcome added income); and composing, twice a week for two years, the periodical essay called *The Rambler* (1750–1752), the most formidable and famous instance of the genre since Addison and Steele had set down the *Spectator* forty years before. Johnson had embarked on the *Dictionary* as a virtual unknown; he emerged from the project with lasting fame and a double measure of celebratory sobriquets: he was widely known as "Dictionary Johnson," and was sometimes referred to simply (without surname) as "the Rambler."

As an epitome of his character the second label was perhaps more apt. A restlessness closely connected with loneliness had marked Johnson's mind since childhood. During the years of the *Dictionary*'s making, the loneliness had deepened. In 1752 Tetty died, and despite the strains in a marriage that had been differently difficult for both of them, Johnson mourned her obsessively for the rest of his days. He also contrived new sources of companionship, at home and in the wider world. He housed under his roof a group of eccentric, often difficult characters, including the ungainly man of medicine Robert Levet; the Jamaican servant Francis Barber; the blind Anna Williams, who waited up late every night to keep him company in his final cup of tea, often after he had spent long hours in more elevated society. He established what amounted to a second residence in the more polished household of the brewer Henry Thrale and his witty wife Hester, who welcomed and pampered not only Johnson but also the accomplished people who now rejoiced to rotate in his orbit: the actor David Garrick (who had been his pupil in the failed school and his companion on the road to London); the painter Joshua Reynolds; the politician and orator Edmund Burke; the writer Oliver Goldsmith; and Johnson's ardent young protégé and future biographer James Boswell. At the Thrales's country seat, and at the London clubs he formed to stave off solitude, Johnson sat surrounded by luminaries, savoring and often dominating the conversation. He talked (as Boswell noted) "for victory," and he generally secured it by a kind of surprise attack, a witty demolition of his companions' most familiar premises and casual assumptions. He won his listeners over by texture as well as text: by the spontaneous clarity and force of his utterance (as lexicographer he had defined every word he spoke); by the depth and energy of his voice.

Writing was by contrast largely solitary. Johnson's work pattern in the decade after the *Dictionary* recapitulated that of the one before: one ambitious, overarching project—this time an edition of all Shakespeare's plays (1765)—punctuated by shorter writings of lasting significance: a new periodical essay called *The Idler* (1758–1760); the philosophical tale *Rasselas, Prince of Abyssinia* (1759). In 1762 Johnson received a royal pension from George III in recognition of the *Dictionary*, assuring him an income of £300 a year for the remainder of his life. The pension brought Johnson a new security, along with the occasional accusation that his subsequent political pamphlets, generally favorable to the regime, amounted to paid propaganda. In fact, Johnson's politics throughout his life correlated fairly well with the views he implicitly espoused in the distinction he once drew for Boswell: "The prejudice of the Tory is for establishment; the prejudice of the Whig is for innovation." Born into a world where Whigs had long prevailed, Johnson early committed himself to Tory ways of thought: he cherished precedent, defended "subordination" (social hierarchy), and opposed Whiggish innovation with seriocomic fervor. What remained most notable about his politics was their compassion. "From first to last," John Wain remarks, Johnson "rooted his life among the poor and outcast"; in his work he argued the causes of prostitutes and slaves, of anyone sunk by the "want of necessaries" into "motionless despondence."

In the wake of his pension, Johnson's writing grew sparser, and markedly more social, compassing gestures to and for people he valued. He continued an ingrained habit of churning out prose for his friends to use under their own names: dictating law briefs for lawyers, composing sermons for preachers. He carried on an abundant and affectionate correspondence with Hester Thrale. With Boswell as companion, he traveled to the Scottish Highlands, and on his return published his account of that gregarious trip, *A Journey to the Western Islands* (1775). His final large work was social in a different sense. He accepted a commission to provide *Prefaces Biographical and Critical* for an anthology of English poets of the past hundred and fifty years. These included predecessors who had influenced him, contemporaries he had known, successors he regarded with admiration or alarm. To write their biographies, to analyze their works, was in a sense to live over his own literary life, and to reenter, at length and for the last time, the world of reading and of writing in which he'd now made his way for almost seven decades.

"Our social comforts drop away," Johnson lamented when his friend Levet died in 1782; his own last years were marred by loss. Successive deaths shrunk his contentious household; his friendship with Hester Thrale disintegrated under the pressure of her passion for a man of whom Johnson disapproved; a stroke temporarily deprived him of speech and ushered in his final difficult illness. At his death, an admirer remarked that Johnson had left "a chasm, which not only nothing can fill up, but which nothing has a tendency to fill up. Johnson is dead. Let us go to the next best:—there is nobody: no man can be said to put you in mind of Johnson." Biographers rushed in to fill the chasm, with the testimony of friends and of detractors, and with transcriptions of the hypnotic talk that many of them (notably Boswell and Thrale) had begun to record decades before. For most of the nineteenth century the fame of Johnson's talk far surpassed that of his writing. In recent decades scholars and readers have redressed the balance, finding in Johnson's prose and verse the richest repositories of his thought. Throughout a life of arduous struggle, prodigious accomplishment, and (in the end) near-matchless celebrity, Johnson wrote most eloquently and most feelingly—even in the *Dictionary*, even in literary criticism—of human vulnerabilities: to hope and disappointment, suffering and loss.

 For additional resources on Johnson, go to *The Longman Anthology of British Literature* Web site at www.myliteraturekit.com.

THE VANITY OF HUMAN WISHES   In his *Life of Pope*, Johnson defines the imitation, a poetic form much in vogue during the late seventeenth and early eighteenth centuries, as a "mode . . . in which the ancients are familiarized by adapting their sentiments to modern topics. . . . It is a kind of middle composition between translation and original design, which pleases when the thoughts are unexpectedly applicable and the parallels lucky." *The Vanity of Human Wishes* is Johnson's most sustained and successful endeavor in the mode. In the second century C.E., the Roman poet Juvenal had written an enduring satire on human ambition and failure, drawing vivid instances from history and from contemporary life. Johnson does the same, replacing the Roman's ancient examples with modern ones, supplanting his Stoic "sentiments" with a Christian credo. Johnson produced his imitation quickly, composing the whole of it in his mind before writing any of it down. It was the first work to appear under his own name, after more than a decade of abundant but anonymous publications. Its title and text sound themes that would preoccupy him for the remainder of his writing life: the dangers of desire, the inevitability of disappointment, the necessity of faith. *The Vanity of Human Wishes* is Johnson's signature poem in more ways than one.

The Vanity of Human Wishes
The Tenth Satire of Juvenal Imitated

    Let Observation, with extensive view,
Survey mankind, from China to Peru;
Remark each anxious toil, each eager strife,
And watch the busy scenes of crowded life;
5   Then say how hope and fear, desire and hate,
O'erspread with snares the clouded maze of fate,
Where wav'ring man, betrayed by vent'rous pride,
To tread the dreary paths without a guide,
As treach'rous phantoms in the mist delude,
10   Shuns fancied ills, or chases airy[1] good;
How rarely reason guides the stubborn choice,
Rules the bold hand, or prompts the suppliant voice;
How nations sink, by darling schemes oppressed,
When vengeance listens to the fool's request.
15   Fate wings with every wish th' afflictive dart,
Each gift of nature, and each grace of art,
With fatal heat impetuous courage glows,

---

1. "Wanting reality; having no steady foundation in truth or nature" (Johnson's *Dictionary*).

With fatal sweetness elocution flows,
Impeachment stops the speaker's pow'rful breath,
20   And restless fire precipitates on death.
       But scarce observed, the knowing and the bold
Fall in the gen'ral massacre of gold;
Wide-wasting pest! that rages unconfined,
And crowds with crimes the records of mankind;
25   For gold his sword the hireling ruffian draws,
For gold the hireling judge distorts the laws;
Wealth heaped on wealth, nor truth nor safety buys,
The dangers gather as the treasures rise.
       Let hist'ry tell where rival kings command,
30   And dubious title shakes the madded land,
When statutes° glean the refuse of the sword,   *tax laws*
How much more safe the vassal than the lord;
Low skulks the hind° beneath the rage of pow'r,   *rural laborer*
And leaves the wealthy traitor in the Tow'r,[2]
35   Untouched his cottage, and his slumbers sound,
Though confiscation's vultures hover round.
       The needy traveler, secure and gay,
Walks the wild heath, and sings his toil away.
Does envy seize thee? crush th' upbraiding joy,
40   Increase his riches and his peace destroy;
Now fears in dire vicissitude invade,
The rustling brake° alarms, and quiv'ring shade,   *thicket*
Nor light nor darkness bring his pain relief,
One shows the plunder, and one hides the thief.
45   Yet still one gen'ral cry the skies assails,
And gain and grandeur load the tainted gales;
Few know the toiling statesman's fear or care,
Th' insidious rival and the gaping heir.
       Once more, Democritus,[3] arise on earth,
50   With cheerful wisdom and instructive mirth,
See motley[4] life in modern trappings dressed,
And feed with varied fools th' eternal jest:
Thou who couldst laugh where want enchained caprice,
Toil crushed conceit, and man was of a piece;
55   Where wealth unloved without a mourner died,
And scarce a sycophant was fed by pride;
Where ne'er was known the form of mock debate,
Or seen a new-made mayor's unwieldy state;
Where change of fav'rites made no change of laws,
60   And senates heard before they judged a cause;
How wouldst thou shake at Britain's modish tribe,
Dart the quick taunt, and edge the piercing gibe?
Attentive truth and nature to descry,°   *discern*

2. The Tower of London.   of humanity.
3. Ancient Greek philosopher who laughed at the follies   4. Multicolored clothes worn by jesters.

And pierce each scene with philosophic eye.
65   To thee were solemn toys or empty show,
The robes of pleasure and the veils of woe:
All aid the farce, and all thy mirth maintain,
Whose joys are causeless, or whose griefs are vain.
     Such was the scorn that filled the sage's mind,
70   Renewed at ev'ry glance on humankind;
How just that scorn ere yet thy voice declare,
Search every state, and canvass every prayer.
     Unnumbered suppliants crowd Preferment's gate,
Athirst for wealth, and burning to be great;
75   Delusive Fortune hears th' incessant call,
They mount, they shine, evaporate, and fall.[5]
On every stage the foes of peace attend,
Hate dogs their flight, and insult mocks their end.
Love ends with hope, the sinking statesman's door
80   Pours in the morning worshiper no more;
For growing names the weekly scribbler lies,
To growing wealth the dedicator flies,
From ev'ry room descends the painted face,
That hung the bright Palladium[6] of the place,
85   And smoked in kitchens, or in auctions sold,
To better features yields the frame of gold;
For now no more we trace in ev'ry line
Heroic worth, benevolence divine:
The form distorted justifies the fall,
90   And detestation rids th' indignant wall.
     But will not Britain hear the last appeal,
Sign her foes' doom, or guard her fav'rites' zeal?
Through Freedom's sons no more remonstrance rings,
Degrading nobles and controlling kings;
95   Our supple tribes° repress their patriot throats,   *of voters*
And ask no questions but the price of votes;
With weekly libels and septennial ale,[7]
Their wish is full to riot and to rail.
     In full-blown dignity, see Wolsey[8] stand,
100   Law in his voice, and fortune in his hand:
To him the church, the realm, their pow'rs consign,
Through him the rays of regal bounty shine,
Turned by his nod the stream of honor flows,
His smile alone security bestows:
105   Still to new heights his restless wishes tow'r,
Claim leads to claim, and pow'r advances pow'r;
Till conquest unresisted ceased to please,

5. The image is that of Fortune's wheel.
6. A statue of Pallas Athena, guardian of Troy.
7. Drink offered to voters as bribes during campaigns for Parliament, held every seven years.

8. Cardinal Wolsey (1475–1530), Henry VIII's Lord Chancellor, who was dismissed and imprisoned for failing to procure the King a divorce from Catherine of Aragon.

And rights submitted, left him none to seize.
At length his sov'reign frowns—the train of state
110   Mark the keen glance, and watch the sign to hate.
Wheree'er he turns he meets a stranger's eye,
His suppliants scorn him, and his followers fly;
At once is lost the pride of awful state,
The golden canopy, the glitt'ring plate,
115   The regal palace, the luxurious board,
The liv'ried army, and the menial lord.
With age, with cares, with maladies oppressed,
He seeks the refuge of monastic rest.
Grief aids disease, remembered folly stings,
120   And his last sighs reproach the faith of kings.
   Speak thou, whose thoughts at humble peace repine,
Shall Wolsey's wealth, with Wolsey's end be thine?
Or liv'st thou now, with safer pride content,
The wisest justice on the banks of Trent?[9]
125   For why did Wolsey near the steeps° of fate,   *precipices*
On weak foundations raise th' enormous weight?
Why but to sink beneath misfortune's blow,
With louder ruin to the gulfs below?
   What gave great Villiers[1] to th' assassin's knife,
130   And fixed disease on Harley's[2] closing life?
What murdered Wentworth, and what exiled Hyde,[3]
By kings protected, and to kings allied?
What but their wish indulged in courts to shine,
And pow'r too great to keep, or to resign?
135   When first the college rolls receive his name,
The young enthusiast[4] quits his ease for fame;
Through all his veins the fever of renown
Burns from the strong contagion of the gown;[5]
O'er Bodley's dome[6] his future labors spread,
140   And Bacon's mansion[7] trembles o'er his head.
Are these thy views? proceed, illustrious youth,
And virtue guard thee to the throne of Truth!
Yet should thy soul indulge the gen'rous heat,
Till captive Science° yields her last retreat;   *knowledge*
145   Should Reason guide thee with her brightest ray,
And pour on misty Doubt resistless day;

9. The river that divides northern from southern England; it is near Lichfield, Johnson's birthplace.
1. George Villiers (1592–1628), first Duke of Buckingham and a favorite of James I, was stabbed to death.
2. Robert Harley (1661–1724), first Earl of Oxford and leading statesman during the reign of Queen Anne, was impeached when George I succeeded to the throne in 1714.
3. Thomas Wentworth (1593–1641), first Earl of Strafford and adviser to Charles I, was executed at the beginning of the English Civil War. Edward Hyde (1609–1674), first

Earl of Clarendon, served Charles II but then fell from favor.
4. "One of hot imagination" (Johnson's *Dictionary*).
5. Scholastic dress (but also a reference to the poisoned garment that killed Hercules).
6. The Bodleian Library, Oxford.
7. "There is a tradition, that the study of friar Bacon [Roger Bacon, a medieval philosopher] built an arch over the bridge, will fall, when a man greater than Bacon shall pass under it" [Johnson's note].

Should no false Kindness lure to loose delight,
Nor Praise relax, nor Difficulty fright;
Should tempting Novelty thy cell refrain,
150   And Sloth effuse her opiate fumes in vain;
Should Beauty blunt on fops her fatal dart,
Nor claim the triumph of a lettered heart;
Should no disease thy torpid veins invade,
Nor Melancholy's phantoms haunt thy shade;
155   Yet hope not life from grief or danger free,
Nor think the doom of man reversed for thee:
Deign on the passing world to turn thine eyes,
And pause awhile from letters, to be wise;
There mark what ills the scholar's life assail,
160   Toil, envy, want, the patron,[8] and the jail.
See nations slowly wise, and meanly just,
To buried merit raise the tardy bust.
If dreams yet flatter, once again attend,
Hear Lydiat's life, and Galileo's end.[9]
165   Nor deem, when learning her last prize bestows,
The glitt'ring eminence exempt from foes;
See when the vulgar 'scape, despised or awed,
Rebellion's vengeful talons seize on Laud.[1]
From meaner minds, though smaller fines content,
170   The plundered palace or sequestered rent;
Marked out by dangerous parts° he meets the shock,   *abilities*
And fatal Learning leads him to the block:
Around his tomb let Art and Genius weep,
But hear his death, ye blockheads, hear and sleep.
175   The festal blazes, the triumphal show,
The ravished standard, and the captive foe,
The senate's thanks, the gazette's pompous tale,
With force resistless o'er the brave prevail.
Such bribes the rapid Greek[2] o'er Asia whirled,
180   For such the steady Romans shook the world;
For such in distant lands the Britons shine,
And stain with blood the Danube or the Rhine;
This pow'r has praise, that virtue scarce can warm,
Till fame supplies the universal charm.
185   Yet Reason frowns on War's unequal game,
Where wasted nations raise a single name,
And mortgaged states their grandsires' wreaths[3] regret,
From age to age in everlasting debt;
Wreaths which at last the dear-bought right convey

---

8. Johnson originally wrote "garret," but changed it to "patron" after enduring the neglect of Lord Chesterfield (see his letter to Chesterfield, page 2744).
9. Thomas Lydiat (1572–1646) was a distinguished but impoverished mathematician. The astronomer Galileo

Galilei (1564–1642) was silenced by the Inquisition.
1. William Laud (1572–1645), Archbishop of Canterbury under Charles I, was beheaded by the Parliamentarians.
2. Alexander the Great.
3. Garlands of victory.

190   To rust on medals, or on stones decay.
                  On what foundation stands the warrior's pride,
             How just his hopes let Swedish Charles[4] decide;
             A frame of adamant, a soul of fire,
             No dangers fright him, and no labors tire;
195   O'er love, o'er fear, extends his wide domain,
             Unconquered lord of pleasure and of pain;
             No joys to him pacific scepters yield,
             War sounds the trump, he rushes to the field;
             Behold surrounding kings their pow'r combine,
200   And one capitulate, and one resign;
             Peace courts his hand, but spreads her charms in vain;
             "Think nothing gained," he cries, "till nought remain,
             On Moscow's walls till Gothic standards fly,
             And all be mine beneath the polar sky."
205   The march begins in military state,
             And nations on his eye suspended wait;
             Stern Famine guards the solitary coast,
             And Winter barricades the realms of Frost;
             He comes, not want and cold his course delay—
210   Hide, blushing Glory, hide Pultowa's day:
             The vanquished hero leaves his broken bands,
             And shows his miseries in distant lands;
             Condemned a needy supplicant to wait,
             While ladies interpose, and slaves debate.
215   But did not Chance at length her error mend?
             Did no subverted empire mark his end?
             Did rival monarchs give the fatal wound?
             Or hostile millions press him to the ground?
             His fall was destined to a barren strand,
220   A petty fortress, and a dubious hand;[5]
             He left the name, at which the world grew pale,
             To point a moral, or adorn a tale.
                  All times their scenes of pompous woes afford,
             From Persia's tyrant[6] to Bavaria's lord.[7]
225   In gay hostility, and barb'rous pride,
             With half mankind embattled at his side,
             Great Xerxes comes to seize the certain prey,
             And starves exhausted regions in his way;
             Attendant Flattery counts his myriads o'er,
230   Till counted myriads soothe his pride no more;

4. Charles XII of Sweden, whose precarious military career ended at the Battle of Pultowa (1709). After his defeat by the Russians, Charles attempted to forge an alliance with the Turks.
5. Charles XII of Sweden was thought to have been killed by one of his own officers during a siege of little military consequence.
6. Xerxes (?519–465 B.C.E.) invaded Greece with a large army and navy. In order to transport his troops, he built a bridge of boats across the Hellespont. When a storm broke up this bridge, Xerxes ordered the wind and water to be punished. The Persian army was defeated at the Battle of Plataea, the navy at the Battle of Salamis.
7. Charles Albert (1697–1745), Elector of Bavaria, was defeated by Empress Maria Theresa, whose army included Austrian colonists from Croatia and Hungarian cavalry called "jussars."

Fresh praise is tried till madness fires his mind,
The waves he lashes, and enchains the wind;
New pow'rs are claimed, new pow'rs are still bestowed,
Till rude resistance lops the spreading god;
235   The daring Greeks deride the martial show,
And heap heir valleys with the gaudy foe;
Th' insulted sea with humbler thoughts he gains,
A single skiff to speed his ligh remains;
Th' encumbered oar scarce leaves the dreaded coast
240   Through purple billows and a floating host.
    The bold Bavarian, in a luckless hour,
Tries the dread summits of Cesarean power,
With unexpected legions bursts away,
And sees defenseless realms receive his sway;
245   Short sway! fair Austria spreads her mournful charms,
The queen, the beauty, sets the world in arms;
From hill to hill the beacon's rousing blaze
Spreads wide the hope of plunder and of praise;
The fierce Croatian, and the wild Hussar,
250   And all the sons of ravage crowd the war;
The baffled prince in honor's flattering bloom
Of hasty greatness finds the fatal doom,
His foes' derision, and his subjects' blame,
And steals to death from anguish and from shame.
255   Enlarge my life with multitude of days,
In health, in sickness, thus the suppliant prays;
Hides from himself his state, and shuns to know,
That life protracted is protracted woe.
Time hovers o'er, impatient to destroy,
260   And shuts up all the passages of joy:
In vain their gifts the bounteous seasons pour,
The fruit autumnal, and the vernal flow'r,
With listless eyes the dotard views the store,
He views, and wonders that they please no more;
265   Now pall the tasteless meats, and joyless wines,
And Luxury° with sighs her slave resigns.   *voluptuousness*
Approach, ye minstrels, try the soothing strain,
Diffuse the tuneful lenitives[8] of pain:
No sounds alas would touch th' impervious ear,
270   Though dancing mountains witnessed Orpheus[9] near;
Nor lute nor lyre his feeble pow'rs attend,
Nor sweeter music of a virtuous friend,
But everlasting dictates crowd his tongue,
Perversely grave, or positively wrong.
275   The still returning tale, and ling'ring jest,
Perplex the fawning niece and pampered guest,

---

8. "Anything medicinally applied to ease pain" (John-son's *Dictionary*).

9. In Greek mythology, the musician Orpheus charmed wild beasts and moved mountains.

While growing hopes scarce awe the gathering sneer,
And scarce a legacy can bribe to hear;
The watchful guests still hint the last° offense,   latest
280   The daughter's petulance, the son's expense,
Improve his heady rage with treach'rous skill,
And mold his passions till they make his will.
        Unnumbered maladies his joints invade,
Lay siege to life and press the dire blockade;
285   But unextinguished Avarice still remains,
And dreaded losses aggravate his pains;
He turns, with anxious heart and crippled hands,
His bonds of debt, and mortgages of lands;
Or views his coffers with suspicious eyes,
290   Unlocks his gold, and counts it till he dies.
        But grant, the virtues of a temp'rate prime
Bless with an age exempt from scorn or crime;
An age that melts with unperceived decay,
And glides in modest innocence away;
295   Whose peaceful day Benevolence endears,
Whose night congratulating Conscience cheers;
The gen'ral favorite as the gen'ral friend:
Such age there is, and who shall wish its end?
        Yet ev'n on this her load Misfortune flings,
300   To press the weary minutes' flagging wings:
New sorrow rises as the day returns,
A sister sickens, or a daughter mourns.
Now kindred Merit fills the sable bier,
Now lacerated Friendship claims a tear.
305   Year chases year, decay pursues decay,
Still drops some joy from with'ring life away;
New forms arise, and different views engage,
Superfluous lags the vet'ran on the stage,
Till pitying Nature signs the last release,
310   And bids afflicted worth retire to peace.
        But few there are whom hours like these await,
Who set unclouded in the gulfs of fate.
From Lydia's monarch should the search descend,
By Solon cautioned to regard his end,[1]
315   In life's last scene what prodigies surprise,
Fears of the brave, and follies of the wise?
From Marlborough's eyes the streams of dotage flow,[2]
And Swift expires a driveler and a show.[3]
        The teeming mother, anxious for her race,
320   Begs for each birth the fortune of a face:
Yet Vane could tell what ills from beauty spring;

1. Solon, Greek philosopher and legislator, warned the wealthy King Croesus of Lydia that no one should count himself happy until reaching the end of life.
2. John Churchill (1650–1722), first Duke of Marlborough,
hero of the War of the Spanish Succession, lived for six years after suffering two paralytic strokes.
3. Jonathan Swift, who declined into senility, was thought to have been exhibited by his servant for money.

And Sedley cursed the form that pleased a king.[4]
Ye nymphs of rosy lips and radiant eyes,
Whom Pleasure keeps too busy to be wise,
325 Whom Joys with soft varieties invite,
By day the frolic, and the dance by night,
Who frown with vanity, who smile with art,
And ask the latest fashion of the heart,
What care, what rules your heedless charms shall save,
330 Each nymph your rival, and each youth your slave?
Against your fame with fondness hate combines,
The rival batters, and the lover mines.
With distant voice neglected Virtue calls,
Less heard and less, the faint remonstrance falls;
335 Tired with contempt, she quits the slipp'ry reign,
And Pride and Prudence take her seat in vain.
In crowd at once, where none the pass defend,
The harmless Freedom, and the private Friend.
The guardians yield, by force superior plied;
340 By Interest, Prudence; and by Flattery, Pride.
Now beauty falls betrayed, despised, distressed,
And hissing Infamy proclaims the rest.
    Where then shall Hope and Fear their objects find?
Must dull Suspense corrupt the stagnant mind?
345 Must helpless man, in ignorance sedate,°   calm
Roll darkling° down the torrent of his fate?   in the dark
Must no dislike alarm, no wishes rise,
No cries attempt the mercies of the skies?
Inquirer, cease, petitions yet remain,
350 Which Heav'n may hear, nor deem religion vain.
Still raise for good the supplicating voice,
But leave to Heav'n the measure and the choice,
Safe in his power, whose eyes discern afar
The secret ambush of a specious prayer.
355 Implore his aid, in his decisions rest,
Secure whate'er he gives, he gives the best.
Yet when the sense of sacred presence fires,
And strong devotion to the skies aspires,
Pour forth thy fervors for a healthful mind,
360 Obedient passions, and a will resigned;
For love, which scarce collective man can fill;
For patience sov'reign o'er transmuted ill;
For faith, that panting for a happier seat,
Counts death kind Nature's signal of retreat:
365 These goods for man the laws of Heav'n ordain,
These goods he grants, who grants the power to gain;
With these celestial Wisdom calms the mind,
And makes the happiness she does not find.

1748   1749

---

4. Anne Vane (1705–1736) was the mistress of the Prince of Wales, Catherine Sedley (1657–1717) of James II.

A Short Song of Congratulation[1]

Long expected one and twenty
    Ling'ring year at last is flown,
Pomp and pleasure, pride and plenty,
    Great Sir John, are all your own.

5   Loosened from the minor's tether,
    Free to mortgage or to sell,
Wild as wind, and light as feather
    Bid the slaves of thrift farewell.[2]

Call the Bettys, Kates, and Jennys
10   Ev'ry name that laughs at care,
Lavish of your grandsire's guineas,
    Show the spirit of an heir.

All that prey on vice and folly
    Joy to see their quarry fly,
15   Here the gamester light and jolly
    There the lender grave and sly.

Wealth, Sir John, was made to wander,
    Let it wander as it will;
See the jockey, see the pander,
20   Bid them come, and take their fill.

When the bonny blade carouses,
    Pockets full, and spirits high,
What are acres? What are houses?
    Only dirt, or wet or dry.

25   If the guardian or the mother
    Tell the woes of willful waste,
Scorn their counsel and their pother,
    You can hang or drown at last.

1780   1794

On the Death of Dr. Robert Levet[1]

Condemned to Hope's delusive mine,
    As on we toil from day to day,
By sudden blasts, or slow decline,
    Our social comforts drop away.

---

1. Written for Sir John Lade (1759–1838), the nephew of Johnson's close friend Henry Thrale.
2. Sir John fulfilled Johnson's predictions: he made a scandalous marriage and then squandered his inheritance.
1. Robert Levet (1705–1782), a friend and dependent of Johnson, had acquired a modicum of medical training while working as a waiter in Paris; he put this training to use by caring for the poorest of the London poor ("Dr." was an honorific title). Many of Johnson's friends wondered why he admired and supported a man whom Boswell described as "an obscure practiser in physick amongst the lower people." Johnson's elegy answers that question.

Well tried through many a varying year,
 See Levet to the grave descend;
Officious,[2] innocent, sincere,
 Of ev'ry friendless name the friend.

Yet still he fills Affection's eye,
 Obscurely° wise, and coarsely kind;   *privately*
Nor, lettered Arrogance, deny
 Thy praise to merit unrefined.

When fainting Nature called for aid,
 And hov'ring Death prepared the blow,
His vig'rous remedy displayed
 The power of art without the show.

In Misery's darkest caverns known,
 His useful care was ever nigh,
Where hopeless Anguish poured his groan,
 And lonely Want retired to die.

No summons mocked by chill delay,
 No petty gain disdained by pride,
The modest wants of ev'ry day
 The toil of ev'ry day supplied.

His virtues walked their narrow round,
 Nor made a pause, nor left a void;
And sure th' Eternal Master found
 The single talent well employed.[3]

The busy day, the peaceful night,
 Unfelt, uncounted, glided by;
His frame was firm, his pow'rs were bright,
 Though now his eightieth year was nigh.

Then with no throbbing fiery pain,
 No cold gradations of decay,
Death broke at once the vital chain,
 And freed his soul the nearest way.

1782   1783

THE RAMBLER   In the midst of working on his *Dictionary*, Johnson took on an ambitious additional task: he wrote *The Rambler*, a twice-weekly periodical essay which he sustained for two full years (1750–1752). The project brought him needed income and also a useful respite from the strains of lexicography. *The Rambler*'s most famous antecedent was Addison and Steele's the *Spectator* (1711–1713), and though Johnson would later praise Addison's prose as a "model of the middle style . . . always equable and always easy," he chose for his own essays a mode more astringent: a large, often Latinate vocabulary, intricately balanced sentences, a steady alertness to the human propensity for self-delusion, a willingness to confront rather than ingratiate. Pressures of production could run high (Johnson later claimed that he sometimes

2. "Kind; doing good offices" (Johnson's *Dictionary*).
3. A reference to Jesus's Parable of the Talents (Matthew

25.14–30), which haunted Johnson throughout his adult life.

wrote his essay with the printer's messenger standing at his side, waiting to take the text to the press), and speed of output may have helped shape the results. Many *Ramblers*, with their formidably wrought prose and surprising turns of thought, manage to seem imposing and improvisatory at the same time. Free to choose his topics, working under relentlessly recurrent deadlines, Johnson drew on four decades dense with reading and thought, during which (in the words of his biographer John Hawkins) he had "accumulated a fund of moral science that was more than sufficient for such an undertaking," and had become "in a very eminent degree qualified for the office of an instructor of mankind in their greatest and most important concerns." Readers proved eager for the instruction. More than any of his earlier writings, *The Rambler* established Johnson's style, his substance, and his fame.

For additional *Ramblers* (no. 170, 171, and 207), go to *The Longman Anthology of British Literature* Web site at www.myliteraturekit.com.

Rambler No. 4
[ON FICTION]

Saturday, 31 March 1750

Simul et jucunda et idonea dicere vitae.

Horace, *Ars Poetica* 1.334

And join both profit and delight in one.

Creech

The works of fiction with which the present generation seems more particularly delighted are such as exhibit life in its true state, diversified only by accidents that daily happen in the world, and influenced by passions and qualities which are really to be found in conversing with mankind.

This kind of writing may be termed not improperly the comedy of romance, and is to be conducted nearly by the rules of comic poetry. Its province is to bring about natural events by easy means, and to keep up curiosity without the help of wonder: it is therefore precluded from the machines[1] and expedients of the heroic romance, and can neither employ giants to snatch away a lady from the nuptial rites, nor knights to bring her back from captivity; it can neither bewilder its personages in deserts, nor lodge them in imaginary castles.

I remember a remark made by Scaliger upon Pontanus,[2] that all his writings are filled with the same images; and that if you take from him his lillies and his roses, his satyrs and his dryads, he will have nothing left that can be called poetry. In like manner, almost all the fictions of the last age will vanish, if you deprive them of a hermit and a wood, a battle and a shipwreck.

Why this wild strain of imagination found reception so long, in polite and learned ages, it is not easy to conceive; but we cannot wonder that, while readers could be procured, the authors were willing to continue it: for when a man had by practice gained some fluency of language, he had no further care than to retire to his closet,[3] let loose his invention, and heat his mind with incredibilities; a book was

---

1. "Supernatural agency in poems" (Johnson's *Dictionary*).
2. The Renaissance humanist Julius Caesar Scaliger (1484–1558) criticized the poetry of Giovanni Pontano

(1426–1503).
3. Study.

thus produced without fear of criticism, without the toil of study, without knowledge of nature, or acquaintance with life.

The task of our present writers is very different; it requires, together with that learning which is to be gained from books, that experience which can never be attained by solitary diligence, but must arise from general converse, and accurate observation of the living world. Their performances have, as Horace expresses it, *plus oneris quantum veniae minus*, little indulgence, and therefore more difficulty.[4] They are engaged in portraits of which every one knows the original, and can detect any deviation from exactness of resemblance. Other writings are safe, except from the malice of learning, but these are in danger from every common reader; as the slipper ill executed was censured by a shoemaker who happened to stop in his way at the Venus of Apelles.[5]

But the fear of not being approved as just copiers of human manners, is not the most important concern that an author of this sort ought to have before him. These books are written chiefly to the young, the ignorant, and the idle, to whom they serve as lectures of conduct, and introductions into life. They are the entertainment of minds unfurnished with ideas, and therefore easily susceptible of impressions; not fixed by principles, and therefore easily following the current of fancy; not informed by experience, and consequently open to every false suggestion and partial account.

That the highest degree of reverence should be paid to youth, and that nothing indecent should be suffered to approach their eyes or ears, are precepts extorted by sense and virtue from an ancient writer, by no means eminent for chastity of thought.[6] The same kind, though not the same degree of caution, is required in every thing which is laid before them, to secure them from unjust prejudices, perverse opinions, and incongruous combinations of images.

In the romances formerly written, every transaction and sentiment was so remote from all that passes among men, that the reader was in very little danger of making any applications to himself; the virtues and crimes were equally beyond his sphere of activity; and he amused himself with heroes and with traitors, deliverers and persecutors, as with beings of another species, whose actions were regulated upon motives of their own, and who had neither faults nor excellencies in common with himself.

But when an adventurer is leveled with the rest of the world, and acts in such scenes of the universal drama, as may be the lot of any other man, young spectators fix their eyes upon him with closer attention, and hope by observing his behavior and success to regulate their own practices, when they shall be engaged in the like part.

For this reason these familiar histories may perhaps be made of greater use than the solemnities of professed morality, and convey the knowledge of vice and virtue with more efficacy than axioms and definitions. But if the power of example is so great, as to take possession of the memory by a kind of violence, and produce effects almost without the intervention of the will, care ought to be taken that, when the choice is unrestrained, the best examples only should be exhibited; and that which is likely to operate so strongly, should not be mischievous or uncertain in its effects.

The chief advantage which these fictions have over real life is, that their authors are at liberty, though not to invent, yet to select objects, and to cull from the mass of mankind those individuals upon which the attention ought most to be

4. Horace, *Epistles* 2.1.170.
5. In his *Natural History*, Pliny the Elder tells this story of the famous painter Apelles.

6. Johnson refers to the opening lines of Juvenal's fourteenth satire.

employed; as a diamond, though it cannot be made, may be polished by art, and placed in such a situation as to display that lustre which before was buried among common stones.

It is justly considered as the greatest excellency of art, to imitate nature; but it is necessary to distinguish those parts of nature, which are most proper for imitation: greater care is still required in representing life, which is so often discolored by passion, or deformed by wickedness. If the world be promiscuously[7] described, I cannot see of what use it can be to read the account; or why it may not be as safe to turn the eye immediately upon mankind, as upon a mirror which shows all that presents itself without discrimination.

It is therefore not a sufficient vindication of a character, that it is drawn as it appears, for many characters ought never to be drawn; nor of a narrative, that the train of events is agreeable to observation and experience, for that observation which is called knowledge of the world will be found much more frequently to make men cunning than good. The purpose of these writings is surely not only to show mankind, but to provide that they may be seen hereafter with less hazard; to teach the means of avoiding the snares which are laid by Treachery for Innocence, without infusing any wish for that superiority with which the betrayer flatters his vanity; to give the power of counteracting fraud, without the temptation to practice it; to initiate youth by mock encounters in the art of necessary defense, and to increase prudence without impairing virtue.

Many writers, for the sake of following nature, so mingle good and bad qualities in their principal personages, that they are both equally conspicuous; and as we accompany them through their adventures with delight, and are led by degrees to interest ourselves in their favor, we lose the abhorrence of their faults, because they do not hinder our pleasure, or, perhaps, regard them with some kindness for being united with so much merit.

There have been men indeed splendidly wicked, whose endowments threw a brightness on their crimes, and whom scarce any villainy made perfectly detestable, because they never could be wholly divested of their excellencies; but such have been in all ages the great corrupters of the world, and their resemblance ought no more to be preserved, than the art of murdering without pain.

Some have advanced, without due attention to the consequences of this notion, that certain virtues have their correspondent faults, and therefore that to exhibit either apart is to deviate from probability. Thus men are observed by Swift to be "grateful in the same degree as they are resentful."[8] This principle, with others of the same kind, supposes man to act from a brute impulse, and pursue a certain degree of inclination, without any choice of the object; for otherwise, though it should be allowed that gratitude and resentment arise from the same constitution of the passions, it follows not that they will be equally indulged when reason is consulted; yet unless that consequence be admitted, this sagacious maxim becomes an empty sound, without any relation to practice or to life.

Nor is it evident, that even the first motions to these effects are always in the same proportion. For pride, which produces quickness of resentment, will obstruct gratitude, by unwillingness to admit that inferiority which obligation implies; and it is very unlikely that he who cannot think he receives a favor will acknowledge or repay it.

---

7. Indiscriminately.
8. In fact, it was Pope who made this observation, in the

Miscellanies he coauthored with Swift.

It is of the utmost importance to mankind that positions of this tendency should be laid open and confuted; for while men consider good and evil as springing from the same root, they will spare the one for the sake of the other, and in judging, if not of others at least of themselves, will be apt to estimate their virtues by their vices. To this fatal error all those will contribute, who confound the colors of right and wrong, and instead of helping to settle their boundaries, mix them with so much art, that no common mind is able to disunite them.

In narratives where historical veracity has no place, I cannot discover why there should not be exhibited the most perfect idea of virtue; of virtue not angelical, nor above probability, for what we cannot credit we shall never imitate, but the highest and purest that humanity can reach, which, exercised in such trials as the various revolutions of things shall bring upon it, may, by conquering some calamities, and enduring others, teach us what we may hope, and what we can perform. Vice, for vice is necessary to be shown, should always disgust; nor should the graces of gaiety, or the dignity of courage, be so united with it, as to reconcile it to the mind. Wherever it appears, it should raise hatred by the malignity of its practices, and contempt by the meanness of its stratagems; for while it is supported by either parts[9] or spirit, it will be seldom heartily abhorred. The Roman tyrant was content to be hated, if he was but feared;[1] and there are thousands of the readers of romances willing to be thought wicked, if they may be allowed to be wits. It is therefore to be steadily inculcated, that virtue is the highest proof of understanding, and the only solid basis of greatness; and that vice is the natural consequence of narrow thoughts, that it begins in mistake, and ends in ignominy.

Rambler No. 5
[ON SPRING]

Tuesday, 3 April 1750

Et nunc omnis ager, nunc omnis parturit arbos,
Nunc frondent silvae, nunc formosissimus annus.

Virgil, *Eclogues* 3.56–57

Now every field, now every tree is green;
Now genial nature's fairest face is seen.

Elphinston

Every man is sufficiently discontented with some circumstances of his present state, to suffer his imagination to range more or less in quest of future happiness, and to fix upon some point of time, in which, by the removal of the inconvenience which now perplexes him, or acquisition of the advantage which he at present wants,[1] he shall find the condition of his life very much improved.

When this time, which is too often expected with great impatience, at last arrives, it generally comes without the blessing for which it was desired; but we solace ourselves with some new prospect, and press forward again with equal eagerness.

---

9. Abilities.
1. The Roman historian Suetonius reports this of the emperor Caligula.
1. Lacks.

It is lucky for a man, in whom this temper prevails, when he turns his hopes upon things wholly out of his own power; since he forbears then to precipitate his affairs, for the sake of the great event that is to complete his felicity, and waits for the blissful hour, with less neglect of the measures necessary to be taken in the mean time.

I have long known a person of this temper, who indulged his dream of happiness with less hurt to himself than such chimerical wishes commonly produce, and adjusted his scheme with such address, that his hopes were in full bloom three parts of the year, and in the other part never wholly blasted. Many, perhaps, would be desirous of learning by what means he procured to himself such a cheap and lasting satisfaction. It was gained by a constant practice of referring the removal of all his uneasiness to the coming of the next spring; if his health was impaired, the spring would restore it; if what he wanted was at a high price, it would fall its value in the spring.

The spring, indeed, did often come without any of these effects, but he was always certain that the next would be more propitious; nor was ever convinced that the present spring would fail him before the middle of summer; for he always talked of the spring as coming 'till it was past, and when it was once past, everyone agreed with him that it was coming.

By long converse with this man, I am, perhaps, brought to feel immoderate pleasure in the contemplation of this delightful season; but I have the satisfaction of finding many, whom it can be no shame to resemble, infected with the same enthusiasm;[2] for there is, I believe, scarce any poet of eminence, who has not left some testimony of his fondness for the flowers, the zephyrs, and the warblers of the spring. Nor has the most luxuriant imagination been able to describe the serenity and happiness of the golden age, otherwise than by giving a perpetual spring, as the highest reward of uncorrupted innocence.

There is, indeed, something inexpressibly pleasing, in the annual renovation of the world, and the new display of the treasures of nature. The cold and darkness of winter, with the naked deformity of every object on which we turn our eyes, make us rejoice at the succeeding season, as well for what we have escaped, as for what we may enjoy; and every budding flower, which a warm situation brings early to our view, is considered by us as a messenger to notify the approach of more joyous days.

The spring affords to a mind, so free from the disturbance of cares or passions as to be vacant to calm amusements, almost every thing that our present state makes us capable of enjoying. The variegated verdure of the fields and woods, the succession of grateful odors, the voice of pleasure pouring out its notes on every side, with the gladness apparently conceived by every animal, from the growth of his food, and the clemency of the weather, throw over the whole earth an air of gaiety, significantly expressed by the smile of nature.

Yet there are men to whom these scenes are able to give no delight, and who hurry away from all the varieties of rural beauty, to lose their hours, and divert their thoughts by cards, or assemblies, a tavern dinner, or the prattle of the day.

It may be laid down as a position which will seldom deceive, that when a man cannot bear his own company there is something wrong. He must fly from himself, either because he feels a tediousness in life from the equipoise of an empty mind, which, having no tendency to one motion more than another but as it is impelled

---

2. "Elevation of fancy; exaltation of ideas" (Johnson's *Dictionary*).

by some external power, must always have recourse to foreign objects; or he must be afraid of the intrusion of some unpleasing ideas, and, perhaps, is struggling to escape from the remembrance of a loss, the fear of a calamity, or some other thought of greater horror.

Those whom sorrow incapacitates to enjoy the pleasures of contemplation, may properly apply to such diversions, provided they are innocent, as lay strong hold on the attention; and those, whom fear of any future affliction chains down to misery, must endeavor to obviate the danger.

My considerations shall, on this occasion, be turned on such as are burdensome to themselves merely because they want subjects for reflection, and to whom the volume of nature is thrown open, without affording them pleasure or instruction, because they never learned to read the characters.

A French author has advanced this seeming paradox, that "very few men know how to take a walk"; and, indeed, it is true, that few know how to take a walk with a prospect of any other pleasure, than the same company would have afforded them at home.

There are animals that borrow their color from the neighboring body, and, consequently, vary their hue as they happen to change their place. In like manner it ought to be the endeavor of every man to derive his reflections from the objects about him; for it is to no purpose that he alters his position, if his attention continues fixed to the same point. The mind should be kept open to the access of every new idea, and so far disengaged from the predominance of particular thoughts, as easily to accommodate itself to occasional entertainment.

A man that has formed this habit of turning every new object to his entertainment, finds in the productions of nature an inexhaustible stock of materials upon which he can employ himself, without any temptations to envy or malevolence; faults, perhaps, seldom totally avoided by those, whose judgment is much exercised upon the works of art. He has always a certain prospect of discovering new reasons for adoring the sovereign author of the universe, and probable hopes of making some discovery of benefit to others, or of profit to himself. There is no doubt but many vegetables and animals have qualities that might be of great use, to the knowledge of which there is not required much force of penetration, or fatigue of study, but only frequent experiments, and close attention. What is said by the chemists of their darling mercury, is, perhaps, true of every body through the whole creation, that, if a thousand lives should be spent upon it, all its properties would not be found out.

Mankind must necessarily be diversified by various tastes, since life affords and requires such multiplicity of employments, and a nation of naturalists is neither to be hoped, or desired; but it is surely not improper to point out a fresh amusement to those who languish in health, and repine in plenty, for want of some source of diversion that may be less easily exhausted, and to inform the multitudes of both sexes, who are burdened with every new day, that there are many shows which they have not seen.

He that enlarges his curiosity after the works of nature, demonstrably multiplies the inlets to happiness; and, therefore, the younger part of my readers, to whom I dedicate this vernal speculation, must excuse me for calling upon them, to make use at once of the spring of the year, and the spring of life; to acquire, while their minds may be yet impressed with new images, a love of innocent pleasures, and an ardor for useful knowledge; and to remember, that a blighted spring makes a barren year, and that the vernal flowers, however beautiful and gay, are only intended by nature as preparatives to autumnal fruits.

Rambler No. 60
[ON BIOGRAPHY]

Saturday, 13 October 1750

—*Quid sit pulchrum, quid turpe, quid utile, quid non,*
Plenius et melius Chrysippo et Crantore dicit.

Horace, *Epistles* 1.2.3–4

Whose works the beautiful and base contain;
Of vice and virtue more instructive rules,
Than all the sober sages of the schools.

Francis

All joy or sorrow for the happiness or calamities of others is produced by an act of the imagination, that realizes the event however fictitious, or approximates[1] it however remote, by placing us, for a time, in the condition of him whose fortune we contemplate; so that we feel, while the deception lasts, whatever motions would be excited by the same good or evil happening to ourselves.

Our passions are therefore more strongly moved, in proportion as we can more readily adopt the pains or pleasures proposed to our minds, by recognizing them as once our own, or considering them as naturally incident to our state of life. It is not easy for the most artful writer to give us an interest in happiness or misery, which we think ourselves never likely to feel, and with which we have never yet been made acquainted. Histories of the downfall of kingdoms, and revolutions of empires, are read with great tranquility; the imperial tragedy pleases common auditors only by its pomp of ornament, and grandeur of ideas; and the man whose faculties have been engrossed by business, and whose heart never fluttered but at the rise or fall of stocks, wonders how the attention can be seized, or the affections agitated by a tale of love.

Those parallel circumstances, and kindred images, to which we readily conform our minds, are, above all other writings, to be found in narratives of the lives of particular persons; and therefore no species of writing seems more worthy of cultivation than biography, since none can be more delightful or more useful, none can more certainly enchain the heart by irresistible interest, or more widely diffuse instruction to every diversity of condition.

The general and rapid narratives of history, which involve a thousand fortunes in the business of a day, and complicate innumerable incidents in one great transaction, afford few lessons applicable to private life, which derives its comforts and its wretchedness from the right or wrong management of things which nothing but their frequency makes considerable, *parva, si non fiant quotidie,* says Pliny,[2] and which can have no place in those relations which never descend below the consultation of senates, the motions of armies, and the schemes of conspirators.

I have often thought that there has rarely passed a life of which a judicious and faithful narrative would not be useful. For, not only every man has, in the mighty mass of the world, great numbers in the same condition with himself, to whom his

---

1. Bring close.
2. "Matters which would be trivial were they not part of a   daily routine" (Pliny the Younger, *Epistles* 3.1).

mistakes and miscarriages, escapes and expedients, would be of immediate and apparent use; but there is such an uniformity in the state of man, considered apart from adventitious and separable decorations and disguises, that there is scarce any possibility of good or ill, but is common to humankind. A great part of the time of those who are placed at the greatest distance by fortune, or by temper, must unavoidably pass in the same manner; and though, when the claims of nature are satisfied, caprice, and vanity, and accident, begin to produce discriminations and peculiarities, yet the eye is not very heedful, or quick, which cannot discover the same causes still terminating their influence in the same effects, though sometimes accelerated, sometimes retarded, or perplexed by multiplied combinations. We are all prompted by the same motives, all deceived by the same fallacies, all animated by hope, obstructed by danger, entangled by desire, and seduced by pleasure.

It is frequently objected to relations of particular lives, that they are not distinguished by any striking or wonderful vicissitudes. The scholar who passed his life among his books, the merchant who conducted only his own affairs, the priest, whose sphere of action was not extended beyond that of his duty, are considered as no proper objects of public regard, however they might have excelled in their several stations, whatever might have been their learning, integrity, and piety. But this notion arises from false measures of excellence and dignity, and must be eradicated by considering that, in the esteem of uncorrupted reason, what is of most use is of most value.

It is, indeed, not improper to take honest advantages of prejudice, and to gain attention by a celebrated name; but the business of the biographer is often to pass slightly over those performances and incidents, which produce vulgar greatness, to lead the thoughts into domestic privacies, and display the minute details of daily life, where exterior appendages are cast aside, and men excel each other only by prudence and by virtue. The account of Thuanus is, with great propriety, said by its author to have been written, that it might lay open to posterity the private and familiar character of that man, *cujus ingenium et candorem ex ipsius scriptis sunt olim semper miraturi,*[3] whose candor and genius will to the end of time be by his writings preserved in admiration.

There are many invisible circumstances which, whether we read as inquirers after natural or moral knowledge, whether we intend to enlarge our science,[4] or increase our virtue, are more important than public occurrences. Thus Sallust, the great master of nature, has not forgot, in his account of Catiline, to remark that "his walk was now quick, and again slow," as an indication of a mind revolving something with violent commotion.[5] Thus the story of Melancthon[6] affords a striking lecture on the value of time, by informing us, that when he made an appointment, he expected not only the hour, but the minute to be fixed, that the day might not run out in the idleness of suspense; and all the plans and enterprises of De Witt are now of less importance to the world, than that part of his personal character which represents him as "careful of his health, and negligent of his life."[7]

---

3. Johnson quotes from a commentary affixed by Nicolas Rigault to the *History of His Own Time* by the French historian Jacques-Auguste de Thou (1553–1617). The Latin is translated by the words that follow.
4. Knowledge.
5. Johnson quotes from an account by the Roman historian Sallust of Catiline's conspiracy against Rome.
6. Johnson quotes from a biography of the Protestant theologian Philip Melancthon (1497–1560) by Joachim Camerarius.
7. Johnson quotes the essayist Sir William Temple's verdict on the Dutch statesman Jan de Witt (1625–1672).

But biography has often been allotted to writers who seem very little acquainted with the nature of their task, or very negligent about the performance. They rarely afford any other account than might be collected from public papers, but imagine themselves writing a life when they exhibit a chronological series of actions or preferments; and so little regard the manners or behavior of their heroes, that more knowledge may be gained of a man's real character, by a short conversation with one of his servants, than from a formal and studied narrative, begun with his pedigree, and ended with his funeral.

If now and then they condescend to inform the world of particular facts, they are not always so happy as to select the most important. I know not well what advantage posterity can receive from the only circumstance by which Tickell has distinguished Addison from the rest of mankind, the irregularity of his pulse:[8] nor can I think myself overpaid for the time spent in reading the life of Malherb,[9] by being enabled to relate, after the learned biographer, that Malherb had two predominant opinions; one, that the looseness of a single woman might destroy all her boast of ancient descent; the other, that the French beggars made use very improperly and barbarously of the phrase "noble gentleman," because either word included the sense of both.

There are, indeed, some natural reasons why these narratives are often written by such as were not likely to give much instruction or delight, and why most accounts of particular persons are barren and useless. If a life be delayed till interest and envy are at an end, we may hope for impartiality, but must expect little intelligence; for the incidents which give excellence to biography are of a volatile and evanescent kind, such as soon escape the memory, and are rarely transmitted by tradition. We know how few can portray a living acquaintance, except by his most prominent and observable particularities, and the grosser features of his mind; and it may be easily imagined how much of this little knowledge may be lost in imparting it, and how soon a succession of copies will lose all resemblance of the original.

If the biographer writes from personal knowledge, and makes haste to gratify the public curiosity, there is danger lest his interest, his fear, his gratitude, or his tenderness, overpower his fidelity, and tempt him to conceal, if not to invent. There are many who think it an act of piety to hide the faults or failings of their friends, even when they can no longer suffer by their detection; we therefore see whole ranks of characters adorned with uniform panegyric, and not to be known from one another, but by extrinsic and casual circumstances. "Let me remember," says Hale, "when I find myself inclined to pity a criminal, that there is likewise a pity due to the country."[1] If we owe regard to the memory of the dead, there is yet more respect to be paid to knowledge, to virtue, and to truth.

---

8. Thomas Tickell prefixed a biography of Joseph Addison to his edition of Addison's *Works* (1721).
9. Johnson refers to the biography of the French poet Francois de Malherbe (1555–1628) by the Marquis de Racan.
1. Johnson quotes from the biography of Sir Matthew Hale (1609–1676), eminent jurist and religious writer, by Gilbert Burnet.

Idler No. 31[1]

[ON IDLENESS]

Saturday, 18 November 1758

Many moralists have remarked, that pride has of all human vices the widest dominion, appears in the greatest multiplicity of forms, and lies hid under the greatest variety of disguises; of disguises, which, like the moon's "veil of brightness," are both its "luster and its shade,"[2] and betray it to others, though they hide it from ourselves.

It is not my intention to degrade pride from this pre-eminence of mischief, yet I know not whether idleness may not maintain a very doubtful and obstinate competition.

There are some that profess idleness in its full dignity, who call themselves the Idle, as Busiris in the play "calls himself the Proud";[3] who boast that they do nothing, and thank their stars that they have nothing to do; who sleep every night till they can sleep no longer, and rise only that exercise may enable them to sleep again; who prolong the reign of darkness by double curtains, and never see the sun but to "tell him how they hate his beams";[4] whose whole labor is to vary the postures of indulgence, and whose day differs from their night but as a couch or chair differs from a bed.

These are the true and open votaries of idleness, for whom she weaves the garlands of poppies, and into whose cup she pours the waters of oblivion; who exist in a state of unruffled stupidity,[5] forgetting and forgotten; who have long ceased to live, and at whose death the survivors can only say, that they have ceased to breathe.

But idleness predominates in many lives where it is not suspected, for, being a vice which terminates in itself, it may be enjoyed without injury to others, and is therefore not watched like fraud, which endangers property, or like pride, which naturally seeks its gratifications in another's inferiority. Idleness is a silent and peaceful quality, that neither raises envy by ostentation, nor hatred by opposition; and therefore nobody is busy to censure or detect it.

As pride sometimes is hid under humility, idleness is often covered by turbulence and hurry. He that neglects his known duty and real employment, naturally endeavors to crowd his mind with something that may bar out the remembrance of his own folly, and does any thing but what he ought to do with eager diligence, that he may keep himself in his own favor.

Some are always in a state of preparation, occupied in previous measures, forming plans, accumulating materials, and providing for the main affair. These are certainly under the secret power of idleness. Nothing is to be expected from the workman whose tools are forever to be sought. I was once told by a great master, that no man ever excelled in painting, who was eminently curious[6] about pencils[7] and colors.

1. *The Idler* (1758–1760) bears a more self-deprecating title than *The Rambler*; other circumstances, too, suggest that Johnson intended a less imposing performance in this series of periodical essay than in its predecessor. The new pieces appeared not twice but once a week, and not as an independent sheet but as a department within a weekly newspaper called *The Universal Chronicle* (which achieved little eminence apart from Johnson's contribution). The *Idlers* were shorter than the *Ramblers*, and dealt more often in light topics and comic touches. Boswell opined that the second series had "less body and

more spirit . . . more variety of real life, and greater facility of language." His judgment is hardly definitive; the comparison has been assayed, with varying results, many times since.

2. Both quotations come from Samuel Butler's poem *Hudibras* (1663–1678) 2.1.905 and 908.

3. *Busiris* (1719) by Edward Young.

4. Milton, *Paradise Lost* 4.37.

5. Stupor.

6. "Difficult to please" (Johnson's *Dictionary*).

7. Brushes.

There are others to whom idleness dictates another expedient, by which life may be passed unprofitably away without the tediousness of many vacant hours. The art is, to fill the day with petty business, to have always something in hand which may raise curiosity, but not solicitude, and keep the mind in a state of action, but not of labor.

This art has for many years been practiced by my old friend Sober,[8] with wonderful success. Sober is a man of strong desires and quick imagination, so exactly balanced by the love of ease, that they can seldom stimulate him to any difficult undertaking; they have, however, so much power, that they will not suffer him to lie quite at rest, and though they do not make him sufficiently useful to others, they make him at least weary of himself.

Mr. Sober's chief pleasure is conversation; there is no end of his talk or his attention; to speak or to hear is equally pleasing; for he still fancies that he is teaching or learning something, and is free for the time from his own reproaches.

But there is one time at night when he must go home, that his friends may sleep; and another time in the morning, when all the world agrees to shut out interruption. These are the moments of which poor Sober trembles at the thought. But the misery of these tiresome intervals, he has many means of alleviating. He has persuaded himself that the manual arts are undeservedly overlooked; he has observed in many trades the effects of close thought, and just ratiocination. From speculation he proceeded to practice, and supplied himself with the tools of a carpenter, with which he mended his coal-box very successfully, and which he still continues to employ, as he finds occasion.

He has attempted at other times the crafts of the shoemaker, tinman, plumber, and potter; in all these arts he has failed, and resolves to qualify himself for them by better information. But his daily amusement is chemistry. He has a small furnace, which he employs in distillation, and which has long been the solace of his life. He draws oils and waters, and essences and spirits, which he knows to be of no use; sits and counts the drops as they come from his retort, and forgets that, while a drop is falling, a moment flies away.

Poor Sober! I have often teased him with reproof, and he has often promised reformation; for no man is so much open to conviction as the idler, but there is none on whom it operates so little. What will be the effect of this paper I know not; perhaps he will read it and laugh, and light the fire in his furnace; but my hope is that he will quit his trifles, and betake himself to rational and useful diligence.

Idler No. 32
[ON SLEEP]

Saturday, 25 November 1758

Among the innumerable mortifications that waylay human arrogance on every side may well be reckoned our ignorance of the most common objects and effects, a defect of which we become more sensible by every attempt to supply it. Vulgar and inactive minds confound familiarity with knowledge, and conceive themselves informed of the whole nature of things when they are shown their form or

---

8. Johnson's friends believed that the portrait of Sober was autobiographical.

told their use; but the speculatist, who is not content with superficial views, harasses himself with fruitless curiosity, and still as he inquires more perceives only that he knows less.

Sleep is a state in which a great part of every life is passed. No animal has been yet discovered, whose existence is not varied with intervals of insensibility; and some late philosophers have extended the empire of sleep over the vegetable world.

Yet of this change so frequent, so great, so general, and so necessary, no searcher has yet found either the efficient or final cause; or can tell by what power the mind and body are thus chained down in irresistible stupefaction; or what benefits the animal receives from this alternate suspension of its active powers.

Whatever may be the multiplicity or contrariety of opinions upon this subject, nature has taken sufficient care that theory shall have little influence on practice. The most diligent inquirer is not able long to keep his eyes open; the most eager disputant will begin about midnight to desert his argument, and once in four and twenty hours, the gay and the gloomy, the witty and the dull, the clamorous and the silent, the busy and the idle, are all overpowered by the gentle tyrant, and all lie down in the equality of sleep.

Philosophy has often attempted to repress insolence by asserting that all conditions are leveled by death; a position which, however it may deject the happy, will seldom afford much comfort to the wretched. It is far more pleasing to consider that sleep is equally a leveler with death; that the time is never at a great distance, when the balm of rest shall be effused alike upon every head, when the diversities of life shall stop their operation, and the high and the low shall lie down together.

It is somewhere recorded of Alexander, that in the pride of conquests, and intoxication of flattery, he declared that he only perceived himself to be a man by the necessity of sleep. Whether he considered sleep as necessary to his mind or body it was indeed a sufficient evidence of human infirmity; the body which required such frequency of renovation gave but faint promises of immortality; and the mind which, from time to time, sunk gladly into insensibility had made no very near approaches to the felicity of the supreme and self-sufficient nature.

I know not what can tend more to repress all the passions that disturb the peace of the world than the consideration that there is no height of happiness or honor from which man does not eagerly descend to a state of unconscious repose; that the best condition of life is such that we contentedly quit its good to be disentangled from its evils; that in a few hours splendor fades before the eye and praise itself deadens in the ear; the senses withdraw from their objects, and reason favors the retreat.

What then are the hopes and prospects of covetousness, ambition and rapacity? Let him that desires most have all his desires gratified, he never shall attain a state which he can, for a day and a night, contemplate with satisfaction, or from which, if he had the power of perpetual vigilance, he would not long for periodical separations.

All envy would be extinguished if it were universally known that there are none to be envied, and surely none can be much envied who are not pleased with themselves. There is reason to suspect that the distinctions of mankind have more show than value when it is found that all agree to be weary alike of pleasures and of cares, that the powerful and the weak, the celebrated and obscure, join in one common wish, and implore from nature's hand the nectar of oblivion.

Such is our desire of abstraction from ourselves that very few are satisfied with the quantity of stupefaction which the needs of the body force upon the mind. Alexander himself added intemperance to sleep, and solaced with the fumes of wine the sovereignty of the world. And almost every man has some art by which he steals his thoughts away from his present state.

It is not much of life that is spent in close attention to any important duty. Many hours of every day are suffered to fly away without any traces left upon the intellects. We suffer phantoms to rise up before us, and amuse ourselves with the dance of airy images, which after a time we dismiss forever, and know not how we have been busied.

Many have no happier moments than those that they pass in solitude, abandoned to their own imagination, which sometimes puts sceptres in their hands or mitres on their heads, shifts the scene of pleasure with endless variety, bids all the forms of beauty sparkle before them, and gluts them with every change of visionary luxury.

It is easy in these semi-slumbers to collect all the possibilities of happiness, to alter the course of the sun, to bring back the past, and anticipate the future, to unite all the beauties of all seasons, and all the blessings of all climates, to receive and bestow felicity, and forget that misery is the lot of man. All this is a voluntary dream, a temporary recession from the realities of life to airy fictions; an habitual subjection of reason to fancy.

Others are afraid to be alone, and amuse themselves by a perpetual succession of companions, but the difference is not great; in solitude we have our dreams to ourselves, and in company we agree to dream in concert. The end sought in both is forgetfulness of ourselves.

Idler No. 84
[ON AUTOBIOGRAPHY]

Saturday, 24 November 1759

Biography is, of the various kinds of narrative writing, that which is most eagerly read, and most easily applied to the purposes of life.

In romances, when the wild field of possibility lies open to invention, the incidents may easily be made more numerous, the vicissitudes more sudden, and the events more wonderful; but from the time of life when fancy begins to be overruled by reason and corrected by experience, the most artful tale raises little curiosity when it is known to be false; though it may, perhaps, be sometimes read as a model of a neat or elegant style, not for the sake of knowing what it contains, but how it is written; or those that are weary of themselves, may have recourse to it as a pleasing dream, of which, when they awake, they voluntarily dismiss the images from their minds.

The examples and events of history press, indeed, upon the mind with the weight of truth; but when they are reposited in the memory, they are oftener employed for show than use, and rather diversify conversation than regulate life. Few are engaged in such scenes as give them opportunities of growing wiser by the downfall of statesmen or the defeat of generals. The stratagems of war, and the intrigues of courts, are read by far the greater part of mankind with the same indifference as the adventures of fabled heroes, or the revolutions of a fairy region. Between falsehood and useless truth there is little difference. As gold which he cannot spend will make no man rich, so knowledge which he cannot apply will make no man wise.

The mischievous consequences of vice and folly, of irregular desires and predominant passions, are best discovered by those relations which are leveled with the general surface of life, which tell not how any man became great, but how he was made happy; not how he lost the favor of his prince, but how he became discontented with himself.

Those relations are therefore commonly of most value in which the writer tells his own story. He that recounts the life of another, commonly dwells most upon conspicuous events, lessens the familiarity of his tale to increase its dignity, shows his favorite at a distance decorated and magnified like the ancient actors in their tragic dress, and endeavors to hide the man that he may produce a hero.

But if it be true which was said by a French prince, "that no man was a hero to the servants of his chamber," it is equally true that every man is yet less a hero to himself. He that is most elevated above the crowd by the importance of his employments or the reputation of his genius, feels himself affected by fame or business but as they influence his domestic life. The high and low, as they have the same faculties and the same senses, have no less similitude in their pains and pleasures. The sensations are the same in all, though produced by very different occasions. The prince feels the same pain when an invader seizes a province, as the farmer when a thief drives away his cow. Men thus equal in themselves will appear equal in honest and impartial biography; and those whom fortune or nature place at the greatest distance may afford instruction to each other.

The writer of his own life has at least the first qualification of an historian, the knowledge of the truth; and though it may be plausibly objected that his temptations to disguise it are equal to his opportunities of knowing it, yet I cannot but think that impartiality may be expected with equal confidence from him that relates the passages of his own life, as from him that delivers the transactions of another.

Certainty of knowledge not only excludes mistake but fortifies veracity. What we collect by conjecture, and by conjecture only can one man judge of another's motives or sentiments, is easily modified by fancy or by desire; as objects imperfectly discerned take forms from the hope or fear of the beholder. But that which is fully known cannot be falsified but with reluctance of understanding, and alarm of conscience; of understanding, the lover of truth; of conscience, the sentinel of virtue.

He that writes the life of another is either his friend or his enemy, and wishes either to exalt his praise or aggravate his infamy; many temptations to falsehood will occur in the disguise of passions, too specious[1] to fear much resistance. Love of virtue will animate panegyric, and hatred of wickedness embitter censure. The zeal of gratitude, the ardor of patriotism, fondness for an opinion, or fidelity to a party, may easily overpower the vigilance of a mind habitually well disposed, and prevail over unassisted and unfriended veracity.

---

1. "Plausible; superficially, not solidly right" (Johnson's *Dictionary*).

But he that speaks of himself has no motive to falsehood or partiality except self-love, by which all have so often been betrayed, that all are on the watch against its artifices. He that writes an apology for[2] a single action, to confute an accusation, or recommend himself to favor, is indeed always to be suspected of favoring his own cause; but he that sits down calmly and voluntarily to review his life for the admonition of posterity, or to amuse himself, and leaves this account unpublished, may be commonly presumed to tell truth, since falsehood cannot appease his own mind, and fame will not be heard beneath the tomb.

Idler No. 97
[ON TRAVEL WRITING]

Saturday, 23 February 1760

It may, I think, be justly observed, that few books disappoint their readers more than the narrations of travelers. One part of mankind is naturally curious to learn the sentiments, manners, and condition of the rest; and every mind that has leisure or power to extend its views, must be desirous of knowing in what proportion Providence has distributed the blessings of nature or the advantages of art, among the several nations of the earth.

This general desire easily procures readers to every book from which it can expect gratification. The adventurer upon unknown coasts, and the describer of distant regions, is always welcomed as a man who has labored for the pleasure of others, and who is able to enlarge our knowledge and rectify our opinions; but when the volume is opened, nothing is found but such general accounts as leave no distinct idea behind them, or such minute enumerations as few can read with either profit or delight.

Every writer of travels should consider that, like all other authors, he undertakes either to instruct or please, or to mingle pleasure with instruction. He that instructs must offer to the mind something to be imitated or something to be avoided; he that pleases must offer new images to his reader, and enable him to form a tacit comparison of his own state with that of others.

The greater part of travelers tell nothing, because their method of traveling supplies them with nothing to be told. He that enters a town at night and surveys it in the morning, and then hastens away to another place, and guesses at the manners of the inhabitants by the entertainment which his inn afforded him, may please himself for a time with a hasty change of scenes, and a confused remembrance of palaces and churches; he may gratify his eye with variety of landscapes; and regale his palate with a succession of vintages; but let him be contented to please himself without endeavor to disturb others. Why should he record excursions by which nothing could be learned, or wish to make a show of knowledge which, without some power of intuition unknown to other mortals, he never could attain.

Of those who crowd the world with their itineraries,[1] some have no other purpose than to describe the face of the country; those who sit idle at home, and are curious to know what is done or suffered in distant countries, may be informed by one of these wanderers, that on a certain day he set out early with the caravan, and in the first hour's march saw, towards the south, a hill covered with trees, then passed over a

---

2. Defense of.   1. Travel books.

stream which ran northward with a swift course, but which is probably dry in the summer months; that an hour after he saw something to the right which looked at a distance like a castle with towers, but which he discovered afterwards to be a craggy rock; that he then entered a valley in which he saw several trees tall and flourishing, watered by a rivulet not marked in the maps, of which he was not able to learn the name; that the road afterward grew stony, and the country uneven, where he observed among the hills many hollows worn by torrents, and was told that the road was passable only part of the year: that going on they found the remains of a building, once perhaps a fortress to secure the pass, or to restrain the robbers, of which the present inhabitants can give no other account than that it is haunted by fairies; that they went to dine at the foot of a rock, and traveled the rest of the day along the banks of a river, from which the road turned aside towards evening, and brought them within sight of a village, which was once a considerable town, but which afforded them neither good victuals nor commodious lodging.

Thus he conducts his reader through wet and dry, over rough and smooth, without incidents, without reflection; and, if he obtains his company for another day, will dismiss him again at night equally fatigued with a like succession of rocks and streams, mountains and ruins.

This is the common style of those sons of enterprise, who visit savage countries, and range through solitude and desolation; who pass a desert, and tell that it is sandy; who cross a valley, and find that it is green. There are others of more delicate sensibility, that visit only the realms of elegance and softness; that wander through Italian palaces, and amuse the gentle reader with catalogues of pictures; that hear masses in magnificent churches, and recount the number of the pillars or variegations of the pavement. And there are yet others who, in disdain of trifles, copy inscriptions elegant and rude, ancient and modern; and transcribe into their book the walls of every edifice, sacred or civil. He that reads these books must consider his labor as its own reward; for he will find nothing on which attention can fix, or which memory can retain.

He that would travel for the entertainment of others should remember that the great object of remark is human life. Every nation has something peculiar in its manufactures, its works of genius, its medicines, its agriculture, its customs, and its policy. He only is a useful traveler who brings home something by which his country may be benefited; who procures some supply of want or some mitigation of evil, which may enable his readers to compare their condition with that of others, to improve it whenever it is worse, and whenever it is better to enjoy it.

A DICTIONARY OF THE ENGLISH LANGUAGE   Johnson's *Dictionary* struck its first readers as a nearly superhuman accomplishment; it seems one still. "A dictionary of the English language," observed one early reviewer, had never before "been attempted with the least degree of success"; the closest antecedents to Johnson's project were the national dictionaries of France and Italy, and these had been composed by whole academies of scholars, working collectively over the course of decades. Here, by contrast, was the seven years' labor of a single author (aided only by six part-time amanuenses): 40,000 words defined with unprecedented exactitude, and illustrated with more than 114,000 passages drawn from English prose and poetry of the previous 250 years. Ninety years earlier, members of the newly founded Royal Society for Improving Natural Knowledge had dreamed of such a resource; Johnson produced it by empirical methods much like the ones they promulgated. He spent his first years on the project accumulating data, rereading the English writers he valued most, marking any passage that strikingly illuminated the workings of a particular word. He then worked from this heap of collected evidence to the fine-honed, sharply distinguished conclusions of his definitions. The results have been variously and accurately described as the first standard English dictionary; as one of the final fruits of Renaissance humanism; as a commonplace-book (or database) of important English writing from Sidney to Pope; as a massive map of its author's mind. The key to that map resides in the *Dictionary's* Preface, where Johnson measures the grandeur of his aspirations against the limitations of his achievement. In this mix of personal memoir and linguistic meditation, lexicography becomes a local instance of the vanity of human wishes. Human language, massive, metamorphic, and intractable, overmatches the human desire to codify and contain it, to fix it once and for all.

from A Dictionary of the English Language
from *Preface*

[ON METHOD]

It is the fate of those who toil at the lower employments of life to be rather driven by the fear of evil than attracted by the prospect of good; to be exposed to censure, without hope of praise; to be disgraced by miscarriage or punished for neglect, where success would have been without applause and diligence without reward.

Among these unhappy mortals is the writer of dictionaries; whom mankind have considered not as the pupil but the slave of science, the pioneer[1] of literature, doomed only to remove rubbish and clear obstructions from the paths through which learning and genius press forward to conquest and glory, without bestowing a smile on the humble drudge that facilitates their progress. Every other author may aspire to praise; the lexicographer can only hope to escape reproach, and even this negative recompense has been yet granted to very few.

I have, notwithstanding this discouragement, attempted a dictionary of the English language which, while it was employed in the cultivation of every species of literature, has itself been hitherto neglected; suffered to spread, under the direction of chance, into wild exuberance; resigned to the tyranny of time and fashion; and exposed to the corruptions of ignorance, and caprices of innovation.

When I took the first survey of my undertaking, I found our speech copious without order, and energetic without rules: wherever I turned my view, there was perplexity to be disentangled and confusion to be regulated; choice was to be made out of boundless variety, without any established principle of selection; adulterations were to be detected without a settled test of purity; and modes of expression to be rejected or received without the suffrages[2] of any writers of classical reputation or acknowledged authority.

Having therefore no assistance but from general grammar, I applied myself to the perusal of our writers; and, noting whatever might be of use to ascertain or illustrate any word or phrase, accumulated in time the materials of a dictionary, which, by degrees, I reduced to method, establishing to myself in the progress of the work such rules as experience and analogy suggested to me; experience, which practice and observation were continually increasing; and analogy, which, though in some words obscure, was evident in others.

---

1. "One whose business is to level the road, throw up works, or sink mines in military operations" (Johnson's *Dictionary*).
2. Votes, testimonies.

[ON DEFINITIONS AND EXAMPLES]

That part of my work on which I expect malignity most frequently to fasten is the explanation; in which I cannot hope to satisfy those who are perhaps not inclined to be pleased, since I have not always been able to satisfy myself. To interpret a language by itself is very difficult; many words cannot be explained by synonyms because the idea signified by them has not more than one appellation; nor by paraphrase, because simple ideas cannot be described. When the nature of things is unknown, or the notion unsettled and indefinite, and various in various minds, the words by which such notions are conveyed or such things denoted will be ambiguous and perplexed. And such is the fate of hapless lexicography that not only darkness, but light, impedes and distresses it; things may be not only too little, but too much known, to be happily illustrated. To explain requires the use of terms less abstruse than that which is to be explained, and such terms cannot always be found; for as nothing can be proved but by supposing something intuitively known and evident without proof, so nothing can be defined but by the use of words too plain to admit a definition.

Other words there are, of which the sense is too subtle and evanescent to be fixed in a paraphrase; such are all those which are by the grammarians termed expletives, and, in dead languages, are suffered to pass for empty sounds, of no other use than to fill a verse or to modulate a period,[1] but which are easily perceived in living tongues to have power and emphasis, though it be sometimes such as no other form of expression can convey. * * *

The solution of all difficulties and the supply of all defects must be sought in the examples subjoined to the various senses of each word, and ranged according to the time of their authors.

When first I collected these authorities, I was desirous that every quotation should be useful to some other end than the illustration of a word; I therefore extracted from philosophers principles of science; from historians remarkable facts; from chemists complete processes; from divines striking exhortations; and from poets beautiful descriptions. Such is design while it is yet at a distance from execution. When the time called upon me to range this accumulation of elegance and wisdom into an alphabetical series, I soon discovered that the bulk of my volumes would fright away the student, and was forced to depart from my scheme of including all that was pleasing or useful in English literature, and reduce my transcripts very often to clusters of words in which scarcely any meaning is retained; thus to the weariness of copying, I was condemned to add the vexation of expunging. Some passages I have yet spared which may relieve the labor of verbal searches, and intersperse with verdure and flowers the dusty deserts of barren philology.

The examples, thus mutilated, are no longer to be considered as conveying the sentiments or doctrine of their authors; the word for the sake of which they are inserted, with all its appendant clauses, has been carefully preserved; but it may sometimes happen, by hasty detruncation, that the general tendency of the sentence may be changed: the divine may desert his tenets, or the philosopher his system.

Some of the examples have been taken from writers who were never mentioned as masters of elegance or models of style; but words must be sought where they are used; and in what pages, eminent for purity, can terms of manufacture or agriculture be found? Many quotations serve no other purpose than that of proving the bare existence of words, and are therefore selected with less scrupulousness than those which are to teach their structures and relations.

1. Clause or sentence.

My purpose was to admit no testimony of living authors, that I might not be misled by partiality, and that none of my contemporaries might have reason to complain; nor have I departed from this resolution but when some performance of uncommon excellence excited my veneration, when my memory supplied me, from late books, with an example that was wanting, or when my heart, in the tenderness of friendship, solicited admission for a favorite name.

So far have I been from any care to grace my pages with modern decorations that I have studiously endeavored to collect examples and authorities from the writers before the Restoration, whose works I regard as "the wells of English undefiled,"[2] as the pure sources of genuine diction. Our language, for almost a century, has, by the concurrence of many causes, been gradually departing from its original Teutonic character, and deviating towards a Gallic structure and phraseology, from which it ought to be our endeavor to recall it by making our ancient volumes the groundwork of style, admitting among the additions of later times only such as may supply real deficiencies, such as are readily adopted by the genius[3] of our tongue, and incorporate easily with our native idioms.

But as every language has a time of rudeness[4] antecedent to perfection, as well as of false refinement and declension, I have been cautious lest my zeal for antiquity might drive me into times too remote and crowd my book with words now no longer understood. I have fixed Sidney's work for the boundary beyond which I make few excursions. From the authors which rose in the time of Elizabeth, a speech might be formed adequate to all the purposes of use and elegance. If the language of theology were extracted from Hooker and the translation of the Bible; the terms of natural knowledge[5] from Bacon; the phrases of policy, war, and navigation from Raleigh; the dialect of poetry and fiction from Spenser and Sidney; and the diction of common life from Shakespeare, few ideas would be lost to mankind for want of English words in which they might be expressed.

It is not sufficient that a word is found unless it be so combined as that its meaning is apparently[6] determined by the tract[7] and tenor of the sentence; such passages I have therefore chosen, and when it happened that any author gave a definition of a term or such an explanation as is equivalent to a definition, I have placed his authority as a supplement to my own, without regard to the chronological order that is otherwise observed.

Some words, indeed, stand unsupported by any authority, but they are commonly derivative nouns or adverbs, formed from their primitives by regular and constant analogy, or names of things seldom occurring in books, or words of which I have reason to doubt the existence.

There is more danger of censure from the multiplicity than paucity of examples; authorities will sometimes seem to have been accumulated without necessity or use, and perhaps some will be found which might, without loss, have been omitted. But a work of this kind is not hastily to be charged with superfluities: those quotations which to careless or unskillful perusers appear only to repeat the same sense will often exhibit to a more accurate examiner diversities of signification or, at least, afford different shades of the same meaning: one will show the word applied to persons,

---

2. Johnson quotes Spenser's praise of Chaucer in *The Faerie Queene* (4.2.2).
3. Native spirit.
4. Barbarism.

5. Science.
6. Clearly.
7. "Continuity; course; manner of process" (Johnson's *Dictionary*).

another to things; one will express an ill, another a good, and a third a neutral sense; one will prove the expression genuine from an ancient author; another will show it elegant from a modern: a doubtful authority is corroborated by another of more credit; an ambiguous sentence is ascertained by a passage clear and determinate; the word, how often soever repeated, appears with new associates and in different combinations, and every quotation contributes something to the stability or enlargement of the language. * * *

I have sometimes, though rarely, yielded to the temptation of exhibiting a genealogy of sentiments, by showing how one author copied the thoughts and diction of another: such quotations are indeed little more than repetitions which might justly be censured, did they not gratify the mind by affording a kind of intellectual history.

[CONCLUSION]

A large work is difficult because it is large, even though all its parts might singly be performed with facility; where there are many things to be done, each must be allowed its share of time and labor in the proportion only which it bears to the whole; nor can it be expected that the stones which form the dome of a temple should be squared and polished like the diamond of a ring.

Of the event of this work, for which, having labored it with so much application, I cannot but have some degree of parental fondness, it is natural to form conjectures. Those who have been persuaded to think well of my design will require that it should fix our language and put a stop to those alterations which time and chance have hitherto been suffered to make in it without opposition. With this consequence I will confess that I flattered myself for a while; but now begin to fear that I have indulged expectation which neither reason nor experience can justify. When we see men grow old and die at a certain time one after another, from century to century, we laugh at the elixir that promises to prolong life to a thousand years; and with equal justice may the lexicographer be derided, who being able to produce no example of a nation that has preserved their words and phrases from mutability, shall imagine that his dictionary can embalm his language and secure it from corruption and decay, that it is in his power to change sublunary nature, and clear the world at once from folly, vanity, and affectation.

With this hope, however, academies have been instituted to guard the avenues of their languages, to retain fugitives and repulse intruders; but their vigilance and activity have hitherto been vain; sounds are too volatile and subtle for legal restraints; to enchain syllables and to lash the wind are equally the undertakings of pride, unwilling to measure its desires by its strength. The French language has visibly changed under the inspection of the Academy,[1] the style of Amelot's translation of Father Paul is observed by Le Courayer to be *un peu passé;*[2] and no Italian will maintain that the diction of any modern writer is not perceptibly different from that of Boccace, Machiavel, or Caro.[3]

---

1. The French Academy, founded in 1635, undertook to preserve the purity of the language.
2. When in the 1730s Le Courayer retranslated Father Paolo Sarpi's *History of the Council of Trent*, he criticized his predecessor Amelot's version (1683) as "a little outdated."

3. Johnson refers to Giovanni Boccaccio (1313–1375), author of *The Decameron;* Niccolo Machiavelli (1469–1527), author of *The Prince;* and Annibale Caro (1507–1566), author of pastoral romances.

Total and sudden transformations of a language seldom happen; conquests and migrations are now very rare; but there are other causes of change which, though slow in their operation, and invisible in their progress, are perhaps as much superior to human resistance, as the revolutions of the sky, or intumescence of the tide. Commerce, however necessary, however lucrative, as it depraves the manners, corrupts the language; they that have frequent intercourse with strangers, to whom they endeavor to accommodate themselves, must in time learn a mingled dialect, like the jargon which serves the traffickers[4] on the Mediterranean and Indian coasts. This will not always be confined to the exchange, the warehouse, or the port, but will be communicated by degrees to other ranks of the people, and be at last incorporated with the current speech.

There are likewise internal causes equally forcible. The language most likely to continue long without alteration would be that of a nation raised a little, and but a little, above barbarity, secluded from strangers, and totally employed in procuring the conveniences of life; either without books or, like some of the Mahometan countries, with very few: men thus busied and unlearned, having only such words as common use requires, would perhaps long continue to express the same notions by the same signs. But no such constancy can be expected in a people polished by arts and classed by subordination, where one part of the community is sustained and accommodated by the labor of the other. Those who have much leisure to think will always be enlarging the stock of ideas, and every increase of knowledge, whether real or fancied, will produce new words or combinations of words. When the mind is unchained from necessity, it will range after convenience; when it is left at large in the fields of speculation, it will shift opinions; as any custom is disused, the words that expressed it must perish with it; as any opinion grows popular, it will innovate speech in the same proportion as it alters practice.

As by the cultivation of various sciences a language is amplified, it will be more furnished with words deflected from their original sense; the geometrician will talk of a courtier's zenith, or the eccentric[5] virtue of a wild hero, and the physician of sanguine expectations and phlegmatic delays.[6] Copiousness of speech will give opportunities to capricious choice, by which some words will be preferred and others degraded; vicissitudes of fashion will enforce the use of new or extend the signification of known terms. The tropes of poetry will make hourly encroachments, and the metaphorical will become the current sense: pronunciation will be varied by levity or ignorance, and the pen must at length comply with the tongue; illiterate writers will at one time or other, by public infatuation, rise into renown, who, not knowing the original import of words, will use them with colloquial licentiousness, confound distinction, and forget propriety. As politeness increases, some expressions will be considered as too gross and vulgar for the delicate, others as too formal and ceremonious for the gay and airy; new phrases are therefore adopted, which must for the same reasons be in time dismissed. Swift, in his petty[7] treatise on the English language,[8] allows that new words must sometimes be introduced, but proposes that none should be suffered to become obsolete. But what makes a word obsolete more

---

4. Merchants.
5. "Deviating from the center" (Johnson's *Dictionary*).
6. "Sanguine" and "phlegmatic" are medical terms relating to the doctrine of the four humors. Those in whom blood predominates are "sanguine" or optimistic, those

ruled by phlegm are dull and sluggish.
7. Little.
8. *A Proposal for Correcting, Improving, and Ascertaining the English Tongue* (1712).

than general agreement to forbear it? and how shall it be continued when it conveys an offensive idea, or recalled again into the mouths of mankind when it has once become unfamiliar by disuse and unpleasing by unfamiliarity?

There is another cause of alteration more prevalent than any other, which yet in the present state of the world cannot be obviated. A mixture of two languages will produce a third distinct from both, and they will always be mixed where the chief part of education, and the most conspicuous accomplishment, is skill in ancient or in foreign tongues. He that has long cultivated another language will find its words and combinations crowd upon his memory; and haste or negligence, refinement or affectation, will obtrude borrowed terms and exotic expressions.

The great pest of speech is frequency of translation. No book was ever turned from one language into another without imparting something of its native idiom; this is the most mischievous and comprehensive innovation; single words may enter by thousands and the fabric of the tongue continue the same, but new phraseology changes much at once; it alters not the single stones of the building but the order of the columns.[9] If an academy should be established for the cultivation of our style, which I, who can never wish to see dependence multiplied, hope the spirit of English liberty will hinder or destroy, let them, instead of compiling grammars and dictionaries, endeavor, with all their influence, to stop the license of translators, whose idleness and ignorance, if it be suffered to proceed, will reduce us to babble a dialect of France.

If the changes that we fear be thus irresistible, what remains but to acquiesce with silence, as in the other insurmountable distresses of humanity? It remains that we retard what we cannot repel, that we palliate what we cannot cure. Life may be lengthened by care, though death cannot be ultimately defeated: tongues, like governments, have a natural tendency to degeneration; we have long preserved our constitution, let us make some struggles for our language.

In hope of giving longevity to that which its own nature forbids to be immortal, I have devoted this book, the labor of years, to the honor of my country, that we may no longer yield the palm[1] of philology without a contest to the nations of the Continent. The chief glory of every people arises from its authors: whether I shall add anything by my own writings to the reputation of English literature must be left to time: much of my life has been lost under the pressures of disease; much has been trifled away; and much has always been spent in provision for the day that was passing over me; but I shall not think my employment useless or ignoble if by my assistance foreign nations and distant ages gain access to the propagators of knowledge, and understand the teachers of truth; if my labors afford light to the repositories of science, and add celebrity to Bacon, to Hooker, to Milton, and to Boyle.

When I am animated by this wish, I look with pleasure on my book, however defective, and deliver it to the world with the spirit of a man that has endeavored well. That it will immediately become popular I have not promised to myself: a few wild blunders and risible absurdities, from which no work of such multiplicity was ever free, may for a time furnish folly with laughter, and harden ignorance in contempt; but useful diligence will at last prevail, and there never can be wanting some

---

9. In classical architecture, the five "orders" are Doric, Ionic, Corinthian, Tuscan, and Composite.

1. Crown (symbol of victory).

who distinguish desert,[2] who will consider that no dictionary of a living tongue ever can be perfect, since while it is hastening to publication some words are budding and some falling away; that a whole life cannot be spent upon syntax and etymology, and that even a whole life would not be sufficient; that he whose design includes whatever language can express, must often speak of what he does not understand; that a writer will sometimes be hurried by eagerness to the end, and sometimes faint with weariness under a task, which Scaliger compares to the labors of the anvil and the mine;[3] that what is obvious is not always known, and what is known is not always present; that sudden fits of inadvertency will surprise vigilance, slight avocations will seduce attention, and casual eclipses of the mind will darken learning; and that the writer shall often in vain trace his memory at the moment of need for that which yesterday he knew with intuitive readiness, and which will come uncalled into his thoughts tomorrow.

In this work, when it shall be found that much is omitted, let it not be forgotten that much likewise is performed; and though no book was ever spared out of tenderness to the author, and the world is little solicitous to know whence proceeded the faults of that which it condemns; yet it may gratify curiosity to inform it, that the *English Dictionary* was written with little assistance of the learned, and without any patronage of the great; not in the soft obscurities of retirement or under the shelter of academic bowers, but amidst inconvenience and distraction, in sickness and in sorrow. It may repress the triumph of malignant criticism to observe that if our language is not here fully displayed, I have only failed in an attempt which no human powers have hitherto completed. If the lexicons of ancient tongues, now immutably fixed and comprised in a few volumes, are yet, after the toil of successive ages, inadequate and delusive; if the aggregated knowledge, and cooperating diligence of the Italian academicians did not secure them from the censure of Beni;[4] if the embodied critics of France, when fifty years had been spent upon their work, were obliged to change its economy and give their second edition another form, I may surely be contented without the praise of perfection, which, if I could obtain, in this gloom of solitude, what would it avail me? I have protracted my work till most of those whom I wished to please have sunk into the grave, and success and miscarriage are empty sounds: I therefore dismiss it with frigid tranquility, having little to fear or hope from censure or from praise.

[Some Entries][1]

FUNK. n[oun] s[ubstantive]. A stink. A low word.

FÚNNEL. n.s. [*infundibulum*, Latin; whence *fundible, fundle, funnel.*]

1. An inverted hollow cone with a pipe descending from it, through which liquors are poured into vessels with narrow mouths; a tundish.

> If you pour a glut of water upon a bottle, it receives little of it; but with a *funnel*, and by degrees, you shall fill many of them.

—Ben. Jonson's *Discoveries*

---

2. Merit.
3. Johnson refers to a poem, *Against the Compilers of the Lexicons*, by the great Renaissance scholar Joseph Justus Scaliger.
4. Paolo Beni criticized the Italian dictionary published

in 1612 by the Accademia della Crusca.
1. All entries are from the fourth edition of Johnson's *Dictionary* (1773), the last that Johnson prepared. Each entry is presented complete, with etymology, definitions, illustrations.

Some the long *funnel's* curious mouth extend,
Through which ingested meats with ease descend.

—Blackmore

The outward ear or auricula is made hollow, and contracted by degrees, to draw the sound inward, to take in as much as may be of it, as we use a *funnel* to pour liquor into any vessel.

—Ray on the Creation

2. A pipe or passage of communication.

Towards the middle are two large *funnels*, bored through the roof of the grotto, to let in light or fresh air.

—Addison

FÚTURE. n.s. [from the adjective.] Time to come; somewhat to happen hereafter.

Thy letters have transported me beyond
This ign'rant present time; and I feel now
The *future* in the instant.

—Shakespeare, *Macbeth*

The mind, once jaded by an attempt above its power, either is disabled for the *future*, or else checks at any vigorous undertaking ever after.

—Locke

IMAGINÁTION. n.s. [*imaginatio*, Lat. *imagination*, Fr. from *imagine*.]

1. Fancy; the power of forming ideal pictures; the power of representing things absent to one's self or others.

Imagination I understand to be the representation of an individual thought. *Imagination* is of three kinds: joined with belief of that which is to come; joined with memory of that which is past; and of things present, or as if they were present: for I comprehend in this imagination feigned and at pleasure, as if one should imagine such a man to be in the vestments of a pope, or to have wings.

—Bacon

Our simple apprehension of corporal objects, if present, is sense; if absent, *imagination*: when we would perceive a material object, our fancies present us with its idea.

—Glanville

O whither shall I run, or which way fly
The sight of this so horrid spectacle,
Which erst my eyes beheld, and yet behold!
For dire *imagination* still pursues me.

—Milton

Where beams of warm *imagination* play,
The memory's soft figures melt away.

—Pope

2. Conception; image in the mind; idea.

Sometimes despair darkens all her *imaginations*; sometimes the active passion of love cheers and clears her invention.

—Sidney

Princes have but their titles for their glories,
An outward honor for an inward toil;
And, for unfelt *imaginations*,
They often feel a world of restless cares.

—Shakespeare, *Richard III*

Better I were distract,
So should my thoughts be severed from my griefs;
And woes, by wrong *imaginations*, lose
The knowledge of themselves.

—Shakespeare, *King Lear*

His *imaginations* were often as just as they were bold and strong.

—Dennis

3. Contrivance; scheme.

Thou hast seen all their vengeance, and all their *imaginations* against me.

—Bible (Lamentations 3.60)

4. An unsolid or fanciful opinion.

We are apt to think that space, in itself, is actually boundless; to which *imagination*,
the idea of space, of itself leads us.

—Locke

JÚDGMENT. n.s. [*jugement*, Fr.]

1. The power of discerning the relations between one term or one proposition and
another.

O *judgment!* thou art fled to brutish beasts,
And men have lost their reason.

—Shakespeare, *Julius Caesar*

The faculty, which God has given man to supply the want of certain knowledge, is
judgment, whereby the mind takes any proposition to be true or false, without perceiving a demonstrative evidence in the proofs.

—Locke

Judgment is that whereby we join ideas together by affirmation or negation; so, this
tree is high.

—Watts

2. Doom; the right or power of passing judgment.

If my suspect be false, forgive me, God;
For *judgment* only doth belong to thee.

—Shakespeare, *Henry VI*

3. The act of exercising judicature; judicatory.

They gave *judgment* upon him.

—Bible (2 Kings)

When thou, O Lord, shalt stand disclosed
In majesty severe,
And sit in *judgment* on my soul,
O how shall I appear?

—Addison's *Spectator*

4. Determination; decision.

Where distinctions or identities are purely material, the *judgment* is made by the imagination, otherwise by the understanding.

—Glanville's *Scepsis*

We shall make a certain *judgment* what kind of dissolution that earth was capable of.

—Burnet's *Theory*

Reason ought to accompany the exercise of our senses, whenever we would form a just *judgment* of things proposed to our inquiry.

—Watts

5. The quality of distinguishing propriety and impropriety; criticism.

Judgment, a cool and slow faculty, attends not a man in the rapture of poetical composition.

—Dennis

'Tis with our *judgments* as our watches, none
Go just alike; yet each believes his own.

—Pope

6. Opinion; notion.

I see men's *judgments* are
A parcel of their fortunes, and things outward
Draw the inward quality after them,
To suffer all alike.

—Shakespeare, *Antony and Cleopatra*

When she did think my master loved her well,
She, in my *judgment*, was as fair as you.

—Shakespeare

7. Sentence against a criminal.

When he was brought again to th' bar, to hear
His knell rung out, his *judgment*, he was stirred
With agony.

—Shakespeare, *Henry VIII*

The chief priests informed me, desiring to have *judgment* against him.

—Bible (Acts 25.15)

On Adam last this *judgment* he pronounced.

—Milton

8. Condemnation. This is a theological use.

> The *judgment* was by one to condemnation; but the free gift is of many offenses unto justification.
>
> —Bible (Romans 5.16)

> The precepts, promises, and threatenings of the Gospel will rise up in *judgment* against us, and the articles of our faith will be so many articles of accusation.
>
> —Tillotson

9. Punishment inflicted by Providence, with reference to some particular crime.

> This *judgment* of the heavens that makes us tremble,
> Touches us not with pity.
>
> —Shakespeare, *King Lear*

> We cannot be guilty of greater uncharitableness, than to interpret afflictions as punishments and *judgments*: it aggravates the evil to him who suffers, when he looks upon himself as the mark of divine vengeance.
>
> —Addison's *Spectator*

10. Distribution of justice.

> The Jews made insurrection against Paul, and brought him to the *judgment* seat.
>
> —Bible (Acts 18.12)

> Your dishonor
> Mangles true *judgment*, and bereaves the state
> Of that integrity which should become it.
>
> —Shakespeare, *Coriolanus*

> In *judgments* between rich and poor, consider not what the poor man needs, but what is his own.
>
> —Taylor

> A bold and wise petitioner goes strait to the throne and *judgment* seat of the monarch.
>
> —Arbuthnot and Pope

11. Judiciary law; statute.

> If ye hearken to these *judgments*, and keep and do them, the Lord thy God shall keep unto thee the covenant.
>
> —Bible (Deuteronomy)

12. The last doom.

> The dreadful *judgment* day
> So dreadful will not be as was his sight.
>
> —Shakespeare, *Henry VI*

KNACK. n.s.

1. A little machine; a petty contrivance; a toy.

> When I was young, I was wont
> To load my she with *knacks:* I would have ransacked
> The peddler's silken treasury, and have poured it
> To her acceptance.
>
> —Shakespeare, *Winter's Tale*

> For thee, fond boy,
> If I may ever know thou dost but sigh
> That thou no more shalt see this *knack*, as never
> I mean thou shalt, we'll bar thee from success.
>
> —Shakespeare

> This cap was moulded on a porringer,
> A velvet dish; fie, fie, 'tis lewd and filthy:
> Why 'tis a cockle, or a walnut shell,
> A *knack*, a toy, a trick, a baby's cap.
>
> —Shakespeare

> But is't not presumption to write verse to you,
> Who make the better poems of the two?
> For all these pretty *knacks* that you compose,
> Alas! what are they but poems in prose!
>
> —Denham

> He expounded both his pockets,
> And found a watch, with rings and lockets;
> A copper-plate, with almanacks
> Engraved upon't, with other *knacks*.
>
> —Hudibras

2. A readiness; an habitual facility; a lucky dexterity.

> I'll teach you the *knacks*
> Of eating of flax,
> And out of their noses
> Draw ribbands and posies.
>
> —Ben. Jonson's *Gypsies*

> The *knack* of fast and loose passes with foolish people for a turn of wit; but they are not aware all this while of the desperate consequences of an ill habit.
>
> —L'Estrange

> There is a certain *knack* in conversation that gives a good grace by the manner and address.
>
> —L'Estrange

> Knaves, who in full assemblies have the *knack*
> Of turning truth to lies, and white to black.
>
> —Dryden

My author has a great *knack* at remarks: in the end he makes another, about our refining in controversy, and coming nearer and nearer to the church of Rome.

—Atterbury

The dean was famous in his time,
And had a kind of *knack* at rhyme.

—Swift

3. A nice trick.

For how should equal colors do the *knack?*
Chameleons who can paint in white and black?

—Pope

LEXICÓGRAPHER. n.s. [λεξικον and γραφειν *lexicographe*, Fr.] A writer of dictionaries; a harmless drudge, that busies himself in tracing the original, and detailing the signification of words.

Commentators and *lexicographers* acquainted with the Syriac language, have given these hints in their writings on scripture.

—Watt's *Improvement of the Mind*

SÚBSTANCE. n.s. [*substance*, Fr.; *substantia*, Lat.]

1. Being; something existing; something of which we can say that it is.

Since then the soul works by herself alone,
Springs not from sense, nor humors well agreeing,
Her nature is peculiar, and her own;
She is a *substance*, and a perfect being.

—Davies

The strength of gods,
And this empyreal *substance* cannot fail.

—Milton

2. That which supports accidents.

What creatures there inhabit, of what mold,
And *substance*.

—Milton

Every being is considered as subsisting in and by itself, and then it is called a *substance*; or it subsists in and by another, and then it is called a mode or manner of being.

—Watts

3. The essential part.

It will serve our turn to comprehend the *substance*, without confining ourselves to scrupulous exactness in form.

—Digby

This edition is the same in *substance* with the Latin.

—Burn

They are the best epitomes, and let you see with one cast of the eye the *substance* of a hundred pages.

—Addison

4. Something real, not imaginary; something solid, not empty.

Shadows tonight
Have struck more terror to the soul of Richard,
Than can the *substance* of ten thousand soldiers
Armed in proof and led by shallow Richmond.

—Shakespeare

He the future evil shall no less
In apprehension than in *substance* feel.

—Milton

Heroic virtue did his actions guide,
And he the *substance*, not th' appearance chose:
To rescue one such friend he took more pride,
Than to destroy whole thousands of such foes.

—Dryden

God is no longer to be worshipped and believed in as a god foreshowing and assuring by types, but as a god who has performed the *substance* of what he promised.

—Nelson

5. Body; corporeal nature.

Between the parts of opaque and colored bodies are many spaces, either empty or replenished with mediums of other densities; as water between the tinging corpuscles wherewith any liquor is impregnated, air between the aqueous globules that constitute clouds or mists, and for the most part spaces void of both air and water; but yet perhaps not wholly void of all *substance* between the parts of hard bodies.

—Newton

The qualities of plants are more various than those of animal *substances*.

—Arbuthnot on Aliments

There may be a great and constant cough, with an extraordinary discharge of phlegmatic matter, while, notwithstanding, the *substance* of the lungs remains sound.

—Blackmore

6. Wealth; means of life.

He hath eaten me out of house and home, and hath put all my *substance* into that fat belly of his, but I will have some of it out again.

—Shakespeare, *Henry IV*

We are destroying many thousand lives, and exhausting our *substance*, but not for our own interest.

—Swift

VACÚITY. n.s. [*vacuitas*; from *vacuus*, Lat. *vacuité*, Fr.]

1. Emptiness; state of being unfilled.

> Hunger is such a state of *vacuity*, as to require a fresh supply of aliment.
>
> —Arbuthnot

2. Space unfilled; space unoccupied.

> In filling up *vacuities*, turning out shadows and ceremonies, by explicit prescription of substantial duties, which those shadows did obscurely represent.
>
> —Hammond's *Fund*

> He, that seat soon failing, meets
> A vast *vacuity*.
>
> —Milton

> Body and space are quite different things, and a *vacuity* is interspersed among the particles of matter.
>
> —Bentley

> God, who alone can answer all our longings, and fill every *vacuity* of our soul, should entirely possess our heart.
>
> —Rogers

> Redeeming still at night these *vacuities* of the day.
>
> —Fell

3. Inanity; want of reality.

> The soul is seen, like other things, in the mirror of its effects: but if they'll run behind the glass to catch at it, their expectations will meet with *vacuity* and emptiness.
>
> —Glanville

THE HISTORY OF RASSELAS, PRINCE OF ABYSSINIA   Johnson wrote *Rasselas* with his customary speed but under particular pressures. He composed the tale probably in late January 1759, possibly (as Boswell reports) during the "evenings of one week." This was the month of his mother's death; he may have made the book in order to help defray expenses and to articulate loss. His friend the painter Sir Joshua Reynolds later praised *Rasselas* for compassing within its few pages as much wisdom as though it had been written "by an angel or some superior being, whose comprehensive faculties could develop and lay open the inmost recesses of the human mind," and who could convey "in a few hours the experience of ages." The experience that *Rasselas* imparts, Johnson had expressed in other forms before. Rasselas is a prince born to a life of ease within the Happy Valley, a sequestered utopia of limitless luxuries; he suffers, though, from an oppressive sense of dissatisfaction, or (in a favorite Johnsonian term) "vacuity." Tantalized by his conviction that true happiness must lie elsewhere, he escapes the valley accompanied by his sister Nekayah and his mentor Imlac, only to find his own propensity for misplaced hopes, unfulfilled plans, and ineffectual wishes mirrored in the unhappy lives of nearly every mortal he meets with. Early in the tale, just before effecting his escape, Rasselas asks Imlac to tell the story of his own life, lived mostly in the larger world. In his reminiscences, Imlac gently sketches the cycles of desire and disillusion that the prince and princess will shortly experience for themselves.

from The History of Rasselas, Prince of Abyssinia
Chapter 8. The History of Imlac

The close of the day is, in the regions of the torrid zone, the only season of diversion and entertainment, and it was therefore mid-night before the music ceased, and the princesses retired. Rasselas then called for his companion and required him to begin the story of his life.

"Sir," said Imlac, "my history will not be long: the life that is devoted to knowledge passes silently away, and is very little diversified by events. To talk in public, to think in solitude, to read and to hear, to inquire, and answer inquiries, is the business of a scholar. He wanders about the world without pomp or terror, and is neither known nor valued but by men like himself.

"I was born in the kingdom of Goiama, at no great distance from the fountain of the Nile. My father was a wealthy merchant, who traded between the inland countries of Africk and the ports of the Red Sea. He was honest, frugal and diligent, but of mean sentiments, and narrow comprehension: he desired only to be rich, and to conceal his riches, lest he should be spoiled[1] by the governors of the province."

"Surely," said the prince, "my father must be negligent of his charge, if any man in his dominions dares take that which belongs to another. Does he not know that kings are accountable for injustice permitted as well as done? If I were emperor, not the meanest of my subjects should be oppressed with impunity. My blood boils when I am told that a merchant durst not enjoy his honest gains for fear of losing them by the rapacity of power. Name the governor who robbed the people, that I may declare his crimes to the emperor."

"Sir," said Imlac, "your ardor is the natural effect of virtue animated by youth: the time will come when you will acquit your father, and perhaps hear with less impatience of the governor. Oppression is, in the Abyssinian dominions, neither frequent nor tolerated; but no form of government has been yet discovered, by which cruelty can be wholly prevented. Subordination supposes power on one part and subjection on the other; and if power be in the hands of men, it will sometimes be abused. The vigilance of the supreme magistrate may do much, but much will still remain undone. He can never know all the crimes that are committed, and can seldom punish all that he knows."

"This," said the prince, "I do not understand, but I had rather hear thee than dispute. Continue thy narration."

"My father," proceeded Imlac, "originally intended that I should have no other education, than such as might qualify me for commerce; and discovering in me great strength of memory, and quickness of apprehension, often declared his hope that I should be some time the richest man in Abyssinia."

"Why," said the prince, "did thy father desire the increase of his wealth, when it was already greater than he durst discover or enjoy? I am unwilling to doubt thy veracity, yet inconsistencies cannot both be true."

"Inconsistencies," answered Imlac, "cannot both be right, but, imputed to man, they may both be true. Yet diversity is not inconsistency. My father might expect a time of greater security. However, some desire is necessary to keep life in motion, and he, whose real wants are supplied, must admit those of fancy."

---

1. Plundered.

"This," said the prince, "I can in some measure conceive. I repent that I interrupted thee."

"With this hope," proceeded Imlac, "he sent me to school; but when I had once found the delight of knowledge, and felt the pleasure of intelligence and the pride of invention, I began silently to despise riches, and determined to disappoint the purpose of my father, whose grossness of conception raised my pity. I was twenty years old before his tenderness would expose me to the fatigue of travel, in which time I had been instructed, by successive masters, in all the literature[2] of my native country. As every hour taught me something new, I lived in a continual course of gratifications; but, as I advanced towards manhood, I lost much of the reverence with which I had been used to look on my instructors; because, when the lesson was ended, I did not find them wiser or better than common men.

"At length my father resolved to initiate me in commerce, and, opening one of his subterranean treasuries, counted out ten thousand pieces of gold. 'This, young man,' said he, 'is the stock with which you must negotiate. I began with less than the fifth part, and you see how diligence and parsimony have increased it. This is your own to waste or to improve. If you squander it by negligence or caprice, you must wait for my death before you will be rich: if, in four years, you double your stock, we will thenceforward let subordination cease, and live together as friends and partners; for he shall always be equal with me, who is equally skilled in the art of growing rich.'

"We laid our money upon camels, concealed in bales of cheap goods, and traveled to the shore of the Red Sea. When I cast my eye on the expanse of waters my heart bounded like that of a prisoner escaped. I felt an unextinguishable curiosity kindle in my mind, and resolved to snatch this opportunity of seeing the manners of other nations, and of learning sciences[3] unknown in Abyssinia.

"I remembered that my father had obliged me to the improvement of my stock, not by a promise which I ought not to violate, but by a penalty which I was at liberty to incur, and therefore determined to gratify my predominant desire, and by drinking at the fountains of knowledge, to quench the thirst of curiosity.

"As I was supposed to trade without connection with my father, it was easy for me to become acquainted with the master of a ship, and procure a passage to some other country. I had no motives of choice to regulate my voyage; it was sufficient for me that, wherever I wandered, I should see a country which I had not seen before. I therefore entered a ship bound for Surat, having left a letter for my father declaring my intention.

Chapter 9. The History of Imlac Continued

"When I first entered upon the world of waters, and lost sight of land, I looked round about me with pleasing terror, and thinking my soul enlarged by the boundless prospect, imagined that I could gaze round for ever without satiety; but, in a short time, I grew weary of looking on barren uniformity, where I could only see again what I had already seen. I then descended into the ship, and doubted for a while whether all my future pleasures would not end like this in disgust and disappointment. 'Yet, surely,' said I, 'the ocean and the land are very different; the only variety of water is rest and motion, but the earth has mountains and valleys, deserts and cities: it is

---

2. "Learning; skill in letters" (Johnson's *Dictionary*).   3. Modes of knowledge.

inhabited by men of different customs and contrary opinions; and I may hope to find variety in life, though I should miss it in nature.'

"With this thought I quieted my mind, and amused myself during the voyage; sometimes by learning from the sailors the art of navigation, which I have never practiced, and sometimes by forming schemes for my conduct in different situations, in not one of which I have been ever placed.

"I was almost weary of my naval amusements when we landed safely at Surat. I secured my money, and purchasing some commodities for show, joined myself to a caravan that was passing into the inland country. My companions, for some reason or other, conjecturing that I was rich, and, by my inquiries and admiration,[4] finding that I was ignorant, considered me as a novice whom they had a right to cheat, and who was to learn at the usual expense the art of fraud. They exposed me to the theft of servants, and the exaction of officers, and saw me plundered upon false pretenses, without any advantage to themselves, but that of rejoicing in the superiority of their own knowledge."

"Stop a moment," said the prince. "Is there such depravity in man, as that he should injure another without benefit to himself? I can easily conceive that all are pleased with superiority; but your ignorance was merely accidental, which, being neither your crime nor your folly, could afford them no reason to applaud themselves; and the knowledge which they had, and which you wanted, they might as effectually have shown by warning, as betraying you."

"Pride," said Imlac, "is seldom delicate, it will please itself with very mean advantages; and envy feels not its own happiness, but when it may be compared with the misery of others. They were my enemies because they grieved to think me rich, and my oppressors because they delighted to find me weak."

"Proceed," said the prince. "I doubt not of the facts which you relate, but imagine that you impute them to mistaken motives."

"In this company," said Imlac, "I arrived at Agra, the capital of Indostan, the city in which the great Mogul commonly resides. I applied myself to the language of the country, and in a few months was able to converse with the learned men; some of whom I found morose and reserved, and others easy and communicative; some were unwilling to teach another what they had with difficulty learned themselves; and some showed that the end of their studies was to gain the dignity of instructing.

"To the tutor of the young princes I recommended myself so much, that I was presented to the emperor as a man of uncommon knowledge. The emperor asked me many questions concerning my country and my travels; and though I cannot now recollect any thing that he uttered above the power of a common man, he dismissed me astonished at his wisdom, and enamored of his goodness.

"My credit was now so high, that the merchants, with whom I had traveled, applied to me for recommendations to the ladies of the court. I was surprised at their confidence of solicitation, and gently reproached them with their practices on the road. They heard me with cold indifference, and showed no tokens of shame or sorrow.

"They then urged their request with the offer of a bribe; but what I would not do for kindness I would not do for money; and refused them, not because they had injured me, but because I would not enable them to injure others; for I knew they would have made use of my credit to cheat those who should buy their wares.

---

4. "Wonder; the act of admiring or wondering" (Johnson's *Dictionary*).

"Having resided at Agra, till there was no more to be learned, I traveled into Persia, where I saw many remains of ancient magnificence, and observed many new accommodations[5] of life. The Persians are a nation eminently social, and their assemblies afforded me daily opportunities of remarking characters and manners, and of tracing human nature through all its variations.

"From Persia I passed into Arabia, where I saw a nation at once pastoral and warlike; who live without any settled habitation; whose only wealth is their flocks and herds; and who have yet carried on, through all ages, an hereditary war with all mankind, though they neither covet nor envy their possessions.

Chapter 10. Imlac's History Continued. A Dissertation upon Poetry

"Wherever I went, I found that poetry was considered as the highest learning, and regarded with a veneration somewhat approaching to that which man would pay to the angelic nature. And it yet fills me with wonder, that, in almost all countries, the most ancient poets are considered as the best: whether it be that every other kind of knowledge is an acquisition gradually attained, and poetry is a gift conferred at once; or that the first poetry of every nation surprised them as a novelty, and retained the credit by consent which it received by accident at first: or whether, as the province of poetry is to describe nature and passion,[6] which are always the same, the first writers took possession of the most striking objects for description, and the most probable occurrences for fiction, and left nothing to those that followed them, but transcription of the same events, and new combinations of the same images. Whatever be the reason, it is commonly observed that the early writers are in possession of nature, and their followers of art: that the first excel in strength and invention, and the latter in elegance and refinement.

"I was desirous to add my name to this illustrious fraternity. I read all the poets of Persia and Arabia, and was able to repeat by memory the volumes that are suspended in the mosque of Mecca. But I soon found that no man was ever great by imitation. My desire of excellence impelled me to transfer my attention to nature and to life. Nature was to be my subject, and men to be my auditors: I could never describe what I had not seen: I could not hope to move those with delight or terror, whose interests and opinions I did not understand.

"Being now resolved to be a poet, I saw every thing with a new purpose; my sphere of attention was suddenly magnified: no kind of knowledge was to be overlooked. I ranged mountains and deserts for images and resemblances, and pictured upon my mind every tree of the forest and flower of the valley. I observed with equal care the crags of the rock and the pinnacles of the palace. Sometimes I wandered along the mazes of the rivulet, and sometimes watched the changes of the summer clouds. To a poet nothing can be useless. Whatever is beautiful, and whatever is dreadful, must be familiar to his imagination: he must be conversant with all that is awfully[7] vast or elegantly little. The plants of the garden, the animals of the wood, the minerals of the earth, and meteors of the sky, must all concur to store his mind with inexhaustible variety: for every idea is useful for the enforcement or decoration of moral or religious truth; and he who knows most will have most power of

5. "Conveniences, things requisite to ease or refreshment" (Johnson's *Dictionary*).
6. Nature: "the constitution and appearance of things"

(Johnson's *Dictionary*); Passion: "violent commotion of the mind" (Johnson's *Dictionary*).
7. Solemnly.

diversifying his scenes, and of gratifying his reader with remote allusions and unexpected instruction.

"All the appearances of nature I was therefore careful to study, and every country which I have surveyed has contributed something to my poetical powers."

"In so wide a survey," said the prince, "you must surely have left much unobserved. I have lived, till now, within the circuit of these mountains, and yet cannot walk abroad without the sight of something which I had never beheld before, or never heeded."

"The business of a poet," said Imlac, "is to examine, not the individual, but the species; to remark general properties and large appearances: he does not number the streaks of the tulip, or describe the different shades in the verdure of the forest. He is to exhibit in his portraits of nature such prominent and striking features, as recall the original to every mind; and must neglect the minuter discriminations, which one may have remarked, and another have neglected, for those characteristics which are alike obvious to vigilance and carelessness.

"But the knowledge of nature is only half the task of a poet; he must be acquainted likewise with all the modes of life. His character requires that he estimate the happiness and misery of every condition; observe the power of all the passions in all their combinations, and trace the changes of the human mind as they are modified by various institutions and accidental influences of climate or custom, from the sprightliness of infancy to the despondence of decrepitude. He must divest himself of the prejudices of his age or country; he must consider right and wrong in their abstracted and invariable state; he must disregard present laws and opinions, and rise to general and transcendental truths, which will always be the same: he must therefore content himself with the slow progress of his name; condemn the applause of his own time, and commit his claims to the justice of posterity. He must write as the interpreter of nature, and the legislator of mankind, and consider himself as presiding over the thoughts and manners of future generations; as a being superior to time and place.

"His labor is not yet at an end: he must know many languages and many sciences; and, that his style may be worthy of his thoughts, must, by incessant practice, familiarize to himself every delicacy of speech and grace of harmony."

Chapter 11. Imlac's Narrative Continued. A Hint on Pilgrimage

Imlac now felt the enthusiastic[8] fit, and was proceeding to aggrandize his own profession, when the prince cried out, "Enough! Thou hast convinced me, that no human being can ever be a poet. Proceed with thy narration."

"To be a poet," said Imlac, "is indeed very difficult." "So difficult," returned the prince, "that I will at present hear no more of his labors. Tell me whither you went when you had seen Persia."

"From Persia," said the poet, "I traveled through Syria, and for three years resided in Palestine, where I conversed with great numbers of the northern and western nations of Europe; the nations which are now in possession of all power and all knowledge; whose armies are irresistible, and whose fleets command the remotest parts of the globe. When I compared these men with the natives of our own kingdom, and those that surround us, they appeared almost another order of beings.

8. "Vehemently hot in any cause" (Johnson's *Dictionary*).

In their countries it is difficult to wish for any thing that may not be obtained: a thousand arts, of which we never heard, are continually laboring for their convenience and pleasure; and whatever their own climate has denied them is supplied by their commerce."

"By what means," said the prince, "are the Europeans thus powerful? or why, since they can so easily visit Asia and Africa for trade or conquest, cannot the Asiatics and Africans invade their coasts, plant colonies in their ports, and give laws to their natural princes? The same wind that carries them back would bring us thither."

"They are more powerful, Sir, than we," answered Imlac, "because they are wiser; knowledge will always predominate over ignorance, as man governs the other animals. But why their knowledge is more than ours, I know not what reason can be given, but the unsearchable will of the Supreme Being."

"When," said the prince with a sigh, "shall I be able to visit Palestine, and mingle with this mighty confluence of nations? Till that happy moment shall arrive, let me fill up the time with such representations as thou canst give me. I am not ignorant of the motive that assembles such numbers in that place, and cannot but consider it as the center of wisdom and piety, to which the best and wisest men of every land must be continually resorting."

"There are some nations," said Imlac, "that send few visitants[9] to Palestine; for many numerous and learned sects in Europe concur to censure pilgrimage as superstitious, or deride it as ridiculous."

"You know," said the prince, "how little my life has made me acquainted with diversity of opinions: it will be too long to hear the arguments on both sides; you, that have considered them, tell me the result."

"Pilgrimage," said Imlac, "like many other acts of piety, may be reasonable or superstitious, according to the principles upon which it is performed. Long journeys in search of truth are not commanded. Truth, such as is necessary to the regulation of life, is always found where it is honestly sought. Change of place is no natural cause of the increase of piety, for it inevitably produces dissipation of mind. Yet, since men go every day to view the fields where great actions have been performed, and return with stronger impressions of the event, curiosity of the same kind may naturally dispose us to view that country whence our religion had its beginning; and I believe no man surveys those awful scenes without some confirmation of holy resolutions. That the Supreme Being may be more easily propitiated in one place than in another, is the dream of idle superstition; but that some places may operate upon our own minds in an uncommon manner, is an opinion which hourly experience will justify. He who supposes that his vices may be more successfully combated in Palestine, will, perhaps, find himself mistaken, yet he may go thither without folly: he who thinks they will be more freely pardoned, dishonors at once his reason and religion."

"These," said the prince, "are European distinctions. I will consider them another time. What have you found to be the effect of knowledge? Are those nations happier than we?"

"There is so much infelicity," said the poet, "in the world, that scarce any man has leisure from his own distresses to estimate the comparative happiness of others. Knowledge is certainly one of the means of pleasure, as is confessed by the natural desire which every mind feels of increasing its ideas. Ignorance is mere privation, by

9. Pilgrims.

which nothing can be produced: it is a vacuity in which the soul sits motionless and torpid for want of attraction; and, without knowing why, we always rejoice when we learn, and grieve when we forget. I am therefore inclined to conclude that, if nothing counteracts the natural consequence of learning, we grow more happy as our minds take a wider range.

"In enumerating the particular comforts of life we shall find many advantages on the side of the Europeans. They cure wounds and diseases with which we languish and perish. We suffer inclemencies of weather which they can obviate. They have engines for the dispatch of many laborious works, which we must perform by manual industry. There is such communication between distant places, that one friend can hardly be said to be absent from another. Their policy removes all public inconveniences: they have roads cut through their mountains, and bridges laid upon their rivers. And, if we descend to the privacies of life, their habitations are more commodious, and their possessions are more secure."

"They are surely happy," said the prince, "who have all these conveniences, of which I envy none so much as the facility with which separated friends interchange their thoughts."

"The Europeans," answered Imlac, "are less unhappy than we, but they are not happy. Human life is every where a state in which much is to be endured, and little to be enjoyed."

Chapter 12. The Story of Imlac Continued

"I am not yet willing," said the prince, "to suppose that happiness is so parsimoniously distributed to mortals; nor can believe but that, if I had the choice of life, I should be able to fill every day with pleasure. I would injure no man, and should provoke no resentment: I would relieve every distress, and should enjoy the benedictions of gratitude. I would choose my friends among the wise, and my wife among the virtuous; and therefore should be in no danger from treachery, or unkindness. My children should, by my care, be learned and pious, and would repay to my age what their childhood had received. What would dare to molest him who might call on every side to thousands enriched by his bounty, or assisted by his power? And why should not life glide quietly away in the soft reciprocation of protection and reverence? All this may be done without the help of European refinements, which appear by their effects to be rather specious[1] than useful. Let us leave them and pursue our journey."

"From Palestine," said Imlac, "I passed through many regions of Asia; in the more civilized kingdoms as a trader, and among the barbarians of the mountains as a pilgrim. At last I began to long for my native country, that I might repose after my travels, and fatigues, in the places where I had spent my earliest years, and gladden my old companions with the recital of my adventures. Often did I figure to myself those, with whom I had sported away the gay hours of dawning life, sitting round me in its evening, wondering at my tales, and listening to my counsels.

"When this thought had taken possession of my mind, I considered every moment as wasted which did not bring me nearer to Abyssinia. I hastened into Egypt, and, notwithstanding my impatience, was detained ten months in the contemplation of its ancient magnificence, and in enquiries after the remains of its

---

1. "Showy; pleasing to the view" (Johnson's *Dictionary*).

ancient learning. I found in Cairo a mixture of all nations; some brought thither by the love of knowledge, some by the hope of gain, and many by the desire of living after their own manner without observation, and of lying hid in the obscurity of multitudes: for, in a city, populous as Cairo, it is possible to obtain at the same time the gratifications of society, and the secrecy of solitude.

"From Cairo I traveled to Suez, and embarked on the Red Sea, passing along the coast till I arrived at the port from which I had departed twenty years before. Here I joined myself to a caravan and re-entered my native country.

"I now expected the caresses of my kinsmen, and the congratulations of my friends, and was not without hope that my father, whatever value he had set upon riches, would own with gladness and pride a son who was able to add to the felicity and honor of the nation. But I was soon convinced that my thoughts were vain. My father had been dead fourteen years, having divided his wealth among my brothers, who were removed to some other provinces. Of my companions the greater part was in the grave, of the rest some could with difficulty remember me, and some considered me as one corrupted by foreign manners.

"A man used to vicissitudes is not easily dejected. I forgot, after a time, my disappointment, and endeavored to recommend myself to the nobles of the kingdom: they admitted me to their tables, heard my story, and dismissed me. I opened a school, and was prohibited to teach. I then resolved to sit down in the quiet of domestic life, and addressed a lady that was fond of my conversation, but rejected my suit, because my father was a merchant

"Wearied at last with solicitation and repulses, I resolved to hide myself for ever from the world, and depend no longer on the opinion or caprice of others. I waited for the time when the gate of the Happy Valley should open, that I might bid farewell to hope and fear: the day came; my performance was distinguished with favor, and I resigned myself with joy to perpetual confinement."

"Hast thou here found happiness at last?" said Rasselas. "Tell me without reserve; art thou content with thy condition? or, dost thou wish to be again wandering and inquiring? All the inhabitants of this valley celebrate their lot, and, at the annual visit of the emperor, invite others to partake of their felicity."

"Great prince," said Imlac, "I shall speak the truth: I know not one of all your attendants who does not lament the hour when he entered this retreat. I am less unhappy than the rest, because I have a mind replete with images, which I can vary and combine at pleasure. I can amuse my solitude by the renovation of the knowledge which begins to fade from my memory, and by recollection of the accidents of my past life. Yet all this ends in the sorrowful consideration, that my acquirements are now useless, and that none of my pleasures can be again enjoyed. The rest, whose minds have no impression but of the present moment, are either corroded by malignant passions, or sit stupid in the gloom of perpetual vacancy."

"What passions can infest those," said the prince, "who have no rivals? We are in a place where impotence precludes malice, and where all envy is repressed by community of enjoyments."

"There may be community," said Imlac, "of material possessions, but there can never be community of love or of esteem. It must happen that one will please more than another; he that knows himself despised will always be envious; and still more envious and malevolent, if he is condemned to live in the presence of those who despise him. The invitations, by which they allure others to a state which they feel to be wretched, proceed from the natural malignity of hopeless misery. They are weary of themselves, and of each other, and expect to find relief in new companions.

They envy the liberty which their folly has forfeited, and would gladly see all mankind imprisoned like themselves.

"From this crime, however, I am wholly free. No man can say that he is wretched by my persuasion. I look with pity on the crowds who are annually soliciting admission to captivity, and wish that it were lawful for me to warn them of their danger."

"My dear Imlac," said the prince, "I will open to thee my whole heart. I have long meditated an escape from the Happy Valley. I have examined the mountains on every side, but find myself insuperably barred: teach me the way to break my prison; thou shalt be the companion of my flight, the guide of my rambles, the partner of my fortune, and my sole director in the *choice of life*."

"Sir," answered the poet, "your escape will be difficult, and, perhaps, you may soon repent your curiosity. The world, which you figure to yourself smooth and quiet as the lake in the valley, you will find a sea foaming with tempests, and boiling with whirlpools: you will be sometimes overwhelmed by the waves of violence, and sometimes dashed against the rocks of treachery. Amidst wrongs and frauds, competitions and anxieties, you will wish a thousand times for these seats of quiet, and willingly quit hope to be free from fear."

"Do not seek to deter me from my purpose," said the prince: "I am impatient to see what thou hast seen; and, since thou art thyself weary of the valley, it is evident, that thy former state was better than this. Whatever be the consequence of my experiment, I am resolved to judge with my own eyes of the various conditions of men, and then to make deliberately my *choice of life*."

"I am afraid," said Imlac, "you are hindered by stronger restraints than my persuasions; yet, if your determination is fixed, I do not counsel you to despair. Few things are impossible to diligence and skill."

1759   1759

THE PLAYS OF WILLIAM SHAKESPEARE   Johnson first proposed a new edition of Shakespeare's plays, without success, in 1745; he finally published one twenty tears later. In the intervening decades, his work on the *Dictionary* had made him (in Bertrand Bronson's phrase) "the greatest living authority on Shakespeare's diction," and had secured him such fame that the booksellers greeted his renewed Shakespeare proposal with enthusiasm rather than indifference. Even so, he found the work slow going; he promised completion in eighteen months and took nine years. Five major editions had appeared since the start of the century, and Johnson was alert to their many inadequacies. Earlier editors displayed a passion for emendation, for finding "printer's errors" everywhere in the text, and replacing them with overconfident conjectures as to what Shakespeare had really "meant" and wrote. Johnson opted more often to let things be: to take a passage as given, to discover its intention, to explain its success, or to analyze its failure. The same kind of scrutiny suffuses his Preface, in which he investigates how plays really operate upon their audience. In the process, he demolishes the critical criteria by which Shakespeare had long been deemed an inferior crafter of drama (albeit an inimitably inspired poet). Johnson's *Shakespeare* is distinctive for the energy of its thought and of its feeling; for the intensity of its grappling with the impact of tiny passages and of towering genius.

from The Plays of William Shakespeare
from *Preface*
["JUST REPRESENTATIONS OF GENERAL NATURE"]

That praises are without reason lavished on the dead, and that the honors due only to excellence are paid to antiquity, is a complaint likely to be always continued by those who, being able to add nothing to truth, hope for eminence from the heresies of paradox; or those who, being forced by disappointment upon consolatory expedients, are willing to hope from posterity what the present age refuses and flatter themselves that the regard which is yet denied by envy will be at last bestowed by time.

Antiquity, like every other quality that attracts the notice of mankind, has undoubtedly votaries that reverence it not from reason, but from prejudice. Some seem to admire indiscriminately whatever has been long preserved, without considering that time has sometimes cooperated with chance; all perhaps are more willing to honor past than present excellence; and the mind contemplates genius through the shades of age, as the eye surveys the sun through artificial opacity. The great contention of criticism is to find the faults of the moderns and the beauties of the ancients. While an author is yet living, we estimate his powers by his worst performance; and when he is dead, we rate them by his best.

To works, however, of which the excellence is not absolute and definite, but gradual and comparative; to works not raised upon principles demonstrative and scientific but appealing wholly to observation and experience, no other test can be applied than length of duration and continuance of esteem. What mankind have long possessed they have often examined and compared; and if they persist to value the possession, it is because frequent comparisons have confirmed opinion in its favor. As among the works of nature no man can properly call a river deep or a mountain high, without the knowledge of many mountains and many rivers; so, in the productions of genius, nothing can be styled excellent till it has been compared with other works of the same kind. Demonstration immediately displays its power and has nothing to hope or fear from the flux of years; but works tentative and experimental must be estimated by their proportion to the general and collective ability of man, as it is discovered in a long succession of endeavors. Of the first building that was raised, it might be with certainty determined that it was round or square, but whether it was spacious or lofty must have been referred to time. The Pythagorean scale of numbers was at once discovered to be perfect; but the poems of Homer we yet know not to transcend the common limits of human intelligence but by remarking that nation after nation, and century after century, has been able to do little more than transpose his incidents, newname his characters, and paraphrase his sentiments.

The reverence due to writings that have long subsisted arises, therefore, not from any credulous confidence in the superior wisdom of past ages or gloomy persuasion of the degeneracy of mankind, but is the consequence of acknowledged and indubitable positions that what has been longest known has been most considered, and what is most considered is best understood.

The poet of whose works I have undertaken the revision[1] may now begin to assume the dignity of an ancient and claim the privilege of established fame and prescriptive veneration. He has long outlived his century, the term commonly fixed as the test of literary merit. Whatever advantages he might once derive from personal allusions, local customs, or temporary opinions have for many years been lost; and every topic of merriment or motive of sorrow which the modes of artificial[2] life afforded him now only obscure the scenes which they once illuminated. The effects of favor and competition are at an end; the tradition of his friendships and his enmities have perished; his works support no opinion with arguments nor supply any

---

1. Edition.   2. "Made by art; not natural" (Johnson's *Dictionary*).

faction with invectives; they can neither indulge vanity nor gratify malignity, but are read without any other reason than the desire of pleasure and are therefore praised only as pleasure is obtained; yet, thus unassisted by interest or passion, they have passed through variations of taste and changes of manners, and, as they devolved from one generation to another, have received new honors at every transmission.

But because human judgment, though it be gradually gaining upon certainty, never becomes infallible; and approbation, though long continued, may yet be only the approbation of prejudice or fashion; it is proper to inquire by what peculiarities of excellence Shakespeare has gained and kept the favor of his countrymen.

Nothing can please many, and please long, but just representations of general nature. Particular manners can be known to few, and therefore few only can judge how nearly they are copied. The irregular combinations of fanciful invention may delight awhile by that novelty of which the common satiety of life sends us all in quest; but the pleasures of sudden wonder are soon exhausted, and the mind can only repose on the stability of truth.

Shakespeare is, above all writers, at least above all modern writers, the poet of nature, the poet that holds up to his readers a faithful mirror of manners and of life. His characters are not modified by the customs of particular places, unpracticed by the rest of the world; by the peculiarities of studies or professions which can operate but upon small numbers; or by the accidents of transient fashions or temporary opinions: they are the genuine progeny of common humanity, such as the world will always supply, and observation will always find. His persons act and speak by the influence of those general passions and principles by which all minds are agitated and the whole system of life is continued in motion. In the writings of other poets a character is too often an individual; in those of Shakespeare it is commonly a species.

It is from this wide extension of design that so much instruction is derived. It is this which fills the plays of Shakespeare with practical axioms and domestic wisdom. It was said of Euripides that every verse was a precept;[3] and it may be said of Shakespeare that from his works may be collected a system of civil and economical prudence.[4] Yet his real power is not shown in the splendor of particular passages, but by the progress of his fable and the tenor of his dialogue; and he that tries to recommend him by select quotations will succeed like the pedant in Hierocles,[5] who, when he offered his house for sale, carried a brick in his pocket as a specimen.

It will not easily be imagined how much Shakespeare excels in accommodating his sentiments to real life but by comparing him with other authors. It was observed of the ancient schools of declamation that the more diligently they were frequented, the more was the student disqualified for the world, because he found nothing there which he should ever meet in any other place. The same remark may be applied to every stage but that of Shakespeare. The theater, when it is under any other direction, is peopled by such characters as were never seen, conversing in a language which was never heard, upon topics which will never arise in the commerce of mankind. But the dialogue of this author is often so evidently determined by the incident which produces it, and is pursued with so much ease and simplicity, that it seems scarcely to claim the merit of fiction, but to have been gleaned by diligent selection out of common conversation and common occurrences.

---

3. This observation was made by Cicero in his *Familiar Letters* (16.8).
4. Public and private duty.

5. The critic Hierocles, writing in the 5th century C.E., tells this story in his commentary on Pythagoras.

Upon every other stage the universal agent is love, by whose power all good and evil is distributed and every action quickened or retarded. To bring a lover, a lady, and a rival into the fable; to entangle them in contradictory obligations, perplex them with oppositions of interest, and harass them with violence of desires inconsistent with each other; to make them meet in rapture and part in agony, to fill their mouths with hyperbolical joy and outrageous sorrow, to distress them as nothing human ever was distressed, to deliver them as nothing human ever was delivered, is the business of a modern dramatist. For this, probability is violated, life is misrepresented, and language is depraved. But love is only one of many passions; and as it has no great influence upon the sum of life, it has little operation in the dramas of a poet who caught his ideas from the living world and exhibited only what he saw before him. He knew that any other passion, as it was regular or exorbitant, was a cause of happiness or calamity.

Characters thus ample and general were not easily discriminated and preserved, yet perhaps no poet ever kept his personages more distinct from each other. I will not say with Pope that every speech may be assigned to the proper speaker, because many speeches there are which have nothing characteristical; but, perhaps, though some may be equally adapted to every person, it will be difficult to find any that can be properly transferred from the present possessor to another claimant. The choice is right, when there is reason for choice.

Other dramatists can only gain attention by hyperbolical or aggravated[6] characters, by fabulous and unexampled excellence or depravity, as the writers of barbarous romances invigorated the reader by a giant and a dwarf; and he that should form his expectations of human affairs from the play, or from the tale, would be equally deceived. Shakespeare has no heroes; his scenes are occupied only by men, who act and speak as the reader thinks that he should himself have spoken or acted on the same occasion. Even where the agency is supernatural, the dialogue is level with life. Other writers disguise the most natural passions and most frequent incidents, so that he who contemplates them in the book will not know them in the world. Shakespeare approximates the remote and familiarizes the wonderful; the event which he represents will not happen but, if it were possible, its effects would probably be such as he has assigned; and it may be said that he has not only shown human nature as it acts in real exigences, but as it would be found in trials to which it cannot be exposed.

This, therefore, is the praise of Shakespeare, that his drama is the mirror of life; that he who has mazed his imagination in following the phantoms which other writers raise up before him may here be cured of his delirious ecstasies by reading human sentiments in human language, by scenes from which a hermit may estimate the transactions of the world and a confessor predict the progress of the passions.

[FAULTS; THE UNITIES]

Shakespeare with his excellencies has likewise faults, and faults sufficient to obscure and overwhelm any other merit. I shall show them in the proportion in which they appear to me, without envious malignity or superstitious veneration. No question can be more innocently discussed than a dead poet's pretensions to renown; and little regard is due to that bigotry which sets candor[1] higher than truth.

---

6. Exaggerated.   1. "Sweetness of temper; kindness" (Johnson's *Dictionary*).

His first defect is that to which may be imputed most of the evil in books or in men. He sacrifices virtue to convenience and is so much more careful to please than to instruct that he seems to write without any moral purpose. From his writings indeed a system of social duty may be selected, for he that thinks reasonably must think morally; but his precepts and axioms drop casually from him; he makes no just distribution of good or evil, nor is always careful to show in the virtuous a disapprobation of the wicked; he carries his persons indifferently through right and wrong and at the close dismisses them without further care and leaves their examples to operate by chance. This fault the barbarity of his age cannot extenuate; for it is always a writer's duty to make the world better, and justice is a virtue independent on time or place.

The plots are often so loosely formed that a very slight consideration may improve them, and so carelessly pursued that he seems not always to comprehend his own design. He omits opportunities of instructing or delighting which the train of his story seems to force upon him, and apparently rejects those exhibitions which would be more affecting, for the sake of those which are more easy.

It may be observed that in many of his plays the latter part is evidently neglected. When he found himself near the end of his work and in view of his reward, he shortened the labor to snatch the profit. He therefore remits his efforts where he should most vigorously exert them, and his catastrophe is improbably produced or imperfectly represented.

He had no regard to distinction of time or place but gives to one age or nation, without scruple, the customs, institutions, and opinions of another, at the expense not only of likelihood but of possibility. These faults Pope has endeavored, with more zeal than judgment, to transfer to his imagined interpolators. We need not wonder to find Hector quoting Aristotle,[2] when we see the loves of Theseus and Hippolyta combined with the Gothic mythology of fairies.[3] Shakespeare, indeed, was not the only violator of chronology, for in the same age Sidney, who wanted not[4] the advantages of learning, has, in his Arcadia, confounded the pastoral with the feudal times, the days of innocence, quiet, and security, with those of turbulence, violence, and adventure.

In his comic scenes he is seldom very successful when he engages his characters in reciprocations of smartness and contests of sarcasm; their jests are commonly gross and their pleasantry licentious; neither his gentlemen nor his ladies have much delicacy nor are sufficiently distinguished from his clowns by any appearance of refined manners. Whether he represented the real conversation of his time is not easy to determine. The reign of Elizabeth is commonly supposed to have been a time of stateliness, formality, and reserve; yet perhaps the relaxations of that severity were not very elegant. There must, however, have been always some modes of gaiety preferable to others, and a writer ought to choose the best.

In tragedy his performance seems constantly to be worse as his labor is more. The effusions of passion which exigence forces out are for the most part striking and energetic; but whenever he solicits his invention or strains his faculties, the offspring of his throes is tumor, meanness, tediousness, and obscurity.

In narration he affects a disproportionate pomp of diction and a wearisome train of circumlocution and tells the incident imperfectly in many words which might have been more plainly delivered in few. Narration in dramatic poetry is naturally tedious, as it is unanimated and inactive and obstructs the progress of the action; it

---

2. *Troilus and Cressida* 2.2.166–67.   4. Did not lack.
3. This combination occurs in A *Midsummer Night's Dream*.

should therefore always be rapid and enlivened by frequent interruption. Shakespeare found it an encumbrance and, instead of lightening it by brevity, endeavored to recommend it by dignity and splendor.

His declamations or set speeches are commonly cold and weak, for his power was the power of nature; when he endeavored, like other tragic writers, to catch opportunities of amplification and, instead of inquiring what the occasion demanded, to show how much his stores of knowledge could supply, he seldom escapes without the pity or resentment of his reader.

It is incident to him to be now and then entangled with an unwieldy sentiment, which he cannot well express and will not reject; he struggles with it awhile and, if it continues stubborn, comprises it in words such as occur and leaves it to be disentangled and evolved by those who have more leisure to bestow upon it.

Not that always where the language is intricate the thought is subtle, or the image always great where the line is bulky; the equality of words to things is very often neglected, and trivial sentiments and vulgar ideas disappoint the attention to which they are recommended by sonorous epithets and swelling figures.[5]

But the admirers of this great poet have most reason to complain when he approaches nearest to his highest excellence and seems fully resolved to sink them in dejection and mollify them with tender emotions by the fall of greatness, the danger of innocence, or the crosses[6] of love. What he does best, he soon ceases to do. He is not long soft and pathetic without some idle conceit[7] or contemptible equivocation. He no sooner begins to move than he counteracts himself; and terror and pity, as they are rising in the mind, are checked and blasted by sudden frigidity.

A quibble[8] is to Shakespeare what luminous vapors are to the traveler; he follows it at all adventures; it is sure to lead him out of his way and sure to engulf him in the mire. It has some malignant power over his mind, and its fascinations are irresistible. Whatever be the dignity or profundity of his disquisition, whether he be enlarging knowledge or exalting affection, whether he be amusing attention with incidents or enchaining it in suspense, let but a quibble spring up before him and he leaves his work unfinished. A quibble is the golden apple for which he will always turn aside from his career or stoop from his elevation.[9] A quibble, poor and barren as it is, gave him such delight that he was content to purchase it by the sacrifice of reason, propriety, and truth. A quibble was to him the fatal Cleopatra for which he lost the world and was content to lose it.

It will be thought strange that in enumerating the defects of this writer I have not yet mentioned his neglect of the unities, his violation of those laws which have been instituted and established by the joint authority of poets and critics.

For his other deviations from the art of writing, I resign him to critical justice without making any other demand in his favor than that which must be indulged to all human excellence: that his virtues be rated with his failings. But from the censure which this irregularity may bring upon him, I shall, with due reverence to that learning which I must oppose, adventure to try how I can defend him.

His histories, being neither tragedies nor comedies, are not subject to any of their laws; nothing more is necessary to all the praise which they expect than that

5. Figures of speech.
6. Obstacles, vexations.
7. Play on words.
8. Pun.

9. Johnson alludes to the story of the runner Atalanta, who lost a race because she was distracted by golden apples tossed in her path.

the changes of action be so prepared as to be understood, that the incidents be various and affecting, and the characters consistent, natural, and distinct. No other unity is intended, and therefore none is to be sought.

In his other works he has well enough preserved the unity of action. He has not, indeed, an intrigue regularly perplexed and regularly unraveled; he does not endeavor to hide his design only to discover it, for this is seldom the order of real events, and Shakespeare is the poet of nature; but his plan has commonly, what Aristotle requires,[1] a beginning, a middle, and an end, one event is concatenated with another, and the conclusion follows by easy consequence. There are perhaps some incidents that might be spared, as in other poets there is much talk that only fills up time upon the stage; but the general system makes gradual advances, and the end of the play is the end of expectation.

To the unities of time and place he has shown no regard; and perhaps a nearer view of the principles on which they stand will diminish their value and withdraw from them the veneration which, from the time of Corneille,[2] they have very generally received, by discovering that they have given more trouble to the poet than pleasure to the auditor.

The necessity of observing the unities of time and place arises from the supposed necessity of making the drama credible. The critics hold it impossible that an action of months or years can be possibly believed to pass in three hours; or that the spectator can suppose himself to sit in the theater while ambassadors go and return between distant kings, while armies are levied and towns besieged, while an exile wanders and returns, or till he whom they saw courting his mistress shall lament the untimely fall of his son. The mind revolts from evident falsehood, and fiction loses its force when it departs from the resemblance of reality.

From the narrow limitation of time necessarily arises the contraction of place. The spectator, who knows that he saw the first act at Alexandria, cannot suppose that he sees the next at Rome, at a distance to which not the dragons of Medea[3] could, in so short a time, have transported him; he knows with certainty that he has not changed his place; and he knows that place cannot change itself; that what was a house cannot become a plain; that what was Thebes can never be Persepolis.

Such is the triumphant language with which a critic exults over the misery of an irregular poet and exults commonly without resistance or reply. It is time, therefore, to tell him by the authority of Shakespeare, that he assumes, as an unquestionable principle, a position which, while his breath is forming it into words, his understanding pronounces to be false. It is false, that any representation is mistaken for reality; that any dramatic fable in its materiality was ever credible, or, for a single moment, was ever credited.

The objection arising from the impossibility of passing the first hour at Alexandria and the next at Rome supposes that when the play opens the spectator really imagines himself at Alexandria and believes that his walk to the theater has been a voyage to Egypt, and that he lives in the days of Antony and Cleopatra. Surely he that imagines this may imagine more. He that can take the stage at one time for the palace of the Ptolemies may take it in half an hour for the promontory of Actium. Delusion, if delusion be admitted, has no certain limitation; if the spectator can be

1. Aristotle, *Poetics*, ch. 8.
2. The French neoclassical dramatist Pierre Corneille published his influential *Essay on the Three Unities* in 1660.
3. After killing her rival and her children, Medea eluded pursuit in a chariot drawn by dragons.

once persuaded that his old acquaintance are Alexander and Caesar, that a room illuminated with candles is the plain of Pharsalia or the bank of Granicus,[4] he is in a state
of elevation above the reach of reason or of truth, and from the heights of empyrean
poetry may despise the circumscriptions of terrestrial nature. There is no reason why a
mind thus wandering in ecstasy should count the clock, or why an hour should not be
a century in that calenture[5] of the brains that can make the stage a field.

The truth is that the spectators are always in their senses and know from the
first act to the last that the stage is only a stage, and that the players are only players.
They come to hear a certain number of lines recited with just gesture and elegant
modulation. The lines relate to some action, and an action must be in some place;
but the different actions that complete a story may be in places very remote from
each other; and where is the absurdity of allowing that space to represent first
Athens and then Sicily which was always known to be neither Sicily nor Athens,
but a modern theater?

By supposition, as place is introduced, time may be extended; the time required
by the fable elapses for the most part between the acts; for, of so much of the action
as is represented, the real and poetical duration is the same. If in the first act preparations for war against Mithridates are represented to be made in Rome, the event of
the war may, without absurdity, be represented in the catastrophe as happening in
Pontus; we know that there is neither war nor preparation for war; we know that we
are neither in Rome nor Pontus; that neither Mithridates nor Lucullus are before us.
The drama exhibits successive imitations of successive actions; and why may not the
second imitation represent an action that happened years after the first if it be so
connected with it that nothing but time can be supposed to intervene? Time is, of
all modes of existence, most obsequious to the imagination; a lapse of years is as easily conceived as a passage of hours. In contemplation we easily contract the time of
real actions and therefore willingly permit it to be contracted when we only see
their imitation.

It will be asked how the drama moves if it is not credited. It is credited with all
the credit due to a drama. It is credited, whenever it moves, as a just picture of a real
original; as representing to the auditor what he would himself feel if he were to do or
suffer what is there feigned to be suffered or to be done. The reflection that strikes
the heart is not that the evils before us are real evils, but that they are evils to which
we ourselves may be exposed. If there be any fallacy, it is not that we fancy the players, but that we fancy ourselves unhappy for a moment; but we rather lament the
possibility than suppose the presence of misery, as a mother weeps over her babe
when she remembers that death may take it from her. The delight of tragedy proceeds from our consciousness of fiction; if we thought murders and treasons real,
they would please no more.

Imitations produce pain or pleasure not because they are mistaken for realities,
but because they bring realities to mind. When the imagination is recreated[6] by a
painted landscape, the trees are not supposed capable to give us shade, or the fountains coolness; but we consider how we should be pleased with such fountains playing beside us and such woods waving over us. We are agitated in reading the history
of *Henry the Fifth*, yet no man takes his book for the field of Agincourt. A dramatic

4. Johnson refers to the site of battles fought by Julius
Caesar and Alexander the Great.

5. Fever.
6. "Delighted, gratified" (Johnson's *Dictionary*).

exhibition is a book recited with concomitants that increase or diminish its effect. Familiar[7] comedy is often more powerful in the theater than on the page; imperial tragedy is always less. The humor of Petruchio[8] may be heightened by grimace; but what voice or what gesture can hope to add dignity or force to the soliloquy of Cato?[9]

A play read affects the mind like a play acted. It is therefore evident that the action is not supposed to be real; and it follows that between the acts a longer or shorter time may be allowed to pass, and that no more account of space or duration is to be taken by the auditor of a drama than by the reader of a narrative, before whom may pass in an hour the life of a hero or the revolutions of an empire.

Whether Shakespeare knew the unities and rejected them by design, or deviated from them by happy ignorance, it is, I think, impossible to decide and useless to inquire. We may reasonably suppose that when he rose to notice, he did not want the counsels and admonitions of scholars and critics, and that he at last deliberately persisted in a practice which he might have begun by chance. As nothing is essential to the fable but unity of action, and as the unities of time and place arise evidently from false assumptions, and, by circumscribing the extent of the drama, lessen its variety, I cannot think it much to be lamented that they were not known by him, or not observed; nor, if such another poet could arise, should I very vehemently reproach him that his first act passed at Venice and his next in Cyprus.[1] Such violations of rules merely positive become the comprehensive genius of Shakespeare, and such censures are suitable to the minute and slender criticism of Voltaire:

> Non usque adeo permiscuit imis
> Longus summa dies, ut non, si voce Metelli
> Serventur leges, malint a Caesare tolli.[2]

Yet when I speak thus slightly of dramatic rules, I cannot but recollect how much wit and learning may be produced against me; before such authorities I am afraid to stand, not that I think the present question one of those that are to be decided by mere authority, but because it is to be suspected that these precepts have not been so easily received but for better reasons than I have yet been able to find. The result of my inquiries, in which it would be ludicrous to boast of impartiality, is that the unities of time and place are not essential to a just drama; that, though they may sometimes conduce to pleasure, they are always to be sacrificed to the nobler beauties of variety and instruction; and that a play written with nice observation of critical rules is to be contemplated as an elaborate curiosity, as the product of superfluous and ostentatious art, by which is shown rather what is possible than what is necessary.

He that, without diminution of any other excellence, shall preserve all the unities unbroken deserves the like applause with the architect who shall display all the orders of architecture[3] in a citadel without any deduction from its strength; but the principal beauty of a citadel is to exclude the enemy, and the greatest graces of a play are to copy nature and instruct life. * * *

---

7. Domestic.
8. The hero of *The Taming of the Shrew*.
9. The protagonist of Addison's tragedy, *Cato* (1713), soliloquizes at the beginning of the final act.
1. Johnson refers to *Othello*.
2. Johnson quotes from the epic poem *Pharsalia* by Lucan:

"Things are not yet so confused that / If the laws were preserved by the voice of Metellus, / They would not prefer to be suppressed by Caesar." Johnson aligns Metellus, a politician of negligible importance, with Voltaire; Caesar correlates with Shakespeare.
3. The five classical styles of architecture.

[SELECTED NOTES ON *OTHELLO*]

> OTHELLO: Wherein of antres vast, and deserts idle,
> Rough quarries, rocks, and hills, whose heads touch heaven . . . (1.3.141–42)

Whoever ridicules this account of the progress of love,[1] shows his ignorance, not only of history, but of nature and manners. It is no wonder that, in any age, or in any nation, a lady, recluse, timorous, and delicate, should desire to hear of events and scenes which she could never see, and should admire the man who had endured dangers, and performed actions, which, however great, were yet magnified by her timidity.

Every mind is liable to absence and inadvertency, else Pope could never have rejected a word so poetically beautiful.[2] "Idle" is an epithet used to express the infertility of the chaotic state, in the Saxon translation of the Pentateuch.

> DESDEMONA: That I did love the Moor to live with him,
> My downright violence and storm of fortunes
> May trumpet to the world. (1.3.249–51)

There is no need of this emendation.[3] "Violence" is not "violence suffered," but "violence acted." Breach of common rules and obligations. The old quarto has, "scorn" of fortune, which is perhaps the true reading.

> DESDEMONA: I saw Othello's visage in his mind,
> And to his honors and his valiant parts
> Did I my soul and fortunes consecrate. (1.3.253–55)

It must raise no wonder, that I loved a man of an appearance so little engaging; I saw his face only in his mind; the greatness of his character reconciled me to his form.

> OTHELLO: Excellent wretch![4] (3.3.91)

The meaning of the word "wretch," is not generally understood. It is now, in some parts of England, a term of the softest and fondest tenderness. It expresses the utmost degree of amiableness, joined with an idea, which perhaps all tenderness includes, of feebleness, softness, and want of protection. Othello, considering Desdemona as excelling in beauty and virtue, soft and timorous by her sex, and by her situation absolutely in his power, calls her "excellent wretch." It may be expressed: "Dear, harmless, helpless excellence."

> OTHELLO: when I love thee not,
> Chaos is come again. (3.3.91–92)

When my love is for a moment suspended by suspicion, I have nothing in my mind but discord, tumult, perturbation, and confusion.

> IAGO: She did deceive her father, marrying you;
> And when she seemed to shake and fear your looks,
> She loved them most. (3.3.206–8)

---

1. As had Thomas Rymer in his *Short View of Tragedy* (1692).
2. In his edition of Shakespeare's works (1725), Alexander Pope had emended "deserts idle" to "deserts wild."
3. A prior editor had emended "violence and storm of fortunes" to "violence to forms, my fortunes."
4. In his edition of Shakespeare's works (1733–1734), Lewis Theobald had emended "wretch" to "wench."

This and the following argument of Iago ought to be deeply impressed on every reader. Deceit and falsehood, whatever conveniences they may for a time promise or produce, are, in the sum of life, obstacles to happiness. Those who profit by the cheat, distrust the deceiver, and the act by which kindness was sought, puts an end to confidence.

The same objection may be made with a lower degree of strength against the imprudent generosity of disproportionate marriages. When the first heat of passion is over, it is easily succeeded by suspicion, that the same violence of inclination which caused one irregularity, may stimulate to another; and those who have shown, that their passions are too powerful for their prudence, will, with very slight appearances against them, be censured, as not very likely to restrain them by their virtue.

> EMILIA: 'Tis not a year or two shows us a man. (3.4.97)

From this line it may be conjectured, that the author intended the action of this play to be considered as longer than is marked by any note of time. Since their arrival at Cyprus, to which they were hurried on their wedding-night, the fable seems to have been in one continual progress, nor can I see any vacuity into which a "year or two," or even a month or two, could be put. On the night of Othello's arrival, a feast was proclaimed; at that feast Cassio was degraded, and immediately applies to Desdemona to get him restored. Iago indeed advises Othello to hold him off a while, but there is no reason to think, that he has been held off long. A little longer interval would increase the probability of the story, though it might violate the rules of the drama. See Act 5, Scene 2

> OTHELLO: It is the cause, it is the cause, my soul.
> Let me not name it to you, you chaste stars!
> It is the cause. (5.2.1–3)

The abruptness of this soliloquy makes it obscure. The meaning I think is this. "I am here," says Othello in his mind, "overwhelmed with horror. What is the reason of this perturbation? Is it want of resolution to do justice? Is it the dread of shedding blood? No; it is not the action that shocks me, but 'it is the cause, it is the cause, my soul; let me not name it to you, ye chaste stars! it is the cause.'"

> OTHELLO: This sorrow's heavenly;
> It strikes where it doth love. (5.2.21–2)

This tenderness, with which I lament the punishment which justice compels me to inflict, is a holy passion.

I wish these two lines could be honestly ejected. It is the fate of Shakespeare to counteract his own pathos.

> OTHELLO: Oh perjured woman! thou dost stone my heart,
> And mak'st me call, what I intend to do,
> A murder, which I thought a sacrifice. (5.2.67–69)

This line is difficult. "Thou hast hardened my heart, and makest me" kill thee with the rage of a "murderer," when "I thought to have sacrificed" thee to justice with the calmness of a priest striking a victim.

It must not be omitted, that one of the elder quartos reads, "thou dost stone *thy* heart"; which I suspect to be genuine. The meaning then will be, "thou forcest me" to dismiss thee from the world in the state of the "murdered" without preparation for death, "when I intended" that thy punishment should have been "a sacrifice" atoning for thy crime.

I am glad that I have ended my revisal of this dreadful scene. It is not to be endured.

The beauties of this play impress themselves so strongly upon the attention of the reader, that they can draw no aid from critical illustration. The fiery openness of Othello, magnanimous, artless, and credulous, boundless in his confidence, ardent in his affection, inflexible in his resolution, and obdurate in his revenge; the cool malignity of Iago, silent in his resentment, subtle in his designs, and studious at once of his interest and his vengeance; the soft simplicity of Desdemona, confident of merit, and conscious of innocence, her artless perseverance in her suit, and her slowness to suspect that she can be suspected, are such proofs of Shakespeare's skill in human nature, as, I suppose, it is vain to seek in any modern writer. The gradual progress which Iago makes in the Moor's conviction, and the circumstances which he employs to inflame him, are so artfully natural, that, though it will perhaps not be said of him as he says of himself, that he is "a man not easily jealous," yet we cannot but pity him when at last we find him "perplexed in the extreme."

There is always danger lest wickedness conjoined with abilities should steal upon esteem, though it misses of approbation; but the character of Iago is so conducted, that he is from the first scene to the last hated and despised.

Even the inferior characters of this play would be very conspicuous in any other piece, not only for their justness but their strength. Cassio is brave, benevolent, and honest, ruined only by his want of stubbornness to resist an insidious invitation. Roderigo's suspicious credulity, and impatient submission to the cheats which he sees practiced upon him, and which by persuasion he suffers to be repeated, exhibit a strong picture of a weak mind betrayed by unlawful desires, to a false friend; and the virtue of Emilia is such as we often find, worn loosely, but not cast off, easy to commit small crimes, but quickened and alarmed at atrocious villanies.

The scenes from the beginning to the end are busy, varied by happy interchanges, and regularly promoting the progression of the story; and the narrative in the end, though it tells but what is known already, yet is necessary to produce the death of Othello.

Had the scene opened in Cyprus, and the preceding incidents been occasionally related, there had been little wanting to a drama of the most exact and scrupulous regularity.[5]

LIVES OF THE POETS   In March 1777, a consortium of booksellers persuaded Johnson to undertake a new endeavor. "I am engaged," he informed Boswell, "to write little Lives and little Prefaces, to a little edition of the English Poets" of the past century and a half. In the end, he produced fifty-two *Prefaces Biographical and Critical*, now better known as *Lives of the Poets*. Some of the lives remained "little" (the booksellers had selected the poets, and Johnson did not consider all of them worthy of sustained attention); but many of them expanded in range and interest far beyond Johnson's initial expectation. As Boswell later observed, Johnson pursued the project "with peculiar delight" because he knew this literary territory so very well. In the longest *Lives* (of Milton, Dryden, Addison, and Pope), Johnson paid complex tribute to the predecessors who had mattered most to him as models in his youth—who had shaped the literary

---

5. I.e., according to the rules of the "unities," which Johnson rejects in the Preface.

world in which he had now found his own place. The three-part structure in which Johnson cast most of the prefaces was well calculated to display the powers and precepts accumulated over a lifetime. In the first part, an account of the poet's life, he fulfilled his own dictum (in *Rambler* No. 60) that biography is most useful when it deals in the "minute details" and "domestic privacies" of the subject's daily life; in the second part, an assessment of the poet's character, he implemented his own conviction that the biographer (unlike the eulogist) should forgo pure praise in favor of complex truth; in the third section, a critical review of the poet's work, he found full scope for the close analysis of literary cause and effect that had always informed his reading. "The biographical part of literature," he had once remarked, "is what I love the most." The *Lives* were that love's last labor. In them, the fusion of a favorite genre with a deeply familiar subject produced, in John Wain's words, "the greatest masterpiece of English eighteenth-century criticism."

from Lives of the Poets
from *The Life of Milton*

[ON PARADISE LOST]

Whatever be his subject he never fails to fill the imagination. But his images and descriptions of the scenes or operations of nature do not seem to be always copied from original form, nor to have the freshness, raciness,[1] and energy of immediate observation. He saw nature, as Dryden expresses it, "through the spectacles of books"; and on most occasions calls learning to his assistance. The garden of Eden brings to his mind the vale of Enna, where Proserpine was gathering flowers. Satan makes his way through fighting elements, like Argo between the Cyanean rocks, or Ulysses between the two Sicilian whirlpools, when he shunned Charybdis "on the larboard." The mythological allusions have been justly censured, as not being always used with notice of their vanity; but they contribute variety to the narration, and produce an alternate exercise of the memory and the fancy.

His similes are less numerous and more various than those of his predecessors. But he does not confine himself within the limits of rigorous comparison: his great excellence is amplitude, and he expands the adventitious[2] image beyond the dimensions which the occasion required. Thus, comparing the shield of Satan to the orb of the moon, he crowds the imagination with the discovery of the telescope and all the wonders which the telescope discovers.

Of his moral sentiments it is hardly praise to affirm that they excel those of all other poets; for this superiority he was indebted to his acquaintance with the sacred writings. The ancient epic poets, wanting the light of revelation, were very unskillful teachers of virtue: their principal characters may be great, but they are not amiable. The reader may rise from their works with a greater degree of active or passive fortitude, and sometimes of prudence; but he will be able to carry away few precepts of justice, and none of mercy. * * *

In Milton every line breathes sanctity of thought and purity of manners, except when the train of the narration requires the introduction of the rebellious spirits; and even they are compelled to acknowledge their subjection to God in such a manner as excites reverence and confirms piety.

---

1. "Strong; flavorous; tasting of the soil" (Johnson's   2. Accidental.
Dictionary).

Of human beings there are but two; but those two are the parents of mankind, venerable before their fall for dignity and innocence, and amiable after it for repentance and submission. In their first state their affection is tender without weakness, and their piety sublime without presumption. When they have sinned they show how discord begins in mutual frailty, and how it ought to cease in mutual forbearance; how confidence of the divine favor is forfeited by sin, and how hope of pardon may be obtained by penitence and prayer. A state of innocence we can only conceive, if indeed in our present misery it be possible to conceive it; but the sentiments and worship proper to a fallen and offending being we have all to learn, as we have all to practice.

The poet whatever be done is always great. Our progenitors in their first state conversed with angels; even when folly and sin had degraded them they had not in their humiliation "the port of mean suitors"; and they rise again to reverential regard when we find that their prayers were heard.

As human passions did not enter the world before the Fall, there is in the *Paradise Lost* little opportunity for the pathetic;[3] but what little there is has not been lost. That passion which is peculiar to rational nature, the anguish arising from the consciousness of transgression and the horrors attending the sense of the Divine Displeasure, are very justly described and forcibly impressed. But the passions are moved only on one occasion; sublimity is the general and prevailing quality in this poem—sublimity variously modified, sometimes descriptive, sometimes argumentative.

The defects and faults of *Paradise Lost,* for faults and defects every work of man must have, it is the business of impartial criticism to discover. As in displaying the excellence of Milton I have not made long quotations, because of selecting beauties there had been no end, I shall in the same general manner mention that which seems to deserve censure; for what Englishman can take delight in transcribing passages, which, if they lessen the reputation of Milton, diminish in some degree the honor of our country?

The generality of my scheme does not admit the frequent notice of verbal inaccuracies which Bentley,[4] perhaps better skilled in grammar than in poetry, has often found, though he sometimes made them, and which he imputed to the obtrusions of a reviser whom the author's blindness obliged him to employ. A supposition rash and groundless, if he thought it true; and vile and pernicious, if, as is said, he in private allowed it to be false.

The plan of *Paradise Lost* has this inconvenience, that it comprises neither human actions nor human manners. The man and woman who act and suffer are in a state which no other man or woman can ever know. The reader finds no transaction in which he can be engaged, beholds no condition in which he can by any effort of imagination place himself; he has, therefore, little natural curiosity or sympathy.

We all, indeed, feel the effects of Adam's disobedience; we all sin like Adam, and like him must all bewail our offenses; we have restless and insidious enemies in the fallen angels, and in the blessed spirits we have guardians and friends; in the Redemption of mankind we hope to be included: in the description of heaven and hell we are surely interested, as we are all to reside hereafter either in the regions of horror or of bliss.

But these truths are too important to be new: they have been taught to our infancy; they have mingled with our solitary thoughts and familiar conversation, and are habitually interwoven with the whole texture of life. Being therefore not new they raise no unaccustomed emotion in the mind: what we knew before we cannot learn; what is not unexpected, cannot surprise.

---

3. "Affecting the passions" (Johnson's *Dictionary*).
4. Richard Bentley, a distinguished classical scholar

whose edition of *Paradise Lost* (1732) incorporates numerous misguided "corrections."

Of the ideas suggested by these awful scenes, from some we recede with reverence, except when stated hours require their association; and from others we shrink with horror, or admit them only as salutary inflictions, as counterpoises to our interests and passions. Such images rather obstruct the career of fancy than incite it.

Pleasure and terror are indeed the genuine sources of poetry; but poetical pleasure must be such as human imagination can at least conceive, and poetical terror such as human strength and fortitude may combat. The good and evil of Eternity are too ponderous for the wings of wit; the mind sinks under them in passive helplessness, content with calm belief and humble adoration.

Known truths however may take a different appearance, and be conveyed to the mind by a new train of intermediate images. This Milton has undertaken, and performed with pregnancy and vigor of mind peculiar to himself. Whoever considers the few radical[5] positions which the Scriptures afforded him will wonder by what energetic operations he expanded them to such extent and ramified them to so much variety, restrained as he was by religious reverence from licentiousness of fiction.

Here is a full display of the united force of study and genius; of a great accumulation of materials, with judgment to digest and fancy to combine them: Milton was able to select from nature or from story, from ancient fable or from modern science, whatever could illustrate or adorn his thoughts. An accumulation of knowledge impregnated his mind, fermented by study and exalted by imagination.

It has been therefore said without an indecent hyperbole by one of his encomiasts, that in reading *Paradise Lost* we read a book of universal knowledge.

But original deficience cannot be supplied. The want of human interest is always felt. *Paradise Lost* is one of the books which the reader admires and lays down, and forgets to take up again. None ever wished it longer than it is. Its perusal is a duty rather than a pleasure. We read Milton for instruction, retire harassed and overburdened, and look elsewhere for recreation; we desert our master, and seek for companions.

from *The Life of Pope*

[POPE AND DRYDEN]

In acquired knowledge the superiority must be allowed to Dryden, whose education was more scholastic, and who before he became an author had been allowed more time for study, with better means of information. His mind has a larger range, and he collects his images and illustrations from a more extensive circumference of science. Dryden knew more of man in his general nature, and Pope in his local manners. The notions of Dryden were formed by comprehensive speculation, and those of Pope by minute attention. There is more dignity in the knowledge of Dryden, and more certainty in that of Pope.

Poetry was not the sole praise of either, for both excelled likewise in prose; but Pope did not borrow his prose from his predecessor. The style of Dryden is capricious and varied, that of Pope is cautious and uniform; Dryden obeys the motions of his own mind, Pope constrains his mind to his own rules of composition. Dryden is sometimes vehement and rapid; Pope is always smooth, uniform, and gentle. Dryden's page is a natural field, rising into inequalities, and diversified by the varied exuberance of abundant vegetation; Pope's is a velvet lawn, shaven by the scythe, and leveled by the roller.

5. Original.

Of genius, that power which constitutes a poet; that quality without which judgment is cold and knowledge is inert; that energy which collects, combines, amplifies, and animates—the superiority must, with some hesitation, be allowed to Dryden. It is not to be inferred that of this poetical vigor Pope had only a little, because Dryden had more, for every other writer since Milton must give place to Pope; and even of Dryden it must be said that if he has brighter paragraphs, he has not better poems. Dryden's performances were always hasty, either excited by some external occasion, or extorted by domestic necessity; he composed without consideration, and published without correction. What his mind could supply at call, or gather in one excursion, was all that he sought, and all that he gave. The dilatory caution of Pope enabled him to condense his sentiments, to multiply his images, and to accumulate all that study might produce, or chance might supply. If the flights of Dryden therefore are higher, Pope continues longer on the wing. If of Dryden's fire the blaze is brighter, of Pope's the heat is more regular and constant. Dryden often surpasses expectation, and Pope never falls below it. Dryden is read with frequent astonishment, and Pope with perpetual delight.

This parallel will, I hope, when it is well considered, be found just; and if the reader should suspect me, as I suspect myself, of some partial fondness for the memory of Dryden, let him not too hastily condemn me; for meditation and enquiry may, perhaps, show him the reasonableness of my determination.

[ON THE RAPE OF THE LOCK]

To the praises which have been accumulated on *The Rape of the Lock* by readers of every class, from the critic to the waiting-maid, it is difficult to make any addition. Of that which is universally allowed to be the most attractive of all ludicrous compositions, let it rather be now inquired from what sources the power of pleasing is derived.

Dr. Warburton, who excelled in critical perspicacity, has remarked that the preternatural agents are very happily adapted to the purposes of the poem. The heathen deities can no longer gain attention: we should have turned away from a contest between Venus and Diana. The employment of allegorical persons always excites conviction of its own absurdity: they may produce effects, but cannot conduct actions; when the phantom is put in motion, it dissolves; thus Discord may raise a mutiny, but Discord cannot conduct a march, nor besiege a town. Pope brought into view a new race of Beings, with powers and passions proportionate to their operation. The sylphs and gnomes act at the toilet[6] and the tea-table, what more terrific and more powerful phantoms perform on the stormy ocean or the field of battle; they give their proper help, and do their proper mischief. * * *

In this work are exhibited in a very high degree the two most engaging powers of an author: new things are made familiar, and familiar things are made new. A race of aerial people never heard of before is presented to us in a manner so clear and easy, that the reader seeks for no further information, but immediately mingles with his new acquaintance, adopts their interests and attends their pursuits, loves a sylph and detests a gnome.

That familiar things are made new every paragraph will prove. The subject of the poem is an event below the common incidents of common life; nothing real is

---

6. Dressing table.

introduced that is not seen so often as to be no longer regarded, yet the whole detail of a female-day is here brought before us invested with so much art of decoration that, though nothing is disguised, every thing is striking, and we feel all the appetite of curiosity for that from which we have a thousand times turned fastidiously away.

[ON *ELOISA TO ABELARD*]

The *Epistle of Eloisa to Abelard* is one of the most happy productions of human wit: the subject is so judiciously chosen that it would be difficult, in turning over the annals of the world, to find another which so many circumstances concur to recommend. We regularly interest ourselves most in the fortune of those who most deserve our notice. Abelard and Eloisa were conspicuous in their days for eminence of merit. The heart naturally loves truth. The adventures and misfortunes of this illustrious pair are known from undisputed history. Their fate does not leave the mind in hopeless dejection; for they both found quiet and consolation in retirement and piety. So new and so affecting is their story that it supersedes invention, and imagination ranges at full liberty without straggling into scenes of fable.

The story thus skillfully adopted has been diligently improved. Pope has left nothing behind him which seems more the effect of studious perseverance and laborious revisal. Here is particularly observable the *curiosa felicitas*,[7] a fruitful soil, and careful cultivation. Here is no crudeness of sense, nor asperity of language.

[ON *AN ESSAY ON MAN*]

The *Essay on Man* was a work of great labor and long consideration, but certainly not the happiest of Pope's performances. The subject is perhaps not very proper for poetry, and the poet was not sufficiently master of his subject; metaphysical morality was to him a new study, he was proud of his acquisitions, and, supposing himself master of great secrets, was in haste to teach what he had not learned. Thus he tells us, in the first Epistle, that from the nature of the Supreme Being may be deduced an order of beings such as mankind, because Infinite Excellence can do only what is best. He finds out that these beings must be "somewhere," and that "all the question is whether man be in a wrong place." Surely if, according to the poet's Leibnitzian reasoning,[8] we may infer that man ought to be only because he is, we may allow that his place is the right place, because he has it. Supreme Wisdom is not less infallible in disposing than in creating. But what is meant by "somewhere" and "place" and "wrong place" it had been vain to ask Pope, who probably had never asked himself.

Having exalted himself into the chair of wisdom he tells us much that every man knows, and much that he does not know himself; that we see but little, and that the order of the universe is beyond our comprehension, and opinion not very uncommon; and that there is a chain of subordinate beings "from infinite to nothing," of which himself and his readers are equally ignorant. But he gives us one comfort which, without his help, he supposes unattainable, in the position "that though we are fools, yet God is wise."

This *Essay* affords an egregious instance of the predominance of genius, the dazzling splendor of imagery, and the seductive powers of eloquence. Never were penury of

---

7. Studied inspiration.
8. Johnson believed that Pope had been influenced by

the deterministic philosophy of Gottfried Wilhelm von Leibnitz (1646–1716).

knowledge and vulgarity of sentiment so happily disguised. The reader feels his mind full, though he learns nothing; and when he meets it in its new array no longer knows the talk of his mother and his nurse. When these wonder-working sounds sink into sense, and the doctrine of the *Essay*, disrobed of its ornaments, is left to the powers of its naked excellence, what shall we discover? That we are, in comparison with our Creator, very weak and ignorant; that we do not uphold the chain of existence; and that we could not make one another with more skill than we are made. We may learn yet more: that the arts of human life were copied from the instinctive operations of other animals; that if the world be made for man, it may be said that man was made for geese. To these profound principles of natural knowledge are added some moral instructions equally new: that self-interest well understood will produce social concord; that men are mutual gainers by mutual benefits; that evil is sometimes balanced by good; that human advantages are unstable and fallacious, of uncertain duration and doubtful effect; that our true honor is not to have a great part, but to act it well; that virtue only is our own; and that happiness is always in our power.

Surely a man of no very comprehensive search may venture to say that he has heard all this before, but it was never till now recommended by such a blaze of embellishment or such sweetness of melody. The vigorous contraction of some thoughts, the luxuriant amplification of others, the incidental illustrations, and sometimes the dignity, sometimes the softness of the verses, enchain philosophy, suspend criticism, and oppress judgment by overpowering pleasure.

This is true of many paragraphs; yet if I had undertaken to exemplify Pope's felicity of composition before a rigid critic I should not select the *Essay on Man*, for it contains more lines unsuccessfully labored, more harshness of diction, more thoughts imperfectly expressed, more levity without elegance, and more heaviness without strength, than will easily be found in all his other works.

Letters

To Lord Chesterfield[1]

My Lord: 7 February 1755

I have been lately informed by the proprietor of *The World* that two papers in which my Dictionary is recommended to the public were written by your Lordship.[2] To be so distinguished is an honor which, being very little accustomed to favors from the great, I know not well how to receive, or in what terms to acknowledge.

When upon some slight encouragement I first visited your Lordship I was overpowered like the rest of mankind by the enchantment of your address, and could not forbear to wish that I might boast myself *le vainqueur du vainqueur de la terre*,[3] that I might obtain that regard for which I saw the world contending; but I found my attendance so little encouraged, that neither pride nor modesty would suffer me to continue

1. Philip Dormer Stanhope (1694–1773), fourth Earl of Chesterfield, a politician and man of letters renowned for his elegant manners and his knowledge of the polite world. In 1747 Johnson had dedicated his *Plan of a Dictionary* to Chesterfield but had received neither financial nor moral support from him during the long years of labor on the *Dictionary*.

2. Chesterfield had contributed two essays to Robert Dodsley's periodical *The World*. In these essays he praised the forthcoming *Dictionary* in such a way as to imply that he had been its enlightened sponsor.
3. "The conqueror of the world's conqueror" (the opening line of the epic *Alaric*, by Georges de Scudéry).

it. When I had once adressed your Lordship in public, I had exhausted all the art of pleasing which a retired and uncourtly scholar can possess. I had done all that I could, and no man is well pleased to have his all neglected, be it ever so little.

Seven years, my lord, have now passed since I waited in your outward rooms or was repulsed from your door, during which time I have been pushing on my work through difficulties of which it is useless to complain, and have brought it at last to the verge of publication without one act of assistance, one word of encouragement, or one smile of favor. Such treatment I did not expect, for I never had a patron before.

The shepherd in Virgil grew at last acquainted with Love, and found him a native of the rocks.[4] Is not a patron, my lord, one who looks with unconcern on a man struggling for life in the water and when he has reached ground encumbers him with help?[5] The notice which you have been pleased to take of my labors, had it been early, had been kind; but it has been delayed till I am indifferent and cannot enjoy it, till I am solitary and cannot impart it, till I am known and do not want it.

I hope it is no very cynical asperity not to confess obligation where no benefit has been received, or to be unwilling that the public should consider me as owing that to a patron, which providence has enabled me to do for myself.

Having carried on my work thus far with so little obligation to any favorer of learning I shall not be disappointed though I should conclude it, if less be possible, with less, for I have been long wakened from that dream of hope, in which I once boasted myself with so much exultation, my lord, your Lordship's most humble, most obedient servant,

S.J.

To Hester Thrale

Dear Madam: Bolt Court, Fleetstreet, 19 June 1783

I am sitting down in no cheerful solitude to write a narrative which would once have affected you with tenderness and sorrow, but which you will perhaps pass over now with the careless glance of frigid indifference.[1] For this diminution of regard however, I know not whether I ought to blame you, who may have reasons which I cannot know, and I do not blame myself who have for a great part of human life done you what good I could, and have never done you evil.

I had been disordered in the usual way, and had been relieved by the usual methods, by opium and cathartics,[2] but had rather lessened my dose of opium.

On Monday the 16 I sat for my picture,[3] and walked a considerable way with little inconvenience. In the afternoon and evening I felt myself light and easy, and began to plan schemes of life. Thus I went to bed, and in a short time waked and sat up as has been long my custom when I felt a confusion and indistinctness in my head which lasted, I suppose about half a minute. I was alarmed and prayed God,

4. Johnson alludes to a pastoral poem by Virgil (*Eclogue* 8), in which Love is described as coming from a land of "flinty crags."
5. In his *Dictionary*, Johnson defines "patron" as "commonly a wretch who supports with insolence, and is paid with flattery."
1. As she became more and more attached to Gabriel Piozzi, an Italian musician, Hester Thrale (correctly sensing how angry Johnson would be) began to disengage from their close friendship. Though he knew something had gone wrong, Johnson did not learn of the love affair until a year later, when Mrs. Thrale wrote to inform him of her marriage.
2. Purgatives.
3. Johnson's portrait was being painted.

that however he might afflict my body he would spare my understanding. This prayer, that I might try the integrity of my faculties, I made in Latin verse. The lines were not very good, but I knew them not to be very good, I made them easily, and concluded myself to be unimpaired in my faculties.

Soon after I perceived that I had suffered a paralytic stroke, and that my speech was taken from me. I had no pain, and so little dejection in this dreadful state that I wondered at my own apathy, and considered that perhaps death itself when it should come, would excite less horror than seems now to attend it.

In order to rouse the vocal organs I took two drams. Wine has been celebrated for the production of eloquence; I put myself into violent motion, and, I think, repeated it. But all was vain; I then went to bed, and, strange as it may seem, I think, slept. When I saw light, it was time to contrive what I should do. Though God stopped my speech he left me my hand, I enjoyed a mercy which was not granted to my Dear Friend Lawrence,[4] who now perhaps overlooks me as I am writing and rejoices that I have what he wanted.[5] My first note was necessarily to my servant, who came in talking, and could not immediately comprehend why he should read what I put into his hands.

I then wrote a card to Mr. Allen,[6] that I might have a discreet friend at hand to act as occasion should require. In penning this note I had some difficulty, my hand, I know not how nor why, made wrong letters. I then wrote to Dr. Taylor[7] to come to me, and bring Dr. Heberden, and I sent to Dr. Brocklesby, who is my neighbor. My physicians are very friendly and very disinterested; and give me great hopes, but you may imagine my situation. I have so far recovered my vocal powers, as to repeat the Lord's Prayer with no very imperfect articulation. My memory, I hope, yet remains as it was. But such an attack produces solicitude for the safety of every faculty.

How this will be received by you, I know not, I hope you will sympathize with me, but perhaps

> My Mistress gracious, mild, and good,
> Cries, Is he dumb? 'tis time he should.[8]

But can this be possible, I hope it cannot. I hope that what, when I could speak, I spoke of You, and to You, will be in a sober and serious hour remembered by You, and surely it cannot be remembered but with some degree of kindness. I have loved You with virtuous affection, I have honored You with sincere esteem. Let not all our endearment be forgotten, but let me have in this great distress your pity and your prayers. You see I yet turn to You with my complaints as a settled and unalienable friend, do not, do not drive me from You, for I have not deserved either neglect or hatred.

To the girls,[9] who do not write often, for Susy has written only once, and Miss Thrale owes me a letter, I earnestly recommend as their guardian and friend, that they remember their Creator in the days of their youth.[1]

---

4. Johnson's favorite physician, Dr. Thomas Lawrence, had died earlier that month after suffering a stroke.
5. Lacked.
6. Johnson's printer and neighbor, Edmund Allen.
7. The clergyman John Taylor, one of Johnson's oldest and closest friends.
8. Johnson adapts a couplet from Swift's Verses on the Death of Dr. Swift: "The Queen, so gracious, mild and good, / Cries, 'Is he gone? 'Tis time he should'" (lines 181–82).
9. Hester Thrale's four surviving daughters: Hester Maria ("Miss Thrale"), Susanna ("Susy"), Sophia, and Cecilia.
1. "Remember now thy Creator in the days of thy youth, while the evil days come not" (Ecclesiastes 12.1).

I suppose You may wish to know how my disease is treated by the physicians. They put a blister upon my back, and two from my ear to my throat, one on a side. The blister on the back has done little, and those on the throat have not risen. I bullied, and bounced, (it sticks to our last sand)[2] and compelled the apothecary to make his salve according to the Edinburgh dispensatory[3] that it might adhere better. I have two on now of my own prescription. They likewise give me salt of hartshorn, which I take with no great confidence, but am satisfied that what can be done, is done for me.

O God, give me comfort and confidence in Thee, forgive my sins, and if it be thy good pleasure, relieve my diseases for Jesus Christ's sake. Amen.

I am almost ashamed of this querulous letter, but now it is written, let it go. I am Madam, Your most humble servant,

SAM. JOHNSON

To Hester Thrale Piozzi

Madam: 2 July 1784

If I interpret your letter right, You are ignominiously married,[1] if it is yet undone, let us once talk together. If You have abandoned your children and your religion, God forgive your wickedness; if You have forfeited your fame, and your country, may your folly do no further mischief.[2]

If the last act is yet to do, I, who have loved you, esteemed you, reverenced you, and served you, I who long thought You the first of humankind, entreat that before your fate is irrevocable, I may once more see You. I was, I once was, Madam, most truly yours,

SAM. JOHNSON

I will come down if you permit it.

To Hester Thrale Piozzi

Dear Madam: London, 8 July 1784

What You have done, however I may lament it, I have no pretense to resent, as it has not been injurious to me. I therefore breathe out one sigh more of tenderness perhaps useless, but at least sincere.

I wish that God may grant You every blessing, that you may be happy in this world for its short continuance, and eternally happy in a better state. And whatever I can contribute to your happiness, I am very ready to repay for that kindness which soothed twenty years of a life radically wretched.

Do not think slightly of the advice which I now presume to offer. Prevail upon Mr. Piozzi to settle in England. You may live here with more dignity than in Italy, and with more security. Your rank will be higher, and your fortune more under your

---

2. "Time, that on all things lays his lenient hand, / Yet tames not this; it sticks to our last sand" (Pope, *Epistle to Cobham*, lines 224–25).
3. Medical manual.
1. Hester Thrale had written on 30 June to inform John- son of her marriage to Gabriel Piozzi.
2. Johnson's objections to Gabriel Piozzi include the fact that he is a musician (and therefore socially inferior), a Catholic, and an Italian.

own eye. I desire not to detail all my reasons; but every argument of prudence and interest is for England, and only some phantoms of imagination seduce you to Italy.

I am afraid, however, that my counsel is vain, yet I have eased my heart by giving it.

When Queen Mary took the resolution of sheltering herself in England, the Archbishop of St. Andrew's attempting to dissuade her,[1] attended on her journey and when they came to the irremeable[2] stream that separated the two kingdoms, walked by her side into the water, in the middle of which he seized her bridle, and with earnestness proportioned to her danger and his own affection, pressed her to return. The Queen went forward.—If the parallel reaches thus far; may it go no further. The tears stand in my eyes.

I am going into Derbyshire,[3] and hope to be followed by your good wishes, for I am with great affection, Your most humble servant,

SAM. JOHNSON

Any letters that come for me hither, will be sent me.

✦ ✦ ⛬ ✦ ✦

James Boswell
1740–1795

"I have discovered," James Boswell announced at age twenty-two in the journal he had just commenced, "that we may be in some degree whatever character we choose." The possibilities opened up by this discovery both exhilarated and troubled him. Neither the "choosing" nor the "being" turned out to be as simple as he expected, in part because some alternate choice always beckoned. In the pages of his journal, Boswell performed his excited choices and anxious reconsiderations. The oscillation did much to drive the intricate comedy and intermittent pathos, the energetic posing and fervent self-scrutiny of the diaries he kept all his adult life, and of the published books he crafted from them.

Boswell's parents had chosen their own characters early, and had stuck to them assiduously. His father was a Scots laird—heir to an ancient family and a landed estate—and a distinguished jurist, serving as justice on Scotland's highest courts. His mother was an impassioned Calvinist, who numbered among her many strictures an abhorrence of the theater; the actors' freedom of character-choice, which made the playhouse for her a place of sinful deception, would make it the site of a lifelong enchantment for her son. Boswell's parents had chosen firmly for their first-born too. James was to become, like his father, an eminent lawyer and respectable landowner.

Boswell chafed at the narrowness of the scheme. Struggling (he later recalled) "against paternal affection, ambition, interest," he ran away to London for a short spell at age eighteen and returned there at twenty-two, seeking a commission as a soldier with the king's personal bodyguard, a post that would have secured him lifelong residence in the city, flashy uniforms, and ample opportunities to display himself in them. While Boswell waited for this prospect to

---

1. Johnson draws on a semifictional account of Mary Queen of Scots' fateful decision to take refuge in England. According to this version, she crossed the river on horseback, attended by John Hamilton, Archbishop of St. Andrews.

2. "Admitting no return" (Johnson's *Dictionary*).

3. The home of John Taylor.

materialize (it never did), he found his real calling. He started to keep a copious journal, narrating each day in succession, dispatching the text in weekly packets to his friend John Johnston back home in Scotland. Here too was self-display, intricately contrived. Boswell managed his journal as a kind of manuscript theater—often written as a play text, complete with dialogue and stage directions—for an audience of one (the performance of his journal texts for a wider reading public would later become his literary life's work). London, the theatrical city, teemed with "characters" living and dead, real and fictional, whom Boswell by turns and in combinations strove to "be": Addison, Steele, and their imaginary paragon of self-possession Mr. Spectator; Captain Macheath from *The Beggar's Opera* (on whose adventures Boswell modeled some of his own sexual exploits); the actors Thomas Sheridan and David Garrick; and most important, Garrick's old teacher Samuel Johnson, whose writings had provided Boswell with a model of moral firmness more attractive than his father's, and who befriended the young diarist six months into his London stay.

The friendship with Johnson gave Boswell's journal a new purpose (to record the conversations of this dazzling talker) and his life a new direction. Reconciled to his father's plan, Boswell studied law in Holland and, as reward for his painfully diligent endeavors, made the Grand Tour of Europe, where he collected the conversation and the counsel of further celebrities: the French iconoclasts Voltaire and Rousseau, and the Corsican rebel leader Pasquale Paoli, then fighting to free his island from foreign domination. Returning to Scotland in 1766, Boswell took up the life his father had mapped for him, settling in Edinburgh, and becoming (as he haughtily informed his disreputable friend John Wilkes) "a Scottish lawyer, a Scottish laird, and a Scottish married man." In each of these roles, though, he repeatedly broke character. He went down to London almost every spring, ostensibly to cultivate his legal practice but really to renew his old absorptions: in theater, in sexual adventure, in the spellbinding company of Johnson and the group of artists, writers, and thinkers who surrounded him.

Boswell yearned to join their number not merely as admirer but as eminent author, and he soon did. Over the ensuing years, he produced much journalism and some verse, as well as three books in which he explored with increasing audacity the potential of his own diary as a public text—as a vehicle of entertainment, instruction, profit, and fame. He pursued for the journal form a print authority it had not previously possessed, devising ways for it to encroach upon, even to colonize, territory and tasks traditionally reserved to other genres: travel book, "character" sketch, biography. In his first attempt, *An Account of Corsica . . . and Memoirs of Pascal Paoli* (1769), he recast his original travel journal (rearranging the entries, dropping the dates) to produce a heroic portrait of his friend the liberator. In his second experiment, *A Journal of a Tour to the Hebrides with Samuel Johnson* (1785), which appeared the year after Johnson's death, the imperative to portraiture was even more pronounced. The public craved accounts of the lost titan, and this time Boswell met that demand a different way. He presented his journal *as* a journal, with scrupulously dated, plentifully narrated consecutive entries rich in the "minute details of daily life" that Johnson himself had stipulated as the criteria for good biography. The book struck readers as startlingly new. Some mocked it for its minutiae ("How are we all with rapture touched," exclaimed one versifier, "to see / Where, when, and at what hour, you swallowed tea!"), while many praised its veracity and abundance.

There was much more where that came from. In *The Life of Samuel Johnson, LL.D.* (1791), Boswell deployed the *Tour*'s techniques on a massive scale. Drawing on his diaries, and on years of arduous research among Johnson's many acquaintances, Boswell built a thousand-page biography that is largely a book of talk, of conversations diligently recorded and deftly dramatized, the culmination of the textual theater that Boswell had long practiced in manuscript. Johnson's capacious mind and imposing presence find embodiment in a text dense with accumulated time, told and retold over the span of almost three decades that stretches from Boswell's first Johnsonian journal entry to the biography's publication. Pleased with the book's commercial success, stung by charges that he had been either too partial to Johnson or too critical of him, Boswell worked at two further editions (in which his footnotes swelled with new information and rebuttals). He died at fifty-five, unmade by alcoholism, by venereal disease, and by the violent depressions that accompanied his ongoing uncertainty as to what he might "be" and had become.

His books sustained his fame, though ever since the *Life*'s first appearance, readers have debated the degree of its accuracy and the merits of its portraiture. Two centuries later, Boswell's biography has become a touchstone text for the problem of the "documentary"—the question of how art and "fact" should merge in representations of historical events. Over the past eighty years the debate has been deepened by the unexpected recovery of Boswell's original papers, including the diaries that he drew on and boasted of in his published books. The papers had long been given up for lost, but masses of them had actually been stashed and forgotten by various descendants in odd receptacles (cabinet, croquet box, grain loft) on estates scattered across Scotland and Ireland. The papers' recovery took more than twenty years; the process of their publication continues. Taken together, Boswell's papers and his published works make it possible to trace the intricate course by which the flux of his energetic, agitated life became fixed in text.

 For additional resources on Boswell, including selections from *A Journal of a Tour to the Hebrides with Dr. Samuel Johnson,* go to *The Longman Anthology of British Literature* Web site at www.myliteraturekit.com.

from London Journal
[A SCOT IN LONDON]

Wednesday, 1 December [1762]. * * * On Tuesday I wanted to have a silver-hilted sword, but upon examining my pockets as I walked up the Strand,[1] I found that I had left the most of my guineas at home and had not enough to pay for it with me. I determined to make a trial of the civility of my fellow-creatures, and what effect my external appearance and address would have. I accordingly went to the shop of Mr. Jefferys, sword-cutter to His Majesty, looked at a number of his swords, and at last picked out a very handsome one at five guineas. "Mr. Jefferys," said I, "I have not money here to pay for it. Will you trust me?" "Upon my word, Sir," said he, "you must excuse me. It is a thing we never do to a stranger." I bowed genteelly and said, "Indeed, Sir, I believe it is not right." However, I stood and looked at him, and he looked at me. "Come, Sir," cried he, "I will trust you." "Sir," said I, "if you had not trusted me, I should not have bought it from you." He asked my name and place of abode, which I told him. I then chose a belt, put the sword on, told him I would call and pay it tomorrow, and walked off. I called this day and paid him. "Mr. Jefferys," said I, "there is your money. You paid me a very great compliment. I am much obliged to you. But pray don't do such a thing again. It is dangerous." "Sir," said he, "we know our men. I would have trusted you with the value of a hundred pounds." This I think was a good adventure and much to my honor. * * *

This afternoon I was surprised with the arrival of Lady Betty Macfarlane, Lady Anne Erskine, Captain Erskine, and Miss Dempster, who were come to the Red Lion Inn at Charing Cross. It seems Lady Betty had written to the laird that if he would not come down, she would come up; and upon his giving her an indolent answer, like a woman of spirit, she put her resolution in practice. I immediately went to them.[2]

To tell the plain truth, I was vexed at their coming. For to see just the plain *hamely*[3] Fife family hurt my grand ideas of London. Besides, I was now upon a plan of

---

1. A major commercial street in the West End of London.
2. With the exception of Miss Dempster, the sister of his friend George, Boswell refers to the daughters and son of

the Fifth Earl of Kellie ("the laird"). The family came from Fife, a county in eastern Scotland.
3. Scots dialect for "homely," home-like.

studying polite reserved behavior, which is the only way to keep up dignity of character. And as I have a good share of pride, which I think is very proper and even noble, I am hurt with the taunts of ridicule and am unsatisfied if I do not feel myself something of a superior animal. This has always been my favorite idea in my best moments. Indeed, I have been obliged to deviate from it by a variety of circumstances. After my wild expedition to London in the year 1760, after I got rid of the load of serious reflection which then burthened me, by being always in Lord Eglinton's company, very fond of him, and much caressed by him, I became dissipated and thoughtless.[4] When my father forced me down to Scotland, I was at first very low-spirited, although to appearance very high. I afterwards from my natural vivacity endeavored to make myself easy; and like a man who takes to drinking to banish care, I threw myself loose as a heedless, dissipated, rattling fellow who might say or do every ridiculous thing. This made me sought after by everybody for the present hour, but I found myself a very inferior being; and I found many people presuming to treat me as such, which notwithstanding of my appearance of undiscerning gaiety, gave me much pain. I was, in short, a character very different from what God intended me and I myself chose. I remember my friend Johnston[5] told me one day after my return from London that I had turned out different from what he imagined, as he thought I would resemble Mr. Addison.[6] I laughed and threw out some loud sally of humor, but the observation struck deep. Indeed, I must do myself the justice to say that I always resolved to be such a man whenever my affairs were made easy and I got upon my own footing. For as I despaired of that, I endeavored to lower my views and just to be a good-humored comical being, well liked either as a waiter, a common soldier, a clerk in Jamaica, or some other odd out-of-the-way sphere. Now, when my father at last put me into an independent situation, I felt my mind regain its native dignity. I felt strong dispositions to be a Mr. Addison. Indeed, I had accustomed myself so much to laugh at everything that it required time to render my imagination solid and give me just notions of real life and of religion. But I hoped by degrees to attain to some degree of propriety. Mr. Addison's character in sentiment, mixed with a little of the gaiety of Sir Richard Steele and the manners of Mr. Digges,[7] were the ideas which I aimed to realize.

Indeed, I must say that Digges has more or as much of the deportment of a man of fashion as anybody I ever saw; and he keeps up this so well that he never once lessened upon me even on an intimate acquaintance, although he is now and then somewhat melancholy, under which it is very difficult to preserve dignity; and this I think is particularly to be admired in Mr. Digges. Indeed, he and I never came to familiarity, which is justly said to beget contempt. The great art of living easy and happy in society is to study proper behavior, and even with our most intimate friends to observe politeness; otherwise we will insensibly treat each other with a degree of rudeness, and each will find himself despised in some measure by the other. As I was therefore pursuing this laudable plan, I was vexed at the arrival of the Kellie family, with whom when in Scotland I had been in the greatest familiarity. Had they not come for a twelvemonth, I should have been somewhat established in my address, but as I had been but a fortnight from them, I could not without the appearance of strong

4. At the age of 18, Boswell had run away to London, where he impulsively converted to Catholicism. The tenth Earl of Eglinton, a charming and generous rake, weaned him from religion by turning him into a libertine.
5. John Johnston of Grange, Boswell's close friend, to whom he was sending the journal in weekly installments.
6. Joseph Addison, author, with Sir Richard Steele, of the *Tatler* and *Spectator* papers. Addison was particularly identified with the character of the silent, all-seeing Mr. Spectator.
7. West Digges, an actor in Edinburgh, particularly known for his portrayal of Macheath in *The Beggar's Opera*.

affectation appear much different from what they had seen me. I accordingly was very free, but rather more silent, which they imputed to my dullness, and roasted me about London's not being agreeable to me. I bore it pretty well, and left them.

* * *

Wednesday, 15 December [1762]. The enemies of the people of England who would have them considered in the worst light represent them as selfish, beef-eaters, and cruel. In this view I resolved today to be a true-born Old Englishman. I went into the City[8] to Dolly's Steak-house in Paternoster Row and swallowed my dinner by myself to fulfill the charge of selfishness; I had a large fat beefsteak to fulfill the charge of beef-eating; and I went at five o'clock to the Royal Cockpit in St. James's Park and saw cockfighting for about five hours to fulfill the charge of cruelty.

A beefsteak house is a most excellent place to dine at. You come in there to a warm, comfortable, large room, where a number of people are sitting at table. You take whatever place you find empty; call for what you like, which you get well and cleverly dressed. You may either chat or not as you like. Nobody minds you, and you pay very reasonably. My dinner (beef, bread and beer and waiter) was only a shilling. The waiters make a great deal of money by these pennies.[9] Indeed, I admire the English for attending to small sums, as many smalls make a great, according to the proverb.

At five I filled my pockets with gingerbread and apples (quite the method), put on my old clothes and laced hat, laid by my watch, purse, and pocketbook, and with oaken stick in my hand sallied to the pit. I was too soon there. So I went into a low inn, sat down amongst a parcel of arrant blackguards, and drank some beer. The sentry near the house had been very civil in showing me the way. It was very cold. I bethought myself of the poor fellow, so I carried out a pint of beer myself to him. He was very thankful and drank my health cordially. He told me his name was Hobard, that he was a watchmaker but in distress for debt, and enlisted that his creditors might not touch him.

I then went to the Cockpit, which is a circular room in the middle of which the cocks fight. It is seated round with rows gradually rising. The pit and the seats are all covered with mat. The cocks, nicely cut and dressed and armed with silver heels, are set down and fight with amazing bitterness and resolution. Some of them were quickly dispatched. One pair fought three quarters of an hour. The uproar and noise of betting is prodigious. A great deal of money made a very quick circulation from hand to hand. There was a number of professed gamblers there. An old cunning dog whose face I had seen at Newmarket[1] sat by me a while. I told him I knew nothing of the matter.[2] "Sir," said he, "you have as good a chance as anybody." He thought I would be a good subject for him. I was young-like. But he found himself balked. I was shocked to see the distraction and anxiety of the betters. I was sorry for the poor cocks. I looked round to see if any of the spectators pitied them when mangled and torn in a most cruel manner, but I could not observe the smallest relenting sign in any countenance. I was therefore not ill pleased to see them endure mental torment. Thus did I complete my true English day, and came home pretty much fatigued and pretty much confounded at the strange turn of this people.

---

8. The older, eastern half of London, which included the centers of finance, law, and journalism.
9. The waiter's tip was one of the 12 pence that made up a shilling.
1. A town in Suffolk famous for horse racing.
2. About betting on cockfighting.

[LOUISA][1]

Wednesday, 12 January [1763]. Louisa and I agreed that at eight at night she would meet me in the piazzas of Covent Garden.[2] I was quite elevated, and felt myself able and undaunted to engage in the wars of the Paphian Queen.[3]

I dined at Sheridan's[4] very heartily. He showed to my conviction that Garrick[5] did not play the great scene in the Second Part of *King Henry*[6] with propriety. "People," said he, "in this age know when particular lines or even speeches are well spoke; but they do not study character, which is a matter of the utmost moment, as people of different characters feel and express their feelings very differently. For want of a knowledge of this, Mr. Barry[7] acted the distress of Othello, the Moorish warrior whose stubborn soul was hard to bend, and that of Castalio, the gentle lover who was all tenderness, in the self-same way. Now Mr. Garrick in that famous scene whines most piteously when he ought to upbraid. Shakespeare has discovered[8] there a most intimate knowledge of human nature. He shows you the King worn out with sickness and so weak that he faints. He had usurped the crown by the force of arms and was convinced that it must be held with spirit. He saw his son given up to low debauchery. He was anxious and vexed to think of the anarchy that would ensue at his death. Upon discovering that the Prince had taken the crown from his pillow, and concluding him desirous of his death, he is fired with rage. He starts up. He cries, 'Go chide him hither!' His anger animates him so much that he throws aside his distemper. Nature furnishes all her strength for one last effort. He is for a moment renewed. He is for a moment the spirited Henry the Fourth. He upbraids him with bitter sarcasm and bold figures. And then what a beautiful variety is there, when, upon young Harry's contrition, he falls on his neck and melts into parental tenderness."

I yielded this point to Sheridan candidly. But upon his attacking Garrick as a tragedian in his usual way, I opposed him keenly, and declared he was prejudiced; because the world thought him a good tragic actor. "So do I, Sir," said he; "I think him the best I ever saw." BOSWELL: "Except yourself, Mr. Sheridan. But come, we shall take this for granted. The world then think him near equal or as good as you in what you excel in." SHERIDAN: "Sir, I am not a bit prejudiced. I don't value acting. I shall suppose that I was the greatest actor that ever lived and universally acknowledged so, I would not choose that it should be remembered. I would have it erased out of the anecdotes of my life. Acting is a poor thing in the present state of the stage. For my own part, I engaged in it merely as a step to something greater, a just notion of eloquence." This was in a good measure true. But he certainly talked too extravagantly.

An old Irish maid, or rather an Irish old maid (O most hideous character!) dined with us. She was indeed a terrible Joy.[9] She was a woman of knowledge and criticism and correct taste. But there came to tea a Miss Mowat who played once on the stage here for a winter or two, a lovely girl. Many an amorous glance did I exchange with her. I was this day quite flashy with love. We often addressed our

---

1. An actress at Covent Garden Theatre, whose real name was Mrs. Lewis.
2. The arcades along the northern perimeter of the square, designed by Inigo Jones and popularly known as "piazzas," were a famous trysting place.
3. Venus.
4. Thomas Sheridan, Irish actor and teacher of elocution; father of Richard Brinsley Sheridan, author of *The School for Scandal*.

5. David Garrick (1717–1779), the most celebrated actor-manager of his age.
6. Shakespeare's *2 Henry IV* 4.5.
7. Spranger Barry, a well-known actor who played the protagonist in Shakespeare's *Othello* and in Otway's *The Orphan*.
8. Revealed.
9. Irishwoman.

discourse to each other. I hope to see her again; and yet what have I to do with any-body but dear Louisa?

At the appointed hour of eight I went to the piazzas, where I sauntered up and down for a while in a sort of trembling suspense, I knew not why. At last my charm-ing companion appeared, and I immediately conducted her to a hackney coach which I had ready waiting, pulled up the blinds, and away we drove to the destined scene of delight. We contrived to seem as if we had come off a journey, and carried in a bundle our nightclothes, handkerchiefs, and other little things. We also had with us some almond biscuits, or as they call them in London, macaroons, which looked like provision on the road. On our arrival at Hayward's[1] we were shown into the parlor, in the same manner that any decent couple would be. I here thought proper to conceal my own name (which the people of the house had never heard), and assumed the name of Mr. Digges. We were shown up to the very room where he slept. I said my cousin, as I called him, was very well. That Ceres and Bacchus might in moderation lend their assistance to Venus,[2] I ordered a genteel supper and some wine.

Louisa told me she had two aunts who carried her over to France when she was a girl, and that she could once speak French as fluently as English. We talked a little in it, and agreed that we would improve ourselves by reading and speaking it every day. I asked her if we did not just look like man and wife. "No," said she, "we are too fond for married people." No wonder that she may have a bad idea of that union, considering how bad it was for her. She has contrived a pretty device for a seal.[3] A heart is gently warmed by Cupid's flame, and Hymen[4] comes with his rude torch and extinguishes it. She said she found herself quite in a flutter. "Why, really," said I, "reason sometimes has no power. We have no occasion to be frightened, and yet we are both a little so. Indeed, I preserve a tolerable presence of mind." I rose and kissed her, and conscious that I had no occasion to doubt my qualifications as a gallant,[5] I joked about it: "How curious would it be if I should be so frightened that we should rise as we lay down." She reproved my wanton language by a look of modesty. The bells of St. Bride's church rung their merry chimes hard by. I said that the bells in Cupid's court would be this night set a-ringing for joy at our union.

We supped cheerfully and agreeably and drank a few glasses, and then the maid came and put the sheets, well aired, upon the bed. I now contemplated my fair prize. Louisa is just twenty-four, of a tall rather than short figure, finely made in person, with a handsome face and an enchanting languish in her eyes. She dresses with taste. She has sense, good humour, and vivacity, and looks quite a woman in genteel life. As I mused on this elevating subject, I could not help being somehow pleasingly confounded to think that so fine a woman was at this moment in my possession, that without any motives of interest[6] she had come with me to an inn, agreed to be my intimate companion, as to be my bedfellow all night, and to permit me the full enjoyment of her person.

When the servant left the room, I embraced her warmly and begged that she would not now delay my felicity. She declined to undress before me, and begged I would retire and send her one of the maids. I did so, gravely desiring the girl to go up

---

1. Fleet Street inn, recommended to Boswell by Digges.
2. Deities of grain, wine, and love, respectively. Boswell refers to the proverb, "without Ceres and Bacchus, Venus grows cold."
3. A personal emblem or insignia, which would be im-pressed on the wax sealing a letter.

4. God of marriage, who traditionally carries a torch.
5. A lover; Boswell jokes that, were he anxious, he might lose his erection, in which case the couple would "rise" from the bed, without consummation.
6. Mercenary motives.

to Mrs. Digges. I then took a candle in my hand and walked out to the yard. The night was very dark and very cold. I experienced for some minutes the rigors of the season, and called into my mind many terrible ideas of hardships, that I might make a transition from such dreary thoughts to the most gay and delicious feelings. I then caused make a bowl of negus,[7] very rich of the fruit, which I caused be set in the room as a reviving cordial.

I came softly into the room, and in a sweet delirium slipped into bed and was immediately clasped in her snowy arms and pressed to her milk-white bosom. Good heavens, what a loose[8] did we give to amorous dalliance! The friendly curtain of darkness concealed our blushes. In a moment I felt myself animated with the strongest powers of love, and, from my dearest creature's kindness, had a most luscious feast. Proud of my godlike vigor, I soon resumed the noble game. I was in full glow of health. Sobriety had preserved me from effeminacy[9] and weakness, and my bounding blood beat quick and high alarms. A more voluptuous night I never enjoyed. Five times was I fairly lost in supreme rapture. Louisa was madly fond of me; she declared I was a prodigy, and asked me if this was not extraordinary for human nature. I said twice as much might be, but this was not, although in my own mind I was somewhat proud of my performance. She said it was what there was no just reason to be proud of. But I told her I could not help it. She said it was what we had in common with the beasts. I said no. For we had it highly improved by the pleasures of sentiment.[1] I asked her what she thought enough. She gently chid me for asking such questions, but said two times. I mentioned the Sunday's assignation,[2] when I was in such bad spirits, told her in what agony of mind I was, and asked her if she would not have despised me for my imbecility. She declared she would not, as it was what people had not in their own power.

She often insisted that we should compose ourselves to sleep before I would consent to it. At last I sunk to rest in her arms and she in mine. I found the negus, which had a fine flavor, very refreshing to me. Louisa had an exquisite mixture of delicacy and wantonness that made me enjoy her with more relish. Indeed I could not help roving in fancy to the embraces of some other ladies which my lively imagination strongly pictured. I don't know if that was altogether fair. However, Louisa had all the advantage. She said she was quite fatigued and could neither stir leg nor arm. She begged I would not despise her, and hoped my love would not be altogether transient. I have painted this night as well as I could. The description is faint; but I surely may be styled a Man of Pleasure.

Thursday, 20 January [1763][3] * * * I then went to Louisa. With excellent address did I carry on this interview, as the following scene, I trust, will make appear:

LOUISA: My dear Sir! I hope you are well today.
BOSWELL: Excessively well, I thank you. I hope I find you so.
LOUISA: No, really, Sir. I am distressed with a thousand things. (Cunning jade, her circumstances![4]) I really don't know what to do.

7. A drink of wine and hot water, sweetened and flavored.
8. What freedom.
9. Impotence.
1. Feelings of affection.
2. During an assignation ten days earlier, Boswell had attempted—unsuccessfully—to consummate the relationship.

3. The day before, Boswell had observed in himself the unmistakable signs of venereal disease: "Too, too plain was Signor Gonorrhoea!" He then visited his doctor, who confirmed the diagnosis and asserted "that the woman who gave it me could not but know about it."
4. During the course of the relationship, Louisa had talked often about her debts, and Boswell had made her a loan.

BOSWELL: Do you know that I have been very unhappy since I saw you?

LOUISA: How so, Sir?

BOSWELL: Why, I am afraid that you don't love me so well, nor have not such a regard for me, as I thought you had.

LOUISA: Nay, dear Sir! [*Seeming unconcerned.*]

BOSWELL: Pray, Madam, have I no reason?

LOUISA: No, indeed, Sir, you have not.

BOSWELL: Have I no reason, Madam? Pray think.

LOUISA: Sir!

BOSWELL: Pray, Madam, in what state of health have you been in for some time?

LOUISA: Sir, you amaze me.

BOSWELL: I have but too strong, too plain reason to doubt of your regard. I have for some days observed the symptoms of disease, but was unwilling to believe you so very ungenerous. But now, Madam, I am thoroughly convinced.

LOUISA: Sir, you have terrified me. I protest I know nothing of the matter.

BOSWELL: Madam, I have had no connection with any woman but you these two months. I was with my surgeon this morning, who declared I had got a strong infection, and that she from whom I had it could not be ignorant of it. Madam, such a thing in this case is worse than from a woman of the town,[5] as from her you may expect it. You have used me very ill. I did not deserve it. You know you said where there was no confidence, there was no breach of trust. But surely I placed some confidence in you. I am sorry that I was mistaken.

LOUISA: Sir, I will confess to you that about three years ago I was very bad.[6] But for these fifteen months I have been quite well. I appeal to God Almighty that I am speaking true; and for these six months I have had to do with no man but yourself.

BOSWELL: But by G-d, Madam, I have been with none but you, and here am I very bad.

LOUISA: Well, Sir, by the same solemn oath I protest that I was ignorant of it.

BOSWELL: Madam, I wish much to believe you. But I own I cannot upon this occasion believe a miracle.

LOUISA: Sir, I cannot say more to you. But you will leave me in the greatest misery. I shall lose your esteem. I shall be hurt in the opinion of everybody, and in my circumstances.

BOSWELL [*to himself*]: What the devil does the confounded jilt mean by being hurt in her circumstances? This is the grossest cunning. But I won't take notice of that at all.—Madam, as to the opinion of everybody, you need not be afraid. I was going to joke and say that I never boast of a lady's *favors*. But I give you my word of honor that you shall not be discovered.

LOUISA: Sir, this is being more generous than I could expect.

BOSWELL: I hope, Madam, you will own that since I have been with you I have always behaved like a man of honor.

LOUISA: You have indeed, Sir.

BOSWELL [*rising*]: Madam, your most obedient servant.

During all this conversation I really behaved with a manly composure and polite dignity that could not fail to inspire an awe, and she was pale as ashes and trembled and faltered. Thrice did she insist on my staying a little longer, as it was

5. Prostitute.　　　　　6. Severely infected.

probably the last time that I should be with her. She could say nothing to the purpose. And I sat silent. As I was going, said she, "I hope, Sir, you will give me leave to inquire after your health." "Madam," said I, archly, "I fancy it will be needless for some weeks." She again renewed her request. But unwilling to be plagued any more with her, I put her off by saying I might perhaps go to the country, and left her. I was really confounded at her behavior. There is scarcely a possibility that she could be innocent of the crime of horrid imposition. And yet her positive asseverations really stunned me. She is in all probability a most consummate dissembling whore.

Thus ended my intrigue with the fair Louisa, which I flattered myself so much with, and from which I expected at least a winter's safe copulation. It is indeed very hard. I cannot say, like young fellows who get themselves clapped in a bawdy house,[7] that I will take better care again. For I really did take care. However, since I am fairly trapped, let me make the best of it. I have not got it from imprudence. It is merely the chance of war.

I then called at Drury Lane for Mr. Garrick. He was vastly good to me. "Sir," said he, "you will be a very great man. And when you are so, remember the year 1763. I want to contribute my part towards saving you. And pray, will you fix a day when I shall have the pleasure of treating you with tea?" I fixed next day. "Then, Sir," said he, "the cups shall dance and the saucers skip."

What he meant by my being a great man I can understand. For really, to speak seriously, I think there is a blossom about me of something more distinguished than the generality of mankind. But I am much afraid that this blossom will never swell into fruit, but will be nipped and destroyed by many a blighting heat and chilling frost. Indeed, I sometimes indulge noble reveries of having a regiment, of getting into Parliament, making a figure, and becoming a man of consequence in the state. But these are checked by dispiriting reflections on my melancholy temper and imbecility of mind. Yet I may probably become sounder and stronger as I grow up. Heaven knows. I am resigned. I trust to Providence. I was quite in raptures with Garrick's kindness—the man whom from a boy I used to adore and look upon as a heathen god—to find him paying me so much respect! How amiable is he in comparison of Sheridan! I was this day with him what the French call *un étourdi* [a scatterbrain]. I gave free vent to my feelings. Love[8] was by, to whom I cried, "This, Sir, is the real scene." And taking Mr. Garrick cordially by the hand, "Thou greatest of men," said I, "I cannot express how happy you make me." This, upon my soul, was no flattery. He saw it was not. And the dear great man was truly pleased with it. This scene gave me a charming flutter of spirits and dispelled my former gloom. * * *

[FIRST MEETING WITH JOHNSON]

Monday, 16 May [1763]. Temple[1] and his brother breakfasted with me. I went to Love's to try to recover some of the money which he owes me. But, alas, a single guinea was all I could get. He was just going to dinner, so I stayed and eat a bit, though I was angry at myself afterwards. I drank tea at Davies's[2] in Russell Street, and about seven came in the great Mr. Samuel Johnson, whom I have so long wished to

---

7. Acquire gonorrhea in a brothel.
8. James Love, actor and longtime friend of Boswell.
1. William Johnson Temple, Boswell's most intimate and

upstanding friend.
2. Thomas Davies, actor and bookseller.

see. Mr. Davies introduced me to him. As I knew his mortal antipathy at the Scotch, I cried to Davies, "Don't tell where I come from." However, he said, "From Scotland." "Mr. Johnson," said I, "indeed I come from Scotland, but I cannot help it." "Sir," replied he, "that, I find, is what a very great many of your countrymen cannot help." Mr. Johnson is a man of a most dreadful appearance. He is a very big man, is troubled with sore eyes, the palsy, and the king's evil.[3] He is very slovenly in his dress and speaks with a most uncouth voice. Yet his great knowledge and strength of expression command vast respect and render him very excellent company. He has great humor and is a worthy man. But his dogmatical roughness of manners is disagreeable. I shall mark what I remember of his conversation. * * *

1762–1763   1950

An Account of My Last Interview with David Hume, Esq.
Partly recorded in my Journal, partly enlarged from my memory, 3 March 1777[1]

On Sunday forenoon the 7 of July 1776, being too late for church, I went to see Mr. David Hume, who was returned from London and Bath,[2] just a-dying. I found him alone, in a reclining posture in his drawing room. He was lean, ghastly, and quite of an earthy appearance. He was dressed in a suit of gray cloth with white metal buttons, and a kind of scratch wig. He was quite different from the plump figure which he used to present. He had before him Dr. Campbell's *Philosophy of Rhetoric*.[3] He seemed to be placid and even cheerful. He said he was just approaching to his end. I think these were his words. I know not how I contrived to get the subject of immortality introduced. He said he never had entertained any belief in religion since he began to read Locke and Clarke. I asked him if he was not religious when he was young. He said he was, and he used to read *The Whole Duty of Man*;[4] that he made an abstract from the catalogue of vices at the end of it, and examined himself by this, leaving out murder and theft and such vices as he had no chance of committing, having no inclination to commit them. This, he said, was strange work; for instance, to try if, notwithstanding his excelling his schoolfellows, he had no pride or vanity. He smiled in ridicule of this as absurd and contrary to fixed principles and necessary consequences, not adverting that religious discipline does not mean to extinguish, but to moderate, the passions; and certainly an excess of pride or vanity is dangerous and generally hurtful. He then said flatly that the morality of every religion was bad, and, I really thought, was not jocular when he said that when he heard a man was religious, he concluded he was a rascal, though he had known some

3. Scrofula, a form of tuberculosis that the king's touch was believed to cure.
1. Boswell was terrified of death, preoccupied with the question of an afterlife, and in doubt as to the sturdiness of his own Christian faith. All these agitations converged at the deathbed of the "infidel" Scots philosopher David Hume (1711–1776), whom he had known (and intermittently exasperated) for about 15 years. Boswell first wrote this account three weeks after the event, and revisited it twice, altering and expanding it in March of the following year, and adding a postscript ten months later. For David Hume, see Perspectives: Mind and God (page 2631) and the conversations recorded in the *Life of John-*

son (page 2763).
2. To his house in Edinburgh.
3. George Campbell (1719–1796), a Scots clergyman, had made his philosophical reputation by a book-length rebuttal to Hume's essay *Of Miracles*, but he cheerfully acknowledged Hume's influence on his thought, and the two men sustained an affectionate relationship. *The Philosophy of Rhetoric*, which would become Campbell's most successful work, was now newly published.
4. A massively popular work of uncertain authorship, first published in 1658, which prescribed a rigorous code of Christian conduct.

instances of very good men being religious. This was just an extravagant reverse of the common remark as to infidels.

I had a strong curiosity to be satisfied if he persisted in disbelieving a future state even when he had death before his eyes. I was persuaded from what he now said, and from his manner of saying it, that he did persist. I asked him if it was not possible that there might be a future state. He answered it was possible that a piece of coal put upon the fire would not burn; and he added that it was a most unreasonable fancy that we should exist forever. That immortality, if it were at all, must be general; that a great proportion of the human race has hardly any intellectual qualities; that a great proportion dies in infancy before being possessed of reason; yet all these must be immortal; that a porter who gets drunk by ten o'clock with gin must be immortal; that the trash of every age must be preserved, and that new universes must be created to contain such infinite numbers. This appeared to me an unphilosophical objection, and I said, "Mr. Hume, you know spirit does not take up space."

I may illustrate what he last said by mentioning that in a former conversation with me on this subject he used pretty much the same mode of reasoning, and urged that Wilkes[5] and his mob must be immortal. One night last May as I was coming up King Street, Westminster, I met Wilkes, who carried me into Parliament Street to see a curious procession pass: the funeral of a lamplighter attended by some hundreds of his fraternity with torches. Wilkes, who either is, or affects to be, an infidel, was rattling away, "I think there's an end of that fellow. I think he won't rise again." I very calmly said to him, "You bring into my mind the strongest argument that ever I heard against a future state"; and then told him David Hume's objection that Wilkes and his mob must be immortal. It seemed to make a proper impression, for he grinned abashment, as a Negro grows whiter when he blushes. But to return to my last interview with Mr. Hume.

I asked him if the thought of annihilation never gave him any uneasiness. He said not the least; no more than the thought that he had not been, as Lucretius observes.[6] "Well," said I, "Mr. Hume, I hope to triumph over you when I meet you in a future state; and remember you are not to pretend that you was joking with all this infidelity." "No, no," said he. "But I shall have been so long there before you come that it will be nothing new." In this style of good humor and levity did I conduct the conversation. Perhaps it was wrong on so awful[7] a subject. But as nobody was present, I thought it could have no bad effect. I however felt a degree of horror, mixed with a sort of wild, strange, hurrying recollection of my excellent mother's pious instructions, of Dr. Johnson's noble lessons, and of my religious sentiments and affections during the course of my life. I was like a man in sudden danger eagerly seeking his defensive arms; and I could not but be assailed by momentary doubts while I had actually before me a man of such strong abilities and extensive inquiry dying in the persuasion of being annihilated. But I maintained my faith. I told him that I believed the Christian religion as I believed history. Said he: "You do not believe it as you believe the Revolution."[8] "Yes," said I; "but the difference is that I am not so much interested in the truth of the Revolution; otherwise I should have anxious doubts concerning it. A man who is in love has doubts of the affection of

5. John Wilkes (1725–1797), radical politician.
6. Titus Lucretius Carus, Roman philosopher and poet; Hume's observation appears to echo more closely an observation by the Stoic philosopher Seneca: "Death is non-existence. What that may be I already know. What

shall be after me is what was before me" (Epistolae 54.4).
7. Solemn.
8. The "Glorious Revolution" of 1688–1689, when the Stuart monarch James II was replaced by William and Mary.

his mistress, without cause." I mentioned Soame Jenyns's little book in defense of Christianity, which was just published but which I had not yet read.[9] Mr. Hume said, "I am told there is nothing of his usual spirit in it."

He had once said to me, on a forenoon while the sun was shining bright, that he did not wish to be immortal. This was a most wonderful[1] thought. The reason he gave was that he was very well in this state of being, and that the chances were very much against his being so well in another state; and he would rather not be more than be worse. I answered that it was reasonable to hope he would be better; that there would be a progressive improvement. I tried him at this interview with that topic, saying that a future state was surely a pleasing idea. He said no, for that it was always seen through a gloomy medium; there was always a Phlegethon[2] or a hell. "But," said I, "would it not be agreeable to have hopes of seeing our friends again?" and I mentioned three men lately deceased, for whom I knew he had a high value: Ambassador Keith, Lord Alemoor, and Baron Mure. He owned it would be agreeable, but added that none of them entertained such a notion. I believe he said, such a foolish, or such an absurd, notion; for he was indecently[3] and impolitely positive in incredulity. "Yes," said I, "Lord Alemoor was a believer." David acknowledged that *he* had *some* belief.

I somehow or other brought Dr. Johnson's name into our conversation. I had often heard him speak of that great man in a very illiberal manner. He said upon this occasion, "Johnson should be pleased with my *History*."[4] Nettled by Hume's frequent attacks upon my revered friend in former conversations, I told him now that Dr. Johnson did not allow him much credit; for he said, "Sir, the fellow is a Tory by chance."[5] I am sorry that I mentioned this at such a time. I was off my guard; for the truth is that Mr. Hume's pleasantry was such that there was no solemnity in the scene; and death for the time did not seem dismal. It surprised me to find him talking of different matters with a tranquillity of mind and a clearness of head which few men posses at any time. Two particulars I remember: Smith's *Wealth of Nations*, which he commended much, and Monboddo's *Origin of Language*, which he treated contemptuously.[6] I said, "If I were you, I should regret annihilation. Had I written such an admirable history, I should be sorry to leave it." He said, "I shall leave that history, of which you are pleased to speak so favorably, as perfect as I can."[7] He said, too, that all the great abilities with which men had ever been endowed were relative to this world. He said he became a greater friend to the Stuart family as he advanced in studying for his history; and he hoped he had vindicated the two first of them so effectually that they would never again be attacked.

Mr. Lauder, his surgeon, came in for a little, and Mr. Mure, the Baron's son, for another small interval. He was, as far as I could judge, quite easy with both. He said

9. Soame Jenyns (1704–1787) had published *A View of the Internal Evidence of the Christian Religion*.
1. Astonishing.
2. In Greek mythology, a river in Hades.
3. In his first version, Boswell had written the milder "improperly."
4. The six-volume *History of Great Britain* (1754–1762); Hume was now revising it, and had noted that his alterations to the portion on the "two first Stuarts" were "invariably to the Tory side" (the view favored by Johnson).
5. "As being a Scotchman," Johnson had gone on to explain, "but not upon a principle of duty; for he has no principle."
6. *The Wealth of Nations* (1776), by Hume's friend Adam

Smith, is the foundation text of modern economics; in *The Origin and Progress of Language* (1773), James Burnett, Lord Monboddo, argued (among other things) that humans and orangutans are of the same species.
7. Once, to entertain Adam Smith, Hume pretended that these revisions might furnish him with an excuse for living longer: "'Allow me a little time,'" he imagined himself saying to the mythic ferryman who conveyed the dead to Hades, "'that I may see how the public receives the alterations.' But Charon would answer, 'When you have seen the effect of these, you will be for making other alterations. There will be no end to such excuses; so, honest friend, please step into the boat.'"

he had no pain, but was wasting away. I left him with impressions which disturbed me for some time.

(Additions from memory, 22 January 1778) Speaking of his singular notion that men of religion were generally bad men, he said, "One of the men" (or "The man"—I am not sure which) "of the greatest honor that I ever knew is my Lord Marischal,[8] who is a downright atheist. I remember I once hinted something as if I believed in the being of a God, and he would not speak to me for a week." He said this with his usual grunting pleasantry, with that thick breath which fatness had rendered habitual to him, and that smile of simplicity which his good humor constantly produced.

When he spoke against Monboddo, I told him that Monboddo said to me that he believed the abusive criticism upon his book in *The Edinburgh Magazine and Review* was written by Mr. Hume's direction. David seemed irritated, and said, "Does the *scoundrel*" (I am sure either *that* or "*rascal*") "say so?" He then told me that he had observed to one of the Faculty of Advocates that Monboddo was wrong in his observation that————and gave as a proof the line in Milton. When the review came out, he found this very remark in it, and said to that advocate, "Oho! I have discovered you"—reminding him of the circumstance.[9]

It was amazing to find him so keen in such a state. I must add one other circumstance which is material, as it shows that he perhaps was not without some hope of a future state, and that his spirits were supported by a consciousness (or at least a notion) that his conduct had been virtuous. He said, "If there were a future state, Mr. Boswell, I think I could give as good an account of my life as most people."

1776–1778   1970

from The Life of Samuel Johnson, LL.D.

[INTRODUCTION; BOSWELL'S METHOD]

To write the Life of him who excelled all mankind in writing the lives of others, and who, whether we consider his extraordinary endowments or his various works, has been equaled by few in any age, is an arduous, and may be reckoned in me a presumptuous task.

Had Dr. Johnson written his own life, in conformity with the opinion which he has given, that every man's life may be best written by himself;[1] had he employed in the preservation of his own history, that clearness of narration and elegance of language in which he has embalmed so many eminent persons, the world would probably have had the most perfect example of biography that was ever exhibited. But although he at different times, in a desultory manner, committed to writing many particulars of the progress of his mind and fortunes, he never had preserving diligence enough to form them into a regular composition. Of these memorials a few have been preserved; but the greater part was consigned by him to the flames, a few days before his death.

As I had the honor and happiness of enjoying his friendship for upwards of twenty years; as I had the scheme of writing his life constantly in view; as he was well apprised of this circumstance, and from time to time obligingly satisfied my inquiries, by communicating to me the incidents of his early years; as I acquired a

---

8. George Keith, tenth Earl Marischal of Scotland, a renowned Jacobite who as an old man had befriended the young Boswell and accompanied him on the German portion of his Grand Tour.

9. The details of the dispute remain obscure; Boswell never filled in the blank or identified the "line in Milton."
1. In *Idler* No. 84.

facility in recollecting, and was very assiduous in recording, his conversation, of which the extraordinary vigor and vivacity constituted one of the first features of his character; and as I have spared no pains in obtaining materials concerning him, from every quarter where I could discover that they were to be found, and have been favored with the most liberal communications by his friends; I flatter myself that few biographers have entered upon such a work as this with more advantages; independent of literary abilities, in which I am not vain enough to compare myself with some great names who have gone before me in this kind of writing. * * *

Instead of melting down my materials into one mass, and constantly speaking in my own person, by which I might have appeared to have more merit in the execution of the work, I have resolved to adopt and enlarge upon the excellent plan of Mr. Mason, in his *Memoirs* of Gray.[2] Wherever narrative is necessary to explain, connect, and supply, I furnish it to the best of my abilities; but in the chronological series of Johnson's life, which I trace as distinctly as I can, year by year, I produce, wherever it is in my power, his own minutes,[3] letters, or conversation, being convinced that this mode is more lively, and will make my readers better acquainted with him, than even most of those were who actually knew him, but could know him only partially; whereas there is here an accumulation of intelligence from various points, by which his character is more fully understood and illustrated.

Indeed I cannot conceive a more perfect mode of writing any man's life than not only relating all the most important events of it in their order, but interweaving what he privately wrote, and said, and thought; by which mankind are enabled as it were to see him live, and to "live o'er each scene"[4] with him, as he actually advanced through the several stages of his life. Had his other friends been as diligent and ardent as I was, he might have been almost entirely preserved. As it is, I will venture to say that he will be seen in this work more completely than any man who has ever yet lived.

And he will be seen as he really was; for I profess to write, not his panegyric, which must be all praise, but his Life; which, great and good as he was, must not be supposed to be entirely perfect. To be as he was, is indeed subject of panegyric enough to any man in this state of being; but in every picture there should be shade as well as light, and when I delineate him without reserve, I do what he himself recommended, both by his precept[5] and his example. * * *

What I consider as the peculiar value of the following work is the quantity that it contains of Johnson's conversation; which is universally acknowledged to have been eminently instructive and entertaining; and of which the specimens that I have given upon a former occasion have been received with so much approbation that I have good grounds for supposing that the world will not be indifferent to more ample communications of a similar nature. * * *

I am fully aware of the objections which may be made to the minuteness on some occasions of my detail of Johnson's conversation, and how happily it is adapted for the petty exercise of ridicule, by men of superficial understanding and ludicrous fancy;[6] but I remain firm and confident in my opinion, that minute particulars are frequently characteristic,[7] and always amusing, when they relate to a distinguished

---

2. William Mason constructed his *Memoirs* of Thomas Gray (1775) around a selection of the poet's letters.
3. Memoranda.
4. "To wake the soul by tender strokes of art, / To raise the genius, and to mend the heart, / To make mankind in conscious virtue bold, / Live o'er each scene, and be what they behold" (lines 1–4 of Pope's prologue to Addison's *Cato*).

5. Boswell proceeds to quote from *Rambler* No. 60 (see page 2694) in which Johnson articulates his biographical principles.
6. Boswell's Hebridean journal had already been parodied in print for its "minuteness" and "detail."
7. Revealing of character.

man. I am therefore exceedingly unwilling that anything, however slight, which my illustrious friend thought it worth his while to express, with any degree of point,[8] should perish. * * *

Of one thing I am certain, that considering how highly the small portion which we have of the table talk and other anecdotes of our celebrated writers[9] is valued, and how earnestly it is regretted that we have not more, I am justified in preserving rather too many of Johnson's sayings than too few; especially as from the diversity of dispositions it cannot be known with certainty beforehand, whether what may seem trifling to some, and perhaps to the collector himself, may not be most agreeable to many; and the greater number that an author can please in any degree, the more pleasure does there arise to a benevolent mind.

To those who are weak enough to think this a degrading task, and the time and labor which have been devoted to it misemployed, I shall content myself with opposing the authority of the greatest man of any age, Julius Caesar, of whom Bacon observes, that "in his book of Apothegms which he collected, we see that he esteemed it more honor to make himself but a pair of tables, to take the wise and pithy words of others, than to have every word of his own to be made an apothegm or an oracle."

Having said thus much by way of introduction, I commit the following pages to the candor of the Public.

[CONVERSATIONS ABOUT HUME]

[21 July 1763] Next morning I found him alone, and have preserved the following fragments of his conversation. Of a gentleman[1] who was mentioned, he said, "I have not met with any man for a long time who has given me such general displeasure. He is totally unfixed in his principles, and wants to puzzle other people." I said his principles had been poisoned by a noted infidel writer,[2] but that he was, nevertheless, a benevolent good man. JOHNSON: "We can have no dependence upon that instinctive, that constitutional goodness which is not founded upon principle. I grant you that such a man may be a very amiable member of society. I can conceive him placed in such a situation that he is not much tempted to deviate from what is right; and as every man prefers virtue, when there is not some strong incitement to transgress its precepts, I can conceive him doing nothing wrong. But if such a man stood in need of money, I should not like to trust him; and I should certainly not trust him with young ladies, for *there* there is always temptation. Hume and other skeptical innovators are vain men, and will gratify themselves at any expense. Truth will not afford sufficient food to their vanity; so they have betaken themselves to error. Truth, Sir, is a cow which will yield such people no more milk, and so they are gone to milk the bull. If I could have allowed myself to gratify my vanity at the expense of truth, what fame might I have acquired. Everything which Hume has advanced against Christianity had passed through my mind long before he wrote. Always remember this, that after a system is well settled upon positive evidence, a few partial objections ought not to shake it. The human mind is so limited that it cannot take in all the parts of a subject, so that there may be objections raised against anything. There are objections against a *plenum*, and objections against a *vacuum*;[3] yet one of them must certainly be true."

8. "Remarkable turn of words or thought" (Johnson's *Dictionary*).
9. E.g., Joseph Spence's *Anecdotes, Observations and Characters of Books and Men, Collected from the Conversation of Mr. Pope*, which (though unpublished until 1820) Johnson drew on for his *Life* of Pope.

1. Boswell's friend George Dempster.
2. The skeptical philosopher David Hume.
3. According to the scientific theory of the *plenum*, all space is full (*plenus*) of matter; the opposing theory postulated that there are parts of space that are empty (*vacuus*) of matter.

I mentioned Hume's argument against the belief of miracles, that it is more probable that the witnesses to the truth of them are mistaken, or speak falsely, than that the miracles should be true. JOHNSON: "Why, Sir, the great difficulty of proving miracles should make us very cautious in believing them. But let us consider; although God has made Nature to operate by certain fixed laws, yet it is not unreasonable to think that he may suspend those laws, in order to establish a system highly advantageous to mankind. Now the Christian religion is a most beneficial system, as it gives us light and certainty where we were before in darkness and doubt. The miracles which prove it are attested by men who had no interest in deceiving us; but who, on the contrary, were told that they should suffer persecution, and did actually lay down their lives in confirmation of the truth of the facts which they asserted. Indeed, for some centuries the heathens did not pretend to deny the miracles; but said they were performed by the aid of evil spirits. This is a circumstance of great weight. Then, Sir, when we take the proofs derived from prophecies which have been so exactly fulfilled, we have most satisfactory evidence. Supposing a miracle possible, as to which, in my opinion, there can be no doubt, we have as strong evidence for the miracles in support of Christianity, as the nature of the thing admits."

At night Mr. Johnson and I supped in a private room at the Turk's Head coffeehouse, in the Strand. "I encourage this house (said he); for the mistress of it is a good civil woman, and has not much business."

"Sir, I love the acquaintance of young people; because, in the first place, I don't like to think myself growing old. In the next place, young acquaintances must last longest, if they do last; and then, Sir, young men have more virtue than old men; they have more generous sentiments in every respect. I love the young dogs of this age: they have more wit and humor and knowledge of life than we had; but then the dogs are not so good scholars. Sir, in my early years I read very hard. It is a sad reflection, but a true one, that I knew almost as much at eighteen as I do now. My judgment, to be sure, was not so good; but I had all the facts. I remember very well, when I was at Oxford, an old gentleman said to me, 'Young man, ply your book diligently now, and acquire a stock of knowledge; for when years come upon you, you will find that poring upon books will be but an irksome task.'"

* * *

[26 October 1769] When we were alone, I introduced the subject of death, and endeavored to maintain that the fear of it might be got over. I told him that David Hume said to me, he was no more uneasy to think he should *not be* after this life, than that he *had not been* before he began to exist. JOHNSON: "Sir, if he really thinks so, his perceptions are disturbed; he is mad: if he does not think so, he lies. He may tell you, he holds his finger in the flame of a candle, without feeling pain; would you believe him? When he dies, he at least gives up all he has." BOSWELL: "Foote,[4] Sir, told me, that when he was very ill he was not afraid to die." JOHNSON: "It is not true, Sir. Hold a pistol to Foote's breast, or to Hume's breast, and threaten to kill them, and you'll see how they behave." BOSWELL: "But may we not fortify our minds for the approach of death?" Here I am sensible I was in the wrong, to bring before his view what he ever looked upon with horror; for although when in a celestial frame, in his *Vanity of Human Wishes*,[5] he has supposed death to be "kind Nature's signal

4. Samuel Foote (1721–1771), actor, playwright, and theatrical manager.

5. Johnson's imitation of Juvenal's tenth satire, lines 363–64 (see page 2685).

for retreat," from this state of being to "a happier seat," his thoughts upon this awful change were in general full of dismal apprehensions. His mind resembled the vast amphitheater, the Colosseum at Rome. In the center stood his judgment, which, like a mighty gladiator, combated those apprehensions that, like the wild beasts of the Arena, were all around in cells, ready to be let out upon him. After a conflict, he drove them back into their dens; but not killing them, they were still assailing him. To my question, whether we might not fortify our minds for the approach of death, he answered, in a passion, "No, Sir, let it alone. It matters not how a man dies, but how he lives. The act of dying is not of importance, it lasts so short a time." He added (with an earnest look), "A man knows it must be so, and submits. It will do him no good to whine."

I attempted to continue the conversation. He was so provoked that he said, "Give us no more of this"; and was thrown into such a state of agitation, that he expressed himself in a way that alarmed and distressed me, showed an impatience that I should leave him, and when I was going away, called to me sternly, "Don't let us meet tomorrow."

I went home exceedingly uneasy. All the harsh observations which I had ever heard made upon his character crowded into my mind; and I seemed to myself like the man who had put his head into the lion's mouth a great many times with perfect safety, but at last had it bit off.

[DINNER WITH WILKES]

[May 1776] I am now to record a very curious incident in Dr. Johnson's life, which fell under my own observation; of which *pars magna fui*,[1] and which I am persuaded will, with the liberal-minded, be much to his credit.

My desire of being acquainted with celebrated men of every description had made me, much about the same time, obtain an introduction to Dr. Samuel Johnson and to John Wilkes, Esq.[2] Two men more different could perhaps not be selected out of all mankind. They had even attacked one another with some asperity in their writings; yet I lived in habits of friendship with both. I could fully relish the excellence of each; for I have ever delighted in that intellectual chemistry which can separate good qualities from evil in the same person.

Sir John Pringle,[3] "mine own friend and my Father's friend," between whom and Dr. Johnson I in vain wished to establish an acquaintance, as I respected and lived in intimacy with both of them, observed to me once, very ingeniously, "It is not in friendship as in mathematics, where two things, each equal to a third, are equal between themselves. You agree with Johnson as a middle quality, and you agree with me as a middle quality; but Johnson and I should not agree." Sir John was not sufficiently flexible, so I desisted, knowing, indeed, that the repulsion was equally strong on the part of Johnson, who, I know not from what cause, unless his being a Scotchman, had formed a very erroneous opinion of Sir John. But I conceived an irresistible wish, if possible, to bring Dr. Johnson and Mr. Wilkes together. How to manage it was a nice[4] and difficult matter.

---

1. "I was no small part." (Virgil, *Aeneid* 2.5).
2. John Wilkes (1727–1797), libertine, satirist, and radical politician, had been expelled from Parliament for blasphemous and seditious libel. Johnson considered Wilkes an unprincipled philanderer and demagogue.

3. John Pringle (1707–1782), distinguished physician and president of the Royal Society. Johnson disliked Pringle's freethinking religious views and his pro-American political convictions.
4. Delicate.

My worthy booksellers[5] and friends, Messieurs Dilly in the Poultry, at whose hospitable and well-covered table I have seen a greater number of literary men than at any other, except that of Sir Joshua Reynolds, had invited me to meet Mr. Wilkes and some more gentlemen on Wednesday, May 15. "Pray," said I, "let us have Dr. Johnson."—"What, with Mr. Wilkes? not for the world," said Mr. Edward Dilly, "Dr. Johnson would never forgive me."—"Come," said I, "if you'll let me negotiate for you, I will be answerable that all shall go well." DILLY: "Nay, if you will take it upon you, I am sure I shall be very happy to see them both here."

Notwithstanding the high veneration which I entertained for Dr. Johnson, I was sensible that he was sometimes a little actuated by the spirit of contradiction, and by means of that I hoped I should gain my point. I was persuaded that if I had come upon him with a direct proposal, "Sir, will you dine in company with Jack Wilkes?" he would have flown into a passion, and would probably have answered, "Dine with Jack Wilkes, Sir! I'd as soon dine with Jack Ketch."[6] I therefore, while we were sitting quietly by ourselves at his house in an evening, took occasion to open my plan thus:—"Mr. Dilly, Sir, sends his respectful compliments to you, and would be happy if you would do him the honor to dine with him on Wednesday next along with me, as I must soon go to Scotland." JOHNSON: "Sir, I am obliged to Mr. Dilly. I will wait upon him:" BOSWELL: "Provided, Sir, I suppose, that the company which he is to have is agreeable to you." JOHNSON: "What do you mean, Sir? What do you take me for? Do you think I am so ignorant of the world, as to imagine that I am to prescribe to a gentleman what company he is to have at his table?" BOSWELL: "I beg your pardon, Sir, for wishing to prevent you from meeting people whom you might not like. Perhaps he may have some of what he calls his patriotic[7] friends with him." JOHNSON: "Well, Sir, and what then? What care I for his patriotic friends? Poh!" BOSWELL: "I should not be surprised to find Jack Wilkes there." JOHNSON: "And if Jack Wilkes should be there, what is that to me, Sir? My dear friend, let us have no more of this. I am sorry to be angry with you; but really it is treating me strangely to talk to me as if I could not meet any company whatever, occasionally." BOSWELL: "Pray forgive me, Sir. I meant well. But you shall meet whoever comes, for me." Thus I secured him, and told Dilly that he would find him very well pleased to be one of his guests on the day appointed.

Upon the much-expected Wednesday, I called on him about half an hour before dinner, as I often did when we were to dine out together, to see that he was ready in time, and to accompany him. I found him buffeting[8] his books, as upon a former occasion, covered with dust and making no preparation for going abroad. "How is this, Sir?" said I. "Don't you recollect that you are to dine at Mr. Dilly's?" JOHNSON: "Sir, I did not think of going to Dilly's: it went out of my head. I have ordered dinner at home with Mrs. Williams."[9] BOSWELL: "But, my dear Sir, you know you were engaged to Mr. Dilly, and I told him so. He will expect you, and will be much disappointed if you don't come." JOHNSON: "You must talk to Mrs. Williams about this."

Here was a sad dilemma. I feared that what I was so confident I had secured would yet be frustrated. He had accustomed himself to show Mrs. Williams such a degree of humane attention, as frequently imposed some restraint upon him; and I

---

5. Publishers.
6. Famous 17th-century hangman.
7. Those in favor of diminishing the power of the monarch and supporting the rights of the American colonists. Johnson had recently written a political tract called The

Patriot (1774) in which he attacked Wilkes and his supporters.
8. Vigorously cleaning.
9. An elderly blind woman who lived in Johnson's house as one of several dependents.

knew that if she should be obstinate, he would not stir. I hastened downstairs to the blind lady's room and told her I was in great uneasiness, for Dr. Johnson had engaged to me to dine this day at Mr. Dilly's, but that he had told me he had forgotten his engagement, and had ordered dinner at home. "Yes, Sir," said she, pretty peevishly, "Dr. Johnson is to dine at home." "Madam," said I "his respect for you is such that I know he will not leave you unless you absolutely desire it. But as you have so much of his company, I hope you will be good enough to forgo it for a day; as Mr. Dilly is a very worthy man, has frequently had agreeable parties at his house for Dr. Johnson, and will be vexed if the Doctor neglects him today. And then, Madam, be pleased to consider my situation; I carried the message, and I assured Mr. Dilly that Dr. Johnson was to come, and no doubt he has made a dinner, and invited a company, and boasted of the honor he expected to have. I shall be quite disgraced if the Doctor is not there." She gradually softened to my solicitations, which were certainly as earnest as most entreaties to ladies upon any occasion, and was graciously pleased to empower me to tell Dr. Johnson, "That all things considered, she thought he should certainly go." I flew back to him, still in dust, and careless of what should be the event,[1] "indifferent in his choice to go or stay";[2] but as soon as I had announced to him Mrs. Williams's consent, he roared, "Frank, a clean shirt," and was very soon dressed. When I had him fairly[3] seated in a hackney coach with me, I exulted as much as a fortune hunter who has got an heiress into a post chaise with him to set out for Gretna Green.[4]

When we entered Mr. Dilly's drawing room, he found himself in the midst of a company he did not know. I kept myself snug and silent, watching how he would conduct himself. I observed him whispering to Mr. Dilly, "Who is that gentleman, Sir?"—"Mr. Arthur Lee."—JOHNSON: "Too, too, too" (under his breath), which was one of his habitual mutterings. Mr. Arthur Lee could not but be very obnoxious to Johnson, for he was not only a *patriot* but an *American*. He was afterwards minister from the United States at the court of Madrid. "And who is the gentleman in lace?"—"Mr. Wilkes, Sir." This information confounded him still more; he had some difficulty to restrain himself, and taking up a book, sat down upon a window seat and read, or at least kept his eye upon it intently for some time, till he composed himself. His feelings, I dare say, were awkward enough. But he no doubt recollected his having rated[5] me for supposing that he could be at all disconcerted by any company, and he, therefore, resolutely set himself to behave quite as an easy man of the world, who could adapt himself at once to the disposition and manners of those whom he might chance to meet.

The cheering sound of "Dinner is upon the table" dissolved his reverie, and we *all* sat down without any symptom of ill humor. There were present, besides Mr. Wilkes, and Mr. Arthur Lee, who was an old companion of mine when he studied physics at Edinburgh, Mr. (now Sir John) Miller, Dr. Lettsom, and Mr. Slater, the druggist. Mr. Wilkes placed himself next to Dr. Johnson and behaved to him with so much attention and politeness that he gained upon him insensibly.[6] No man eat[7] more heartily than Johnson, or loved better what was nice and delicate. Mr. Wilkes

---

1. Not caring how the matter turned out.
2. Boswell adapts a line from Addison's *Cato*: "Indiff'rent in his choice to sleep or die" (5.1).
3. Securely.
4. A village just across the border in Scotland; it was the common destination of eloping couples, who could thereby bypass the formalities and restrictions of the Anglican Church.
5. Chided.
6. Imperceptibly.
7. Ate (pronounced "ett").

was very assiduous in helping him to some fine veal. "Pray give me leave, Sir—It is better here—A little of the brown—Some fat, Sir—A little of the stuffing—Some gravy—Let me have the pleasure of giving you some butter—Allow me to recommend a squeeze of this orange, or the lemon, perhaps, may have more zest."—"Sir, Sir, I am obliged to you, Sir," cried Johnson, bowing, and turning his head to him with a look for some time of "surly virtue,"[8] but, in a short while, of complacency.

Foote being mentioned, Johnson said, "He is not a good mimic." One of the company added, "A merry Andrew, a buffoon." JOHNSON: "But he has wit[9] too, and is not deficient in ideas, or in fertility and variety of imagery, and not empty of reading;[1] he has knowledge enough to fill up his part. One species of wit he has in an eminent degree, that of escape. You drive him into a corner with both hands; but he's gone, Sir, when you think you have got him—like an animal that jumps over your head. Then he has a great range for his wit; he never lets truth stand between him and a jest, and he is sometimes mighty coarse. Garrick is under many restraints from which Foote is free." WILKES: "Garrick's wit is more like Lord Chesterfield's." JOHNSON: "The first time I was in company with Foote was at Fitzherbert's.[2] Having no good opinion of the fellow, I was resolved not to be pleased; and it is very difficult to please a man against his will. I went on eating my dinner pretty sullenly, affecting not to mind him. But the dog was so very comical, that I was obliged to lay down my knife and fork, throw myself back upon my chair, and fairly laugh it out. No, Sir, he was irresistible. He upon one occasion experienced, in an extraordinary degree, the efficacy of his powers of entertaining. Among the many and various modes which he tried of getting money, he became a partner with a small-beer brewer, and he was to have a share of the profits for procuring customers among his numerous acquaintance. Fitzherbert was one who took his small beer;[3] but it was so bad that the servants resolved not to drink it. They were at some loss how to notify[4] their resolution, being afraid of offending their master, who they knew liked Foote much as a companion. At last they fixed upon a little black boy, who was rather a favorite, to be their deputy and deliver their remonstrance; and having invested him with the whole authority of the kitchen, he was to inform Mr. Fitzherbert, in all their names, upon a certain day, that they would drink Foote's small beer no longer. On that day Foote happened to dine at Fitzherbert's, and this boy served at table; he was so delighted with Foote's stories, and merriment, and grimace,[5] that when he went downstairs, he told them, 'This is the finest man I have ever seen. I will not deliver your message. I will drink his small beer.'"

Somebody observed that Garrick could not have done this. WILKES: "Garrick would have made the small beer still smaller. He is now leaving the stage; but he will play Scrub[6] all his life." I knew that Johnson would let nobody attack Garrick but himself, as Garrick once said to me, and I had heard him praise his liberality; so to bring out his commendation of his celebrated pupil, I said, loudly, "I have heard Garrick is liberal." JOHNSON: "Yes, Sir, I know that Garrick has given away more money than any man in England that I am acquainted with, and that not from ostentatious views. Garrick was very poor when he began life; so when he came to

---

8. Boswell quotes from Johnson's poem *London*.
9. Intelligence, cleverness.
1. Devoid of learning.
2. William Fitzherbert (1712–1772), landowner and politician.
3. Weak beer.

4. Express.
5. Exaggerated facial expressions (Foote specialized in caricatures of his contemporaries).
6. A character in George Farquhar's comedy, *The Beaux' Stratagem*.

have money, he probably was very unskillful in giving away, and saved when he should not. But Garrick began to be liberal as soon as he could; and I am of opinion, the reputation of avarice which he has had, has been very lucky for him and prevented his having many enemies. You despise a man for avarice, but do not hate him. Garrick might have been much better attacked for living with more splendor than is suitable to a player: if they had had the wit to have assaulted him in that quarter, they might have galled him more. But they have kept clamoring about his avarice, which has rescued him from much obloquy and envy."

Talking of the great difficulty of obtaining authentic information for biography, Johnson told us, "When I was a young fellow I wanted to write the *Life of Dryden*, and in order to get materials, I applied to the only two persons then alive who had seen him; these were old Swinney, and old Cibber.[7] Swinney's information was no more than this, "That at Will's coffeehouse Dryden had a particular chair for himself, which was set by the fire in winter, and was then called his winter-chair; and that it was carried out for him to the balcony in summer, and was then called his summer-chair." Cibber could tell no more but "that he remembered him a decent old man, arbiter of critical disputes at Will's." You are to consider that Cibber was then at a great distance from Dryden, had perhaps one leg only in the room, and durst not draw in the other." BOSWELL: "Yet Cibber was a man of observation?" JOHNSON: "I think not." BOSWELL: "You will allow his *Apology* to be well done." JOHNSON: "Very well done, to be sure, Sir. That book is a striking proof of the justice of Pope's remark:

> Each might his several province well command,
> Would all but stoop to what they understand."[8]

BOSWELL: "And his plays are good." JOHNSON: "Yes; but that was his trade; *l'esprit du corps*: he had been all his life among players and play-writers. I wondered that he had so little to say in conversation, for he had kept the best company, and learnt all that can be got by the ear. He abused Pindar[9] to me, and then showed me an ode of his own, with an absurd couplet, making a linnet soar on an eagle's wing. I told him that when the ancients made a simile, they always made it like something real."

Mr. Wilkes remarked, that "among all the bold flights of Shakespeare's imagination, the boldest was making Birnam Wood march to Dunsinane,[1] creating a wood where there never was a shrub; a wood in Scotland! ha! ha! ha!" And he also observed that "the clannish slavery of the Highlands of Scotland was the single exception to Milton's remark[2] of 'The mountain nymph, sweet Liberty,' being worshipped in all hilly countries." "When I was at Inverary," said he, "on a visit to my old friend, Archibald, Duke of Argyle, his dependents congratulated me on being such a favorite of his Grace. I said, 'It is then, gentlemen, truly lucky for me; for if I had displeased the Duke, and he had wished it, there is not a Campbell among you but would have been ready to bring John Wilkes's head to him in a charger. It would have been only

---

7. Owen Mac Swiney and Colley Cibber, actors from the first half of the 18th century. Cibber was also a poet, playwright, and the author of a widely read autobiography (his *Apology*).
8. Pope, *Essay on Criticism*, lines 66–67.
9. Spoke disparagingly of the ancient Greek poet Pindar, famous for his odes.
1. In Act 5 of *Macbeth*. In his *Journey to the Western Islands* (1775), Johnson had commented repeatedly on the treelessness of Scotland.
2. In his poem *L'Allegro* (36).

Off with his head! So much for Aylesbury.[3]

I was then member[4] for Aylesbury." * * *

Mr. Arthur Lee mentioned some Scotch who had taken possession of a barren part of America, and wondered why they should choose it. JOHNSON: "Why, Sir, all barrenness is comparative. The *Scotch* would not know it to be barren." BOSWELL: "Come, come, he is flattering the English. You have now been in Scotland, Sir, and say if you did not see meat and drink enough there." JOHNSON: "Why yes, Sir; meat and drink enough to give the inhabitants sufficient strength to run away from home." All these quick and lively sallies were said sportively, quite in jest, and with a smile, which showed that he meant only wit. Upon this topic he and Mr. Wilkes could perfectly assimilate; here was a bond of union between them, and I was conscious that as both of them had visited Caledonia,[5] both were fully satisfied of the strange narrow ignorance of those who imagine that it is a land of famine. But they amused themselves with persevering in the old jokes. When I claimed a superiority for Scotland over England in one respect, that no man can be arrested there for a debt merely because another swears it against him; but there must first be the judgment of a court of law ascertaining its justice; and that a seizure of the person, before judgment is obtained, can take place only if his creditor should swear that he is about to fly from the country, or, as it is technically expressed, is *in meditatione fugae*. WILKES: "That, I should think, may be safely sworn of all the Scotch nation." JOHNSON (to Mr. Wilkes): "You must know, Sir, I lately took my friend Boswell and showed him genuine civilized life in an English provincial town. I turned him loose at Lichfield, my native city, that he might see for once real civility: for you know he lives among savages in Scotland, and among rakes in London." WILKES: "Except when he is with grave, sober, decent people like you and me." JOHNSON (smiling): "And we ashamed of him."

They were quite frank and easy. Johnson told the story of his asking Mrs. Macaulay[6] to allow her footman to sit down with them, to prove the ridiculousness of the argument for the equality of mankind; and he said to me afterwards, with a nod of satisfaction, "You saw Mr. Wilkes acquiesced." Wilkes talked with all imaginable freedom of the ludicrous title given to the Attorney General, *Diabolus Regis*,[7] adding, "I have reason to know something about that officer; for I was prosecuted for a libel."[8] Johnson, who many people would have supposed must have been furiously angry at hearing this talked of so lightly, said not a word. He was now, *indeed*, "a good-humored fellow."

After dinner we had an accession[9] of Mrs. Knowles, the Quaker lady, well known for her various talents, and of Mr. Alderman Lee. Amidst some patriotic groans, somebody (I think the Alderman) said, "Poor old England is lost." JOHNSON: "Sir, it is not so much to be lamented that Old England is lost, as that the Scotch

---

3. Wilkes adapts Colley Cibber's popular version of Shakespeare's *Richard III*, which contains the line, "Off with his head. So much for Buckingham."
4. Of Parliament.
5. Scotland (from the Roman name for North Britain).
6. Catherine Macaulay, author of a controversial *History of England* (1763–1783). In order to test her egalitarian principles, Johnson had proposed that she invite her footman to join them at dinner. "I thus, Sir, showed her the

absurdity of the leveling doctrine," he told Boswell. "She has never liked me since."
7. The King's Devil.
8. See n. 2, page 2765.
9. I.e., these additional guests arrived: Mary Morris Knowles (1733–1807), a highly accomplished needlewoman whose "sutile pictures" Johnson praised in a letter to Mrs. Thrale; and William Lee (1739–1795), merchant, diplomat, and the only American ever elected an alderman of London.

have found it."[1] Wilkes : "Had Lord Bute governed Scotland only, I should not have taken the trouble to write his eulogy, and dedicate *Mortimer* to him."[2]

Mr. Wilkes held a candle to show a fine print of a beautiful female figure which hung in the room, and pointed out the elegant contour of the bosom with the finger of an arch connoisseur. He afterwards, in a conversation with me, waggishly insisted that all the time Johnson showed visible signs of a fervent admiration of the corresponding charms of the fair Quaker.

This record, though by no means so perfect as I could wish, will serve to give a notion of a very curious interview, which was not only pleasing at the time, but had the agreeable and benignant effect of reconciling any animosity, and sweetening any acidity, which in the various bustle of political contest, had been produced in the minds of two men, who though widely different, had so many things in common— classical learning, modern literature, wit, and humor, and ready repartee—that it would have been much to be regretted if they had been forever at a distance from each other.

Mr. Burke gave me much credit for this successful *negotiation* and pleasantly said that "there was nothing to equal it in the whole history of the *Corps Diplomatique*."

I attended Dr. Johnson home, and had the satisfaction to hear him tell Mrs. Williams how much he had been pleased with Mr. Wilkes's company, and what an agreeable day he had passed.

[CONVERSATIONS AT STREATHAM AND THE CLUB][1]

[30 March 1778] I mentioned that I had in my possession the Life of Sir Robert Sibbald, the celebrated Scottish antiquary, and founder of the Royal College of Physicians at Edinburgh, in the original manuscript in his own handwriting; and that it was I believed the most natural and candid account of himself that ever was given by any man. As an instance, he tells that the Duke of Perth, then Chancellor of Scotland, pressed him very much to come over to the Roman Catholic faith; that he resisted all his Grace's arguments for a considerable time, till one day he felt himself, as it were, instantaneously convinced, and with tears in his eyes ran into the Duke's arms, and embraced the ancient religion; that he continued very steady in it for some time, and accompanied his Grace to London one winter, and lived in his household; that there he found the rigid fasting prescribed by the church very severe upon him; that this disposed him to reconsider the controversy, and having then seen that he was in the wrong, he returned to Protestantism. I talked of some time or other publishing this curious life. MRS. THRALE: "I think you had as well let alone that publication. To discover[2] such weakness exposes a man when he is gone." JOHNSON: "Nay, it is an honest picture of human nature. How often are the primary motives of our greatest actions as small as Sibbald's, for his re-conversion." MRS. THRALE: "But may they not as well be forgotten?" JOHNSON: "No, Madam, a man loves to review his own

---

1. Soon after succeeding to the throne in 1760, George III made his former tutor, the Scottish Earl of Bute, Prime Minister of Britain. The appointment unleashed a flood of anti-Scottish propaganda.
2. As part of a sustained campaign against Bute's government, Wilkes had chosen to reprint a 1731 play called *The Fall of Mortimer* and had prefaced it with a mockre-

spectful dedication to the prime minister.
1. These were two of Johnson's favorite venues of conversation. Streatham was the country estate of Henry and Hester Thrale, where Johnson and his friends were often guests. The Club was a group of distinguished thinkers, writers, artists, and statesman that met weekly.
2. Reveal.

mind. That is the use of a diary, or journal." LORD TRIMLESTOWN: "True, Sir. As the ladies love to see themselves in a glass, so a man likes to see himself in his journal." BOSWELL: "A very pretty allusion." JOHNSON: "Yes, indeed." BOSWELL: "And as a lady adjusts her dress before a mirror, a man adjusts his character by looking at his journal." I next year found the very same thought in Atterbury's *Funeral Sermon on Lady Cutts,* where, having mentioned her *Diary,* he says, "In this glass she every day dressed her mind." This is a proof of coincidence, and not of plagiarism; for I had never read that sermon before.

Next morning, while we were at breakfast, Johnson gave a very earnest recommendation of what he himself practiced with the utmost conscientiousness: I mean a strict attention to truth, even in the most minute particulars. "Accustom your children," said he, "constantly to this; if a thing happened at one window, and they, when relating it, say that it happened at another, do not let it pass, but instantly check them; you do not know where deviation from truth will end." BOSWELL: "It may come to the door: and when once an account is at all varied in one circumstance, it may by degrees be varied so as to be totally different from what really happened." Our lively hostess, whose fancy was impatient of the rein,[3] fidgeted at this, and ventured to say, "Nay, this is too much. If Mr. Johnson should forbid me to drink tea, I would comply, as I should feel the restraint only twice a day; but little variations in narrative must happen a thousand times a day, if one is not perpetually watching." JOHNSON: "Well, Madam, and you *ought* to be perpetually watching. It is more from carelessness about truth than from intentional lying, that there is so much falsehood in the world."

In his review of Dr. Warton's *Essay on the Writings and Genius of Pope,* Johnson has given the following salutary caution upon this subject:

"Nothing but experience could evince[4] the frequency of false information, or enable any man to conceive that so many groundless reports should be propagated, as every man of eminence may hear of himself. Some men relate what they think, as what they know; some men of confused memories and habitual inaccuracy ascribe to one man what belongs to another; and some talk on, without thought or care. A few men are sufficient to broach falsehoods, which are afterwards innocently diffused by successive relaters."

Had he lived to read what Sir John Hawkins and Mrs. Piozzi have related concerning himself[5] how much would he have found his observation illustrated. He was indeed so much impressed with the prevalence of falsehood, voluntary or unintentional, that I never knew any person who upon hearing an extraordinary circumstance told, discovered more of the *incredulus odi.*[6] He would say, with a significant look and decisive tone, "It is not so. Do not tell this again." He inculcated upon all his friends the importance of perpetual vigilance against the slightest degrees of falsehood; the effect of which, as Sir Joshua Reynolds observed to me, has been, that all who were of his *school* are distinguished for a love of truth and accuracy, which they would not have possessed in the same degree, if they had not been acquainted with Johnson.

---

3. Whose imagination did not like to be restrained.
4. Prove, serve as evidence of.
5. Boswell refers to the two rival biographies, Sir John Hawkins's *Life of Samuel Johnson LL.D.* (1787) and Hes-

ter Thrale Piozzi's *Anecdotes of the Late Samuel Johnson LL.D.* (1786).
6. Hostile incredulity.

Talking of ghosts, he said, "It is wonderful that five thousand years have now elapsed since the creation of the world, and still it is undecided whether or not there has ever been an instance of the spirit of any person appearing after death. All argument is against it; but all belief is for it."

He said, "John Wesley's[7] conversation is good, but he is never at leisure. He is always obliged to go at a certain hour. This is very disagreeable to a man who loves to fold his legs and have out his talk, as I do."

On Friday, April 3, I dined with him in London, in a company where were present several eminent men, whom I shall not name, but distinguish their parts in the conversation by different letters.[8]

F: "I have been looking at this famous antique marble dog of Mr. Jennings, valued at a thousand guineas, said to be Alcibiades's dog."[9] JOHNSON: "His tail then must be docked.[1] That was the mark of Alcibiades's dog." E: "A thousand guineas! The representation of no animal whatever is worth so much. At this rate a dead dog would indeed be better than a living lion." JOHNSON: "Sir, it is not the worth of the thing, but of the skill in forming it which is so highly estimated. Everything that enlarges the sphere of human powers, that shows man he can do what he thought he could not do, is valuable. The first man who balanced a straw upon his nose; Johnson,[2] who rode upon three horses at a time; in short, all such men deserved the applause of mankind, not on account of the use of what they did, but of the dexterity which they exhibited." BOSWELL: "Yet a misapplication of time and assiduity is not to be encouraged. Addison, in one of his *Spectators*, commends the judgment of a king, who, as a suitable reward to a man that by long perseverance had attained to the art of throwing a barleycorn through the eye of a needle, gave him a bushel of barley." JOHNSON: "He must have been a king of Scotland, where barley is scarce." F: "One of the most remarkable antique figures of an animal is the boar at Florence." JOHNSON: "The first boar that is well made in marble should be preserved as a wonder. When men arrive at a facility of making boars well, then the workmanship is not of such value, but they should however be preserved as examples, and as a greater security for the restoration of the art, should it be lost."

E: "We hear prodigious complaints at present of emigration. I am convinced that emigration makes a country more populous." J: "That sounds very much like a paradox." E: "Exportation of men, like exportation of all other commodities, makes more be produced." JOHNSON: "But there would be more people were there not emigration, provided there were food for more." E: "No; leave a few breeders, and you'll have more people than if there were no emigration." JOHNSON: "Nay, Sir, it is plain there will be more people, if there are more breeders. Thirty cows in good pasture will produce more calves than ten cows, provided they have good bulls." E: "There are bulls enough in Ireland."[3] JOHNSON (smiling): "So, Sir, I should think from your argument." BOSWELL: "You said, exportation of men, like exportation of other commodities, makes more be produced. But a bounty is given to encourage the exportation of corn, and no bounty is given for the exportation of men, though, indeed,

---

7. Co-founder (1703–1791) of the Methodist movement.
8. "F" stands for John Fitzpatrick, Earl of Upper Ossory, an Irish nobleman; "E" for Edmund Burke, statesman and political theorist; "R" for Richard Brinsley Sheridan, playwright; "C" for George Fordyce, a chemist; "P" for Sir Joshua Reynolds ("Painter").

9. A marble statue purchased in Rome by the collector Henry Jennings, it was called after an antique sculpture in the Uffizi, Florence.
1. Clipped.
2. An acrobatic rider (no relation).
3. An "Irish bull" was a foolish blunder.

those who go, gain by it." R: "But the bounty on the exportation of corn is paid at home." E: "That's the same thing." JOHNSON: "No, Sir." R: "A man who stays at home gains nothing by his neighbors emigrating." BOSWELL: "I can understand that emigration may be the cause that more people may be produced in a country; but the country will not therefore be the more populous, for the people issue from it. It can only be said that there is a flow of people. It is an encouragement to have children, to know that they can get a living by emigration." R: "Yes, if there were an emigration of children under six years of age. But they don't emigrate till they could earn their livelihood in some way at home." C: "It is remarkable that the most unhealthy countries, where there are the most destructive diseases, such as Egypt and Bengal, are the most populous." JOHNSON: "Countries which are the most populous have the most destructive diseases. *That* is the true state of the proposition." C: "Holland is very unhealthy, yet it is exceedingly populous." JOHNSON: "I know not that Holland is unhealthy. But its populousness is owing to an influx of people from all other countries. Disease cannot be the cause of populousness, for it not only carries off a great proportion of the people, but those who are left are weakened and unfit for the purposes of increase."

R: "Mr. E., I don't mean to flatter, but when posterity reads one of your speeches in Parliament, it will be difficult to believe that you took so much pains, knowing with certainty that it could produce no effect, that not one vote would be gained by it." E: "Waiving your compliment to me, I shall say in general, that it is very well worthwhile for a man to take pains to speak well in Parliament. A man, who has vanity, speaks to display his talents; and if a man speaks well, he gradually establishes a certain reputation and consequence[4] in the general opinion, which sooner or later will have its political reward. Besides, though not one vote is gained, a good speech has its effect. Though an act which has been ably opposed passes into a law, yet in its progress it is modeled, it is softened in such a manner that we see plainly the Minister[5] has been told that the Members attached to him are so sensible of its injustice or absurdity from what they have heard that it must be altered." JOHNSON: "And, Sir, there is a gratification of pride. Though we cannot out-vote them we will out-argue them. They shall not do wrong without its being shown both to themselves and to the world." E: "The House of Commons is a mixed body. (I except the Minority, which I hold to be pure [smiling][6] but I take the whole House.) It is a mass by no means pure; but neither is it wholly corrupt, though there is a large proportion of corruption in it. There are many members who generally go with the Minister, who will not go all lengths. There are many honest well-meaning country gentlemen who are in Parliament only to keep up the consequence of their families. Upon most of these a good speech will have influence." JOHNSON: "We are all more or less governed by interest.[7] But interest will not make us do everything. In a case which admits of doubt, we try to think on the side which is for our interest, and generally bring ourselves to act accordingly. But the subject must admit of diversity of coloring;[8] it must receive a color on that side." * * * In the House of Commons there are members enough who will not vote what is grossly unjust or absurd. No, Sir, there must always

---

4. Importance, social standing.
5. Prime minister.
6. The party to which Burke belonged was out of power.

7. Self-interest.
8. Legitimately have two sides to it.

be right enough, or appearance of right, to keep wrong in countenance." BOSWELL: "There is surely always a majority in Parliament who have places, or who want to have them, and who therefore will be generally ready to support government without requiring any pretext." E: "True, Sir; that majority will always follow

> *Quo clamor vocat et turba faventium.*"[9]

BOSWELL: "Well now, let us take the common phrase, Place-hunters.[1] I thought they had hunted without regard to anything, just as their huntsmen, the Minister, leads, looking only to the prey." J: "But taking your metaphor, you know that in hunting there are few so desperately keen as to follow without reserve. Some do not choose to leap ditches and hedges and risk their necks, or gallop over steeps, or even to dirty themselves in bogs and mire." BOSWELL: "I am glad there are some good, quiet, moderate political hunters." E: "I believe, in any body of men in England, I should have been in the Minority; I have always been in the Minority." P: "The House of Commons resembles a private company. How seldom is any man convinced by another's argument; passion and pride rise against it." R: "What would be the consequence, if a Minister, sure of a majority in the House of Commons, should resolve that there should be no speaking at all upon his side." E: "He must soon go out. That has been tried; but it was found it would not do."

E: "The Irish language is not primitive; it is Teutonic, a mixture of the northern tongues: it has much English in it." JOHNSON: "It may have been radically Teutonic; but English and High Dutch have no similarity to the eye, though radically the same. Once, when looking into Low Dutch, I found, in a whole page, only one word similar to English; *stroem*, like *stream*, and it signified *tide*." E: "I remember having seen a Dutch sonnet, in which I found this word, *roesnopies*. Nobody would at first think that this could be English; but, when we inquire, we find *roes*, rose, and *nopie*, knob; so we have *rosebuds*."

JOHNSON: "I have been reading Thicknesse's travels, which I think are entertaining." BOSWELL: "What, Sir, a good book?" JOHNSON: "Yes, Sir, to read once; I do not say you are to make a study of it and digest it; and I believe it to be a true book in his intention. All travelers generally mean to tell truth; though Thicknesse observes, upon Smollett's account[2] of his alarming a whole town in France by firing a blunderbuss, and frightening a French nobleman till he made him tie on his portmanteau, that he would be loath to say Smollett had told two lies in one page; but he had found the only town in France where these things could have happened. Travelers must often be mistaken. In everything, except where mensuration can be applied, they may honestly differ. There has been, of late, a strange turn in travelers to be displeased."

E: "From the experience which I have had—and I have had a great deal—I have learnt to think *better* of mankind." JOHNSON: "From my experience I have found them worse in commercial dealings, more disposed to cheat, than I had any notion of; but more disposed to do one another good than I had conceived." J: "Less just and more beneficent." JOHNSON: "And really it is wonderful, considering

---

9. Amid the plaudits of the noisy crowd (Horace, *Odes* 3.24.46).
1. Those who sought political sinecures ("places").

2. Philip Thicknesse, *A Year's Journey through France and Spain* (1777); Tobias Smollett, *Travels in France and Italy* (1766).

how much attention is necessary for men to take care of themselves, and ward off immediate evils which press upon them, it is wonderful how much they do for others. As it is said of the greatest liar, that he tells more truth than falsehood; so it may be said of the worst man, that he does more good than evil." BOSWELL: "Perhaps from experience men may be found *happier* than we suppose." JOHNSON: "No, Sir; the more we inquire, we shall find men the less happy." P: "As to thinking better or worse of mankind from experience, some cunning people will not be satisfied unless they have put men to the test, as they think. There is a very good story told of Sir Godfrey Kneller, in his character of a justice of the peace. A gentleman brought his servant before him, upon an accusation of having stolen some money from him; but it having come out that he had laid it purposely in the servant's way, in order to try his honesty, Sir Godfrey sent the master to prison." JOHNSON: "To resist temptation once is not a sufficient proof of honesty. If a servant, indeed, were to resist the continued temptation of silver lying in a window, as some people let it lie, when he is sure his master does not know how much there is of it, he would give a strong proof of honesty. But this is a proof to which you have no right to put a man. You know, humanly speaking, there is a certain degree of temptation which will overcome any virtue. Now, in so far as you approach temptation to a man, you do him an injury; and, if he is overcome, you share his guilt." P: "And, when once overcome, it is easier for him to be got the better of again." BOSWELL: "Yes, you are his seducer; you have debauched him. I have known a man resolve to put friendship to the test by asking a friend to lend him money merely with that view, when he did not want it." JOHNSON: "That is very wrong, Sir. Your friend may be a narrow man, and yet have many good qualities: narrowness may be his only fault. Now you are trying his general character as a friend, by one particular singly, in which he happens to be defective, when, in truth, his character is composed of many particulars."

E: "I understand the hogshead³ of claret, which this society was favored with by our friend the Dean, is nearly out; I think he should be written to, to send another of the same kind. Let the request be made with a happy ambiguity of expression, so that we may have the chance of his sending *it* also as a present." JOHNSON: "I am willing to offer my services as secretary on this occasion." P: "As many as are for Dr. Johnson being secretary hold up your hands.—Carried unanimously." BOSWELL: "He will be our Dictator." JOHNSON: "No, the company is to dictate to me. I am only to write for wine; and I am quite disinterested, as I drink none; I shall not be suspected of having forged the application. I am no more than humble *scribe*." E: "Then you shall *prescribe*." BOSWELL: "Very well. The first play of words today." J: "No, no; the *bulls* in Ireland." JOHNSON: "Were I your Dictator you should have no wine. It would be my business *cavere ne quid detrimenti Respublica caperet*,⁴ and wine is dangerous. Rome was ruined by luxury" (smiling). E: "If you allow no wine as Dictator, you shall not have me for your master of horse."⁵

1791

---

3. A large barrel.
4. "To ensure that no harm befall the republic." Johnson quotes from the *Senatus Consultum Ultimum*, a declaration of public emergency by the Roman senate. This declaration suspended ordinary laws and appointed a dictator for the duration of the emergency.
5. Under the emergency decree, the master of the horse served as second in command to the dictator.

Oliver Goldsmith
1730–1774

Goldsmith's cluster of famous friends never tired of describing and diagnosing what they saw as the baffling discrepancy between his success in writing and his oddity in conversation. Samuel Johnson put the problem succinctly: "No man was more foolish when he had not a pen in his hand, or more wise when he had." The actor David Garrick compacted the same paradox into the second line of an imaginary epitaph, composed while its outraged subject was present in the room: "Here lies Nolly Goldsmith, for shortness called Noll, / Who wrote like an angel, and talked like poor Poll"—that is, like a parrot, noisily spouting verbiage mimicked from minds better furnished than his own. Always quick to take offense, Goldsmith took so much at this that he devoted the remaining months of his short life to a *Retaliation* in which he took vengeance, in the form of caustic verse epitaphs, on the many people from whom he thought he had suffered slights.

Goldsmith's awkwardness, competitiveness, and defensiveness arose partly from discomfort as to humble origins and scattershot education. Born in Ireland to an eccentric curate, he had come to London in 1756 after a checkered academic career spent in Dublin, Edinburgh, and on the Continent, half-heartedly pursuing degrees (never obtained) in divinity and medicine. Upon arriving in London, Goldsmith took a series of odd jobs (druggist, physician, schoolteacher) before establishing himself as a reviewer, translator, essayist, and editor. His work brought him to the attention of the eminent, in whose company he launched that precarious social strategy which his closest friend, the painter Joshua Reynolds, later analyzed: "He had a very strong desire, which I believe nobody will think very peculiar, to be liked, to have his company sought after by his friends. To this end, for it was a system, he abandoned his respectable character as a writer or a man of observation to that of a character [in whose presence] nobody was afraid of being humiliated." As Reynolds acknowledges, the "system" often backfired, because Goldsmith wanted desperately to be impressive as well as "liked." Friends found his mystery worth probing because of the almost palpable preponderance of his merits: alongside irascibility, Goldsmith possessed a compelling charm and generosity; and an amazing *feeling* (Reynolds's emphatic term) for what made writing work.

To support spendthrift habits and a love of gambling, Goldsmith undertook much compendious hackwork—*A History of England* (1764); *Roman History* (1769); *Grecian History* (1774); and a *History of the Earth, and Animated Nature* (1774). At the same time, he managed to score more successes in more genres than almost any of his contemporaries save Johnson: periodical essay (*The Citizen of the World*, 1760–1761); biography (*The Life of Richard Nash*, 1762); novel (*The Vicar of Wakefield*, 1766); stage comedy (*The Good Natured Man*, 1768; *She Stoops to Conquer*, 1773); and poetry (*The Traveller*, 1764; and *The Deserted Village*, 1770). *The Deserted Village* was the work most celebrated in his own lifetime. Two years in the making, the poem recasts an argument Goldsmith had voiced earlier in an essay against the acquisition of rural acreage by merchants who, having acquired their wealth by the commerce of empire and the trade in luxuries, were now bent on converting their new-bought lands from productive communal pasture into pretty pleasure grounds: "In almost every part of the kingdom the laborious husbandman [farmer] has been reduced, and the lands are now either occupied by some general undertaker, or turned into enclosures destined for the purposes of amusement or luxury." Such encroachment, Goldsmith contended, was driving farm families from their villages and annihilating centuries of graceful country tradition. In his poem, Goldsmith mingled nostalgia for a rural past with dread of a commercial future. Contemporary critics promptly ushered *The Deserted Village* into the poetic canon by sundering those elements Goldsmith had worked hard to fuse: they dismissed the poem's economic doctrine and praised its imaginative power. Like the poet's friends, the poem's readers are left to sort out and savor Goldsmith's characteristic complexity: a "sentimental radicalism" (the phrase is John Barrell's) whereby the conservative defense of old values produces a new and volatile empathy with the plight of the poor.

The Deserted Village
TO SIR JOSHUA REYNOLDS[1]

Dear Sir,

I can have no expectations in an address of this kind, either to add to your reputation, or to establish my own. You can gain nothing from my admiration, as I am ignorant of that art in which you are said to excel; and I may lose much by the severity of your judgment, as few have a juster taste in poetry than you. Setting interest therefore aside, to which I never paid much attention, I must be indulged at present in following my affections. The only dedication I ever made was to my brother,[2] because I loved him better than most other men. He is since dead. Permit me to inscribe this poem to you.

How far you may be pleased with the versification and mere mechanical parts of this attempt, I don't pretend to inquire; but I know you will object (and indeed several of our best and wisest friends concur in the opinion) that the depopulation it deplores is nowhere to be seen, and the disorders it laments are only to be found in the poet's own imagination. To this I can scarce make any other answer than that I sincerely believe what I have written; that I have taken all possible pains, in my country excursions, for these four or five years past, to be certain of what I allege; and that all my views and inquiries have led me to believe those miseries real, which I here attempt to display. But this is not the place to enter into an inquiry, whether the country be depopulating, or not; the discussion would take up much room, and I should prove myself, at best, an indifferent politician, to tire the reader with a long preface, when I want his unfatigued attention to a long poem.

In regretting the depopulation of the country, I inveigh against the increase of our luxuries; and here also I expect the shout of modern politicians against me. For twenty or thirty years past, it has been the fashion to consider luxury as one of the greatest national advantages; and all the wisdom of antiquity in that particular, as erroneous.[3] Still however, I must remain a professed ancient on that head, and continue to think those luxuries prejudicial to states, by which so many vices are introduced, and so many kingdoms have been undone. Indeed so much has been poured out of late on the other side of the question, that, merely for the sake of novelty and variety, one would sometimes wish to be in the right.

I am,
Dear Sir,
Your sincere friend,
and ardent admirer,
OLIVER GOLDSMITH.

---

1. Reynolds (1723–1792) was one of England's leading portrait painters and first president of the Royal Academy; his close friendship with Goldsmith had begun in the mid-1760s.
2. Goldsmith had dedicated his previous long poem, *The*

Traveller (1764), to his brother Henry, who died in 1768.
3. A long line of ancient authors—Horace, Seneca, and Pliny among them—had warned that the traffic in luxuries was sapping Rome's health, and had urged moderation.

Sweet Auburn, loveliest village of the plain,[4]
Where health and plenty cheered the laboring swain,
Where smiling spring its earliest visit paid,
And parting summer's lingering blooms delayed:
5 Dear lovely bowers of innocence and ease,
Seats of my youth, when every sport could please,
How often have I loitered o'er thy green,
Where humble happiness endeared each scene;
How often have I paused on every charm,
10 The sheltered cot,° the cultivated farm,   *cottage*
The never-failing brook, the busy mill,
The decent church that topped the neighboring hill,
The hawthorn bush, with seats beneath the shade,
For talking age and whispering lovers made.
15 How often have I blessed the coming day,
When toil remitting lent its turn to play,
And all the village train, from labor free,
Led up their sports beneath the spreading tree,
While many a pastime circled in the shade,
20 The young contending as the old surveyed;
And many a gambol frolicked o'er the ground,
And sleights of art and feats of strength went round.
And still as each repeated pleasure tired,
Succeeding sports the mirthful band inspired;
25 The dancing pair that simply sought renown
By holding out to tire each other down;
The swain mistrustless of his smutted face,
While secret laughter tittered round the place;
The bashful virgin's sidelong looks of love,
30 The matron's glance that would those looks reprove.
These were thy charms, sweet village; sports like these,
With sweet succession, taught even toil to please;
These round thy bowers their cheerful influence shed,
These were thy charms—But all these charms are fled.

35   Sweet smiling village, loveliest of the lawn,
Thy sports are fled, and all thy charms withdrawn;
Amidst thy bowers the tyrant's hand is seen,
And desolation saddens all thy green:
One only master grasps the whole domain,
40 And half a tillage[5] stints° thy smiling plain;   *sets limits to*
No more thy glassy brook reflects the day,
But choked with sedges, works its weedy way.
Along thy glades, a solitary guest,
The hollow sounding bittern guards its nest;
45 Amidst thy desert walks the lapwing flies,

---

4. "Auburn" is fictitious; it may be based in part on the
Irish village of Lissoy, Goldsmith's childhood home.   5. Piece of tilled land.

And tires their echoes with unvaried cries.
Sunk are thy bowers, in shapeless ruin all,
And the long grass o'ertops the mouldering wall,
And trembling, shrinking from the spoiler's hand,
50   Far, far away thy children leave the land.

    Ill fares the land, to hastening ills a prey,
Where wealth accumulates and men decay:
Princes and lords may flourish or may fade;
A breath can make them, as a breath has made;
55   But a bold peasantry, their country's pride,
When once destroyed, can never be supplied.

    A time there was, ere England's griefs began,
When every rood° of ground maintained its man;   *quarter acre*
For him light labor spread her wholesome store,
60   Just gave what life required, but gave no more:
His best companions, innocence and health;
And his best riches, ignorance of wealth.

    But times are altered; trade's unfeeling train
Usurp the land and dispossess the swain;
65   Along the lawn,° where scattered hamlets rose,   *open countryside*
Unwieldy wealth and cumbrous pomp repose;
And every want to opulence allied,
And every pang that folly pays to pride.
These gentle hours that plenty bade to bloom,
70   Those calm desires that asked but little room,
Those healthful sports that graced the peaceful scene,
Lived in each look, and brightened all the green;
These far departing seek a kinder shore,
And rural mirth and manners are no more.

75   Sweet Auburn! parent of the blissful hour,
Thy glades forlorn confess the tyrant's power.
Here as I take my solitary rounds,
Amidst thy tangling walks, and ruined grounds,
And, many a year elapsed, return to view
80   Where once the cottage stood, the hawthorn grew,
Remembrance wakes with all her busy train,
Swells at my breast, and turns the past to pain.

    In all my wanderings round this world of care,
In all my griefs—and God has given my share—
85   I still had hopes my latest hours to crown,
Amidst these humble bowers to lay me down;
To husband out life's taper[6] at the close,
And keep the flame from wasting by repose.
I still had hopes, for pride attends us still,

---

6. Candle. "To husband out" means to maintain something thriftily, so that it lasts long.

90   Amidst the swains to show my book-learned skill,
     Around my fire an evening group to draw,
     And tell of all I felt, and all I saw;
     And, as an hare whom hounds and horns pursue,
     Pants to the place from whence at first she flew,
95   I still had hopes, my long vexations past,
     Here to return—and die at home at last.

     O blest retirement, friend to life's decline,
     Retreats from care that never must be mine,
     How happy he who crowns in shades like these
100 A youth of labor with an age of ease;
     Who quits a world where strong temptations try,
     And, since 'tis hard to combat, learns to fly.
     For him no wretches, born to work and weep,
     Explore the mine, or tempt the dangerous deep;
105 No surly porter stands in guilty state
     To spurn imploring famine from the gate,
     But on he moves to meet his latter end,
     Angels around befriending virtue's friend;
     Bends to the grave with unperceived decay,
110 While resignation gently slopes the way;
     And, all his prospects brightening to the last,
     His Heaven commences ere the world be past!

     Sweet was the sound when oft at evening's close
     Up yonder hill the village murmur rose;
115 There as I passed with careless steps and slow,
     The mingling notes came softened from below;
     The swain responsive as the milkmaid sung,
     The sober herd that lowed to meet their young,
     The noisy geese that gabbled o'er the pool,
120 The playful children just let loose from school,
     The watchdog's voice that bayed the whispering wind,
     And the loud laugh that spoke the vacant° mind,   *carefree*
     These all in sweet confusion sought the shade,
     And filled each pause the nightingale had made.
125 But now the sounds of population fail,
     No cheerful murmurs fluctuate in the gale,
     No busy steps the grass-grown footway tread,
     For all the bloomy flush of life is fled.
     All but yon widowed, solitary thing
130 That feebly bends beside the plashy⁷ spring;
     She, wretched matron, forced, in age, for bread,
     To strip the brook with mantling° cresses⁸ spread,   *growing*
     To pick her wintry faggot° from the thorn,   *firewood*
     To seek her nightly shed, and weep till morn;
135 She only left of all the harmless train,
     The sad historian of the pensive plain.

7. Abounding in pools.   8. Leafy, edible plants.

Near yonder copse, where once the garden smiled,
And still where many a garden flower grows wild;
There, where a few torn shrubs the place disclose,
140 The village preacher's modest mansion rose.
A man he was, to all the country dear,
And passing rich with forty pounds a year;
Remote from towns he ran his godly race,
Nor e'er had changed, nor wished to change his place;
145 Unpracticed he to fawn, or seek for power,
By doctrines fashioned to the varying hour;
Far other aims his heart had learned to prize,
More skilled to raise the wretched than to rise.
His house was known to all the vagrant train,
150 He chid their wanderings, but relieved their pain;
The long remembered beggar was his guest,
Whose beard descending swept his aged breast;
The ruined spendthrift, now no longer proud,
Claimed kindred there, and had his claims allowed;
155 The broken soldier, kindly bade to stay,
Sat by his fire, and talked the night away;
Wept o'er his wounds, or tales of sorrow done,
Shouldered his crutch, and showed how fields were won.
Pleased with his guests, the good man learned to glow,
160 And quite forgot their vices in their woe;
Careless their merits or their faults to scan,
His pity gave ere charity began.

Thus to relieve the wretched was his pride,
And even his failings leaned to virtue's side;
165 But in his duty prompt at every call,
He watched and wept, he prayed and felt, for all.
And, as a bird each fond endearment tries,
To tempt its new fledged offspring to the skies,
He tried each art, reproved each dull delay,
170 Allured to brighter worlds, and led the way.

Beside the bed where parting life was laid,
And sorrow, guilt, and pain by turns dismayed,
The reverend champion stood. At his control,
Despair and anguish fled the struggling soul;
175 Comfort came down the trembling wretch to raise,
And his last faltering accents whispered praise.

At church, with meek and unaffected grace,
His looks adorned the venerable place;
Truth from his lips prevailed with double sway,
180 And fools, who came to scoff, remained to pray.
The service past, around the pious man,
With steady zeal each honest rustic ran;
Even children followed with endearing wile,

And plucked his gown, to share the good man's smile.
185 His ready smile a parent's warmth expressed,
Their welfare pleased him, and their cares distressed;
To them his heart, his love, his griefs were given,
But all his serious thoughts had rest in Heaven.
As some tall cliff that lifts its awful form,
190 Swells from the vale, and midway leaves the storm,
Though round its breast the rolling clouds are spread,
Eternal sunshine settles on its head.

    Beside yon straggling fence that skirts the way,
With blossomed furze° unprofitably gay,   *thorny bushes*
195 There, in his noisy mansion, skilled to rule,
The village master taught his little school;
A man severe he was, and stern to view,
I knew him well, and every truant knew;
Well had the boding tremblers learned to trace
200 The day's disasters in his morning face;
Full well they laughed with counterfeited glee,
At all his jokes, for many a joke had he;
Full well the busy whisper circling round,
Conveyed the dismal tidings when he frowned;
205 Yet he was kind, or if severe in aught,
The love he bore to learning was in fault;
The village all declared how much he knew;
'Twas certain he could write, and cipher too;
Lands he could measure, terms and tides presage,[9]
210 And even the story ran that he could gauge.[1]
In arguing too, the parson owned° his skill,   *acknowledged*
For even though vanquished, he could argue still;
While words of learned length, and thundering sound,
Amazed the gazing rustics ranged around;
215 And still they gazed, and still the wonder grew,
That one small head could carry all he knew.

    But past is all his fame. The very spot,
Where many a time he triumphed, is forgot.
Near yonder thorn, that lifts its head on high,
220 Where once the signpost caught the passing eye,
Low lies that house where nut-brown draughts° inspired,   *drinks*
Where gray-beard mirth and smiling toil retired,
Where village statesmen talked with looks profound,
And news much older than their ale went round.
225 Imagination fondly stoops to trace
The parlor splendors of that festive place;
The whitewashed wall, the nicely sanded floor,

9. "Terms" were the days when payments of rents and wages were due; "tides" were holidays like Easter that shifted date from year to year; information on both was readily available in the annual almanacs.
1. Calculate the capacity of barrels and other containers.

The varnished clock that clicked behind the door;
The chest contrived a double debt to pay,
230   A bed by night, a chest of drawers by day;
The pictures placed for ornament and use,
The twelve good rules,[2] the royal game of goose;[3]
The hearth, except when winter chilled the day,
With aspen boughs, and flowers, and fennel gay,
235   While broken teacups, wisely kept for show,
Ranged o'er the chimney, glistened in a row.

　　Vain transitory splendors! Could not all
Reprieve the tottering mansion from its fall!
Obscure it sinks, nor shall it more impart
240   An hour's importance to the poor man's heart;
Thither no more the peasant shall repair
To sweet oblivion of his daily care;
No more the farmer's news, the barber's tale,
No more the woodman's ballad shall prevail;
245   No more the smith his dusky brow shall clear,
Relax his ponderous strength, and lean to hear;
The host himself no longer shall be found
Careful to see the mantling° bliss go round;   *foaming*
Nor the coy maid, half willing to be pressed,
250   Shall kiss the cup to pass it to the rest.

　　Yes! let the rich deride, the proud disdain,
These simple blessings of the lowly train;
To me more dear, congenial to my heart,
One native charm, than all the gloss of art;
255   Spontaneous joys, where nature has its play,
The soul adopts, and owns their first born sway;
Lightly they frolic o'er the vacant mind,
Unenvied, unmolested, unconfined.
But the long pomp, the midnight masquerade,
260   With all the freaks of wanton wealth arrayed,
In these, ere triflers half their wish obtain,
The toiling pleasure sickens into pain;
And, even while fashion's brightest arts decoy,
The heart distrusting asks, if this be joy.

265   　　Ye friends to truth, ye statesmen, who survey
The rich man's joys increase, the poor's decay,
'Tis yours to judge, how wide the limits stand
Between a splendid and an happy land.
Proud swells the tide with loads of freighted ore,
270   And shouting Folly hails them from her shore;
Hoards, even beyond the miser's wish abound,

---

2. This list of simple life lessons ("Keep no bad company"; "Encourage no vice"), supposedly compiled by Charles I, was displayed, beneath a picture of his execution, in many country inns and houses.
3. A game in which dice determine the movement of the pieces across the board.

And rich men flock from all the world around.
Yet count our gains. This wealth is but a name
That leaves our useful products still the same.
275 Not so the loss. The man of wealth and pride
Takes up a space that many poor supplied;
Space for his lake, his park's extended bounds,
Space for his horses, equipage, and hounds;
The robe that wraps his limbs in silken sloth
280 Has robbed the neighboring fields of half their growth;
His seat, where solitary sports are seen,
Indignant spurns the cottage from the green;
Around the world each needful product flies,
For all the luxuries the world supplies.
285 While thus the land adorned for pleasure all
In barren splendor feebly waits the fall.

   As some fair female unadorned and plain,
Secure to please while youth confirms her reign,
Slights every borrowed charm that dress supplies,
290 Nor shares with art the triumph of her eyes;
But when those charms are past, for charms are frail,
When time advances, and when lovers fail,
She then shines forth, solicitous to bless,
In all the glaring impotence of dress.
295 Thus fares the land, by luxury betrayed;
In nature's simplest charms at first arrayed;
But verging to decline, its splendors rise,
Its vistas strike, its palaces surprise;
While scourged by famine from the smiling land,
300 The mournful peasant leads his humble band;
And while he sinks without one arm to save,
The country blooms—a garden, and a grave.

   Where then, ah where, shall poverty reside,
To scape the pressure of contiguous pride?
305 If to some common's⁴ fenceless limits strayed,
He drives his flock to pick the scanty blade,
Those fenceless fields the sons of wealth divide,
And even the bare-worn common is denied.

   If to the city sped—What waits him there?
310 To see profusion that he must not share;
To see ten thousand baneful arts combined
To pamper luxury, and thin mankind;
To see those joys the sons of pleasure know
Extorted from his fellow-creature's woe.
315 Here, while the courtier glitters in brocade,
There the pale artist° plies the sickly trade;   *artisan*

---

4. Grazing land once shared by all the villagers.

Here, while the proud their long-drawn pomps display,
There the black gibbet glooms beside the way.
The dome° where Pleasure holds her midnight reign,   *lavish house*
320 Here, richly decked, admits the gorgeous train;
Tumultuous grandeur crowds the blazing square,
The rattling chariots clash, the torches glare.
Sure scenes like these no troubles e'er annoy!
Sure these denote one universal joy!
325 Are these thy serious thoughts?—Ah, turn thine eyes
Where the poor houseless shivering female lies.
She once, perhaps, in village plenty blest,
Has wept at tales of innocence distressed;
Her modest looks the cottage might adorn,
330 Sweet as the primrose peeps beneath the thorn;
Now lost to all; her friends, her virtue fled,
Near her betrayer's door she lays her head,
And pinched with cold, and shrinking from the shower,
With heavy heart deplores that luckless hour
335 When idly first, ambitious of the town,
She left her wheel and robes of country brown.

     Do thine, sweet Auburn, thine, the loveliest train,
Do thy fair tribes participate° her pain?   *partake of*
Even now, perhaps, by cold and hunger led,
340 At proud men's doors they ask a little bread!

     Ah, no. To distant climes, a dreary scene,
Where half the convex world intrudes between,
Through torrid tracts with fainting steps they go,
Where wild Altama⁵ murmurs to their woe.
345 Far different there from all that charmed before,
The various terrors of that horrid shore;
Those blazing suns that dart a downward ray,
And fiercely shed intolerable day;
Those matted woods where birds forget to sing,
350 But silent bats in drowsy clusters cling,
Those poisonous fields with rank luxuriance crowned,
Where the dark scorpion gathers death around;
Where at each step the stranger fears to wake
The rattling terrors of the vengeful snake;
355 Where crouching tigers wait their hapless prey,
And savage men, more murderous still than they;
While oft in whirls the mad tornado flies,
Mingling the ravaged landscape with the skies.
Far different these from every former scene,
360 The cooling brook, the grassy vested green,
The breezy covert of the warbling grove,
That only sheltered thefts of harmless love.

5. The Altamaha River, in Georgia (then a colony).

Good Heaven! what sorrows gloomed that parting day,
That called them from their native walks away;
365   When the poor exiles, every pleasure past,
Hung round their bowers, and fondly looked their last,
And took a long farewell, and wished in vain
For seats like these beyond the western main;
And shuddering still to face the distant deep,
370   Returned and wept, and still returned to weep.
The good old sire the first prepared to go
To new-found worlds, and wept for others' woe.
But for himself, in conscious virtue brave,
He only wished for worlds beyond the grave.
375   His lovely daughter, lovelier in her tears,
The fond companion of his helpless years,
Silent went next, neglectful of her charms,
And left a lover's for a father's arms.
With louder plaints the mother spoke her woes,
380   And blessed the cot° where every pleasure rose;   *cottage*
And kissed her thoughtless babes with many a tear,
And clasped them close in sorrow doubly dear;
Whilst her fond husband strove to lend relief
In all the silent manliness of grief.

385   O luxury! Thou curst by Heaven's decree,
How ill exchanged are things like these for thee!
How do thy potions, with insidious joy,
Diffuse their pleasures only to destroy!
Kingdoms, by thee to sickly greatness grown,
390   Boast of a florid vigor not their own;
At every draught more large and large they grow,
A bloated mass of rank unwieldy woe;
Till sapped their strength, and every part unsound,
Down, down they sink, and spread a ruin round.

395   Even now the devastation is begun,
And half the business of destruction done;
Even now, methinks, as pondering here I stand,
I see the rural virtues leave the land.
Down where yon anchoring vessel spreads the sail,
400   That idly waiting flaps with every gale,
Downward they move, a melancholy band,
Pass from the shore, and darken all the strand.
Contented toil, and hospitable care,
And kind connubial tenderness are there;
405   And piety, with wishes placed above,
And steady loyalty, and faithful love:
And thou, sweet Poetry, thou loveliest maid,
Still first to fly where sensual joys invade;
Unfit, in these degenerate times of shame,
410   To catch the heart, or strike for honest fame;

Dear charming nymph, neglected and decried,
My shame in crowds, my solitary pride;
Thou source of all my bliss, and all my woe,
That found'st me poor at first, and keep'st me so;
415   Thou guide by which the nobler arts excel,
Thou nurse of every virtue, fare thee well.
Farewell, and O where'er thy voice be tried,
On Torno's[6] cliffs, or Pambamarca's[7] side,
Whether where equinoctial fervors[8] glow,
420   Or winter wraps the polar world in snow,
Still let thy voice, prevailing over time,
Redress the rigors of the inclement clime;
Aid slighted truth, with thy persuasive strain
Teach erring man to spurn the rage of gain;
425   Teach him that states of native strength possessed,
Though very poor, may still be very blest;
That trade's proud empire hastes to swift decay,
As ocean sweeps the labored mole° away;   breakwater
While self-dependent power can time defy,
430   As rocks resist the billows and the sky.[9]

1770

⌒∞⌒

Responses
George Crabbe [1]from *The Village*

The village life, and every care that reigns
O'er youthful peasants and declining swains;
What labor yields, and what, that labor past,
Age, in its hour of languor, finds at last;
5   What forms the real picture of the poor,
Demand a song—the Muse can give no more.

* * *

I grant indeed that fields and flocks have charms
40   For him that grazes or for him that farms;
But when amid such pleasing scenes I trace
The poor laborious natives of the place,
And see the midday sun, with fervid ray,
On their bare heads and dewy temples play;
45   While some, with feebler heads and fainter hearts,

6. The Tornio, a river in Sweden.
7. A mountain in Ecuador.
8. Equatorial heat.
9. Samuel Johnson supplied the poem's last two couplets.
1. Physician, clergyman, poet (1754–1832). Reacting against Goldsmith's poetic nostalgia in *The Deserted Village*, and against the larger tradition of pastoral poetry which conceived the countryside as an Arcadia abounding in simple pleasures, Crabbe tried to depict realistically the benighted lives of the rural poor. Within the long compass of his own lifetime, his work found favor among readers of widely divergent convictions and generations, across the cusp of centuries and revolutions. Johnson, Reynolds, and Burke encouraged him early; Jane Austen reckoned him her favorite poet; Lord Byron praised him as "Nature's sternest painter yet the best." The first three excerpts given here are from Book 1 of *The Village*.

Deplore their fortune, yet sustain their parts,
Then shall I dare these real ills to hide
In tinsel trappings of poetic pride?

* * *

Ye gentle souls who dream of rural ease,
Whom the smooth stream and smoother sonnet please;
Go! if the peaceful cot your praises share,
175   Go, look within, and ask if peace be there;
If peace be his—that drooping weary fire,
Or theirs, that offspring round their feeble sire,
Or hers, that matron pale, whose trembling hand
Turns on the wretched hearth th' expiring brand.

* * *

See the stout churl, in drunken fury great,
Strike the bare bosom of his teeming mate![2]
35   His naked vices, rude and unrefined,
Exert their open empire o'er the mind;
But can we less the senseless rage despise,
Because the savage acts without disguise?

* * *

And hark! the riots of the green begin,
That sprang at first from yonder noisy inn;
65   What time° the weekly pay was vanished all,   once
And the slow hostess scored the threatening wall;[3]
What time they asked, their friendly feast to close,
A final cup, and that will make them foes;
When blows ensue that break the arm of toil,
70   And rustic battle ends the boobies' broil.

* * *

Yet why, you ask, these humble crimes relate,
Why make the poor as guilty as the great?
90   To show the great, those mightier sons of Pride,
How near in vice the lowest are allied;
Such are their natures and their passions such,
But these disguise too little, those too much:
So shall the man of power and pleasure see
95   In his own slave as vile a wretch as he;
In his luxurious lord the servant find
His own low pleasures and degenerate mind;
And each in all the kindred vices trace
Of a poor, blind, bewildered, erring race;

2. From Book 2. In this section of *The Village* Crabbe is describing (according to rubrics he published with the poem) "the repose and pleasure of a summer Sabbath, interrupted by intoxication and dispute"; in the next excerpt he proceeds to "the evening riots."

3. At taverns, the running debts of the drinkers were often recorded by means of marks ("scores") on the wall. Compare Goldsmith's description of the village tavern (*Deserted Village* 217–220).

100   Who, a short time in varied fortune past,
             Die, and are equal in the dust at last.
1780–1783   1783

George Crabbe: from *The Parish Register*

             The year revolves, and I again explore
             The simple annals of my parish poor;[1]
             What infant members in my flock appear,
             What pairs I blessed in the departed year;
5   And who, of old or young, of nymphs or swains,
             Are lost to life, its pleasures and its pains.
                     No Muse I ask, before my view to bring
             The humble actions of the swains I sing.—
             How passed the youthful, how the old their days;
10   Who sank in sloth, and who aspired to praise;
             Their tempers, manners, morals, customs, arts,
             What parts° they had, and how they employed their parts;   *talents*
             By what elated, soothed, seduced, depressed,
             Full well I know—these records give the rest.
15   Is there a place, save one the poet sees,
             A land of love, of liberty and ease,
             Where labor wearies not, nor cares suppress
             Th' eternal flow of rustic happiness;
             Where no proud mansion frowns in awful state,
20   Or keeps the sunshine from the cottage gate;
             Where young and old, intent on pleasure, throng,
             And half man's life is holiday and song?
             Vain search for scenes like these! no view appears,
             By sighs unruffled or unstained by tears;
25   Since vice the world subdued and waters drowned,
             Auburn and Eden can no more be found.
c. 1802–1806   1807

‿∞‿

---

1. The speaker is a parish priest.

══╫ PERSPECTIVES ╫══
Novel Guises

The noun *novel*, at its root, means "a new thing," and for a long while the thing in question was so new that no one knew for certain what to call it. *Novel* highlighted the genre's breaks with precedent, but at first other more familiar labels occupied the title pages and the reviewer's columns. *History* emphasized the new form's equivocal relation to truth and fact; *adventures* its affinity for the wayward, the risky, and the picaresque; *romance* its lingering linkage with an older, more fantastical form of fiction whose conventions it radically reworked but whose fairy-tale components it often managed, mysteriously, to retain. Late in the century, in her literary history *The Progress of Romance* (1785), the novelist Clara Reeve drew up a distinction between the old form and the new that helped establish *novel* as the latter's name:

> The Romance is an heroic fable, which treats of fabulous persons and things. The Novel is a picture of real life and manners, and of the times in which it was written. The Romance, in lofty and elevated language, describes what never happened nor is likely to happen. The Novel gives a familiar relation of such things as pass every day before our eyes, such as may happen to our friend, or to ourselves; and the perfection of it is to represent every scene in so easy and natural a manner, and to make them appear so probable, as to deceive us into a persuasion (at least while we are reading) that all is real, until we are affected by the joys or distresses of the persons in the story, as if they were our own.

Reeve gives voice to what had oft been thought but never quite so lucidly expressed: that one of the genre's chief claims to novelty lay in a new relationship between the written and the real.

But not its only claim. Reeve's definition, for example, echoes almost word for word Samuel Johnson's famous pronouncement, in Rambler No. 60, on the power of biography (see page 2694). One of the newest things about the novel was its magpie capacity to mimic and make use of many other genres which had themselves been recently invented, or prodigiously reworked, to provide fresh representations of the real: biography and autobiography; diaries and letters; newspapers and essays; histories, legal and fiscal documents, statistical studies; satire; drama; and even lyric poetry. A comparable heterogeneity marked the genre's authors, and its readers, who occupied a wider social spectrum than had the makers and consumers of any previous literary mode. "What was unusual about the appeal of novels," J. Paul Hunter has remarked, "was the way it spanned the social classes and traditional divisions of readers" and of authors, compassing servants as well as masters, the entrepreneurial as well as the entitled, and, most pivotally, women as well as men. Well over a century before Henry James, in 1907, lamented the "large loose baggy monster" that the novel in some hands had become, the genre was already providing ample evidence of its appetite for absorbing whole categories of writing, writers, and audiences.

That capaciousness extends too to the genre's explicators. The past half century has produced varied explanations of why the novel began where and when it did. As chief cause, Ian Watt pinpoints the rise of literacy and of the middle class; Lennard Davis the impact of news and the appetite for fact; Nancy Armstrong the confinement, and empowerment, of women within a newly configured domestic sphere; Michael McKeon the competing discourses concerning truth and virtue to which a newly secular, commercial, and motile culture gave rise; J. Paul Hunter the amalgam of earlier literary forms and functions for which the novel came to serve as crucible. Though the explanations sometimes conflict, they also converge; they tell more truth in concert than apart. What's more, the explaining, and the debating, began long ago, with the early novelists themselves, who often felt prompted to declare their intents, propound their methods, distinguish themselves from their predecessors, and defend their work against the frequent charges that it was morally corrupting and aesthetically debased. Such discourse appeared not only (as might be expected) in the prefaces, but also within the narratives. Among the most striking features of the novel is its capacity to talk about itself, even when ostensibly bent on other business. Whether the story concerns a man on an island, a servant-girl under siege, or a solitary eccentric oddly recapturing his prenatal past, the prose will focus, often and obsessively, on the phenomena with which the novelists themselves are always, intrinsically engaged: the experience of writing and the impact of reading.

The novel by its nature is impossible to anthologize; it is itself an anthology. What follows is a series of short extracts (DNA samples from the baggy monster) in which makers of the new fiction discuss and demonstrate what they think they're up to, and how they hope it works.

 For additional resources on the novel, including texts by Mary Carleton, Daniel Defoe, Samuel Richardson, and Henry Fielding, go to *The Longman Anthology of British Literature* Web site at www.myliteraturekit.com.

Daniel Defoe
1660–1731

Daniel Defoe, long notable for his ubiquity, has already cropped up at two points in this anthology (pages 2293–2309; and 2314–15). And for good reason. Relentlessly inventive, he worked transformations in many of the modes of writing that mattered most during the eighteenth century: journalism, satire, travel literature, criminal biography, political commentary. But he worked no innovations so productive as those he undertook, on the verge of his seventh decade, and after accumulating some 300 previous publications, in the realm of prose fiction. Narrating, in *Robinson Crusoe*, "the life of a man in an island" (as he described it in that first novel's second sequel), Defoe hit on something that struck readers as wholly new, and became hugely popular—making *Crusoe* one of the bestselling books of its moment, its century, and all time. The newness consisted not in the mysteries of the self disguised, but in the astonishments of the self stripped down, shorn of civilized props and privileges, but intent on re-creating them by a process so painstaking that everything Crusoe's readers take for granted (shelter, furniture, pen and paper) becomes, in his calloused hands and plain prose, new, strange, and surprising. Crusoe, like Defoe, knows the novelty of what he's doing; early on, he promises a tale "such as was never heard of in the world before." That sense, of story emerging urgently out of long sequestration, suffuses most of the novels Defoe produced over the next five years, whose narrators have led secret lives which now, with a mix of pain, pride, and pressing need, they choose to put upon the page. In all his subsequent fictions, Defoe rang changes on *Crusoe*'s core preoccupations: the tribulations of individuals as they make their way precariously through new and dangerous worlds (economic as well as geographic); an irresolvable tension between the practical and the pious; and an intrinsic human isolation, almost inseparable from the imperatives of survival, which crops up insistently (like so many of Defoe's peripatetic characters) everywhere on the globe.

from The Life and Strange Surprizing Adventures
of Robinson Crusoe
The Preface

If ever the story of any private man's adventures in the world were worth making public, and were acceptable when published, the editor of this account thinks this will be so.[1]

The wonders of this man's life exceed all that (he[2] thinks) is to be found extant, the life of one man being scarce capable of greater variety.

This story is told with modesty, with seriousness, and with a religious application of events to the uses to which wise men always apply them, *viz.*, to the instruction of others by this example, and to justify and honor the wisdom of Providence in all the variety of our circumstances, let them happen how they will.

The editor believes the thing to be a just history of fact; neither is there any appearance of fiction in it. And whoever thinks, because all such things are dispatched,[3] that the improvement of it, as well to the diversion as to the instruction of the reader, will be the same; and as such, he thinks, without farther compliment to the world, he does them a great service in the publication.

[FIRST DAYS ON THE ISLAND]

I now began to consider seriously my condition, and the circumstance I was reduced to, and I drew up the state of my affairs in writing, not so much to leave them to any that were to come after me, for I was like to have few heirs, as to deliver my thoughts from daily poring upon them, and afflicting my mind; and as my reason began now to master my despondency, I began to comfort myself as well as I could, and to set the Good against the Evil, that I might have something to distinguish my case from worse, and I stated it very impartially, like debtor and creditor, the comforts I enjoyed, against the miseries I suffered, thus:

EVIL	GOOD
I am cast upon a horrible desolate island, void of all hope of recovery.	But I am alive, and not drowned as all my ship's company were.
I am singled out and separated, as it were, from all the world to be miserable.	But I am singled out too from all the ship's crew to be spared from death; and he that miraculously saved me from death can deliver me from this condition.
	But I am not starved and perishing on a barren place, affording no sustenance.
I am divided from mankind, a solitaire, one banished from human society.	
I have not clothes to cover me.	But I am in a hot climate, where if I had clothes I could hardly wear them.
I am without any defense or means to resist any violence of man or beast.	But I am cast on an island, where I see no wild beasts to hurt me, as I saw on the coast of Africa: and what if I had been shipwrecked there?

1. As in his earlier piece of journalism, *A True Relation of the Apparition of* Mrs. *Veal,* Defoe warrants the authenticity of his narrative by presenting himself not as fictive author, but as editor of a real-life narrator's firsthand account.
2. I.e., the editor.

3. I.e., read quickly, so that their power over the reader, whether to amuse or to instruct, is limited. (In the remainder of the sentence, the syntax doesn't quite hold together; Defoe is asserting the value of his narrative against anticipated accusations of triviality).

I have no soul to speak to, or relieve me.   But God wonderfully sent the ship in near enough to the shore, that I have gotten out so many necessary things as will either supply my wants, or enable me to supply myself even as long as I live.

Upon the whole, here was an undoubted testimony, that there was scarce any condition in the world so miserable, but there was something *negative* or something *positive* to be thankful for in it; and let this stand as a direction from the experience of the most miserable of all conditions in this world, that we may always find in it something to comfort ourselves from, and to set in the description of Good and Evil, on the credit side of the accompt.

Having now brought my mind a little to relish my condition, and given over looking out to sea to see if I could spy a ship, I say, giving over these things, I began to apply myself to accommodate my way of living, and to make things as easy to me as I could.

I have already described my habitation, which was a tent under the side of a rock, surrounded with a strong pale of posts and cables, but I might now rather call it a wall, for I raised a kind of wall up against it of turfs, about two foot thick on the outside, and after some time, I think it was a year and a half, I raised rafters from it leaning to the rock, and thatched or covered it with bows of trees, and such things as I could get to keep out the rain, which I found at some times of the year very violent.

I have already observed how I brought all my goods into this pale, and into the cave which I had made behind me. But I must observe too, that at first this was a confused heap of goods, which as they lay in no order, so they took up all my place, I had no room to turn myself; so I set myself to enlarge my cave and works farther into the earth, for it was a loose sandy rock, which yielded easily to the labor I bestowed on it; and so when I found I was pretty safe as to beasts of prey, I worked sideways to the right hand into the rock, and then turning to the right again, worked quite out and made me a door to come out, on the outside of my pale or fortification.

This gave me not only egress and regress, as it were a back way to my tent and to my storehouse, but gave me room to stow my goods.

And now I began to apply myself to make such necessary things as I found I most wanted, as particularly a chair and a table, for without these I was not able to enjoy the few comforts I had in the world: I could not write, or eat, or do several things with so much pleasure without a table.

So I went to work; and here I must needs observe, that as reason is the substance and original of the mathematics, so by stating and squaring everything by reason, and by making the most rational judgment of things, every man may be in time master of every mechanic art.[4] I had never handled a tool in my life, and yet in time, by labor, application, and contrivance, I found at last that I wanted nothing but I could have made it, especially if I had had tools; however, I made abundance of things, even without tools, and some with no more tools than an adze[5] and a hatchet, which perhaps were never made that way before, and that with infinite labor. For example, if I wanted a board, I had no other way but to cut down a tree, set it on an edge before me, and hew it flat on either side with my axe, till I had brought it to be thin as a plank, and then dub[6] it smooth with my adze. It is true, by this method I could make but one board out of a whole tree, but this I had no remedy for but patience, any

4. Manual craft.
5. A kind of axe, used for rough-shaping timber.

6. Beat.

more than I had for the prodigious deal of time and labor which it took me up to make a plank or board. But my time or labor was little worth, and so it was as well employed one way as another.

However, I made me a table and a chair, as I observed above, in the first place, and this I did out of the short pieces of boards that I brought on my raft from the ship. But when I had wrought out some boards, as above, I made large shelves of the breadth of a foot and half one over another, all along one side of my cave, to lay all my tools, nails, and iron-work, and in a word, to separate everything at large in their places, that I might come easily at them; I knocked pieces into the wall of the rock to hang my guns and all things that would hang up.

So that had my cave been to be seen, it looked like a general magazine[7] of all necessary things, and I had everything so ready at my hand, that it was a great pleasure to me to see all my goods in such order, and especially to find my stock of all necessaries so great.

And now it was when I began to keep a journal of every day's employment, for indeed at first I was in too much hurry, and not only hurry as to labor, but in too much discomposure of mind, and my journal would have been full of many dull[8] things. For example, I must have said thus:

Sept. the 30th. After I got to shore and had escaped drowning, instead of being thankful to God for my deliverance, having first vomited with the great quantity of salt water which was gotten into my stomach, and recovering myself a little, I ran about the shore, wringing my hands and beating my head and face, exclaiming at my misery, and crying out, I was undone, undone, till tired and faint I was forced to lie down on the ground to repose, but durst not sleep for fear of being devoured. Some days after this, and after I had been on board the ship, and got all that I could out of her, yet I could not forbear getting up to the top of a little mountain and looking out to sea in hopes of seeing a ship, then fancy at a vast distance I spied a sail, please myself with the hopes of it, and then after looking steadily till I was almost blind, lose it quite, and sit down and weep like a child, and thus increase my misery by my folly.

But having gotten over these things in some measure, and having settled my household stuff and habitation, made me a table and a chair, and all as handsome about me as I could, I began to keep my journal, of which I shall here give you the copy (though in it will be told all these particulars again) as long as it lasted, for having no more ink I was forced to leave it off.

THE JOURNAL

September 30, 1659. I poor miserable *Robinson Crusoe*, being shipwrecked, during a dreadful storm, in the offing, came on shore on this dismal unfortunate island, which I called *the Island of Despair*, all the rest of the ship's company being drowned, and myself almost dead.

All the rest of that day I spent in afflicting myself at the dismal circumstances I was brought to, *viz.* I had neither food, house, clothes, weapon, or place to fly to, and in despair of any relief, saw nothing but death for want of food. At the approach of night, I slept in a tree for fear of wild creatures, but slept soundly though it rained all night.

1719

For selections from Defoe's *Roxana*, go to *The Longman Anthology of British Literature* Web site at www.myliteraturekit.com.

---

7. Storehouse.   8. Stupid.

+→ ≡✦≡ ←+

Eliza Haywood
ca. 1693–1756

Eliza Haywood, as Clara Reeve observed, "was one of the most voluminous female writers that England ever produced." Over the course of four decades, she published more than sixty works, in a vast variety of genres ranging from comedies to conduct books. But she achieved her first fame by pioneering a form of fiction that dwelt along the highly eroticized (and very lucrative) cusp between reality as the novel was beginning to figure it, and romance as Reeve would later define it: "an heroic fable, which treats of fabulous persons and things." In Haywood's fictions, the fabulousness inheres not in heroic exploits but in sexual ardor. Her female protagonists pursue their desires so intensely and so successfully that she was dubbed by one admirer "the Grand Arbitress of Passion." Her first novel, bearing the expressive title *Love in Excess* (1719), appeared in the same year as *Crusoe*, and vied with it in popularity. *Fantomina* (1724), the novel reprinted here, appeared simultaneously with *Roxana*, and explores some of the same issues, but in Haywood's characteristic register of an overtly heightened reality. Fantomina runs through a sequence of disguises that push deception beyond the plausible towards the preposterous, and her tactics differ diametrically from Roxana's in their motivation. They are directed at one man rather than many, and grounded in an intense desire for risk and sex rather than security and wealth. In Haywood's early fiction, her female adventurers, her lovers in excess, pursue their pleasures at variable cost, paying sometimes with their lives, and sometimes not at all. In *Fantomina* Haywood celebrates, as usual, her protagonist's erotic energies, ingenuities, and appetites, and at the same time partly anticipates the more domesticated and didactic novels of her later years, wherein (as Reeve remarks) "she had the good fortune to recover a lost reputation, and the yet greater honor to atone for her errors." (For a sample of such atonement, see the introductory self-portrait Haywood wrote for her pioneering periodical, *The Female Spectator* pages 2322–23.)

Fantomina: Or, Love in a Maze
Being a Secret History of an Amour Between Two Persons of Condition[1]

> In love the victors from the vanquished fly.
> They fly that wound, and they pursue that die.

> —Waller[2]

A young lady of distinguished birth, beauty, wit, and spirit, happened to be in a box one night at the playhouse; where, though there were a great number of celebrated toasts,[3] she perceived several gentlemen extremely pleased themselves with entertaining a woman who sat in a corner of the pit,[4] and, by her air and manner of receiving them, might easily be known to be one of those who come there for no other purpose than to create acquaintance with as many as seem desirous of it. She could not help testifying her contempt of men who, regardless either of the play or circle, threw away their time in such a manner, to some ladies that sat by her: but they, either less surprised by being more accustomed to such sights than she who had

---

1. Upper-class rank.
2. The final lines of Edmund Waller's "To a Friend, on the different success of their loves" (1645), in which a man describes how his infatuation with a proud woman named Celia met with her rejection, while his subsequent loss of interest turned the tables and made her solicitous of him. "To die" here also means "to experience orgasm."

3. Belles, fine young ladies (whose health was commonly drunk by gentlemen in toasts).
4. The area below the stage generally occupied by gentlemen, law students, professional or literary types, and (in this case) prostitutes. Aristocracy generally sat in the boxes above.

been bred for the most part in the country, or not of a disposition to consider any-thing very deeply, took but little notice of it. She still thought of it, however; and the longer she reflected on it, the greater was her wonder that men, some of whom she knew were accounted to have wit,[5] should have tastes so very depraved.—This excited a curiosity in her to know in what manner these creatures were addressed,[6]—she was young, a stranger to the world, and consequently to the dan-gers of it; and having nobody in town at that time to whom she was obliged to be accountable for her actions, did in everything as her inclinations or humors rendered most agreeable to her: therefore thought it not in the least a fault to put in practice a little whim which came immediately into her head, to dress herself as near as she could in the fashion of those women who make sale of their favors, and set herself in the way of being accosted as such a one, having at that time no other aim, than the gratification of an innocent curiosity.—She no sooner designed this frolic than she put it in execution; and muffling her hoods over her face, went the next night into the gallery-box, and practicing as much as she had observed at that distance the behavior of that woman, was not long before she found her disguise had answered the ends she wore it for.—A crowd of purchasers of all degrees and capacities were in a moment gathered about her, each endeavoring to outbid the other in offering her a price for her embraces.—She listened to 'em all, and was not a little diverted in her mind at the disappointment she should give to so many, each of which thought him-self secure of gaining her. She was told by 'em all that she was the most lovely woman in the world; and some cried, *Gad, she is mighty like my fine Lady Such-a-one*—naming her own name. She was naturally vain, and received no small pleasure in hearing herself praised, though in the person of another, and a supposed prosti-tute; but she dispatched as soon as she could all that had hitherto attacked her, when she saw the accomplished *Beauplaisir*[7] was making his way through the crowd as fast as he was able, to reach the bench she sat on. She had often seen him in the drawing-room, had talked with him; but then her quality[8] and reputed virtue kept him from using her with that freedom she now expected he would do, and had dis-covered something in him which had made her often think she should not be dis-pleased, if he would abate some part of his reserve.—Now was the time to have her wishes answered:—he looked in her face, and fancied, as many others had done, that she very much resembled that lady whom she really was; but the vast disparity there appeared between their characters prevented him from entertaining even the most distant thought that they could be the same.—He addressed her at first with the usual salutations of her pretended profession, as, *Are you engaged, Madam?—Will you permit me to wait on you home after the play?—By Heaven, you are a fine girl!—How long have you used this house?*—and such like questions; but perceiving she had a turn of wit, and a genteel manner in her raillery, beyond what is frequently to be found among those wretches, who are for the most part gentlewomen but by necessity, few of 'em having had an education suitable to what they affect to appear, he changed the form of his conversation, and showed her it was not because he understood no better that he had made use of expressions so little polite.—In fine, they were infi-nitely charmed with each other: he was transported to find so much beauty and wit in a woman, who he doubted not but on very easy terms he might enjoy; and she

5. Intelligence, good taste, judgment.
6. Creatures: common term of disrespect for women of low birth or reputation. Addressed: approached, solicited.

7. Lovely pleasure (French).
8. High social station.

found a vast deal of pleasure in conversing with him in this free and unrestrained manner. They passed their time all the play with an equal satisfaction; but when it was over, she found herself involved in a difficulty, which before never entered into her head, but which she knew not well how to get over.—The passion he professed for her, was not of that humble nature which can be content with distant adorations:—he resolved not to part from her without the gratifications of those desires she had inspired; and presuming on the liberties which her supposed function allowed of, told her she must either go with him to some convenient house of his procuring, or permit him to wait on her to her own lodgings.—Never had she been in such a *dilemma*: three or four times did she open her mouth to confess her real quality; but the influence of her ill stars prevented it, by putting an excuse into her head, which did the business as well, and at the same time did not take from her the power of seeing and entertaining him a second time with the same freedom she had done this.—She told him, she was under obligations to a man who maintained her, and whom she durst not disappoint, having promised to meet him that night at a house hard by[9]—This story so like what those ladies sometimes tell was not at all suspected by *Beauplaisir*; and assuring her he would be far from doing her a prejudice,[1] desired that in return for the pain he should suffer in being deprived of her company that night, that she would order her affairs, so as not to render him unhappy the next. She gave a solemn promise to be in the same box on the morrow evening; and they took leave of each other; he to the tavern to drown the remembrance of his disappointment; she in a hackney-chair[2] hurried home to indulge contemplation on the frolic she had taken, designing nothing less on her first reflections than to keep the promise she had made him, and hugging herself with joy, that she had the good luck to come off undiscovered.

But these cogitations were but of a short continuance; they vanished with the hurry of her spirits, and were succeeded by others vastly different and ruinous:—all the charms of *Beauplaisir* came fresh into her mind; she languished, she almost died for another opportunity of conversing with him; and not all the admonitions of her discretion were effectual to oblige her to deny laying hold of that which offered itself the next night.—She depended on the strength of her virtue, to bear her fate through trials more dangerous than she apprehended this to be, and never having been addressed by him as Lady——was resolved to receive his devoirs[3] as a townmistress, imagining a world of satisfaction to herself in engaging him in the character of such a one, observing the surprise he would be in to find himself refused by a woman, who he supposed granted her favors without exception.—Strange and unaccountable were the whimsies she was possessed of—wild and incoherent her desires—unfixed and undetermined her resolutions, but in that of seeing *Beauplaisir* in the manner she had lately done. As for her proceedings with him, or how a second time to escape him, without discovering who she was, she could neither assure herself, nor whether or not in the last extremity she would do so.—Bent, however, on meeting him, whatever should be the consequence, she went out some hours before the time of going to the playhouse, and took lodgings in a house not very far from it, intending, that if he should insist on passing some part of the night with her, to carry him there, thinking she might with more security to her honor entertain him at a place where she was mistress, than at any of his own choosing.

9. Nearby.
1. Injury.

2. Hired sedan chair carried by two men.
3. Respects.

The appointed hour being arrived, she had the satisfaction to find his love in his assiduity: he was there before her; and nothing could be more tender than the manner in which he accosted her: but from the first moment she came in, to that of the play being done, he continued to assure her no consideration should prevail with him to part from her again, as she had done the night before; and she rejoiced to think she had taken that precaution of providing herself with a lodging, to which she thought she might invite him, without running any risk, either of her virtue or reputation.—Having told him she would admit of his accompanying her home, he seemed perfectly satisfied; and leading her to the place, which was not above twenty houses distant, would have ordered a collation[4] to be brought after them. But she would not permit it, telling him she was not one of those who suffered themselves to be treated at their own lodgings; and as soon she was come in, sent a servant, belonging to the house, to provide a very handsome supper, and wine, and everything was served to table in a manner which showed the director neither wanted money, nor was ignorant how it should be laid out.

This proceeding, though it did not take from him the opinion that she was what she appeared to be, yet it gave him thoughts of her, which he had not before.—He believed her a *mistress*, but believed her to be one of a superior rank, and began to imagine the possession of her would be much more expensive than at first he had expected; but not being of a humor to grudge anything for his pleasures, he gave himself no farther trouble than what were occasioned by fears of not having money enough to reach her price, about him.

Supper being over, which was intermixed with a vast deal of amorous conversation, he began to explain himself more than he had done; and both by his words and behavior let her know he would not be denied that happiness the freedoms she allowed had made him hope.—It was in vain; she would have retracted the encouragement she had given:—in vain she endeavored to delay, till the next meeting, the fulfilling of his wishes:—she had now gone too far to retreat:—*he* was bold;—he was resolute: *she* fearful—confused, altogether unprepared to resist in such encounters, and rendered more so, by the extreme liking she had to him.—Shocked, however, at the apprehension of really losing her honor, she struggled all she could, and was just going to reveal the whole secret of her name and quality, when the thoughts of the liberty he had taken with her, and those he still continued to prosecute, prevented her, with representing[5] the danger of being exposed, and the whole affair made a theme for public ridicule.—Thus much, indeed, she told him, that she was a virgin, and had assumed this manner of behavior only to engage him. But that he little regarded, or if he had, would have been far from obliging him to desist;—nay, in the present burning eagerness of desire, 'tis probable, that had he been acquainted both with who and what she really was, the knowledge of her birth would not have influenced him with respect sufficient to have curbed the wild exuberance of his luxurious wishes, or made him in that longing—that impatient moment, change the form of his addresses. In fine, she was undone; and he gained a victory, so highly rapturous, that had he known over whom, scarce could he have triumphed more. Her tears, however, and the distraction she appeared in, after the ruinous ecstasy was past, as it heightened his wonder, so it abated his satisfaction:—he could not imagine for what reason a woman, who, if she intended not to be a *mistress*, had counterfeited the part of one, and taken so much pains to engage him, should lament a con-

4. Light meal.   5. By calling to mind.

sequence which she could not but expect, and till the last test, seemed inclinable to grant; and was both surprised and troubled at the mystery.—He omitted nothing that he thought might make her easy; and still retaining an opinion that the hope of interest had been the chief motive which had led her to act in the manner she had done, and believing that she might know so little of him, as to suppose, now she had nothing left to give, he might not make that recompense she expected for her favors: to put her out of that pain, he pulled out of his pocket a purse of gold, entreating her to accept of that as an earnest of what he intended to do for her; assuring her, with ten thousand protestations, that he would spare nothing, which his whole estate could purchase, to procure her content and happiness. This treatment made her quite forget the part she had assumed, and throwing it from her with an air of disdain, Is this a reward (*said she*) for condescensions,[6] such as I have yielded to?— Can all the wealth you are possessed of make a reparation for my loss of honor?— Oh! no, I am undone beyond the power of heaven itself to help me!—She uttered many more such exclamations; which the amazed *Beauplaisir* heard without being able to reply to, till by degrees sinking from that rage of temper, her eyes resumed their softening glances, and guessing at the consternation he was in, No, my dear *Beauplaisir*, (*added she*) your love alone can compensate for the shame you have involved me in; be you sincere and constant, and hereafter shall, perhaps, be satisfied with my fate, and forgive myself the folly that betrayed me to you.

Beauplaisir thought he could not have a better opportunity than these words gave him of inquiring who she was, and wherefore she had feigned herself to be of a profession which he was now convinced she was not; and after he had made her a thousand vows of an affection, as inviolable and ardent as she could wish to find in him, entreated she would inform him by what means his happiness had been brought about, and also to whom he was indebted for the bliss he had enjoyed.— Some remains of yet unextinguished modesty, and sense of shame, made her blush exceedingly at this demand; but recollecting herself in a little time, she told him so much of the truth, as to what related to the frolic she had taken of satisfying her curiosity in what manner *mistresses*, of the sort she appeared to be were treated by those who addressed them; but forbore discovering her true name and quality, for the reasons she had done before, resolving, if he boasted of this affair, he should not have it in his power to touch her character: she therefore said she was the daughter of a country gentleman, who was come to town to buy clothes, and that she was called *Fantomina*. He had no reason to distrust the truth of this story, and was therefore satisfied with it; but did not doubt by the beginning of her conduct, but that in the end she would be in reality, the thing she so artfully had counterfeited; and had good nature enough to pity the misfortunes he imagined would be her lot: but to tell her so, or offer his advice in that point, was not his business, at least, as yet.

They parted not till towards morning; and she obliged him to a willing vow of visiting her the next day at three in the afternoon. It was too late for her to go home that night, therefore contented herself with lying there. In the morning she sent for the woman of the house to come up to her; and easily perceiving, by her manner, that she was a woman who might be influenced by gifts, made her a present of a couple of broad pieces,[7] and desired her, that if the gentleman, who had been there the night before, should ask any questions concerning her, that he should be told, she was lately come out of the country, had lodged there about a fortnight, and that her

---

6. Unworthiness, vice.   7. Gold coins.

name was *Fantomina*. I shall (*also added she*) lie but seldom here; nor, indeed, ever come but in those times when I expect to meet him: I would, therefore, have you order it so, that he may think I am but just gone out, if he should happen by any accident to call when I am not here; for I would not, for the world, have him imagine I do not constantly lodge here. The landlady assured her she would do everything as she desired, and gave her to understand she wanted not the gift of secrecy.

Everything being ordered at this home for the security of her reputation, she repaired to the other, where she easily excused to an unsuspecting aunt, with whom she boarded, her having been abroad all night, saying, she went with a gentleman and his lady in a barge, to a little country seat of theirs up the river, all of them designing to return the same evening; but that one of the bargemen happening to be taken ill on the sudden, and no other waterman to be got that night, they were obliged to tarry till morning. Thus did this lady's wit and vivacity assist her in all, but where it was most needed.—She had discernment to foresee, and avoid all those ills which might attend the loss of her *reputation*, but was wholly blind to those of the ruin of her *virtue*; and having managed her affairs so as to secure the *one*, grew perfectly easy with the remembrance she had forfeited the *other*.—The more she reflected on the merits of *Beauplaisir*, the more she excused herself for what she had done; and the prospect of that continued bliss she expected to share with him took from her all remorse for having engaged in an affair which promised her so much satisfaction, and in which she found not the least danger of misfortune.—If he is really (*said she, to herself*) the faithful, the constant lover he has sworn to be, how charming will be our amor?—And if he should be false, grow satiated, like other men, I shall but, at the worst, have the private vexation of knowing I have lost him;—the intrigue being a secret, my disgrace will be so too:—I shall hear no whispers as I pass—She is forsaken:—the odious word *forsaken* will never wound my ears; nor will my wrongs excite either the mirth or pity of the talking world:—it would not be even in the power of my undoer himself to triumph over me; and while he laughs at, and perhaps despises the fond, the yielding *Fantomina*, he will revere and esteem the virtuous, the reserved lady.—In this manner did she applaud her own conduct, and exult with the imagination that she had more prudence than all her sex beside. And it must be confessed, indeed, that she preserved an economy in the management of this intrigue beyond what almost any woman but herself ever did: in the first place, by making no person in the world a confidant in it; and in the next, in concealing from *Beauplaisir* himself the knowledge who she was; for though she met him three or four days in a week, at that lodging she had taken for that purpose, yet as much as he employed her time and thoughts, she was never missed from any assembly she had been accustomed to frequent.—The business of her love has engrossed her till six in the evening, and before seven she has been dressed in a different habit, and in another place.—Slippers, and a night-gown loosely flowing, has been the garb in which he has left the languishing *Fantomina*;—laced and adorned with all the blaze of jewels has he, in less than an hour after, beheld at the royal chapel, the palace gardens, drawing-room, opera, or play, the haughty awe-inspiring lady—a thousand times has he stood amazed at the prodigious likeness between his little mistress and this court beauty; but was still as far from imagining they were the same as he was the first hour he had accosted her in the playhouse, though it is not impossible but that her resemblance to this celebrated lady might keep his inclination alive something longer than otherwise they would have been; and that it was to the thoughts of this (as he supposed) unenjoyed charmer she owed in great measure the vigor of his latter caresses.

But he varied not so much from his sex as to be able to prolong desire to any great length after possession: the rifled charms of *Fantomina* soon lost their potency, and grew tasteless and insipid; and when the season of the year inviting the company to the *Bath*,[8] she offered to accompany him, he made an excuse to go without her. She easily perceived his coldness, and the reason why he pretended her going would be inconvenient, and endured as much from the discovery as any of her sex could do: she dissembled it, however, before him, and took her leave of him with the show of no other concern than his absence occasioned: but this she did to take from him all suspicion of her following him, as she intended, and had already laid a scheme for.—From her first finding out that he designed to leave her behind, she plainly saw it was for no other reason, than that being tired of her conversation, he was willing to be at liberty to pursue new conquests; and wisely considering that complaints, tears, swoonings, and all the extravagancies which women make use of in such cases, have little prevalence over a heart inclined to rove, and only serve to render those who practice them more contemptible, by robbing them of that beauty which alone can bring back the fugitive lover, she resolved to take another course; and remembering the height of transport she enjoyed when the agreeable *Beauplaisir* kneeled at her feet, imploring her first favors, she longed to prove the same again. Not but a woman of her beauty and accomplishments might have beheld a thousand in that condition *Beauplaisir* had been; but with her sex's modesty, she had not also thrown off another virtue equally valuable, though generally unfortunate, *constancy:* she loved *Beauplaisir*; it was only he whose solicitations could give her pleasure; and had she seen the whole species despairing, dying for her sake, it might, perhaps, have been a satisfaction to her pride, but none to her more tender inclination.—Her design was once more to engage him, to hear him sigh, to see him languish, to feel the strenuous pressures of his eager arms, to be compelled, to be sweetly forced to what she wished with equal ardor, was what she wanted, and what she had formed a stratagem to obtain, in which she promised herself success.

She no sooner heard he had left the town, than making a pretense to her aunt, that she was going to visit a relation in the country, went towards *Bath*, attended but by two servants, who she found reasons to quarrel with on the road and discharged: clothing herself in a habit she had brought with her, she forsook the coach, and went into a wagon, in which equipage she arrived at *Bath*. The dress she was in was a round-eared cap,[9] a short red petticoat, and a little jacket of gray stuff,[1] all the rest of her accoutrements were answerable to these, and joined with a broad country dialect, a rude unpolished air, which she, having been bred in these parts, knew very well how to imitate, with her hair and eye-brows blacked, made it impossible for her to be known, or taken for any other than what she seemed. Thus disguised did she offer herself to service in the house where *Beauplaisir* lodged, having made it her business to find out immediately where he was. Notwithstanding this metamorphosis she was still extremely pretty; and the mistress of the house happening at that time to want a maid was very glad of the opportunity of taking her. She was presently received into the family; and had a post in it (such as she would have chose, had she been left at her liberty), that of making the gentlemen's beds, getting them their breakfasts, and waiting on them in their chambers. Fortune in this exploit was extremely on her side; there were no others of the male-sex in the house than an old gentleman, who had lost the use of his limbs with the rheumatism, and had come thither for the benefit of the waters, and her beloved *Beauplaisir*; so that she was in no apprehensions of any amorous violence, but where she wished to find it. Nor were her designs disappointed: He was fired with the

---

8. Town in southwestern England, popular as a resort because of its hot springs.

9. Style of cap associated with country women.
1. Coarse wool fabric.

first sight of her; and though he did not presently take any farther notice of her, than giving her two or three hearty kisses, yet she, who now understood that language but too well, easily saw they were the prelude to more substantial joys.—Coming the next morning to bring his chocolate, as he had ordered, he catched her by the pretty leg, which the shortness of her petticoat did not in the least oppose; then pulling her gently to him, asked her, how long she had been at service?—How many sweethearts she had? If she had ever been in love? and many other such questions, befitting one of the degree she appeared to be: all which she answered with such seeming innocence, as more enflamed the amorous heart of him who talked to her. He compelled her to sit in his lap; and gazing on her blushing beauties, which, if possible, received addition from her plain and rural dress, he soon lost the power of containing himself.—His wild desires burst out in all his words and actions: he called her little angel, cherubim, swore he must enjoy her, though death were to be the consequence, devoured her lips, her breasts with greedy kisses, held to his burning bosom her half-yielding, half-reluctant body, nor suffered her to get loose, till he had ravaged all, and glutted each rapacious sense with the sweet beauties of the pretty *Celia*,[2] for that was the name she bore in this second expedition.—Generous as liberality itself to all who gave him joy this way, he gave her a handsome sum of gold, which she durst not now refuse, for fear of creating some mistrust, and losing the heart she so lately had regained; therefore taking it with an humble courtesy, and a well counterfeited show of surprise and joy, cried, O law, Sir! what must I do for all this? He laughed at her simplicity, and kissing her again, though less fervently than he had done before, bad her not be out of the way when he came home at night. She promised she would not, and very obediently kept her word.

His stay at *Bath* exceeded not a month; but in that time his supposed country lass had persecuted him so much with her fondness, that in spite of the eagerness with which he first enjoyed her, he was at last grown more weary of her, than he had been of *Fantomina*; which she perceiving, would not be troublesome, but quitting her service, remained privately in the town till she heard he was on his return; and in that time provided herself of another disguise to carry on a third plot, which her inventing brain had furnished her with, once more to renew his twice-decayed ardors. The dress she had ordered to be made, was such as widows wear in their first mourning, which, together with the most afflicted and penitential countenance that ever was seen, was no small alteration to her who used to seem all gaiety.—To add to this, her hair, which she was accustomed to wear very loose both when *Fantomina* and *Celia*, was now tied back so straight, and her pinners[3] coming so very forward, that there was none of it to be seen. In fine, her habit and her air were so much changed, that she was not more difficult to be known in the rude country *girl*, than she was now in the sorrowful *widow*.

She knew that *Beauplaisir* came alone in his chariot to the *Bath*, and in the time of her being servant in the house where he lodged, heard nothing of any body that was to accompany him to *London*, and hoped he would return in the same manner he had gone: She therefore hired horses and a man to attend her to an inn about ten miles on this side of *Bath*, where having discharged them, she waited till the chariot should come by; which when it did, and she saw that he was alone in it, she called to him that drove it to stop a moment, and going to the door saluted the master with these words:

---

2. In Renaissance literature the name Celia is frequently associated with vanity or pride, as in Lyly's *Love's Metamorphosis* as well as Waller's "To Phyllis" and "To a Friend" (quoted in the epigraph); similarly, in Swift's "The Lady's Dressing Room" (see page 2346), Celia is the woman who spends five hours in her dressing room each day in an effort to conceal her natural nastiness.

3. The side flaps of a close-fitting hat, usually worn by women of higher rank.

The distressed and wretched, Sir (*said she*), never fail to excite compassion in a generous mind; and I hope I am not deceived in my opinion that yours is such:—You have the appearance of a gentleman, and cannot, when you hear my story, refuse that assistance which is in your power to give to an unhappy woman, who without it, may be rendered the most miserable of all created beings.

It would not be very easy to represent the surprise, so odd an address created in the mind of him to whom it was made.—She had not the appearance of one who wanted charity; and what other favor she required he could not conceive: but telling her she might command any thing in his power gave her encouragement to declare herself in this manner: You may judge (*resumed she*), by the melancholy garb I am in, that I have lately lost all that ought to be valuable to womankind; but it is impossible for you to guess the greatness of my misfortune, unless you had known my husband, who was master of every perfection to endear him to a wife's affections.—But, notwithstanding, I look on myself as the most unhappy of my sex in out-living him, I must so far obey the dictates of my discretion, as to take care of the little fortune he left behind him, which being in the hands of a brother of his in *London*, will be all carried off to *Holland*,[4] where he is going to settle; if I reach not the town before he leaves it, I am undone for ever.—To which end I left *Bristol*, the place where we lived, hoping to get a place in the stage at *Bath*, but they were all taken up before I came; and being, by a hurt I got in a fall, rendered incapable of traveling any long journey on horseback, I have no way to go to *London*, and must be inevitably ruined in the loss of all I have on earth, without you have good nature enough to admit me to take part of your chariot.

Here the feigned widow ended her sorrowful tale, which had been several times interrupted by a parenthesis of sighs and groans; and *Beauplaisir*, with a complaisant and tender air, assured her of his readiness to serve her in things of much greater consequence than what she desired of him; and told her it would be an impossibility of denying a place in his chariot to a lady who he could not behold without yielding one in his heart. She answered the compliments he made her but with tears, which seemed to stream in such abundance from her eyes, that she could not keep her handkerchief from her face one moment. Being come into the chariot, *Beauplaisir* said a thousand handsome things to persuade her from giving way to so violent a grief; which, he told her, would not only be destructive to her beauty, but likewise her health. But all his endeavors for consolement appeared ineffectual, and he began to think he should have but a dull journey, in the company of one who seemed so obstinately devoted to the memory of her dead husband, that there was no getting a word from her on any other theme:—but bethinking himself of the celebrated story of the *Ephesian* matron,[5] it came into his head to make trial, she who seemed equally susceptible of *sorrow*, might not also be so too of *love*: and having began a discourse on almost every other topic, and finding her still incapable of answering, resolved to put it to the proof, if this would have no more effect to rouse her sleeping spirits:—with a gay air, therefore, though accompanied with the greatest modesty and respect, he turned the conversation, as though without design, on that joy-giving passion, and soon discovered that was indeed the subject she was best pleased to be entertained with; for on his giving her a hint to begin upon, never any tongue run more voluble than hers, on the prodigious power it had to influence the souls of those possessed of it, to actions even the most distant from their intentions, principles, or humors.—From that she passed to a description of the happiness of mutual affection;—the

---

4. Holland had been a frequent destination for English religious dissenters in exile.
5. In Petronius's *Satyricon*, the Ephesian matron is a faithful wife who stays by her dead husband's burial vault day and night until she is seduced by a soldier who guards the nearby bodies of crucified criminals. When one of the bodies is stolen, the matron gives her own husband's body to the soldier to save him from punishment.

unspeakable ecstasy of those who meet with equal ardency; and represented it in colors so lively, and disclosed by the gestures with which her words were accompanied, and the accent of her voice so true a feeling of what she said, that *Beauplaisir,* without being as stupid, as he was really the contrary, could not avoid perceiving there were seeds of fire, not yet extinguished, in this fair widow's soul, which wanted but the kindling breath of tender sighs to light into a blaze.—He now thought himself as fortunate, as some moments before he had the reverse; and doubted not, but, that before they parted, he should find a way to dry the tears of this lovely mourner, to the satisfaction of them both. He did not, however, offer, as he had done to *Fantomina* and *Celia,* to urge his passion directly to her, but by a thousand little softening artifices, which he well knew how to use, gave her leave to guess he was enamored. When they came to the inn where they were to lie, he declared himself somewhat more freely, and perceiving she did not resent it past forgiveness, grew more encroaching still:— he now took the liberty of kissing away her tears, and catching the sighs as they issued from her lips; telling her if grief was infectious, he was resolved to have his share; protesting he would gladly exchange passions with her, and be content to bear her load of *sorrow,* if she would as willingly ease the burden of his *love.*—She said little in answer to the strenuous pressures with which at last he ventured to enfold her, but not thinking it decent, for the character she had assumed, to yield so suddenly, and unable to deny both his and her own inclinations, she counterfeited a fainting, and fell motionless upon his breast.—He had no great notion that she was in a real fit, and the room they supped in happening to have a bed in it, he took her in his arms and laid her on it, believing, that whatever her distemper was, that was the most proper place to convey her to.—He laid himself down by her, and endeavored to bring her to herself; and she was too grateful to her kind physician at her returning sense, to remove from the posture he had put her in, without his leave.

It may, perhaps, seem strange that *Beauplaisir* should in such near intimacies continue still deceived: I know there are men who will swear it is an impossibility, and that no disguise could hinder them from knowing a woman they had once enjoyed. In answer to these scruples, I can only say, that besides the alteration which the change of dress made in her, she was so admirably skilled in the art of feigning, that she had the power of putting on almost what face she pleased, and knew so exactly how to form her behavior to the character she represented, that all the comedians at both playhouses[6] are infinitely short of her performances: she could vary her very glances, tune her voice to accents the most different imaginable from those in which she spoke when she appeared herself.—These aids from nature, joined to the wiles of art, and the distance between the places where the imagined *Fantomina* and *Celia* were, might very well prevent his having any thought that they were the same, or that the fair *widow* was either of them: it never so much as entered his head, and though he did fancy he observed in the face of the latter, features which were not altogether unknown to him, yet he could not recollect when or where he had known them;—and being told by her, that from her birth, she had never removed from *Bristol,* a place where he never was, he rejected the belief of having seen her, and supposed his mind had been deluded by an idea of some other, whom she might have a resemblance of.

They passed the time of their journey in as much happiness as the most luxurious gratification of wild desires could make them; and when they came to the end of it, parted not without a mutual promise of seeing each other often.—He told her to what place she should direct a letter to him; and she assured him she would send to let him know where to come to her, as soon as she was fixed in lodgings.

6. Comedians are actors. There were only two public playhouses in London, established by royal decree in 1660.

She kept her promise; and charmed with the continuance of his eager fondness, went not home, but into private lodgings, whence she wrote to him to visit her the first opportunity, and inquire for the Widow *Bloomer*.—She had no sooner dispatched this billet,[7] than she repaired to the house where she had lodged as *Fantomina*, charging the people if *Beauplaisir* should come there, not to let him know she had been out of town. From thence she wrote to him, in a different hand, a long letter of complaint, that he had been so cruel in not sending one letter to her all the time he had been absent, entreated to see him, and concluded with subscribing herself his unalterably affectionate *Fantomina*. She received in one day answers to both these. The first contained these lines:

To the Charming Mrs. Bloomer,

It would be impossible, my Angel! for me to express the thousandth part of that infinity of transport, the sight of your dear letter gave me.—Never was woman formed to charm like you: never did any look like you.—write like you,—bless like you;—nor did ever man adore as I do.— Since yesterday we parted, I have seemed a body without a soul; and had you not by this inspiring billet, gave me new life, I know not what by tomorrow I should have been.—I will be with you this evening about five:—O, 'tis an age till then!—But the cursed formalities of duty oblige me to dine with my lord—who never rises from table till that hour;—therefore adieu till then sweet lovely mistress of the soul and all the faculties of

Your most faithful,
Beauplaisir.

The other was in this manner:

To the Lovely Fantomina,

If you were half so sensible as you ought of your own power of charming, you would be assured, that to be unfaithful or unkind to you, would be among the things that are in their very natures impossibilities.—It was my misfortune, not my fault, that you were not persecuted every post with a declaration of my unchanging passion; but I had unluckily forgot the name of the woman at whose house you are, and knew not how to form a direction that it might come safe to your hands.—And, indeed, the reflection how you might misconstrue my silence, brought me to town some weeks sooner than I intended—If you knew how I have languished to renew those blessings I am permitted to enjoy in your society, you would rather pity than condemn

Your ever faithful,
Beauplaisir.

P.S. *I fear I cannot see you till tomorrow; some business has unluckily fallen out that will engross my hours till then.—Once more, my dear, Adieu.*

Traitor! (*cried she*) as soon as she had read them, 'tis thus our silly, fond, believing sex are served when they put faith in man: so had I been deceived and cheated, had I like the rest believed, and sat down mourning in absence, and vainly waiting recovered tendernesses.—How do some women (*continued she*) make their life a hell, burning in fruitless expectations, and dreaming out their days in hopes and fears, then wake at last to all the horror of despair?—But I have outwitted even the most subtle of the deceiving kind, and while he thinks to fool me, is himself the only beguiled person.

7. Note, brief letter.

She made herself, most certainly, extremely happy in the reflection on the success of her stratagems; and while the knowledge of his inconstancy and levity of nature kept her from having that real tenderness for him she would else have had, she found the means of gratifying the inclination she had for his agreeable person, in as full a manner as she could wish. She had all the sweets of love, but as yet had tasted none of the gall, and was in a state of contentment, which might be envied by the more delicate.

When the expected hour arrived, she found that her lover had lost no part of the fervency with which he had parted from her; but when the next day she received him as *Fantomina,* she perceived a prodigious difference; which led her again into reflections on the unaccountableness of men's fancies, who still prefer the last conquest, only because it is the last.—Here was an evident proof of it; for there could not be a difference in merit, because they were the same person; but the Widow *Bloomer* was a more new acquaintance than *Fantomina,* and therefore esteemed more valuable. This, indeed, must be said of *Beauplaisir,* that he had a greater share of good nature than most of his sex, who, for the most part, when they are weary of an intrigue, break it entirely off, without any regard to the despair of the abandoned nymph. Though he retained no more than a bare pity and complaisance for *Fantomina,* yet believing she loved him to an excess, would not entirely forsake her, though the continuance of his visits was now become rather a penance than a pleasure.

The Widow *Bloomer* triumphed some time longer over the heart of this inconstant, but at length her sway was at an end, and she sunk in this character, to the same degree of tastelessness, as she had done before in that of *Fantomina* and *Celia.*— She presently perceived it, but bore it as she had always done; it being but what she expected, she had prepared herself for it, and had another project in embryo, which she soon ripened into action. She did not, indeed, complete it altogether so suddenly as she had done the others, by reason there must be persons employed in it; and the aversion she had to any confidants in her affairs, and the caution with which she had hitherto acted, and which she was still determined to continue, made it very difficult for her to find a way without breaking through that resolution to compass what she wished.—She got over the difficulty at last, however, by proceeding in a manner, if possible, more extraordinary than all her former behavior:—muffling herself up in her hood one day, she went into the park about the hour when there are a great many necessitous gentlemen,[8] who think themselves above doing what they call little things for a maintenance, walking in the *Mall,*[9] to take a *Camelion* Treat,[1] and fill their stomachs with air instead of meat. Two of those, who by their physiognomy she thought most proper for her purpose, she beckoned to come to her; and taking them into a walk more remote from company, began to communicate the business she had with them in these words: I am sensible, gentlemen (*said she*), that, through the blindness of fortune, and partiality of the world, merit frequently goes unrewarded, and that those of the best pretentions meet with the least encouragement:—I ask your pardon (*continued she*), perceiving they seemed surprised, if I am mistaken in the notion, that you two may, perhaps, be of the number of those who have reason to complain of the injustice of fate; but if you are such as I take you for, I have a proposal to make you, which may be of some little advantage to you. Neither of them made any immediate answer, but appeared buried in consideration for some moments. At length, We should, doubtless, madam (*said one of them*), willingly come into any

---

8. Poor men.
9. A popular walk in St. James's Park.

1. Chameleons were thought to subsist on air.

measures to oblige you, provided they are such as may bring us into no danger, either as to our persons or reputations. That which I require of you (*resumed she*), has nothing in it criminal: All that I desire is *secrecy* in what you are entrusted, and to disguise yourselves in such a manner as you cannot be known, if hereafter seen by the person on whom you are to impose.—In fine, the business is only an innocent frolic, but if blazed abroad, might be taken for too great a freedom in me:—Therefore, if you resolve to assist me, here are five pieces to drink my health, and assure you, that I have not discoursed you[2] on an affair, I design not to proceed in; and when it is accomplished fifty more lie ready for your acceptance. These words, and, above all, the money, which was a sum which, 'tis probable, they had not seen of a long time, made them immediately assent to all she desired, and press for the beginning of their employment: but things were not yet ripe for execution; and she told them, that the next day they should be let into the secret, charging them to meet her in the same place at an hour she appointed. 'Tis hard to say, which of these parties went away best pleased; *they*, that fortune had sent them so unexpected a windfall; or *she*, that she had found persons, who appeared so well qualified to serve her.

Indefatigable in the pursuit of whatsoever her humor was bent upon, she had no sooner left her new-engaged emissaries, than she went in search of a house for the completing of her project.—She pitched on one very large, and magnificently furnished, which she hired by the week, giving them the money beforehand, to prevent any inquiries. The next day she repaired to the park, where she met the punctual 'squires of low degree; and ordering them to follow her to the house she had taken, told them they must condescend to appear like servants, and gave each of them a very rich livery. Then writing a letter to *Beauplaisir*, in a character vastly different from either of those she had made use of, as *Fantomina*, or the fair Widow *Bloomer*, ordered one of them to deliver it into his own hands, to bring back an answer, and to be careful that he sifted out nothing of the truth.—I do not fear (*said she*), that you should discover to him who I am, because that is a secret, of which you yourselves are ignorant; but I would have you be so careful in your replies, that he may not think the concealment springs from any other reasons than your great integrity to your trust.—Seem therefore to know my whole affairs; and let your refusing to make him partaker in the secret, appear to be only the effect of your zeal for my interest and reputation. Promises of entire fidelity on the one side, and reward on the other, being past, the messenger made what haste he could to the house of *Beauplaisir*; and being there told where he might find him, performed exactly the injunction that had been given him. But never astonishment exceeded that which *Beauplaisir* felt at the reading this billet, in which he found these lines:

> To the All-conquering Beauplaisir.
>
> *I imagine not that 'tis a new thing to you, to be told, you are the greatest charm in nature to our sex: I shall therefore, not to fill up my letter with any impertinent praises on your wit or person, only tell you, that I am infinite in love with both, and if you have a heart not too deeply engaged, should think myself the happiest of my sex in being capable of inspiring it with some tenderness.—There is but one thing in my power to refuse you, which is the knowledge of my name, which believing the sight of my face will render no secret, you must not take it ill that I conceal from you.—The bearer of this is a person I can trust; send by him your answer; but endeavor not*

to dive into the meaning of this mystery, which will be impossible for you to unravel, and at the same time very much disoblige me:—But that you may be in no apprehensions of being imposed on by a woman unworthy of your regard, I will venture to assure you, the first and greatest men in the kingdom would think themselves blessed to have that influence over me you have, though unknown to yourself, acquired.—But I need not go about to raise your curiosity, by giving you any idea of what my person is; if you think fit to be satisfied, resolve to visit me tomorrow about three in the afternoon; and though my face is hid, you shall not want sufficient demonstration, that she who takes these unusual measures to commence a friendship with you, is neither old, nor deformed. Till then I am,

Yours,
Incognita[3]

He had scarce come to the conclusion, before he asked the person who brought it, from what place he came;—the name of the lady he served;—if she were a wife, or widow, and several other questions directly opposite to the directions of the letter; but silence would have availed him as much as did all those testimonies of curiosity: no *Italian Bravo,*[4] employed in a business of the like nature, performed his office with more artifice; and the impatient inquirer was convinced, that nothing but doing as he was desired, could give him any light into the character of the woman who declared so violent a passion for him; and little fearing any consequence which could ensue from such an encounter, resolved to rest satisfied till he was informed of everything from herself, not imagining this *Incognita* varied so much from the generality of her sex, as to be able to refuse the knowledge of anything to the man she loved with that transcendency of passion she professed, and which his many successes with the ladies gave him encouragement enough to believe. He therefore took pen and paper, and answered her letter in terms tender enough for a man who had never seen the person to whom he wrote. The words were as follows:

To the Obliging and Witty Incognita.

Though to tell me I am happy enough to be liked by a woman, such, as by your manner of writing, I imagine you to be, is an honor which I can never sufficiently acknowledge, yet I know not how I am able to content myself with admiring the wonders of your wit alone: I am certain, a soul like yours must shine in your eyes with a vivacity, which must bless all they look on.—I shall, however, endeavor to restrain myself in those bounds you are pleased to set me, till by the knowledge of my inviolable fidelity, I may be thought worthy of gazing on that heaven I am now but to enjoy in contemplation.—You need not doubt my glad compliance with your obliging summons: there is a charm in your lines, which gives too sweet an idea of their lovely author to be resisted.— I am all impatient for the blissful moment, which is to throw me at your feet, and give me an opportunity of convincing you that I am,

Your everlasting slave,
Beauplaisir.

Nothing could be more pleased than she, to whom it was directed, at the receipt of this letter; but when she was told how inquisitive he had been concerning her character and circumstances, she could not forbear laughing heartily to think of the tricks she had played him, and applauding her own strength of genius, and force of resolution, which by such unthought-of ways could triumph over her lover's inconstancy, and render that very temper, which to other women is the greatest curse, a means

---

3. Unknown woman (Latin); i.e., a woman in disguise.   4. Hired assassin.

to make herself more blessed.—Had he been faithful to me (*said she, to herself*), either as *Fantomina*, or *Celia*, or the Widow *Bloomer*, the most violent passion, if it does not change its object, in time will wither: possession naturally abates the vigor of desire, and I should have had, at best, but a cold, insipid, husband-like lover in my arms; but by these arts of passing on him as a new mistress whenever the ardor, which alone makes love a blessing, begins to diminish, for the former one, I have him always raving, wild, impatient, longing, dying.—O that all neglected wives, and fond abandoned nymphs would take this method!—Men would be caught in their own snare, and have no cause to scorn our easy, weeping, wailing sex! Thus did she pride herself as if secure she never should have any reason to repent the present gaiety of her humor. The hour drawing near in which he was to come, she dressed herself in as magnificent a manner, as if she were to be that night at a ball at court, endeavoring to repair the want of those beauties which the vizard[5] should conceal, by setting forth the others with the greatest care and exactness. Her fine shape, and air, and neck appeared to great advantage; and by that which was to be seen of her, one might believe the rest to be perfectly agreeable. *Beauplaisir* was prodigiously charmed, as well with her appearance, as with the manner she entertained him: but though he was wild with impatience for the sight of a face which belonged to so exquisite a body, yet he would not immediately press for it, believing before he left her he should easily obtain that satisfaction.—A noble collation being over, he began to sue for the performance of her promise of granting everything he could ask, excepting the sight of her face, and knowledge of her name. It would have been a ridiculous piece of affectation in her to have seemed coy in complying with what she herself had been the first in desiring: she yielded without even a show of reluctance: and if there be any true felicity in an amour such as theirs, both here enjoyed it to the full. But not in the height of all their mutual raptures, could he prevail on her to satisfy his curiosity with the sight of her face: she told him that she hoped he knew so much of her, as might serve to convince him, she was not unworthy of his tenderest regard; and if he could not content himself with that which she was willing to reveal, and which was the conditions of their meeting, dear as he was to her, she would rather part with him for ever, than consent to gratify an inquisitiveness, which, in her opinion, had no business with his love. It was in vain that he endeavored to make her sensible of her mistake; and that this restraint was the greatest enemy imaginable to the happiness of them both: she was not to be persuaded, and he was obliged to desist his solicitations, though determined in his mind to compass what he so ardently desired, before he left the house. He then turned the discourse wholly on the violence of the passion he had for her; and expressed the greatest discontent in the world at the apprehensions of being separated;—swore he could dwell for ever in her arms, and with such an undeniable earnestness pressed to be permitted to tarry with her the whole night, that had she been less charmed with his renewed eagerness of desire, she scarce would have had the power of resisting him; but in granting this request, she was not without a thought that he had another reason for making it besides the extremity of his passion, and had it immediately in her head how to disappoint him.

The hours of repose being arrived, he begged she would retire to her chamber, to which she consented, but obliged him to go to bed first; which he did not much oppose, because he supposed she would not lie in her mask, and doubted not but the morning's dawn would bring the wished discovery.—The two imagined servants

5. Mask or veil.

ushered him to his new lodging; where he lay some moments in all the perplexity imaginable at the oddness of this adventure. But she suffered not these cogitations to be of any long continuance: she came, but came in the dark; which being no more than he expected by the former part of her proceedings, he said nothing of; but as much satisfaction as he found in her embraces, nothing ever longed for the approach of day with more impatience than he did. At last it came; but how great was his dis-appointment, when by the noises he heard in the street, the hurry of the coaches, and the cries of penny-merchants,[6] he was convinced it was night nowhere but with him? He was still in the same darkness as before; for she had taken care to blind the win-dows in such a manner, that not the least chink was left to let in day.—He com-plained of her behavior in terms that she would not have been able to resist yielding to, if she had not been certain it would have been the ruin of her passion:—she, there-fore, answered him only as she had done before; and getting out of the bed from him, flew out of the room with too much swiftness for him to have overtaken her, if he had attempted it. The moment she left him, the two attendants entered the chamber, and plucking down the implements which had screened him from the knowledge of that which he so much desired to find out, restored his eyes once more to day:—they attended to assist him in dressing, brought him tea, and by their obsequiousness, let him see there was but one thing which the mistress of them would not gladly oblige him in.—He was so much out of humor, however, at the disappointment of his curios-ity, that he resolved never to make a second visit.—Finding her in an outer room, he made no scruple of expressing the sense he had of the little trust she reposed in him, and at last plainly told her, he could not submit to receive obligations from a lady, who thought him uncapable of keeping a secret, which she made no difficulty of let-ting her servants into.—He resented—he once more entreated—he said all that man could do, to prevail on her to unfold the mystery; but all his adjurations were fruitless; and he went out of the house determined never to re-enter it, till she should pay the price of his company with the discovery of her face and circumstances.—She suffered him to go with this resolution, and doubted not but he would recede from it, when he reflected on the happy moments they had passed together; but if he did not, she com-forted herself with the design of forming some other stratagem, with which to impose on him a fourth time.

She kept the house, and her gentlemen-equipage[7] for about a fortnight, in which time she continued to write to him as *Fantomina* and the Widow *Bloomer*, and received the visits he sometimes made to each; but his behavior to both was grown so cold, that she began to grow as weary of receiving his now insipid caresses as he was of offering them: she was beginning to think in what manner she should drop these two characters, when the sudden arrival of her mother, who had been some time in a foreign country, obliged her to put an immediate stop to the course of her whimsical adventures.—That lady, who was severely virtuous, did not approve of many things she had been told of the conduct of her daughter; and though it was not in the power of any person in the world to inform her of the truth of what she had been guilty of, yet she heard enough to make her keep her afterwards in a restraint, little agreeable to her humor, and the liberties to which she had been accustomed.

But this confinement was not the greatest part of the trouble of this now afflicted lady: she found the consequences of her amorous follies would be, without almost a miracle, impossible to be concealed:—she was with child; and though she

---

6. Street vendors of cheap wares.   7. Retinue of footmen.

would easily have found means to have screened even this from the knowledge of the world, had she been at liberty to have acted with the same unquestionable authority over herself, as she did before the coming of her mother, yet now all her invention was at a loss for a stratagem to impose on a woman of her penetration:—by eating little, lacing prodigious straight, and the advantage of a great hoop-petticoat, however, her bigness was not taken notice of, and, perhaps, she would not have been suspected till the time of her going into the country, where her mother designed to send her, and from whence she intended to make her escape to some place where she might be delivered with secrecy, if the time of it had not happened much sooner than she expected.—A ball being at court, the good old lady was willing she should partake of the diversion of it as a farewell to the town.—It was there she was seized with those pangs, which none in her condition are exempt from:—she could not conceal the sudden rack which all at once invaded her; or had her tongue been mute, her wildly rolling eyes, the distortion of her features, and the convulsions which shook her whole frame, in spite of her, would have revealed she labored under some terrible shock of nature.—Everybody was surprised, everybody was concerned, but few guessed at the occasion.—Her mother grieved beyond expression, doubted not but she was struck with the hand of death; and ordered her to be carried home in a chair, while herself followed in another.—A physician was immediately sent for: but he presently perceiving what was her distemper, called the old lady aside, and told her, it was not a doctor of his sex, but one of her own, her daughter stood in need of.— Never was astonishment and horror greater than that which seized the soul of this afflicted parent at these words: she could not for a time believe the truth of what she heard; but he insisting on it, and conjuring her to send for a midwife, she was at length convinced of it.—All the pity and tenderness she had been for some moment before possessed of now vanished, and were succeeded by an adequate[8] shame and indignation:—she flew to the bed where her daughter was lying, and telling her what she had been informed of, and which she was now far from doubting, commanded her to reveal the name of the person whose insinuations had drawn her to this dishonor.—It was a great while before she could be brought to confess anything, and much longer before she could be prevailed on to name the man whom she so fatally had loved; but the rack of nature growing more fierce, and the enraged old lady protesting no help should be afforded her while she persisted in her obstinacy, she, with great difficulty and hesitation in her speech, at last pronounced the name of *Beauplaisir*. She had no sooner satisfied her weeping mother, than that sorrowful lady sent messengers at the same time, for a midwife, and for that gentleman who had occasioned the other's being wanted.—He happened by accident to be at home, and immediately obeyed the summons, though prodigiously surprised what business a lady so much a stranger to him could have to impart.—But how much greater was his amazement, when taking him into her closet, she there acquainted him with her daughter's misfortune, of the discovery she had made, and how far he was concerned in it?—All the idea one can form of wild astonishment, was mean to what he felt:— he assured her, that the young lady her daughter was a person whom he had never, more than at a distance, admired:—that he had indeed, spoke to her in public company, but that he never had a thought which tended to her dishonor.—His denials, if possible, added to the indignation she was before enflamed with:—she had no longer patience; and carrying him into the chamber, where she was just delivered of

8. Equal.

a fine girl, cried out, I will not be imposed on: the truth by one of you shall be revealed.—*Beauplaisir* being brought to the bedside, was beginning to address himself to the lady in it, to beg she could clear the mistake her mother was involved in; when she, covering herself with the cloths, and ready to die a second time with the inward agitations of her soul, shrieked out, Oh, I am undone!—I cannot live, and bear this shame!—But the old lady believing that now or never was the time to dive into the bottom of this mystery, forcing her to rear her head, told her, she should not hope to escape the scrutiny of a parent she had dishonored in such a manner, and pointing to *Beauplaisir,* Is this the gentleman (*said she*), to whom you owe your ruin? or have you deceived me by a fictitious tale? Oh! no (*resumed the trembling creature*), he is, indeed, the innocent cause of my undoing:—Promise me your pardon (*continued she*), and I will relate the means. Here she ceased, expecting what she would reply, which, on hearing *Beauplaisir* cry out, What mean you, madam? I your undoing, who never harbored the least design on you in my life, she did in these words, Though the injury you have done your family (*said she*), is of a nature which cannot justly hope forgiveness, yet be assured, I shall much sooner excuse you when satisfied of the truth, than while I am kept in a suspense, if possible, as vexatious as the crime itself is to me. Encouraged by this she related the whole truth. And 'tis difficult to determine, if *Beauplaisir,* or the lady, were most surprised at what they heard; he, that he should have been blinded so often by her artifices; or she, that so young a creature should have the skill to make use of them. Both sat for some time in a profound reverie; till at length she broke it first in these words: Pardon, sir (*said she*),[9] the trouble I have given you: I must confess it was with a design to oblige you to repair the supposed injury you had done this unfortunate girl, by marrying her, but now I know not what to say:—The blame is wholly hers, and I have nothing to request further of you, than that you will not divulge the distracted folly she has been guilty of.—He answered her in terms perfectly polite; but made no offer of that which, perhaps, she expected, though could not, now informed of her daughter's proceedings, demand. He assured her, however, that if she would commit the newborn lady to his care, he would discharge it faithfully. But neither of them would consent to that; and he took his leave, full of cogitations,[1] more confused than ever he had known in his whole life. He continued to visit there, to inquire after her health every day; but the old lady perceiving there was nothing likely to ensue from these civilities, but, perhaps, a renewing of the crime, she entreated him to refrain; and as soon as her daughter was in a condition, sent her to a monastery in *France,* the abbess of which had been her particular friend. And thus ended an intrigue, which, considering the time it lasted, was as full of variety as any, perhaps, that many ages have produced.

Samuel Richardson
1689–1761

"From my earliest youth," Samuel Richardson once recalled, "I had a love of letter-writing." That love, coupled with his high achievements as a printer and his marked predilection for inculcating virtue, enabled him to reroute the course of fiction at a single stroke, with his first

---

9. I.e., the elder lady.   1. Anxious thoughts.

novel. *Pamela; or, Virtue Rewarded* (1740), was rapidly written and promptly published by a man who, now fifty years old, had never really intended to become an author at all. Nonetheless, he was drawing on a lifetime of epistolary experience, as he makes clear in his sole surviving autobiography—itself a long letter to his inquisitive Dutch translator. In his teens, Richardson explains, at the request of the "young women of taste and reading in the neighborhood," he composed "answers to their lovers' letters," and observed intently the conflicting emotions that his prose was to capture or conceal: "I have been directed to chide, and even repulse, when an offence was either taken or given, at the very time that the heart of the chider or repulser was open before me, overflowing with esteem and affection—and the fair repulser dreading to be taken at her word, directing *this* word, or *that* expression, to be softened or changed." A little later, during his arduous apprenticeship, Richardson found solace in his copious correspondence with "a gentlemen greatly my superior in degree, . . . a master of the epistolary style," from whom, he implies, he derived his most authentic and valuable education. Finally, years after he had established himself as one of London's most efficient and prosperous printers, Richardson received a commission from two publishers who "entreated me to write for them a little volume of letters, in a common style, on such subjects as might be of use to those country readers who were unable to indite [i.e., compose letters] for themselves. 'Will it be any harm,' said I, 'in a piece you want to be written so low, if we should instruct them how to think and act in common cases, as well as indite?' . . . I set about it, and in the progress of it, [wrote] two or three letters to instruct handsome girls" who worked as house servants "how to avoid the snares that might be laid against their virtue" by men of the household seeking to seduce them. "And hence," Richardson concludes, "sprung Pamela"—a servant who finds herself, at sixteen years old, beset by just such advances from her master Mr. B. and, in the novel that bears her name, writes up her ordeal in a series of letters and journals addressed to her anxious parents. What struck readers most about the novel's content was its double argument, familiar in outline but freshly dramatized: that virtue was of paramount importance for its own sake; but that if zealously sustained, it might yield impressive earthly rewards—even to the point of dissolving the barriers of class and wealth. What struck readers most about the novel's form was its intrinsic intensity: the way each letter slowed down time and heightened experience, as Richardson sought to capture complex emotional oscillations of the kind that he had first observed in those ardent, agitated "young women" years earlier. After *Pamela*, the epistolary mode dominated novel-writing for decades. Richardson, meanwhile, though still assiduous in his work as printer, wrote a sequel to *Pamela*, and two much longer novels, *Clarissa* (1747–48) and *Sir Charles Grandison* (1753–54), in which he continued to explore and expound the fictional method that, to his obvious delight, he had improbably invented.

from Pamela; or, Virtue Rewarded
Preface by the Editor[1]

If to *divert* and *entertain*, and at the same time to *instruct*, and *improve* the minds of the *youth* of *both sexes*:

> If to inculcate *religion* and *morality* in so easy and agreeable a manner, as shall render them equally *delightful* and *profitable* to the *younger class* of readers, as well as worthy of the attention of persons of *maturer* years and understandings:
>
> If to set forth in the most exemplary lights the *parental*, the *filial*, and the *social* duties, and that from *low* to *high* life:

---

1. Richardson, like Defoe, presents himself in his novels not as author but as editor of authentic manuscripts which have come into his hands. Richardson's pointed emphases have been retained (in italics) throughout the preface.

If to paint *vice* in its proper colors, to make it *deservedly odious*; and to set *virtue* in its own amiable light, to make it *truly lovely*:

If to draw characters *justly*, and to support them *equally*:

If to raise a distress from *natural* causes, and to excite compassion from *proper* motives:

If to teach the man of *fortune* how to *use* it; the man of *passion* how to *subdue* it; and the man of *intrigue*,[2] how, gracefully, and with honor to himself, to *reclaim:*[3]

If to give *practical* examples, worthy to be followed in the most *critical* and *affecting* cases, by the modest *virgin*, the chaste *bride*, and the obliging *wife*:

If to effect all these good ends, in so probable, so natural, so *lively* a manner, as shall engage the passions of every sensible[4] reader, and strongly interest them in the edifying story:

And all without raising a *single idea* throughout the whole, that shall shock the exactest purity, even in those tender instances where the exactest purity would be most apprehensive:

If these (embellished with a great variety of entertaining incidents) be laudable or worthy recommendations of any work, the editor of the following letters, which have their foundation in *truth* and *nature*, ventures to assert, that all these desirable ends are obtained in these sheets. And as he is therefore confident of the favorable reception which he boldly bespeaks for this little work, he thinks any further *preface* or *apology*[5] for it unnecessary, and rather for two reasons: First, because he can appeal from *his own* passions (which have been uncommonly *moved* in perusing these engaging scenes) to the passions of *everyone* who shall read them with the least attention; and, in the next place, because an *editor* may be reasonably supposed to judge with an impartiality which is rarely to be met with in an *author* towards his own works.

The Editor

[A Dreadful Trial][6]

My dear parents,

O let me take up my complaint, and say, never was poor creature so unhappy, and so barbarously used, as your Pamela! O my dear father and mother, my heart's just broke! I can neither write as I should do, nor let it alone, for to whom but you can I vent my griefs, and keep my poor heart from bursting! Wicked, wicked man! I have no patience left me! But yet, don't be frighted—for—I hope—I hope, I am honest! But if my head and my heart will let me, you shall hear all. Is there no constable nor headborough,[7] though, to take me out of his house? For I am sure I can safely swear the peace against him.[8] But, alas! he is greater than any constable, and is a Justice himself;[9] such a Justice, deliver me from! But God Almighty, I hope, in time, will right me! For he knows the innocence of my heart!

---

2. Amorous schemes and affairs.

3. Reform.

4. Sensitive; capable of "being easily or strongly affected" (Johnson's *Dictionary*).

5. Defense.

6. Mr. B., finding his attempts at seduction energetically defied, has promised Pamela that she may soon return to her parents; he now tries out a new tactic of attack. "I have been rallied [teased]," Richardson remarked, "on a

warm [i.e. potentially erotic] scene or two in *Pamela*"; this is one of them. (For Henry Fielding's unsparing parody, see pages 2821–22).

7. "A subordinate constable" (Johnson's *Dictionary*); a parish officer.

8. I.e., have him restrained on the grounds that he has threatened bodily harm.

9. I.e., Mr. B. is himself a Justice of the Peace, possessing the highest legal authority within the parish.

John went your way in the morning, but I have been too much distracted to send by him;[1] and have seen nobody but Mrs. Jervis, and Rachel,[2] and one I hate to see. And indeed I hate now to see anybody. Strange things I have to tell you, that happened since last night, that good Mr. Jonathan's letter, and my master's harshness put me into such a fluster.[3] But I will no more *preambulate*.[4]

I went to Mrs. Jervis's chamber; and Oh! my dear father and mother, my wicked master had hid himself (base gentleman as he is!) in her closet,[5] where she has a few books, and chest of drawers, and such-like. I little suspected it, though I used, till this sad night, always to look into that closet, and another in the room, and under the bed, ever since the summer house trick,[6] but never found anything; and so I did not do it then, being fully resolved to be angry with Mrs. Jervis for what had happened in the day,[7]and so thought of nothing else.

I sat myself down on one side of the bed, and she on the other, and we began to undress ourselves; but she on that side next the wicked closet, that held the worst heart in the world. "So," said Mrs. Jervis, "you won't speak to me, Pamela! I find you are angry with me." "Why, Mrs. Jervis," said I, "so I am, a little; 'tis a folly to deny it. You see what I have suffered by your forcing me in to my master! And a gentlewoman of your years and experience must needs know that it was not fit for me to pretend to be anybody else for my own sake, nor with regard to my master."[7]

"But," said she, "who would have thought it would have turned out so?" "Aye," said I, little thinking who heard me, "Lucifer always is ready to promote his own work and workmen. You see, presently, what use he made of it, pretending not to know me, on purpose to be free with me. And when he took upon himself to know me, to quarrel with me, and use me hardly—and you too," said I, "to cry, 'Fie, fie, Pamela!,' cut me to the heart, for that encouraged him."

"Do you think, my dear, that I would encourage him? I never said so to you before, but since you force it from me, I must tell you, that ever since you consulted me, I have used my utmost endeavors to divert him from his wicked purposes, and he has promised fair; but, to say all in a word, he dotes upon you; and I begin to see it is not in his power to help it."

I luckily said nothing of the note from Mr. Jonathan; for I began to suspect all the world almost. But I said, to try Mrs. Jervis, "Well then, what would you have me do? You see he is for having me wait on Lady Davers now."[8]

"Well, I'll tell you freely, my dear Pamela," said she, "and I trust to your discretion to conceal what I say: my master has been often desiring me to put you upon asking him to let you stay."

1. John, Mr. B's footman, has earned Pamela's trust by carrying letters back and forth between her and her parents.

2. Rachel is a housemaid; Mrs. Jervis is Mr. B's housekeeper, supervisor of his household staff. Pamela at first found her sympathetic ("the best friend I have in the world"), and asked permission to sleep in her room for the sake of security. She has now begun to suspect, wrongly, that Mrs. Jervis is complicit in Mr. B's schemes.

3. Jonathan, a fellow servant, has sent Pamela a short note warning her that, despite her expectation of being allowed to return to her parents, Mr. B. has declared that "By G— I will have her!"

4. I.e., write this preface to the main narrative.

5. "A small room of privacy and retirement" (Johnson's

Dictionary).

6. When Mr. B, cornering Pamela in his garden gazebo, for the first time forced a kiss upon her, and made clear his intention that she become his mistress.

7. Earlier in the day, after Pamela had changed into simple "homespun" garb in expectation of soon returning to her parents, Mr. B. failed to recognize her, and took her for some unknown and perhaps seducible local beauty. Perceiving his mistake, Mrs. Jervis took the opportunity to inveigle Pamela into yet another unwanted and uncomfortable encounter with her master.

8. In order to retain access to Pamela, Mr. B. has proposed that she become a servant in his sister's household, rather than return home to her parents.

"Yes," said I, "Mrs. Jervis, let me interrupt you. I will tell you why I could not think of that. It was not the pride of my heart, but the pride of my honesty.[9] For what must have been the case? Here my master has been very rude to me, once or twice; and you say he cannot help it, though he pretends to be sorry for it. Well, he has given me warning to leave my place, and uses me very harshly, mayhap to frighten me to his purposes, as he supposes I would be fond of staying (as indeed I should, if I could be safe; for I love you and all the house, and value him, if he would act as my master). Well then, as I know his designs, and that he owns he cannot help it, must I not have asked to stay, knowing he would attempt me again? For all you could assure me of, was, he would do nothing by *force*; so I, a poor weak girl, was to be left to my own strength, God knows! And was not this to allow him to tempt me, as one may say? and to encourage him to go on in his wicked devices? How then, Mrs. Jervis, could I ask or wish to stay?"

"You say well, my dear child," says she, "and you have a justness of thought above your years; and for all these confederations, and for what I have heard this day, after you run away (and I am glad you went as you did) I cannot persuade you to stay; and I shall be glad, which is what I never thought I could have said, that you was well at your father's; for if Lady Davers will entertain[1] you, she may as well have you from thence as here." "There's my good Mrs. Jervis!" said I. "God will bless you for your good counsel to a poor maiden that is hard beset. But pray what did he say," said I, "when I was gone?" "Why," said she, "he was very angry with you." "But he would hear it!"[2] said I. "I think it was a little bold, but then he provoked me to it. And had not my honesty been in the case, I would not by any means have been so saucy. Besides, Mrs. Jervis, consider, it was the truth: if he does not love to hear of the summer house and the dressing room,[3] why should he not be ashamed to continue in the same mind?" "But," said she, "when you had muttered this to yourself, you might have told him anything else."[4] "Well," said I, "I cannot tell a willful lie, and so there's an end of it. But I find you now give him up, and think there's danger in staying! Lord bless me, I wish I was well out of the house, though it was at the bottom of a wet ditch, on the wildest common in England!"

"Why," said she, "it signifies nothing to tell you all he said; but it was enough to make me fear you would not be so safe as I could wish; and upon my word, Pamela, I don't wonder he loves you; for, without flattery, you are a charming girl! And I never saw you look more lovely in my life than in that same new dress of yours. And then it was such a surprise upon us all! I believe truly, you owe some of your danger to the lovely appearance you made." "Then," said I, "I wish the clothes in the fire. I expected no effect from them, but if any, a quite contrary one.—Hush!" said I, "Mrs. Jervis, did you not hear something stir in the closet?" "No, silly girl," said she! "Your fears are always awake!" "But indeed," says I, "I think I heard something rustle!" "Maybe," says she, "the cat may be got there. But I hear nothing."

I was hush, but she said, "Prithee, my good girl, make haste to bed. See if the door be fast." So I did, and was thinking to look in the closet. But hearing no more noise, thought it needless, and so went again and sat myself down on the bedside, and went on undressing myself. And Mrs. Jervis, being by this time undressed, stepped into bed, and bid me hasten, for she was sleepy.

---

9. Chastity.
1. Employ.
2. I.e., he created a situation in which he was forced to

listen to my refusal.
3. Another site of Mr. B's recent attempts.
4. I.e., you ought not have confronted him so directly.

I don't know what was the matter; but my heart sadly misgave me; but Mr. Jonathan's note was enough to make it do so, with what Mrs. Jervis had said. I pulled off my stays,[5] and my stockens, and my gown, all to an under-petticoat, and then hearing a rustling again in the closet, I said, "God protect us! but before I say my prayers I must look into this closet." And so was going to it slipshod,[6] when—O dreadful!—out rushed my master, in a rich silk and silver morning gown.[7]

I screamed, and run to the bed; and Mrs. Jervis screamed too; and he said, "I'll do you no harm, if you forbear this noise; but otherwise take what follows."

Instantly he came to the bed; for I had crept into it, to Mrs. Jervis, with my coat on, and my shoes. And taking me in his arms, said, "Mrs. Jervis, rise, and just step upstairs, to keep the maids from coming down at this noise. I'll do no harm to this rebel."

"O, for God's sake! for pity's sake! Mrs. Jervis," said I, "if I am not betrayed, don't leave me; and I beseech you, raise[8] all the house." "No," said Mrs. Jervis, "I will not stir, my dear lamb; I will not leave you. I wonder at you, Sir," said she, and kindly threw herself upon my coat, clasping me round the waist. "You shall not hurt this innocent," said she, "for I will lose my life in her defense. Are there not," said she, "enough wicked ones in the world, for your base purpose, but you must attempt such a lamb as this!"

He was desperate angry, and threatened to throw her out of the window, and to turn her out of the house the next morning. "You need not, sir," said she, "for I will not stay in it. God defend my poor Pamela till tomorrow, and we will both go together." Says he, "Let me but expostulate a word or two with you, Pamela." "Pray, Pamela," said Mrs. Jervis, "don't hear a word, except[9] he leaves the bed, and goes to the other end of the room." "Aye, out of the room!" said I. "Expostulate tomorrow, if you must expostulate!"

I found his hand in my bosom, and when my fright let me know it, I was ready to die; and I sighed, and screamed, and fainted away. And still he had his arms about my neck; and Mrs. Jervis was about my feet, and upon my coat. And all in a cold, clammy sweat was I. "Pamela, Pamela!" said Mrs. Jervis, as she tells me since. "O—h"—and gave another shriek—"my Pamela is dead for certain!" And so, to be sure, I was for a time; for I knew nothing more of the matter, one fit following another, till about three hours after, as it proved to be, I found myself in bed, and Mrs. Jervis sitting up one side, with her wrapper about her, and Rachel on the other, and no master, for the wicked wretch was gone. But I was so overjoyed that I hardly could believe myself; and I said, which were my first words, "Mrs. Jervis, Mrs. Rachel, can I be sure it is you? God be praised! God be praised! Where have I been?" "Hush, my dear," said Mrs. Jervis. "You have been in fit after fit. I never saw anybody so frightful in my life!"

By this I judged Mrs. Rachel knew nothing of the matter; and it seems my wicked master had, upon Mrs. Jervis's second noise on my going away, slipped out, and, as if he had come from his own chamber, disturbed by the screaming, went up to the maids' room (who, hearing the noise, lay trembling, and afraid to stir) and bid them go down and see what was the matter with Mrs. Jervis and me. And he charged Mrs. Jervis, and promised to forgive her for what she had said and done, if she would

---

5. Corset; stiff undergarment.
6. Wearing slippers.
7. "A loose gown worn before one is formally dressed"

(Johnson's *Dictionary*).
8. Wake.
9. Unless.

conceal the matter. So the maids came down; for the men lie in the outhouses;[1] and all went up again, when I came to myself a little, except Rachel, who stayed to sit up with me, and bear Mrs. Jervis company. I believe they all guess the matter to be bad enough, though they dare not say anything.

When I think of my danger, and the freedoms he actually took, though I believe Mrs. Jervis saved me from worse, and she says she did (though what can I think, who was in a fit, and know nothing of the matter?), I am almost distracted.[2]

At first I was afraid of Mrs. Jervis; but I am fully satisfied she is very good, and I should have been lost but for her; and she takes on grievously about it. What would have become of me, had she gone out of the room, to still the maids, as he bid her? He'd certainly have shut her out, and then, Mercy on me! what would have become of your poor Pamela!

I must leave off a little, for my eyes and my head are sadly bad.—O this was a dreadful trial! This was the worst of all! God send me safe from this dreadful wicked man! Pray for

For an additional selection from *Pamela*, see *The Longman Anthology of British Literature* Web site at www.myliteraturekit.com.

Your distressed daughter.

from *The Preface to* Clarissa. Or, The History of a Young Lady[1]

* * * All the letters are written while the hearts of the writers must be supposed to be wholly engaged in their subjects (the events at the time generally dubious);[2] so that they abound not only with critical situations, but with what may be called *instantaneous* descriptions and reflections (proper to be brought home to the breast of the youthful reader); as also with affecting conversations, many of them written in the dialogue or dramatic way. "Much more lively and affecting," says one of the principal characters,[3] "must be the style of those who write in the height of *present* distress; the mind tortured by the pangs of uncertainty (the events then hidden in the womb of Fate); than the dry, narrative, unanimated style of a person relating difficulties and dangers surmounted can be; the relater perfectly at ease; and if himself unmoved by his own story, not likely greatly to affect the reader." * * *

1747

from *The Preface to* The History of Sir Charles Grandison, Baronet[4]

* * * The nature of familiar letters, written, as it were, to the *moment*, while the heart is agitated by hopes and fears, on events undecided, must plead an excuse for the *bulk* of a collection of this kind.[5] Mere facts and characters might be comprised in a much smaller compass: but, would they be equally interesting? It happens fortunately, that an account of the juvenile years of the principal person is narratively

---

1. Buildings located elsewhere on the estate.
2. Driven mad.
1. In the prefaces to all three of his novels, Richardson defended the morality of his writing. In his prefaces to the last two, he celebrated the method also: the power of the epistolary mode.
2. I.e., the outcome being doubtful.
3. Richardson quotes his fictional creation John Belford,

friend and aid to the novel's villain Robert Lovelace. Like Mr. B. before him, Belford takes pleasure in reading the letters of the suffering protagonist.
4. Earlier in the preface, Richardson has declared the new topic of his third novel: "the character and actions of a man of true honor."
5. In its original, multivolume editions, *Grandison* ran about 2,400 pages.

given in some of the letters. As many, however, as could be spared, have been omitted. There is not one episode in the whole; nor, after Sir CHARLES GRANDISON is introduced, one letter inserted, but what tends to illustrate the principal design. Those which precede his introduction, will not, it is hoped, be judged unnecessary on the whole, as they tend to make the reader acquainted with persons, the history of whom is closely interwoven with that of Sir Charles.

1753

Henry Fielding
1707–1754

Richardson's *Pamela; or, Virtue Rewarded* prompted a huge response, ranging from praise to parody. Eliza Haywood authored the *Anti-Pamela; or, Feigned Innocence Detected* (1741), which makes good on its title by tracing the adventures of its heroine, the decidedly unchaste Syrena Tricksy, who pursues by sexual manipulation the ascent in wealth and standing that Richardson's Pamela attains by virtue alone. Syrena's lascivious exploits constitute Haywood's farewell to the amorous, sensual fiction she had so profitably pioneered. Like many other novelists, she soon veered in Richardson's overtly moralistic direction, first in the short fictions of *The Female Spectator*, and then in her last novels.

For Henry Fielding, by contrast, parody of *Pamela* produced a fresh start, from which followed his life's most lasting work. Fielding's fame had long preceded Richardson's; he had spent the 1730s as a prolific and celebrated satiric playwright, until strict new measures of censorship proscribed him from the playhouse, and prompted him to search for something new. In *Shamela*, his first foray into fiction, Fielding compresses a Haywood-like exposé into his heroine's very name: she is a sham—libidinous, cunning, and shameless—from start to finish. But in the long title of his short parody—*An Apology for the Life of Mrs. Shamela Andrews*—Fielding widens his satiric scope. He echoes the rubric of *An Apology for the Life of Colley Cibber*, the autobiography of a widely known actor, which had appeared in the same year as *Pamela*, and which had appalled Fielding, among others, for its loquacity, seeming shapelessness, and shameless vanity; no actor hitherto had seen fit to recount at such length what was still deemed an intrinsically low career.

In *Shamela*, then, Fielding mocks not only the most influential novel of the century, but also the tradition of autobiography—copiously particularized, inherently self-centered—which had shadowed the whole genre, like a sometimes indistinguishable twin, from its inception. In *Joseph Andrews*, his first full-length novel, Fielding took *Shamela*'s key jokes further, but also much deeper. As target, Cibber remains much in view, and the titular Joseph Andrews, brother to Richardson's Pamela, undergoes a gendered inversion of her predicament; he is beset by his *female* employer, the lustful Lady Booby (sister to Richardson's more discreetly named Mr. B.). But in *Joseph Andrews*, and more expansively in his next novel *Tom Jones*, Fielding pushes past the straightforward reversals of parody to declare himself "the founder of a new province of writing," whose newness consisted partly in a theory of the "ridiculous" at once mocking and humane; partly in the Quixote-like mix of innocence and ineptitude variously and endearingly embodied in his fiction's central characters; but especially in the foregrounding of a component largely excluded from Richardson's fiction: the voice of an omnipresent and observant author, who views his characters, and addresses his readers, with an ironic acuity designed to enhance audience access to those two abiding desiderata of eighteenth-century literature, instruction and delight.

from An Apology for the Life of Mrs. Shamela Andrews[1]

SHAMELA ANDREWS TO HENRIETTA MARIA HONORA ANDREWS

O Madam, I have strange things to tell you! As I was reading in that charming book about the dealings,[2] in comes my master—to be sure he is a precious one. Pamela, says he, what book is that, I warrant you Rochester's poems.[3]—No, forsooth, says I, as pertly as I could. Why how now saucy chops, boldface, says he—Mighty pretty words, says I, pert again.—Yes (says he) you are a d—d, impudent, stinking, cursed, confounded jade, and I have a great mind to kick your a—. You, kiss— says I. A—gad,[4] says, he, and so I will; with that he caught me in his arms, and kissed me till he made my face all over fire. Now this served purely, you know, to put upon the fool for anger.[5] O! What precious fools men are! And so I flung from him in a mighty rage, and pretended as how I would go out at the door; but when I came to the end of the room, I stood still, and my master cried out, Hussy, slut, saucebox, boldface, come hither.—Yes to be sure, says I. Why don't you come, says he. What should I come for, says I. If you don't come to me, I'll come to you, says he. I shan't come to you I assure you, says I. Upon which he run up, caught me in his arms, and flung me upon a chair, and began to offer to touch my under-petticoat. Sir, says I, you had better not offer to be rude. Well, says he, no more I won't then; and away he went out of the room. I was so mad to be sure I could have cried.

Oh what a prodigious vexation it is to a woman to be made a fool of.

Mrs. Jervis, who had been without, harkening, now came to me. She burst into a violent laugh the moment she came in. Well, says she, as soon as she could speak, I have reason to bless myself that I am an old woman. Ah, child! If you had known the jolly blades of my age, you would not have been left in the lurch in this manner. Dear Mrs. Jervis, says I, don't laugh at one; and to be sure I was a little angry with her.—Come, says she, my dear honeysuckle, I have one game to play for you; he shall see you in bed; he shall, my little rosebud, he shall see those pretty, little, white, round, panting——; and offered to pull off my handkerchief. —Fie, Mrs. Jervis, says I, you make me blush, and upon my fackins,[6] I believe she did. She went on thus: I know the squire likes you, and notwithstanding the awkwardness of his pro-ceeding, I am convinced hath some hot blood in his veins, which will not let him rest, 'till he hath communicated some of his warmth to thee, my little angel. I heard him last night at our door, trying if it was open. Now tonight I will take care it shall be so; I warrant that he makes the second trial; which if he doth, he shall find us ready to receive him. I will at first counterfeit sleep, and after a swoon; so that he will have you naked in his possession: and then if you are disappointed, a plague of all young squires, say I.—And so, Mrs. Jervis, says I, you would have me yield myself to him, would you; you would have me be a second time a fool for nothing.[7] Thank

---

1. Letter 6. The multiple names of Shamela's mother sug-gest pretensions to which the parents in *Pamela* (plain John and Elizabeth Andrews) would never aspire. Field-ing's letter closely tracks, and mocks, the nighttime alarms narrated in *Pamela*'s letter 25, above (pages 2815–19).

2. The book that Shamela has just received from her mother: *A Short Account of God's Dealings with the Rev-erend Mr. George Whitefield, from his Infancy, to the Time of his Entering into Holy Orders* (174), written by White-field himself (1714–1770), a prominent Methodist preacher whose autobiographical writings prompted widespread charges of sinful pride and rampant egomania. In counting Shamela and her mother among Whitefield's enthusiastic readers, Fielding sustains his attack on self-indulgent self-inscribers, for which his chief target, throughout *Shamela* and *Joseph Andrews*, is the secular autobiography of the actor Colley Cibber.

3. John Wilmot, Earl of Rochester (1647–1680), notori-ous for the obscenity of his verse (see pages 2202–13).

4. By God

5. I.e., deceive him into thinking I was angry.

6. By my faith.

7. Shamela alludes to her first liaison, with the sexually skillful but penniless Parson Williams, with whom she has had an illegitimate child. In Richardson's novel, Williams is a virtuous but at times ineffectual clergyman, who tries hard to provide Pamela with practical and spiri-tual succor; in Fielding's parody, he is a seductive rascal.

you for that, Mrs. Jervis. For nothing! Marry forbid, says she, you know he hath large sums of money, besides abundance of fine things; and do you think, when you have inflamed him, by giving his hand a liberty with that charming person; and that you know he may easily think he obtains against your will, he will not give anything to come at all?[8] —This will not do, Mrs. Jervis, answered I. I have heard my Mamma say (and you know, Madam, I have) that in her youth, fellows have often taken away in the morning what they gave overnight. No, Mrs. Jervis, nothing under a regular taking into keeping, a settled settlement,[9] for me, and all my heirs, all my whole lifetime, shall do the business—or else cross-legged, is the word, faith, with Sham; and then I snapped my fingers.

Thursday night, twelve o'clock

Mrs. Jervis and I are just in bed, and the door unlocked; if my master should come— odsbobs![1] I hear him just come in at the door. You see I write in the present tense, as Parson Williams says.[2] Well, he is in bed between us, we both shamming a sleep, he steals his hand into my bosom, which I, as if in my sleep, press close to me with mine, and then pretend to awake.—I no sooner see him, but I scream out to Mrs. Jervis, she feigns likewise but just to come to herself; we both begin, she to becall, and I to bescratch very liberally. After having made a pretty free use of my fingers, without any great regard to the parts I attacked, I counterfeit a swoon. Mrs. Jervis then cries out, Oh, Sir, what have you done, you have murdered poor Pamela: she is gone, she is gone.—

Oh what a difficulty it is to keep one's countenance, when a violent laugh desires to burst forth.

The poor booby, frightened out of his wits, jumped out of bed, and, in his shirt,[3] sat down by my bedside, pale and trembling, for the moon shone, and I kept my eyes wide open and pretended to fix them in my head. Mrs. Jervis applied lavender water and hartshorn,[4] and this, for a full half hour; when, thinking I had carried it on long enough, and being likewise unable to continue the sport any longer, I began by degrees to come to myself.

The squire, who had sat all this while speechless, and was almost really in that condition which I feigned, the moment he saw me give symptoms of recovering my senses, fell down on his knees; and Oh Pamela, cried he, can you forgive me, my injured maid? By heaven, I know not whether you are a man or a woman, unless by your swelling breasts. Will you promise to forgive me? I forgive you! D—n you (says I) and d—n you, says he, if you come to that. I wish I had never seen your bold face, saucy sow, and so went out of the room.

Oh what a silly fellow is a bashful young lover!

He was no sooner out of hearing, as we thought, than we both burst into a violent laugh. Well, says Mrs. Jervis, I never saw anything better acted than your part: but I wish you may not have discouraged him from any future attempt; especially since his passions are so cool, that you could prevent his hands going further than your bosom. Hang him, answered I, he is not quite so cold as that I assure you; our hands, on neither side, were idle in the scuffle, nor have left us any doubt of each other as to that matter.

---

8. I.e., to take full possession of you.
9. I.e., Shamela will not consent to consummation until she is offered full status as a "kept" mistress, with a legal contract spelling out payments and compensations.
1. A compression of "Ods bodkins": [by] God's little body!
2. Fielding echoes, and mocks, Richardson's doctrine of

writing "to the *moment*" (see page 2819).
3. Nightshirt.
4. An herb used (like the lavender water) as a smelling salt.

Friday Morning

My master sent for Mrs. Jervis, as soon as he was up, and bid her give an account of the plate and linen in her care; and told her, he was resolved that both she and the little gipsy (I'll assure him[5]) should set out together. Mrs. Jervis made him a saucy answer; which any servant of spirit, you know, would, though it should be one's ruin; and came immediately in tears to me, crying, she had lost her place on my account, and that she should be forced to take to a house,[6] as I mentioned before; and that she hoped I would, at least, make her all the amends in my power, for her loss on my account, and come to her house whenever I was sent for. Never fear, says I, I'll warrant we are not so near being turned away as you imagine; and, i'cod,[7] now it comes into my head, I have a fetch[8] for him, and you shall assist me in it. But it being now late, and my letter pretty long, no more at present from

Your dutiful daughter,
SHAMELA

1741   1741

from *The Preface to* The History of the Adventures of Joseph Andrews

As it is possible the mere *English* reader may have a different idea of romance[1] with the author of these volumes; and may consequently expect a kind of entertainment not to be found, nor which was even intended, in the following pages; it may not be improper to premise a few words concerning this kind of writing, which I do not remember to have seen hitherto attempted in our language.

The *epic* as well as the *drama* is divided into tragedy and comedy. *Homer*, who was the father of this species of poetry, gave us a pattern of both these, though that of the latter is entirely lost; which *Aristotle* tells us, bore the same relation to comedy which his *Iliad* bears to tragedy.[2] And perhaps, that we have no more instances of it among the writers of antiquity, is owing to the loss of this great pattern, which, had it survived, would have found its imitators equally with the other poems of this great original.

And farther, as this poetry may be tragic or comic, I will not scruple to say it may be likewise either in verse or prose: for though it wants one particular, which the critic enumerates in the constituent parts of an epic poem, namely meter; yet, when any kind of writing contains all its other parts, such as fable, action, characters, sentiments, and diction, and is deficient in meter only; it seems, I think, reasonable to refer to the epic; at least, as no critic hath thought proper to range it under any other head, nor assign it a particular name to itself * * *

Now a comic romance is a comic epic-poem in prose; differing from comedy, as the serious epic from tragedy; its action being more extended and comprehensive; containing a much larger circle of incidents, and introducing a greater variety of characters. It differs from the serious romance in its fable and action, in this: that as in the one these are grave and solemn, so in the other they are light and ridiculous.

---

5. I.e., "as he dares to call me (and as I am in fact)."
6. I.e., a brothel. Mrs. Jervis is eager to set up in the business, and Shamela's mother has offered to help.
7. By God.
8. Trick.
1. The word's meaning varied widely in the eighteenth century. Johnson's *Dictionary* offers these definitions: "A tale of wild adventures in war and love; . . . a lie; a

fiction." For Johnson's own ideas on the much-discussed question of romance's relation to newer modes of fiction, see his Ramber No. 4 (pages 2688–91); for Clara Reeve's lapidary contrast between the two terms, see page 2791.
2. Aristotle (*Poetics*, 4.10–12) mentions a burlesque called *Margites* ("madman") of which only a small fragment now survives; the claim for Homeric authorship is unsubstantiated.

It differs in its characters by introducing persons of inferior rank, and consequently of inferior manners, whereas the grave romance sets the highest before us; lastly in its sentiments and diction, by preserving the ludicrous instead of the sublime. In the diction I think burlesque itself may be sometimes admitted; of which many instances will occur in this work, as in the descriptions of the battles, and some other places, not necessary to be pointed out to the classical reader; for whose entertainment those parodies or burlesque imitations are chiefly calculated.

But though we have sometimes admitted this in our diction, we have carefully excluded it from our sentiments and characters. For there it is never properly introduced, unless in writings of the burlesque kind, which this is not intended to be. Indeed, no two species of writing can differ more widely than the comic and the burlesque: for as the latter is ever the exhibition of what is monstrous and unnatural, and where our delight, if we examine it, arises from the surprising absurdity, as in appropriating the manners of the highest to the lowest, or *é converso*;[3] so in the former, we should ever confine ourselves strictly to nature, from the just imitation of which will flow all the pleasure we can this way convey to a sensible reader. And perhaps, there is one reason why a comic writer should of all others be the least excused for deviating from nature, since it may not be always so easy for a serious poet to meet with the great and the admirable; but life everywhere furnishes an accurate observer with the ridiculous * * *[4]

But to return: the ridiculous only, as I have before said, falls within my province in the present work. Nor will some explanation of this word be thought impertinent by the reader, if he considers how wonderfully it hath been mistaken, even by writers who have professed it. For to what but such a mistake can we attribute the many attempts to ridicule the blackest villainies; and what is yet worse, the most dreadful calamities? What could exceed the absurdity of an author who should write the *Comedy of Nero* with the merry incident of ripping up his mother's belly?[5] Or what would give a greater shock to humanity than an attempt to expose the miseries of poverty and distress to ridicule? And yet, the reader will not want much learning to suggest such instances to himself.

Besides, it may seem remarkable that Aristotle, who is so fond and free of definitions, hath not thought proper to define the ridiculous. Indeed, where he tells us it is proper to comedy, he hath remarked that villainy is not its object;[6] but he hath not, as I remember, positively asserted what is. Nor doth the Abbé Bellegarde, who hath writ a treatise on this subject,[7] though he shows us many species of it, once trace it to its fountain.

The only source of the true ridiculous (as it appears to me) is affectation. But though it arises from one spring only, when we consider the infinite streams into which this one branches, we shall presently cease to admire[8] at the copious field it affords to an observer. Now affectation proceeds from one of these two causes, vanity or hypocrisy: for as vanity puts us on affecting false characters, in order to purchase applause; so hypocrisy sets us on an endeavor to avoid censure by concealing our vices under an appearance of their opposite virtues. And though these two causes

3. *Vice versa.*
4. In the section omitted here, Fielding analyzes the workings of burlesque.
5. When the Roman emperor Nero (37–68 C.E.) commanded that his mother be killed, she urged her executioner to stab her in the womb that had given birth to her matricidal son.
6. *Poetics,* 5.1–2.
7. Jean Baptiste Morvan de Bellegarde, *Reflexions sur le ridicule* (*Reflections on the Ridiculous*, 1696).
8. Marvel.

are often confounded (for they require some difficulty in distinguishing), yet, as they proceed from very different motives, so they are as clearly distinct in their operations: for indeed, the affectation which arises from vanity is nearer to truth than the other; as it hath not that violent repugnancy of nature to struggle with, which that of the hypocrite hath. It may be likewise noted that affectation doth not imply an absolute negation of those qualities which are affected: and therefore, though, when it proceeds from hypocrisy, it be nearly allied to deceit; yet when it comes from vanity only, it partakes of the nature of ostentation. For instance, the affectation of liberality in a vain man differs visibly from the same affectation in the avaricious; for though the vain man is not what he would appear, or hath not the virtue he affects, to the degree he would be thought to have it; yet it sits less awkwardly on him than on the avaricious man, who is the very reverse of what he would seem to be.

From the discovery of this affectation arises the ridiculous—which always strikes the reader with surprise and pleasure; and that in a higher and stronger degree when the affectation arises from hypocrisy, than when from vanity. For to discover any one to be the exact reverse of what he affects is more surprising, and consequently more ridiculous, than to find him a little deficient in the quality he desires the reputation of. I might observe that our Ben Jonson,[9] who of all men understood the ridiculous the best, hath chiefly used the hypocritical affectation.

Now from affectation only, the misfortunes and calamities of life, or the imperfections of nature, may become the objects of ridicule. Surely he hath a very ill-framed mind who can look on ugliness, infirmity, or poverty as ridiculous in themselves: nor do I believe any man living who meets a dirty fellow riding through the streets in a cart is struck with an idea of the ridiculous from it; but if he should see the same figure descend from his coach and six, or bolt from his chair[1] with his hat under his arm, he would then begin to laugh, and with justice. In the same manner, were we to enter a poor house, and behold a wretched family shivering with cold and languishing with hunger, it would not incline us to laughter (at least we must have very diabolical natures if it would), but should we discover there a grate, instead of coals, adorned with flowers, empty plate or china dishes on the side-board, or any other affectation of riches and finery either on their persons or in their furniture; we might then indeed be excused for ridiculing so fantastic an appearance. Much less are natural imperfections the objects of derision: but when ugliness aims at the applause of beauty, or lameness endeavors to display agility, it is then that these unfortunate circumstances, which at first moved our compassion, tend only to raise our mirth.

The poet carries this very far:

> None are for being what they are in fault,
> But for not being what they would be thought.[2]

Where if the meter would suffer the word *ridiculous* to close the first line, the thought would be rather more proper. Great vices are the proper objects of our detestation, smaller faults of our pity: but affectation appears to me the only true source of the ridiculous.

But perhaps it may be objected to me that I have against my own rules introduced vices, and of a very black kind into this work. To which I shall answer: first,

---

9. Poet and playwright (1573?–1637).
1. I.e., a sedan chair, carried through the streets: a comparatively luxurious mode of London transportation.

2. William Congreve (1670–1729), from "Of Pleasing: An Epistle to Sir Richard Temple."

that it is very difficult to pursue a series of human actions and keep clear from them. Secondly, that the vices to be found here are rather the accidental consequences of some human frailty, or foible, than causes habitually existing in the mind. Thirdly, that they are never set forth as the objects of ridicule but detestation. Fourthly, that they are never the principal figure at that time on the scene; and lastly, they never produce the intended evil.

Having thus distinguished *Joseph Andrews* from the productions of romance writers on the one hand, and burlesque writers on the other, and given some few very short hints (for I intended no more) of this species of writing, which I have affirmed to be hitherto unattempted in our language: I shall leave to my good-natured reader to apply my piece to my observations, and will detain him no longer than with a word concerning the characters in this work.

And here I solemnly protest I have no intention to vilify or asperse anyone: for though everything is copied from the book of nature, and scarce a character or action produced which I have not taken from my own observations and experience, yet I have used the utmost care to obscure the persons by such different circumstances, degrees, and colors, that it will be impossible to guess at them with any degree of certainty; and if it ever happens otherwise, it is only where the failure characterized is so minute that is a foible only which the party himself may laugh at as well as any other.

As to the character of *Adams*,[3] as it is the most glaring in the whole, so I conceive it is not to be found in any book now extant. It is designed a character for perfect simplicity; and as the goodness of his heart will recommend him to the good-natured; so I hope it will excuse me to the gentlemen of his cloth; for whom, while they are worthy of their sacred order, no man can possibly have a greater respect. They will therefore excuse me, notwithstanding the low adventures in which he is engaged, that I have made him a clergyman; since no other office could have given him so many opportunities of displaying his worthy inclinations.

1741–1742   1742

from The History of Tom Jones, a Foundling[1]

Showing What Kind of a History This Is;
What It Is Like, and What It Is Not Like.[2]

Though we have a properly enough entitled this our work, a History, and not a Life;[3] nor an Apology for a Life,[4] as is more in fashion; yet we intend in it rather to pursue the method of those writers who profess to disclose the revolutions of countries than

---

3. Parson Abraham Adams, Joseph's benevolent, beleaguered, deeply lovable mentor and companion, and Fielding's first great comic creation.

1. The title of Fielding's second novel compasses some of its comedy. A "foundling" is a bastard child; "Tom Jones" is as plain a name as English affords. Such creatures were not deemed worthy of a "history," and the novel's comedy consists partly in the incongruity, and the mesh, between the grandeur of its design and language, and the lowliness of its generous, bumbling, often estimable hero's origins and predicaments.

2. Book 2, Chapter 1. *Tom Jones* includes 18 prefatory essays, one for each of the multichaptered "books" into which Fielding divides his long narrative. The 18th

century was much in love with prefaces, but Fielding took the genre to a new pinnacle of critical and comic artistry. He makes it the means for imparting his opinions, his ambitions, and his affections, both for the protagonists who people his narrative and the readers who engage with it. In this, the second of the 18, he takes pains to explain to his readers just how he has structured his book to serve, and sustain, their interests.

3. I.e., an ordinary biography.

4. This is another of Fielding's many satiric slaps at the actor whose garrulous, digressive, self-congratulatory autobiography, *An Apology for the Life of Mr. Colley Cibber, Comedian* (1740), provided a paradigm, for Fielding and other mockers, of everything a book should not be.

to imitate the painful and voluminous historian, who, to preserve the regularity of his series, thinks himself obliged to fill up as much paper with the detail of months and years in which nothing remarkable happened, as he employs upon those notable eras when the greatest scenes have been transacted on the human stage.

Such histories as these do, in reality, very much resemble a newspaper, which consists of just the same number of words, whether there be any news in it or not. They may likewise be compared to a stagecoach, which performs constantly the same course, empty as well as full. The writer, indeed, seems to think himself obliged to keep even pace with time, whose amanuensis he is; and, like his master, travels as slowly through centuries of monkish dullness, when the world seems to have been asleep, as through that bright and busy age so nobly distinguished by the excellent Latin poet.[5]

> Ad configendum venientibus undique paenis;
> Omnia cum belli trepido concussa tumultu
> Horrida contremeuere sub altis aetheris auris:
> In dubisque fait sub utrorum regna cadendum
> Ominibus humanis esset, terraque marique.

Of which we wish we could give our reader more adequate translation than that by Mr. Creech:[6]

> When dreadful Carthage frighted Rome with arms,[7]
> And all the world was shook with fierce alarms;
> Whilst undecided yet, which part should fall,
> Which nation rise the glorious lord of all.

Now it is our purpose in the ensuing pages to pursue a contrary method. When any extraordinary scene presents itself (as we trust will often be the case) we shall spare no pains nor paper to open it at large to our reader; but if whole years should pass without producing anything worthy his notice, we shall not be afraid of a chasm in our history; but shall hasten on to matters of consequence, and leave such periods of time totally unobserved.

These are indeed to be considered as blanks[8] in the grand lottery of time. We therefore who are the registers of that lottery, shall imitate those sagacious persons who deal in that which is drawn at Guildhall, and who never trouble the public with the many blanks they dispose of;[9] but when a great prize happens to be drawn, the newspapers are presently filled with it, and the world is sure to be informed at whose office it was sold: indeed, commonly two or three different offices lay claim to the honor of having disposed of it; by which, I suppose, the adventurers[1] are given to understand that certain brokers are in the secrets of Fortune, and indeed of her cabinet council.

---

5. Lucretius, *De Rerum Natura (On the Nature of Things)*, 3.833–7.
6. Thomas Creech (1659–1700), classical scholar whose translation of the reputedly "atheistic" Lucretius caused a sensation on its first appearance (1682) and remained current for well over half a century.
7. I.e., during the Punic Wars (third century B.C.E.), when Roman dominance in the Mediterranean was threatened by the possibility of Carthaginian conquest.
8. Worthless tickets.
9. Guildhall was in effect the city hall of London, and the site of lottery drawings; Fielding's point is that the ticket sellers, in order to sustain their customers' hopes and their own income, never speak of all the "blanks" they profit by.
1. Risk-takers; gamblers.

My reader then is not to be surprised if, in the course of this work, he shall find some chapters very short, and others altogether as long; some that contain only the time of a single day, and others that comprise years; in a word, if my history sometimes seems to stand still, and sometimes to fly. For all which I shall not look on myself as accountable to any court of critical jurisdiction whatever: for as I am, in reality, the founder of a new province of writing, so I am at liberty to make what laws I please therein. And these laws, my readers, whom I consider as my subjects, are bound to believe in and to obey; with which that they may readily and cheerfully comply, I do hereby assure them that I shall principally regard their ease and advantage in all such institutions: for I do not, like a *jure divino* tyrant,[2] imagine they are my slaves, or my commodity.[3] I am, indeed, set over them for their own good only, and was created for their use, and not they for mine. Nor do I doubt, while I make their interest the great rule of my writings, they will unanimously concur in supporting my dignity, and in rendering me all the honor I shall deserve or desire.

For an additional chapter from *Tom Jones*, go to *The Longman Anthology of British Literature* Web site at www.myliteraturekit.com.

Laurence Sterne
1713–1768

Unlike Richardson and Fielding, the Yorkshire parson and proud eccentric Laurence Sterne commenced his masterpiece, *The Life and Opinions of Tristram Shandy, Gentleman*, without so much as a paragraph of preface. Instead he plunged right into the opening chapter with an emphatic "I wish." For *Tristram*'s earliest readers, this abruptness would have been only the first, and maybe the mildest, of the innumerable astonishments to follow, in a novel that unfolded in two-volume increments published at irregular intervals throughout the ensuing decade, and that displayed so odd and elusive a narrative shape that critics have debated for centuries whether, in the final volume (published shortly before the author's death) Sterne actually completed the work, or simply meant to keep it going. No text of the period presented itself so insistently, on every page, as new and strange; the narrative simply revels in its seeming discontinuities, with its predecessors and with itself. Yet, just as the ubiquitous dashes that split Sterne's prose into tiny fragments conceal the integrities of his phenomenally well-made sentences, the novel itself traffics slyly in continuities too. From favorite writers, Sterne absorbed favored tactics: Rabelais's antic obscenity and copious scope; Montaigne's acutely particularized self-scrutiny; Cervantes's ironies; Quixote's sweetness; Swift's satiric debunking of specious learning. From the novel's two most pressing precedents, Richardson and Fielding, Sterne devised a combinatorial game that percolates through his text as a playful question. What if an autobiographer were to pursue Fielding's objectives—an ongoing, thought-rich, conversational colloquy with the reader—by Richardson's means, exponentially intensified: a practice of writing "to the moment" so thorough, and so insistent, that it seeks to encompass literally all the agitations (distractions, digressions, preoccupations, puzzlements) *of the*

2. An oppressor who rules by assertion of divine right; Fielding here strikes a glancing blow at the Jacobites, who held that their leader Charles Stuart (1720–1788) possessed such a claim to the throne, and who had recently been decisively defeated at the Battle of Culloden (1746).
3. "Wares; merchandise; goods for traffic" (Johnson's *Dictionary*).

moment, including those entailed by the act of writing itself? In such a case, the autobiographer might find that his *Opinions* so define his *Life*, but at the same time intrude so emphatically on his narration, that he might need, say, four volumes and two years simply (or intricately) to recount the day of his birth. In *Tristram Shandy*, he does.

from The Life and Opinions of Tristram Shandy, Gentleman
[INTERRUPTIONS[1]]

I wish either my father or my mother, or indeed both of them, as they were in duty both equally bound to it, had minded what they were about when they begot me; had they duly considered how much depended upon what they were then doing;— that not only the production of a rational Being was concerned in it, but that possibly the happy formation and temperature of his body, perhaps his genius and the very cast of his mind;—and, for aught they knew to the contrary, even the fortunes of his whole house might take their turn from the humors and dispositions which were then uppermost:[2]—Had they duly weighed and considered all this, and proceeded accordingly,—I am verily persuaded I should have made a quite different figure in the world, from that, in which the reader is likely to see me.——Believe me, good folks, this is not so inconsiderable a thing as many of you may think it; ——you have all, I dare say, heard of the animal spirits,[3] as how they are transfused from father to son, &c. &c.——and a great deal to that purpose:——Well, you may take my word, that nine parts in ten of a man's sense or his nonsense, his successes and miscarriages in this world depend upon their motions and activity, and the different tracks and trains you put them into, so that when they are once set a-going, whether right or wrong, 'tis not a halfpenny matter,[4]—away they go cluttering like hey-go mad; and by treading the same steps over and over again, they presently make a road of it, as plain and as smooth as a garden walk, which, when they are once used to, the Devil himself sometimes shall not be able to drive them off.

Pray, my dear, quoth my mother, *have you not forgot to wind up the clock?*—— *Good G—!* cried my father, making an exclamation, but taking care to moderate his voice at the same time, —*Did ever woman, since the creation of the world, interrupt a man with such a silly question?* Pray what was your father saying?——Nothing.[5]

1759–1760   1760

---

1. Volume 1, Chapter 1.
2. In the long-accepted theory of the humors, each person's character was thought to be determined by whichever of four fluids (blood, phlegm, choler, and black bile) was "uppermost" (that is, existed in the highest proportion) within his or her body. If black bile predominated, for example, the person would be melancholic (Greek: *melan* [black] + *chol* [bile]).
3. Vapors or fluids thought to course through the body, directing its sensations and actions. "The animal spirits," explained Robert Burton in *The Anatomy of Melancholy*, ". . . brought up to the brain, and diffused by the nerves to the subordinate members, give sense and motion to them all."
4. Trivial.
5. This question-and-answer punch line, initially obscure, encapsulates much of Tristram's predicament. As he will

explain a little later, his father, "one of the most regular men in everything he did," made it his practice to wind up the household clock on the first Sunday of every month, and at the same time to take care of "some other little family concernments" (i.e., marital intercourse), so that he would "be no more plagued and pestered with them the rest of the month." So, at the moment narrated, his father is saying nothing but doing something: begetting Tristram. His mother, similarly engaged, jumps by "an unhappy association of ideas" to her question about the clock, with which she interrupts the current, crucial activity. Meanwhile, as Tristram starts to tell his story, a nameless and confused reader (the first of many in the text) interrupts *him* with a question ("what was your father saying?") based, like so much in the book to come, on an incomplete understanding of data waywardly supplied.

[CALCULATIONS[6]]

Holla![7]——you chairman![8]——here's sixpence——do step into that bookseller's shop, and call me a day-tall critic.[9] I am very willing to give any one of 'em a crown to help me with this tackling,[1] to get my father and my uncle Toby off the stairs, and to put them to bed.——

——'Tis even high time; for except a short nap, which they both got whilst Trim was boring the jackboots—and which, by the by, did my father no sort of good upon the score of the bad hinge—they have not else shut their eyes, since nine hours before the time that Doctor Slop was led into the back parlor in that dirty pickle by Obadaiah.[2]

Was every day of my life to be as busy a day as this,——and to take up,—— truce——

I will not finish that sentence till I have made an observation upon the strange state of affairs between the reader and myself, just as things stand at present——an observation never applicable before to any one biographical writer since the creation of the world, but to myself——and I believe will never hold good to any other, until its final destruction——and therefore, for the very novelty of it alone, it must be worth your worships attending to.

I am this month one whole year older than I was this time twelve-month;[3] and having got, as you perceive, almost into the middle of my fourth volume——and no farther than to my first day's life——'tis demonstrative that I have three hundred and sixty-four days' more life to write just now, than when I first set out; so that instead of advancing, as a common writer, in my work with what I have been doing at it——on the contrary, I am just thrown so many volumes back——was every day of my life to be as busy a day as this——And why not?——and the transactions and opinions of it to take up as much description——And for what reason should they be cut short? as at this rate I should just live 364 times faster than I should write——It must follow, an'[4] please your worships, that the more I write, the more I shall have to write——and consequently, the more your worships read, the more your worships will have to read.

Will this be good for your worships' eyes?

It will do well for mine; and, was it not that my OPINIONS will be the death of me, I perceive I shall lead a fine life of it out of this self-same life of mine; or, in other words, shall lead a couple of fine lives together.

As for the proposal of twelve volumes a year, or a volume a month, it no way alters my prospect——write as I will, and rush as I may into the middle of things, as Horace advises,[5]——I shall never overtake myself——whipped and driven to the

---

6. Volume 4, Chapter 13. Still narrating the day of his birth, Tristram finds himself in a predicament. As the long day wanes, his father and his uncle Toby, lost in conversation, are stranded on the staircase; as narrator, Tristram is trying to find a way to get them off the stairs and into bed.

7. "You there!"

8. Carrier of a sedan chair (i.e., the eighteenth-century equivalent of a taxi driver, idling on the street while waiting for a fare).

9. A hack writer, so called because his prose is reckoned (tallied) and paid for by the day rather than by its merits.

1. Equipment: ropes and pulleys.

2. Tristram catalogues just a few of the day's catastrophes, to each of which he has already devoted whole chapters:

his father Walter's favorite pair of boots has been appropriated and destroyed by Uncle Toby's well-meaning servant Corporal Trim; both father and uncle have been woken from their nap by a door-hinge that has stayed squeaky for the past ten years; the Shandys' servant Obadaiah, sent on horseback to fetch the "man-midwife" Dr. Slop, has collided with that beleaguered obstetrician and sent him sprawling into deep mud.

3. I.e., a year ago, when the first two volumes of *Tristram Shandy* were published.

4. If it.

5. The ancient Roman poet advised authors to imitate Homer's practice in the *Iliad*: not to begin their stories at the very start, but instead to plunge their readers in *medias res*, "into the middle [of] things" (*Ars Poetica*, 11.146ff.).

last pinch, at the worst I shall have one day the start of[6] my pen——and one day is enough for two volumes——and two volumes is enough for one year.——

Heaven prosper the manufactures of paper under this propitious reign, which is now opened to us,[7]——as I trust its providence will prosper everything else in it that is taken in hand.——

As for the propagation of geese[8]——I give myself no concern——Nature is all bountiful——I shall never want[9] tools to work with.

——So then, friend! you have got my father and my uncle Toby off the stairs, and seen them to bed?——And how did you manage it?——You dropped a curtain at the stairs' foot[1]——I thought you had no other way for it——Here's a crown[2] for your trouble.

1760   1761

✦ ✦ ✦

Frances Burney
1752–1840

In the preface to her first novel, *Evelina* (1778), Frances Burney praises "the pathetic powers of Richardson," "the wit of Fielding," and the skills of several other fiction-makers, before making what amounts to a modest boast: "I yet presume not to attempt pursuing the same ground which they have tracked; whence, though they may have cleared the weeds, they have also culled the flowers." Like so many of her predecessors, she wants to make clear that she has chosen a newer route, sketched in the novel's subtitle. Her book will chronicle the six-month "history of a young lady's entrance into the world."

In fact, *Evelina* enacted two such entrances, the heroine's and the author's. Throughout her writings, Burney remained preoccupied with the precarious dynamics of entrance—with the peculiarly "female difficulties" (to quote the subtitle of her last novel) encountered by a young woman who tries to make her way into a world seemingly bent, whether through indifference or hostility, on the suppression of her autonomy, the obstruction of her desires, even the eradication of her identity. "Why," Burney famously asks at the age of sixteen, in her very first journal entry, " . . . must a *female* be made Nobody?" Over the seven ensuing decades, in her copious journals, revelatory letters, and four increasingly ambitious novels, Burney sought answers to the "why" and set down challenges to the "must." In the selections here, from her earliest journals, from *Evelina*, and from her final novel *The Wanderer*, Burney makes clear how writing can register the difficulties of being female in England during the late eighteenth century—and how it can inflect, alter, and at times perhaps resolve them, too.

from **The Early Journals**
[FIRST ENTRY]

Poland Street, London [27 March 1768][1]

To have some account of my thoughts, manners, acquaintance and actions, when the hour arrives at which time is more nimble than memory is the reason which induces

---

6. I.e., be one day ahead of.
7. George III had become king the year before, in 1760.
8. Whose feathers furnished quill pens.
9. Lack.
1. I.e., did it as a dramatist might, dropping a curtain over one scene in order to indicate a shift in time and space

before the next scene commences.
2. A coin worth 5 shillings, or 60 pence: ten times what Tristram paid the chairman to fetch the critic.
1. Burney, who will turn 16 in 11 weeks, now lives with her three sisters, two brothers, father and stepmother in a prosperous district of London.

me to keep a journal: a journal in which I must confess my *every* thought, must open my whole heart! But a thing of this kind ought to be addressed to somebody—I must imagine myself to be talking—talking to the most intimate of friends—to one in whom I should take delight in confiding, and feel remorse in concealment: but who must this friend be?—to make choice of one to whom I can but *half* rely would be to frustrate entirely the intention of my plan. The only one I could wholly, totally confide in, lives in the same house with me, and not only never *has*, but never *will*, leave me one secret *to* tell her.[2] To whom, then *must* I dedicate my wonderful, surprising and interesting adventures?—to *whom* dare I reveal my private opinion of my nearest relations? the secret thoughts of my dearest friends? my own hopes, fears, reflections and dislikes—Nobody!

To Nobody, then, will I write my journal! since To Nobody can I be wholly unreserved—to Nobody can I reveal every thought, every wish of my heart, with the most unlimited confidence, the most unremitting sincerity to the end of my life! For what chance, what accident can end my connections with Nobody? No secret can I conceal from No—body, and to No—body can I be *ever* unreserved. Disagreement cannot stop our affection, Time itself has no power to end our friendship. The love, the esteem I entertain for Nobody, No-body's self has not power to destroy. From Nobody I have nothing to fear, the secrets sacred to friendship, Nobody will not reveal, when the affair is doubtful, Nobody will not look towards the side least favorable.—

I will suppose you, then, to be my best friend: though God forbid you ever should! My dearest companion—and a romantic girl, for mere oddity may perhaps be more sincere—more *tender*—than if you were a friend in propria personae[3]—in as much as imagination often exceeds reality. In your breast my errors may create pity without exciting contempt; may raise your compassion, without eradicating your love.

From this moment, then, my dear girl—but why, permit me to ask, must a *female* be made Nobody? Ah! my dear, what were this world good for, were Nobody a female? And now I have done with *preambulation*.[4]

["I CANNOT HELP IT"]

Cabin, Saturday [30 July 1768][5]

And so I suppose you[6] are staring at the torn paper, and unconnected sentences—I don't much wonder—I'll tell you how it happened. Last Monday I was in the little parlor, which room my papa generally dresses in—and writing a letter to my grandmamma Sleepe—You must know I always have the last sheet of my journal in my pocket, and when I have wrote it half full—I join it to the rest, and take another sheet—and so on. Now I happened unluckily to take the last sheet out of my pocket with my letter—and laid it on the piano forte, and there, negligent fool!—I left it.[7] Unfortunately while we were at Mrs. Allen's on Sunday evening, I wrote about half a page in which I

---

2. Burney's 13-year-old sister Susanna (1755–1800), in whom she confided, through talk and long letters, throughout the ensuing decades.
3. In one's own person (Latin); i.e., if you were an actual, living person.
4. Preface-making. In using (and emphasizing) this somewhat unusual word, Burney may just possibly be echoing *Pamela* (see above, page 2816).
5. Burney spent summers with her family in King's Lynn, the Norfolk port town where she was born. The "cabin"

stood on her stepmother's property, with a view of the nearby river. Burney liked the place for its privacy, and often wrote her journal there: "I always spend the evening, sometimes all the afternoon, in this sweet cabin . . . I cannot express the pleasure I have in writing down my thoughts, at the very moment—" (13 July 1768).
6. I.e., "Nobody."
7. Burney's father Charles was an eminent teacher and historian of music; the piano was therefore a center of household life—and of his attention.

mentioned poor Susan [xxx 2 words][8] teasing me with *particular* questions, on a *particular* subject, which related to a *particular* case, concerning Mama—Can you not guess *what?*[9]—[xxx 1 line] and besides this, I mentioned several other little matters—Well, as ill fortune would have it, papa went into the room—took my poor journal—read and pocketed it! Mama came up to me and told me of it. O dear! I was in a sad distress—I could not for the life of me ask for it—and so *dawdled* and fretted the time away 'till Tuesday evening. Then, gathering courage—Pray, Papa—have you got—any *papers* of mine?—Papers of yours?—said he—how should I come by papers of yours?—I'm sure—I don't know—but—Why do you leave your papers about the house? asked he, gravely—I could not say another word—and he went on playing on the piano forte. Well, to be sure, thought I these same dear journals are most shocking plaguing things—I've a good mind to resolve never to write a word more.—However, I stayed still in the room, working and looking wistfully at him for about an hour and a half. At last, he rose to dress—again I looked wistfully at him—he laughed—what, Fanny, said he, kindly—are you in sad distress?—I half laughed—Well—I'll give it you, now I see you are in such distress—but take care, my dear, of leaving your writings about the house again—Suppose anybody else had found it—I declare I was going to read it loud—Here—take it—but if ever I find any more of your journals, I vow I'll stick them up in the market place! And then he kissed me so kindly—Never was parent so *properly*, so *well-judged* affectionate.

I was so frightened that I have not had the heart to write since, 'till now, I should not but that—in short, but that I cannot help it!—As to the *paper*, [xxx 1/2 line] I destroyed it[1] the moment I got it. We have had several little parties of pleasure since I wrote last but they are not worth mentioning.

["The Most Dangerous Employment Young Persons Can Have"]

[King's Lynn, August 1768]

I have been having a long conversation with Miss Young[2] on journals. She has very seriously and earnestly advised me to give mine up—heigho-ho! Do you think I can bring myself to oblige her? What she says has great weight with me: but, indeed, I should be very loath to *quite* give my poor friend up. She says that it is the most dangerous employment young persons can have—it makes them often record things which ought not to be recorded, but instantly forgot. I told her, that as *my* journal was *solely* for my own perusal, nobody could in justice, or even in sense, be angry or displeased at my writing anything.

"But how can you answer," said she, "that it is only for your perusal? That very circumstance of your papa's finding it shows you are not so very careful as is necessary for such a work. And if you drop it, and any improper person finds it, you know not the uneasiness it may cost you."

"Well but, dear ma'am, this is an 'if' that may not happen once in a century."

"I beg your pardon, I know not how often it may happen; and even once might prove enough to give you more pain than you are aware of."

"Why, dear ma'am, papa never prohibited my writing, and he knows that I *do* write, and *what* I do write."

---

8. Later in life, Burney edited and excised her journals by many means: crossing words out, pasting them over, cutting whole pages. In this case, she crossed out the entire passage beginning at "Unfortunately" and ending in "matters"; the square brackets indicate words and lines that editors have been unable to recover.

9. Probably her stepmother's ("Mama's") pregnancy.
1. Burney inserted this phrase decades later, perhaps as replacement for the excised half-line.
2. Dorothy Young, a resident of King's Lynn, and best friend of Burney's mother.

"I question that. However, 'tis impossible for you to answer for the curiosity of others. And suppose anybody finds a part in which they are extremely censured."

"Why then, they must take it for their pains. It was not wrote for *them*, but *me*, and I cannot see any harm in writing to *myself*."

"It was very well whilst there were only your sisters with you to do anything of this kind; but, depend upon it, when your connections are enlarged, your family increased, your acquaintance multiplied, young and old *so* apt to be curious—depend upon it, Fanny, 'tis the most dangerous employment you can have. Suppose now, for example, your favorite wish were granted, and you were *to fall in love,* and then the object of your passion were to get sight of some part which related to himself?"

"Why then, Miss Young, I must take a little trip to Rosamond's Pond."[3]

"Why, ay, I doubt[4] it would be all you would have left."

"Dear Miss Young!—But I'm sure, by your earnestness, that you think worse of my poor journal than it deserves."

"I know very well the nature of these things. I know that in journals, thoughts, actions, looks, conversations—*all* go down; do they not?"

The conclusion of our debate was that if I would show her some part of what I had wrote she should be a better judge, and would then give me her best advice whether to proceed or not. I believe I shall accept her condition; though I own I shall show it with shame and fear, for such nonsense is so unworthy her perusal.

I'm sure, besides, I know not what part to choose. Shall I take at random?

from **Evelina;**
or, the History of a Young Lady's Entrance into the World

EVELINA TO THE REVEREND MR. VILLARS[1]

Howard Grove, March 26

This house seems to be the house of joy; every face wears a smile, and a laugh is at everybody's service. It is quite amusing to walk about, and see the general confusion; a room leading to the garden is fitting up for Captain Mirvan's study.[2] Lady Howard does not sit a moment in a place; Miss Mirvan[3] is making caps; everybody so busy!—such flying from room to room!—so many orders given, and retracted, and given again!—nothing but hurry and perturbation.

Well but, my dear Sir, I am desired to make a request to you. I hope you will not think me an encroacher; Lady Howard insists upon my writing!—yet I hardly know how to go on; a petition implies a want,—and have you left me one? No, indeed.

I am half ashamed of myself for beginning this letter. But these dear ladies are so pressing—I cannot, for my life, resist wishing for the pleasures they offer me,—provided you do not disapprove them.

---

3. Located in London's St. James's Park, Rosamond's Pond was a popular place for lovers' meetings and (Burney's joke here) for lovers' suicides; because of those dark associations, it was filled in (and thereby eradicated) two years later.
4. Expect.
1. Volume 1, letter 8. *Evelina* is made up mostly of letters written by the 16-year-old heroine to her guardian and surrogate father Arthur Villars, from whom she has not been separated since infancy, when he took on the task of caring for her after her mother's death and her father's

refusal to acknowledge her his daughter. Now, with Villars's reluctant consent, she has left on an extended visit to the family of his friend Lady Howard, who hopes to help Evelina establish the legitimacy of her birth and standing. Here, in the first of her many letters home, Evelina is charged with making a further request, and discovers something of how writing can inflect desire.
2. Captain Mirvan is the brutish husband of Lady Howard's kindly daughter. *Fitting up for:* being remodeled as.
3. Lady Howard's granddaughter; Evelina's contemporary and friend.

They are to make a very short stay in town.[4] The Captain will meet them in a day or two. Mrs. Mirvan and her sweet daughter both go;—what a happy party! Yet I am not *very* eager to accompany them: at least, I shall be contented to remain where I am, if you desire that I should.

Assured, my dearest Sir, of your goodness, your bounty, and your indulgent kindness, ought I to form a wish that has not your sanction? Decide for me, therefore, without the least apprehension that I shall be uneasy, or discontented. While I am yet in suspense, perhaps I may *hope*, but I am most certain, that when you have once determined, I shall not repine.

They tell me that London is now in full splendor. Two playhouses are open,— the Opera-House,—Ranelagh,[5]—the Pantheon.[6]—You see I have learned all their names. However, pray don't suppose that I make any point of going, for I shall hardly sigh to see them depart without me; though I shall probably never meet with such another opportunity. And, indeed, their domestic happiness will be so great,—it is natural to wish to partake of it.

I believe I am bewitched! I made a resolution when I began, that I would not be urgent; but my pen—or rather my thoughts, will not suffer me to keep it—for I acknowledge, I must acknowledge, I cannot help wishing for your permission.

I almost repent already that I have made this confession; pray forget that you have read it, if this journey is displeasing to you. But I will not write any longer; for the more I think of this affair, the less indifferent to it I find myself.

Adieu, my most honored, most reverenced, most beloved father! for by what other name can I call you? I have no happiness or sorrow, no hope or fear, but what your kindness bestows, or your displeasure may cause. You will not, I am sure, send a refusal, without reasons unanswerable, and therefore I shall cheerfully acquiesce. Yet I hope—I hope you will be able to permit me to go.

I am,

With the utmost affection,

gratitude, and duty,

Your

EVELINA ————

I cannot to *you* sign *Anville*, and what other name may I claim?[7]

[A RIDICULOUS AND REJECTED WOOER][8]

Mr. Smith teased me[9] till I was weary of resistance; and I should at last have been obliged to submit, had I not fortunately recollected the affair of Mr. Lovel, and told my persecutor that it was impossible I should dance with him, even if I wished it, as I had refused several persons in his absence.[1]

---

4. London.
5. A well-known pleasure garden.
6. An elegant assembly room, used for concerts and balls.
7. "Anville," an anagram of Evelina's own first name, is the surrogate surname her guardian has contrived for her. She cannot write it to him because they both know it for a fiction; as a purportedly illegitimate child, she possesses no other last name.
8. From volume 2, letter 19: Evelina to the Rev. Mr. Villars. Throughout the novel, Evelina is beset by suitors. Mr. Smith, the man of "low-bred vivacity" who pursues her here at a downmarket London dance, is one of the more transitory, but he provides Evelina with an opportu-

nity to review how much she's learned, and how much she's changed, since arriving in London only four months earlier.
9. Pestered (not mocked); he wants to dance with her.
1. At her first, more elegant London ball, Evelina had declined the odious Mr. Lovel's invitation to dance, but nervously assured him that she had no other partner, and that she simply did not wish to "dance at all"; she was later mortified when he found her dancing with a far more attractive partner, to whom she'd assented out of the same agitation. What she experienced as awkwardness then, she deploys as tactic now.

He was not contented with being extremely chagrined, but took the liberty, openly and warmly, to expostulate with me upon not having said I was engaged.[2]

The total disregard with which, involuntarily, I heard him, made him soon change the subject. In truth, I had no power to attend to him, for all my thoughts were occupied in retracing the transactions of the two former balls at which I had been present. The party—the conversation—the company—O how great the contrast!

In a short time, however, he contrived to draw my attention to himself, by his extreme impertinence;[3] for he chose to express what he called his *admiration* of me, in terms so open and familiar, that he forced me to express my displeasure with equal plainness.

But how was I surprised, when I found he had the temerity—what else can I call it?—to impute my resentment to doubts of his honor; for he said, "My dear Ma'am, you must be a little patient; I assure you I have no bad designs, I have not upon my word; but, really, there is no resolving upon such a thing as matrimony all at once; what with the loss of one's liberty, and what with the ridicule of all one's acquaintance,—I assure you, Ma'am, you are the first lady who ever made me even demur[4] upon this subject; for, after all, my dear Ma'am, marriage is the devil!"

"Your opinion, Sir," answered I, "of either the married or the single life, can be of no manner of consequence to me, and therefore I would by no means trouble you to discuss their different merits."

"Why, really, Ma'am, as to your being a little out of sorts, I must own I can't wonder at it, for, to be sure, marriage is all in all with the ladies; but with us gentlemen it's quite another thing! Now only put yourself in my place,—suppose you had such a large acquaintance of gentlemen as I have,—and that you had always been used to appear a little—a little smart among them,—why now, how should you like to let yourself down all at once into a married man?"

I could not tell what to answer; so much conceit, and so much ignorance, both astonished and silenced me.

"I assure you, Ma'am," added he, "there is not only Miss Biddy,—though I should have scorned to mention her, if her brother had not blabbed, for I'm quite particular in keeping ladies' secrets,[5]—but there are a great many other ladies that have been proposed to me,—but I never thought twice of any of them,—that is, not in a *serious* way,—so you may very well be proud," offering to take my hand, "for I assure you, there is nobody so likely to catch me at last as yourself."

"Sir," cried I, drawing myself back as haughtily as I could, "you are totally mistaken, if you imagine you have given me any pride I felt not before, by this conversation; on the contrary, you must allow me to tell you, I find it too humiliating to bear with it any longer."

I then placed myself behind the chair of Madame Duval;[6] who when she heard of the partners I had refused, pitied my ignorance of the world, but no longer insisted on my dancing.

---

2. I.e., not having used the alternate tactic of telling unwanted partners that, in effect, her dance card was already full.
3. "Troublesomeness; intrusion" (Johnson's *Dictionary*).
4. "To pause in uncertainty" (Johnson's *Dictionary*).
5. Mr. Smith alludes to the vulgar Branghton family, with

whom Evelina is remotely connected and reluctantly entangled; brother Tom has just revealed that his sister Biddy wants Smith for herself.
6. Evelina's maternal grandmother, intent on seeing her married off.

Indeed, the extreme vanity of this man makes me exert a spirit which I did not, till now, know that I possessed; but I cannot endure that he should think me at his disposal.

from **The Wanderer; or, Female Difficulties**
from *the Preface*[1]

* * * With regard to the very serious subject[2] treated upon, from time to time, in this work, some—perhaps many—may ask, "Is a novel the vehicle for such considerations, such discussions?"

Permit me to answer: whatever, in illustrating the characters, manners, or opinions of the day, exhibits what is noxious or reprehensible, should scrupulously be accompanied by what is salubrious, or chastening. Not that poison ought to be infused merely to display the virtues of an antidote; but that, where error and mischief bask in the broad light of day, truth ought not to be suffered to shrink timidly in the shade.

Divest, for a moment, the title of Novel from its stationary standard of insignificance, and say! What is the species of writing that offers fairer opportunities for conveying useful precepts? It is, or it ought to be, a picture of supposed, but natural and probable human existence. It holds, therefore, in its hands our best affections; it exercises our imaginations; it points out the path of honor; and gives to juvenile credulity knowledge of the world, without ruin, or repentance; and the lessons of experience, without tears.

And is not a novel, permit me, also, to ask, in common with every other literary work, entitled to receive its stamp as useful, mischievous, or nugatory, from its execution? Not necessarily, and in its changeless state, to be branded as a mere vehicle for frivolous, or seductive amusement? If many may turn aside from all but mere entertainment presented under this form, many, also, may, unconsciously, be allured by it into reading the severest truths, who would not even open any work of a graver denomination.

What is it that gives the universally acknowledged superiority to the epic poem? Its historical truth? No: the three poems,[3] which, during so many centuries, and till Milton arose, stood unrivalled in celebrity, are, with respect to fact, of constantly disputed, or rather, disproved authenticity. Nor is it even the sweet witchery of sound: the ode, the lyric, the elegiac, and other species of poetry have risen to equal metrical beauty.

'Tis the grandeur, yet singleness of the plan: the never broken, yet never obvious adherence to its execution; the delineating and support of character; the invention of incident; the contrast of situation; the grace of diction and the beauty of imagery, joined to a judicious choice of combinations, and a living interest in every partial detail, that give to that sovereign species of the works of fiction its glorious preeminence.

Will my dear father smile at this seeming approximation of the compositions which stand foremost, with those which are sunk lowest in literary estimation? No; he will feel that it is not the futile presumption of a comparison that would be preposterous, but a fond desire to separate (with a high hand!) falsehood, that would deceive to evil, from fiction, that would attract another way—and to rescue from ill opinion the sort of production (call it what we may) that his daughter ventures to lay at his feet, through the alluring but awful[4] tribunal of the public.

---

1. Burney addresses this preface, part theoretical and part autobiographical, to her father Charles, now 87 years old; he died two weeks after the novel's publication.
2. The aftermath of the French Revolution, which had rendered Burney's husband, like the heroine of the *Wanderer*, an exile in England.
3. Homer's *Iliad* and *Odyssey*; Virgil's *Aeneid*.
4. I.e., awe-inspiring.

He will recollect, also, how often their so mutually honored Dr. Johnson has said to her, "Always aim at the eagle—even though you expect but to reach a sparrow!"

The power of prejudice annexed to nomenclature is universal: the same being who, unnamed, passes unnoticed,[5] if preceded by the title of a hero, or a potentate, catches every eye, and is pursued with clamorous praise or (its common reverberator!) abuse. But in nothing is the force of denomination more striking than in the term *novel*: a species of writing which, though never mentioned, even by its supporter, but with a look that fears contempt, is not more rigidly excommunicated from[6] its appellation, in theory, than sought and fostered, from its attractions, in practice.

So early was I impressed myself with ideas that fastened degradation to this class of composition, that at the age of adolescence, I struggled against the propensity which, even in childhood, even from the moment I could hold a pen, had impelled me into its toils; and on my fifteenth birthday, I made so resolute a conquest over an inclination at which I blushed, and that I had always kept secret, that I committed to the flames whatever, up to that moment, I had committed to paper.[7] And so enormous was the pile, that I thought it prudent to consume it in the garden.

You, dear Sir, knew nothing of its extinction, for you had never known of its existence. Our darling Susanna,[8] to whom alone I had ever ventured to read its contents, alone witnessed the conflagration; and—well I remember!—wept, with tender partiality, over the imaginary ashes of Caroline Evelyn, the mother of Evelina.

The passion, however, though resisted, was not annihilated: my bureau was cleared, but my head was not emptied; and, in defiance of every self-effort, Evelina struggled herself into life. * * *

[CODA][9]

Here, and thus felicitously, ended, with the acknowledgment of her name, and her family, the DIFFICULTIES of the WANDERER; —a being who had been cast upon herself; a female Robinson Crusoe, as unaided and unprotected, through the midst of the world, as that imaginary hero in his uninhabited island; and reduced either to sink, through inanition, or to be rescued from famine and death by such resources as she could find, independently, in herself.

How mighty, thus circumstanced, are the DIFFICULTIES with which a FEMALE has to struggle! Her honor always in danger of being assailed, her delicacy of being offended, her strength of being exhausted, and her virtue of being calumniated!

Yet even DIFFICULTIES such as these are not insurmountable, where mental courage, operating through patience, prudence, and principle, supply physical force, combat disappointment, and keep the untamed spirits superior to failure, and ever alive to hope.

1814

5. The phrasing here well describes the initially nameless heroine of *The Wanderer*, whose predicament (by the ensuing logic in Burney's sentence) becomes analogous to that of the genre that depicts her.
6. I.e., because of the stigma associated with.
7. Burney partly discloses to her father, perhaps for the first time, the story of her earliest writing. During her early teens, in the wake of her beloved mother's sudden death and her worshipped father's troubling remarriage, Burney wrote a novel, "The History of Carolyn Evelyn," and then, on her fifteenth birthday, burned it, out of fear that her father, and the world at large, would frown at the audacity and impropriety frequently imputed to women who wrote fiction. *Evelina*, composed a decade later, was in effect a sequel to the immolated work; it tells the story of Carolyn's daughter.
8. Burney's younger sister and closest confidant, whose death in 1800 haunted Burney for the remainder of her own long life; she died 40 years to the day after Susanna.
9. In these, the final paragraphs of her career as novelist, Burney reworks her book's subtitle, touches on concerns that have beset all her female protagonists as they strive to establish both name and identity, and harkens back, with a significant shift in gender, to a narrative published 95 years earlier.

CREDITS

TEXT CREDITS

Addison, Joseph and Richard Steele. From *The Spectator, Volume I* (1987), edited by Donald Bond. By permission of Oxford University Press.

Excerpt from *Amazons, Savages, and Machiavels travel and colonial writing in English, 1550–1630: an anthology* edited by Andrew Hadfield. Copyright © 2001. Reprinted by permission of Oxford University Press.

Burney, Fanny. From *The Early Journals and Letters of Fanny Burney, Volume I, 1768–1773*, ed. by Lars E. Troide. Montreal: McGill-Queen's University Press, 1988. Reprinted by permission of the publisher. Entries from *Selected Journals and Letters of Frances Burney*, edited with an introduction and notes by Peter Sabor and Lars E. Troide, with the assistance of Stewart J. Cooke and Victoria Kortes-Papp. London: Penguin Books, 2001. Reproduced by permission of Penguin Books Ltd.

Dryden, John. "The Secular Masque" from *John Dryden* (1987), edited by Keith Walker. By permission of Oxford University Press. From "Preface to Fables Ancient and Modern" and "Alexander's Feast" from *The Poems and Fables of John Dryden* (1962) edited by James Kinsley. By permission of Oxford University Press.

Evelyn, John. Excerpt from *The Diary of John Evelyn*, edited by E.S. DeBeer. By permission of Oxford University Press.

Pepys, Samuel. From *The Diary of Samuel Pepys*, edited and translated by Robert Latham and William Matthews. Copyright © 1972–1986. The Master, Fellows and Scholars of Magdalen College, Cambridge, Robert Latham, and the Executors of William Matthews. Reprinted by permission of the University of California Press.

ILLUSTRATION CREDITS

Page 1980: © Copyright The British Museum; 1981: © Historical Picture Library/Philip de Bay/CORBIS All Rights Reserved; 1982 (top): Erich Lessing/Art Resource, NY; 1982 (bottom): Art Resource, NY; 1983 (top): National Portrait Gallery, London; 1983 (middle): Robert Walpole; 1983 (bottom): Guidhall Art Gallery, London, GB/HIP/Art Resource, NY; 1984: Guidhall Art Gallery, London, GB/HIP/Art Resource, NY; 2009: The Bridgeman Art Library International; 2010: Lebrecht Music & Arts Photo Library; 2050: © Rare Books Division, The New York Public Library, Astor, Lenox and Tilden Foundations; 2053: HIP/Oxford Science Archive, Oxford, GB/Art Resource, NY; 2074: National Portrait Gallery, London; 2125: National Portrait Gallery, London; 2304–05: Museum of London; 2329: Courtesy of Washington University Libraries; 2331: Guildhall Library, Corporation of London; 2337: National Portrait Gallery, London; 2438: National Portrait Gallery, London; 2605: Dover Publications, Inc.; 2606: Dover Publications, Inc.; 2607: Dover Publications, Inc.; 2608: Dover Publications, Inc.; 2609: Dover Publications, Inc.; 2610: Dover Publications, Inc.; 2611: Dover Publications, Inc.; 2612: Dover Publications, Inc.; 2674: National Portrait Gallery, London

COLOR PLATE CREDITS

Color Plate 20: The Royal Collection © 2005, Her Majesty Queen Elizabeth II.; Color Plate 21: The Royal Collection © 2005, Her Majesty Queen Elizabeth II.; Color Plate 22: The Bridgeman Art Library International.; Color Plate 23: Picture Desk, Inc./Kobal Collection.; Color Plate 24: Derby Museums and Art Gallery.; Color Plate 25: © National Gallery, London/Art Resource, NY.; Color Plate 26: The Bridgeman Art Library International.; Color Plate 27: Copyright © Tate Gallery, London/Art Resource, NY.; Color Plate 28: Cincinnati Art Museum, Given in honor of Mr. and Mrs. Charles F. Williams by their children. Accession #: 1948.173.

INDEX